Contents

Watching wildlife color section following p.264

Alaska in winter color section following p.488

◀◀ Sunset in Denali National Park ◀ Savonoski Loop, Katmai National Park

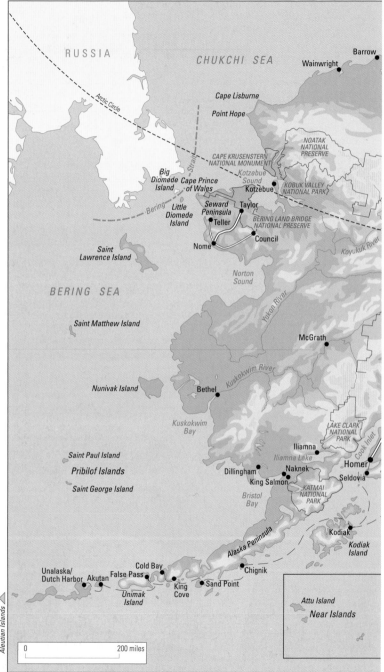

RUSSIA

CHUKCHI SEA

Barrow

Wainwright

Arctic Circle

Cape Lisburne

Point Hope

NOATAK
NATIONAL
PRESERVE

CAPE KRUSENSTERN
NATIONAL MONUMENT

Kotzebue
Sound

KOBUK VALLEY
NATIONAL PARK

Big
Diomede Cape Prince
Island of Wales

Kotzebue

Bering Strait

Little
Diomede
Island

Seward
Peninsula

Teller

Taylor

BERING LAND BRIDGE
NATIONAL PRESERVE

Koyukuk River

Nome

Council

Saint
Lawrence Island

Norton
Sound

BERING SEA

Yukon River

Saint Matthew Island

McGrath

Kuskokwim River

Nunivak Island

Bethel

Kuskokwim
Bay

LAKE CLARK
NATIONAL
PARK

Iliamna

Cook Inlet

Saint Paul Island

Pribilof Islands

Iliamna Lake

Naknek

Homer

Dillingham

Seldovia

Saint George Island

King Salmon

KATMAI
NATIONAL
PARK

Bristol
Bay

Kodiak

Alaska Peninsula

Kodiak
Island

Cold Bay

Chignik

Unalaska/
Dutch Harbor

False Pass

Akutan

Sand Point

Unimak
Island

King
Cove

Attu Island

Near Islands

Aleutian Islands

0   200 miles

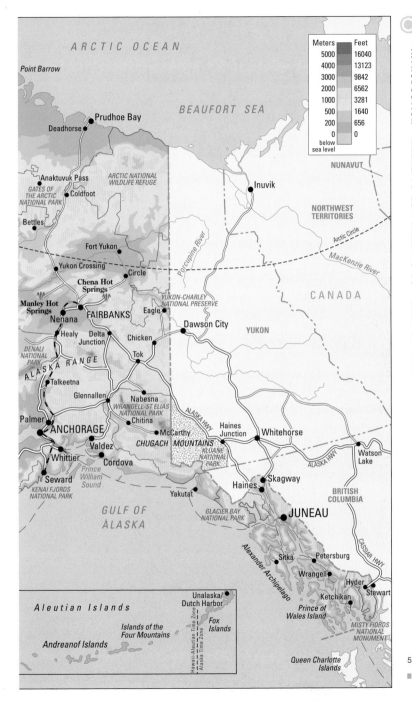

ARCTIC OCEAN

Point Barrow

BEAUFORT SEA

Prudhoe Bay
Deadhorse

Meters	Feet
5000	16040
4000	13123
3000	9842
2000	6562
1000	3281
500	1640
200	656
0	0
below sea level	

NUNAVUT

Anaktuvuk Pass
GATES OF THE ARCTIC NATIONAL PARK
Coldfoot
ARCTIC NATIONAL WILDLIFE REFUGE

Inuvik

NORTHWEST TERRITORIES

Bettles

Fort Yukon

Porcupine River

Arctic Circle

MacKenzie River

Yukon Crossing
Circle

Chena Hot Springs

YUKON-CHARLEY NATIONAL PRESERVE

CANADA

Manley Hot Springs
Nenana
FAIRBANKS
Eagle

Healy
Delta Junction
Chicken

Dawson City

YUKON

DENALI NATIONAL PARK

Tok

ALASKA RANGE

Talkeetna

Glennallen
Nabesna
WRANGELL-ST ELIAS NATIONAL PARK

Palmer
Chitina

ANCHORAGE
McCarthy
CHUGACH MOUNTAINS

ALASKA HWY

Haines Junction

Whitehorse

Valdez
Whittier
Cordova
KLUANE NATIONAL PARK

ALASKA HWY

Watson Lake

Seward
KENAI FJORDS NATIONAL PARK
Prince William Sound

Yakutat

Haines
Skagway

BRITISH COLUMBIA

GULF OF ALASKA

GLACIER BAY NATIONAL PARK

JUNEAU

CASSIAR HWY

Alexander Archipelago

Sitka
Petersburg

Wrangell

Hyder
Stewart

Ketchikan

Prince of Wales Island

MISTY FIORDS NATIONAL MONUMENT

Aleutian Islands

Unalaska/ Dutch Harbor

Fox Islands

Islands of the Four Mountains

Andreanof Islands

Hawaii-Aleutian Time Zone

Alaska Time Zone

Queen Charlotte Islands

5

Introduction to
Alaska

Hardly anywhere in the world conjures up sharper images than Alaska, and the name itself – a derivation of *Alyeska*, an Athabascan word meaning "great land of the west" – fires the imagination of many a traveler. Few who see this land of gargantuan ice fields, sweeping tundra, glacially excavated valleys, lush rainforests, deep fjords, and active volcanoes leave disappointed. Wildlife here is equally oversized and abundant, with Kodiak bears reaching heights of eleven feet, moose stopping traffic in downtown Anchorage, wolves howling through the night, bald eagles soaring above the trees, and fifty-plus-pound salmon jamming rivers.

Alaska's sheer size alone is hard to comprehend – its vast expanse is more than twice that of Texas, and its coastline is almost as long as the rest of the United States'. The nation's sixteen highest peaks are all found within Alaska's boundaries, along with its two largest national parks, and two most extensive national forests. There are more active glaciers here than in the rest of the inhabited world.

Little more than half a million people live in this huge state, around 42 percent residing in Anchorage. Altogether, only a twentieth of one percent of the land area is developed, the rest remaining almost entirely untouched. In many ways Alaska mirrors the American West of the nineteenth century, not surprising for a place often referred to as the **Last Frontier**: an endless wonderland in which to stake a claim and escape the world at large. Or at least that's how many Alaskans would like it to be. Throughout

Traveling around Alaska demands a spirit of adventure

the twentieth century tens of thousands have been lured here by the promise of wealth, first by gold and then by fishing, logging, and, most recently, oil.

Alaska is the kind of place folks become obsessive about, and the obsessed fall into two camps. Most love it, but treat it as a boundless treasure trove so far from Washington DC that federal jurisdiction is irrelevant. Any truth to this has long since passed, but the myth persists and many Alaskans believe in their right to do whatever they want, bitterly resenting anyone who suggests otherwise.

Fact file

• Disconnected from the rest of the United States, Alaska borders Canada's Yukon Territory and straddles the **Arctic Circle**. The western tip of the 1100-mile **Aleutian Chain** almost touches the Russian mainland and is on the same longitude as New Zealand.

• With 572,000 square miles, Alaska is the **largest state** in the union, over twice the size of Texas, a fifth the size of the entire Lower 48, and six times the size of Britain.

• Alaska's **landscape** is hugely varied, from swampy, lake-pocked lowlands to the 20,320-foot summit of **Mount McKinley**, the loftiest point on the continent. Evergreen forests swathe much of the southern half of the state, thinning to the barren tundra of the north. Altogether there are estimated to be **100,000 glaciers**.

• With only 665,000 people, Alaska is one of the US's **least populated** states. Almost half the people congregate around the biggest city, **Anchorage**; Sitka, the fourth-largest city, has fewer than ten thousand residents, and of the 348 locales listed in the 2000 census almost seventy percent have fewer than five hundred inhabitants.

• The **state economy** is heavily reliant on **oil**, which provides around eighty percent of general revenue. Current oil production is only half what it was in the late 1980s peak, though recent high world oil prices have boosted depleted coffers.

Alaska's Native peoples

Native Alaskans make up around fifteen percent of the state's population, and most lead a semi-subsistence lifestyle in small rural villages on the fringes of the mainstream economy. Tradition remains strong, with fishing and whale-hunting still important pursuits and totem pole-building in a resurgence. Natives live fundamentally modern lives, though: they've replaced paddles with outboard motors, and many receive annual dividends from **Native corporations**, which have their fingers in tourism, forestry, fishing, oil, and more besides.

There are four broad groupings of Native peoples. The **Tlingit** traditionally occupied the lush forests of Southeast Alaska, making best use of the mild climate, rich plant life, and abundant fish and game. The bounty provided the time to develop a complex culture characterized by bright ceremonial costume, totem poles, and gorgeous buttoned blankets. The Interior is the preserve of **Athabascans**, close kin of the Navajo and Apache of the American Southwest. They had to learn to cope with a very short growing season and turned to fishing for salmon and tracking caribou and moose. The north and west of Alaska is the homeland of the Yup'ik and Iñupiat peoples, collectively known as **Eskimos** – a term not generally considered offensive in these parts. Aside from a few roots and berries gathered during the short, cool summer, the Eskimo mainly hunted sea mammals – seals, walruses, and small whales – taking to the water in skin-covered kayaks and larger umiaks. The final major grouping is the **Aleut**, who populate the Aleutian Islands and much of the Southwest. They became accomplished traders and raiders, paddling in their skin-covered canoes, or bidars, and relying on a constant supply of sea mammals for sustenance and trading.

Others came to Alaska for its pristine qualities and want to keep it that way. With growing pressure from these green-minded activists and the federal government, environmental issues have increasingly made front-page news. Current controversies include the practice of clear-cutting in the national forests, the prospect of oil exploration in the Arctic National Wildlife Refuge, over-fishing, and wolf-culling which, according to animal rights groups, is primarily to ensure that there are more caribou for hunters.

Most infamous is the unholy mess created by the *Exxon Valdez* oil tanker in 1989, although little visible evidence of the spill remains today.

Long before Alaska became involved in national politics, it was inhabited by Native peoples, whose 86,000 descendants are today largely marginalized from mainstream society. Most choose to live in remote communities, known as "Native villages," where services are often limited and earning a living can be entirely dependent on the number of salmon running that year. Very few live in the larger towns, and those that do usually endure conditions that are harsh at best. Natives have largely been left behind by the state's periodic boom times, though a hefty land claim settlement in the 1970s paved the way for relatively wealthy Native corporations to provide much-needed income for their people.

Alaska is a land of mythic proportions, and costs are often similarly monumental. Thanks to pricey rental cars and long distances between attractions, **transport** is far from cheap, and **eating and drinking** are, at best, about twenty percent more expensive than in the Lower 48. Still, experiencing Alaska without spending a fortune is possible with a bit of planning. Traveling outside the peak summer season will save you money on accommodation, as will **campgrounds** and **hostels**, the latter found mostly in the major towns. On the other hand, a couple nights at a luxury fly-in lodge can be well worth the price tag; rates typically cover all amenities and the quality of the lodging and included tours is exceptional.

Alaska is a land of mythic proportions

Alaskan gold

From a white American per-spective, **gold** created Alaska, driving its transition from neglected territory towards eventual statehood. A sequence of gold strikes in progressively less accessible locales first brought steamers into the Inte-rior along two thousand miles of the Yukon River, then precipi-tous railroads, and finally the all-weather roads that replaced the dog-sled routes. Initial gold strikes were wildly exaggerated

on the Outside, precipitating a mass arrival of argonauts ill-equipped for the rigors of the North. A few fortunes were made, but most prospectors returned penniless to the Lower 48 after a season or two, having blown their earnings in the bars and brothels that sprang up in the towns along-side the diggings.

Lonely miners are still out there shoveling away at their "rocker" or using suction dredges to collect ore-bearing gravel from riverbeds. Wherever you go in rural Alaska, you'll find claims fiercely protected and meet pros-pectors happy to tell you just how much they're going to make next year.

Public claims dotted around the state allow visitors to try their hand. Most only do it for fun and a few flakes, but some stay all summer hop-ing to collect enough to forge their wedding ring.

Where to go

Traveling around Alaska demands a spirit of adventure, as well as patience. Unless you are flying in, there are only two **approaches**: the **Alaska Highway**, which cuts across British Columbia and the Yukon on its way to the Alaskan Interior and the Arctic North, and the **Marine Highway ferries**, which skirt elegiac fjords, glaciers, and mountains border-ing the Pacific from Washington State to **Southeast Alaska**. From there a dozen small towns are starting points for salmon-fishing, whale-watching, and glacier-viewing trips. Highlights include the former Russian capital of **Sitka**; the current state capital, **Juneau**; the gold-rush town of **Skagway**; and the pristine wonderland of **Glacier Bay National Park**.

Flights from out of state almost all land in **Anchorage**, the largest city, and just as much an Alaskan experience as the great outdoors. From here, it's easy to get to the glacier-bound and wildlife-rich waters of **Prince William Sound** and the **Kenai Peninsula**, a kind of Alaska in miniature. When you tire of the excellent hiking, head to laid-back **Homer** for its halibut-fishing trips, kayaking around **Kachemak Bay**, and day-trips to pretty **Seldovia** and the tiny boardwalk community of **Halibut Cove**.

Further west, **Southwest Alaska** contains historic **Kodiak** and the host of tiny **Alaska Peninsula** communities most easily accessed by the Aleutians ferry trip, which terminates at Dutch Harbor, the largest town in the **Aleutian Islands**. Perhaps the area's most alluring destination is **Katmai National Park**, with peerless lake canoeing, hiking amid a volcanic wasteland, and one of the best places to watch brown bears catching salmon as they leap up a waterfall.

North from Anchorage, the **Interior** is the most road-accessible part of the state with highways reaching **Wrangell–St Elias National Park**, containing the twin settlements of **McCarthy** and **Kennicott**, and mammoth **Denali National Park**, home to the nation's highest mountain, the 20,320-foot **Mount McKinley** (aka Denali). These parks highlight what is perhaps the state's greatest appeal: the unparalleled opportunity to get away from civilization and experience the natural world. Some visitors base an entire sojourn around a major backcountry trek or a canoeing expedition on one of the many river systems, fishing along the way and camping out each night (see box, p.32).

Fairbanks, 358 miles north of Anchorage, is Alaska's second-largest town and the gateway to the endless tundra and remote villages of the **Arctic North**. The **Dalton Highway** covers most of the five hundred miles north to Deadhorse, almost on the edge of the Arctic Ocean. Pretty much everywhere else in the region requires a flight, though from **Nome** you can use a few hundred miles of road to explore gold dredges, an abandoned train, and some rural hot springs.

▼ Glory Hole Road near Chilkoot Lake

◀ Full moon, Wrangell–St Elias National Park

When to go

Alaska has a very short tourist season. For guaranteed long daylight hours and the greatest likelihood of fairly warm weather, you'll need to travel in the **peak season** from Memorial Day weekend (the last in May) until Labor Day weekend (the first in September). During this time, the climate in Southeast Alaska, Anchorage, and the Kenai Peninsula is mild (45–65°F) and much more rain (in some towns 180-plus inches per year) falls than snow. Remarkably, the Interior in summer often gets as hot as 80°F.

You'll be far from alone in Alaska at this time, when hotel availability is at its tightest and prices go up accordingly. Being there with everyone else has its advantages, though; you'll have an incredibly wide range of tours, restaurants, and lodging to choose from, unlike in the winter when most establishments shut down. If you want to avoid the crowds and still find most businesses operating, try the last two weeks in May and first two in September – Alaska's **shoulder seasons**.

Daily temperatures and average rainfall

	Jan	Feb	Mar	Apr	May	June	July	Aug	Sept	Oct	Nov	Dec	Avg/ Total
Anchorage													
max °F	19	26	34	45	54	63	64	64	57	43	30	19	43
min °F	5	9	12	27	36	45	48	46	39	28	16	7	27
max °C	-7	-3	1	7	12	17	18	18	14	6	-1	-7	6
min °C	-15	-13	-11	-3	2	7	9	8	4	-2	-9	-14	-3
rain (inches)	0.8	0.7	0.6	0.4	0.5	0.7	1.6	2.6	2.6	2.2	1	0.9	14.6
rain (mm)	20	18	15	10	13	18	41	66	66	56	25	23	371
Barrow													
max °F	-9	-11	-8	7	25	39	46	45	34	21	7	-4	16
min °F	-22	-26	-22	-8	12	28	34	34	27	12	-6	-17	4
max °C	-23	-24	-22	-14	-4	4	8	7	1	-6	-14	-20	-9
min °C	-30	-32	-30	-22	-11	-2	1	1	-3	-11	-21	-27	-16
rain (inches)	0.2	0.1	0.1	0.1	0.1	0.3	0.9	0.8	0.5	0.5	0.3	0.2	4.1
rain (mm)	5	3	3	3	3	8	23	20	13	13	8	5	107
Fairbanks													
max °F	-2	10	41	43	59	72	72	66	54	36	12	1	39
min °F	-20	-9	-4	18	36	46	48	45	34	18	-6	-17	16
max °C	-19	-12	5	6	15	22	22	19	12	2	-11	-17	4
min °C	-29	-23	-20	-8	2	8	9	7	1	-8	-21	-27	-9
rain (inches)	0.9	0.5	0.7	0.3	0.6	1.3	1.9	2.1	1.3	0.8	0.7	0.6	11.7
rain (mm)	23	13	18	8	15	33	48	53	33	20	18	15	297
Juneau													
max °F	27	34	37	17	54	63	64	63	54	17	39	32	42
min °F	16	21	25	31	37	46	48	46	45	36	28	21	33
max °C	-3	1	3	8.5	12	17	18	17	12	8.5	4	0	8
min °C	-9	-6	-4	-0.5	3	8	9	8	7	2	-2	-6	1
rain (inches)	3.5	3.7	3.3	3.2	3.3	2.7	4.1	4.8	6.1	7.2	4.8	4.6	51.3
rain (mm)	90	95	84	81	84	69	105	123	156	183	123	117	1310
Unalaska/Dutch Harbor													
max °F	37	37	39	41	46	52	57	59	54	47	43	39	46
min °F	28	27	29	31	37	42	46	48	43	37	32	30	36
max °C	3	3	4	5	8	11	14	15	12	8	6	4	8
min °C	-2	-3	-2	-1	3	6	8	9	6	3	0	-1	2
rain (inches)	3.0	2.4	2.4	2.1	2.1	2.0	2.4	3.3	3.9	4.1	4.3	3.7	35.7
rain (mm)	77	60	61	53	54	50	61	84	100	104	109	94	907

The weather at this time can be just as warm as midsummer, and you've got the added bonus of watching trees transform from bare to full foliage in a matter of days, or experiencing the boreal forest in its autumnal plumage.

There is some regional variation, but in general anyone here before mid-May or after mid-September will find their options limited: there will be few glacier and whale-watching cruises; kayaking operations will have locked away their paddles; Denali shuttle buses will have stopped running; flightseeing trips will be grounded; and even whole towns (admittedly tiny ones like Chicken and McCarthy) will have shut up shop for the winter.

The moderating effects of the ocean (and the more southerly latitude) mean that the season in **Southeast Alaska** is a little longer, with a few of the cruise-ship companies extending their seasons to include early May and late September. In **Anchorage** the mid-May to mid-September rule holds true, though the first serious snowfall probably won't come until mid-October, making this a good place to finish a late-season trip. In **Fairbanks and the Arctic North** your movements at the periphery of the season may be more limited, particularly in the coastal towns of Nome, Kotzebue, and Barrow, where the sea ice may remain frozen until mid-June or later. It is often late May before the roads on the Seward Peninsula near Nome are plowed, so if you are planning to explore up here, go later.

Hikers should avoid May and early June unless they like high-stepping through snow on the trail; late August and September are generally a much better bet, and considerably drier underfoot.

Visitors traveling to Alaska after mid-September, particularly around Fairbanks, have a good chance of seeing the **aurora borealis**, but keen watchers need to come in winter. However, even the tourist promoters admit that for most visitors November, December, and January are just too cold and dark to enjoy. March and the first week in April are generally best for winter activities – from aurora-watching to dog-mushing – with a thick layer of snow on the ground, lengthening days, and temperatures that are just about bearable. The rest of April, early May, and October are neither winter nor summer and not very conducive to activity in most parts of the state: the snow isn't thick enough for winter pursuits, but it's too thick for summer ones.

Beyond the myths

Mention you are off to Alaska and people react as though the whole state is snow and ice year-round. In fact, if you go in June, July, or August (as most visitors do), then about the only snow you'll see will be on the mountaintops and the only ice will be in glaciers. Landscapes of green trees, grass, wildflowers, and salmonberries are the typical visitor experience, and you'll often be in shorts and a T-shirt during the day.

Some arrive expecting to see **igloos**, and although it is true that Alaska's native Eskimos may have once used igloos as temporary shelters on hunting trips, with the advent of snowmobiles they now just drive back to town. Some places in the Far North do get visits from **polar bears** in winter, but you're not going to see any roaming through downtown Anchorage. That said, moose are pretty common in the city, and traffic sometimes has to stop for them.

Most people have figured out that the long winter nights equate to almost endless summer days, but many fail to realize that long hours of dusk make viewing the **northern lights** unlikely any time from April to mid-September. Another enduring misperception is that there are seven men for every woman in Alaska. This may still be true in small fishing and mining communities where the extreme male domination becomes really evident, but Alaska's population is now 48.3 percent women (against a national average of 50.9).

What to take

n Alaska formal clothing is out, but you need to be prepared for the physical demands of a trip to the state, and your comfort will largely be affected by **what you wear**. Multiple thin **layers** are warmer than a couple of thick ones and give you the freedom to strip off one or two as the day heats up. In June, July, and August, you'll get by happily with normal clothing (including shorts and T-shirts), plus a fleece jacket, a waterproof coat, hat, gloves, and strong shoes. If you are heading to the north before the end of May or after the end of August, take thermal underwear and an extra warm layer. Winter visitors to Southeast Alaska need take no extra precautions, but in the Interior or Arctic, bring down jackets, insulating pants, and specialist footwear, or buy once you arrive. Special considerations for **campers** are discussed on p.66.

Besides clothing, you'll want to bring a camera and binoculars and, rather more mundanely, bug spray – the **mosquito** is often referred to as the "Alaska State bird."

26

things not to miss

It's not possible to see everything that Alaska has to offer in one trip – and we don't suggest you try. What follows is a selective and subjective taste of the state's highlights: wondrous landscapes, rugged excursions, and distinctive towns among them. They're arranged in five color-coded categories to help you find the very best to see, do, and experience. All highlights have a page reference to take you straight into the guide, where you can find out more.

01 Glacier Bay National Park Page **176** ● Alaska's most celebrated icy wonderland is one of the state's best places to witness hunks of glacier thundering into the sea. Fabulous kayaking too.

02 Hiking Page **65** • You can hardly expect to visit Alaska and not do some hiking; choice spots to hit include the Chugach Mountains, Denali, and the Kenai Peninsula.

03 Sitka Page **138** • Set on an island-dotted bay, the old Russian colonial capital is the jewel of Southeast, with an onion-domed cathedral and a striking Tlingit totem park.

04 McCarthy and Kennicott Page **457** • Wrangell-St Elias National Park's enormous ice fields and dense cluster of lofty peaks are most easily accessed from quirky McCarthy and neighboring Kennicott, with its elegantly decaying copper-mill buildings.

17

05 **College Fjord Cruise** Page 314 • Major cruise liners and Whittier-based day cruises offer unparalleled glacier views, plus a chance to see seals and sea otters up close.

06 **Moose Dropping Festival, Talkeetna**

Page **402** • Make time for this eccentric summer festival, where you can win prizes by tossing moose droppings, watch "mountain mothers" race around a wood-chopping and fly-casting course, or just revel in the revelry.

07 **Aleutian ferry trip** Page 363 • Ride the "Trusty Tusty" to remote Unalaska/Dutch Harbor, passing the snow-capped volcanoes of the Alaska Peninsula, calling at isolated fishing ports, and scanning the horizon for whales on the three-day journey.

08 **Independence Mine** Page **395** • A wonderfully evocative collection of old mine buildings set high up in an alpine bowl, surrounded by snowy peaks.

10 Aurora borealis Page **506** •
Seeing the northern lights should be on everyone's lifetime list. Head for Fairbanks after mid-September or make a special winter visit.

09 Sea kayaking Page **69** •
Don't miss the chance to experience Alaska by kayak. It may be just a gentle paddle along the shore or near the face of a glacier, but even for beginners, several days exploring Kenai Fjords National Park, Prince William Sound, or any of Southeast's myriad waterways isn't a stretch.

11 Denali National Park Page **412** • Nowhere else in Alaska are you virtually assured of seeing brown and black bears, moose, caribou, and even wolves in a single day's sightseeing. Add in views of ice-capped Mount McKinley and this will be a highlight of any trip.

I ACTIVITIES I CONSUME I **EVENTS** I NATURE I SIGHTS I

13 **Salmon** Page **604** • Follow their upstream journey from the oceans to freshwater spawning grounds; later, sink your teeth into a lightly pan-fried steak or Native-style, air-dried jerky.

12 **Stay in a fly-in cabin** Page **52** • Fly in by float-plane, then fish, canoe, and relax.

20

14 **Seldovia** Page **302** • Soak in the secluded beauty of this delightful little community, with its boardwalks perched on stilts above the water, welcoming B&Bs, and views across Kachemak Bay.

15 **Drive (or cycle) the Denali Highway** Page **439** • Fabulous scenery, ease of access, and no permits make the Denali Highway an excellent alternative to its namesake national park.

16 **Million Dollar Bridge** Page **336** • Nearly swallowed by the Childs Glacier during construction and wrecked by the 1964 earthquake, the Million Dollar Bridge is a fitting finale to the Copper River Highway.

17 **White Pass & Yukon Route railway** Page **198** • It's not cheap, but this thrilling ride past stupendous Southeast scenery is a must if you're anywhere near Skagway.

18 **Museum of the North**
Page **509** • With its striking modern expansion, this already excellent Fairbanks museum has gotten even better with outstanding art, natural history, and science exhibits.

19 **Canoeing** Page **483** • Launch an epic canoe adventure down the Yukon River from the former fort town of Eagle.

20 **Combat fishing** Page **224** • Try your luck in a salmon-fishing derby, stand shoulder to shoulder with other anglers in what's known as "combat fishing," or hire a guide to get you closer to the big catch.

21 **Chilkoot Trail** Page **200** • Embark on Alaska's finest multiday mountain hike through what is effectively an outdoor gold-rush museum.

22 **Chicken** Page **481** • A slice of the Alaska you've been looking for: rustic, rural, and just a little off the wall.

24 Native crafts Page 245 •
Pass on the tacky miniature totem poles in favor of finely crafted Tlingit button blankets, Iñupiat and Yup'ik spirit masks, and bentwood boxes from Southeast.

23 Katmai National Park Page 356 • Come to watch bears catching salmon at Brooks Falls, but leave time to explore the otherworldly Valley of 10,000 Smokes and canoe the 86-mile Savonoski Loop.

25 Halibut-fishing Page 299 •
You may never catch a big salmon, but go halibut-fishing from Homer or one of numerous other Alaskan ports and you're almost guaranteed a thirty-pounder.

26 Trains to Nowhere Page 563 • These rusting steam locomotives once hauled gold, but they have now been left to sink slowly into the coastal plain just outside Nome.

Basics

Basics

Getting there

Traveling to Alaska can be just as much of an adventure as being there. The quickest and easiest way to get there is to fly; it's also often the cheapest way to reach Anchorage and the Interior. Most flights to Anchorage go through Seattle, though there are direct flights from other parts of the world. Flights run throughout the year, but are most frequent during the main summer tourist season from late May to early September. From North America, there are also several ways to arrive either overland or by sea.

Anchorage was a major refueling stop for transpolar flights between Europe and Asia throughout the late twentieth century, but with the advent of longer-range jets it has become something of a backwater on the international circuit. **Anchorage International Airport (ANC)** does receive some international flights, principally from Taipei and Seoul, and from late May to late September both Anchorage and Fairbanks have direct flights from Frankfurt with German airline Condor. ANC also accepts a number of direct flights from US cities, including Chicago, Denver, Los Angeles, Las Vegas, Minneapolis/St Paul, Phoenix, Portland (OR), Salt Lake City, and San Francisco. **Fairbanks** receives a few long-haul flights in summer, mainly from Chicago, Minneapolis/St Paul, and Seattle. **Airfares** always depend on the season, with the highest usually between June and August, when the weather is best. Fares drop during the "shoulder" seasons – May and September – and you'll get the best prices during the low season, October to April (excluding Christmas and New Year's, when seats are at a premium and prices are hiked up). Fares on the airlines' own websites are generally as good as anything you'll find elsewhere, but discount agents may offer special student and youth fares plus other travel-related services, such as insurance, car rental, tours, and the like.

If Alaska is only one stop on a longer journey, you might be able to include it as part of an off-the-shelf **Round-the-World (RTW) ticket**, though due to the scarcity of international flights this may be difficult unless you are very flexible. Skyteam (which includes Korean Airlines and Northwest Airlines), and Star Alliance (Japan Airlines and United) are the most likely of the global alliances to provide an RTW routing via Alaska.

From North America

The fastest, and often least expensive, way to get to Alaska is to **fly**. Those after adventure can **drive** (or even ride a series of **buses**) along the Alaska Highway right up through Canada's Yukon Territory and into Alaska. For a more scenic approach, join a **cruise** or take state-run **ferries** up through the sheltered and supremely scenic Inside Passage. Better still, combine the overland and sea routes into one big loop.

By air

Almost all the major American carriers fly to Alaska, most to Anchorage and some to Fairbanks. From Anchorage, Alaska Airlines and smaller carriers fan out to the rest of the state, often by propeller-driven **"bush flights."** The vast majority of flights reach Alaska via Seattle, which also offers direct access to the Southeast towns of Ketchikan, Juneau, and Sitka with Alaska Airlines.

Special deals on airfares are occasionally listed online and in the weekend papers; otherwise, the cheapest fares are with APEX (Advanced Purchase Excursion Fare) tickets, which have to be purchased between 7 and 21 days ahead of departure. APEX prices vary, but those we've quoted below are for summer round-trips including taxes; winter fares can be a little lower but not hugely. Flights to Anchorage are available from $370 from Seattle, $520 from Los Angeles,

$540 from Chicago, $580 from Minneapolis/St Paul, and $590 from New York. From Canada, prices are around Can$700 from Toronto and Can$930 from Vancouver (from where it may be cheaper to go via Seattle). Many flights continue on from Anchorage to Fairbanks, often for only an extra $60, so you may want to make Fairbanks your first stop and work south from there. Many operators run all-inclusive packages that combine plane tickets and accommodation with activities like whale-watching, kayaking, hiking, or tours of Denali National Park. Even if the "package" aspect isn't necessarily your thing, these deals can work out to be more convenient and more economical than arranging the same trip yourself, and tour operators often have access to remote areas unknown to most visitors. With such a vast range of packages available, it's impossible to give a complete picture, but the list on pp.34–35 should get you started.

By car

The most adventurous way to approach Alaska is along the **Alaska Highway** (also known as the ALCAN Highway), two lanes of blacktop that stretch 1422 miles through remote, forested, and frequently mountainous scenery from Dawson Creek, on the BC/Alberta border, north to Delta Junction in Alaska. As daunting as this may sound, over a hundred thousand people make the pilgrimage each summer, braving limited and **sporadic services**, occasionally difficult weather, and a lot of frost heaves. Despite sometimes significant delays due to summer road repairs, it is not a particularly difficult drive. If you put your foot down it can be done in four or five days, though it is much more enjoyable to spread the journey over twice that. The Alaska Highway, its sights, and towns are covered in detail in *The Rough Guide to the Pacific Northwest* and *The Rough Guide to Canada*.

Most people who drive to Alaska take their own vehicle. Very few rental companies allow one-way drop-offs, and those that do charge astronomical prices. If you really want to drive up there and back and see something of Alaska, you'll need a month and look at charges of around $60 a day for a compact, $110 for a 4WD. American citizens planning

to drive their own cars into Canada should be certain to carry proper owner **registration** and proof of insurance coverage, and no guns. The Canadian Non-Resident Inter-Provincial Motor Vehicle Liability **Insurance** Card, available from any US insurance company, is accepted as evidence of financial responsibility in Canada. See Getting around, p.47, for car rental agencies.

With fortuitous timing, luck, and a degree of flexibility, you may be able to get a **driveaway**, thereby avoiding trashing your own rig. Look in the *Yellow Pages* under "Auto-transporters & Driveaway Companies," or contact Auto Driveaway (☎1-800/346-2277, ⊛www.driveaway.com), which lists regional offices and vehicles that currently need delivering on its website. Typically, there's no charge, but you'll be required to cover 300–400 miles a day and must pay for fuel. The same sort of deal applies with rental companies, who sometimes need cars and RVs delivered to Alaska at the beginning of the summer (especially in May), and back south in September and October; call around if you're interested.

Drivers who don't want to do the long haul in both directions can have their vehicle shipped between Anchorage and Tacoma, Washington, in about five days with Totem Ocean Trailer Express (in Tacoma ☎1-800/426-0074, in Alaska ☎1-800/234-8683, ⊛www.totemocean.com). In summer the northbound rates are $1209 for any passenger car or small truck, and $1829 for a camper or smallish RV, including taxes and charges. Summer southbound rates are $968 and $1407 for the same vehicle types.

The highway remains open all year, with gas, food, and lodging every twenty to fifty miles in summer, though by early September places start to close, frequently leaving hundred-mile gaps between services. Consequently, you'll want to be certain your vehicle is in decent condition before you set out. When planning your travels, consider the size of vehicle: a couple of people, camping gear, spares, and a stack of food can soon overload a small car. Make sure you have a jack and wheel brace suitable for installing your spare tire, preferably ones that will perform well in adverse conditions. You'll need new windscreen wipers and plenty of washer detergent to protect from dirt and

Fly less – stay longer! Travel and climate change

Climate change is the single biggest issue facing our planet. It is caused by a build-up in the atmosphere of carbon dioxide and other greenhouse gases, which are emitted by many sources – including planes. Already, flights account for around 3–4% of human-induced global warming: that figure may sound small, but it is rising year on year and threatens to counteract the progress made by reducing greenhouse emissions in other areas.

Rough Guides regard travel, overall, as a global benefit, and feel strongly that the advantages to developing economies are important, as are the opportunities for greater contact and awareness among peoples. But we all have a responsibility to limit our personal "carbon footprint". That means giving thought to how often we fly and what we can do to redress the harm that our trips create.

Flying and climate change

Pretty much every form of motorized travel generates CO_2, but planes are particularly bad offenders, releasing large volumes of greenhouse gases at altitudes where their impact is far more harmful. Flying also allows us to travel much further than we would contemplate doing by road or rail, so the emissions attributable to each passenger become truly shocking. For example, one person taking a return flight between Europe and California produces the equivalent impact of 2.5 tonnes of CO_2 – similar to the yearly output of the average UK car.

Less harmful planes may evolve but it will be decades before they replace the current fleet – which could be too late for avoiding climate chaos. In the meantime, there are limited options for concerned travellers: to reduce the amount we travel by air (take fewer trips, stay longer!), to avoid night flights (when plane contrails trap heat from Earth but can't reflect sunlight back to space), and to make the trips we do take "climate neutral" via a carbon offset scheme.

Carbon offset schemes

Offset schemes run by ⓦ www.climatecare.org, ⓦ www.carbonneutral.com, and others allow you to "neutralize" the greenhouse gases that you are responsible for releasing. Their websites have simple calculators that let you work out the impact of any flight. Once that's done, you can pay to fund projects that will reduce future carbon emissions by an equivalent amount (such the distribution of low-energy lightbulbs and cooking stoves in developing countries). Please take the time to visit our website and make your trip climate neutral.

www.roughguides.com/climatechange

bugs. Assorted spares – headlamp, hoses, and belts – and the tools to fit them are a good idea; even if you don't have the requisite mechanical knowledge, it's wise to carry the parts, as local mechanics may not be able to get supplies quickly.

To find out about the latest road conditions and travel advisories, call ☎511 in Alaska, ☎1-866/282-7577 elsewhere, or see ⓦ511.alaska.gov; for Yukon road conditions call ☎1-867/456-7623 or 1-877/456-7623 (toll-free in YT), or see ⓦwww.gov.yk.ca/roadreport.

By bus

Traveling by **bus** is the least appealing way to reach Alaska. There is none of the expedition

feel of driving yourself, and you won't save much time over using the AMHS ferries. If you just want to get to Anchorage or Fairbanks, then flying is usually just as cheap.

There is no direct bus service to Alaska. Greyhound (☎1-800/229-9424 or 402/330-8552, ⓦwww.greyhound.com) runs frequent buses (roughly every 3hr) from Seattle to Vancouver (4hr), where you can transfer to Greyhound Canada (☎1-800/661-8747, ⓦwww.greyhound.ca) for their service to Whitehorse, Yukon (44hr; mid-June to early Sept daily except Sat; early Sept to mid-June Tues, Thurs, Sun). The standard one-way Seattle–Vancouver–Whitehorse fare is US$169, though a non-refundable seven-day advance purchase costs only US$107.

The AlaskaPass

Foot passengers planning on traveling up the Inside Passage to Anchorage, Denali, and Fairbanks may make considerable savings by purchasing the AlaskaPass, which allows unlimited ferry, train, and bus travel for a certain period. Currently, only the Alaska Marine Highway System ferries, the Alaska Railroad, the White Pass & Yukon Route railway, and Holland-America Motorcoaches are members, but that may change; check to see if any other services have joined.

There are four passes: 15 consecutive days of travel ($829); 8 travel days out of 12 ($699); 12 days out of 21 ($849); and a land-only pass from Skagway to Anchorage ($399). Kids (2 to 11) travel half-price, except for the land-only pass. You'll also have to factor in a $75 booking fee, which is charged per itinerary (not per person). Passes are available from AlaskaPass Inc, PO Box 351, Vashon, WA 98070 (☎1-800/248-7598, ⓦwww.alaskapass.com).

This usually works out cheaper than catching a Greyhound from Seattle to Vancouver (US$24.50) and then buying another ticket to Whitehorse, though, with **exchange-rate** fluctuations, it's worth calculating the difference. From Vancouver to Whitehorse there is a walk-on fare of Can$287 (return Can$535), reduced to Can$171 (return Can$310) if booked seven days in advance. Despite selling advance tickets, Greyhound Canada does not guarantee space will be available, so you could conceivably find yourself on a later service – which could be quite inconvenient, given Greyhound's limited operations in the low season.

In summer, there is service from Whitehorse into Alaska with Alaska/Yukon Trails (☎1-800/770-7275, ⓦwww.alaskashuttles .com), which runs to Dawson City, Yukon (7hr 30min; US$143) three days a week (Mon, Wed & Fri). You'll have to spend a couple of nights in Dawson, as buses to Fairbanks (8hr 15min; US$162) leave on the same days of the week.

A completely different approach is to join the slightly countercultural Green Tortoise (☎1-800/867-8647, ⓦwww.greentortoise.com), which runs a converted sleeper bus to Alaska, with one 28-day trip (starting mid-June; $1700 + $290 for food) from San Francisco to Prince Rupert, taking ferries from there to Ketchikan, Juneau, and Haines, and continuing overland to Fairbanks, Denali, and Anchorage. They also operate a couple of Anchorage-based 14-day loop trips (starting mid-July & early Aug; $700 + $190 for food), which visit the Kenai Peninsula and Interior Alaska.

By train

There is **no direct rail** connection to Alaska from the rest of North America, although rail can be combined with sea travel to reach the 49th state, most easily by catching Amtrak to Bellingham, WA, then taking an AMHS ferry (see p.40). In Canada, Via Rail (☎1-888/842-7245, ⓦwww.viarail.ca) runs trains from Jasper (on the trans-Canada route) three days a week (Wed, Fri & Sun) through the Rockies to Prince Rupert, which is an AMHS ferry port; a five-day advance purchase costs around Can$220 including taxes, though you have to spend a night in Prince George along the way. In summer you should try to reserve a couple of months in advance, especially if you want the luxury of the Totem dome-car.

By boat

Most coastal towns are connected by the **Alaska Marine Highway System (AMHS)**, state-funded vehicular ferries discussed in detail in "Getting around" (see p.40). Always reserve as far in advance as you can if you want to travel by ferry.

The ferries also serve two ports outside Alaska, the more convenient being Bellingham, in Washington State, 87 miles north of Seattle. Sailings are on Fridays at 6pm (plus Tuesdays at 6pm in peak season) and skip all Canadian ports, making straight for the southernmost Alaskan port of Ketchikan (37hr), followed by Wrangell (44hr), Petersburg (48hr), Juneau (59hr), Haines (65hr), and Skagway (66hr). Note that if you have a vehicle, you'll still have to pass through Canada if you wish to continue beyond Skagway, unless you wait for the **"Cross-Gulf"** service to Whittier, which sails every two weeks in summer only. For this route, booking as early as April isn't unreasonable, particularly if you are taking a vehicle; cabins book out within four hours of going on sale, usually early in the previous November. Although it may sound much less convenient than the standard AMHS ferry services, especially for travelers without vehicles, it's a fantastic journey; see p.158. To reach the Bellingham ferry dock, take exit 250 (Fairhaven Parkway) off I-5, and follow signs for the Fairhaven Transportation Center (also served by frequent buses and trains from Seattle, Vancouver, and further afield; their schedules are well integrated with that of the ferries). Ferry passengers should arrive at the dock two hours before departure time.

One way of cutting costs on the journey to Alaska (particularly if you are taking a vehicle on the ferries) is to make your way **overland** to Prince Rupert and link up with Alaska's AMHS ferries there (typically 3–5 weekly; see pp.42–43 for details of fares). The initial Bellingham-to-Prince Rupert section of the ferry journey is the least interesting, so traveling overland to Prince Rupert may save you both time and money without losing you much in the way of scenic grandeur. You can reach Prince Rupert by car, air, train (see p.30), and Greyhound Canada, which, in summer, operates one or two buses a day on the twenty-four-hour run from Vancouver (one-way Can$208, 14-day advance purchase Can$138).

By combining a couple of ferry systems it is also possible – though less convenient – to reach Alaska by sea directly from Seattle. The simplest sequence involves catching the vehicular *Victoria Clipper* (in summer 3 daily; 3hr; $77 one-way for foot passengers; ☎1-800/888-2535, ⓦwww .victoriaclipper.com) from Seattle to Victoria on Vancouver Island. From Victoria, take a Laidlaw Coach Lines/Greyhound Canada bus (daily 5.30am; 10hr; Can$94; ☎250/385-4411, ⒺÏnit@island.net) to Port Hardy at the northern tip of the island; you'll have to spend the night here. BC Ferries

(☎1-888/223-3779, ⓦwww.bcferries.com) leaves Port Hardy every two or three days in summer (7.30am; high-season Can$172, small car Can$297; low-season Can$78–99/Can$180-227), taking around eighteen hours to reach Prince Rupert.

From the UK and Ireland

There are currently no direct routes from Britain or Ireland to Alaska; all flights require at least one change of plane, sometimes two or three. The main hub for international flights to Alaska is Seattle, though there are also routings via Chicago, Houston, Portland, Oregon, or Minneapolis/St Paul. In summer there's also the option of flying from London to Vancouver and then connecting directly to Alaska.

The **best selection** of flights is available between June and August, although flights run all year. Conversely, fares tend to be lowest in winter, and highest from June to August, though there is considerable variation depending on short-term demand and how far ahead you book. Peak-season fares from London to Anchorage are around £750, though you may find something as low as £600. There are also flights direct to New York and Chicago from Birmingham, Manchester, Glasgow, and Dublin, but prices are usually £150–300 higher than from London, so it makes sense to go via Heathrow or Gatwick. Ryanair and Aer Lingus have flights from Ireland to London for as little as £25 one-way.

From Australia and New Zealand

There are no direct flights from Australia or New Zealand to Alaska: all routes require at least one change of plane. The most popular route is across the Pacific to a West Coast city (Los Angeles, San Francisco, or Vancouver) followed by a connecting flight to Anchorage or a flight or ferry ride to one of the Southeast towns. Savings can be made by skipping the Lower 48 entirely and flying to Anchorage via Asia, though there are far fewer flights, and you may have to spend a night, or the best part of a day, in the airline's home city. Korean Air offers convoluted routes via Seoul, Tokyo, and Seattle; a better bet is China Airlines, which flies three times a week from Brisbane and Sydney to Anchorage via Taipei.

Fares don't vary greatly with season, though you may find they jump up by around $200 or so in July. The fares quoted below can often be undercut by short-term specials and discounts offered through airline websites and travel agents.

Multiday adventure tours

As a destination, Alaska encourages the grand gesture. Elsewhere, you might spend an afternoon rafting or hiking around some wooded area, but in Alaska you can build your entire vacation around a single float trip down an Arctic river or spend a week exploring Prince William Sound by sea kayak. In this box, we have brought together some of the best full-commitment adventure trips available.

As well as the activity-specific operators listed below, it is worth researching the Sierra Club (℡415/977-5522, ⓦwhistler.sierraclub.org/TripSearch), which organizes around two dozen trips a year, ranging from dog mushing (7 days; $3000) to backpacking (8–14 days; $2000–2325) to yachting (7 days; $4000). See also ⓦwww.alaska.sierraclub.org for day outings.

Many of the trips detailed here only run a few times a year (sometimes only once), and numbers are limited, so plan as far in advance as possible.

Sea kayaking

Anadyr Adventures ℡1-800/865-2925, ⓦwww.anadyradventures.com. Valdez-based kayaking company running assorted camping excursions in Prince William Sound (7 days; up to $1645), trips where you're based at a remote lodge (3 days; $1045), and "mothership" adventures involving kayaking during the day but spending the night on a motor yacht (6 days; $3600).

Pangaea ℡1-800/660-9637, ⓦwww.alaskasummer.com. Valdez-based tours, including guided camping excursions (two days around Shoup Glacier $410; eight days around Prince William Sound $1795) and "mothership" trips using either a sailboat (6 days; $1600 per day for a group of four) or motor yacht (4 days; $1800 per day for a group of four). They also offer hiking and ice climbing, as well as an eight-day multisport trip ($2060).

Southeast Sea Kayaks ℡1-800/287-1607, ⓦwww.kayakketchikan.com. Inclusive guided kayaking trips into Misty Fiords National Park from Ketchikan (4 nights; $1400), plus plenty of advice if you'd rather go alone.

Rafting and canoeing

Chilkat Guides ℡1-888/292-7789, ⓦwww.raftalaska.com. Haines-based company running trips on two rivers on the US/Canada border: the Alsek (13 days; $3395) and the Tatshenshini (10 days; $2895). They also run the Kongakut (11 days; $3995) in the Arctic National Wildlife Refuge.

GoNorth ℡1-866/236-7272, ⓦwww.paratours.net. Fairbanks-based operation organizing trips throughout the north. Particularly good for rafting and canoeing in the Brooks Range – North Fork of the Koyukuk (10 days; $2550) or the Middle Fork (5 days; $1640); Kobuk River (10 days; $2870); Noatak River (21 days; $3165); Sheenjek River in the Arctic National Wildlife Refuge (9 days; $2900); also hiking to the Arrigetch Peaks (6 days; $1975; add-on 6-day float trip $920).

Sourdough Outfitters ℡692-5556, ⓦwww.sourdough.com. Bettles-based five- to ten-day rafting trips in the southern Brooks Range – including the Noatak, John, and the North Fork of the Koyukuk. $2095–3100; shorter trips can be arranged from $350–450 per day plus flights.

Too-loó-uk River Guides ℡683-1542, ⓦwww.akrivers.com. Extended Denali-based wilderness raft trips, including the gentle Kongakut River through the Arctic

Seat availability on most international flights out of Australia and New Zealand is limited, so it's best to book as far in advance as possible.

Almost all the major US airlines, as well as Qantas, Air New Zealand, Air Canada, and others have flights or code-share flights across the Pacific, usually with connections

National Wildlife Refuge (10 days; $3800), the Class III–IV Chitina/Copper rivers (12 days; $2600), and the continuous Class III–IV Talkeetna (5 days; $1300).

Wilderness Birding Adventures ☎694-7442, ⓦwww.wildernessbirding.com. Based in Eagle River and operating five trips in ANWR in June, July, and August: rafting the Marsh Fork and Canning River (12 days; $3400) or the Kongakut River (10 days; $3400); canoeing the Lower Kongakut River and the Arctic Coast (9 days; $3200); six days at a base camp ($2850); and the Gray-headed Chickadee Float down the Canning River (7 days; $2600). Also kayaking off Kodiak Island and birding trips to Gambell and the Pribiloffs.

Dog-sledding

Denali Dog Sled Expeditions ☎683-2863, ⓦwww.earthsonglodge.com. Get deep into the heart of Denali National Park on tours run by former park ranger Jon Nierenberg in the November to January sledding season. Usually limited to two or three customers, trips range from basic day outings ($75–200 per person) and overnight jaunts ($600 per person per day), to multiday epics along the Stampede Trail (5 days; $2750–2900) and the Toklat River Loop (7 days; $4060).

Sourdough Outfitters (see above). Winter dog-sledding trips in the Brooks Range (4 days; $2100, or 7 days; $2800), around Arrigetch Peaks (11 days; $4000), and on the North Slope (April only; 7 days; $3100).

Cycling

Alaska Backcountry Bike Tours ☎1-866/354-2453, ⓦwww.mountainbikealaska .com. Single-track adventures in the Chugach National Forest near Anchorage – two days for $345–495, four days for $595–895, and six days for $995–1195, depending on accommodation choices; also multisport trips (6 days; $1595).

Alaska Cycling Adventures ☎245-2175, ⓦwww.alaskabike.com. Anchorage-based outfit mainly offering bike trips through the Interior, averaging 65 miles a day and staying in lodges and cabins with all meals provided (8 days; $2695).

Backroads ☎1-800/462-2848, ⓦwww.backroads.com. Active tours worldwide, including Alaska (July/August; 8 days cycling $3100; 6 days hiking $2400; 6 days multisports $1900–2700).

Multisport

Alaska Alpine Adventures ☎1-877/525-2577, ⓦwww.alaskaalpineadventures .com. Based in Port Alsworth (in Lake Clark NP), they operate trips to all of Alaska's National Parks.

Alaska Outdoors ☎1-800/320-2494, ⓦwww.travelalaskaoutdoors.com. Wasilla-based company offering hiking, rafting, and multisport trips; 7 days from $975, 10 days $1425–1645, 14 days Grand Combo $1945, 17 days $2400.

Mountain Travel-Sobek ☎1-888/687-6235, ⓦwww.mtsobek.com. Kayaking, rafting and multisport adventure tours worldwide, including Alaska trips operated under the name of **Alaska Discovery** (in Juneau; ☎1-800/586-1911, ⓦwww.alaskadiscovery .com). These include kayaking (3 days; $2195), multisport (8 days; $2790–3090), Denali National Park (4–8 days; $1200–2800), the Chilkoot Trail (7 days; $1990), a Wrangell-St Elias Glacier Expedition (8 days; $2690), Kongakut River (in ANWR; 8 days $3790; 10 days $4390), and rafting and hiking along the Hulahula River (21 days; $4700).

on to Anchorage. From **Australia**, fares to Alaska from eastern cities start around Aus$2500, while from Perth you'll pay at least Aus$2800. From **New Zealand** you'll pay around NZ$3000 to get to Alaska.

Airlines, agents, and tour operators

Online booking

ⓦ www.expedia.co.uk (in UK), ⓦ www.expedia .com (in US), ⓦ www.expedia.ca (in Canada)
ⓦ www.lastminute.com (in UK)
ⓦ www.opodo.co.uk (in UK)
ⓦ www.orbitz.com (in US)
ⓦ www.travelocity.co.uk (in UK), ⓦ www .travelocity.com (in US), ⓦ www.travelocity .ca (in Canada)
ⓦ www.zuji.com.au (in Australia), ⓦ www .zuji.co.nz (in New Zealand)

Airlines in the US and Canada

Air Canada ☎ 1-888/247-2262,
ⓦ www.aircanada.com.
Air France US ☎ 1-800/237-2747,
Canada ☎ 1-800/667-2747, ⓦ www.airfrance.com.
Alaska Airlines ☎ 1-800/252-7522,
ⓦ www.alaskaair.com.
All Nippon Airways (ANA) ☎ 1-800/235-9262,
ⓦ www.anaskyweb.com.
American Airlines ☎ 1-800/433-7300,
ⓦ www.aa.com.
America West See US Airways (now merged).
British Airways ☎ 1-800/247-9297,
ⓦ www.ba.com.
China Airlines ☎ 907/248-3603 or 1-800/227-5118, ⓦ www.china-airlines.com.
Condor ☎ 1-800/364-1667,
ⓦ www.condor.com.
Continental Airlines ☎ 1-800/523-3273,
ⓦ www.continental.com.
Delta ☎ 1-800/221-1212, ⓦ www.delta.com.
Frontier Airlines ☎ 1-800/432-1359,
ⓦ www.flyfrontier.com.
JAL (Japan Air Lines) ☎ 1-800/525-3663,
ⓦ www.jal.com or ⓦ www.japanair.com
KLM (Royal Dutch Airlines) See Northwest/KLM.
Korean Air ☎ 1-800/438-5000,
ⓦ www.koreanair.com.
Lufthansa US ☎ 1-800/645-3880, Canada
☎ 1-800/563-5954, ⓦ www.lufthansa.com.
Northwest/KLM US ☎ 1-800/225-2525,
ⓦ www.nwa.com, ⓦ www.klm.com.

United Airlines US ☎ 1-800/864-8331,
ⓦ www.united.com.
US Airways ☎ 1-800/428-4322,
ⓦ www.usairways.com.

Travel agents and tour operators in the US and Canada

Adventures Abroad ☎ 1-800/665-3998, ⓦ www .adventures-abroad.com. "Soft adventure" specialists with trips through western Canada to Alaska.
Alaska Discovery ☎ 1-800/586-1911, ⓦ www .akdiscovery.com. Experienced Alaska tour provider offering kayaking, hiking, bear-watching, whale-watching, and more.
Explore Tours ☎ 1-800/523-7405, ⓦ www .exploretours.com. A thorough, well-organized tour agent serving all of Alaska.
STA Travel US ☎ 1-800/781-4040, Canada
☎ 1-888/427-5639, ⓦ www.statravel.com. Worldwide specialists in independent travel; also student IDs, travel insurance, car rental, rail passes, and more. Good discounts for students and under-26s.

Airlines in the UK and Ireland

Aer Lingus UK ☎ 0870/876 5000, Republic of Ireland ☎ 0818/365 000, ⓦ www.flyaerlingus .com.
Air Canada UK ☎ 0871/220 1111, Republic of Ireland ☎ 01/679 3958, ⓦ www.aircanada.com.
American Airlines UK ☎ 0845/778 9789, Republic of Ireland ☎ 01/602 0550, ⓦ www .aa.com.
bmi UK ☎ 0870/607 0222, from Republic of Ireland ☎ +44 1332 648181, ⓦ www.flybmi.com.
British Airways UK ☎ 0870/850 9850, Republic of Ireland ☎ 1890/626 747, ⓦ www.ba.com.
Continental UK ☎ 0845/607 6760, Republic of Ireland ☎ 1890/925 252, ⓦ www.continental.com.
Delta UK ☎ 0845/600 0950, Republic of Ireland ☎ 1850/882 031 or 01/407 3165, ⓦ www.delta .com.
KLM/Northwest UK ☎ 0870/507 4074, Republic of Ireland ☎ 1850/747 400, ⓦ www.klm.com.
SAS Scandinavian Airlines UK ☎ 0870/607 2727, Republic of Ireland ☎ 01/844 5440,
ⓦ www.scandinavian.net.
United Airlines UK ☎ 0845/844 4777,
ⓦ www.unitedairlines.co.uk.
US Airways UK ☎ 0845/600 3300, Republic of Ireland ☎ 1890/925 065, ⓦ www.usairways .com
Virgin Atlantic UK ☎ 0870/380 2007, ⓦ www .virgin-atlantic.com.

Travel agents and tour operators in the UK and Ireland

Apex Travel Republic of Ireland ☎ 01/241 8000, ⓦ www.apextravel.ie. Specialists in flights to the US and consolidators for BA, American, and SAS Scandinavian.

Bridge the World UK ☎ 0870/443 2399, ⓦ www.bridgetheworld.com. Specialists in long-haul travel, with good-value flight deals, round-the-world tickets, and tailor-made packages, all aimed at the backpacker market.

Discover the World UK ☎ 8700/603 288, ⓦ www.discover-the-world.co.uk. Well-established wildlife holiday specialist, with groups led by naturalists to Alaska, among other places. Also offers small-ship cruises in Southeast Alaska.

ebookers UK ☎ 0870/010 7000, ⓦ www.ebookers.com; Republic of Ireland ☎ 01/241 5689, ⓦ www.ebookers.ie. Low fares on an extensive selection of scheduled flights and package deals.

Exodus UK ☎ 0870/240 5550, ⓦ www.exodus.co.uk; Republic of Ireland ☎ 01/804 7153, ⓦ www.abbeytravel.ie. Adventure tour operators taking small groups on specialist programs in countries around the world that take in walking, biking, overlanding, adventure, and cultural trips.

Flightcentre UK ☎ 0870/890 8099, ⓦ www.flightcentre.co.uk. Rock-bottom fares worldwide.

Flights4Less UK ☎ 0871/222 3423, ⓦ www.flights4less.co.uk. Good discount airfares. Part of Lastminute.com.

Flynow UK ☎ 0870/444 0045, ⓦ www.flynow.com. Large range of discounted tickets.

Holidays4Less UK ☎ 0871/222 3423, ⓦ www.holidays4less.co.uk. Discounted package deals worldwide. Part of Lastminute.com.

Joe Walsh Tours Republic of Ireland ☎ 01/676 0991, ⓦ www.joewalshtours.ie. Long-established general budget fares and holidays agent.

Lee Travel Republic of Ireland ☎ 021/427 7111, ⓦ www.leetravel.ie. Flights and holidays worldwide.

Maxwells Travel Republic of Ireland ☎ 01/679 5700, ⓔ maxwellstravel@eircom.net. Agent for a wide array of deals from adventure operators worldwide.

McCarthys Travel Republic of Ireland ☎ 021/427 0127, ⓦ www.mccarthystravel.ie. General flight agent.

North South Travel UK ☎ 01245/608 291, ⓦ www.northsouthtravel.co.uk. Friendly, competitive travel agency, offering discounted fares worldwide. Profits are used to support projects in the developing world, especially the promotion of sustainable tourism.

Rosetta Travel UK ☎ 028/9064 4996, ⓦ www.rosettatravel.com. Flight and holiday agent, specializing in deals direct from Belfast.

STA Travel UK ☎ 0870/160 0599, ⓦ www.statravel.co.uk.

Thomas Cook UK ☎ 0870/750 0512, ⓦ www.thomascook.co.uk. Long-established one-stop travel agency for package holidays, city breaks, or flights, with bureau de change issuing Thomas Cook branded travelers' checks, plus travel insurance and car rental.

Trailfinders UK ☎ 020/7938 3939, ⓦ www.trailfinders.com; Republic of Ireland ☎ 01/677 7888, ⓦ www.trailfinders.ie.

Travel Bag UK ☎ 0870/890 1456, ⓦ www.travelbag.co.uk. Discount deals worldwide.

Trek America UK ☎ 01295/256 777, ⓦ www.trekamerica.com. Walking and soft adventure tours all over North America including Alaska.

USIT Northern Ireland ☎ 028/9032 7111, ⓦ www.usitnow.com; Republic of Ireland ☎ 0818/200 020, ⓦ www.usit.ie. Specialists in student, youth, and independent travel – flights, trains, study tours, visas, and more.

World Travel Centre Republic of Ireland ☎ 01/416 7007, ⓦ www.worldtravel.ie. Excellent fares to Europe and worldwide.

Airlines in Australia and New Zealand

Air Canada Australia ☎ 1300/655 767, New Zealand ☎ 09/969 74702, ⓦ www.aircanada.com.

Air New Zealand Australia ☎ 132 476, New Zealand ☎ 0800/737 000, ⓦ www.airnewzealand.com.

Air Pacific Australia ☎ 1800/230 150, New Zealand ☎ 0800/800 178, ⓦ www.airpacific.com.

American Airlines Australia ☎ 1300/650 747, New Zealand ☎ 0800/887 997, ⓦ www.aa.com.

China Airlines Australia ☎ 02/9231 5588, ⓦ www.china-airlines.com.

Korean Air Australia ☎ 02/9262 6000, New Zealand ☎ 09/914 2000, ⓦ www.koreanair.com.

Qantas Australia ☎ 131 313, New Zealand ☎ 0800/808 767 or 09/357 8900, ⓦ www.qantas.com.

United Airlines Australia ☎ 131 777, ⓦ www.united.com.

Travel agents and tour operators in Australia and New Zealand

Adventure World Australia ☎ 02/8913 0755, ⓦ www.adventureworld.com.au; New Zealand ☎ 09/524 5118, ⓦ www.adventureworld.co.nz. Individual and small-group trips with small-boat cruises and packages combining train trips, and kayaking and wilderness experiences.

Canada & America Travel Specialists Australia ☏ 02/9922 4600, ⊛ www.canada-americatravel .com.au. North American specialists with Alaska expertise in accommodation, train travel, adventure sports, car and motorhome rentals, cruises, escorted tours, independent travel, and more.

STA Travel Australia ☏ 1300/733 035, New Zealand ☏ 0508/782 872, ⊛ www.statravel.com. **Trailfinders** Australia ☏ 1300/780 212, ⊛ www .trailfinders.com.

Cruising Alaska

The most relaxed way to experience Alaska's stupendous scenery is undoubtedly on a cruise. With accommodation, transport, meals, and activities mostly taken care of, you can just lie back and take in the sights, or join in with all manner of on-ship and on-shore fun. It is possible to spend a small fortune on a cruise, but the major operators are fiercely competitive, and there are bargains to be had.

What you gain in ease of travel on a cruise you lose in flexibility, with most routes being a fairly similar circuit of the main Southeast and Southcentral ports. Usually the boats sail overnight, then stop to allow passengers to explore on shore during the day before gliding off again in the evening. The **cruise season** is essentially late May to early September, though a few boats venture north a couple of weeks either side of the main rush. If you want a blend of cruise luxury and independence, you'd be wise to travel north by land and return with one-way fare on a southbound ship, against the flow of most visitor traffic.

Types of cruises

The majority of Alaska's visitors arrive on a **big-boat cruise**, sailing on some of the world's largest pleasure craft. While fares may seem quite high, remember that they generally include all accommodation, 24-hour dining, nightly entertainment, and full use of ship's facilities (pools, gyms, and the like). Several ships carry 3000 passengers and over 1000 crew, and place as much emphasis on the on-board experience as the place you're visiting. When one (or several) of these behemoths arrives in a tiny Southeast port the whole dynamic of the town changes, giving a somewhat distorted impression of what the place is about. Shore visits can be very packaged and perfunctory, though there's usually a huge array of activities on offer (for a fee) – from whale-watching to flightseeing over a nearby glacier to town tours in a horse-drawn carriage. The same tours (or more relaxed independent ones) are usually available at a far lower cost on the dockside, although the ship won't wait if you're delayed. In addition, the cruises themselves now continue on shore, with luxury trains and road coaches whisking passengers directly from the dock to hotels owned by the cruise companies; this is especially the case in Denali National Park.

A less commercial alternative is a casual **small-ship cruise**, typically with 50 to 150 fellow passengers. The range of on-board facilities and distractions is narrower than on the big boats, but comfort isn't sacrificed, and the focus tends to be more on the destination. Companies such as American Safari, Clipper, CruiseWest, Glacier Bay Cruises, Polar Cruises, and Tauck sometimes stop in remote places, giving a more intimate view of Alaska; they can enter smaller waterways and get closer to wildlife. Some even head around the coast up into Arctic waters or over to the Russian Far East. These activities are more likely to be naturalist-led trips ashore than the big-boat excursions are.

Schedules and fares

Generally, you cruise in one direction and fly into or out of Anchorage for the other leg. There are some circular cruises, and occasionally people simply stay on board for both legs. Although many cruises start from Vancouver, British Columbia, there are now ships that can fit in a two-week circuit from Seattle (a week each way). Most routes are variations on the standard cruise: a seven-night run up the Inside Passage with stops in Ketchikan, Sitka, Juneau, Skagway, and at one of the big tidewater glaciers, before finishing the run in Seward or Whittier.

Fares vary enormously. Shop around and you'll see newspaper and Internet offers for seven-night big-boat cruises for as little as $700. You can book these directly through the cruise lines' websites, or through agents and cruise brokers. The standard fares offered by cruise lines for a week-long trip start around $1800 for a twin-share in an interior cabin. Ocean-view room rates start at $2300, and for balcony rooms you'll be looking at $3000–9000. There are usually **discounts** for early- and late-season sailings, and a saving of thirty percent or more can be had for bookings made several months in advance. Small-ship cruises are generally more expensive, though because of the size of ship all rooms usually have ocean views. One-week trips start around $3000, but there are three-night trips for $1100, and plenty of two-week expeditions with rates from around $5000, often including a one-way flight from Seattle to Juneau or Sitka.

Cruise companies

American Safari Cruises ☎1-888/862-8881, ⓦwww.amsafari.com.

Celebrity Cruises ☎1-800/647-2251 (North America), ☎0800/018 2525 (UK), ⓦwww.celebritycruises.com.
Clipper Cruise Line ☎1-800/325-0010, ⓦwww.clippercruise.com.
CruiseWest ☎1-888/851-8133, ⓦwww.cruisewest.com.
Glacier Bay Cruises ☎1-800/451-5952, ⓦwww.glacierbaytours.com.
Holland America ☎1-877/724-5425, ⓦwww.hollandamerica.com.
Norwegian Cruise Line ☎1-800/327-7030 (USA), 0845/658 8010 (UK), ⓦwww.uk.ncl.com.
Polar Cruises ☎1-888/484-2244, ⓦwww.polarcruises.com.
Princess ☎1-800/7746-2377, ⓦwww.princess.com.
Royal Caribbean ☎1-866/562-7625, ⓦwww.royalcaribbean.com.
Tauck ☎1-800/788-7885, ⓦwww.cruise-travel.tauck.com.

Cruise brokers

Alaska Cruise Center ☎1-800/977-9705, ⓦwww.akcruises.com.
American West Steamboat Company ☎1-800/434-1232, ⓦwww.americanweststeamboat.com.
Cruise Holidays of Anchorage ☎1-800/566-7447, ⓔcruiseholidays@customcpu.com.
Cruise Holidays of Vancouver ☎1-800/565-2784, ⓦwww.alaskacruiseexperts.com.
Cruise Planners, Inc. ☎1-888/275-3788, ⓦwww.greatcruising.com.
The Cruise Web, Inc. ☎1-800/377-9383 (ext 286), ⓦwww.cruiseweb.com.
GalaxSea Cruises ☎1-800/357-9393 or 1-800/544-4009, ⓦwww.galaxseacr.com
Richmond Cruiseshipcenter ☎1-888/237-0111 (free in the US or Canada), ⓦwww.richmondcruiseship.com.

Getting around

When traveling around Alaska it is not unusual to ride ferries, buses, and trains, drive a rental car, cycle, fly, or hike. Come winter, and you may well ski, ride a snowmobile, or drive a dog team. Whatever your mode of transportation, getting around is liable to take up a fair bit of your time and money, but don't treat it as a hardship – often the journey is as enjoyable as the destination.

All of Alaska's mountain ranges, glaciers, and vast stretches of boggy wilderness put up significant barriers to ground transportation, ones only surmounted by taking to the air or water. Consequently, Alaskans **fly** more than anyone else in the world – you should follow suit if you want to reach remote villages, or even just do some flightseeing. Although much of Alaska is inaccessible to road traffic, the Kenai Peninsula, the Interior, and the region around Fairbanks all have a fair **highway** network, though some sections are best viewed from the **train** line. For many visitors, the highlight of their trip is making use of the **ferry system**, which links over thirty ports, mostly in the Southeast "panhandle," but also around Prince William Sound, the Kenai Peninsula, and west to the Aleutian Islands. Thoroughly relaxing, they leisurely thread their way through narrow channels and across deep sounds where whales and dolphins make regular appearances.

If you stick to the roads and ferries, **transportation costs** won't be especially high, considering the distances involved. Start flying out to remote bush communities, though, and you'll soon start racking up the bills. A tour of Anchorage, the Kenai Peninsula, Denali, and Fairbanks can be done cheaply on buses and trains, though if you ever want to get off the beaten path you'll need to rent a car. Expect to pay $50–70 a day for a compact – perhaps more if your own vehicle insurance doesn't cover you; this can be a good investment, as it enables you to stay in cheaper out-of-town motels, or perhaps pull off the road and camp for nothing. **Savings** can also be made by investing in an **AlaskaPass** (see box, p.30), which combines Alaska Marine Highway System (AMHS) ferries, the Alaska Railroad, the White Pass & Yukon Route railway, and Holland-America Motorcoaches.

Domestic flights

The statistics for small planes in Alaska are astounding: roughly one in every sixty Alaskans is a certified pilot, and almost all of these pilots own their own planes. That is something like six times as many pilots and fourteen times as many planes per capita as the rest of the United States.

Clearly, flying is the quickest – and sometimes only – way to get around, since surface travel is hampered by long distances, impassable mountain ranges, and inconveniently sited bodies of water. **Short flights** can save you a lot of time, and, sometimes, money. For example, to get from Juneau to Anchorage you can wait for the twice-monthly ferry to Whittier and then catch the bus or train (taking two days in all), or fly for ninety minutes at a lower cost. Services between the larger towns are mostly run by Alaska Airlines, though in some areas flights are contracted out to partners such as ERA and PenAir. If any of these carriers fly to your destination, this will almost certainly be the cheapest way to go. Otherwise it is difficult to pin down exact **fares**, which vary enormously depending on demand and how far in advance you can reserve. In general, the most expensive fares are those bought less than two weeks in advance: a fourteen-day advance purchase will save perhaps thirty percent. On some routes buying a ticket 21 days in advance will cut almost forty percent off the walk-up rate. **One-way tickets** are generally half the round-trip fare, and it is always worth checking for specials on the Alaska Airlines website.

Anchorage is very much the hub of operations; if you stick with Alaska Airlines, you'll be continually shuttling back to the big city. Sometimes, though, smaller airlines work out to be more convenient. For example, if you want to get from Kotzebue to Barrow, you could fly via Anchorage on Alaska Airlines or more directly by taking local bush flights.

Scheduled services from Anchorage and Fairbanks to the larger remote communities, such as Nome, Barrow, and Dutch Harbor, carry mail, newspapers, and essential supplies. These places rely so heavily on air deliveries that you may well find yourself on a 737 Combi almost entirely given over to freight, with only two dozen seats left for passengers.

Scheduled airlines

Alaska Airlines/Horizon Air ☎1-800/252-7522, ⓦwww.alaskaair.com. The main regional airline, with flights to all major towns in Alaska and frequent out-of-state flights to Chicago, Denver, Los Angeles, Portland, San Franciso, and Seattle, plus from Seattle to Boston, Dallas, Miami, and New York, as well as Puerto Vallarta and eight other Mexican destinations. Also maintains an extensive Pacific Northwest network through Horizon Air.
Andrew Airways ☎907/487-2566, ⓦwww .andrewairways.com. Flights from Anchorage to Kodiak.
ERA Aviation ☎1-800/866-8394, ⓦwww .flyera.com. Alaska Airlines partner, with flights from Anchorage to Cordova, Homer, Iliamna (summer only), Kenai, Kodiak, and Valdez.
Frontier Flying Service ☎1-800/478-6779, ⓦwww.frontierflying.com. Major bush operator (not to be confused with Frontier Airlines, which flies from Denver to Anchorage), with regular services to small communities all over Alaska's north and west – Anaktuvuk Pass, Barrow, Deadhorse, Dillingham, Fort Yukon, Kotzebue; also Anchorage–Fairbanks 3 or 4 times a day.
Grant Aviation ☎1-888/359-4726, ⓦwww .flygrant.com. Flights from Anchorage to Homer and Kenai.
Hageland Aviation ☎1-866/239-0119, ⓦwww .hageland.com. Flights from Anchorage to Barrow, Barter Island, Bethel, Deadhorse, Kotzebue, and Nome.
PenAir ☎1-800/448-4226, ⓦwww.penair.com. Alaska Airlines partner covering the Southwest and Aleutians with flights from Anchorage to Dillingham, Dutch Harbor, King Salmon, the Pribilof Islands, Unalakleet, and lots of regional feeders.

Bush planes

You cannot truly appreciate Alaska without experiencing the workhorse of Alaskan transportation: the **bush plane**. It sometimes seems that there isn't a place in the state that these planes won't land, and hair-raising stories of pioneering touchdowns on postage-stamp lakes and crevasse-riddled glaciers are legion. Some planes have floats for lake and river landings or bulbous tundra tires for rough-field and gravel-bar touchdowns, while others have skis for snow and glaciers, with ordinary wheels to land on gravel airstrips. Even international airports like Anchorage and Fairbanks are designed to cope with all types of landing gear: the main tarmac runway is flanked by another for light planes and a float pond.

Many bush flights run on regular schedules, using larger towns as hubs for services to tiny villages. Timetables are more flexible, and **fares** more stable, than on the intercity routes. You'll also come across dedicated mail flights that briefly visit three or four communities and often have a few seats for passengers.

Apart from these regular services, **chartered bush planes** are the only way to get to some of the real gems of the great Alaskan outdoors. Some operators charge an hourly rate (typically $350–400 per hour for a five-seater), some a flat rate even if they have to try again due to bad weather, so it pays to look at costs and conditions when planning a bush flight. The price is usually for the plane and pilot, with little or no extra cost for additional passengers. Pack your gear in relatively small bags as weight distribution is crucial; heavy items and bear spray, camping fuel, etc, will often be stowed in the floats.

Arranging a flight is usually no problem, given the long hours of daylight in summer, but reserving in advance is always a good idea. Companies aim to fill their flights, and if you are going somewhere popular, the outfit may well do this for you; the more remote the destination, however, the more you'll have to organize this yourself. Remember that unless they have found a return fare, you are paying for the plane until it gets back to base, though when flying to USFS cabins you can almost always share the cost with the previous occupants flying out.

There are a number of **precautions** to consider when arranging to be picked up. Firstly, make sure you can get to the designated spot. Hiking across tundra is slow going and apparently benign rivers can turn out to be impassable. Weather can make it impossible for your pilot to reach you at the arranged time and, with supplies running low, it is comforting to know when subsequent attempts will be made. Your pilot will probably return to the designated spot later on (or the next day), but it is essential to have a clear **contingency plan** understood by all parties. With this in mind, make sure you don't have any pressing engagements (like international flights) immediately after bush trips.

Pilots know their patch very well and will only arrange to pick you up somewhere they know they can land, but it always pays to check. Spring break-up (mid-April to late May) severely limits water landings in the Interior, and around the coast you should consider the **tides** to ensure the pilot can get close in to the shore.

Ferries

Traveling through Southeast Alaska, you'll almost certainly make extensive use of the **Alaska Marine Highway System** (AMHS; see box for contact info). This state-run network of eleven vehicular ferries provides the principal means of transport between 34 ports in Southeast and Southcentral Alaska. Our chapter maps (p.92, p.254, p.310, and p.342) show the routes and ports of call. In general, the ferry system has daily departures from major ports and perhaps one or two a week in each direction from smaller places. The main problem with the AMHS system is that it operates in two separate sections: Southeast, which extends from Bellingham, WA, to Haines and Skagway, and Southcentral/Southwest, which covers Prince William Sound, the Kenai Peninsula, Kodiak Island, and the Aleutians. One ferry does make connecting **"cross-gulf" trips** between Juneau and Whittier, continuing to Kodiak, but only every two weeks from May to mid-September. If you don't catch these, you'll have to fly or go by road through Canada to make the link.

Ferries tend to be in port for only a short time (1–3hr) and many of the Southeast ferry docks are inconveniently sited several miles from the heart of town, making it difficult (if not impossible) to get a feel for the place if you're traveling onward. To this end, building **stopovers** into your itinerary is fairly necessary, and should be done in advance; buy a series of journeys between your chosen ports of call rather than, say, Bellingham to Juneau. If you have bought such a ticket and then decide to make extra stopovers, alterations can be made for a fee, which varies according to the changes. This will also affect your reservations, an important consideration in the busy summer months.

For details of ferry connections from Bellingham, WA, and through British Columbia, see pp.30–31.

AMHS ferry contact numbers

To plan and reserve your ferry travel contact the Alaska Marine Highway System, 6858 Glacier Hwy, Juneau, AK 99801-7909 (☎1-800/642-0066 Mon-Fri 7.30am–4.30pm), or consult their website ⊛www.ferryalaska.com or www.dot.state.ak.us/amhs/index.html, which has schedule and fare information along with details of how to make reservations. Locally, call the numbers listed below:

Anchorage	☎272-7116	**Petersburg**	☎772-3855
Bellingham, WA	☎360/676-8445	**Prince Rupert, BC**	☎250/627-1744
Cordova	☎424-7333	**Seldovia**	☎234-7868
Haines	☎766-2113	**Sitka**	☎747-3300
Homer	☎235-8449	**Skagway**	☎983-2229
Juneau	☎465-3940	**Valdez**	☎835-4436
Ketchikan	☎225-6181	**Wrangell**	☎874-3711
Kodiak	☎486-3800		

New and fast ferries

In 2004 AMHS began a modernization program and introduced catamaran ferries. These still carry vehicles but travel twice as fast as the classic vessels, with the result that visitors now have more flexibility when touring Southeast Alaska and Prince William Sound.

The first of the new ferries serves Juneau, Haines, Skagway, and Sitka; the second, Whittier, Valdez, and Cordova. There are also plans for a road up the east side of the Lynn Canal to a new terminal at the Katzehin River, 90 miles north of Juneau, from where ferries would make frequent short hops to Skagway and Haines.

In addition, the long-standing AMHS monopoly on Alaskan ferry service is being broken. Prince of Wales Island now runs its own routes from Ketchikan, Wrangell, and South Mitkof, near Petersburg (see pp.93, 121, and 137), operated by the Inter-Island Ferry Authority; and the Chilkat Cruise Fast Ferry runs between Haines and Skagway, up to 26 times a day. A similar fast ferry should be operating from Anchorage to Point Mackenzie by mid-2008, and then possibly to the Kenai Peninsula.

On-board facilities

All vessels carry vehicles and passengers, though other facilities depend on the boat in question. The new fast ferries do not operate at night and have no **cabins**; instead they have airline-style seats, an external **solarium**, work/study areas, satellite phones, and a snack bar.

The older ferries are more oriented towards leisurely cruising, all having coin-operated lockers for your valuables and somewhere to lay down a sleeping roll. All except the *LeConte* and *Aurora* have cabins, most with private bathrooms, from $15 for a two-person roomette (Skagway–Haines) to $562 for a two-berth with sitting room (Bellingham–Skagway). If you can't afford a cabin on the longer journeys, obtaining a good place to sleep becomes critical, to the point that in Bellingham it can be a mad dash for the top-deck solarium, widely regarded as a prime spot for its fresh air, good views, and nighttime peace. Some people even erect tents on the upper deck; if you attempt this, make sure you secure it firmly against the stiff breezes that come up when underway. Except for brief visits to attend to pets, passengers are not allowed on the vehicle deck when sailing, so sleeping in your RV is not an option.

Lounges have reclining seats, and pillows and blankets can be rented for a modest fee on most sailings. There are hot **showers** (either free or coin-operated), and some boats even have a laundry room. In addition, there are usually free educational programs run by "interpreters" from the Tongass National Forest, as well as films and Alaska videos. The ferries have GPS position displays, and trials are under way with WiFi Internet access.

The **meals** available in the ship's buffet-style restaurant are pretty good and reasonably priced by Alaskan standards. The larger boats also have a bar. You are welcome to lug aboard your own supplies (they provide free hot water or a microwave) but use of backpacking stoves is strictly prohibited.

Timetables, reservations, and fares

When it comes to planning your travels it is imperative that you get hold of up-to-date **timetables**, which depend on the tides. The May to September summer schedule is published early in the year: download it from the website or pick up a free brochure locally. Even so, you will find that mechanical and logistical issues and, occasionally, industrial action can play havoc with the schedule; it always pays to check departure times with the nearest office.

During the summer, vehicle space and cabins fill up quickly, so reserve a place as far in advance as possible. In practice, foot passengers can often wend their way through the Southeast without making any **reservations**, though it is still wise to book ahead. The AMHS website allows **online booking**, though if you have a complex itinerary it may be quicker to call the toll-free number, or send in your requirements by fax or mail. Print out the reservation form on the website, or simply list the relevant details: the journeys required; number, names, and ages (if under 12) of those in the party; width, height, and overall length

Ferry fares

			Kodiak 284	Seldovia 346 78
Ketchikan*	232	58		
Wrangell	252	84	36	
Petersburg	270	96	58	32
Sitka	292	124	80	58
Juneau	316	152	104	84
Haines	342	172	130	104
Skagway	352	184	142	118
Tenakee	316	152	104	84
	Bellingham	**Pr. Rupert**	**Ketchikan***	**Wrangell**

Prices are in US dollars and valid for ages 12 and older.
* Metlakatla is a side trip from Ketchikan, $24 each way.

of any vehicles; a mailing address and phone number; alternate travel dates; and the date you plan to leave home. Ask to be put on a waitlist if your requested itinerary is full. Cabin waitlists exist for trips north from Bellingham, Juneau to Whittier, and west to the Aleutians; vehicles can only be wait-listed on the latter two.

We've included 2007 passenger fares on the accompanying chart, but prices are subject to change – check the AMHS website (see box, above) for the latest info. The total fee is arrived at by adding together the various components – passenger fares, **cabins**, vehicles, and so forth. **Kids'** fares (6–11 inclusive) are roughly half of the adult fare, and kids under 6 travel free. Cabins start with a two-berth room (0.8 times the adult fare) and range up to a large four-berth affair (1.4–1.7 times the adult fare). A small **car** (up to fifteen feet long) will cost twice the adult passenger fare, something up to 21 feet will be three times, and a **bicycle** travels for one-sixth of the adult fare. On cross-gulf trips, adult passengers travel from Juneau to Whittier for $214.

Trains

Mention that you are traveling on the **Alaska Railroad** and Alaskans will usually mumble something about never having gotten around to riding it. This is largely because train travel in Alaska is something of a luxury, except for the few hundred people who live close to tracks and rely on the train for access to town, and because there is just one passenger line,

a 470-mile run through the heart of the Interior from Seward to Fairbanks. Nonetheless, riding the Alaska Railroad is an experience cherished by the state's summer visitors, who make up the vast majority of the passengers. As with the ferries, there has been considerable investment in the railroad in the last few years, with GoldStar first-class service introduced on the *Denali Star* in 2005, new stations at Anchorage airport, Denali Park, and Fairbanks, some track realignment, and plans to rebuild the downtown Anchorage station by 2011, possibly leading to an Anchorage/Mat-Su suburban service at some point.

Services along the line are both infrequent and slow, pretty much precluding their use as practical transport, but the stately pace and matchless scenery make the Alaska Railroad the most pleasurable way to get to the few places it does reach. Note though that **fuel** cannot be taken on trains, so campers will need to purchase it between disembarking from the train and heading into the wild. With so much of Alaska's tourist industry tied in to the major cruise and package companies it comes as no surprise to find that most trains are largely made up of luxurious, dedicated Princess, Royal Celebrity, and Holland America carriages. Independent travelers will find themselves getting jounced along in less salubrious cars; they're still very spacious, air-conditioned, and comfortable, but with high-back seats set so low you'll have to stand up to get a good view of the scenery. The upper-deck **observation car** (for twenty minutes at most at one time), and the **dining**

Homer	Whittier	Valdez	Cordova	
340	440	408	408	Unalaska
72	88	142	142	Kodiak
32	158	200	200	Seldovia
	154	196	196	Homer
		86	86	Whittier
44			48	Valdez
64	44			
86	64	36		
98	74	48	30	
64	34	34	58	70
Petersburg	Sitka	Juneau	Haines	Skagway

car, which sells good food at reasonable prices (snacks and drinks $2–5, meals $11), also have good views. Don't try to hang out in the dining car at lunchtime, though – it fills up quickly. The journey is accompanied by a running commentary, and there's also a gift shop. In GoldStar class you ride in reclining seats in a full-length dome (with no time limit, but hand luggage is restricted) with an open platform at the rear; free drinks and a gift bag are provided, and there's a restaurant with the same menu and prices as the regular restaurant car. **Tickets** can be bought in advance by mail, by phone, or online from Alaska Railroad Corporation, PO Box 107500, Anchorage, AK 99510-7500 (☎1-800/544-0552, ⓦwww.alaskarailroad. com), but seats are not allocated until just before you travel; check in (with photo ID) at the station half an hour early.

Alaska's only other train service is the **White Pass & Yukon Route railway**, used primarily by sightseeing day-trippers, which climbs the mountains behind Skagway as it follows a route used by Klondike gold seekers. It is covered in detail on p.198.

Anchorage to Denali and Fairbanks

The main train between Anchorage and Fairbanks is the **Denali Star** (daily mid-May to mid-Sept), which departs Anchorage at 8.15am, stops at Wasilla (9.45am), Talkeetna (11.25am), Denali Park (3.45pm), and Nenana (5.45pm; flag-stop only) before arriving in Fairbanks at 8.15pm. In the opposite direction the daily service leaves Fairbanks at 8.15am and calls at Nenana (10am; flag-stop only), Denali Park (noon), Talkeetna (4.40pm), Wasilla (6.05pm), and Anchorage (8.15pm). The **Hurricane Turn** "flag-stop" service also runs during the summer (mid-May to mid-Sept Thurs–Sun plus holiday Mondays), but only the 55 miles from Talkeetna (departing 12.15pm) to Hurricane and back (arriving 5.45pm). Designed to fit the needs of bush dwellers, this service claims to be the last of its kind in the US – would-be passengers pull up their canoes and off-road buggies next to the tracks and wave a white sheet to get the train to stop. The route runs through pretty swampy country, and is therefore of little use to hikers, but good for anglers.

Two services also run in winter; firstly the **Aurora** (mid-Sept to mid-May), a flag-stop train – usually just two carriages with luggage and buffet cars – running from Anchorage to Fairbanks on Saturday, returning south on the Sunday. In addition, the *Hurricane Turn* (Oct to May first Thurs of the month only) runs round-trip from Anchorage to Talkeetna and Hurricane. There are no other weekday trains.

Fares are one-way and depend on whether you travel during the peak season (early June to Aug), the value season (mid-May to early June and the first two weeks in Sept), or in winter, when there are discounts for those over 65. Children aged 2–11 travel for about half-price all year. From Anchorage to Fairbanks the fares are $185 peak, $148 value, $130 winter. There are also section fares: Anchorage–Talkeetna ($108,

$63, $50); Anchorage–Denali ($129, $103, $86); Talkeetna–Denali ($75, $61, $50); Talkeetna–Fairbanks ($106, $85, $80); and Denali–Fairbanks ($56, $45, $38). *The Hurricane Turn* costs up to $39 each way ($30 in winter). You're allowed one carry-on bag and two free checked bags (up to 50lb each, plus two more at a price). Bikes, canoes, and kayaks are carried at a cost of $20 per trip (free in winter). If these prices seem too steep, consider making only the run from Talkeetna to Denali, the most spectacular section. If, on the other hand, you want a bit more comfort, GoldStar service costs $105 extra from Anchorage to Fairbanks, and $85 for all intermediate segments.

Alternatively, you can book with **Alaska Rail Tours** (☎1-800/628-3843, ⒲www .alaskarailtours.com) and ride on the same train in 1950s dome cars (beautifully restored, with satellite-controlled audio commentary), with the option of returning by bus; fares can actually be less than regular ARR coach fares.

Anchorage to Seward

If you head **south from Anchorage**, the line passes the wildlife-viewing area of Potter Marsh along Turnagain Arm to Portage Junction, from where the Whittier Spur runs through a couple of tunnels to Whittier. The main line continues through the Placer River valley and into the Kenai Mountains before following the broad Resurrection Valley to Seward.

The **Coastal Classic** (mid-May to mid-Sept daily) runs south from Anchorage, leaving at 6.45am and arriving in Seward at 11.05am. The return service leaves Seward at 6pm and arrives back in Anchorage at 10.15pm, giving day-trippers almost seven hours in Seward; fares are $62 one-way or $103 round-trip, bikes $5.

A separate service, the **Glacier Discovery** (mid-May to mid-Sept daily), leaves Anchorage at 10am for Whittier arriving at 12.20pm. It continues to Spencer and Grandview, where rafting packages are available. Returning, it leaves Whittier at 6.45pm and gets into Anchorage at 9.30pm. The fare is $55 one-way, $68 round-trip, and $5 for bikes. Unlike the *Coastal Classic* and *Denali Star*, this train has no dome car. In summer special trains

carry cruise passengers from Seward or Whittier to Anchorage airport, and, for Princess passengers, to Denali Park. There are no services south of Anchorage in winter.

Buses

Most of the blacktop roads in Southcentral and Interior Alaska have **scheduled services** on the blacktop roads from early May to mid-September. There is usually only one bus a day in each direction (if that), making bus travel possible but not very flexible. The main exception is the 360-mile run from Anchorage to Denali National Park, which is plied by several buses each day. Companies are notoriously short-lived, so it pays to check who is operating and pick up the relevant timetables from visitor centers when you reach Alaska. Detailed coverage of routes, frequency, and journey times is given in "**Travel details**" at the end of each chapter. Bus stops (usually visitor centers, major hotels, and hostels) are noted in town accounts.

Almost all companies use minibuses seating 20–30 passengers. Competition along the Anchorage–Denali–Fairbanks route keeps fares low, with most operators offering similarly priced tickets. Nonetheless, it is worth shopping around, as there are bargains to be had, and companies have different timetables. Expect to pay $90 between Anchorage and Fairbanks; $45 from Fairbanks to Denali; $65 from Anchorage to Denali; $100 from Fairbanks to Valdez; $165 from Fairbanks to Dawson City, Yukon; $45 from Anchorage to Seward; and $60 from Anchorage to Homer. Round-trip rates are usually twice the one-way fare, or at best about ten percent less. Most services will call at Anchorage airport, for a supplement of about $5.

Bus companies and their routes

Alaska Direct Bus Line ☎1-800/770-6652, in Anchorage ☎277-6652, ⒲www.tokalaska.com. One service (mid-May to Sept 3 days a week) from Anchorage to Whitehorse via Palmer, Glennallen, Tok, and Haines Junction, where you can transfer onto a bus to Haines. A service from Fairbanks meets the Whitehorse-bound bus at Tok, and another bus connects Whitehorse to Skagway.
Alaska Park Connection ☎1-800/266-8625, ⒲www.alaskacoach.com. A daily run in each

direction (mid-May to mid-Sept) between Seward, Anchorage, Talkeetna, and Denali; a daily run from Anchorage to Seward and back (mid-May to mid-Sept); and an express run from Anchorage to Denali and back (June to early Sept).

Alaska/Yukon Trails ☎1-800/770-7275, ⓦwww.alaskashuttle.com. From May to September, daily runs along the Parks Highway. Southbound buses stop around Fairbanks (8–9am), and at Denali Park (noon), Talkeetna, and Anchorage (6pm; the airport at 6.30pm). Northbound buses stop around Anchorage (6.30–7am) and arrive in Fairbanks by 4pm. From October to April, southbound services on Sunday, Tuesday, and Friday; northbound on Monday, Wednesday, and Saturday. There are also services from Fairbanks to Dawson City (Canada) (mid-May to mid-Sept Sun, Tues, and Thurs; returns Mon, Wed, Fri), via Tok and Chicken; and from Dawson City to Whitehorse (Sun, Tues, and Thurs; returns Mon, Wed, and Fri), connecting with Greyhound Canada (☎1-867/667-2223 or 1-800/661-8747, ⓦwww .greyhound.ca).

Homer Stage Line Anchorage ☎868-3914 or 563-0800, Homer ☎235-2252, Soldotna ☎262-4584, ⓦwww.homerstageline.com. Round-trips between Anchorage and Homer (June–Aug daily; May & Sept Mon, Wed, & Fri; Oct–April Mon & Thurs to Anchorage, Tues, & Fri to Homer) and Anchorage and Seward (mid-May to mid-Sept Mon–Fri).

The Magic Bus ☎268-6311, ⓦwww .themagicbus.com. Daily runs from Anchorage (leaves the *Captain Cook Hotel* at noon, also picks up at the visitor center) to Whittier and Girdwood.

Seward Bus Line Seward ☎224-3608, Anchorage ☎563-0800, ⓦwww.sewardbuslines .net. Year-round, daily: departs Seward 9.30am, arrives Anchorage noon; departs Anchorage 2.30pm, arrives Seward 5.30pm.

Talkeetna Shuttle Service ☎1-888/288-6008, ⓦwww.denalicentral.com. Door-to-door service between Anchorage and Talkeetna, once daily in summer and more frequently during the mid-April to mid-June mountaineering season.

Driving

Whether you make the epic journey up the Alaska Highway, or simply rent a vehicle on arrival, **driving** is the best way to explore Southcentral Alaska, the Interior, and parts of the North. You can visit places beyond the reach of public transport, set your own timetable, and access points of interest in the larger towns much more easily. What's more, two or more people traveling together and renting a car can save a fair bit of money by staying in cheaper but less central accommodation, or camping out pretty much anywhere.

Road conditions (☎511 or 282-7577, ⓦwww.511.alaska.gov) vary enormously, from six-lane freeways in Anchorage and Fairbanks to remote gravel roads with a hundred miles between settlements. If you come in summer and stick to the paved highways, you'll find driving pretty easy,

---

Tips for foreign drivers

In most cases, a **driver's license** from your home country is valid for ninety days in the United States; check with your national motoring organization if you have any questions. Driving is on the **right**; you can turn **right on red** at intersections provided there is no oncoming traffic, unless signage specifically prohibits it. **Seatbelts** are compulsory for all passengers (but helmets are not required on motorbikes). The **speed limit** ranges from 25–45mph in urban areas to 55–65mph on major highways. Driving with **headlights on** during daytime is required only along the Seward Highway between Anchorage and Seward, but many people light up as a matter of course. You must stop when you come upon a **school bus** with its lights flashing, disgorging passengers.

If the **police** flag you down, don't get out of the car or start searching for your license; simply sit with your hands on the wheel and wait for an officer to approach. Of course, **driving while intoxicated** (DWI) is a very serious offense, and if you are carrying any alcohol it should be kept unopened in the trunk.

Foreign drivers who are members of motoring organizations may find they can get reciprocal membership at the **American Automobile Association** (AAA; main AK office: 1005 E Dimond Blvd, Suite 2A, Anchorage 99501 ☎1-888/391-4222; also at 3409 Airport Way, Fairbanks 99709 ☎479-4442, ⓦwww.aaa-mountainwest.com); check with your home organization.

with broad highways and shoulders and lots of left- and right-turn lanes. Stray onto dirt roads and you need to slow down and take some precautions against moose and frost heaves – though you should keep your eyes peeled wherever you drive. **Snow** is possible any month of the year, especially on a few high passes, namely Thompson Pass (p.469), Isabel Pass (p.471), and Broad Pass (p.412); the asphalt roads are kept open year-round, but many of the gravel highways are impassable by September, when winter really begins to show its face. If in doubt, don't travel. If you must, then take it slow and be sure you have survival gear in case of an accident or breakdown.

Gas is priced about the same as in the Lower 48 – basic unleaded (fine for most rental vehicles) is currently around $2.70 a US gallon in Anchorage and Fairbanks, $3 further out, and over $3.50 in remote spots. At most gas stations you can use a credit card to pay at the pump, even if it is unattended.

Renting a car

Renting a car in Alaska is not cheap, but the freedom it affords is worth the price. The competition in Anchorage keeps the rates there low, but you can rent a car in almost any town – this can be handy if you are using public transportation but want to take a side trip somewhere otherwise inaccessible, like the hotsprings around Fairbanks.

Reserve well in advance for a summer rental: a month should be enough. Arrive in June without a reservation and you'll be lucky to find anything available, let alone affordable. Plan to drop off your rental where you picked it up: few places allow one-way rentals, and those that do charge high **relocation fees** ($200 between Anchorage and Fairbanks; $400 between Anchorage and Haines or Skagway). Some companies don't allow you to go into **Canada**, so make sure you are clear on this when you make your reservation. Note that Canadians are not allowed to drive a US rental car into Canada, either.

The biggest factor to consider when renting is whether you will want to drive on **gravel roads**. Most agencies refuse to insure or provide logistical backup once you stray from paved highways, but seeing many of Alaska's finest features requires travel along unpaved roads, like the road to McCarthy in the Wrangell-St Elias National Park, Taylor Highway to Chicken and Eagle, Elliott Highway to Manley Hot Springs, and Denali Highway along the southern side of the Alaska Range.

There are a few ways around this potential sticking point: the best is to rent a car from Affordable Rentals (listed in our Anchorage and Fairbanks accounts) or a camper from GoNorth in Fairbanks (see p.523), which rent almost-new cars at affordable prices and allow them to be used (and insured) on all roads except the Dalton Highway north of the Yukon River and the Top of the World Highway from Chicken to Dawson City in the Canadian Yukon.

A second alternative is to simply ignore the rental company's rules. This is a common enough practice, but remember that even if you have insurance independent of the rental agency, the fact that you are breaking the rental agreement by driving off the paved highways is likely to invalidate your insurance: should you get in trouble, no one is going to organize a mechanic for you, and you'll have to pay any costs out-of-pocket. The last option is to **rent a 4WD** vehicle, some of which can be insured for gravel roads. The downside here is that you'll pay at least twice the daily rate of an ordinary compact (say, $100–130 a day). Car rental agencies fall into two main groups. The **majors** – Avis, Budget, Dollar, Hertz, National, Payless, and Thrifty – all rent new compacts for around $45–55 a day plus tax with unlimited mileage in summer. **Local companies** are usually about $5–10 a day cheaper in return for slightly (sometimes substantially) older vehicles and a poorer backup network. We've listed the best of these at the end of major town accounts (especially Anchorage on p.247 and Fairbanks on p.523), and you'll find more in the local *Yellow Pages*. Many companies offer **weekly rates** (typically seven days for the price of six), though in peak season the savings may be less. Rental companies advertise prices exclusive of **local taxes**: expect to have 10–20 percent added to listed prices (29 percent at Anchorage airport).

Insurance may raise your car rental fees further. If you have your own vehicle insurance at home, it is worth checking if it provides any coverage for rentals (either with or without some extension fee). There are no hard-and-fast rules, but most US policies will cover you in Alaska. It's also worth checking to see if your credit card provides any cover. Quite likely you will find you have available a collision damage waiver (CDW, sometimes called Liability Damage Waiver), a form of insurance well worth considering, as it covers you for damage to your vehicle. It may cost $12–30 a day (around $16 average), but otherwise you are liable for every scratch to the car – even those that aren't your fault. Often CDW comes with several levels of coverage, the cheaper ones leaving you liable for, say, the first $1000–2000 of any claim, while the more expensive policies cover you for everything. Always make sure you understand the fine print.

You'll need to be 21 or over to rent a vehicle, and many places won't rent you one if you're under 25. Even if they do, you will have to pay an additional $5–10 a day.

Car rental companies

Alamo ☎1-800/462-5266, ⊛www.alamo.com.
Avis ☎1-800/331-1212, ⊛www.avis.com.
Budget ☎1-800/527-0700, ⊛www.budget.com.
Dollar ☎1-800/800-4000, ⊛www.dollar.com.
Enterprise ☎1-800/261-7331, ⊛www. enterprise.com.
Hertz ☎1-800/654-3131, ⊛www.hertz.com.
National ☎1-800/227-7368, ⊛www .nationalcar.com.
Payless ☎1-800/729-5377, ⊛www .paylesscarrental.com.
Rent-A-Wreck ☎1-800/944-7501, ⊛www .rent-a-wreck.com.
Thrifty ☎1-800/367-2277, ⊛www.thrifty.com.

Renting an RV

In summer Alaskan roads and campgrounds are thick with **RVs** (recreational vehicles). Some have been driven up the Alaska Highway or transported by ferry up the Inside Passage, but most are rented in Alaska (principally Anchorage) from any of a dozen or so agencies, although a good number are actually owned by Alaskans, who use them as bases for their hunting and fishing trips.

Deciding to rent an RV isn't something to be undertaken lightly: summer rental rates (based on a minimum one-week rental period) start at around $130 a day for a model that's comfortable for two – plus a lot of gas (some RVs achieve under ten miles per gallon).

Some companies charge premium all-in rates, while others cut corners on their basic rates but add assorted extra charges – it is always worth asking. You might get fifty or a hundred **free miles** (especially during shoulder season) but most likely you'll pay 15–20¢ a mile. Insurance is often included, but there may be a $1500 deductible on accidents; a collision damage waiver ($12–15 a day) will reduce this to a couple of hundred dollars or less.

Unless you've lugged half your kitchen with you, there may also be a fee for a "housekeeping" kit of pans, plates, bedding, and towels; this might cost a few dollars a day or just a $100 flat fee, and TVs, deck chairs, fishing rods, and bike racks may be included or extra. All this is offset, of course, by the reduction in accommodation costs. Instead of $70–100 a night in a motel you can get away with $20–30 a night in a campground, or nothing at all parked by the side of the road. Some RV-rental companies include 24-hour roadside assistance, and may even offer a free pass for camping in state parks and selected commercial campgrounds around Alaska.

RVs, or motorhomes, come in several sizes: some are lumbering behemoths that are the bane of everyone else on the road, while others, though less spacious, are relatively nimble. Generally, the smallest RV offered is the camperhome (roughly $130–180), essentially an eighteen-foot pickup truck with a camper strapped onto the back. These sleep two adults reasonably comfortably (and perhaps one child) and have a toilet and cooking stove, though not much wiggle room. A compact ($140–200) measures around 21ft and sleeps two adults and two kids in some comfort. The 23-foot **standard models** ($150–215) are more spacious, with a higher level of fittings and appliances. Two (or even three) couples traveling together might prefer a 26-foot intermediate ($180–230) or 30-foot large ($200–240) model. The prices quoted above are for summer high season; rates drop by twenty to thirty percent in May and September, and are reduced a little further in winter. You'll pay around ten percent more if your rental is for less than a week. AAA and AARP members (American Association of Retired People; ⓦwww.aarp.org) typically get a five percent discount. The **minimum age** for drivers varies from 21 to 25. If five or more vehicles are following you, Alaska law requires you to move over at the first pullout to let them pass.

As with car rentals, you'll need to make **reservations** early (three months ahead isn't ridiculous at peak times). **One-way rentals** are not usually worthwhile, though some companies will let you pick up or drop off a vehicle in Fairbanks for a $750 fee, or Skagway for $1200. If you are headed north in May, it is worth calling around for a delivery run (try ABC to start with); you may be able to drive a new RV from the Lower 48 at around seventy percent of the normal rate. If you are bringing your own RV to Alaska but don't want to drive both ways, consider shipping your rig (see p.28).]

All of the companies listed below are based in Anchorage (phone code ☎907), where there's an eleven percent tax; all offer airport transfer.

RV rental companies

ABC Motorhome & Car Rentals 3875 W Old International Airport Rd ☎1-800/421-7456, ⓦwww.abcmotorhome.com. Large company renting late-model RVs. Summer rates (including everything but gas) are $190 a day for an upscale camper with shower and toilet, $210 for a compact, $240 for a standard, and $270 for an intermediate model. One-way rentals available from Elkhart, Indiana, and Seattle, Washington, in May (from $130 per day), and back from mid-Sept to mid-Oct (from $90, both with a ten-day minimum and unlimited mileage).

Alaska Camper Adventures 801 E 82nd Ave ☎1-888/552-5238, ⓦwww.alaskacamperadventures .com. Small pickup-based campers (fits a family of four). $125 per day in May and early June and Sept–Oct; $160 from mid-June to Aug, plus tax.

Alaska Motor Home Rental 4900 Homer Drive ☎1-888/660-5115. New motorhomes with good shoulder-season and winter discounts. Standard models from $170 in peak season, intermediate $190, and huge 34-foot beasts for $255 a day, plus tax and $0.17 a mile (or $30 per day unlimited mileage).

Alaska Motorhome Rentals at Ship Creek Landing RV Park, 150 N Ingra ☎1-800/254-9929, ⓦwww.alaskarv.com. Compact models from $95 per day (for 21-plus days mid-April to mid-May and mid-Sept to mid-Oct) to $199 (six days or less in Aug), intermediate RVs for $105–205, large RVs $115–215. Also one-way Skagway drop-offs.

Alaska Vacation Motorhome Rentals 8825 Runamuck Place, no.3 ☎1-800/648-1448 ⓦwww.alaskavacationmotorhomerentals.com. Pickup-based campers: $70 per day in May and from mid-Sept to mid-Oct, $100 in early June and from mid-Aug to mid-Sept, and $155 from mid-June to mid-Aug; mid-size vehicles cost $80/110/165 or $90/120/185, and the largest 29-foot vehicles cost $100/130/195, all plus tax, $0.17 per mile (or $30 per day unlimited mileage), and $90 for rentals of less than a week.

Clippership Motorhome Rentals 5401 Old Seward Hwy ☎1-800/421-3456 ⓦwww .clippershiprv.com. Standard campers cost $160–190 per day for 4–6 days, $150–180 for 7–17 days, and $145–175 for 18 days or more, plus tax and $0.15 per mile (or $185–215, $175–205 and $170–200 with unlimited mileage). Economy rigs cost $20 per day less and luxury ones $15 per day more; from Sept to May there's a discount of $30 per day plus 100 free miles per day. One-way rentals available

---

Addresses and mileposts

Larger Alaskan towns follow the grid system used elsewhere in the country, whereby the Anchorage address 3901 Old Seward Highway would be at the intersection of Old Seward Highway and 39th Avenue. In rural areas every Alaskan highway – Alaska, Richardson, Glenn, George Parks, Taylor, and so on – is demarcated by mileposts marking the distance from the town regarded as the beginning of that highway. Addresses along that highway are simply given as the milepost reading to the nearest tenth of a mile. Also, in the US, what would be the ground floor in Europe is the first floor, the first floor the second floor, and so on; Suite #801 will be on the eighth floor.

from Anchorage to Fairbanks ($550), Seward ($380), and Whitehorse, Skagway, or Haines ($1150).

Cruise America 8850 Runamuck Place
☎1-800/671-8042 or 1-800/327-7799 (one-ways), ⓦwww.cruiseamerica.com. One of the biggest operators in the business with a huge range of vehicles at relatively high prices.

Great Alaskan Holidays 9800 Old Seward Hwy
☎1-888/225-2752, ⓦwww.greatalaskanholidays .com. Rigs with all the extras included. Rates can be with unlimited mileage (compact $100–190, large $128–230) or charged at $0.17 a mile ($70–160/$103–205).

Murphy's RV Rentals 5300 Eielson St
☎1-800/582-5123, ⓦwww.alaskaone.com /murphyrv/reservations.htm. Rates range from $150 to $225 per day plus $0.20 per mile and tax.

Cycle touring

You can also get around Alaska by **bicycle**. Cycling can be a wonderful experience, giving you plenty of time to savor the stunning scenery and long summer days, but it can also be a major slog – it all depends on where you go and how ambitious your plans are. Southeast Alaska is especially well suited for cycle touring since you can take your bike on the **ferries**, then easily explore the few miles of road around each port of call. You have to be a bit more dedicated to cycle in the Interior, where points of interest are further apart and surfaces can be rough once you get off the main roads. However, major road construction projects must now include **bike paths**, so increasingly long sections of path exist beside main highways.

You can rent bikes in the state's larger towns ($20–30 a day), but if you're planning on doing extensive touring it's better to bring your own wheels. Most international airlines will carry bicycles either free or for a small charge. Some companies will ask you to remove the pedals, deflate the tires, lower the saddle, and turn the handlebars ninety degrees; others will demand you break your bike down to fit into a cardboard bike delivery box (usually available free from your friendly local bike dealer) – ask before you fly. Surprisingly, Alaska Airlines is not bike-friendly, insisting on the box approach and charging US$50 per bike for each day you fly, so take this into consideration if planning multiple flights throughout the state. You can usually take your bike with you on public

---

Rough Guide favorites: cycle touring routes

Copper River Trail p.456
Denali Highway p.439
Denali Park Road p.427
Hatcher Pass p.395
McCarthy Road p.454
Prince of Wales Island p.113
Top of the World Highway p.483

---

transportation, where it exists (buses free in the cities, around $10 per long-distance trip; trains $5–20 per journey), which means you don't need to pedal every mile just to get to the good bits.

If you plan to stick entirely to **paved roads**, you'll do well with either a touring bike or an ATB fitted with narrower tires. Of the paved road routes, the Kenai Peninsula is probably the most rewarding, with wonderful scenery, challenging terrain, and relatively short distances between towns. For something longer, try going from Anchorage to Valdez (with a possible side-trip to McCarthy), followed by a ferry ride to Whittier, Seward, or Homer and some time on the Kenai Peninsula. The George Parks Highway from Anchorage to Fairbanks is perhaps the busiest and least appealing main route, though you can skip sections by taking a bus or train; from Wasilla (take a Mascot bus from Anchorage) there's a good cycle track as far as Willow, well engineered and away from the highway. Many points of interest require you to do a little off-roading, or at least spend some time on the state's myriad gravel roads. In both cases, fat-tired mountain bikes should be your two-wheeled conveyance of choice. You'll appreciate good suspension and forgiving frame dimensions on prime routes like those listed in our favorites box (see above) and on long gravel stretches, like the Steese and Elliott highways around Fairbanks, the Taylor Highway up to Eagle on the Yukon River, and even the Dalton Highway to Prudhoe Bay (lengthy and esoteric but possible).

To be fully prepared, you should be kitted out for rain in the coastal areas, cold in the Interior, and bugs whenever you stop. **Spare parts** are thin on the ground outside

Anchorage and Fairbanks, so be sure to carry anything you might reasonably need – tubes, cables, spokes, and the like. One thing you probably won't need if you are here in the middle of summer is lights: it barely ever gets dark.

For more detailed information on cycling through Alaska, consult the *Alaska Bicycle Touring Guide* by Pete Praetorius and Alys Culhane (Denali Press), and Richard Larson's *Mountain Bike Alaska* (Glacier House).

Hitching

Unlike the rest of the US, Alaska enjoys a reputation for relative safety among hitchhikers. The official advice remains "**don't hitch**," but with the state's skeletal public transport network many choose to do so anyway, if only to get back to their car at the end of a long hike. Alaskan drivers are generally well disposed to pick up hitchers, and finding a good hitching spot is usually just a matter of walking towards the edge of town and using your common sense: pick a spot where you

can be clearly seen and drivers can stop safely. That said, there just aren't many drivers, and along gravel roads (where hitching is more common) you could wait hours without seeing anyone.

Keep in mind that despite its hitcher-friendly image, Alaska, like anywhere else, has its share of unpleasant individuals. To this end, always travel in pairs (no guarantee of avoiding trouble, but safer than going solo). **Women**, especially, should trust their instincts. It is better to refuse a lift than regret it later; there will always be another vehicle at some point. Always ask the driver where they are going, rather than telling them where you are headed, and keep your gear with you so you can make a quick getaway if it becomes necessary. Remember, too, that even the most helpful driver may drop you in the middle of nowhere with the weather deteriorating. You should really be fully equipped for a night out by the roadside or make sure you can be dropped somewhere you can seek food and shelter.

Accommodation

Accommodation in Alaska is generally warm, welcoming, and often comes with a superb view and maybe even a moose or bear strolling past your bedroom window. Unfortunately, accommodation prices are quite steep year-round, and especially in July and August, when high demand allows hotels to ratchet the rates up even higher. If money is tight, consider spending a few nights in one of the increasing number of hostels or a US Forest Service cabin. Camping, too, is a big money-saver, and nowhere near as cold as you might expect, particularly in the middle of summer, when you've got close to 24-hour daylight. Off-season rates can be half the summer rate, and even May and September can offer some savings.

Roadhouses, hotels, and motels

The backbone of Alaska's accommodation has traditionally been the **roadhouse** (❸–❹) – all-in-one hotel, bar, restaurant, and stable establishments that cropped up along the trails used by miners and mail carriers. Most

have closed now, but a few still fly the flag in rural areas, typically offering warped floors, shaky beds, thin walls, a shared hall bath, and bags of character. Several have been taken over by proprietors who really care about institutional legacy, and have gone to some lengths to provide hearty food and a

Accommodation price codes

Accommodation listed in this book has been price-coded using the symbols below. The rates quoted represent the **cheapest** double or twin **room** in high season. Single rooms generally cost only 10 to 20 percent less. Fees for **tent sites** and cabins are quoted, and are for the site or cabin unless otherwise stated. **Hostel** bed prices are also quoted. Additionally, in most Alaskan towns there will be local and bed taxes, which typically add 4 to 12 percent to the quoted price.

In **winter** you can generally expect prices to drop by one (or possibly two) price codes except for hostels and campgrounds, which generally don't vary much, if at all.

❶ up to $50	❹ $80–100	❼ $160–200
❷ $50–65	❺ $100–130	❽ $200–250
❸ $65–80	❻ $130–160	❾ $250 and over

convivial common area. After campgrounds and hostels, these are often the cheapest places to stay, at around $70–90 per room.

As communities in the fledgling territory consolidated, roadhouses were replaced by **hotels** (❻–❾). A few original, independent operations still exist in the larger towns, but these days the market is dominated by faceless corporate chains catering to businesspeople and package tourists. Standards are as high as you would expect, but prices are higher: in peak summer months you won't get a room in a top-line Anchorage hotel for under $200, sometimes $250. Off-season, and especially on winter weekends, such places are almost empty and prices drop dramatically: haggle a bit, and you might find yourself with a tremendous bargain.

Almost invariably, though, you are better off in a **motel** (❹–❻). These tend to string out along approach roads into urban areas, but since most towns are pretty small this isn't much of an inconvenience. A few belong to chains, but most are independently run, with standards varying little. All offer private bathrooms, cable TV, phone, Internet access, and, increasingly, free WiFi, all for $90–140 a room. Pay a little more, and everything will be newer, larger, and you may possibly have a kitchenette or hot tub. That said, if you've got that sort of money then there is usually somewhere nicer to stay.

Hostels

For a roof over your head at minimal cost, **hostels** (❶–❷) are your only viable option. With dorm beds going for as little as $10

($20–25 is more normal) and some establishments offering basic double rooms for under $60, you can't go wrong. The only hitch is that hostels are thin on the ground: Anchorage and Fairbanks are reasonably well supplied and several smaller towns have a hostel, but in many regions you can go for hundreds of miles without finding one.

Historically, some Alaskan hostels have been members of the worldwide organization Hostelling International (ⓦ www.hiusa .org), though none are currently members. All hostels are operated independently, though many promote themselves through the **Alaska Hostel Association** (ⓦ www .alaskahostelassociation.org).

For the most part, hostels are very simple, with each having its own distinct character and rules. Some close during the day (usually 10am to 5pm), maintain a curfew (typically 11pm), have separate men's and women's dorms, or expect you to do a small morning chore. Others are part of people's homes, so their character and quality are dependent on the owner, and the restrictions are often looser with similarly varied effects. In general, though, the standard is high and many stay open all day.

You'll usually be allowed to use your own sleeping bag, though a few places insist on **sheets**, which can be rented on site. No Alaskan hostels currently offer meals, but all provide **cooking facilities**. As with any other accommodation, **reserve** well in advance, directly with the hostel, especially during the summer.

B&Bs

If you're on a budget but tents and hostel bunks aren't for you, **B&Bs** (❹–❼) may be your best bet. They're usually cheaper than hotels or motels and the host may well be your best introduction to the region, either helping plan your travels or just clueing you in to more about the state's idiosyncracies. And of course there's breakfast – many establishments offer substantial meals that can keep you going past lunchtime. Summer room **rates** start around $80 (with genuinely swanky places charging perhaps $120–150), although there is occasionally a small supplement for stays of only one night. In winter many places close, but those that stay open might drop their rates by around thirty percent.

As ever, it is usually advisable to **book a few days ahead** (weeks if you want one particular B&B), though if you'd rather remain flexible you can get help from visitor centers, which often call around the local area on the day and know what's available. We've picked many of the best B&Bs, but for a wider selection consider browsing specialist websites such as Ⓦwww.bbonline.com/ak and Ⓦwww.bedandbreakfast.com/Alaska.html.

Campgrounds

It is quite possible to see most of Alaska without going near a campground, but spending nights out of doors is so much part of the Alaskan experience that it seems unsporting to spend every night in comfort. Although you may plan on sticking to more rigid forms of shelter, it is still worth bringing a tent: it's the best way to feel in tune with all that wilderness, and besides, the high price of everything else might just force your hand.

Though backcountry camping (see "Outdoor activities," p.65) draws its share of visitors to Alaska, it's not the only way to camp – there are some wonderful campgrounds strung along the highway system for those not ready to head out across the tundra. You'll occasionally come across free campgrounds, with pit toilets and nearby river water (which needs to be treated), but most campgrounds cost between $6 and $12 per site – typically allowing up to two vehicles and as many as ten or a dozen

people. These grounds are usually separated into campsites, with picnic tables, fire rings, a hand pump for drawing water, and an outhouse (not traditional wooden shacks over holes, but concrete structures cleverly designed to minimize odors).

Most places have car parking next to the site, but a few campgrounds have peaceful **walk-in sites**, where you must leave your vehicle a few yards away. During the summer, many of the more popular places have a campground host, who will come around and make sure you've paid your fees – though sometimes you just drop the money in an "iron ranger," a metal post with a slot in it. The more spacious campgrounds are large enough to cope with all but the biggest **RVs**, and offer "dry parking" – basically just a place to park with water and toilets accessible nearby. From there you can step up to private campgrounds with proper showers and toilet blocks and varying degrees of connectedness: electrical hookup, piped water, and finally full hookup with wastewater pipe, cable TV, and a modem jack or WiFi. Full RV hookup usually costs $28–35, but those using tents can also stay in such places for just $15–20.

Cabins

Though a tent will undoubtedly give you maximum flexibility in the wilderness, spare yourself lugging the thing around by staying in **public-use cabins** (❶). They're not intended to be used for a sequence of overnight stops, but rather as a short-term base, with users flying or boating in, then exploring the area on foot or by canoe, with an arrangement to be picked up several days later: a true wilderness experience without much struggle.

Several land-management authorities operate cabins, but the **US Forest Service** (USFS) leads the pack, maintaining over 200 throughout the Southeastern panhandle (in the Tongass National Forest) and South-central Alaska (in the Chugach National Forest). Usually, the cabins are in scenic or remote spots, sometimes beside a trail, but frequently only accessible by float-plane or boat. Ketchikan, Petersburg, Sitka, Juneau, Cordova, and Seward are the closest access points to the majority of cabins, several of

Reserving campsites and cabins on public land

With so many authorities managing public lands in Alaska, booking cabins and campsites can be confusing. To simplify the task, we've listed the main players below. All agencies that manage cabins on public lands throughout the state can be accessed from the APLIC website at ⑩ www.nps.gov/aplic/cabins.

Campgrounds

Bureau of Land Management All campgrounds on BLM land are first-come, first-served; there is no booking system.

Denali National Park See "Reserving in advance" box, p.418.

National Forests There are a handful of campgrounds in the Chugach and Tongass national forests that can be booked through the National Recreation Reservation Service (see cabins information below).

State Parks and **State Recreation Areas** With the exception of Eagle River campground (see p.222) there is no reservation system for campgrounds in state parks. All others are first-come, first-served.

Cabins

Bureau of Land Management The BLM's eleven public cabins ($20 per night on weekends, $15 during the week; credit cards accepted) in the White Mountains north of Fairbanks can be booked up to 30 days in advance by phone (☎472-2251 or 1-800/437-7021). Alternatively, write or turn up in person at BLM Public Room, 1150 University Ave, Fairbanks, AK 99709. Stays are limited to three consecutive nights. Only one of these cabins (and the nearby Fred Blixt cabin; see p.534) are available in summer. Information about the cabins can be found at the White Mountains website (⑩ www.blm.gov/ak/whitemountains/cabins.htm).

National Forests Chugach and Tongass. Roughly 200 cabins ($25–45 a night, mostly $35 in summer, $25 in the off-season) can be booked using a credit card up to 180 days in advance through the National Recreation Reservation Service. Call ☎1-877/444-6777 or 518/885-3639 (daily April–Aug 8am–midnight, Sept–March 10am–7pm EST) or see ⑩ www.reserveusa.com. The website also has some details about the cabins.

State Parks and **State Recreation Areas** Around 55 recreational cabins all over the state, sleeping three to eight people for $25–75 a night (mostly $45 peak and $30 off-peak). Peak rates apply on Friday and Saturday throughout the year, daily from May to September and over Christmas, New Year's, and Easter. The state parks website (⑩ www.alaskastateparks.org) has stacks of information on location, facilities, and cost. There are no phone reservations, so book online (up to six months in advance), or go in person or write to the Department of Natural Resources office (DNR Public Information Center, 550 W 7th Ave, Suite 1260, Anchorage, AK 99501-3557; ☎269-8400). Booking forms can be printed out from the website, payment should be by check or money order made out to "State of Alaska," and there's a maximum stay of between three and seven days.

which are listed in the text. A full rundown of cabins, their features, access, and availability can be found on the Internet (see box, above) or through the various USFS ranger district offices, which we've listed in the text for each town.

The cabins themselves ($25–45 per night) tend to be clean but fairly primitive, typically sleeping four to six on wooden bunks

and coming equipped with a wood-burning stove for heating. There'll be an outhouse, water nearby that needs treating, and possibly a canoe or rowboat. You bring everything you'd need for camping except a tent. The cabins are very popular with Alaskans, and many are in great demand during hunting and fishing seasons. Ideally you should book several months in advance, but with some flexibility and a willingness to visit the less popular areas, you can usually find something pretty amazing, especially midweek.

Wilderness lodges

Throughout this book you'll read about large pieces of wilderness without so much as a managed trail. This is all true, except for the presence of dozens of **wilderness lodges** built on the dream of a charmed life in the Alaskan backcountry. The great majority cater to the rod-and-gun set, who hunt and fish in barely charted territory but stay in beautifully sited lodges or in cabins around a central lodge where gourmet meals are served. Access is usually by float-plane, with average stays of 3–7 days, often on a package with everything thrown in, including fishing guides and daily flights to remote rivers.

Of course, all this pampering comes at a price, which can be anywhere from $200 to $800 per person per day, with many places offering three-day packages in the $1200–2500 range, and seven-day packages for around twice that. We've listed a few in the appropriate sections of the Guide, but if you are especially interested in this kind of experience then check out websites like Ⓦwww.theoutpostmall.com/alaska.htm and Ⓦwww.alaskafishguides.com, which have links to dozens of such places.

A few lodges wear the **ecotourism** badge, though many of these are fishing lodges going by another name. For guidance here, contact the Alaska Wilderness Recreation and Tourism Association, 2207 Spenard Rd, Suite 201, Anchorage, AK 99503 (☎258-3171, Ⓦwww.awrta.org).

Food and drink

Salmon, halibut, and king crab, lightly cooked, simply dressed, and served within hours of being hauled from cold Alaskan waters, is a culinary highlight worth traveling for. Catch it yourself, and the pleasure is doubled. After that things go downhill pretty rapidly, and in many parts of Alaska it seems like there is only one menu endlessly recycled, with the prices getting higher the further away you get from the transport lines. You'd better like burgers, sandwiches, pizza, and clam chowder.

There is no hiding it: food in Alaska is expensive. The growing season is short but intense, and despite the high latitude people do manage to grow **huge vegetables**. The trouble is, few can grow things reliably enough to suit wholesalers, so most of what you (and restaurants) buy comes direct from Seattle either by barge up the Inside Passage, or by air freight. This adds to **costs** that are already inflated because of high wages. Additionally, the range is often limited; most Alaskan communities are small – even large dots on the map might only represent a thousand people – and can't support establishments that

cater to anything other than the mainstream demands. Still, for short visits the selection is varied enough, and at its best the quality can be outstanding.

Alaskan specialties

Alaska doesn't have a distinctive cooking style, but its cuisine stands apart in its use of local ingredients. The biggest treat is the abundance of **fresh seafood** plucked from the waters around the coast or hauled out of the super-rich inland rivers. Mention Alaska and many foodies' thoughts quickly turn to **salmon**: for over a century, the five species of Pacific salmon (see Contexts, p.604, for further discussion of salmon) have been canned in Alaska and shipped all around the world. As salmon stocks have declined, so has the number of canneries, though a few still exist at remote locations. Most salmon is now vacuum-packed for export or frozen ready for delivery to restaurants, the main exception being the **Copper River kings**, the early-season catch (at the beginning of June) being whisked off to Seattle restaurants where they're on a plate within hours of being caught. The better restaurants around the state serve salmon fresh, usually simply prepared, perhaps grilled over alder. It is listed on the menu along with the species – typically **king (chinook), red (sockeye), or silver (coho)** – and sometimes the river where the fish was caught. Freezing robs the fish of some of its delicacy, but if you are sticking to cheaper places and diners, that's what you're likely to get, often stuffed in a burger or even as salmon balls, batter-dipped and deep-fried.

Of equal importance on every Alaskan menu is **halibut**, a white-meat flat fish that grows to enormous proportions (over 400 pounds is possible), though it's the meat from twenty- to forty-pound specimens (known as "chicken halibut" for its tender flesh) that ends up on dinner plates, typically as a char-grilled fillet or wedged into a sandwich. Either way, the delicate flesh is superb. You'll also find more exotic fruits of the sea, such as clams, most commonly in a chowder, and crab, sometimes king or, more likely, Dungeness.

Most Alaskans spend at least some of the year dining on the fruit of their hunting expeditions, principally moose, caribou, and, to a much lesser degree, bear. Though largely absent from restaurant menus, you may taste these meats at a private barbecue or salmon bake, or one of the tourist-oriented dinner shows, where the gold-rush stage entertainment is accompanied by tasty morsels designed to mimic the pioneer diet.

Gold prospectors and early trappers aimed to lighten their hard and tasteless bread by using a **sourdough culture**, a yeasty concoction passed from one generation to the next. There are people in the state who claim their sourdough is a distant relative of one that some ancestor carried over the Chilkoot Pass or Valdez Glacier. Sourdough bread remains popular and can be wonderful dunked into a steaming pot of clam chowder. Almost any diner will give you the option of sourdough bread for your sandwich and will also have sourdough pancakes served up for breakfast. One local delicacy to look out for in May is the **fiddlehead**, the still-unopened head of a fern that is used in salads and even as a pizza topping in some of the more adventurous restaurants.

You are more likely to hear about **Eskimo delicacies** than taste them. Unlike most Alaskans, Natives are permitted a subsistence harvest of sea mammals, such as seals and whales. If you are in a northern coastal town like Barrow or Kotzebue during the spring or fall hunting seasons, you may see a kill. Once a whale has been butchered, it is brought in from the sea ice, and some of the blubber, or muktuk, is distributed in the community, and sometimes to visitors. Seal oil was once a staple in the North and still gets used in Native villages, sometimes for Eskimo ice cream, or akutug, a confection in which it is combined with caribou or reindeer fat (though often vegetable oil these days), sugar, and water, fluffed up into a sorbet and served in a sea of ice and berries – something of an acquired taste.

Restaurants

The **diner** is pretty much the mainstay of the Alaskan culinary scene. This is where you'll come for **breakfast** ($5–10), the most filling and often the best-value meal of the day. The most common dish is eggs cooked any way you like, though pancakes are another favorite. More upmarket joints may also offer French toast, eggs Benedict, or *huevos rancheros*. Most meals come with as much weak **filter coffee** as you can stomach.

Breakfast is sometimes available all day, but often stops at 11am when the **lunch** menu takes over. Midday staples are soups – usually clam chowder plus one other – sandwiches, and burgers, in a variety of guises. **Sandwiches** are often served with a packet of chips (not fries), though of course fries are always available. Most diners offer a soup and sandwich combo ($8–10) or the more manageable soup and half-sandwich ($6–8). Favorite sandwiches include BLTs, tuna melts, and the French dip – a chunk of toasted French bread with meat *au jus*.

In larger towns diners often close around 4 or 5pm, but in small communities diners are the social center, and tend to stay open much later, serving plates of steak, salmon, and halibut ($16–25), usually with potatoes and vegetables. The main course is typically preceded by salad topped with a choice of dressings – blue cheese, Italian, ranch, and thousand island being the most common. If you see something described as a **dinner**, you'll get soup as well as the main course. There will probably also be Caesar salad ($8–12), pasta dishes ($13–18), and pizza ($10–16) with a huge variety of toppings. **Dessert** is typically fruit pie ($3), sometimes homemade, with a fabulous range of fillings – cherry, blueberry, chocolate, lemon meringue. The only significant difference between diners and Alaskan restaurants is that the latter are liquor-licensed, though sometimes just for beer and wine (about $4 a glass and up). Meals are usually delivered in huge portions, but most places are happy to "box up" your leftovers.

Relief from diner-fare boredom can be found at a **salmon bake**, sometimes just a restaurant with a menu heavy on salmon and halibut dishes, but more likely an outdoor venue, or well-ventilated but bug-proof enclosure, where they dish up an all-you-can-eat salmon and halibut feast which extends to ribs, caribou stew, baked potatoes, and a salad bar, usually for $18–25. These are most common in the tourist haunts of the Southeast, though Anchorage, Fairbanks, and a few other places sometimes get in on the act. Relatively small numbers of **ethnic restaurants** are scattered around the state, many of them very authentic and run by native Mexicans, Chinese, Thai, and Vietnamese. In smaller towns they may well feel compelled to augment their menu with burgers, pizza, and pasta dishes, and sometimes lose their focus entirely. Chinese and some Thai places can be especially good value with heaped plates for $8–10, and feature all-you-can-eat lunchtime buffets for much the same price.

Fast-food culture is now fairly well established in Alaska, and towns of any size all have at least one of the major chains represented;

Anchorage and Fairbanks have most of the familiar names.

If you just want to cut down on red meat, the Alaskan diet is ideal, but **vegetarians** are less well catered for. Even sandwiches rarely come meat-free. Still, diner breakfasts are varied, meat-free pizza is almost always available, and you can survive for ages on salads and pasta dishes. **Vegans** will find things much harder and may want to spend at least some of their time self-catering.

Self-catering

The lure of money-sucking whale-watching trips and flightseeing around Denali may fuel your desire to **economize** on food expenses. If you are camping, driving an RV, staying in hostels, or seeking out motels with kitchens, you can cut costs (and avoid an overly fatty or meat-laden diet) by cooking your own meals. With the appropriate license, you might even gather your own ingredients; it is easy enough to **catch your own fish** (salmon and halibut are the prize species), or even gather a bucket of razor clams. Berries – salmonberries, blueberries, wild strawberries, high- and low-bush cranberries – are also good from midsummer to fall and, if you know what you are looking for, there are mushrooms and fiddlehead ferns to be found.

For the less adventurous there are always **supermarkets** – Safeway/Carr's, Fred Meyer, and IGA are the major names. Every town has one. Larger places may also have an extensive deli, in-shop bakery, fresh-fish counter, and useful buy-as-much-as-you-need bulk food bins. In smaller towns they don't just sell groceries, but also act as the video rental outlet, Western Union counter, and have a liquor store immediately adjacent; in truly remote communities the supermarket may have fast-food outlets and sell everything from Carhartt clothing to snowmobiles. Near popular hiking areas you may also find **freeze-dried meals**, though you can often prepare something tastier for less money.

Prices depend mostly on location. In Anchorage non-perishable items are only ten or twenty percent more expensive than in the Lower 48, though items like **milk** and **produce** might be fifty percent more, or even twice what you'd expect. Stores in main towns on the highway system and the larger ports of the Southeast will charge a little more, again with perishable products the worst affected. Visit places such as Dutch Harbor, Kotzebue, and Barrow, and you'll find prices get seriously inflated: $4 for a half-gallon of milk isn't unheard of and the range of fresh vegetables may be seriously depleted. Lastly, don't expect grocery-store seafood to come cheaply. It may be plentiful, but local wages are high and the prices correspondingly so.

Drink

Nights spent chatting in historic roadhouses or spit-and-sawdust wayside bars are likely to be some of the most enjoyable (though poorly remembered) times you'll have in Alaska. The best of these are dimly lit, convivial places where the owner feels compelled to string up as many moose racks, stuffed salmon, ancient snowshoes, and fly-fishing rods as possible. As often as not, you'll find a line of beards in baseball caps deep in conversation about hunting and fishing. In towns, drinking establishments tend to be a bit more cosmopolitan, with Anchorage even boasting a couple of sleek and fashionable cocktail bars, and a slew of excellent microbreweries. But, on the whole, consumption prevails over style. Something to look out for is **the bell**, prominently displayed above the bar in some establishments: ring it and you're signaling your intention to buy a drink for everyone in the bar.

Sadly, Alaska has one of the highest rates of alcoholism in the US, a figure boosted by frighteningly high rates among Alaskan Natives. In an attempt to combat this problem, many rural communities **ban alcohol** sales (see box, below) and in some cases forbid the transportation of any booze to that

Dry Alaska

Most Native authorities recognize that excessive alcohol consumption is a major problem among their people, not just for its antisocial effects but as a serious health risk. Some estimate that approaching fifty percent of adult Natives have some form of alcohol problem, a state of affairs undoubtedly exacerbated by the erosion of traditional values.

After the American purchase in 1867, the sale of alcohol to Natives – who already had a reputation for drunkenness – was banned, a selective prohibition which continued until 1953, when federal laws overruled such discrimination. Drunkenness again became rampant, and in 1980 village councils were given the power to restrict sales within their own communities in an effort to contain the (self-)destructive behavior. Many communities decided that the route to redemption was through outlawing alcohol in the village altogether, and they became dry. A few chose to manage sales through stores owned or controlled in some way by the community, but remained wet. Some felt that problems could be dealt with more openly if they were damp, with drink sales proscribed, but importation of supplies allowed. Barrow and other villages chose to be soggy, periodically voting on their status. Whatever the moral benefits, dry towns appear to have lower instances of assault, homicide, and suicide.

Of course, any form of prohibition is of only minimal use. Alcohol does get in (or is made) and obtaining supplies can become more of an obsession than drinking the stuff ever was. Bootleggers can make huge profits on bottles of whisky, which can change hands for ten times the retail price. There is also an effect on "wet" airline-hub communities, particularly Fairbanks, which sell huge quantities of alcohol to those on a binge during infrequent town visits. The sight of the terminally drunk around the downtown bar quarter is a sad one, and it can only be hoped that, as Native communities regain their self-respect and revive their culture, the drive for binge drinking will subside and the necessity of managing alcohol availability will cease to exist.

town. Elsewhere the **drinking age** is 21, and anyone who could conceivably be thought to be underage (however remotely) may be asked to produce picture ID on entry to a bar. Ordinances also prevent supermarkets from selling alcohol, though there is almost always a liquor store next door (or even as part of the supermarket with a separate checkout system). **Bar hours** are more lenient and vary depending on who is in that night; only the most inveterate late-night drinker will have trouble finding a bar to lean on.

American beers fall into two camps: wonderful and tasteless. You may be familiar with the latter, which are found throughout Alaska: light, fizzy brands such as Budweiser, Miller, Michelob, and Rainier, costing around $4 a pint. The alternative is a fabulous range of microbrewed beers, some arriving from California and the Pacific Northwest, while others are brewed locally. Juneau's Alaskan Brewing Co is the major regional brewer, and its golden, medium-weight Amber Ale is excellent. Look out, too, for beers from Silver Gulch Brewing & Bottling Co near Fairbanks (which claims to be the world's northernmost brewery), whose brews even have the Anchorage beer cognoscenti taking notice.

Increasingly, Alaskan brewers are setting up shop in their home towns, brewing their own beer, and selling it through **brewpubs**, where you'll find crisp pilsners, amber ales, wheat beers, and stouts on tap, at prices only marginally above those of the national brews (say, $5 a pint). Anchorage is especially well catered for in this regard, though anywhere with the population to support it will have somewhere with some stainless-steel tanks in the corner. Most bars also stock a fair range of **foreign brews**, particularly European and Canadian beers, and Mexican beers such as Corona, Dos Equis, and the excellent Bohemia.

Wine drinking is largely confined to restaurants, where menus are dominated by Californian varietals at fairly high prices. **Cocktails** are always popular, though you'll always be paying full price since Alaskan law forbids happy hours.

Coffee and tea

With Alaska's long-standing economic and cultural ties to the Pacific Northwest, **coffee** culture has become almost as highly developed here as in Seattle. The terms espresso, cappuccino, and latte have nearly become meaningless in themselves, and require half a dozen qualifiers before you'll get served anything: size, strength, regular or decaf, type of milk, amount of froth, additional syrup flavors, and so forth. It can all seem baffling at first, but most baristas are happy to explain, and the coffee is almost always excellent. Good coffee can also be found in bookshop cafés, drive-in kiosks beside city streets, and in cybercafés, where the purchase of a coffee (or any of the snacks and specialty teas on offer) may get you half an hour's free surfing.

Diner **coffee** is filtered, almost tasteless, and keeps coming as long as you sit there. For those who don't like it black, there is usually a basket of whiteners on the table ranging from non-dairy powders to half-and-half.

Restaurants also serve **tea**, though visitors from countries where tea drinking is more a religion than a way of quenching thirst will undoubtedly find what's on offer insipid, and may be induced to head straight for a coffee shop selling specialist teas, or try one of the herbal infusions also widely available. No matter what you go for it is likely to be inelegantly served by dropping a teabag into a mug of hot water.

Entertainment

Thanks to Alaska's **long evenings**, the tourist day doesn't need to stop at 6pm. Strolling along a Southeast boardwalk after dinner, or along a sub-Arctic beach at midnight with the sun still in the sky can prove to be one of your trip's highlights. In small towns and anywhere off the beaten path, the sun may be your only evening entertainment, though there will always be a bar or movie theater around. If you are lucky, you might find a **band** playing, though your chances are greater in the bigger towns where a few well-known names have a loyal following. The music is likely to be a solid rock or blues band churning out reliable danceable tunes, though you may also come across acoustic sets by Alaska's coterie of singer-songwriters. Out-of-state bands occasionally make it up here to play big venues in Anchorage and

Fairbanks, and perhaps one of the summer festivals (see p.74).

In some of the most popular destinations you'll find events laid on especially for tourists. In areas with significant Native populations – particularly in coastal areas – groups perform **traditional dance**, usually in full costume and often in a replica of a traditional house. In the Interior and parts of the Southeast it is the gold-mining heritage that holds sway, and mock saloons play host to music-hall shows, typically with performers in period costume.

Health

Alaska is a fairly safe place to visit. There is some physical danger from the sheer hostility of the environment, but nothing you can't learn to handle (or avoid altogether). There have been some fatal sightseeing accidents in recent years, and road conditions can pose a challenge, but on balance the risks are few.

Travelers from Europe and Australasia do not require **inoculations** or special health certification to enter the US. Once in Alaska, if you have a serious **accident**, emergency medical services (dial ☏**911**) will get to you quickly and charge you later.

Should you need to see a **doctor**, lists can be found in the *Yellow Pages* under "Clinics" or "Physicians and Surgeons," and there'll be a basic consultation fee of $75–150, payable in advance. Medication isn't cheap either – keep all your receipts for later claims on your insurance policy.

Most **minor ailments** can be remedied at **drugstores**. Foreign visitors should bear in mind that many pills available over the counter at home need a prescription in the US – most codeine-based painkillers, for example. Local brand names can be confusing; ask for advice at the **pharmacy** in any drugstore.

The tap **water** in Alaska is perfectly drinkable, and many rural campsites have potable water from hand pumps. If you are drinking water from rivers or lakes, however, it should be boiled, filtered, or chemically treated (see box on p.61 for more).

At some time you'll probably find yourself on a ferry or day-cruise and will be glad that most boats travel in protected waters. Nonetheless, those prone to **motion sickness** can improve their chances of feeling good by remaining close to the center of the ship, getting plenty of fresh air, and avoiding reading. As a precaution, use one of the motion sickness patches or pills available over the counter at drugstores.

Cold, rain, wind, and sun

You are not likely to come down with any unpleasant diseases in Alaska, but dealing with the physical demands of the environment will be a day-to-day concern. During the main May to September summer season, temperatures are likely to be warmer than you might expect, and you're not going to need Arctic-type clothing, though **hypothermia** is still a threat. You will need two or three warm layers (wool, fleece, and synthetic thermals are good; cotton is not), a hat, and some gloves. Always be prepared: a vehicle breakdown on a remote road in September could quickly turn into a nightmare if you are underdressed. Hypothermia isn't just about temperature – it's also about staying dry. Protection from the **rain** can be a big issue, especially in Southeast Alaska where you are bound to encounter a downpour at some point. **Wind**, too, can be a problem in coastal areas (and on whale-watching cruises and the like), so a good waterproof

Bears

Alaska's brown (grizzly) and black bears don't think of us as food and are seldom a problem (with perhaps one human death every two or three years), though they are inquisitive animals and have learned that humans often have snacks stashed away in tents. More than anything else, they don't like surprises, so the best way to **avoid bear encounters** is by making plenty of noise: whistle, clap, sing, or strap a **bear bell** onto your pack. In open country try to walk with the wind at your back – a bear's sense of smell is better than its sight or hearing. **If you see a bear** and it hasn't seen you, move away, keeping downwind if possible. If the bear has seen you, **don't run** – as this tells the bear that you are worth chasing – but stand still, gently waving your arms while talking firmly but calmly and avoiding any aggressive behavior, such as staring at the bear. If you look slightly away and move slowly backwards the bear will probably move off, but if it follows, hold your ground. Very rarely, they will charge: if they do, it is usually a bluff and if you stand firm (or as firm as you can manage), the bear will probably veer away at the last moment. Never, ever get between a mother and her cub.

Advice varies about what you should do if a bear gets so close it can touch you, and much of what is offered depends on you being able to tell a brown from a black (which doesn't have a shoulder hump; see p.601 for more on bear identification) in a very stressful situation.

The best, though not easiest, thing to do is to try to determine the bear's motivation. If it appears mostly interested in feeding or protecting its young, it may see you as a threat, in which case you should "play dead": lie on your front with your pack on, your hands behind your neck, and your legs splayed to prevent the bear rolling you over. If the bear seems to be hunting, fight back with sticks, rocks, bear spray, or whatever: the bear will (hopefully) be so surprised it will back off.

Don't **camp** beside salmon streams or near paths worn by bears (usually identifiable by their tracks and scat). Learn to recognize droppings, which are always large but vary in content: grass in spring, animal hair and bones any time, and berries in fall. Be sure to prevent bears getting at your food. Where they've been provided, use bear poles to hang your food or lockers to store it. Otherwise hang your food fifteen feet up a tree (carry rope), or, preferably, from a rope strung between two trees. Any **smelly items**, such as sunscreen, toothpaste, and mosquito repellent, should stay with the food; you're better off doing without soap and deodorant for a couple of days. Once bears get the idea that humans equal free food they become a problem and are sometimes shot: as they say up here, "A Fed Bear is a Dead Bear."

In open areas with no substantial trees, follow the **triangle principle** in which your tent, cooking spot, and food storage area are at the points of an equal-sided triangle with sides at least a hundred yards (preferably 200yds) long. Your tent should be the most upwind of the three spots, so a bear that does seek out your kitchen or pantry won't go past your tent to get to it. Choose **low-odor food** (not tuna, sardines, or bacon) and keep it stored in airtight containers or Ziploc-style bags. In areas with high bear concentrations you should use a **bear-resistant food canister**, a hard plastic cylinder that holds enough food for about four days. These can be bought for

and windproof coat is pretty much essential along with decent shoes and warm socks.

Visitors often forget that the sun also shines in Alaska – with potentially twenty hours of sunshine a day through much of the summer **sunburn** is a real risk. Despite the low angle of the sun you should still slap on some sunscreen during the day, especially near snow and water where the reflection can catch you unawares; don't forget to cover the underside of your chin and nose. A peaked hat or baseball cap is a good idea, and be sure to wear glacier goggles or very dark sunglasses if spending time on or around glaciers.

around $80 from sports and outdoor stores or rented locally for $4 a day. In Denali and Wrangell–St Elias the National Park Service will provide them free. Take all your **garbage** out with you.

Many Alaskans carry a **gun** for bear protection, though unless you have specifically come to hunt you probably won't have a gun and can survive just as well with the kind of good bushcraft described above; if you have no experience with guns this is not the time to learn. A compromise is to carry a can of **pepper spray** or mace, which can be effective though you need to be careful not to use it directly upwind of yourself, and the range is only around six yards (rather closer than you really want to be). A can costs around $40, has a limited shelf life, and won't be allowed on scheduled flights, so you may feel that you can manage without.

In Arctic Alaska you are no longer at the top of the food chain. **Polar bears** have been known to stalk humans over several miles, so in their territory you want to be in a very strong vehicle or equipped with a powerful rifle and the ability to shoot straight under pressure. Fortunately, unexpected encounters are rare, and polar bears only really come onshore in the very far north – Kotzebue, Barrow, and Prudhoe Bay for example – when the pack ice is solid, anywhere from October through to May.

Hypothermia

Hikers are usually aware of the possibility of hypothermia, though most cases occur under relatively benign conditions (say, 30–50°F) when people are least prepared. Always dress in layers: synthetic materials – polypropylene and fleeces – are best as they are warm, lightweight, and dry quickly. Avoid cotton (including denim) as it provides little warmth when dry, and none at all when wet. A windproof and waterproof layer (preferably breathable) is also essential. Beware of wet clothing – change after a river crossing and keep your wet gear to use for the next one. It is also a good idea to keep feeding yourself warm food and drinks, so a portable stove is quite important.

If anyone in your party exhibits symptoms such as lethargy, irrational behavior, muscle cramps, and even taking off clothing claiming they are hot, they should be treated for hypothermia. Keep them out of wind and rain, ensure they are wearing dry clothing, and feed them high-energy foods and hot drinks. A sleeping bag and human warmth are the next stage. In extreme conditions, send for medical assistance.

Water purification

Water from a spigot or pump in a campground should be safe to drink, but any water gathered from streams and lakes (no matter how clean it looks or how remote the area) should always be purified to kill the parasites that cause giardia. Many people carry a **water filter**, which must be rated down to five microns. Though convenient, filters are just one more thing to carry and easily clog up in silt-laden glacial waters. You should let any silty water settle overnight before filtering. **Iodine** tablets and solutions are just as effective, if properly used, and weigh next to nothing. (With very cold water you may need to leave it for twenty minutes before drinking.)

Bugs, bears, and other nasties

In Alaska you don't need to worry about snakes, spiders, or poison oak, but **bears** and, particularly, **mosquitoes** can be troublesome. The size and number of mosquitoes is legendary and with good reason – they're everywhere. At various points throughout the summer you'll also have to contend with **no-see-ums** (very small bitey things) and **white socks** (small black flies with white feet). They are seldom all around at the same time, but each has its few weeks of infamy, so always carry some maximum-potency bug dope. Anything with around 25 to 35 percent DEET is optimal; anything higher than that doesn't increase effectiveness much. One application should last at least four hours, but DEET is pretty nasty stuff, so to reduce reliance on it wear long-sleeved shirts buttoned up to the neck, tuck your pants into your socks, and use citronella candles if you are sitting outside in the evening. Broad-brimmed hats with nets covering your face are only really necessary in extreme circumstances, usually on remote rafting, canoeing, and fishing trips.

Bears are all over Alaska – town centers excepted – though it is only brown (grizzly) and black bears that are widespread; polar bears are rarely seen apart from in Arctic towns such as Barrow and Kotzebue, and even there summer sightings are rare. Despite the number of grizzly stories you might hear, the risk of a bear attack is

extremely low and, with a small amount of knowledge and some common sense, there is no need to let fear get the better of you. We've covered bear encounters in more detail in the box on p.60.

Alaska is full of smaller mammals, though most of them won't bother you. Should for any reason you get bit, however, definitely seek immediate medical treatment, and consider a series of **rabies** shots.

If you are a fan of shellfish, you need to be aware of **paralytic shellfish poisoning** (PSP), which attacks a handful of people each year and occasionally results in death. Shellfish sold commercially are routinely tested and are safe for consumption, but if you have collected your own, particularly from unmonitored beaches where there may be no warning signs, seek medical help if you sense tingling or numbness in the lips and tongue and loss of muscle coordination, dizziness, weakness, or drowsiness.

The media

The standard of media coverage in Alaska is much as you'd expect elsewhere in the United States but on a smaller scale. There are fewer TV and radio stations than in the Lower 48, though some towns have such poor reception that almost everyone, and almost every hotel, has cable (or satellite), with the usual fifty-plus channels. Locally produced shows are rare, with the exception of weather, news, and current affairs. In smaller villages you may come across the Rural Alaska Communications Service, which serves almost 250 rural communities with commercial content from Anchorage stations, material from the Alaska Public Broadcasting Service (PBS), and some local or regional programming.

Radio varies greatly throughout the state with only the serious, publicly funded Alaska Public Radio Network (FM frequencies 87–92MHz) having wide coverage; much of its content is straight from **National Public Radio**. The bigger towns have a selection of niche stations (alternative rock, classic rock, Seventies, country, etc), but smaller places might have just one, often an evangelical Christian station, and it is on these that you

should listen out for "bushlines," a kind of radio bulletin board for people who don't have phones. The whole town, and particularly those in cabins out in the bush, will listen to the messages, usually prosaic instructions for someone to meet somewhere, or sending thanks for the side of moose delivered Tuesday. Between towns there may be nothing at all: bring CDs for those long hauls, or an adaptor for your MP3 player.

The widest-circulation **newspaper** is the *Anchorage Daily News* (ⓦwww.adn.com), which provides Alaska's most comprehensive coverage of local and world events. It is pretty much the de facto state newspaper, much to the chagrin of a good portion of the state's residents, not just because they resent Anchorage's dominance, but because of its left-leaning, liberal politics (at least by Alaskan standards). Some years back it absorbed the city's afternoon paper, the *Anchorage Times*, and as a sop to its former owner and readers and "in the interests of preserving a diversity of viewpoints in the community," the *Anchorage Daily News* prints the "Voice of the Times," a daily half-page of right-wing Libertarian views. Anchorage also has the excellent weekly *Press* (ⓦwww.anchoragepress.com), an alternative views and listings tabloid. The *Press* has some coverage of and distribution in Fairbanks, which also has the less excellent *Fbx Square* (ⓦwww.fbxsquare.com).

The *Fairbanks Daily News-Miner* (ⓦwww.news-miner.com) and *Juneau Empire* (ⓦwww.juneauempire.com) are the two other papers with large regional followings, the former covering much of the Interior and the North, the latter found all over Southeast. None is likely to win you over with outstanding journalism, but they're quite adequate, and the weekend magazine sections offer interesting insights into aspects of the state you may not otherwise come across. In addition, each sizeable town produces its own local-interest rag – the *Arctic Sounder*, the *Tundra Drums*, the *Nome Nugget*, and a dozen more around the state – though the content often fails to live up to the promise of the title.

Supermarket magazine stands in the bigger towns might stock the major dailies from the Lower 48, but most likely you'll be reduced to *Time* and *Newsweek* for wider coverage. Alaska-specific **magazines** are rare, though you might look for the monthly *Alaska* (ⓦwww.alaskamagazine.com), which tries for a wide coverage of outdoor issues but fails to disguise its hunting and fishing heritage. Women looking to spend a lot more time in Alaska should seek out *AlaskaMen* (ⓦwww.alaskamen-online.com), a matchmaking magazine that claims to feature "interesting and exciting men whose individualism, spirit and vitality make them unique among men of the world."

Culture and etiquette

In many respects Alaska, especially urban Alaska, is now part of the North American mainstream and you should behave much as you would anywhere else. However, pioneer attitudes do survive in the bush, and you should be sure to respect subsistence hunting and property rights; in particular be sure not to barge past a "No Entry" sign into someone's gold claim, as these are zealously guarded. Shooting is not allowed within a quarter-mile of a cabin, road, or the pipeline, but you can never be sure.

The biggest hot-button issue in Alaska is currently the **great outdoors**: most residents agree it's what makes the state special, though beyond that, attitudes toward nature are highly polarized. Many see the outdoors as a place to hunt, fish, and otherwise exploit, while others are all for preserving it and hiking, biking, or kayaking as unobtrusively as possible. The two camps coexist surprisingly well, but visitors should be tactful in expressing their opinions.

Minorities

As a state, Alaska tends to celebrate individuality – those forging a path away from the mainstream may find that their choices are unexpectedly celebrated. **Gay** men and women will find support groups and even a small scene in Anchorage, Fairbanks, and Juneau (we've listed contacts throughout the book). Same-sex marriage was banned in 1998, but in 2005 the Alaska Supreme Court required some same-sex benefits for state employees. Nonetheless, prejudice does exist; it's best for gays to keep a low profile in rural areas. Harassment will seldom be more than a little verbal abuse, but overtly homosexual behavior, for example, is liable to elicit a more vigorous response.

Alaskan women have been decidedly liberated since the days of pipeline construction, when they showed they could work shoulder to shoulder with men. **Racism** is not much of a problem, with large numbers of minorities arriving with the military and in some cases staying on. Native Alaskans do have to contend with some prejudice, but it cuts both ways, as whites can be made to feel unwelcome in some bush villages.

Shoes

To avoid traipsing mud, snow, and road grit everywhere many Alaskans (B&B hosts included) ask that you remove your **outdoor footwear** upon coming inside.

Smoking

The legal age for smoking in Alaska is 19. The practice is widely considered antisocial and, as in many other states, is banned in most public areas. Restaurants must provide a **nonsmoking** section; from July 2007 smoking will be banned altogether in Anchorage restaurants.

Tipping

You should always **tip** the waitstaff in a bar or restaurant at least fifteen percent. A similar percentage should be added to taxi fares. A hotel porter should get roughly $1 for each bag carried to your room.

Wilderness etiquette

Pack it in, pack it out – you should leave **no trace** of your visit to the backcountry. Make sure fires are extinguished, leave no food or trash, and if using a public cabin you should replenish the supply of firewood and leave dry kindling. Private cabins are traditionally left open, and you can help yourself to food in a survival situation.

Sports and outdoor activities

Alaska has more outdoors than just about anywhere else, and a large portion of the time you spend in the state is likely to be spent in it. This might involve something as gentle as whale-watching in Prince William Sound or wandering along a paved path to the face of a glacier, but could just as easily include a ten-day rafting trip in the Arctic or hiking the famed Chilkoot Trail.

With such a vast expanse of territory and a limited transportation infrastructure, access to the **wilderness** can be an issue, especially if you haven't the money for frequent bush-plane flights or water taxis to remote bays. If you can afford such adventures, it is important to try not to do too much: decide instead on a couple of areas you most want to visit and concentrate your energy (and resources) on those.

River crossings

When hiking away from formed trails you may well find yourself needing to cross a river, something which causes more hiker deaths than bear attacks. Most rivers in Alaska are **glacial rivers**, which means they are very cold, contain silt (which makes it hard to pick your route across), and are subject to rising water levels as the sun increases meltwater late in the day – early morning is the best time to cross and you should plan your trip accordingly. If in doubt, wait a few hours (or overnight) and try again, or go back. Pick the widest section of river you can find (it is likely to be the shallowest) and shuffle across facing the opposite shore keeping your feet apart to provide a secure brace. Groups should link up (with arms around waists or shoulders) to form a line parallel to the current with the strongest person upstream; lone hikers should find a stout stick to use as a "third leg," which allows you to always keep two points of contact. If you do get swept off your feet, don't panic: rid yourself of your pack (some recommend wearing the pack loosely with the waist belt unbuckled), then float on your back with your feet pointing downstream and swim across the current to the bank. Don't put your feet down; ankles can get trapped.

Much of the outdoors (and almost all the hiking territory covered in this book) is classed as public land, managed by a combination of state and federal authorities; the National Park Service focuses on conservation, while the state's Departments of Natural Resources and of Fish and Game, and the federal Forest Service and Bureau of Land Management are all pro-exploitation, with rather less concern for sustainability. In the middle is the federal Fish and Wildlife Service (which runs Alaska's sixteen National Wildlife Reserves), which will allow sustainable use of the land. Though there are **charges** for camping and parking, access to the park is free, with the exception of Denali National Park, which is run by the National Park Service. The entrance fee to Denali is $10 per person for 7 days; the NPS also offers the Golden Eagle Passport ($65 for one year from date of purchase), which gives free entry for the holder and immediate family into almost all national parks, preserves, monuments, historic sites, and wildlife refuges in the United States. US citizens and permanent residents age 62 and older are eligible for a Golden Age Passport ($10), which is valid for life and also gives free entry to federal areas as well as a fifty percent reduction on camping and boat-launch fees. Disabled US citizens and permanent residents (of any age) are eligible for a free Golden Access Passport giving the same benefits. An annual day-use/parking permit for state parks is available to all from the DNR for $40.

Hiking

Hiking in Alaska is no walk in the park, but it is the easiest and least expensive way of getting out into the wilderness. For many, it is the main reason to come to Alaska, and with good reason: there are few spots on earth where it is so easy to walk for days without seeing a soul, and fewer still with such wonderful wildlife. The range of hikes varies enormously from short strolls along a hard-packed trail to see a glacier to multi-day fly-in epics. Many people stick to the former, and even if you think you are in this category, it is worth trying something slightly harder. You may find yourself captivated by stunning vistas of snowcapped mountains, dense dripping forests, or vast stretches of tundra rolling away to the horizon.

Most of your hiking is likely to be along formed trails, but in theory you can stop almost anywhere – take a compass and set off for days across ranges of hills, fording rivers when necessary and camping when you get tired. The reality can be very different, however. In Southeast dense forest restricts your passage, and in the boggy terrain of the Interior and North, it is all too obvious why Native Alaskans and early pioneers traveled in winter, when the rivers were frozen and skis, snowshoes, and dog teams could be put to good use. Off-trail hiking can be an

Rough Guide favorites: hikes

arduous task, watching every step to avoid bog-filled holes, high-stepping onto spongy mounds and then wrestling with low willow and blueberry bushes. For more on hiking in tundra see the Hiking and camping practicalities on p.431.

With a short summer **hiking** season, picking the right time for a visit is very important. Except for the odd lowland walk, don't even think about hiking in May, when large sections of the trails are still covered in snow. Similar conditions persist well into June in some areas – strong waterproof boots and gaiters are essential. By July, most hikes are free of snow and starting to dry out, but bugs can be at their worst. Generally, the best time for hiking is late summer (mid-Aug to Sept), when the days are still long, the ground is as dry as it is going to get, and the nights aren't that cold. In the North you might even see the aurora at this time.

With the exception of Denali's complex rules and the Chilkoot Trail's booking system, there is **no reservation system** for trails in Alaska, though restrictions exist for campsites and cabins (see Accommodation, p.53).

No matter where you are going, you should always leave a reasonably detailed **trip plan** with someone responsible and be sure to check in when you return. Besides a few short walks close to town, most of the hikes in this book may be more of a wilderness experience than you are used to. Conditions can be harsh, you can go without seeing other humans for days, cell phones won't work, and no one is going to look for you until after you are due back, which may be a couple of days away. Since you will need

to be entirely self-sufficient, we've included a few helpful pointers below, but they are no substitute for discussing your plans with local park and forest service rangers, making sure your map-reading skills are well honed, and using a good deal of common sense.

Equipment

Alaska's backcountry cabins are seldom sited along hiking trails, so to hike for any length of time in most areas you'll need to bring a fair amount of equipment. If you live outside the US, it is worth considering buying gear once you arrive. Anchorage has a good stock of outdoor stores selling competitively priced gear (particularly American-manufactured goods) and there is no sales tax.

Put some thought into your choice of **tent**. A freestanding dome-style tent (or some variation on that theme) allows you to avoid pounding pegs into rocky ground, boggy tundra, or the loose gravel of river bars. Something rated for three seasons is a minimum requirement – high winds and driving rain can strike at any time of year; a four-season model is better still. Remember that it can snow in any month in Denali, and tents injudiciously pitched in river valleys are frequently blown inside out throughout the summer. If you want to get any sleep at all, make sure your tent is completely mosquito-proof, and equipped with an ample expanse of fine-mesh netting.

You'll need to carry a **cooking stove** and fuel, as many areas do not permit campfires, and the few huts and shelters you'll come across will only have heating stoves. Something burning efficient, widely available, and cheap white gas (also known as Coleman fuel; around $5.50 a gallon) is a good option. Canisters for propane and butane stoves – such as Camping Gas, Primus, MSR, and Snowpeak – are only sporadically available (although bulk propane is available at most gas stations). EPIgas canisters and methylated spirits (denatured alcohol in US parlance) can be even harder to come by; the latter can be found at REI in Anchorage and in some hardware stores but costs roughly four times as much as Coleman fuel. You'll also go through it quicker – a serious consideration if you're spending a few nights in the backcountry. Traveling by train and scheduled flight is off-limits if you're carrying any kind of fuel. If you charter a bush plane, provision will be made for flying fuel in (often in the plane's floats), but if you are on a scheduled service to a bush town, check that you can buy fuel when you get there. The best bet is to carry a stove that will burn standard unleaded gasoline (petrol). MSR and several other manufacturers make compact models that burn both Coleman fuel and unleaded gasoline without modification.

You'll also want some form of insulated sleeping mat, a warm sleeping bag, some reliable method of purifying water (see box, p.61), a detailed map, compass, insect repellent, and an insect-proof head net (not stylish but you won't care). Extra items might include waterproof matches and a lighter; a first-aid kit; a signaling device such as a whistle, light, or flare; and strong plastic bags for keeping clothes and sleeping bags dry.

Minimum-impact hiking and camping

Nowhere is the practice of **minimum-impact** hiking and camping more important than in Alaska. Like all Arctic and sub-Arctic regions, the landscape here is very fragile and a small amount of damage can take a long time to recover: tundra plants grow so slowly that vehicle tracks can take decades to disappear, and ten-foot-high trees only a few inches in diameter might be a hundred years old.

How you go about minimizing your impact depends on where you are hiking. On well-formed trails you'll probably be following familiar rules: stick to the trail, walk in single file, don't cut switchbacks, and only camp at designated sites. When hiking in Denali or anywhere away from managed trails, you do the exact opposite, the idea being that in trackless areas you should do what you can to avoid creating tracks. We've discussed this in more detail in our Denali account (see p.431), but essentially you walk in small groups fanned out across the landscape, each group finding its own route, then camp where there is no evidence of previous campers, being sure to move on every day or so. Make sure you leave nothing behind, avoid lighting fires, and where possible camp on **river bars** where the evidence is washed away in spring floods. The breeze on river bars often keeps the bugs down as well, but you need to be prepared to move if rains cause the river to rise. Some people even carry light comfortable shoes to minimize the impact around the campsite.

Maintaining personal hygiene can adversely affect the fragile environment. Burn used toilet paper; bury it and any **human waste** in a shallow hole at least a hundred feet away from a watercourse. If you bury it too deep, the permanently cold ground won't support decomposition. **Soap** should be used sparingly if at all – even biodegradable soaps take a long time to decompose up here and hikers downstream may be using the river for drinking water. Pots can be cleaned with river sand and hot water; any sudsy water you do create should be discarded well away from streams and standing water.

Mountain biking

Many of the trails listed as hiking trails are equally (if not more) suited to **mountain biking**, offering long stretches with relatively easy gradients and only short technical sections. Most of the best riding is relatively distant from places you can rent bikes, so unless you are prepared to stump for fairly expensive long-term rental it definitely pays to have your own machine; if you're driving up here, consider strapping your bike on.

Throughout the Guide we've indicated which trails are most suited to biking, but there are numerous gravel roads that can

Rough Guide favorites: mountain biking

be fun – the longer ones are listed under "Cycle touring" on p.49. Except on trails where bikes are banned, there are no special rules, but common courtesy demands you ride within your ability and pull over for hikers. You should also be aware of **bears**. They tend to move away from approaching hikers, but bikes travel faster and often more quietly, so be especially wary when rounding blind corners.

Rafting, canoeing, and kayaking

Most people shy away from immersing themselves in Alaskan waters, but that doesn't rule out rafting, canoeing, and kayaking. These activities seldom require getting wet – except on commercial whitewater-rafting trips – as the emphasis is mostly on gentle appreciation of the surroundings, and maybe a bit of fishing. People do kayak the inland rivers, but by far the majority of people kayaking in Alaska restrict themselves to coastal regions, where you can paddle among whales in sight of huge tidewater glaciers.

Rafting

Rafting trips in Alaska fall into two broad categories: float trips, usually on gentle water where you'll spend your time admiring the scenery and spotting wildlife; and whitewater trips, where the focus is on getting wet, though the scenery is usually spectacular as well. We've listed some of our favorites in both categories in the box below.

In a few places along the highway system, and even in Southeast, you'll find short **float trips** only a couple of hours long, perhaps finishing off with a barbecue beside the river. Many more, however, are specialist multiday

affairs through genuinely remote wilderness areas, such as in the Gates of the Arctic National Park, the Noatak National Preserve, or the Arctic National Wildlife Refuge. Some trips even run up to two weeks long and may make up your entire vacation. Your options are wide open.

Whitewater-rafting trips exist mostly in a few road-accessible areas in the Interior and on the Kenai Peninsula. If you have been whitewater rafting outside the US, you may be used to small rafts entirely controlled by paddle-wielding customers. Here, larger rafts are the norm, with the guide maneuvering the raft using oars, leaving the customers pretty much as passengers. Although this is undoubtedly a very safe way of running rafting trips, it does take the edge off the excitement of pulling together as a team to get through the rapids. The main rivers for short trips are Sixmile River near Hope, the Matanuska River near Chickaloon, and the Nenana River by Denali National Park. There are also multiday trips; the pick of these are the Talkeetna River near Talkeetna and the Alsek and Tatshenshini rivers, which are rafted from Haines.

If you can get a group together and have some backcountry experience, you might want to **rent a raft**, then charter a plane to fly you into the headwaters of some remote river and float down to a prearranged meeting point. Multiday trips usually involve a lot of drifting and occasional stretches of whitewater, which you can often portage. It can be a tiring job, so it is good to learn how to **line** your vessel, allowing the raft to follow the river while you walk the bank holding on by a rope. Companies running such trips are listed in the relevant sections of the Guide. There's also a good listing of Alaska river-rafting guides at ⓦalaskan .com/outdoors/rafting.htm.

Rough Guide favorites: river trips

Sixmile Creek p.263
Savonoski Loop p.360
Delta River p.443
Lion Head on the Matanuska River p.464
Yukon River from Eagle to Circle p.486
Chena River p.526
North Fork of the Koyukuk River p.32

Canoeing and river kayaking

Alaska has over a hundred rivers suitable for canoeing and kayaking, ranging in difficulty from flat water to some of the wildest water anywhere (see the box on p.71 for river grading). Some of these rivers are road-accessible, but there are often long distances between put-in and take-out points, and access can still be difficult since car rental agencies don't like renters putting racks on their cars and often don't allow driving on gravel roads. Consequently, keen river-paddlers are better off driving up from the Lower 48 or Canada and bringing their own gear. Rental kayaks and canoes are available but most companies have strict rules as to what rivers you put them in.

Some of Alaska's finest inland paddling is on **lakes**, particularly sequences of several lakes and easy rivers that can be combined into overnight or week-long trips. Much of the best lake paddling is not accessible by road, requiring bush flights to the access points. Rigid shell canoes and kayaks don't lend themselves to easy transport and those pilots who do fly them in – usually strapped to the floats of a float-plane – will often insist on a separate passenger-free flight for the boats, thereby adding to the overall cost of the trip. To get around this, many people opt for a **folding kayak** (sometimes known as a Klepper, one of the most common brand names), typically a slot-together aluminum frame with an outer coating of plasticized canvas. These can be surprisingly rigid and hold enough gear for a two-week trip or longer. Rentals are sometimes available, but if you are doing an extended trip it often works out better to buy one and make sure it is comfortable and equipped to your specifications.

No matter where you are going, you'll need to do a little **advance planning**, best done by reading the river guidebooks listed in the Contexts section of this book (see p.611) and contacting one of the Public Lands Information Centers (see p.85), where you can also obtain the free *Planning a River Trip in Alaska* leaflet. There are 25 National Wild and Scenic Rivers in Alaska (thirteen "Wild" ones administered by the National Park Service) and there may be detailed leaflets and other facilities for exploring these; see (w)www.nps.gov/rivers/wildriverslist.html#ak).

You should also keep in mind the potential **dangers**, and remember that you'll need to be totally self-reliant; it may be days before anyone comes looking for you. Most Alaskan rivers are fed by snowmelt and are incredibly cold. You should never underestimate how quickly a dunking can turn into a serious situation. To reduce the chances of a swim, you should lower your estimate of your abilities, so if you normally paddle Class III, then you shouldn't be looking at anything harder than Class II in Alaska. There's no substitute for getting sound advance information about the river, but you should also **scout ahead**, even if you think you can cope with upcoming obstacles. Remember that damaging a boat or losing a paddle can mean a very long, arduous, and possibly life-threatening walk out. Keep in mind that rapids aren't the only problem: rivers often meander through forested river valleys, cutting away at the outside banks until trees along the river fall in and create perhaps the biggest threat of all, **sweepers** (also known as strainers). Sweepers drag their branches in the water: you don't get washed around them like you would a rock, but get sucked under into an impenetrable tangle of branches. If anything, they are more common on easier-class rivers, posing a particular challenge to the inexperienced. Always steer well clear. Where there are log jams or harder rapids than you are prepared to tackle, you'll have to portage around the obstacle or line your boat through (see "Rafting," p.68, for more on both terms).

Sea kayaking

For most visitors the majority of Alaska's stupendously scenic coastline – longer than that of the rest of the US put together – remains inaccessible. The solution to this is sea kayaking (sometimes known here as **blue-water paddling**). Huge expanses of water sheltered from ocean swells by protective islands make Alaska a perfect sea-kayaking destination, and enthusiasts turn up with their own gear to spend weeks paddling along the coast, particularly around Misty Fiords National Park, Sitka, Glacier Bay, Prince William Sound, Resurrection

Bay, Kachemak Bay, and Kodiak Island. For beginners, it needn't be as daunting as it might at first sound, and every summer hundreds of people with no paddling experience join guided trips ranging from a few hours to several days.

At their most basic, commercial trips might depart the harbor of a Southeast port and paddle around the wharves and along the nearby coastline, but it is only a small step up to transport a kayak to the face of some nearby glacier and paddle around. Longer trips may extend to several days, spending each day moving on to the next campsite – a bit like hiking without a pack.

If you already have some experience you may want to **go it alone**, either with your own equipment or gear rented locally. A double kayak always works out much cheaper than two singles, and it allows you to move more quickly. You'll need to show the rental agency some evidence of your abilities and should also have a solid knowledge of **winds and tides**, both of which can be treacherous, even during the main mid-May to August paddling season. Be prepared for all eventualities no matter how benign the conditions are when you set out, and always carry a couple of days' extra food and fuel in case you are delayed. Almost the entire Alaskan coastline experiences a wide tidal range, so you should always haul your boat well above the high-water mark.

For kayak camping trips, put everything in small waterproof bags that will fit in the kayak; if you get wet and cold, the last thing you need is a sodden sleeping bag. Always file a **trip plan** with friends or the agency managing the area, try to stick to it whenever possible, and let them know when you get back. Cell phones probably won't work, but you might take a satellite phone or radio. Lifejackets are known as PFDs (personal flotation devices) and are strongly recommended. Lastly, if you've arranged for a boat

or plane to pick you up at a particular time, be sure to have a contingency plan in case something turns against you.

Fishing

In some circles Alaska is synonymous with fishing, and many people base their whole vacation around the pursuit of the fighting **salmon** and **trout** (see Contexts, p.604, for a discussion of fish species) in the rivers of Southcentral and the Interior. Armed with a license and suitable tackle, you won't have much trouble finding a place to fish – and there are a lot of fish out there waiting to be caught. That said, fishing is popular, and there's a good deal of competition beside the more accessible rivers. Keen anglers can improve their chance of a full catch bag by hiring **fishing guides** ($17–200 for half a day) or staying in isolated **fishing lodges**, where the remote locations have kept the fish-per-angler quotient high. You can still catch fish without going the big-money route simply by fishing in rivers you pass on your travels, such as when you are out hiking or on a backcountry trip. If you've got a lightweight rod at home, bring it along, or purchase one of the compact models that you can keep in your day-pack. Your chances of catching trophy-size fish are slim, but if you are just after something for your evening meal then a quiet hour or two by the riverside could hardly be better spent.

Winter visitors might try their hand at ice fishing, generally from early December to late March. It's a slightly bizarre pastime, usually involving sitting huddled in a hut out on a frozen lake dangling a line through a hole in the ice hoping to land king salmon, rainbow trout, Dolly Varden, arctic char, or arctic grayling.

Regulations

The **regulations** about where and when you can fish, bag limits, and so forth are complex

River grading

Both rivers and rapids are graded according to the six-level system below. The river class is dictated by the most demanding rapid. This lends itself to some creative marketing, since a river hyped as Class V might be almost entirely Class III with one Class V rapid. For those looking for an adventure, the expression to look out for when browsing brochures is "Continuous Class IV." Float trips, where the emphasis is more on the scenery and wilderness experience, tend to be on Class I and II rivers.

I Moving water and a few small waves.

II Choppier wave patterns and easily avoided rocks increase the dunking potential for inexperienced kayakers, though they are no problem in a raft.

III Bigger but still easily ridden waves make this class bouncy and fun, though there may be more technical sections. Good proving ground for first-time rafters.

IV Long rapids with much larger, bouncier, and less predictable waves churned up by rocks midstream demand greater boat control and teamwork. This makes for excellent fun but dramatically increases the chance of a swim.

V Serious stuff with chaotic standing waves, narrow channels, and huge holes ready to swallow you up. Best avoided by first-time rafters but thrilling for the experienced.

VI Dicing with death. Grade V taken to new heights; commercially unraftable and only tackled by the most experienced of paddlers.

and changeable. For the latest information, consult the Alaska Department of Fish and Game, Division of Sport Fishing, PO Box 115526, Juneau, AK 99802-5526 (☎465-4100, ⓦwww.sf.adfg.state.ak.us/statewide/sf_home.cfm). Their very informative website lists all the rules, links to handy publications, the latest fishing news, and feature stories.

You'll need to get an Alaska State **sport-fishing license** for nonresidents, which costs $20 for one day, $35 for three days, $55 for a week, $80 for two weeks, and $145 for the full year. If you are planning to fish for chinooks (and you are over 16), you'll also need a king salmon stamp ($10/20/30/50/100), which should be attached to your fishing license. If you are only fishing for kings, this will almost double your license cost. Limit your expenses by buying a two-week general license, with a daily **king salmon stamp** for the days you're fishing for that species.

Licenses can be bought all over the state, primarily from tackle shops but also from general stores and even campgrounds – just ask around. You can also buy licenses online at ⓦwww.admin.adfg.state.ak.us/license.

In Anchorage you can inquire at the Sport Fish Information Center, 333 Raspberry Rd ☎267-2218 (Mon–Fri 8am–5pm), 24hr

recorded info ☎267-2510; you can call ten other local offices including Fairbanks ☎459-7385.

Fishing derbies

Just about every coastal town has a **fishing derby** at some point during the summer, or sometimes just for the few weeks a particular salmon species makes its run for the breeding grounds. Usually, there are daily prizes for the biggest fish, a prize for the biggest caught during the entire derby, and one or more tagged fish, often with prizes of $100,000 or more on their head. Most derby tickets only cost about $10 to enter for the few days you're likely to be in town. Even if you don't participate, it is fun to wander down to the dockside in the late afternoon for the daily weigh-in.

We mention several such derbies throughout the text; there are more detailed listings at ⓦalaskaoutdoorjournal.com/Derbies/derbies.html and under the fishing section of ⓦwww.alaska.com. The state also issues **trophy fish certificates** for fish over a specified weight, for example 250lb for halibut or 50lb for king salmon (75lb in the Kenai River); see ⓦwww.sf.adfg.state.ak.us/statewide/trophy/form.cfm.

Combat fishing

Alaska may be huge and have miles of productive salmon streams, but most of the people are concentrated fairly close to Anchorage and only have access to rivers along the limited road system. The result is combat fishing, with anglers standing shoulder to shoulder trying to avoid snagging their neighbor with each cast. If this is what you're after (or you just want to see this freak show in action), head down to **Ship Creek**, right in the heart of Anchorage; **Bird Creek**, along the Seward Highway 25 miles to the south; or the Russian and Kenai rivers, another 30 miles south. To avoid tangled lines, cast slightly upstream and synchronize with your neighbors so that the lines drift downstream together. When someone else has a "fish-on," reel in your line so that the other fisher has a fair chance of landing the fish.

Hunting

For hunting you'll need a registered guide (or a cousin or closer relative aged 19 or older and resident in Alaska); a **license** costs $85, plus $30 for wolf or $500 for brown bear. For more information and a list of guides see ⓦwww.dced.state.ak.us/occ/pgui.htm.

Winter sports

Anyone wanting to undertake winter activities should come between **November** and **March**, when the days are reasonably long but there is enough darkness to coax out the aurora borealis. At this time, temperatures aren't that bad, but it's still cold enough for you to appreciate retiring to a warm fire at the end of the day. Otherwise, early-summer visitors might get in a few days of downhill skiing near Anchorage or some fly-in snowmobiling or cross-country skiing, and later in the summer helicopters can whisk you up to do some dog-sledding on glaciers above Seward, Skagway, and Juneau, but that's about it.

Skiing

To Alaskans, skiing means cross-country; although there are plenty of mountains and snow, there are very few places dedicated to **downhill skiing**. The only real resort is

Alyeska Resort at Girdwood (see p.257), forty miles southeast of Anchorage. There's also exciting heli-skiing near Valdez (see p.327). After that you're down to tiny fields such as Alpenglow (ⓦwww.skialpenglow .com) and Hilltop (ⓦwww.hilltopskiarea.org), both in Anchorage; Cleary Summit (ⓦwww .skiland.org, ⓦwww.mt-aurora.com), twenty miles north of Fairbanks; Eaglecrest in Juneau (ⓦwww.juneau.org/ecrestftp); and the Mount Eyak Ski Area in Cordova (see p.334).

However, there is virtually no limit to where you can go for **cross-country skiing**. The boggy lakeland that fills much of the Interior is virtually impenetrable in summer, but it's fair game when frozen and snow-covered. Most people head for recognized cross-country ski areas around Anchorage, on the Kenai Peninsula, throughout the Interior, and north of Fairbanks. Good places to kick off are Anchorage's Kincaid Park, site of the 1994 Olympic Trials, the area around Chena Hot Springs outside Fairbanks, and the Hatcher Pass Recreation Area near Palmer.

Dog-mushing and ski-joring

Dog-mushing is the official sport of Alaska, so it is appropriate that the one event for which Alaska is known worldwide is the **Iditarod** (see box, p.392), a 1100-mile dog-sled race across the state's frozen Interior. You'll see compounds throughout the state, with dogs chained to their kennels impatiently waiting their turn "in the traces" of a sled. A few dog-mushers offer summertime rides behind a wheeled sled, and there are expensive trips on glaciers in the peak visiting season, but both are pale substitutes for the real thing. Kennels offer widely differing experiences, but a good place to start is the Big Lake area, where you can visit the Buser, Plettner, and Halter kennels (see p.398).

Alaskans love their dogs so much they have found a way to take them skiing: **ski-joring**. Put on your cross-country skis, strap your dog into a harness, and hang on. It certainly makes uphill sections a good deal easier. There are only limited possibilities for experiencing this, unless you bring all your own equipment (including dog), but you may be able to hook up with people who will show you the ropes through the Alaska Skijoring & Pulk Association (☎457-5456 in Anchorage, ⊛www.sleddog.org/skijor).

Snowmobiling

Snowmobiles are almost as popular as dogs, and it sometimes seems that every yard has one hiding under a blue tarp. They're not just for fun, either – anyone living away from the road system relies on them for getting around in winter.

There are spots all over the state where you can see machines in action: generally, areas for mechanized shenanigans are separate from those designated for quieter pursuits. Modern snowmobiles are very fast, topping 100mph, and, not surprisingly, there are about twenty deaths a year, not just from crashing at speed, but also going through thin ice or triggering avalanches

while hotdogging on steep slopes. The summer equivalent, for yahoo recreation and for bringing in that essential moose, is the ATV or All-Terrain Vehicle, a quadbike that ploughs up hiking trails and is banned from national parks (except Wrangell-St Elias, although that may change) and from most urban roads,

In popular areas like Cantwell, Summit Lake, and Eureka, you can often rent snowmobiles (from $165 a day for a 550cc model), though unless you know what you're doing it is far better to join a guided tour. Try Alaska Snow Safaris, 6543 Brayton Drive, Anchorage (☎1-888/414-7669, ⊛www.snowmobile-alaska.com), which does rentals as well as introductory trips (3hr; $169), backcountry runs (5hr; $229), and full-day tours (from $329). There are numerous other companies offering similar deals: look for advertisements during the snowy months.

Shopping

Other than birch syrup and moose nuggets (usually chocolate, unless you buy the real thing in Talkeetna – see p.400), there's not a lot to buy that's specifically Alaskan. The exception is the superb range of Native crafts available all over the state.

It's always more satisfying to buy direct from the artist, and there's often a financial benefit, too, though this is offset by the cost of flying out to remote villages where most of the artists live. If you can't buy from the artist you'll want to be sure of what you are buying and its authenticity. Ask questions: a reputable dealer should know the artist's cultural background, the materials used and maybe even have some sort of biography of the artist. Look, too, for signatures and consider the feel of the piece; for example, genuine ivory will feel a lot heavier than any plastic imitation. If something is cheap, it's probably fake. Carved ivory usually costs at least $100 an inch, and woven grass baskets are just as pricey.

Also keep an eye out for the **Silver Hand** logo, which indicates traditional artwork made by an Alaskan Native currently residing in the state. Many genuine artists don't participate in the scheme, however. Silver Hand stickers bear a permit so you can call for verification (☎269-6610 in Anchorage or 1-888/278-7424). Legally, any item produced after 1935 can be marketed as "Indian," "Native American," or "Alaska Native" only if it was made by a member of a recognized tribe or a certified Indian artisan. A polar bear symbol or "Made in Alaska" sticker only means that it is made in the state. For information or complaints contact the Federal Trade Commission (☎1-877/382-4357, ⊛www.ftc.gov) or the Alaska

Attorney General's Office (☎269-5100, ⓦwww.law.state.ak.us/consumer).

Taking stuff home

In an attempt to preserve traditional lifestyles, particularly in remote villages, Native Alaskans are allowed to trade in raw materials otherwise proscribed by the Convention on International Trade in Endangered Species (CITES). Although it is perfectly legal to buy Native artifacts such as walrus-tusk cribbage boards, spirit masks, whalebone sculpture, etched pieces of baleen, and the pelts of wolves, otters, walruses, seals, and bears, the customs people back home may take a dim view of your bringing such things in with you.

It is illegal to export from the US products containing parts of bears (black, brown, and polar), cormorants, eagles, loons, puffins, ravens, sea lions, snowy owls, waterfowl, and whales of any kind. Canada, the United Kingdom, Australia, New Zealand, and many other countries also ban the import of such products, along with those made from lynx, otters, walruses, wolves, and wolverines. However, it is possible to import some items into some countries with the appropriate paperwork, and any reputable shop will provide a US Department of the Interior CITES Personal Property Exemption form and preferably documentation of who made the item and where. If you think you are likely to buy Native crafts, the best bet is to check import restrictions before you leave home. One publication worth checking out is *A Customs Guide to Alaska Native Arts* (online at ⓦwww.dced.state.ak.us/oed/nag/nativearts.htm), which includes a country-by-country list of which species are legal, permissible with paperwork, or illegal.

Export and import restrictions are irrelevant for **US residents**, except that they can't take banned goods into Canada, even in transit.

Festivals

Between Memorial Day weekend (the last in May) and Labor Day weekend (the first in September) Alaskans make the best of the long summer days with some sort of festival happening pretty much every weekend. Things are quieter in spring and fall, but winter throws up its own array of wondrous events, many worth planning a trip around. For information on public holidays, see p.83.

January

Russian Orthodox Christmas (Jan 7). Solemn services held in Kodiak, Sitka, and elsewhere.

February

Yukon Quest International Sled Dog Race (second week). Starts or finishes in Fairbanks. ⓦwww.yukonquest.org.
Iceworm Festival in Cordova (first full weekend). Giant model iceworm paraded through the streets and general carousing. ⓦwww.iceworm.org.
Fur Rendezvous in Anchorage (second to third weekend). Ten-day citywide "Fur Rondy," packed with uniquely Alaskan activities, costume ball, sled-dog races, snow sculpture competition, etc. ⓦwww.furrondy.net.

March

World Ice Art Championships in Fairbanks (first two weeks). Major competition with fabulous, larger-than-life sculptures. ⓦwww.icealaska.com.
Nenana Ice Classic tripod raising (first weekend). ⓦwww.nenanaakiceclassic.com.
Iditarod Trail Sled Dog Race from Anchorage to Nome (for 12 days from first Sat). ⓦwww.iditarod.com.
Miners & Mushers Ball in Nome (second Sat). A black-tie ball coinciding with the Iditarod.

Ice Festival Valdez (middle week). Games and festivities in town plus competitive ice climbing in Keystone Canyon. See p.327.

Bering Sea Ice Golf Classic in Nome (third Sat). Fund-raising 6-hole par-41 golf on ice.

Seward's Day (last Mon). Public holiday. Commemorates the signing (on March 30, 1867) of the treaty by which the United States bought Alaska from Russia.

Pillar Mountain Golf Classic (last weekend, or first in April). One-hole par-70 cross-country golf. See p.350.

April

Good Friday and Easter Monday (late March or early April).

Big Mountain Master Extreme Snowboard Competition in Valdez (first two weeks). Major snowboarding events. See p.327.

Alaska Folk Festival in Juneau (second week). A real musicians' festival. ⓦ www.akfolkfest.org.

Stikine River Garnet Festival in Wrangell (fourth weekend). Five days primarily celebrating the mass arrival of bald eagles. ⓦ www.wrangellchamber.org.

May

Copper River Delta Shorebird Festival in Cordova (first weekend). Serious bird-watching and associated events. ⓦ www.cordovachamber.org.

Kachemak Bay Shorebird Festival in Homer (first or second weekend). All sorts of shorebird-watching, activities for kids, and a Wooden Boat Festival. ⓦ www.homeralaska.org/shorebird.htm.

Little Norway Festival in Petersburg (third full weekend).

Kodiak Crab Festival (Memorial Day weekend). General crab-themed festivities and weird races. ⓦ www.kodiak.org/crabfest.html. See p.351.

Kachemak Bay Kayak Festival (last week). Sea kayak instruction and workshops for all ages and skill levels, plus assorted social events. ⓦ www.kachemakkayakfest.com.

Great Alaska Craftbeer & Homebrew Festival in Haines (fourth weekend). Tasting, jazz, blues, and a Saturday-night banquet.

June

Kachemak Bay Writers' Conference in Homer (second weekend Thurs–Sun). Lectures, workshops, panel presentations, and readings with nationally recognized writers. ⓦ www.writersconference.homer.alaska.edu.

Colony Days in Palmer (second weekend Fri–Sun). Craft fair, wagon rides, bicycle rodeo, etc.

Blues on the Green in Anchorage (second Sat). Alaska's premier blues festival (along with soul and bluegrass) held in Anchorage's Kincaid Park. ⓦ www.bluescentral.biz.

Sitka Summer Music Festival (first or last three weeks). Mostly classical and chamber music. See p.152.

Summer Solstice Celebrations in Fairbanks (third week, culminating on June 21). Fun run, midnight basketball, and other like-minded events. See p.513.

Seldovia Music Festival (solstice weekend). See p.302.

Midnight Sun Festival in Nome (weekend nearest to June 21). Complete with Polar Bear Swim. ☎443-6624, ⓦ www.nomealaska.org.

Mayor's Marathon in Anchorage (Saturday nearest June 21). Alaska's biggest marathon (3500 strong) held along Anchorage's trail system, attracts runners from around the world.

Nalukataq in Barrow (mid-June to early July). Celebration of the end of the spring whale hunt.

Last Frontier Theatre Conference in Valdez (third or last week). ⓦ www.pwscc.edu/conference. See p.328.

Gold Rush Days in Juneau (fourth weekend). Competitive logging and mining events plus food and family fun. ☎780-6075.

Southeast Alaska State Fair in Haines (last weekend). Logging show, fiddle contest, horseshoe tournament, etc. ⓦ www.seakfair.org.

July

Mount Marathon Race in Seward (July 4). See p.270.

Girdwood Forest Fair (July 4th weekend). Crafts, music, and entertainment. ⓦ www.girdwoodforestfair.com. See p.259.

Moose Dropping Festival in Talkeetna (second weekend). Street vendors, music, plays, food, and the fabled Mountain Mother contest. See p.402.

World Eskimo-Indian Olympics in Fairbanks (second or third week). ⓦ www.weio.org. See p.513.

Anderson Bluegrass Country Music Festival Mile 283 Parks Hwy (last weekend). See p.436.

Prince of Wales Island Fair and Logging Show Thorne Bay, PoW Island (last weekend). See p.120.

August

Talkeetna Bluegrass Festival at Mile 102 Parks Hwy (first weekend). Major summer bash with top Alaskan bands all weekend plus camping and family areas. ⓦ www.talkeetnabluegrass.com. See p.402.

Tanana Valley State Fair in Fairbanks (second week). ☎452-3750, ⓦwww.tananavalleyfair.org.
Blueberry Arts Festival in Ketchikan (first or second weekend). ⓦwww.ketchikanarts.org.
Sandhill Crane Festival in Fairbanks (third weekend). Celebration of the fall migration of Sandhill cranes. ⓦwww.creamersfield.org.
Alaska State Fair in Palmer (late Aug to early Sept). The biggest of the five state fairs, held over ten days ending on Labor Day. See p.386.

September

Totem Pole Raising in Klawok, PoW Island (Labor Day). See p.116.
Rubber Duck Race in Nome (Labor Day). Sub-Arctic pooh-sticks. ☎443-5221.

Bathtub Race in Nome (Labor Day). A wheeled bathtub push. ☎443-2919.
Equinox Marathon in Fairbanks (nearest Sat to Sept 21). ⓦwww.equinoxmarathon.org.

October

Alaska Day (Oct 18). Public holiday. Anniversary of the formal transfer of the territory from Russia and the raising of the US flag at Sitka in 1867.
Alaska Day Festival (Oct 18). Week-long festivities in Sitka. ⓦwww.cityofsitka.com/alaskaday.

December

Bachelor Ball and Wilderness Woman Contest in Talkeetna (first weekend). ⓦwww.talkeetnachamber.org. See p.402.

Travel essentials

Costs

Alaska's **high prices** are legendary; the reputation stems mostly from the mid-1970s, when pay packets bulging from pipeline construction pushed prices into the stratosphere. Alaska remains one of the most expensive states to visit, but in recent years prices have moderated, and Anchorage now doesn't seem much more costly than any other American city.

There's no hiding from the fact that you are going to spend a fair bit of money on your travels here. If you are used to Lower 48 prices, you can safely assume that in the bigger towns you'll be paying 10 to 20 percent more for groceries and meals, and in remote communities anything up to double the usual cost. There is also a general trend for the towns of Southeast Alaska (which are closer to the supply entrepôt of Seattle) to be marginally cheaper than elsewhere.

Your **daily budget**, if you are camping, hitching, or cycling, preparing most of your own food, and keeping a tight rein on tours and activities, would be in the region of $30 each (£16, €23), rising to $40–60

(£21–32, €31–46) if you stay in hostels, use buses, trains, and ferries, and indulge in the odd meal out. Couples staying in cheaper motels, eating at unpretentious restaurants and not skimping on the main attractions and activities are looking at around $70–90 each (£37–47, €54–69); and if you rent a car for at least some of your stay, sleep in comfortable B&Bs, and eat well, you should reckon on at least $120 a day (£63, €92). All these figures can be ramped up dramatically if you start flying out to remote communities or staying at wilderness lodges, though this can be offset by abstemious days hiking and backcountry camping when you'll spend nothing.

Adults generally pay full price for tours, activities, and museum entry, but small **discounts** of around ten percent are available to military, seniors, and sometimes (though not often) students.

Unlike most US states, Alaska imposes no statewide **sales tax**; instead, each community sets its own tax rate. In many places (including Anchorage) this is nothing at all, but when it does occur it's usually between four and seven percent of your purchase price (especially in Southeast). **Tipping** is expected in restaurants, bars, and taxis, and a guide or tour host will welcome a similar appreciation; leave around fifteen percent of the bill.

Crime and personal safety

Alaska has more than its fair share of **violent crime**, but much of this takes place behind closed doors or in places you are not going to visit, so as a visitor you are unlikely to be affected. You are more likely to be a victim of **theft**, though instances of bag snatching and personal assault are rare. Avoid carrying around and flaunting huge wads of cash, stash your valuables in the hotel safe (if there is one), and keep a photocopy of the important pages of your passport along with a record of the travelers' checks you haven't spent. Because of an increase in **theft from vehicles** at trailheads, especially those close to town, you should avoid leaving valuables in your car or truck. In practice, this is difficult to do, but at least store stuff out of sight.

Assuming you don't fall victim to any of this, you'll probably spend your entire time in Alaska without coming into contact with any of Alaska's various law enforcement agencies. Perhaps the easiest way to attract their attention is to fail to buy the appropriate hunting or **fishing license** or to infringe on the bag-limit rules in some way. Rules vary throughout the state, so always be sure to know what you are allowed to take. **Drugs** are, of course, totally illegal.

Disabled travelers

Travelers with physical disabilities are fairly well catered for in Alaska and are likely to experience a minimum of discrimination. Cruises, whale-watching trips, trains, Denali Park buses, and many other things have ways to facilitate disabled access. Even out in the wilderness you'll increasingly find the authorities have installed accessible walkways and trails, and some popular fishing areas have provision for wheelchairs. For state parks (including cabins and campgrounds) check out ADA Facilities at Ⓦwww.dnr.state.ak.us/parks.

The Americans with Disabilities Act (ADA) means that all new or substantially upgraded accommodation will have easy-entry rooms with adapted bathrooms. Unfortunately this often doesn't cover some of the most distinctive B&Bs and hostels, so you're likely to find yourself in comfortable but undistinguished motels and hotels.

Also consider contacting Accessible Alaska Adventures (Ⓣ1-800/349-6301 or 907/349-6301, Ⓦwww.accessiblealaska.com) who book appropriate tours and organize independent travel.

Electricity

Alaska uses the same power supply as the rest of the US: 110 volts at 60Hz. North Americans can use appliances with no modification; pretty much everyone else will need a plug adaptor. Some form of transformer may also be needed, though electronic goods (laptops, camera chargers, and the like) are increasingly capable of running on a wide range of voltages.

Entry requirements

US and Canadian citizens do not require passports to enter Alaska, though they are encouraged to do so. If you cross a national border, you must carry some form of notarized identification, such as a birth certificate or naturalization papers.

Citizens of all other countries must have a valid passport, and citizens of countries not covered by the Visa Waiver Program (see blow) or people who don't fulfill the scheme's requirements need a **non-immigrant visa**. Forms are available from your nearest embassy or consulate (see p.79), and can be downloaded from Ⓦtravel.state.gov/visa. You'll need a passport valid until six months after your return date, a passport photo, and US$100.

Visa Waiver Program

Under the **Visa Waiver Program** citizens of 27 countries – Andorra, Australia, Austria, Belgium, Brunei, Denmark, Finland, France, Germany, Iceland, Ireland, Italy, Japan, Liechtenstein, Luxembourg, Monaco, Netherlands, New Zealand, Norway, Portugal, San Marino, Singapore, Slovenia, Spain, Sweden, Switzerland, and the United Kingdom – need only a full passport and a **visa** waiver form (provided by your travel agent or your airline) to enter the United States for a period of less than ninety days.

Note that **passports** must be **machine-readable** (most issued in the past ten years will be) and if yours was issued after October 26, 2005 it must have a digital photo rather than a normal photo laminated in place. Additionally, passports issued on or after October 26, 2006 must have an integrated chip (e-passport) on the data page. For more information visit Ⓦwww.cbp.gov.

If you intend to work, study, or stay in the country for more than ninety days, you must apply for a visa in advance. You should also apply for a visa in advance if you are a convicted felon, have a communicable disease – HIV/AIDS or TB in particular – or admit to being a communist or a fascist.

Canadian formalities

Anyone approaching Alaska through Canada (either overland or on BC Ferries) will need to complete **Canadian formalities**: for full details check Citizenship and Immigration Canada (Ⓦwww.cic.gc.ca). British citizens, as well as citizens of the European Union (EU), Norway, and most Commonwealth countries (including Australia and New Zealand) only need a valid passport, though visitors from South Africa will need a visa. If you are traveling on the Alaska Marine Highway System (AMHS) ferries from Bellingham, WA, your first stop will be in Ketchikan, Alaska, so although you will be traveling through Canadian waters, for immigration purposes you are not considered to be entering Canada.

Overland travelers shouldn't expect the rules to be relaxed by the Canadian border guards just because you need to pass through their country to get to Alaska, and it is worth keeping in mind that Canadian customs officials may also ask you to prove you have sufficient funds for the journey. **Motorists** driving through Canada will be asked to show some proof of vehicle ownership and liability insurance cover.

Immigration control

The standard immigration regulations apply to all foreign visitors, whether or not they are using the Visa Waiver Program. During the flight to your first US port of call (which may not be in Alaska), you'll be handed an immigration form (and a customs declaration; see below), which must be given up at immigration control once you land. This **I-94 form** requires details of your length of stay and where you are staying on your first night. Writing "transit" or the name of some random hotel you picked out of this guide is increasingly unlikely to be accepted. If at all possible, get the full address of the place you are going to stay, including the zip code. On arrival, officials will take a photograph and **electronic fingerprints**: it sounds like Orwell's *1984* but it is all fairly quick and painless.

You probably won't be asked, but you should be able to prove that you have enough money to support yourself while in the US – $300–400 a week is usually considered sufficient – as anyone revealing the slightest intention of working while in the country is likely to be refused admission. Part of the immigration form will be attached to your passport, where it must stay until you leave, when an immigration or airline official will detach it.

Customs

Foreign visitors flying to Alaska via another US airport will have to retrieve their bags and pass through customs at the first point of entry. Unless you subsequently leave the US you will not need to complete customs or immigration procedures on arrival in Alaska.

The adult **duty-free allowance** is 200 cigarettes or 100 cigars (not Cuban), and 34 ounces (1 liter) of spirits, and goods up to a total of $800. Foodstuffs (particularly fresh fruit, vegetables, and seeds) can be brought in but need to be declared and inspected.

Exports are also restricted, particularly antiquities and anything made from endangered species (for more on this, see p.73). **Hunters and anglers** wanting to take home their trophies or just a freezer-shelf-full of salmon, halibut, or moose steaks will usually find that their guides can make the necessary arrangements.

US embassies and consulates

Websites and contact details for all US embassies and consulates abroad can be found at ⓦusembassy.state.gov.

Australia Canberra ⓣ02/6214 5600, ⓦcanberra .usembassy.gov; consulates in Melbourne, Perth, and Sydney.

Canada Ottawa ⓣ613/238-5335, ⓦcanada .usembassy.gov; consulates in Calgary, Halifax, Montreal, Quebec, Toronto, Vancouver, and Winnipeg

Denmark Copenhagen ⓣ35 55 31 44, ⓦwww .usembassy.dk.

Ireland Dublin ⓣ01/668 8777, ⓦdublin .usembassy.gov.

Netherlands The Hague ⓣ070/310 2209, ⓦnetherlands.usembassy.gov; consulate in Amsterdam.

New Zealand Wellington ⓣ04/462 6000, ⓦwellington.usembassy.gov; consulate in Auckland.

Norway Oslo ⓣ22 44 85 50, ⓦnorway .usembassy.gov.

South Africa Pretoria ⓣ12/431-4000, ⓦpretoria.usembassy.gov; consulates in Cape Town, Durban, and Johannesburg.

Sweden Stockholm ⓣ08/783 53 00, ⓦstockholm.usembassy.gov.

UK London ⓣ020/7499 9000, premium-rated visa hotline ⓣ09042/450100, ⓦlondon .usembassy.gov; consulates in Belfast and Edinburgh.

Insurance

It is always advisable to take out a travel **insurance policy**. Before paying for a new policy, check whether you are already covered: some all-risks home insurance policies may cover your possessions when overseas, and many private medical schemes include cover when abroad. Students will often find that their student health coverage extends during the vacations and for one term beyond the date of last enrollment.

After exhausting the possibilities above, you might want to contact a specialist travel insurance company, or consider the travel insurance deal we offer (see below). A typical travel insurance policy usually provides cover for the loss of baggage, tickets and – up to a certain limit – cash or checks, as well as cancellation or curtailment of your journey. Most of them exclude so-called dangerous sports unless an extra premium is paid for, say, whitewater rafting or skiing. Many policies can be chopped and changed to exclude coverage you don't need – for example, sickness and accident benefits can often be excluded or included at will. If you do take medical coverage, ascertain whether benefits will be paid as treatment proceeds or only after return home, and whether there is a 24-hour medical emergency number. When securing baggage cover, make sure that the per-article limit – typically $500–1000 – will cover your most valuable possessions. If you need to make a claim, you should keep receipts for medicines and medical treatment, and in the event you have anything stolen you must obtain an official statement from the police.

Rough Guides has teamed up with Columbus Direct to offer you **travel insurance** that can be tailored to suit your needs. Products include a low-cost **backpacker** option for long stays; a **short break** option for city getaways; a typical **holiday package** option; and others. There are also annual **multi-trip** policies for those who travel regularly. Different sports and activities (trekking, skiing, etc) can usually be covered if required.

See our website (ⓦwww.roughguides insurance.com) for eligibility and purchasing options. Alternatively, UK residents should call ⓣ0870/033-9988; US citizens ⓣ1-800/ 749-4922; Australians ⓣ1-300/669 999; all other nationalities ⓣ+44 870/890 2843.

Internet

Alaska is extremely well connected. Wherever you go (even tiny communities) you'll find Internet access, usually free at the local library. High summer demand (especially in popular tourist areas) means you sometimes have to wait hours to get on, but that is alleviated by more libraries offering free **WiFi**, allowing those with a laptop or PDA to get online without waiting for the library's computers.

For more immediate needs there is almost always a shop (or café) nearby offering Internet access at $5–6 for half an hour.

Most mid- to upper-end hotels and motels now also have dataports in all rooms and WiFi is increasingly common everywhere – sometimes unsecured, often secured but still free once you obtain the password. Hostels will sometimes have a coin-op machine in the corner.

Kids

Traveling with kids in Alaska is pretty easy. Most restaurants are fairly family oriented and kids are welcomed at most accommodation, although a few top-end B&Bs might discourage youngsters.

Traveling distances are long and whale-watching cruises might take all day so it pays to take toys, books, DVDs, games, etc to keep the young ones entertained.

In summer, ordinary precautions should keep any babies and toddlers warm and dry, but if you are traveling before mid-May or after mid-September, be sure to take extra warm clothing.

You'll find baby-changing facilities in restaurants and public buildings, though these will obviously be less common in remoter areas.

Generally, **kids go free** if they're under 5, and will pay around half the adult fare if under 12 or so.

Laundry

Almost every town has a laundromat, typically with self-serve machines, service washes, and **showers** ($3–4 plus 50¢ or $1 for use of a towel). Most hotels and motels also have a laundry room with coin-op machines and a powder dispenser.

Living and working in Alaska

Stories of astonishing wages in Alaska still hang wilting on the travelers' grapevine; in reality you are unlikely to earn a bundle. Some people do get rich quick, though more frequently they spend the summer up here working hard in unpleasant conditions and going home with little more than what they came with, having spent their meager earnings quickly. Nonetheless, it is one way of spending time in Alaska without blowing your savings, and you may end up with an experience you'll cherish for a lifetime.

Visas

US citizens have no legal difficulties living and working in Alaska, but if you are **not a US citizen** you will need to plan ahead.

Visitors who enter the US on the Visa Waiver Program cannot extend their stay beyond the allocated ninety days, so if you suspect you may want to stay longer it is advisable to obtain a suitable visa before leaving home. If you enter on a non-immigrant visa you may be able to **extend your stay** beyond your allocated time by applying to the Department of Homeland Security's US Citizenship and Immigration Service (USCIS; Ⓦwww.uscis .gov). They will automatically assume that you're working illegally, and it's up to you to convince them otherwise. Do this by providing evidence of ample finances, and, if you can, bring along an upstanding American citizen to vouch for you. Start the process as early as possible, but at least 30 days before your visa expires.

Foreigners planning to work should apply for a special **working visa** at any American embassy before setting off. Different types of visas are issued, depending on your skills and length of stay, but, unless you've got relatives (parents or children over 21) or a prospective employer to sponsor you, your chances are slim at best. In practice, it is almost impossible to get one for the sort of seasonal work typically on offer in Alaska. Most visas go to foreigners working in summer camps in the Lower 48, and to those sponsored by an employer, who needs to prove that there is no US citizen available to take the job. Even in the traditionally more casual establishments like restaurants and bars, things have really tightened up, and if you do find work it's likely to be of the less visible, poorly paid kind – dishwasher rather than waiter. If you are still keen, the best bets are usually with the smaller restaurants and tourism operators who are prepared to pay cash-in-hand.

Working

Most high-earning legends stem from the late 1970s construction of the Alaska Pipeline, or from good fishing seasons when fishermen returned with a share of the profits that amounted to a small fortune. Such hauls are rare these days, and your chances of getting a good slice of the action are slim. There are plenty of experienced old-hands who will always get first pick over first-timers with no proven track record.

This kind of hierarchy can work in your favor if you are prepared to work more than one season up here; those who make it through one summer are almost guaranteed work the following year, often in a better position with greater earning potential. You can also improve your chances of getting something worthwhile by **planning ahead**. Most employers want their new employees to work the full season from May to sometime in September, and they recruit between December of the previous year and February. You can get work by just turning up and asking around in May, but many positions will already be taken, and you'll be hoping to fill in for no-shows and early sackings.

Securing a position in advance also opens up the possibility that your employer may pay for, or subsidize, your travel to Alaska, though this is more usual if you've worked for that employer before. More frequently, you'll get free or cheap accommodation, and maybe meals, especially if you are working away from town.

Types of jobs

Many of the jobs on offer in Alaska are in coastal regions, particularly in **salmon canneries** and other fish-processing plants. They usually offer around $9–11 an hour for standing beside a noisy and wet canning line gutting or filleting fish. If you can hack the arduous and boring work, it is possible to earn a packet doing long shifts with plenty of overtime, and keeping living costs down by bringing a tent or staying in cannery-owned bunkhouses. The season in each place is often short and the catch uncertain, so you'll need to be flexible enough to cope with early lay-offs and may have to move towns several times during the summer. You can sometimes land jobs by turning up at canneries early in the morning – Ketchikan, Petersburg, Pelican, Cordova, and Kodiak are all worth trying – but it is far better to contact companies well in advance, preferably in January or February. Try companies such as Trident Seafoods (ⓦwww.tridentseafoods.com) and

Unisea (ⓦwww.unisea.com), or specific jobs websites like Fishjobs (ⓦwww.fishjobs .com) and the Alaska Department of Labor's seafood industry job bank (ⓦalexsys.labor .state.ak.us).

Working offshore on **fish-processing ships** is more of a lottery. In a good season rewards can be higher than for onshore workers (around $14 an hour or a percentage of the catch), but it is dirty, miserable, and dangerous work with no relief from the pitching seas; boats often stay at sea for weeks at a time.

There's more fun and profit working with the **tourism industry**, often in the most beautiful parts of Alaska. Jobs might include driving buses (either between towns or on city tours), hotel reception, expediting, tour narrator, or hotel work. Rates around $8 an hour are normal in jobs where tips are common, more like $9–13 an hour where no tips are likely. If you've got specialist skills, you might even get a position as a rafting guide or leading mountain-bike trips, though these are seldom offered to first-time Alaska workers. The biggest operators are Holland America subsidiary Gray Line of Alaska (ⓦwww.graylinealaska.com), and Princess Tours (ⓦwww.princessjobs.com), who both accept online applications. You might want to try smaller companies we've listed throughout the Guide, or approach the bigger hotels directly.

There is also the possibility of working for the **federal government** through one of their land management agencies – the National Park Service (ⓦwww.nps.gov /personnel), the Forest Service (ⓦwww .fs.fed.us/fsjobs), the Fish and Wildlife Service (ⓦwww.fws.gov), or the Bureau of Land Management (ⓦwww.ak.blm .gov). You can log on to each organization's website, but eventually they all lead to the federal government's Office of Personnel Management site (ⓦwww.usajobs.opm .gov), which handles most positions.

For a wide listing of jobs available throughout the state, visit the Department of Labor's Alaska Jobs Bank at ⓦwww.jobs.state.ak.us.

Volunteer work

For those not legally allowed to work in the US, the only chance of working for the federal government is as a **volunteer**. Even US citizens might want to consider this option, as it is much easier to land a volunteer position than a paid job. Volunteers will probably get free accommodation and food, and may even have some transportation costs taken care of, but do not usually receive wages. In return for this poor remuneration, you may get to work in fabulous places learning valuable skills working alongside professionals conducting wildlife surveys or helping restore salmon breeding areas. Then again, you may end up doing fairly dull work, such as cleaning up campgrounds, or find yourself working in rugged conditions doing something physically demanding; always make sure you know what you are letting yourself in for. The websites of the federal agencies listed on p.81 will take you to information on their volunteer programs – the most active is the one run by the Forest Service.

Mail

With the sophistication of the US phone network and the ease of sending emails you may want to bypass the US Postal Service altogether. Compared with the mail in Britain and Australasia, it is both slow and careless, though things tend to turn up eventually. **Stamps** can also be bought from automatic vending machines, the lobbies of larger hotels, and many retail outlets and newsstands. Blue **mail boxes** stand on city street corners but are less common in rural areas.

Ordinary **mail** costs 39¢ for a letter (weighing not more than one ounce) sent within the US; postcards are 24¢. The international rate for letters weighing up to an ounce is 63¢ to Canada and Mexico, and 84¢ elsewhere. Postcards are 50¢, 55¢, and 75¢ respectively. Other rates are available at ⊛www.usps.com.

Letters can be sent c/o **General Delivery** (what's known elsewhere as **poste restante**) to the main post office in each town and must be addressed using AK, for the state of Alaska, followed by the five-digit **zip code**. We've included zip codes of larger towns in "Directory" at the end of their section.

Maps

For general navigation, you should be able to get by using the maps in this book. Should you feel the need for extra direction, specialist travel booksellers should have general maps of Alaska. Once in the state you'll find that gas stations sell tolerably useful and cheap maps, the best of which is the one by Rand McNally ($4), which at an inch to 75 miles gives only a broad sweep but does have handy enlargements of most of the areas where you are likely to spend time. Map enthusiasts won't be able to resist the weighty DeLorme *Alaska Atlas and Gazetteer* ($20), which covers most of the state at an inch to five miles, marks all hikes, huts, peaks, landing strips, and comes complete with contour lines and GPS grids. There's little worthwhile in between these two extremes, though there are regional maps available in each area.

If you are planning to do some serious hiking, you'll need a **topographic map**. These are sold by visitor centers in popular hiking areas, such as Denali National Park, at the Alaska Public Lands Information Centers. The *National Geographic Trails Illustrated* series has excellent maps ($10 each) covering all the major National Parks and area you'll likely to be hiking in – Denali, Kenai Fjords, Katmai, Chilkoot Trail, Gates of the Arctic, etc. For greater detail consider the US Geological Survey topo maps available online or by mail order (Box 25286, Denver, CO 80225 ☏1-888/275-8747, ⊛ask.usgs.gov). An order form can be downloaded from their website.

Measurements

The US has yet to go metric, so measurements are in inches, feet, yards, and miles; weight in ounces, pounds, and tons. American pints and gallons are four-fifths of Imperial ones. Clothing sizes are always two figures less than they would be in Britain – a British woman's size 12 is a US size 10 – while British shoe sizes are half a size below American ones for women, and one size below for men.

Public holidays

For most visitors to Alaska the important **public holidays** are Memorial Day, which marks the beginning of the main summer tourist season; Independence Day; and Labor Day, which marks the end of the summer season.

New Year's Day (Jan 1)
Martin Luther King, Jr Day (3rd Mon in Jan)
Presidents' Day (3rd Mon in Feb)
Seward's Day (March 27)
Memorial Day (4th Mon in May)
Independence Day (July 4)
Labor Day (1st Mon in Sept)
Columbus Day (2nd Mon in Oct)
Alaska Day (Oct 18)
Veterans' Day (Nov 11)
Thanksgiving Day (4th Thurs in Nov)
Christmas Day (Dec 25)

Money

Alaska is a US state and you'll be using US currency; its proximity to Canada does not mean that Canadian dollars will be accepted. **US currency** comes in **bills** of $1, $5, $10, $20, $50, and $100, plus various rarely seen larger denominations. The dollar is made up of 100 cents, with **coins** of 1 cent (known as a penny), 5 cents (a nickel), 10 cents (a dime), 25 cents (a quarter). For phones, vending machines, and buses it always pays to keep a stack of quarters handy.

If you don't already have a **credit card** you should seriously think about getting one before traveling to Alaska; it will make your life much easier – when checking into a hotel or renting a car, kayak, etc, you're likely to be asked for an imprint to establish your creditworthiness. Paying by plastic is accepted almost everywhere and 24-hour **ATMs** are now so common (even in tiny, remote communities) that you can always get a **cash advance** when you need it. Visa and MasterCard (known elsewhere as Access), and to a lesser extent American Express, Discover, and Diners Club, are all widely accepted. You should also carry an **ATM card** that works on either Cirrus or Plus, international systems widely established in Alaska that enable you to obtain money from your home account.

US-dollar traveler's checks are still the safest way to carry money and can be used as cash in restaurants and shops. Don't be put off by "no checks" signs in the window: that only refers to personal checks. Except for Canadian currency, exchanging **foreign traveler's checks** and bills is almost impossible outside Anchorage and Fairbanks. Wells Fargo banks are your best bet.

International **exchange rates** seem to fluctuate more wildly every year, but as we go to press one US dollar trades for Aus$1.30, Can$1.14, €0.78, £0.53, and NZ$1.50.

Opening hours and public holidays

Few places are as seasonal as Alaska. You'll find shops, cruises, tour offices, and restaurants have long opening hours every day of the summer, the only exceptions being public holidays when some businesses may close. **Banks** (Mon–Fri 9am–4.30pm) and **post offices** (Mon–Fri 9am–5pm and in some places Sat 9am–1pm) tend to operate the same hours year-round.

In summer (Memorial Day to Labor Day), shops and museums are generally open daily 9am to 5pm, though in tourist centers many stay open an hour or two longer in the evening. Supermarkets and superstores might remain open until midnight or even 24 hours. During the **winter months** most tourist-related businesses (and some museums) operate with vastly reduced hours or shut down altogether. Always call

Calling home from Alaska

Note that the initial zero is omitted from the area code when dialing the UK, Ireland, Australia, and New Zealand from abroad.

Canada just dial the number.
Australia 011 + 61 + city code.
New Zealand 011 + 64 + city code.
UK 011 + 44 + city code.
Republic of Ireland 011 + 353 + city code.
South Africa 011 + 27 + city code.

ahead to check opening hours and off-season schedules.

Phones

North American travelers will generally find their **mobile phone** works fine in Alaska, and many foreign visitors are also adequately served, though it always pays to check in advance with your provider. **Reception** is good in most towns, but there are long gaps between communities where you will be incommunicado, and as soon as you get out into bush you are on your own. For long periods out of range, such as epic kayaking trips, it may pay to rent a handheld **satellite phone**. A quick Internet search will show several companies renting phones for around $75 a week. You can expect to pay around $2 a minute for calls – cheap if something bad happens when you're five days from civilization.

Public phones are still plentiful in Alaska. **Local calls** cost 25–50¢, but since virtually the whole of Alaska has the same ☎**907 area code** this is no indication of what constitutes a long-distance call. **Call rates** for non-local and long-distance calls are much lower on weekends and between 6pm and 8am. Calls from motel and **hotel rooms**

are usually much more expensive, though local calls are usually free.

If you are making a lot of long-distance calls, it works out much cheaper if you buy a **phone card**, usually available in denominations of $5, $10, $20, and $50 from convenience stores, supermarkets, post offices, and motel front desks.

Photography

Wherever you go you'll find somewhere happy to burn your **digital photos** onto a CD for around $7. You might find it more convenient (and cheaper) to upload your images to one of the Web-based photo storage sites, though libraries and cybercafés might not look too kindly on you using up their bandwidth.

Film is still reasonably widely available, but if you need anything other than standard print film you might have to go looking or stock up in the bigger towns.

Photography in Alaska has special demands, requiring a lens as wide as 28mm to really capture the magnificent scenery, but something as long as 300mm (and consequently a tripod) if you don't want to have to explain that the distant brown smudge is a bear. Most point-and-shoot cameras will

Useful phone numbers

Emergencies ☎911; ask for the appropriate emergency service: fire, police, or ambulance.
Directory assistance ☎411 (press 1 after the listed number to be connected).
Directory assistance for 800 numbers out of state ☎1-800/555-1212
Long-distance directory assistance within Alaska ☎1-907/555-1212, outside Alaska ☎1-(area code)/555-1212
Operator ☎0

Trip-planning resources

Alaska Department of Fish and Game 1255 W 8th St, PO Box 115525, Juneau, AK 99811-5526 ☎907/465-4100, ⊛www.adfg.state.ak.us.

Alaska Marine Highway System 6858 Glacier Hwy, Juneau, AK 99801-7909 ☎907/465-3941 or 1-800/642-0066 in US, ⊛www.ferryalaska.com.

Alaska Public Lands Information Centers ⊛www.nps.gov/aplic. Anchorage: 605 W 4th Ave, #105, AK 99501 ☎907/271-2737; Fairbanks: 250 Cushman St, #1a, AK 99701 ☎907/456-0527; Ketchikan: Southeast Alaska Discovery Center, 50 Main St, AK 99901 ☎907/228-6234; Tok: PO Box 359, AK 99780 ☎907/883-5667.

Alaska Tourism Industry Association 2600 Cordova St, Suite 201, Anchorage, AK 99503 ⊛www.travelalaska.com.

Alaska Wilderness Recreation and Tourism Association 2207 Spenard Rd, Suite 201, Anchorage, AK 99503 ☎907/258-3171, ⊛www.awrta.org.

not return decent wildlife shots. The best time for seeing animals is around dawn and dusk, when light levels are low and shadows are long. Low light levels increase the need for faster film settings, usually 400 or higher.

Senior travelers

Alaska doesn't present any particular problems for senior travelers. Indeed, the abundance of older people on cruise ships means that seniors make up the bulk of all Alaska tourists. Trips and tours occasionally offer small discounts for seniors, though nothing to get excited about.

Taxes

There is no statewide tax on goods or services. Some communities (particularly in Southeast) impose their own sales tax (typically four to seven percent), and many cities charge an additional bed tax of two to eight percent. In Juneau, for example, these combined taxes add twelve percent to the quoted price of hotel beds. Tourists are also stung with extra taxes for rental cars starting with a ten percent statewide tax. Other taxes vary, but in Anchorage you can expect to pay a further eight percent on the quoted price if you use one of the airport-based rental companies.

Departure taxes are included in your ticket price and there are no additional airport fees.

Time

Alaska Standard Time is observed throughout the whole state (except for a few far western Aleutian Islands not covered in this book). **Daylight saving** is observed from the first Sunday in April to the last Sunday in October – the same as in most of the rest of the US and Canada. In summer when it is noon in Anchorage it is 1pm in Vancouver, 1pm in Seattle, 4pm in New York, 9pm in London, 6am (the next day) in Sydney, and 8am (the next day) in Wellington.

Tourist information

Alaska does relatively little to promote itself at a state level, preferring to let individual businesses and local tourism organizations conduct their own promotions. Nonetheless, for advance information a good starting point is the *Alaska Vacation Planner*, glossy promotion material on Alaska and the Yukon. It can be ordered online (⊛www.travelalaska.com) and is free in the US and Canada (otherwise $10).

Visitor centers

Every town of any size has a **visitor center** (the term we've used throughout the book), which might be officially known as the visitor information center, Chamber of Commerce, or Convention and Visitors Bureau (CVB). At best they're well-stocked places laden with info on just about everything in the state and staffed by knowledgeable personnel; in many cases they are small offices with a handful of leaflets, or just a simple rack of advertising in the corner of the village store. Hours are equally varied – most are open daily in summer from 9 or 10am to 5pm or later. In general, they don't make bookings for tours or accommodation, but will often have a phone you can use.

In small towns the visitor center is likely to be your first contact for information about local hikes and cabins, though occasionally there is a separate visitor center run by the US Forest Service. National parks also have visitor centers, but by far the best sources of information about the outdoors are the four interagency **Alaska Public Lands Information Centers** (APLIC) – in Anchorage, Fairbanks, Ketchikan, and Tok. Run jointly by the authorities responsible for national parks, state parks, national forests, and national wildlife refuges, along with the Bureau of Land Management (BLM), they will provide just about everything you need to plan hiking, camping, canoeing, fishing, or wildlife-viewing trips.

Guide

Guide

Southeast Alaska

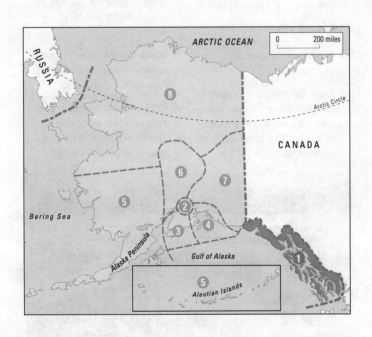

CHAPTER 1 # Highlights

✳ **Blue-water kayaking**
Explore the region by kayak
for fabulous scenery and
the chance to see marine
mammals up close: Misty
Fiords National Monument,
Tracy Arm Fjord, and Glacier
Bay National Park are three
of many worthy candidates.
See p.109, p.173, and p.176

✳ **Kasaan Totem Park** The
most enigmatic of Southeast's
totem parks is well worth the
trip. See p.117

✳ **Anan Wildlife Observatory**
Watch black and brown bears
fishing for salmon in a beautiful setting by a small waterfall
south of Wrangell. See p.128

✳ **Sitka** This immensely
appealing town has a
sublime island-studded
coastal setting, superb totem
poles, and a fascinating
Russian heritage. See p.138

✳ **Glacier Bay National Park**
An impressive concentra-
tion of tidewater glaciers set
amid magical scenery.
See p.176

✳ **White Pass & Yukon Route
railway** Ride the rails on this
historic line. See p.198

✳ **Chilkoot Trail** Alaska's most
celebrated multiday hike
and an evocative Gold Rush
history lesson. See p.200

△ Float-planes docked, Ketchikan

Southeast Alaska

V
isitors arriving in **Southeast Alaska** have a treat in store, a landscape writ on a grand scale, stretching four hundred miles along the coast. This is the **Alaskan Panhandle**, flanked by impenetrable snow-capped coastal mountains and incised by hairline fjords that create an interlocking archipelago of over a thousand densely forested islands. Along its length runs the continuous thread of calm waterways known as the Inside Passage. So narrow are some of the glacier-carved channels that on larger boats you could reach out and touch the steeply shelving rocks. Sheltered beaches are rare, and out of necessity towns are crammed onto whatever flat land can be found, often spilling out over the sea on a network of boardwalks; shops, streets, and even whole salmon canneries are perched picturesquely along the waterside on spruce poles.

Like much of Alaska, Southeast is defined by its weather, though here the moderator is **rain** rather than cold. With a maritime climate and a latitude similar to Scotland, Southeast seldom gets really cold in the winter, and summer highs are tempered by incessant low cloud and heavy rainfall, which can top two hundred inches a year in places. It is quite feasible to visit Southeast at any time, even for late-season events like Sitka's Alaska Day in October. The mountains still get covered with snow, though, and this lingers well into late June, making late summer and fall the best times for hiking.

The dripping leaves, sodden mosses, and wispy mist seem to suit ravens and bald eagles, which are everywhere, and it comes as no surprise that they became the prime crest symbols of the native **Tlingit** people. The Tlingit (*thling-get*), along with the Haida (*HI-da*) and Tsimshian (*SIM-shee-an*), have left an enduring legacy: **totem poles**, typically found clustered around replicas of the clan houses in which their creators once lived. Their original village sites were located to exploit the abundance of plunderable sea-life: as they say here, "When the tide's out, dinner's in." The early Russian fur traders and American gold seekers didn't disrupt the social fabric too much, but with the arrival of the missionaries the Tlingit abandoned their villages in favor of the schools and churches of the white towns that sprang up around gold mines, forts, canneries, and fishing ports. Suddenly, the motto changed to "We eat what we can, and can what we can't."

The importance of canneries gradually declined with the rise of logging in the 1960s. Almost the entirety of Southeast falls within the immense **Tongass National Forest**, and for decades cutting rights ensured the profitability of pulp and saw mills and guaranteed extensive clear-cutting of old-growth spruce and hemlock forests. Since the early 1990s, however, logging has rapidly declined. This is partly due to changes in world markets, but families

SOUTHEAST ALASKA

0   50 miles

FAIRWEATHER RANGE

Whittier

(3)   (2)   (7)

Skagway

Haines

GLACIER BAY
NATIONAL PARK

CANADA

Gustavus

COAST MOUNTAINS

Hoonah

Pelican

Mendenhall
Valley

Chichagof
Island

JUNEAU

Douglas

N

Tenakee
Springs

Admiralty
Island

Kruzof
Island

Mount
Edgecumbe

Baranof
Island

Chatham Strait

Angoon

TRACY ARM/
FORD'S TERROR
WILDERNESS

Sitka

Goddard
Hot Springs

TONGASS
NATIONAL
FOREST

Whitehorse

Kake

Kuiu
Island

Kupreanof
Island

Devil's
Thumb

Petersburg

(37)

Mitkof
Island

Zarembo
Island

Wrangell

Coffman
Cove

Etolin
Island

Wrangell
Island

Anan Wildlife
Observatory

Alexander Archipelago

Prince of
Wales
Island

Klawock

Craig   Hollis

Revillagigedo
Island

Mountain View

(37A)

Hyder   Stewart

Hydaburg

Dall
Island

Ketchikan

MISTY FIORDS
NATIONAL
MONUMENT

Prince George

Metlakatla

CANADA

Prince Rupert, BC and Bellingham, WA

Ferry fares

The prices of AMHS ferry journeys are given in the chart in Basics, p.42.

1

SOUTHEAST ALASKA | Ketchikan and around

of unemployed loggers and mill workers often blame eight years of Clinton government. During this time restrictions were imposed on building new logging roads into pristine forests. Loggers' hopes were raised when George W. Bush passed legislation that reopened some areas, but the industry remained stubbornly flat and in 2006 further legislation severely restricted uneconomic road-building subsidies. The battle for how the Tongass will be used looks likely to run for some time.

With mills closing or downsizing, small communities feel under siege and are turning to tourism as their savior. They hope to tap into the rich vein of the **cruise-ship industry**, which conditions almost every element of tourist life in Southeast. When a boat ties up (and many towns see at least one per day, sometimes four or five), it feels as if the circus is in town. Tour buses line the dock, helicopters and planes buzz the skies, and the gift shops and restaurants brace themselves for the onslaught of visitors who bring much-needed cash but swamp towns like Ketchikan, Juneau, and Skagway.

Yet even in the most popular ports of call, a little imagination and judicious timing can leave you in pristine environments without a soul in sight. **Ketchikan** is rightly celebrated for its wonderful examples of native culture, but if you find its totem parks too busy, head for **Prince of Wales Island**, where similar sites are well off the tourist trail. Kayaking is a superb way of seeking a little solitude, and the glacial granite masterpiece of **Misty Fiords National Monument** is a prime destination for a paddling expedition, although it's more commonly visited on a day-trip. Up the coast the beachside petroglyphs of Wrangell can be visited on a short stopover, though the town's totem parks and fine hikes take a little longer. The constricting Wrangell Narrows are just wide enough for ferries to reach the lively Norwegian fishing town of Petersburg, a base for visiting the LeConte Glacier, the southernmost of the dozens of glaciers that regularly calve into the waters of the Inside Passage. The jewel in Southeast's crown is **Sitka**, where Native and Russian cultures come together in beautiful surroundings. The state capital, **Juneau**, puts up a good fight for your attention with its cosmopolitan edge, a fascinating gold-mining history, and unparalleled access to the marvelous **Glacier Bay National Park**. From here, Lynn Canal runs north to two towns: Haines, with its low-key charms and unusual wintertime congregation of bald eagles, and the gold-rush town of Skagway, the start of the **White Pass & Yukon Route railway (WP&YR)** as well as the challenging **Chilkoot Trail**.

Throughout Southeast you'll find boat captains eager to take you out fishing, sightseeing, or, most of all, **whale-watching**, in the hopes of catching a breaching humpback or the prominent dorsal fin of an orca.

Ketchikan and around

Ketchikan, almost seven hundred miles north of Seattle, likes to bill itself as Alaska's "first city," the initial Alaskan port of call for northbound AMHS ferries and cruise ships. With over fifteen thousand people it ranks as Alaska's fourth largest city, and yet on arrival you are struck not so much by the town itself

KETCHIKAN

0   800 yds

N

ACCOMMODATION

Alderhouse	B
Captain's Quarters B&B	F
Clover Pass Resort	A
Eagle View Hostel	D
Gilmore Hotel	I
Ketchikan Youth Hostel	G
The Landing	C
New York Hotel	J
Super 8 Motel	E
WestCoast Cape Fox Lodge	H

RESTAURANTS & BARS

Annabelle's	5
Arctic Bar	3
Bar Harbor	1
Chico's	4
Diaz Café	8
First City Saloon	2
Pioneer Café	6
Steamers	9
That One Place	7
WestCoast Cape Fox Lodge	H

Hatchery & Eagle Center
City Park
Totem
Heritage Center
Tatsuda's
Supermarket
Laundromat

Deer Mountain Trail

KETCHIKAN LAKES RD

SCHOENBAR STREET
STEDMAN STREET
S. TONGASS HWY

Saxman Totem Park (2 miles)

BROWN DEER RD.
FAIRY CHASM ROAD
SCHOENBAR ROAD
PARK AVE.
SUMMIT TERR.
FOREST AVENUE
FAIRY CHASM
GRANT STREET

see inset for detail

T o n g a s s   N a r r o w s

Pennock Island

MILLER ST

WATER STREET
TONGASS AVENUE

2ND AVE
AUSTIN ST
WASHINGTON ST
ADAMS ST
JEFFERSON ST
1ST AVENUE

Southeast
Sea Kayaks

Plaza Mall

5TH AVENUE
4TH AVENUE
3RD AVE
MONROE ST
JACKSON STREET

DENALI AVE
LAKE ROAD
CARLANNA AVE
6TH AVENUE
BRYANT ST
ALDER STREET
HILL ROAD
BARANHOF
ALASKA AVENUE
HILLSIDE ST
3RD AVENUE

Forest Service
District Office

IFA
Ferry Dock

AMHS
Ferry Dock

TONGASS AVENUE

Airport
Shuttle
Ferry Dock

Gravina Island

Airport (200yds)
Totem Bight (8 miles)

DOWNTOWN KETCHIKAN

0   200 yds

N

Council of
the Clans

Dolly's
House

Fish
Ladder

Married
Man's Trail

PARK AVENUE
HARRIS ST
VENETIA AVE
EDMOND ST
CREEK ST
STEDMAN STREET

Tongass
Historical
Museum
& Library

Discovery
Center

Lumberjack
Show

Salmon Landing

PINE ST
GRANT STREET
BAWDEN STREET
EDMOND ST
MAIN STREET
MISSION ST
DOCK ST
FRONT STREET
SPRUCE MILL
MILL STREET

Cruise Ship
Docks

TUNNEL

Tongass Narrows

but by its insignificance after the miles of dense forest you've just sailed past or flown over. On most summer days downtown Ketchikan disappears behind a white wall of cruise ships which feed up to five thousand tourists into the compact town center, affecting almost every activity you take part in and quite possibly souring your opinion of this otherwise likeable community.

Shoehorned onto the southwestern edge of **Revillagigedo Island** (correctly, *ruh-vee-uh-hih-HAY-do*, but usually just "Revilla"), Ketchikan is – like most Southeast towns – squeezed tightly between forested hills and the plunging depths of the Inside Passage, in this case the waters of Tongass Narrows. Land is in such demand that precipitous hillsides have been put to residential use, the houses linked by long staircases that are significant enough to have street names. Some people lack vehicular access to their residences, while others drive home on streets that are really just wide boardwalks. Climb up to the wooden Warren, G, and Harding streets – jointly named for the 29th president, who visited in 1923 – from where it is apparent just how much of the waterfront is on stilts. The other face of Ketchikan is the historic downtown core, now overdeveloped with flashy diamond and fur shops, cheek by jowl with tacky souvenir emporia.

Nonetheless, Ketchikan remains one of Southeast's more interesting towns. Nowhere else can you get such a broad sweep of Southeast Native culture, starting with one of the world's finest collections of authentic nineteenth-century totem poles in the **Totem Heritage Center**. A few miles along Ketchikan's limited road system, the Totem Bight State Historic Park and Saxman Totem Park both exhibit exquisite replicas in a more natural, outdoor setting; the latter runs a carving center where you can watch new totem poles being worked. The celebrated boardwalks of **Creek Street**, now somewhat sanitized of their red-light past, are still a good place to stroll while checking out the craft and book shops and the salmon in the waters below.

To escape the crowds, make use of some of the area's hiking trails, though bear in mind Ketchikan is a strong contender to be the nation's wettest town – annual precipitation averages over 160 inches (and has topped 200).

Although you may want to spend only a day or two in Ketchikan itself, there's no shortage of intriguing destinations a short flight or ferry trip from the city. Flightseeing and boat-charter companies are eager to take you into the granite wonderland of **Misty Fiords National Monument**, a trip that can be extended by staying in Forest Service cabins or camping out beside your kayak.

For a less intense approach to the grandeur of Southeast Alaska, spend a few days on **Prince of Wales Island** (see p.113), or pay a visit to the Tsimshian community of **Metlakatla**, the only Native reservation in the state. If it's **bears** you want to see, you've got a fair chance of spotting one from a drive around Prince of Wales Island, but there's more structured viewing at Anan Creek (see "Wrangell," on p.128, although it's accessible from Ketchikan) and at **Hyder** (see box, p.111), a tiny piece of Alaska that feels a lot more like Canada.

Arrival and information

Near-daily AMHS **ferries** (☎225-6181) and twice-daily Inter-Island Ferry Authority ferries from Prince of Wales Island (☎826-4848 or 1-866/308-4848, ⓦwww.interislandferry.com) pull in at separate docks two miles north of downtown on N Tongass Highway; city buses (see p.96) stop outside. Ketchikan's **airport** (with frequent Alaska Airlines flights from Seattle and Juneau, and occasional links to the smaller Southeast towns; ☎225-6800) is on

Gravina Island, separated from the town by the 200-yard channel of Tongass Narrows. A vehicular **shuttle ferry** (every 15–30min whenever there are flights; $5 same-day round-trip, vehicles $6 each way) plies the gap and drops you two miles north of downtown (close to the AMHS ferry terminal) where you can catch a bus into town. Alternatively, hop aboard the frequent Airporter (☎225-5429) right outside the airport terminal for a combined ferry ride and drive into town for $20. The Airporter meets all planes and picks up and drops off at hotels around town.

Stacks of leaflets and information on the town are available at the **visitor center**, 131 Front St (Mon–Fri 8am–5pm, plus extended hours and Sat & Sun opening whenever cruise ships are in; ☎225-6166 or 1-800/770-3300, ⓦwww .visit-ketchikan.com). For anything related to the outdoors, you're better off at the **Southeast Alaska Discovery Center**, 50 Main St (early May–Sept daily 8am–5pm; Oct to early May Tues–Sat 10am–4.30pm; free entry to visitor center portion; ☎228-6220, ⓦwww.fs.fed.us/r10/tongass), where the unstaffed Alaska Room comes stuffed with Alaska videos, plenty of brochures on trails, camping, and kayaking, and a computer and direct phone line for reserving Forest Service cabins. For something more specific, call the Forest Service's District Office, 3031 N Tongass Hwy (Mon–Fri 8am–4.30pm; ☎225-2148), out towards the ferry dock.

Getting around and tours

Getting around the downtown area is very easy on foot, though to get to the ferry terminal and airport (and perhaps to your accommodation) you might need the **bus** services provided by "The Bus" (daily 6.15am–7pm roughly hourly; ☎225-8726, ⓦwww.borough.ketchikan.ak.us; $2 per journey). The most useful of the three routes is the Blue Line (Mon–Fri only), which makes an hour-long loop from downtown, past the AMHS and airport ferry docks, out to Totem Bight State Park, and back. The Green Line replaces the Blue Line's Totem Bight leg with a loop through the suburbs but also calls at the airport and AMHS ferry docks and town center. The Red Line loops from the airport ferry dock through town to Saxman and back. These options are satisfactory if you plan ahead, but for more impulsive moves or to visit the totem parks you may want to **rent a car** (good value for two or more), rent a **bike**, or grab a **taxi** (see Listings, p.107).

Ketchikan has at least a dozen land-based **tours**, most of them geared up to deal with the waves of passengers spilling off the cruise ships each day. In fact, many of the tours are only sold on the ships and independent travelers are either ignored or vastly outnumbered by ship passengers. Horse-drawn buggy circuits, Hummer tours, amphibian adventures, and many more are all available; call at the tour reservation area of the visitor center if you are interested.

With Saxman and Totem Bight both accessible by city bus, you may feel no need to take a tour, though joining up with an agency makes it all a bit easier. Rainbird Deluxe Tours (☎1-888/505-8810, ⓦwww.alaskarainbird .com) does a tour of the sights of town and visits Saxman (2hr; $35), and also offers a Saxman and Totem Bight combo (3hr; $40). Northern Tours of Alaska (☎1-877/461-8687, ⓦwww.northerntoursofalaska.com) has a similar tour (2hr; $30) focusing on Totem Bight. For something a little different, look out for the enthusiastic Lois Munch, who runs Classic Tours (☎225-3091, ⓦwww.classictours.com), using a restored 1955 Chevy to visit Saxman (2hr; $84) or, additionally, a section of forest, which includes a stop at an eagle's nest (3hr; $99).

Accommodation

Ketchikan's modest range of accommodation sets the pattern for what you'll find all the way up the coast: downtown hotels and B&Bs, a couple of motels, a hostel or two, and some wooded campgrounds out of town. There are few genuinely luxurious places, but in general standards are high and prices tolerable, despite the additional thirteen percent tax charged on hotel beds. Most of the hotels are downtown, with B&Bs scattered along the road system.

The closest **campgrounds** to town are in the attractive Ward Lake Recreation Area, five miles northwest of the ferry terminal. Although these spots accept RVs, there are no hookups, and motorhome drivers wanting power and cable TV will have to stay fourteen miles north of downtown at *Clover Pass Resort*.

You should book directly with the establishments as far in advance as you can manage in summer, but if you're in real difficulty contact the visitor center or Ketchikan Reservation Service (☎247-5337 or 1-800/987-5337, ⓦwww.ketchikan-lodging.com), which can arrange accommodation.

There are also dozens of Forest Service **cabins** around Ketchikan, some of which we've listed in the boxes on pp.104 and 108. If you're geared up for camping, then you've everything you need for staying in a cabin – those less well equipped can rent everything they need from Alaska Wilderness Outfitting, 3857 Fairview Ave (☎225-7335, ⓦwww.latitude56.com/camping), including a complete cooking kit for $22 a day.

Hotels, motels, and B&Bs

Alderhouse 420 Alder Street ☎247-2537, ⓦwww.alderhousebnb.com. Comfortable and very welcoming B&B an easy walk from the AMHS ferry dock and close to buses running between downtown and Totem Bight. Attention to detail makes everything, especially the breakfast, a treat. Free WiFi. Open June–Sept; two night minimum. ❺

Captain's Quarters B&B 325 Lund St ☎225-4912, ⓦwww.ptialaska.net/~captbnb. Three spacious rooms separate from the owner's house, all with queen-sized beds and cable TV – and one with a kitchen – in a nautically themed hillside house with some great views over the town. Continental breakfast included. ❺

Gilmore Hotel 326 Front St ☎1-800/275-9423, ⓦwww.gilmorehotel.com. Despite recent remodeling, this 1927 establishment retains the tenor of an old-style hotel, with a range of rooms from poky doubles without a view, to larger water-view rooms and much more spacious queen suites with a tub in the bathroom. Suites ❻, standard & water view ❺

The Landing 3434 Tongass Ave ☎1-800/428-8304, ⓦwww.landinghotel.com. Comfortable, well-appointed *Best Western* hotel two miles north of downtown, right opposite the AMHS ferry terminal and within walking distance of the airport ferry. There's cable TV, free WiFi, a fitness center, a restaurant and bar, a courtesy van into town, and some spacious suites for not much more than the room rate. Reserve well in advance. Suites and room ❼

New York Hotel 207 Stedman St ☎1-866/225-0246, ⓦwww.thenewyorkhotel.com. Excellent-value older hotel that's tastefully refurbished with black-and-white-tiled bathrooms and an antique vanity or armoire in each room. Most rooms are fairly small, but if you reserve in time you may be able to get the large harbor-view rooms at the front. Alternatively, step up to the spacious suites attractively sited on the Creek Street boardwalks above the river. Each comes with a small sunny balcony, DVD and VCR, spa bath, and full kitchen, which can make them an economic option for small groups. Free WiFi. Suites ❼, rooms ❺

Super 8 Motel 2151 Sea Level Drive ☎1-800/800-8000, ⓦwww.super8.com. The cheapest motel in town, fairly uninspiring but decent enough, with all the facilities you'd expect. Large rooms. Suites ❻, rooms ❺

WestCoast Cape Fox Lodge 800 Venetia Way ☎225-8001 or 1-800/325-4000, ⓦwww.westcoasthotels.com. The top hotel in town, attractively sited on the hill behind the downtown area, featuring comfy, well-equipped, but slightly bland rooms, many with water views glimpsed through the spruce and hemlock. Suites ❾, water-view rooms ❽, mountain view ❼

Hostels and campgrounds

Clover Pass Resort At Knudson Cove, 14 miles north along Tongass Hwy ☏ 1-800/410-2234, ⓦ www.cloverpassresort.com. The only RV site around Ketchikan with hookups. No tent sites. They also rent skiffs from $65 a day. $29.

Eagle View Hostel 2303 5th Ave ☏ 225-5461, ⓦ www.eagleviewhostel .com. Great views of the Narrows from this converted suburban house, which has a male dorm sleeping five with its own shower, plus a double and a women's triple, which share a bathroom. The $28 rate includes tax, bed linens,

Totem poles

Despite the teachings of early missionaries, **totem poles** – the enduring image of the Alaskan (and whole Pacific Northwest) coast – were never intended as objects of worship or religious veneration but stood as cultural symbols recording the lineage, legends, history, and lore of a people: silent storytellers in a land with no written language. Equally, they were visual statements of a clan's wealth: the cost of employing highly esteemed carvers added greatly to the commissioner's prestige. The raising of a pole was always accompanied by a **potlatch**, a kind of feast where the clan could give away a vast portion of its property. In contrast to modern values, status was determined by how much a person gave away rather than how much they accumulated.

A little history

Totem poles exist from Puget Sound in Washington State right through the Alaskan Panhandle, exactly the range of the western red cedar, whose timber is preferred for its easy-to-work straight grain and unusual rotting characteristics. It decomposes from the inside out, thus lasting longer in the eternally damp climate (though still only sixty to seventy years).

Every element in the preparation of a pole – the selecting and felling of the tree, the carving, the painting, and finally the raising – was marked by ceremony, culminating with the singing, dancing, and drumming of the final potlatch given by the patron's clan. While the assembled throng dug a six-foot hole and, using a scaffold and ropes, eased the pole's base into it, the head of the clan would recite the history represented on the pole to publicly validate the clan's right to use the crests and associated songs and dances. Once erected, the poles were not changed or repaired but allowed to decay until they finally fell over and rotted into the undergrowth. The raising of totem poles reached its **"golden age"** in the latter half of the nineteenth century, peaking around 1860. Wealth bolstered by the fur trade and a thriving culture unleashed a great burst of creativity, enhanced by access to abundant iron for carving tools and newly available artificial pigments. Hundreds of poles sprouted up along the coast, and photos from that time show whole forests of poles clustered around traditional clan houses.

This era ended with the arrival of missionaries who discouraged pole raising, built schools and churches, and encouraged the Natives to abandon many of the old traditions. Meanwhile, late nineteenth-century tourists were fascinated with totem poles as an art form, and many poles were relocated to sites closer to the steamer routes, breaking the tradition of leaving them *in situ*. From around 1875 onwards, private and museum collectors began removing them from abandoned villages. With the exception of the replicas described below, there were very few poles carved between the late 1880s and the 1970s.

A brief resurgence of interest came in the late 1930s when the Civilian Conservation Corps (CCC) undertook an unemployment-relief program to salvage poles and employ skilled carvers to create replicas. Honoring tradition, artists used handmade tools as close as possible in design to pre-European models, and matched colors by combining natural pigments with chewed, dry salmon eggs. These replica totems have survived intact and can be seen in totem parks on Prince of Wales Island, Saxman and Totem Bight in Ketchikan, Shakes Island in Wrangell, and in Sitka.

and towel as well as use of the kitchen, barbecue, and sauna. No lockout or curfew. When he's
in the mood, owner Dale runs sightseeing trips,
and won't let you get bored even on the wettest
days. Follow Jefferson off Tongass Hwy, then turn
right onto 5th. Open April–Oct and by reservation.
Doubles ❷

Ketchikan Youth Hostel 400 Main St ☏ 225-
3319, ⓔ ktnyh@eagle.ptialaska.net. Very basic
and rigidly managed hostel in the United
Methodist Church with simple dorm beds for
$15 and a reasonable kitchen. Bring a sleeping
bag and expect a daytime lockout (9am–6pm),
an 11pm curfew, and a chore requirement. For

The skills retained by older carvers were passed on to a younger generation of
artisans who still carve poles. Inspired by contemporary conservation efforts such
as the Totem Pole Survey and Retrieval Project, Ketchikan's Totem Heritage Center,
and Saxman's Carving Center, these artists adhere to traditional forms and color
schemes but incorporate brighter paints and other modern elements (including
the use of steel tools) as expressions of a renewed sense of cultural identity and
tribal pride.

Pole types

Totem poles fall into five main categories. Perhaps the best known are **heraldic
poles**, also known as crest or story poles for the complex series of designs showing
the matrilineal genealogy and history of the clan or family that commissioned them.
Some of the same elements are incorporated into **house posts**, which support the
roof beams in clan houses, and the entrance poles built into Haida clan houses.

Mortuary poles were designed to honor the dead and usually topped with the
crest symbol of that person. Many originally had a recess in the back where ashes
could be placed, but missionaries strongly discouraged cremation and this practice
died away, the mortuary pole being replaced by the **memorial pole**. These often had
only a couple of crest figures in a simple design, and were usually placed adjacent to
the village or around the house of the deceased.

Another feature to look out for are watchmen crouched on top of some Haida
totems to protect the clan with their supernatural powers. Their high status is often
marked by a potlatch hat (hence the name **potlatch poles**) – otherwise reserved for
memorial poles – with the number of rings around the hat denoting the number of
potlatches the person hosted.

Finally, there are ridicule or **shame poles**, the least common type but usually
prominently placed where they could poke the most fun. Erected to discredit someone who had failed to clear a debt, behaved dishonorably, or broken his word, these
would be cut down when amends were made.

Interpretation

Totem poles often come without any explanation of their meaning, partly because
the story associated with the pole belongs to the clan concerned. Nonetheless,
something can be gleaned from the design elements, which are based on interlinking
ovoids – rounded rectangles – depicting anything from a whole head or torso down
to teeth. This geometrical approach encourages a high degree of stylization that can
make detecting which creatures are represented difficult at first, though it gets easier
with a few clues. First, **animals** always have ears on top, while **humans** have theirs
on the side. The most common representations are of Eagle and Raven, which are
easily confused, though the **Eagle** always has a hooked beak-tip. Bear and Wolf both
have a rounder shape to their mouths, the latter sporting sharper teeth and a more
slender snout. Whales crop up fairly often, particularly **Killer Whale** with his straight
dorsal fin, sometimes created by adding a plank to the totem rather than carving it
into the main body of the pole. **Beaver** always has two prominent front teeth and
usually a flat, cross-hatched tail.

advance bookings send a money order for the first night's fee (and an SAE if you want confirmation) to PO Box 8515, Ketchikan, AK 99901. Open June–Aug.

Settlers Cove State Recreation Site Mile 18.2 N Tongass Hwy. First-come, first-served campground and picnic area overlooking Clover Passage that is probably the nicest, least crowded, and most distant site from Ketchikan. No hookups, but there's a beach and a mile-long loop trail to Upper Lunch Creek Falls. $10.

Ward Lake Recreation Area ☎1-877/444-6777, ⊛www.reserveusa.com. Two Forest Service campgrounds in the temperate rainforest with easy access to scenic lakes and gentle trails. They are all located on (or just off) Revilla Rd, which cuts inland six miles north of Ketchikan. Ward Lake Rd leads off Revilla Rd at Mile 1.4 and runs to *Signal Creek Campground* (May to late Sept), with lots for small RVs. Go 2.3 miles along Revilla Rd to get to *Last Chance Campground* (late May to mid-Sept), amid old-growth forest with designated RV lots. Both cost $10.

The town and totem parks

Ketchikan's popularity as a tourist destination is due in part to its concentrated collection of sights around a central core of **historic streets**, notably Creek Street, now wiped clean of its seedy origins. It's an appealing spot for a stroll along the boardwalks, stopping to peek into one of the galleries or gaze over the bridge to watch the salmon make their way to the Deer Mountain Tribal Hatchery. Perhaps Ketchikan's most compelling claim to greatness is its unmatched expression of Southeast Native culture through the superb **Totem Heritage Center**, assorted totem poles around town, and the two **totem parks** just outside town: the Totem Bight State Historic Park of replica poles and clan house, and the Saxman Totem Park at the Native village of Saxman.

Downtown Ketchikan

If Ketchikan is your introduction to Alaska, your first stop should be the **Southeast Alaska Discovery Center**, 50 Main St (early May–Sept daily 8am–5pm; Oct–early May Tues–Sat 10am–4.30pm; $5, winter free), a striking cedar-framed building with absorbing displays on the region's natural ecosystems, resources, and Native culture. A fish-cam even lets you watch salmon migrating up Ketchikan Creek. Those who have already spent time in the state may find it a little simplistic, even promotional. It can be all too obvious that the Forest Service has provided much of the funding here, and you might wonder why they've bothered replicating a temperate rainforest when there are seventeen million acres of the real thing right outside the door. It also operates as an outdoor information center (see "Arrival and information," p.96).

For local flavor visit the small and well-laid-out **Tongass Historical Museum**, 629 Dock St (May–Sept daily 8am–5pm; Oct–April Wed–Fri 1–5pm, Sat 10am–4pm, Sun 1–4pm; $2, winter free), which is full of fascinating old photos of the town and its happenings, mining paraphernalia, and a great corner filled with Native artifacts: a carved bowl from the 1880s and large, carved bentwood boxes, watertight storage vessels whose sides are formed from a single piece of wood shaped by steaming and bending. There are also old "coppers" – essentially large sheets of copper that, in the early years of trade with Europeans, gave their owners great status and were accordingly the ultimate item to give away at potlatches (see box, p.98).

The prettiest section of town lies along **Creek Street**, a rickety-looking boardwalk perched high above the tidal waters of Ketchikan Creek, where salmon head upstream (July–Oct) often pursued by seals. This was Ketchikan's red-light district from 1903 until 1954, when the brothels were closed down. Its notoriety was enhanced during prohibition, when boats laden with illicit liquor were floated up at high tide, the contraband being fed up through trapdoors in the floors of the houses. Today the former houses of ill repute have been smartened up, painted in bright colors and mostly used as gift shops, though there are a few higher-quality galleries and an excellent bookshop (see Shopping, p.106). The main destination for those fancying a glimpse of the old days is **Dolly's House**, 24 Creek St (generally daily 8am–5pm though dependent on cruise ships; $5), once the home and workplace of Dolly Arthur, the town's most famous prostitute, and now a small museum with original decor and saucy memorabilia. Ignoring the fact that Dolly ceased her trade here only half a century back, the guides have gone for the Victorian look, and "ladies" dressed in puffy gold-rush dresses will usher you in for a tour and headful of anecdotes from Dolly's intriguing life.

A short **inclined tramway** ($2) climbs the bluff behind Creek Street to the lobby of the *WestCoast Cape Fox Lodge* (see pp.97 and 107), which has a small display of quality Native crafts and commands a great view of the town and Tongass Narrows. In front of the hotel stands the "Council of the Clans" ring of short totem poles commissioned by the Cape Fox Native Corporation, which owns the hotel. From here, Venetia Avenue leads down to Park Avenue and City Park.

An alternative route to City Park is known as the **Married Man's Trail** for the secretive escape route it provides from Creek Street. It follows a narrow boardwalk upstream past some small rapids and beside a fish ladder where, throughout the summer, you'll see salmon fighting the current. This brings you to Park Avenue, which runs inland to **City Park**, a small but attractive area of grass, small streams, and summer blooms. Tall cages on the west side of the park mark the **Deer Mountain Tribal Hatchery and Eagle Center** (May–Sept daily 8.30am–4.30pm; $9, combo ticket with Totem Heritage Center $12), where a couple of injured bald eagles are kept to educate the public about these majestic birds. You may be more interested in the hatchery, concrete tanks with fish at different stages in their development. Follow the guided tour to learn about the king and coho salmon that find their way up Ketchikan Creek to breed here. Outside, a footbridge over the creek leads to the Totem Heritage Center (see p.102).

For something a little less serious, return to the waterfront behind the Discovery Center where you'll find the **Great Alaskan Lumberjack Show** (usually three shows daily, call for times; $31.80; ☎1-888/320-9049). The ninety-minute extravaganza is coaxed along by an MC who whips the audience into a lighthearted frenzy of US–Canadian rivalry as "frontier woodsmen" are put

Bear-viewing and flightseeing

Several spots around Ketchikan are known for their exemplary bear-viewing. Anan Wildlife Observatory (see "Around Wrangell," p.128) and Fish Creek Wildlife Viewing Area (see "Hyder," p.111) are both possibilities, but the most accessible is **Margaret Bay**, a twenty-minute float-plane flight from Ketchikan. Here, black bears actively fish from late July until September, which you can witness with Taquan Air (☎1-800/770-8800, ⓦwww.taquanair.com) on its Traitors Cove Bear Adventure (2hr 30min; $409), a tour that involves a flight, a short van ride, and a quarter-mile walk to a viewing platform beside a waterfall.

As well as scheduled flights and dedicated flightseeing trips, Taquan Air also runs a number of Alaska Bush Pilot tours (1–2hr; $139–169), which follow a different route each day depending on the day's schedule. If the weather is good, don't miss the chance to go on the mail run and freight flight (Mon & Thurs; $172) from Ketchikan to Hyder (see p.111), a trip that passes over Misty Fiords. Although not as good as a dedicated Misty flightseeing trip, it's just about the cheapest way to see the park.

through their paces chopping and sawing wood, rolling logs, felling trees, and speed-treeclimbing with spiked shoes. It has the tenor of a circus sideshow and, when it opened in 2000, put a few noses out of joint. The local pulp mill had only recently closed, and unemployed loggers – they don't really call themselves lumberjacks around here – were understandably put out by the tourist industry appearing to cash in on a dying way of life.

Totem Heritage Center

The wonderful ☀ **Totem Heritage Center**, 601 Deermount St (May–Sept daily 8am–5pm; Oct–April Mon–Fri 1–5pm; $5, combo ticket with hatchery $12), was set up in 1976 to preserve and exhibit the largest collection of original totem poles in the US, 33 in all. Most of the poles you'll see around town and elsewhere in Southeast are replicas (see box, p.98), many of them based on the poles, house posts, and fragments gathered here. For much of the twentieth century, cultural preservationists had recognized that unless something was done, the nation's rapidly dwindling stock of original nineteenth-century totem poles would rot away and be lost forever. So, in 1973, the Totem Pole Survey and Retrieval Project was established to collect the remaining poles from abandoned Tlingit and Haida villages within fifty miles of Ketchikan. Of the hundreds noted and photographed previously by explorers and early steamship tourists, only 44 remained, eleven of which were unsalvageable.

Before entering the building, pause a moment to see how modern themes and techniques have been incorporated into the vibrantly painted "Honoring Those Who Give" pole, raised in 1999 to recognize those who helped fund the center. It was created by renowned carver **Nathan Jackson**, whose first pole, "Raven-Frog Woman" (1978), stands nearby. There's yet more of his work at Totem Bight State Park and in public places all over town.

Inside the center you are confronted with five magnificent poles from the "golden age" of totem-pole carving – two memorial, one heraldic, one potlatch, and one mortuary – all over a century old. Greatly weathered and often missing parts of various appendages, they are mostly free of any coloring, although under the beaver's chin on the Haida potlatch pole you can still see a hint of green, made from copper oxide mixed with crushed salmon eggs. For all their crumbling fragility, they still retain a menacing power, something robbed from the remaining poles and house posts that are too delicate to display upright. Almost a dozen such poles occupy an adjacent room, many of them broken and laid down in cradles, but still impressive. Panels around the walls have photos of how the poles appeared in their original locations and explain almost all you ever wanted to know about this art form. Museum staff is on hand to fill in the gaps and conduct ad hoc tours.

The poles provide inspiration for the off-season **Native Arts Classes**, a series of courses covering anything from cedar-bark weaving, regalia-making, and introductory carving to more advanced techniques such as bentwood-box manufacture and drum making. Courses run from mid-September to April, and typically cost $150 for a one- or two-week course, which does not include accommodation. For details, click to the museum's website from ⓦ www.city.ketchikan.ak.us/departments/museums/tongass.html.

North of town: Totem Bight State Historic Park

Following the Tongass Highway north of the AMHS and airport ferry docks, Ketchikan begins to thin out. The road hugs the coast to Ward Cove, an unsightly industrial wasteland occupied until 1997 by the Ketchikan Pulp Mill. A road heads inland from here to the **Ward Lake Recreation Area**, a wooded site of attractive picnic areas, two campgrounds, and several good local hikes (see box, p.104).

A couple of miles on, **Totem Bight State Historic Park** (unrestricted access) comprises a replica Native village breathtakingly set on a forested strip of coast overlooking the Narrows, ten miles north of town. Fourteen of the finest replica totem poles and a re-created tribal house look majestically out over the water, making this about the best place to easily get a sense of what a Tlingit village looked like a hundred or more years back. Although it is unlikely that the site was ever permanently settled – it was originally a summer fish camp – in the late 1930s the Civilian Conservation Corps (see box, p.98) reconstructed an entire Native village here. Lack of money and manpower during World War II stunted initial ambition, but the result still includes a very fine **clan house**. The front is strikingly painted in a Raven design flanked by squat figures wearing potlatch hats and centered on the large "Raven Stealing the Sun" entrance pole. The hole in this pole would have been the sole way to get into the house, thus an important security feature. Up to fifty people could live inside, with separate family areas on the raised platforms around the central fire pit and belongings stored underneath the planks.

Eleven of the totem poles are clustered in a couple of semicircles beside the clan house, almost all of them executed in the late 1930s, though a couple have had to be replicated again. (This third generation was completed in the 1990s, mostly by Nathan Jackson; see p.102.) There's a great variety: Tlingit and Haida – despite this being a traditionally Tlingit area – mortuary poles, grave markers, heraldic poles, and the lovely "Sea Monster" pole, topped by a human figure representing the village watchman.

On arrival, call at the Alaska Natural History Association bookstore (Tues–Sat 9am–4.45pm, Mon & Sun 9am–2pm), which stocks an excellent leaflet ($1 donation requested) explaining what the poles depict and has an original section of a pole wedged into one corner. By visiting the park in the evening (the bus runs to 7pm) you'll miss the bulk of the bus tours, but may not be able to see inside the clan house.

The Tongass Highway continues for another eight miles past Knudson Cove marina to *Settlers Cove Campground* on the shores of Clover Passage.

△ Ketchikan totem poles and clan house, Totem Bight State Historic Park

South of town: Saxman Native Village

Just under three miles along South Tongass Highway from downtown Ketchikan, the Tlingit village of **Saxman** centers on the **Saxman Totem Park** (always open; $3 entry whenever there is someone around to take your money), which encompasses the world's largest collection of replica totem poles, a replica clan house, and an active carving center. Most people visit on a tour (see p.96) but it is possible to drive, cycle, or catch "The Bus" there and simply wander round the poles by yourself, listening to the spiels of assorted tour guides. The walking tour leaflet ($1 from the Co-op store) aids interpretation. The store is at the start of the approach avenue where a dozen Tlingit poles lead up to the main arc of poles. Look out for the famous Abraham Lincoln pole surmounted by an image of Honest Abe, who has been carved with stunted legs, apparently because the

Ketchikan hikes

Extremely high rainfall and what can sometimes seem like constant clouds and drizzle may put some people off hiking around Ketchikan, but if you strike it lucky – or are feeling especially hardy – it can be very rewarding. Four local trails are particularly worthwhile. Only Deer Mountain Trail is readily accessible from town, but it is best hiked from late June to September as snow cover limits access to the alpine sections during the rest of the year. The remaining three can be hiked in any season, but you'll need to get out to Ward Cove and hike inland from there to the trailheads. All hikes are marked on the "Around Ketchikan" map (see opposite). Pick up the useful and free *Ketchikan Area Hiking Guide* from the Discovery Center.

Connell Lake Trail (4.5 miles round-trip; 2–3hr; 100ft ascent). Easy trail mostly beside Connell Lake and running to Talbot Lake with good birding, excellent berries in summer and fall, and fishing access to both lakes. The trail starts on Connell Lake Road, which spurs off Revilla Road just past the entrance to *Last Chance Campground*.

Deer Mountain Trail (10 miles one way; 1–2 days; 3350ft ascent). Easily accessible trail that makes a perfect escape from the daytime crowds for a couple of hours, switchbacking up across the face of Deer Mountain through old-growth Sitka spruce, hemlock, and red cedar. It takes an hour or so to reach a wooded overlook (1500ft) with a wonderful view over the city, Pennock, Gravina, Annette, and Prince of Wales islands, and close to three hours to reach the 3000-foot alpine summit of Deer Mountain. Deer Mountain Trail can be extended as an overnight one-way trek to the Beaver Falls Powerhouse on George Inlet – either camp beside Blue Lake or stay in either the four-bunk Deer Mountain Shelter on the upper flank of Deer Mountain or the three-bunk Blue Lake Shelter just beyond (both first-come, first-served; free). This alpine section of the hike is exposed to bad weather and is steep in places, remaining high for several hours before a final steep descent past Silvia Lakes. The trail starts on Ketchikan Lakes Road, off Deermount Street near the junction of Fair Street (see "Ketchikan" map, p.94) and finishes fourteen miles out along S Tongass Highway. There is very little traffic out this way, so it is best to arrange a ride back to town before you start – or do the whole thing in reverse and finish in town.

Perseverance Lake Trail (4.5 miles round-trip; 2–3hr; 450ft ascent). An easy but enjoyable (partly boardwalk) trail up to Perseverance Lake through temperate rainforest and muskeg. It starts on Ward Lake Road, 2.5 miles off the N Tongass Highway at Ward Cove.

Ward Lake Nature Trail (1.3-mile loop; 1hr; negligible ascent). Gentle stroll round Ward Lake on an easy gravel path, past panels on the region's flora and fauna. The trailhead is seven miles along N Tongass Highway to Ward Cove, then 2.5 miles inland along Ward Lake Road.

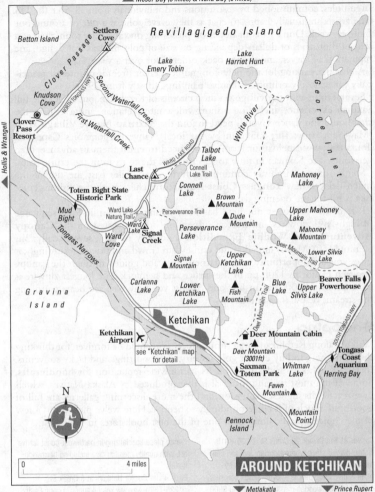

▲ *Moser Bay (3 miles) & Naha Bay (6 miles)*

R e v i l l a g i g e d o   I s l a n d

Betton Island

Settlers Cove

Clover Passage

Lake Emery Tobin

Lake Harriet Hunt

G e o r g e   I n l e t

Knudson Cove

NORTH TONGASS HWY

Second Waterfall Creek

White River

Clover Pass Resort

First Waterfall Creek

WARD LAKE ROAD

Talbot Lake

Connell Lake Trail

Hollis & Wrangell ◄

Last Chance

Connell Lake

Mahoney Lake

Totem Bight State Historic Park

Ward Lake Nature Trail

Brown Mountain ▲

Perseverance Trail

Upper Mahoney Lake

Mud Bight

Ward Lake

▲ *Dude Mountain*

Mahoney Mountain ▲

Signal Creek

Perseverance Lake

Ward Cove

Tongass Narrows

Signal Mountain ▲

Upper Ketchikan Lake

Deer Mountain Trail

Lower Silvis Lake

G r a v i n a   I s l a n d

Carlanna Lake

Lower Ketchikan Lake

Fish Mountain ▲

Blue Lake

Upper Silvis Lake

Beaver Falls Powerhouse ◄

Ketchikan

Ketchikan Airport ✈

see "Ketchikan" map for detail

Deer Mountain Trail

SOUTH TONGASS HWY

Ketchikan

■ **Deer Mountain Cabin**

Tongass Coast Aquarium

N

Deer Mountain (3001ft)

Saxman Totem Park

Whitman Lake

Herring Bay

Fawn Mountain ▲

Pennock Island

Mountain Point

| 0 | 4 miles |

AROUND KETCHIKAN

▼ *Metlakatla*   ▼ *Prince Rupert*

only image the carvers had of him was in a photo which cut him off at the knees. There's also a shame pole to William Seward, who attended four potlatches during a visit to Alaska without ever throwing one in return, a dishonorable omission that earned him the distinctive red ears, nose, and lips on his pole.

Unless you are on a tour, you won't get to see inside the cedar-scented **Beaver Clan House**. Here the **Cape Fox Dancers** put on a diverting performance, during which you'll learn a little Tlingit and can join one of the dances alongside a troupe made up of adults, kids, and even babes in arms, many wearing superb blankets and robes.

Possibly the most interesting bit of all is the nearby **Carving Center**, which is officially only open to those on tours, though you can peer through the window and at quiet times may be invited in. Here, highly respected Haida and Tlingit craftsmen (Nathan Jackson among them) can be seen at work on large poles, commissioned by institutions and individuals from all over the US. The artists are usually happy to chat as they carve poles at a rate of around one foot per week. Don't set your hopes on possessing one any time soon; they cost tens of thousands of dollars depending on size of pole, intricacy of design, and reputation of carver, and they're back-ordered for over a year.

Across the parking lot the new community center (free) is of interest principally for its lovely primitivist Native paintings, mostly from 1970.

Several tours visit the village on their circuits of Ketchikan, but to get the full Saxman experience, including a short video, interpretation, and a visit to the clan house and dancers, you'll need to join the **Saxman Native Village Tour** (May–Sept daily; 1hr; $35) run by the local Native corporation's Cape Fox Tours (ⓦ www.capefoxtours.com). You'll need to email them in advance, then get yourself to Saxman in time to meet one of the tours from the cruise ships.

South Tongass Highway continues a further ten miles past the site of the much-delayed new **Tongass Coast Aquarium**; check with the visitor center (see p.96) for the opening date.

Part of the rainforest out here has been strung with a mile-long sequence of high-level zipwires and treetop suspension bridges visited on the **Canopy Adventures and Wildlife Expedition** (mid-May to Sept, several daily; 3hr 30min; $160). Mainly aimed at the cruise-ship crowd and priced accordingly, it gives you the opportunity to get harnessed up and guided through the canopy between platforms 120ft up in the spruce and hemlock. The longest zipwire is an impressive 850ft, and in July and August you may well see bears patrolling the streams below for salmon.

Shopping

Walking along Ketchikan's waterfront streets, you could be forgiven for thinking there's nothing to buy except gold jewelry, diamond rings, and tacky souvenirs. In fact, Ketchikan prides itself on its nationwide reputation for **handicrafts**. Some of the most striking material is that produced by Alaska Natives, which here reaches its highest expression, and the more discerning galleries are full of good stuff, much of it correspondingly expensive. Here we've picked out a few of the choicest places along with one of the best bookstores in Southeast.

Carver at the Creek 28 Creek St ☎ 225-3018. Native-owned place where Norman Jackson can be seen executing fine carving amid work by other Native craftspeople – lovely Tlingit blankets ($2000–4000), wooden masks from around $800, cedar-bark hats, silverwork, and fine prints, some excellent ones for around $140.

Crazy Wolf Studio 607 Mission St ☎ 1-888/331-9653, ⓦ www.crazywolfstudio.com. Aiming for the middle ground, this shop has plenty of gift shop tack interspersed with a few quality artworks at modest prices.

Eagle Spirit Gallery 310 Mission St ☎ 1-866/867-0976, ⓦ www.eaglespiritalaska.com.

Classy place specializing in northwest-coast Native art, with quality merchandise including bentwood boxes.

Parnassus Books Upstairs at 5 Creek St ☎ 225-7690, ⓦ www.ketchikanbooks.com. Easily the best bookstore in town with a matchless selection of Alaskana, alternative topics, and more mainstream titles.

Soho Coho 5 Creek St ☎ 225-5954, ⓦ www .trollart.com. Nicely sited gallery that's particularly good for prints, paintings, and original work by local artists, some at quite modest prices. Look out for owner Ray Troll's entertaining cartoonish work and the raven prints of Evon Zebkez.

Eating, drinking, and entertainment

Although cosmopolitan by Alaskan standards, Ketchikan is still a small town and its attempts at sophistication are limited. That said, it does have a range of good and inexpensive choices and it supports most of the major fast-food franchises.

For **supermarkets** check out Tatsuda's, 633 Steadman St (daily 7am–11pm), which is fairly central, or the bigger Safeway at the Plaza Mall about a mile north of downtown.

Ketchikan empties in the late afternoon. The cruise passengers all shuffle back to their floating hotels, which almost imperceptibly slip away, leaving the town peaceful, but somehow drained of its lifeblood. Still, there's plenty of hard **drinking** to be done at several downtown bars. Teetotalers could try the Coliseum Twin Theater, on Mission Street at Main Street, which shows first-run **movies**.

Annabelle's Keg & Chowder House 326 Front St ⊤ 225-6009. Venerable restaurant done in grand style with dark paneling, pressed-tin ceilings, and formal dining chairs in the nonsmoking section, and a more relaxed atmosphere in the bar. The sourdough pancake breakfasts and famed clam chowder lunches are moderately priced; dinner gets more spendy, maxing out at crab entrees ($20 for snow crab, $35 for jumbo kings).

Arctic Bar 509 Water St ⊤ 225-6959. Basic, dark, boozing bar with a great view over the water once the cruise ships have left.

Bar Harbor 2813 Tongass Ave ⊤ 225-2813. Lovely little restaurant a mile or so north of town where you can sit inside or out on the spacious deck, tucking into the likes of Grandma's meatloaf ($15), chicken teriyaki ($15), pasta dishes ($15–17), and steaks ($18–24) as the sun sets over the adjacent float-plane base. Dinner nightly.

Chico's 435 Dock St ⊤ 225-2833. Bargain authentic Mexican food and pizza with dinners starting at $10, or just grab a $6.50 burrito to eat in or take out.

Diaz Café 335 Stedman St ⊤ 225-2257. Some of the finest inexpensive food in town with widely acclaimed burgers and fries rounding out a menu specializing in Chinese and tasty Filipino dishes: fried rice for $9, chow mein and chicken adobo for around $14. Open to 8pm. Closed Mon.

First City Saloon 830 Water St. Straightforward boozing bar occasionally featuring bands and shows. Probably the most likely place to indulge in a little dancing.

Pioneer Café 617 Mission St ⊤ 225-1600. Downtown diner where they do everything well. Open 24hr on weekends.

Steamers 76 Front St, above Dockside Trading ⊤ 225-1600. Spacious, bustling restaurant opposite the cruise-ship dock with great views, a stack of microbrews on tap, and occasional live music. The food's good too – try their heaped plate of snowcrab legs ($22).

That One Place 211 Stedman St ⊤ 225-0246. Nonsmoking restaurant and bar where you can perch on bentwood chairs as harbor light streams through the big windows and choose from a menu loaded with excellent soups, burgers, wraps, and salads (mostly $9–12), plus some sumptuous desserts. Also open evenings when there's an excellent tapas menu with most plates $5–7. Closed Sun.

WestCoast Cape Fox Lodge 800 Venetia Way ⊤ 225-8001. Fairly upmarket dining in the town's best hotel with great views over town. Lunch is somewhat casual with manageable prices for sandwiches ($9–12) or the excellent halibut and chips ($11). Dinner is more formal, with dishes ranging from chicken fettuccini ($18) to baked salmon ($24) and king crab ($32).

Listings

Banks Several downtown, all with ATMs, including First Bank, 331 Dock St.

Bike rental Downtown at the Lumberjack Show (see p.101) for $8 an hour or $25 a half-day.

Boat charters There are dozens of boat-charter operators keen to take you out fishing or sightseeing in Misty Fiords National Monument, or who will drop you off at some remote cabin. With a group of four or five, this option can work out to be a flexible and cost-effective alternative to the cruise boats. Northern Lights Charters (⊤ 1-888/550-8488, ⓦ www.ketchikanfishing.net), which has a booth at the visitor center, is particularly good and runs fishing trips from $99 for 3hr.

Car rental Alaska Car Rental, 2828 Tongass Ave (⊤ 1-800/662-0007, ⓦ www.akcarrental.com), and Budget, 4950 N Tongass Hwy (⊤ 225-8383 or 1-800/478-2438, ⓦ www.budget.com), both have desks at the airport and offer similar rates of around $55 a day.

Internet access Crow's Nest, 308 Grant St, is central and offers fast machines, laptop connections, and WiFi at good rates. The library (see p.108) has free use for members. Membership is

Kayaking around Revillagigedo Island and Misty Fiords

Wherever you are in Southeast Alaska, the range of places you can go paddling is only limited by your imagination and your budget. Dozens of possibilities present themselves, but from Ketchikan the most common destinations are relatively short paddles close to town and trips into Misty Fiords National Monument, which can take on the feeling of an expedition without requiring really long periods away from civilization.

The simplest approach is to hook up with Southeast Sea Kayaks, 1007 Water St (☎225-1258 or 1-800/287-1607, ⓦwww.kayakketchikan.com), which is fully geared toward independent visitors, offering personal treatment, small groups, and no minimum numbers. For a taster, try the Pennock Paddling Adventure (2hr 30min; $79) in the channel in front of Ketchikan; for a good deal more peace and quiet step up to the Orcas Cove trip (4hr; $139), which starts with a short boat ride and then takes you kayaking along the shore with fabulous wildlife-viewing and gorgeous scenery. Custom full-day trips cost $189 including lunch.

Guided trips to **Misty Fiords National Monument** start with the Full Day Adventure ($389), which includes a cruise out there and four to five hours of paddling in fabulous scenery. Two-night weekend trips using fixed campsites start around $700 and longer trips go up from there.

Going it alone

Southeast Sea Kayaks rents at daily rates that decrease for longer rental periods, and will drop you along the road system for a small fee; expect to pay $30–40 a day for a plastic single kayak, $40–45 for a fiberglass single, and $50–60 for a fiberglass double. You don't need much prior experience to be let loose around the Ketchikan waterfront, but for longer journeys you'll have to be a moderately competent paddler and have some knowledge of tides and backcountry camping. Don't be put off, though – the generally sheltered waters in these parts can be tackled by people of quite modest ability (see below for suggested trips). Wherever you go, get the latest information (maps, tide tables, and so forth) from the rental company, pick up the free *Ketchikan Area Kayak Guide* from the Discovery Center, and be sure you leave the company an itinerary of your likely movements.

George Inlet (1–2 days). Pretty coves, loads of small islands, and the old George Inlet cannery embellish this trip to the south and west of Ketchikan. Either paddle from downtown or get a ride out to the Hole-in-the-Wall marina (7.5 miles south on Tongass Highway).

available for a $10 fee plus a $20 deposit refundable when you leave town – worthwhile for stays of a few days.

Laundry and showers The Mat, 989 Stedman (daily 7am–10pm; ☎225-0628), is half a mile south of downtown.

Left luggage There is no formal left luggage in town, but *The Landing* (see p.97) opposite the ferry terminal holds bags for meal or room guests. If you've just got a day in Ketchikan, pop in for breakfast, then leave your bag all day.

Library Ketchikan Public Library, 629 Dock St (Mon–Wed 10am–8pm, Thurs–Sat 10am–6pm, Sun 1–5pm; ☎225-3331).

Medical assistance Ketchikan General Hospital, 3100 N Tongass Ave, near the AMHS ferry dock (☎1-888/890-8301), has daytime clinics and 24hr ER.

Pharmacy Downtown Drugstore, 300 Front St ☎225-3144.

Photographic supplies Schallerer's, 2414 Tongass Ave near the Plaza Mall (☎225-4210, ⓦwww.schallerers.com), is the best around though their limited downtown shop at 449 Mill St is more convenient.

Post office The main post office, 3609 Tongass Ave (☎225-9601), by the AMHS ferry dock (Mon–Fri 8.30am–5pm) has **General Delivery** (zip code 99901). There's a more convenient suboffice at 422 Mission St (Mon–Sat 9am–5.30pm).

Taxes City sales tax is 6 percent, and hotel rooms incur an additional 7 percent tax, additional to our quoted accommodation prices.

Taxis Sourdough (☎225-5544) and Yellow Cab (☎225-5555) are both fine.

Gravina Island Circumnavigation (3–4 days). Sixty miles of rocky shoreline with abundant wildlife, all easily accessible from Ketchikan. Note that one ten-mile section offers almost no protection from the weather.

Naha Bay (2–4 days). With great scenery, plenty of wildlife, and excellent salmon and trout fishing along the Naha River, this excursion provides a wonderful opportunity to get a real wilderness feel without straying too far from Ketchikan. The trip can also work out to be pretty inexpensive, as you can start your paddle right from town and camp out every night. If you'd like to save time, catch a ride out to Knudson Cove marina (14.5 miles north of town) for around $35 per person. Aside from the pleasures of gentle paddling, you can hike the 5.4-mile Naha River National Recreation Trail, which leads from Naha Bay past Jordan Lake to Heckman Lake. Both lakes have gorgeous Forest Service cabins ($35). You don't need to paddle into the nearby Roosevelt Lagoon to access the trail, but if you do want to paddle in the lagoon be warned that racing tides make its entrance very dangerous – portaging beside the picnic shelter is a better bet. There is also a lot of black bear activity during the salmon runs: good for viewing as long as you are careful.

Tatoosh Islands (1–4 days). Easily accessible islands just north of Ketchikan, with beautiful beaches where seals haul out on the rocks to rest and plenty of opportunity for camping and exploring.

Misty Fiords

The most ambitious kayaking destination is **Misty Fiords National Monument**, for which Southeast Sea Kayaks sells a superb trip-planning kit ($20) complete with topographic maps, tide tables, and plenty of itinerary suggestions. It can be reached directly by kayak from Ketchikan, though it is at least two days' paddle each way and requires open-water kayaking skills.

Most paddlers get a ride with Southeast Sea Kayaks, which charges around $150 each way depending on location. Once there, the scope is enormous, with some people happily spending three or four weeks in the monument. The main northern arm of Behm Canal is a little exposed for most paddlers, who aim for narrow corners such as Rudyerd Bay, Punchbowl Cove, and Walker Cove, typically camping or making use of a Forest Service cabin or shelter (see p.110).

Misty Fiords National Monument

The essential excursion from Ketchikan is to the Connecticut-sized **MISTY FIORDS NATIONAL MONUMENT**, an awe-inspiring tranche of narrow fjords flanked by sheer, 3000-foot glacially scoured granite walls strung with gossamer waterfalls and surrounded by dense rainforest. Located between twenty and sixty miles east of Ketchikan, Misty Fiords drapes partly over the eastern side of Revillagigedo Island but is primarily defined by the mountainous terrain between two fjords, the 117-mile Behm Canal and the 72-mile hairline thread of Portland Canal, which marks the US–Canada border.

At its most stirring when wreathed in low clouds, Misty, as it is often known, was created by presidential proclamation in 1978 and remains almost entirely undeveloped. No roads lead here. There aren't even any airstrips, so access is by cruise boat, float-plane, or kayak. As with so many vast areas of wilderness, most people visit roughly the same area, though it is quite possible to get air-charter companies to fly you anywhere you want. Day cruises and scheduled flightseeing trips concentrate on the area around **Rudyerd Bay**, off Behm Canal some twenty minutes by plane or fifty sea miles from Ketchikan. Here the cliffs plunge as far below the surface as they soar above it, notably in **Punchbowl Cove**, widely regarded as the highlight of the monument and an obligatory stop on every boat trip. Along the way you pass the volcanic plug of **New Eddystone Rock**, a 237-foot pillar rising from the middle of Behm Canal, which Captain Vancouver, exploring here in 1793, obviously thought was reminiscent of the lighthouse-topped namesake off the southern English coast. The trees around its base are almost swamped at high tide, but there is just enough room for kayakers to pitch a tent, provided the waves aren't too high.

Wildlife-spotting opportunities are plentiful, with seals, porpoises, and orca in the fjords, and bears, deer, mountain goats, and more on land, all watched over by bald eagles.

Cruises, flights, and cabins

The most convenient way to see something of Misty Fiords is a **cruise** with Misty Fjords & Wilderness Explorer ($149; ☎1-877/6868-8100, ⓦwww .mistyfjordswildlifequest.com), which runs several trips a day on a fast boat taking just over four hours round-trip. Alaska Cruises (☎1-800/228-1905, ⓦwww.mistyfjord.net) offers a more leisurely six-hour **cruise** (early May to Sept, daily hours vary; $130) and four-hour cruise and flight packages ($260, occasional evening specials $200). Trips are geared around the combo packages, so if you can afford the extra cash, go for the cruise/fly option (preferably in that order), not only to take in the excellent airborne views, but to avoid the identical itinerary and commentary on the return journey.

If time is limited you can **fly** both ways with Promech Air (☎1-800/860-3845, ⓦwww.promechair.com) for $195. The outfit can also fly you and your supplies to one of the fourteen rustic **cabins** rented out by the Forest Service ($25–45; ☎1-877/444-6777), two of which are beside salt water, with the remaining twelve on freshwater lakes, often linked to the fjord by a short trail.

Alternatively, you can kayak here (see box, p.108) and gain access to some cabins and shelters that way. Shelters are first-come, first-served and free. Possibilities include: Alava Bay Cabin; following the mile-long trail at the back of Punchbowl Bay up the face of a solidified lava flow to Punchbowl Lake and the three-sided Punchbowl Lake Shelter; hiking a mile from Rudyerd Bay to Nooya Lake Shelter; hiking the 2.3-mile Winstanley Lake Trail to Winstanley Lake Shelter; Winstanley Island Cabin; Manzanita Bay Shelter; and Manzanita Lake Cabin, reached by the steep 3.5-mile Manzanita Lake Trail from near the shelter. See the "Southern Inside Passage" map (p.118) for cabin and shelter locations.

Metlakatla

If you arrive by float-plane at the small Native village of **Metlakatla** (ⓦwww .metlakatla.com), twelve miles southeast of Ketchikan on the western shore of Annette Island, you'll set foot on the very spot where Anglican missionary **William Duncan** landed in 1887 along with 823 followers, all Tsimshian Natives. They were on the run from the authorities in British Columbia, where Tsimshian land claims weren't respected, and from the more threatening Canadian bishops of the Church Missionary Society (CMS), with whom Duncan had fallen out. Fortunately, he had friends in high places in New York – Henry Wellcome and Thomas Edison among them – who pulled strings for him in Washington and coaxed the US government to grant the community Annette Island, site of a largely abandoned Tlingit settlement. Many Alaskan Natives live

Hyder

The remote outpost of **Hyder** (pop. 130) is so entirely isolated from the rest of Alaska that it might as well be part of Canada. Indeed, it is far more closely linked with its immediate British Columbian neighbor, Stewart, with which it shares a Canadian phone code (☏250), time zone, Canadian currency (though greenbacks are also accepted), and Canadian national holidays. Even the police are of the Mountie variety.

This easternmost of Alaskan towns is a ramshackle place that has traditionally only attracted people visiting Stewart, just two miles away by road, who come here so that they can say they've been to Alaska. But in recent years the biggest draw has become **bears**, which congregate at the Forest Service's **Fish Creek Wildlife Observation Site** (daily 6am–10pm; free), three miles east of Hyder along Salmon Glacier Road. Throughout July, August, and September (best mid-July to early Sept), both black and brown bears come down to the stream to feast on spawning chum and pink salmon, occasionally observed by bald eagles, which also fancy an easy fish snack. Come early in the morning or towards dusk for the best viewing, though you'll still have to compete for the best spots with professional photographers and a gaggle of other tourists.

At some point during your visit, you'll probably find yourself in one of Hyder's two bars, where if you toss back a shot of overproof liquor you'll receive an "I've Been Hyderized" card. At the *Glacier Inn* an additional tradition is to pin a dollar to the wall in case you return broke and need a drink. Although it's a fairly common pastime in northern bars, the effect here is particularly spectacular, with many thousands of dollars creating the "world's most expensive wallpaper."

It sounds a bit of a tourist carry-on, but if you arrive out of season there's a genuine warmth about the place that warrants its claims to be the "Friendliest Ghost Town in Alaska."

Accommodation and eating

Hyder has a modest range of **accommodation**, including the rustic *Hyder Base Camp Hostel* (✉hostel@hyderstewart.com, ⊛www.hyderhostel.com, booking by email only; open mid-May to mid-Sept; bunks $20), and the budget *Sealaska Inn and Camp Run-a-Muck* (☏1-888/393-1199, ⊛www.sealaskainn.com; ❷), which offers tent sites ($12–15), RV sites (dry $15, full hookup $22), and modest hotel rooms. The *Grand View Inn* (☏250/636-9174, ⊛www.grandviewinn.net; ❷) has slightly nicer units, all with microwave and fridge, plus some with full kitchen for which there is a small additional charge. There's more accommodation across the border in Stewart, mostly more expensive, and some very appealing; consult ⊛www.stewart-hyder.com.

After a hard morning's bear-viewing, follow the **breakfast** crowds to the excellent ⚘ *Wildflour Coffee Shop* (☏250/636-2875), which also does tasty baked goods. Later in the day you'll have to make do with the limited offerings at the *Sealaska Inn* or head across to Stewart.

The only **road access to Hyder** is through Canada along the especially beautiful Glacier Highway, which is strung with hanging glaciers that appear about to calve right onto the road at the slightest provocation.

Contact with the rest of Alaska is by air with Taquan Air (☏225-8800 or 1-800/770-8800, ⊛www.taquanair.com), which flies here from Ketchikan for $157 each way; alternatively, you can get a quick sense of the place on one of the twice-weekly mailruns (Mon & Thurs; $172), which won't give you any time to explore but will provide you superb views of Misty Fiords National Monument.

in remote villages largely populated by their own people, but Annette Island became the only Native reservation in Alaska.

Under the leadership of Father Duncan, Alaska's sole Tsimshian settlement grew into one of the most successful CMS missions, a model of religious, social, and economic independence that became a template for similar communities elsewhere. Duncan had already spent thirty years working with the Tsimshian in British Columbia and continued his efforts to get rid of intertribal slavery while keeping the church in control of secular as well as religious activities. He also became something of a patriarch, allegedly siring dozens of children to Native women.

The group's landing point proved highly suitable, with a waterfall (close to the modern ferry dock) that could be harnessed for power and water, a sloping beach that made an ideal site for a cannery, and enough timber to start a sawmill and build frame houses and the church. What is known as the **Duncan Memorial Church**, on 4th Avenue, is a replica of the original that burned down in 1949 and is guarded by Duncan's grave. Although Duncan is well remembered, his religion has failed to flower. None of Metlakatla's eight churches is now Anglican.

There's more to be seen in the single-story wooden-frame **Duncan Cottage Museum**, Jail Street, close to the small boat harbor (mid-May to mid-Sept Mon–Fri 2–6pm and during scheduled tours, or by appointment; $5; ☎886-8687), in the house where Duncan lived from 1894 until his death in 1914. It contains plenty of photos and material on the life and times of Duncan and the people of Metlakatla, along with the Bible Duncan brought with him from England, a very early Edison phonograph, a prominent portrait of Queen Victoria, and Duncan's bedroom complete with his personal effects and a couple of large safes. There's also discussion of World War II, when Annette Island became an important military base.

Once you've seen the museum, there's not a great deal to do. Entry to the tribal longhouse and Native dancing are only for those visiting with Metlakatla Tours (see below), and an hour or two is enough to wander the waterfront with its cannery, the dilapidated former sawmill, and the only **fish traps** left in the state, none in very good order. With time on your hands, stroll half a mile out along Western Avenue until you reach Pioneer Park, a small nub of land threaded by rough boardwalks with great sea views. Alternatively, hike a mile and a half out along Airport Road to the sandstone outcrop of **Yellow Hill**, which affords a superb view over the town and Prince of Wales Island. **Cyclists** and anyone bringing a car over have the run of the island's fairly extensive road system, giving access to more hiking along the **Purple Lake Trail**, four miles south of town, and to the appropriately named **Sand Dollar Beach**.

Practicalities

Ferry access to Metlakatla is on the AMHS **Metlakatla Shuttle** (daily except Tues & Wed, 2 per day; $24 each way), which runs between the Ketchikan AMHS ferry dock and the Metlakatla ferry dock a mile from town. Plans are well advanced for a much shorter crossing from Saxman to Walden Point on the northern tip of Annette Island; a ferry service may start operating in 2008 or 2009. You find faster and more frequent transit by **float-plane** with Promech Air (☎1-800/860-3845, ⓦwww.promechair.com), which flies several times daily and charges $80 round-trip.

Call in advance to synchronize your visit with one of the four-hour **Metlakatla Tours** (May–Sept twice weekly; $40, reservations essential; ☎886-8687, ⓦwww.metlakatlatours.net), which include a town tour detailing the stories behind the town's numerous totem poles, a tribal dance in full regalia, and a visit to the carvers and craftspeople at the Artists' Village.

Unless you are on the tour, your Metlakatla experience will be more rewarding with a local contact, most easily obtained by staying at *Tuck 'em Inn* on Oceanview (☎886-6611 or 886-7853, ⓦwww.alaskanow.com/tuckem-inn; ❹), which has

rooms with private bath and continental breakfast. They can also organize charter halibut-fishing trips. A reasonable alternative is *Metlakatla Inn* (☎886-3456; ❹). There are no formal campgrounds and **camping** isn't encouraged.

The *Metlakatla Inn* has about the only real **restaurant** in town, with sandwiches and burgers at reasonable prices, though you might just want to grab a burger, donut, or espresso at the Laesk Mini-Mart on Milton Street, which is your best bet for **groceries**. Note that this is a dry community, so **no alcohol** is allowed.

Prince of Wales Island

Prince of Wales Island is the third largest in the US (after Kodiak and Hawaii's Big Island), over 135 miles long and threaded by more miles of road than the rest of Southeast put together – over 1500 in total, though less than a hundred are paved. Many are dead-end logging roads, but they provide unparalleled access to this mountainous landscape shaped by ancient glaciers and subsequently flooded to create a deeply indented coastline pocked by small bays and rocky coves. **Wildlife** is abundant, and everywhere you go there are streams thick with salmon – indeed, the **fishing** is legendary, and many of the island's visitors are here to haul in prize specimens while staying in the exclusive fishing lodges that line the coast. Below ground, the underlying limestone has been eroded to form Alaska's only sizeable **cave system**.

The spruce and hemlock forests that cloaked the steep island's hillsides for millennia have, in recent decades, become the most savagely logged area of the Tongass National Forest. Forestry has downsized drastically of late, but scars left by clear-cuts can appear unsightly for thirty years or more after cutting. Still, the forest seems to recover quickly and without trees crowding in on all

△ Sitka black-tailed deer, Prince of Wales Island

sides the long views are excellent. What's more, the logging legacy makes this a wonderful place to explore by 4WD, by mountain bike, or more carefully in an ordinary car.

With the exception of the limestone caves in the north of the island and several excellent collections of replica totem poles, there are few sights, but POW (as it is often known) is a great place to unwind for a few days. It's not the sort of place that rewards a quick visit; you really need time to explore and slip into the pace of life here, resting up in one of the more than twenty Forest Service cabins (many of which have lake access and good fishing), spending a few days paddling one of the canoe routes, or just strolling the driftwood-strewn beaches. The island is also a big hunting destination and, in late April and May, **bear hunters** hog the roads and rental vehicles can be hard to get.

Traditionally, Prince of Wales Island was Tlingit territory, but around three hundred years ago – and a hundred years before European contact – Haida from Canada's Queen Charlotte Islands got a toehold and gradually occupied much of the island. They continued to trade with their kin on the Nass River in British Columbia and, during the fur-trade years under Russian rule, amassed great wealth. At this time the potlatch reached its peak and totem-pole raising was at its height, a tradition remembered in the **totem parks** at Hydaburg, Klawock, and, most notably, Kasaan.

By the late nineteenth century, Presbyterian missionaries and fishing interests were well entrenched here, the former suppressing Native traditions and the latter bringing disease and altering the economic dynamic. Haida numbers

Hiking and paddling on Prince of Wales Island

Although Prince of Wales Island has a couple of well-known short trails, it isn't especially noted for its hiking; serious outdoors fans might be better off considering the two excellent **canoe routes**, best tackled from May to September. The coastline lends itself superbly to **kayaking**. Although no formal routes have been mapped out, there's scope for anything from a paddle of a couple of hours to a several-week circumnavigation. The best source for suggestions and boats is Alaska Kustom Kayaks in Klawock (see p.116).

One Duck Trail (2.5 miles round-trip; 2hr; 1200ft ascent). Moderately steep but rewarding hike with magnificent views from the small shelter and open muskeg at the top. Starts on Hydaburg Road, two miles south of the Craig–Hollis Highway.

Soda Lake Trail (5 miles round-trip; 3hr; negligible ascent). Fairly easy walking across muskeg and through forest, ending at Soda Lake and some bubbling mineral springs with good bird- and wildlife-spotting. Starts on Hydaburg Road, twelve miles south of the Craig–Hollis Highway.

Honker Divide Canoe Route (30 miles; 3–4 days; 150ft elevation gain). A rugged and strenuous route formerly used by early trappers and requiring good canoeing and backcountry camping skills. Long sections may need lining unless there has been recent rain, and waterfalls and rapids need to be portaged. There will also be sweepers to avoid (see Basics, p.69). It is a rewarding experience, though, and the Forest Service's *Honker Lake Cabin* (only accessible through this route; $25) may be available for the first or second night.

Sarkar Lake Canoe Route (15-mile loop; 6–8hr; negligible ascent). Easy route through a roadless area linking six lakes by means of stream and short board-walk portages, often spread over two to three days. Good fishing and wildlife viewing. There's a Forest Service cabin ($35) beside Sarkar Lake, two miles from the put-in.

dropped from an estimated ten thousand to around eight hundred as canneries were set up around the coast. The importance of these gradually gave way to logging, which for the second half of the twentieth century was the mainstay of the local economy. With the 1999 closure of a large pulp mill in Ketchikan, logging has declined drastically, leading to high unemployment in some areas. Poor global prices for timber products undoubtedly contributed, but in these parts the Clinton administration's policies received a lot of flak. Environmentalist is a dirty word around here, though hopes that George W. Bush would be the loggers' savior have come to nothing.

Planning, arrival, and getting around

Before you head to Prince of Wales Island, visit Ketchikan's Discovery Center, a good starting point for detailed information on campgrounds, canoe routes, hikes, and Forest Service cabins. It also stocks the comprehensive *Prince of Wales Island Guide* (free) and the *Prince of Wales Island Forest Service Road Guide* ($7), a detailed though slightly dated map.

POW is served by Island Ferry Authority (℡1-866/308-4848, Ⓦwww .interislandferry.com), which operates vehicle-carrying **ferries** along two routes, making it possible to loop through the island on your way through Southeast: ideal for cyclists. One runs from **Ketchikan to Hollis** (1–2 daily all year; 3hr; adult one-way $37, bikes & kayaks $27, vehicles $72–85 for most normal sizes); the other is from **Coffman Cove to Wrangell** (mid-May to mid-Sept Thurs–Sun; 3hr; adult one-way $37, bikes & kayaks $27, vehicles $72–85 for most normal sizes), with continuing service from Wrangell to South Mitkof, near Petersburg (see p.130). Both docks on POW have new terminal buildings but public transportation is limited. Prince of Wales Transportation (℡826-5555) meets ferries at Hollis but only runs as far as Klawock or Craig ($25). A separate shuttle service (℡826-5556) operates to Coffman Cove on a reservation-only basis ($75 per person).

Alternatively, catch a **float-plane** from Ketchikan to Craig or Klawock, where you can pick up a rental car without the delivery fee. Pacific Airways (℡1-877/360-3500, Ⓦwww.flypacificairways.com) flies to Craig or Klawock for $135 one way; Promech Air (℡1-800/860-3843, Ⓦwww.promechair.com) flies three to four times daily to Craig for $135 ($235 round-trip).

To **get around** you really need a car. For long stays it may be worth bringing one over from Ketchikan, but **rental vehicles** can be had on the island. Most are SUVs or trucks designed for the more rugged island roads and costing close to $100 a day; call early to get smaller, cheaper vehicles. For the best selection try Klawock-based Wilderness Rent-a-Car (℡1-800/949-2205, Ⓦwww.wildernesscarrental.com), which offers compact 4WDs (from $69 a day plus 15 percent tax), 4WD Ford Explorers ($89), and four-berth RVs ($200). It's an extra $50 to pick up and drop off the vehicle at the ferry. Craig-based Alaska Rentals (℡1-800/720-3468, Ⓦwww.alaskarentals.com) has similar prices. Remember to fill up where you can: **gas** is only available at Craig, Klawock, Thorne Bay, Coffman Cove, and Naukati. If you're looking to get out on the water, almost everywhere you go on Prince of Wales Island you'll find someone keen to rent you a **boat** or take you fishing.

Once out of town you can **camp** on any Forest Service land: the map in the *Prince of Wales Island Guide* shows where private land is located and also pinpoints several popular "dispersed" camping sites, where it's legal to camp but no facilities are available. On the other end of the price scale, exclusive **fly-in lodges** dot the coast, some in abandoned canneries and most charging four-figure sums for the privilege of spending two or three days there: all have comprehensive websites, and the visitor center in Craig can point you in the right direction.

❶ Hydaburg and Klawock

Apart from a new ferry terminal, there is nothing at Hollis, where the ferry from Ketchikan arrives. From Hollis (Mile 31) an asphalt road runs ten miles west to the Harris River junction. Turning south, Hydaburg Road heads for twenty miles past the trailhead for One Duck Trail (Mile 2), the Cable Creek Fish Pass (Mile 8), and the trailhead for Soda Lake Trail (Mile 12) to **Hydaburg**. This small waterside Haida town, established in 1911 when three local villages combined, is devoted to preserving its culture and isn't particularly interested in visitors, although you might call in to inspect the Civilian Conservation Corps totem park constructed in the late 1930s.

Instead, most people head north at the Harris River intersection to Klawock and beyond. At Mile 19.7 there's the first-come, first-served *Harris River Campground* ($8 per vehicle), an attractive and organized site with toilets, pump water, and pleasant walks through the forest. Ten miles on, you can stop to see the workings of the community-run Prince of Wales Hatchery (daily 7am–7pm; ☎755–2231), where you are welcome to wander around the tanks and fish ladder outside, or stick around for one of the guided tours (Mon–Sat 1–6pm and by arrangement; donations appreciated).

It is a mile on to **Klawock**, which serves as the island's main intersection where Boundary Road heads north. The junction is marked by a modern Bell Tower mall with a post office, liquor store, supermarket, and the island's Chamber of Commerce **visitor center** (Mon–Fri 10am–3pm; ☎755-2626, Ⓦ www.princeofwalescoc.org).

Nearby on Big Salt Lake Road, Alaska Kustom Kayaks (☎755-2800, Ⓦ www.alaskakustomkayaks.com) rents bikes ($20 for 8hr, $30 for 24hr) and top-quality fiberglass kayaks (singles $60 a day, doubles $70). They also have plastic canoes ($45) and will advise on the best places to suit your needs. Camping gear may also be available to rent, and they'll run guided trips to order ($120 per day; two-person minimum).

There's accommodation nearby at *Log Cabin Resort & RV Park*, Big Salt Lake Road (☎1-800/544-2205, Ⓦ www.logcabinresortandrvpark.com; camping $8.50 per person, cabins ❸, suites ❺), gravel pads suitable for RVs, simple two-berth cabins, fairly luxurious suites, and assorted canoe and boat rentals and fishing charters. For more luxury, try the fishing-oriented *Fireweed Lodge*, Hollis–Craig Highway (☎755-2930, Ⓦ www.fireweedlodge.com), where you'll pay around $225 each per night for room, hot tub, meals, and saltwater fishing gear rental. Eat at *Dave's Diner* (☎755-2986) near the start of Big Salt Lake Road.

Across the highway from the Bell Tower mall, look out for Tlingit carver John Rowan working on totem poles in The Carving Shed. He is usually around weekdays until 2pm and, if not too busy, often happy to chat about his work. Most of his recent poles have been recarvings of poles from the Tlingit Native village of Klawock, a mile or so to the west. This was a very important place in the early years of American Alaska; the state's first cannery was set up here in 1878, and two of Alaska's first three sawmills were constructed nearby. Now it is chiefly known for the collection of fifteen totem poles erected under the auspices of the CCC and displayed on a sloping hill beside a couple of roads. New poles have been added in the past few years, underscoring the continued importance of totem carving in Tlingit community life. New poles are usually erected around Labor Day each year.

Craig

South of Klawock, the highway runs seven miles to **Craig**, the island's largest town, although it has fewer than two thousand residents. With a couple of fish-processing plants, boats bobbing in the harbor, and the hard-bitten tenor of a real working town, it is a likeable place and is pretty enough to wander round on a sunny afternoon. There are no real sights, however, and apart from making use of the island's densest concentration of hotels, restaurants, and services (banks, library with free Internet access, etc), you'll soon find yourself wanting to move on. Before you do, call in at Stone Arts of Alaska, 118 JT Brown St (daily 10am–5pm; ☎826-3571, ⓦ www.stoneartsofalaska.com), where Gary McWilliams produces some beautiful **stone carvings**, mostly using local rock.

It's easy to overlook that Craig sits on its own eponymous island, linked by a short bridge to Prince of Wales Island. As you approach over the bridge from Prince of Wales Island you find yourself on Water Street passing the town's cluster of mini-malls, where you'll find a supermarket, the post office, a bank (with ATM), and *Papa's Pizza*. A couple of hundred yards further on, Voyageur Bookstore at 7th and Water streets (☎826-2333) is the best place on the island to relax over an espresso and muffin or check your email. The older commercial heart of Craig is a couple of blocks straight on beside the picturesque remains of an old cannery.

Craig has easily the largest range of **accommodation** on Prince of Wales Island, much of it booked up with fishing parties. There's nothing particularly cheap, though you'll be well housed at ✹ *Dreamcatcher*, 1405 Hamilton Drive (☎826-2238, ⓦ www.dreamcatcherbedandbreakfast.com; ❺), a lovely three-room B&B in a wooded setting close to town that has great sea views. All rooms have private bath, and a continental breakfast is included. For hotel rooms, try *Ruth Ann's Hotel* on Water Street (☎826-3378, ⓔ ruthanns @aptalaska.net; suites ❻, rooms ❹), with spacious modern rooms equipped with TV, microwave, refrigerator, and coffeepot, plus older and smaller rooms that have a bit more character.

For **eating**, the *Bait Box*, 510 Water St (☎826-2303; closed Sun), does wraps, subs, and burgers to go, but the locals' favorite is *Ruth Ann's* with a bar and restaurant built on pilings over the water by the dock. The adjacent *Hill Bar* is always animated and has **live music** whenever they can coax a band over here.

Kasaan

Until fairly recently, the roads north of Klawock were all unpaved, but the advent of the new ferry terminal at Coffman Cove has set construction wheels in motion. Miles of smooth, broad asphalt link Klawok with Thorne Bay and by 2008 they should reach Coffman Cove. The rest of the northern roads are single-lane and often potholed: take things steady and be sure to have a good spare tire.

Leaving Klawock, the road heads north past Klawock airport through some open hill country sixteen miles to a road junction: turn left to Coffman Cove and the caves, or right to Kasaan and Thorne Bay. A couple of miles along the Klawock–Thorne Bay road you reach the lovely first-come, first-served *Eagle Nest Campground* ($8 per vehicle), with well-spaced sites, some of which are walk-in platforms with lake views. Take a few minutes to stroll along the half-mile boardwalk around **Balls Lake**.

Beyond the campground a bone-shaking seventeen-mile road cuts southeast to the tiny waterside Haida village of **Kasaan**, one of Southeast's best (if least

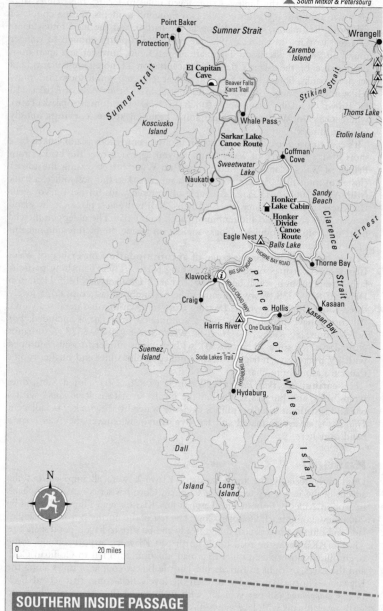

SOUTHEAST ALASKA

SOUTHERN INSIDE PASSAGE

Point Baker
Sumner Strait
Wrangell
Port Protection
Zarembo Island
El Capitan Cave
Beaver Falls Karst Trail
Stikine Strait
Sumner Strait
Whale Pass
Thoms Lake
Kosciusko Island
Etolin Island
Sarkar Lake Canoe Route
Coffman Cove
Sweetwater Lake
Sandy Beach
Naukati
Clarence
Honker Lake Cabin
Ernest
Honker Divide Canoe Route
Eagle Nest ✕
Balls Lake
THORNE BAY ROAD
Thorne Bay
Klawock ⓘ BIG SALT ROAD
Prince
Strait
Craig
Hollis
Kasaan
HOLLIS CRAIG HWY
Harris River △ One Duck Trail
of
Kasaan Bay
Suemez Island
Soda Lakes Trail
Wales
Hydaburg
Dall
Island
Island
Long Island

N

0   20 miles

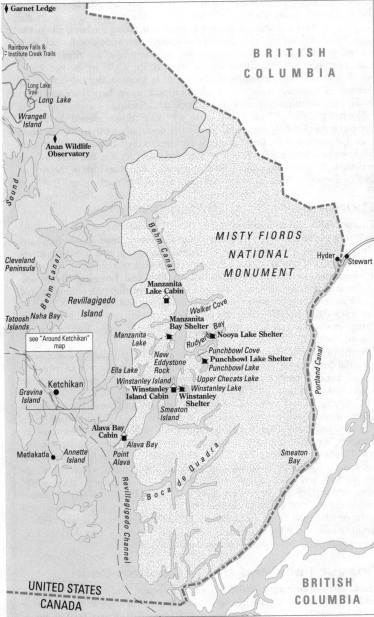

Garnet Ledge

Rainbow Falls & Institute Creek Trails

Long Lake Trail

Long Lake

Wrangell Island

Anan Wildlife Observatory

Sound

BRITISH COLUMBIA

Behm Canal

MISTY FIORDS NATIONAL MONUMENT

Hyder Stewart

Cleveland Peninsula

Behm Canal

Revillagigedo Island

Tatoosh Islands Naha Bay

Manzanita Lake Cabin

Walker Cove

Manzanita Bay Shelter Bay

Rudyerd

Nooya Lake Shelter

Manzanita Lake

New Eddystone Rock

Punchbowl Cove

Punchbowl Lake Shelter

Punchbowl Lake

Portland Canal

see "Around Ketchikan" map

Ella Lake

Upper Checats Lake

Ketchikan

Winstanley Island

Gravina Island

Winstanley Island Cabin

Winstanley Lake

Winstanley Shelter

Smeaton Island

Alava Bay Cabin

Metlakatla Annette Island

Alava Bay

Point Alava

Boca de Quadra

Smeaton Bay

Revillagigedo Channel

UNITED STATES

CANADA

BRITISH COLUMBIA

Whitehorse & Prince George

Prince Rupert, BC & Bellinghams WA

convenient) places to see totem poles. It was originally founded a century back when the lure of mining and fishing jobs attracted Haida here from the now-abandoned village of Old Kasaan. The only reason to come here is to visit the abandoned **totem park**, a mile west of the village. Leave your car by the Community Hall and walk back towards the beach, taking the last track on the right. Follow this for twenty minutes or so through beachside woods to the next bay, where you'll find what is perhaps the finest setting of any Alaskan totem park. The poles and clan house are the work of the CCC in the late 1930s, but its neglected state, the authentic feeling of its location, and the lack of any commercial trappings make it a wonderful spot. If you're here alone, especially in the early morning or at dusk, it is particularly affecting.

The beach is backed by the clan house, with its platforms around the sunken fire pit and powerfully carved roof supports now only partly achieving their intended purpose as the forest gradually reclaims its own. In front, a superb pole faces out to sea, four feet thick at its base and over fifty feet tall, with bulbous eyes set in four-foot-high faces. Nearby, several other poles lurk in the woods, four of them in a ring almost swallowed by the undergrowth.

Thorne Bay and Coffman Cove

Thorne Bay Road runs, not surprisingly, to **Thorne Bay**, which from 1962 to 2001 was the site of the Ketchikan Pulp Company's main log-sorting yard. Once described as the world's largest logging camp, it is now mostly of interest to anglers. If you're on the island around the last weekend in July, be sure to check out the **Prince of Wales Island Fair and Logging Show**, one of the last of these traditional events with ax-throwing, pole-climbing, and chainsaw-handling competitions. The *Welcome Inn B&B* (☏1-888/828-3940, Ⓦwww.lodginginnalaska.com; ❹) offers shared-bath rooms with breakfast; **campers** should stock up at the Thorne Bay Market before making for the bays to the north.

North of Thorne Bay, the road hugs the coast for ten miles, passing some beautiful little bays with numerous camping possibilities, none of which is formal. **Sandy Beach**, six miles out, is the most popular spot, with picnic table, toilets, and fire rings.

Occupying an idyllic bay around thirty miles north of Thorne Bay, **Coffman Cove** (Ⓦwww.coffmancove.org) is the former site of a Tlingit village and a 1950s logging camp. There's a library, post office, liquor store, and terminal for ferries to Wrangell, but there's not a great deal to do except beachcomb and fish. This is perhaps best done while **staying** at *Oceanview RV Campgrounds and Lodging* (☏329-2226, Ⓦwww.coffmancove.org/rvpark), which has camping for $15, and full hookup for $25. For fully self-contained cabins you're better off at *Coffman Cove Cabin Rentals* (☏329-2251, Ⓦwww.coffmancove .org/cccabins.html; ❷), or try *Whale Watchers B&B*, located just as you enter town on the road from the south (☏329-2272, Ⓦwww.whalewatchersbnb .com), where the $130 per person rate includes ferry or float dock pickup, very comfortable beachside accommodation, and all meals.

Beaver Falls and the El Capitan Cave

Much of the north of the island is karst landscape, underlain by limestone riddled with dozens of caves, most of them barely explored. A sense of what lies below can be gleaned on the accessible **Beaver Falls Karst Trail**, an interpretive network of boardwalks located 31 miles north of the Coffman Cove road junction. Set aside at least half an hour to wander across muskeg and into dripping forest to depressions in the forest floor marking sinkholes, some of which swallow small streams.

As appealing as the boardwalk is, the prize exhibit around here is **El Capitan Cave**, used by Native peoples as early as 3400 years ago judging by charcoal left from torches. Modern speleologists only started extensively mapping the caves in the late 1980s and have since discovered the El Cap Pit, which is the deepest known natural pit in the US, with an initial drop of almost six hundred feet. The Forest Service runs **guided tours** (late May to early Sept daily at 9am, noon & 2pm; free; ☎ 828-3304): numbers are limited so book a few days in advance. Taking about an hour and a half and penetrating some six hundred feet into the cave, the tours take in the usual limestone formations along with hollows where otters hibernate, crevices where bats roost, and even spots where bears once spent the winter. Bring along a flashlight, warm clothing to combat the cave's constant 40°F temperatures, and some reasonably sturdy footwear. Note that you'll have to make your own way to the site, which is almost a hundred miles from the Hollis ferry dock and a three- to four-hour drive.

A locked gate fifty yards in prevents freelance exploration, but you are welcome to explore the entrance area after negotiating the gorgeous fifteen-minute forest access trail and its 370 steps.

Wrangell and around

Eighty miles north of Ketchikan, the small fishing town of **WRANGELL** occupies a strategically significant spot on the northern tip of Wrangell Island, just seven miles south of the mouth of the **Stikine River**, the only passable break in the Coastal Range between Prince Rupert and Skagway. The area became a major conduit for prospectors bound for the early gold rushes, first during the stampede to central British Columbia in the early 1860s and later during the Yukon rush in 1897, when the Stikine became the so-called back-door route to the Klondike.

Although for many visitors Wrangell is just a forty-minute ferry stop on the run from Ketchikan, the town, altogether quieter and more old-fashioned than its bustling rival, is not without appeal. There are just a few relatively minor sights, all easily accessible on foot. **Chief Shakes Island**, right in the busy harbor and accessible by a short boardwalk, holds an excellent collection of totem poles and a replica tribal house filled with Tlingit artifacts, and about a mile to the north lies **Petroglyph Beach**, where ancient rock carvings defy explanation and have proven difficult to date.

Though Wrangell is by no means an unfriendly place, you sometimes feel there is a grudging acceptance of your presence in what is a fiercely independent town still smarting from the loss of many of the town's jobs with the closure of the local sawmill in 1994. People round here believe in the right of Alaskans to make whatever use they can of the land, and the loss of both jobs and a third of the town's income have come as a shock both economically and psychologically. Always comfortable with its blue-collar workaday existence, the town now wrestles with the notion that tourism might be its savior.

Some people have no difficulty with the concept, and half a dozen tour companies are happy to take you out, either south to watch **bears** gorging on salmon at Anan Creek, or north and inland along the churning waters of the Stikine River, perhaps calling at the **Garnet Ledge**, where local children

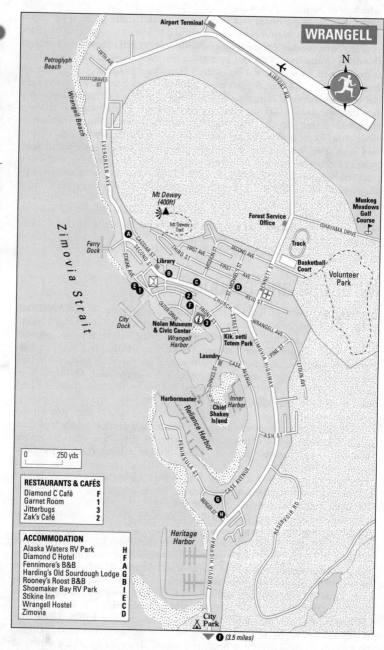

WRANGELL

N

Airport Terminal

Petroglyph Beach

FIFTH AVE

GRAVES ST

AIRPORT RD

Wrangell Beach

EVERGREEN AVE

Muskeg Meadows Golf Course

ISHAYAMA DRIVE

Zimovia Strait

Mt Dewey (400ft)

Mt Dewey Trail

Forest Service Office

Track

Ferry Dock

CASSIAR ST

SECOND ST

THIRD ST

FIRST AVE

SECOND AVE

Basketball Court

Volunteer Park

Library

STIKINE AVE

SECOND ST

FIRST AVE

MISSION ST

ST MICHAEL'S ST

BENNETT S

A

B

C

D

E

1

2

F

3

OUTER DRIVE

FRONT ST

CHURCH STREET

REID ST

WRANGELL AVE

City Dock

Nolan Museum & Civic Center
Wrangell Harbor

Kik. setti Totem Park

ZIMOVIA HIGHWAY

PINE ST

ETOLIN AVE

Laundry

CASE AVENUE

Harbormaster

SHAKES ST

Inner Harbor

Reliance Harbor

Chief Shakes Island

ASH ST

PENINSULA ST

0   250 yds

BERGER ST

G

H

CASE AVENUE

RESERVOIR RD

Heritage Harbor

ZIMOVIA HIGHWAY

City Park

1 (3.5 miles)

RESTAURANTS & CAFÉS

Diamond C Café	F
Garnet Room	1
Jitterbugs	3
Zak's Café	2

ACCOMMODATION

Alaska Waters RV Park	H
Diamond C Hotel	F
Fennimore's B&B	A
Harding's Old Sourdough Lodge	G
Rooney's Roost B&B	B
Shoemaker Bay RV Park	I
Stikine Inn	E
Wrangell Hostel	C
Zimovia	D

gather garnets for sale to tourists, or **Chief Shakes Hot Springs**, a perenni-
ally popular weekend destination for locals. Visitor numbers are still low here,
however – they only get one medium-size cruise ship every week or two – and
it can sometimes be difficult to gather enough people for a trip since they are
arranged by demand. If you can get a group of four or six together, you'll find
that your options (and prices) improve dramatically.

Some history

Wrangell claims to have been ruled by four nations: that of the Tlingit, Russia,
the UK, and the US. In the early nineteenth century, the Tlingit were trading
with the Russian-American Company, which feared the expansionism of the
Hudson's Bay Company. To protect their rights to the sea otters hereabouts,
in 1834 the Russians established Redoubt St Dionysius, a small fort that soon
drew local Native villagers to settle in and around Chief Shakes Island in the
middle of Wrangell Harbor. To quell a trading dispute in 1840, the Russians
leased the fort to the Hudson's Bay Company, which renamed it Fort Stikine
and helped establish it as a supply post for fur traders and the first batch of
gold seekers, who headed up the Stikine River in 1861. When the United
States purchased Alaska in 1867, the Americans renamed the settlement
Wrangell in honor of Baron Ferdinand Wrangel, a former manager of the
Russian-American Company. The Canadian Cassiar gold rush came in the
1870s and thousands of miners brought heady days to this rural outpost, a
situation repeated on a smaller scale with the Klondike gold rush of 1897.
Canneries and logging followed and proved to have greater staying power,
though Wrangell has long ceased to be a major fishing port, and now the
mill has gone.

Arrival, information, and getting around

Wrangell is served by two ferry systems: AMHS (☎874-3711), with almost
daily service to Ketchikan and Petersburg, and IFA (☎1-866/308-4848,
ⓦwww.interislandferry.com), which runs to Coffman Cove at the north end
of Prince of Wales Island (mid-May to mid-Sept Thurs–Sun; 3hr; $37), and to
South Mitkof (mid-May to mid-Sept Thurs–Sun; 1hr; $25), which has road
access to Petersburg.

AMHS usually stops for about forty minutes while IFA stops for an hour,
giving you a better chance of a very quick look at the petroglyphs: walk fast or
call Star Cab, ☎874-3622.

All ferries dock at the northern edge of downtown Wrangell, from where
you can easily walk into town and to most of the accommodation. The **airport**
(☎874-3308), a mile and a half north of town, has daily connections to
Ketchikan, Petersburg, and Juneau, and offers **car rental** from Practical Rent-
A-Car (☎874-3975) for around $60 a day with unlimited mileage.

The town's **visitor center** (Mon–Fri 10am–4pm and when cruise ships
are in; ☎874-3699 or 1-800/367-9745, ⓦwww.wrangellalaska.org) is in
the Nolan Centre at 296 Outer Drive. It has expensive Internet access and
stocks the free *Wrangell Guide*. For information on hikes, cabins, and anything
else in the surrounding Tongass National Forest, visit the Wrangell Ranger
District **Forest Service Office**, 525 Bennett St (Mon–Fri 8am–4.30pm;
☎874-2323).

Though it is easy enough to wander around the main sights in Wrangell,
you might want to **rent a bike** from Rainwalker Expeditions (☎874-2549,
ⓦwww.rainwalkerexpeditions.com), which charges $20 a day. Rainwalker also

runs a series of naturalist-guided walking and van **tours**, among them a visit to Petroglyph Beach (1hr 30min; $15), a tour of historic downtown and Chief Shakes Island (1hr 30min; $12), and a half-day island exploration ($89).

Accommodation

For such a tiny place, Wrangell is fairly well supplied with accommodation, including a simple hostel, a couple of motels, and several B&Bs. Camping is good, too, with half a dozen designated places to camp along the road system. In addition to the **campgrounds** and RV parks listed below, there are several more free sites further along Zimovia Highway at Miles 11, 14, 17, 23, and 28. The best is Three Sisters Overlook, at Mile 14, with long views from its high vantage point.

Alaska Waters RV Park 241 Berger St ☎874-2378. Small and not especially attractive lot with just seven power and water hookup sites for $25. Drop rubbish at the city dump station on Shakes St at Case Ave.

City Park 1.5 miles south on Zimovia Highway. The nearest campground to town, well sited in woods beside the channel, with first-come, first-served sites available for a one-night maximum stay. There are shelters to cook under and marginal toilets but no showers. Free.

Diamond C Hotel 223 Front St ☎874-3322. Budget motel with fairly spacious phone- and shower-equipped rooms (ask for one with an external window), each with cable TV, WiFi, and some with refrigerator. ❸

Fennimore's B&B 312 Evergreen Ave ☎874-3012, ⓦwww.fennimoresbbb.com. Comfy and friendly B&B conveniently located by the ferry dock. Two upstairs rooms with shared bath and three downstairs rooms with private entrances and their own bathrooms, all of which are pleasantly furnished, have cable TV, fridge, and microwave, and include a continental breakfast served in your room. Free bikes for guests. ❸

Harding's Old Sourdough Lodge 1104 Peninsula St ☎1-800/874-3613, ⓦwww.akgetaway.com. Large cedar log building at the southern edge of town with high-standard rooms in various sizes to suit individuals and small groups. The best deals are the wilderness and adventure packages, such as two nights with one day spent on the Stikine River, viewing bald eagles, whale-watching, or visiting the Anan Wildlife Observatory ($429 per person); two nights with car rental and green fees for Wrangell's nine-hole golf course ($298); and six nights, with

five days spent kayaking the Stikine and flightseeing the LeConte Glacier ($1485). Homestay meals for guests only (breakfast and lunch $10, dinner $24). Suites ❼, standard rooms ❺

Rooney's Roost B&B 206 McKinnon St ☎874-2026, ⓦwww.rooneysroost.com. Attractive B&B, close to town, with modernized rooms, phones, TV, antique furniture, clawfoot baths in the rooms with bathrooms, a large lounge, and a full sit-down breakfast. Private bath ❹, shared bath ❸

Shoemaker Bay RV Park 4.5 miles south on Zimovia Highway. First-come, first-served RV and tent campground with 26 spaces, toilets, picnic tables, and shelters, plus beach fishing. Handy for the Rainbow Falls Trail. Electricity hookup sites are $25, dry sites $15.

Stikine Inn 107 Stikine Ave ☎1-888/874-3388, ⓦwww.stikineinn.com. Wrangell's largest hotel, a little dated but right on the waterfront, with spacious rooms all with cable TV and coffeemakers. The waterside rooms are worth the extra few dollars. Suites ❻, rooms ❺

Wrangell Hostel 220 Church St ☎874-3534, ⓔpresby@aptalaska.net. Eighteen dollars seems like a lot for an inflatable mattress on the floor of a room in the First Presbyterian Church, but if you want a cheap roof over your head this is your best bet. It is clean and central with a good kitchen, hot showers, and no daytime lockout. There is an 11pm curfew, but this is flexible. Open June to early Sept.

Zimovia 319 Webber St ☎1-866/946-6842, ⓦwww.zimoviabnb.com. Excellent-value, comfortable, and convenient B&B offering pleasant rooms with kitchenette, access to a sauna, and continental breakfast. ❹

The Town

Young garnet-sellers clustered on the docks usually greet arriving ferry passengers with their red jewels from the Garnet Ledge (see p.128). Although many visitors get no further, you can see a little of what Wrangell has to offer – either

Petroglyph Beach or the Kik.setti Totem Park – while the ferry is in port. You'll need more time to view the museum and Chief Shakes Tribal House or explore the town's hiking trails.

Petroglyph Beach and the Wrangell Museum

By grabbing a taxi (or walking very quickly) it is possible for ferry passengers to blitz **Petroglyph Beach**, just over half a mile north of the ferry dock off Evergreen Avenue at Graves Street. Of course, it is better to stay overnight and give yourself more time to explore the extensive boardwalk, which guides you down to the beach where Southeast's most concentrated array of ancient petroglyphs is etched onto the rocks. Little is known about the purpose of these forty-odd shapes – spirals, birds, orca, faces, and masks – and even the age is uncertain, with numbers ranging from a thousand to ten thousand years bandied about. The range of designs – from simple human forms to more detailed images resembling modern Tlingit iconography – indicate that the petroglyphs were produced in several eras, many predating the relatively modern Tlingit culture. Since they are located on an active beach, stratification studies to determine age are impossible.

It sometimes takes a few minutes to spy your first image, but then you seem to see them everywhere. The most concentrated batch is found around the high-tide line thirty to fifty yards to the right (north) of the boardwalk steps; don't miss the orca and owl forms close to the grass. The best time is usually as the high tide is receding and the glyphs are shiny and more visible (and photogenic). The low light of morning and evening is also helpful. Taking rubbings from the originals is strongly discouraged, and some replicas have been installed on the boardwalk for this purpose.

Some of the more portable glyphs have been removed for safekeeping to the **Wrangell Museum**, in the Nolan Center (May–Sept Mon–Sat 10am–5pm and Sun whenever cruise ships are in port; Oct–April Tues–Sat 1–5pm; $5). Only opened in 2004, this modern building welcomes you with two fine totems and a quartet of carved house posts. These are thought to be the oldest Tlingit house posts in existence, having probably been carved between 1775 and 1790 (and possibly as early as 1740). They're less stylized and more naturalistic in execution than many of the later models seen throughout Southeast; they're also heavily weathered from the years they spent outdoors before being incorporated into the Chief Shakes Tribal House (see p.126).

There's also a slab of rock from the Garnet Ledge with the garnets firmly embedded, as well as extensive coverage of the Cassiar gold rush, Wrangell's logging past, and an opportunity to feel the pelts of otter, beaver, lynx, wolverine, and more.

The Totem Park and Tribal House

Right downtown, on Front Street at Episcopal Street, you'll pass the **Kik .setti Totem Park**, a tiny grassed area created in 1987 on the original site of a long-lost pole known as Kik.setti. Noted carvers Steve Brown and Wayne Price used only traditional hand tools to re-create the Kik.setti totem – depicting the symbols of the Kik.setti people who settled Wrangell Island – which now stands in pride of place, backed by three other replicas of highly regarded poles. Among them is the **Raven totem**, with the Raven creator at the top, just above what is known as the chief's box, which is said to have spiritual powers. Below, a young Raven clasps a man between its wings, signifying how Raven could change into a man at will. The lowest figure is Ha-ya-shon-a-gu, described as the "Native American Atlas" holding up the Earth.

Hikes from Wrangell

Although a couple of easy walks are close at hand, the more challenging **hikes** require some means of getting out along the road system: either rent a vehicle, try hitching out to the relatively accessible hikes off Zimovia Highway, or engage the services of Rainwalker Expeditions. Listed below is a taste of what's on offer in the area; for more information seek out the free *Wrangell Guide* which lists the more popular trails. The Forest Service is also helpful with suggestions and sells topographic maps for $5. If they're closed, try Alaska Vistas, at the foot of the City Dock.

Long Lake Trail (1.2 miles round-trip; 30–40min; negligible ascent). Easy boardwalk to a lake where there's a shelter and a skiff with oars that's perfect for a little trout fishing. The trailhead is 27 miles southeast of Wrangell in the center of the island on Forest Road 6270.

Mount Dewey Trail (1 mile round-trip; 30–40min; 300ft ascent). Pleasant, at times steep, hike through woods to the top of the hill that rises behind downtown Wrangell. There's a good observation point overlooking the town, undoubtedly also used by John Muir when he made the ascent in 1879. The trail starts on 3rd Street.

Rainbow Falls Trail (2 miles round-trip; 1hr; 300ft ascent). Moderate and sometimes boggy trail through the rainforest to the top of a waterfall. From here, keen and fit hikers can continue up what's known as **Institute Creek Trail** (4.5 miles round-trip; 2–4hr; 1200ft ascent) to the three-sided Shoemaker Bay Overlook Shelter atop a high ridge with long views. The trailhead is almost five miles south along Zimovia Highway, opposite the Shoemaker Bay Recreation Site.

Volunteer Park Trail (800yd loop; 20min; flat). Easy nature walk along the edge of a spruce forest, with interpretive panels along the way. Starts near the basketball courts opposite the Forest Service office.

Front Street continues south as Shakes Street to **Chief Shakes Island**, a small grass plot and the heart of the inner harbor, linked to the docks by a short boardwalk. Dominated by the Chief Shakes **Tribal House** ($3) and ringed by a forest of **totem poles**, it makes a wonderfully peaceful place to while away an hour or two. Open only when cruise ships are in port, it is worth calling ☎874-2023 for a private viewing ($20 per group). The replica high-caste clan house was rebuilt as part of the Civilian Conservation Corps project (see box, p.98) on the site of an ancient house and dedicated in 1940 at one of the largest gatherings of Native people seen for many years. With the decline in traditional Tlingit ways in the early part of the twentieth century, there hadn't been a Chief Shakes (overall chief hereabouts) since 1916, and the potlatch – attended by the territorial governor – was seen as an opportunity to inaugurate the nephew of the last chief as Chief Shakes VII. Some 1500 people and several war canoes arrived from all over Southeast for what is generally regarded as the last great potlatch of the Tlingit people. Ancient house posts were incorporated into the building and only removed to the Wrangell Museum in 1982 when replicas were carved to replace them. If the house is open, nose around the adze-beamed interior as the guide explains traditional life inside a clan house. Otherwise you'll have to make do with the intricately carved exterior and half a dozen poles, including the **Three Frogs totem**, a shame totem erected to mock the Frog clan, who married slaves decades ago. The Frog clan was distinctly put out by its controversial raising in 2000.

Outdoor activities

Wrangell has plenty of good hiking (see box, above) and serves as a base for some excellent **kayaking**. (For bear viewing, jetboat trips, and visits to the

Garnet Ledge, see "Around Wrangell," p.128). Half a day spent bobbing around the harbor and along the coast to Petroglyph Beach can be satisfying, but a multiday trip along the sheltered Eastern Passage to Anan Wildlife Observatory is also worth considering. Despite the current, you can also kayak up the mighty Stikine River as far as the Canadian border by utilizing eddies and the slack-water sloughs marked on the Forest Service's schematic *Stikine River Canoe/Kayak Route Map* ($4), which also marks tent sites, cabins, and log jams. You can even pay to be transported upriver and paddle gently back down over several days (for more on the river, see "Around Wrangell," p.129).

Alaska Vistas (T1-866/874-3006, Wwww.alaskavistas.com) runs **guided trips** for around $150 a day and multiday excursions such as a six-day paddle to LeConte Glacier ($1300). **Going it alone**, you can rent kayaks from the same outfit, which offers singles ($45 a day) and doubles ($55) and does drop-offs at good starting points.

Eating, drinking, and entertainment

There's nothing special about **eating** in Wrangell, but you won't go hungry and there's enough variety for the night or two you'll be here. Bob's IGA supermarket on Campbell Drive is reasonably well stocked and has an in-store bakery.

Castle Mountain Theater In the Nolan Center. First-run movies on Fri & Sat nights. Proceeds go to the school sports program.
Diamond C Café 223 Front St T874-3677. Standard diner that's popular with locals for its good-quality food at fair prices.
Garnet Room Inside the *Stikine Inn* T1-888/874-3388. About the best restaurant in town with good sea views, serving the usual menu of burgers, sandwiches, and Caesar salads. Dinners of pasta

($14), steak ($20–22), or halibut ($19) are tasty and well presented.
Jitterbugs 309 Front St T874-3350. Espresso to go.
Zak's Café 316 Front St T874-3355. The fairly antiseptic interior seems about right for a place that tries for a wide-ranging menu but only achieves tolerable quality. It is fairly cheap, though, with entrees at $8–13. Closed Sun.

Listings

Banks First Bank, 204 Brueger St, has an ATM.
Festivals The Stikine River Garnet Festival, 3rd week in April, celebrates the coming of spring and the gathering of bald eagles on the Stikine River with special boat trips and various events that have nothing to do with garnets; there's a king salmon derby from mid-May to mid-June; and a 4th of July celebration with the usual fireworks and parade, plus a log-rolling competition in the harbor.
Internet access Free at the library.
Laundry and showers There's a laundry with showers (daily 8am–8pm) on Shakes St. The Community Center, next to the High School on 2nd

St (T874-2444; closed Sat & Sun), has a pool, weight room, and showers ($2.25).
Library Irene Ingle Public Library on 2nd St (Mon & Fri 10am–noon & 1–5pm, Tues–Thurs 1–5pm & 7–9pm, Sat 9am–5pm).
Medical assistance Wrangell Medical Center, 310 Bennett St T874-7000, Wwww.wrangellmedicalcenter.com.
Post office On Federal St. The General Delivery zip code is 99929.
Taxes There's a seven percent city sales tax, plus a six percent bed tax, neither included in our prices.

Around Wrangell

Wrangell is well positioned to make the best of the local scenery and wildlife. Bear viewing is usually near the top of most people's lists, and there are few places in Alaska you can get close as cheaply as at the **Anan Wildlife Observatory**, little more than a hide and viewing platform but nonetheless a wonderful spot to commune with these fearsome beasts.

Wrangell sits seven miles south of the mouth of the **Stikine River** ("the Great River"), which is said to be the fastest navigable river in North America, with peak flows around six miles per hour. Riverboats that started during the gold rushes continued to run regularly on the river until 1969, a tradition now continued by jetboats that whisk tourists as far upstream as Telegraph Creek in British Columbia. Several companies in Wrangell run trips on the Stikine and to Anan; *Harding's Old Sourdough Lodge* offers competitive packages (see Accommodation, p.124).

Jetboats also run from Wrangell to the **LeConte Glacier** (see p.137), typically taking five to eight hours and costing around $150.

Anan Wildlife Observatory

Easily one of the most rewarding outings from Wrangell is to see the **bears feeding** at the Anan Wildlife Observatory, located on the mainland some thirty miles south of town and only accessible by boat or plane. Here, a waterfall a few hundred yards inland from the gorgeous Anan Lagoon slows the progress of one of the state's largest runs of "humpies," or pink salmon, and black bears (and a few browns) come to dine on the floundering fish. To provide more comfortable viewing conditions and limit the risk of bear–human contact, the Forest Service has constructed an open-sided observation platform reached by a half-mile-long trail from the beach. On arrival, photographers will want to sign up for half an hour in the adjacent viewing hide (free), where being close to the stream gives you a better angle on the bears feeding.

Such is the rise in Anan's popularity that from July 5 to August 25 you now need a **visitor pass** ($10): 48 for any given day are available for early reservation and a further 12 become available three days in advance of your visit. If you sign up for a guided trip the operator will procure the pass for you; if you're organizing your own trip, book online following the Anan Creek links from Ⓦwww.fs.fed.us/r10/tongass. There are no limitations outside the quota period, but bear numbers during this period are likely to be low.

Half a mile north of the landing point is the Forest Service's *Anan Bay Cabin* (book months in advance on Ⓣ1-877/444-6777, Ⓦwww.reserveusa.com; $35), which is perfect if you want to stay a few days, perhaps watching bald eagles or harbor seals out in the lagoon. Up to four people can stay in the cabin, and a reservation here acts as a visitor pass – though you still need to pay the $10.

Access to Anan is by fifteen-minute flight, one-hour boat journey or at least two days by kayak. About the cheapest trips are with Breakaway Adventures (Ⓣ1-888/385-2488, Ⓦwww.breakawayadventures.com), which offers an unguided full-day trip for $160. But unless you are experienced in dealing with bears (or avoiding doing so), it is much safer to visit on a guided trip where a guide stays with you the whole time (and usually has bear spray and a gun). Their guided trips are $195 and compete directly with those run by Stikine Wilderness Adventures (Ⓣ1-800/874-2085, Ⓦwww.akgetaway.com), which charges $200 with up to six hours at the observatory.

Sunrise Aviation (Ⓣ1-800/874-2311, Ⓦwww.sunriseflights.com) sells reasonable flights for a total of $560 per round-trip for up to four people, with as much time as you want at Anan, though you won't get a guide.

Garnet Ledge

Wrangell's dockside garnet-selling industry is one of Southeast's more curious tales. In the 1860s garnets were found on the mainland, seven miles northeast of Wrangell, alongside a creek in an area that has become known as the **Garnet Ledge**. From 1907 to 1923, the Alaska Garnet Mining and Manufacturing

Company – said to be the world's first corporation entirely run by women – was commercially mining the gems from the soft mica schist and making hat pins, watch fobs, and the like.

By the 1930s, deft political maneuvering had left ownership in the hands of Wrangell mayor Fred Hanford, who in 1962 deeded the Garnet Ledge to the local Boy Scouts, with local children having the right to take garnets "in reasonable quantities." They decreed that children under 16 had the sole right to gather and sell the sub-jewelry-quality garnets. When "mining" they must be accompanied by an adult, and enthusiastic parents often take their kids over to the Ledge in their skiff and let them fossick around, mining by hand. After all, a good session of selling to cruise-ship and ferry passengers can easily net $200.

You can join the fun provided that you pay $10 and commit ten percent of your find to the Scouts: ask at the visitor center. Visitors are not allowed to sell their finds, however. Most of the boat operators running trips up the Stikine River, which passes by Garnet Ledge, can drop you off and will be happy to relieve you of your money. An hour will be enough for most people, but you can **stay** at the Forest Service's *Garnet Ledge Cabin* (☎1-877/444-6777; $25) should you wish to extend your visit.

Exploring the Stikine River

From the mountains of British Columbia, the Stikine River threads its way almost four hundred miles to the sea, with only the last thirty miles running through the Stikine–LeConte Wilderness in Alaska. It is a spectacular journey, with dramatic mountains, canyons, glaciers, forests, and matchless wildlife, all visible from jetboat trips or fly-in rafting, canoeing, and kayaking expeditions.

The river reaches tidewater at the **Stikine Flats**, a broad and shallow delta full of small islands sprouting willows and cottonwoods. The surrounding mudflats are covered in spring and fall with **birds** – ducks, geese, sandhill cranes – resting along their migration route (known as the Pacific Flyway). The area around Mallard Slough, and the *Mallard Slough Cabin* (☎1-877/444-6777; $35), is particularly good in late April and early May for spotting shorebirds, including huge flocks of western sandpipers. From late March to early May, small oily fish

△ AMHS ferry, Wrangell Narrows

called eulachon (usually bowdlerized to "hooligan") flood up the river, chased by the state's second largest concentration of **bald eagles** (after Haines), often numbering well over a thousand.

The delta is a popular destination in summer, when it can seem as though half of Wrangell is out here fishing, sightseeing, visiting the Garnet Ledge, or making for **Chief Shakes Hot Springs**, 28 miles by boat from Wrangell, for a soak in one of the redwood tubs (one of which is protected from the elements).

The river is navigable for 160 miles upstream from the hot springs, to the small British Columbian Native town of **Telegraph Creek**, cutting through some wonderful scenery that John Muir favorably compared to his beloved Yosemite. Jetboat trips either stick to the delta and lower river or head right up to Telegraph Creek (about six hours from Wrangell). Most operators are prepared to take you and your kayaks, canoes, or rafts up there and leave you to float back down to Wrangell. Breakaway Adventures runs a slew of trips, including one around the delta that visits the Garnet Ledge, hot springs, and glaciers (7hr; $145), and multiday trips upstream, charged at $1200 a day for a twelve-person boat. Alaska Vistas (☎1-866/874-3006, ⓦwww.alaskavistas.com) has a comparable local trip (6hr; $145) and a couple of times a year runs guided nine-day rafting trips ($2400) with a flight to Telegraph Creek and a gentle float out camping along the river.

These trips should be booked well in advance, giving operators plenty of time to get clearance from **Canadian customs**.

Petersburg and around

One of the highlights of riding the Inside Passage ferries from Wrangell is sitting up front to watch the boat negotiate the 46 slalom-course turns of the 22-mile-long **Wrangell Narrows** between Mitkof and Kupreanof islands. It's a beautiful run by day, when it feels like you can reach out and touch the steep-walled shore and crumbling wooden piers, and doubly so at night, when it is baffling how the captain can pilot a course through the maze of lights from the marker buoys.

As the passage broadens, the starboard shore sprouts a straggle of jetties and wharves that run for a mile along the waterfront of **Petersburg**, with its canneries perched above the water on forests of poles on the northern tip of Mitkof Island. No prizes for guessing that Petersburg is primarily a fishing port. The citizens are more interested in salmon, halibut, black cod, shrimp, crab, and herring than they are in tourists, which is a good part of the appeal. The larger cruise ships can't negotiate the Narrows, thus making Petersburg a bit calmer than other Southeast towns; no one is out to sell you anything, and it is refreshing to just saunter around the docks and gaze across Frederick Sound at the summit of **Devil's Thumb** on the US–Canada border.

Petersburg gets its name from Peter Buschmann, the Norwegian fisherman who, in 1897, decided that the abundant fish, free ice from the nearby LeConte Glacier, and relative proximity to markets made this a good place to found a fishing port. He proved to be very right, and many of his countryfolk followed his lead, giving some credence to Petersburg's claim to be "Alaska's Little Norway." Unless you are here on the third full weekend in May (nearest Norwegian Independence Day on May 17) for the **Little Norway Festival**, when a model Viking longboat is trundled down the street, evidence of Petersburg's heritage

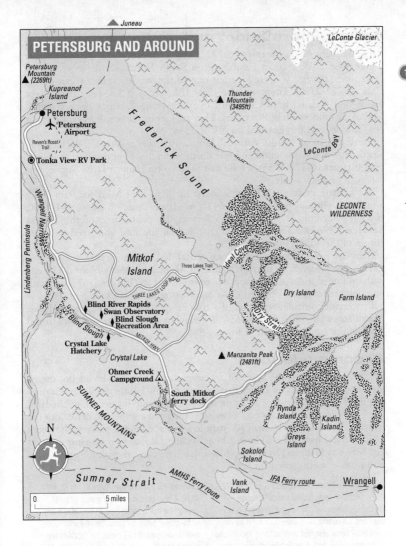

PETERSBURG AND AROUND

Juneau

LeConte Glacier

Petersburg
Mountain
(2269ft)

Kupreanof
Island

Petersburg

Petersburg
Airport

Raven's Roost
Trail

Tonka View RV Park

Frederick Sound

Thunder
Mountain
(3495ft)

LeConte Bay

Wrangell Narrows

Lindenberg Peninsula

LECONTE
WILDERNESS

Mitkof
Island

Three Lakes Trail

THREE LAKES LOOP ROAD

Blind River Rapids
Swan Observatory
Blind Slough
Recreation Area

Blind Slough

MITKOF HWY.

Ideal Cove

Dry Island

Dry Strait

Farm Island

Crystal Lake
Hatchery

Crystal Lake

Ohmer Creek
Campground

South Mitkof
ferry dock

Manzanita Peak
(2481ft)

SUMNER MOUNTAINS

N

Rynda
Island

Kadin
Island

Greys
Island

Sokolof
Island

Sumner Strait

AMHS Ferry route

Vank
Island

IFA Ferry route

Wrangell

0   5 miles

is fairly scant, though several buildings have the Norwegian-style scrolled detailing known as "rosmaling" around their windows, and the general store on Main Street does a nice line in Norwegian sweaters and knick-knacks. Otherwise it's just a busy Alaskan fishing port, where the streets are often filled with the thousand or so temporary cannery workers, who significantly swell the ranks of this town of three thousand in summer.

Sights are fairly thin on the ground, though anyone with a taste for the work of ancient civilizations shouldn't miss the easily accessible **fish traps** and **petroglyphs** at Sandy Beach. Further exploration requires transport: along the road system to some gentle hikes, across Wrangell Narrows to the small settlement of Kupreanof, from where more serious hikes begin, or by boat across the **whale-rich waters** of Frederick Sound to the **LeConte Glacier**.

Arrival, information, and getting around

Roughly daily AMHS **ferries** (T772-3855) from Sitka and Wrangell arrive a mile west of downtown Petersburg on South Nordic Drive, an easy walk from town, though you could catch one of the waiting taxis, or call Metro Cabs (T772-2700). There are also daily IFA ferries (mid-May to mid-Sept Thurs–Sun; 1 daily) from Coffman Cove and Wrangell, which dock at South Mitkof, 25 miles south of Petersburg. They are met by the South Mitkof Express bus ($23; reservations essential on T772-3818).

Petersburg is on Alaska Airlines' Juneau–Petersburg–Wrangell–Ketchikan–Seattle run: one southbound and one northbound flight per day land at Petersburg **airport** (T772-4255), a mile east of town on Haugen Drive. Again, you can walk or catch a cab.

The **visitor center**, 17 Fram St at 1st St (May–Sept Mon–Sat 9am–5pm, Sun noon–4pm; Oct–April Mon–Thurs 10am–2pm; T1-866/484-4700, Wwww.petersburg.org), which also acts as the public face of the **Forest Service** (Wwww.fs.fed.us/r10/tongass), has all the info you need and free copies of the *Viking Visitor Guide*.

There are no city buses, and no **car rental** desks at the airport, though you can arrange for a vehicle through Allstar Car Rentals at *Scandia House* ($52 a day with unlimited mileage; see opposite), or from Avis at *Tides Inn* ($67 a day with unlimited mileage; see opposite). No one is currently doing bike rental.

If your visit coincides with that of a cruise ship, consider joining up with See Alaska Tours (3hr; $39; T772-4656, Ehendyhut@gci.net) for an **educational walk** in the rainforest south of town.

Accommodation

Petersburg is small so the range of accommodation isn't that broad, but there's one hostel and plenty of places that sit very prettily beside the water. **Camping** in town isn't appealing, and although you can camp for free on public land, city limits stretch out seventeen miles, so you'll need a vehicle to drive "out the highway." With only one small RV park in town and limited parking, the needs of RV drivers have been addressed by providing a downtown **staging area** on 2nd Street at Haugen Drive ($1 per hour), where you can park for up to eight hours while waiting for your ferry.

Alaska Island Hostel 805 Gjoa St T772-3632, Wwww.alaskaislandhostel.com. Welcoming hostel handily located between downtown and the airport, with three four-bunk rooms, each bunk being supplied with bedding, locker, and a private reading light. There's free Internet access, stacks of info on the local area, and plenty of games and books to entertain you on wet evenings. Reservations recommended in summer (mid-April to mid-Sept) and essential in winter. $20 per person. Call 5–8pm.
Broom Hus 411 S Nordic Drive T772-3459, Wwww.broomhus.com. Well-equipped apartment (sleeping up to six) in the half-basement of an original 1920s house (with a separate entrance for guests). Continental breakfast is provided, and there's a lovely flower-filled deck out back for those occasional sunny afternoons. ④

LeConte RV Park Haugen Drive at 4th St T772-4680. A cramped and scruffy gravel lot large enough for half a dozen RVs; there's also a tiny, semi-grassy patch for tents. Some traffic noise, and showers are $1.25 extra, but facilities are clean and it is central. Water and electricity $15, dry RV $10, tents $8.
Nordic House B&B 806 S Nordic Drive T772-3620, Wwww.nordichouse.net. Appealing B&B superbly sited close to the ferry dock with six comfortable rooms, some with private bath. There's free use of the kitchen and large lounge, which hangs right over the water, as well as buffet breakfast and free local calls and Internet access for guests. If you catch any fish, they'll handle them for you – or you can just grill on the sunny deck. Courtesy van from the airport or ferry, plus bargain bikes for rent. Apartment ⑤, rooms ④

Ohmer Creek Campground Mile 22 Mitkof Hwy. Picturesque and very appealing Forest Service site on the southern shores of Mitkof Island with fire rings, a canopy of trees, stream water, and space for RVs and tents. First-come, first-served. May–Sept $6, Oct–April free.

Scandia House 110 N Nordic Drive ☎772-4281 or 1-800/722-5006, ⓦ www.scandiahousehotel.com. The best hotel in town, with clean, modern rooms, all with cable TV, phone, and coffeemaker, plus there's a light continental breakfast. Some rooms come with water views, others have kitchenettes, and some are suites with Jacuzzis. There's also a courtesy van. Suites ❼, kitchen rooms and standard rooms ❺

Tides Inn Dolphin St at 1st St ☎772-4288 or 1-800/665-8433, ⓦ www.tidesinnalaska.com.

Ordinary motel made more appealing if you can get a room with a view. All rooms come with bathtubs, cable TV, and WiFi. Free Internet access for guests. ❹

Tonka View RV Park 126 Scow Bay Loop Rd, 3 miles south of town ☎772-4814. Look away from the container terminal and you've great views of Wrangell Narrows from this gravel lot where electricity and water hookups cost $20.

Waterfront B&B 1004 S Nordic Drive ☎772-9300, ⓦ www.alaska.net/~h2Ofrbnb. Great place overlooking the narrows and close to the ferry dock. Five comfy rooms with private bath, continental breakfast, access to a fully-equipped kitchen, and use of a hot tub overlooking the water. ❹

The Town

If the weather behaves, there's nothing better to do in Petersburg than just wander the waterfront boardwalks as the fishing boats come and go and the ferry glides silently through the Wrangell Narrows. From the aptly named **Eagle's Roost Park**, north of downtown, it's all canneries and wharves through the center of town down to the single most striking section, **Sing Lee Alley**, a boardwalk built entirely over the water and named for a Chinese merchant who had his premises here in the early days. The boardwalk is lined by shops and a couple of cafés on one side, and on the other by the town's only real bookshop and the large white clapboard **Sons of Norway Hall**, built in 1912 as a meeting place for this fraternal organization. With its double-pitched roof design and subtle use of "rosmaling" around the windows, it is easily the most distinctly Norwegian building in town. As though to further underline the connection, the adjacent parking lot is home to a model Viking longboat, which is used in the annual Little Norway Festival. Nearby, the ten-foot-tall bronze Bojer Wikan Fisherman's Memorial is the centerpiece of a small boardwalk "park" and was commissioned according to the will of one Bojer Wikan, a local fisherman deeply involved with the Sons of Norway. Both hall and "park" stand on poles above **Hammer Slough**, a narrow estuary lined by brightly painted houses that seem to glow in the evening light.

Although there are two major canneries on and over the waterfront, if you'd like a peek inside the industry you'll have to settle for the hour-long tour around the specialist **Tonka Seafoods** on Sing Lee Alley (Mon–Sat 1.30pm; $5; and by appointment on ☎772-3662 with a minimum $30 fee; ⓦ www .tonkaseafoods.com). Not exclusively a cannery, Tonka also smokes and dries fish in what is really just two small rooms. The equipment isn't especially interesting to look at, but the tours are personal enough that you can direct the discussion to whatever interests you most, be it the life cycle of the fish, means of catching, fishery management, boat type, or processing. Of course, there are free samples of the product and the opportunity to buy what you like.

Moving away from the waterfront, call in at the **Clausen Memorial Museum**, 203 Fram St at 2nd St (May to early Sept Mon–Sat 10am–5pm; $3), marked by the distinctive steel sculpture of salmon, halibut, and herring entitled *Fisk* – Norwegian for fish. There's not a great deal inside, but the staff are usually eager to help you interpret the small collection of Tlingit artifacts (particularly a large bentwood storage box), some great old photos of early Petersburg life,

PETERSBURG

RESTAURANTS & BARS

Coastal Cold Storage	2
Harbor Bar	1
Java Hús	3
La Fonda	4
Northern Lights	3
Papa Bear's Pizza	5

ACCOMMODATION

Alaska Island Hostel	B
Broom Hus	G
LeConte RV Park	D
Nordic House B&B	E
Scandia House	C
Tides Inn	A
Tonka View RV Park	H
Waterfront B&B	F

0   800 yds

Kupreanof Island

Sasby Island

Narrows

Wrangell Narrows

Hungry Point

Eagle's Roost Park

Outlook Park

Cannery

North Boat Harbor

Cannery

Middle Boat Harbor

Tonka Seafoods

Sons of Norway Hall

South Boat Harbor

State Dock

Ferry Dock

Ballfield

Clausen Memorial Museum

RV Staging Area

Supermarket

BOARDWALK

Airport Terminal

Water tower

SANDY BEACH

Public access

Petroglyphs

Fish traps

Sandy Beach Park

N NORDIC DRIVE

VALKYRIE AVENUE

LAKE AVE

EIGHTH ST

5TH ST

3TH ST

DOLPHIN ST

FRAM ST

EXCEL ST

2ND ST

1ST ST

LLOYD ST

NATWICK ST

DRIVE

HAUGEN

MAIN

RAIL ST

KISENO ST

HAMMET

LANSING ST

LUMBER ST

NOSEUMAM ST

ANGLEE ALLEY

Hammet Slough

SANDY BEACH ROAD

HAUGEN DRIVE

12TH ST

11TH ST

DRIVE

1ST ST

WRANGELL AVENUE

WRANGELL ST

UNIMAK ST

SKYLARK WAY

S NORDIC DR (MITKOF HWY)

CABIN CREEK ROAD

▶ South Mitkof ferry dock (25 miles), ① (2 miles), & Ohmer Creek Campground (21 miles)

▶ Raven's Roost Trail (100yds)

PETERSBURG LAKE TRAIL

N

and the story behind the largest salmon ever caught, though no one thought to weigh it before it was gutted (estimates put it at 126 pounds).

Sandy Beach fish traps and petroglyphs

If you don't fancy tackling one of the more robust walks (see box, p.137), consider strolling north along the roads past Hungry Point to **Sandy Beach**, a pleasant little park-backed cove that's best visited at low tide when it is possible to see ancient **Tlingit fish traps** on the mud of the bay. They're not especially obvious to the untrained eye, but with some imagination you can pick out low ridges of rock formed into the shape of thirty-foot-diameter hearts. The pointy ends face the sea, and it is thought that as the tide rapidly receded, fish swimming close to the beach would be guided into the traps and find themselves caught at the sharp end as the water level dropped. The rock formations are probably about two thousand years old and are unique to the immediate area around Petersburg. Later models used hemlock stakes, some of which are occasionally dislodged by the tide, and researchers claim that they are so well preserved by the mud that they still smell of fresh wood.

At the northern end of Sandy Beach, a large rock close to the high-tide line bears the marks of some poorly understood, but certainly old, **petroglyphs**. If you've already seen the petroglyphs at Wrangell you might be a little underwhelmed by what's on show here, but there are five faces etched onto the rock, one partly removed by vandalism a few years back. The petroglyphs can be seen at all water levels except high tide.

Eating and drinking

Apart from a few jars of **pickled herring** sold at Coastal Cold Storage, Petersburg doesn't flaunt its Norwegian culinary heritage.

The best place for groceries is the Hammer & Wikan **supermarket** on the edge of town on Haugen Drive, with a bakery, hot snacks, and a deli. Beyond that, there's a tolerable range of cafés, restaurants, and bars, but nothing special.

Coastal Cold Storage 306 N Nordic Drive ☎772-4177. An unusual establishment combining live-shellfish sales with takeout burgers and espresso. Tanks of live oysters, clams, and Dungeness crabs surround a couple of cramped tables where you can munch on breaded oysters and fries ($9), a crab melt ($7), or a shrimp wrap ($8). Better still, take your haul next door to the Harbor Bar or up to Eagle's Roost Park for an outdoor dinner.

Harbor Bar 310 N Nordic Drive. A foot-to-the-floor drinker's bar that's always full of salmon canners and fishermen.

Java Hüs 110 N Nordic Drive ☎772-2626. Daytime espresso café also serving bagels and donuts.

La Fonda Inside *Kito's Cave* bar, Sing Lee Alley at John Lott St ☎772-4918. Simple but tasty

Mexican fare in this Mexican-run joint inside one of Petersburg's bars. Expect the likes of *carne asada* ($10) and halibut tacos ($8).

Northern Lights 28 Sing Lee Alley ☎772-2900. Reliable restaurant perched on stilts over the water with great views of the fishing boats and dazzling evening sun through the big window, weather permitting. Burgers and sandwiches start at $8; there are also pasta dishes ($13), fish and chips ($19), and prime rib ($24). Alcohol served. Daily 6am until late.

Papa Bear's Pizza Opposite the ferry terminal on S Nordic Drive ☎772-3727. A takeout pizza joint with a few tables inside. Ideal for that quick dash from the ferry if you're passing through. Good ice-cream cones, too.

Listings

Banks There are a couple of banks downtown, including First Bank, 103 N Nordic Drive, which has an ATM.

Bookshop Sing Lee Alley Books, 11 Sing Lee Alley (Mon–Sat 9.30am–5.30pm, Sun noon–4pm; ☎772-4440).

Festivals The Little Norway Festival on the third full weekend in May is the town's celebration of its heritage. The Salmon Derby follows on Memorial Day weekend.

Internet access Free access at the library is in heavy demand, so you may prefer the convenience of the pricey machines at Prime Media Services, 15 N Nordic Drive (Mon–Fri 9.30am–5pm; ☏772-2050).

Laundry and showers Take a swim and shower at the High School pool (☏772-3304); laundry is best done at Glacier Laundry, 313 N Nordic Drive (daily 6am–9pm; ☏772-4144), where they also have showers ($2).

Library Petersburg Public Library, 12 S Nordic Drive (Mon–Thurs noon–9pm, Fri & Sat noon–4pm; ☏772-3349).

Medical assistance Petersburg Medical Center, 2nd & Fram sts (Mon–Fri 9am–5pm and 24hr ER; ☏772-4299).

Post office 1400 Haugen Drive. The **General Delivery** zip code is 99833.

Taxes Petersburg imposes a six percent sales tax plus a four percent bed tax, not included in our accommodation price codes.

Travel agency Viking Travel, 101 N Nordic Drive ☏772-3818.

Around Petersburg

The simplest way to get out of town is to rent a car and drive out along **Mitkof Highway**, seventeen miles of paved two-lane asphalt from which a couple of roads fan out across the island. Fishing streams, easy boardwalk trails, picnic sites, a hatchery, and a seasonal swan-viewing area are the main draws here, along with more serious hikes (see box, opposite).

Getting off the island typically involves joining some kind of tour, either **kayaking**, **whale-watching**, visiting the **LeConte Glacier**, or fishing. As tourists are few, acquiring numbers to make trips viable can be difficult; befriending like-minded travelers on your way here and fronting up as a ready-to-go group of four or more can be a big time-saver. Conversely, when the occasional small cruise ship is in town you may find it hard to get a place on trips pre-booked by the ship. Many tours can be arranged through Viking Travel at 101 N Nordic Drive (☏772-3818); a quick visit here can save you a lot of phoning around. They're particularly helpful for hooking you up with one of the many fishing charters run from town.

Along the road system

Petersburg has a reasonably extensive road system, and if you rent a car there's a fair bit to keep you entertained, though nothing that's essential viewing. Almost everything is along, or just off, the mostly paved Mitkof Highway, which follows Wrangell Narrows for around fourteen miles, then cuts inland to finish on the southern shores of Mitkof Island.

There are no specific sights until you reach **Blind River Rapids**, Mile 14, where there's a quarter-mile-long boardwalk to a tidal stream where salmon come in to spawn and work their way up the gentle rapids. Beyond here, the highway cuts inland along Blind Slough to the **Swan Observatory**, Mile 16, where a kind of primitive hide beside the highway aids in viewing trumpeter swans, which call here on their way south from mid-October to December, a few dozen wintering until around April. During summer, salmon cruise the waters. At Mile 18 you can wander around **Crystal Lake Hatchery** (Mon–Fri 8am–4pm, Sat & Sun 8am–2pm; free) and learn a little of what's going on from the staff on hand. The adjacent **Blind Slough Recreation Area** is good for picnics and swimming (for the thick-skinned). Beyond the hatchery you're on gravel, though there are immediate plans to pave the road as far as the ferry dock. At Mile 20, Man-Made Hole Lake offers a pleasant boardwalk around a small pond that looks far from man-made; if you want to camp, push on to *Ohmer Creek Campground* (see p.133), Mile 22, which acts as the trailhead for a mile-long path along a good trout and salmon fishing stream with some interpretive panels.

The road continues to the South Mitkof ferry dock and beyond, an uneventful few miles along the island's south coast. You're better off backtracking to a mile before Ohmer Creek and heading northeast on Three Lakes Loop Road (Road 6235), which, after 21 miles, rejoins Mitkof Highway at Mile 11. Roughly midway around the loop, you come to a series of three trailheads all interlinked as the **Three Lakes Trail** (30min–3hr), where any number of boardwalk variations allow you to visit one or more of Crane, Hill, and Sand lakes, and access the sea along Ideal Cove Trail. A mile or so north of here, the road passes the **LeConte Overlook**, the only place on the island where you can get a direct view across Frederick Sound to the face of the LeConte Glacier.

Kayaking, whale-watching, and the LeConte Glacier

At some point during their stay, most people want to get out on the water. One prime destination is the **LeConte Glacier**, which peels off the Stikine Icefield, fifteen miles southeast across Frederick Sound. It is the southernmost tidewater glacier in the northern hemisphere, and sometimes surging ninety feet a day, is

Hikes in and around Petersburg

There are a dozen or more good **hikes** around Petersburg, but few are especially convenient unless you've got transport. Although drivers and cyclists can get the best from several short trails out along Mitkof Highway (see opposite), serious hikers should think about two excellent trails a few hundred yards across Wrangell Narrows on Kupreanof Island. People have traditionally tried to hitch a ride across the water, but as local hospitality has been strained over the years you should arrange transport over and back before you head out – or risk being stranded over there. Rent a skiff from the *Scandia Hotel*, contact Craig Curtis (℡772-2425), who charges $25 there and back, or ask the staff at the visitor center who will help you call likely boat-charter companies. Remember that there is no camping on the immediate Kupreanof side of the Narrows as it's private property, but Forest Service cabins can be booked on ℡1-877/444-6777.

Petersburg Lake Trail (10.5 miles one-way; 4hr; 200ft ascent). Moderately difficult trail on Kupreanof Island leading left (west) over a low saddle, then gradually ascending to Petersburg Lake and the *Petersburg Lake Cabin* ($35), which is a good base for salmon- and trout-fishing and bear-viewing in fall. If you use the upper trailhead, which is only accessible at high tides greater than fourteen feet, you can shorten the hike by four miles. Keen adventurers can continue beyond Portage Lake to a couple more cabins, though it is tough going and you'll need the latest information from the visitor center.

Petersburg Mountain Trail (7 miles round-trip; 4–6hr; 2750ft ascent). Challenging trail on Kupreanof Island leading right (east) from the dock opposite Petersburg to the summit of Petersburg Mountain, from where there are long, long views down the Wrangell Narrows and across Frederick Sound to the coastal mountains and glaciers. The final section is a bit of a scramble.

Raven's Roost Trail (8 miles round-trip; 5–6hr; 2000ft ascent). An initial boardwalk leads to an at times steep trail, climbing up to alpine country and eventually to the Forest Service's six-berth *Raven's Roost Cabin* ($35), which has lovely views. Best done from mid-July to September when the likelihood of snow cover is least, though lack of water at the cabin means it is good to have some snow around. The trailhead is by the orange-and-white water towers just south of the airport.

Town Loop (30min–1hr 30min). A number of possibilities exist using the short boardwalks and the gravel path to Hungry Point (see map, p.134). A loop out past the airport to Sandy Beach and back past Hungry Point takes around ninety minutes.

one of the world's fastest moving. Frederick Sound is usually dotted with small icebergs (especially in spring) that get bigger the closer you are to the glacier, some with seals on them idling their day away.

Often LeConte Bay is so packed with ice that you can't even penetrate far enough to see the face of the glacier, which means that you probably won't be able to see calving. If it's any consolation, extended tours also continue a few miles south and visit the delta of the Stikine River (see "Wrangell," p.129). Wherever you go, there is a chance of seeing whales, particularly the humpback whales that usually pass through Frederick Sound from late June to early September.

About the most peaceful way to get on the water is by **kayak** with Tongass Kayak Adventures (℡772-4600, Ⓦwww.tongasskayak.com), which runs four-hour trips ($70) around the Petersburg waterfront and across the Narrows to Petersburg Creek. Though very enjoyable, these half-day trips are really just a taster for the outfit's multiday whale-watching trips – relatively gentle affairs involving three to five hours' paddling per day that need to be booked well in advance. Their Base Camp trips (3 nights for $880, 8 nights for $1980) fly you to sites beside Frederick Sound and near the LeConte Glacier from where you explore by day; the eight-night Explorer Tours ($1480–1880) tend to move on to a new camp each day. The company also rents single ($55 a day) and double ($65) kayaks with a three-day minimum.

If you'd rather someone else do the work, join marine biologist Barry Bracken of Kaleidoscope Cruises (℡1-800/868-4373, Ⓦwww.petersburglodgingandtours.com), who runs entertaining half-day trips to LeConte Glacier in a comfortable 28-foot boat ($175) and full-day **whale-watching** trips ($250), which include listening to the whales' calls through a hydrophone.

The visitor center has information about several other operators who do similar trips; alternatively, go your own way with a skiff and forty-horse motor from *Scandia Hotel* (guests $135 a day, non-guests $160 a day).

Sitka and around

Perched on the seaward edge of the Inside Passage, **SITKA** ranks as one of Alaska's prettiest and most historic towns, with a bay chock-full of tiny islands plumed with hemlock and spruce, and the looming presence of the near-conical **Mount Edgecumbe** volcano rising menacingly across Sitka Sound.

The appeal of the outdoors – hiking and kayaking in particular – is hard to pass up, but Sitka also revels in its sixty-year reign as the political and cultural hub of Russian America. This is where Imperial Russian colonists established their capital, Novo Arkhangel'sk (New Archangel) in 1808, and their legacy is a major draw. When the United States bought Alaska, New Archangel became Sitka (a contraction of the Tlingit Shee Atiká), and development since then has been relatively benign, with the skyline still dominated by **St Michael's Cathedral**, just as it was when General Jefferson Davis came here to formally receive the territory on Castle Hill in 1867.

Although it's the third largest town in Southeast, Sitka is small enough to retain a compact and walkable core as well as a relaxed and friendly ambience. Better still, it isn't as crowded as you'd expect, being off the main Inside Passage cruise-ship lanes and lacking a dock deep enough for the bigger vessels (passengers have to come ashore in lifeboats). Large ships still

▲ Whale Park (3 miles)

SITKA

N

▲ Ferry Dock (6 miles)

ACCOMMODATION

Alaska Ocean View	A
Finn Alley Inn B&B	E
Sealing Cove RV Parking	H
Shee Aitka Totem Square Inn	F
Sheldon Jackson College	D
Sitka Hotel	C
Sitka Youth Hostel	G
Super 8 Motel	B

RESTAURANTS & BARS

Backdoor	6
Bayview Restaurant	3
The Galley Deli	8
Highliner Coffee Co	2
Ludwig's Bistro	4
Market Center	1
Pioneer Bar	5
Sheldon Jackson	
College Dining Room	D
Victoria's Pour House	7

SITKA NATIONAL HISTORIC PARK

SNHP Visitor Center and Museum

Trail of Young Lovers Lane

⊙ Totem Pole

Alaska Raptor Center

Indian River

Indian River Trail

SAWMILL CREEK

INDIAN RIVER ROAD

RAPTOR

Sheldon Jackson Museum

Hames PE Center

JEFF DAVIS STREET

LINCOLN STREET

SHELDON JACKSON DR

JEFF DAVIS STREET

PARK STREET

FINN ST

Marine Wet Lab

Crescent Harbor Marina

Crescent Bay

GEODETIC WAY

Russian Bishop's House

Ceremonial Canoe

Harrigan Centennial Hall

Library

CVB

Cathedral

Pioneer Home

Castle Hill

Tribal Dancers

Blockhouse

ETOLIN STREET

LINCOLN ST

BARANOF STREET

MERRILL STREET

BIORKA

DE GROFF STREET

LAKE STREET

MONASTERY STREET

PHERSON STREET

CHARLES STREET

VERSTOVIA STREET

SIRSTAD STREET

LAKE STREET

ARROWHEAD STREET

IGNINA STREET

PETERSON AVENUE

HALIBUT POINT

LAKEVIEW DRIVE

Swan Lake

Swan Lake Park

Moller Park

Sitka Community Hospital

Sitka Ranger District Office

Thomsen Boat Harbor

Russian Orthodox Cemetery

Lutheran Cemetery

FINCH STREET

MARINE STREET

OSPREY STREET

KOGWANTON STREET

KATLIAN STREET

KATLIAN STREET

Sitka Channel

Harbor Island

Aleutski Island

Sealing Cove Marina

Japonski Island

AIRPORT DRIVE

SEWARD AVENUE

TONGASS DRIVE

ALICE LOOP ROAD

CHARCOAL DRIVE

OSPREY DRIVE

Terminal Building

Rocky Gutierrez Airport

AIRPORT ROAD

The Causeway

0   500 yds

139

visit most days in summer, though, ensuring steady interest in the tacky "Russiocana" – you'll find more nesting dolls here than in the rest of the US put together.

Ambling around is half the pleasure in Sitka, but focus is provided by the historic **Russian Bishop's House**, the densely packed **Sheldon Jackson Museum**, a magnificent array of totem poles in the **Totem Park**, and the popular **Raptor Center**, with its bald eagles.

Some history

Sitka's Kiks.ádi Tlingit clan has probably lived for nine thousand years at their settlement Shee Atiká, meaning "village on the outside of Shee," the Tlingit word for Baranof Island. In 1799 the Russian-American Company came to pursue fur trading and established the first European settlement in Southeast Alaska, seven miles west of Sitka just beyond the AMHS ferry dock. They continued to trade in sea otter pelts until the Kiks.ádi, living on the site of modern Sitka, got tired of their presence and stormed their fort, killing nearly all the Russians. Alexandr Baranov, the chief manager of the Russian-American Company in Kodiak, got wind of this and, in 1804, returned with four ships and several *baidarkas*. The Kiks.ádi, under their leader Katlian, had established a fort at what is now the Totem Park, and the Russians sent a landing party of 150 to conduct the **Siege of Shiskeenu**. Tsarist ships pounded the stockade for six days. On the sixth night the Russians heard strange chanting and, on the next day, discovered ravens hovering over the fort. Though there were ample provisions, suggesting that the Tlingit could have held out for a while, the fort was empty except for the bodies of dead children – allegedly murdered so the Tlingit could retreat in complete silence. The Russians razed the fort, looted and burned the Tlingit community of Shee Atiká, and on the ashes of the village built the stockaded settlement of New Archangel. The Tlingit didn't return for twenty years but eventually settled outside the palisades in a strained but workable relationship with the Russians.

In 1808 Novo Arkhangel'sk became the colonial capital, with food imported from Fort Ross in California and a social scene of dress balls and grand receptions. Still, those who described it as the "Paris of the Pacific" had obviously never been to Paris.

Sitka's status survived the transfer of ownership to the United States, with the town continuing as the capital of the territory of Alaska. As soon as America got hold of Alaska, adventurers flocked north, but gold drew people elsewhere. Capital status passed to Juneau in 1906, and Sitka was left to grow steadily on its fishing, and later logging. As fishing receipts ebb and flow, and logging returns are greatly diminished since the closure of the pulp mill here in 1993, tourism is increasingly filling the gaps.

Arrival, information, and getting around

A few AMHS **ferries** call at Sitka on their Ketchikan–Juneau run, their schedules timed with the tides to allow passage through Segius Narrows and Peril Strait, narrow twisting watercourses that need to be negotiated at slack tide. Ferries often have to wait for three or more hours at the dock, seven miles northwest of town, for the tide to turn. Call the Sitka terminal (℡747-8737) for details of particular sailings and see the box (opposite) for possible diversions during a brief stay.

The bulk of AMHS ferry sailings are on the passenger- and vehicle-carrying *Fairweather* **fast ferry** between Sitka and Juneau, which isn't restricted by tides.

1

Just an hour or two in Sitka?

The vagaries of the ferry timetable mean you're quite likely to have a couple of hours to spare at the Sitka dock, seven miles northwest of town. Most people who come ashore join one of the Sitka Tours buses that do a one- to two-hour circuit of the town's main sights for $12. If this is your only visit to Sitka, it's an opportunity that's hard to pass up. On a fine day, however, you might prefer to stroll fifteen minutes west from the dock to the Starrigavan area, where you'll find a network of easy walks (see box, p.148) – through wetlands and muskeg and along the shoreline – on which there are several well-placed benches with panoramic views.

It doesn't stay in port long enough to allow shore excursions. The **airport**, on Japonski Island a mile or so from downtown, sees Alaska Airlines (☏966-2926) jets direct from Juneau, Ketchikan, and Seattle.

Shuttle buses operated by Sitka Tours (☏747-8443) meet arriving ferries and flights, and run downtown as well as to your accommodation ($6 one-way from dock or airport, $8 round-trip including ferry, downtown, and airport). They also conduct short **tours** (see box, above).

There's a visitor **information desk** (summer daily 8am–5pm; ☏747-5940, ☒www.sitka.org) inside the Harrigan Centennial Hall on Harbor Drive. It is generally staffed only when large cruise ships hit town, but loads of free literature on the town are always available. For anything more complicated, call at the Convention & Visitors Bureau (Mon–Fri 9am–5pm) upstairs at 303 Lincoln St. For information on the surrounding Tongass National Forest, contact the Sitka Ranger District Office, 204 Siganaka Way (Mon–Fri 8am–4.30pm; ☏747-6671, ☒www.fs.fed.us/r10/tongass).

Once in town, **getting around** is easy. You can walk just about anywhere you're likely to want to go, plus there's a visitor transit bus (late May to early Sept Mon–Fri only; $10 all-day pass) that runs a loop through town every half-hour. The bus is perhaps most useful for the run out to the Raptor Center ($5 round-trip), though you might want to walk the mile back through the Totem Park. Alternatively, rent a bike (see Listings, p.152), or call a cab, such as Sitka Taxi (☏747-5001), which charges around $15 to the ferry terminal and $5 to the airport. Rental cars are available for about $65 a day from North Star Rent-A-Car at the airport (☏1-800/722-6927), with your mileage limited only by the extent of the road system.

Accommodation

Sitka has a good range of accommodation, with a fine hotel, a hostel, several B&Bs, and a variety of **campgrounds**. If you're looking for a hideaway, there is a solid selection of Forest Service **cabins** on islands in Sitka Sound; some of the more convenient are listed below (for bookings contact ☏1-877/444-6777 or ☒www.reserveusa.com). To get there, either take a water taxi or rent a kayak for a few days and explore.

Hotels, motels, and B&Bs

Alaska Ocean View B&B Inn 1101 Edgecumbe Drive ☏1-888/811-6870 & 747-8310, ☒www .sitka-alaska-lodging.com. Very high-standard B&B with all rooms featuring cable TV and VCR, CD stereo, dataport, bathrobes, and slippers. Guests also have the use of a patio spa pool and espresso machine, and there are facilities for business travelers. Beds are large and comfortable, the breakfasts generous, and the atmosphere cheerful. **G**

Finn Alley Inn B&B 711 Lincoln St ☎747-3655, ⓦwww.finnalleybedandbreakfast.com. Large, centrally located half-basement apartment with private entrance, full kitchen, and a continental breakfast served in the dining room. ⑤

Shee Atika Totem Square Inn 201 Katlilan St ☎1-866/300-1353, ⓦwww.totemsquareinn.com. Sitka's best hotel, with comfortable and well-appointed rooms made a little more interesting with Native paintings and trimmings. Business center, small gym, and free continental breakfast. Harbor-view rooms are only slightly more expensive. ⑥

Sheldon Jackson College Sheldon Jackson Drive ☎747-2518. Simple college rooms with two single beds (including bedding), shared bathroom, and breakfast supplied are a steal. Mid-June to Aug. ③–④

🏃 Sitka Hotel 118 Lincoln St ☎747-3288, ⓦwww.sitkahotel.com. Renovated historic hotel in the town center, offering good-value rooms with and without bathrooms, and a touch of old-fashioned style. Some of the modern rooms at the back have good views and tubs. Rooms ④, shared bath ③

Super 8 Motel 404 Sawmill Creek Rd ☎747-8804 or 1-800/800-8000, ⓦwww.super8.com. Spacious rooms, large TVs, free local calls, breakfasts of toast, donuts and coffee, as well as the use of a big Jacuzzi make this motel worth your dollar. ⑤

Hostels and campgrounds

Sawmill Creek Campground Blue Lake Rd. Wooded Forest Service site seven miles east of Sitka and at the start of the Beaver Lake Trail. There's only creek water (treat it), pit toilets, and fire rings – and no sea views – but it's free. Late-April to Nov.

Sealing Cove RV Parking Airport Rd, Japonski Island ☎747-3439. Asphalt parking lot a ten-minute walk from downtown beside a fishing boat harbor, with water and electrical hookups and a dump station for $21. May–Sept.

Sitka Sportsman's Association RV Park 5211 Halibut Point Rd ☎747-6033. Parking lot next to the ferry dock with electrical and water hookups for $22. All year.

Sitka Youth Hostel 109 Jeff Davis St, near Sheldon Jackson College ☎747-8661. Brand-new hostel opening in June 2007 and open June, July, and August thereafter. There's a daytime lockout (9.30am–6pm) and evening curfew (11pm), and check-in finishes at 10pm. Bunks $24.

Starrigavan Campground Halibut Point Rd. Gorgeous Forest Service campground 0.7 miles north of the ferry dock, with secluded sites, shore fishing, easy hiking trails, water, and pit toilets. There's a range of walk-in (and kayak-in) tent sites, plus plenty of RV- and car-accessible spots. Some of all site types are first-come, first-served, while others are reservable. Prices start at $12 per site but the prime waterside locations are $16. Tents year-round, RVs May–Nov.

Boat-access accommodation

Allan Point Cabin Nakwasina Passage, 14 miles north of Sitka. Large two-story Forest Service cabin sleeping up to fifteen, located on a sheltered shore in an area with plenty of deer and brown bears. Take fuel oil for heating. $45.

Camp Coogan Bay Hideaway 6 miles southeast of Sitka ☎747-6375. A secluded and private 72ft float house sleeping up to ten ($170) and supplied with a kitchen, propane stove, living room with wood stove, bunks, futons and cots, an outhouse, sauna, and a double kayak for guest use (as well as others available for rent). ⑦

Fred's Creek Cabin Southeast shore of Kruzof Island, ten miles west of Sitka. Brand-new Forest Service cabin at the base of Mount Edgecumbe. A good base for the summit hike. $35.

Kanga Bay Cabin 12 miles south of Sitka. This chalet-style Forest Service cabin, equipped with a wood-burning stove, rests beside a beautiful cove and makes a good stopping point on the way to Goddard Hot Springs. Day trips to the springs are possible from here, although you may prefer to continue three miles beyond the springs and stay at the Forest Service's Seven Fathoms cabin. $35.

Middle Island Recreation Cabin Middle Island, 5 miles southwest of Sitka ☎747-5169, ⓦwww.kruzofventures.com. Four-berth cabin ($75 for two, plus $10 per extra person) on a small island, with everything provided except food, stove fuel, and sleeping bags. A water taxi costs around $70 each way. ③

Samsing Cove Cabin 6 miles south of Sitka. Easily accessible, rustic, two-story Forest Service cabin set by a sandy gravel beach. Take fuel oil for heating. $45.

Shelikof Cabin Kruzof Island. A-frame Forest Service cabin located at Kruzof Island's gorgeous Shelikof Bay, an oceanside beach most easily accessed by a six-mile hike across the island from sheltered Mud Bay. Equipped with a wood-burning stove. $35.

The town and around

Nowhere in Southeast Alaska has as many diverting cultural and historic sights as Sitka. What's more, the attractions are easily accessible on foot and located conveniently along the waterfront. At Sitka's western end, the downtown area is overlooked by the rebuilt onion-domed St Michael's Cathedral, which, along with the immaculately restored Russian Bishop's House nearby, captures something of the spirit of Russian Alaska. Further east along the waterfront, the Sheldon Jackson Museum brings together a wonderful collection of Native crafts from around the state and leads directly to the Totem Park, which forms the major component of the Sitka National Historic Park. Save time, too, for the Raptor Center, one of your few chances to get close and personal with a bald eagle, and some of Sitka's scenic hikes.

Downtown Sitka

Sitka's Russian past is immediately accessible, and the best place to start is from the vantage point of **Castle Hill**, a rocky knob that was the original site of Tlingit Shee Atiká. It subsequently became the site of Baranov's Castle, not

△ Pioneer Home, Sitka

a castle at all but a large wooden residence that was the nerve center of the Russian town and the place where US official Jefferson Davis came for the formal transfer of ownership of Alaska from Russia to the US on October 18, 1867. Baranov's Castle burnt down in 1894, but a plaque marks the spot, and the US, Alaskan, and Russian-American Company flags flutter above.

Vying with Castle Hill for dominance on the city skyline is **St Michael's Cathedral**, Lincoln Street (May–Sept Mon–Fri 9am–4pm, when ships are in port, and by appointment; $2; ☎747-3560), with its teardrop spire bearing a gold triple-bar cross. This fine piece of Russian architecture was built for Bishop Innocent, whose watchmaking skills were put to good use in the design of the church clock. It is, in fact, a faithful replica of the 1848 original, which burned down on January 2, 1966, when a fire spread from a neighboring building to the cathedral tower. In the spirit of cooperation, the townspeople rallied to form a rescue line along which almost all the church's icons and religious treasures were passed in twenty minutes, although the irreplaceable library of books in Russian, Tlingit, and Aleut was lost. They did save the chandelier, however, and eventually even the melted heap of bronze from the church bells was gathered up and recast as new bells. Inside is a priceless collection of icons, thought to be the best in the US, all of which are touched upon on the short tour. You are welcome to attend services (Sat 6.30pm, Sun 10am), which are held in English with elements of Tlingit and Old Slavonic.

Continue your explorations of the old Russian town by calling at the replica blockhouse (not open to the public), a two-story octagonal fort of thick logs on the site of one of the three that guarded the palisades that kept the Russians safe. They feared the Kiks.ádi, whose land they'd stolen but who lived in an uneasy peace in the *ranche*, an area outside the stockade from where they traded furs and food and accepted the benefits of education and religion. On the hill behind, the **Lutheran Cemetery** reveals a few triple-bar crosses and the grave of Princess Maksoutov, the daughter of the last Russian governor of Alaska.

Easily the most significant non-Russian building in town, the 1934 **Pioneer Home**, on Lincoln Street, gives Sitka the architectural solidity that is lacking from so many Alaskan towns. It is really just an old folk's home, and you'll see sourdoughs of both sexes sunning themselves on the porch. Outside, a bronze statue of *The Prospector* stands resolute with staff, gun, pick, shovel, and the obligatory passage of Robert Service poetry (see box, p.204).

Walk back past the cathedral to get to the Harrigan Centennial Hall, which contains the visitor center and the **Isabel Miller Museum**, 300 Harbor Drive (May–Sept Mon–Fri and some weekends 8am–5pm; Oct–April Tues–Sat 10am–noon & 1.15–4pm; donations welcome), full of a little bit of everything, including a model of Sitka as it was at the time of the transfer. Also on display are lots of personal tales of early life in the town, which quickly draw you in once you start reading. Outside, the fifty-foot-long Tlingit ceremonial canoe, with an Eagle at one end and a Raven at the other, was carved in 1967 as part of the centennial of the transfer.

The Russian Bishop's House

With the loss of Sitka's original cathedral, there are now just four buildings left in America from the Russian past: the Log Cache gift shop at 206 Lincoln St in Sitka, the museum in Kodiak, one building at Fort Ross in California, and the large mustard-colored **Russian Bishop's House** on Lincoln Street (May to late Sept daily 9am–5pm; rest of year by appointment on ☎747-0110). Now part of Sitka National Historic Park (see p.148), the house was completed in 1843 from Sitka spruce logs by Finnish shipwrights (who were then subjects of

Russian Alaska and the US purchase

With a post–Cold War mindset it is easy to forget that Alaska – firmly part of the US in the American psyche – was once part of the Czarist Russian Empire. For well over a hundred years, from 1741 to 1867, Russia was the dominant power in the North Pacific, as it oversaw the near extinction of sea otters for their valuable pelts. The impetus for the colonizing drive was not territorial expansionism, but rather a desire to top up the ever-draining coffers of the Imperial court. Though the Russian government enlisted Danish captain Vitus Bering to explore whatever was east of the Kamchatka Peninsula, it didn't subsequently run the show, leaving it up to *promyshleniki* – private fur traders – to reap huge profits under license. The Russian-American Company had already secured control of the entire coast from the Aleutians to Southcentral Alaska when, in 1799, Czar Paul granted it exclusive rights to Alaska and effectively granted permission to subjugate the Aleut people.

About the only limitation put on the Russian-American Company was that it assist the Russian Orthodox Church in its proselytizing. And so began a symbiotic relationship between the two, with the company providing logistical support and housing for the Church and the priests educating and converting the Natives – thereby keeping them subservient and providing an underclass of semi-skilled workers. From 1790 to 1818 Chief Manager **Alexandr Baranov** (1747–1819) oversaw the region, having arrived in Pavlovsk (Kodiak) as a failed Siberian fur businessman but ready to put his aggressive political skills to work. With extremely long supply routes and no military backing from St Petersburg, Baranov was forced to cultivate cordial relations with British and American captains trading in the area. Nonetheless, in short order he expanded the company's domain along the coast. When the profitability of the fur trade declined around Kodiak in the early nineteenth century, he decamped to fresh killing fields around Novo Arkhangel'sk, now Sitka. With untold riches at his behest, he turned Sitka into the envy of the North Pacific. In his early seventies he retired, but never made it back to Russia, dying of fever on the ship home.

Under the second chief manager, **Ferdinand Wrangel**, and others, the sea otter and seal populations continued to decline. Meanwhile, with its government distracted by the Crimean War, Russia began to look less favorably on its North American possessions. With the British-owned Hudson's Bay Company encroaching on Russia's territory from the east and American traders sailing out of the new settlements on the West Coast, it became increasingly obvious that Russia wouldn't be able to hold on much longer. It found a willing buyer in the United States, still a relatively minor country politically and one just recovering from the horrors of the Civil War. Many Americans thought that the $7.2 million the US paid was too much for this unexplored wasteland and dubbed it **"Seward's Folly,"** after the secretary of state, William Seward.

The sale of land didn't cover private dwellings, warehouses, businesses, or the property of the Orthodox Church – including St Michael's Cathedral and the Bishop's House in Sitka – which kept its clergy in Alaska and continued to fund them from Russia until the Marxist Revolution in 1917. Russian residents were offered US citizenship but most left, taking their chattels with them and leaving behind only the racially mixed children with their Native mothers.

With around fifteen thousand believers, Russian Orthodoxy has turned out to be the most durable legacy of the Russian past in Alaska. Apart from a couple of museums in Sitka and Kodiak, however, the only significant reminders of Russia's century-long presence here are the onion-domed churches, filled with exquisite icons and topped with triple-bar gold crosses.

the Russian Czar) in a style and color scheme aimed to create a little piece of St Petersburg in the North Pacific. The Russian Orthodox Church maintained a bishop here until 1969, but after the building had nearly collapsed from the rot induced by ninety inches of rain a year, it was sold to the National Park Service in 1972. The NPS then began a sixteen-year restoration to recapture the atmosphere of Russian nobility in which the incumbent bishop lived. Reproduction wallpaper and sleigh beds as well as original pieces of furniture, including a sofa that could be dismantled to travel flat, give a sense of the comforts of home.

The house's first occupant, Ivan Veniaminov, who became Bishop Innocent of the Kamchatka Peninsula and the Russian-American Company's holdings on the Pacific Coast, rarely experienced such luxuries. He would often travel for months on end, spreading the good word while learning Aleut and Tlingit. Back home in Sitka he wrote a Russian–Aleut dictionary, recorded weather patterns, and became a skilled mason, blacksmith, and carpenter.

You can wander freely around the lower level of the house, which was used at various times as a grade school, seminary, orphanage, and apartment, and now contains a model of New Archangel as it was in 1845 as well as several cases of artifacts and icons. Note the sections of the actual wall and floor that are cut away to reveal the ingenious insulation – sawdust in the walls and draft-preventive joints. Guided tours (usually every 30min; $4) lead you upstairs to the bishop's private apartments, a small library of original books, and the ornate one-room **chapel** that is still consecrated and is used occasionally.

The Sheldon Jackson Museum

Half a mile east along Lincoln Street, Sheldon Jackson College's octagonal **Sheldon Jackson Museum**, 104 College Drive (mid-May to mid-Sept daily 9am–5pm; mid-Sept to mid-May Tues–Sat 10am–4pm; $4, winter $3; ⊤747-8981, ⓦwww.museums.state.ak.us), contains a compact but fascinating collection of Native artifacts. It was put together by the Reverend Dr Sheldon Jackson (see box, below) who, along with his friends, collected more than five thousand examples of Native work, always meticulously recording where and how the pieces – be they utilitarian, ceremonial, or decorative – were acquired. The first shack he built to house the items soon filled up and, in 1897, he constructed the current museum building, the first concrete structure in Alaska.

Sheldon Jackson

New York-born **Sheldon Jackson** (1834–1909) was a Presbyterian missionary who became Alaska's first general agent for education – although he turned out to be much more. Russian Orthodoxy had only ever gained acceptance along the coast, so on his wide-ranging travels throughout Alaska, Jackson took it upon himself to divide the state up into a dozen broadly equivalent sections and encourage any interested Protestant communities to accept a kind of ecclesiastical monopoly within those regions. The Presbyterians took the Arctic North and much of Southeast, Philadelphia Quakers got Kotzebue and a patch near Juneau, and Methodists took the Aleutian Islands; these and other such divisions survived for a considerable time. Jackson also noticed that the European presence had affected hunting patterns and significantly changed the Eskimo lifestyle. Believing that Native culture could be preserved by fostering economic independence, he pushed for the introduction of reindeer on the Seward Peninsula near Nome. The government initially wasn't interested, but Jackson went ahead anyway and shipped 171 reindeer from Siberia in 1892. Acknowledging the positive effect of Jackson's initiative on Native life, the government joined in ten years later and brought over an additional 1280 beasts.

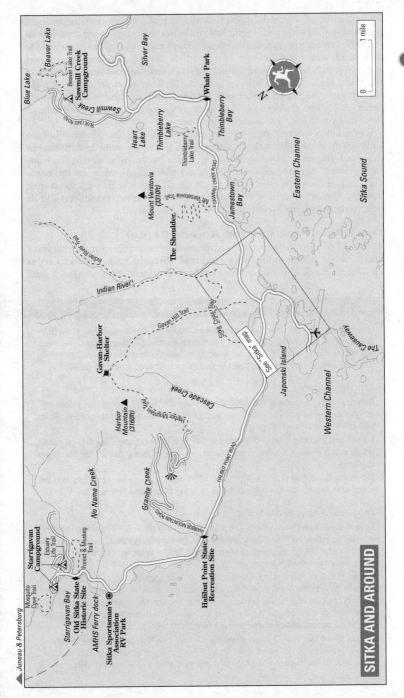

SOUTHEAST ALASKA | Sitka and around

SITKA AND AROUND

Though small and a little old-fashioned with its ranks of glass cases, the museum is packed to the rafters with exemplary works from throughout the state. Totems form the centerpiece, but all around are Tlingit items such as feast bowls made from alder, maple, and birch in bird and bear designs with decorative pieces picked out in bone. The wood and fur **Raven battle helmet** worn by the Kiks .ádi leader Katlian in the 1804 conflict with the Russians vies for pride of place with armor made from leather and wooden slats, an Athabascan birch-bark canoe, an Eskimo reindeer sled, and drawers full of smaller and more delicate items that could keep you occupied for hours.

Across Lincoln Street from the museum, don't miss the Sheldon Jackson College's **Marine Wet Lab & Aquarium** (Mon–Fri 9am–3pm; donations welcome), effectively a biology classroom with a handful of small tanks containing specimens collected locally and three wet tables filled with weird and beautiful creatures you can touch, pick up, or simply watch as they go about their business. Mussel beds, clams, anemones, tube worms, and sea cucumbers all pale next to the wonderfully colorful starfish.

The Totem Park and the Raptor Center

At the end of Lincoln Street, in a verdant copse between ocean and creek, you'll find the main section of the **Sitka National Historic Park**, known locally as the "Totem Park." This wooded area bordered by totem poles occupies a small

---

Hikes around Sitka and Mount Edgecumbe

Sitka is unusually well served with good **hikes**, from easy strolls (especially in the Starrigavan area, eight miles west of town) to harder climbs up Gavan Hill and the steep Mount Verstovia. Most of them are directly accessible from town, although others require transport to the trailhead and Mount Edgecumbe requires boat access.

Starrigavan area

Estuary Life Interpretive Trail (200yd one way; 10min; flat). Accessible boardwalk around an area of wetland with numerous spurs to picturesque seating areas. Good salmon viewing through August.

Forest and Muskeg Trail (1 mile one way; 45min; 100ft ascent). Easy trail on raised gravel paths through the forest and boardwalk over muskeg. Accessible but steep in places.

Mosquito Cove Trail (1.2-mile loop; 1 hr; 100ft ascent). Fairly easy trail following the coast past several lovely viewpoints, then looping back through forest.

Other road-accessible trails

Beaver Lake Trail (3 miles round-trip; 1hr 30min; 400ft ascent). Popular trail climbing steadily from *Sawmill Creek Campground* through temperate forest, then on a boardwalk across muskeg, dropping gently to scenic Beaver Lake, which it then encircles. Good mountain views, if the clouds lift.

Gavan Hill Trail (6 miles round-trip; 4–7hr; 2400ft ascent). Beginning in town off Baranof Street (see map, p.147), this moderate trail leads to subalpine tops where you can hook up with the Harbor Mountain Trail. The Gavan Hill and Harbor Mountain trails meet at the free-use Gavan–Harbor Shelter, which has no stove and is best treated as an emergency shelter; bring a tent if you want to stay up here.

Harbor Mountain Trail (8 miles round-trip; 4–6hr; 1500ft ascent). The narrow gravel Harbor Mountain Road twists five miles off Halibut Point Road to subalpine country at around two thousand feet. Follow the road past an excellent overlook and a

peninsula where the Kiks.ádi Tlingits established a fort shortly after driving off early Russian settlers in their 1802 attack. Returning two years later, the Russians destroyed the fort, and today all that's left is a grassy patch around a particularly striking totem pole. Somehow this area seems a little out of character with the rest of the park, all brooding spruce and hemlocks swathed in almost incessant mist, out of which loom the poles gazing balefully out to sea. As elsewhere in Southeast, most are replicas of nineteenth-century totems.

Set aside in 1890 by President Benjamin Harrison, the park was later developed by Alaska Governor John Brady, who chose the area as the resting place for poles rounded up around Southeast for the St Louis World's Fair of 1904. None had actually come from here (most were from Haida villages on Prince of Wales Island), but with land already set aside this seemed the most sensible place for them. As the poles continued to rot, the Civilian Conservation Corps began a program to replicate the originals, accounting for most of the thirteen poles now present. A couple are more recent creations, however, most notably the colorful pole nearest the visitor center, which was ceremoniously raised in 1996 after considerable debate within the Tlingit community about Raven and Eagle appearing on the same pole.

In addition to inspecting the poles along the foreshore, check in at the **visitor center**, at the end of Lincoln Street (May–Sept daily 8am–5pm; Oct–April Mon–Sat 8am–5pm; $4; ☎747-6281, ⓦwww.nps.gov/sitk), which has a small

couple of picnic areas to the trailhead proper, from where it is two miles up to the Gavan–Harbor Shelter (see opposite).

Indian River Trail (11 miles round-trip; 6–8hr; 500ft ascent). Long but fairly gentle and relaxing trail following the Indian River valley to the eighty-foot Indian River Falls below the Three Sisters Mountains. Lovely rainforest, and there's salmon in the river from midsummer. The trail starts in town off Indian River Road (see map, p.147).

Mount Verstovia Trail (5 miles round-trip; 4–5hr; 2500ft). Arduous hike that's rewarding on a clear day. Beginning a couple of miles east of town off Sawmill Creek Road, it starts gently through an area logged by the Russians in the 1860s; there's still some evidence of the charcoal pits they built. The trail soon climbs with ever-longer views to "the shoulder," which is as far as most people go. Enthusiasts can continue along the ridge to the northeast to the true 3310-foot summit, roughly another hour on.

Thimbleberry–Heart Lakes Trail (2 miles round-trip; 30min–2hr; 50ft ascent). Broad gravel path to Thimbleberry Lake, which is good for fishing. The trailhead is at Mile 4 of Sawmill Creek Road.

Mount Edgecumbe

The near-conical **Mount Edgecumbe**, at the southern end of Kruzof Island, is temptingly visible on Sitka's western horizon, separated by only seventeen miles of Sitka Sound. Part with round-trip water taxi fees of around $160 for up to six people and you've got the place to explore, notably the **Mount Edgecumbe Trail** (13.5 miles round-trip; 7–10hr; 3200ft ascent). This climbs the peak from the Forest Service's *Fred's Creek Cabin* (☎1-877/444-6777; $35), a new shoreline affair where the water taxis drop off. The trail crosses muskeg rising gently for four miles, arriving at a three-sided emergency shelter. From there the path steepens to the tree line at two thousand feet, then follows a line of poles, though if the weather is clear you're encouraged to make your own route to avoid wearing a path. If there is low cloud, follow the poles to get down.

△ Bald eagle, Sitka

museum with well-chosen displays on what is commonly called the "Battle of Sitka," a twelve-minute video on the town's significance to Tlingits during the Russian era and since the area became part of the US, and workshops where you can chat to the Native craftspeople as they work. A room just past the craftspeople contains an impressive collection of primarily **Haida poles** from the early twentieth century; of particular interest is the central Wolf Pole in dramatic high relief. Some summers the outside carving shelter is home to artisans at work on a full-size totem pole.

Before returning to town, consider a visit to the wooded, streamside confines of the nonprofit **Alaska Raptor Center**, 1000 Raptor Way (May–Sept daily 8am–4pm; $12; ☎1-800/643-9425, ⓦwww.alaskaraptor.org). Here, wounded birds of prey – owls, hawks, peregrine falcons, and bald eagles – are cared for and released back into the wild, except for those unable to fly or hunt, which are kept as "raptors in residence." The birds stay in large and thoughtfully constructed compounds and are introduced by the enthusiastic and well-informed staff members, who guide you around the compound and the flight-training center where soon-to-be-released birds are put through their paces. It pays to come on a day when there's a cruise ship in town: for large groups they'll even bring out one of the bald eagles, providing a rare chance to come face-to-beak with one of these regal birds.

Along the road system

Unless you are camping or trying to reach distant trailheads, there is little point in renting a car in Sitka; there are only about seven or eight miles of road in each direction from town, and not a great deal along them. Heading east along Sawmill Creek Road, you pass the trailhead for Mount Verstovia Trail at James-town Bay about three miles out; a mile further is **Whale Park**, three covered observation platforms linked by boardwalks. Another mile or so further west, the site of the pulp mill that closed in 1993 marks Blue Lake Road, which leads to *Sawmill Creek Campground* and Beaver Lake Trail. Cars are banned beyond the end of the paved road, but **bikers** can continue a further six miles past the Medvejie Hatchery to the dammed Green Lake, which provides power and water for Sitka.

Four miles west along Halibut Point Road you hit Halibut Point State Recreation Site, where there are some picnic tables as well as some short trails. More robust hikes can be found at the top of Harbor Mountain Road, which heads inland almost opposite the recreation site. From here, Halibut Point Road continues to the AMHS ferry dock and, half a mile beyond, the **Old Sitka State Historic Site**, where barely discernable remains mark the original site of the Russian settlement in 1799. Cross Starrigavan Creek to reach the *Starrigavan Campground*, a very pleasant area open for day-use and with a selection of easy trails threading along boardwalks and raised gravel paths through the forest. Strategically sited seats make great spots for watching waterbirds wading or salmon jumping.

Cruises, kayaking, and fishing

Sitka's setting, open to the ocean and yet hemmed in by myriad islands, is so beguiling that almost all your time on land is spent wishing you were on the water. That's easily rectified with Sitka Wildlife Quest (late May to early Sept; ☎1-888/747-8101, ⓦwww.allenmarinetours.com), which runs educational and entertaining **wildlife tours** (Tues & Thurs 6–8pm, Sat & Sun 9am–noon; $59, $79 weekends) out on Sitka Sound, with every chance of seeing humpback whales (especially in late summer), sea otters, and seals, as well as bears and deer along the banks of numerous islands. Weather permitting, the trips go out to the sheer volcanic **St Lazaria Island**, a federal wildlife refuge at the mouth of Sitka Sound with cliffs that, during the summer months, are black with seabirds, notably murres, petrels, and comical puffins. The cliffs plunge so steeply into the sea that you can get within a few feet of the creatures. Trips leave from Crescent Harbor Marina.

Sitka has some of the best **sea kayaking** in Southeast, with mile upon mile of sheltered waterways, narrow channels, gorgeous coves, and tide pools. Paddle beyond the swanky homes that dot the islands near Sitka, and you can camp anywhere, or stay in one of the couple of dozen saltwater-accessible cabins (see Accommodation, p.142). In as little as a few hours you can explore **the Causeway**, a series of small islands south of the airport that were linked together during World War II to provide access to gun emplacements. Remnants of the emplacements are still visible, but as they can be hard to find it pays to ask whoever is renting you a kayak before you set out.

One popular destination is **Goddard Hot Springs**, seventeen miles to the south, where two covered hot-tubs face out to sea. Don't expect to have the place to yourself, as it is a popular rest spot for commercial fishermen, but it makes an excellent destination for a kayak expedition (3–4 days round-trip from Sitka). The Forest Service's *Kanga Bay* cabin is on the way, and at Goddard there's the new city-owned *Tom Young Memorial Cabin* (ⓦwww.cityofsitka.com), which can only be booked in person in Sitka. Since it is likely to be reserved, be prepared to camp, best done on offshore islands where the mosquitoes are found in smaller numbers.

Sitka Sound Ocean Adventures (☎747-6375, ⓦwww.ssoceanadventures .com) **rents kayaks** (half-day $30 single, $40 double; full-day $52/$62; multi-day roughly $42/$52 per day) and conducts guided kayak tours, with two-hour paddles around the Totem Park shoreline and out to the closer islands ($63), full-day trips ($132) and multiday affairs ($150 per day). They work out of a blue bus parked by Harrigan Centennial Hall.

The high nutrient content of Sitka Sound means it is one of the best places for saltwater **salmon-fishing** – kings in June, silvers in late July and August. Apparently, it takes an average of two hours to catch a king salmon here, less than half the time it takes in most places around the state. Try A Whale of a Tale Charters (☎738-3647, ⓦwww.sitkasalmon.com), which offers a half-day trip ($150) and full-day trips ($250), all requiring a minimum of three people.

Eating, drinking, and entertainment

With one exception – the excellent *Ludvig's Bistro* – Sitka's **restaurants** aren't exactly going to set gourmet tongues wagging, though you can eat well enough for a few days. You can buy **groceries** at the convenient Market Center (see p.152).

A couple of good **bars** are pretty much the extent of evening activity, but daytime **entertainment** is more varied, with a couple of local **dance troupes** vying for your attention. The choice venue would have to be the Community House, 200 Katlian St, where the Sheet'ka Kwaan Naa Kahidi Dancers (May–Sept; $7; ℡1-888/270-8687, ☻www.sitkatribe.org) perform for half an hour in traditional costume and with a narration of local legends. Performance times (which are dependent on cruise-ship sailings) are posted outside the 1997 replica clan house, beside the stridently painted Eagle- and Raven-design screen. The alternative is the New Archangel Dancers, Harrigan Centennial Hall (generally May–Sept; $8; ℡747-5516), who also do a half-hour show scheduled around the cruise ships, but concentrate on authentic Russian folk dances performed by local women.

Fans of chamber **music** will want to time their visit to coincide with the Sitka Summer Music Festival (℡747-6774, ☻www.sitkamusicfestival.org), which takes place throughout most of June. The festival includes around eight evening concerts, mostly in Harrigan Centennial Hall, and features up to twenty artists of international renown. Call for tickets or drop by Old Harbor Books, 201 Lincoln St (℡747-8808); book in advance or you'll have to be content with sitting in on rehearsals, which are free.

Backdoor 104 Barracks St ℡747-8856. Daytime café with great coffee, plus tasty sandwiches, pastries, and light lunches. Access through Old Harbor Books.

Bayview Restaurant Upstairs at 407 Lincoln St ℡747-5440. Good restaurant with great sea views and a standard, but well prepared, range of burgers, salads, and sandwiches, plus the likes of chicken quesadillas ($9).

The Galley Deli 2a Lincoln St ℡747-9997. Tasty deli selling great chowder and freshly made sandwiches on home-baked bread in a building also housing the Evergreen Natural Foods store. Come early for fresh loaves. Open Mon–Sat 10am–3pm.

Highliner Coffee Co. Seward Square Mall, Seward St ℡747-4924. Daytime coffee shop with relaxing sofas, espresso, good cakes, bagels, and Internet access at commercial rates.

Ludvig's Bistro 256 Katlian St ℡966-3663. If it weren't for the 10pm sunset outside and the fish canneries down the street, you could easily imagine yourself in a tiny Mediterranean bistro dining on a scallop Caesar salad ($18) or Alaskan paella ($29). Everything on the mostly Spanish, French, and Italian menu is cooked

to perfection, and the old-world wines, ports, and sherries served are all available by the glass. It's not cheap, but be sure to make it part of your Sitka plans and reserve ahead. Closed Sun.

Market Center 210 Baranof St ℡747-6686. Central grocery store with good line in prepared sandwiches and salads, plus espresso. Open until midnight in summer.

Pioneer Bar 212 Katlian St ℡747-3456. Down-to-earth spot with boozing at the bar or in booths surrounded by hundreds of black-and-white photographs of fishing boats.

Sheldon Jackson College Dining Room David Sweetland Hall. The best bargain in town for diners on a budget. A simple, cafeteria-style place with all-you-can-eat breakfast (6.30–8am; $5.50), lunch (11.30am–1pm; $8.25), and dinner (5–6pm; $11). On Sunday breakfast and lunch become brunch (11.30am–1pm; $10). Follow the road opposite the entrance to the Sheldon Jackson Museum.

Victoria's Pour House 118 Lincoln St. Convivial nonsmoking bar with a changing roster of draft beers and a kind of Mughal-themed snug out the back.

Listings

Banks The First National Bank at 318 Lincoln St has an ATM.

Bicycle rental and repair The handiest spot is Yellow Jersey Cycle Shop, 329 Harbor Drive (℡747-6317, ☻www.yellowjerseycycles.com), which rents bikes at $25 a day ($30 for 24hr).

Bookshop Old Harbor Books, 201 Lincoln St ℡747-8808, ℮oldharbr@ptialaska.net.

Festivals Apart from the Summer Music Festival (see above), there's a salmon derby on the last weekend of May and first weekend in June; a lively Fourth of July parade and fireworks;

a period-costume ball, parade, and dinners to celebrate the lead-up to Alaska Day and the anniversary of the transfer on Oct 18; and a celebration of all things cetacean in the Sitka WhaleFest (🕸 www.sitkawhalefest.org) in the first week of Nov. It is also worth noting that the Russian Orthodox Church follows the Julian (rather than the standard Gregorian) calendar, so religious festivals – Christmas and Easter in particular – are celebrated twice here, roughly twelve days apart.

Internet access Reservable free access by the hour or half-hour at the library, which also has WiFi. For more immediate needs try Alaska Computer Center, 205 Harbor Drive (Mon–Sat 10am–5pm; ☏747-0600), or *Highliner Coffee* (see opposite).

Laundry and showers The Hames PE Center at Sheldon Jackson College (early May to early Sept Mon–Fri 6am–9pm, Sat noon–8pm, Sun noon–6pm; ☏747-5231) has a pool, racquetball courts, and showers for $4. Super 8 Laundromat, 404 Sawmill Creek Rd (☏747-8804), is the handiest for laundry.

Left luggage Nothing formal, but the information desk in the Harrigan Centennial Hall will often hold bags.

Library The Kettleson Memorial Library, Harbor Drive (Mon–Fri 10am–9pm, Sat & Sun 1–9pm), makes a perfect place to while away a rainy day, with plenty to read, Internet access, and superb picture windows with views of the bay.

Medical assistance Sitka Community Hospital, 209 Moeller Drive (☏747-3241), has emergency medical services and outpatient clinics.

Pharmacy Harry Race Pharmacy, 106 Lincoln St ☏747-8006.

Post office There's a sub-post office downtown at 338 Lincoln St (Mon–Sat 8.30am–5.30pm) and the main on Sawmill Creek Rd out by the Raptor Center. The **General Delivery** zip code is 99835.

Taxes There's a five percent sales tax and an additional six percent bed tax, not included in our price codes.

Water taxis Ester G Sea Taxi (☏747-6481, 🕸 www.puffinsandwhales.com) charges about $140 an hour for up to six people in a fast boat.

Minor ports

All over Southeast Alaska there are small settlements of a few hundred people, some of which are Native villages that have survived intact, some former logging camps or canneries that have developed enough momentum to exist beyond the death of the industry that spawned them. Many of these places are off the main sea lanes plied by the AMHS ferries, while others get regular (though not especially frequent) visits; it is the latter we have covered here. None really warrants a special visit, and in most cases the town you'll spend at the ferry dock is ample. Kayakers, however, may want to paddle to one of these ports, and then catch the ferry back to their starting point. Trips to consider include Petersburg to Kake and Sitka to Tenakee Springs.

Wherever you plan to stop, be sure to study the ferry schedule carefully to ensure you don't end up spending five nights in a place you only intended to spend two.

Kake

Roughly two southbound and two northbound AMHS ferries call in each week at **Kake** (pronounced "cake"), an 800-strong Tlingit village on the northwest coast of Kupreanof Island, between Petersburg and Sitka. Fishing and subsistence hunting keep the town afloat, with the occasional visitor using the town as a springboard for kayak trips to Kuiu Island, or as a destination for a paddling expedition from Petersburg. Ferries dock a mile and a half from town, so if you're here on layover you probably won't have long enough to closely inspect the town's 132-foot **totem pole**, carved for the 1970 World's Fair in Japan and said to be the tallest in the world. On a longer visit, you can **stay** at the *Waterfront Lodge* (☏785-3472, 🕸 www.waterfrontlodgekake.com; ❹), **eat** at the *Nugget Inn* (☏785-6469), and buy groceries from several stores.

Angoon

The Tlingit village of **Angoon**, sixty miles southeast of Juneau, is the only significant settlement on Admiralty Island and occupies one of Southeast's warmest and driest locations on the island's western coast, facing Chatham Strait. Its seven hundred residents survive on fishing and subsistence hunting and do nothing to encourage tourism, which only touches their lives when the AMHS ferries arrive every few days, and since the ferry dock is three miles from town, the impact is very slight. About the only reason to stop is to do a little fishing or kayaking using *Favorite Bay Inn* (☎1-800/423-3123, ⓦwww .favoritebayinn.com; ◎) as your base.

Tenakee Springs

Schedules do change, but currently AMHS ferries visit **Tenakee Springs**, sixty miles southeast of Juneau on the eastern side of Chichagof Island, only once a week. The short stop in port doesn't really give you enough time to wallow in the soothing, no-clothes **hot pool** (men daily 2–6pm & 10pm–9am, women at all other times) at the end of the dock, just fifty yards from the boat. Besides, you may not find yourself warmly welcomed by the locals. They're far from hostile; it's just that most of the hundred residents came here for a quiet life and can be easily overwhelmed by the masses. A case in point was the 1997 visit of a cruise ship, the *World Discoverer*, that disgorged a hundred-plus passengers onto the single, car-free dirt path that serves as the town's main street. The residents shut up shop and effectively hid until the ship went away and promised never to return.

Individuals will feel much more welcome, yet there's not a great deal to do except fall into the pattern of daily baths, perhaps do a little fishing, or hike eight miles east along the single road to the site of the old cannery, whose workers initially popularized the springs in the late nineteenth century.

The only facilities are groceries from Snyder Mercantile (☎736-2205) and simple dining at the venerable *Blue Moon Café*.

Hoonah

A couple of ferries a week briefly visit **Hoonah**, a beachside Huna Tlingit fishing village on the northeast side of Chichagof Island, forty miles west of Juneau.

With around nine hundred residents, Hoonah is the largest Native village in Southeast and has until recently survived on fishing and logging, as the surrounding denuded hillsides attest. Now both industries are almost defunct and in desperation the local community has turned to tourism. Since 2004, large cruise ships have been pulling in to view the partially restored remains of the Hoonah Packing Company **cannery**, which sits picturesquely on the shore around a mile north of town. One of the few intact canneries left in Alaska, it still has some of the old canning lines, but in the tradition of Southeast cruise-ship tourism, space has been made for upscale shops and restaurants. Only one cruise ship is allowed per day but even this seems daunting for such a tiny town. Still, the place is thriving and you can visit the Hoonah Indian Association **Cultural Center and Museum** (Mon–Fri 8am–4.30pm; free), on the hill behind the town, for displays of local history and Native culture, including some interesting totem poles.

Pelican

The cheapest way to visit **Pelican**, seventy miles west of Juneau, deep within Lisianski Inlet on the northeast corner of Chichagof Island, is to come from the capital on the AMHS ferry, which makes its run about every two weeks in summer, always on a Sunday ($48 one-way, $96 round-trip). A stroll along the town's three-quarter-mile boardwalk during the two-hour stopover here is enough to give you a flavor of the place. The real appeal of the trip, however, is the five-hour ferry journey (each way), which passes close to Glacier Bay, through Icy Strait, and around **Point Adolphus**, regarded as one of the world's best places for **watching humpback whales**. This can be the cheapest whale-watching trip you are likely to get.

This tiny fishing village takes its name from the boat belonging to Finnish immigrant fisherman Charlie Raatikianen, who, with a few mates, established the town in 1938 to more conveniently process his catch. The setting proved favorable and the settlement added a post office in 1939, a cannery by 1943, and subsequently a school, a small sawmill, and a hotel. Most of the ramshackle buildings stand on piles over the water, linked by boardwalks, with only a couple of miles of roads.

If the ferry schedule doesn't suit, you can fly here daily from Juneau with Alaska Seaplane Service (☎789-3331, ⓦwww.akseaplanes.com) for $145 each way. The best **place to stay** is the comfortable *Highliner Lodge*, on the boardwalk (☎1-877/386-0397, ⓦwww.highlinerlodge.com; ❺). There are few places to **eat** and **drink**, but most visitors seem to gravitate towards *Rose's Bar and Grill*, on the boardwalk (☎735-2288, ⓦwww.rosesbarandgrill.com), which has a bar that's usually full of commercial fishermen. For more information, visit ⓦwww.pelican.net.

Juneau and around

The sophisticated and vibrant city of **JUNEAU** (JUNE-oh) is unlike any other state capital in the nation. Accessible only by sea and air, it is exceptionally picturesque, hard against the **Gastineau Channel**, with steep, narrow roads clawing up into the rainforested hills behind. With no flat land to speak of and a giant ice field blocking off any chance of direct land access to the interior, it would be hard to think of a less practical site for a state capital, but the vagaries of history and man's lust for gold tipped the balance.

Waste rock from the town's gold mines was dumped into the channel to create the flat downtown area, where a ragged gold-rush town sprang up in the 1880s with the usual complement of bars, churches, and brothels. Juneau had the good fortune to avoid a major fire, a common occurrence in northern towns built entirely of timber where wood-burning stoves raged many months of the year. Most of the older buildings remain, leaving a viable sense of history and creating a harmonious focus for what has to be one of the most physically beguiling town centers in Alaska.

The trouble is, much of the beauty is often obscured by the weather. It is not so much the annual ninety-plus inches of rain, but the consistency with which it comes – two out of every three days on average. Even when not raining, it is often cloudy. That hasn't stopped Juneau from becoming one of the busiest cruise-ship ports in Alaska, and the result is a frenetic atmosphere in which huge floating hotels loom over narrow central streets where diamond and emerald jewelry, handmade Swiss watches, and immaculately cut fur coats vie for shelf space with salmon refrigerator magnets and mini-totem poles. Still, tourism keeps the place lively and makes for a dramatic contrast on those languid evenings when the ships glide away, the streets empty out, and the buildings take on a glossy sheen as the low sun casts its last rays under the blanket of cloud.

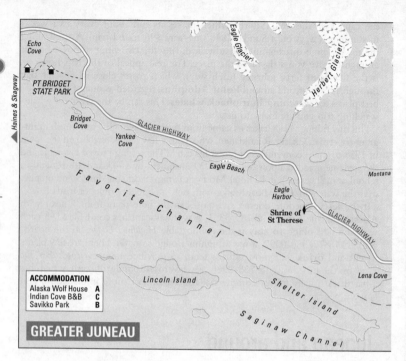

GREATER JUNEAU

ACCOMMODATION	
Alaska Wolf House	A
Indian Cove B&B	C
Savikko Park	B

A couple of excellent **museums**, a pretty Russian Orthodox church, and a tramway ride to some easy subalpine hikes provide the bulk of the diversions downtown, though the environs, which include some old gold mines, hold your interest as well. Further out, there's an educational salmon hatchery, tasting at one of Alaska's premiere breweries, and close-up viewing of the majestic **Mendenhall Glacier**.

Some history

Juneau was founded on gold. No one took much notice of the Auk Tlingit fishing village on Gastineau Channel until 1880, when George Pilz, a mining engineer from Sitka, dispatched Joe Juneau and Dick Harris there with Auk chief Kowee. Kowee had responded to Pilz's offer of a reward for divulging the whereabouts of gold, but these hapless, drunken prospectors were unable to find much. The chief insisted there was ore to be found and, on the second attempt, they unearthed what Harris described as "little lumps as large as peas and beans" at the head of Gold Creek. In no time Alaska had its first gold rush, and Harrisberg became the first American-established town in the new territory. Miners became disenchanted with Harris's dubious claim-staking practices and briefly switched the name to Rockwell before settling on Juneau in 1881.

Gold in the streams quickly ran out, but reef gold – locked in the hard rock below ground – was abundant. There were three main mines. The first and most enduring was the Alaska Juneau Mine (1887–1944), which hollowed out a hundred miles of tunnels in the hillside just south of downtown Juneau. You can still clearly see the scars left by its mill house where twelve thousand

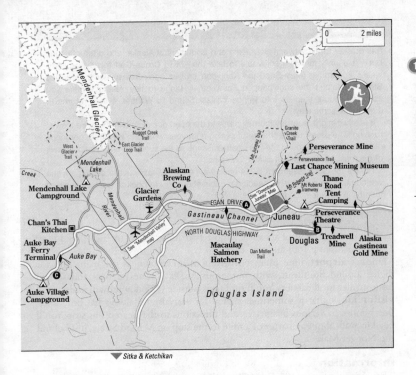

▼ Sitka & Ketchikan

tons of ore could be crushed in a single day by a thousand employees. Next was the Treadwell Mine (1899–1922), in Douglas, which was briefly the most profitable of them all. Finally, there was the short-lived Alaska Gastineau Mine (1915–21), four miles south of Juneau. Early efforts at extraction from a lesser source, Perseverance Mine (1885–1921), soon exhausted the best-grade ore, and throughout most of Juneau's sixty-year gold-mining era, the town's massive mines and crushing mills had to content themselves with low-grade ore. In order to be profitable, mining had to be done on a massive scale: sometimes 28 tons of rock had to be crushed to yield a single ounce of gold.

Unlike the gold rushes elsewhere in Alaska, the feverish activity around Juneau was long-lived, and by 1906 the territorial capital had moved here from Sitka. As the gold became less profitable, the city shifted its focus to its current legislative and administrative role, which has remained despite periodic attempts to move it elsewhere.

Arrival, information, and getting around

Although cruise ships dock conveniently downtown, most Juneau arrivals are inconvenient. The AMHS **ferry terminal**, on Glacier Highway (open for ferry arrivals; ☎789-7453), is fourteen miles northwest of downtown at Auke Bay, and since ferries often arrive at unearthly hours, getting into town can be a problem. There is no public transportation into town, so you either have to grab a taxi (see Listings, p.173), which costs around $40 into town, or walk a mile and a half to the nearest bus stop at the highway junction with Mendenhall Loop Road by DeHarts grocery (for details on buses, see p.158). Late-arriving

The Cross-Gulf ferry

It is quicker to fly between Southeast and Southcentral Alaska, and often cheaper, but it is usually far more enjoyable to take the AMHS **Cross-Gulf ferry**. Every two weeks in summer (May–Sept) the *Kennicott* cruises from Juneau out through Icy Strait and along the snowcapped Fairweather Range to tiny Yakutat (where you spend an hour), then on into Prince William Sound to Whittier. It then returns to Juneau the same way.

It is a two-night, one-day journey partly in the open ocean so there may be a swell running. The payoff is the chance of seeing numerous whales in Icy Strait, gorgeous mountain scenery around the Fairweather Range as the sun sets, and magical views of the massive Wrangell-St Elias mountains.

Tickets for foot passengers ($214 each way) are fairly easily available, but anyone wanting to take a vehicle or needing a cabin should try to book at least a couple of months in advance, longer if possible.

backpackers might want to walk almost two miles north to the *Auke Village Campground* (see p.160) and stay there.

Juneau's **airport**, nine miles northwest of downtown, is the main hub for flights around Southeast, with numerous Alaska Airlines arrivals and several from smaller local carriers. You'll find taxis outside ($25 downtown) and a small **visitor kiosk** that is sometimes staffed for arrivals and always has brochures, free phones to various businesses, and directions to the nearest bus stop. You'll need to walk about a quarter of a mile to the stop on Mallard Street, just behind the Nugget Mall.

Information

The **visitor center**, 101 Egan Drive (May–Sept Mon–Fri 8.30am–5pm, Sat & Sun 9am–5pm; Oct–April Mon–Fri 9am–4pm; ☎1-888/581-2201, ⓦwww .traveljuneau.com), is inside Centennial Hall. Also here is an unstaffed desk devoted to brochures about the Tongass National Forest, including material on Glacier Bay, Tracy Arm Fjord, and the trails and cabins in Juneau's wooded surroundings. For more details, call at the Tongass National Forest District **Ranger Office**, 8461 Old Dairy Rd (Mon–Fri 8am–5pm; ☎586-8800, ⓦwww.fs.fed.us/r10/tongass). You'll find additional daytime **information booths** at Marine Park on the waterfront and by the cruise-ship dock.

Getting around

Juneau's main points of interest (with the exception of the ferry terminal) can all be reached using city **buses** operated by Capital Transit (☎789-6901), which has four routes, all costing $1.50, exact fare required. Buses run every thirty to sixty minutes depending on the time of day. The main routes – #3 and #4 (Mon–Sat 7am–11pm, Sun 9am–5pm) – travel from downtown along the waterfront past Lemon Creek to the airport and then loop through the Mendenhall Valley. Capital Transit also operates services to Douglas (Mon–Sat 7.30am–10.30pm, Sun 9.30am–6pm) from downtown Juneau over the bridge; change from either #3 or #4 to this line at the Federal Building stop on Glacier Avenue (transfers are free). There's also an hourly **express service** (Mon–Fri 7.30am–6pm) between downtown and Auke Bay, about a mile and a half from the AMHS ferry terminal.

Also useful as a means of getting around, MGT (☎789-5460, ⓦwww .mightygreattrips.com) offers a couple of **bus tours** cheap enough to regard as public transportation. Check out their Glacier Express ($6 each way), which is effectively a bus service between the cruise-ship dock downtown and the Mendenhall Glacier visitor center. Last Frontier Tours (☎1-888/396-8687, ⓦwww.lastfrontiertours.com) does a similar Mendenhall Glacier trip ($6 each way), with an optional stop at the hatchery.

The bus system is infrequent enough and the road system extensive enough that it makes sense to **rent a car** (see Listings, p.172) for at least part of your stay. **Cycling** can also work well, with a number of dedicated bike routes that hit all the main destinations; bikes travel free on buses. Pick up the free *Biking in Juneau* leaflet from the visitor center and rent bikes for around $25 a day from *Driftwood Lodge* (see below).

City, glacier, and gold-mine tours

Being a major cruise-ship destination, Juneau offers dozens of city tours primarily geared towards giving cruise passengers a quick look at the main sights and delivering them back in time for their departure. If you have the time you probably won't bother with a tour, but if you're in a rush, MGT's two-hour-plus City & Glacier Tour (early May to late Sept; $22; ☎789-5460) provides low-cost access to the Mendenhall Glacier, allowing forty minutes at the glacier visitor center. With prior notice (and suitable interest) they'll also take in the salmon hatchery ($29 total).

One sight you can't see on your own is the Alaska Gastineau gold mine, four miles south of Juneau. Access is only on the pricey three-hour Alaska Gastineau Mill & Gold Mine Tour ($63; ☎1-800/820-2628), where staggering facts about the size of the mine and anecdotes about the people who worked there keep you entertained as you walk underground along a 360-foot flat tunnel, troop around the old buildings, and drive up the mountainside to a small mining museum.

Accommodation

Juneau has the widest range of accommodation in Southeast, from beautiful campgrounds and a conveniently sited hostel to luxurious B&Bs. Unless you have your own transport, it makes sense to stay downtown, though you might want to stay in Mendenhall Valley for proximity to the airport, access to hiking trails, or just to avoid the bustle of the center of town. **Campers** should pick up the free and very useful *Tent Camping & RV Facilities and Services* leaflet from the visitor center.

Hotels and motels

Alaskan Hotel 167 S Franklin St, downtown ☎1-800/327-9374, ⓦwww.thealaskanhotel.com. Juneau's oldest hotel dates to 1913 and, with the cheapest rooms in town, makes good on its claim, "Styles & rates of a bygone era." Rooms all have antique furniture of some sort, and around half of them have private bathrooms. TVs and kitchenettes are more randomly scattered, and some rooms are pretty small. Avoid the second-floor rooms above the bar if you fancy an early night. Suites and private bath ④, shared ③

Baranof Hotel 127 N Franklin St, downtown ☎586-2660 or 1-800/544-0970, ⓦwww .westmarkhotels.com. Now over sixty years old,

this is Juneau's grandest hotel, though the rooms have become somewhat sanitized now that it's part of the statewide *Westmark* chain. All rooms are slightly different, so ask to look at a few. Suites ⑨, rooms ⑦

Driftwood Lodge 435 Willoughby Ave, downtown ☎1-800/544-2239, ⓦwww.driftwoodalaska.com. Three-story motel one block from the waterfront, with large rooms that include kitchenettes and some one-bedroom and two-bedroom apartments. Courtesy bus to airport and ferry, and bikes available for rent (see p.172). Suites ⑤, rooms ④

Prospector Hotel 375 Whittier St, downtown ☎586-3737 or 1-800/331-2711, ⓦwww .prospectorhotel.com. Probably the nicest business hotel in town, featuring modernized suites and rooms – many with water views – with cable TV (including HBO). Prices are reasonable for its central location. Suites ⑦, rooms ⑥

🏃 **Silverbow Inn** 120 2nd St, downtown ☎1-800/586-4146, ⓦwww.silverbowinn .com. Attractive, small hotel linked to the café and bakery of the same name, with smallish but nicely furnished and tastefully decorated rooms, each with TV, phone, and WiFi, and with a good continental breakfast included. Reasonable off-season rates. ⑥

Super 8 Motel 2295 Trout St, Mendenhall ☎789-4858 or 1-800/800-8000, ⓦwww.super8.com. The cheapest option near the airport, they run a free shuttle, though it is only about five hundred yards away. Rooms are unexciting but well equipped. ⑤

B&Bs

Alaska Wolf House 1900 Wickersham Ave, downtown ☎1-888/425-9653, ⓦwww .alaskawolfhouse.com. Spacious and very comfortable B&B in a large, cedar-log house with views of Gastineau Channel. The hosts excel at helping their guests explore Juneau, inviting them onto their nine-berth, 36-foot wooden boat for a day-long cruise (half-day $750 for the boat, full day $1500 including food and drink) viewing glaciers, shipwreck sites, and wildlife. Back at the B&B there's a range of individually styled suites and tastefully decorated rooms, two with shared bath, and all with plenty of good books. Breakfasts are delicious. Suites ⑦, rooms ⑥

🏃 **Alaska's Capital Inn** 113 W 5th St, downtown ☎586-6507 or 1-888/588-6507, ⓦwww.alaskacapitalinn.com. Elegantly restored 1906 mansion hosts downtown Juneau's most luxurious B&Bs, with a range of mostly large rooms, all with original Arts & Crafts features, beautiful fittings, and either clawfoot or Jacuzzi baths. Some have great views, particularly the attic Governor's suite ($320), a wonderful room that justifies the extra cost. There's also an outdoor hot tub, free WiFi, and a five-course sit-down breakfast. Governor's suite ⑨, rooms ⑥

🏃 **Gold Street Inn** 303 Gold St, downtown ☎586-9863, ⓦwww.goldstreetinn.com. Quiet B&B with five comfortable and attractively decorated rooms (one of them a spacious suite), all with self-catering facilities, satellite TV, and free WiFi. They are in a centrally located two-story house and there's an extensive self-serve continental breakfast. Open all year. Suite ⑥, rooms ④

Indian Cove B&B Glacier Hwy, a mile north of Auke Bay ☎789-2726, ⓦwww.indiancovebb.com. The main attraction at this lovely, waterside B&B

with good views is its proximity to the ferry dock. Continental breakfast. ⑤

Pearson's Pond Luxury Inn 4541 Sawa Circle, Mendenhall ☎789-3772 or 1-888/658-6328, ⓦwww.pearsonspond.com. Sumptuous rooms in a spacious, modern house a mile from Mendenhall Glacier, with CD and VCR, personal gyms, Internet access, kitchenettes with self-serve breakfasts, hot tubs, boating, bikes, in fact just about every amenity you can think of. Each room has a water or garden view and leads out to two communal hot tubs. Summer prices start at $280 a double. ⑨

Hostels and camping

Auke Village Campground Mile 15 Glacier Hwy. First-come, first-served Forest Service campground almost two miles north of the Auke Bay ferry terminal and close to a scenic beach. RVs and tent sites have pit toilets and water and new facilities in 2007. $8.

🏃 **Juneau Hostel** 614 Harris St, AK 99801 ☎586-9559, ⓦwww.juneauhostel.org. At $10 a bunk this is an Alaskan bargain, but in return you have to put up with a daytime lockout (9am–5pm), an evening curfew (midnight), and limited office hours (7–9am & 5pm–midnight). Still, it is a comfortable, relaxed, and central place set in an old Juneau home with separate floors for men and women, a spacious kitchen and lounge, a family room (①), free Internet access, and laundry facilities. Reservations (necessary at least June–Aug) can only be made by mail and should include the first night's fee for each person. They'll reply by SAE or email.

Mendenhall Lake Campground Montana Creek Rd, off Mendenhall Loop Rd, 13 miles from downtown. The place to camp if you have transport. A gorgeous first-come, first-served Forest Service campground within sight of the Mendenhall Glacier and with space for RVs (full hookup $28, water and electricity $26, dry $10) and some lovely lakeside walk-in tent sites ($10). Mid-May to mid-Sept.

Savikko Park Savikko Rd, Douglas. Free space for four RVs to park with water and toilets nearby, located in Douglas, two miles south of the Douglas Bridge. Call for a free permit at the Harbormaster's office, 1600 Harbor Way (☎586-5255), on the waterside of Egan Expressway in Juneau. Maximum three-day stay.

Thane Road Tent Camping Mile 1 Thane Rd. Small, primitive site with chemical toilets and stream water located just fifteen minutes' walk south of downtown. First-come, first-served sites are only $5, but you'll have to put up with the all-night clatter from the docks nearby. Open mid-April to mid-Oct.

The City

Despite its relative sophistication and incontestable scenic qualities, **downtown Juneau** is a faintly incongruous place, torn between the demands of herd tourism and the more prosaic needs of long-standing residents. Though largely populated by elderly cruise-ship passengers window-shopping and poking around, the tiny downtown core is also where you're likely to spend most of your time, especially on wet days when a couple of excellent museums, the State Capitol, and the Russian Orthodox church provide suitably protected distraction. On better days the Mount Roberts Tramway gives instant access to the high country above town, and it is easy to while away an afternoon wandering the precipitous streets and perhaps strolling out to the Last Chance Mining Museum.

Much of Juneau's real commercial life has moved nine miles northwest to **Mendenhall Valley**, the largest piece of flat land around, left behind by the shrinking Mendenhall Glacier; you may well arrive here at the airport, and will likely return to visit the glacier and go hiking. Glacier Highway and the roughly parallel Egan Drive freeway link downtown Juneau with Mendenhall, passing the fascinating salmon hatchery and Alaska's largest and most exalted brewery.

You'll have to cross Gastineau Channel by the Juneau–Douglas Bridge to reach the ruins of the **Treadwell Mine**, the most accessible of all Juneau's gold-mining remains.

Downtown: the historic district

By avoiding the fires that plagued the communities of Sitka, Metlakatla, and elsewhere, Juneau has retained much of its original architecture, particularly in the **South Franklin Street Historic District**, where the ageing upper frontages are in marked contrast to the glitz below. You could follow the self-guided walking tour outline in the *Discover Juneau* leaflet (available free from the visitor center), but a quick whip around the highlights should satisfy most people.

The town's two museums (see p.163) are both well worth visiting, but they're perhaps best saved for a wet day. In better conditions direct your wandering to the marble-porticoed entrance of the **State Capitol**, on Main at 4th Street (mid-May to late Aug Mon–Fri 8.30am–4.30pm, Sat 9.30am–4.30pm), a six-story brick monster built in 1931 as the Territorial Capitol. Follow a self-guided tour (leaflet from reception) or join the free, guided tour (30min) around the corridors of power. You'd have to have a deep interest in Alaskan politics to appreciate seeing the Finance Committee Room, where they passed legislation establishing the Permanent Fund Dividend, or the chamber where, in 1945, Natives were given the right to sit in restaurants with whites, but it is made all the more interesting by a superb collection of Alaskan photos lining the walls. Outside, there's a replica Liberty Bell which, at statehood, was struck seven times by seven people to denote the creation of the 49th state.

Follow Fifth Street inland from the State Capitol to reach the octagonal, onion-domed **St Nicholas** Russian Orthodox Church, 326 5th St at Gold St (mid-May to Sept Mon 9am–6pm, Tues & Thurs 9am–5pm, Fri 10am–noon & 3–5pm, Sat 11am–3pm, Sun 1–5pm; $2 donation), perhaps the most striking building in the city. Originally built in 1894, it was mainly used by Slavic immigrants and by Tlingits who, when virtually forced to accept Christianity, chose the only church with services in Tlingit. It was restored in the 1970s and continues in use today with Divine Liturgy sung in English, Tlingit, and Slavonic (Sat 6pm & Sun 9am). At other times guides will explain the significance of the assorted icons and religious treasures.

162

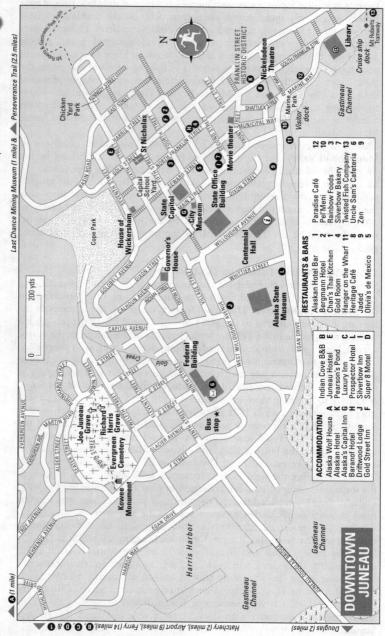

DOWNTOWN JUNEAU

Last Chance Mining Museum (1 mile) & Perseverance Trail (2.5 miles)

▲ A (1 mile)

Hatchery (2 miles), Airport (9 miles), Ferry (14 miles), ▶ 1 & C, D, E, B, 8

Douglas (2 miles) ▼

Douglas (2 miles)

Harris Harbor

Gastineau Channel

Gastineau Channel

Mt Roberts Tramway

Cruise ship dock

Gastineau Channel

Visitor Park dock

ACCOMMODATION
Alaska Wolf House	A
Alaskan Hotel	K
Alaska's Capital Inn	G
Baranof Hotel	H
Driftwood Lodge	J
Gold Street Inn	F
Indian Cove B&B	B
Juneau Hostel	E
Pearson's Pond	C
Luxury Inn	I
Prospector Hotel	L
Silverbow Inn	J
Super 8 Motel	D

RESTAURANTS & BARS
Alaskan Hotel Bar	1
Bergmann Hotel	2
Chan's Thai Kitchen	4
Gold Room	1
Hanger on the Wharf	11
Heritage Café	8
Jaded	9
Olivia's de Mexico	5
Paradise Café	12
Pel'Meni	10
Rainbow Foods	3
Silverbow Bakery	7
Twisted Fish Company	13
Uncle Sam's Cafeteria	6
Zen	9

Up the hill at 213 7th St, the **House of Wickersham** State Historical Site is the historic home of James Wickersham, Alaska's pioneering judge, statehood advocate, and general polymath. The house is currently closed for remodeling, though they hope to open it in summer 2007 with renewed interpretation of the man and the times in which he lived.

Weave down Dixon Street, off Goldbelt Avenue, and you could ring the doorbell at the 1912 **Governor's House**, 716 Calhoun Avenue, a Greek Revival–style antebellum affair that's easily the grandest house on the downtown skyline.

While you're up this way, head over to **Evergreen Cemetery**, which contains a monument to Chief Kowee (next to Glacier Ave) and the graves of Joe Juneau and Richard Harris (opposite each other near Irwin St). Following Glacier Highway back to town, you pass the Federal Building, 709 W 9th St, which contains the main post office, the bargain *Uncle Sam's Cafeteria*, a tiny and uninteresting museum, and a small room set aside as a time capsule. You can peer inside, but since it was only encapsulated in 1994 there's little that is surprising.

Downtown: the museums

One of Juneau's essential sights is the **Alaska State Museum**, 395 Whittier St (mid-May to mid-Sept daily 8.30am–5.30pm; mid-Sept to mid-May Tues–Sat 10am–4pm; $5, winter $3; Ⓦ www.museum.state.ak.us), which rivals the main museums in Anchorage and Fairbanks for its broad coverage of Alaska's culture and history. Much of the content is similar to what you'll see in museums all over Alaska, but nowhere is it better displayed or interpreted. The Russian era is especially well covered, balanced between the historical perspective – they have the logbook in which Bering reported his first sighting of Alaska – and the domestic, with samovars, period furniture, and some luminous icons. Panels explaining the circumpolar distribution of Eskimos (as far east as Greenland) stand beside a hunter seated in his kayak and decked out in a seal-gut parka. The Eskimo carvings, very expressive in their simplicity, are especially beautiful. Elsewhere, the powerfully carved Frog House replicates one from Klukwan, the last Chilkat village, with the meaning of each element in the design clearly explained. To reach the museum's upper level you follow a ramp that curls around a tree with an eagle's nest. The birds are stuffed, but this is likely to be your best chance to appreciate the immense size of the homes these birds make. None of this is overwhelming, but you might want to take the kids to the hands-on Children's Room, where they can dress up and play on the one-third-scale model of the *Discovery*, the ship George Vancouver used to explore the Alaskan coast.

Outside stands *Nimbus*, a modern sheet-metal sculpture in an off shade of green. Originally located on 4th Street at Main Street, it was so reviled that the citizens eventually had it removed and replaced with *Windfall Fisherman*, a bronze sculpture of that Alaskan archetype, the bear fishing for salmon.

You can see the bear on your way up to the **Juneau–Douglas City Museum**, Main Street at 4th Street (mid-May to Sept Mon–Fri 9am–5pm, Sat & Sun 10am–5pm; Oct to mid-May Fri & Sat noon–4pm; summer $4, winter by donation), which gives a vivid picture of how Juneau's past fits into the broader statewide picture. Drills, crucibles, ore samples, carbide lamps, assay scales, and a scale model of the fourteen underground levels of the Perseverance Mine reflect the institution's origins as a mining museum. It is an impression reinforced by the excellent and repeatedly screened *Juneau: City Built on Gold* documentary detailing the early history of Juneau, with a particular focus on hard-rock gold mining. But this is more than a mining museum. In addition to major temporary exhibitions and displays of local artwork, there's also a wonderfully accurate

△ Mount Roberts Tramway, Juneau

relief model of Juneau's landscape in 1967 (witness the extent of the Mendenhall Glacier just forty years ago) and plenty on the city's maritime past.

Take a look at the Montana Creek fish trap, a delicately preserved Native device unearthed in the early 1990s in the Mendenhall Valley. Somewhere between 500 and 700 years old, it is constructed from hemlock staves and spruce-branch hoops all tied together with spruce-root twine. A modern replica shows how it would have looked in action.

If all the mining history has sparked your imagination, consider buying the useful leaflets covering the Perseverance Trail and the Treadwell Mine – then go exploring.

The Tramway and Last Chance Mining Museum

For a bird's-eye view of downtown and much more, take the **Mount Roberts Tramway**, 490 S Franklin St (early May to late Sept daily 9am–9pm; $24; Ⓦwww.goldbelttours.com), which deposits you on a relatively level area 1800ft up Mount Roberts. Here, several gentle and moderate walks fan out from a restaurant and nature center where an 18-minute-long film, *Seeing Daylight*, focuses on Tlingit culture (the tramway is run by Goldbelt, the local Native corporation). Your ticket is valid for as many rides as you want all day, but you still might prefer to hike up (see box, p.168), then pay just $5 to ride down, or make $5 worth of purchases at the tram-top restaurant and bar. Buying a beer effectively pays your fare.

You'll have to go a couple of miles inland to see the **Last Chance Mining Museum** (mid–May to late Sept daily 9.30am–12.30pm & 3.30–6.30pm; $4), around forty minutes' walk from downtown at the end of Basin Road. The hands-on museum features tools, machines, and infrastructure from what was once the world's largest and most advanced hard-rock gold mine. Buildings that once held the assay office, blacksmith shops, and locomotive repair shops now contain displays, antiques, minerals, and the 3-D glass map of the mine tunnels and massive "glory holes" inside the mountain.

The salmon return, but not the profits

Returns are not what they once were in the salmon industry. Every year swarms of salmon of all five Pacific species struggle from the ocean to their birthplace in the headwaters of northern rivers to spawn, and dozens of Alaskan communities rely on the annual bounty. Some years the numbers are low, and whenever small returns occur in consecutive years the newspapers are full of hand-wringing articles about the demise of the wild salmon population. These years always seem to be followed by a bumper harvest the next season, and the trawlers are back in business.

But recently everyone has been hurting, no matter how abundant the fish. Diminished sales to the once-lucrative but now depressed Japanese market don't help, but prices are down across the board. And the blame is laid squarely on the salmon-farming industry, now thriving in Chile and Canada. Throughout Alaska, bumper stickers urge "Friends don't let friends eat farmed fish," as concerned citizens try to stem the seemingly inevitable switch to the farmed product. Wild salmon is pure, natural, tastes great, and doesn't have to be fed dye-laden food to make the flesh pink. But its farmed cousin is available fresh throughout the year, always looks and tastes the same (even if it isn't quite as succulent and firm), and most of all is cheap. And that suits the restaurant and supermarket trade just fine, thank you very much.

Salmon farming has been banned in Alaska since 1990, so even if you stick to the farmed stuff at home, the least you can do when in Alaska is support the small fishing communities and eat plenty of local wild salmon.

Towards Mendenhall Valley and the Mendenhall Glacier

Three miles north of downtown, Egan Drive charges past the **Macaulay Salmon Hatchery**, 2697 Channel Drive (May–Sept Mon–Fri 10am–6pm, Sat & Sun 10am–5pm; $3.25; ☎1-877/463-2486, ⊛www.dipac.net), one of the best places in the state to learn the intricacies of artificially rearing salmon. Although it is very much a working hatchery, responsible for stocking streams throughout the region, the site was partly designed with visitors in mind.

Inside, large saltwater aquariums are filled with local sea creatures in something akin to their natural environment, while outside you can follow walkways overlooking the entire hatchery process, from pink and chum salmon struggling up the 450-foot-long fish ladder (the longest in the state), through various stages of development, up to "ready for release." The fish only run from late June to October, so in the early part of the season you are shown the incubation room instead. If you've got your own fishing gear (and the appropriate state license), you can dip a line in the water with a fair chance of bagging the limit in double-quick time. If you're arriving by bus, ask the driver the best spot to get off and reboard.

City buses also pass through the suburb of Lemon Creek, five miles north of downtown, where you'll find the **Alaskan Brewing Co**, 5429 Shaune Drive (May–Sept daily 11am–4.30pm; Oct–April Thurs–Sat 11am–4.30pm; free; ☎780-5866, ⊛www.alaskanbeer.com), which was one of the first microbreweries in the United States (it was founded in 1986) and is now Alaska's largest brewer. The twenty-minute tour mostly involves looking at half a dozen stainless-steel tanks while a guide explains the brewing process, but it does entitle you to a free tasting of the award-winning suds.

A couple of miles further out, adversity has been channeled to good effect at **Glacier Gardens Rainforest Adventure**, 7600 Glacier Way (May–Sept daily 9am–6pm; $20; ☎790-33778, ⊛www.glaciergardens.com), the site of a devastating mudslide in 1984 and now a landscaped woodland garden. The entry price seems high for what's mostly a golf-cart ride up a spruce- and hemlock-wooded hillside to a good viewpoint high above Gastineau Channel. Still, it costs nothing to visit the parking lot, where the signature display of upturned tree trunks (salvaged from the mudslide) is festooned with brightly colored begonias, petunias, and fuchsias in hanging baskets – a curiously arresting sight.

There are certainly bigger and more spectacular glaciers in Alaska, but the twelve-mile-long, one-and-a-half-mile-wide **Mendenhall Glacier**, thirteen miles north of downtown, is one of the most accessible. You can drive within a mile of the face and gaze across Mendenhall Lake at the huge sheet of white creeping down from the immense Juneau Icefield. When John Muir saw the glacier in 1879, it ended halfway down the valley where the suburb of Mendenhall now lies, but like most glaciers in Alaska it has been retreating rapidly, leaving behind all sorts of geological evidence of its passage. Should your knowledge of cirques and striations be a little rusty, there's detailed explanation, along with a wonderful relief map of the Juneau Icefield and an entertaining ten-minute video, inside the Forest Service's Mendenhall Glacier **Visitor Center** (May–Sept daily 8am–7.30pm; Oct–April Thurs–Sun 10am–4pm; $3, winter free; ☎789-0097), located on a point occupied by the glacier as recently as 1940. If this inspires, consider joining one of the Forest Service's hour-plus **nature hikes** (late May to early Sept daily at 10am plus Tues–Sun at 2pm; free). The morning option is the better of the two excursions and follows the educational Moraine Ecology Trail (1.5-mile loop; 40min–1hr; negligible ascent). This trail and the handicap-accessible Photo Point Trail (0.6 miles round-trip;

MENDENHALL VALLEY

Mendenhall Glacier

Mendenhall Lake

MONTANA CREEK RECREATION AREA

West Glacier Trail

MONTANA CREEK RD.

SKATERS CABIN RD.

Mendenhall Lake Campground

Visitor Center

Photo Point Trail

Moraine Ecology Trail

East Glacier Long Trail

MENDENHALL LAKE RECREATION AREA

MENDENHALL LOOP ROAD

RIVER RD

Pearson's Pond

Cross Country Ski Area

GLACIER SPUR HWY

MENDENHALL LOOP ROAD

TAKU BLVD

ASPEN AVE

MENDENHALL LOOP ROAD

RIVERSIDE DRIVE

Mendenhall River

Montana Creek

TONGASS NATIONAL FOREST

◄ Auke Bay ferry dock (5 miles)

WEST MENDENHALL VALLEY GREENBELT/ BROTHERHOOD PARK

◄ Auke Bay ferry dock (5 miles)

RIVERSIDE DRIVE

Safeway supermarket

MENDENHALL LOOP ROAD

EGAN DRIVE

Super 8 Motel

GLACIER HWY

Nugget Mall

★ **Bus stop**

Glacier Gardens

EGAN DRIVE

Airport Terminal

Tongass National Forest District Ranger Office

Juneau (7 miles) ►

MENDENHALL WETLANDS STATE GAME RESERVE

N

0   500 yds

20min; negligible ascent) are the shortest of the local walks and therefore the most popular. Three longer trails are listed in the box below.

Getting to the glacier without your own transport isn't too difficult: Capital Transit buses leave hourly from downtown and pass Glacier Spur Road, where you need to get off and walk the final mile or so. A visit to Mendenhall Glacier is also pretty much *de rigueur* on any of the Juneau city tours (see p.158); cheapest is probably with MGT (☎789-5460), which offers a two-hour tour for $22 and also provides a $6 (each way) shuttle service from downtown.

Glacier Highway

Beyond the suburb of Mendenhall Valley and the airport, Glacier Highway continues past Auke Lake and the University of Alaska Juneau campus to the AMHS ferry dock at Auke Bay.

Beyond here, the highway is worth exploring only if you've got your own transport, in which case you could call in at the **Shrine of St Therese**, Mile 23 (generally open daily 8.30am–10pm in summer; donations appreciated), an attractive little church on a promontory accessed by a five-minute walk along a narrow spit. Built from beach stones in the 1930s and surrounded by the Stations of the Cross, the church is now very popular for weddings, and the

---

Hikes around Juneau

Juneau is unmatched in Southeast for the number of top-quality **trails** accessible from the road system, many of which are easily approached either from downtown or by the city bus out to Mendenhall Valley. Glaciers, forests, alpine high country, the remains of gold mines, and abundant wildlife make for a varied selection of trails, some easy and some fairly demanding.

If you are planning to spend a few days **hiking** in the area, it is definitely worth purchasing the plasticized inch-to-a-mile *Juneau Area Trails Guide* ($10); otherwise make do with the free leaflets from the Forest Service visitor center.

Only one of the hikes listed below passes a Forest Service cabin, but there are loads of them in the area. The more accessible cabins – whether you're arriving on foot, on skis, by float-plane, or by boat – are all frequently used by Juneau residents. Getting one on short notice should be possible during the week, but weekends will be more difficult. The Forest Service desk at the main visitor center (see p.158) has good information about the location of cabins, but for availability and reservations contact ReserveUSA (☎1-877/444-6777, ⓦwww.reserveusa.com).

From Downtown Juneau

Perseverance Trail, **Granite Creek Trail**, and **Mount Juneau Trail** (1–10hr). The most popular and easily accessed system of trails in Juneau, suitable for a couple of hours of easy valley strolling or an overnight hike along a rugged alpine ridge with stupendous views. The Perseverance Trail (3 miles round-trip; 2–4hr; 700ft ascent; $1 historic trail guide from the City Museum) follows Perseverance Creek to Silverbow Basin, where the Perseverance Mine operated intermittently from 1885 to 1921. Be very careful when exploring the old mine workings. The Granite Creek Trail and Mount Juneau Trail both spur off the Perseverance Trail and can be linked up using the Mount Juneau Ridge Route, creating a ten-hour expedition. There are no cabins along the way, but Granite Creek has a couple of lovely places to camp. The trailhead is 2.5 miles from downtown at the end of Basin Road. There's no public transport but you could grab a taxi or just walk from town.

Mount Roberts Trail (9 miles round-trip; 5–6hr; 3800ft ascent). A moderately difficult trail to the summit of Mount Roberts, switchbacking and climbing all the way, with increasingly good views and plenty of wildlife. You don't have to do the whole thing,

spit is a favored spot for anglers keen to bag kings, silvers, and pinks from the shore.

The highway currently stops around forty miles north of Juneau at Cascade Point but looks set to soon be extended as part of a planned, but controversial, **Juneau Access Road**. Boosters have long campaigned for road access to Skagway, but just as many (if not more) Juneau residents favor no road access. Until leaving office in December 2006, Governor Frank Murkowski had been pushing hard for the road, not least to provide access to the new **Kensington gold mine**. But a combination of enormous costs and the need to push the road through a designated "roadless" section of the Tongass National Forest saw the project scaled back.

The current plan sees the road stopping seventeen miles short of Skagway at the Katzehin River mouth, where shuttle ferries would make the connection to Haines and Skagway. Opponents see this as simply "extending the dead end." But obtaining Federal funding still looks uncertain and even the most hopeful boosters don't expect the road–ferry combo to be complete before 2010.

Douglas and the Treadwell Mine

Downtown Juneau is connected by a road bridge to **Douglas Island**, a mountainous, forest-clad place that partly acts as a dormitory suburb for

since the trail passes the upper station for the Mount Roberts Tramway (2 miles one-way; 1hr to 1hr 30min; 1800ft ascent), where there's a nature center and a possible ride down in the tram for $5 (or $5 worth of purchases at the tram-top restaurant and gift shop). Continue a little further on and you come to a wooden cross, a replica of one erected up here in 1908 by a local Jesuit priest, Father Brown. The trail starts downtown from the top of 6th Street.

From Mendenhall Valley
East Glacier Loop Trail (3.5-mile loop; 2–3hr; 400ft ascent). Moderate trail from the Mendenhall Glacier Visitor Center around the east of Mendenhall Lake, with good views of the glacier, though more distant than those from the West Glacier Trail. The upper portion of the trail passes the remains of an old wooden flume and rail tram left over from a Nugget Creek hydropower project that was designed to provide energy to the Treadwell Mill in 1911. A 600-foot tunnel drilled for the project (which was taken over by the Alaska-Juneau Mine) spews the water that creates the A-J waterfall, visible from the trail. Midway round the **Nugget Creek Trail** (add 5 miles round-trip; 3hr; 300ft ascent) spurs up Nugget Creek to the free-use Vista Creek Shelter.

West Glacier Trail (7 miles round-trip; 4–6hr; 1300ft ascent). Excellent moderate-to-difficult hike that skirts the northwestern side of Mendenhall Lake before climbing through alder and willow to a scenic overlook. There are great views of icefalls and even access to ice caves on the glacier (don't explore unless you know what you're doing and have the proper equipment). The trail is generally in good condition but deteriorates into a series of tape markers near the end. You can continue steeply for another couple of miles to the summit of Mount McGinnis, making it a full-day outing. The trailhead is on Skaters Cabin Road, about a mile from the Capital Transit bus stop at the junction of Montana Creek Road and Mendenhall Loop Road.

On Douglas Island
Dan Moller Trail (6.5 miles round-trip; 3–5hr; 1800ft ascent). A moderate trail ending high in an alpine cirque and the Forest Service's *Dan Moller Cabin* (☎1-877/444-6777; $35). The trail starts close to the junction of Cordova and Foster streets (bus stop); follow Pioneer Street and the trailhead is by the fifth house.

Juneau. There was a brief time around 1910 when the city of **Douglas** was the largest in Southeast Alaska because of the employment opportunities at the local Treadwell Mine. Like all of Juneau's mines, the Treadwell relied on economies of scale to turn a profit, processing huge quantities of low-grade ore to extract the valuable metal – $67 million worth between 1882 and 1922. At one stage it was the most extensive gold-mining operation in the world, supporting a town of 15,000 people and burrowing 2800ft below Gastineau Channel. In 1917 a serious cave-in and the subsequent flooding closed all but one shaft, and work ceased entirely by 1922, just four years before the whole place was destroyed by fire. Today most of the mine buildings have been enveloped by the regenerating alder and spruce forest, with saplings sprouting from the moldering concrete shells of buildings, hulks of old machinery rusting quietly, and several rows of pilings from long-gone wharves running out into the channel. The remains are threaded by the **Treadwell Mine Historic Trail**, a network of paths and numbered markers that are meaningless without the *Treadwell Mine Historic Trail* explanatory leaflet (50¢) available from the City Museum.

Capital Transit's Douglas **bus** runs every half-hour to downtown Douglas, from where you can wander past the Douglas boat harbor to **Sandy Beach Park**, a small strand created from the tailings from the mine. The Treadwell Mine Historic Trail starts at the southern end of the park. There are a couple of cafés in Douglas if you can't wait until you get back to Juneau, but the only real reason to stick around is to attend a performance at the Perseverance Theatre (see p.172).

Flightseeing, rafting, and kayaking

A visit to the Mendenhall Glacier only gives you a tiny sense of what lies behind the immense 1500-square-mile Juneau Icefield, which feeds close to forty glaciers, some creaking down the hills behind Juneau, others flowing the other way into Canada. The easiest and cheapest way to see all this is on a scenic plane flight with Wings of Alaska (☎789-0790, ⓦwww.wingsofalaska .com), which charges $155 for a 40-minute flight. **Helicopter flights** are an increasingly popular way to tour the area. Temsco (☎1-877/789-9501, ⓦwww .temscoair.com) offers a 55-minute Mendenhall Glacier Tour ($219), including a 25-minute glacier landing, and a 90-minute variation ($349) with two glacier landings. Coastal Helicopters (☎789-5600, ⓦwww.coastalhelicopters.com) does one-hour flyovers ($192) and 90-minute trips with glacier landing ($315), and also offers dog-sled tours ($395) involving two scenic flights sandwiching a spin across the glacier on a sled towed by six dogs. North Star Trekking (☎790-4530, ⓦwww.glaciertrekking.com) offers a helicopter flight with time spent hiking across a glacier and provides crampons and trekking poles. The gentle Walkabout ($295) gives about an hour on the ice, though you can double this on the slightly more strenuous Trek ($359) or opt for up to four hours on the Extended Trek ($459), which includes some roped ice climbing.

If you're heading to Skagway and fancy some tremendous **flightseeing** over Glacier Bay National Park (see p.176), go with Skagway Air Service (☎789-2006, ⓦwww.skagwayair.com), which will include a diversion over Glacier Bay on the scheduled flight between Juneau and Skagway ($250).

Closer to Juneau, the Mendenhall River offers the only **rafting** in these parts, with a little low-grade whitewater and a good deal of even gentler stuff with guides explaining the local natural history. Auk Ta Shaa (mid-May to Sept; $99; ☎586-8687 or 1-800/820-2628) and Alaska Travel Adventures (May–Sept; $99;

T789-0052 or 1-800/478-0052, W www.alaskaadventures.com) both run trips spending a couple of hours on the water.

Out on the Inside Passage, several opportunities exist for **kayaking**, either on guided tours or on your own, just paddling around the islands in Auke Bay with kayaks rented locally (see p.172). Alaska Travel Adventures runs gentle 3.5-hour trips around the bay (May–Sept; $85), mainly geared to cruise-ship passengers, while Auk Ta Shaa organizes six-hour trips ranging slightly further for $138. For more dedicated kayaking, go with Alaska Discovery (T1-800/586-1911), which has a good selection of multiday trips to Tracy Arm and Pack Creek (see "Around Juneau," p.173).

Eating, drinking, and entertainment

As the largest town in Southeast Alaska, not to mention the state capital, you'd expect a decent range of restaurants and bars, but this is still only a town of 30,000 and your choices are fairly limited. Most of the worthwhile places are downtown, and there's little reason to go elsewhere, except perhaps to Douglas for the Perseverance Theatre. That said, there are enough **restaurants** to keep you well fed for a few days. South Franklin and Front streets have so far resisted the downtown gentrification and retain a number of dark **bars** where back-slapping camaraderie prevails. Of these, you may find the places we've listed more convivial than most.

For **entertainment listings**, the best source is the "This Week" section of Thursday's *Juneau Empire*. One regular piece of entertainment is the free **organ recital** on Fridays at noon in the State Office Building, 333 Willoughby Ave, home to numerous Alaskan government departments and always referred to as the SOB (which locals seem to think is amusing, if not a little risqué).

Cafés and restaurants

Chan's Thai Kitchen 11280 Glacier Hwy T789-9777. No-frills eatery dishing out excellent Thai dishes for under $10. Reasonably handy for the ferry terminal, a mile to the west. Closed Sun & Mon.

Gold Room 127 N Franklin St T586-2660. One of Juneau's finest restaurants in a subdued sky-lit room in the heart of the *Baranof Hotel*, all white-linen tablecloths and refined atmosphere. Start with grilled rock shrimp skewers ($10) and follow with a seafood sample platter ($21) or pan-seared game hen with caramelized pears and onions ($21).

Heritage Café Emporium Mall, 174 S Franklin St T586-1087. About the best café in Juneau, with good espresso, lunch specials, soups, and sandwiches.

Olivia's de Mexico 222 Seward St T586-6870. Juneau's most authentic Mexican may be tucked away in a basement, but it produces excellent *mole* and *fajitas* along with the expected staples. Closed Sun.

Paradise Café 245 Marine Way. Stylish little café and bakery with excellent soups, salads, filo rolls and wraps, all made from scratch and eaten at tables in an adjacent room. A little pricey but worth it. Open for breakfast and lunch to 3pm.

Pel'Meni 2 Marine Way T463-2630. This place serves just one item, a $5 helping of the Russian dish that gives this restaurant its name. These mini-dumplings are made from spicy ground sirloin wrapped in fresh pasta dough, which is boiled and topped with hot sauce, curry powder, and cilantro – they're good any time but especially after a drinking session at one of the Front Street bars. The varied clientele also hangs out, making selections from the eclectic collection of vinyl. Daily 11.30am to around 2am.

Rainbow Foods 224 4th St T586-6476. Whole-food and organic grocery that also serves a limited selection of light lunches (Mon–Fri), including salad bar, homemade cookies, and espresso. There's also an extensive notice board full of holistic classes and massage workshops.

Silverbow Bakery 120 2nd St T586-4146. Relaxed eat-in bakery and coffee bar with big windows that, on a good day, catch the morning sun. Bagels and superb pastries bolster a menu of homemade breads used in hot and cold deli sandwiches ($6–11).

Twisted Fish Company 550 S Franklin St T463-5033. Bustling waterfront restaurant with a cosmopolitan feel, an extensive wine list, and a wide-ranging menu centered on fish and

gourmet pizzas. Salmon and halibut naturally get a high billing, whether you eat inside or out at the salmon bake on the dockside. Personal pizzas and appetizers around $8–12, main courses $18–28.
Uncle Sam's Cafeteria 2nd floor, 709 W 9th St ☏586-3430. Low-cost dining with a view, inside the Federal Building. Open for breakfast (7–10.30am; $5), then lunch including daily specials (noon–4pm; $7) such as taco salad and chicken-fried steak.
Zen In the *Goldbelt Hotel*, 51 Egan Drive ☏586-5075. Classy, modern restaurant giving an Asian twist to Alaskan cuisine – lemongrass salmon ($18) or Thai coconut curry shrimp ($20). The $9 lunch specials are well worth it.

Bars

Alaskan Hotel Bar 167 S Franklin St. Ancient bar dating back to 1913 and still exuding a raucous atmosphere, with live music most nights (especially weekends), which might be anything from funk to bluegrass, an open-mic night on Thursday, and plenty of bar propping any time.
Bergmann Hotel 434 3rd St, downtown ☏586-1690. Dark basement bar tucked up a nondescript side-street in the bowels of one of Juneau's oldest hotels. Well off the main tourist beat.

The Hanger on the Wharf Merchants Wharf ☏586-5018. Renovated, historic float-plane hanger right on the wharf, with one glass wall that gives a tremendous view of the waterfront. There are over twenty beers on tap, pool tables on the mezzanine, and a lively atmosphere, especially on weekends when there's live rock or jazz. Also serves wraps and burgers at lunch and the likes of jambalaya and halibut tacos ($10–12) at dinner.
Jaded In the *Goldbelt Hotel*, 51 Egan Drive ☏586-5075. Chic, modern bar where wine and cocktail sipping prevails over back-slapping beer swilling.

Theaters and shows

20th Century Theater 222 Front St ☏586-4055. Shows first-run movies nightly.
Gold Town Nickelodeon Theater Emporium Mall, 171 Shattuck Way ☏586-ARTS. Artsy place with showings Thurs–Sun evenings.
Perseverance Theatre 914 3rd St, Douglas ☏364-2421, ⓦwww.perseverancetheatre.org. Alaska's largest professional theater and one of the nation's foremost regional houses, presenting revisions of classic texts, cutting-edge works, and new plays by Alaskan playwrights. Paula Vogel's Pulitzer Prize-winning *The Mineola Twins* premiered here in 1996. Sadly, summer is usually a quiet time for the theater.

Listings

Banks Several with 24hr ATMs in the downtown area, including Wells Fargo, 123 Seward St (☏586-3324). There is nowhere to exchange foreign currency.
Bike rental from *Driftwood Lodge*, 435 Willoughby Ave, downtown (☏1-800/544-2239), for $15 per half-day, $25 per day.
Bookshops The most extensive selection is at Hearthside Books, either downtown at 254 Front St (☏586-1726, ⓦwww.hearthsidebooks.com) or in the Nugget Mall close to the airport (☏789-2750), the latter good for whiling away an hour between flights. Rainy Day Books, 113 N Seward St (☏463-2665, ⓦwww.juneanbooks.com), is good for new and used books.
Car rental Almost all the rental agencies are located at the airport, but most will drop off downtown. Some of the cheapest deals are with Rent-A-Wreck (☏789-4111 or 1-888/843-4111, ⓦwww.rentawreck.com), which is $40 a day plus local taxes. All offerings by Budget (☏790-1086) cost roughly $55 per day.
Climbing wall Looking for a wet-day diversion? Try the Rock Dump, 1310 Eastaugh Way (☏586-4982, ⓦwww.rockdump.com), Alaska's largest climbing

gym, which charges $10 all day until 10pm and rents gear at bargain prices. About a mile south of town along S Franklin St.
Ferries The AMHS's main ticket office is at 6858 Glacier Hwy (Mon–Fri 8am–5pm; reservations ☏465-3941, schedule info ☏465-3940).
Festivals The Alaska Folk Festival (☏364-3316, ⓦwww.alaskafolkfestival.org) in mid-April involves a week of performances, workshops, jams, and dances, mostly in Centennial Hall. The Juneau Jazz and Classics Festival (☏463-3378, ⓦwww.jazzandclassics.org) takes place during the third week of May. On July 3 Juneau sets off its fireworks to celebrate the arrival of July 4 and the ensuing parade and carnival.
Internet access The library (see opposite) has non-bookable, free-use machines with 15 & 30min sessions, plus free WiFi.
Kayak rentals Alaska Boat & Kayak (☏789-6886, ⓦwww.juneaukayak.com) rents out top-quality kayaks (single $45 a day, double $60) and skiffs with a 40-horse outboard ($160).
Laundry and showers Harbor Washboard, 1114 Glacier Ave, downtown (Mon–Fri 7.30am–9pm, Sat 9am–9pm, Sun 9am–6pm; ☏586-1133), has

a laundry facility and showers ($2). You can also shower at the Augustus Brown Swimming Pool, 1619 Glacier Ave, near the north end of Douglas Bridge (☎586-5325), which has showers for $3.25.

Left luggage No lockers downtown or at the Auke Bay AMHS terminal, but the *Juneau Hostel*, 614 Harris St (☎586-9559), will store bags.

Library The Juneau Public Library, 292 Marine Way (Mon–Thurs 11am–9pm, Fri–Sun noon–5pm; ☎586-5249), has an extensive range of books and newspapers, Internet access, and a great view of Gastineau Channel.

Medical assistance Bartlett Regional Hospital, 3260 Hospital Drive, 3 miles north of downtown (☎796-8900).

Outdoor equipment Foggy Mountain Shop, 134 N Franklin St (☎586-6780), stocks top-brand gear and unloads it at slightly inflated prices.

Pharmacy Juneau Drug Co, Front St at Seward St (Mon–Fri 9am–9pm, Sat & Sun 9am–6pm).

Post office Inside the Federal Building, 709 W 9th St (Mon–Fri 9am–5pm). The **General Delivery** zip code is 99801.

Taxes Juneau has a six percent sales tax plus a further six percent bed tax, neither included in our accommodation price codes.

Taxis Juneau Taxi & Tours ☎790-4511; Capital Cab ☎586-2772.

Travel agency US Travel, 127 N Franklin St ☎463-5446 or 1-800/478-2423, ⊛www.ustravelak.com.

Around Juneau

Though two or three days might suffice for seeing Juneau, you could easily use it as a base from which to make frequent forays into its hinterland by boat and plane. Day cruises head south to the hairline fjord of **Tracy Arm**, a vast granite and ice wonderland that also lends itself to extended exploration by kayak. When the salmon are running, brown bears find themselves sharing **Pack Creek** with humans eager to watch them gnaw on fish and fatten up for winter. Either drop in for a few hours during the day or visit by kayak and spend a couple days in the area camping nearby.

For extended trips away from Juneau, the prime destination is **Glacier Bay National Park**, around which many visitors build their entire Alaskan vacation. We cover it, along with the humpback whale-watching territory of **Point Adolphus**, in the section beginning on p.176.

Tracy Arm Fjord

If you would like to visit Glacier Bay but don't really have the time or money, consider the cost-effective eight-hour trip to Tracy Arm Fjord, which cuts

△ Tracy Arm Fjord

deeply into the Coast Mountains 45 miles south of Juneau. The glaciers may not be quite as spectacular, but the scenery is definitely on a par with its more exalted neighbor. There's never more than a mile between the sheer waterfall-fringed cliffs that frame your approach to the head of the thirty-mile-long fjord and the North Sawyer and South Sawyer glaciers. At any time these may be calving, but even if they're not there are always seals basking on the ice floes, mountain goats high up on the almost barren hills, and possibly dolphins and whales frolicking in the channels. John Muir was impressed when he visited in 1879; he said it reminded him of his beloved Yosemite, but then much of Southeast had the same effect on him.

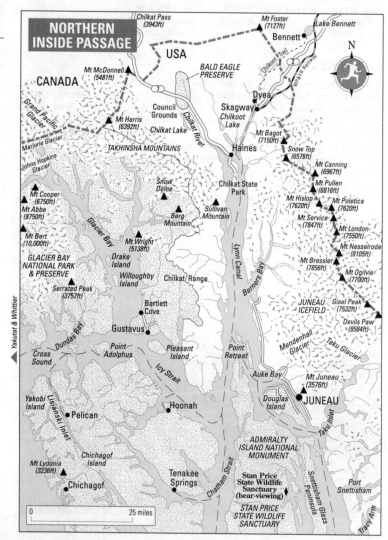

The most popular way to visit is on the Tracy Arm Fjord Glacier Cruise (mid-May to mid-Sept, 4 weekly; $148; ☎1-800/820-2628, ⓦwww.goldbelttours.com), a fast catamaran that departs from beside the downtown cruise-ship dock at 9am, returning eight hours later. For a slightly more personal touch, go with Adventure Bound Alaska (☎1-800/228-3875, ⓦwww.adventureboundalaska.com; $120), which runs a smaller, single-hulled boat from the north end of Marine Park. Being smaller, the boat can get in a little closer through the densely packed icebergs, but the single hull means it goes more slowly, extending the day from 8.30am to 6pm.

Bear-viewing at Pack Creek

Douglas Island separates Juneau from the northern tip of Admiralty Island, a hundred-mile-long landmass of rugged 4000-foot-high mountains cloaked in temperate forests known to the Tlingit as Kootznoowoo, or "fortress of the bears." There is said to be a greater concentration of brown bears here than anywhere else in the world, and despite the town of Angoon sharing the island with them, the bears outnumber the humans. That's not to say you fall over them wherever you go – there is still only one per square mile – so in an effort to guarantee a sighting, most people head straight to the Stan Price State Wildlife Sanctuary at **Pack Creek**, 27 miles south of Juneau on the east side of the island. From June to mid-September (best early July to late August) the pink and chum salmon are running and up to 25 brown bears flock to the tidal flats around the Seymore Canal and to Pack Creek itself. Hunting was banned here back in the 1930s and, in what is considered a textbook case of low-stress habituation, the bears have become used to people watching them fish. The number of float-planes landing each day does drive away some of the bears, but you can still expect to see a handful at any one time.

To help preserve this benign situation, the area has been designated for day-use only, so most people visit from Juneau on a day trip. During the bear season (June–Sept 10) you'll need a viewing **permit** (June 1 to July 5 & Aug 26 to Sept 10, $20 a day; July 6 to Aug 25, $50 a day) from the Forest Service in Juneau (see p.158), which is valid for three days. Outside these dates no permit is needed, but then there are no fish and no bears. Permits are offered from March 1, and you'll need to reserve early to choose specific dates, though four permits for each day become available only three days prior to that date. Due to the fierce competition, it is often more effective to reserve early with one of the float-plane operators, such as Ward Air (☎789-9150, ⓦwww.wardair.com) who drop you off and pick you up later that day, charging around $600 round-trip for a planeload of up to four people. For permit application, write to Admiralty National Monument, 8465 Old Dairy Rd (☎586-8800, downloadable at ⓦwww.fs.fed.us/r10/tongass/districts/admiralty/packweb/applcatn.htm).

One of the best approaches is on a kayaking tour run by Alaska Discovery (see Basics, p.34). On the one-day trip ($550), you fly in by float-plane, then kayak to Pack Creek for bear-viewing and maybe hike a mile and a half inland to the bear-viewing tower on Upper Pack Creek. The 2.5-day trip ($1095) follows the same pattern but includes two nights camped out near Pack Creek. Trips run only on certain dates and fill fast.

If you have your own boat or want to rent a kayak and paddle to Pack Creek, you'll need one of the permits described above. Kayakers need to be moderately experienced, particularly for the potentially rough crossing of Stephens Passage to Admiralty Island. Before setting off, ask for details of the hand-operated tramway, which aids your portage at Oliver Inlet and saves you having to paddle right around the Glass Peninsula. Once here, you can hang around for a few days by camping half a mile away on the east side of Windfall Island, or by staying at the Alaska State Parks' *Seymour Canal Cabin* (☎465-4563, ⓦ www.alaskastateparks.org; $35) at the south end of the portage.

Pack Creek falls within the Kootznoowoo Wilderness, a section of the **Admiralty Island National Monument**, which covers most of the island. If you miss out on a Pack Creek permit, there are several other areas where bears congregate, and the adventure of going somewhere less populated can make your visit that much more appealing. The Forest Service in Juneau can provide details of recommended destinations.

Glacier Bay National Park

When Captain George Vancouver sailed through Icy Strait in 1794, he didn't name Glacier Bay, largely because it didn't exist. Two hundred years ago this 65-mile-long branched fjord, sixty miles west of Juneau, was entirely taken up by the **Grand Pacific Glacier**, which was calving prodigious quantities of icebergs from its twenty-mile-wide, 4000-foot-high face, almost choking the strait. Today, the seaward end of Glacier Bay seldom sees bergs because the Grand Pacific has reeled back 65 miles, its retreat creating Glacier Bay in the process. Nowhere in the world have glaciers retreated so fast, a phenomenon noted by John Muir when he came up by canoe in 1879, finding it an "icy wilderness unspeakably pure and sublime." In the 85 years between

Glaciers for beginners

The existence of a glacier is always a balancing act between snow accumulation and melt rate. Snowfall dozens of feet thick at the **névé**, the source high in the mountains, gradually compacts to form clear blue ice, which feeds the glacier and flows downhill under its own weight. Meanwhile, ice is rapidly melting at the **terminal** of the glacier lower down the valley; the victor between these two processes determines whether the glacier will advance or retreat.

As the glacier moves down the valley, friction against the walls slows its sides, while its center charges headlong down the valley, creating the characteristic scalloped effect on the surface. Where a riverbed steepens, it forms a rapid; under similar conditions glaciers break up into an **icefall**, full of towering blocks of ice known as seracs, separated by crevasses.

In interior Alaska the long, slow-moving glaciers are often discolored because rock debris from the valley walls has accumulated on the surface; it's sometimes so thick that small forests can grow there. This material is deposited at the lowest point of the glacier, forming a **terminal moraine**.

But in much of Southeast and Southcentral Alaska the snowfall is so great that glaciers are still a thick tongue of ice when they reach the sea. These **tidewater glaciers** are perhaps the most spectacular of all, with faces sometimes three miles wide, rising three hundred feet or more above the water and stretching hundreds more below sea level. As the glacier creeps forward, the buoyancy of the seawater becomes insufficient to support the enormous weight of ice and chunks are **calved** off, littering the bay with bobbing white hunks. Anything rising more than fifteen feet above the water is classed as a full-fledged **iceberg**; smaller pieces are known as bergy bits; those between three and seven feet high are growlers; and anything smaller is just brash ice. Another term you'll hear bandied around on ferries and glacier cruises is a shooter, which breaks off from the underside of the glacier and bobs up to the surface.

Vancouver's and Muir's visits, the Grand Pacific had already receded 48 miles. In 1925 Calvin Coolidge designated it a National Monument; Congress upgraded its status to **Glacier Bay National Park** in 1980; and twelve years later the United Nations declared it a World Heritage Site.

All this receding ice has left behind a tranquil land of deep fjords lined by rock walls and encircled by towering mountains, in particular the 15,000-foot **Fairweather Range**, the tallest coastal mountains in the world. The various arms of Glacier Bay are fed by sixteen tidewater glaciers, a dozen of them calving on a regular basis. Huge sections of these intimidating walls of ice periodically come crashing down, captured by hundreds of video cameras onboard the cruise ships that make regular visits. In fact, if you've ever seen an image of a cruise ship dwarfed by the pure white face of a huge glacier, chances are that it was taken here in front of the **Margerie Glacier**, which flows down the slopes of Mount Fairweather. It travels so swiftly it has little time to pick up the surface rubble typical of Alaskan glaciers, making this the most pristine in the state. It shares the barren West Arm of Glacier Bay with two other glaciers: the **Johns Hopkins Glacier**, which calves so much ice that boats can seldom approach within two miles of its white cliffs; and the still-majestic remains of the Grand Pacific Glacier, which in the 1920s receded to the point where boats viewing the face from close quarters were technically in Canada. It has since advanced back into the US.

The glaciers' recession hasn't just left a strikingly beautiful landscape, it has created a living classroom for the mechanics of **plant succession** and **glacial rebound**. As the earth sheds the immense weight of the glaciers, it breathes a sigh of relief, and measurements reveal that the land is rising at a rate of an inch and a half per year. At the same time, the newly uncovered land acts as a blank canvas for progressive colonization by plant species. Near Bartlett Cove the earth was uncovered two centuries back and has a full cover of near-mature spruce forest, though the hemlocks seen elsewhere in Southeast are yet to establish themselves in any numbers.

You can see the succession process in reverse as you cruise up the bay, the spruce initially giving way to alder and cottonwoods, then stunted willows and finally the mosses and lichens that are the first to begin the colonization process. Animals have also been quick to populate the new habitat. In the water, humpback whales, porpoises, seals, and sea otters are often seen, while the shores occasionally reveal glimpses of brown and black bears, moose, mountain goats, and the colorful array of birds that have quickly made the area their home.

Over eighty percent of the park's visitors drift through on the limited number of mainstream cruise ships, while smaller numbers visit on a day cruise from Bartlett Cove and a few hardy souls make the effort of getting out there by kayak. But the action isn't just limited to the park, with worthwhile **whale-watching trips** leaving Bartlett Cove for Point Adolphus, on the south shore of Icy Strait.

Getting there, arrival, and information

A trip to Glacier Bay may well be one of the most memorable parts of your time in Alaska, but immaculate environments with almost complete solitude don't come cheap. Even a brief visit to Glacier Bay – spending perhaps one night in the settlements of either Gustavus or Bartlett Cove and one day exploring the bay either on a day cruise or by kayak – will be a minimum of $350, more likely $500. Perhaps the best **one-day package** is with Gold-belt Tours (☎1-800/820-2628), which offers round-trip flights from Juneau,

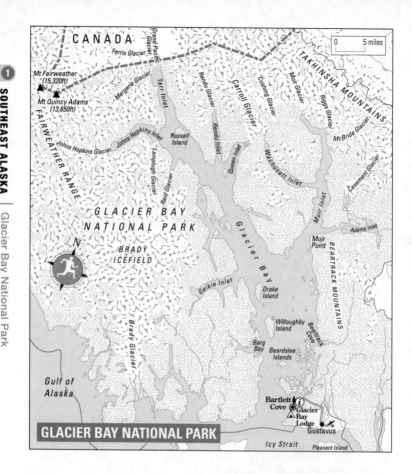

GLACIER BAY NATIONAL PARK

transfers, and the full-day cruise for $380. If money is tight, you might get a better return for your dollar by visiting Tracy Arm (see p.173), spending time around Prince William Sound, or viewing the glaciers on a flightseeing trip from Juneau, Haines, or Skagway.

The main access into Glacier Bay is from **Bartlett Cove**, home to *Glacier Bay Lodge*, a campground, a Park Service visitor center, and a dock for small cruise boats. Everything else happens ten miles away at **GUSTAVUS** (Gust-AY-vus), a thinly scattered former homesteading settlement that now boasts an airport, a ferry dock, and a host of luxury inns. There is **no entrance fee** for the park.

At one time there was a ferry service between Juneau and Gustavus, and this may run again one day, but in the meantime the only way to get to Gustavus and Bartlett Cove is to **fly**. Alaska Airlines has one thirty-minute flight from Juneau each afternoon in summer (late May to mid-Sept) from as little as $90 round-trip (though $120 is more likely). Smaller operators, such as LAB (℡789-9160, ⓦlabflying.com), charge around $60 each way between Gustavus and Juneau, but have more flights.

Arrival

On arrival you'll probably be met by someone who will take you straight to your lodge or B&B. Campers should call *Glacier Bay Lodge* to see which flights will be met by their shuttle bus. If you get stuck, hitching usually works, or call TLC Taxi (☏697-2239). Gustavus lodges usually run their guests to Bartlett Cove for the Glacier Bay cruise, kayaking companies pick up around Gustavus, and many lodges have free bicycles, but if you need a little more flexibility you can rent a car from BW Enterprises Rent-a-Car (around $60 a day; ☏697-2403).

With the limited scope for independent travel, it makes sense to consider the **inclusive packages** offered by lodges (particularly *Glacier Bay Lodge*) and kayak companies.

Information

Gustavus has no visitor center, though it is worth checking out the community website (ⓦwww.gustavus.com). At Bartlett Cove there's a **National Park visitor center**, upstairs in the *Glacier Bay Lodge* (late May to mid-Sept daily noon–8.45pm; ☏697-2661, ⓦwww.nps.gov/glba), which is a mine of general information and has some interesting natural history displays. Rangers lead daily hikes around Bartlett Cove and present several excellent **films** in the afternoon and evening (all free).

Anyone kayaking independently or staying at the campground must visit the **visitor information station**, by the dock in Bartlett Cove (late May to mid-Sept daily 7am–9pm; ☏697-2627), where you'll be put through a short orientation program.

Although there is a **post office** in Gustavus, there are **no banks** or ATMs anywhere around here.

Accommodation

The only indoor accommodation in the park is Glacier Bay Lodge at Bartlett Cove, where you'll also find a campground. Many more people stay at one of two dozen or more **lodges and B&Bs** in Gustavus, most of which cost at least $90 a night for two. Most offer packages including transport, Glacier Bay cruise, accommodation, and meals, typically starting at $600 for two days and one night.

Alaska Discovery Inn Gustavus ☏1-800/586-1911, ⓦwww.akdiscovery.com. If you are kayaking with Alaska Discovery, you'll probably be staying at this welcoming lodge with comfortable en-suite rooms, a hearty breakfast, free use of bikes, and transport to the airport. ❺

Annie Mae Lodge Gustavus ☏1-800/478-2346, ⓦwww.anniemae.com. A large house close to the Good River with attractive wood-paneled rooms, superb meals, free use of bikes, and free local transportation. Shared bath ❹, private bath ❺

Bartlett Cove Campground Bartlett Cove. Waterside first-come, first-served campground, 400 yards from the dock, with wheelbarrows to transport your gear, a warming hut, firewood, and bear-resistant food caches. There are no showers, but bag storage ($6) is available at *Glacier Bay Lodge*. Free.

Bear's Nest B&B Gustavus ☏697-2440, ⓦwww.gustavus.com/bearsnest. One of the best deals, featuring a self-contained, fully furnished circular cabin with a double bed upstairs, a single bed down, and breakfast ingredients provided. There's also a small cabin that comes with a fully-equipped kitchen but no breakfast ingredients, and a spacious and well-appointed room. You'll have to bring cooking supplies from Juneau or wander next door to the *Bear's Nest Café*. Small cabin ❹, cabin and room ❺

Budget Rentals State Dock Road ☏697-3080, ⓔmorgand@realtyagent.com. Simple, low-cost cabins beside the golf course, each with a double and three single beds plus a limited kitchen and shared bathroom and barbecue area. $60 for two people, $80 for three or more. ❷

Glacier Bay Country Inn Gustavus ☎1-800/628-0912, ⓦwww.glacierbayalaska.com. The pick of the top-end places, this lodge comes with its own airstrip and concentrates on saltwater and fly-fishing. Accommodation is either in very comfortable guestrooms in the main lodge or in one of the luxury cabins nearby; rates are around $400 a double including three wonderful meals a day. ❾

Glacier Bay Lodge Bartlett Cove ☎1-888/229 8687, ⓦwww.visitglacierbay.com. Easily the largest of the lodges hereabouts and boasting a big, cozy lounge with a large stone fireplace and a suitably stately restaurant with a great deck overlooking the cove. The rooms are comfortable, if a little uninspired, although some have views of Bartlett Cove. It is also worth considering the one night plus meals and cruise package ($395), though you still need to get yourself to Gustavus. Open mid-May to mid-Sept. Rooms ❼, water view ❽

Good River B&B Gustavus ☎697-2241, ⓦwww.glacier-bay.us. At the cheaper end of the range, this four-room lodge also has a rustic cabin nearby, serves a wholesome continental breakfast, and has free use of bikes. Rooms ❺, cabin ❹

Exploring the park

It would be perverse to come out this way and not explore Glacier Bay National Park, most easily done on the day-cruise run from Bartlett Cove, which visits several of the most spectacular glaciers. Sitting on a boat all day and viewing from a distance is a little limited, so there's a lot to be said for going kayaking, poking around little bays, investigating narrow fjords and camping out on rocky beaches. After a few days of that you'll welcome a return to the comforts and easy pace of Gustavus.

Cruises and kayaking

The principal way of experiencing the park's wonders is the **Glacier Bay day cruise** (8hr; $170), a large launch that leaves Bartlett Cove at 7.30am and makes its way through miles of bergs to the faces of the Margerie and Grand Pacific glaciers. There's an NPS ranger on board and lunch is provided; book through *Glacier Bay Lodge*.

Everyone else goes kayaking which, if you're up for it, has to be the finest way to see Glacier Bay. **Guided day-trips** don't get anywhere near the glaciers, instead sticking close to Bartlett Cove or Gustavus, perhaps venturing into the **Beardslee Islands**, a small archipelago immediately north of Bartlett Cove. Six-hour tours usually involve instruction for the small group followed by gentle paddling, learning something of the flora, fauna, and tidal patterns while hoping to catch sight of moose, black bears, deer, sea otters, and more. The main kayak companies (see opposite) also do multiday trips further up the bay

Hiking around Bartlett Cove

In the entire 3.3 million acres of Glacier Bay National Park, the only formed trails are three gentle affairs around *Glacier Bay Lodge* at Bartlett Cove.

Bartlett Lake Trail (8 miles round-trip; 3–5hr; 100ft ascent). A half- to full-day hike through temperate rainforest, gradually climbing moraine to reach the solitude of Bartlett Lake.

Bartlett River Trail (4 miles round-trip; 1hr 30min to 3hr; negligible ascent). Lovely, popular hike along the intertidal lagoon, where you might see shorebirds, waterfowl, and even bears.

Forest Loop Trail (1-mile loop; 30min–1hr; negligible ascent). A delightful stroll through hemlock forest, past several small ponds and the campground, much of it on a boardwalk.

into glacier-calving territory; five days with float-plane access is likely to cost around $2500.

If you are confident about camping for several days in potentially inclement weather, you may want to **go it alone** with rental kayaks. No prior kayaking experience is needed, but you will need to attend one of the park rangers' orientation programs at the visitor information station at Bartlett Cove (see p.179). You'll also want to bring all your food supplies from Juneau.

Again, the Beardslee Islands make a good and easily accessible destination with excellent beach camping, plenty of wildlife for the patient, and gentle, sheltered paddling with only the tidal currents (which need constant attention) to contend with. More ambitious paddlers will prefer to be dropped off close to the more distant sections of Glacier Bay where motorized traffic is banned. To avoid potentially hazardous open-water crossings, organize transport with the Glacier Bay day cruise, which sets kayakers down at several designated locations in the upper reaches of Glacier Bay – exact locations are frequently changed to avoid excessive impact on particular sites. The charge for kayaker drop-off or pickup is $95, perfect if you want to do a one-way drop-off and then paddle back to Bartlett Cove over a week or so.

Alaska Discovery (☎ 1-800/586-1911, ⓦ www.akdiscovery.com) has permits to go into Glacier Bay and runs full-day ($140), half-day ($90), and two-hour evening paddles ($70) from Bartlett Cove. The Glacier Bay trip (5 days, $2195; 8 days, $2395) travels much deeper into the park, and there's also a three-day trip ($895) specifically aimed at humpback whale-watching around Point Adolphus.

Spirit Walker (☎ 1-800/529-2537, ⓦ www.seakayakalaska.com) conducts very worthwhile trips elsewhere in the area, mostly out into Icy Strait from the Gustavus Dock. Rare one-day trips cost $135 and four-day trips are $1270–1580, depending on numbers.

To go at your own pace, **rent kayaks** from Glacier Bay Sea Kayaks (☎ 697-2257, ⓦ www.glacierbayseakayaks.com) at Bartlett Cove; a fiberglass double costs $80 a day and a single is $40, reducing to $50/$35 for two- to nine-day rentals. Sea Otter Kayak (☎ 697-3007, ⓦ www .he.net/~seaotter) also does rentals (double $50 a day, single $40) and delivers to both Gustavus beach and Bartlett Cove.

Gustavus

Glacier Bay is very much the area's trump card, but **GUSTAVUS** can be a wonderfully peaceful spot with none of the frenetic activity engendered by cruise ship and major ferry arrivals. Unusually for Southeast Alaska, the area has a very spacious feel, with plenty of flat ground on an alluvial fan, cut by a couple of meandering tidal rivers. There's very little specific to

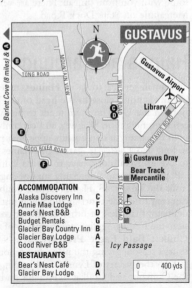

ACCOMMODATION	
Alaska Discovery Inn	C
Annie Mae Lodge	F
Bear's Nest B&B	D
Budget Rentals	G
Glacier Bay Country Inn	B
Glacier Bay Lodge	A
Good River B&B	E
RESTAURANTS	
Bear's Nest Café	D
Glacier Bay Lodge	A

see, but it is a great place to simply hang out at your lodge, perhaps borrowing a bike or going for a stroll in the evening. You might wander down to the small boat harbor by the Salmon River or past the **Gustavus Dray**, a modern gas station beautifully fashioned in 1930s style.

Aside from the Glacier Bay cruises and kayaking, there are also a few Gustavus-based activities to tempt those with more time on their hands. Even those who seldom play **golf** might fancy a round at Gustavus's nine-hole Mount Fairweather Golf Course, on State Dock Road, where you just stick your $15 in the honesty box, plus another few dollars if you need to borrow one of the bags of clubs leaning up against the shed. You can tee off with the setting sun glinting off the distant snowcap of Mount Fairweather, but remember that respecting the wildlife is one of the course rules, even if a moose blocks the fairway or a raven steals your ball.

And, as always, you'll have no shortage of offers to take you fishing.

Eating and drinking

The *Glacier Bay Lodge* offers the only **eating** in Bartlett Cove, with buffet breakfasts ($13), burgers and sandwiches all day ($10), and nicely prepared dinners strong on Alaskan seafood (mains $15–25).

In Gustavus dining mainly centers on the lodge restaurants (usually open to non-guests if booked in advance), which try to outdo each other and offer some of the best eating in Southeast. *Annie Mae Lodge* (see p.179) does superb three-course homestyle dinners for around $35; meals at *Glacier Bay Country Inn* are possibly even more outstanding for a similar price. The only stand-alone **café** worth its salt is the *Bear's Nest Café* (call ☎679-2440 to make sure they are open), good for coffee, cakes, and home-baked bread. They also prepare a limited range of delicious meals from chicken burgers ($9) to Dungeness crab ($24), using organic ingredients and vegetables from the garden. Several of the larger lodges are licensed to serve **alcohol**, but smaller places aren't, and no stores sell it in Gustavus, so if you fancy a glass of wine with your meal, bring some with you from Juneau. There are very limited **groceries** at the Bear Track Mercantile on State Dock Road.

Haines and around

The small service town of **Haines**, ninety miles north of Juneau, occupies a narrow isthmus close to the head of the **Lynn Canal**, the longest and deepest fjord in the US. The town tends to be overshadowed by its more immediately arresting neighbor, Skagway, and certainly sees far fewer cruise ships, but in its own quiet way it's an equally appealing place to spend a few days. Indeed, not so long ago, *Outside* magazine put Haines on its list of top ten "outdoors" towns to live in if you don't have to earn a living.

Populated by an interesting mix of rugged individualists and urban escapees from the Lower 48, Haines leads a double life, constantly vacillating between catering to cruise tourism and being just a sleepy small town. Its history is less dramatic than that of other Southeast communities, and its only major attraction, the mind-boggling congregation of up to four thousand bald eagles in the **Chilkat Bald Eagle Preserve** each November, happens well outside of the tourist season, giving the place an unspoilt authenticity.

With the waters of Lynn Canal lapping its shores and glaciers spilling out of the Chilkoot and Chilkat mountains on both sides, its location is nothing short

HAINES

RESTAURANTS & BARS

Bamboo Room	2
Chilkat Restaurant	1
The Commanders Room	H
Fireweed	6
Fogcutter Bar	3
Haines Brewing Company	5
Mountain Market & Café	4

Battery Point Trail (1.5 miles), Mt Riley Trails (1.5 miles), Portage Cove Campground & ❶ (1 mile)

Skagway (35min)

Portage Cove

Small Boat Harbor

Lookout Park

Chilkat Cruises dock

Tlingit Park

N

Airport (3 miles), Bald Eagle Preserve (20 miles), & Canada (40 miles)

Fairgrounds

Dalton City set

Tsirku Canning Company

Hammer Museum

Howser's Supermarket

Library

Sheldon Museum

Bald Eagle Foundation

Sockeye Cycles

Chilkat Tribal House

Alaska Indian Arts

Storytelling Theater Show

ACCOMMODATION

Beach Roadhouse	H
Bear Creek Cabins and Hostel	I
Captain's Choice Motel	B
Fort Seward B&B	G
The Guardhouse	E
Hotel Hälsingland	F
Mountain View Motel	C
Port Chilkoot Camper Park	D
Summer Inn B&B	A

Chilkat Inlet

Chilkat State Park Campground (7 miles) & Seduction Point Trail

❶ (1 mile)

0   500 yds

of spectacular, particularly on a clear day when some of the town's hiking trails reveal wonderfully long views.

History hasn't completely passed Haines by, either; its days as a military fort protecting the US border from marauding Canadians left behind **Fort William H. Seward**, with its row of green-trimmed white mansions lending a certain weight to what would otherwise be a typically ragged Alaskan townscape.

Some history

Before the arrival of Europeans, this site at the mouth of the Chilkat River protected access to the Chilkat Valley, one of the very few glacier-free corridors to the interior. Chilkat Tlingit fiercely guarded their trading rights along the route, setting themselves up as middlemen between the Russian, American, and British traders along the coast and the Athabascans of the interior. This relationship continued into the early 1880s, but as the Klondike gold rush picked up speed, one Jack Dalton decided to ignore traditional trading rights along the route and took it upon himself to charge prospectors a toll to use the Chilkat Pass. No formal trading treaties existed, and the lack of a well-defined border with Canada led to considerable unrest at local and diplomatic levels.

Into this scene stepped the US military, which chose Haines for the site of a new fort in 1903. The army's presence soon calmed things down, and the fort never saw any military action. Troops grew bored, and Haines became one of the least sought-after postings, though prospects improved during World War II, when the fort played an important role as a logistical base in the construction of the Haines Highway over the Chilkat Pass to the newly built Alaska Highway. Connection to the North American highway system didn't radically affect the town's fortunes, however, and Haines has since bumbled along, surviving off fishing and, more recently, tourism.

Arrival, information, and getting around

In summer frequent AMHS **ferries** (℡766-2113) make a daily run from Juneau to Haines, with connection to Skagway, an hour up the Lynn Canal. The boats – both traditional and fast catamarans – dock at the terminal five miles north of downtown Haines. If you've booked accommodation, you'll probably be met. There is currently only one taxi company, Haines Shuttles and Tours (℡766-3138), which has been known to grossly overcharge the expected $10 per person fare into town; agree on the fare before getting in.

From Skagway you'll find it quicker and more flexible (though fractionally more expensive) to travel with Chilkat Cruises & Tours (℡1-888/766-2103, Ⓦwww.chilkatcruises.com; reservations recommended), which runs a passenger-only **fast ferry** (mid-May to mid-Sept, 3–12 daily, 35min; $25 one-way, $45 round-trip) to the shuttle dock near Fort Seward.

Drivers can reach Haines along the 151-mile Haines Highway, which runs south from Haines Junction, Yukon, on the Alaska Highway, and crosses from Canada into the US (for immigration details see box, p.190). Currently there are **no buses** plying the route.

Although Alaska Airlines doesn't fly to Haines' tiny **airport**, three miles north of town on Haines Highway, you can get here with Skagway Air Service, 211 Willard St (℡766-3233, Ⓦwww.skagwayair.com), from Skagway ($50 one-way, $85 round-trip) and Juneau ($95/$175). LAB (℡766-2222) flies to and from Gustavus ($170/$300).

Information

The **visitor center**, 122 2nd Ave (June to mid-Sept Mon–Fri 8am–7pm, Sat & Sun 9am–6pm; mid-Sept to May Mon–Fri 8am–5pm; ℡1-800/458-3579, Ⓦwww.haines.ak.us), has material on everything you need to know about the district, including campgrounds and Forest Service cabins and trails. They also stock the free *Haines Vacation Planner* booklet, the *Haines Visitor's Guide* newspaper, and the *History and Walking Tour* leaflet for Fort Seward.

Getting around and tours

If you are staying close to town, you can walk to most of the places you're likely to be interested in, though having your own transport opens up the fabulous road-accessible wilderness that's close at hand and provides access to the Chilkat Bald Eagle Preserve. **Bikes** can be rented from Sockeye Cycle Co, 24 Portage St (℡766-2869, Ⓦwww.cyclealaska.com), which charges $12 for two hours, $20 per half-day, and $30 per eight-hour day, with discounts offered for two- and three-day rentals. **Cars** can be rented from Eagle's Nest Rental Car (℡1-800/354-6009, Ⓦwww.alaskaeagletours.com), which charges $45 a day, plus 35¢ a mile after the first hundred. The *Captain's Choice Motel* (see opposite) has unlimited-mileage vehicles for around $70 a day. Note that Canadian citizens are not allowed to drive vehicles rented outside Canada into Canada; all others should have no trouble driving rental vehicles through the Yukon.

When there's a cruise ship in town, Haines explodes with a couple of dozen companies keen to take you on **tours** of some description, most of which are entertaining and educational enough, but overpriced and a bit staged. Alaska Nature Tours (☎766-2876, ⊛www.kcd.com/aknature) offers two good alternatives: a nature tour (several daily; 3hr; $60), which goes either to Chilkoot Lake or the Chilkat Bald Eagle Preserve, and the Chilkat Rainforest Nature Hike (4hr; $70), which takes you to the Battery Point trailhead for an educational walk with naturalists.

Sockeye Cycle Co runs a number of easy to moderate **bicycle tours**: the Chilkoot Lake Bicycle Tour (3hr; $85) dawdles for eight miles around some flat dirt roads that are good for wildlife-viewing; Chilkat Bicycle Tour (1hr 30min; $45) is a little more strenuous, with the emphasis on local history; Chilkat Pass Cycle Tour (full day; $127) is tougher again and heads up into the Yukon's Tatshenshini/Alsek Provincial Park, with an overnight camping option ($380).

Accommodation

Though Haines has no real luxury hotels, there is a reasonable selection of mid-range **places to stay** as well as a welcoming hostel. For some reason, many of the hotels and B&Bs have an overly casual feel, but the hosts manage to carry the day either by going out of their way to help, or by just being entertaining characters. As an incentive to visit, during the bald eagle-watching season (mid-Oct to Jan) prices drop by a third and the *Captain's Choice Motel* does a room and rental-car deal. There is also an abundance of excellent campgrounds, the best of which we've listed below.

Hotels, motels, and B&Bs

Beach Roadhouse Beach Road, a mile south of Fort Seward ☎1-866/736-3060, ⊛www.beachroadhouse.com. Attractive cluster of buildings in a quiet forest setting offering spacious rooms with kitchenette and fully self-contained cabins. Free ferry pickups and low-cost car rental. Cabins ⑥, rooms ④

Captain's Choice Motel 108 2nd Ave ☎766-3111 or 1-800/478-2345, ⊛www.capchoice.com. The nicest and most modern of Haines' motels – although not the cheapest – with forty comfortable rooms and suites, featuring fridge, coffeemaker, and cable TV, and a great view across the fjord from the sun deck. Jacuzzi suite ⑦, standard suites ⑥, rooms ⑤

Fort Seward B&B 1 Officer's Row ☎1-800/615-6676, ⊛www.fortsewardbnb.com. Engaging B&B in what used to be the Chief Surgeon's house in Fort Seward, a three-story clapboard affair with a great veranda out front. There are courtesy ferry transfers, free use of basic bikes, a hearty breakfast included, and a range of rooms. Rooms ⑤, shared bath ④

The Guardhouse Fort Seward Drive ☎1-866/290-7445, ⊛www.alaskaguardhouse.com. Welcoming gay-run B&B with a range of rooms including one with a full kitchen (⑤). Everyone has access to the indoor hot tub, and there are

a couple of friendly dogs. Shared bath ③, private bath ④

Hotel Hälsingland 13 Fort Seward Drive ☎1-800/542-6363, ⊛www.hotelhalsingland.com. Though no longer the *grande dame* of Haines' accommodation scene, this renovated hotel in converted Fort Seward houses is once again a fine place to stay. Modernized rooms come with TV and phone and some still have original features; ask for one with a clawfoot bath, an original fireplace, or just a good view (though none has all three). Private bath ⑤, shared bath ③

Mountain View Motel 57 Mud Bay Rd ☎766-2900 or 1-800/478-2902, ⊛www.mtviewmotel.com. Nine comfortable rooms with cable TV and free coffee; most also feature functional kitchenettes. ④

Summer Inn B&B 117 2nd Ave ☎766-2970, ⊛www.summerinnbnb.com. Immaculately kept and nicely decorated downtown B&B with shared-bath rooms, some with sea views and all including a good cooked breakfast. It has a very homey feel with clawfoot baths, quilts, and fresh flowers. ④

Camping and hostels

Bear Creek Cabins and Hostel Just over a mile south of Fort Seward on Small Tract Rd ☎766-2259, ⊛bearcreekcabinsalaska.com. This small collection of cabins – a couple of which function as single-sex dorms – makes up for its inconvenient location with a coin-op laundry, a well-equipped kitchen, and no lockout or curfew. Rates in the two dorms are $18, cabins cost $48 for two, and there's camping ($12 for one, $14 for two), which includes use of the hostel facilities. May–Oct. ●

Chilkat State Park 8 miles south of Haines on Mud Bay Rd. Thirty first-come, first-served spaces for tents and RVs, with three beachside tent sites, pump water, toilets, and a summertime campground host, in a beautiful setting near the south end of the Haines Peninsula, looking west towards the Takhinsha Mountains and the Davidson and Rainbow glaciers. $10.

Chilkoot Lake State Recreation Site Off Lutak Rd, 11 miles north of downtown. Fairly large site for RVs and tents, with a location beside the Dolly Varden-rich Chilkoot Lake, pump water, toilets, and a boat ramp. First-come, first-served. $10.

Port Chilkoot Camper Park Mud Bay Rd beside Fort Seward ☎1-800/542-6363, ⓦwww .hotelhalsingland.com. The best of the full-hookup sites ($25), right in the heart of things but still peacefully located among the spruce trees. Also suitable for dry RV camping ($16) and tents ($10). Pay-showers and a laundry on site.

Portage Cove State Recreation Site Beach Rd, half a mile southeast of Fort Seward. A small first-come, first-served tent-only site designed for backpackers and cyclists only. It's right by the beach and has great views and potable water. No overnight parking. $5.

Salmon Run RV Campground Lutak Rd, 7 miles north of downtown ☎723-4229, ⓦwww.salmon-runadventures.com. Wooded RV park two miles north of the AMHS ferry dock, with dry camping ($14), camping cabins ($55–65), and showers ($2), but no hookups.

The town and around

Much of the early prosperity of Haines was founded on the half-dozen canneries that sprouted along the coast nearby. The only way you can get a sense of what went on is to visit the **Tsirku Canning Company**, 422 Main St at 5th Ave (roughly daily, times vary according to cruise-ship schedule, ask at the visitor center; $10; ☎766-3474, ⓦwww.cannerytour.com), an authentic canning line briefly operated for tours to illustrate the process. Rescued from an abandoned cannery in Kodiak in the 1990s, the line is now fired up to produce empty cans. The demonstration is followed by a ten-minute video.

Just down the street is Haines' one essential indoor sight, the ⚔ **Sheldon Museum & Cultural Center**, 11 Main St (mid-May to mid-Sept Mon–Fri

△ Haines, at the foot of towering peaks

10am–5pm, Sat & Sun 1–4pm, extended when cruise ships are in port; mid-Sept to mid-May daily except Sat 1–4pm; $3; ℡766-2366, ⓦwww .sheldonmuseum.org), which does a great job of showing how Haines fits into its Chilkat environment and the wider Tlingit world. In few other places (if any) can you see such fine examples of the distinctive yellow and black Chilkat blanket in Wolf, Raven, and Killer-Whale designs, as well as an intriguing example trimmed with pearl buttons and small "coppers." There are also bent-wood boxes superbly carved from a single cedar plank made pliable by steaming with seaweed and hot rocks. Look, too, for the Tlingit armor, comprised of a moose-hide shirt with wooden slatted breastplate plus a thick wooden collar and wooden hat, the two elements merging to leave just a narrow slit unprotected. When threatened by some projectile, the warrior's natural reaction is to duck his head down between his shoulders, thereby closing this gap. For ceremonial headgear it is hard to beat the Murrelet Hat, which is loosely dated to 1740 but may be as much as a hundred years older. The bird figure atop the hat moves rhythmically when its wearer dances, a ceremony performed a few years ago when the hat was repatriated from a Lower 48 private collection. Also worth a look is the small Tsimshian box made from porcupine quills as well as the excellent artworks for sale in the store. Downstairs, there is less diverting coverage of Fort Seward and town life.

Across the street the **Hammer Museum**, 108 Main St (Mon–Fri 10am–5pm; $3; ℡766-2374, ⓦwww.hammermuseum.org), spins a surprisingly interesting tale of the development of this most basic of tools, with some 1400 hammers from the American colonial era to the present.

A stroll along the typically bustling Beach Road and up through Tlingit Park brings you to the home of the **American Bald Eagle Foundation**, 113 Haines Hwy at 2nd Ave (May–Sept daily 10am–6pm; Oct–April call for hours; $3; ℡766-3094, ⓦwww.baldeagles.org), a nonprofit organization dedicated to maintaining the sanctity of the Chilkat Bald Eagle Preserve. Their public face is this wildlife museum, essentially just one large room with stuffed specimens of over 180 species found in the immediate vicinity – bears, moose, seals, sea lions, mountain goats, even lynx. It's not particularly exciting but some enjoy seeing such creatures up close and danger-free.

A couple of hundred yards south is **Fort William H. Seward**, less a fort than a large, sloping, grassy rectangle commonly known as the Parade Ground, which is surrounded by a dozen grand houses. It was established in 1903 in response to the general lawlessness of the gold-rush era and territorial disputes with Canada. With the limited resources at their disposal, the army fashioned a formal military outpost that seems more California than Alaska – rows of huge, white-clapboard houses with shingle roofs and broad verandahs. The Canadian threat receded, and by the end of World War II the fort had outlived its usefulness. Fortunately, five war veterans and their families bought all 85 surplus buildings and proceeded to renovate them. Most are now put to good use as B&Bs, hotels, and condominiums, but you can wander around outside, equipped with the free *History and Walking Tour* leaflet from the visitor center.

At the far southeast corner of the Parade Ground, a former hospital now operates as **Alaska Indian Arts** (Mon–Fri 9am–5pm and for cruise ships; free; ℡766-2160), with a gallery for locally produced sculpture, photos, and carving, and a back room where you can watch and chat with carvers as they work on huge totem poles. The center of the Parade Ground is dominated by the replica **Chilkat Tribal House**, used for the Chilkat Dancers Storytelling (see p.189).

In 1989 Haines was chosen as the location for the filming of Jack London's *White Fang*. A set of Dalton City – really just one short section of street – was created and later moved to the fairgrounds where it remains, partly put to use with a couple of shops and a microbrewery (see p.189).

Haines doesn't just brew beer: Great Land Wines (☎766-2698, ⌨www.greatlandwines.com) makes its own wines from just about anything that will grow – rhubarb, strawberries, blueberries, rose petals, dandelions, even fireweed – and sells the product around town. Call for a tour and free tasting.

Chilkat Bald Eagle Preserve

The heralded annual congregation of bald eagles occurs at the "Council Grounds" in the **Chilkat Bald Eagle Preserve**, around twenty miles north of town along the Haines Highway. Visit between early October and January (especially Nov) and you'll see the world's largest gathering of bald eagles, perhaps four thousand, and up to two dozen in a single cottonwood tree, all here to feed on the extremely late run of chum salmon. By this time of year, most salmon rivers in Alaska are frozen and the fish long gone, but here water collects in alluvial gravels to form an underwater reservoir during the summer and, over time, percolates back into the river to keep it from freezing. The fish come to breed, the eagles come to eat them, and the people come armed with cameras and binoculars. The only problem is that, if you come at any other time of year, there really isn't a great deal to see. You might spot a few resident eagles, but you can see a handful of bald eagles any day of the week in coastal Alaska – so there is little point in making a special journey.

Around the second weekend in November, the American Bald Eagle Foundation promotes the five-day **Bald Eagle Festival** (☎766-3094, ⌨www.baldeaglefestival.org), a series of photographic workshops, naturalist-guided

Hikes around Haines

Haines is blessed with several good trails right on its doorstep. The following hikes are all discussed more fully in the free *Haines is for Hikers* leaflet available from the visitor center.

Battery Point Trail (4 miles round-trip; 2hr; negligible ascent). Shoreline walk from the end of Beach Road, just south of Fort Seward, to Kelgaya Point. It initially parallels the beach through spruce, then traverses meadows to headland where you are free to camp for up to two weeks.

Mount Riley Trails (8 miles round-trip; 4–5hr; 1760ft ascent). A forest and muskeg walk to the summit of Mount Riley, starting about two-thirds of the way along the Battery Point Trail. By using one of several different routes down you can turn it into a long and varied day out, walking all the way from town.

Mount Ripinski Trail (10 miles round-trip; 5–7hr; 3650ft ascent). An exhausting but very worthwhile all-day undertaking, following the distinctive skyline ridge to the north of town. Pick a clear day to get the best views, and if you want to avoid hiking through patches of snow, don't even consider it until late July. Experienced hikers can avoid having to retrace their steps by continuing beyond the North Peak of Mount Ripinski and following the exposed ridgetop Skyline Trail to Peak 3920, from where you can descend to 7 Mile Saddle and the Haines Highway. This extended hike takes ten hours; you'll finish about ten miles from town, so either arrange for a lift, or get down early enough to hitch.

Seduction Point Trail (13.6 miles round-trip; 8–10hr; negligible ascent). Long but relatively easy beach and forest walk from Chilkat State Park (see "Camping," p.186) to Seduction Point, occasionally walking below the high-tide line (consult tide tables before starting). Camping is permitted along the route so you can make it an overnighter, and the mountain and forest scenery is gorgeous.

excursions, and the like that takes place during the greatest gathering of eagles.

The preserve starts nine miles north of Haines and runs for thirty miles along the highway, but the main interpretive exhibits and the best viewing are around 21 miles north of Haines. During the summer, several of the city tours visit the Bald Eagle Preserve, but many people prefer to see the area from the water on a raft. There's no whitewater, so these are very much **float trips** specializing in a pleasant morning or afternoon looking for a few bald eagles and other wildlife along the shore. The very professional Chilkat Guides (T766-2491, W www.raftalaska.com) runs half-day trips (early May to late Sept; $79). Chilkat Guides also offers major multiday expeditions on the wild Alsek and Tatshenshini rivers to the north (see Basics, p.32).

Eating, drinking, and entertainment

Considering its diminutive size, Haines has a decent offering of restaurants and cafés (at least in summer, anyway), with a number of good places both downtown and around Fort Seward. **Groceries** are best sought at Howser's Supermarket at 211 Main St.

Bars tend to be straightforward drinking joints with little sophistication, though for something cultural you could attend the Chilkat Dancers' **Storytelling Theater Show** (generally when cruise ships are in; $10; T766-2540), with dances and tales based on Chilkat life and legends. It takes place in the Tribal House in the Fort Seward's Parade Ground.

While here you should try to sample some birch syrup, a poor relation to its maple-sourced cousin, that's tapped from local trees and is available in many town gift shops.

Bamboo Room 11 2nd Ave near Main T766-2800. Standard diner always popular for its well-prepared meals (especially the locally caught halibut and chip dinner, $18) and fresh-baked pies.

Chilkat Restaurant and Bakery 5th Ave at Dalton St T766-3653. A great spot for baked goods with an espresso, or more substantial fare. They do everything from tasty breakfasts, salads, and halibut sandwiches to regular Thai lunches for $10, all beautifully cooked.

The Commanders Room In the *Hotel Hälsingland*, 13 Fort Seward Drive T766-2000. Haines' finest dining in convivial surroundings with the chance to sample the likes of blackened tiger prawns with cilantro pita bread ($12) followed by braised lamb shank ($20) or duck breast marinated in cilantro and soy ($19).

Fireweed Restaurant Building 37, Blacksmith Rd T766-3838. Fine restaurant, only open in the evenings when this convivial, wood-floored place dishes up the likes of mushroom ravioli ($18) and grilled mahi mahi ($21). Closed Sun & Mon.

Fogcutter Bar 122 Main St. Favorite late-night drinking hole for locals and visitors, with pool tables and sports on TV.

Haines Brewing Company Southeast Alaska Fairgrounds T766-3823. Local microbrewery producing four mostly English-style bottled ales for $10 a half-gallon or on draft at the *Fogcutter Bar*. Closed Sun.

Mountain Market & Café 151 3rd Ave at Haines Hwy T766-3340. Combined natural-food grocery and espresso bar (with coffee roasted on site) that's one of the best places in town for a $6 bagel breakfast, a $7 tortilla wrap (the falafel is especially good), or just a muffin with your mocha.

Listings

Banks First National Bank, 1st Ave at Main St, has an ATM.

Bookshop The Babbling Book, 225 Main St (T766-3356), is the best in town.

Festivals The Alaska Craft Beer and Homebrew Festival takes place in the third week of May

(T766-2476); cyclists racing in the 160-mile Kluane to Chilkat International Bicycle Relay descend on Haines on the Sat nearest the summer solstice in late June; there are the usual parades and fireworks for the Fourth of July; and the cookouts, crafts, and log-rolling of the Southeast State

Crossing the border

Those traveling on into Canada, or continuing to northern Alaska through the Yukon, need to be aware that **Canadian border controls** are no less strict just because you are in transit. Everyone should carry a passport, including North Americans, who from 2007 on will probably find that neither a birth certificate nor driver's license will do. You are also supposed to carry sufficient funds to cover your expenses while in Canada and, although $200 is recommended, they'll let you in with a lot less than this (a credit card will often do the trick). As long as you look reasonably tidy, you probably won't even be asked.

The Klondike Highway border between Skagway and Fraser, BC, is open around the clock in summer and daily 7am–11pm in winter; if in doubt call US customs (☎983-2325) or Canadian customs in Fraser (☎867/821-4111). The Haines Highway crossing is open around the clock when Alaska-bound, but only 7am–11pm (Alaska time) when Canada-bound.

Fair (⊛www.seakfair.org) take place at the end of July along with the Bald Eagle Music Festival, which draws blues and bluegrass players from all over the state. The annual highlight is November's Bald Eagle Festival (see p.188).
Internet access Free at the library (see below).
Laundry and showers The Fort Chilkoot Camper Park has public coin-op showers (min 50¢) and washing machines (7am–9pm).
Library The excellent Haines Public Library, 103 3rd Ave (Mon & Tues 10am–9pm, Wed & Thurs

noon–9pm, Fri 10am–6.30pm, Sat & Sun 12.30–4.30pm), has free Internet access.
Medical assistance Haines Medical Center, 131 1st Ave ☎766-2521.
Post office Haines Hwy opposite Tlingit Park (Mon–Fri 8.30am–5pm, Sat 1–3pm). The **General Delivery** zip code is 99827.
Taxes Haines imposes a 5.5 percent sales tax and an additional 4 percent bed tax, not included in our quoted accommodation prices.

Skagway and around

The northernmost Inside Passage stop on the AMHS ferries, **SKAGWAY** ranks as one of the best-preserved gold-rush towns in the US, a tiny kernel of century-old buildings that has a history to match. Throw in the superb **White Pass and Yukon Route** mountain train trip, a relatively dry climate, and the opportunity to emulate the Klondike gold prospectors hiking the challenging **Chilkoot Trail** (see box, p.200), and you've the makings of an enormously popular tourist destination.

But even when suitably forewarned, most people arrive unprepared for a place where, on a normal summer day, four or five huge boats will be moored at the foot of Broadway disgorging up to eight thousand passengers into a town with a year-round population of only eight hundred. In fact, there are now ten times more people visiting Skagway each year than there were coming through during the Klondike gold rush, and it is not unusual to have the buzz of five choppers and assorted fixed-wing planes in your ears. Still, for most, the pleasures far outweigh the downsides.

This narrow, steep-sided valley at the mouth of the Skagway River was known to the Chilkoot Tlingit as Shgagweí, meaning "wind-ruffled water," though that didn't stop the town springing up overnight to satisfy the needs of stampeders bound for the Klondike. Having grown from one cabin to a town of twenty thousand in three months during 1897, Skagway, rife with disease and desperado violence, won the reputation of "hell on earth." The town, which boasted over

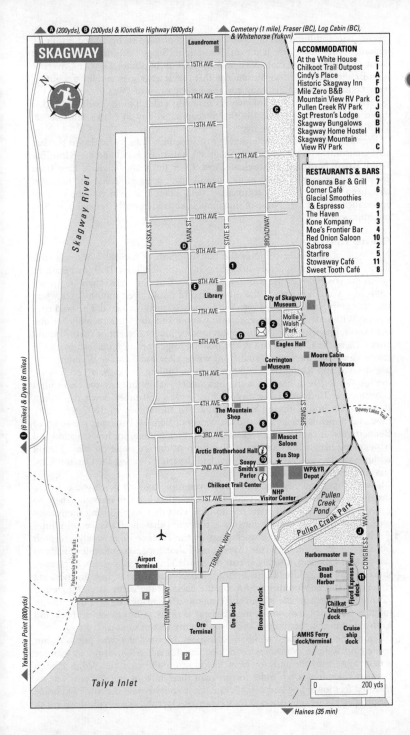

SKAGWAY

▲ **Ⓐ** (200yds), **Ⓑ** (200yds) & Klondike Highway (600yds) ▲ Cemetery (1 mile), Fraser (BC), Log Cabin (BC), & Whitehorse (Yukon)

Laundromat

15TH AVE

14TH AVE

13TH AVE

Ⓒ

12TH AVE

11TH AVE

10TH AVE

Ⓓ

9TH AVE

①

8TH AVE

Ⓔ
Library

City of Skagway Museum

7TH AVE

Ⓕ **②**
Mollie Walsh Park

Ⓖ
6TH AVE

Eagles Hall

Moore Cabin
Moore House

Corrington Museum

5TH AVE

⑥ **③** **④**

⑤

4TH AVE
The Mountain Shop

⑦

⑨ **⑧**

3RD AVE
Ⓗ

Mascot Saloon

Arctic Brotherhood Hall *i*

Soapy Smith's Parlor *i*

⑩

Bus Stop ★

WP&YR Depot

2ND AVE

Chilkoot Trail Center

1ST AVE

NHP Visitor Center

Pullen Creek Pond

Pullen Creek Park

Ⓙ

Airport Terminal

Harbormaster

Small Boat Harbor

Fjord Express Ferry dock

⑪

Chilkat Cruises dock

Ore Terminal

Broadway Dock

Ore Dock

AMHS Ferry dock/terminal

Cruise ship dock

Taiya Inlet

0   200 yds

▼ Haines (35 min)

ACCOMMODATION

At the White House	E
Chilkoot Trail Outpost	I
Cindy's Place	A
Historic Skagway Inn	F
Mile Zero B&B	D
Mountain View RV Park	C
Pullen Creek RV Park	J
Sgt Preston's Lodge	G
Skagway Bungalows	B
Skagway Home Hostel	H
Skagway Mountain View RV Park	C

RESTAURANTS & BARS

Bonanza Bar & Grill	7
Corner Café	6
Glacial Smoothies & Espresso	9
The Haven	1
Kone Kompany	3
Moe's Frontier Bar	4
Red Onion Saloon	10
Sabrosa	2
Starfire	5
Stowaway Café	11
Sweet Tooth Café	8

Skagway River

ALASKA ST
MAIN ST
STATE ST
BROADWAY
SPRING ST

N

◀ **Ⓘ** (6 miles) & Dyea (6 miles)

◀ Yakutania Point (800yds)

Yakutania Point Trails

TERMINAL WAY
CONGRESS WAY

Dewey Lakes Trail

seventy bars and hundreds of prostitutes, was controlled by organized criminals, including the notorious Jefferson Randolph "Soapy" Smith, renowned for cheating hapless prospectors of their gold (see box, opposite). District Governor John Brady complained to Washington that "gamblers, thugs, and lewd women" were taking control of Skagway and the nearby town of Dyea. In response, the government sent the 14th Infantry to maintain order. Things gradually settled down and Skagway became the first incorporated city in Alaska on June 28, 1900, beating Juneau by one day.

Skagway retains a remarkable number of structures from its heyday in the late 1890s, encompassed by downtown Skagway's historical district and the **Klondike Gold Rush National Historical Park**. Over the years, buildings have been restored, long-removed wood-plank sidewalks have been reinstalled, and frontages have been gussied up to try to maintain (and increasingly reinvent) the original appearance of the town. None of this, though, detracts from the general harmonious impression.

Some history

No single image better conjures the human drama of the 1897–98 gold rush than the lines of prospectors struggling over the Chilkoot Trail, desperate to get to the goldfields of the Klondike. Gold was first discovered there in August 1896, but word didn't reach the outside world until eleven months later when the steamship *Excelsior* pulled into San Francisco laden with gold. The gold rush was on. Within days every passage north was booked, and Seattle rapidly became the main supply entrepôt for the routes used by ninety percent of Yukon-bound gold seekers, the Chilkoot and White passes. Prospectors took steamships up the Inside Passage to the Lynn Canal, from where they had a choice of disembarking at Dyea and taking the Chilkoot Trail, or landing at Skagway and following the White Pass route. Once through the coastal mountains, the two routes converged at **Bennett Lake**, from where it was 550 miles down the Yukon River to Dawson City and the Klondike. In the winter of 1897–98, thirty thousand hopefuls reached the frozen waters of Bennett Lake, and the town of Bennett grew up as the gold seekers set about felling trees for miles around and whipsawing planks for their boats. Break-up of the ice came on May 29, and within two days seven thousand boats had departed Bennett for Dawson City, leaving the place almost deserted.

It was a tough journey, one that seems even more difficult when you consider that, in the face of harsh winter conditions, travelers had few maps, nowhere to get supplies en route, and generally no idea what they were getting themselves into. About the only reliable news was the word that the Canadian Mounties – who established ad hoc border posts in the absence of a widely accepted frontier – were enforcing a rule that required all stampeders entering Canada to carry a year's supplies, roughly a **"ton of goods."** Introduced because of chronic shortages in the goldfields, the ruling probably saved many lives in the long run, but it laid enormous hardship on the backs of the stampeders. Altogether 22,000 prospectors made it over the Chilkoot Pass, many carrying their ton of supplies on their backs, sometimes making as many as fifty journeys back and forth through temperatures of -60°F and eighty feet of snowfall.

Before the rush, Skagway (then known as Mooresville) was just one hut owned by William Moore, who helped the Canadian Government pioneer a new route into the interior from Skagway, up and over the White Pass to Bennett Lake. It was ten miles longer than the Chilkoot, but the pass was six hundred feet lower and had a gentler gradient, so it became the route of choice for prospectors wealthy enough to buy horses. Overuse, along with sharp rocks,

The reign of Soapy Smith

Jefferson Randolph "Soapy" Smith and his gang of con men and cut-throats had a short but lucrative career preying on gullible gold stampeders until Soapy got his comeuppance nine months after his arrival in Skagway. Soapy came by his name after a con trick he'd pulled years before in Colorado where he sold $5 bars of soap, some molded around large-denomination bills. From the skeptical crowd of onlookers, Soapy's accomplices emerged to buy the first few bars which, miraculously, contained a $20 or even $50 bill. The ensuing buying frenzy revealed that few of the remaining bars contained even a $1 bill.

In Skagway Soapy established a saloon from which he ran his empire of up to a hundred henchmen, who posed as newspaper reporters, priests, or savvy sourdoughs to ensnare greenhorns arriving at the docks. Victims would soon be swindled at one of Soapy's businesses: crooked gambling halls, bogus freight companies that simply commandeered their consignment, and an army enlistment tent where they'd steal newcomers' clothes and possessions while they visited the "doctor." There was also a telegraph office that received requests for money from loved ones back home but, in fact, had no telegraph link at all. Soapy could, of course, arrange to have the money wired for you.

Soapy got his cronies to do the dirty work and established himself as a solid, philanthropic citizen, funding Skagway's first church and starting an adopt-a-dog program at a time when Skagway was full of discarded, pull-nothing pooches. Many saw through the veneer, but he had the support of much of the business community, and he even stood next to the governor of Alaska during the 1898 Independence Day parade.

Things came to a head four days later when the vigilante "Committee of 101" gathered to discuss the situation at the Juneau Company wharf, led by one Frank Reid. Fearful of mob rule, Soapy went to address the meeting and found himself in a gun battle with Reid. Soapy was shot in the heart and died immediately; Frank Reid died twelve agonizing days later from a gunshot wound to the groin. Both are buried in the Gold Rush Cemetery and, though Reid was no saint, it is obvious from the relative size of the monuments where the town's allegiances lay.

boulder fields, and muskeg, made it very heavy going and over three thousand horses died on what soon became known as the "Dead Horse Trail." Neither trail was the slightest bit appealing, and as one experienced stampeder put it, "It didn't matter which one you took, you'd wished you'd taken the other."

Everything changed with the July 1900 completion of the White Pass & Yukon Route railway, which roughly followed Moore's White Pass Trail. As one local newspaper noted, "What was formerly an all-winter's job for the gold seeker can now be achieved in four hours, for less than one tenth the financial outlay." By the time of the line's completion, however, the gold rush had subsided, but Skagway survived by maintaining the railroad and supporting the tourists who came to see this gold-rush town, the first tour boat arriving in 1900. Skagway got a new lease on life as a supply route for the construction of the Alaska Highway during World War II and continued as the main port for Yukon mineral-ore exports. Low returns for metals eventually closed the railroad in 1982 but the rising influence of tourism saw it revived in 1988.

Arrival, information, and getting around

Regular AMHS **ferries** (☎983-2229) from Juneau and Haines arrive two hundred yards from the main thoroughfare, Broadway. This is marginally the cheapest way to get here from Haines, though the Native-owned Chilkat

Cruises and Tours (mid-May to mid-Sept, 3–12 daily; 35min; ☎1-888/766-2103, ⓦwww.chilkatcruises.com) are a bit quicker and charge $25 one-way and $45 round-trip.

You probably won't have use for the fast connection between Skagway, Haines, and Juneau with Fjord Express ($139 round-trip; ☎1-800/320-0146, ⓦwww.alaskafjordlines.com). It is aimed at those wanting a full-day round-trip to Juneau with a city tour included.

Bus routes to Skagway all pass through Whitehorse in the Yukon. The cheapest to Whitehorse is Yukon Alaska Tourist Tours (reservations essential ☎1-866/626-7383, ⓦwww.yatt.ca), which charges $40 one way ($65 round-trip) and runs daily. The company also offers a Whitehorse–Skagway combo with the WP&YR trains ($95), changing modes of transport at Fraser, BC.

The best source of general information is the **visitor center**, Broadway at 2nd Avenue (May–Sept daily 8am–6pm; Oct–April Mon–Fri 8am–5pm; ☎1-888/762-1898, ⓦwww.skagway.com), though there is also the Klondike Gold Rush National Historic Park visitor center, Broadway at 2nd Avenue (see opposite), and the Trail Center (see box, p.200).

The downtown area is eminently manageable on foot, but the SMART **bus** (May–Sept; ☎983-2743) tours downtown ($1.50 per journey; correct change needed) and is useful for a run up to 22nd Street (on demand), a ten-minute walk from the cemetery.

Accommodation

Growth in tourism has meant a rise in standards for Skagway's accommodation. Prices tend to be quite high, but they generally offer good value. It is pretty much essential to reserve in advance in July and August and advisable a month on either side.

As well as the **campgrounds** listed here, you can camp on the trails out of town, though if you are still within city limits (such as at Lower Dewey Lake) you are required to alert the Skagway police (see p.199) of your presence. There are also two Forest Service **cabins** on the trails hereabouts (see box, p.199).

Hotels, motels, B&Bs, and cabins

At the White House 475 8th Ave at Main St ☎983-9000, ⓦwww.atthewhitehouse.com. High-standard B&B in one of Skagway's original homes, restored from its fire-damaged state and now with fully modernized rooms, some particularly spacious. All have phone, cable TV, ceiling fans, and super-comfy beds. A continental breakfast buffet is served and there's always tea, coffee, and home-baked cookies on hand. Large rooms ⑥, otherwise ⑤

Chilkoot Trail Outpost Dyea ☎983-3799, ⓦwww.chilkoottrailoutpost.com. Comfortable, modern log cabins in the woods cluster around a fire pit and mosquito-free gazebo at this welcoming B&B, located almost 9 miles from Skagway and half a mile from the start of the Chilkoot Trail. Cabins sleep up to four and come with bedding, TV, microwave, fridge, and coffeemaker. Cheaper Hikers' cabins come with bunks and bedding but lack microwave and fridge. Free bikes, WiFi, and breakfast are included for all guests. Hikers' cabins ⑤, cabins ⑥

Cindy's Place Mile 0.2 Dyea Rd, two miles from downtown Skagway ☎1-800/831-8095, ⓦwww.alaska.net/~croland. Three cabins set in a beautiful spot in the woods, two of which are more luxurious, log-built cabins – with private bathrooms (one with a wood-burning stove), phone, and cooking equipment – while the budget third cabin is small but good value, with an indoor toilet, sink, microwave, fridge, kettle, and toaster, but no shower. It sleeps two ($49), but is perfect for one ($35); save $5 per person by using your own bedding and towels. All guests have free use of the hot tub. Thoughtful little touches like fresh baking in the afternoon, a dozen varieties of tea and coffee in the cabins, and homemade jams and jellies for breakfast make this place special. Slight reductions for stays of two nights or more. May–Sept. Deluxe ⑤, budget ❶–❷

The Historic Skagway Inn Broadway at 7th Ave ☎1-888/752-4929, ⓦwww.skagwayinn.com.

Turn-of-the-century former bordello now operating as a boutique B&B hotel with a dozen tastefully modernized rooms, each decorated with antique-style furniture and bearing the name of an erstwhile occupant. Accommodation varies considerably: small rooms with shared bathroom (⑤), larger rooms with private bath down the hall (⑦), and spacious en-suite rooms such as the lovely street-front "Alice" (⑧). A delicious hot breakfast is served, and there's a restaurant on site.

Mile Zero B&B Main St at 9th Ave ☎983-3045, Ⓦwww.mile-zero.com. Modern, purpose-built B&B with large rooms, each with a private entrance. A continental buffet breakfast is served in the communal lounge area, which is where you'll find the TV. ⑤

Sgt Preston's Lodge 6th Ave at State St ☎1-866/983-2521, Ⓦsgtprestons.eskagway.com. Decent downtown motel with standard, and much nicer deluxe, rooms, all with cable TV, DVD players, and pickups by courtesy van. Deluxe ⑤, standard ④

Skagway Bungalows Mile 0.2 Dyea Rd ☎1-877/983-2986, Ⓦwww.aptalaska.net/~saldi. A couple of large cabins in the woods next to *Cindy's Place*, each with king or queen bed, futon couch, an inside bathroom, and a big deck out front. March–Nov. ⑤

Hostels and campgrounds

NPS Dyea Campground at Dyea, 9 miles northeast of Skagway. Simple and attractive first-come,

first-served Park Service campground (not recommended for large RVs) beside the Taiya River, with fire rings, picnic tables, pit toilets, and water that should be treated. $6 per site.

Pullen Creek RV Park Congress Way ☎1-800/936-3731, Ⓦwww.pullencreekrv.com. RV and tent park right by the harbor, with a dozen waterside RV sites. Showers $1.25 extra. Mid-April to mid-Sept. Tent $14, tent and car $20, dry RV $20, water, electricity, and dump $28.

Skagway Home Hostel 3rd Ave at Main St ☎983-2131, Ⓦwww.skagwayhostel.com. Traditionally run hostel in a century-old building, with bunks in a mixed dorm ($15), fairly spacious single-sex dorms ($20), and one private room ($50). Meals are shared, with an honesty box for your contribution for breakfast ($3) or a (typically) vegetarian dinner ($5; free if you cook), plus there's often fresh bread and fruit for a small contribution. Free bikes, basic supplies for cooking, a spacious yard, and no daytime lockout, but office hours are 5.30–10.30pm, and there is an 11pm curfew. Sheets are included in rates. Book using a credit card (particularly in July and Aug, and essential in winter) through the website, or try to catch them on the phone, though they are often unavailable. ②

Skagway Mountain View RV Park Broadway at 12th Ave ☎1-888/778-7700, Ⓦwww.alaskarv.com. Large RV-dominated spot with all the expected facilities, water and electricity hookup ($30) and dry ($20) sites, and a few wooded tent sites ($17) that are in high demand.

The town and around

Almost everything in **downtown Skagway** happens on, or just off, Broadway, a half-mile-long strip lined with hotels, restaurants, a few bars, old buildings restored as museums, and a lot of swanky shops. It is a slightly unsettling blend, though you can come to terms with it all using the free and widely available *Skagway Walking Tour* leaflet. This is where you'll spend your time between forays on the White Pass & Yukon Route railway, out to the **Gold Rush Cemetery**, and further afield to the scant remains of Dyea, the starting point for the multiday Chilkoot Trail hiking path.

Downtown Skagway

Most people arrive by boat and find themselves at the foot of Broadway, an area typically dominated by passengers disgorging from the White Pass & Yukon Route railway. A small park by the tracks contains an old rotary snowplow once used on the line, as well as a statue of a Tlingit guide and prospector built to commemorate the town's centennial in 1998.

Many of Skagway's important historic buildings come under the auspices of the Klondike Gold Rush National Historical Park, including the **NPS visitor center**, Broadway at 2nd Avenue (May–Sept daily 8am–6pm; ☎983-9223, Ⓦwww.nps.gov/klgo), in what was the original WP&YR depot. Here you'll find plenty of information panels and park rangers ready to answer any questions,

△ Broadway in Skagway

but it is best to time your visit to coincide with the excellent thirty-minute *Days of Adventure, Dreams of Gold* video (8am, 9am, 11am, noon, 1pm, 2pm, 4pm & 5pm; free), which tells the tale of the gold-rush prospectors' struggles over the passes to the Klondike. The center also runs ranger presentations (10am & 3pm; free) and walking tours of the downtown historic district (9am, 10am, 11am, 2pm & 3pm; free, but obtain tickets early in the day to be sure of a place). In a separate room there are great photos of those heady days a century back, along with a sample "ton of goods" – a lot more than you'd fancy hauling over the Chilkoot Trail.

Opposite the visitor center, a small building contains the **Chilkoot Trail Center** (see box, p.200), the first stop for all modern-day Chilkoot Trail aspirants, but otherwise of little interest. Around the corner stands **Soapy Smith's Parlor**, from where he ran his short-lived empire. The building is an 1890s original, though it was moved to this site in 1964 and is not currently open to the public. Across 2nd Avenue, the **Red Onion Saloon** is another transported building, though it is very much open for business (see p.205). Liquor was only one of the commodities formerly sold here, and you can now join the fifteen-minute **Brothel Tour** (May–Sept daily, roughly hourly 11am–4pm; $5), a tongue-in-cheek but historically accurate walk through what is left of the upstairs rooms (one of them restored) guided by "girls," suitably dressed in push-up bodices and feather boas, who stay in character throughout and tell a stack of entertaining tales.

Pressing on along Broadway you pass the eye-catching facade of the **Arctic Brotherhood Hall**, decorated with almost nine thousand pieces of driftwood nailed to the front. Built in 1899 by gold miners who paid their dues in nuggets, the hall now houses the town's main visitor center. Across the road is the **Mascot Saloon** (May–Sept daily 8am–6pm; free), which had its heyday as a bar and gambling den from 1897 to 1916, finally closing under Prohibition. It's been renovated to its 1910 state, complete with a tableau of a bar scene, the marvelous mirror-backed bar patronized by several mannequins.

A couple of blocks up Broadway, turn right on 5th Avenue and head to the birthplace of Skagway, marked by Moore Cabin and **Moore House**, 5th Avenue

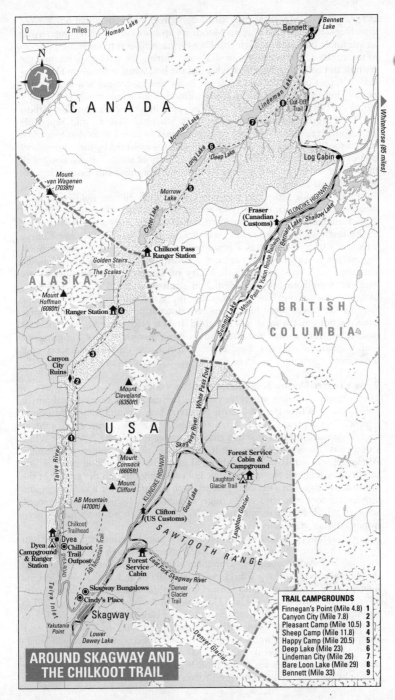

0   2 miles

N

CANADA

Homan Lake

Bennett Lake

Bennett **9**

Lindeman Lake

Cut-Off Trail **8**

7

Mountain Lake

Log Cabin

Long Lake

6
Deep Lake

5

Morrow Lake

Crater Lake

Mount van Wagenen
(7038ft)

Fraser
(Canadian
Customs)

KLONDIKE HIGHWAY

Bernard Lake   Shallow Lake

Chilkoot Pass
Ranger Station

Golden Stairs

The Scales

ALASKA

Mount
Hoffman
(6080ft)

Ranger Station **4**

Summit Lake

White Pass & Yukon Route Railway

BRITISH

COLUMBIA

3

Canyon
City
Ruins

2

Mount
Cleveland
(6350ft)

Whitehorse (85 miles)

USA

White Pass Fork

Taiya River

Mount
Cormack
(6605ft)

Mount
Clifford

Skagway River

AB Mountain
(4700ft)

KLONDIKE HIGHWAY

Goat Lake

Forest Service
Cabin & Campground

Laughton Glacier Trail

Laughton Glacier

1

Clifton
(US Customs)

AB Mountain Trail

SAWTOOTH RANGE

Chilkoot Trailhead

Dyea
Chilkoot
Trail Outpost

Forest
Service
Cabin

East Fork Skagway River

Dyea
Campground
& Ranger
Station

DYEA ROAD

Skagway Bungalows

Cindy's Place

Denver
Glacier
Trail

Taiya Inlet

Skagway

Yakutania
Point

Lower
Dewey Lake

Denver Glacier

**AROUND SKAGWAY AND
THE CHILKOOT TRAIL**

TRAIL CAMPGROUNDS	
Finnegan's Point (Mile 4.8)	**1**
Canyon City (Mile 7.8)	**2**
Pleasant Camp (Mile 10.5)	**3**
Sheep Camp (Mile 11.8)	**4**
Happy Camp (Mile 20.5)	**5**
Deep Lake (Mile 23)	**6**
Lindeman City (Mile 26)	**7**
Bare Loon Lake (Mile 29)	**8**
Bennett (Mile 33)	**9**

at Spring Street (May–Sept daily 10am–5pm; free). It was here that 65-year-old founding settler Captain William Moore set up his cabin in 1887, prophesying an imminent gold rush, though he'd have to wait ten years to see it. Despite tales to the contrary, Moore made a small fortune during the gold rush, running the sawmill and collecting dues from what was the best wharf in Skagway. The original cabin (not open), and a much larger house that started out as a simple cabin in 1897 but by 1901 had grown to accommodate his whole family, still stand.

Back on Broadway, it is worth briefly popping into the craft store that harbors the **Corrington Museum**, Broadway at 5th (mid-May to mid-Sept daily 9am–6pm; free), with its six-foot mammoth tusk, fossilized mastodon tooth, and spruce-root and baleen basketware, all thoroughly upstaged by the huge collection of engraved walrus tusks. There are over forty of these artifacts, along with the custom-made carving tools used to conjure scenes from Eskimo legends and European adventures.

Seventh Avenue spans the spectrum of cultural life in gold-rush Skagway. Northwest of Broadway you are in what became the town's red-light district after brothels were consolidated here in the early twentieth century; to the southeast of Broadway lies the granite, mock-Gothic McCabe College building, which was built as a private school in 1899, before public schooling arrived in Skagway. After roles as a courthouse, a jail, and City Hall, the building now houses the refurbished **City of Skagway Museum** (May–Sept Mon–Fri 9am–5pm, Sat 10am–5pm, Sun 10am–4pm; $2; ☎983-2420, ⓦwww .skagwaymuseum.org). There's plenty here on Soapy Smith, of course, including the tiny Derringer pistol he kept in his waistcoat pocket and a roulette table allegedly from his parlor, as well as a good deal on Native culture, with intricate basketware from around the state and an impressive thirty-foot Tlingit canoe with a beautifully painted bow. Don't overlook the unusual, iridescent quilt made from cured duck necks or the videos on Skagway during World War II.

The White Pass & Yukon Route railway

Undoubtedly the most stately way to see the dazzling scenery hereabouts is aboard the ↗**White Pass & Yukon Route** railway (around May 10 to around Sept 20, 2–3 departures daily; ☎1-800/343-7373, ⓦwww.wpyr.com), a three-foot-wide narrow-gauge line that climbs from sea level to the 2865-foot White Pass in just twenty miles, making it one of the world's steepest train routes. Along the way it follows the tumbling Skagway River, trundling over precarious bridges, hugging precipitous cliffs, and tunneling through the granite of the Sawtooth Range. It is a stunning journey with waterfalls, ice-packed gorges, and a thousand-foot wooden trestle bridge, all seen from 1890s-style rolling stock, some of which is very recent, some older than the railroad itself, having been imported from elsewhere.

As with almost everything else around here, the railroad's construction was driven by gold. The relatively easy gradient of the White Pass (though still uniquely steep for a railroad) made it amenable to the construction of a train line, and as thousands slogged their way to the goldfield over the Chilkoot and White passes, private interests were at work on Alaska's first railroad. In the two months following May 1898, four miles of track were laid. Things slowed considerably as workers had to be slung from ropes on the steep terrain to place blasting charges, and enormous bridges had to be built. Nonetheless, the entire 110 miles to Whitehorse were completed in just 26 months. Altogether 35,000 workers were employed building the railroad, but never more than 2000 at once, ample evidence of just how transient the population was at this time. It had cost its backers $10 million, but despite being completed after the great Yukon stampede was over, the railroad soon

Hikes around Skagway

To enjoy the good hiking available around Skagway, equip yourself with the useful *Skagway Trail Map*, available free from the visitor center, with detailed descriptions of nine walks in the area, the best of which are described below. Some of the trails are within an easy walk of downtown, while others can be reached via the WP&YR railway's summer hiker flag-stop service (mid-May to mid-Sept). These trails can all be tackled in a day, though you could make use of the two Forest Service cabins in the area. Note that the Forest Service doesn't have an office in Skagway, so you'll need to book through their reservation service (T 1-877/444-6777, W www.reserveusa.com). Camping along the local trails is also possible, though you need to be fully self-sufficient and must register in person at the local police station, State Street at 1st Avenue (T 983-2232).

AB Mountain Trail (9.5 miles round-trip from downtown; 6–8hr; 4700ft ascent). Strenuous hike up the southwest ridge of the prominent mountain immediately north of town which provides panoramic views from the alpine meadows near the summit. The trailhead on Dyea Road is most easily reached by the Yakutania Point Trail (see below). Some claim the mountain's name comes from the Arctic Brotherhood, while others contend it is for the letters A and B, which were once picked out in the melting snow; you can see them on old photos and on a post-card in the *Mascot Saloon* on Broadway. Recent tree growth means you'll need a lot of imagination to see them these days, your best chance being in May and early June.

Denver Glacier Trail (6 miles round-trip; 4–6hr; 1200ft ascent). Moderate hike in the shadow of the magnificent Sawtooth Range to the scrubby terminal moraine of the Denver Glacier. Ice cliffs at the end of the glacier itself hang high above. The trailhead is six miles north of downtown Skagway and is accessed by the WP&YR railway's summer flag-stop service ($30 round-trip) departing from Skagway daily at 8am and 12.30pm, with Skagway-bound services passing the trailhead at 11.45am and 3.55pm. By the trailhead there is an old railroad caboose, which operates as a Forest Service cabin ($35).

Dewey Lakes Trails (1–8 miles round-trip; 40min–6hr; 500–3600ft ascent). A varied system of trails that starts near the end of 3rd Avenue and straggles up the hills to the south of Skagway to pretty, subalpine lakes and tumbling waterfalls. A steep ten-minute walk gets you to a great viewpoint over town, though it is worth continuing to Lower Dewey Lake (0.7 miles). If you're fairly fit, press on to the muskeg meadows around Upper Dewey Lake (3 miles), where there's a primitive free-use cabin, and the new Upper Dewey Lake cabin (sleeps 8; $35; T 983-2679, E reccenter@aptalaska.net). You could even press on to Devil's Punchbowl (4.2 miles), where there's a small alpine lake.

Laughton Glacier Trail (3 miles round-trip; 1hr to 1hr 30min; 200ft ascent). Easy stroll following the Skagway River ending in a wonderful rocky amphitheater surrounded by hanging glaciers. It is a short walk, but consider staying overnight, either camping or in the Forest Service cabin ($35) about half a mile from the trailhead and a mile from the glacier. The trailhead is fourteen miles north of Skagway and is accessed by the WP&YR railway's summer flag-stop service ($54 round-trip), depart-ing from Skagway daily at 8am and 12.30pm, with Skagway-bound services passing the trailhead at 11.10am and 3.15pm.

Yakutania Point Trails (1.5 miles; 30–40min round-trip; negligible ascent). Gentle stroll to the pleasant picnic area at Yakutania Point or to another at Smuggler's Cove, a few minutes further. Start by following the path and footbridge by the airport build-ings at the southwestern corner of town.

Alaska's most famous and popular hike, the 33-mile **Chilkoot Trail** (ⓦwww.nps .gov/klgo/chilkoot.htm and ⓦwww.pc.gc.ca/chilkoot) is a three- or four-day journey through a giant wilderness museum, tracing the footsteps of Klondike-bound prospectors from the coast at **Dyea** through temperate rainforest, alpine tundra, and the bare rocks of the Chilkoot Pass to **Bennett Lake** in British Columbia. The entire route is littered with haunting reminders of the past: ancient boilers that once drove aerial tramways, twisted metal fittings, collapsed huts, glass bottles, old boots, wooden tramway pylons, and even a stash of canvas and wood boats that were never used. Leave everything as you found it and try not to step on fragile relics.

The trail has an iconic status in the North and is consequently used by over three thousand hikers a year, many of whom would never consider any other multiday hike. Keen hikers shouldn't find it too challenging, though the less fit find it tough going, especially the much-hyped 37-degree scramble from the former tent city of "the Scales" to the top of the pass – 2500ft of ascent in one nine-mile day – which some people struggle to finish in twelve or fourteen hours. All this is made considerably more intimidating if the weather turns inclement, as it can do in any month of the year.

You need to be entirely self-sufficient and must camp in one of the nine approved **campgrounds**, each equipped with demarcated sites (sometimes on wooden platforms), pit toilets, and a central eating area overlooked by twenty-foot poles for hanging food out of bears' reach. With the exception of the one long day mentioned above, most campgrounds are spaced less than four hours apart, so you can take the whole trail at a leisurely pace.

The route

Most people hike from Dyea to Bennett, which keeps the strong prevailing winds at your back and makes for an easier scramble up the slippery rocks to the pass. From the trailhead you hike through temperate rainforest, following the Taiya River past campgrounds at Finnegan's Point (Mile 4.8), Canyon City (Mile 7.8), and Pleasant Camp (Mile 10.5) before reaching **Sheep Camp** (Mile 11.8), the last before the big day over the pass. Get an early start from Dyea and it is easy enough to hike to Sheep Camp in one day; late risers should aim to cover the distance in two days. Leaving Sheep Camp at 4am or 5am ensures that you get over the pass and past an avalanche danger zone early in the day when it is safest. You initially climb through forest and tundra to "the Scales," where prospectors marshaled their gear before the arduous ascent of "Golden Stairs," a 500-foot, hands-and-feet clamber over rocks to the top. At the pass there's an occasionally manned **Canadian border post** and a warming hut where you can brew up and gather your strength for the long hike down to **Happy Camp** (Mile 20.5). In June you'll have to cross extensive snowfields, but the stunning alpine scenery easily compensates. If you've got the strength you might want to continue on to the campground at Deep Lake (Mile 23), beautifully set beside some rapids, or even on to the lakeside campground at Lindeman City (Mile 26), where some prospectors built their boats. An early start from here takes you along a ridge parallel to Lindeman Lake and gets you to Bennett (Mile 33) in time for the train back to Skagway, though it is worth spending an extra day here exploring what is left of Bennett, basically a wooden church, a Parks Canada visitor center, and a lot of junk the prospectors left behind.

From Bennett it is a seven-mile hike along the railroad tracks to the highway at Log Cabin, where shuttle buses can pick you up for a ride back to Skagway. You can, however, take a **Cut-Off Trail** by Bare Loon Lake before reaching Bennett, along which there is a campground at Mile 29, midway between Lindeman City and Bennett. This option saves you about four miles of walking, but means you'll never see Bennett.

Reservations and permits

The trail is open all year, though most visit during the **hiking season** (early June to early Sept) when rangers patrol the trail, warming huts are open, and poles mark the route.

You can still expect to encounter snow, however, up until the first or second week of July. Throughout the hiking season Parks Canada limits the number of hikers crossing the Chilkoot Pass into Canada to fifty per day. Of these spots, 42 places can be booked in advance, while the remainder are offered on a first-come, first-served basis from the Skagway **Trail Center**, Broadway at 1st Avenue (early June to early Sept daily 8.30am–4.30pm; ☏983-3655), after 1pm on the day before you plan to start the trail. **Reservations** (Can$12) are advised and are virtually essential during the peak season (July to mid-Aug). In the off-season call the reservation system (☏867/667-3910 or 1-800/661-0486 between 8.30am and 4pm Pacific Standard Time, which is one hour ahead of Alaska time); from early June to early September reserve through the Trail Center. Be sure to have on hand your desired hiking itinerary, including a list of the nights you intend to spend in each campground, and an alternative schedule.

All hikers (either with or without reservations) need to go to the Trail Center to buy a **permit** (Can$55), sign a register (for customs purposes), and consult the weather forecast. You'll need to present and carry a **passport** (from 2007 on it is likely that a birth certificate won't do, and a driver's license is definitely not acceptable) for each hiker. You may be required to deal with Canadian customs at the Chilkoot Pass ranger station, but more likely you'll do it after your hike at the Alaska–Canada border post at Fraser or in Whitehorse.

Though it isn't really necessary, you may want to buy the Canadian Parks Service's *Chilkoot Trail* **map** ($4.10 from the Trail Center), which is about the best available.

Transport and supplies

To get to the start of the trail, nine miles northwest of Skagway at Dyea, you could arrange a lift or walk. As road walks go it is a very pleasant hike, though you might be able to thumb a lift if you get bored. Otherwise you'll have to engage the services of one of the **shuttle buses** ($10): Dyea Dave (☏983-2731 or mobile ☏209-5031) or Frontier Excursions (☏1-877/983-2512, ⓦwww.frontierexcursions.com).

The trail finishes at Bennett from where you can **return to Skagway** on the WP&YR railway's Chilkoot Trail Hikers Service (June–Aug Sat, Sun & Mon at 1pm Alaska time; generally $40 one-way to Fraser, $80 to Skagway, but on Sat $50/$90), which is one carriage of the Lake Bennett Excursion that's specially designated for smelly hikers. Remember to buy your **tickets** at the WP&YR office in Skagway before you set off on the trail – otherwise you'll have a $15 fee added to the ticket price for the convenience of buying your ticket on the train (note that for customs reasons the train doesn't stop at Log Cabin). Riding the rails is the perfect complement to the hike, giving a sense of how important the train was to the prospectors.

Alternatively, hike the eight miles along the tracks from Bennett to the highway at Log Cabin and meet up with one of the shuttle buses ($25–30 for a combined drop-off and pickup). It isn't much fun walking along the tracks, so consider the cut-off trail mentioned opposite, which avoids Bennett.

Continuing on to Whitehorse involves getting yourself to Log Cabin (by train or on foot), then picking up Yukon Alaska Tourist Tours (4.30pm Alaska time; $34; ☏1-866/626-73383).

When setting out from Skagway be sure to take wet-weather gear, matches, some method of water treatment, sunscreen, sunglasses, a flashlight, and **thirty feet of rope** so that you can sling your food, toothpaste, and any scented items over the bear poles at each campground. Campgrounds on the US side all have bear-proof storage boxes but you'll need rope for the Canadian side. Rope is available from Skagway Hardware Co, Broadway and 4th Avenue. Early in the season when there's plenty of snow about, consider **gaiters** and **hiking poles**, which can be rented from the Mountain Shop in Skagway (see Listings, p.205).

Almost all accommodation in Skagway offers free **gear storage** for guests.

recouped the capital as ever-hopeful prospectors abandoned both the Chilkoot and White Pass trails in favor of the railroad.

As the flood of gold seekers abated, the WP&YR settled into a more staid existence shipping metal ores from mines around Whitehorse to the sea at Skagway and acting as a supply route during the wartime construction of the Alaska Highway. Service along the route was suspended in 1982, only to be revived six years later with a view to tapping the cruise-ship market. Since then services have been progressively expanded, with trains now running as far as Bennett Lake, forty miles from Skagway. Unfortunately, this unmissable trip doesn't come cheap, and with heavy bookings from the cruise ships you seldom have the luxury of waiting for a fine day and traveling on the spur of the moment. The most popular run – the one that most cruise passengers are funneled onto – is the three-hour White Pass Summit Excursion (around May 10 to Sept 20, 2–3 daily; $95 round-trip), which runs from the **train station** at the junction of Broadway and 2nd Avenue to the Canadian border at the top of White Pass and back; sit on the left going up. All services are diesel-hauled except for the eight-hour Bennett Lake Adventure (early June to late Aug, Sat, Sun & Mon only), which on Sunday and Monday is diesel-hauled ($150) but on Saturday ($180) is drawn by a steam engine. The Adventure continues beyond the pass to Bennett Lake, British Columbia (the end of the Chilkoot Trail hiking route), where stampeders built boats before launching them five hundred miles down the Yukon to Dawson City. You get a couple of hours by the lake to eat your packed lunch (included) and poke around the evidence of those frenetic two years. In addition, there is the steam-hauled Fraser Meadows trip (June to early Sept, Sun at noon; $125). To reach Whitehorse use the Skagway–Whitehorse Rail+Bus service (mid-May to mid-Sept daily; $95 one-way to Whitehorse) on which you ride the train as far as Fraser (the Canadian border), then transfer to a bus for the run past Carcross to Whitehorse.

Gold Rush Cemetery and Dyea

No exploration of Skagway's gold-rush heritage would be complete without a visit to the **Gold Rush Cemetery**, the final resting place of many of the stampeders. Among them are Skagway's most famous outlaw, Soapy Smith (see box, p.193), and his nemesis, Frank Reid, who according to his gravestone "gave his life for the honor of Skagway." Local prostitute Ella Wilson is also interred here, though her cheeky epitaph – "She gave her honor for the life of Skagway" – has now been removed. Still, it fit nicely in a cemetery full of gentle conceits; most of the signs marking graves are modern additions put here when the cemetery was revamped for the benefit of tourists. It is a pleasant enough place to idle away half an hour; while here, be sure to take the short stroll to the 300-foot-high **Reid Falls**, which cascade down the hills behind the graveyard. The cemetery is about two miles from downtown; follow Alaska Street and keep heading northeast.

Those prospectors who weren't in Skagway trying to cheat death on the White Pass route to the Klondike were chancing their luck at the start of the Chilkoot Trail (see box, p.200), nine miles away at the mouth of the Taiya River in **Dyea** (Dy-EE). At the height of the rush this was a bustling town of over five thousand where gold seekers stopped off just long enough to prepare for the three-month journey ahead, ferrying goods over the Chilkoot Pass. Initially favored over Skagway by prospectors, Dyea once ranked as the largest town in Alaska, but it fell into rapid decline after the opening of the WP&YR railway. Most of the town's buildings have long since been torn down, but a few foundations remain, along with rotting stumps from the two-mile-long wharf and the **slide cemetery**, a mass burial place for the victims of a Chilkoot Trail avalanche that took sixty-odd lives at the former tent city of "the Scales" in April 1898. There's little else to show for the place, but it is a lovely spot to wander around, admiring the wildflowers and spotting birds, guided by interpretive panels and paths constructed by the Park Service. There's also a simple campground here and a sporadically attended ranger station, which runs free **guided walks**, including a Dyea townsite tour (June–Aug Fri, Sat & Sun 10am & daily 2pm; 1hr 30min), which meets at the Dyea town site. Call the Park Service (☏983-9223) to confirm times.

Local tours and outdoor activities

Although it's easy enough to stroll around the downtown area and even hike out to the Gold Rush Cemetery, for more extensive exploration you might want to join one of the dozen or so cruise passenger-oriented **local tours**. They come and go rapidly and change their itineraries seemingly annually. Frontier Excursions, Broadway at 7th Avenue (☏1-877/983-2512, ⓦwww .frontierexcursions.com), does a White Pass Summit and City Tour (2hr 30min; $45), which also visits the cemetery, and a Dyea tour (3hr; $55).

Sockeye Cycle Co, 5th Avenue at Broadway (☏983-2851, ⓦwww.cyclealaska .com), offers a couple of guided **cycling tours**, neither requiring much effort: the Dyea Bicycle Adventure (2hr 30min; $75) starts with a van ride to the start of the Chilkoot Trail, followed by ninety minutes of gentle riding on the dirt roads around Dyea; the Klondike Bicycle Tour (2hr 30min; $75) involves a narrated van ride up to the 3300-foot White Pass and then a fairly steep descent back to Skagway with negligible pedaling. A train and bike combo ($175) replaces the van ride with a trip on the WP&YR.

To get on the water, contact Skagway Float Tours (☏983-3688, ⓦwww .skagwayfloat.com), which runs **rafting trips**. Their staples are the Scenic Float Tour (3hr; $75) and the Hike & Float (4hr; $85), both involving about 45 minutes floating down the Taiya River at Dyea, plus plenty of natural history, and in the latter case a two-mile nature walk.

Flightseeing trips from Skagway are understandably popular; the glacial scenery immediately around town is certainly impressive, and you're only a few minutes' flight from the majestic wonder of Glacier Bay. Some of the most popular local trips are with Temsco Helicopters (☏983-2900, ⓦwww .temscoair.com), which does a flightseeing circuit with forty minutes stopped on a flat section at the foot of one of the local glaciers (1hr 20min; $249). They will also whisk you up onto the Denver Glacier (2hr; $449), where they've installed several dog teams that will take you on a half-hour sled ride.

Planes lack the agility of choppers, but because they are cheaper to run and have a longer range, you tend to get a longer trip for your money. They're also able to fly over Glacier Bay. Three companies operate tours, including Skagway Air Service, 420 Broadway (☏983-2218, ⓦwww.skagwayair.com), which has a Gold Rush Tour (45min; $100) around the White and Chilkoot passes, Bennett Lake, and the Juneau Icefield, as well as an excellent Glacier Bay Tour (1hr 30min; $150), with views down to the main glaciers and sometimes straying as far as the Fairweather Range. This outfit also flies to Skagway from Juneau (direct 45min, $100; with a Glacier Bay flyover 2hr, $250), and from Gustavus ($130).

Eating, drinking, and entertainment

Most of Skagway's **bars** and **restaurants** lie in the touristy part of Broadway, where a five-minute stroll will reveal almost everything the town has to offer. As befits such a heavily visited locale, the range is pretty decent, though the fast-food

Robert Service: poet of the gold rush

With the possible exception of Jack London, no literary figure is more closely associated with the sub-Arctic North than English-born poet **Robert Service** (1874–1958), whose lilting, well-crafted rhymes captured the essence of the Klondike gold rushes. This "Bard of the Yukon" had only tenuous contact with Alaska – he traveled through Skagway and on the WP&YR railway to Whitehorse – but the material he dealt with, and the spirit with which he imbued his poetry, rings just as true in Alaska as it does in the Yukon. Accordingly, Service has been wholly adopted by the Alaskan tourist machine. In several spots around the state you'll find crowds of visitors flocking to hear performers reciting Service's more crowd-pleasing Klondike works: *The Shooting of Dan McGrew*, *The Cremation of Sam McGee*, and *The Spell of the Yukon*.

Service's work is often derided by the literary establishment, who barely consider him a "real" poet let alone a "great" one, but, despite the unfamiliarity of his subject matter, he spoke to the average reader in language understood by all, his vibrant imagery delivered with a dramatic, almost metronomic intensity. Undoubtedly a people's poet, he once claimed, "The only society I like, is that which is rough and tough – and the tougher the better. That's where you get down to bedrock and meet human people." His sympathies certainly rested with the common people, but he was never the archetypal starving poet, and after the publication of his Yukon poems he quickly became very wealthy, some claiming that *The Shooting of Dan McGrew* alone brought in half a million dollars.

His three most famous poems were written in Whitehorse during a prolific few months at the end of 1906, eight years after the Klondike rush, a phenomenon that Service had missed entirely as he drifted around the southwestern US and Mexico. By 1904 he had returned to his original profession as a bank clerk and been transferred to Whitehorse, a town in decline as prospectors had moved on to richer Alaskan strikes, leaving the old claims to be worked over by mechanical dredges. Still, there were enough sourdoughs left to tell the tale, and when the local paper, which knew of his poetic leanings, asked for "something about our own bit of earth," he quickly tapped into a rich vein. Overheard yarns, shaggy-dog stories, and snippets gleaned from every source were woven together and soon became his first and most celebrated book, *Songs of a Sourdough*.

Numerous other books followed, some even being turned into films, but none of his later work captured the zeitgeist to the same degree, nor have any had the same enduring popularity. Service spent the rest of his long life pursuing all manner of interests and doing pretty much as he pleased, freed by the nest egg he had created in those few months in Whitehorse. He traveled the world, worked as a war correspondent, settled in Paris with a Frenchwoman, flirted with Marxism, narrowly escaped the German army after mocking Hitler in a poem he wrote for a newspaper, and died of a heart attack at his retreat in Lancieux at the age of 84.

franchises haven't moved in yet. For **groceries** and trail supplies head to the Fairway Market, State Street at 4th Avenue, or for more exotic (and healthy) goods, visit You Say Tomato, State Street at 21st Avenue (☎983-2784).

Evening **entertainment** mainly revolves around the bars (all on Broadway), though you may want to catch some Robert Service poetry in the Eagle Hall at the *Days of '98 Show*, Broadway at 6th Avenue (May–Sept daily at 10.30am, 2.30pm & 8pm; $16; ☎983-2545), where the story of Soapy and Frank is acted out in a gold-rush saloon atmosphere (only without the drinking). The evening show is preceded by an hour of fake gambling.

Bonanza Bar & Grill Broadway at 3rd Ave ☎983-6214. Bustling sports bar with a range of microbrews and a select menu of burgers, sandwiches, and salads (all $9–12).

Corner Café State St at 4th Ave ☎983-2155. Often smoky daytime diner that's much favored by Skagway's locals and a good break from the press of people on Broadway just a couple of blocks away. Stuffed croissants with salad or soup for $7, or salmon burger for $9.

Glacial Smoothies & Espresso 336 3rd Ave ☎983-3074. A good coffee spot also serving a limited range of bagels and wraps. Internet access.

The Haven State St at 9th Ave ☎983-3553. Relaxed coffee shop with sofas and stacks of magazines, serving good espresso, egg or granola breakfasts, mouthwatering panini, and fresh salads – Santa Fe, Greek, Caesar, and more ($8.50). WiFi available.

Kone Kompany 485 Broadway ☎1-800/664-2370. Ever-popular little store selling homemade fudge, ice cream, yogurt, and excellent shakes.

Moe's Frontier Bar Broadway at 4th Ave ☎983-2238. Locals' bar that's *the* place for straightforward drinking.

🏃 Red Onion Saloon Broadway at 2nd Ave ☎983-2222. An 1898 wood-floored bar and former bordello where the bar staff don period dress and engage in role play that would be horribly cheesy if it wasn't done with such enthusiasm. It is an approach much loved by cruise-ship passengers, who flock in during the day, often with the ship's band in tow, ready to strike up a few jazz tunes. The girls who once plied their trade upstairs have unwittingly given their names to the excellent pizza, a theme followed with the named sandwiches washed down with the town's best selection of draft beers. Evenings bring out the locals, with bands several nights a week in summer.

🏃 Sabrosa Broadway at 6th Ave ☎983-2469. Daytime café and bakery, tucked in behind the gift shops, that's great for breakfast (from $5) and lunches of burritos ($8), vegetarian chili (cup $4, bowl $6), and tarragon, pecan, and chicken salad ($9). Shaded outdoor seating for those hot days.

Starfire 4th Ave at Broadway ☎983-3663. Quality Thai with sheltered outdoor seating for those fine summer evenings. Kick off with a plate of pot stickers ($6.50) perhaps followed by one of their curry, noodle, or stir-fry dishes ($16–18).

🏃 Stowaway Café 205 Congress Way ☎983-3463. About the best evening dining in Skagway, with a congenial atmosphere and lovely views of the small boat harbor. Expect the likes of lemongrass halibut ($22), baby back ribs ($22), and peach bread pudding ($6). Open nightly 4pm–10pm.

Sweet Tooth Café Broadway at 3rd Ave ☎983-2405. Popular nonsmoking diner-style café, serving breakfast along with lunches featuring Reuben sandwiches ($8.50), halibut burgers ($9), and ice cream. Daily 6am–2pm.

Listings

Banks Wells Fargo, Broadway at 6th Ave (Mon–Fri 9.30am–5pm), has a 24hr ATM.

Bicycle rental Sourdough Car Rentals (see below) rents basic runabouts for $10 a day; Sockeye Cycle Co, 381 5th Ave at Broadway (☎983-2851, ⓦwww.cyclealaska.com), charges $12 for 2hr, $20 a half-day, and $30 an eight-hour day, with discounts offered for two- and three-day rentals.

Bookshop Skagway News Depot, Broadway at 3rd Ave (☎983-3354, ⓦwww.skagwaybooks.com), has lots of Alaskana, a small selection of other books and magazines, and out-of-state newspapers.

Car rental The cheapest cars are offered by Sourdough Car Rentals, 350 6th Ave at Broadway (☎983-2523, ⓦwww.geocities.com/sourdoughcarrentals), which has compacts for $60 with 125 miles a day.

Festivals and events The Buckwheat Ski Classic (3rd weekend in March) is a cross-country ski race following the route of the stampeders over the White Pass; the lively Independence Day celebrations (July 4) are a good day to be in town, as is the Klondike Trail of '98 International Road Relay (first weekend in Sept; ☎1-867/668-4236, ⓦwww.sportyukon.com), during which almost 200 teams of runners leave Skagway for Whitehorse, racing through the night.

Internet access Free for half an hour at the library (see below); commercially at Alaska Cruiseship Services, 2nd Ave at State St, *Glacial Smoothies & Espresso*, 3rd Ave at Broadway, and *The Haven*, State St at 9th Ave, which has WiFi.

Laundry and showers Pay-by-the-quarter showers next to the Harbormaster's office on Congress Way. Laundry at Services Unlimited, on State at 2nd (daily 7am–9pm), and at *Garden City RV Park*, State St at 16th St.

Left luggage Hands Free, 4th Ave & State St, offers bag storage for $1 an hour or $5 a day. When hiking the Chilkoot you can often leave bags with your hotel or hostel; most are amenable but it pays to ask.

Library Skagway Public Library, State St at 8th Ave (Mon–Fri noon–9pm, Sat 1–5pm).

Medical assistance Dahl Memorial Medical Clinic, Main St at 15th Ave ☎983-2255.

Outdoor gear The Mountain Shop, 355 4th Ave (☎983-2544, ⓦwww.packerexpeditions.com), sells major brands and rents tents (first night $20, subsequent nights $10), sleeping bags ($16/$8), cooking stoves ($6/$3), packs ($14/$7), sleeping pads ($6/$3), trekking poles ($5/$3), and snowshoes ($5). Post office Broadway at 6th Ave (Mon–Fri 8.30am–5pm and summer Sundays 10am–4pm). The General Delivery zip code is 99840.

Taxes There's a four percent sales tax in Skagway; the tax on hotels amounts to eight percent and isn't included in our quoted accommodation prices.

Travel details

With the exception of the 372-mile loop between near neighbors Haines and Skagway, none of the towns in Southeast is connected by road, so ferries and planes take the load. The following ferry frequencies apply only from late May to early September, though there are limited services throughout the winter.

Alaska Airlines links most of the main Southeast towns using Juneau as the main hub. It runs several frequent-stop "milk runs" daily, such as Juneau–Petersburg–Wrangell–Ketchikan–Seattle, Anchorage–Juneau–Sitka–Seattle, and Anchorage–Cordova–Yakutat–Juneau–Seattle.

Buses

Skagway to: Whitehorse (1 daily; 3–4hr).

Ferries

Angoon to: Juneau (2 weekly; 6hr).
Bellingham, WA to: Juneau (2 weekly; 60hr); Ketchikan (2 weekly; 37hr).
Coffman Cove, POW to: Wrangell (4 weekly; 3hr).
Haines to: Juneau (1–2 daily; 2hr 30min–6hr); Skagway (several daily; 1hr).
Hollis to: Ketchikan (2 daily; 3hr).
Hoonah to: Juneau (2 weekly; 3–7hr); Tenakee Springs (1 weekly; 2hr 30min).
Juneau to: Angoon (2 weekly; 6hr); Bellingham, WA (2 weekly; 60hr); Haines (1–2 daily; 2hr 15min–4hr); Hoonah (2 weekly; 3hr); Ketchikan (roughly daily; 20hr); Petersburg (roughly daily; 8hr); Prince Rupert, BC (4–5 weekly; 26–29hr); Sitka (4–5 weekly; 4–8hr); Skagway (1–2 daily; 2hr 30min–7hr); Tenakee Springs (weekly; 5hr); Whittier (2 monthly; 38hr); Wrangell (roughly daily; 14hr).
Ketchikan to: Bellingham, WA (2 weekly; 37hr); Hollis (2 daily; 3hr); Metlakatla (2 daily Mon–Thurs; 1hr 30min); Petersburg (roughly daily; 10hr); Prince Rupert, BC (4–5 weekly; 6–7hr); Wrangell (roughly daily; 6hr).
Metlakatla to: Ketchikan (2 daily Mon–Thurs; 1hr 30min).
Petersburg to: Juneau (roughly daily; 8hr); Sitka (1–3 weekly; 11hr); Wrangell (roughly daily; 3hr).
Prince Rupert, BC to: Juneau (4–5 weekly; 26–29hr); Ketchikan (4–5 weekly; 6–7hr).
Sitka to: Juneau (4–5 weekly; 4–8hr); Petersburg (1–3 weekly; 11hr).
Skagway to: Haines (several daily; 1hr); Juneau (1–2 daily; 2hr 30min–8hr).
South Mitkof to: Wrangell (4 weekly; 1hr).

Tenakee Springs to: Hoonah (1 weekly; 2hr 30min); Juneau (2 weekly; 5–7hr).
Wrangell to: Coffman Cove, POW (4 weekly; 3hr); Juneau (roughly daily; 14hr); Ketchikan (roughly daily; 7hr); Petersburg (roughly daily; 3hr); South Mitkof (4 weekly; 1hr).

Flights

Glacier Bay/Gustavus to: Juneau (3–5 daily; 25–40min).
Juneau to: Anchorage (4 daily; 1hr 40min); Cordova (1 daily; 2hr 15min); Gustavus (3–5 daily; 25–40min); Ketchikan (2 daily; 1–2hr); Petersburg (1 daily; 40min); Seattle (6–9 daily; 3hr 20min–4hr 30min); Sitka (2–3 daily; 40min); Wrangell (1 daily; 1hr 40min); Yakutat (1 daily; 45min).
Ketchikan to: Anchorage (1 daily; 4hr 30min); Craig (3 daily; 45min); Juneau (2 daily; 1–2hr); Metlakatla (15 daily; 10min); Petersburg (1 daily; 1hr 45min); Seattle (5 daily; 2hr); Sitka (1 daily; 1hr 50min); Wrangell (1 daily; 40min).
Petersburg to: Anchorage (1 daily; 3hr); Juneau (1 daily; 40min); Ketchikan (1 daily; 1hr 45min); Seattle (1 daily; 5hr); Wrangell (1 daily; 20min).
Seattle to: Juneau (6–9 daily; 3hr 20min–4hr 30min); Ketchikan (5 daily; 2hr); Petersburg (1 daily; 5hr); Sitka (4 daily; 4–5hr); Wrangell (1 daily; 2hr 30min); Yakutat (1 daily; 3hr).
Sitka to: Anchorage (1 daily; 3hr); Juneau (2–3 daily; 40min); Ketchikan (1 daily; 50min); Seattle (4 daily; 4–5hr).
Wrangell to: Anchorage (1 daily; 4hr); Juneau (1 daily; 1hr 40min); Ketchikan (1 daily; 40min); Petersburg (1 daily; 20min); Seattle (1 daily; 2hr 30min).
Yakutat to: Anchorage (1 daily; 2hr); Cordova (1 daily; 45min); Juneau (1 daily; 45min); Seattle (1 daily; 3hr).

Anchorage

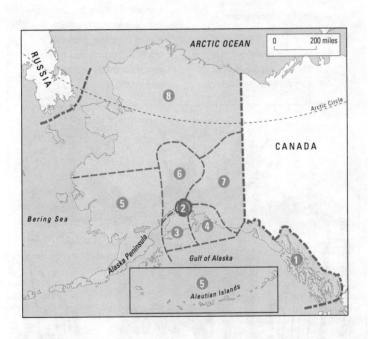

CHAPTER 2   # Highlights

* **Ride the Coastal Trail** Explore the bike trails of Kincaid Park, then ride back in the evening sun along the Tony Knowles Coastal Trail. See p.217

* **Hooking kings downtown** Fish for king and silver salmon in Ship Creek, virtually in the shadow of downtown skyscrapers. See p.224

* **Museum of History & Art** A first-class exploration of Alaska's culture and history, plus the state's best collection of fine art. See p.226

* **Hike the Crow Pass Trail** An excellent overnight hike around eastern Anchorage through the Chugach Mountains. See p.233

* **Alaska Native Heritage Center** A pricey but welcome introduction to Alaska's Native peoples. Especially worth it if you're not going to visit their tribal homelands. See p.235

△ An unexpected visitor

2

Anchorage

Now over a quarter of a million strong, **ANCHORAGE** is Alaska's only true city. It is home to 42 percent of Alaskans, is five times the size of its nearest challenger, Fairbanks, and is the state capital in all but name. Alaska's lifeblood, oil, plays a big part. Black gold is neither tapped, shipped, nor pumped anywhere near the city, but oil companies have established offices here, and oil-generated wealth has a tangible presence. In many ways it is the very antithesis of all things archetypally Alaskan, with gleaming cars, designer labels, and gourmet goodies present in a way you won't find anywhere else in the state. On these grounds alone Anchorage is loathed, or at least resented, by just about everyone who doesn't live in the big city. Whenever talk turns to moving the state capital away from Juneau to somewhere more central and accessible, Anchorage is the obvious choice, but for fear of concentrating even more power here, the rest of the state will never let that happen.

Flying into the **Anchorage Bowl** – the region encompassing the city and its immediate surroundings – you're instantly struck by the majesty of the setting, seated at the foot of the snowcapped Chugach Mountains on the edge of a great wilderness and girt by the shimmering water of Cook Inlet. Trouble is, the civic planners seem to have turned their backs on the location and managed to produce a replica of just about any American city west of the Great Plains: a couple of clusters of glass office blocks set in a fabric of shopping malls, all cemented together by fast-food and family restaurants. "Condensed, instant Albuquerque," John McPhee called it in his 1977 classic *Coming into the Country*, and that's probably truer today (when some call it "Los Anchorage") than it was then. Some seventy percent of current residents were not here in 1980. Indeed, until very recently, Anchorage was always considered a stepping-stone to somewhere better (usually more remote, or warmer). Even today, it's likely you won't be in Anchorage long before some wag tells you that the great thing about the city is that Alaska is only half an hour away. It is certainly true that you have to travel only a short distance to experience glaciers, precipitous mountains, and wild bush country, but Anchorage itself has its charms. What other city has moose grazing alongside the highways and chomping through suburban flower gardens, Beluga whales breaching within yards of the coastal bike trail, twenty hours of midsummer sunlight, and magnificent hiking trails just a couple of miles from downtown?

Thanks to the warming effect of the Japan Current and the rain-shadowing beneficence of the Kenai and Chugach mountains, you can spend the summer days in shorts and a T-shirt cycling the coastal bike trail, hiking to hilltops with fabulous views of the Alaska Range, or even swimming in one of

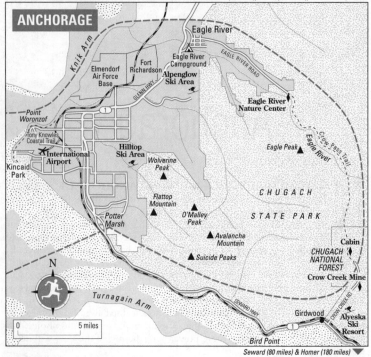

Palmer (30 miles), Denali (230 miles), & Fairbanks (350 miles)

ANCHORAGE

Eagle River

Knik Arm

EAGLE RIVER ROAD

Eagle River
Campground

Elmendorf
Air Force
Base

Fort
Richardson

Eagle River
**Alpenglow
Ski Area**

Eagle River
Nature Center

GLENN HWY

Point
Woronzof

Crow Pass Trail

Eagle River

Tony Knowles
Coastal Trail

**Hilltop
Ski Area**

Eagle Peak

International
Airport

Wolverine
Peak

Kincaid
Park

Flattop
Mountain

O'Malley
Peak

C H U G A C H

S T A T E   P A R K

Potter
Marsh

Avalanche
Mountain

Suicide Peaks

Cabin

*CHUGACH
NATIONAL
FOREST*

Crow Creek Mine

N

CROW CREEK RD

Turnagain Arm

SEWARD HWY

Girdwood

**Alyeska
Ski
Resort**

0   5 miles

Bird Point

Seward (80 miles) & Homer (180 miles)

ANCHORAGE

2

the city's small lakes. There are more urban attractions, too, not least the state's most cosmopolitan, and tolerably affordable, dining and drinking scene, and a coffee culture as strong as that of any West Coast city. That alone is enough to justify stopping for a few nights, but there are also a couple of excellent museums – the Anchorage Museum of History & Art and the Alaska Heritage Museum – and the ground-breaking Alaska Native Heritage Center.

Some history

The banks of Cook Inlet were first discovered around five thousand years ago when proto-Eskimos occupied sites along Turnagain Arm. Dena'ina Athabascans had taken their place by the time early Russian explorers came to exchange copper and iron for fish and furs, and in 1778 these Native Alaskans traded with British captain **James Cook** who was here in search of the Northwest Passage, a mythical short-cut for ships from the Atlantic to the Pacific. This waterway is now known as Cook Inlet in his honor, though he himself dubbed one branch **Turnagain Arm** as he about-faced and tacked off to search further west.

By Cook's time, the **Russians** were well established in the region, particularly in Eklutna, twenty miles north of Anchorage, where a Russian Orthodox church still stands. It wasn't until 1912 that Congress sensed the need for greater access to strategic inland coalfields and sanctioned the construction of a railroad linking the port of Seward and the navigable rivers of the Interior. Construction was centered on the ice-free shores of Cook Inlet, a flat and barren spot that soon sprouted the fledgling city of Anchorage. Within weeks the tent city on the north shore of Ship Creek was home to two thousand construction hopefuls. Five months later the land south of the creek was auctioned off in gridded lots, leaving the site of the tent city as home to rail yards and docks. Some 650 lots were sold with the stipulation that any lots used for gambling, prostitution, or liquor production would be forfeited. The US Post Office used a literal description of the site and called the place Anchorage, a name which the residents failed to dislodge despite holding a referendum and picking Alaska City as the name for their new home.

Since then Anchorage has been characterized by rapid but sporadic growth. By the beginning of the 1940s, the city still had only 3500 residents, but it was soon to see the effect of a developing infrastructure and a spin-off from the influx of New Deal settlers in the Matanuska–Susitna Valley. With the arrival of the military during World War II, Anchorage was firmly established as Alaska's dominant city, and statewide developments – such as the construction of the Alaska Highway – only served to reinforce this position. The population had jumped to 47,000 by the completion of the road link to Seward in the early 1950s, just in time for the discovery of oil on the Kenai Peninsula. This, statehood in 1959, and the establishment of Anchorage's international airport – which, being equidistant from New York and Tokyo, soon became

The Permanent Fund Dividend

Alaskans pay no state income tax, and on top of that they reap the benefits of the **Permanent Fund Dividend** (🖥 www.pfd.state.ak.us), the result of a 1976 state constitutional amendment that set aside a quarter of all oil royalties as a kind of nest egg to be used as oil revenues declined. Very quickly the account reached embarrassing proportions, and in 1982 the state made its first payment to residents, distributing ten percent of the annual interest gained (averaged over the preceding five years) among those who qualified. Initially there was to be a payment of $50 to each adult for each year of residency, but that was overthrown by the US Supreme Court, and there is now an equal payment in the first week in October each year to every man, woman, and child who has spent ten months of the previous calendar year in Alaska. Even a vagrant can claim it, if he can come up with a viable address.

Having peaked at $1963 per resident in 2000, the PFD gradually fell to $846 due to recession and the state's growing population; however, in 2006 soaring oil prices sent it back up to $1107, with bigger payouts forecast for the next few years. For a family of five it might form a quarter of their annual income and provide an opportunity to stash some away for the kids' education or to just get frivolous. By mid-September Alaskan companies start tapping into the mini-boom, luring customers with attractive offers: airlines advertise multiflight trips, and with winter approaching snowmobile dealers do a roaring trade discounting their latest models. For people eking out a hand-to-mouth existence in the woods from hunting, trapping, and a little gold panning, it is even more important. For them PFD season is the only time of year they have enough cash to stock up on spare parts, fishing lures, ammunition, fuel, and basic groceries.

The payment has become a staple of the Alaskan year – a strange situation in a state where anything that has the faintest whiff of socialism is widely reviled and ridiculed. It was long considered political suicide to drop or substantially cut the PFD, but recent state budget shortfalls meant that even this icon of the North was briefly under threat. Despite the bear markets of recent years having lowered the PFD's value from $28 billion to around $22 billion, however, skyrocketing oil prices subsequently pushed it up to $34 billion in 2006. Its investment income now generates more wealth than the state earns from its oil, gas, and mineral royalties.

a kind of subpolar crossroads for Great Circle flights – set an optimistic tone for the new decade. Confidence was soon rocked by the 1964 **Good Friday earthquake** (see box, p.590), which destroyed an entire suburb, wrecked the city, and imprinted itself on the memories of a generation.

During the 1950s, a small oil-drilling operation had been established on the Kenai Peninsula, so when enormous quantities of the commodity were discovered at Prudhoe Bay in Alaska's Arctic North, it made sense for oil companies to consolidate their operations in Anchorage. Fairbanks was the base for the construction of the Trans-Alaska Pipeline (see box, p.538), but Anchorage continued to benefit from the new pool of skilled workers, who increased the workforce and justified further city development in order to accommodate them. When the state's oil revenues started pouring in so fast they couldn't be spent, the benefits were divided proportionally to population, so it was Anchorage that got a slew of new and grandiose buildings downtown – library, sports arena, civic center, and more. But much of the money was diverted into the Permanent Fund (see box, opposite), which helped ease the hardships brought on by low oil prices in the late 1980s. Today, Anchorage continues to grow, gradually shaking off its boom-and-bust persona and gaining a level of maturity as it copes with the economic difficulties thrown up by the decline in oil output.

Arrival, information, and city transportation

As Alaska's major gateway city, Anchorage sees a sizeable portion of the state's international arrivals. If you're not driving the Alaska Highway or cruising up through the Inside Passage you'll almost certainly arrive here. Most domestic **flights** arrive from Seattle; get a right-side window seat for views of the Inside Passage, fjords, and glaciers prior to the magnificent descent into Anchorage airport (ANC), renamed Ted Stevens Anchorage International Airport a few years back for Alaska's senior senator (see box, p.593).

Direct flights from outside North America and all Delta and US Airlines flights arrive at the North (international) Terminal, which has only a small visitor desk (open for flight arrivals) and an ATM; to get to the main terminal or parking lots board the free Airport Shuttle that runs every fifteen minutes around the clock. All other flights arrive at the main South (domestic) Terminal which, along with the usual restaurants and shops, has a **visitor information** desk (daily 9am–4pm) in the baggage claim area, ATMs (but no foreign exchange facilities), courtesy phones to some hotels, and luggage storage (see Listings, p.248). For arrivals information see Ⓦwww.dot.state.ak.us/anc or check with the airline concerned.

The airport is only five miles southwest of central Anchorage, so **getting downtown** is quick and fairly painless. Taxis cost about $20 and line up outside the terminal; the city's **People Mover bus** #7 runs downtown every hour (Mon–Fri 7am–10.20pm, Sat 9am–7.40pm, Sun 10am–6pm; $1.50) from both terminals; hotels, hostels, and car rental companies almost all provide shuttles. Alaska Shuttle Service (Ⓣ388-8888 or 694-8888) charges $10 to take you downtown ($5 each for three or more passengers), $20 (around $10 each for three or more) to other parts of the Anchorage Bowl, and $30 to Eagle River ($10 each for three or more). Similar service is provided by Shuttle Man (Ⓣ677-8537), while Eagle River Shuttle (Ⓣ694-8888) and Talkeetna Shuttle (Ⓣ1-888/288-6008) specialize in transport to their respective offices.

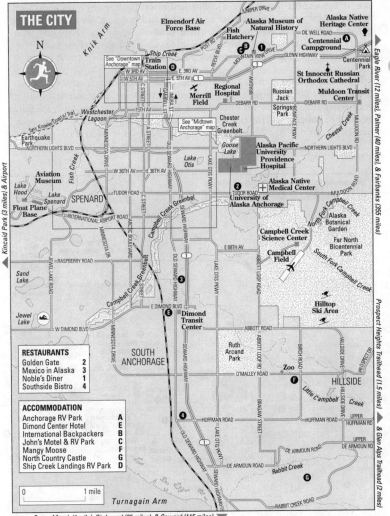

Knik Arm

JUNIPER DRIVE

Elmendorf Air Force Base

Fish Hatchery

Alaska Museum of Natural History

Alaska Native Heritage Center

OIL WELL ROAD

Centennial Campground **A**

C **B** **1**

MOUNTAIN VIEW DRIVE

POST RD

REEVE BLVD

GLENN HIGHWAY

Centennial Park

Eagle River (12 miles), Palmer (40 miles), & Fairbanks (355 miles)

Ship Creek Train Station **D**

See "Downtown Anchorage" map

E. 3RD AV

E. 5TH AV

W 3RD AV

W 5TH AV

C STREET

GAMBELL ST

INGRA ST

Merrill Field

Regional Hospital

St Innocent Russian Orthodox Cathedral

Muldoon Transit Center

Westchester Lagoon

15TH AV

DEBARR RD

Russian Jack Springs Park

BONIFACE PKWY

DEBARR RD

Chester Creek Greenbelt

See "Midtown Anchorage" map

MULDOON RD

Tony Knowles Coastal Trail

Earthquake Park

NORTHERN LIGHTS BLVD

MINNESOTA DRIVE

C STREET

LAKE OTIS PKWY

Goose Lake

Chester Creek

NORTHERN LIGHTS BLVD

Kincaid Park (3 miles) & Airport

Fish Creek

Lake Otis

Alaska Pacific University Providence Hospital

Aviation Museum

Lake Hood

Lake Spenard

SPENARD

W 36TH AV

36TH AV

Alaska Native Medical Center

MULDOON ROAD

North Fork Campbell Creek

Float Plane Base

INTERNATIONAL AIRPORT ROAD

TUDOR ROAD

C STREET

ARCTIC BOULEVARD

Campbell Creek Greenbelt

SEWARD HIGHWAY

TUDOR ROAD **2**

University of Alaska Anchorage

Alaska Botanical Garden

Far North Bicentennial Park

South Fork Campbell Creek

JEWEL LAKE ROAD

RASPBERRY ROAD

MINNESOTA DR.

OLD SEWARD HIGHWAY

LAKE OTIS PKWY

E 68TH AV

Campbell Creek Science Center

Campbell Field

Prospect Heights Trailhead (1.5 miles)

Sand Lake

Jewel Lake

3

ABBOTT LOOP ROAD

PROSPECT DR

Hilltop Ski Area

Campbell Creek Greenbelt

E DIMOND BLVD

E Dimond Transit Center

ABBOTT ROAD

HILLSIDE DRIVE

& Glen Alps Trailhead (2 miles)

W DIMOND BLVD

MINNESOTA DRIVE

SOUTH ANCHORAGE

OLD SEWARD HIGHWAY

SEWARD HIGHWAY

Ruth Arcand Park

ABBOTT LOOP RD

BRAGAW STREET

BIRCH RD

Zoo

O'MALLEY ROAD

F

HILLSIDE DRIVE

Little Campbell Creek

HILLSIDE

4

HUFFMAN ROAD

LAKE OTIS PKWY

HUFFMAN ROAD

UPPER HUFFMAN RD

UPPER DE ARMOUN RD

DE ARMOUN ROAD

DE ARMOUN ROAD

Rabbit Creek

G

RABBIT CREEK ROAD

Turnagain Arm

0 — 1 mile

RESTAURANTS
Golden Gate   2
Mexico in Alaska   3
Noble's Diner   1
Southside Bistro   4

ACCOMMODATION
Anchorage RV Park   **A**
Dimond Center Hotel   **E**
International Backpackers   **B**
John's Motel & RV Park   **C**
Mangy Moose   **F**
North Country Castle   **G**
Ship Creek Landings RV Park **D**

Potter Marsh (1 mile), Girdwood (25 miles), & Seward (115 miles) ▼

ANCHORAGE | Arrival, information, and city transportation

Cruise lines provide trains to take passengers directly from the airport to their ships, but there are currently no plans for passenger trains to downtown. From mid-2008 there should be fast ferry service across the Knik Arm from near the mouth of Ship Creek to Point Mackenzie. For your first night's accommodation (or last night before departure), it may be worth staying at one of the places closest to the airport (see Midtown and Spenard accommodation, p.218), which offer courtesy airport pickup and drop-off.

Drivers picking up **rental cars** will find desks for the major car rental agencies – Alamo, Avis, Budget, Dollar, Hertz, National, Payless, and Thrifty – in the South Terminal (see opposite), while the smaller companies will meet you at the airport if you have a confirmed reservation – always a good idea in the summer when vehicles are in demand, and booking ahead will usually get you better deals. Also note that these smaller companies frequently offer much lower rates in return for slightly older cars and that off-airport agencies can charge slightly lower prices by avoiding a city tax on car rental at the airport.

The **train station** is at 411 1st St, a fairly easy walk from downtown hotels; dating from 1948, it is now being expanded, but this should not interfere greatly with schedules. Services are limited to a couple of trains a day (and are fully detailed in Basics, p.42); the ticket office (mid-May to mid-Sept daily 5am–4pm; mid-Sept to mid-May Mon–Fri 9am–4pm; ☏265-2494 Mon–Fri 7am–5pm,

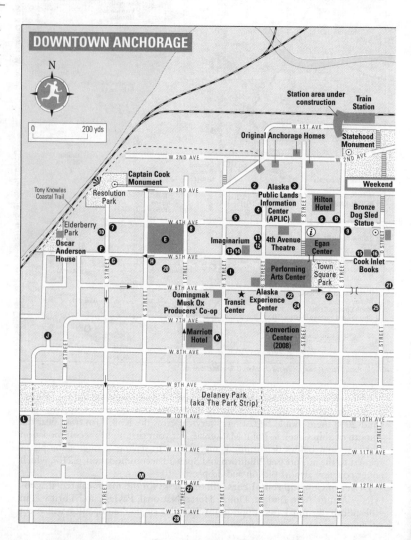

DOWNTOWN ANCHORAGE

Sat & Sun 8am–4pm) fields inquiries and sells tickets to Seward, Denali, and Fairbanks. Taxis meet all arriving trains.

Various **long-distance buses** serve Anchorage and pick up at the airport and around town (for more details see p.218 & p.247). Cruise passengers should usually check in at the Egan Conference Center (on 5th Avenue between E and F streets) for buses to their ships.

Orientation

The grid-plan **downtown** area is at the city's northern limit, with avenues running east–west and increasing numerically as you go south. Streets run north–south, progressing alphabetically as you travel west from A Street (though

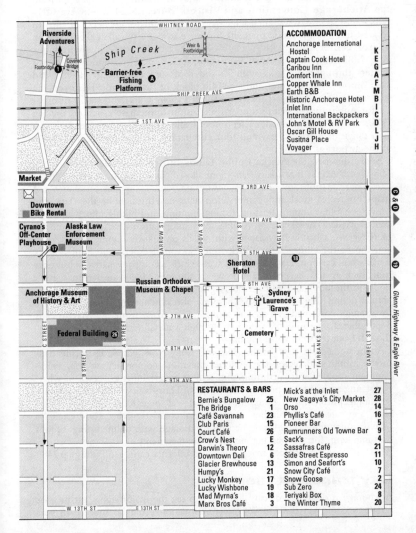

ACCOMMODATION

Anchorage International Hostel	K
Captain Cook Hotel	E
Caribou Inn	G
Comfort Inn	A
Copper Whale Inn	F
Earth B&B	M
Historic Anchorage Hotel	B
Inlet Inn	I
International Backpackers	C
John's Motel & RV Park	D
Oscar Gill House	L
Susitna Place	J
Voyager	H

RESTAURANTS & BARS

Bernie's Bungalow	25	Mick's at the Inlet	27
The Bridge	1	New Sagaya's City Market	28
Café Savannah	23	Orso	14
Club Paris	15	Phyllis's Café	16
Court Café	26	Pioneer Bar	5
Crow's Nest	E	Rumrunners Old Towne Bar	9
Darwin's Theory	12	Sack's	4
Downtown Deli	6	Sassafras Café	21
Glacier Brewhouse	13	Side Street Espresso	11
Humpy's	21	Simon and Seafort's	10
Lucky Monkey	17	Snow City Café	7
Lucky Wishbone	19	Snow Goose	2
Mad Myrna's	18	Sub Zero	24
Marx Bros Café	3	Teriyaki Box	8
		The Winter Thyme	20

there is no J Street), and carrying alphabetized names – Barrow, Cordova, Denali, and so on – as you travel east from A Street. Addresses along streets increase going south so that number 320 is between 3rd and 4th.

The Chester Creek Greenbelt marks the boundary between downtown and **midtown**, an amorphous smear of malls and broad streets bounded on the east by the city's two universities and to the west by Spenard Road and the airport.

Beyond Tudor Road, **South Anchorage** comprises the whole southern half of the city, and stretches up onto the wealthier suburb of the **Hillside**.

Information

Advance information on Anchorage and its vicinity is available from the **Anchorage Convention and Visitors Bureau**, 524 W 4th Ave (☎1-800/478-1255, ⓦwww.anchorage.net, ⓦwww.anchorage.net/454.cfm to request free visitors guide by mail), but once in the city call at the log-cabin **visitor center**, 546 W 4th Ave at F St (daily: May & Sept 9am–6pm; June–Aug 7.30am–7pm; Oct–April 9am–4pm; ☎274-3531), a model for visitor centers throughout Alaska with its sod roof sprouting Jacob's ladder and wild onions in springtime, and a 5114lb block of jade outside. Here you can pick up the free, listings-packed *Anchorage Visitors Guide* and stacks of other visitor publications. In the modern extension immediately behind the log cabin you can find a broader selection of leaflets, plus free direct-dial phones to a range of places to stay and tour companies. The center has an outpost at the airport as well.

Across the road, the **Alaska Public Lands Information Center** (APLIC), 605 W 4th Ave at F St (daily 9am–5pm, closed Sat & Sun from early Sept to late May; ☎1-866/869-6887, ⓦwww.nps.gov/aplic), supplies brochures and maps on recreational and conservation activities throughout the state, and provides cabin, camping, boating, fishing, hunting, and hiking information for central Alaska. There's also an AMHS ferry information desk, and free copies of *Ridgelines*, a handy newspaper with details on hikes, camping, and day-use activities in the Chugach State Park which surrounds Anchorage. Stuffed bears, musk oxen, caribou, Dall sheep, and wolverines accompany native subsistence tools such as nets, harpoons, and bows; in summer, videos are screened every hour on the hour, and staff members give free talks (2pm Sun–Wed) and live animal demos (2pm Thurs–Sat). There are also downtown walking tours, led by a ranger costumed as Captain Cook, at 11am daily from late May to early September. To get in you need to go through a metal detector and (in theory) show ID, but it's well worth the hassle.

Anchorage's main paper is the *Anchorage Daily News*, which also prints daily movie listings and on Friday publishes the more comprehensive *Play* entertainment supplement. For listings and offbeat, entertaining coverage of what's happening around town pick up a free copy of Thursday's weekly *Press* (ⓦwww.anchoragepress.com) at bookshops and cafés all over town: something of a clubs and cafés newsletter, but a refreshing alternative to the *ADN*. Craigslist (ⓦwww.anchorage.craigslist.org) covers Anchorage, with online listings of jobs, housing, items for sale, and community announcements.

For more on Anchorage's map outlets and Internet cafés, see Listings, p.248.

City transportation

Anchorage is designed for cars, but you can see the major sights, eat in good restaurants, and get back to your accommodation using no more than your

Anchorage's main roads are four-lane drag strips hogged by drivers whose lack of bike-awareness threatens cyclists: wear a helmet. Fortunately, green "Bike Route" signs herd riders onto the sidewalk – it's not exactly a bike path but the total absence of pedestrian obstacles makes it safer than the car-dominated road. All People Mover buses are equipped with bike racks, and bikes ride free.

Cycling in Anchorage is best following one of the **bike trails** – smooth, paved affairs also open to walkers, rollerbladers, and rollerskiers – though they're seldom the shortest route between two points. Foremost among them is the **Tony Knowles Coastal Trail** (see p.228), which runs eleven miles from the western end of 2nd Avenue downtown to Kincaid Park, itself laced with more than forty miles of trails. On any fine day you'll have plenty of company, with everyone making the best of the long views over tidal flats to **Mount Susitna**, locally known as The Sleeping Lady (it takes some imagination, but apparently she has her arms crossed over her chest).

At Westchester Lagoon, a mile south of downtown, the **Lanie Fleischer Chester Creek Trail** cuts inland through the Chester Creek Greenbelt, a streamside meander through midtown verdure to the university campuses and the Campbell Tract. With a bit of on-street riding you could then pick up the **Campbell Creek Trail**, heading southwest to Turnagain Arm south of Kincaid Park. North of downtown, the new **Ship Creek Trail** leads east to the regeneration area of Mountain View.

Mountain bikers are also well served, with scope for exploring the Chugach Mountains (see box, p.232) and a heap of cross-country ski trails, which make excellent bike routes from mid-May to mid-October. Pick up the *Anchorage Cross Country Ski Trails Map* ($8 from the visitor center) for details on miles of trails (for skiing in winter, biking in summer) primarily in the moose-infested **Kincaid Park**, through the undulating landscape, beaver pools, and mud of **Far North Bicentennial Park**, or in the more limited terrain of **Russian Jack Springs Park**. Hilltop Park, just south of Far North Bicentennial Park, boasts some world-class single-track trails, such as the Spencer Loop and Brown Bear trails; it's also possible to find a way from the Spencer Loop Trail to the Chugach State Park's Prospect Heights Trail by following either the rough right-of-way of an old gas pipeline or the narrow Canyon Trail along Campbell Creek.

There are several **bike rental** places around town, most offering fairly decent machines for about $30 a day, including helmet, lock, and a map of good routes. The most convenient outlet downtown is Downtown Bicycle Rental, 333 W 4th Ave (mid-May to mid-Sept daily 9am–7pm; sporadically in winter; ℡279-5293, ⓦwww.alaska-bike-rentals.com), which rents bikes on a first-come, first-served basis and requires a major credit card; rates are $15 for three hours and $29 for 24 hours, and tandems go for $43 a day. Pablo's Bike Rentals at 5th Ave and L St (May–Sept daily 8am–7pm; ℡250-2871) has bikes for $15 for four hours and $5 per additional hour to a maximum of $30 for 24 hours. In midtown the Bicycle Shop, 1035 W Northern Lights Blvd (℡272-5219), sells and repairs bikes and also offers bargain rental of mid-range mountain bikes for $20 for the first 24 hours then $15 a day thereafter.

Bike tours from Anchorage are run by Alaska Backcountry Bike Tours (May–Sept daily; ℡1-866/354-2453, ⓦwww.mountainbikealaska.com), which has a number of day-trips, ranging from ninety minutes on the Coastal Trail ($69) to sixteen miles of technical single-track riding over Johnson Pass ($129), plus multiday expeditions.

Horse-riding is also catered for by Turnagain Trails (mid-May to mid-Oct; ℡336-4077, ⓦwww.turnagaintrails.com), off Abbott Road in Hilltop Park, offering rides at $75 for ninety minutes, $125 for half a day, or $200 for a day, plus overnight trips.

own feet and the city bus system. Try to do anything in a hurry, though, and you're out of luck – possibly the best argument for **renting a car** in Anchorage. Once equipped with a vehicle, getting used to Anchorage's traffic is rarely a problem. **Parking** is easy; every mall has a huge lot, and even downtown you'll find low-cost parking meters within a couple of blocks of where you need to be. Free two-hour parking is available pretty close to downtown, south of the Park Strip.

Cycling is also viable and can be the most pleasant way to get around, especially using some of the city's excellent bike trails (see box, p.217).

Buses

For such a spread-out and thinly populated city, Anchorage's "People Mover" **bus system** (ⓦwww.peoplemover.org) does a remarkably good job of covering a lot of ground, though the limited hours of operation (Mon–Fri 6am–10pm, Sat 8am–8pm, Sun 9.30am–6.30pm) can be frustrating, with some less popular routes shutting down as early as 7pm. Drivers take single fares ($1.75, no change given, bills accepted) and sell passes for a day ($4) or month ($50).

Routes generally start at the Downtown **Transit Center**, 6th Avenue and G Street, where you can obtain *The Ride Guide* ($1) with a route map and timetables for all services; staff can advise you here or on ⓣ343-6543 Monday through Friday, 8am–5pm (at other times this number reaches the automated Rideline). South Anchorage is served by the **Dimond Transit Center**, behind the Dimond Center Mall, five miles south of downtown, and East Anchorage by the **Muldoon Transit Center**, on Muldoon at DeBarr. People Mover also runs the Ship Creek Shuttle ($1.50), which loops through the downtown area, past the train station and to Ship Creek – though unless you're carrying heavy bags you may find it quicker and easier to walk. DART dial-a-ride buses (ⓣ277-3278) serve outlying areas of Eagle River, South Anchorage, and the Hillside.

You might also find some use for the **4th Avenue Trolley Tours**, 630 W 4th Ave (mid-May to mid-Sept, 8am–5.30pm every 30min; one tour $10, all-day pass $16; ⓣ257-5679), which leave from the 4th Avenue Theater and offer highly orchestrated bus tours which at least provide transport to a few places ill-served by city buses: Lake Hood, the Alaskan Aviation Heritage Museum, Earthquake Park, and Westchester Lagoon. Tours include a visit to the Art Deco 4th Avenue Theatre itself, and from early June to mid-September you can combine them with the *Hullabaloo* show (8pm; $15 alone or $20 combined with the tour; ⓣ257-5678). The same outfit also does 75-minute tours on wobbly Segway two-wheelers for $49 (ⓣ411-1124, ⓔsegtours@gci.net). **Anchorage City History Trolley Tours**, similar in style, leave from 612 W 4th Ave (ⓣ276-5603, ⓦwww.alaskatrolley.com); a one-hour tour is $10, leaving on the hour from 9am to 5pm.

Accommodation

Anchorage must have more **places to stay** than the rest of Alaska put together, but since most visitors to the state spend at least a couple of nights here, places fill up fast. From the beginning of June until the end of August it is critical to have something booked a few days (or even weeks) in advance. Late May can be busy too, but by mid-September things quiet down considerably. The city's hotel tax has been raised from eight to twelve percent for a period of four years to pay for the construction of the new Convention Center; it has to be quoted separately and not included in the room rate. There is no tax for RVs or tents.

Campers and RV drivers will find sites scattered all around the city, but everyone else ends up **downtown**, in **Spenard** near the airport, or on the **Hillside**, Anchorage's swanky suburb and home to some of the best B&Bs.

Prices strictly follow demand. In summer, hotels can pretty much charge what they like, and they do. Even quite modest motels go for over $100 a night, while the big hotels let their most basic room for upwards of $200, the same price you'd pay for the presidential suite in winter. B&Bs vary their prices less, but they play by the same rules: expect thirty to forty percent reductions on peak rates once winter rolls around. Visitors in early May, late September, and October can expect shoulder-season prices somewhere between these extremes. Hostels and campgrounds tend to hold their prices year-round, making them less competitive in the off-season, especially for a small group; in winter four people can stay at the *Sheraton* for little more than the cost of a dorm bed each at a hostel.

The price codes in this section represent the **cheapest** double or twin **room** in high season. Single rooms generally cost only ten to twenty percent less. Fees for **camping** are quoted and are for the tent site unless otherwise stated. **Hostel** bed prices are also quoted. Anchorage has raised its hotel **tax** from eight to twelve percent, and it may change again in 2009. This is not included in our accommodation price codes, and you should remember that locally quoted prices will be exclusive of these taxes as well.

In **winter** you can generally expect prices to drop by one (or possibly two) price codes except for hostels, which generally don't vary.

Hostels

Anchorage has Alaska's best range of hostels, from the basic-but-cheap to something approaching B&B luxury. Only the *Anchorage International Hostel* is downtown.

Anchorage Guesthouse 2001 Hillcrest Drive ☎274-0408, ⓦ www.akhouse.com. Just over a mile from downtown, this suburban house, run as sustainably as possible by musician-activist Andy Baker, is handy for midtown and the Coastal Trail (bikes available for $2.50 per hour with lock and helmet). Other perks include sheets, towels, breakfast, use of kitchen, free gear storage, free local calls, laundry, and Internet access ($2 for 15 minutes). There is (deliberately) just one small TV/video player. On offer are dorms with bunks and single beds ($30 June to mid-Oct/$27 off-peak) as well as private rooms with two doubles or one king-sized bed ($84/73), all sharing bathrooms.
Anchorage International Hostel 700 H St ☎276-3635, ⓦ www.anchorageinternationalhostel .org. A functional hostel in a great downtown location – a block from the Transit Center – though the daytime lockout (10am–5pm) and 1am curfew are less appealing. Kitchen, laundry, Internet access ($1 per 10min), and luggage storage ($1 a day per bag). There's a five-night maximum stay in summer. Reserve well in advance for dorm beds ($20) and private rooms ($55 for two).

International Backpackers Hostel 3523 Peterkin Ave ☎274-3870. The cheapest beds in Anchorage are at this group of houses which double as long-term accommodation. A couple of miles east of downtown in a rough but friendly neighborhood, there's no lockout or curfew. Take the #45 bus (every 40min, hourly at weekends) to Bragaw and Peterkin, and walk west three blocks. Laundry and bikes are available, and there's a huge TV with theater seating. Camping costs $10, beds in dorms (two are female-only; max three per room) are $15, and there are two private rooms for $30.
Jason's Anchorage Midtown International Youth Hostel 3324 Eide ☎562-0263. International backpackers gather here because of the free Internet and international phone calls on Skype, as well as the cooked breakfast. Washing machines are available, and some bus companies pick up here. Beds in four-bed rooms cost $20 in winter or $25 in summer.
Spenard Hostel International 2845 W 42nd Ave ☎248-5036, ⓦ www.alaskahostel.org. Friendly hostel about 1.5 miles from the airport and four from downtown with bikes for rent ($10 a day

without gears, $15 a day for mountain bikes). Most dorms are single-sex, there are no private rooms (unless you pay for four beds), and you'll be invited to do a small chore, but at $21 a bunk it's good value. Also features a garden with barbecue, spacious communal areas (including three kitchens), free hot drinks, low-cost baggage storage and laundry, Internet access ($0.10/min or $5/hr, or WiFi at $5/day), and no lockout. You may even be able to do three hours' work in return for your night's stay.

Hotels and motels

There are two major concentrations of hotels and motels. In the heart of the **downtown** area business hotels predominate, some all-out five-star affairs, some more modest but still attractive. Most other places – a couple of large hotels and lots of smaller motels – are in the **Spenard** neighborhood, close to much of the city's nightlife and the airport; all offer airport pickups.

Downtown and north

Captain Cook 4th Ave at K St ☎1-800/843-1950, ⓦwww.captaincook.com. The oil man's hotel of choice, the *Captain Cook* boasts every luxury – four restaurants with well-stocked bars, fabulous views (the best goes for $1500 in the penthouse suite), and a health club with pool. Suites $20 above normal room rates of $255. ❾

Caribou Inn 501 L St at 5th Ave ☎1-800/272-5878, ⓦwww.cariboubnb.com. These small and ageing but reasonably comfortable rooms are worth the price, coming with complimentary airport and train station shuttle, cable TV, off-street parking, and breakfast. Private and shared bath both ❹

Comfort Inn 111 W Ship Creek Ave ☎1-800/424-6423, ⓦwww.anchoragecomfortinn.com. Modern chain hotel with spacious, comfortable rooms (all with fridge, microwave, and cable TV) and abundant amenities including indoor pool, gym, hot tub, laundry, free wireless Internet access, plenty of parking, and a substantial continental breakfast. It is only ten minutes' walk from downtown but they run a 24hr free shuttle, and another to the airport. ❼

Historic Anchorage Hotel 330 E St at 4th Ave ☎1-800/544-0988, ⓦwww.historicanchoragehotel .com. This friendly little hotel, once frequented by renowned Alaskan painter Sydney Laurence, has been around since the birth of Anchorage (when it had a basement kennel for 100 dogs) and acts as a counterpoint to the top-notch business hotels surrounding it. The fascinating historic photos offset the understated decor, and it has business facilities plus complimentary newspaper and continental breakfast. ❼

Inlet Inn 539 H St at 6th Ave ☎277-5541, ⓔinletinn@ak.net. Undoubtedly the cheapest hotel rooms downtown, and the complimentary airport and train station shuttle, cable TV, and free local calls make it a bargain, though it can be noisy. The public areas and some of the decor leave a fair bit to be desired, and the presence of long-term guests doesn't help matters, but all rooms have private bath. ❹

Voyager 501 K St at 5th Ave ☎1-800/247-9070, ⓦwww.voyagerhotel.com. The best of the mid- to upper-range hotels, featuring spacious rooms (with kitchenette) plus most of the amenities of the business hotels without the stuffiness. There's a laundry, WiFi in the lobby, and free parking. Entirely nonsmoking and with a light breakfast included. Reserve well in advance for summer, when rates are almost double those in winter. ❼

Midtown and Spenard

Arctic Inn Motel 842 W International Airport Rd at Arctic Blvd ☎561-1328, ⓕ562-8701. Affordable motel that's close to the airport (about $8 by cab) and local restaurants, as well as Anchorage's main biker bar. The spacious and clean (if plain) rooms come with cable TV, phone, microwave, and fridge, although those near the front can be a little noisy. ❹

Dimond Center Hotel 700 E Dimond Center Blvd ☎1-866/770-5002, ⓦwww.dimondcenterhotel .com. Owned by the Seldovia Native Corporation (and with signs in Yupik as well as English), this new hotel has huge, lovely rooms (with giant tubs and TVs plus microwave, fridge, coffeemaker, dataport, and WiFi), a gym, and laundry. Although at South Anchorage's main transit interchange and well placed for transfer between the airport (free shuttle hourly) and the Kenai Peninsula, it's a little in the wilds otherwise, with no decent restaurant in the hotel or nearby. ❽

Millennium Alaskan Hotel 4800 Spenard Rd ☎1-800/544-0553, ⓦwww.millenniumhotels.com /anchorage. With perhaps the city's best collection of stuffed beasts and its own floatplane dock, plus 248 rooms (with coffeemakers and dataports), gym, and sauna, this is one of the most reliable stopovers near the airport. The *Fancy Moose Lounge* (serving food all day) and *Flying Machine Restaurant* offer the best dining in the immediate area. **9**

Puffin Inn 4400 Spenard Rd at Turnagain Blvd Ⓣ 1-800/478-3346, Ⓦ www.puffininn.net. The most appealing of the mid-priced motels close to the airport. Well maintained with simple but attractive economy rooms (all now air-conditioned) and a new deluxe wing. Free local calls, cable TV, gym, complimentary newspaper, coffee and muffins, and free airport transfers. Deluxe **7**, economy **6**

Qupqugiac Inn 640 W 36th Ave at Arctic Blvd Ⓣ 563-5633, Ⓦ www.qupq.com. Excellent small hotel that offers simply furnished but attractively decorated rooms (some with private shower and toilet) each with satellite TV and phones with voice mail. Unusually, there's also a common room equipped with a full kitchen, free tea and coffee, big TVs and free Internet access. Roadside rooms can be a little noisy. Private **4**, shared **3**

B&Bs

Anchorage's B&B market is booming, with new places opening all the time to cater to the massive summer influx, including semi-underground networks of gay, Christian, and suchlike B&Bs. They range from modest houses to palaces where the attention to detail borders on fanatical. The two main concentrations of B&Bs are **downtown**, within easy walking distance of just about everywhere (including the Transit Center for ventures further afield), and in the **Hillside** area, over five miles southeast of the center on the flanks of the Chugach Mountains and close to the hiking trailheads. You really need a car to stay out here, but if you have one this is the place to be – scenic and quiet. It is worth bearing in mind that city ordinances limit the size and location of B&Bs' signs, so you may need to look hard to find your bed for the night. Also, there is an increasing tendency to charge a premium (around $20) for one-night stays: ask when you book. All those listed here are open all year.

Downtown and north

Copper Whale Inn 440 L St Ⓣ 1-866/258-7999, Ⓦ www.copperwhale.com. Large and welcoming B&B ideally situated in the center of downtown. Rooms are comfortably furnished and have fitted blackout shades – a boon on the long summer evenings – but (intentionally) come without phones or TVs. An extensive buffet-style breakfast is served in the lounge, which overlooks Cook Inlet. Winter rates are less than half those for summer. **7**

Earth B&B 1001 W 12th Ave Ⓣ 279-9907, Ⓦ www.earthbb.com. Enthusiastically and liberally run, this is home away from home for Denali-bound climbers. It's fairly basic but very accommodating, with a garage for drying and sorting gear, a barbecue out back, and flexible deals for groups (particularly anyone doing anything adventurous or happy to share a room). Continental breakfast included. Bus #3, #36, or #60 from downtown. Private bath **5**, shared bath **4**

Oscar Gill House 1344 W 10th Ave Ⓣ 279-1344, Ⓦ www.oscargill.com. Lovely B&B in a historic house moved from Knik in 1916, comprehensively restored while maintaining character and understated elegance. Common areas are strewn with intriguing bric-a-brac plus books, mags, and photos. Two rooms share a bath and the largest has its own Jacuzzi; all are tastefully done

and looked after by very welcoming hosts, Mark and Susan Lutz, who lay on a very full breakfast and offer free laundry and bikes. Private bath **6**, shared bath **5**

Susitna Place 727 N St Ⓣ 274-3344, Ⓦ www.susitnaplace.com. Central lodge with a comfortable communal area overlooking Cook Inlet and Mount Susitna. Recently remodeled, rooms range from smallish shared-bath affairs to larger rooms with private baths, some with sundeck and water views, to the huge and always popular Susitna Suite, with magnificent views, whirlpool tub, and a private deck with views of Denali. Suite **7**, sea view **6**, shared bath **4**

The Hillside and around

Mangy Moose 5560 E 112th St Ⓣ 346-8052, Ⓦ www.alaskamangymoose.com. Neither the prominent moose's head in the lounge nor the rest of the house is the slightest bit mangy; in fact, this is one of the nicest B&Bs around. Attractive wood-paneled rooms all have private facilities and open onto a lovely deck, and everyone meets in the communal lounge with satellite TV, VCR, PC, and a self-serve kitchenette. Good breakfasts, too. **7–9**

North Country Castle 14600 Joanne Court Ⓣ 345-7296, Ⓦ www.castlealaska.com. Excellent value, if a little distant from the sights, this modern, informal home (as little like a castle as you could imagine) is tucked in among the white spruce at the southern limit of Anchorage. One suite has views of Flattop Mountain; the other sports a wonderful view over Turnagain Arm

from its private deck and has its own fireplace. There's WiFi and DSL Internet access; see their website for a map. Summer rates for two people are $209 for one suite, $229 for the other; Winter rates $149/$169.

Camping and RV parks

Campers are not well catered for in Anchorage; the nearest place that is at all pleasant to pitch a tent is *Centennial Campground*. With your own vehicle you might find it more pleasant commuting into the city from *Eagle River Campground* or the wooded sites 27 miles south at Bird Creek. **RV drivers** are better served with several full-service (and pricey) places close to town.

Anchorage RV Park 1200 N Muldoon Rd ☎1-800/400-7275, ⊛www.anchoragervpark.com. Very large, well-organized, and well-appointed RV park with wooded landscaping and pull-through sites with cable TV, WiFi, and laundry. No tents (this is bear country) but there is a cabin for $75–85 off-peak/$95–105 peak for two to four persons. Mid-May to mid-Sept. From $32 per day off-peak, $34 peak ($201/214 per week).

Centennial Campground 8300 Glenn Hwy off Boundary Ave ☎343-6986. Leafy first-come, first-served site five miles east of downtown with sites for $17 (tents) or $20 (RVs) and free showers. Bus #3 from downtown stops within half a mile or so.

Eagle River Campground Glenn Hwy, Eagle River ☎694-7982 or 746-4644. An Alaska State Parks campground twelve miles north of Anchorage

with fire pits, water, and outhouses, plus fishing, whitewater rafting, and short hiking trails right on the doorstep. Exploration opportunities include a shuttle to Eklutna Lake ($5) and a cycle trail to Anchorage. $15. Take the Hiland Rd exit off the expressway.

John's Motel & RV Park 3543 Mountain View Drive ☎1-800/478-4332, ⊛www.johnsmotel .com. Although it's mostly a gravel lot next to a busy road, *John's* offers good value with laundry and free showers. No tents; full hookup $25.

Ship Creek Landing RV Park 150 N Ingra ☎1-888/778-7700, ⊛www.alaskarv.com. Very central RV park and campground that's quite secluded despite being close to the train tracks. Tent sites on specially constructed sand pads ($16) and RV sites from dry ($19) to full hookup pull-through ($40); reductions in May and September.

△ Looking across Cook Inlet to downtown Anchorage

The City

In their eagerness to hightail it into the "real" Alaska, visitors tend to overlook Anchorage, but it's well worth spending some time here experiencing the only big-city taste that the state has to offer. Those who do will find that there are plenty of things to occupy two or three days – even a week isn't unreasonable, if you fancy using the city as a base for day-trips and local hikes. For the best introduction to Anchorage, simply wander around **downtown**, getting a flavor of a city grown too fast, whose blend of old and new, urban blight and rural parks can still conjure something of a shantytown feel. You can't miss the evidence of Anchorage's boom-and-bust development, with prefabricated clapboard houses and abandoned lots lying in the shadow of the glitzy high-rise ConocoPhillips oil building, which critics half-jokingly refer to as the city's capitol. The impact of oil revenue is equally visible in the Performing Arts Center and the **Anchorage Museum of History & Art**. In fact there's a new boom underway now, thanks to the soaring price of oil, with a $110 million convention center due for completion in 2008, followed by extensions to the museum and railroad station, not to mention $70 million of road improvements and regeneration projects in the Ship Creek and Mountain View districts. Other key sights to take in while walking around the downtown area include the salmon waters of **Ship Creek**, on the north side of which the original tent city sprung up, and the cemetery full of the headstones of prominent sourdoughs.

Just south of the central business district is the **Park Strip** (also known as Delaney Park), cleared to make an airfield in 1923, when, it's said, bottles of bootleg whiskey were hidden under tree stumps to encourage the workforce; it has also been a golf course and the site of the fifty-ton statehood bonfire in 1959. Today, it mainly supports summer-evening softball and soccer games and is home to a preserved Alaska Railroad steam loco, built in 1943 to European gauge. Head further south, and you're into the malls of **midtown**. You'll most likely find yourself here during the day buying books, renting outdoor equipment, eating, and visiting the **Heritage Museum**, and again at night for the bars of the Spenard district.

Immediately north of downtown, the city butts up against Elmendorf Air Force Base and Fort Richardson Military Reservation, both flanked by the Glenn Highway heading north past the celebrated **Alaska Native Heritage Center**.

One of the best things about the city is the opportunity to be outdoors. On a fine day it's hard to beat a late afternoon stroll (or cycle) along the waterside **Tony Knowles Coastal Trail** or, more adventurously, a stiff hike up Flattop Mountain or Wolverine Peak in the encircling Chugach Mountains. Hidden in the wilder country beyond is the city's hiking gem, the two-day **Crow Pass Trail**, which ends by the delightful Eagle River Nature Center. There's plenty more to do in and around the city, including rock climbing, swimming (see Listings, p.249), and salmon-fishing (see box, p.224).

The big city peters out beyond the limits of the Anchorage Bowl, but there are a few places you might consider as **day-trips from Anchorage**: to the south, Girdwood (p.257) and Portage Glacier (p.260) lie within an hour's drive along Turnagain Arm; and to the north Eklutna (p.381), Palmer (p.383), and the Independence Mine at Hatcher Pass (p.395) are also all easily accessible by car.

Downtown Anchorage

Immediately west of the visitor center is Anchorage's major Art Deco building, the **4th Avenue Theatre**, 630 W 4th Ave. Already architecturally dated when it opened in 1947, it remains a fine example of the style, all mahogany and Italian marble, ziggurats and chevron friezes, and a proscenium flanked by floor-to-ceiling relief panels depicting Old and New Alaska scenes – uplifting and positive in true Deco fashion. It spent much of its life as Anchorage's premier cinema and, though now used for an evening dinner–theater show, it can be visited as part of a city tour (see p.218).

On the corner of 4th Avenue and D Street is the striking **Wendler Building**, Anchorage's only corner turret structure, which overlooks a bronze sculpture of a sled dog – the ceremonial kickoff point of the Iditarod (see box, p.392) and the real start for numerous dog-sled races. As E Street heads north, the road slopes down a dozen feet – a consequence of the 1964 quake – to 3rd, where a parking lot between here and C Street transforms into the **weekend market** (mid-May to late-Sept Sat & Sun 10am–6pm; Ⓦ www.anchoragemarkets.com), selling everything from oversized Mat-Su vegetables to arts and crafts, some of them really good, some just cheap souvenirs; there's also music and entertainment. A block north is the **Statehood Monument**, a bronze statue depicting Eisenhower's head being attacked by a bald eagle – or so it seems from some angles. Below, the hillside drops away to Ship Creek and the site of the original tent city, now occupied by rail yards and the restrained Art Deco form of the **train station**.

From the monument, 2nd Avenue runs west past a handful of Anchorage's original homes – numbers 542, 605, 610, and 618 (none open to the public) – to the start of the Tony Knowles Coastal Trail. There's more to be seen at the corner of 3rd Avenue and L Street, where a nest of steps and viewing platforms known as **Resolution Park** is crowned by the **Captain Cook Monument**, a regal statue of the great navigator. The waters that once bore his ship, the *Resolution*, now bear his name and stretch away to Mount Susitna and the Alaska Range. On a clear day the dominant peaks of Mount Foraker and Denali can be seen presiding over the city in the distance.

Below the monument is the 1915 **Oscar Anderson House Museum**, 420 M St (June to mid-Sept Mon–Fri noon–5pm; $3; Ⓦ www .anchoragehistoricproperties.org), a lovely two-story that was once the home

---

Downtown fishing

Visitors to Alaska often spend thousands of dollars to fly to a remote lodge and hire a guide to help them catch a trophy specimen, but all the while there are kings and silvers five minutes' walk from downtown Anchorage just waiting to be hooked. Some city office workers even cast away their lunch hour at **Ship Creek**, where for under $50 a day you can obtain the appropriate license (for details see Basics, p.71) and rent rod, reel, and waders from a creekside shack run by Riverside Adventures (☎258-7773).

The creek no longer supports a natural run, but fishery-raised salmon returning to the Elmendorf Hatchery provide ample sport. There's no guarantee of a good catch but it isn't unreasonable to expect to catch **king salmon** weighing 45lb (though 15–25lb is more common; season mid-May to mid-July), and **silver salmon** topping 20lb (7–12lb is typical; July–Sept). Two hours either side of high tide is generally regarded as the best time.

Through the summer, Ship Creek hosts two **salmon derbies** (Ⓦ www .anchoragederbies.com): a king salmon derby (second week of June; entry tickets $7 for one day, $30 for the week) with a first prize of $5000 and the bonus chance of landing a pre-tagged fish for $10,000; and a silver salmon derby (second week of August; $7 for one day, $30 for the duration) with a $3000 top prize.

of Oscar Anderson, a Swedish butcher and Anchorage's eighteenth resident. Guides lead you through period-furnished rooms of what was the city's first privately built wood-frame residence, completed soon after the town's lots were auctioned off. You can buy a combined ticket for the Historic Downtown Anchorage walking tour (June–Aug Mon–Fri 1pm; $5, or $6 with the Oscar Anderson House), leaving from the **Historic City Hall** at 524 W 4th Ave; built in 1936, this included a library, phone exchange, three cells, and the "tank room" for holding drunks overnight.

Back in the center of town, the **Alaska Experience Theater**, 705 W 6th Ave at G St (daily on the hour: mid-May to mid-Sept 9am–9pm; mid-Sept to mid-May noon–6pm; ☎276-3730, ⓦwww.alaskaexperiencetheatre.com), projects an eminently missable movie on the state and its wonders onto a 180-degree wraparound screen (40min; $7). There's also a considerably more diverting earthquake exhibit ($6, joint entry with film $10), with displays on the 1964 quake (see box, p.590), and a fifteen-minute film (and jolting quake simulation) featuring a wonderfully Germanic-sounding professor expounding the geophysics of it all and poignant tales from Anchorage residents. Kids will be better off at the nearby **Imaginarium Science Discovery Center**, 737 W 5th Ave at G St (Mon–Sat 10am–6pm, Sun noon–5pm; $5.50; ☎276-3179, ⓦwww.imaginarium.org), packed with hands-on experiments using prisms, pendulums, gears, and a contraption that makes giant soap bubbles around you. A touch-tank full of local marine life, instructional material on earthquakes and the northern lights, and, of course, dinosaurs, make this a worthwhile diversion for youngsters.

The **Bear & Raven Adventure Theater**, opposite the *Hilton* at 315 E St (☎1-800/770-4545, ⓦwww.bearandraventheater.com), puts on a half-hour interactive sled-simulator show, *Anchorage to Nome – The Amazing Trail*, with so-called butt-kicker seats and storm, white-out, and aurora effects, on the hour and half-hour daily.

Big shows that make it to Alaska often play the acoustically impressive **Alaska Center for the Performing Arts**, 6th Avenue between F and G streets (aka PAC; ☎263-2900, ⓦwww.alaskapac.org), where you might consider seeing *Aurora, The Great Northern Lights* (late May–August daily 9am–9pm on the hour; $8.75; ⓦwww.thealaskacollection.com/summershow.htm), an audiovisual show on the aurora, including views from space and of comets and planets. Out front is the **Town Square Park**, a riot of blooms in summer, overlooked by a whales-in-the-Arctic mural by renowned environmental artist Wyland. Two blocks east at 245 W 5th Ave, the **Alaska Law Enforcement Museum** (Mon–Fri 10am–4pm, Sat noon–4pm; free; ☎279-5050, ⓦwww.alaskatroopermuseum.com) has a ragtag collection ranging from a 1952 Hudson Hornet car, a polygraph lie-detector, and miscellaneous guns to police caps and helmets from Britain and Germany, as well as interesting displays on firefighting, the role of women in the police, and the construction and protection of the pipeline. They don't tell you the more lurid stories, such as how Anchorage's first police chief was killed in an alley with his own gun after being on the job six weeks (the department's oldest unsolved homicide), or how one police captain was fired after calling in sick and being found in a brothel. In the late 1940s almost the entire department, including the chief, was fired at one time for corruption (mainly taking kickbacks from bars).

Heading east past the Anchorage Museum of History & Art (see p.226) you come to the **Anchorage Memorial Park Cemetery** (daily: May–Oct 8am–8pm; winter 8am–5pm), where Alaskans of note have sought to be buried since 1915. Respected pioneers have ended up along the north perimeter together with artist Sydney Laurence. Elsewhere the upright whalebone ribs marking Iñupiat graves mix with propeller blades of pioneer aviators and triple-bar Russian Orthodox crosses. It would be a peaceful place to idle away half an hour were it not for the constant drone of small planes from nearby **Merrill Field**, one of the nation's busiest airfields – only a mile from downtown – with more than 230,000 takeoffs and landings annually and up to 1200 on a busy summer's day.

At 605 A St, opposite the Anchorage Museum of History & Art, a long and low green wooden building houses the **Russian Orthodox Museum** (mid-May to mid-Sept Mon–Fri 10am–6pm, Sat 10am–5pm, Sun 1–5pm; mid-Sept to mid-May Mon–Fri 10am–5pm, Sat 9am–4pm; free; ☎276-7257) as well as a chapel (with around four services a week in Old Church Slavonic), gift shop, and the *Cupola Café* (closed Sun). It has a well-presented collection of vestments (including Tlingit beadwork), icons and silverware, plus information on figures such as St Iakov Netsvetov, the first priest of Aleut descent (although his father was Russian), who in the 1840s founded the parish of Interior Alaska, four thousand miles across and larger than Texas. St Innocent Veniaminov, first resident bishop of Alaska who designed and built the Orthodox cathedral of St Michael in Sitka and translated the gospels and liturgy into his own Cyrillic-based version of Aleut, is also profiled. While in the Orthodox groove you might also wish to visit the **cathedral of St Innocent**, built in 1993 towards the north end of Turpin Avenue; it has a wood-planked exterior and blue onion domes, but a light modern interior with all-American features such as wheelchair ramps and water fountains, so that the iconostasis, with its icons of the Mother of God and St Iakov to the right and Father Herman and St Peter the Aleut to the left, seems rather out of place.

Anchorage Museum of History & Art

Even if you're spending only a night or two in Anchorage, be sure to drop by the ✈ **Anchorage Museum of History & Art**, 121 W 7th Ave at A St (mid-May to mid-Sept daily 9am–6pm, 9pm on Thurs; mid-Sept to mid-May Tues–Sat 10am–6pm, Sun noon–5pm; $8; ☎343-4326, ⓦ www .anchoragemuseum.org), a visit best timed to coincide with one of the free **museum tours** (hourly 10am–2pm) or one of the free **films** showing in the auditorium. It's easy to devote several hours to the collection and, if you find yourself lingering, you might want to take a break in the excellent atrium café, an offshoot of downtown's *Marx Bros Café* (see p.238). The museum is currently expanding westwards to gain a frontage facing the newly baptised SoNo ("south of Nordstrom's") district, home to various trendy boutiques and bars; this will increase exhibition and retail space and incorporate a planetarium and the Imaginarium (see p.225). The Smithsonian Institution's Arctic Studies Center will also open its Sharing Knowledge gallery, on Alaska's indigenous cultures, here in 2010.

Upper floor

The legacy of the 1970s oil windfall is immediately apparent in the museum's opulent atrium with its fine-grained wood, preserved totem pole, and arresting sculptures, mainly by Native Alaskan artists. Upstairs, after passing an array of photos of pioneer families, you'll enter the museum's history displays in the Alaska Gallery, moving chronologically through the state's history, beginning with exquisite dioramas of Native village life. These lead to full-size re-creations of Native houses along with an 1830s Russian blockhouse, relocated from where it once defended the town of St Michael near the Yukon delta, mock-ups of a gold-miner's hut, a 1920s Anchorage home, and a wartime Quonset hut, as well as a kayak, an umiak, and a Bristol Bay sailing gill-netter. All this is given some context in well laid out displays that illustrate the changes Alaska has undergone during the past two centuries. You'll also find gorgeous examples of carved walrus ivory, including cribbage boards, candleholders, and even an engraved map of the Yukon. Alongside there's a small but instructive collection of Native **basketware** illustrating the open-weave Yup'ik coiled-grass style, Tlingit spruce-root weaves, Kobuk River woven birch-bark designs, super-fine Aleut baskets with up to 1000 stitches per square inch, and Iñupiat vessels constructed from whale baleen, a material that is traditionally worked only by men. Note the presence of Russian, and later American, influence as European patterns get worked into the designs. There are informative displays on the Orthodox Church, fishing and whaling, earthquakes and tsunamis, and the Aleutian campaign of World War II.

The upper-floor exhibits come close to the present with thorough coverage of the roles of telecommunications and air travel in modern Alaska, logging displays with a rather camp-looking timber worker, and, inevitably, paeans to the oil industry including a short section of the pipeline and an explanation of the *Exxon Valdez* disaster (see box, p.322). It ends (more or less) as it began, with a diorama of a 1980s rural village with its Bureau of Indian Affairs frame houses.

Lower floor

The lower floor is given over to **Alaskan art**, mostly works by Alaskan (or adoptive Alaskan) artists, but first there's a small gallery of sketches and paintings by artists and others on the early voyages of exploration, such as an Aleut man and woman painted by Johann Wäber, the Swiss artist on Cook's third voyage (known here as John Webber). Art-loving Alaskans all but genuflect at mention of **Sydney Laurence** (1865–1940), widely regarded as the most accomplished historical painter of the Alaskan landscape. Born in Brooklyn in 1865, Laurence spent time developing his style in Europe, then came to Alaska in 1904 to prospect for gold. Limited success gradually forced him into photography, his Anchorage studio supporting frequent painting forays into the wilds. By the mid-1920s his reputation, built on a lifelong passion for painting Mount McKinley, effectively gave him a monopoly on the mountain's depiction in oil. He died in 1940 and is buried in the Anchorage Memorial Park Cemetery (see p.225). There are more than two dozen Laurence works on display, along with his portable painting kit. His most iconic painting of *Mount McKinley*, the ice-white peak of Denali shining back at you through the alpenglow, has pride of place in the Alaska Landscapes gallery.

The museum has a good selection of works by Laurence's Detroit-born near-contemporary, **Eustace Ziegler** (or "Zieg" as he was usually known; 1881–1969). His landscapes are less the subject than the frame in which to set his subjects – trappers, fishermen, Native Alaskans – who are often shown outside the stereotypical roles for them common in Alaskan art of the time. His vibrant *Alaska Fishermen* is a fine example.

Fred Machetanz (1908–2002), probably the most popular Alaskan artist of recent times, owed his ascendancy during the 1970s, at least in part, to purchases of his work by large corporations who found his anodyne canvases – with their recurrent motifs of polar bears, blue water and sky, and alpenglow – perfect for large public spaces and company boardrooms. *Serenity*, *Where Men and Dogs Seem Small*, and others can seem little more than adult painting-by-numbers, but it is helpful when viewing them to look at some of his earlier works to see how his painting developed from early oils of sourdoughs and Native life.

A side gallery houses a small collection of striking works by twelve artists, including Austin Mecklem, Prescott Jones, Merlin Pollock, and Carl Saxild, sent to Alaska in 1937 by the WPA, part of the Great Depression public works program. More modern painters to look out for in the contemporary gallery include **Spence Guerin**, represented by his luminous cloudscape *Moon over Matanuska*, and **Rosemary Redmond**, whose abstract landscape *Somewhere East of the Sun and West of the Moon* stands in stark contrast to Laurence's *Mount McKinley* just along the wall. Look, too, for paintings and sculpture by Native Alaskans displaying a very imaginative use of multimedia and all available dimensions, particularly Lawrence Beck's humorous *Punk Walrus Spirit* and Lawrence Ullaq Ahvaliana's more sensitive *Waiting for the Wolf Dance*. Four works by John (Jay) Hoover, whose art can also be seen in Anchorage's Egan Center, the Alaska Native Heritage and Medical centers, and the garden of the White House in Washington, DC, hang here as well.

Midtown and the Coastal Trail

The Chester Creek Greenbelt runs east–west across the city a mile or so south of downtown, demarcating the northern limit of midtown Anchorage. Much of midtown is made up of sprawling malls, but the western shoreline is traced by the excellent **Tony Knowles Coastal Trail**, which runs down to Kincaid Park, the airport, and **Lake Hood**, the focus of the city's float-plane activity. The nearby district of **Spenard** is short on sights in the usual sense, but you may find yourself gravitating here to get stuff done or to sleep near the airport. The junction of Northern Light Boulevard and Spenard Road is especially handy in this respect, with loads of places to buy or rent outdoor gear, one of the city's best bookshops, some excellent restaurants, bars, and clubs, and a post office and travel agent.

To the east Anchorage's universities, a couple of large parks, and the Alaska Botanical Garden stand between the city's commercial heart and the snowy heights of the Chugach Mountains beyond.

Along the Coastal Trail

Provided you're not in a tearing hurry, the best approach to midtown is along the **Tony Knowles Coastal Trail** which, a mile south of downtown, weaves around **Westchester Lagoon**, a waterfowl sanctuary usually alive with ducks and geese, or with skaters on winter evenings. A little further south, **Bootleggers' Cove** is where stills supplied Anchorage's speakeasies from the city's founding until the end of Prohibition in 1933. This whole coastline was affected by the 1964 Good Friday earthquake, but nowhere more so than **Earthquake Park**, three miles from downtown, the site of Anchorage's most extensive and destructive landslide. Ninety seconds into the quake the clays underlying the Turnagain Heights suburb effectively liquefied, destroying 75 homes and killing four people. There is a blockish sculpture, fence posts, and concrete barriers, all designed in jagged forms, alluding to the effects of the quake. Nearby, explanatory panels fill in the details, but to actually see the results you'll need to ferret among the birch trees, where the ground looks like scrunched paper on a grand scale. The Coastal Trail continues past the teenage hangout of **Point Woronzof** and on to Kincaid Park, but if you are midtown-bound you'll need to cut inland from Earthquake Park following Northern Lights Boulevard (the fairly frequent bus #7A comes within half a mile of Earthquake Park). The long-sought-after extension of the coastal trail to Potter Marsh remains blocked

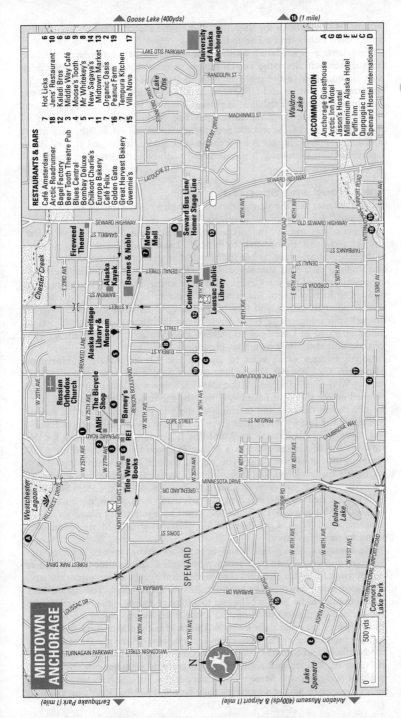

▲ Goose Lake (400yds)　　　▲ **16** (1 mile)

MIDTOWN ANCHORAGE

0 | 500 yds

N

RESTAURANTS & BARS

Café Amsterdam	7
Arctic Roadrunner	18
Bagel Factory	12
Bear Tooth Theatre Pub	3
Blues Central	4
Bombay Deluxe	5
Chikoot Charlie's	1
Europa Bakery	11
Café Felix	7
Golden Gate	16
Great Harvest Bakery	7
Gwennie's	15
Hot Licks	6
Jens' Restaurant	10
Kaladi Bros	6
Middle Way Café	6
Moose's Tooth	9
Mr Whitekey's	8
New Sagaya's	14
Midtown Market	13
Organic Oasis	2
Peanut Farm	19
Tempura Kitchen	7
Villa Nova	17

ACCOMMODATION

Anchorage Guesthouse	A
Arctic Inn Motel	G
Jason's Hostel	B
Millennium Alaska Hotel	F
Puffin Inn	E
Qupqugiac Inn	C
Spenard Hostel International	D

229

by property owners, to the disgust of those who prefer to enjoy the scenery from a bike rather than a Laz-E-Boy.

The relatively new **Planet Walk**, a scale model of the solar system, stretches from downtown along the coastal trail to Kincaid Park; a leisurely walking pace is equivalent to the speed of light, so that one step equals the distance light travels in one second (186,000 miles). It therefore takes eight minutes to walk from the sun to Earth, just as photons from the sun take on their journey, and five and a half hours to reach Pluto. The symbol representing the sun is at 5th Avenue and G St and the first five planets are all on W 5th, with Mars at Elderberry Park; Jupiter is by Westchester Lagoon, Saturn at Lyn Ary Park, Uranus at Point Woronzoff, Neptune at the north end of the runway, and Pluto at Kincaid chalet.

Lake Hood and Spenard

Anchorage now has the world's third busiest cargo airport; with 45,950 cargo planes and 2.6 billion tons of goods passing through in 2005, as well as 49,993 passenger planes and five million passengers, it accounts for ten percent of the city's employment. Immediately to its north, **Lake Hood** is believably claimed as the busiest float-plane harbor in the world, with over eight hundred takeoffs and landings on a peak summer day. Any time the water isn't frozen there is a constant drone of taxiing Cessnas, and on a sunny day it can be surprisingly pleasant to hang out here and dream of the planes' exotic destinations: remote lakes, wilderness cabins, and tiny Native villages, transport to which may be beyond your budget. The *Fancy Moose* bar in the *Millennium Alaskan* hotel at the eastern end of Lake Spenard makes for comfortable plane-watching, with its patio near the hotel's own float-plane dock.

Aircraft fanatics won't want to pass up the **Alaska Aviation Heritage Museum**, 4721 Aircraft Drive (June to mid-Sept daily 9am–5pm; mid-Sept to May Wed–Sun 9am–5pm; $10; ℡248-5325, ⓦ www.alaskaairmuseum.com), perched on the shores of Lake Hood right by the airport. Three linked hangars are devoted to the lives and machines of the pilots who played such a pivotal role in Alaska's history, with credit given to the state's many female fliers. Extensive coverage of Alaska's role in World War II provides the framework for the crown jewels of Alaskan aviation, a couple of dozen mostly restored pre-1950 planes in the hangar next door (you can ask to look inside if anything's going on, mostly on weekdays, and the volunteers are usually welcoming and talkative). Above you as you enter is the museum's pride and joy, the 1928 Stearman C2B that carried diphtheria serum in 1931, made the first landing and rescue on Mount McKinley in 1932, and was flown by a roll call of Alaska's aviation pioneers: Noel Wien, Carl Ben Eielson, Wiley Post, and Merle "Mudhole" Smith, to name just a few.

The contiguous lakes Hood and Spenard form the western limit of the **Spenard** district, a region once synonymous with sleaze that's still the raunchiest part of town. In 1916 a chancer called Joe Spenard established a resort at the lake, but it soon burnt down and he left for California the next year. Though the land turned out not to be his – it belonged to a forestry reserve – the district's future was decided. To the east of Minnesota Drive it shades into the newer midtown district, where the main sight is the ⚑ **Alaska Heritage Museum & Library** on the ground floor of the Wells Fargo Bank building at the corner of C Street and Northern Lights Boulevard (Mon–Fri noon–4pm; free). It's a compact room of Native Alaskan artwork and artifacts that perfectly complements the contextual slant of downtown's Museum of History & Art. The emphasis here is on the pieces themselves, almost all exceptionally beautiful works. Don't miss the bird parka made from the skins of over fifty murres, or the fragile-looking kayak and bleached seal-gut parka trimmed with auklet feathers and beaks. Though brittle when dry, seal gut becomes soggy and clingy in the sea but remains breathable – Eskimo Gore-Tex, and only three ounces in weight. Blankets sold to Tlingit people by the Hudson's Bay Company were also turned into clothing, here fashioned into a ceremonial coat used for potlatches with the owner's crest picked out in buttons. Basketware is also well represented, along with matchless ivory carving, from simple, stylized seals to whaling scenes depicted along the length of a walrus tusk. Look, too, for the ivory scale model of the *Bear*, a locally famous revenue cutter (effectively the Alaskan coast guard in the late nineteenth century) that patrolled Alaskan waters for forty years and first brought reindeer to the territory in 1885. Elsewhere there's a small collection of Russian icons as well as oils by leading Alaskan artists such as Laurence, Ziegler, and Machetanz. More contemporary native art and crafts can be seen at the **Alaska Native Medical Center** (4315 Diplomacy Drive, off Tudor Rd ⓦ www.anmc.org), where display cases line the main staircase of the north building, with wonderful pieces such as walrus and seal-gut parkas and Athabascan beaded moosehide; there's also contemporary native art in the public spaces, plus a fine craft shop (see p.246) and even a cafeteria where you can sample native foods such as reindeer sausage and fried bread.

Eastern midtown

Northern Lights Boulevard continues east until it meets the Chester Creek Greenbelt near **Goose Lake** on the northern flank of Anchorage's two universities, the University of Alaska Anchorage and Alaska Pacific University. Neither is of special interest to visitors except for occasional events, for instance, at UAA's Wendy Williamson Auditorium. North of the universities lie the urban hiking and biking trails of **Russian Jack Springs Park** (named after moonshiner and murderer Jack Marchin), which also contains the municipal greenhouse known as the Mann Leiser Memorial Greenhouses, 5200 DeBarr Rd (daily 8am–3pm; free; ⓣ 343-4717). Keen horticulturists, however, are better off south of the universities at the **Alaska Botanical Garden**, Campbell Airstrip Road (June–Aug daily 9am–9pm; $5 donation; ⓦ www.alaskabg.org), boasting pleasant paths around perennial and herb gardens, wildflower walks, and trails into the nearby woods; bus #75 passes fairly close.

The Botanical Garden lies within **Far North Bicentennial Park**, a vast forested area butting up against Chugach State Park and an ideal spot for mountain bikers. Immediately to the west is the Campbell Tract, 730 acres of wilderness that's home to moose, black and brown bears (especially in salmon season), coyote, lynx, spruce grouse, and various raptors. It surrounds the Campbell Airstrip, built as a dispersal field in case of Japanese raids on Elmendorf AFB and now used by the BLM's smokejumpers or parachuting firefighters. The **Campbell Creek Science Center** (reached from 68th/Abbott Loop Rd) hosts school programs, walks, talks and so on, and you can hike or bike trails around the airstrip, linking Campbell Airstrip Road, Tudor Road, and Abbott Loop Road. This must be the only place in the world where you'll see a flyover carrying a cycle trail over a dog-mushing trail; races start from Tozer Park, just north on Tudor Road, most winter weekends.

South Anchorage

It's not that hard to see Alaskan animals in the wild, but if you're not feeling too adventurous you can always check out the **Alaska Zoo**, 4731 O'Malley Rd

Contrary to expectations, Alaska is not overly endowed with good, maintained hiking trails. Much of the state is too remote, too steep, or too boggy, but the **Chugach Mountains**, rising immediately behind Anchorage, are one major exception. Their western end forms part of the Chugach State Park which, at half a million acres, is the third largest state park in the country. The **major hikes** – all with fabulous views over the city, Cook Inlet, and north to the Alaska Range – all start from trailheads within half an hour's drive of Anchorage. Most can be tackled in a day and some can be combined into multiday affairs. The best source of information is the *Ridgelines* newspaper (free from APLIC; see p.216), which contains the latest trail information; for more details consult *55 Ways to the Wilderness of Southcentral Alaska* (The Mountaineers), which covers all walks in the Chugach State Park, including some south of Anchorage along Turnagain Arm, or Shawn Lyons' *Walk-about Guides to Alaska*. Volume One covers the Kenai and Turnagain Arm; Volume Two the Chugach Mountains.

Hiking season begins in May, but most trails aren't free of snow until early June, staying clear until early October. The Flattop Mountain Shuttle runs from 333 W 4th Ave ($29 round-trip; ☏279-3334, ⓦwww.alaska-bike-rentals.com) to the Glen Alps trailhead at 10.30am, 1pm, 3.30pm, and 6.30pm, returning at 1.30pm, 4pm, and 9pm (with midtown pickups and drop-offs at the Loussac library; see Listings, p.248). Without a car or bicycle, your access to other trailheads is limited: ride a bus to the Dimond Transit Center in South Anchorage (routes #2, #7, #9, and #60 from downtown) and take a taxi from there.

Bikes are not generally allowed along these trails with the exception of the 0.3-mile run from the Glen Alps parking lot to the Powerline Trail, the 13 miles along the Powerline Trail from Prospect Heights to Indian, and the three-mile Near Point Trail from Prospect Heights; hikers always have right of way. There are also popular cycle trails along Turnagain Arm, notably the new 7.5-mile Bird-to-Gird (Bird Point to Girdwood) route – see p.259.

From the Eagle River Nature Center

The nature center is the base for a couple of gentle nature trails (see p.236), and the finishing point for the Crow Pass Trail (see opposite). Sections of the Crow Pass Trail can be walked from this end: for example, the relatively easy **Heritage Falls Trail** (10 miles round-trip; 4–5hrs; 100ft ascent) and the stiffer **Twin Falls Trail** (19 miles round-trip; 8–10hrs; 300ft ascent), which involves some stream crossings but rewards with beaver ponds and the Twin Falls themselves. To reach the center follow the Glenn Highway twelve miles north of Anchorage, turn onto Eagle River Loop Road, then follow Eagle River Road ten miles east. There is a parking fee of $5 for every twelve hours.

From Prospect Heights Trailhead

The Prospect Heights Trailhead (1050ft) is a 25-minute drive south of downtown Anchorage, reached by following O'Malley Road east until it becomes Upper O'Malley Road, then turning left onto Prospect Drive and following it 1.3 miles to the parking lot, which has a $5 per day parking fee.

Middle Fork Trail (13 miles round-trip; 8–10hr; 1600ft ascent). Easy-to-moderate trail which starts on the Near Point Trail, then cuts right after 1.3 miles. It can get muddy underfoot as you gently climb through mountain hemlock and spruce towards beautiful alpine lakes set amid the open tundra under the precipitous face of Mount Williwaw. Anyone not needing to return to a vehicle can vary the return journey by descending via a different path to the Glen Alps Trailhead. Gets the early sun but is in shadow later in the day.

Wolverine Peak Trail (10.5 miles round-trip; 8–10hr; 3400ft ascent). Moderately strenuous trail that initially follows the Near Point Trail for two miles, then spurs up towards the bush line. The way up to the triangular, 4450-foot summit of Wolverine Peak is clear enough but you need to be sure where the path re-enters the bush on the way down. Besides the fabulous views and possible animal sightings – moose, sheep, and arctic ground squirrel – you can spot parts of a wrecked plane near the summit.

From the Glen Alps Trailhead

The Glen Alps Trailhead (2250ft) is located near the tree line above the swanky Hillside suburb, twenty minutes' drive south of downtown Anchorage: turn east off Hillside Drive and follow Upper Huffman Road for 2.6 miles to the parking lot. There is a $5 per day parking fee.

Flattop Mountain (3.5 miles round-trip; 2–3hrs; 1500ft ascent). Good views over Anchorage and to the Alaska Range from Alaska's most-hiked peak. It's a fairly steep haul through mountain hemlocks and out onto the tundra and requires some attention, as hikers higher up can dislodge rocks.

Powerline Trail to Indian (11 miles one-way; 5–6hr; 1300ft ascent). Easy-to-moderate walking gradually gaining open tundra that's good for berry picking in fall. Start early in the day as it goes into shadow in the afternoon.

Ship Pass (10 miles round-trip; 5–6hr; 2000ft ascent). Easy-to-moderate walk forking left off the Powerline Trail to climb south of O'Malley Peak to the pass, from where you can scramble north to The Ramp (5240ft), south to The Wedge (4660ft), or drop down to Ship Lake.

Williwaw Lakes (14 miles round-trip; 6–8hr; 740ft ascent). Easy-to-moderate walk that's best started early in the day to catch the sun. It climbs through spruce woods and mountain hemlock, joining the Middle Fork Trail (see opposite) for the climb above the tree line to Williwaw Lakes.

The Crow Pass Trail

The single best hike in the Anchorage area, the **Crow Pass Trail** (26 miles one-way; 2–3 days; 2500ft ascent, 3500ft descent) is a dramatic grind up a steep pass overhung by glaciers, then down a narrow, wildlife-rich wooded valley strung with waterfalls. Along the way the trail passes the magnificent Raven Gorge where the fledgling Raven Creek plunges into a chasm sculpted into channels, chutes, and cauldrons. The Crow Pass Trail is part of the Historic Iditarod Trail, recognizing the days prior to the completion of the railroad in 1918 when miners used it as a winter track to get from the north side of Turnagain Arm to Knik. The hike is best done in summer and fall when avalanche danger is negligible.

The trail starts forty miles southeast of Anchorage and five miles inland from Girdwood at the end of Crow Creek Road, finishing at Eagle River Nature Center 22 miles north of Anchorage. Unless you can arrange for people to drop you off and pick you up at the other end, it makes sense to use the limited public transportation. Take one of the Kenai-bound buses to Girdwood, then either walk or hitch the five miles to the trailhead. At the other end hitch from the nature center to Eagle River and pick up bus #75, #77, or #102 back to Anchorage.

Despite the trail's length it isn't an especially arduous hike, though bad weather can turn it into a nightmare for the ill-prepared. Black bears are commonly seen but pose little threat as long as you follow the advice on p.60. The one objective difficulty is crossing the glacial Eagle River at the trail's midpoint – a simple but cold calf-deep wade that can turn into a wide and impassable waist-high torrent, especially after a series of warm days when glacial run-off is greatest. Call the nature center (☎694-2108) for the latest information. Memorize the route before you leave and you're unlikely to get lost, but if you've any doubts at all, obtain the inch-to-a-mile Anchorage A6 and A7 quad maps.

For maximum flexibility (and the pick of the campsites) carry a stove, although there are numerous primitive **campsites** where campfires are allowed, as well as a six-berth **cabin** atop Crow Pass at Mile 3 (June–Sept; $35 for the cabin; book up to six months in advance ☎1-877/444-6777, ⓦwww.reserveusa.com).

△ Biking the Coastal Trail

(daily: May–Sept 9am–6pm; Oct–April 10am–5pm; $9; ℡346-3242 ⓦwww
.alaskazoo.org), which specializes in Alaskan fauna but also has a few camels
and Siberian tigers, plus Maggie the elephant, focus of a dogged campaign
(ⓦwww.friendsofmaggie.net) to get her moved somewhere warmer. Since
2004 $1 million has been spent on improving her conditions, but, alas, she's not
interested in her purpose-built treadmill. A free shuttle runs from the visitor
center via the *Hilton* and *Captain Cook* hotels at 10.20am, 11.40am, 1.10pm,
and 2.20pm. Beyond the zoo, O'Malley Road continues to climb through the
plush houses of the Hillside to the open flanks of the Chugach Mountains. The
Prospect Heights and Glen Alps trailheads (see box, p.232) give access to
the widest range of hikes, and the latter offers expansive city and sea views from
a viewing platform.

Twelve miles south of downtown, the railroad, built in 1916 and now paralleled by New Seward Highway (Mile 115), arcs away from the Chugach foothills, effectively creating a sea wall between Turnagain Arm and the 540 acres of
Potter Marsh (unrestricted entry). Since 1971 the marsh has been part of the
Anchorage Coastal Wildlife Refuge, which (particularly late May to early
June and late Aug to early Sept) acts as a stopover for more than two hundred
species of migratory birds: Canada geese, mallards, pintails, green-winged teal,
widgeons, canvasbacks, shovelers, and scaup are common, and trumpeter swans,
bald eagles, northern harrier, snow geese, and short-eared owls are also occasionally present. A boardwalk with interpretive displays provides a vantage point
for viewing king salmon running below, but is too close to the highway to be
really relaxing. It's to be increased in length by half again, with restrooms at last,
and there are plans for a Bird Treatment and Learning Center ("Bird-TLC")
facility on the bluff over Potter Marsh to allow public programs and displays.

For details on the Potter Section House and the drive south along Turnagain Arm,
see the Kenai Peninsula chapter (p.255).

North Anchorage: the Alaska Native Heritage Center and Eagle River

The city's northern boundary is marked by the original townsite on Ship Creek, which, during the salmon runs, is lined with anglers eager to land the fish returning to the **Elmendorf State Fish Hatchery**, 941 N Reeve Blvd (daily 8am–4.30pm). Every year over a million king salmon are raised here for sportfishing around the state and, while there's not a lot to see, there are spawning salmon aplenty visible from the adjacent **Salmon Viewing Area** on Post Road (late June–Oct daily 8am–10pm).

Both Ship Creek, now a largely postindustrial area of train yards, and Mountain View, a deprived residential area just northeast, have been targeted for regeneration as designated Arts and Culture Districts. In Ship Creek the Alaska Railroad has some potentially attractive 1940s warehouses which are touted to become something like Seattle's iconic Pike Street Market, while Mountain View is to be home to the Anchorage Opera, the Alaska Dance Theater, and Special Olympics Alaska. The standard-bearer is the **Alaska Museum of Natural History** (summer Tues–Sat 10am–5pm, Sun noon–5pm; winter Wed–Sat 10am–4pm, Sun noon–4pm; closed holidays; $5; ℡274-2400, ⓦwww .alaskamuseum.org), which recently moved to 201 N Bragaw, a block and a half north of the Glenn Highway (reached by bus #45). It's very child-oriented, with touchy-feely displays and lots on dinosaurs, but actually gives quite a lot of detail that adults might appreciate – the evolutionary importance of Chinese bird-dinosaurs, for instance. It also plans to stir things up soon with special shows on climate change.

Heading out of town along the Glenn Highway, you notice an abrupt transition from the activity of downtown Anchorage to a rather rural stretch of sparsely populated military bases. But before leaving the city completely, there's one essential – if expensive – sight: the ⚑ **Alaska Native Heritage Center**, 8800 Heritage Center Drive (mid-May to late Sept daily 9am–6pm; Nov–April Sat 10.30am–4.30pm; $21, Alaskans $9; infoline ℡330-8000 or 1-800/315-6608, ⓦwww.alaskanative.net). The center, which opened in 1999, celebrates the traditions of Alaska's five main Native groups (for more on this, see the Contexts section of this book). Although the center takes a fairly broad, almost simplistic, approach and barely addresses some key issues in modern tribal life, as an introduction to the people and their lives it is hard to beat – not least because it is staffed almost entirely by Native Alaskans.

Kick off your visit with the excellent twenty-minute film, *Stories Given, Stories Shared*, which gives insight into groups whose cultures are finally starting to be accorded the respect they deserve. After the film explore the center's small museum, a sparse display of lovely artifacts – ivory work, spirit masks, and beadwork – interpreted by case studies and images that evoke what it is like to be a Native in modern Alaska. Outside, you'll find the main body of the center, five outdoor compounds arranged around a small lake, each representing a major tribal group – Athabascan, Yup'ik, Iñupiat, Aleut, and Tlingit/Haida/Tsimshian. The focus of each area is a house, built in the style appropriate for that particular group, using traditional materials and surrounded by plants typical of the group's region. Guides interpret the lifestyles of their people, though this sometimes has an artificial tone as much of the knowledge has been specially learned, rather than passed down as it once was. Look out, too, for the themes being pursued each summer, each chosen to focus on a particular aspect of Alaskan Native culture. During your visit try to catch one of the cultural performances – Native dance, storytelling, music – held in the main auditorium.

For details on the drive north past Eklutna to Palmer, see Chapter Six (p.377).

The center is seven miles northwest of the city; there's a free shuttle from the Heritage Center's downtown shop at 333 W 4th Ave via the Anchorage Museum of History & Art, or you can take the Glenn Highway to the Muldoon exit. Alternatively, ride city bus #4, which takes almost an hour to arrive here from downtown.

Eagle River

The Glenn Highway, twelve miles north of Anchorage, hurtles straight through **EAGLE RIVER**, a strip-mall suburb mainly of interest for the **Eagle River Nature Center** (June–Aug Sun–Thurs 10am–5pm, Fri & Sat 10am–7pm; May & Sept Tues–Sun 10am–5pm; Oct–April Fri, Sat & Sun 10am–5pm; parking $5 per day; ☎694-2108, ⓦ www.ernc.org), twelve miles east of Eagle River at the end of Eagle River Road. Take in its gorgeous setting, nestled below 7000-foot peaks and surrounded by dense forest, from extensive outdoor decking. A cozy, telescope-equipped lounge lets you view Dall sheep, eagles, coyote, and occasionally bears; moose come so close there's no need for magnification. The center sells coffee, a very limited supply of snacks, and maps and guides, and offers bountiful information on surrounding **walks**. The easiest of these is the gentle **Rodak Nature Trail** (half-mile loop; 15–30min; 50ft ascent), which slopes down to an attractive salmon-viewing deck on stilts over a small lake. For something a little more strenuous, try the **Albert Loop Trail** (3-mile loop; 1–2hr; 100ft ascent; closed from late summer) through the forest and across gravel bars of the glacial Eagle River, or the **Crow Pass Trail** (see box, p.233). The center also provides daily guided nature walks and weekend programs.

A few options are available if you choose to spend a night or two in Eagle River. There is plenty of **free camping** at very basic sites (really just wide patches) along the Crow Pass Trail, and the nature center manages a modern eight-berth **cabin** and two **yurts** (one four-berth, one six-berth), deep in the woods just over a mile from the center, with sleeping platforms, wood stoves, firewood, and a lake for water. They each cost $65 a night ($55 for nature center members) and are often booked well in advance, especially on weekends and school vacations; check availability through the ERNC website.

Eating

Nowhere in Alaska will you find a more diverse range of places to eat than Anchorage. That's not to say you'd make a special journey for its culinary wonders, but after a week or two in the Interior it can seem like heaven. As the state's population (and sophistication) has increased, so has the enthusiasm of food importers, to the point where the stock in exotic supermarket-cum-delis (such as New Sagaya's City and Midtown Markets) ranks with the best in the Northwest. Add to that the bounty of Alaska's seas and rivers, and you've got the basis for some pretty wonderful eating. And competition means that prices here are some of the lowest in the state, though newcomers to Alaska will still get a shock.

There are superb places to eat all over the city, which is liberally dotted with cafés, diners, ethnic restaurants, brewpubs, and fine-dining establishments. You'll

Winter in Anchorage

Once the tourists have gone, the days start getting shorter, and the bike trails begin to grow thick with rollerski enthusiasts, you know that winter is approaching. When people talk skiing in Anchorage, they mean cross-country – and for good reason. **Cross-country skiers** are spoilt for choice, with backcountry skiing trails in and around the city. The eleven-mile-long Tony Knowles Coastal Trail is flat and groomed, with excellent views of Cook Inlet and the city, all the way to **Kincaid Park**, where over forty miles of well-maintained trails await both classic and skate skiers. In less busy areas – east Anchorage's Bicentennial Park, for example – you'll find people **ski-joring**, a variation on cross-country skiing in which a dog, harnessed to your chest, takes the strain. There are also two **downhill skiing** venues in town: Hilltop, in South Anchorage (ⓦwww.hilltopskiarea.org), and Alpenglow, just north of downtown (ⓦwww.skialpenglow.com). Both charge $24 for a day pass, but neither is particularly challenging. Instead, most people head to Alyeska Resort (see p.257) 35 miles south. Backcountry skiing (including telemarking) is popular at Hatcher Pass, Turnagain Pass (off the Seward Highway), and on Peaks 2 1/2 and 3, behind Flattop (reached from the De Harmoun Trailhead).

Lakes freeze to produce eight outdoor **ice-skating** rinks, and occasionally paths are cleared across the ice of Westchester Lagoon. **Snowmobile** riders head for the five areas of Chugach State Park set aside for their noisy activities; more retiring types huddle over holes in local lakes for **ice fishing**.

Spectator-oriented events focus on the citywide Anchorage Fur Rendezvous (also known as **Fur Rondy**, ⓦwww.furrondy.net), which runs two weeks from the third weekend in February and stems from the city's early days when trappers made one of their rare appearances out of the bush to sell their furs. But the highlight of the winter calendar is the ceremonial start of the 1100-mile **Iditarod** (see box, p.392) at 10am on the first Saturday in March. Also at the start of March, the **Tour of Anchorage** (ⓦwww.tourofanchorage.com) involves forty- and fifty-kilometer ski marathons from Hillside (and a 25km course from Russian Jack) with over two thousand participants converging via the Coastal Trail on Kincaid Park. Winter draws near its end in April with the Alaskan Native Youth Olympics, celebrating the activities devised to pass the long winter nights, such as the ear-pull and the one- and two-foot high kicks.

find the largest overall concentration of restaurants in the **downtown** area, which has seen a burst of activity in recent years with new places popping up every few months. Midtown has a good stock, too, and there are a few places worth seeking out in the south of the city.

Buying **groceries** is easy enough with your own wheels, but without a car you're a bit stuck. There is nowhere to buy ordinary groceries downtown, only the gourmet New Sagaya's City Market. There's a midtown Sagaya's too, plus Alaska Game and Gourmet for imported cheeses you won't find anywhere else in Alaska. For lower prices and 24-hour shopping head to Carrs at the junction of Northern Lights Boulevard and Minnesota Drive (bus #3, #4, or #36) or in several other locations noted in the listings below. The quality of produce is slightly better at Fred Meyers supermarkets; again, see listings for locations.

Downtown

The Bridge 221 W Ship Creek Ave ⓣ677-6771, ⓦwww.thebridgealaska.com. On a bridge across Ship Creek, this is a great place to watch combat fishing while enjoying imaginative Asian-influenced dishes such as crab and rock shrimp cakes with Thai chili butter sauce, lamb tagine, or the usual halibut, salmon, and filet mignon; starters cost $9–12, mains $17–30, desserts $5–7. Closed Sundays.

Café Savannah 508 W 6th Ave ☏ 646-9121. A new tapas place with a relaxed vibe and an imaginative use of glass and cutlery in the decor. Tapas $4–5 (fried calamari, omelettes, meatballs), larger *platillos* $16–20, and an extensive choice of wines. Mon–Fri 11am–3pm, 5–10pm (Fri to 11pm), Sat & Sun 5pm–midnight.

Carrs 13th Ave at Gambell St and in Northway Mall, 3101 Penland Pkwy (east of downtown). Find low prices (for Alaska, anyway) and 24-hour shopping at this grocery chain.

Club Paris 417 W 5th Ave, between D and E sts ☏ 277-6332, ⓦ www.clubparisrestaurant.com. Anchorage institution that survived the 1964 earthquake and flourished during the oil-boom years, specializing in what are undoubtedly Alaska's finest steaks ($21 "mini"-sirloin to the $34 four-inch-thick filet mignon), served in the dim recesses of leather booths. Alaskan seafood is top-notch, too. Lunches (Mon–Sat only) come in at modest prices and you can follow with Key lime pie or *crème brûlée*.

Court Café In the Federal Building, 222 W 7th Ave, at C St ☏ 277-6736. Breakfast and lunch cafeteria that's about the best budget eating downtown, and certainly a cut above the fast-food joints around, if you can be bothered with the security checks (bring ID). A large bowl of clam chowder or one of their entrees from a daily-changing menu will set you back only $5 or so.

Downtown Deli 525 W 4th Ave ☏ 276-7116. The city's premier diner, owned by former mayor and governor Tony Knowles (seldom seen serving these days), and a long-standing Anchorage favorite for bagels, sandwiches, and the full range of breakfasts. Reasonable prices, and in summer there are seats outside.

Glacier Brewhouse 737 W 5th Ave ☏ 274-2739, ⓦ www.glacierbrewhouse.com. Typically rowdy, hectic, and hugely popular restaurant, bar, and microbrewery that serves wonderful food and drink. There are always at least half a dozen toothsome house-brewed beers on tap (a shot-glass "brewery tour" of five of them costs about $5), and the brewing grains go on to *Europa Bakery* (see p.240), returning as scrumptious bread served with an olive oil dip. Try the amber ale-battered halibut ($10), alderwood-baked gourmet pizza ($11), the spit-grilled three-peppercorn prime rib ($25), or the steamed Alaskan king crab legs ($37), but leave room for outstanding bread pudding ($6.50) and something from their selection of ports.

Humpy's Great Alaskan Alehouse 610 W 6th Ave ☏ 276-2337, ⓦ www.humpys.com. Though it functions primarily as a bar (see p.243), *Humpy's*

also turns out some of the best-value meals in town. Charbroiled salmon, burgers, soups, and salads are all much better than you'd expect from a bar – and the halibut burger with a small Caesar salad is only about $10.

Lucky Monkey 258 W 5th Ave ☏ 258-0505. A simple eatery popular with teenagers, serving meat and veggie dumplings (though it's hard to tell the difference), soup, teas, and coffees. Mon–Thurs 8am–midnight, Fri 8am–2.30am, Sat 11am–2.30am, Sun 11am–6pm.

Lucky Wishbone 1033 E 5th Ave ☏ 272-3454. Anchorageites have been coming to "the Bone" since 1955 for its classic diner decor and a menu chiefly noted for its lightly battered, pan-fried chicken (dishes mostly around $8). For the real enthusiast, they often serve gizzards, livers, and giblets.

The Marx Bros Café 627 W 3rd Ave ☏ 278-2133, ⓦ www.marxcafe.com. The best all-around fine dining downtown: gourmet cuisine served up in a historic house with views of the water. Start with the likes of Kachemak Bay oysters with pepper vodka and ginger sorbet ($13) or Neapolitan seafood mousse ($15), and follow it up with roast pheasant breast with couscous and carrot purée ($32), or their signature dish, baked halibut rolled in a macadamia-nut crust with curry sauce and chutney ($30). Dinner only (closed Mon in winter); at lunchtime they run the museum's café.

Mick's at the Inlet 1200 L St ☏ 276-0110. A fine wine bar (with good beers, too) which also serves – at the bar or in the restaurant section – starters such as wild mushroom cheesecake ($8), prosciutto-wrapped jumbo scallops ($10), salads ($7), or main courses such as sirloin or elk chop ($25), ahi tuna ($27), or filet mignon ($28). Open Mon–Fri 11.30am–2pm, 5.30–10pm.

New Sagaya's City Market 900 W 13th Ave at I St. *The* place to get your groceries and deli takeouts, with prices to match its trendiness. But the choice is great – varied organic selection, unusual vegetables, great cheeses, on-site bakery – and it's about the only place to buy such things anywhere near downtown. There's also a café for eat-in meals (around $8) with Thai dishes, sushi and sashimi, pizza, wraps, sandwiches, and good coffee. Mon–Sat 6am–10pm, Sun 8am–9pm. See p.240 for their midtown branch.

Noble's Diner 4133 Mountain View Drive at Park ☏ 770-3811, ⓦ www.noblesdiner.com. This place claims to specialize in Alaskan/Southern comfort food such as red beans and rice with reindeer sausage, Noble's Delight (pasta and ground buffalo with caramelized onions), or barley vegetable risotto, all around $13. But it's also one of Anchorage's more vegetarian-friendly options, with delicately flavored soups ($3–5), appetizers such as a roast veggie bowl ($4.50) or mozzarella and herb tomatoes ($7.50), salads such as tabouleh ($8.50), not to mention sandwiches such as tuna melt, grilled eggplant, Reuben, or meatloaf ($7–9.50). Great imported beers, too. Mon–Sat 11am–3pm, 5–9pm.

🏃 **Orso** 737 W 5th Ave ☎ 222-3232. Fine dining in a baronial setting where smartly dressed staff serve tempting Northern Italian dishes, plus Alaskan staples of fish and steak. *Crostini di funghi* is done well, as are the wild mushroom ravioli ($19) and the chocolate torte with sambuca syrup. Appetizers cost $5–13, pasta $14–22, seafood $20–28, and steaks $25–32. There's a $10 lunch Monday to Friday (with bar menu on summer afternoons). Mon–Fri 11.30am–4pm (winter to 2pm), Sun–Thurs 5–10pm (winter to 9pm), Fri & Sat 5–11pm.

Phyllis's Café and Salmon Bake 436 D St, at 5th Ave ☎ 274-6576. Outdoor seating and bustling atmosphere make this an essential summer stop for mounds of salmon or ribs for under $20, halibut for $22, or just a bowl of chowder with sourdough bread for $5, as well as beef and buffalo burgers, ribs etc. 11am–midnight.

Sack's 328 G St ☎ 274-4022 or 276-3546, Ⓦ www.sackscafe.com. An appealing and modestly priced favorite. Everything is made with care from the Caesar salad ($8.50) and sandwiches ($10–13) to the poached eggs and scallop crab cakes ($13). Entrees might include deconstructed pork tamale ($24) or rack of NZ lamb ($32), and they do Sunday brunch (11am–3pm) with a south-of-the-border variation on eggs Benedict ($10). Lunch 11am–2.30pm (Sat & Sun to 3pm), dinner 5–9.30pm (Fri & Sat to 10.30pm).

Sassafras Café 343 W 6th Ave, at D St ☎ 222-2512. An arty little place serving espresso and smoothies, plus a daily quiche ($4), salads ($5–7), wraps ($8–9), and sandwiches (some veggie; $7.50–9); add soup or salad for $3 extra. Good desserts, too. Tues–Sat 10am to 5–7pm.

Side Street Espresso 412 G St. Coffee is pretty much all they do, and they attract a loyal following for doing it right. Have your caffeine and browse the magazines and community notice board. Occasional live music. Mon–Sat 7am–3pm.

Simon and Seafort's 420 L St ☎ 274-3502. Consistently one of Anchorage's better restaurants, serving meals such as beer-battered fish and chips ($11) in the bar (see p.243) and beautifully prepared American favorites – steaks, ribs, salmon, and such, plus more interesting dishes like halibut asiago, and luscious desserts such as wildberry ice cream and bread pudding – in a *c.*1900-style saloon with wonderful views of Cook Inlet. Expect to pay $40–50 for three courses. Closed for weekend lunches.

🏃 **Snow City Café** 1034 W 4th Ave, at L St ☎ 272-2489, Ⓦ www.snowcitycafe.com. Probably the city's best breakfast spot – eggs Benedict or Florentine for $9.50, yogurt, fruit & granola for $5 – and great for relaxing over a pot of Earl Grey and a slice of cake. Soups and salads pad out a lunch menu that might include pesto chicken pasta ($9) and tofu stir-fry ($9). Not open for dinner except for soup and sandwiches on Wednesday, when there's an Irish music session (7–11pm).

Tempura Kitchen 3826 Spenard, at Oregon ☎ 277-2741. Long-established Japanese place specializing in superb sushi – try Alaskan side-striped shrimp if they're in season. Lunch Mon–Fri, dinner daily.

Teriyaki Box 401 I St ☎ 248-4011. Great little eat-in and takeout place that speedily serves tasty dishes such as wonton noodle soup ($6.50), shrimp yakisoba noodles ($8.50), and teriyaki halibut with rice and stir-fry veggies ($10), plus espresso coffees. Closed Sundays.

The Winter Thyme 930 W 5th near K St ☎ 677-3843, Ⓔ thewinterthyme@fastmail.fm. A new place promising "fine comfort food," much like *Noble's Diner*, in a similar casual setting. What they mean is starters like salmon or vegetable wontons ($4–12) or naan pizza ($7), and entrees such as cedar plank-roasted Idaho trout with chives ($10), halibut parmesan ($13), buffalo meatloaf in puff pastry with *chevre* cheese ($20), or king salmon with savory fennel bread pudding ($18). They do desserts too, if you can manage. Thurs–Mon 11.30am–midnight.

Midtown

Alaska Game and Gourmet 1021 W Northern Lights Blvd ☎ 278-8500. Stocks imported cheeses and other delicacies hard to come by in Alaska.

Arctic Roadrunner 5300 Old Seward Hwy, at International Airport Rd ☎ 561-1245. Few fancy trimmings, just good no-nonsense burgers ($5) regularly voted the best in town. An eat-in and takeout Anchorage staple since 1964. Closed Sun.

Bagel Factory 100 W 34th Ave, (between A and C sts ☎ 561-8871. The best bagels in town, also breakfasts and deli sandwiches. Mon–Sat 6.30am–3pm.

🏃 **Bear Tooth Theatre Pub** 1230 W 27th Ave ☎ 276-4200, Ⓦ www.beartooththeatre .net. Top-notch combination restaurant, bar, and cinema, where for $3 on top of your meal price you can dine while watching a movie (see Listings, p.247). The menu has a wide range – halibut chowder ($4), Caesar salads ($6), burritos and tacos ($5–8), and gourmet pizzas ($15 for a 16-inch pie) – and the microbrews are excellent.

Bombay Deluxe 555 W Northern Lights Blvd ☎277-1200, ⊛www.bombaydeluxe.com. The best of Anchorage's limited range of curry houses, reliably dishing up the standard Punjabi (despite the name) range of biryanis, vindaloos, and tikka masalas. There's a $10 all-you-can-eat lunch buffet plus easy online ordering. Mon–Fri 11am–10pm, Sat 5–10pm, Sun noon–9pm.

Café Amsterdam 530 E Benson (Metro Mall) ☎274-0074. Known for its good bottled beers (Belgian, Bavarian, and the like) as much as for food, but you can have breakfast from 7am and the beer bar is open 10am–10pm.

Café Felix 530 E Benson in Metro Book & Music (see p.244) ☎279-8500. Arty nook serving a soup of the day, bagel sandwiches, and savory and dessert crêpes, plus teas, organic coffees, and smoothies, and putting on music and events Wed to Sat at about 7pm. Mon–Sat 9am–9pm, Sun 10.30am–5pm.

Carrs Three locations on Northern Lights Blvd: at Minnesota Drive, Denali St, and Muldoon Rd (east of Midtown). Find low prices (for Alaska, anyway) and 24-hour shopping at this grocery chain.

Europa Bakery 601 W 36th Ave ☎563-5704, ⊛www.europabakery.com. Superb bakery producing all manner of loaves, including a spent-grain variety using the leftovers from the *Glacier Brewhouse*'s beer-brewing. Excellent sandwiches ($7) to take out or eat in as well as fine pastries, cakes, and coffee. It's also a popular place for an omelette breakfast on weekends. Mon–Fri 5.30am–7pm, Sat 7am–7pm, Sun 9am–6pm.

Fred Meyers Northern Lights Blvd at Seward Hwy, and Muldoon Rd at Debarr Rd (east of Midtown). Supermarket chain carrying produce of a slightly higher quality than Carrs. 7am–11pm.

Golden Gate 3471 E Tudor Rd ☎561-4274. Basic Chinese joint that's inconveniently located but well worth seeking out for heaving plates at bargain prices. The Mongolian beef ($7 starter/$11 main) is excellent, and they do combination dinners for one from $13. Closed Sunday lunchtime.

Great Harvest Bakery In Metro Mall, 530 E Benson ☎274-3331, ⊛www.greatharvestalaska .com. For very pricey but very tasty bread (white chocolate and cherry, anyone?) and free samples, just walk through the door. Mon–Sat 7am–6pm.

Gwennie's Old Alaska Restaurant 4333 Spenard Rd, at Forest Rd ☎243-2090. Something of an

institution, with two busy floors decorated with Alaskan memorabilia and old photos providing a family setting for all-day breakfasts – the sourdough pancakes are outstanding– as well as the usual range of burgers and sandwiches. Daily 6am–11pm in summer.

Hot Licks 1340 W Northern Lights ☎929-5425. Alaska's finest ice cream (also coffee and free WiFi). Tues–Sat noon–10pm, Sun 1–9pm.

Jens' Restaurant 701 W 36th Ave, at Arctic Blvd ☎561-5367, ⊛www.jensrestaurant.com. Highly fashionable fine-dining restaurant and wine bar with a well-heeled crowd and a convivial atmosphere. The menu, which reflects the chef-patron's Danish heritage, varies daily but you might expect to start with gravadlax or spinach ravioli ($11) followed by pan-fried medallions of marlin on mango, jalapeño, and citrus *beurre blanc* ($20). From 4pm you can snack on appetizers ($10–16) or Alaska oysters ($2.75 each) at the bar. The wine list is equally impressive. Closed Sat lunch, all day Sun, and all January.

Kaladi Bros 1360 W Northern Lights Blvd ☎344-5483. Excellent coffee and a relaxed environment in a café attached to Title Wave Books. There's Internet access for $7/hr, plus free wireless access. There are a couple of other branches around town, and you'll find their coffee sold across Alaska.

Middle Way Café 1200 W Northern Lights Blvd ☎272-6433. Low-key café specializing in low-fat, healthy, and mostly vegetarian food, particularly soups, sandwiches, wraps, and salads (mostly under $7), plus espresso, organic juices, and smoothies including one offering "inner balance." Breakfast daily, kitchen open to 4.30pm Mon–Sat, café open daily 'til early evening.

Moose's Tooth 3300 Old Seward Hwy, at 33rd Ave ☎258-2537, ⊛www.moosestooth .net. A perennial favorite, always alive with diners tucking into some of the town's best gourmet pizza (in 38 variations, from $6.50 to $26) or imbibing one of a dozen or so house-brewed beers at the bar. On the first Thursday of the month they celebrate First Tap Thursday (9pm–1am), offering a band, a party, and an opportunity to meet the brewer over a glass of that month's new creation. To 11pm daily.

New Sagaya's Midtown Market 3700 Old Seward Hwy. Like their *City Market* downtown, this is an upmarket deli with a café for eat-in meals (around $8) with Thai dishes, sushi and sashimi, pizza, wraps, sandwiches, and Kaladi coffee; across the road is *Natural Pantry* (Mon–Sat 9am–9pm), a health-food supermarket.

Organic Oasis 2610 Spenard Rd ☎277-7882. Earthy and reasonably priced spot that's great for soups and organic dishes, mostly (though not exclusively) vegetarian or vegan. Try their wraps, sandwiches, and mini-pizzas (mostly $9–11) washed down with a shot of wheatgrass, fruit smoothie, or (if you must) an espresso or organic beers and wines. From 7pm Tues to Sat there's usually some form of civilized live music. Closed Mon in winter.

Villa Nova 5121 Arctic Blvd ℡561-1660. Anchorage's best Italian restaurant, its secret being to take the finest Alaskan ingredients such as scallops and halibut and turn them into something quintessentially Mediterranean. As appetisers, try the *caponata* (eggplant relish) or *bruschetta* ($11 each), followed by halibut filet stuffed with crab ($25) or veal *valdostana* ($21). There are also wonderful desserts and ice cream, all made on the premises, and a fine wine list. Mon–Sat 5–10pm.

South Anchorage

Carrs Huffman Rd at Seward Hwy. Find low prices (for Alaska, anyway) and 24-hour shopping at this grocery chain.

Fred Meyers Abbott Rd at Lake Otis Pkwy. Super-market chain carrying produce of a slightly higher quality than Carrs. 7am–11pm.

Mexico in Alaska 7305 Old Seward Hwy, at 73rd Ave ℡349-1528. Anchorage's most authentic Mexican restaurant. Although the food is slightly sanitized for northern tastes, you won't find better dishes than the *camarones Veracruzana* ($20) or chicken in a savory *mole* sauce ($12). For the non-carnivore there's a good range of veggie dishes ($13–15), for the budget-conscious the $11 weekday lunch buffet is a good bet, and there are always bottles of the excellent Bohemia beer. Closed Sun lunch.

Southside Bistro 1320 Huffman Park Drive ℡348-0088, ⓦwww.southsidebistro.com. Some of the finest dining in the south of the city, this stylish spot is particularly noted for its seafood and fresh pasta on the restaurant side (mains $9–14 lunch, $15–33 dinner) and a good wine list. The adjacent bistro has excellent hardwood-baked flatbread pizza. Closed Sun & Mon.

Drinking and entertainment

Good bars abound in downtown Anchorage, and the atmosphere varies as much as the clientele. You don't need to dig far to find dark, block-built hideaway lounges left over from the oil-boom Seventies when they were meeting places for shady deals, and late at night the main drag of **4th Avenue** can seem like a surreal slalom course as you swerve to avoid the terminally drunk. But the downtown area also harbors half a dozen or more genuinely appealing places to drink, and even a little **live music**, most reliably at *Humpy's*, as well as jazz at *Sullivan's Steakhouse*, 320 W 5th Ave at C Street (℡258-2882).

The other lively area is **Spenard** – along Spenard Road between Northern Lights Boulevard and International Airport Road – which has long since shaken its reputation for sleazy excess, earned during the freewheeling oil days of the late 1970s, but still retains an edge. It can be a lot of fun as long as you are sensible, though women travelers may not find the wilder side of macho Anchorage quite as endearing as many locals seem to think it is, evident in some innocent-looking bars turning out to be strip joints (there are even alcohol-free strip clubs for those innocent under-21s). Here, too, you'll find live music, at *Blues Central* and *Chilkoot Charlie's*.

Beer drinkers should be very happy in Anchorage, which must have more top-quality microbreweries than any city of comparable size in the US. Breweries worth trying are the *Moose's Tooth*, *Bear Tooth*, *Glacier Brewhouse*, *Snow Goose*, and even *Humpy's*, which doesn't brew its own, but has a vast range on tap.

There isn't a great deal of live **theater** in Anchorage, particularly during the summer when it takes something really special to lure Alaskans indoors. For the rest of the year, the Alaska Performing Arts Center (℡263-2900, ⓦwww.alaskapac.org) puts its exemplary acoustics to the test with a variety of shows, plays, and concerts, and hosts both the Anchorage Opera (℡279-2557, ⓦwww.anchorageopera.org) and the Anchorage Symphony Orchestra (℡274-8668,

△ Downtown Anchorage

www.anchoragesymphony.org). Look out, too, for the Anchorage Festival of Music (℡272-1471, www.anchorageconcerts.org), which takes place in mid-June.

It's a major step down in formality, though not ambition or invention, to the quirky Cyrano's Off Center Playhouse, 413 D St at 4th Ave (℡274-2499, www.cyranos .org), which puts on a play each month (Thurs–Sat 7pm, Sun 3pm; $15), ranging from locally penned pieces to the more edgy classics (notably Albee, Miller, Chekhov, and Shakespeare), frequently performed by their resident troupe, the Eccentric Theater Company. Scared Scriptless, an improv comedy session, performs at 10pm on the second Saturday of each month.

To find out what's on at any of the places listed below, consult the *Anchorage Daily News* – particularly Friday's comprehensive *Play* entertainment supplement (www.play.adn.com) – or Thursday's free weekly *Press*, a more alternative listings mag found all over town. Both also give a rundown of the blockbusters showing at the profusion of multiscreen **cinemas** in suburban malls and more interesting films at the Bear's Tooth Theatre Pub, Out North Arts Center, and the museum and universities (see Listings, p.247). The "All About Anchorage" recorded activity infoline is ℡276-3200.

Tickets for almost any major show can be bought from the CenterTix office in the foyer of the Performing Arts Center (Mon–Fri 10am–5pm, Sat noon–5pm and prior to evening events; ℡263-2787 or 1-800/278-7849, www.centertix.net), and in any Carrs supermarket.

First Friday, held of course on the first Friday of each month, from about 5 to 8pm, is a sort of huge promenade around town, when art galleries all launch their new shows and lay on free drinks, nibbles, and perhaps music.

Downtown

Bernie's Bungalow 626 D St, at 7th Ave ℡276-8808, www.berniesbungalowlounge.com. Very un-Alaskan, chic martini bar fashioned from an old wooden house that shimmies to cool Latin and jazz grooves. They have an ever-expanding deck for the long summer evenings, but indoor seating is in short supply so come early and dress up. Breakfast, lunch, and dinner are also served (appetizers $7–10, burgers $8–14, pasta $9–12).

Crow's Nest Atop the *Captain Cook Hotel*, 939 W 5th Ave ℡276-6000. Folks come here for the fantastic views of city and inlet, elegant service, fine wine list, and recherché drinks such as pomegranate vodka, as well as exquisite hors d'oeuvres such as citrus-cured salmon gravadlax, tartare of ahi tuna with avocado, or horseradish-marinated Dungeness crab. There's also a stylish French restaurant, with the same views, and Anchorage's swishest Sunday brunch. Daily in summer, may close Tues or Wed in winter; dinner Mon–Sat.

Darwin's Theory 426 G St at 4th Ave ℡277-5322. Straightforward bar for moderately priced boozing, a great jukebox, and beery encounters with colorful local characters.

Humpy's Great Alaskan Alehouse 610 W 6th Ave at F St ℡276-2337; see p.238. An ever-popular watering hole with a college-bar feel and what must be Alaska's widest selection of Pacific Northwest microbrews (over 30) as well as some expensive English and Belgian bottled beers. Whisky drinkers are also well catered for with more than thirty single malts, and there is live music nightly (free), often acoustic or Irish.

Mad Myrna's 530 E 5th Ave ℡276-9762, www.alaska.net/~madmyrna. Anchorage's main gay dance club, usually open Mon–Sat from 3pm, with karaoke (Wed & Thurs) and drag nights (Fri 9pm). Small cover charge at weekends and when there's someone special performing.

Pioneer Bar 739 W 4th Ave ℡276-7996. Traditional, dark downtown bar that has swapped its seedy reputation in favor of boisterous youthful drinking and pool.

Rumrunners Old Towne Bar and Grill 4th Ave at E St ℡278-4493. Hugely popular bar attracting a young crowd with DJ-led dance most nights and showy cocktail-mixing.

Simon and Seafort's 420 L St ℡274-3502. Mainly an upmarket restaurant (see p.239), but the saloon bar is a great spot for cocktails or scotches and bourbons (over 100 varieties), especially if you can steal a seat close to the picture windows, which boast unsurpassed views of Cook Inlet and Mount Susitna.

Snow Goose 717 W 3rd Ave ℡277-7727, www.alaskabeers.com. Good restaurant and microbrewery chiefly noted for its wonderfully spacious deck that's perfect for those long summer evenings. From 11.30am.

Sub Zero 612 F St. Currently the place to be seen, all steel and ice-blue lighting, and nonsmoking to boot.

Midtown

Blues Central 825 W Northern Lights Blvd, at Arctic Ave ☏ 272-1341, ⊛ www.bluescentral .net. A restaurant mainly notable as Anchorage's premier venue for blues (plus a little soul), operating every night until 2am, with a very popular jam session on Sunday nights. $3–5 cover charge.

Chilkoot Charlie's 2435 Spenard Rd ☏ 272-1010, ⊛ www.koots.com. OK, so it's not everyone's idea of a good night out, and can be a cattle market,

but "Koots" is Alaskan through and through. Every night this sawdust-strewn barn of a place packs them in for a wide range of pricey drinks (10 bars in total), pool, foosball, multiple floors of DJ-led dance and a band from 9.30pm, or comedy on Thursdays. "We screw the other guy and pass the savings on to you!" they claim, but still have a cover charge, usually $2–6.

Peanut Farm 5227 Old Seward Hwy, at International Airport Rd ☏ 563-3283. Straightforward sports bar, always lively and open from 8am (6am for football games) to very late. Their "burgers as big as your head" are best consumed on their spacious deck, watching salmon or beaver in Campbell Creek on a warm evening. It's the home of Alaska's very own Duck Fart cocktail (mainly Bailey's and Kahlua).

Shopping

For Alaskans, Anchorage offers the best shopping this side of Seattle, and is often the only place you can get your hands on the goods. As a visitor, shopping is likely to be fairly low on your list of priorities, though with no state sales tax to pay, it can be a good place to buy **books** and **outdoor equipment**. Consider putting some cash aside for **Native craftwork**, such as spirit masks, ivory carving, and etched baleen (though see our comments on transporting restricted goods on p.74). Some of what's available can be tasteless souvenir junk, but much of it is beautiful and superbly made with prices to match. Some judicious shopping around, however, can turn up affordable pieces.

Books

Wherever you are in Alaska you'll have no problem finding books about the state or by Alaskan authors, but if you've got specific needs Anchorage is by far your best bet. Also see the Books section of Contexts for specific recommendations.

A Novel View 415 L St ☏ 278-0084. Literature and art (new and second-hand) are the specialties. Mon–Fri 11am–7pm, Sat 10am–5pm, Sun noon–4pm.

Barnes & Noble 200 E Northern Lights Blvd ☏ 279-7323. The chain bookshop has its usual solid selection of new books and newspapers. Daily 9am–11pm.

Borders Books and Music 1100 E Dimond Blvd ☏ 344-4099. South Anchorage equivalent of Barnes & Noble. Mon–Thurs 10am–10pm, Fri & Sat 10am–11pm, Sun 10am–9pm.

C&M Used Books 215 E 4th Ave ☏ 278-9394. Second-hand bookshop just east of downtown where, amid the apparent chaos, they've got some good books available at half the cover price (or quarter price with a similarly priced trade). Mon–Sat 9am–5pm, closed Sun.

Campus Center Bookstore UAA, 3211 Providence Drive ☏ 786-1151. Plenty of good Alaskana as well as academic texts. Summer Mon–Fri 8.30am–6pm.

Cook Inlet Book Co 415 W 5th Ave, at D St ☏ 240-4148, ⊛ www.cookinlet.com. Anchorage's handiest source for new and used books, magazines and newspapers, that's particularly strong on Alaskan titles. Daily 9am–10pm in summer.

Cyrano's 413 D St ☏ 274-2599. Specialist bookshop with a good line in the arts, literary fiction, the classics, and Alaskan titles; mostly second-hand. Mon–Sat 9am–5.30pm.

Metro Book & Music 530 E Benson ☏ 279-8500 Mon–Sat 9am–9pm, Sun 10.30am–5pm. A pleasant, arty store offering Internet access as well as live music and other events from Wed to Sat at about 7pm.

Title Wave 1360 W Northern Lights Blvd ☎1-888/598-9283, ⓦwww.wavebooks.com. Wondrous midtown emporium with the widest selection of used books in the city, a large and well-chosen selection of remaindered and new titles, plus new and used CDs. *Kaladi* Bros Internet café (see p.247) on site.

Several readings and other events each week. Mon–Thurs 9am–9pm, Fri & Sat 9am–10pm, Sun 11am–7pm.
Twice Told Tales 1231 W Northern Lights Blvd ☎561-3828. Friendly second-hand store opposite REI.

Camping and outdoor equipment

If you're planning to spend a fair bit of time in the Alaskan outdoors, you'll need the right gear. Your best bet is to head to Anchorage's outdoor-supply ghetto – at the junction of Spenard Road and Northern Lights Boulevard, in midtown – where you'll find pretty much everything you need: canoes, tents, climbing tackle, fishing gear, and bicycles, some of it also available for rent (see Listings, p.248).

Alaska Kayak 2605 Barrow St, between Northern Lights and Fireweed blvds ☎522-7710. Anchorage's specialist canoe and kayak store, which rents canoes and whitewater kayaks from $60 for 2 days, as well as kiteboarding gear.
Alaska Mountaineering & Hiking 2633 Spenard Rd ☎272-1811, ⓦwww.alaskamountaineering.com. Rock climbers and mountaineers are best served here at AMH, which also covers hiking needs, rents mountaineering and ski equipment at competitive rates, and has a used equipment board. Mon–Fri 9am–7pm, Sat 9am–6pm, Sun noon–5pm.
Barney's Sport Chalet 906 W Northern Lights Blvd ☎561-5242. A little more personal than the bigger REI, strong on top-quality tents, backpacking equipment and, in winter, cross-country ski equipment. Mon–Fri 10am–7pm, Sat 10am–5pm.
The Bicycle Shop 1035 W Northern Lights Blvd ☎272-5219. Open daily for sales, parts, and servicing.
Chain Reaction Cycles 1100 Huffman Park Drive Unit 2 ☎235-0750. The new pretenders, more into hardcore mountainbiking than neighboring Paramount.

Great Outdoor Clothing Co 1200 W Northern Lights Blvd ☎277-6664. The best spot for low-cost fleeces, hats, and thermal underwear. Mon–Fri 10am–6pm, Sat & Sun 10am–8pm.
Paramount Cycles 1320 Huffman Park Drive ☎336-2453. An especially female-friendly bike shop with a good range of bikes and parts, plus local info and contacts. Service from $40, labor $50/hr. Mon–Fri 11am–7pm , Sat 6pm close, Sun 5pm close.
REI 1200 W Northern Lights Blvd ☎272-4565, ⓦwww.rei.com/anchorage. This one-stop specialist store stocks Alaska's widest selection of camping, hiking, canoeing, climbing, cycling, and skiing gear plus clothing, footwear, and freeze-dried foods. They also do an extensive range of rentals. A single lifetime family payment of $15 gives you membership in the co-op and substantial discounts on retail and rental gear. Mon–Sat 10am–9pm, Sun 10am–6pm.
Skinny Raven 800 H St ☎274-7222, ⓦwww.skinnyraven.com. Best downtown source for running and outdoor gear. Mon–Fri 10.30am–6.30pm, Sat 10am–6pm.

Crafts

Most of the tourist-oriented shops in Anchorage stock the usual array of T-shirts and overpriced knick-knacks, not much of it even kitschy enough to be enticing. Amongst the dross you will find some excellent **Native crafts** – Anchorage has the best selection in the state since craftspeople visiting the big city from outlying villages tend to bring in their work for sale. When buying here you lose some of the satisfaction of dealing directly with the artisan and will probably pay more than you would at the source. Before buying anything containing parts of endangered animals, read the box on taking your purchases out of the state.

Alaska hasn't quite shaken its Russian influence and accordingly there are several shops downtown stocking **Russian-made goods**. Look for porcelain tea sets from Lomonosov in St Petersburg and nested *matryoshka* dolls – the wooden ones that fit into each other – in traditional designs and modern variations: American football teams, *South Park* characters, and political genealogies from Lenin to Putin. The strip of G St between 3rd and 5th is home to the artier shops and the center of the First Friday scene.

Alaska Native Medical Center 4315 Diplomacy Drive, off Tudor Rd ☎ 729-1122, ⓦ www.anmc.org. Serious buyers should definitely make for the craft shop on the ground floor of this hospital. Items are brought in by folk from Native villages when they come to visit recuperating friends and relatives. Good range and fair (though not cheap) prices. Mon–Fri 10am–2pm and first and third Saturday of the month 11am–2pm.

Alaskan Ivory Exchange 700 W 4th Ave ☎ 272-3662. A small shop chock-full of carved walrus ivory and fossilized whalebone products; some simple and fairly cheap, others more intricate and pricey.

Anchorage Museum of History & Art 121 W 7th Ave at A St ☎ 343-4326. The museum shop in the foyer (no entrance fee) stocks a wide selection of quality Native crafts along with Russian lacquerwork and Alaska books.

Antique Gallery 1001 W 4th Ave, Suite B ☎ 276-8986, ⓦ www.theantiquegallery.com. A real treasure trove, packed to the rafters with pre-twentieth-century artifacts you'd normally see only in museums – and everything's for sale. Avoid sticking your foot through the thousand-dollar canvases that line the aisles and browse through $1500 baskets woven from whale baleen, Tiffany lamps, suits of armor, ormolu clocks, stacks of shotguns and pistols, Russian icons, and even the occasional $40,000 oil by Laurence, Ziegler, or Machetanz.

Antique 314 G St ☎ 277-1663, ⓦ www.artiqueltd.com. On the strip of G St that's home to the artier gift shops, this is also the heart of the First Friday scene; going strong for 35 years, Artique has Alaskan paintings, sculptures, pottery, and glassware.

Aurora 713 W 5th Ave, at G St ☎ 274-0234, ⓦ www.aurorafineart-alaska.com. Colorful store with a wide range of arts and crafts (with a particular niche in big giclée prints), much of it quite expensive but top quality.

Heritage Gifts Downtown 333 W 4th, at C St ☎ 272-5048. The downtown outlet of the Alaska Native Heritage Center (linked by a free shuttle), with fine pieces by all Alaska's Native peoples, plus from June to August craft demonstrations and dancing (11am and 1pm).

Kobuk Coffee Company 504 W 5th Ave ☎ 272-3626, ⓦ www.kobukcoffee.com. Mainly a coffee and tea emporium, the Kobuk also sells beautiful Russian tea services and offers free samples of samovar tea.

Oomingmak Musk Ox Producers' Co-operative 604 H St ☎ 272-9225, ⓦ www.qiviut.com. Small shop selling garments knitted from qiviut, the under-fur of the musk ox, by natives of western Alaska, where each village has its own distinctive design. Most products are fawn, with caps going for $120–180, headbands for $150, scarves for $245–330, *nachaqs* or circular scarves for $175, and hats for $85–185. (For more on this organization and these ancient beasts, see p.387.)

Russian Orthodox Museum gift shop 605 A St ☎ 276-7257. Lomonosov porcelain, lacquer boxes, icons, and CDs of church music.

Listings

Airlines (See Basics, p.34, for more airlines serving Anchorage.); Bering Air, ☎ 907/624-3175, ⓦ www.beringair.com; ERA Aviation ☎ 1-800/866-8394, ⓦ www.flyera.com; Frontier Flying Service ☎ 1-800/478-6779, ⓦ www.frontierflying.com; Grant Aviation ☎ 1-888/359-4726, ⓦ www.flygrant.com; Hageland Aviation ☎ 1-866/239-0119, ⓦ www.hageland.com; Hawaiian ☎ 1-800/367-5320, ⓦ www.hawaiianair.com; Mavial Magadan Airlines ☎ 907/248-2994; PenAir 1-800/448-4226, ⓦ www.penair.com; Reeve Aleutian Airways ☎ 907/243-1112; WestJet ☎ 1-888/ 937-8538 or 1-800/538-5696, ⓦ www.westjet.com

Airport Ted Stevens International Airport ☎ 266-2526, ⓦ www.dot.state.ak.us/anc. For details of flights, see Basics, p.27.

American Express American Express Travel Service, 700 G St, Suite 128 (☎ 274-5588), and 5011 Jewel Lake Rd (☎ 266-6666), operates as a travel agency, exchanges foreign currency, and handles client mail.

Banks and currency exchange Banks are located all over town, many of them drive-thru. ATMs are even more abundant, mostly indoors in malls, gas stations, and some even in bars. Downtown there's a First National Bank branch at 646 W 4th Ave between F and G sts and a Wells

Fargo outpost in the Fifth Avenue Mall at D St (Mon–Sat 10am–6pm), which handles foreign exchange.

Buses (long-distance) The following services operate roughly from mid-May to mid-Sept, though it pays to book ahead at the end of the season when services may not run if there are too few customers. (See Basics on p.44 for route details.) Alaska Direct Bus Line (☎1-800/770-6652; in Anchorage ☎277-6652) departs from *Days Inn*, 321 5th Ave, and the *Anchorage International Hostel* for Whitehorse, Yukon (Wed, Fri, and Sun only) via Palmer, Glennallen, and Tok; Alaska Park Connection (☎1-800/266-8625 ⓦwww .alaskacoach.com) picks up at the *Dimond Center Hotel* and outside the Egan Convention Center on 5th Ave for the morning runs to Talkeetna and Denali, and outside the *Best Western Golden Lion* (Seward Hwy and 36th) for the afternoon run north, and for runs to Seward; Alaska/Yukon Trails (☎1-800/770-2725) picks up at the airport, *Jason's Hostel*, *Anchorage International Hostel*, and the Egan Center and goes to Fairbanks; Anchorage Denali Shuttle (☎301-5436, ⓦwww .anchoragedenalishuttle.com) leaves daily to Denali Park from 4th Ave at B St; from mid-May to end of Aug, Denali Transport (☎1-877/272-1346) runs daily to Denali Park from 306 G St (at 3rd Ave); The Magic Bus (☎441-8420, ⓦwww .the magicbus.com) does a run to Whittier, leaving the *Captain Cook Hotel* at noon, and to Girdwood leaving the visitor center at 4.30pm daily. Homer Stage Line (☎868-3914, ⓦwww.homerstageline .com) and the Seward Bus Line (☎563-0800, ⓦwww.sewardbuslines.net) both leave from 3333 Fairbanks St in midtown for the runs to Homer and Seward respectively, via the airport if pre-booked.

Camping and outdoor equipment rental REI (see p.245; rentals ☎272-4564) rents tents from $15 for the first day, $7 thereafter; sleeping bags $15/$7; stoves $5/$2; kayaks $25/12, canoes $40/$15; and more. In summer a lot of this stuff is reserved in advance, so phone early. Nonmembers pay double these prices so start by paying the $15 lifetime membership fee.

Car rental Renting a car from one of the desks at the airport operated by Alamo, Avis, Budget, Dollar, Hertz, National, Thrifty, and Payless incurs an additional eleven percent tax on top of all other taxes, so for anything other than a very brief rental it works out cheaper to rent off-airport, although opening hours are more restricted. Budget, Thrifty, and numerous local agencies have depots close to the airport, but they can't pick you up, so grab a cab (around $8; refundable with some agencies), or go to your hotel and they'll drop a vehicle

off when you're ready for it free of charge. The cheapest (and oldest) vehicles are from Denali Car Rental, 1209 Gambell St (☎276-1230 or 1-800/757-1230, @raycinjsc@yahoo.com; Mon–Fri 8am–6pm, Sat 10am–4pm, Sun noon–4pm), which has 2- to 3-year-old compacts, some with manual gears, from $45 a day with 150 free miles a day (25¢ a mile thereafter). Winter rates start at $30 for a weekend with 150 miles/day free mileage. CDW is only $12 a day with $1000 deductible. They're a fair way from the airport so go to your lodging and they'll pick you up; an airport drop-off costs $25. For one- or two-year-old vehicles starting at around $50 a day try: Advantage, 421 Spenard Rd (☎1-888/877-3585, ⓦwww .ineedacarrental.com); Affordable New Car Rentals, Spenard Rd at Breezewood (☎1-800/248-3765, ⓦwww.ancr.com); Airport Car Rental, 502 W Northern Lights Blvd (☎562-0897, ℻561-1437, ⓦwww.alaskan/airportcarrental); Alaska Car & Van Rentals, 3934 Spenard Rd at Macrae (☎1-800/243-4832, ⓦwww.alaskacarandvan .com), which doesn't take reservations; Arctic (aka Payless), 1130 W International Airport Rd (☎1-888/714-4690, ⓦwww.arcticrentacar.com); Midnight Sun Rentals, 4211 Spenard Rd (☎243-8806); or Value Car Rental, 420 W International Airport Rd (☎1-877/561-7368, ⓦwww .rentalcaralaska.com). Local details for the majors are: Avis – airport ☎249-8260 (Mon–Fri 5.30am–2.30am); 5th Ave at B St ☎277-4567 (Mon–Fri 7am–7pm, Sat & Sun 9am–5pm); Budget – airport ☎243-0150 (6am–2am); near airport, 5011 Spenard ☎243-0150 (7am–8pm); 802 Gambell ☎274-1002 or 278-7825 (7am–8pm); Dollar – airport ☎248-5338 (6am–2am); near airport ☎279-5275 (8am–10pm); Enterprise – near airport 5000 W International Airport Rd ☎1-800/261-7331, ⓦwww.enterprise.com (daily 6am–midnight); 926 E 4th Ave at Ingra ☎277-1600 (Mon–Fri 7.30am–6pm, Sat 9am–noon); Hertz– airport ☎243-3308 (5.30am–3am); 414 K St ☎562-4594 (Mon–Fri 8am–5pm, Sat 9am–2pm); Thrifty– near airport ☎276-2855 (7am–11pm summer/8pm winter); and Payless – near airport ☎243-3616, 1-800/729-5377 (Mon–Fri 8am–6pm, Sat/Sun 8am–4pm).

Cinemas The Anchorage Museum of History & Art (see p.226) shows two or three films a day on Alaskan life and culture (mid-May to mid-Sept 11.30am, 2.30 & 4.30pm; free), plus classic or arthouse movies at weekends (all year Sat & Sun 6pm; $6); the *Bear Tooth Theatre Pub* (see p.239) plays movies a couple of months old and often has film festivals and classic-movie nights, all for $3. The remaining movie theaters are suburban multiplexes: closest to downtown is the Fireweed Theater, 661 E Fireweed at Gambell (☏ 566-3328); otherwise try Century 16, 301 E 36th Ave (☏ 929-FILM; $8.50, early shows $5.50), or the Regal Dimond Center (☏ 1-800/3263-2646). Check the *Press* for listings and other movie houses.

Consulates Canada, 3512 Campbell Airstrip Rd ☏ 333-1400; UK, 3211 Providence Drive ☏ 786-4848.

Festivals and events All major (and many minor) events are listed at ⓦ www.anchorage.net /events. The pick are: Anchorage Fur Rendezvous, a ten-day winter festival held in March (ⓦ www .furrondy.net); the start of the Iditarod Trail Sled Dog Race (see p.392) in early March; the Blues on the Green Festival held in Kincaid Park in mid-June (☏ 1-800/478-7328); and the Anchorage Festival of Music, a classical music celebration held over a week in late June (ⓦ www.festivalmusic.org).

Gay and lesbian helpline ☏ 258-4777; daily 6–11pm.

Internet access Sign up and wait for your free hour at the main Loussac Library (see below), or use the free WiFi if you have a laptop. Also Cook Inlet Book Company, 415 W 5th Ave ($2/15min, $5/hr); Cyber City, 1441 W Northern Lights Blvd; Kaladi Bros at 1360 W Northern Lights Blvd and 6921 Brayton Drive ($1.75/15min, also free WiFi at both sites); Perfect Cup, Level 2, Dimond Center; and The UPS Store, 645 G St. There's free WiFi at Bernie's Bungalow, Café Sassafras, Cupola Café, Glacier Brewhouse, Hot Licks, Lucky Monkey, and Sub Zero cafés/bars plus most hotels and B&Bs and at UAA's Campus Center/student union.

Laundry Arctic Laundry, 3607 Arctic (daily 10am–10pm); Home Style, 701 W 36th (Mon–Fri 9am–7pm, Sat & Sun 9am–4pm); K-Speed Wash, 600 E 6th Ave at Cordova (open Mon–Sat 7am–8pm); Surf Laundry, 3833 Mountain View Drive at Bragaw.

Left luggage There is luggage storage (daily 5am–2am) at the airport's main South (domestic) Terminal. For up to 24 hours storage they charge $5–7 for a suitcase or backpack and $15 for a set of antlers.

Library ZJ Loussac Library, 3600 Denali St at 36th St (Mon–Thurs 10am–9pm, Fri & Sat 10am–6pm, Sun 1–5pm; closed Sun in summer), has a huge selection of books with plenty on Alaska as well as free Internet access (see above) and a café. Buses #2 and #60 are most convenient from downtown.

Maps Topographical and geotechnical maps, as well as books such as the Sibley bird guide, are available from USGS Earth Science Information Center, 4230 University Drive, Room 101 Grace Hall at Alaska Pacific University (☏ 786-7011, ℻ 786-7050; Mon–Fri

8.30am–5pm); you can also custom-print National Geographic and USGS maps at REI (see p.245).

Markets In addition to the weekend market downtown (see p.224), there's the Anchorage Farmers Market (May to early Oct Sat 9am–2pm), which is temporarily at Clark Middle School, between the Glenn Hwy and Mountain View Drive – contact the visitor center to check the venue. There's another in South Anchorage at the same times, in the sports center at 11111 O'Malley Center Drive, at the Old Seward Hwy. In July and Aug there's also a Wed market (11am–5pm) at the Northway Mall, 3101 Penland Pkwy (☏ 272-5634), with stalls selling crafts, clothes, food and more, and entertainment too.

Medical assistance Alaska Health Care Clinic, 3600 Minnesota Drive at 36th Ave (Mon–Fri 8am–7pm, Sat 10am–4pm ☏ 279-3500); Anchorage Medical & Surgical Clinic, 718 K St (Mon–Fri 8am–5.30pm ☏ 272-2571); and Providence Alaska Medical Center (☏ 562-2211, ⓦ www .providence.org/Alaska/default.htm).

Newspapers The *Anchorage Daily News* and the free weekly *Press* are available all over town. For papers from the Lower 48, your best bet downtown is Cook Inlet Book Co (see p.244).

Pharmacy Fred Meyer's, 1000 E Northern Lights Blvd (☏ 264-9633), has a pharmacy open daily 8am–11pm; there's another (9am–9pm) in Carrs, on Minnesota Drive at Northern Lights Blvd (☏ 297-0560).

Photographic supplies Stewart's Photo Shop, 531 W 4th Ave between E and F sts (Mon–Sat 8.30am–6pm; ☏ 272-8581), caters to pretty much all film and camera needs.

Post office The most central post office (Mon–Fri 10am–5.30pm) is located downstairs in the Ship Creek mall on W 4th Ave between C and D sts and is the best place to use as General Delivery (zip code 99510). Fed Ex (☏ 1-800/463-3339, ⓦ www .fedex.com) is at 410 K St (Mon–Fri 10am–5pm), also at Kinko's, 2210 E Northern Lights (24hr) and 300 E Dimond; the UPS Store is at 100 W 34th Ave (☏ 561-4410, ⓦ www.theupsstore.com).

Rock climbing The nearest rock climbing to the city is the quarried embankment alongside the Seward Highway and train line between fifteen and thirty miles south of the city. It is close enough for locals to pop out after work – if you want to join them just drive along and look for likely spots or purchase the local guidebook *The Scar* (see Books, p.611). The Portage Valley and Hatcher Pass are also popular spots, as is the Wookie Wall eight miles beyond Chickaloon, a two-hour drive out on the Glenn Highway. Indoors, there's the Alaska Rock Gym, 4840 Fairbanks St (daily noon–10pm or thereabouts; ☎ 562-7265, ⓦ www.alaskarockgym .com), which charges $14 a visit.

RV rental See our general comments about RV rentals in Basics (p.47).

Swimming Cook Inlet isn't suitable for swimming but a couple of lakes are: Goose Lake, near the universities (bus #3), has a beach with picnic tables, beach volleyball, and a café, and lifeguards on duty from noon to 9pm (early June to late Aug); Jewel Lake, at the west end of 88th Ave, has similar facilities (bus #7). To swim indoors, try any high school pool (typically $3.50). Numbers are listed in the *Yellow Pages* under Schools – High and the pool usually has a separate number. There's also H2Oasis Indoor Waterpark, 1520 O'Malley Rd at the New Seward Hwy (daily 10am–10pm; $20, kids $15; ☎ 1-888/426-2747, ⓦ www.h2oasiswaterpark.com), with wave pool, lazy river, hot tubs, pirate ship lagoon, and water coaster, among other aquatic delights.

Taxes There is no sales tax in Anchorage, but the city does impose a twelve percent bed tax, which is additional to our quoted accommodation prices.

Taxis Alaska Cab ☎ 929-9999; Anchorage Checker Cab ☎ 276-1234; Anchorage Yellow Cab ☎ 272-2422. Expect $6 for a journey downtown, $8–10 between downtown and midtown, and $18–20 from downtown to the airport.

Travel agency New World Travel, 1200 W Northern Lights Blvd ☎ 276-7071.

Travel details

As Anchorage is the heart of Alaska's land and air transport networks, you'll almost certainly find yourself passing through, even if you're not interested in the city. The following journey frequencies all apply to the summer season and are greatly reduced in winter.

Trains make one round-trip a day each to Seward and Whittier, and there's one service a day in each direction between Anchorage and Fairbanks, via Talkeetna and Denali. Bus routes are slightly more extensive, with individual lines fanning out to Seward, Homer, Tok, and Denali, with one service continuing to Fairbanks. Most planes follow simple there-and-back flight schedules, though the strung-out nature of Southeast Alaska and the importance of Seattle make long multistop runs more suitable. Major towns – especially Juneau, Ketchikan, and Seattle – have direct nonstop services, while smaller places are reached on multistop routes such as: Anchorage–Juneau–Sitka–Ketchikan–Seattle; Anchorage–Cordova–Yakutat–Juneau–Seattle; and Anchorage–Juneau–Petersburg–Wrangell–Ketchikan–Seattle.

Trains

Anchorage to: Denali Park (daily; 7hr); Fairbanks (daily; 12hr); Seward (daily; 4hr 20min); Talkeetna (daily; 3hr); Wasilla (daily; 1hr 20min); Whittier (daily; 2hr 20min).

Buses

Anchorage to: Denali Park (4 daily; 5–6hr); Fairbanks (1 daily in summer, 3/week in winter; 9–10hr); Girdwood (3 daily; 1hr 15min); Glennallen (3 weekly; 4hr 30min); Homer (2 daily; 5hr 30min); Nenana (1 daily; 7hr 30min); Ninilchik (1 daily; 4hr 30min); Palmer (3 daily; 1hr); Seward (4 daily; 2hr 30min–3hr 30min); Soldotna (1 daily; 3hr 45min); Talkeetna (2–3 daily; 2hr); Talkeetna Junction (4 daily; 3hr); Tok (3 weekly; 8hr 30min); Wasilla (4 daily; 1hr 50min); Whitehorse (3 weekly; 18hr).

Flights

Anchorage to: Barrow (2 daily; 3hr); Cordova (2–3 daily; 50min); Dutch Harbor (4–6 daily; 3hr); Fairbanks (10–12 daily; 1hr); Homer (4–6 daily; 50min); Iliamna (1–2 daily; 1hr); Juneau (4 daily; 1hr 40min); Kenai (14–18 daily; 25min); Kenai (14–18 daily; 25min); Ketchikan (1 daily; 4hr 30min); King Salmon (5–8 daily; 1hr–1hr 20min); Kodiak (7–10 daily; 1hr); Kotzebue (3 daily; 1hr 30min); Nome (3 daily; 1hr 30min–3hr); Petersburg (1 daily; 3hr); Prudhoe Bay/Deadhorse (1 daily; 1hr 40min); St George (4 weekly; 4hr 30min); St Paul (4 weekly; 3hr); Seattle, WA (16 daily; 3hr 20min); Seldovia (4 weekly; 1hr 15min); Sitka (1 daily; 3hr); Valdez (2–3 daily; 40min); Wrangell (1 daily; 4hr); Yakutat (1 daily; 2hr).

The Kenai Peninsula

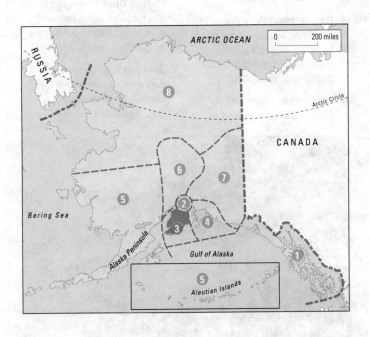

CHAPTER 3   # Highlights

* **Sixmile Creek** Brace yourself for rafting some of the wildest whitewater in the state. See p.263

* **Kenai Fjords National Park** Seeing whales seems like a bonus on cruises past calving glaciers and a Steller's sea lion colony. See p.265

* **Resurrection Pass** Follow in the steps of gold prospectors along the region's premier multiday hiking and mountain biking trail. See p.279

* **Kenai River kings** Stop in Soldotna and try to land a bigger salmon than you ever thought possible. See p.281

* **Homer Spit** Visit this oddly compelling gravel bank for the fabulous sea views, sparkling light, and opportunities to go halibut fishing and kayaking. See p.292

* **Halibut Cove** Cruise out for lunch at *The Saltry* followed by a boardwalk stroll past the art galleries. See p.300

* **Seldovia** A gorgeous and supremely relaxing little town beautifully set on Kachemak Bay. See p.302

△ Boardwalk on Homer Spit

The Kenai Peninsula

The **Kenai Peninsula**, a 150-by-120-mile hunk of land immediately south of Anchorage, is sometimes lauded as Alaska in a nutshell. It is certainly true that a lot of what is great in the state can be found here shoehorned into what, by Alaskan standards, is a tiny area. You miss out on the extreme conditions of the Interior, the towering mountains of the Alaska Range, the full span of the state's cultural mix, and a lot more besides, but the Kenai (KEEN-eye) packs in a little of almost everything Alaska has to offer: tidewater glaciers, whale-watching, outstanding halibut and salmon fishing, entertaining small towns, accessible hiking, and much more. In short, if you can only spend time in one part of Alaska, then this is probably your best bet.

Before the arrival of Europeans, most of the Kenai Peninsula was Dena'ina country, populated by the Kenaitze sub-tribe. Whatever balance they had achieved with surrounding peoples was turned upside down by the arrival of Russians, who established a small town on the Kenai Peninsula in 1791. Once under US control the area was virtually ignored until gold was found along **Turnagain Arm** in 1897. After the gold played out, Seward became an important port at the southern end of the Alaska Railroad, but much of the peninsula was ignored until 1957, when oil and gas deposits were discovered along the northwestern coast. That small find was soon overshadowed by far greater finds elsewhere, but Kenai retains its gas-production platforms and oil refinery.

Proximity to Anchorage has helped make the Kenai one of the most populated rural areas of the state, as well as one of the best connected, with a train line, a relatively dense network of roads, and good ferry services. These factors combine to make this one of the most popular parts of Alaska, and the pressure on accommodation can be a problem in summer. But having a lot of people around can be a benefit as the increased demand for all kinds of trips – flightseeing, cruises, kayaking, and the like – means you'll find more companies running a wider range of trips to more unusual destinations.

Leaving Anchorage, the **Seward Highway** follows Turnagain Arm, a broad finger off Cook Inlet that provided access for late nineteenth-century prospectors. The only town that has seen much activity in recent times is **Girdwood**, an easygoing place that is home to Alaska's premier downhill **ski resort** and the best-preserved of the old gold mines. Continuing south you've a choice: take Portage Road past **Portage Glacier** and head for Whittier or continue around the head of Turnagain Arm onto the Kenai Peninsula proper.

The old gold town of **Hope** makes a good base for hiking the wonderful Resurrection Trail and whitewater rafting down the thunderous Sixmile Creek. Crossing through the heart of the mountains, the Seward Highway continues to the south-coast port of **Seward**, where you can stand next to a

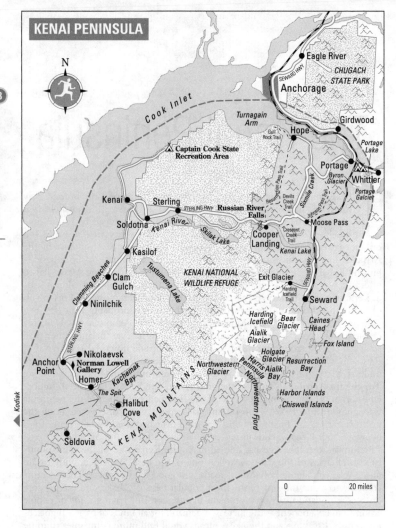

KENAI PENINSULA

N

Eagle River

CHUGACH STATE PARK

SEWARD HWY

Anchorage

Cook Inlet

Turnagain Arm

Girdwood

Hope

Gull Rock Trail

Portage Lake

△ Captain Cook State Recreation Area

Portage

Byron Glacier

Whittier

Portage Galcier

Resurrection Pass Trail

Skilak Creek

Kenai

Sterling

STERLING HWY **Russian River Falls**

Devils Creek Trail

Johnson Pass Trail

Soldotna

Kenai River

Skilak Lake

Cooper Landing

Crescent Creek Trail

Moose Pass

Kasilof

Tustumena Lake

KENAI NATIONAL WILDLIFE REFUGE

Kenai Lake

Exit Glacier

Harding Icefield Trail

SEWARD HWY

Clamming Beaches

Clam Gulch

Harding Icefield

Bear Glacier

Seward

Caines Head

Ninilchik

Aialik Glacier

Fox Island

STERLING HWY

Nikolaevsk

Holgate Glacier

Harris Aialik Bay

Anchor Point

▲ Norman Lowell Gallery

Northwestern Glacier

Northwestern Peninsula

Resurrection Bay

Homer

Kachemak Bay

The Spit

Halibut Cove

KENAI MOUNTAINS

Northwestern Fiord

Harbor Islands

Chiswell Islands

Seldovia

◄ *Kodiak*

0   20 miles

glacier or cruise about as icebergs calve into the fjord nearby. Whale-watching is another popular pastime, though at Seward's classy SeaLife Center, the aquatic world doesn't wait for you to spot it; it will come right to you. Stay in the mountains and there are hundreds of miles of first-class **hiking trails** just waiting for you to strap on your boots, and peaceful campgrounds where you can while away a warm afternoon. Follow the Sterling Highway south, and you enter serious **salmon-fishing** territory where some of the world's largest and most combative salmon are caught, particularly around the towns of **Soldotna** and **Kenai**. The whole peninsula is alive with moose, bears, mountain goats, and other large game, but few places boast greater concentrations than the **Kenai National Wildlife Refuge**, good canoeing and hunting territory.

Further south, the **razor-clamming** beaches of Clam Gulch and Ninilchik are marginal distractions from the main goal, easy-paced **Homer**, with its bohemian air and great halibut-fishing trips. It sits beside Kachemak Bay, a beautiful mountain-backed sound where water taxis and short cruises provide access to great hiking and the gorgeous village of **Seldovia**.

All of this is within five hours' drive of the big city, and therein lies a problem. With so much to do and such ease of access, everyone gets the same idea, and you can sit on the highway for two hours behind a line of RVs only to end up at a packed campground. Keep this in mind when you visit, but remember also that it only takes a little imagination to beat the crowds.

Turnagain Arm, Girdwood, and Portage Glacier

Drive twelve miles south of downtown Anchorage, and you are already a world away from the city, hemmed in between the Chugach Mountains and **Turnagain Arm**, a 45-mile-long tendril of Cook Inlet that separates the Chugach range from the Kenai Peninsula. Road and train line run parallel along the shore, a superb route between snow-capped mountains and glistening, opaque waters. The tidal range here is the second greatest in North America (after Nova Scotia's Bay of Fundy), something that helps create a **tidal bore** (see box, p.256) that sweeps up the arm on extremely low tides. The bore is best seen from roadside pull-outs also used as vantage points for spotting the white **Beluga whales** that can occasionally be seen chasing salmon. At low tide the broad expanse might look enticing, but the **mudflats** are dangerous, and you should steer well clear of them. The glacial silt here is so fine that once you break the surface crust your leg sinks in and is almost impossible to remove; then the tide comes in, quickly.

Turnagain Arm first saw white men in the 1890s when a small gold rush erupted, with bursts of activity at Independence Mine, Sunrise City, Resurrection Creek, and Hope City. By the summer of 1901 the strike in Nome had lured miners elsewhere, but a couple of small mines remain as testaments to the dreams of prospectors in an unmapped and untamed land. The best of these is just outside **Girdwood**, a growing dormitory community for Anchorage with its own downhill **ski resort** – Alyeska – and enough rat-race refugees to give it a bohemian character.

Turnagain Arm finally narrows to a point at the old town of Portage, now abandoned after the land around here dropped by six to eleven feet as a result of the 1964 earthquake. From here a road runs inland to the relatively unspectacular but always popular **Portage Glacier**, and continues through a combined road and rail tunnel to Whittier (see p.312).

Tide tables

If you want to fish, spot Turnagain Arm's bore tide, go clamming along the Kenai's western shore, or simply stroll along the shore at low water, you'll need to know the state of the region's thirty-foot-plus tides. The free annual **Southcentral Alaska Tide Tables** booklet is available from fishing tackle shops, visitor centers, grocery stores, and many banks. Along with details of tide times around the region, tide heights, and good fishing days, they handily include sunrise and sunset times, expected salmon run dates, notes on clam-digging techniques, fishing knots, and a guide to gauging a halibut's weight from its length.

The Seward Highway

From Potter Marsh Wildlife Refuge, twelve miles south of Anchorage, the **Seward Highway** runs for nearly forty miles along the shore of Turnagain Arm to Portage and the junction for Portage Glacier and Whittier. Just as you leave the Potter Marsh wetlands behind, an ancient railway snowplow marks the Potter Section House Historic Site, where the 1929 section house, once a maintenance depot for a stretch of the railroad, now serves as the **Chugach State Park Headquarters** (Mon–Fri 10am–noon & 1–4.30pm; T345-5014, Wwww.dnr.state.ak.us/parks/units/chugach; $5 parking after 30min).

All along the highway there are great views across the water to the snow-capped Kenai Mountains, but none better than from **McHugh Creek Wayside**, Mile 112, some four miles south of Potter Marsh (daily 9am–9pm; parking $5), where a refreshing waterfall cascades past the start of several hiking trails (see box, p.258) and some barbecue areas.

In recent years, the numbers of Beluga whales in Cook Inlet has rapidly decreased, perhaps as part of a natural cycle, though some blame overzealous Native hunting. With only around three hundred left, the frequency of sightings has dropped accordingly, but your best chance of spotting them as they chase salmon up the inlet from May to August is at the **Beluga Point Interpretive Site**, Mile 110. This is also a prime location for viewing Turnagain Arm's tidal bore (see box, below).

Anchorage rock climbers hone their skills on the roadside cliffs on the way to the tiny settlement of **Indian**, Mile 104. The Indian Valley Trail (see box, p.258) also begins here, as does a coastal **bike trail** that follows the old undulating road the remaining fifteen miles to Girdwood. It can be windy along here in the afternoons, so ride early if you can.

Indian is also the site of the **Indian Valley Mine** (mid-May to mid-Sept daily 9am–9pm; $1; Wwww.indianvalleymine.com), which captures the area's mining history from 1920 to 1939 through a small collection of artifacts found at the site and displayed (along with a gift shop) in the original assay office. You can pan for gold (from $3) and see the old underground mine entrances, but little else.

A mile south of Indian, the trailhead for the Bird Ridge Trail heralds **Bird Creek**, scene of frenetic summer "combat fishing" where anglers stand shoulder to shoulder along the riverbank, casting for silver and pink salmon (mid-July to

---

Turnagain's tidal bore

When low tides are extremely low, it is possible to see Turnagain Arm's **tidal bore**, a broken wave of foaming whitewater up to six feet high that sweeps up the arm towards Portage once every tide. It is a rare phenomenon that occurs at perhaps only sixty places around the world, two of them in Alaska – a smaller one is found on Knik Arm, just to the north of Anchorage. Bores are caused by a combination of extreme tidal variation (almost 39ft in Turnagain Arm) and the local marine geography, here accentuated by the arm's funneling effect. It is at its most impressive a day or so either side of full moon, when the tidal variation is at its greatest. Under less auspicious conditions the bore is barely noticeable. At Beluga Point the best time for viewing – and possibly seeing keen board-riders surf the bore – is an hour and a quarter after low tide in Anchorage (2hr 15min at Bird Point, 3hr at Girdwood); check tide times in the *Anchorage Daily News* (Wwww.adn.com/weather) and look for a low tide of minus 4.5ft or lower.

Aug). The *Bird Creek Campground*, Mile 101, just east of the Bird Creek bridge ($10; pump water), has tent sites away from the RV parking, but you'll need to arrive early to get a site away from the highway. The excellent *Bird Ridge Café and Bakery*, Mile 101, renowned for its burgers, espresso, and fruit pies, is handily less than a mile further on.

From here, the highway continues to hug the coast four miles to the **Bird Point Scenic Overlook** (parking $5 a day), an elaborate series of viewpoints and walkways with information panels telling you when to expect the tidal bore to sweep past.

Girdwood and Alyeska Resort

Almost forty miles southeast of Anchorage, Turnagain Arm and the Chugach Mountains briefly release their grip on the Seward Highway, which now runs across broad wetlands. The wetlands were the original site of Girdwood, abandoned after it sank six to eight feet during the 1964 earthquake. In the process the roots of hundreds of black spruce were immersed in the brackish waters of Turnagain Arm. They soon died, but remain standing in a semi-petrified state and are now afforded some degree of legal protection.

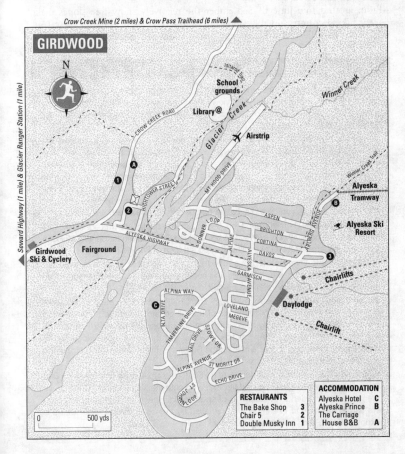

Crow Creek Mine (2 miles) & Crow Pass Trailhead (6 miles)

GIRDWOOD

Seward Highway (1 mile) & Glacier Ranger Station (1 mile)

S. Crow Creek Road

Iditarod Trail

School grounds

Library @

Glacier Creek

Winner Creek

Airstrip

Hightower Street

Mt Hood Drive

Donner Loop

Aspen

Brighton

Cortina

Davos

Alyeska Avenue

Garmisch

Winner Creek Trail

Alyeska Tramway

Ritberg Avenue

Alyeska Ski Resort

Chairlifts

Girdwood Ski & Cyclery

Fairground

Alyeska Highway

Alpine

Alpina Way

Alta Drive

Timberline Drive

Vail Drive

Loveland

Megeve

Stowe Dr

Daylodge

Chairlift

Alpine Avenue

St Moritz Dr

Echo Drive

St John Loop

0   500 yds

RESTAURANTS	
The Bake Shop	3
Chair 5	2
Double Musky Inn	1

ACCOMMODATION	
Alyeska Hotel	C
Alyeska Prince	B
The Carriage House B&B	A

Girdwood relocated a couple of miles inland and has developed into a modest and active woodland community populated by neo-hippies, outdoor enthusiasts, and escapees from Anchorage. It sits among the spruce below the 3939-foot summit of Mount Alyeska, the low-rise sprawl given some focus by the presence of the **Alyeska Resort** (T 1-800/880-3880, snow report T 754-7669, W www.alyeskaresort.com), Alaska's premier downhill ski complex. This is the lowest-elevation ski resort in the world, with tows that start just 250ft above sea level, and yet it manages a five-month season (late Nov to mid-April, and weekends through to the first weekend in June) courtesy of an average annual snowfall of nearly fifty feet. Factor in a healthy range of runs (including half a dozen perilously steep, double-black-diamond descents), stupendous views, relatively mild temperatures (usually in the twenties), plus the chance to see the aurora borealis, and an Alaskan skiing holiday here takes on considerable appeal. Until 1993 Alyeska resembled one of the small municipal resorts in the Rockies, but a huge influx of cash has given it many new downhill runs, a first-class hotel, and an extensive night-skiing operation (Christmas to New Year and weekends mid-Dec to mid-March, until 9.30pm). Lift **tickets** cost $52 a day ($22 at night) and you can rent basic downhill equipment for $32 a day; quality ski gear or snowboard and boots cost $35.

From around mid-June to September the relatively snow-free slopes make decent hiking country, notably along the ridge-crest Alyeska Glacier View Trail, which can be followed as far as your fitness allows. To get to the trail, head to

Hikes from Turnagain Arm

With the Kenai Peninsula drawing you on it is tempting to skip the hikes beside the Seward Highway, but the sparkling views from sea level, and steep slopes rising straight from the road, do make these a worthwhile venture. Hikes are listed in order of distance from Anchorage.

Turnagain Arm Trail (9.4 miles one way; 5–6hr; negligible ascent). Easy coastal trail following a path forged by Dena'ina Natives and consolidated by gold-miners. The views of Turnagain Arm are tremendous, and you might see spring wildflowers or Dall sheep among the crags. It runs from the Potter Section House to Windy Corner, passing numerous access points that make it easy to do in shorter stretches. Since this trail runs along the highway, you can easily make this a one-way hike, arranging for someone to pick you up or hitching a ride back to the trailhead.

McHugh Lake Trail (14 miles round-trip; 6–8hr; 2750ft ascent). Moderately stiff hike that leads from the McHugh Creek Wayside up McHugh Creek to the tundra-girt McHugh Lake and the larger Rabbit Lake below the rugged form of Suicide Mountain.

McHugh Scenic Overlook (2 miles round-trip; 1hr; negligible ascent). Wheelchair-accessible paved path with handrails and seating, offering views of Turnagain Arm and wind-sculpted trees. Parking $5 a day.

Indian Valley Trail (12 miles round-trip; 5–7hr; 2100ft ascent). An easy to moderate trail on a well-graded path climbing out of the tall coastal woods to a pass among alpine tundra and back. Hardy hikers can continue beyond the pass and link up with the Ship Creek Trail behind Anchorage (in winter this becomes a cross-country ski trail). The trailhead is just over a mile off the Seward Highway (Mile 103.1) at the end of a gravel road.

Bird Ridge Trail (8 miles round-trip; 4–6hr; 2500ft ascent). A steep trail following Bird Ridge from a trailhead parking lot (Mile 102.1) up onto the alpine tundra. Once again, the views are wonderful, the chances of spotting Dall sheep are high, and wildflowers carpet the ground in early spring, replaced by berries in the fall. Note that it is exposed above the tree line and can be windy. Parking $5 a day.

the *Alyeska Prince* resort and take the **Alyeska Tramway** gondola (late May to mid-Sept daily 10.30am–9.30pm; $16), which swoops you up to the *Seven Glaciers* and *Glacier Express* restaurants perched high on the mountain. If you are also planning to dine up here, expensive menus can be offset to some degree by buying a Tram & Lunch Combo ($22), which includes a bite to eat in the *Glacier Express*. Should you choose to hike up, the ride down is free. The top of the tramway also serves as a launch pad for rides with **Alaska Paragliding** (June–Sept; $185; ☎301-1215, ⊛www.alaskaparagliding.com).

Low-level hiking is possible a mile back towards the Seward Highway from Alyeska along the unimproved Crow Creek Road, which penetrates five miles further into the heart of the Chugach Mountains. After three hundred yards you pass the *Double Musky Inn*, an excellent restaurant, and press on three miles to **Crow Creek Mine** (mid-May to mid-Sept daily 9am–6pm; $3, gold panning $5 extra; ☎278-8060). The mine was established here in 1898 and soon became the most productive of the Turnagain Arm gold strikes. The so-called Crow Creek Boys instituted hydraulic mining operations to scour away the gold-bearing gravels and left in their wake all manner of detritus, which today litters the valley. It is still worked on a small scale but is mostly set up for tourists, with eight of the mine buildings still on their original foundations and prettied up with planters, moose racks, and ageing artifacts.

Another option is the **Winner Creek Trail** (7 miles round-trip; 3hr; 100ft ascent), which heads east from the base of the tramway and weaves through moss-carpeted hemlock and spruce to the plunging Winner Creek gorge. You eventually come to a primitive hand-hauled high-wire tram across the gorge, which gives access to the Crow Creek Mine. Return a short way along Crow Creek Road and pick up the Iditarod Trail back to town.

The trailhead for the **Crow Pass Trail** lies four miles beyond the mine up Crow Creek Road (for more on the trail, see p.233).

If you're in the vicinity around the Fourth of July weekend, head to the Girdwood Fairgrounds, Alyeska Highway Mile 2.2, for the **Girdwood Forest Fair** (free; ⊛www.girdwoodforestfair.com), originally an arts and crafts fair but now as much a music festival, which seems to draw out every artist and neo-hippy in Southcentral Alaska.

Practicalities

Trains between Anchorage and Seward make a request stop on Brudine Road a couple of miles from Girdwood, where the Alyeska Highway to Girdwood spurs off the Seward Highway. If you need to get here by public transportation, it makes more sense to come by bus: Homer Stage Line (☎868-3914, ⊛www .homerstageline.com) and the Magic Bus (☎268-6311) both drop off in town on request.

The closest thing to a visitor center in these parts is the Forest Service's **Glacier Ranger Station** (Mon–Fri 8am–5pm; ☎783-3242), at the start of Alyeska Highway, which concentrates on hiking and outdoor activities in the region. Alternatively, log on to ⊛www.girdwoodalaska.com. Since there is limited public transportation, anyone without a car should visit Jim at Girdwood Ski and Cyclery, Mile 1.5 (☎783-2453; closed Mon & Tues), who rents city **bikes** ($5/hr, $25/day) that are adequate for the immediate surroundings and as much as you fancy of the coastal bike path to Indian, fifteen miles away. In winter and spring Jim rents telemark and backcountry equipment for $30 a day.

Accommodation and **eating** choices are limited in number but wide in scope.

Accommodation

Alta House Vacation Rentals ☎770-0482, ⓦwww.thealtahouse.com. A range of self-catering cabins, chalets, and cottages dotted around Girdwood, all available by the night and some sleeping up to eight. Chalet ❼, cottage ❻, cabin ❺

Alyeska Hostel Alta Drive ☎783-2222, ⓦwww.alyeskahostel.com. Tiny, year-round hostel with mountain views, cooking facilities, and a relaxed atmosphere. There's just one mixed dorm for $15 a person, a $40 room, and a separate cabin for $60.

Alyeska Prince ☎754-1111 or 1-800/880-3880, ⓦwww.alyeskaresort.com. Rack rates at this eight-story resort are outside most budgets, but throughout the summer there are deals offering one night plus a tramway ride for $209 per room including tax. Even if you can't afford a room, you may want to treat yourself to a meal in one of the restaurants or check out the health spa ($10) complete with pool, hot tub, and views up to Mount Alyeska. ❽

The Carriage House B&B Mile 0.2 Crow Creek Road ☎1-888/961-9464 & 783-9464, ⓦwww.thecarriagehousebandb.com. Attractive B&B with comfy rooms and a fully equipped guest kitchen.

They even offer carriage rides around town. Suite ❼, rooms ❺

Crow Creek Mine Mile 3.5 Crow Creek Road. Good basic camping with stream water and longdrop loo. $5.

Eating and drinking

🥢 **The Bake Shop** Olympic Mountain Loop at the base of the ski tows ☎783-2831. Skiers, mountain bikers, in fact just about anyone with a hunger for tasty low-cost food comes here for legendary soup and sourdough bread, and great breakfasts served until 1pm. Open daily 7am–7pm.

Chair 5 Lindblad Avenue ☎783-2500. Lively restaurant that's good for moderately priced gourmet pizza, burgers, fresh seafood, and microbrews.

🥢 **Double Musky Inn** Crow Creek Road. The restaurant that really draws the Anchorage foodies is this evening-only place that has been an institution since 1962. Its dark bar and airy conservatory are always bustling with diners eager to get their lips around the Louisiana Cajun cuisine and tender steaks. Expect halibut *ceviche*, scallop-stuffed mushroom Rockefeller, rack of lamb, and salmon in green peppercorns and brandy, and set aside $40 apiece. Closed Mon; no reservations.

Portage Glacier

The five-mile-long, mile-wide **Portage Glacier** is the single most visited sight in the state. The impressive calving which earned its reputation is a thing of the past, but proximity to Anchorage – just fifty miles to the northwest – and assiduous promotion by Gray Line Tours ensure that it remains *the* destination for day-trips from the city. Not so many years ago visitors could see the glacier from the access road, but its recession has been so profound that it can now only be seen by taking an hour-long **cruise** across the lake its retreat has created. Throughout the summer, tour buses decant their passengers onto the *Ptarmigan* (mid-May to mid-Sept 10.30am–4.30pm, every 1hr 30min; $29, day-trip from Anchorage with Gray Line $68; ☎277-5581 or 1-800/478-6388), which shoulders its way through small icebergs and spends half an hour patrolling the face of the glacier as everyone hopes for a display of calving. A measure of how much it has retreated can be gauged by the location of the **Begich, Boggs Visitor Center**, Mile 5.5 (June–Sept daily 9am–6pm; Oct–May Sat & Sun 10am–5pm; ☎783-2326), built on the moraine which marks the furthest extent of glacial advance a century ago, now three and a half miles from the face. Even when the visitor center was built in the mid-1980s you could spot the glacier from the huge picture windows, something no longer true. Though the center

The road to Whittier and Prince William Sound

Until summer 2000 Portage Glacier was the end of the line, but a single-lane road and rail tunnel (see box, p.313) now continues to Whittier. When there are delays, you will have to wait in the staging area a mile on from the Begich, Boggs Visitor Center.

△ The visitor center at Portage Glacier

still screens its glacier-oriented *Voices from the Ice* film (hourly; $1), it has been revamped to spread its coverage to include the ecology of the whole Portage and Whittier region, with interactive displays offering plenty to see, touch, and listen to.

Still, the center is a sheltered spot from which to admire the surrounding glaciers, mostly bearing the names of British poets – Burns, Shakespeare, and Byron. For closer inspection, strike out along the trail to the base of **Byron Glacier** (0.7 miles one way), where you can sometimes see slender, black **ice worms** living on the surface of the glacier. To learn more about this intriguing wee beastie – which many believe only exists in a poem by Robert Service – you can join the free, two-hour **Iceworm Safari** (July & Aug usually on Sat and one weekday afternoon; call in advance) from the visitor center.

Without joining the cruise, the best views of Portage Glacier are now from the approach road to the Whittier tunnel: drive through the first short tunnel (free) to a large viewing area about half a mile on.

Practicalities

Portage Glacier lies six miles off the Seward Highway (Mile 79) and is reached from a junction marked by a copse of salt-damaged trees, which make an especially picturesque backdrop for a couple of dilapidated buildings slowly sinking into the mire, both victims of the 1964 earthquake. From here, Portage Road runs up the Portage Valley passing two **campgrounds**: the tent-only, first-come, first-served *Black Bear*, Mile 3.7 ($10; pump water), and the very pleasant *Williwaw*, Mile 4.2 ($13; reserve through ⓦ www.reserveusa.com; pump water). Next to the latter, reds and chums come up to spawn from mid- to late summer below a platform at the **Williwaw Salmon Viewing Area** (Mile 4.3). Williwaw is also a good place to start the **Trail of the Blue Ice**, a three-mile loop of boardwalks and flat trails through the valley.

Alongside Portage Lake there's the visitor center and boat dock (roughly a mile apart) and the *Portage Glacier Lodge* (mid-May to mid-Sept daily 9am–7pm), a gift shop and decent **café** with hearty soup, sandwich, and drink lunch specials for under $10. Just behind, the 400-yard **Moraine Nature Trail** is an easy way to get away from the crowds and has a fine viewpoint for a picnic. In spring and fall it is also a good place for **bird-watching**, since the forested and steeply sided valley is used as a flyway for birds spending the summer in western Alaska.

③ Northeastern Kenai Peninsula

The northeastern third of the Kenai Peninsula is mostly mountainous country with the Chugach and Kenai mountains meeting around the head of Turnagain Arm. Numerous peaks top four thousand feet and a few soar up over five thousand, creating a near-impenetrable barrier to the lusher flatlands to the south. Only the Seward Highway finds a passage by climbing Turnagain Pass and continuing to Seward, while the Sterling Highway peels off west through the Central Kenai to Homer. In summer the high country beside the highway is used by hikers and bikers here to tackle some of the excellent trails, and nearby **Sixmile Creek** gets crowded with rafters risking some superb whitewater.

The only real destination in the region is **Hope**, a former gold town on the shores of Turnagain Arm that's great for just kicking back for a couple of days, perhaps doing a little **gold-panning** in Resurrection Creek.

Turnagain Pass and Sixmile Creek

Where the road to Portage Glacier and Whittier splits off from the Seward Highway, a copse of salt-ravaged trees marks the **Alaska Wildlife Conservation Center**, Mile 79 Seward Hwy (daily: summer 8am–8pm; winter 10am–4pm; $7.50; ☎783-2025, ⓦwww.alaskawildlife.org), a 140-acre nonprofit clinic where injured and orphaned animals are brought for rehabilitation. Most can't be returned to the wild and are kept here in fairly naturalistic grassland enclosures, which can be toured either by car or on foot. This may be the easiest place in Alaska to see moose, bison, elk, musk oxen, caribou, deer, and bears all in under an hour.

Continuing on, the Seward Highway loops around the head of Turnagain Arm and hugs the water for a few more miles before turning inland for the steady five-mile climb up to the 1000-foot **Turnagain Pass** (Mile 68). The altitude and shadowing effect of the surrounding 4000-foot peaks means that spring comes late up here. Even into mid-June you may see Anchorage weekenders cross-country skiing and snowmobiling: motorized on the west side of the road, human-powered on the east.

It is a broad and fast road through here with nothing in the way of services, so it is tempting to hurry on straight to Hope, Seward (about 60 miles away), or Homer (around 170 miles). Still, the scenery is striking, with highway-side alpine meadows crisscrossed by glacial streams, so you might want to stop a night or two in one of the campgrounds and consider tackling some of the long hikes (see box, p.278). Summer wildflowers abound; you may well see false hellebore, valerian, wild geranium, chocolate lily, and shooting stars, all occasionally visited by a hoary marmot.

Descending from Turnagain Pass, milepost numbers continue to decrease towards Seward, the highway passing a couple of first-come, first-served Forest Service campgrounds in the next five miles – *Bertha Creek*, Mile 65 ($10), and *Granite Creek*, Mile 63 ($10) – both handy for one-day forays up part of the **Johnson Pass Trail**, which leaves the highway between the two.

Rafting the Sixmile

Just off the Seward Highway, a mile along the road to Hope, rafters amass for the wildest stretch of commercially rafted whitewater in Alaska that doesn't require expedition logistics. With a maximum descent of fifty feet per mile, the **Sixmile Creek** is thrilling stuff, and justly popular. The river's three canyons – all beautiful with crisp, clear, and very cold water – increase progressively in difficulty, and rafting companies accommodate all comers, tailoring trips to suit. The **rafting season** runs from May to September but peaks from mid-June to August. Sometimes in July high water levels mean trips have to be canceled.

The **first canyon** (Class III; 1hr 30min on the water) is suitable for beginners and families, but still has one section that kicks up to Class IV in high flows. This bit can be avoided by a short walk. Trips often combine the first with the **second canyon** (Class III–IV; 1hr on the water), which ups the ante a little with four major drops in succession. Most companies have a higher minimum age limit (usually 16) and require some kind of swimming test before letting customers down the exciting **third canyon** (Class IV–V; 1hr on the water) with its long sequences of tough rapids. Companies generally use paddle rafts, which means you'll be expected to paddle – hard.

Chugach Outdoor Center, Mile 7.5 on Hope Highway (☎277-7238 or 1-866/277-7238, ⊛ www.chugachoutdoorcenter.com) offers rides in the first and second canyons (9am & 2pm; $99), and all three (9am & 2pm; $145); while Nova (☎1-800/746-5753, ⊛ www.novalaska.com) meets near the junction of the Seward and Hope highways for either the top two canyons (9am & 2pm; $90) or all three (9am & 2pm; $135).

At Mile 57 the Seward Highway sweeps high across the whitewater-rafting currents of **Sixmile Creek**, and then the Hope Highway branches right to run sixteen miles to the small town of Hope, passing the negligible remains of the gold-rush town of Sunrise at Mile 8.

Hope

At the end of a sixteen-mile asphalt branch off the Seward Highway, the small, former gold-rush town of **Hope** sits quietly beside the south shore of Turnagain Arm. It is mostly populated by loners and nine-to-five escapees but is close enough to Anchorage to draw in hikers, anglers after salmon (particularly pinks from mid-July to mid-August), and even gold seekers. There may be fewer than two hundred residents now, but in the last five years of the nineteenth century, this whole area was alive with gold prospectors. The town survived long after the gold as a dusty collection of picturesque, weatherworn log buildings. To get a sense of what it was like at its peak, visit the small **Hope and Sunrise Historical Museum** in the old town (late May to early Sept daily noon–4pm; free), full of old-time photos and gold-mining paraphernalia. There's still **gold** in the creeks, too, and you're free to make use of the Forest Service's claim close to the start of the Resurrection Pass Trail (see box, p.279).

Hikers who aren't up for something as taxing as the Resurrection Pass Trail should drive to the *Porcupine Campground* (see p.264) at the end of the Hope Highway, which marks the beginning of the gentle and heavily used **Gull Rock Trail** (10 miles round-trip; 4–6hr; constantly undulating). This path follows a narrow old wagon road along Turnagain Arm through spruce, birch, and aspen woods, and past the scant remains of an old sawmill to a viewpoint atop Gull Rock where there are some primitive camping spots. The trail can be tackled any time from May to October, though late summer is good for low-bush cranberry picking. From the beginning of July, the trail is also open to **mountain bikes**. Moderately skilled riders should be able to handle the first three miles and last mile without too much difficulty, but abundant rocks and tree roots in the middle section dictate more pushing and carrying than riding.

Practicalities
At the first road junction as you drive into town along the Hope Highway, a left turn leads five miles up Resurrection Road to the start of the Resurrection Trail. Straight on at the junction, *Tito's Discovery Café* marks the start of the old town, reached down the road on the right. This eventually rejoins the Hope Highway for the final mile to the road-end *Porcupine Campground*.

Eating is best either at the *Seaview* (see below), *Bowmans Bear Creek Lodge*, Mile 15.7 Hope Hwy (☎782-3141, ⓦwww.bowmansbearcreeklodge.com), or *Tito's Discovery Café*, Mile 16 Hope Hwy (☎782-3274), with great breakfasts and a tasty halibut and chips ($13).

Accommodation
Discovery Cabins ☎782-3730, ⓦwww .adventurealaskatours.com/cabins.htm. Simple but comfortable and appealing streamside cabins with access to a hot tub. ❹
HHH of Hope 19209 Discovery Drive, opposite *Discovery Cabins* ☎782-9733, ⓔricharddovie @acsalaska.net. Basic hostel with a dorm ($20 per bunk), a couple of private rooms, and full cooking facilities. ❷
Hope Gold Rush B&B 64932 2nd St ☎782-3436, ⓔfayrene@alaska.net. Accommodation in a very comfortable, fully equipped cabin sleeping a five-person party, with a hearty breakfast included. ❹
Porcupine Campground Just over a mile beyond Hope. Neatly tended sites among the woods with fire rings, picnic tables, pump water, and even some Turnagain Arm views. Often full in summer; no fees or water in winter. $11.

Resurrection Road camping Budget tenters who don't mind being over four miles inland from Hope can camp near the start of the Resurrection Pass Trail. This area has been set aside for recreational gold-panning, and you are free to try your hand, though you'll need your own pan. Free.
Seaview Café Main Street in the old town ☎782-3300, ⓦhome.gci.net/~hopeak. About the best place to stay and eat, in a cluster of 1896 buildings nicely sited close to Turnagain Arm. There are rustic cabins without running water but sleeping up to four, a rather exposed campsite ($15 for power hookup, $10 for tents), a great restaurant noted for its baked goods, especially the apple pie, and a bar that stays open to midnight. They even have a sunny deck outside and frequent live music in summer. May–Sept. ❷

The Seward Highway: south from Turnagain Pass

South of Hope, the Seward Highway continues past the first-come, first-served *Tenderfoot Creek Campground*, Mile 46 ($10), with creekside sites and pump water. It then reaches **Tern Lake**, Mile 37, an important migration stop for waterfowl, including arctic terns, for which the lake is named. From the waterside viewing platform you might also spot common loons, pintails, bald eagles, and even a beaver. Here, two highways part company: the Sterling Highway turns right and runs 143 miles through the central Kenai Peninsula to Homer, while the Seward Highway carries straight on towards Seward, 37 miles distant.

Around five miles on from Tern Lake, the Seward Highway passes the trail-head for the Johnson Pass Trail (see p.278), then runs a couple of miles to the scattered community of **Moose Pass** (ⓦwww.moosepassalaska.com), originally established along the first Iditarod Trail in a favorite spot for moose. It comprises little more than a few cabins in the woods and a post office, all beautifully set beside Upper Trail Lake. A few of the cabins operate as B&Bs, and there's even

Watching wildlife

Alaska has some of the finest wildlife-watching opportunities in the world, and few people visit without joining a whale-watching cruise or attempting to see bears at a riverside salmon feed. Dedicated tours are undoubtedly rewarding, but abiding wildlife experiences are just as often unplanned – perhaps a moose crossing a four-lane highway in Fairbanks, a pure-white Dall sheep balancing on a crag outside your train window, or whales breaching alongside your ferry. Here's how to track down some of Alaska's most conspicuous residents; for further coverage of the state's fauna, see Contexts, p.600.

Top bear-viewing sites

Anan, Southeast Close-up viewing of black and a few brown bears dining on pink salmon. Relatively cheap boat access from Wrangell. Early July to late August. p.128

Brooks Camp, Southwest Probably the best site not regulated by lottery. Here the world's top wildlife photographers come to shoot bears that stand atop Brooks Falls, trying to catch jumping salmon in their mouths. July & September. p.359

Kodiak Island, Southwest This is the place to see the world's largest bears (some up to 1500 pounds) in their natural habitat. Four-hour fly-in trips give at least two hours on the ground. June to mid-September. p.354

McNeil River, Southwest Alaska's ultimate viewing spot, where brown bears are so accustomed to humans they'll happily walk right by you in their pursuit of salmon. You can camp amongst them but a lottery greatly limits visitor access. Early July to mid-August. p.362

Pack Creek, Southeast Great viewing made even better by joining a kayak trip from Juneau, with camping nearby. June to mid-September. p.175

Bears: black, brown, and white

Bears live all over Alaska, but seeing one still feels like a privilege. Hikers may amble quite comfortably through bear territory, singing and talking to prevent unexpected encounters, but most people prefer to observe the critters from the safety of a sturdy vehicle. Many visitors head straight for Denali National Park, where buses traveling the Park Road make perfect viewing platforms for sighting brown (aka **grizzly**) and **black** bears. With forty-odd pairs of eyes scanning the tundra, someone is bound to spot something, and the driver will make the obligatory photo stop until the animal gets bored or spooked and moves away.

Few people get the chance to see **polar bears** in Alaska. They only exist in the Far North where the sea ice meets land in winter. You really need to make a dedicated trip, most likely to Point Barrow or Kaktovik, where whale entrails are dumped after a successful Native hunt (typically May and September). Tours visit the sites in suitably strong vehicles.

▲ Moose

Moose, caribou, and reindeer

Few tour companies offer trips specifically designed to spot **moose**; they're fairly abundant and your chances of seeing one are good, particularly if you're attentive to your surroundings. That said, these enormous beasts, weighing up to 1200 pounds, are surprisingly elusive and thrilling to behold. You may see them from the road, usually belly-deep in shallow lakes and chomping on aquatic weeds. At other times you might drive hundreds of miles without seeing any, then nearly hit one on a city street. They're obstinate things, and if one is standing in your path you're best advised to backtrack.

Smaller members of the deer family are less frequently seen, though caribou are common enough in northern Alaska. Denali is a good place to spot them, the open tundra and sweeping panoramas from the Park Road providing optimal views. You might also see them from your car while driving the Taylor, Richardson, or Glenn highways through the Interior.

Caribou's domesticated cousins, reindeer, are mostly restricted to the Seward Peninsula north of Nome, where the Iñupiat still round them up annually for their meat and hides.

▲ Caribou

Whales, sea lions, and sea otters

If you spend any time on Alaska's coast you're sure to see the telltale puff of a venting whale, the arch of its back, and then its tail flukes as it dives. With luck you may also catch one breaching, launching its thirty tons skyward and then crashing back into the water. Grey whales, humpbacks, and orca are the state's most commonly spotted large sea mammals, and numerous day cruises leave the ports of Southeast and Southcentral Alaska with whale-watching high on the agenda. Such trips target prime locales, but can't guarantee sightings; you'll often do just as well by keeping your eyes skinned as your AMHS ferry chugs through sheltered waters.

▶ A sea otter enjoys a tasty snack

Though over-fishing of pollock is taking its toll on Alaska's Steller's sea lion population, accessible colonies can still be visited, often on trips combined with whale-watching. With luck you'll observe several one-ton bulls slathered over the rocks, each maintaining its harem of females.

You don't need to make any special effort to see sea otters, among Alaska's cuter animals. Almost clubbed into extinction by fur traders, the population has since rebounded, and you'll often see them in coastal waters floating on their backs, perhaps trying to crack open a scallop with a stone they always keep secreted under one arm.

Hints for watching wildlife

Take binoculars Trip organizers supply several pairs, but these have to be passed around and are seldom top quality. A pocket-sized 7x20 pair is perfect for most people; larger models are unwieldy for casual use and higher magnifications can cause difficulty in finding your subject and keeping the image steady when you do. Buy the best you can afford; quality makes a big difference and the close-up views will amaze.

Be patient Movement scares off most creatures, so it's best to find a likely spot, keep quiet and still, and let them come to you. A little prior knowledge about an animal's habits (and the shape of its tracks and scat) should help you choose the right area for viewing. Provided you're not upwind of them, animals may draw very near without even knowing you're there.

Don't get too close When approaching an animal, keep a safe distance away and watch it closely for signs of anxiety. Mammals tend to raise their heads and look toward you with perked ears; step closer and they'll either run away or challenge you. Birds will keep an eye on you and cry out when they feel threatened. You should never approach so close that you cause an animal to flee (or worse, attack), especially if your actions force it to abandon or aggressively protect its young.

▲ A brown bear stands its ground

a grocery, a couple of places to eat, a lodge, and an RV park, but not much action except at summer solstice when the town holds the Moose Pass Summer Festival, with cookouts, craft stalls, and all sorts of kids' games. If you fancy staying, try *Spruce Moose B&B* (℡288-3667, Ⓦwww.seward.net/sprucemoose; ◐), where you get a whole self-contained chalet complete with satellite TV, hot tub, sauna, and full kitchen.

Along the last half-hour of the drive into Seward, you'll pass *Snow River Hostel* (see p.268), a few more fine campgrounds, and the trailheads for a couple of hikes listed in the box on p.278.

Seward and the Kenai Fjords National Park

Charming **Seward** (SOO-erd) lies nestled between the shores of Resurrection Bay and the icy wastes of the Kenai Fjords National Park, 130 miles south of Anchorage. It is a small town, with a good deal less bustle than Homer and yet a perfect balance of distractions. It is also a strategic spot as the southern terminus of the Alaska Railroad and a major port (at least by Alaska's standards) with cruise ships coming and going on a fairly regular basis, though seldom altering the slow pace of life.

Along with a couple of other diversions, among them the informative SeaLife Center, it is mainly Seward's proximity to the **Kenai Fjords National Park** that makes it so appealing. Only created in 1978, it remains a little-known expanse almost entirely covered in ice, much of its western portion composed of the **Harding Icefield**, a vast, frozen tableland thought to be up to four thousand feet thick in places and spreading over almost three hundred square miles. The ice at the edges spills over the mountains as steep glaciers – 32 of them in all – which forge paths down U-shaped valleys. **Exit Glacier** comes so close to Seward that a road has been built to its terminus. Despite the spectacular views this road affords, few can resist joining one of the **cruises** visiting some of the eight tidewater glaciers that regularly calve icebergs into the fjords along the park's southeast flank. Cruising the waterways only nibbles at the fecund edges of the park, and to really get a sense of its barren, icy immensity you need to fly over it (see Listings, p.275), or hike up beside Exit Glacier for a glimpse of this sheet of white punctuated by bare pyramidal mountains known as nunataks, an Eskimo word meaning "lonely peaks."

Close to where the SeaLife Center stands today, John Ballaine established a railroad in 1903 to serve a new port on the shores of Resurrection Bay. Ballaine called the place Seward, in honor of the man who was responsible for the US purchase of Alaska from Russia. Although there were already two towns called Seward in Alaska, Ballaine's petitioning prevailed, and this became the true Seward. Around the same time Seward was the gold-shipping port at the end of the Iditarod Trail, with huge quantities arriving by sled from Nome and the Interior. The railroad went through several incarnations before being incorporated into the construction of the Alaska Railroad in 1915, after which Seward continued to prosper as a railhead and port for both goods and commercial fishing. Everything looked set to change when the 1964 earthquake set the town ablaze and caused whole chunks of the waterfront to slide into the bay, but Seward was rebuilt, and the town continues, building on its fishing and tourism industries.

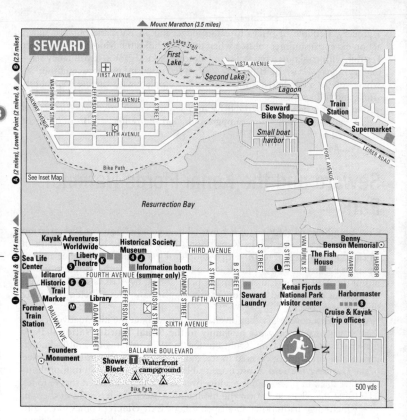

Arrival, information, and getting around

Seward is remarkably well connected, with buses, trains, a good highway, and even a network of long-distance hiking trails ending not far from town. The four-hour **train** journey from Anchorage (see Basics, p.44) pulls in at Seward's desolate platform, a couple of hundred yards north of the small boat harbor.

It is a little cheaper and quicker to travel by **bus**, and three companies run daily from Anchorage in summer: Seward Bus Line, at *Hotel Seward*, 217 E 5th Ave ($45 one way, $85 round-trip; in Anchorage ☎563-0800, in Seward ☎224-3608, ⑩www.sewardbuslines.net); the slightly more expensive Park Connection ($54 each way; ☎1-800/266-8625, ⑩www.alaskacoach.com), which also has service from Denali and drops off around town; and Homer Stage Line ($45 one way, $80 round-trip; in Seward ☎224-3608, in Homer ☎235-2252, ⑩www.homerstageline.com). Homer Stage Line also makes a weekday run between Homer and Seward in summer ($50 one way, $95 round-trip).

Information

The **visitor center** (mid-May to mid-Sept daily 8am–6pm; mid-Sept to mid-May Mon–Fri 8am–5pm; ☎224-8051, ⑩www.seward.com), on the approach to town at Mile 2 on the Seward Highway, holds a broad range of general

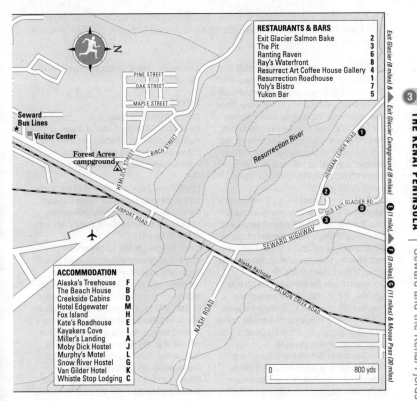

Exit Glacier (8 miles) & ▶ Exit Glacier Campground (8 miles) ◗ (1 mile), ▶ ◗ (3 miles), ◗ (11 miles) & Moose Pass (30 miles)

RESTAURANTS & BARS

Exit Glacier Salmon Bake	2
The Pit	3
Ranting Raven	6
Ray's Waterfront	8
Resurrect Art Coffee House Gallery	4
Resurrection Roadhouse	1
Yoly's Bistro	7
Yukon Bar	5

PINE STREET
OAK STREET
MAPLE STREET

Seward
Bus Lines
Visitor Center

Forest Acres
campground

HEMLOCK STREET
BIRCH STREET

Resurrection River

HERMAN LEIRER ROAD

OLD EXIT GLACIER RD

AIRPORT ROAD

SEWARD HIGHWAY

Alaska Railroad

SALMON CREEK ROAD

NASH ROAD

ACCOMMODATION

Alaska's Treehouse	F
The Beach House	B
Creekside Cabins	D
Hotel Edgewater	M
Fox Island	H
Kate's Roadhouse	E
Kayakers Cove	I
Miller's Landing	A
Moby Dick Hostel	J
Murphy's Motel	L
Snow River Hostel	G
Van Gilder Hotel	K
Whistle Stop Lodging	C

0   800 yds

information. For outdoor-oriented advice, visit the **Kenai Fjords National Park Visitor Center**, 1212 4th Ave, in Seward's small boat harbor (daily: May & Sept 9am–5pm; June–Aug 8.30am–7pm; ☎224-2125, ⊛www.nps.gov/kefj), which provides maps, shows a couple of worthwhile videos, and has details on regional hikes.

City transportation

Once in Seward, **getting around** the central sights is easy on foot, though downtown and the small boat harbor are almost a mile apart. To visit Exit Glacier, you could make use of the **Exit Glacier Shuttle** run by Exit Glacier Guides (☎224-5569), which runs every hour (late May to mid-Sept 9am–5pm; $9 round-trip), or **rent a bike** (see Listings, p.275).

Accommodation

Seward has **accommodation** to suit most tastes. There are three **hostels** (one in town, one more rural, and a third sixteen miles north along the highway to Anchorage), a wide selection of **campgrounds** (one conveniently right in the center beside Resurrection Bay), motels, and several good B&Bs, some downtown, though many of the best places are inconveniently sited for those without a car.

A bit further out, Resurrection Bay and the shores of Kenai Fjords National Park have **cabins** and even a couple of more formal lodges accessible by kayak, water taxi, or cruise.

Hotels, motels, and B&Bs

Alaska's Treehouse Rainforest Circle ☏224-3867, ⊛www.seward.net/treehouse. Very attractive and welcoming B&B in a large timber house seven miles out along the Seward Highway (turn into Timber Lane Drive then Rainforest Circle). There's one room with a private (but separate) bathroom and a suite which sleeps up to five. Everyone gets a full sourdough pancake breakfast and access to a hot tub out on the deck among the spruce trees. Suite ❺, room ❹

The Beach House Lowell Point, 2.5 miles south of Seward ☏224-7000, ⊛www.beachhousealaska .com. Two two-bedroom self-catering houses with space for up to seven, though compact enough to be comfortable for two, plus a one-bedroom apartment. Good bay views, peaceful location, and good walking to Caines Head nearby. ❻

Creekside Cabins Old Exit Glacier Rd, 3.5 miles from town ☏224-1996, ⊛www.welovealaska .com. Four attractively set log cabins in the woods, each with heating, refrigerator, coffeemaker (coffee and juice provided), and outdoor fire pit, as well as access to a streamside sauna. ❹

Hotel Edgewater 200 5th Ave ☏224-2700 or 1-888/793-6800, ⊛www.hoteledgewater.com. Modern hotel with a range of comfortable rooms with in-room dataports, WiFi, cable, and VCR. Other amenities include hot tub, sauna, and mini-gym room, plus free shuttle to railroad and harbor. View rooms ❽, queen rooms ❼, atrium rooms ❻

Murphy's Motel 911 4th Ave ☏224-8090 or 1-800/686-8191, ⊛www.murphysmotel.com. Well-kept motel close to the small boat harbor with great bay and mountain views from many rooms, especially those in the new block. All come with microwave, fridge, dataport, and cable TV, though older rooms are smaller. New rooms ❼, older ❺

Van Gilder Hotel 308 Adams St ☏224-3079 or 1-800/204-6835, ⊛www.vangilderhotel.com. Original 1916 hotel right in the heart of town that's been fully restored. The small but modernized rooms are mostly decorated in Victorian style and have cable TV and dataports; those with a full bath are better value than the budget rooms. Suites ❾, rooms with bath ❼, shared bath ❺

Whistle Stop Lodging 411 Port Ave ☏224-5050, ⊛www.sewardak.net/ws. Just two rooms unusually sited in a reconstructed World War II railcar close to the small boat harbor. The rooms, which have great views of the fjord, aren't luxurious but are comfortable and come with private bath.

A kitchenette costs $10 extra. Open mid-May to mid-Sept. ❺

Hostels and campgrounds

Exit Glacier Campground At Exit Glacier, 13 miles northwest of Seward. Attractively set first-come, first-served walk-in tent sites with outhouse, pump water, fire rings, and bear-resistant food storage. Free.

Forest Acres Campground Hemlock Ave, a mile north of the small boat harbor. Pleasant wooded site with some grass but no views. Reasonably convenient, if *Waterfront Campground* is full. Tents $8, dry RV sites $12.

Kate's Roadhouse Mile 5.5 Seward Hwy ☏224-5888, ⊛www.alaskakatesroadhouse.com. Comfortable and welcoming hostel with a six-bed hostel room (no bunks; $20) and two private doubles (❷) in the house, plus four lovely cabins out back ($39 for one person, otherwise ❸) each with its own little outdoor seating area. Bedding is included and everyone has access to the kitchen with use of garden herbs, a barbecue area with free charcoal, and freezer space for your catch. Internet access; no credit cards. ❷–❸

Miller's Landing Lowell Point, 2 miles south of Seward ☏224-5739 or 1-866/541-5739, ⊛www .millerslandingak.com. One of the best-organized campgrounds around with RV spots ($28) beside the beach and tent camping ($23) in the woods, plus cozy cabins and rooms (❶–❹), fishing charters, kayak rental, and indoor seating for when you need to escape the rain. April–Sept. ❶–❹

Moby Dick Hostel 432 3rd Ave ☏224-7072, ⊛www.mobydickhostel.com. Slightly cramped downtown hostel with bunks ($19), limited kitchen facilities, and small private rooms ($55; some with kitchenettes, $66). Mid-April to Sept. ❷

Snow River Hostel 22634 Seward Hwy, 15.7 miles out from Seward ☏440-1907, ⊛www .snowriverhostel.org. Fairly rustic but attractive and welcoming hostel with men's and women's dorms ($15), a private room sleeping five, and a separate, quaint cabin, all supplied with bedding and breakfast fixings. All have access to a well-stocked kitchen and there are several nearby trails to keep you entertained. Open year-round. ❶

Waterfront Campground Ballaine Blvd ☏224-4055, ⊛www.cityofseward.net/sprd. Excellent central campground that's so close to the shores of Resurrection Bay you can almost fish from inside your tent. There are separate designated tent sites ($8) away from the RVs (dry $12, power and water $25) and coin-operated showers ($2), but open fires and alcohol are banned. Mid-April to Sept.

Boat-accessible accommodation

Fox Island 14 miles southeast of Seward in Resurrection Bay. Operated by Kenai Fjords Tours (see p.274). Comfortable but rustic wilderness lodge (there's only electricity when they fire up the generator), visited daily by Kenai Fjords Tours, which calls in for salmon lunch and a stroll on the pebble beaches. You get a cozy cabin with proper beds, wood stove, bathroom, and solar-powered lighting, plus all meals and the chance to go on a guided kayaking trip (from $89). A one-night stay with whale-watching cruise goes for $349; two nights including all meals and a full-day guided sea kayaking tour is $687. June–Aug.

Kayakers Cove On the Resurrection Peninsula, 12 miles southeast of Seward ☎ 224-8662, ⓦ www .geocities.com/kayakerscove_99664. A lovely rustic lodge (no electricity) that makes a great retreat for a couple of days' hiking, paddling, fishing, and reading. Accommodation is in either a 12-bunk dorm (bring a sleeping bag or rent bedding) or a private three-berth cabin, and there's a full kitchen along with dining and sitting areas in the main lodge. You can paddle out there, but most arrive by water taxi ($58 round-trip with *Miller's Landing*), then rent kayaks at the lodge (singles $20 a day; doubles $30). Mid-May to mid-Sept. Cabin $60, bunks $20 per person.

The town and around

The center of town is small and short on sights except for the superb **SeaLife Center**; from there it's a stroll down to the small boat harbor, site of most of the companies running cruises and kayaking trips out onto Resurrection Bay and into the glacier-fed waters of the **Kenai Fjords National Park**, a prime spot for **whale-watching**. At some point, everyone finds their way to **Exit Glacier**, one of the few glaciers in Alaska that you can walk right up to. Fewer people make it out to the World War II gun emplacements at Caines Head State Recreation Area, partly because of the long walk and the need to monitor the tide times.

One activity not normally associated with Seward is **dog-sledding**, but Godwin Glacier Dog Sled Tours (late May–early Sept; $413; ☎ 224-8239,

△ On Mount Marathon, Seward

The event of the year in Seward is the Fourth of July footrace up **Mount Marathon**, the big chunk of rock that looms more than 3022ft above Seward. Over ten thousand visitors pack the town center for the race, for which up to nine hundred competitors from all over the state and beyond train to tackle the steep, taxing, and frequently dusty conditions. The winner usually features on the front page of the next day's *Anchorage Daily News*.

The event allegedly started with a barroom wager in 1909 (or maybe 1911), when a couple of sourdoughs speculated as to whether it was possible to climb the mountain and return in under an hour. They just failed, but the event soon became an annual fixture with times rapidly dropping to under 53 minutes by 1928. Eight-time winner Bill Spencer set the current record of 43 minutes 23 seconds in 1981. The women's record holder is Nancy Pease, who took 50 minutes 30 seconds in 1990, and in 2003 Nina Kemppel became the first competitor to win nine titles, eight of these consecutive.

The race route starts and finishes at the junction of 4th and Adams and follows Jefferson Street before beginning the climb up the steep ridge, averaging 38 degrees. The route returns down an obvious line of loose rock and scree. A gentler and more **scenic route** up Mount Marathon (3.5 miles round-trip; 3–4hr; 3000ft ascent) starts by a gate at the western end of Monroe Street and follows a Jeep track up to the town's former reservoir, then skirts north around the flank of the mountain to Scheffler Creek waterfall. You can also cut to the skyline ridge that runs up to "Race Point," where competitors turn back. You'll probably want to follow their example, but it is possible to hike higher to the true 4603-foot summit of Mount Marathon.

Other hikes

There are a few interesting trails in Seward's immediate vicinity, ranging from the short and gentle Two Lakes Trail right in town to the stiff Harding Icefield Trail. In addition to those listed below, there is a coastal trail from Lowell Point to Caines Head (see p.273) and a stack more a few miles back up the Seward Highway around Moose Pass and Cooper Landing (see box, p.278).

Harding Icefield Trail (7.8 miles round-trip; 5–8hr; 3000ft ascent). A taxing but superbly gratifying hike up a steep and occasionally slippery trail on the north side of Exit Glacier, providing wonderful views of the glacier and, once you get high enough, of the Harding Icefield itself. The trail can usually be hiked from late June to mid-October, but upper sections have snow until late July. The trail starts near the base of Exit Glacier at the end of the paved trail and finishes at an excellent viewpoint half a mile past the Harding Icefield emergency shelter. Take water and be prepared for all kinds of weather.

Lost Lake Trail (7 miles one way; 3hr; 1800ft ascent). Moderately difficult and very scenic trail starting in Lost Lake subdivision at Mile 5.3 of the Seward Highway and winding through spruce forest. Four miles along there is a 1.5-mile side-path to *Clemens Memorial Cabin* ($35), though day-hikers should continue up above the tree line at Mile 5 to Lost Lake. From here you can either return the way you came, or follow the **Primrose Trail** (8 miles one way; 3–4hr; 1500ft descent) north, mostly following an old mining road to *Primrose Campground* ($10) beside Kenai Lake, rejoining the Seward Highway at Mile 17. This makes a good loop but leaves you twelve miles along the Seward Highway from where you started; hitch back or plan your hike to coincide with the bus schedule.

Two Lakes Trail (1-mile loop; 20–30min; 100ft ascent). Easy and enjoyable downtown trail encircling two small lakes and passing a salmon-spawning creek. Starts at the back of a parking lot near the junction of 2nd Avenue and B Street.

@www.alaskadogsled.com) will gladly whisk you by helicopter up to the Godwin Glacier, where you'll spend about ninety minutes with the dogs, part of it being towed around on a sled. It is great fun, but cost may force you to opt for the snow-free equivalent with IdidaRide Sled Dog Tours (June–Aug; $49; ☎1-800/478-3139, @www.ididaride.com) involving a look around the kennels and a short ride on a wheeled sled out in the forest by the *Resurrection Roadhouse*.

Alaska SeaLife Center

Before taking a cruise to the Kenai Fjords National Park, consider spending a couple of hours on Seward's waterfront at the 🐾 **Alaska SeaLife Center**, 301 Railway Ave (daily: mid-April to mid-Sept 8am–7pm; mid-Sept to mid-April 10am–5pm; $15; ☎1-800/224-2525, @www.alaskasealife.org), a unique attempt to integrate research, rehabilitation, and public education under one roof. It owes its genesis to the *Exxon Valdez* oil spill (see box, p.322), which highlighted the need for a coldwater marine research facility in the western hemisphere. When marine mammals and seabird populations were severely harmed by the spill, the lack of baseline information hampered attempts to measure just how severely. Altogether some $37 million was diverted from the various civil and criminal settlements against Exxon and funneled into this nonprofit facility.

The SeaLife Center opened in 1998 and, despite years of funding difficulties, has since firmly established itself on the tourist circuit, not as some bells-and-whistles marine circus, or even an aquarium in the traditional sense, but as a genuine educational and research facility. It can sometimes feel too earnest, but generally balances its priorities well. Certainly there are nicely displayed tanks of fish, but all the marine specimens are native to this part of Alaska and displayed in context, usually to illustrate some facet of the local marine environment. The impact of the oil spill is covered, along with the conflict between commercial fishing and the well-being of marine mammals, and the need for habitat protection in old-growth forests to protect the purity of salmon-spawning streams. As you stroll around you'll pass windows overlooking wet labs and outdoor compounds where you might see sea lions recovering from illness or measurements being taken from coho salmon, which swim up a fish ladder from Resurrection Bay. There's also simple and tactile child-friendly coverage of the Bering Sea, which, in addition to providing a monstrous proportion of the seafood consumed in the US, also supports a severely declining population of Steller's sea lions now being studied by the center.

The main concession to entertainment is a series of tanks with underwater viewing windows: one containing Steller's sea lions, another harbor seals, and a third captive-bred pigeon guillemots, cute "underwater swimming" tufted puffins, and common murres. There are no shows as such, but aquarium habits die hard, and everyone flocks to the appropriate tank or window when feeding is announced. If closer views of a working research facility seem enticing, call in when you first hit town to book a spot on the hour-long **Behind the Scenes Tour** (daily in summer; $12). Other tours include the Octopus Experience ($49), Puffin Encounter ($49), and the Mysteries of Survival ($10).

The rest of downtown and the small boat harbor

From the waterfront, follow 3rd Avenue a couple of blocks north to the **Seward Museum**, 336 3rd Ave (May–Oct daily 9am–5pm; $3), which is full of moderately interesting displays on Seward's early days, including its role as a Russian shipyard in the early nineteenth century, treatment of its rail heyday, and coverage of the devastating effects of the 1964 earthquake. More detail can be gleaned a few blocks away at the **library**, 238 5th Ave, where slides of the 1964 earthquake are shown (Mon–Sat 2pm; $3). Returning to the SeaLife Center, notice a small marker indicating the start of the **Iditarod Trail**, a route now mostly associated with the Anchorage to Nome sled-dog race, though at the beginning of the twentieth century it was the overland trail to the goldfields of the Interior. The distinctive green 1917 building nearby was the train station until the 1964 earthquake, and now languishes unused.

From here, follow the bike path along the shore past a concrete obelisk to Seward's founders, taking in the bay views all the way to the small boat harbor, which is often livelier than downtown. The only sight at the harbor is the **Benny Benson Memorial** (see box, above), but this is where you'll come to organize trips out onto Resurrection Bay and to the tidewater glaciers (see opposite). You'll also find a few places to eat, and it can be a pleasant place to spend an afternoon planning the rest of your stay and watching the day's catch come in.

If you want to catch something yourself, call at Miller's Landing at Lowell Point (see opposite), which charges $15 for an eight-hour rod hire.

Exit Glacier

One of the most popular activities in Seward is to drive thirteen miles to **Exit Glacier** (never closed; free), a three-mile-long tongue of ice poking out from the Harding Icefield that is one of the few glaciers in the state you can approach by car. During early explorations of the Harding Icefield in the 1960s, the glacier was found to be convenient as an "exit" route from the icy wastes above.

To get there, follow the Seward Highway four miles north, then turn onto the nine-mile Herman Leirer Road (snow-free mid-May to mid-Oct) beside the Resurrection River. Along the final mile, date markers beside the road indicate the location of the glacier's terminus as it retreats at an average of fifty feet a year (though only twenty feet a year recently); the 1790 marker is two miles from the current face of the glacier. Though the ice moves forward at roughly two feet per day, it melts back slightly more, leaving a broad outwash plain of gravel in its wake.

The road ends at the *Exit Glacier Campground* (see p.268) and **Exit Glacier Nature Center** (late May to early Sept daily 9am–8pm) with interpretive displays on the glacier, Harding Icefield, and local ecosystems. From here an easy half-mile trail leads to the glacier. Compared to the calving glaciers out in the fjords it is not especially impressive, but there are wildlife-viewing opportunities – moose, bears, and mountain goats especially – and a couple of other short loop trails giving a more elevated view into deep-blue crevasses. Rangers lead free **nature walks** (late May to early Sept daily at 10am, 2pm, & 4pm) around the base of the glacier, and occasionally (usually July & Aug Sat 9am, but call ☎224-3175 to check) guide all-day treks up the Harding Icefield Trail (see box, p.270).

Those without a car may want to cycle (see p.275 for rentals), walk, or engage the services of the Exit Glacier Shuttle (see p.267).

Lowell Point and Caines Head State Recreation Area

South of downtown, Lowell Point Road runs a couple of miles south along the fjord to **Lowell Point**, a small scattered community with the *Miller's Landing Campground*, some B&Bs, and a couple of kayak-rental places. Just as you enter Lowell Point, the Lowell Point State Recreation Area marks the start of a 4.5-mile tide-dependent hiking trail following old army roads to **Caines Head State Recreation Area**, a site occupied by **Fort McGilvray** during World War II. On a strategic headland 650ft above the tide with mountains and alpine meadows all about, the fort still has the remains of gun emplacements and ammunition magazines used to defend the southern terminus of the Alaska Railroad. *Miller's Landing* will water-taxi you there ($40 one way, $50 round-trip), and it is possible to kayak there in a couple of hours from Seward. If you choose to **hike** (4.5 miles one way; 2–3hr; 700ft ascent), you'll need to take into account the tide, which must be at its lowest ebb on the middle section of the hike: set off two hours before low tide and you should be able to get there and back before the water level cuts off your return. Alternatively, stay overnight either at one of several free campsites, or at one of the two **cabins** ($65 each; reservations ☎262-5581, ⓦwww.alaskastateparks.org), *Derby Cove* or *Callisto Canyon*, both at the northern end of the recreation area around four miles from the trailhead.

Resurrection Bay and beyond

A visit to Seward wouldn't be complete without time spent on the water. The shorter and generally cheaper cruises and kayak trips travel around **Resurrection Bay**, where you might expect to see Dall's and harbor porpoises, sea lions, sea otters, mountain goats on the hillsides, and large numbers of birds – bald eagles, puffins, black-legged kittiwakes, murres, and more. It is definitely worth the extra expense and time to go beyond the limit of the bay into the **Kenai Fjords National Park**, where the larger open bodies of water improve your chances of seeing humpback and gray whales, orcas, and maybe the huge fin whales. These trips also visit the **Chiswell Islands** in the Alaska Maritime National Wildlife Refuge, at the mouth of Aialik Bay, a major summer nesting site for fifty thousand birds from eighteen species, such as tufted and horned puffins, storm petrels, common murres, and auklets. The refuge is also the only Steller's sea lion pupping area in Alaska that you can legally approach and observe. This is particularly special since, for reasons as yet undetermined, the number of Steller's sea lions has dropped rapidly in recent years and they are now protected under the Endangered Species Act.

Slightly longer trips venture into Aialik Bay for a close encounter with the Holgate Glacier, an impressive example of a calving **tidewater glacier**, with the chance to see towers of ice crashing into the water. The longest trips go further into the park into **Northwestern Fjord**, where three glaciers all calve into the same bay.

Cruising

Several companies offer cruises, running a total of four basic circuits; all the following prices are subject to a six percent city tax plus $9 harbor tax.

THE KENAI PENINSULA | Seward and the Kenai Fjords National Park

The biggest and most popular of the cruise companies is Kenai Fjords Tours (☎276-6249 or 1-888/478-3346, ⓦwww.kenaifjords.com), which offers a huge array of trips from the basic Resurrection Bay (3hr; $59) up to the mighty Northwestern Fjord (9hr; $159). Several cruises call at their simple wilderness lodge on **Fox Island** (see Accommodation, p.269) for lunch or dinner, adding around $10 to the cost. Trips run from late May to early September, with a couple of them extending a week or two at either end of the season. Early-season visitors can enjoy the Gray Whale Watch Cruise (late March to early May; 5hr; $69), which hopes to sight some of the twenty thousand California gray whales as they pass on their spring migration to the Arctic.

Under the guise of Mariah Tours, Kenai Fjords Tours also runs **small-boat cruises**, trading some boat stability and speed for more personal attention. Their main trip is to Northwestern Fjord (10hr; $169).

The main competition is Major Marine Tours (☎224-8030 or 1-800/764-7300, ⓦwww.majormarine.com), which has national park rangers on board their cruises to Resurrection Bay (4hr; $59) and Holgate Glacier (8hr; $119), both with a worthwhile option of a salmon and chicken lunch buffet ($15). Renown Tours (☎224-3806 or 1-888/514-8687, ⓦwww.renowntours.com) offers a Resurrection Bay taster (3hr; $69) and an Aialik Bay trip (6hr; $129) and specializes in early-season whale-watching trips (April to mid-May; 4hr; $69).

Kayaking

Resurrection Bay offers wonderful **sea-kayaking** territory, often with far less cruise-boat traffic than you would expect. Further afield there's even more spectacular paddling around the fjord-indented coast of Kenai Fjords National Park, particularly around Aialik Bay. The more remote Northwestern Fjord is less visited, though possibly less varied unless you are skilled enough to venture out onto more open waters at the fjord's mouth. The best approach is to get a charter boat to deliver you and your kayak: typical fares are $300 per person round-trip for Aialik Bay, and closer to $350 for Harris Bay or Northwestern Fjord. You can then spend several days either hopping from one campsite to another or basing yourself at one of several water-accessible **cabins** ($35; reserve through APLIC in Anchorage ☎271-2737). The Kenai Fjords visitor center (see p.267) has a stack of good advice to help your trip planning.

Lowell Point's Sunny Cove Sea Kayaking Co (☎224-4426 or 1-800/770-9119, ⓦwww.sunnycove.com) offers a wide range of tours direct from its base, with guided paddles on Resurrection Bay (3hr for $59; 8hr for $125 including lunch) and a three-hour evening paddle at 7pm. The company also team ups with Kenai Fjord Tours to offer a cruise, a meal at Fox Island, and three to six hours of kayaking ($149–179). To paddle among icebergs you'll need the cruise-and-paddle trip to Aialik Bay (10hr; $299), or stay overnight, either two nights in Aialik Bay ($900), or four nights in Northwestern Fjord ($1300).

There's a more personal and flexible feel paddling with Kayak Adventures Worldwide, 328 3rd Ave (☎224-3960, ⓦwww.kayakak.com), which also has guided trips around Resurrection Bay (4hr for $65; 7hr for $120). Utilizing water taxis to extend range, they run day-trips to Aialik Bay ($375) with an overnight variation ($650), and even do fly-in paddling trips to Bear Glacier ($400), with its huge icebergs. Those suitably experienced can **rent kayaks** (single $60/day; double $75) and explore at will. Relatively close destinations include Caines Head State Recreation Area, which has two cabins, and *Kayakers Cove* (see Accommodation, p.269).

Eating, drinking, and entertainment

A healthy tourist industry raises Seward's culinary scene a notch above the Alaskan small-town norm, with several worthwhile **restaurants** spanning the spectrum. Most are downtown, though there are a few around the small boat harbor worth seeking out. The majority of the restaurants listed below are licensed, but a handful of good **bars** also exist around the waterfront end of 4th Avenue. Entertainment is limited to second-run **movies**, nightly at the Liberty Theatre, 305 Adams St, though most people are content to eat and then spend the long evenings wandering along the waterfront or paying a late visit to Exit Glacier.

For **groceries**, there's virtually nothing downtown, but the big Safeway supermarket at Mile 2 on the Seward Highway has a good selection.

Exit Glacier Salmon Bake Mile 0.3 Exit Glacier Rd ☏ 224-2204. Their claim to being the "home of cheap beer and lousy food" is wide of the mark. The beer's not especially cheap and the food is pretty good. In fact the place is usually packed with locals tucking into breadcrumbed jumbo prawns ($22) or grilled salmon ($20).

The Pit Mile 3.5 Seward Hwy ☏ 224-3006. Seward's liveliest and latest-closing bar that's perfect for an evening of pool, shuffleboard, or just slotting money into the jukebox. Closes 2am weekdays, later on weekends.

Ranting Raven 238 4th Ave ☏ 224-2228. Gift shop with attached bakery and café serving tasty and inexpensive quiches, pastries, croissants, bagels, and espresso in a sunny, wooden-floored room.

Ray's Waterfront 1316 4th Ave ☏ 224-5606. Fine dining by the small boat harbor in a building distinctively topped by a fake lighthouse. Take in the great mountain views as you devour the likes of roasted elephant garlic ($9), crab cakes ($13), pan-seared Thai scallops ($24), and prime rib ($24), all beautifully cooked. April–Oct.

Resurrect Art 320 3rd Ave ☏ 224-7161. Seward's best café inhabits a former

church, with seating on the main floor, surrounded by quality local arts and crafts, and up in the choir, where there are sofas, books, and board games. Good coffee and cakes at agreeable prices, plus occasional acoustic music and book readings in the evening. Open daily to 6pm or later.

Resurrection Roadhouse Mile 0.7 Exit Glacier Rd ☏ 224-7116. Large, modern log-built restaurant and bar offering daylong smart-casual dining for a dollar or two more than you'd pay downtown. It is worth the drive for daytime burgers and sandwiches, gourmet pizza ($15), and more substantial mains, such as reindeer ragout ($22) and tiger prawns ($23), plus a decent range of microbrews and wines, all available by the glass.

Yoly's Bistro 220 4th Ave ☏ 224-3295. The pick of the lunch and casual dinner places downtown with great soups, burgers, and sandwiches (around $10), plus dinners such as lemongrass chicken ($15), wasabi halibut ($20), and ribeye steak ($22). Also a bar with live music at weekends.

Yukon Bar 201 4th Ave at Washington St ☏ 224-3063. Lively bar with a good range of beers and live music throughout the summer – jam session (Mon), karaoke (Wed), live bands (Thurs–Sat), and usually a set or two from Kenai Peninsula legend Hobo Jim on Sunday.

Listings

Banks There are several around town with 24hr ATMs, including First National Bank, 303 4th Ave.
Bike rental Seward Bike Shop (☏ 224-2448) in the railcars at Fourth and Port has cruisers ($14/half-day; $23/day) and full-suspension mountain bikes ($21/38).
Car rental Hertz, 604 Port Ave ☏ 224-4378.
Flightseeing Scenic Mountain Air (☏ 288-3646, ⓦ www.scenicmountainair.com) runs flightseeing trips from Seward airport out over Kenai Fjords and the Harding Icefield (45min; $139, min 2).

Internet access The free sessions at the library are in high demand, so you might find it easier to visit Grant Electronics, 222 4th Ave (closed Mon; ☏ 224-7015), where rates are reasonable, or one of several other places that spring up each summer.
Laundry Seward Laundry and Dry Cleaning, 804 4th Ave (Mon–Sat 8am–8pm; ☏ 224-5727), has coin-op and service laundry. Also Suds n' Swirl, 335 Third Ave (Mon–Fri 7am–5pm, Sat 9am–5pm; ☏ 224-3111).

Library Seward Community Library, 238 5th Ave (Mon–Wed 9am–6pm, Thurs 9am–8pm, Fri 9am–5pm, Sat 9am–noon; ☎224-3646), has free Internet access.

Medical assistance Providence Seward Medical Center, 417 1st Ave at Jefferson St ☎224-5205.

Post office 507 Madison St at 6th Ave. The General Delivery zip code is 99664.

Showers The Harbormaster's office by the small boat harbor has coin-op showers for $2, and

Seward Laundry (see above) has showers with towel and soap for $5.

Taxes The six percent city tax is charged on all purchases. With an additional four percent bed tax, ten percent is added to hotel bills, not included in our quoted accommodation prices.

Water taxi Miller's Landing at Lowell Point ☎224-5739, ⊛www.millerslandingak.com.

Western Kenai Peninsula

Few places in Alaska exhibit a more dramatic change of scenery than the transition from the tight-bound, almost claustrophobic, mountains of the northeastern peninsula to the flatlands of the **western Kenai Peninsula** just twenty-odd miles away. Almost the entire western half of the landmass is low and swampy country studded with shallow, spruce-ringed lakes. In fact, this region is one of the largest areas of flat, useable land in Alaska; only the Mat-Su Valley and the territory around Fairbanks have comparable acreages. This has its benefits, with numerous interconnected lakes and level portages forming superb canoe routes, but it has also left the region open to unfettered development. Much of the area around the towns of Kenai and Soldotna was developed with no thought of town planning. The coast north of Kenai is also one of Alaska's most industrialized on account of the oil and natural gas sucked out of the ground underneath Cook Inlet.

Depressing though that may sound, it mars only a small area, and the vast majority of the region is wonderfully pristine, much of it falling under the control of the **Kenai National Wildlife Refuge**. A tranche running through the center of the peninsula from the far northern tip to Kachemak Bay was originally set aside by Franklin D. Roosevelt in 1941 as a moose-hunting preserve, and then expanded into the Kenai National Wildlife Refuge in 1980. Very little has highway access, making its trails and lakes some of the least-visited in the region, though it does get busy in the campgrounds along the Skilak Lake Loop Road. The best source of detailed information on the area is the park visitor center in Soldotna.

In summer **Soldotna** is overrun by Alaskans and outsiders seeking some of the world's best **king salmon fishing**. Nearby **Kenai** is popular for its fish, but it has some history, too, best seen in its beautiful Russian Orthodox church. Get anywhere near the coast on a fine day and it is hard to be unimpressed by the sight of the two conical volcanoes – Redoubt and Iliamna – across the water, though the best views are south of Soldotna where the highway runs close to the clifftops past the state's finest razor-clam beaches.

Cooper Landing and around

Tern Lake Junction marks the point where the Sterling Highway splits off from the Seward Highway. Mileposts for Homer-bound traffic confusingly start at Mile 37, reflecting the distance from Seward in the days before these roads were connected to Anchorage. With the exception of a couple of campgrounds, there is very little in the way of facilities along the Sterling Highway until **Cooper Landing**, another of those strung-out Alaskan

KENAI

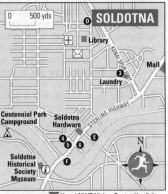

SOLDOTNA

Kenai NWR Visitor Center (1 mile)

ACCOMMODATION

Beluga Lookout Lodge & RV Park	B
Best Western	D
Harborside Cottages	C
Hooligans Lodge	F
Kenai Merit Inn	A
Soldotna B&B Lodge	E

RESTAURANTS & BARS

BJ's	5
Kaladi Brothers Coffee Co	4
Mykel's	3
Old Town Village Restaurant	2
Sal's Klondike Diner	6
Veronica's Café	1

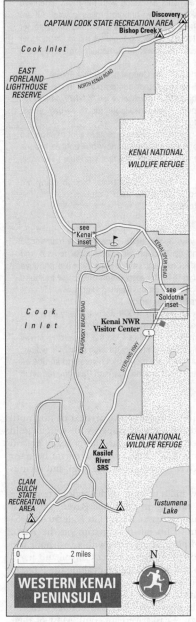

WESTERN KENAI PENINSULA

Hiking and biking in northern Kenai

The mountains of the northern Kenai Peninsula are laced with the most extensive network of multiday hiking trails in Alaska, over two hundred miles in total. All are fairly long, and none finish close to where they start, but it is quite possible for experienced hikers to spend a week or ten days piecing together a circular loop, or hiking across the peninsula from Hope, on the shores of Turnagain Arm, to Seward on Resurrection Bay.

The whole region falls within the bounds of the Chugach National Forest, which manages over a dozen first-come, first-served forest campgrounds in the region, along with almost twenty public-use cabins ($35–45; reserve on ☏1-877/444-6777, ⓦwww.reserveusa.com), the more popular being available for three-day stays, though you can stay in others for a week.

It is worth remembering that the Kenai mountains typically receive a lot of snow, so don't expect the upland sections of any of these trails to be snow-free until early June or later. The main **hiking season** is from mid-June until the first significant snowfall, usually in late September.

Mountain biking is also a possibility on the smoother trails, though many are closed to bikers from April to June and under snow from October to April. The months to go are July, August, and September.

Trails

Crescent Creek Trail (6.4 miles one way; 3–4hr; 860ft ascent). Well-maintained trail with great mountain views, climbing up through birch and alder forests and wildflower meadows, and finishing beside Crescent Lake where there's a primitive campground and the *Crescent Lake Cabin* ($45; by reservation only). The trailhead is at Mile 3.5 on Quartz Creek Road, which turns off the Sterling Highway at Mile 45. Also one of the best **mountain biking trails** in the region.

Johnson Pass Trail (23 miles one way; 2–3 days; 1000ft ascent). Fairly easy and particularly beautiful trail with a predominance of treeless subalpine country with wondrous long views. From the north trailhead at Mile 64 on the Seward Highway (close to the *Granite Creek Campground*), it climbs steeply through hemlock, willow, and alder, and then, as the trail levels out, there are more wildflowers and shrubs as well as great camping spots. At the highest point around Johnson Pass the terrain is

---

highway towns where you're never quite sure if you've arrived or not, until you've passed through. It was named for Joseph Cooper, who sought gold here in 1884 and set up a trading post, though the place never really got off the ground until **salmon-fishing** enthusiasts began to congregate here for the red-salmon run on the Russian River (mid-June to late Aug), and various runs on the Kenai River.

You might prefer to hike the first few miles of some of the region's trails (see box, above), or try some fairly gentle **rafting** on the Kenai River, with great opportunities for spotting eagles and moose. Alaska Rivers Co, Mile 50 (☏595-1226, ⓦwww.alaskariverscompany.com), runs raft-fishing trips on the Kenai River (half-day $97, full day $180) and pure rafting trips, with a two-hour trip (Class II; $49) or a seven-hour run through the Kenai River Canyon and across Skilak Lake (Class III; $120). They also run $40 guided hikes along the Russian Lakes Trail (see box, above) and rent rustic but comfortable cabins (⑤), one by the river. There's nothing shoddy about Alaska Rivers' trips, but there's an altogether slicker approach to those run by Alaska Wildland Adventures, Mile 50 (☏595-1279 or 1-800/478-4100, ⓦwww.alaskarivertrips.com). Most of their business comes from all-inclusive packages, such as three nights staying in their

open enough for you to explore away from the trail pretty much as you please. The route finishes just west of Moose Pass at Mile 32.5 on the Seward Highway. This is a very popular mountain biking trail.

Resurrection Pass Trail (39 miles one way; 2–4 days; 2100ft ascent). Superb and justly popular trail following the long valley of Resurrection Creek up to Resurrection Pass, then down to the Sterling Highway near Cooper Landing. It was the scene of frenetic activity in 1888, when this was the site of a brief but intense gold rush, during which the prospectors forged the trail now used by hikers. Most of the trail is fairly easy going, well maintained and with a gradual grade, though it can be boggy with June snowmelt. Apart from the superb mountain scenery – about a third of the path is above the tree line – there's abundant wildlife and good fishing in three lakes towards the southern end of the trail; take a rod and a license. You can camp in the many designated spots (usually just off the trail), though there are also eight **cabins**, evenly distributed along the route.

Without an amenable driver, you'll have to hitch from the Seward Highway fourteen miles into Hope, then hitch again (or more likely, walk) the four miles up Resurrection Road to the trailhead. The southern trailhead is at Mile 52 on the Sterling Highway near Cooper Landing, from where you can pick up passing buses to your next destination, hitch back to Hope if your car is there, or continue hiking along the Russian Lakes Trail. **Mountain bikers** can also tackle the Resurrection Pass Trail in around ten to twelve hours, making it doable in a day by leaving your gear with someone who can meet you at the other end. Bikes are banned from April to June, making July, August, and September the only feasible months.

Russian Lakes Trail (21 miles one way; 2–4 days; 1100ft ascent). A less arduous alternative to the Resurrection Pass Trail that's fairly gently graded and well maintained, most of it through spruce forests well below the timberline. It may not be as dramatic as some of the other hikes, but it's good for spotting moose, bears, Dall sheep, and even wolves. Fishing is rewarding, especially for rainbow trout in Upper and Lower Russian lakes. Without transport, access is a problem as the best starting point is twelve miles off the Sterling Highway (Mile 48) at Cooper Lake, where there's the *Cooper Lake Campground* ($13 camping, $6 trailhead parking). The trail finishes at Mile 52 of the Sterling Highway, close to Cooper Landing.

comfortable lodge ($850) with the option of two days spent fishing for salmon and trout, although they also do rafting (2hr float, $49; 7hr canyon, $125) and day-fishing trips on the upper Kenai (8hr; $210).

Fishing trips are also available from *Gwin's Lodge*, Mile 52 (☎595-1266, ⓦwww.gwinslodge.com), a classic roadhouse that has been serving diner meals for over fifty years, around the clock during the red-salmon run. Their driftboat fishing trips are either half-day ($150–175) or full-day ($200–225) and they also do popular fly-in salmon-fishing and bear-viewing trips for $295. *Gwin's* has **accommodation** in the form of salubrious cabins with plumbing and proper beds (❹–❻).

Meanwhile, **campers** are well served with campgrounds beside red-salmon spawning grounds: *Cooper Creek*, Mile 50.7 ($11), which has riverside sites, and the larger *Russian River*, Mile 52.6 (RVs $22, day-parking $8), which is enormously popular with fishers, but because of recent bear incidents no longer accepts tents: hard-sided vehicles only.

Russian River marks the start of the handicap-accessible **Russian River Falls Trail** (5 miles round-trip; 2–3hr; 200ft ascent), which winds through the forest to a viewing platform that's perfect for watching salmon leaping a series of falls.

They aren't exactly high, but are fast-flowing enough to make you wonder how the sockeye can get up them.

Frugal types not wanting to pay for parking can leave their vehicle half a mile down the road at the trailhead for the **Resurrection Pass Trail** (see box, p.278). Even if you're not up for the whole thing, consider hiking the first four miles to sixty-foot Juneau Falls, and perhaps a couple of hundred yards beyond to a bridge over the creek and a nice little primitive camping spot.

A little further on you enter the **Kenai National Wildlife Refuge** and pass the campground at *Kenai-Russian River Access Area*, Mile 55, typically full of RVs and anglers, who use a small passenger **ferry** ($8 round-trip) to get to favored spots on the far bank. A couple of miles on, the trailhead for the **Fuller Lakes Trail**, Mile 57 (6 miles round-trip; 4–6hr; 1400ft ascent), heralds the Kenai National Wildlife Refuge **contact station** (mid-May to mid-Sept daily 10am–4pm), where you can pick up information on Skilak Lake Loop Road.

Skilak Lake Loop Road

From Russian River Falls the Sterling Highway barrels west through forested lake country; rather than sticking with the highway, consider taking **Skilak Lake Loop Road**, a nineteen-mile diversion past Skilak Lake and several lakeside campgrounds. Leaving the Sterling Highway at Mile 58, stop after half a mile and follow the easy, signposted **Kenai River Trail** for about fifteen minutes to a nice little viewpoint high above the swirling waters of the Kenai River Canyon.

Most people come to Skilak Lake to hang out at one of the five **campgrounds**, maybe do a little swimming in the shallows, and mess about in boats on the lake. Although there are no formal facilities – bring everything with you – it is worth the detour, even for just a night camped beside water. *Hidden Lake* ($10) and *Upper Skilak* campgrounds (tents $5, RVs $10) are the most popular, leaving *Lower Skilak*, *Lower Ohmer*, and *Engineer Lake* (all free) for those after more seclusion.

The Swan Lake and Swanson River canoe routes

Skilak Lake Loop Road rejoins the Sterling Highway at Mile 75. The highway then runs through dull **Sterling**, which sprawls for eight miles along the highway with no focus. There's little of interest except for Swanson River Road which runs around 25 miles north to the start (and finish) of a couple of excellent canoe routes which involve sequences of small lakes and short portages. The **Swan Lake Canoe Route** (2–3 days) is the most popular of the two and has several variations allowing you to add another day or two. The **Swanson River Canoe Route** (1–3 days) is a little more complex and can include some river paddling, though that leaves you about ten miles from where you started. Both routes are mainly popular with locals, as you really need to bring your own gear or else rent canoes elsewhere and bring them with you. Kenai National Wildlife Refuge visitor centers stock free maps to both routes and can help with planning.

Soldotna

There is hardly anywhere in Alaska where fishing isn't a big deal, but nowhere is it quite so all-consuming as in **Soldotna**, 47 miles west of Cooper Landing. The town sits on the banks of the Kenai River which, in summer, is the most heavily fished salmon river in Alaska, and for good reason: it regularly produces some of the largest **king salmon** ever caught. The current record, caught in 1985, is a 97-pound monster now mounted and on display in the visitor center. Elsewhere a fifty-pound king would be considered a trophy, but here you'll have to land a fish over 75 pounds, something done fairly frequently.

Fishing aside, Soldotna is a dull place characterized by a strip-mall sprawl of supermarkets and fast-food restaurants, having developed since being homesteaded by returning World War II soldiers in the late 1940s. Veterans were given first preference of homesteading land, and they flocked here despite the lack of roads and the need to either fly in or make the difficult hike from the coast at Kenai.

It is this homesteading legacy that provides Soldotna's only tangible sight, the **Soldotna Historical Society Museum** (mid-May to mid-Sept Tues–Sat 10am–4pm, Sun noon–4pm; donations appreciated), around the corner from the visitor center, a classic example of showcasing Alaskan "history" that mostly happened less than half a century back. It occupies six original log cabins that have been moved to the site, their interiors arranged to illustrate homesteading life with everything from beds and stoves to oil lamps and preserving jars. One cabin was the former schoolhouse, built by the teacher and pupils' parents.

Though the Kenai National Wildlife Refuge is scattered over the peninsula's western lowlands, Soldotna is home to the main KNWR **visitor center** (June to early Sept Mon–Fri 8am–5pm, Sat & Sun 9am–pm; early Sept to May Mon–Fri 8am–4.30pm, Sat & Sun 10am–5pm; ☎262-7021, ⓦkenai.fws.gov), a mile off the Sterling Highway at Mile 96, near the Soldotna visitor center. Pop in for the extensive displays about the region, wildlife videos in the theater, and the opportunity to stroll along a couple of easy **woodland trails**.

Further wildlife-watching opportunities are available across Cook Inlet in the form of **bear-viewing** trips. Most leave from Homer, but there are sometimes bargain flights from here.

Fishing the Kenai

Salmon-fishing is king in Soldotna, but it may not be the wilderness experience you expect. With kings, reds, silvers, pinks (in significant numbers only in even-numbered years), rainbow trout, and Dolly Varden all spawning in the river, it is busy throughout most of the summer. The peak is from mid-May to early July, when the first run of kings comes in. The combination of the Kenai River's dimensions and the sheer size of the fish means that they keep to the middle, so successful anglers fish from boats, and the river can be thick with people zipping back and forth in their outboard skiffs. On average, it takes 31 hours of amateur fishing to land a king, though odds can be improved threefold with a guide. Not only do they know the best spots and techniques, they're also up with the Kenai's Byzantine regulations (which differ from the rules on other rivers).

To learn more about the river's bounty, join the visitor center's twenty-minute **Fish Walk** tour (mid-June to mid-Aug daily at 11.30am; free) which visits the wheelchair-accessible boardwalk just in front of the visitor center.

For a recorded fishing report (and the latest regs) call ☎262-9097. The visitor center can put you in touch with fishing guides (typically $175–225 a day) and boat-rental places, but if this all sounds too complicated and expensive you could always just wet a line from the boardwalk, or fish the Kasilof River, fifteen miles south, where the fish are a little smaller but can be caught from the bank.

Fishing guides can be found using links from the chamber of commerce website (ⓦwww.visitsoldotna.com), but before committing in advance, be sure to ask lots of pertinent questions – hours of fishing, tackle supplied, fish-cleaning services and so forth – to be sure you're getting what you want. Generally, the more experience the guide has on the Kenai, the better your chances will be. For further advice as well as tackle, contact Soldotna Hardware, 44648 Sterling Hwy (☎262-4655).

Timing is everything, and you want to be sure you're here in the **season** for your target species: kings (first run mid-May to July, second run last two weeks of July); reds (first run late May to early June, second run mid-July to early Aug); silvers (late July to late Aug); pinks (late July to late Aug in even years only); rainbow trout (mid-June to Oct); and Dolly Varden and lake trout (all year). For a bit of spectacle, arrive during the **Kenai River Classic** (two days at the start of July), an invitational fishing tournament with 180 participants that's dedicated to raising funds for the preservation of the local fishery – past tournaments have raised over $1 million.

Practicalities

Homer Stage Line (☎262-4584 in Soldotna) passes through Soldotna (daily in summer) and drops off at the **visitor center**, 47900 Sterling Hwy (May–Sept daily 9am–7pm; mid-Sept–April Mon–Fri 9am–5pm, Sat noon–5pm; ☎262-1337, ⊛www.visitsoldotna.com), beside the Kenai River at Mile 69. They have all you need to know about fishing in the area and hold brochures for dozens of B&Bs scattered around.

You'll find **banks** along the highway, laundry and showers at Soldotna Wash & Dry, 121 S Frontage Rd (daily 8am–10pm, and 24hr in peak summer), and a **library** at 235 Binkley St with free **Internet** use.

Most of the accommodation is geared towards the fishing set and is consequently booked solid and more expensive in the season. There's a good selection of **places to eat**, including many of the major fast-food chains, almost all visible along the highway.

Accommodation

Best Western 35546 Kenai Spur Hwy ☎1-888/262-5857. Straightforward motel with free HBO. ⑤, July ⑥

Centennial Park Campground Kalifornsky Beach Rd. Large, wooded first-come, first-served campground close to the Kenai River. Fills up early in the day in July, though they'll usually fit everyone in their "overflow" lots. Open May–Sept. $13

Hooligans Lodge 44715 Sterling Hwy ☎262-9951, ⊛www.hooliganslodge.com. Central hotel with spacious but soulless rooms, though it is fairly cheap. ⑤, July ⑥

Soldotna Bed & Breakfast Lodge 399 Lovers Lane ☎1-877/262-4779, ⊛www.soldotnalodge .com. Very comfortable fishing-oriented lodge but with plenty of activities such as canoeing, berry-picking, and ecotours to keep you entertained. ⑧

Eating and drinking

BJ's 44695 Sterling Hwy ☎262-1882. Traditional bar with live bands, including Soldotna's resident troubadour, Hobo Jim (Thurs to Sat).

Kaladi Brothers Coffee Co 315 S Kobuk St ☎262-5980. Good espresso and free WiFi.

Mykel's 35041 Kenai Spur Rd ☎262-4305, ⊛www.mykels.com. Upscale dining with walnut-crusted salmon in raspberry *beurre blanc*, deep-fried halibut (both $22), and other such delicacies.

Sal's Klondike Diner 44619 Sterling Hwy ☎262-2220. In truth it is nothing special, but somehow everyone ends up at this popular diner – with waitresses in tarty gold-rush dresses – serving biscuits, gravy, and two eggs ($5), veggie skillet ($9), a half-pound Yukon burger ($9), and more. Famous for its sticky cinnamon rolls (huge $4, ridiculously huge $5). Open 24hr.

Kenai and around

On initial acquaintance, **Kenai**, eleven miles northwest of Soldotna, is little rosier than its southern sibling, suffering from the same unplanned development – in fact, both have spread so far they almost join. That said, it can be a pretty place, especially on clear days when there are wonderful views of Iliamna and Redoubt volcanoes across Cook Inlet. There is also a tangible sense of history, though perhaps less than you would expect in what is the second oldest permanent European settlement in the state.

The Russians arrived in 1791 looking to obtain sea otter pelts and built Redoubt Nikolaevsk (Fort St Nicholas) to protect their interests. Despite a battle over fur trading with the local Dena'ina Athabascans in which a hundred people were killed, the Russians stuck around, building a productive brickworks in 1841 and a school in 1864, just three years before they sold Alaska to the United States.

Apart from a few homesteaders and fishermen, no one took much notice of the place until 1957, when oil was discovered along the Swanson River. Subsequently, natural gas was found under Cook Inlet, and today over a dozen production platforms send oil and gas to the refinery north of town.

On arrival, stop first at the **Kenai Visitors and Cultural Center**, on Kenai Spur Highway at Main Street (June–Aug Mon–Fri 9am–7pm, Sat & Sun 10am–6pm; Sept–May Mon–Fri 9am–5pm, Sat 11am–4pm; ☎283-1991, ⓦwww.visitkenai.com), which has free WiFi but no computers. The Cultural Center ($3) section usually has a top-quality exhibition to bolster the already fascinating coverage of local history, with good examples of baleen and ivory baskets and an Athabascan necklace fashioned from shells and Russian trade beads. The star exhibit is a complete set of both the first and second printings of Captain Cook's journals.

You can also pick up the free *Old Town Kenai Walking Tour* leaflet, and then stroll a quarter of a mile to the historic part of town, on a bluff overlooking Cook Inlet and the mouth of the Kenai River. This is the remains of the Russian settlement built around the striking **Holy Assumption of the Virgin Mary Orthodox Church**, Mission Street (June–Aug Mon–Sat 11am–4pm; donation appreciated; ☎283-4122 for other visiting times), with its three blue onion domes representing the Father, Son, and Holy Spirit. The ornate interior, dominated by a huge chandelier that came from Irkutsk in 1875, contains an ancient Bible brought here by Father Nicolai, much loved locally for his dedication in administering the smallpox vaccine while Natives in other communities were dying by the hundreds. Icons and religious images, some dating back two hundred years, cover the walls; look particularly for the image of Russian patriot and hero Alexandr Nefsky on the doorway to the left of the altar.

Nearby, you'll find the bare-wood **Chapel of Saint Nicholas**, built in 1906 over the grave of Father Nicolai, who apparently presided over such a wide area that it would take two years to complete his "circuit" of baptisms.

Across the road from the church is the site of the US army barracks of **Fort Kenay**, Mission Avenue, though the buildings (closed to the public) are reconstructions built in 1967 for the Alaska Centennial. Continuing southeast along Mission Avenue you come to Eric Hansen Scout Park, on Mission Avenue at Main Street, a clifftop viewing platform ideal for **Beluga whale-watching**, though the sight of them chasing salmon is increasingly rare these days.

Practicalities

Homer Stage Line **buses** (☎262-4584 in Soldotna) stop in Kenai once in each direction on their run between Seward and Homer, dropping off at the visitor center on request. With Homer (or Seward, or even Anchorage) beckoning, there is really not much reason to **stay** in Kenai, although there are some decent possibilities (see below). **Campers** are better served at the Captain Cook

State Recreation Area (see below). For other practical needs, you'll find **banks** across the road from the visitor center, and **Internet** access at the Kenai Public Library, 163 Main St Loop (Mon–Thurs 10am–8pm, Fri & Sat 10am–5pm, Sun noon–5pm; ☏283-4378).

Accommodation

Beluga Lookout Lodge & RV Park 929 Mission Ave ☏283-5999, ⓦwww.belugalookout.com. RV drivers at the end of a long day might want to hook up here, right by the Russian church. Sites with sea views $40, otherwise $30.

Harborside Cottages 813 Riverview Drive ☏283-6162 or 1-888/283-6162, ⓦwww .harborsidecottages.com. Lovely spot where you stay in simply-furnished, self-contained cottages with great views of the Kenai River mouth. ⑥

Kenai Merit Inn 260 S Willow St ☏283-6131 or 1-800/227-6131. Motel with comfortable rooms, complimentary breakfast, and a restaurant. ④

Eating and drinking

Veronica's Café 604 Peterson Way ☏283-2725. Classy yet casual place well-sited opposite the church that has seating outdoors and inside, where you can read magazines over a good coffee or excellent soups, sandwiches, and quiches. Evening live music is currently folk (Tues), open-mike (Thurs), jazz (Fri), bands (Sat).

Captain Cook State Recreation Area

North of Kenai, the suburban sprawl bleeds easily into **Nikiski**, which in turn fades out as the highway briefly brushes the coast. Take a quick look at the volcanoes across Cook Inlet before your view is blocked by the oil refinery and the fertilizer plant, which uses natural gas from the rigs dotted out to sea. The road then weaves inland through trees until, 25 miles north of Kenai, it hits the **Captain Cook State Recreation Area**, a peaceful refuge with road access to lake swimming and camping.

Clamming on the Kenai

At almost any low tide along the western shores of the Kenai Peninsula, you'll see dozens of people up to their knees in mud digging out **razor clams** (Siliqua patula). These sharp-edged bivalves, which burrow a foot or two under the sand, make especially good eating, if you can catch them. As they're typically around three to four inches long (though sometimes up to seven), you only need a dozen or so each for a good meal, served up either lightly pan-fried or in clam chowder. The best source of information about the rules and necessary skills for clamming is the free Kenai Peninsula Razor Clams leaflet, available widely but specifically from the Soldotna Office of Fish and Game at 34828 Kalifonsky Beach Rd. Essentially, you need to equip yourself with a state sportfishing license (see Basics, p.71), knee-high rubber boots, rubber gloves, a narrow-bladed shovel, and a bucket, all available to buy or rent locally. Once you're kitted out, wait for a low tide (the lower the better), look for a dimple in the sand and quickly dig just on the seaward side of it to avoid breaking the mollusk's fragile shell. After two or three shovels, dig around with your hand and grab the clam before it scuttles away. Dump your prizes in salt water, and they'll naturally clear themselves of sand, saving you a lot of trouble.

Clams can be harvested the entire year, but the most succulent are found during the early summer before spawning season. The best digging is usually an hour before and two hours after a low tide. Generally, the daily limit is 60, though on the most popular beaches you can only take the first 45 dug, and no throwing back those with broken shells. You should also be aware of paralytic shellfish poisoning (PSP), a buildup of natural toxins, which sometimes happens towards the end of summer; if it occurs, there will be warnings posted widely advising you not to eat.

For more information on clamming, visit ⓦwww.dnr.state.ak.us/parks/units /clamglch.htm.

△ Russian Orthodox church, Ninilchik

You first encounter the small *Bishop Creek Campground* ($10), which has walk-in tent sites, paths down to the beach, and potable water, and is an easy walk from the **swimming** beach on **Stormy Lake**. Three miles on, the larger *Discovery Campground* ($10) has the best Cook Inlet views and spacious drive-in campsites among the trees. Limited supplies are available at the *Bishop Creek Bar* and liquor store, a couple of miles back down the highway, but it is best to stock up with supplies in Soldotna or Kenai.

South of Soldotna

The Sterling Highway makes its final 84-mile run to Homer mostly following the western coast of the Kenai Peninsula along the shores of Cook Inlet, a wonderful drive on a clear day when the snowcapped volcanic peaks of Iliamna and Redoubt dominate the views. There is a handful of small settlements along the way – the most interesting being **Ninilchik** with its Russian Orthodox church – but the coast is really known for its **clamming beaches**.

Kasilof and Clam Gulch

The Sterling Highway and Kalifonsky Beach Road converge at **Kasilof**, fourteen miles south of Soldotna, a small fishing community. It's mainly of interest for its collection of simple **campgrounds** beside lakes or fishing streams, the best being the small *Kasilof River State Recreation Site*, Mile 109 ($10).

Ten minutes further south, **Clam Gulch**, Mile 117, is really just a post office and a few cabins beside the most northerly of the major clamming beaches. With its broad, gently shelving strand, Clam Gulch is widely regarded as one of the best hunting grounds, and has the added convenience of the *Clam Gulch State Recreation Area* (day-use $5, camping $10) right by the beach, and *Clam Shell Lodge*, Mile 118 (☎262-4211), where they'll rent you a shovel for $5 and sell you tasty bowls of clam chowder.

Ninilchik

Down the coast another seventeen miles you reach **Ninilchik**, a loosely defined community spreading a couple of miles along the highway and centered on the mouths of two rivers: the Ninilchik River to the north, and Deep Creek a mile to the south. Most visitors come for the exemplary **clamming**, but there is interest, too, in the picturesque **Russian Orthodox church** (usually closed) and cemetery superbly set atop the hill overlooking town. The church was built in 1901, some eighty years after employees of the Russian-American Company first established a town here. Unlike many Russian communities, Ninilchik wasn't deserted when the Russians sold Alaska to the US, and the descendants still live hereabouts.

After admiring the exterior of the church, head down the highway to **Old Ninilchik Village**, a collection of cabins and engagingly dilapidated shacks bounded on three sides by a bend in the Ninilchik River where old fishing boats rest on the shore. Much of the village was lost when the ground sank three feet during the 1964 earthquake, but you can still visit the restored nineteenth-century cabin known as the **Village Cache**, now a quality craft shop where you can pick up the free *Tour of Ninilchik Village* leaflet. Spend a few minutes here before walking around to the main beach where the best of the clamming happens.

Practicalities

When the weather is good, Ninilchik is certainly appealing enough to entice you to stay the night, and if you're here for the clamming it seems in the spirit

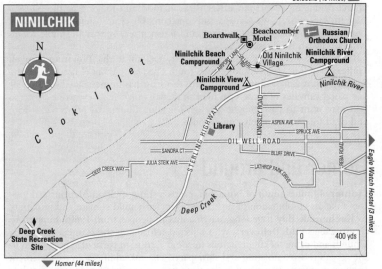

Soldotna (40 miles)

NINILCHIK

N

Boardwalk
Beachcomber Motel
Russian Orthodox Church
Ninilchik Beach Campground
Old Ninilchik Village
Ninilchik River Campground
Ninilchik View Campground

Ninilchik River

C o o k   I n l e t

AIRPORT LANE - VILLAGE ROAD

KINGSLEY ROAD
Library
ASPEN AVE
OIL WELL ROAD
SPRUCE AVE
STERLING HIGHWAY
SANDRA CT
BLUFF DRIVE
REBA ROAD
JULIA STEIK AVE
DEEP CREEK WAY
LATHROP PARK DRIVE

Eagle Watch Hostel (3 miles)

Deep Creek
State Recreation
Site

Deep Creek

0   400 yds

Homer (44 miles)

of the enterprise to **camp** by the beach. This is easily done either on gravel sites at the exposed *Ninilchik Beach Campground* ($10) or a mile south at the larger *Deep Creek State Recreation Site* ($10), which is heavily used by clammers (day-use $5). There are also more sheltered and secluded $10 sites inland and close to the highway at *Ninilchik River* and also at the small *Ninilchik View Campground*, high up and with great volcano views from some sites.

Right on the beach, there are simple **rooms** at the *Beachcomber Motel* (☎567-3417; ❸, RV sites $25), and about three miles inland there's 🏕 *The Eagle Watch* **hostel**, Mile 3 Oilwell Rd (mid-May to mid-Sept; office 8–10am & 5–10pm; ☎567-3905, ⓦhome.gci.net/~theeaglewatch; dorms $13, rooms ❶), sited on a high bluff above a meandering creek where moose often graze. It is a spotless and well-organized hostel in a family home with separate men's and women's dorms plus a couple of private rooms, and a communal kitchen. Tea, coffee, and some kitchen necessities are supplied, they'll sometimes pick up from the highway with prior warning, and they run clamming sessions ($5 if you stay at the hostel the night before) when the tides are low enough and four people can be rounded up.

There isn't much choice for **eating**, but about the best place is the *Boardwalk* (no phone), almost opposite the *Beachcomber*, where you can sit inside or out admiring the view as you dine on build-your-own subs, burgers, halibut dishes and, of course, clam chowder, all at moderate prices. Most of Ninilchik's limited services are a mile south of here, including the **library** (☎567-3333), which stocks some local information (ⓦwww.ninilchikchamber.com if you want more), an **ATM** at the Ninilchik General Store, and not a lot else.

Anchor Point and Nikolaevsk

South from Ninilchik the only significant settlement is the fishing town of **Anchor Point**, hardly noteworthy itself, though you might want to drive ten miles east along North Fork Road to reach **Nikolaevsk**. This small community founded by Russian Old Believers (see p.288) as recently as 1968 still sees women dressed in traditional garb, has a pretty blue and white onion-dome church (built in 1983), and offers Russian food and lodging at the *Samovar Café* (T 235-6867, W www.russiangiftsnina.com; ❷), clearly signposted in town. Drop in for *borscht, pirozhki, pel'meni*, and Russian tea, or **stay** in simple rooms with a Russian breakfast included.

If you're in no hurry, you could briefly call in at the **Norman Lowell Gallery**, Sterling Highway, four miles south of Anchor Point (May–Sept Mon–Sat 9am–7pm, Sun 1–5pm; free), where the artist has homesteaded since 1959. His pastel canvases of archetypal Alaskan scenes won't be to everyone's taste, so you may want to pass straight through the shop (unframed prints $250–750) and head for Homer, twelve miles south.

Homer and around

Homer, 44 miles south of Ninilchik, exerts a strong pull on Alaskans and visitors alike. Its combination of superb location, fairly mild climate, and proximity to **Kachemak Bay** have long drawn a mix of people, from 1960s dropouts to the so-called **Old Believers**, who rejected reforms of the Russian Orthodox Church and came seeking religious freedom. Artists, in particular, have taken to the town's relative isolation and slow-paced charms, adding a creative element to the community that seems at the same time more varied and integrated than those you find elsewhere in Alaska.

If you arrive on a cloudy day, the town's beauty can seem over-hyped, but you can easily fall under its relaxed spell by hanging out on the **Spit**, a distinctive four-mile gravel bank where everyone comes to fish for salmon, charter halibut boats, or simply admire the backdrop of snowcapped mountains across Kachemak Bay. A water-taxi ride to the opposite shore gives access to a wondrous array of hikes, as well as a welcome retreat in places like **Seldovia** and **Halibut Cove**.

The first whites to come to Kachemak Bay were Russians who arrived in search of sea otters. They found plenty and nearly wiped them out, but the otters have rebounded in such numbers that you'll likely see several on any bay cruise. No significant settlements were established until the end of the nineteenth century, when an English company developed a mine to exploit coal seams on the north shore of the bay.

Homer was founded in 1898 at the tip of the Spit by Homer Pennock, something of a conman who had convinced a fifty-strong party of men to come here to look for gold. Little was discovered, but they stayed on and set up an isolated community based on herring-fishing and coal. As the herring-salting industry took off in the early years of the twentieth century, communities sprang up around Kachemak Bay, notably Seldovia, which soon became the main town of the region. After 1951, when new gravel roads connected Homer to the rest of the state highway system, it began to take over that mantle, a position consolidated by the effects of the 1964 earthquake, which virtually destroyed Seldovia. Homer Spit sank six feet, swamping a stand of spruce and the fields where cows once grazed, and making the end of the Spit an island at high tide. It has since taken considerable effort to restore and maintain road access along its length, something justified by the thriving commercial port and tourism based around the small boat harbor.

Arrival, information, and getting around

You'll most likely arrive in Homer by car or on one of the **buses** run by Homer Stage Line (T 235-7009, W www.homerstageline.com), which through the

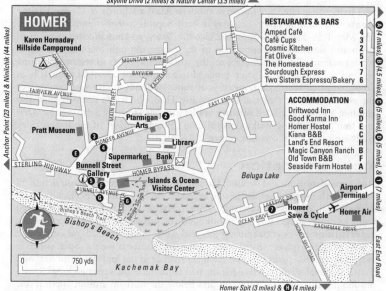

Skyline Drive (2 miles) & Nature Center (3.5 miles) ▲

HOMER

Karen Hornaday Hillside Campground

MOUNTAIN VIEW

BAYVIEW

FAIRVIEW AVENUE

Pratt Museum

Ptarmigan Arts ❷

PIONEER AVENUE

Library

Supermarket **Bank**

STERLING HIGHWAY

Bunnell Street Gallery

BUNNELL AVENUE

HOMER BYPASS

Islands & Ocean Visitor Center

Beluga Lake

LAKESIDE DR.

Airport Terminal

OCEAN DRIVE

Homer Saw & Cycle

Homer Air

KACHEMAK DRIVE

Bishop's Beach Trail

Bishop's Beach

N

0   750 yds

Kachemak Bay

Anchor Point (23 miles) & Ninilchik (44 miles) ◀

EAST HILL ROAD

KACHEMAK WAY

MAIN STREET

EAST END ROAD

HOMER SPIT ROAD

Homer Spit (3 miles) & ⑭ (4 miles) ▼

Ⓐ (4 miles), Ⓑ (4.5 miles), Ⓒ (5 miles), Ⓓ (5 miles) & Ⓔ (7 miles) ▶

East End Road ▶

❸ **3 THE KENAI PENINSULA** | Homer and around

RESTAURANTS & BARS

Amped Café	4
Café Cups	3
Cosmic Kitchen	2
Fat Olive's	5
The Homestead	1
Sourdough Express	7
Two Sisters Espresso/Bakery	6

ACCOMMODATION

Driftwood Inn	G
Good Karma Inn	D
Homer Hostel	E
Kiana B&B	C
Land's End Resort	F
Magic Canyon Ranch	B
Old Town B&B	H
Seaside Farm Hostel	A

---

summer has a daily service from Anchorage and a weekday run from Seward. It is an impressive approach with sweeping views of Kachemak Bay, the Spit, and Homer itself from high on a bluff just before you enter town. The highway continues almost five miles out to the end of the Spit, the western limit of the continuous US highway system. The terminal here (☎235-8449) is where the **AMHS ferries** leave for Kodiak and Seldovia. Visitors in a hurry might want to **fly** from Anchorage to Homer's airport on FAA Drive with Grant Aviation (☎1-888/359-4726, ⓦwww.flygrant.com) who charge $105 one way, or ERA Aviation (☎235-5205 or 1-800/866-8394, ⓦwww.flyera.com), which is usually a touch more expensive.

Once here it is quite possible to walk around downtown and around the Spit, but to span the four miles between the two you'll need to hitch, call a taxi (see p.295), or **rent a bike** from Homer Saw and Cycle, 1532 Ocean Drive, at the head of the Spit road (☎1-800/478-8405, ⓔhomersaw@xyz.net), which charges $25 a day for quality off-road machines. There's a handy bike path beside the road along the Spit.

Car rental is best through Adventure Alaska Car Rentals, 1368 Ocean Drive (☎1-800/882-2808 or 325-4022), which offers compact cars for $60 a day with 150 free miles and free pickup.

Information

The town's **visitor center**, 201 Sterling Hwy (late May to early Sept Mon–Fri 9am–7pm, Sat & Sun 10am–6pm; early Sept to late May Mon–Fri 9am–5pm; ☎235-7740, ⓦwww.homeralaska.org), is the place to pick up free advertising-laden magazines, consult with the knowledgeable staff, and make reservations on their free phone service. Homer is also the headquarters for the Alaska Maritime National Wildlife Refuge, a vast tract of land covering large sections of the Alaska Peninsula, the Aleutian Islands, and the Pribilof Islands that was set up mainly to protect seabirds – all forty million of them. Although the refuge isn't particularly close to Homer, its modern **Alaska Islands & Ocean Visitor Center**, 95 Sterling Hwy (late May to early Sept daily 9am–6pm; early Sept to late May Tues–Sat 10am–5pm; ☏235-6961, ⊛www.islandsandocean.org), is in town and showcases various facets of the refuge through interactive exhibits, replica seabird cliffs, and displays on the work of biologists in remote locations, all approached through a foyer designed to resemble an intertidal zone. It is an engaging place worth an hour of your time, especially if you sit in on one of the wildlife movies that run continuously. Throughout the summer they also run free hour-long guided **birding walks** (late May to early Sept, variable days) and free tide-pooling walks along Bishop's Beach on days of the lowest tides; dates are posted at the visitor center.

Accommodation

Accommodation in and around Homer is about as diverse as you'll find in Alaska, with camping on the beach, excellent B&Bs boasting spectacular views of the Kenai Mountains, waterside cabins in Kachemak Bay State Park, and even some exclusive lodges just half an hour away by water taxi. For B&Bs and hotels, **reservations** are essential during July and worthwhile a month on either side.

For many, the quintessential place to stay in Homer is on the **Spit**, either in one of several RV parks that line the main road or in the tent sites with the "Spit Rats," seasonal workers who live in makeshift tents all summer long. Sitting around a driftwood fire as the sun dips below the horizon around 10pm is one of the pleasures of time spent in Homer; getting nearly washed off the beach in heavy rain is not.

In addition to places listed in the camping section, RV drivers should check out the *Driftwood Inn*. It is also worth looking at the accommodation around Kachemak Bay (in our account starting on p.295). Although the location may not be good for exploring Homer, the bay may form a large component of your time in the area.

Hotels, motels, and B&Bs

🏃 **Driftwood Inn** 135 W Bunnell Ave ☏235-8019 or 1-800/478-8019, ⊛www.thedriftwoodinn.com. Charismatic and welcoming beach-front hotel with a wide range of rooms, from smallish shared-bath rooms and "ship's quarters" rooms with a nautical feel to large modern rooms in a separate building with its own communal lounge and cooking area. There's also an on-site RV park with full hookup ($35) as well as plenty of space for cleaning fish and then cooking them up on the sunny deck. Lodge rooms ⓺, private bath ⓸, shared bath ⓷

Good Karma Inn 57480 Clover Ave, 5 miles east ☏1-866/435-2762, ⊛www.goodkarmainn.com. Modern Scandinavian-style log-house with fabulous glacier views and comfortable, tastefully furnished en-suite rooms, all with TV, VCR, and local artwork adorning the walls. A hearty, self-serve continental breakfast sets you up for the day, and there's a barbecue to cook your catch and freezer space for what's left. ⓺

Kiana B&B Mile 5 East End Rd ☏1-866/235-8824 or 235-8824, ⊛www.akms.com/kiana.

Very hospitable B&B occupying the upper floor of a modern house with great views from the guest lounge and some rooms. There's also a great little cabin out the back, a hot tub under the stars, and a full continental breakfast. En suite ⓺, private bath outside room ⓹

Land's End Resort 4786 Homer Spit Rd ☏235-0400 or 1-800/478-0400, ⊛www.lands-end-resort.com. It is all about location here at the end of Homer Spit, an incomparable spot that means there's little point going for a landside room. Opt for the comfortable bayside rooms, which all have a petite deck, full bath, and TV. Guests have access to a lap pool, small gym, and beachside hot tub, plus there's a restaurant and bar. Sea-view suites ⓼, sea-view rooms ⓻, land-view rooms ⓺

🏃 **Magic Canyon Ranch** Mile 5.5 East End Rd ☏235-6077, ⊛www.magiccanyonranch.com. Welcoming B&B surrounded by peaceful countryside (with llamas) and great Kachemak Bay views. Rooms are quite comfortable and tastefully decorated, all having en-suite or semi-private bathrooms. The Glacier View Suite, with its antique four-poster, clawfoot bath, and good view of Grewingk Glacier, is the best of the lot. Breakfasts to remember. ⑤

Old Town B&B 106 W Bunnell Ave ☎235-7558, ⓦwww.oldtownbedandbreakfast.com. Beautiful, three-room B&B in a 1936 building in the oldest part of Homer. The rooms have wooden floors and a restrained decor of antiques, quilted bed-covers, and old-fashioned bathroom fittings; two have tremendous sea views (one with a private bathroom). All are reached by a seriously crooked staircase. Breakfast (included) is at *Panarelli's* downstairs. ⑥

Hostels and camping

🏃 **Homer Hostel** 304 W Pioneer Ave ☎235-1463, ⓦwww.homerhostel.com. Conven-ient, centrally located hostel in a converted home where you sleep in comfy doubles or made-up beds and bunks ($23) in 4- to 6-bed dorms and relax in a big lounge with a great view of the mountains. There's no curfew or lockout, and bikes and fishing rods can be rented for $10 and $5 a day respectively. ②

Homer Spit Camping ☎235-1583. Several loca-tions, mostly along the western shore of the Spit with spots on the beach (mostly tents) and round the fishing hole (mostly RVs). Within a short walk of

each site, you'll find drinking water, toilets, and fish-cleaning tables – dump stations are also nearby. Fees of $8 per tent and $15 per RV are payable at the office by the fishing hole. Rules forbid late-night rowdiness, generator use, and homemade tents – though "Spit Rats" add extensions of driftwood and blue-plastic tarps all the same.

Karen Hornaday Hillside Campground Camp-ground Rd ☎235-1583. Wooded sites (some with views) on the slopes above Homer and away from the bustle of the Spit. The campground has potable water, toilets, picnic tables, and fire rings on hand, but no hookups or showers. Tents $8 per site, RVs $15.

🏃 **Seaside Farm Hostel** Mile 5 East End Rd ☎235-7850, ⓦwww.xyz.net/~seaside. One of the best hostels in Alaska, set on a small farm that runs down to the shores of Kachemak Bay. Bunks ($20) are tucked away under the main house in a slightly poky hostel section, so it is better to go for the lovely private rooms and quirky cabins scattered around the grounds, including the almost waterside Sea Shell Cabin, which has a small deck. There's even camping ($10 per tent; heat your own shower water), with the use of an outside kitchen area. Cabins ③, rooms ②, dorms $20, camping $10. Open May–Sept.

The Town

Apart from the **Islands & Ocean Visitor Center** (see opposite), the only real sight in town is the **Pratt Museum of Homer**, 3779 Bartlett St (mid-May to mid-Sept daily 10am–6pm; mid-Sept to mid-May Tues–Sun noon–5pm; $6; ⓦwww.prattmuseum.org), a highly informative and well-presented trawl through local and natural history provided primarily by the "Kachemak Bay: An Exploration of People and Place" exhibit. Wide-ranging displays teach and entertain by encouraging you to question your perceptions. Elsewhere, mounted examples of sea mammals, tide pools, and the handiwork of the peninsula's Native peoples enhance features on major issues over the years. One exhibit, for example, is devoted to the *Exxon Valdez* oil spill, where you can hear the deadpan communication between Captain Hazelwood and the US Coast Guard immediately after the ship struck the Bligh Reef and listen to Natives' reactions to the mess. One of the best sections covers Kachemak birdlife, particularly that of **Gull Island** (see p.296), which is equipped with a remote-controlled camera giving unsurpassable close-ups of nesting glaucous-winged gulls, murres, puffins, and cormorants. A control panel allows you to pan and zoom in on whichever birds attract your attention. A similar technique is used to screen live footage of the bears at McNeil River (see p.362) with interpretation by a National Park Service ranger at scheduled times throughout July and early August.

Outside, the historic **Homestead Cabin** hosts old-timers telling tales of bygone days. The museum also runs hour-long **walking tours** of the Homer harbor (June–Sept Thurs–Sat 3pm; $5) starting at a kiosk by the *Salty Dawg Saloon*.

Elsewhere, the work of Homer's community of artists, potters, sculptors, and craftspeople fills numerous **galleries**. Pick up the free *Homer, Alaska Art Galleries* leaflet and choose from such long-standing favorites as the nonprofit Bunnell Street Gallery, 106 W Bunnell St (℡235-2662, ⓦwww .bunnellstreetgallery.org), which exhibits work by a changing roster of cutting-edge artists, and Ptarmigan Arts, 471 Pioneer Ave (℡235-5345), which takes a more commercial and craft-oriented approach, often with artists in residence.

With your own transport, it is also worth taking a drive five miles from downtown up East Hill Road to Skyline Drive, which runs along the top of a series of bluffs a thousand feet above town. The views across the glistening waters of the bay to the glaciers and mountains beyond can be tremendous, but even when clouds are low it is worth calling in at the **Carl E. Wynn Nature Center**, East Skyline Drive (mid-June to early Sept daily 10am– 6pm; $5; ⓦwww.akcoastalstudies.org). Here, the Center for Alaskan Coastal Studies has gone to considerable lengths to interpret the local flora and fauna, both through displays in their small visitor center and outside along gentle and well-formed trails, wildflower meadows, and spruce forests. To appreciate more of the mushrooms, lichens, and mosses, or learn to identify the animal tracks you come across, join one of the naturalist-led **tours** (10am & 2pm).

Further afield, you might fancy a slice of pie at the board-floored **Fritz Creek General Store**, Mile 8, East End Rd, a great little piece of living Alaskana. It is a general store in the truest sense of the word, complete with a video-rental joint, liquor store, gas station, general community meeting place, and ancient post office boxes. The café serves pizza slices and espresso in addition to excellent fresh fruit pie.

Homer Spit

Homer's defining feature is the **Spit**, a narrow bank of gravel that runs over four miles out into Kachemak Bay, almost cutting off the inner bay from Cook Inlet. For a place that is one of Alaska's most powerful tourist magnets, it is oddly ugly: the shimmer of the water is often outdone by the sheet-metal glare of

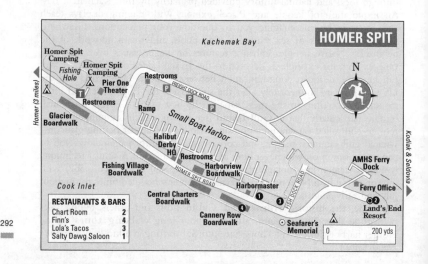

HOMER SPIT

Kachemak Bay

Homer Spit Camping
Fishing Hole
Homer Spit Camping
Pier One Theater
Restrooms
Glacier Boardwalk
Homer (3 miles)
FREIGHT DOCK ROAD
Ramp
Small Boat Harbor
Halibut Derby HQ
Restrooms
Fishing Village Boardwalk
Harborview Boardwalk
HOMER SPIT ROAD
Harbormaster
AMHS Ferry Dock
Kodiak & Seldovia
Ferry Office
Cook Inlet
Central Charters Boardwalk
Cannery Row Boardwalk
FISH DOCK ROAD
Land's End Resort
Seafarer's Memorial
N
0   200 yds

RESTAURANTS & BARS	
Chart Room	2
Finn's	4
Lola's Tacos	3
Salty Dawg Saloon	1

Hiking and biking around Homer

The most exalted hikes hereabouts are those in the Kachemak Bay State Park on the south side of the bay, but if you just want a good walk and don't fancy paying $55 for the water-taxi ride to the trailhead, there are a couple of moderately interesting hikes right on Homer's doorstep. Starting at the eastern end of Bunnell Avenue, the **Beluga Slough Trail** (200yd) runs along a boardwalk beside some wetlands, then continues as the **Bishop Beach Trail** (as long as you want to make it), which heads north along the beach and is best done at low tide when hiking is easier and tide pools more numerous. The beach is passable for around eleven miles, with good sea views all the way; three miles along is a popular spot for sea otters to raft up offshore, and at seven miles there's access to the highway.

The visitor center has free leaflets detailing how to reach the **Homestead Trail** (7.2 miles one way; 3hr), a route mostly on car-free dirt roads that link Roger's Loop Road to Skyline Drive near the Bridge Creek Reservoir. You gain height quickly and get great views to the west and south, but it is a fairly long walk and you may have to do it twice unless you can talk someone into driving your car to the end trailhead.

A **bicycle** is an ideal way to get around Homer, and you can flog those thigh muscles riding up to the bluff-crest Skyline Drive, which is relatively flat once you get up there. There is no biking in the Kachemak Bay State Park, but you can take your machine over to Seldovia or Jakolof Bay and ride to Red Mountain Valley (15 miles round-trip; 3hr; 1200ft ascent), an old mining area.

hundreds of RVs, and the snowy mountains have to compete with the rusting machinery of a working port.

Nonetheless, it has become activity-central for Kachemak Bay: this is where you'll come to catch ferries to Seldovia or Halibut Cove, and to organize day cruises, halibut-fishing trips, and kayak rentals (all covered in our Kachemak Bay account starting on p.295). Charter-company offices, fishing-tackle shops, espresso bars, restaurants, and small fish-processing operations are arranged in a series of short rows raised off the beach on pilings and linked by boardwalks. You can spend a good part of the day wandering around here, though there are no real sights. Perhaps the biggest lure is the **Fishing Hole** (mid-May to mid-Sept), a small man-made harbor stocked with hatchery-raised salmon, which return here to spawn. Visitors stand cheek by jowl hoping to land one of the late-run kings (late July to early Aug), known to have topped sixty pounds (but averaging half that), or smaller pinks and silvers. Fish the incoming tide as if it were a river, or relax on the beach and try a bobber and bait.

Towards the end of the Spit stands the **Seafarer's Memorial**, a statue remembering Homer residents lost at sea, but there's considerably more interest nearby at the *Salty Dawg Saloon*. Comprising three relocated huts from the early days of Homer and topped by a wooden lighthouse tower, the saloon is a spit-and-sawdust kind of place with the emphasis on drinking and telling tall tales, although it's also firmly on the tourist tick list.

Eating, drinking, and entertainment

Homer has a better range of **restaurants** than most Alaskan small towns, some of them located out on the Spit, where you can sit and watch the sun go down over a late dinner. If you catch a huge halibut, you may just want to cook up your own feast with **groceries** bought from the Safeway supermarket close to the beginning of the Sterling Highway.

△ *Salty Dawg Saloon*, Homer

On long summer evenings it is a pleasure just to stroll around and take it easy, though if you're looking for nightlife, there are a few bars, none of them very fancy. Likewise, you could visit the Pier One Theater (late May to early Sept Thurs–Sun; $13; ☏235-7333, Ⓦwww.xyz.net/~lance), a quality **community theater** that occasionally sees touring shows.

Downtown and around

Amped Café 111 W Pioneer Ave ☏226-2671. Chilled-out espresso and bagel hangout with free Internet access and WiFi. Occasionally opens evenings for touring bands.

Café Cups 162 W Pioneer Ave ☏235-8330. Justly popular licensed restaurant, unmissable with its huge sculpted cups above the door, and good for lunch or dinner inside or on the small deck. Come during the day for their Cosmic Halibut sandwich ($8.50), and later for a tofu coconut curry ($16), or perhaps breaded prawns with a honey *habañero* dip ($18).

Cosmic Kitchen 510 E Pioneer Ave ☏235-6355. Budget eat-in and takeout joint specializing in

Mexican dishes (burritos $8), burgers ($7), and breakfasts. Try the *fajita* omelette ($7.50) and an espresso.

Fat Olive's 276 Olsen Lane ☏235-3448. Chic, modern Italian-ish restaurant in a former bus garage, suitably funked up with corrugated iron sheeting and a lively color scheme. Kick off with roasted sweet garlic ($8) or a seafood salad ($14) and follow with an excellent gourmet pizza ($15–27; also sold to take away). A good selection of microbrews goes well with the convivial atmosphere.

The Homestead Mile 8.2 East Rd ☏235-8723. One of Homer's top restaurants, open nightly for dinner, which might be Kachemak Bay oysters

($14) followed by scallop, halibut, and shrimp linguine ($28), Alaskan bouillabaisse ($30), or a steak and Tanner crab surf & turf plate ($36). **Sourdough Express** 1316 Ocean Drive ☏235-7571, ⊕www.freshsourdoughexpress.com. Excellent on-site bakery and restaurant justly noted for its down-home breakfasts ($6–9), buffalo and falafel burgers ($9), and salmon and halibut dinners ($18). Probably the best place to have lunch made up for your day out on the water. Serves Homer Brewing Company beer.

🏃 **Two Sisters Espresso/Bakery** 233 E Bunnell Ave ☏235-2280. Great little spot for that morning coffee, either inside the bakery or at tables out on the small deck. Good for pizza, soups, and quiches, and especially cinnamon rolls, all at moderate prices.

The Spit

Chart Room *Land's End Resort*, 4786 Homer Spit Rd ☏235-0400. Tasty, well-presented meals at reasonable prices come with great views of

Kachemak Bay from the end of the Spit. Good-value breakfasts (eggs Benedict for $11), sandwiches and salad lunches, and dinners that might start with a seafood *quesadilla* ($11) and feature grilled halibut ($23) or rack of ribs ($24).

🏃 **Finn's** Cannery Row Boardwalk ☏235-2878. Low-key pizza joint with great sea views upstairs and a select range of salads, local beer, wine and, of course, pizza – the Greek is particularly good.

Lola's Tacos Homer Spit Rd ☏235 6542. Diminutive takeout with tables outside by the small boat harbor, serving delicious tacos, burritos, and enchilladas at modest prices. Closed Tues.

🏃 **Salty Dawg Saloon** Homer Spit Rd. No self-respecting drinker should pass up a few jars in the *Dawg*, with its dark sawdust-floored interior, thousands of dollar bills and assorted ephemera pinned to the walls, and what is reliably claimed to be the only surveyors' benchmark located in a bar in the US. Usually an energetic mix of locals and tourists.

Listings

Banks Branches of Wells Fargo at 203 Pioneer Ave and 4014 Lake St; and First National Bank on the Homer Bypass at Heath St. All have 24hr ATMs.
Bookshop Homer Bookstore, 332 Pioneer Ave (Mon–Sat 10am–7pm, Sun noon–5pm). A good selection of books with a focus on Alaskana.
Festivals The Kachemak Bay Shorebird Festival (☏235-7740), over the first weekend of May, coincides with the Wooden Boat Festival, but they are really only worth the journey if you're a keen birder or wooden-boater. The last week of May sees the Kachemak Kayak Fest (☏235-7740, ⊕www.kachemakkayakfest.com), with workshops, demos, instruction, and guided trips.
Horseback riding Trails End Horse Adventures, Mile 11.2 E End Rd (☏235-6393), has horseback rides ($25/hour, $75/4hr, and $130/day) along the river flats and the shores of Kachemak Bay.

Internet access There's free email at the library in half-hour blocks, and for unlimited time at *Amped Café* (see p.294); for pay access go to Tech Connect, 432 E Pioneer Ave (☏235-5248).
Laundry Washboard Laundromat, 1204 Ocean Drive (☏235-8586), has laundry and showers.
Library The Homer Public Library is in a flash new building at 500 Hazel St (Tues & Thurs 10am–8pm, Mon, Wed, Fri & Sat 10am–6pm; ☏235-3180, ⊕library.ci.homer.ak.us).
Medical assistance South Peninsula Hospital, 4300 Bartlett St ☏235-8101. Also the much cheaper Seldovia Village Tribe Health Clinic, 880 East End Road ☏226-2228.
Post office on Sterling Hwy at Lake St. The General Delivery zip code is 99603.
Taxi Kache Cab ☏235-1950.

Around Homer: Kachemak Bay

Even tourists on a busy schedule often spend a week around Homer, not so much for what the town offers, but for its access to wonderful country nearby. Most people's focus is **Kachemak Bay**, a forty-mile-long and eight-mile-wide tongue of water with a southern shore that has been carved by the glaciers that still peel off the Kenai Mountains behind.

Kachemak Bay is almost divided in two by Homer Spit, its central position and deep harbor making it the nerve center for activities around the bay and a staging point for day cruises, ferries, and water taxis. Boats crossing the bay almost always spend a few minutes bobbing around in the waters off

Gull Island, a guano-encrusted rock three miles off the tip of the Spit that is typically alive with up to sixteen thousand squawking, screeching seabirds: glaucous-winged gulls, black-legged kittiwakes, tufted puffins, and pelagic and red-faced cormorants, and perhaps common murres congregating offshore before they wing in and lay their eggs among the rocks. The boats get right up close to the steep cliffs, so you get a great view, aided by the binoculars many companies make available. The birds almost certainly appreciate the super-rich waters of the bay, also dear to the hearts of anglers who have made Homer something of a **halibut-fishing** mecca.

The surrounding mountains give Kachemak Bay a relatively mild and dry climate with conditions further enhanced by Homer Spit, which provides some protection from swells. Nonetheless, **kayakers** largely stick to the even more sheltered fjords of the **Kachemak Bay State Park**, which encompasses most of the southern shoreline and the hill country inland. Easy multiday trips are possible by making use of several free campsites along the shore and kayak-accessible cabins, which are also used by **hikers** (see box, below).

Just outside the state park lie the two most popular and highly pictur-esque destinations around Homer: **Halibut Cove**, with its tiny boardwalk community, art galleries, and *The Saltry* restaurant; and the larger **Seldovia**, a peaceful, former herring-canning town where there is not a great deal to do, and that's just perfect.

Hiking in Kachemak Bay State Park

The south side of Kachemak Bay has some wonderful hiking along a forty-mile series of interlinked trails, none penetrating far into the interior of the Kenai Mountains, but most providing access to shoreline walks, fishing streams, small lakes, seasonal berry-picking, and the Grewingk Glacier. Those listed here are just a taster of the sixteen trails currently included on the *Kachemak Bay State Park Hiking Trails* leaflet ($2), which also pinpoints a dozen simple, trail-accessible **campsites** (first-come, first-served; no permits required; free) and five **cabins** ($65; sleeping 6–8). Three of these (*Lagoon Overlook*, *Lagoon East*, and *Lagoon West*) are at the head of Halibut Cove Lagoon, the *China Poot Lake Cabin* is next to China Poot Lake, and the *Sea Star Cove Cabin* sits on the western shore of Tutka Bay. All are bookable through the state park office or website (℗ 269-8400, ⓦ www.alaskastateparks.org). Access is by water taxi (see below) and costs $60–70, depending on the distance between Homer Spit and your destination.

Keen hikers might also buy Trails Illustrated's *Kachemak Bay State Park* map ($10) from the Homer visitor center and elsewhere.

Glacier Lake Trail (2.2 miles one way; 1hr to 1hr 30min; negligible ascent). A very easy trail with good Grewingk Glacier views that links the Glacier Spit and Saddle trailheads and has a number of potential (longer) variations. *Rusty's Lagoon Campsite* is close to the Glacier Spit trailhead.

Grewingk Glacier Trail (13 miles round-trip; 4–6hr; 500ft ascent). Easy and relatively flat trail with superb views of the glacier and surrounding area. Makes a good day-trip from Homer – get dropped at Glacier Spit with an evening pickup at the Saddle Trailhead – though there are good campsites along the way.

Wosnesenski River Trail (11 miles one way; 8–10hr; 300ft ascent). One of the long-est hikes in the park and one of the most scenic, starting from the Haystack Trailhead in China Poot Bay and following a broad river valley through cottonwoods before climbing over a low ridge to a series of three lakes. It finishes at China Poot Lake, where there is a cabin and a choice of trails to reach Halibut Cove Lagoon.

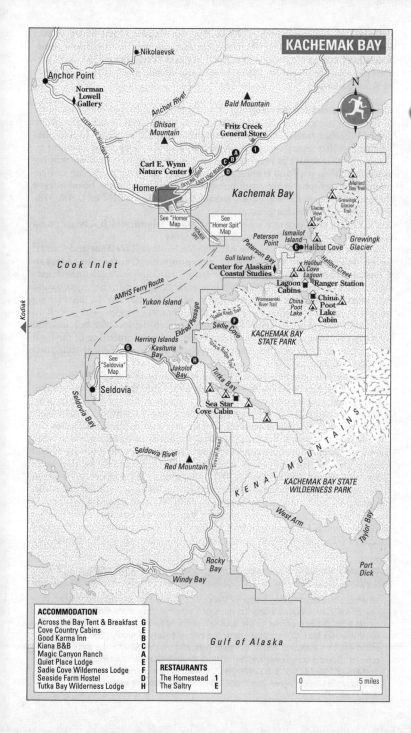

KACHEMAK BAY

N

Nikolaevsk

Anchor Point

Norman
Lowell
Gallery

STERLING HIGHWAY

Anchor River

Bald Mountain

Ohlson
Mountain

Fritz Creek
General Store

Carl E. Wynn
Nature Center

SKYLINE DRIVE   EAST END ROAD

A
C B
D

1

Homer

Kachemak Bay

See "Homer
Map"

See
"Homer
Spit"
Map

HOMER SPIT

Cook Inlet

AMHS Ferry Route

Mallard
Bay Trail

Grewingk
Glacier Trail

Glacier
View X
Trail

Peterson Point

Peterson Bay

Ismailof
Island
E Halibut Cove

Grewingk
Glacier

Gull Island

Center for Alaskan
Coastal Studies

Halibut
Cove
Lagoon

Halibut Cove Creek

Lagoon
Cabins

Ranger Station

Yukon Island

Wosnesenski
River Trail

China
Poot
Lake

China
Poot
Lake
Cabin

Kodiak

Eldred Passage

Sadie Knob Trail

Sadie Cove

Grace Ridge Trail

KACHEMAK
BAY
STATE
PARK

Herring Islands

Kasituna
Bay

G

See
"Seldovia
Map"

Jakolof
Bay

H

Tutka Bay

Seldovia

Sea Star
Cove Cabin

Seldovia Bay

Seldovia River

Red Mountain

KENAI MOUNTAINS

JAKOLOF BAY RD

KACHEMAK BAY STATE
WILDERNESS PARK

West Arm

Rocky
Bay

Port
Dick

Windy Bay

Taylor Bay

ACCOMMODATION

Across the Bay Tent & Breakfast	G
Cove Country Cabins	B
Good Karma Inn	C
Kiana B&B	A
Magic Canyon Ranch	F
Quiet Place Lodge	E
Sadie Cove Wilderness Lodge	D
Seaside Farm Hostel	F
Tutka Bay Wilderness Lodge	H

RESTAURANTS

The Homestead	1
The Saltry	E

Gulf of Alaska

0   5 miles

Beyond the confines of Kachemak Bay, the Katmai Coast of the Alaska Peninsula offers great bear-watching; in fact, Homer is the closest road-accessible base for excursions to Katmai National Park (see p.356), and bear-viewing from here can be better value than visiting the park via the town of King Salmon.

Cruises and kayaking

Homer Spit is packed with companies keen to get you out on the water. We've covered halibut-fishing (opposite), transport to Halibut Cove (p.300), and Seldovia (p.302) separately, but there are also several cruises, some operated by companies that double as water taxis, as well as a handful of companies running guided paddling trips and renting kayaks. Most of the people offering services operate through one of the small number of agencies along the boardwalks at the end of the Spit; the biggest is Central Charters (☎235-7847 or 1-800/478-7847, ⓦ www.centralcharter.com).

The most visited spot in Kachemak Bay is **Gull Island**, which is best seen on one of the boat trips to Seldovia or Halibut Cove.

Commit the whole day on the excellent-value Low Tide Tour and Coastal Forest Hike (7–8hr; $100) run by the nonprofit **Center for Alaskan Coastal Studies** (☎235-6667), reservations through St Augustine's Charters (2hr; $45; ☎299-1894, ⓦ www.homerkayaking.com). The organization promotes appreciation and conservation of Kachemak Bay by broadening people's understanding of the marine and forest ecosystems with a visit to their field station in Peterson Bay. Here, you can explore the beaches and intertidal ecosystem, walk through the forest, or learn something of the local flora, fauna, and first peoples. You can even stay over in their dorm-style yurts for $25 a night.

Kayaking gives you a chance to connect more intimately with your surroundings, and True North Kayak Adventures (☎235-0708, ⓦ www.truenorthkayak .com), makes a point of being ecologically sensitive. They do half-day ($90) and three-quarter-day ($120) taster trips but it pays to step up to their basic full-day trip ($135), which involves a water-taxi ride to their base across the bay on Yukon Island, followed by around six hours of paddling and a break for a tasty lunch. More ambitious explorers should opt for the two-day Eldred Passage Overnight ($350) with extended paddling around Tutka Bay, Sadie Cove, and Eldred Passage (see p.301) and camping somewhere on a beach selected by the guide (you save $40 if you have your own camping and cooking gear). Custom multiday wilderness expeditions cost around $350 for two days and $135 for each extra day. Similarly priced kayaking trips can be booked through Central Charters (see box, below) and Seaside Adventures Ecotours (☎235-6672), both of which water-taxi you across the exposed Kachemak Bay

Water taxis and bookings

Whether you are just going hiking for the day, spending time kayaking, or staying in one of the luxury lodges along the edge of Kachemak Bay State Park, you'll need to get from the Spit across to the southern shore of Kachemak Bay. For this you'll need a **water taxi**. Competition keeps the prices steady at around $55 per person round-trip to the closest bits of the state park and roughly $65 for the more distant corners. Several companies can be booked through Central Charters, 4241 Homer Spit Rd (☎235-7847 or 1-800/478-7847, ⓦ www.centralcharter.com), but a reliable alternative is Mako's Water Taxi (☎235-9055, ⓦ www.makoswatertaxi.com).

and into the sheltered waters of the far shore. Experienced paddlers can **rent kayaks** (doubles $65, singles $45); those less sure of their abilities can join a one-day trip and head off solo afterwards.

Halibut-fishing

The waters around Homer have become inextricably tied to halibut-fishing. The very biggest ones aren't caught here, but a combination of good halibut waters close to town and the lucrative summer-long halibut derby have created enough of a buzz that it seems every RV driver wants an ice chest full of the succulent white flesh. Wander along the Spit in the late afternoon, and you'll see small groups of people lined up for photos behind their boat's catch of the day. Two-hundred-pound fish are relatively common, and three-hundred-pounders get landed each summer, but something in the twenty- to forty-pound range is more common. Even at this size it can be quite a strain reeling the thing in.

Every year there are sob stories about people who bagged a huge halibut that would have claimed a $50,000 jackpot prize in the annual **Halibut Derby** (May 1 to Sept 30; ⓦ www.homerhalibutderby.com), but had failed to buy a derby ticket. With prizes for landing various previously tagged fish, as well as monthly prizes and an overall biggest-fish jackpot, you really should buy a $10 ticket either from your charter operator or from the Derby Headquarters (daily 5.30–8am & 3–7pm), a log cabin by Ramp 4 at the small boat harbor on the Spit.

Trips are typically all-day affairs with boats powering an hour or two out into the bay, then bobbing around for about six hours, with some anglers using herring to land their two-fish limit and (on rougher days) others hanging over the back laying down ground bait. The going rate for these outings is $190–230 depending on the season (mid-June to mid-Aug being the most expensive); add $30–35 if you also want to go after saltwater king salmon as they make their way towards the spawning streams. With all the charter companies located close to each other on the Spit, spend a few minutes wandering around to get the best deals, asking about the size, speed, and comfort of the boat, the number of other customers, the amount of fish cleaning and filleting the company does for you, lunch, and so on.

There is really no need to book anything in advance, but if you're the call-ahead type you could try Homer Ocean Charters (ⓣ1-800/426-6212, ⓦ www.homerocean.com) or Rainbow Tours (ⓣ235-7272, ⓦ www.rainbowtours.net), which does a half-day trip for $95.

Bear-viewing

Homer makes a convenient starting point for bear-viewing trips to Katmai National Park (see p.356) and McNeil River State Game Sanctuary (see box, p.362), both on the Alaska Peninsula, around sixty to ninety minutes' float-plane flight away. From mid-May to September, there are always bears to be found somewhere, either clamming and grazing on sedge in the early season, or gorging themselves on salmon swimming up their spawning streams from July onwards. The air-charter companies always know the best spots. Trips typically cost $500–600 per person for a round-trip flight and around six hours on the ground viewing, and there's usually a two- or three-person minimum. Try Bald Mountain Air Service (ⓣ235-7969 or 1-800/478-7969, ⓦ www.baldmountainair.com), which charges upwards of $550, or the comparably priced trips run by Emerald Air Service (ⓣ235-6993, ⓦ www.emeraldairservice.com). For a cut-price deal, consider backtracking to Soldotna, home of Talon Air (☎262-8899, ⓦwww.talonair.com), which sometimes has trips for around $300.

Halibut Cove

One of the most popular day-trips from Homer is to the small private community of **Halibut Cove** (ⓦwww.halibutcove.com), a gorgeous enclave of boardwalks, art galleries, a restaurant, and some accommodation (but no roads), on Ismailof Island, eight miles east of the tip of Homer Spit on the southern shore of Kachemak Bay. The island was once the site of a herring industry, which peaked in the 1920s when there were over a thousand people here working 36 salteries. The community had diminished to just a few old bachelors when, in the late 1940s, fisherman Clem Tillion and his watercolorist wife Diana were spellbound by the isolation and beauty and decided to stay. Their presence encouraged others to remain, and the community revived. By the late 1970s other artists began to arrive, and today a creative tenor prevails in the hundred-strong population.

It is hard not to be enchanted as you stroll the boardwalks, follow the paths through Sitka spruce forests, or just mooch around the three high-quality **art galleries**. Those who aren't buying tend to spend time at the only **restaurant**, *The Saltry* (late May to early Sept; reservations recommended ☎235-7847), where you can sit on the deck on pilings over the water and dine on a bowl of clam chowder ($8.50), caramelized goat cheese salad ($10), or pesto halibut ($19), all washed down with wine or microbrews.

Almost everyone arrives direct from Homer on the *Danny J* (book through Central Charters; see p.298), a quaint old fishing boat that leaves from behind the *Salty Dawg Saloon* twice a day. One sailing leaves at noon (returns 5pm; $48 round-trip) and takes in Gull Island en route to Halibut Cove, where you

△ Wooded seclusion in Halibut Cove

get two and a half hours to lunch and wander the boardwalks. The second sailing, which skips the Gull Island diversion, is at 5pm (returns 10pm; $25) and is limited to visitors with dinner or accommodation reservations in Halibut Cove, but the savings on this later journey just about pays for your dinner (typically $15–25). In the middle of summer, the press of visitors during the day can rob the place of some of its tranquility, so staying at Halibut Cove and enjoying the quieter evenings may be preferable. The cheapest option is the self-catering *Cove Country Cabins* (☎296-2257, ⊛www.xyz.net/~ctjones; ⑥), perfectly comfortable accommodation with no indoor plumbing but access to a shared shower house. If you've got the budget, go for the *Quiet Place Lodge* (☎235-1800, ⊛www.quietplace.com; ⑨), where four-day, four-night packages (around $2000) include a luxurious cabin, all meals, and free use of their kayaks and rowboats.

Ismailof Island, on which the community of Halibut Cove perches, sits in a body of water also known as Halibut Cove. The head of the cove is Halibut Cove Lagoon, part of Kachemak Bay State Park and a popular spot for the hiking trails that surround it and the three state park cabins – *West, East,* and *Overlook* – on its southern shore. Water taxis, though barred from delivering you to other parts of the cove (including *The Saltry*), can bring you here (around $50 round-trip), dropping you at the trailhead close to the **Halibut Cove Lagoon Ranger Station**, which is staffed full-time from late May to early September.

Sadie Cove, Tutka Bay, and Eldred Passage

Moving further southwest along the southern shores of Kachemak Bay, you'll pass **Peterson Bay** with its Center for Alaskan Coastal Studies field station, accessible on day cruises (see p.298). The wide mouth of the bay opens onto Gull Island, visited on just about every local cruise, and provides access to **China Poot Bay**, a sheltered spot for paddling and the starting point of some good hiking trails (see box, p.296). To get around to **Sadie Cove** and **Tutka Bay**, you have to pass through **Eldred Passage**, a broad channel with the mainland on one side and Cohen Island, Yukon Island, and Hesketh Island on the other. This is some of the most gorgeous paddling and cruising territory in Alaska, with plenty of wildlife (especially sea otters, seals, and sea lions), steep beaches for camping, and even some caves around the high-tide line on the north shore of Yukon Island.

Exploring the region doesn't necessarily mean camping out. The state park maintains *Sea Star Cove Cabin* ($65) on the western shore of Tutka Bay, and there are a couple of **luxury lodges** only accessible by sea or float-plane. The slightly cheaper of the two is the elegant yet rustic *Sadie Cove Wilderness Lodge* (☎235-2350 or 1-888/283-7234, ⊛www.sadiecove.com; ⑨), where the nightly fee of $300 includes all meals, lodging in a private cabin, and use of fishing tackle and a kayak, though you'll have to pay for the water taxi to get here ($90 round-trip). You'll pay the same access cost and be required to stay a minimum of two nights at the *Tutka Bay Wilderness Lodge* (☎235-3905 or 1-800/606-3909, ⊛www.tutkabaylodge.com; ⑨), which ranks as one of the finest wilderness lodges in Alaska, with comfortable cabins linked by a series of boardwalks in a beautiful setting. Plenty of beach walking, tide pooling, and fishing and sightseeing excursions are also available, all for $740 per person for a two-night stay, including all meals and assorted activities.

Just around the point from Tutka Bay is **Jakolof Bay**, linked to Seldovia by the only road on the south side of Kachemak Bay.

Seldovia

Although it's just fifteen miles across Kachemak Bay, **Seldovia** seems a world away from the bustle of Homer. This maze of peninsulas, waterways, lakes, and steeply raked beaches manages to balance seclusion with sophistication, and superb B&Bs and a couple of good places to eat ensure your comfort as you slow to the pace of local life. Draped around its small boat harbor, it is a tremendously picturesque town, with snow-clad mountains behind, a view of Redoubt and Iliamna volcanoes across the bay, and a few vestiges of the boardwalks that once made the place famous. In the quaintest section, brightly painted houses are artistically perched on pilings over the slough, and when the weather plays ball there's nothing better to do than sit on the boardwalk trying to spot sea otters, or lean over the rails of the bridge coaxing a salmon onto your hook.

This is the oldest port on Kachemak Bay, and was named Zaliv Seldovoy, or Herring Bay, by a Russian captain in 1852. Initially, the trade was in sea otter pelts, but the bay's namesakes soon had their day and several canneries sprang up during the 1920s. The activity brought a wave of Scandinavians, who stayed for the next forty years to fish for salmon, halibut, and crab. Wooden boardwalks along the waterfront were built during this time to facilitate travel between the dozens of buildings standing on pilings. With the closure of most of the canneries due to stock depletion, Seldovia went into a decline hastened by the 1964 earthquake, which dropped the land around here by four feet and destroyed much of the town. The town was rebuilt on landfill, and although only short sections of the original boardwalk survived, much of Seldovia's character was retained.

If you're in the vicinity around June 21, consider making it here for the **Seldovia Music Festival** (☏234-7614, ⓦ www.xyz.net/~seldarts), an intimate two-day affair costing $20 a day, $35 for both.

Arrival, information, and getting around

Almost everyone reaches Seldovia by boat or plane from Homer. The cheapest way is on the car-carrying AMHS **ferry** *Tustumena* ($32 each way), which makes the ninety-minute crossing two or three times a week, usually staying in Seldovia for around five hours, long enough for a quick look around. You'll be able to explore a lot more of the surrounding countryside by taking the hour-long boat shuttle by Rainbow Tours ($35 round-trip; ☏235-7272, ⓦ www .rainbowtours.net), which leaves Homer at 9am and gives you seven hours in Seldovia. Alternatively, go with the *Discovery* ($48; book through Central Charters, see p.298), which leaves at 11am and visits Gull Island on the way, but only gives you three hours in Seldovia. Both the Rainbow Tours shuttle and the *Discovery* allow you to split your journey and spend as many nights as you wish in Seldovia.

Water taxis do not run from Homer to Seldovia, but do go to Jakolof Dock ($45 round-trip), twelve miles by road from Seldovia, which may be handy if you are planning to do some cycling over here. Bikes usually travel for $5, or free on some boats.

Mako's Water Taxi (☏235-9055, ⓦ www.makoswatertaxi.com) offers a couple of ways to see Seldovia. Simplest is a scenic trip to Jakolof Bay, a water taxi to Seldovia, lunch there, then a flight back to Homer for $95. If you fancy some aquatic activity, opt instead for the excellent Day on Kachemak Bay combo ($180), which adds in half a day kayaking with *Across the Bay Tent & Breakfast* (see p.304). Boats and flights are frequent enough to allow you to tailor your stay for as long as you wish at *Across the Bay* or in Seldovia.

Locals who can't hitch a ride on a neighbor's fishing boat usually **fly** from Homer, a scenic twelve-minute flight best done with Smokey Bay Air ($35 each way; ☎1-888/482-1511, ⓦwww.smokeybayair.com), which flies almost hourly in summer and offers an extended detour over the Grewingk Glacier for an additional $30. Great Northern Airlines (☎243-1968 or 1-800/243-1968, ⓦwww.gnair.com) runs direct flights from Anchorage for $155 each way.

Nowhere in Seldovia is more than half a mile from the dock or airstrip, so **getting around** is easy on foot, but there are dozens of miles of gravel roads in the vicinity, and you may want to **rent a bike** from the *Boardwalk Hotel*, which rents mountain bikes ($15 a half-day, $25 for 8hr, $35 overnight). Alternatively, bring a bike with you from Homer: it will cost you $5 each way with Rainbow Tours.

There is currently no **visitor center**, but everything you need to know is on the widely available *Map of the City of Seldovia* leaflet, and you can check out the happenings online at ⓦwww.seldovia.com. In town you'll find a **post office**, on Main Street at Seldovia Street, and a sporadically open **library**, 260 Seldovia St, but **no bank or ATM**; most businesses accept credit cards.

Accommodation

Seldovia specializes in quality B&Bs, and staying at one sets the perfect tone for taking in the area at a leisurely pace. There's great **camping**, too, at the *Wilderness Park*, Mile 1.5 Jakolof Bay Rd, where RVs get sites ($8) among the trees. Tent campers are better off at tent sites ($5) scattered along the foreshore a quarter-mile from the RV sites or along Outside Beach. You'll find pump water and outhouses near the RV sites. Before heading out to camp, register and pay at the City Office, 346 Dock St (☎234-7643) by the AMHS ferry dock. The 6.5 percent local **tax** has not been included in our price codes.

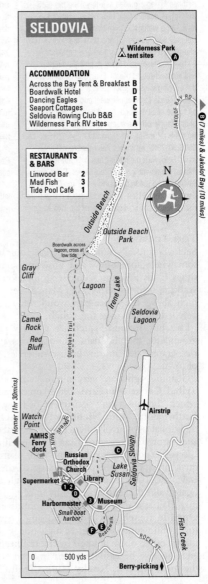

SELDOVIA

ACCOMMODATION
Across the Bay Tent & Breakfast B
Boardwalk Hotel   D
Dancing Eagles   F
Seaport Cottages   C
Seldovia Rowing Club B&B   E
Wilderness Park RV sites   A

RESTAURANTS & BARS
Linwood Bar   2
Mad Fish   3
Tide Pool Café   1

Wilderness Park tent sites A

▲ B (7 miles) & Jakolof Bay (10 miles)

Outside Beach

Outside Beach Park

Boardwalk across lagoon, cross at low tide

Gray Cliff

Lagoon

Irene Lake

Seldovia Lagoon

Camel Rock

Red Bluff

Otterbahn Trail

Homer (1hr 30mins) ◄

Watch Point

Airstrip

AMHS Ferry dock

Main St

Russian Orthodox Church

Lake Susan

Seldovia Slough

Supermarket

Library

Harbormaster

Museum

Small boat harbor

Boardwalk

Rocky St

Fish Creek

0   500 yds

Berry-picking ▼

Across the Bay Tent & Breakfast Kasitsna Bay, Mile 8 Jakolof Bay Rd May–Sept ☎ 235-3633, Oct–April ☎ 345-2571, ⊛ www.tentandbreakfastalaska .com. A collection of canvas-walled platform tents (with carpet, fresh flowers, hot showers, outhouse toilets with stained-glass window, and a wood-fired sauna) beside the beach eight miles east of Seldovia that is a great place to hang out for a while, perhaps taking a guided sea-kayaking trip ($85 for 4hr), or doing a little bike riding (rentals $25 a day). Get a water taxi from Homer to Jakolof Dock (roughly $45 round-trip) or a boat to Seldovia. They charge $75 per person for tent and breakfast, or $110 if you also want them to provide their excellent seafood-based meals. Everyone chips in with the evening entertainment, and it is worth checking their website for summer weekend workshops on topics such as yoga, travel writing, and nature photography. Bring a sleeping bag. ❻

Boardwalk Hotel 243 Main St ☎ 234-7816 or 1-800/238-7862, ⊛ www.seldoviaboardwalkhotel .com. Seldovia's main hotel has only fourteen rooms, many with great harbor views. There are savings to be made by taking either the One-Night Package (from $159), which includes a cruise from Homer and a scenic flight back, or the Two-Night

Kayak Special (from $329), adding a day of kayaking and an extra night at the hotel. ❻

🏃 **Dancing Eagles** ☎ 234-7627, ⊛ www .dancingeagles.com. Superbly sited B&B, perched on rocks right above the water. The rooms (shared-bath) in the lodge are great value, but the real star is the fully self-contained "cabin" with fabulous views and enough room for six ($50 extra per person). A breakfast basket is provided to either take to your room or eat on the secluded deck. Cabin ❼, rooms ❺

Seaport Cottages 313 Shoreline Drive ☎ 234-7483, ⊛ www.acsalaska.net/~seaportcottages. A little cluster of ageing, but attractive and well-priced, fully self-contained cottages that are perfect for longer stays, plus one that's great for families. Although there are no sea views, it's a short walk to the harbor, and you can explore using the free bikes. Suite sleeping five ❺, cottages ❹

Seldovia Rowing Club B&B The Boardwalk ☎ 234-7614, ⊛ www.seldoviarowingclub.com. Floral rooms in a friendly boardwalk B&B, built on stilts overlooking the slough and run by watercolor artist Susan Mumma. Just two suites, each with sitting room, deck, and private bath, plus a huge gourmet breakfast. ❻

The Town

Seldovia is ideally suited for hanging out: strolling around the harbor, stopping somewhere for coffee, and browsing some of the better-than-average craft shops. Easily the most scenic section is along what's left of the **original boardwalks** at the southern end of Main Street, where you can walk the plank streets high above the water past wonderfully picturesque, brightly painted houses perched on stilts over the slough.

Late July to mid-September is berry-picking time, and the best hunting ground for the abundant salmonberries and blueberries, as well as mossberries, cranberries, and lowbush cranberries, is along Rocky Road to the south of town.

Genuine sights are very minor, but you should call briefly at the **Alaska Tribal Cache Museum**, 206 Main Street (Mon–Sat 10.30am–4.30pm; free), which contains a tiny assortment of ivory, a whalebone bowl, and a samovar. Further along, **Saint Nicholas Russian Orthodox Church** is Seldovia's only traditional sight, idyllically set on a knoll above the harbor. It was built in 1891, and restored ninety years later, but is usually closed.

If you're looking to do some light exercise, follow Main Street north and duck up Spring Street to the start of the **Otterbahn Trail** (1.5 miles one way; 1hr; 100ft ascent), a track through the coastal forest and over lagoon boardwalks diligently created by local high school students. It reaches Kachemak Bay at a steeply shelving, diminutive beach, then rounds a headland to **Outside Beach**, reached by crossing a tidal slough which may be impassable (or require some wading) at high tide. Check the tide tables at the Harbormaster office or on a board by the trailhead. Outside Beach has a day-use area and can also be easily reached by road (see map, p.303). You could also try the more vigorous **Rocky Ridge Trail** (2.5-mile loop; 2–3hr; 800ft ascent), which is steep in places and slick underfoot but rewards with great views over the town and across Cook Inlet to Mount Iliamna. The trailhead is half a mile east of town along Rocky Street.

Outdoor activities

With miles of protected bays, coves, and islands to explore, especially around Eldred Passage, Sadie Cove, and Tutka Bay, **kayaking** from Seldovia is something not to be missed. Kayak'atak (T234-7425, Wwww.alaska.net/~kayaks) runs guided day-trips (3hr for $80, 5hr for $120), as well as overnight outings ($180 each, discounts for three or more) for which you'll need your own sleeping bag and rain gear. Departures are designed with the ferry schedules in mind. More confident paddlers can rent kayaks at $50 for a single and $80 for a double ($35 and $50 respectively for second and subsequent days).

With several miles of former logging roads, **mountain biking** is also great, either with a bike rented here or one brought over from Homer. The road to Jakolof continues south to the Gulf of Alaska coast via **Red Mountain**, a huge lump of chromium ore that was once mined and is now cloaked in stunted vegetation, rather than the huge trees found elsewhere. It is about 35 miles to the end of the road, and while it can be done in a long Alaskan day an overnight trip is better. Ask about local conditions before you go.

For a little **fishing**, consider a full-day halibut trip with Alaskan Grace Charters ($200; T234-7811), or just hang off the bridge over the slough where there is always something running after mid-May; consult the sportfishing regulations posted at the head of the gangway to the boat harbor.

Eating and drinking

With all the day-trippers (and a fair number of overnight visitors) Seldovia's **eating** scene has boomed in recent years. For **groceries**, head along Main Street to Main Street Market, which has fairly limited supplies.

Linwood Bar 257 Main St. Long sunny evenings in Seldovia are best admired outdoors, but for a change of scenery, duck into this bar's dark interior for a beer or three.

Mad Fish Restaurant 221 Main St T234-7676. A great place to watch harbor life while savoring roasted garlic, white bean, and sun-dried tomato dip ($7) or Szechwan seafood noodle salad ($14.50), followed perhaps by local salmon in a delicate ginger orange sauce ($18). They make great desserts, too. Closed Wed.

The Tide Pool Café 267 Main St T234-7502. The pick of the restaurants for good espresso, breakfast, lunch, and weekend dinners. The excellent Santa Fe chicken salad ($11), a marinated steak with chilies wrap ($11), halibut and chips ($13), and more are all served on a deck that's almost overhanging the harbor, or inside among sea fans, starfish, and shells.

Travel details

Trains

Seward to: Anchorage (daily; 4hr 20min).

Buses

Girdwood to: Anchorage (3 daily; 1hr 15min);
Seward (2 daily; 2hr).
Homer to: Anchorage (2 daily; 5hr 30min); Ninilchik
(2 daily; 1hr); Seward (daily; 5hr); Soldotna (2 daily;
2hr 30min).
Ninilchik to: Anchorage (1 daily; 4hr 30min);
Homer (2 daily; 1hr).
Seward to: Anchorage (4 daily; 2hr 30min–3hr
30min); Girdwood (2 daily; 2hr); Homer (daily; 5hr).
Soldotna to: Anchorage (1 daily; 3hr 45min);
Homer (2 daily; 2hr 30min).

Ferries

Homer to: Kodiak (3–4 weekly; 7–13hr); Port
Lions (1–3weekly; 10hr); Seldovia (2–4 weekly;
1hr 30min).
Seldovia to: Homer (2–4 weekly; 1hr 30min).

Flights

Homer to: Anchorage (4–6 daily; 50min); Seldovia
(several daily; 12min).
Kenai to: Anchorage (14–18 daily; 25min).
Seldovia to: Anchorage (4 weekly; 1hr 15min);
Homer (several daily; 12min).

Prince William Sound

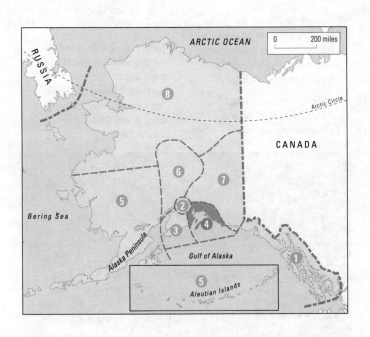

CHAPTER 4

Highlights

PRINCE WILLIAM SOUND | Highlights

4

* **Whittier** More a curiosity than a highlight, this long-isolated town provides an excellent base for kayaking. See p.312

* **Kayaking the Sound** Paddle in front of calving glaciers, camp on remote beaches, and keep watch for whales and seals. See p.315

* **Columbia Glacier** Cruise to the area's largest tidewater glacier, which spews icebergs into the sound from its three-mile-wide face. See p.325

* **Blueberry Lake State Recreation Site**. Spend a night or two at this ridgeline campground, amid the jagged, snowy peaks of the Chugach Mountains. See p.329

* **Copper River Delta** Drive the Copper River Highway through this gorgeous network of ponds, sloughs, and wetlands, alive with birds and the odd moose or bear. See p.337

* **Million Dollar Bridge** This earthquake-wrecked relic of the Copper River & Northwestern Railway still spans the Copper River, defiant in front of the Childs Glacier. See p.338

△ Boats in harbor, Valdez

Prince William Sound

I f you've come to Alaska hoping to see huge chunks of ice crashing into deep fjords where harbor seals loll on icebergs and mountain goats dot the hillsides, then **PRINCE WILLIAM SOUND** is the place for you. It's perfect for sea kayaking: bobbing around the faces of tidewater glaciers while scanning the horizon for breaching whales, you'll quickly understand why it's hard to surpass these sheltered waters, with their three thousand miles of convoluted coastline and countless uninhabited islands. The sound itself is a ragged bite out of the northern reaches of the Gulf of Alaska, ninety miles long and 15,000 square miles in area – roughly the size of Switzerland or twice that of Massachusetts. This expanse provides plenty of elbow room for the sound's rich **wildlife**, which includes seven resident pods of orca, several fifty-ton humpback whales, numerous Dall's porpoises, thirteen thousand sea otters, and over two hundred species of birds.

Many compare the sound favorably with Southeast's Glacier Bay, citing a larger number of glaciers and ease of access, though that same accessibility robs Prince William Sound of some of the isolated qualities possessed by Glacier Bay. This is also where the *Exxon Valdez* went aground on Bligh Reef in 1989, spilling millions of gallons of oil and killing thousands of birds and sea mammals. Many species have yet to fully recover, but there are no longer any visual reminders of those appalling times, just sparkling blue water and abundant animal life.

You'll likely approach the sound from one of the three towns on its shores: **Whittier**, a strange former military port connected by road and rail to Anchorage; the port of **Valdez**, with its massive oil terminal, extreme skiing, and superb kayaking opportunities; or isolated **Cordova**, which stands as a gateway to the **Copper River Delta**, with its vast wetlands, glaciers feeding icebergs into the Copper River, and the famed Million Dollar Bridge. It hardly matters which town you choose as your base, but each one's cruises and kayak trips tend to focus on a particular area of the sound. Around Whittier the prize destinations are **College Fjord**, with its aptly named tidewater glaciers, Harvard and Yale, and the nearby **Harriman Fjord**, almost entirely encircled by glacier-white mountains. King of all the Prince William Sound glaciers is the **Columbia Glacier**, the largest tidewater glacier in Southcentral Alaska, named for New York's Columbia University and best accessed from Valdez. It is an astonishing sight, protruding 34 miles from the peaks of the snowbound Chugach Mountains to the sound, where its three-mile-wide face is forever calving off huge bergs. Actually, icy chunks are falling off faster than they are being replaced, and the glacier has retreated seven miles since 1984, leaving behind a huge new fjord choked with bobbing hunks of ice. Although it's usually impossible to get close enough to see any impressive calving, this is a brilliant place to spend time

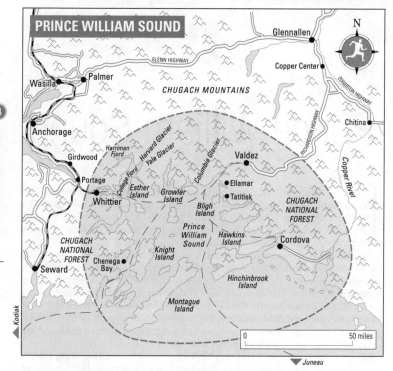

▼ Juneau

listening to the popping of melting ice. Around Cordova much of the interest focuses on the Copper River Delta, though glaciers also feature here, with the Childs Glacier looming large above the Million Dollar Bridge.

Money, time, and your taste for adventure will determine how you explore the sound. Even an experience as brief as a ferry trip between Whittier and Valdez gives a sense of the region's beauty, affords distant views of glaciers, and may offer a few sightings of seals and perhaps whales. If you have the time, go **kayaking**, which can be as easy-going as you wish and gives a much more realistic sense of the scale of everything than you would get from a big cruise boat.

Some history

In pre-European times, the Prince William Sound area was primarily occupied by the Chugach people, who settled around its shores, and the Eyak, who lived further east around the Copper River Delta and traded inland with the Ahtna. Russians were the first whites to arrive: **Vitus Bering** and his crew set foot on Alaskan soil in 1741, on Kayak Island near present-day Cordova.

One of the first Europeans to gain a sense of what lay behind the sheltering band of islands here was **James Cook**, who sailed through in 1778 when searching for the Northwest Passage. He named it Sandwich Sound in honor of his patron, the Earl of Sandwich, but on Cook's return to England the earl was out of favor and the House of Lords changed the name to recognize the king's son, William Henry, who later became King William IV. Spanish explorer **Don Salvador Fidalgo** arrived in 1790 also looking for the Northwest Passage. He took longer to decide he hadn't found it, and in the process named Galena Bay, Puerto Fidalgo, and Puerto Valdes, renamed Valdez during the Spanish-American War at the end of the nineteenth century. He approached Columbia Glacier but turned away, as he thought the loud roar and spray of calving icebergs was the action of a live volcano. The Russians continued to be an active presence during these European explorations, finding the mouth of the Copper River in 1781 and establishing a settlement for hunting and trading sea otters at Fort Constantine, on Hinchinbrook Island, in 1793.

Portuguese and French sailors followed, but it was Americans who brought the first real changes to the area, flocking to Valdez during the Klondike gold rush in the late nineteenth century. The discovery of copper inland at Kennicott drove the development of Cordova, and World War II effectively created Whittier, as the US needed a deep-water port kept safe from Japanese bombers by low cloud cover.

A very different instinct was at work in 1907 when President Theodore Roosevelt established one of the country's first national forests, the **Chugach National Forest**, which cloaks the entire coast of Prince William Sound, and much of Southcentral Alaska as well. After Southeast's Tongass National Forest, it is America's largest and, as with Tongass, the issue of logging is highly controversial. Clear-cutting does take place, but in most of the areas you're likely to visit, all you'll see is untouched wilderness running down to the steep gravel beaches.

Getting around the sound

Whittier and Valdez, two of Prince William Sound's three main towns, are accessible by road, though roads do not directly connect them to each other.

The Harriman Expedition

At the end of the nineteenth century, the Klondike gold rush sparked interest in the previously ignored territory of Alaska. Railroad magnate Edward H. Harriman was more proactive than most; when told by his doctor to take a holiday, he financed the **Harriman Expedition**, a grand scientific tour along the Alaskan coast with the support of the US Biological Survey. Harriman quickly marshaled resources, refitted the SS *George W Elder* within weeks, laid out a route up the panhandle to the Bering Strait, and recruited leading scientists. The group included **John Muir**, already a recognized expert on Alaska from his two previous visits in 1879–80 and 1890, who described the territory in a 1901 letter as "one of the richest, most glorious mountain landscapes I ever beheld." Their departure in May 1899 was front-page news all over the world.

Though only two months long, the expedition was deemed a great success, vastly increasing knowledge of Alaskan flora and fauna and yielding surveys of long sections of coastline. Perhaps its most evident legacy is Prince William Sound's **College Fjord**, where the glaciers ranged along each side are named after Eastern US colleges. Along the south side are the original Seven Sisters women's colleges – including Wellesley, Vassar, Bryn Mawr, and Smith – while those along the northern side were once men's schools – Dartmouth, Amherst, and Williams among them – with Yale and Harvard at the head of the fjord. Naturally, Harvard was the biggest, its face over two miles wide and four hundred feet high. Around the corner from College Fjord, the expedition's leader let his mark with **Harriman Fjord**, the sound's most popular multiday kayaking destination, with plenty of opportunities for camping on beaches. On a kayak, short paddles give you access to interesting glaciers, particularly Harriman Glacier and Surprise Glacier, the latter tending to exhibit the most calving activity in the area.

Consequently, the best way to travel in the region is by boat. Not only is it quicker than driving, it's also the easiest path to a true understanding of the area.

The cheapest passage between the three towns, and the only option if you have a vehicle, is the AMHS **fast ferry** *Chenega* that links the Prince William Sound ports most days.

If you are not planning to take one of the dedicated glacier cruises (see p.314), you should at least take the ferry between Whittier and Valdez, which passes within sight of the Columbia Glacier. It is a popular run and, while foot passengers seldom have trouble getting a space, drivers should **reserve in advance**. Ferry fares are roughly half the cruise fares and are listed in Basics (see p.42).

Whittier

The tiny port of **WHITTIER**, sixty miles southeast of Anchorage, is in effect a sprawling rail-yard hemmed in by heavily glaciated mountains. Almost all of the town's two hundred permanent residents live either in the Begich Tower apartments or the scruffy, low-rise Whittier Manor. Until June 2000 the town had only been reachable by sea or train, a state of isolation shattered by the conversion of the rail tunnel into a road and train combined-use throughway. The upgrade cost the state $80 million, and at two and a half miles it was, until 2007, the longest highway tunnel in the US; it is still the longest combined rail and highway tunnel in North America.

Many of the townsfolk opposed road access, fearing a flood of tourists, but since the tunnel first opened to vehicular traffic their fears seem to have been unfounded. Still, visitor numbers have been slowly increasing, due in part to the abolition in 2003 of a $1-per-passenger cruise-ship tax that had, for the previous ten years, enticed ships to Seward instead. In 2004 a floating bridge near Seattle was moved to Whittier to become its new cruise dock, and was soon bringing in six ships a week.

To adapt to these changes, the town has graveled over railroad sidings to make parking lots and established new businesses along the waterfront. The Forest Service is doing its part by creating a network of hiking trails so that people have some reason to be here other than to get on a cruise. The new road may yet signal Whittier's renaissance, though as one tourist put it, "I went through the longest tunnel in North America and all I got was Whittier."

Some history

Whittier was founded as an alternative ice-free port during World War II, when the profusion of boats waiting to unload cargo onto the Alaska Railroad at Seward was seen as an easy target for Japanese bombers pressing eastward from the Aleutians. Whittier's location at the head of Passage Canal and almost permanent cloud cover made it an ideal location for a secret base. Two tunnels of 5000ft and 13,000ft were bored through the surrounding mountains, and by 1943 a rail link was established to Portage and Anchorage. Soon after the end of the war, the army began consolidating its position by building the six-level **Buckner Building**, now a hollow shell, but once the largest building in Alaska, known as the "city under one roof" with living quarters, shops, rifle range, hospital, morgue, cinema, bowling alley, and swimming pool. The all-in-one design dramatically reduced snow-removal problems in an area notorious for heavy dumps (but offered no protection

The Whittier Tunnel

To drive in or out of Whittier you have to negotiate the single-lane Whittier Tunnel (officially, the Anton Anderson Memorial Tunnel; daily: May–Sept 5.30am–11.15pm; April & Oct 8.30am–8.15pm; Nov–March 8.30am–6.45pm; cars, motorbikes and RVs under 28ft $12, RVs over 28ft $20; toll only charged when Whittier-bound), a previously rail-only passage that was converted to accommodate road traffic as well. The tunnel only handles traffic in one direction at a time. Typically, traffic from Whittier comes through for the first 15 minutes of each hour, and traffic to Whittier from 30 to 45 minutes after each hour, but breaks in the schedule to accommodate trains and maintenance mean that if you turn up at a bad time you may have to wait two hours to get through. Therefore, be sure to check schedules, locally, by phone (☎611-2586 or 472-2640) or online (⊛www.dot.state.ak.us/creg/whittiertunnel), or by tuning to AM530 in Whittier and AM1610 in Portage.

from the 1964 tsunami, which reached the building's third floor). The same principle was applied when the army built the fourteen-story, pastel-toned **Begich Tower**, which is now home to more than half the town's residents. The army pulled out in 1960, and the town passed the days by serving the railroad, the AMHS ferries to Valdez and Cordova, and a few tourists looking to take glacier cruises.

The town, cruises, and kayaking

Whittier's mountains, glaciers, and glistening fjord make a dramatic first impression, but there isn't a great deal to do in town. The only conventional sight is the **Prince William Sound Gateway Museum**, opened in 2005 in the *Anchor Inn* at 100 Whittier St (May to early Sept 9am–10pm, rest of year 11am–5pm; $3); dealing mainly with the military's influence in Alaska, it covers the construction of the tunnel, Lend-Lease flights from Alaska to Siberia, the wreck of the SS *Yukon* off Cape Fairweather in 1946, and the

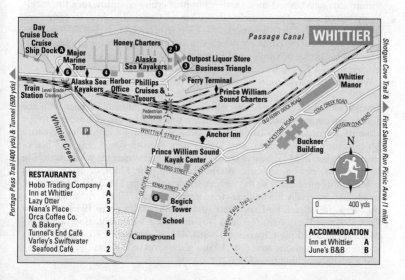

RESTAURANTS	
Hobo Trading Company	4
Inn at Whittier	A
Lazy Otter	5
Nana's Place	3
Orca Coffee Co. & Bakery	1
Tunnel's End Café	6
Varley's Swiftwater Seafood Café	2

ACCOMMODATION	
Inn at Whittier	A
June's B&B	B

Cold War stand-off, when Tupolev bombers probed the US's air defenses and over seventy American spy flights were shot down by the Soviets. Most striking, however, is the display on the Aleutian campaign, with Japanese military photos of the air raid on Dutch Harbor and the occupation of Attu, the westernmost of the Aleutian islands; in May 1943 over 11,000 US troops landed to recapture the island from its garrison of 2600 Japanese, very few of whom survived – many, including the wounded, killed themselves by holding grenades to their chests. The museum consists mainly of photos and text, with relatively few artifacts, but it's quite neatly presented. Once you tire of being indoors, it is worth setting aside an hour or two to enjoy some of the local hikes (see box, p.317), but otherwise you'll want to get out on the water. The AMHS ferry, and almost all of the cruises and kayak trips, initially head across Passage Canal to **Kittiwake Rock**, where ten thousand black-legged kittiwakes nest beside several waterfalls cascading right into the fjord.

Cruises

Biggest and slickest of the local cruises is waterfront-based Phillips' Cruises & Tours' five-hour 26 Glacier Cruise (mid-May to mid-Sept; $109 May & Sept, $129 June–Aug plus tax; ☎472-2416 (Whittier), 276-8023 (Anchorage), or 1-800/544-0529, ⓦwww.26glaciers.com), which makes a 135-mile tour of all of the glaciers in Harriman and College fjords on a remarkably speedy and stable catamaran. Stops are necessarily brief, but you see a lot and have a good chance of spotting wildlife. A snack lunch is included with free tea and coffee, and there's a full bar and gift shop.

Among the slightly less hectic big-boat cruises is Prince William Sound Cruises & Tours (mid-May to mid-Sept; 6hr; $109 plus tax; ☎472-2410 (Whittier), 277-2131 (Anchorage) or 1-800/992-1297, ⓦwww.princewilliamsound.com), at the east corner of the small boat harbor. The tour visits the world's second-largest salmon hatchery, winds through the hairline Esther Passage, and loiters around the tidewater glaciers in Barry Arm, where there are lots of critters to see. From June to early September there's also a four-hour trip ($79) to Blackstone glacier, an active tidewater glacier with a massive face and abundant wildlife in its vicinity. Major Marine Tours, another big-boat cruise company, runs the excellently priced and more leisurely Glacier Lovers Cruise (late May to early Sept; 5hr; $109; ☎472-2356 (Whittier), 274-7300 (Anchorage), or 1-800/764-7300, ⓦwww.majormarine.com), on which you can pay $15 extra for the hearty all-you-can-eat buffet of salmon and prime rib as you visit Blackstone and Beloit glaciers, with a Forest Service ranger on board.

Whereas the above tours all tend to be fairly crowded and cursory, marine wildlife biologist Gerry Sanger of Sound Eco Adventures (☎1-888/471-2312, ⓦwww.soundecoadventure.com) offers much more intimate contact with the aquatic environment, and more time on the water. Using a small boat able to get close in and make beach landings, he covers the main glacier-calving territory on trips into College Fjord (8hr; $165), Barry Arm (5–6hr; $145), and Blackstone Bay (5–6hr; $145), and also plies more peaceful waters for whale-watching (10hr; $195), viewing seabirds on remote islands (8hr; $165), or catching fjord wildlife at its most active in the early morning (over 4hr; $117). It's best to book in advance, especially for multiday trips (from around $750 a day). Similar small-boat trips are offered by Lazy Otter (☎472-6887), who go to Blackstone Bay (3hr; $99) and Barry Arm (4–6hr; $149) and host a whale-watching outing (8–11hr; $199); and Epic Charters (☎1-888/472-3742, ⓦwww.epicchartersalaska .com), who do a glacier tour (3hr; $95), a glacier and wildlife tour (4–6hr; $155), and a whale-watching trip ($195).

Kayaking

In the calm waters of Prince William Sound, you really need no prior experience to join a guided sea-kayaking trip such as those run by ⚓ Prince William Sound Kayak Center on Billings St (☎1-877/472-2452, ⓦwww.pwskayakcenter.com), which runs a number of guided day-trips with an emphasis on passing on skills and preparing customers for future unguided trips. Take the tour across the bay to the Kittiwake Rookery (3hr; from $70 depending on numbers), which provides instruction in the first part of the day and then sends you off to explore the coastline on your own. The full-day Blackstone Bay trip (from $210 each) involves a water-taxi ride, lunch, and plenty of paddling on berg-filled waters. Overnight trips (from $130/person for two days to $210 for four days), bringing your own food and camping gear, are well worth the cost. Those suitably skilled can **rent kayaks** for the day (single $50, double $80), two days ($100/$160), three days ($140/$210), or more.

Alaska Sea Kayakers, at the west end of the harbor, and at the Business Triangle (☎1-877/472-2534, ⓦwww.alaskaseakayakers.com), is a little less instruction-oriented and runs several day-trips: the Kittiwake trip (3hr; $79); the Passage Canal trip (6hr; $120), which heads further out into the fjord; the Shotgun Cove trip (5hr; $175), a five-mile paddle with a return by watertaxi; and the Blackstone Bay trip (full day; $300), using a watertaxi for part of the way in both directions, which gives you the opportunity to paddle around calving tidewater glaciers. They also do kayak rentals at rates comparable to the Prince William Sound Kayak Center's.

The waters of Harriman Fjord, College Fjord, and Blackstone Bay make for one of the most easily accessible and rewarding places for **extended paddling trips** hereabouts. To save a bit of slog getting there, it may be worth loading your boat onto a water taxi. Sound Eco Adventures will oblige: they often try to consolidate parties to reduce costs and will recommend another outfit if they're not available. It is also worth trying Honey Charters (☎1-888/477-2493, ⓦwww.honeycharters.com) down at the Business Triangle, Lazy Otter, Epic Charters, or Whittier Marine Charters (by the *Inn at Whittier*, ☎440-9510, ⓦwww.fishwhittier.com). See opposite page for more information.

Practicalities

With your own vehicle it is now easy enough to **drive to Whittier** through the tunnel (see box, p.313). Cyclists and pedestrians are prohibited, but are catered for by Whittier Shuttle Services (☎632-5974, ⓦwww.myspace.com/whittiershuttle), who pop through the tunnel on the half-hour (Mon–Fri 8am–6pm) to Bear Valley (fare $35 per person, $5 per bike or large backpack), fares including admission to the Begich, Boggs Visitor Center (see p.260) and free coffee at the *Portage Glacier Lodge* (see p.261). The shuttle also runs to Anchorage for $100 ($150 return) by reservation only. All-day **parking** in Whittier costs $5 ($10 overnight).

Transport from Anchorage is available from the major cruise companies (see Basics, opposite) at about $44–45 round-trip by bus, $60–68 by rail. Bus transfers (80min) are provided by The Magic Bus (☎268-6311, ⓦwww.themagicbus.com), leaving the *Captain Cook Hotel* in Anchorage at 11am and returning from the Whittier day-cruise dock at 6pm. The **train** (mid-May to mid-Sept; ☎265-2494 or 1-800/544-0552, ⓦwww.alaskarailroad.com) runs from Anchorage's downtown station (leaving 10am, arriving Whittier 12.20pm) and makes a stop in Girdwood (11.15am en route to Whittier, 7.35pm return to Anchorage). The return train leaves Whittier at 6.45pm, arriving in Anchorage at 9.15pm.

△ Train leaving downtown Whittier

Rental cars are available from Avis at the Harbor Store (☏472-2348 or 1-800/331-1212), where there's also an ATM. In addition, Harley's Rental (☏317-8500, ⓦwww.harleysrentalaska.com) specializes in one-way rentals between Anchorage and Whittier, although these only become worthwhile for three or more days, due to high drop-off fees.

The Alaska Marine Highway System (☏472-2378/2471) operates the new fast **ferry** *Chenega* to Valdez and Cordova on a more or less daily circuit.

The US Forest Service sets up its Backcountry Information Yurt by the small boat harbor from June to mid-Sept (daily 9am–5pm), issuing information on hikes and campsites, maps, and bearproof canisters on loan.

Most cruise and kayak trip departures are timed to coincide with the train and bus schedules, so it is unlikely you'll have to spend more than a couple of hours in town. If you find you need **to stay**, the best bets are: the **campground** ($10 per site; showers at the Harbor Office for $4; early June to Sept), tucked in behind the Begich Tower; *June's B&B* (☏1-888/472-2396, ⓦwww.breadnbuttercharters .com, or c/o the Bread and Butter Charters office by the harbor; ❹), spread over several condos inside the Begich Tower; and, on the waterfront, the new and very flash *Inn At Whittier* (☏1-866/472-5757, ⓦwww.innatwhittier.com; ocean-view rooms with queen-size bed ❽, mountain-view with king-size bed ❾). A new public-use cabin in Squirrel Cove, eight miles east of Whittier in Decision Point State Marine Park and accessible by boat or kayak, is available for $65 per night for up to six people, but needs to be booked in Anchorage.

Most businesses and **restaurants** cluster along the waterfront, either at the Triangle Business Park or behind the small boat harbor. ⚓ *Orca Coffee Co. and Bakery* (☏472-2450) has great views up the fjord and a deck for enjoying salmon chowder, burgers, and espresso. *Varley's Swiftwater Seafood Café* (☏472-2550) serves super-fresh halibut and chips ($10.50) along with bottled microbrews and good coffee (☏472-2550; May–Sept 11.30am–9pm, to 10pm Fri & Sat). Nearby, *Nana's Place* (11am–9pm May to end Oct) is a decent greasy spoon, serving seafood, burgers, and sandwiches. The *Lazy Otter* (☏472-6887)

Make sure you set aside a couple of hours to explore Whittier's developing range of trails. **Hike** ten minutes beyond any trailhead and you won't believe Whittier is just half a mile away.

Horsetail Falls Trail (2 miles round-trip; 1hr to 1hr 30min; 700ft accent). Beautiful trail climbing into an alpine bowl up behind Whittier, mostly on boardwalks and steps. At the treeline you've got great views over the town and across the fjord to Billings Glacier. The trailhead is up behind the Buckner Building, reached by following Cove Creek Road and turning right.

Portage Pass Trail (3 miles round-trip; 2hr; 750ft ascent). A trailhead close to the entrance of the tunnel marks the start of a fairly steep route once followed by gold prospectors, who would climb to the pass and descend across Portage Glacier (a route no longer feasible as the glacier has receded to form Portage Lake). Hike up to Divide Lake and a little further to the top of the pass, from where there are great views back down the fjord, superseded only by those down to the Portage Glacier.

Shotgun Cove Trail (go as far as you want; gently undulating). The first mile along Salmon Run Road east of Whittier is gravel but vehicle-accessible and takes you to the **First Salmon Run** picnic area (1 mile from Whittier), a lovely spot with glacier and fjord views. Beyond there the road becomes impassable to vehicles, so you'll need to strike out on foot along a narrow gravel road to the trailhead proper (3 miles from Whittier). From here the trail sticks more or less to the shoreline with occasional access to the water, with one good viewpoint only fifteen minutes from the trailhead. That's far enough for many people, although the trail just goes on and on, enabling you to make a full day of it if you wish.

has a friendly little café serving good coffee, soups, sandwiches, and pastries. Local renegade and political activist Babs serves burgers, sandwiches, pies, and ice cream (among other treats) from a glassed-in cabin known as the *Hobo Trading Company* (☎472-2374; mid-May to mid-Sept; closed Tues), overlooking the small boat harbor. Further west at 12 Harbor Loop Rd, the *Tunnel's End Café* (☎472-3000) serves espresso, breakfasts of eggs (around $5) or pancakes, lunches of soups, Philly cheesesteak sandwich ($7.50), or halibut burger ($8), and dinners such as chicken alfredo, tempura shrimp (both $11), or halibut cake (starter $8/main $30). The *Inn At Whittier* has a swanky restaurant with great fjord views.

There is a **post office** (Mon, Wed, Fri 9am–3pm) on the first floor of the Begich Tower, together with the *Rolling Pin Bakery* (☎472-2562; 7am–noon daily; also Fri & Sat 5–8pm for pizza and dessert); a grocery store (9am–10pm in summer) and laundry at the *Anchor Inn* on Whittier Street; and **ATMs** in the Outpost Liquor Store at the Business Triangle and the Harbor Store. Whittier does not have a bank. A **health clinic** is on the third floor of the Begich Tower (Mon, Tues, Thurs, Fri 10am–1pm, 2–6pm; ☎472-2303/2485, after-hours 632-7225, emergency 911 or 472-7999).

Valdez and around

VALDEZ possesses one of the most remarkably picturesque settings in Alaska, nestled under some of the world's tallest coastal mountains on the shores of Valdez Arm, a curving tentacle threading twelve miles north off Prince William Sound. A small town without a great deal to actually see, Valdez (Val-DEEZ) easily makes up for its nondescript nature by its proximity to some wonderful cruising and sea-kayaking waters and the stupendous **Columbia Glacier**.

There are fewer than five thousand residents in Valdez but its status as North America's northernmost ice-free port has brought it considerable prosperity, largely as the southern terminus for the trans-Alaska oil pipeline. Tankers seem almost perpetually moored across the water at the Alyeska Marine Terminal, a constant reminder that the **Exxon Valdez disaster** (see box, p.322) happened just a few miles away.

But the oil spill was only the latest chapter in a catalog of grim events to have befallen Valdez over the years. The first was in 1897, when the Klondike gold rush inspired thousands of ill-prepared prospectors to set off north from Valdez Arm, an arduous journey that rewarded precious few (see box, opposite). Soon after, a potential boost came with the 1900 discovery of huge deposits of copper at Kennicott (see p.457), a hundred miles to the northeast. When a railroad was proposed to transport the copper to a port, Cordova and Valdez battled over the privilege, with a gunfight even taking place in Keystone Canyon between rival rail companies. Valdez eventually lost the battle and life passed by quietly until 1964, when the area was struck by the **Good Friday earthquake**, the most powerful on record in North America (see box, p.590). The ensuing tsunami claimed 33 lives and destroyed the town, which was subsequently rebuilt on more stable ground four miles to the west. Although a few interesting, original buildings were relocated to the new site, the modern, characterless town you see today is one of the quake's legacies. Valdez's fortunes momentarily improved when it was selected as the southern terminus of the Trans-Alaska Pipeline, whose construction began in 1974. The building of the pipeline and the huge oil terminal brought boom times to the town, but everything was about to change. On Good Friday 1989, the *Exxon Valdez* catapulted the town into world headlines, when the fully laden tanker struck Bligh Reef at the entrance to Valdez Arm, exactly 25 years after the 1964 earthquake. Since then, Valdez has settled back into a fairly sleepy existence, trying to lure visitors as a hedge against the day when the oil stops flowing; cruise liners no longer call, due to the town's poor infrastructure, but there's hope that small ships will return as the Wrangell-St Elias National Park becomes a greater attraction.

Although the main attraction for visitors is the Columbia Glacier and the surrounding islands and bays of Prince William Sound, there is interest on land with a couple of diverting museums and a few spots for salmon-viewing. Inland the Richardson Highway heads through the rafting waters of Keystone Canyon towards the glacial heights of Thompson Pass. The scattered nature of these land-based sights means you really need your own vehicle to get around. If you prefer to travel by skis, snowboard, or other snow-sports equipment, you've come to the right place: the 7000-foot barrier of the Chugach Mountains encourages storms to dump an average of 27ft of snow – and a record 46ft in 1989–90 – on the town each winter.

Arrival and information

AMHS **ferries** from Valdez and Cordova cruise past the amazing Columbia Glacier and right up Valdez Arm and dock at the ferry terminal (T835-4436), a quarter of a mile west of downtown Valdez. Arriving **by road** from Glennallen is equally spectacular on the most dramatic section of the Richardson Highway, where it negotiates the towering Chugach Mountains; our account starts on p.468. Alaska/Yukon Trails (T1-800/770-7275, Wwww .alaskashuttle.com) will run a charter bus down the Richardson Highway from Fairbanks to Valdez if enough people book.

Valdez's first ice climbers

During the Klondike gold rush of 1897, American gold-seekers quickly became wary of Canadian regulations and taxes on the White Pass and Chilkoot trails from Skagway to the Yukon. So there was a ready audience when the *Seattle Post-Intelligencer* reported that the **All-American Route** from Valdez Arm to the Interior was not only two hundred miles shorter than other routes but "altogether in American territory . . . and said to be not difficult." No one mentioned that Valdez was just a handful of tents set on mudflats, or the need to cross the Valdez and Klutina glaciers over a twenty-mile route riddled with killer crevasses. Roughly 3500 prospectors set off from Valdez, and as one gold seeker put it, "It was a wonderful sight to stand on the summit of that glacier five thousand feet above the sea and look back eighteen miles to the coast and see the black serpent of humanity winding its way over the snow and ice like a huge snake." Gold fever outweighed prudence, and most set off entirely unprepared, with hundreds dying of starvation and scurvy. Those who tried to hike during the day struggled desperately through the soft snow or succumbed to snow blindness and groped unseeing into gaping crevasses. Most were forced to travel at night with minimal protection from the terrible cold. Relatively few prospectors reached the Klondike in time to stake a paying claim, and of those, many arrived in such bad health that they died before breaking ground. The All-American Route remained in use until 1899, when it was replaced by more sensible alternatives.

The fast **ferry** *Chenega* comes almost daily from Whittier, often continuing to Cordova; the AMHS booking office is at the ferry terminal at the end of Hazelet Avenue (☎835-4436). The only scheduled **flights** into Valdez are with ERA Aviation (☎1-800/866-8394, ⓦwww.flyera.com), which flies direct from Anchorage (from $90 plus tax each way) three times daily to Valdez airport, four miles east of town along Airport Road. A **taxi** into town with Valdez Yellow Cab (☎835-2500) will cost around $10. For more flexibility, visit the airport **rental car** office of Valdez-U-Drive (☎835-4402 or 1-800/478-4402 in Alaska, ⓦwww.valdezudrive.com), which charges around $50 a day for a compact.

Once in town, you can access everything on foot from the central **visitor center**, 200 Fairbanks St (mid-June to mid-Sept Mon–Fri 8am–7pm, Sat 9am–6pm, Sun 10am–5pm; ☎1-800/770-5954, ⓦwww.valdezalaska .org), which has a free map of town and informational flyers, and can answer questions and book accommodation for you. Outside there's a free phone linked to some of the town's B&Bs. In winter, information is available from the **CVB** (year-round Mon–Fri 8.30am–5pm) in the same building. Valdez Accommodations & Attractions (owned by Stan Stephens Cruises; ☎835-4731, 1-866/867-1297, ⓦwww.valdez-alaska.com) is a local booking service for accommodation, sights, and tours, including their own cruises. Bikes are available for rent in Valdez; see p.328.

Accommodation

Traditional **accommodation** is fairly expensive in Valdez, though you'll find more satisfying and cheaper rooms at the assortment of downtown and neighborhood **B&Bs**, the descendants of the city's first crop, which sprang up during the *Exxon Valdez* clean-up when there weren't enough beds to go round for the hordes of volunteers. In high summer downtown is swamped with RVs occupying soulless, if well-placed, gravel lots. The nearest leafy **campground** is five miles away; signs downtown discourage free camping, but for one-night stays creative campers should find a quiet spot a mile or so west of the center along

Mineral Creek. If the recommendations below prove fruitless, try contacting the handy Independent Network of B&Bs (Ⓦ www.valdezbnbnetwork.com). There's a six percent tax on accommodation, not included in our price codes.

Hotels and B&Bs

Aspen Hotel 100 Meals Ave ⓣ 1-800/478-4445, Ⓦ www.aspenhotelsak.com. Behind the boxy exterior are 102 spacious rooms, all with fridge, coffeemaker, microwave, VCR, hairdryer, WiFi, and dataport; breakfast is included, and there's an indoor swimming pool and spa, gym, and laundry. The hotel website gives far cheaper deals than the rack rate quoted here. ⓺

Downtown B&B Inn 113 Galena Drive ⓣ 1-800/478-2791, Ⓦ www.alaskaone.com/downinn. Small, reasonably priced hotel open all year with a handy downtown location and a substantial continental breakfast (mid-May to mid-Sept only). A little shabby in places, but there's cable TV and some of the newer rooms have private bath. Private bath ⓹, shared ⓸

Keystone Hotel 401 W Egan Drive ⓣ 1-888/835-0665, Ⓦ www.keystonehotel.com. Modern hotel with steel-clad exterior and well-appointed but small rooms, all of which come with private bathrooms, TV, and a complimentary continental breakfast. ⓸

L&L's B&B 533 W Hanagita St ⓣ 835-4447, Ⓦ www.lnlalaska.com. Comfortable five-room B&B with shared bathrooms in a modern home a ten-minute walk from the center. There are bikes for getting around and a good self-serve breakfast. ⓷

Lake House Lake House Rd, Mile 5.9 Richardson Hwy ⓣ 835-4752, Ⓦ www.geocities.com/lakehousevaldez. Lovely and very welcoming B&B about ten miles east of Valdez, run by John Devens, who was mayor of Valdez when the *Exxon Valdez* went aground. The comfortable rooms are all en suite, and most have balconies overlooking Robe Lake. There's also a hot tub and a good help-yourself continental breakfast. ⓺

Valdez Harbor Inn 100 N Harbor Drive ⓣ 1-888/222-3440, Ⓦ www.valdezharborinn.com. A *Best Western*, this has 88 recently renovated rooms with cable TV, DVD player, microwave and fridge, and king business rooms with desk and DSL Internet access; there's free WiFi, a gym, laundry, and a great waterside location. The best views are reserved for the restaurant/bar. ⓺

Hostels and camp-grounds

Allison Point Ocean Front Campground Mile 5 Dayville Rd ⓣ 835-2282, Ⓦ www.valdezcampgrounds.com. Gravel RV sites ($10) with water and outhouses, and most sites wedged between Dayville Rd and the bay. Oil-terminal traffic makes it less than peaceful, but the view is great. Late May to early Sept.

Bear Paw Camper Park 101 N Harbor Drive ⓣ 835-2530, Ⓦ www.bearpawrvpark.com. Not the cheapest of the downtown RV parks ($20 dry, $25 full hookup), but it's in a great location and has a heated, indoor sitting area with modem jacks. There's also a more sedate, adult-only area ($5 extra), plus a tent section ($17–20) in the alders away from the RVs.

Valdez Glacier Campground Mile 2.3 Airport Rd ⓣ 835-2282, Ⓦ www.valdezcampgrounds.com. Spacious and leafy, Valdez's only rural campground is located five miles east of town, by the airport. Sites ($10) are well spaced with picnic tables and fire rings. Mid-May to mid-Sept.

The town and around Valdez Arm

Perched beside a deep fjord in its mountain-ringed setting, Valdez can be a great place just to walk around, perhaps along the Overlook Trail or the Dock Point Trail (see box, p.326) to gain a better vantage or heading for the small boat harbor later in the day when huge halibut are landed and strung up.

About the only distraction in town is the **Valdez Museum**, 217 Egan Drive (mid-May to early Sept daily 9am–6pm; early Sept to mid-May Mon–Fri 1–5pm, Sat noon–4pm; $5; Ⓦ www.valdezmuseum.org), sitting behind one of the pipeline's ubiquitous scraper pigs (a hefty pipe-cleaning tool), a fire bell, and two boats. It's an eclectic regional collection with the old Fresnel lens from the Hinchinbrook Lighthouse at the entrance to Prince William Sound, a field gun from Fort Liscum, which closed in 1922 and is now the Alyeska Marine Terminal, and the superb, mirror-backed Pinzon Bar from a pre-quake Valdez saloon. Notice the copper panel covering the holes in the bar that were cut for soda siphons during Prohibition. Photos of yesteryear on display show prospectors crossing the Valdez Glacier in 1898 and the effect of the 1964 earthquake, while others from the big-snow winter of 1989–90 illustrate just how much of a problem snow clearance can be. There's even a .75-inch-thick piece of the hull from the *Exxon Valdez*, which was all that stood between 53 million gallons of crude and a pristine marine environment; now all tankers coming into Valdez are double-hulled. A new exhibit on the area's native cultures is due to open; check the website for further information.

The **Remembering Old Valdez** exhibit, in an annex at 436 S Hazelet Ave (June–Aug daily 9am–6pm, winter by appointment; $1.50), is more focused than the Valdez Museum, dominated by a huge and historically accurate model of Valdez as it was in 1963, before the earthquake. It's worth watching the whole of the 45-minute *Though the Earth Moved* video, of the 1964 earthquake, if only to see the 8mm footage shot from aboard the oil tanker *Chena*, which was moored at Valdez dock. Despite being buffeted by huge waves, then having the sea sucked out from under them, two crew members somehow managed to keep filming throughout.

Once upon a time you could tour the Alyeska Marine Terminal across the bay, but due to security concerns you now have to make do with the **Alaska Pipeline Media Tour and Exhibit** (May to mid-Sept daily 9.30am, 11.30am & 1.30pm; $5, or $7 in combination with the Whitney Museum; T834-1600) at the Community College, 303 Lowe St. Along with coverage of the pipeline and oil terminal, there is material on the tankers and the wildlife of Prince William Sound. On a warm afternoon it's a pleasant half-mile wander along East Egan Drive to the **Crooked Creek Salmon Viewing Platform** (unrestricted access). Located on the site of a former hatchery, it's still a good place to spot pink and chum salmon, especially during spawning season from mid-July to October. In summer the Forest Service installs a temporary cabin (T835-4680; late May to early Sept 9am–6pm) with a ranger and a book and gift shop.

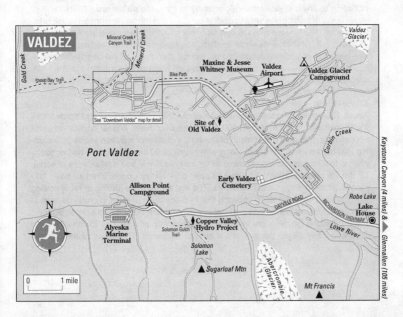

In the American public consciousness the name Valdez isn't so much associated with the town as with the 987-foot oil tanker *Exxon Valdez*, which struck Bligh Reef, 25 miles to the southwest of Valdez, in 1989. It spilled almost eleven million gallons of North Slope crude over ten thousand square miles of Prince William Sound, rapidly becoming the biggest and most catastrophic **oil spill** in US history. Images of oil-smothered birds and slick black beaches flashed around the globe, and the State of Alaska looked on as if paralyzed. More than a decade later, Prince William Sound seems as unspoiled as ever, but scratch below the surface (at least on the beaches) and evidence of the ongoing effects – oil beneath a layer of sand and rocks – is easy to find, a realization revived every time a new round of legal wrangling over settlement hits the media outlets.

The spill

On the evening of Good Friday, March 23, 1989, the *Exxon Valdez* left port with a full load, and within a couple of hours had to take evasive action to avoid an iceberg that had calved off the Columbia Glacier. After issuing instructions, hot-shot tanker captain **Joseph Hazelwood** had gone below – a common enough practice, considering all the paperwork he had to complete – leaving an inexperienced third mate in charge. At 12.04am Hazelwood reported, "We've fetched up hard aground north of Goose Island off Bligh Reef, and evidently leaking some oil." As soon as the disaster happened, Exxon hired a PR company, which locked onto Hazelwood as a convenient scapegoat, especially when it was reported that he had been drinking at the *Pipeline Inn* immediately before taking command. Remedial action would have been more useful, but the sole response barge was under fourteen feet of snow, delaying the clean-up team for three days. In 1993 a report on the incident by the State of Alaska described the response as "botched"; a tenth-anniversary report stated that:

Eleven million gallons of oil spread slowly over open water during three days of flat calm seas. Despite the opportunity to skim the oil before it hit the shorelines, almost none was scooped up . . . Even if [the response barge] had responded, there were not enough skimmers and booms available to do an effective job. Dispersants were applied, but were determined to be ineffective because of prevailing conditions. Even if dispersants had been effective, however, there was not enough dispersant on hand to make a dent in the spreading oil slick.

The effects

About 1300 miles of coastline were befouled – 200 miles badly – and some slicks found their way to shore almost 500 miles from Bligh Reef. Animal population studies estimate, that as a direct result of the spill, a quarter of a million seabirds, including 200 bald eagles, perished, along with nearly 3000 sea otters, 300 harbor seals, and up to 22 orcas. Salmon streams as far away as Kenai and Kodiak were affected. Of the 28 species affected by the oil spill, only two are considered to have fully recovered: bald eagles and river otters. The rest are all still suffering or recuperating in some way, with one study showing that hydrocarbons present in crude oil even at concentrations as low as one part per billion can harm herring and salmon eggs.

Ten thousand people were involved in the clean-up at a cost to Exxon of around $2 billion. Only eleven percent of the oil was recovered. The futility of the process was highlighted by Alutiiq village chief Walter Meganack, who described spending "all day cleaning one huge rock, and the tide comes in and covers it with oil again. Spend a week wiping and spraying the surface, but pick up a rock and there's four inches of oil underneath."

In Native villages, subsistence-hunting for seals and the harvest of herring eggs from kelp were ruined for years, and many residents fled to Valdez, some getting jobs on oil-spill response crews. The 1989 commercial fishing season never began, and fish stocks were hurt for years. The $12 million herring fishery was closed from 1993 to 1996 – a rash of ulcers and a virus causing the harvest to crash from an all-time high in 1992 to an all-time low the next year – and again in 1999.

Although some say fish stocks are still showing signs of damage, with the passage of time and widespread over-fishing, among other factors, it is increasingly difficult to blame the oil spill for the woes of the local industry. In 1994 the state produced a Restoration Plan, allocating $22 million for a Sound Ecosystems Assessment project, which has produced interesting results showing that the Gulf of Alaska began to experience a decadal climate shift back in 1978, its waters warming and becoming dominated by cod and pollock in place of shrimp; from around 1996–98 the waters began cooling again and the cod and pollock are declining. This further complicates the science of assessing the spill's effects.

The current situation

Change has been forced by federal and state laws and newly created monitoring organizations, such as the Prince William Sound Regional Citizens' Advisory Council (@www.pwsrcac.org), a permanent, industry-funded citizens' group which struggles to maintain its independence from industry lobbyists. Prince William Soundkeeper (℡835-5503, @www.pwsoundkeeper.org) is more independent and more effective. Today Prince William Sound has more weather buoys than any similar body of water in the world, the coast guard monitors a much wider area, and the oil companies, under the eye of the Advisory Council, are testing an innovative submerged-iceberg detection system. Other changes include the introduction of a powerful and highly maneuverable escort tug to guide boats in from as far as the entrance to Prince William Sound, drug and alcohol tests for tanker captains before sailing, improved oil skimming and storage capability, and regular response drills.

Meanwhile, Exxon has wrestled in the courts over restitution. In 1991 Exxon, the federal government, and the State of Alaska reached an out-of-court settlement requiring Exxon to pay the other two parties $100 million in criminal restitution for fish, wildlife, and lands, and $900 million as a **civil settlement** with payments spread over ten years. Forty thousand commercial fishers and other parties who suffered as a result of the spill then joined forces in a class-action suit against Exxon. In 1994 a jury awarded them $5.2 billion. Exxon immediately appealed and, though this money has been put in escrow and is gaining interest, the fishers have seen little of it. In December 2002 an appeals judge reduced the award to $4 billion, but still the fishermen, or the 30,000 who are still alive, wait. In 2006 the case again went before the US Court of Appeals in San Francisco, which further reduced the payment to $2.5 billion, partly in an effort to end the ongoing deliberations. Though Exxon Mobil (as it's now named) continues to make appeals and to salvage its sullied public image, there's little sympathy for the corporation, which made a world-record profit of $36 billion in 2005.

From Valdez waterside roads run along both sides of Valdez Arm, providing access to a few minor sights and plenty of great views. Drive along East Egan Drive four miles to Mile Zero of the Richardson Highway, where Alaska Avenue runs down to the **Old Townsite**, little more than a couple of building foundations and a memorial plaque. On the other side of the Richardson Highway, Airport Road runs a mile to the airport, where you'll find the **Maxine & Jesse Whitney Museum** (May to mid-Sept daily 9.30am–7pm; winter by appointment; $5, or $7 in combination with the Pipeline Media Tour; ☎834-1614, ⓦ www.pwscc.edu/museum.shtml), which contains one of the finest collections of sculpted ivory and Eskimo artifacts in the state. The enormous stuffed bull moose, caribou, bison, and polar bear loom over beautifully made mukluks, a parka of ground-squirrel pelts, another of murre skins, and a large umiak with ribs of whale baleen. Two moose hides decorated with mountain scenes are hung next to each other to illustrate the changing Alaskan landscape. The images are thought to be of the same subject: the first (undated) of a cabin in the newly tamed wilderness, and the second a few years later (1913) of the cabin in disrepair and moose reclaiming the territory. The ivory room is crammed with pieces veering well away from the typical walrus-tusk cribbage boards, ranging from grotesque figures traditionally used to ward off evil spirits to a model of a PanAm 747 carved in the 1970s.

Some seven miles out of town along the Richardson Highway (Mile 2.9), Dayville Road cuts around the head of the bay and, four miles on, reaches the **Solomon Gulch Hatchery** and the diminutive **Copper Valley Hydro Project**, which channels water from high-country lakes through turbines, providing power to Valdez and Glennallen. The penstocks above the power station can be seen on the **Solomon Gulch Trail** (see box, p.326), which starts a mile further on by the *Allison Point* RV park. The road finishes at the Alyeska Marine Terminal (no access), built on the site of the former Fort Liscum, the terminus of the WAMCATS telegraph wire to Eagle (see box, p.484) from 1900 to 1923.

△ Oil tanker loading at the pipeline terminus, Valdez

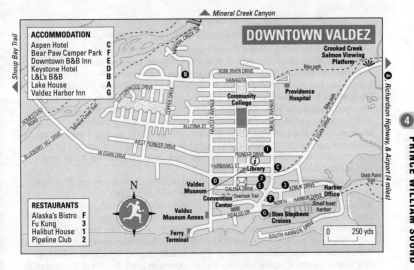

DOWNTOWN VALDEZ

ACCOMMODATION
Aspen Hotel C
Bear Paw Camper Park F
Downtown B&B Inn E
Keystone Hotel D
L&L's B&B B
Lake House A
Valdez Harbor Inn G

RESTAURANTS
Alaska's Bistro F
Fu Kung 3
Halibut House 1
Pipeline Club 2

Mineral Creek Canyon

Crooked Creek
Salmon Viewing
Platform

Bike path

ROBE RIVER DRIVE

HANAGITA

MINERAL CREEK DR.

Providence
Hospital

Community
College

MEALS AVENUE

COPPER DRIVE

HAZELET AVENUE

COTTONWOOD DRIVE

KLUTINA ST.

E EGAN DRIVE

Bike path

WEST PIONEER DRIVE

PIONEER DRIVE

W EGAN DRIVE

FAIRBANKS ST.

Library

GALENA DRIVE

KOBUK DRIVE

Harbor
Office

Valdez
Museum

Convention
Center

Overlook Trail

NORTH HARBOR DRIVE

Small boat
harbor

FIDALGO DR.

Stan Stephens
Cruises

Valdez
Museum Annex

SOUTH HARBOR DRIVE

Ferry
Terminal

N

HOMESTEAD ROAD

BLUEBERRY HILL DRIVE

Mineral Creek Trail

Shoup Bay Trail

Richardson Highway & Airport (4 miles)

Dock Point
Trail

0   250 yds

4

PRINCE WILLIAM SOUND | Valdez and around

Cruises and outdoor activities

You really haven't experienced the best of Valdez until you've been out on the water, either on a cruise to Prince William Sound and the Columbia Glacier or on a kayak trip around Valdez Arm and beyond. Fishing and whitewater rafting round out the aquatic activities, or you could just take a helicopter flight over the whole lot. On land there are some pleasant, short-ish hikes (see box, p.326), and if you come in winter, the extreme skiing and boarding is second to none (see box, p.327).

Cruises

Valdez is superbly placed for cruises out to Prince William Sound. The most popular are those with Stan Stephens Glacier & Wildlife Cruises, based at the *Valdez Harbor Inn* (T 1-866/867-1297, W www.stanstephenscruises.com), which offers two options. The Columbia Glacier Cruise (mid-May to mid-Sept daily; 6–7hr; $90) mainly visits the glacier, but there's usually plenty of time for watching whales or whatever else makes an appearance. The Columbia and Meares Glacier Cruise (June to Aug daily; 9hr; $130) also takes in the advancing Meares Glacier.

For a small boat, a more leisurely approach, and plenty of whale-watching, try a five-hour cruise ($75) aboard the *Lu-Lu Belle* with Glacier Charter Service (Kobuk Drive; T 1-800/411-0090, W www.lulubelletours.com), which also visits Columbia Glacier. There's even an opportunity to attend the Chapel of the Sea, a one-hour cruise (Sun 8am) with a nondenominational service at sea (free, but a collection is taken).

Kayaking

Although the cruises in the area are excellent, there's an undeniably more intimate feel aboard a kayak. One of the most popular destinations is **Shoup Glacier**, which drains out into Valdez Arm eight miles west of Valdez. Like most Alaskan glaciers, it is currently retreating, but over the centuries it has made two significant advance-and-retreat cycles, leaving two terminal moraines and

325

Hiking and biking around Valdez

Much of the best hiking around Valdez requires a vehicle for access, but there are a couple of good hikes that start right in town. These should be largely snow-free from early June to late September. **Mountain bikers** can explore the first mile of the Shoup Bay Trail, but are better off on the approach to Mineral Creek Canyon.

Dock Point Trail (1 mile loop; 30min; 100ft ascent). A peaceful nature walk on gravel trails and boardwalks with interpretive signs. It leads from the east end of the small boat harbor to a knoll and a couple of viewpoints looking across the bay.

Mineral Creek Canyon Trail (2 miles round-trip; 1hr; 100ft ascent). Pretty decent trail leading up to the abandoned gold stamp mill of Hercules Mine near the base of the Johnson Glacier. Drive the rough six-mile road up to the trailhead, if you have a high-clearance vehicle, or bike up there.

Overlook Trail (100 yards; 5min; mostly steps). A flight of steps running off Clifton Drive leads up to a shelter with great views over town and Valdez Arm.

Shoup Bay Trail (20 miles round-trip; 1–2 days; mostly flat). Beautiful, easy (but long) hike along the shores of Port Valdez to Shoup Bay, where the face of Shoup Glacier is the view for three beautifully sited, eight-bunk state park **cabins** ($50 off-peak/$65 peak; book through the Department of Natural Resources in Anchorage ☎269-8400, check availability on ⓦwww.dnr.state.ak.us/parks/cabins/pws.cfm). The hike is particularly good for keen birders, although direct access to the shores of the fjord is limited.

Solomon Gulch Trail (3.8 miles round-trip; 1hr 30min to 2hr 30min; 620ft ascent). Starting thirteen miles from Valdez on the road to the pipeline terminal, the trail initially follows the gravel road laid atop the penultimate mile of the oil pipeline as far as Solomon Gulch. Surplus tubing from the pipeline was used for hydro-station penstocks, which are followed to the glacial waters behind the Solomon Gulch Dam, overlooked by Sugarloaf Mountain (3484ft) and a distant glacier at the end of the lake.

creating Shoup Bay. At high tide you can paddle up from Shoup Bay to the lake immediately below the glacier and come close (but not too close) to the face. As you bob around on the opaque, gray-green water, thick with brash ice, it feels like you're floating on a giant frozen margarita. Through most of the summer, one prominent rock is completely covered by some twenty thousand black-legged **kittiwakes** that nest here. It is even possible to stay in one of the three Alaska State Parks cabins nearby, which share an outstanding view (see box, above).

Two companies, both with offices along North Harbor Drive, offer nearly identical **kayaking** trips: Anadyr Adventures at no 225 (☎1-800/865-2925, ⓦwww.anadyradventures.com), and Pangaea Adventures at no 107 (☎1-800/660-9637, ⓦwww.alaskasummer.com). Visit both to see which company has the best deals and a schedule that fits your timetable.

Anyone after a gentle paddle with opportunities for spotting seals, sea lions, and shorebirds should opt for the Duck Flats trip (3–4hr; $55), or the more ambitious coastal paddle to Gold Creek (6–7hr; $75–80). It is really worth dedicating the time and money to reach distant paddling destinations, principally Shoup Glacier (8hr; $150) and Columbia Glacier (10hr; $185–199), access to which can be assisted by water taxi.

Both companies also offer **kayak rentals** (single $45 per day, double $65, triple $80), the rates for which reduce by $5–10 a day after the first or second day. Anadyr and Pangaea also have multiday guided trips, either camping out, based at a remote lodge, or using a mother ship for sleeping and getting between paddling spots: for more details see the company websites and Basics (p.32).

Fishing, rafting, and helicopter flightseeing

During summer Valdez holds two **fishing derbies** (ⓦwww.valdezfishderbies
.com) – one for halibut (mid-May to Aug), the other for silver salmon (Aug)
– both with prizes of $15,000 for the biggest fish caught during the derby
period, as well as daily prizes. Both end with the Spawn 'til Dawn party the first
weekend in September. To participate, you'll need a ticket ($10 a day or $50 a
season per species), available from several stores and campgrounds around town.
The small boat harbor is full of boats ready to take you out to catch that winner;
try Northern Comfort Charters (Kobuk Drive at Meals Ave; ☎1-800/478-
9884, ⓦwww.northerncomfortcharter.com), which charges a competitive $125
for a half-day of salmon fishing and $225 for the full day necessary to get out
to good halibut waters.

Keystone Raft & Kayak Adventures (☎1-800/328-8460, ⓦwww
.alaskawhitewater.com) runs **whitewater-rafting** trips on the Lowe River
through Keystone Canyon (June–Aug; $45) with an hour on the water tack-
ling predominantly Class III–IV rapids and floating under dramatic waterfalls,
and longer trips in Class IV rivers including the Tsaina (3hr; $85), the Tonsina
(all day; $125), and the Tana, in the Wrangell Mountains (4 days; $1200).

For **flightseeing**, go with ERA Helicopters, at the airport (☎1-800/843-1947,
ⓦwww.alaskaone.com/eracopters), whose Prince William Sound Safari (1hr;
$240) heads out over the Columbia Glacier and lands briefly beside Shoup Bay.

Eating and drinking

Valdez has several perfectly adequate eateries, some with harbor views, and
a couple of dark bars to keep you entertained in the evening. **Groceries**,

---

Winter in Valdez

Valdez likes to promote itself as "Snow Capital of Alaska," and with good reason:
with an average of 27ft of snowfall per year, it gets more than any other town in
Alaska and more than any other seaside town in the world. A few miles inland in
the Chugach Mountains, that number almost triples, and the dense, wet quality
of coastal snow makes this perfect territory for extreme skiing in ludicrously steep
chutes. There's also some wonderful heli-skiing on more forgiving slopes. No one has
built any permanent downhill skiing facilities, but there is plenty of scope for snowmobiling, backcountry skiing, and dog-mushing around Valdez, or ice climbing on
the waterfalls of Keystone Canyon. The main heli-skiing operators are Alaska Backcountry Adventures (☎1-888/283-9354, ⓔbcountry@ptialaska.net), Alaska Rendezvous Heli-Guides (☎822-3300, reservation 307/734-0721, 1-888/634-0721, ⓦwww
.airlinc.com), H2O Heli-Guides (☎835-8418, ⓦwww.h2oguides.com), and Valdez
Heli-Camps (☎783-3243, ⓦwww.alaska.net/~heliski). For a list of other operators,
obtain the free annual *Valdez Vacation Guide* from the Valdez visitor center (or visit
ⓦwww.valdezalaska.org).

A good way to organize a winter trip to Valdez is to synchronize your visit with
one of the town's **winter festivals**, which start in early March with the Valdez Ice
Climbing Festival (ⓦwww.alaskagold.com/ice), continue in late March with the Alaskan Local Snowboarding Championships, and conclude with the Mountain Master
Extreme Snowboard Competition during the first two weeks of April. Although it's
nearly impossible to see any of the extreme skiing or snowboarding up close, just
being in town for the associated activities and partying is excuse enough for a visit.
Snowmobile fans will want to check out some of the regular events run by the Valdez
Snowmachine Club (ⓦwww.valdezsnow.com) from January to April, especially the

along with deli selections, baked goods, and espresso are available from the two supermarkets, the better being the Eagle Quality Center (a Safeway; open 4.30am–midnight), on Pioneer Drive at Meals Avenue.

Alaska Halibut House 208 Meals Ave ☎ 835-2788. Budget halibut sandwiches, salmon wedges, chicken nuggets, and assorted fried goodies, mostly for under $6 and served in spartan surroundings.

Alaska's Bistro In the *Valdez Harbor Inn* ☎ 835-5688, ⓦ www.alaskasbistro.com. Tasty, well-presented food in a range of styles, and a wonderful harbor-view setting make this the pick of Valdez's restaurants. Loosely Mediterranean in style, the menu ranges from deluxe burgers and bar snacks to crab-stuffed halibut ($25) and shrimp and scallops over pasta ($22). There's an extensive wine list, too. Closed in winter for lunch and Mon & Tues nights.

Fu Kung 207 Kobuk St ☎ 835-5255. Korean-run restaurant dishing up mainstream Mandarin,

Szechwan, Cantonese, and Japanese, plus several set dinners for $14–19 per person.

The Pipeline Club 112 W Egan Drive ☎ 835-4444. Dim booths in a room off the main bar create a suitable ambience for this oil-boom survivor. It's still a favorite of the tanker crews, who come for the menu of top-quality steak and seafood that features a 12oz filet mignon dinner ($28), a salmon, shrimp, halibut, and scallop combo ($23), and the Pipeline Pu Pu house special – sliced steak sautéed with onion, bell pepper, tomatoes, and soy sauce on a bed of rice that's a bargain at $16. Burgers and sandwiches can be had at the bar, which is the most likely place in town to find live bands and dancing.

Listings

Banks and exchange Valdez has only two banks: Wells Fargo, 337 Egan Drive (☎ 835-4745), and First National Bank, 101 Egan Drive (☎ 834-4800). Both have 24hr ATMs (also at the airport).

Bike rental Anadyr Adventures on N Harbor Drive (☎ 835-2814) offers bikes for $8/hr or $30/day.

Camping equipment The Prospector, 141 Galena Drive (Mon–Fri 9am–8pm, Sat 9am–7pm, Sun noon–6pm; ☎ 835-3858), targets the hunting and fishing set but also stocks good standard gear that can be a bargain.

Festivals Most of the major annual events happen in winter (see box, p.327), but the May Day Fly-In is an air show on the last weekend of April or the first of May, with cheap scenic flights from $25 and events like flour-bombing competitions. The Last Frontier Theater Conference (☎ 834-1615, ⓦ www .pwscc.edu/conference), in late June, is earning a reputation beyond the state border, especially for its long-standing association with noted playwright Edward Albee, who usually attends. New plays by Alaskan writers are read and performed along with an Albee piece or two.

Internet access Free access at the library (see below); there's WiFi at Anadyr Adventures, some RV parks, and the *Valdez Harbor Inn*.

Laundry and showers Like Home Laundromat, Valdez Mall, 121 Egan Drive (daily 8am–9pm, to 8pm winter; ☎ 835-2913), has washers, dryers, and showers; the Habormaster's office on N Harbor Drive (Sept to mid-May 8.30am–5pm; mid-May to Aug 8am–10.30pm) offers ten-minute showers for $4.

Library Valdez Library, 200 Fairbanks St (Mon & Fri 10am–6pm, Tues–Thurs 10am–8pm, Sat noon–5pm; ⓦ www.ci.valdez.ak.us/library), has a good selection of books and free Internet access by the hour.

Medical assistance Providence Valdez Medical Center, 911 Meals Ave at E Hanagita (☎ 835-2249, ⓦ www.providence.org/alaska/valdez).

Pharmacy Village Pharmacy, in the Eagle Quality Center, Pioneer Drive at Meals Ave (Mon–Thurs 9am–6pm, Fri 9am–7pm, Sat 10am–noon).

Post office Galena Drive at Tatitlek St (Mon–Fri 9am–5pm, Sat 10am–noon; ☎ 835-4449). The **General Delivery** zip code is 99686.

Taxes There is no sales tax in Valdez; there is a hotel tax of six percent, additional to our quoted prices for accommodation.

North along the Richardson: Keystone Canyon and Thompson Pass

The site of old Valdez marks the beginning of the **Richardson Highway** (for more on the origins of this important artery, see box, p.470), sections of

Our account of places further north along the Richardson Highway begins on p.468.
Wrangell-St Elias National Park coverage starts on p.446.

which constitute some of the finest road in the state, particularly the southern forty miles or so where it winds from Valdez, between the steep rock walls of Keystone Canyon, and up over Thompson Pass through the seemingly impenetrable rock-and-ice barrier presented by the Chugach Mountains.

Keystone Canyon

The Richardson Highway initially traces the right bank (if you're facing downstream) of the Lowe River, a wide expanse of water, heavily braided at first and then, thirteen miles outside Valdez, constrained by **Keystone Canyon**, a narrow, three-mile-long passage cutting through angled bedrock. During the gold rush, the canyon proved one of the most difficult obstacles prospectors faced on the route into the Interior, with many preferring the hazardous journey across the Valdez Glacier. All this changed in 1899 when the army cut the **Goat Trail** high on the cliffs, 200–300ft above the north bank, a path just wide enough for two horses to pass. Today most drive straight through, pausing only long enough to photograph **Horsetail Falls** (Mile 13.6) and the five-leap, 400-foot **Bridal Veil Falls** (Mile 13.8). If you feel like stretching your legs, you can follow part of the Goat Trail for up to six miles from two hundred feet south of the Bridal Veil Falls turnout. The best section is the short climb up to the Bridal Veil Falls overlook (400yd each way), though the trail continues along for a couple of miles high above the west side of the canyon.

While pleasant enough, the trail is less exciting than it might be, with restricted views and no convenient way to walk it in a loop. There isn't much in the way of gold-rush relics, either: just the remains of a hand-cut tunnel, to the east at Mile 15, left over from an attempt to install a train line along the floor of the canyon after the successful completion of the Goat Trail.

Thompson Pass

As you emerge from Keystone Canyon the country opens up again, this time into broad river flats hemmed in by mountains spilling glaciers down their flanks towards the road. The highway then begins its climb towards **Thompson Pass**, a 2771-foot alpine saddle between 6000-foot craggy peaks. Midway up, a mile-long access road leads to *Blueberry Lake State Recreation Site*, Mile 24.1 ($12; pump water), one of the finest campgrounds in the state, with ten popular sites high on a ridge with 360-degree views of sawtooth mountains and creaking crystalline glaciers – though many sites remain snow-covered well into June. From here it is only a couple of miles to the crest of the pass at Mile 26.5, where grayling and rainbow trout fill a number of small lakes. The low tundra surrounding the water is spotted with stunted willow and makes inviting territory for a half-hour **hike**, which should bring you to the snow line even in late summer. The majesty of the area is only spoilt by maintenance sheds for the pipeline, which crosses the pass underground, and road-clearing equipment needed to keep the Richardson Highway open in winter, when it sees some of the heaviest snowfall in the state (a record 81ft in the winter of 1952–53), but rarely avalanches. If you are traveling south, the pass will give you a first glimpse of the mountains in that direction, but little indication that Valdez and the sea are only twenty miles away.

The descent through the northern foothills of the Chugach Mountains is more gradual, initially passing the three-pronged **Worthington Glacier**, Mile

28.7, which threatens to envelop the highway. It is part of a day-use-only state recreation site where you can drive within three hundred yards of the glacier, then follow a paved path to a viewpoint or a short trail along the lateral moraine almost to its face.

Cordova and around

On the eastern shores of Prince William Sound, yet seemingly a world apart from the day-cruise bustle of Whittier and Valdez, **CORDOVA** can feel like a town displaced. The town was tenuously linked to the Interior by a railroad up the Copper River Valley, but you can now get here only by boat or plane. Even its waterfront canneries and large fishing fleet seem out of place, more characteristic of Southeast Alaska, four hundred miles away.

Cordova's 2500 residents (whose ranks are doubled in summer) go quietly about their business, balancing the day-to-day needs of a small town with the demands of a busy port and fledgling tourist industry. Half the population is dependent on fishing, above all the massive runs of red and king salmon from mid-May, the first of which are flown directly to Seattle where they command astounding prices and produce media coverage similar to that of the arrival of Beaujolais Nouveau. With less than one cruise-ship visit a week in summer, Cordova has remained off the main tourist circuit. There's a definite charm to wandering the streets (some still with wooden boardwalks) that straggle up the hillside, or strolling past the waterside canneries perched on rows of forty-foot stilts, their rusted, corrugated iron sides spot-painted with patch jobs. Much of the time all of this is blanketed in low cloud and damp mist, giving a suitably ethereal atmosphere to the spruce-specked islands off the coast.

Much of downtown dates back to 1906 when Irish railroad engineer Michael J. Heney selected this cannery site as the export base for copper from the mines at Kennicott and began forging a railroad between the two outposts. Cordova, which Heney named after his favorite Spanish city, prospered thanks to its docks, railroad, and canneries until 1939, when the mines and railroad closed for good due to falling copper prices caused by the Great Depression. The 1964 earthquake

△ Old cannery on Eyak River, Cordova

moved the town 46ft southeast, causing damage worth $1.7 million but taking no lives. In recent years the biggest threat to the town's livelihood came when a big slick from the *Exxon Valdez* destroyed most of the fishery.

Long after the railroad closed down, the route was turned into the Copper River Highway, which provides access to the immense birding wetlands of the **Copper River Delta**, the partly destroyed **Million Dollar Bridge** over the Copper River, and the **Childs Glacier**.

Arrival and information

Arriving by **ferry** (☎424-7333 in Cordova) from Valdez or Whittier, you'll be dropped an easy fifteen-minute walk north of the town center. If you can't be bothered, call Wild Hare (☎424-3939) or Cordova **taxi** services (☎424-5151). The new Cordova-based fast ferry, *Chenega*, and the older *Aurora* make daily runs to Valdez and Whittier.

Alaska Airlines (☎1-800/225-2752) runs daily scheduled **flights** from Anchorage, and from Seattle via the Southeast towns of Yakutat and Juneau; ERA Aviation (☎1-800/426-0333) also flies daily from Anchorage, landing at the Merle K. "Mudhole" Smith International Airport (☎424-7151), named for an early bush pilot and located thirteen miles east of town along the Copper River Highway. The airport shuttle ($12 each way; ☎424-3272) meets each plane and runs into town, and there are also taxis. Local bush fliers include Alaska Wilderness Air (☎424-5553), Copper River Air (☎424-5371), Cordova Air Service (☎424-3289/7611), and Silverado Air Taxi (☎424-7893).

Those looking to fully explore the Copper River Highway will want to **rent a car** from either Chinook Auto Rentals (in the *Airport Depot Diner* or at the *Northern Nights Inn* in town; ☎424-5279 or 1-877/424-5279, @www.chinookautorentals.com), which has cars from $55 plus 22 percent tax; or Cordova Auto Rental, at the airport (☎424-5982, @www.ptialaska.net/~cars), which has new cars for $85 a day, plus slightly older ones for $75. **Bikes** are also a viable option, even for exploring the Copper River Highway; rent from Cordova Coastal Outfitters ($15 a day; see p.334).

The main **visitor center** is the Chamber of Commerce, 404 1st St (all year Mon–Fri 9am–4pm, occasionally on Sat; ☎424-7260, @www.cordovachamber.com). If it's not open, check out the booth at the museum. Information on hikes, cabins, and wildlife is best sought at the Forest Service's **Cordova Ranger District Office**, 610 2nd St (Mon–Fri 8am–5pm; ☎424-7661), which has a few mildly interesting displays on the local natural history and an aquarium with native fish.

Accommodation

Cordova's accommodation is fairly varied, and most people should find somewhere that suits. There are lots of B&Bs but most are tiny (and don't actually serve breakfast); the Chamber of Commerce keeps full details of availability. There is no hostel, however, and **camping** close to town is limited – although there are plenty of good places along the Copper River Highway for those with transport. The Forest Service plans to open a campground at the Childs Glacier by mid-2007.

Alaskan Hotel 600 1st St ☎424-3299, @hotelak@yahoo.com. Old and fairly low-standard hotel in one of the town's original buildings. The price is right, however, with shared-bath rooms at $44 and ones with private bath and TV for $66. Go for the rooms on the right to minimize noise and smoke from the bar below. ❶

City Camper Park Whitshed Rd ☎424-6200. Just a gravel lot with token-operated showers and a view of town. It's fine for RVs ($18) but neither well priced nor pleasant for campers ($18).

Cordova Lighthouse Inn Nicholoff Way ☎424-7080, @www.cordovalighthouseinn.com. Small, modern inn right by the small boat harbor with six well-appointed rooms, some with great views, plus cable TV, WiFi, and morning coffee and pastries (not included) in the café downstairs (see p.335). ⑤ **Cordova Rose Lodge** 1315 Whitshed Rd ☎424-7673, ⓦwww.cordovarose.com. Unusual B&B a mile south of downtown that's been imaginatively converted from a barge landlocked by the shores of Odiak Slough. They've kept the nautical theme throughout, the eleven rooms feeling somewhat like cabins, each with its own character and all sharing a communal lounge with library, TV/VCR, WiFi, and a great view. There's also a separate three-room, self-contained annex with a fishing theme. Hearty breakfast and dinner can be arranged. With breakfast ⑤ , without ④

🏃 **Northern Nights Inn** 501 3rd Ave ☎424-5356, ⓦwww.northernnightsinn.com. Four spacious and antique-flavored rooms in one of Cordova's original homes (built in 1910), all with private bathroom, cable TV, WiFi, and phone, and most with kitchenettes and harbor views. The owners don't provide breakfast, though you can prepare your own. They do car-rental and low-cost airport pickups for guests. ③–④

🏃 **Orca Adventure Lodge** Orca Rd ☎1-866/424-6722, ⓦwww.orcaadventurelodge.com. In a former cannery (dating from 1886) a mile and a half north of the ferry dock, this place specializes in fishing packages (with three remote fly-in lodges), as well as other activities, including heli-skiing, but you can also stay here, rent bikes and kayaks, and enjoy the sea otters and birds right outside. There are no TVs in the rooms (you can watch videos in the refectory) but there is WiFi; kayak/canoe rentals cost $65/day, or you can sign up for their adventure package, with full board, transfers, and use of kayaks, canoes, bikes, and fishing gear, from $155 a day. ⑥ **Prince William Motel** 501 2nd St ☎424-3201 or 1-888/796-6835, ⓔpwmotel@yahoo.com. Modern, spacious motel, all rooms with cable TV, microwaves, and fridges (kitchenettes $20 extra). ⑤ **Reluctant Fisherman** 407 Railroad Ave ☎424-3272 or 1-877/770-3272, ⓔreluctantfishermaninn@ak.net. An oldish motel (now being revamped) but the largest in town, although even this may be full in fishing season. Rooms have cable TV and dataports, and there's a PC and WiFi in the lobby. ⑤

The town and around

The self-guided **Cordova Historic Walking Tour** (pick up the free leaflet – and CD, if it's available – at the Chamber of Commerce) is a pleasant way to spend an hour, getting a sense of how rapidly the town developed as the railhead for the Copper River & Northwestern Railway (CR&NW Railway). The town center still has plenty of original buildings from 1908 that give Cordova a fairly harmonious architectural flavor. When the weather fouls, make for the **Cordova Historical Museum**, 620 1st St (June to early Sept Mon–Sat 10am–6pm, Sun 2–4pm; early Sept to May Tues–Fri 10am–5pm, Sat 1–5pm; $1 donation appreciated), and spend half an hour watching the ageing but still relevant thirty-minute video on the region's history (ask if it isn't already playing). You then have the context for a few minutes' poking around the eclectic collection spanning Aleut and Tlingit artifacts, the local fishing and mining industries, the evolution of the little **ice worm** that lives in the glaciers and the funky festival that celebrates its existence each mid-February, and minor paintings by Eustace Ziegler and Sydney Laurence (see p.227), who both lived here during the early years of the twentieth century. Be sure to also check out the display on the railroad, with plenty of photos and a couple of lovely aquatints (one showing a waterside section of track, another the mill at Kennicott), track-laying equipment, and jewelry cut from high-grade copper ore.

Entering the new **Ilanka Cultural Center**, opposite the Fisherman's Memorial at 110 Nicholoff Way (late May to mid-Sept Tues–Sat 9am–5pm; rest of year Tues–Fri 10am–4pm; donation appreciated; ☎424-7903, ⓔiccilanka @nveyak.org) you'll pass below one of just five fully-articulated orca skeletons in the world, recovered from a stranding in 2000. There's a small exhibit of local Native art, including work by John Jay Hoover, whose family runs the Hoover's Movers gas station on 1st Street and a Gift Gallery, selling Native and Made in Alaska (see Basics, p.73) craftwork and books. Representing the local Eyak,

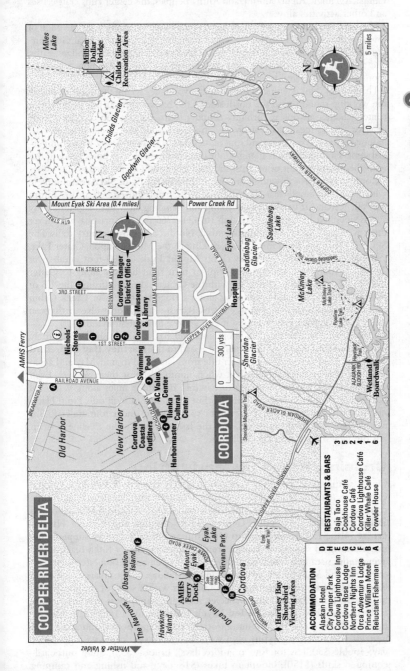

COPPER RIVER DELTA

The Narrows
Hawkins Island
Observation Island
Orca Inlet
Eyak Lake
Nirvana Park

Mount Eyak
POWER CREEK ROAD

AMHS Ferry Dock
Cordova
See inset map

Hartney Bay Shorebird Viewing Area

WHITSHED ROAD
COPPER RIVER HIGHWAY

Eyak River Trail

◄ Whittier & Valdez

ACCOMMODATION
Alaskan Hotel	D
City Camper Park	H
Cordova Lighthouse Inn	E
Cordova Rose Lodge	C
Northern Nights Inn	G
Orca Adventure Lodge	F
Prince William Motel	B
Reluctant Fisherman	A

RESTAURANTS & BARS
Baja Taco	3
Cookhouse Café	5
Cordova Café	2
Cordova Lighthouse Café	4
Killer Whale Café	1
Powder House	6

CORDOVA

◄ AMHS Ferry
Old Harbor
New Harbor

BREAKWATER AVE
RAILROAD AVENUE

Nichols' Stores

Cordova Coastal Outfitters
Harbormaster
AC Value Center
Ilanka Cultural Center

Swimming Pool

NICHOLOFF WAY
1ST STREET
2ND STREET
3RD STREET
4TH STREET
6TH STREET

BROWNING AVENUE
ADAMS AVENUE
LAKE AVENUE

▲ Mount Eyak Ski Area (0.4 miles)
Power Creek Rd ▶

Cordova Ranger District Office
Cordova Museum & Library

COPPER RIVER HIGHWAY
CHASE ROAD
Eyak Lake
Hospital

0 — 300 yds

Childs Glacier
Goodwin Glacier
Miles Lake

Million Dollar Bridge
Childs Glacier Recreation Area

COPPER RIVER HIGHWAY

Saddlebag Glacier
Saddlebag Lake
McKinley Lake
McKinley Lake Trail
Pipeline Lakes Trail
Saddlebag Glacier Trail

Sheridan Glacier
SHERIDAN GLACIER ROAD
Sheridan Mountain Trail
ALAGANIK SLOUGH RD
Haystack Trail
Wetland Boardwalk

0 — 5 miles

333

Chugach, Tlingit, Aleut/Alutiiq, and Ahtna peoples, the center runs craft classes and other activities all year.

Nirvana Park, a former Eyak cemetery in a patch of rainforest at the edge of town on Power Creek Road, was taken over in the 1920s by a local German-born Buddhist (now buried there), who added wooden gates and bridges, paths, and a fountain; it was restored and rededicated in 1988, and is now a popular spot for swimming and boating.

That's about it for genuine sights, though if you fancy seeing the inside of one of the working canneries on the north side of the harbor, you can ask at the visitor center whether anyone is currently running tours. Equally, you can get a sense of what fishing means to Cordova by strolling around the extensive small boat harbor, very much the heart and soul of the town and always abuzz with commercial seiners and gill-netters going about their business, charter boats heading out with their complement of tourists, and bald eagles waiting for scraps.

Cordova even has a downhill ski slope at the **Mount Eyak Ski Area**, complete with an antique single-seat chairlift built in 1936 and moved here in 1974 from Sun Valley, Idaho. It works in a chunking and grinding, slow but magisterial way and is operated by the local ski club (T 424-7766), after Christmas whenever there is enough snow, accessing downhill, Nordic, and cross-country trails. The Ski Hill Trail starts from the ski area, linking to the Mount Tripod, Crater Lake, and Power Creek trails. You can climb Mount Eyak (a 400-foot climb over 2.5 miles, taking 4.5 hours round-trip) or turn right halfway along to Crater Lake in its alpine bowl, joining up with the Crater Lake Trail (from Mile 1.5 of Power Creek Road) and continuing along a ridge to the Power Creek Cabin (4.2 miles from Mile 6.9 of Power Creek Road) – a total of twelve or thirteen miles and a very long day's hiking if you choose to do it all in a day.

Anyone who is interested in shorebirds and has a vehicle should definitely drive the five miles out along Whitshed Road to the **Hartney Bay Shorebird Viewing Area**, especially near high tide from late April to mid-May and again from September through October, when numbers are at their greatest. Even without wheels it's worth hiking to Sawmill Bay, three miles along Whitshed Rd, where there's also good birding within two hours of high tide. From Hartney Bay the Heney Ridge Trail climbs to 1850ft in under four miles (5.5hr round-trip); it's muddy in places, and the last mile above the treeline is steep, but the views make it worth the effort.

Cruising, kayaking, and rafting

One essential stop for any active visitor to Cordova is 🜲 Cordova Coastal Outfitters (T 424-7424, W www.cordovacoastal.com), located in a multi-colored cabin floating in the small boat harbor off Nicholoff Way (and also at the rear of the AC Value Center). Their Wildlife and Natural History **cruise** (4hr; $150) heads out into Orca Inlet, with local history supplementing sightings of sea otters, seals, seabirds, and occasionally Sitka black-tailed deer, Steller's sea lions, and maybe orca. Keen birders will be better served by the Birds and Mud tour (early May only; 4hr; $65), which floats down Eyak River and spends time sitting by the mudflats within sight of the mountains hoping to spot as many as thirty species, including sandpipers, dunlins, jaegers, and harriers. They also do **guided kayak tours** on Orca Inlet (half-day $75; full-day $115), paddling among sea otters, harbor porpoises, and maybe sea lions. If you'd rather go your own way, they **rent sea kayaks** (single $35 a day; double $50; less for four or more days), canoes ($35), 30hp outboard-equipped skiffs ($150), mountain bikes ($18/day), and fishing and camping gear ($30 per day, $175 per week for the two-person "Cabin Package"; $45 per day, $275 per week for the two-person "Camping Package").

An excellent way to see something of the Copper River Delta and get in a little **rafting** is to join one of the trips run by Alaska River Expeditions (℡1-800/776-1864, Ⓦwww.alaskarafters.com), based at the Cordova airport. There's immediate appeal in the half-day Sheridan Glacier Adventure (late May to Aug; $75), paddling among icebergs in the moraine lake and then rafting the Class II–III water, but the company also does multiday trips on the Copper River (5 days $1350, and 10 days all the way from McCarthy for $2150) plus a half-day's iceclimbing for $95 (minimum 2 persons).

Eating and drinking

If you are cooking your own meals or surviving on snacks, make use of the large AC Value Center **supermarket** on Nicholoff Way, which has the best selection as well as a good deli counter and bakery, and is open to 9pm or later nightly. Nichols' Frontdoor Store at 512 1st Ave (Mon–Sat 8am–9pm, Sun 9am–7pm) and Nichols' Backdoor Store on 2nd St (Mon–Sat 10am–7pm, Sun 9am–7pm) are more convenient but stock less. For more substantial **meals** there's a reasonable selection of eateries in town, and the *Powder House* a mile "out the road," but nothing beyond that.

Baja Taco Nicholoff Way ℡424-5599. Order your taco ($3), *huevos rancheros* ($7.75), or chicken *mole* ($9.50) from the bright-red school bus and hang out on the sunny deck, retreat to the Mexicana-filled dining room, or wander across the street to watch the fishermen return to the small boat harbor. Mon–Sat 8am–9pm, Sun 10am–9pm.

Cookhouse Café 1 Cannery Rd ℡424-5920. Half a mile north in a charmingly restored cannery mess hall, serving breakfast and lunch, with huge piles of pancakes a specialty. June–Sept from 5.30am.

Cordova Café 604 1st St ℡424-5543. Windowless greasy spoon that looks closed most of the time but is open 7am–midnight and usually full of fishermen dismantling $4 stacks of sourdough pancakes and other diner favorites.

Cordova Lighthouse Café Nicholoff Way ℡424-7080. Superb breakfasts (to 10.30am), lunches, salads, and sandwiches, plus freshly baked artisan breads, gourmet pizzas (mainly weekends; $17–22), and rich cakes – all homemade and served in convivial surroundings. Closed Mon.

Killer Whale Café 507 1st St ℡424-7733. A favorite with Cordova's slackers (despite being run by the ex-mayor), where you'll find three-egg omelette breakfasts ($8.50) till 11am, sandwiches on a choice of French stick, whole wheat, or croissant ($9), burgers, soup, imaginative salads ($7–9), and good coffee. Open to 4pm; closed Sun.

Powder House Mile 1.5 Copper River Hwy ℡424-3529. Restaurant and bar built in a former gunpowder storage shed from the CR&NW Railway days, now with a deck overlooking Eyak Lake. They do ribs on Wednesday nights, sushi on Fridays, and a grill (salmon, steak, etc) from Wednesday to Saturday.

Listings

Banks Wells Fargo, 510 1st St (℡424-3258), and First National, 528 1st St (℡424-6700), have ATMs, as does the AC Value Center supermarket.
Bookshop Orca Books and Sound, 507 1st St ℡424-5305.
Festivals The Cordova Iceworm Festival (Ⓦwww.iceworm.org) takes place the first full weekend of Feb with the annual march of the ice worm (a 100ft-long costume with dozens of feet sticking out) down the main street; the Copper River Delta Shorebird Festival (Ⓦwww.ptialaska.net/~midtown) attracts birders from all over on the first weekend of May.

Internet access At the library, Orca Books and Sound, plus WiFi at *Baja Taco* and the *Lighthouse Café.*
Library Cordova Public Library, 620 1st St (Tues–Fri 10am–8pm, Sat 1–5pm; ℡424-6667), has free Internet access (terminals and WiFi).
Medical assistance Cordova Community Medical Center, 602 Chase Ave ℡424-8000; 24hr emergency room.
Post office Railroad Ave and Council Ave (Mon–Fri 10am–5.30pm, Sat 10am–1pm). The **General Delivery** zip code is 99574.

Showers Harbormaster Office ($4 for 10min,
token available; Mon–Fri 8am–5pm); the Bob Korn
Memorial Pool on Railroad Ave (☎ 424-7200) is
only a dollar more, and you get a swim as well.

Taxes Cordova imposes a six percent sales tax,
plus a six percent bed tax, not been included in our
accommodation price codes.

The Copper River Delta and the Million Dollar Bridge

You should really spend at least one of your days in Cordova driving the fifty-mile-long **Copper River Highway**, and if you are equipped for camping then two or three days would be better: pick up the Chugach National Forest's free *Copper River Delta* and *Take A Hike!* leaflets from the ranger center. There's plenty to explore, not least the **Copper River Delta**, the largest intact wetland on the Pacific coast, stretching for sixty miles east of Cordova. It is a wonderfully rich area of marshes, ponds, and sloughs fed by the outwash from half a dozen glaciers, myriad channels of the mighty Copper River, and more than 160 inches of rainfall. Almost every stream offers opportunities for patient **fishers**, with Dolly Varden and cutthroat trout biting throughout the summer (cutthroat from mid-June), and more seasonal runs of red (late May to mid-July) and silver salmon (Aug to mid-Sept). **Bird-watchers** are even more generously rewarded, especially in spring (late April to late May) during the massive migration of around twenty million waterfowl and shorebirds, including over six million western sandpipers (almost the entire world population), and 3.5 million dunlin. In

---

Hiking and biking from the Copper River Highway

Don't just drive the highway to the Million Dollar Bridge; take time out to explore some varied trails. Most offer the best **hiking** from June to September, and all can be muddy after rain. **Mountain bikers** are poorly served by the typically soggy terrain, but the Saddlebag Glacier Trail is usually a good bet. Trails are listed below in order of their distance from Cordova.

Eyak River Trail (4.4 miles round-trip; 5hr; negligible ascent). This easy but sometimes mushy trail follows the river to the former Crystal Falls cannery, built in 1934 and closed after the 1964 quake. The trailhead is at Mile 5.6, just before the Eyak River boat launch.

Sheridan Mountain Trail (6 miles round-trip; 4–5hr; 2000ft ascent). A frequently wet trail which climbs gradually up through the forest to open country for tremendous views of Sheridan and Sherman glaciers. Go late in the season, preferably after a dry spell. The trailhead is four miles north of the highway at Mile 13.7.

Haystack Trail (1.6 miles round-trip; 1hr; 100ft ascent). Easy hike mostly over boardwalks, taking you to a small glacier-carved knoll from where the whole delta and parts of the coast spread out before you. The trailhead is at Mile 19.1.

McKinley Lake/Pipeline Lake trails (5 miles round-trip; 2–3hr; negligible ascent). Gentle rainforest hike to McKinley Lake and the *McKinley Lake Cabin* (see opposite), where a rough trail leads to the remains of the 1920s Lucky Strike Mine. About halfway back, turn right onto the Pipeline Lakes Trail, which follows an abandoned pipeline once used to supply water for the Copper River & Northwestern Railway's locomotives. It reaches the highway at Mile 21.4, just west of the McKinley Lake Trailhead at Mile 21.6.

Saddlebag Glacier Trail (6 miles round-trip; 2–3hr; 100ft ascent). A pleasant and easy walk through moss-hung Sitka spruce forest and cottonwoods to Saddlebag Lake, where the glacier is visible among steep cliffs. Watch for mountain goats. The trailhead is a mile north of the highway at Mile 24.9.

PRINCE WILLIAM SOUND | Cordova and around

summer this is nesting ground for the entire world population of dusky Canada geese (an endangered subspecies, helped out by artificial nest sites).

The highway is laid on the old bed of the **Copper River & Northwestern Railway** (see box, p.453), which linked the ice-free port of Cordova with the copper mines at Kennicott by way of the Copper River Valley. When the mines closed in 1938, the railroad was pulled up, and Cordova boosters have since promoted the idea of using the trackbed to connect their town with the outside world. Congress appropriated funds to lay a road on the old trackbed in 1954, but ten years later, before work really started, the Good Friday earthquake partially destroyed the crucial Million Dollar Bridge. Despite numerous attempts to revive the plan, proponents are still waiting.

For maximum freedom you really need a car, though it is also rewarding (if often wet) to explore by bike, which can be rented in Cordova (see p.331). Allow at least a day in each direction to the end of the Copper River Highway and back, or use Cordova Coastal Outfitters' shuttle service to drop you off and ride back ($100 to the road end for up to three people). Alternatively, organize your trip to be in Cordova on Wednesday afternoon when Copper River and Northwest Tours (late May to early Sept; $45; ☎424-5356) runs a five-hour sightseeing and wildlife-spotting outing by minibus, complete with a box lunch at road's end.

The road to the airport is always kept open and will usually be **snow-free** to the Copper River by late April, though the last few miles to the Million Dollar Bridge may not be cleared until mid-May or later; there's always a chilly wind off the glaciers here in any case.

Along the Copper River Highway

The Copper River Highway leaves Cordova past Eyak Lake, then bursts out of the mountains that hem in the town. From here on there are broad views on all sides as you drive across outwash fans from the Scott, Sheridan, and Sherman glaciers, all named after Union generals and visible off to the left. Just before Mile 11 there's a Forest Service interpretive kiosk, which is worth a quick look. With streams and ponds (many with resident beavers) all about, you seldom seem to be on firm ground for long prior to Cordova's airport (Mile 12), at which point the asphalt gives out onto a good, fast, but unpaved road. A couple of miles on, Sheridan Glacier Road runs four miles inland to the trailhead for the **Sheridan Mountain Trail**, where there's an attractive little streamside picnic site with fire rings, tables, and stream water.

Back on the highway you'll soon come to Alaganik Slough Road (Mile 16.9), a three-mile easement among lily ponds to a picnic area (with restrooms and boat launch) and a 300-yard-long **wetland boardwalk**, which leads to raised platforms perfect for viewing waterfowl, notably nesting trumpeter swans, ducks and grebes in summer. Just before the parking lot, the Alaganik Slough Trail follows geotextile laid over bog for half a mile to a beaver dam. Between highway miles 18 and 26 you are again on firm ground, and a couple of side roads provide access to interesting hiking trails. A couple of rare, foot-accessible public-use **cabins** sit along the trail that starts at Mile 21.6: *McKinley Trail Cabin*, a hundred yards along, and *McKinley Lake Cabin*, right by the water almost three miles from the trailhead; both sleep six and cost $35 (booking ☎1-877/444-6777, ⊛www.reserveusa.com).

Soon the highway crosses to Long Island, where you'll probably see many bald eagles in trees and a few of their huge nests. After several miles of island-hopping across the Copper River's multiple broad, gray channels, the final few miles run (washouts permitting) along the eastern bank of the river and end at a point unnervingly close to two glaciers, the Miles and the Childs, both of which feed icebergs into the river. This is where railroad maestro Michael Heney chose to build his huge, four-span, steel and concrete **Million Dollar Bridge**, one of the biggest engineering headaches during the 1908–10 construction of the CR&NW Railway. Heney was undaunted, boasting "give me enough dynamite and snoose and I'll build a road to hell." He did manage to build a railroad to Kennicott, though only just, and died of exhaustion just months before its completion. As his workers battled temperatures of -60°F, winds reaching 95mph, and 34ft of snow a year, the Childs Glacier unexpectedly began advancing at around 35ft per day, threatening to destroy the bridge. By feverish hacking away at the ice and a fortuitous halt in the glacier's advance, the bridge was saved, only to succumb to the 1964 earthquake. The northernmost span was dislodged so that the trackbed now drags in the river, though a ramp was rigged up so that pedestrians, bikes, and even high-clearance vehicles could cross the downed span and explore about three miles of unmaintained road on the other side. From 2004 to 2005 the span was replaced, but plans to extend the road along the railroad trackbed are on hold. Should you wish to explore further, the North Childs Glacier Trail (2 miles), South Childs Glacier Trail (3 miles), Miles Lake Trail (3 miles), and Goodwin Glacier Trail (1.5 miles) all start from near the bridge.

The highway ends at the south side of the bridge (Mile 48) from where the Copper River Trail (and parallel road) lead west for half a mile to the **Childs Glacier Recreation Area**, separated from the three-mile-wide face of the Childs Glacier only by the quarter-mile-wide river. Enormous snowfalls in the Chugach Mountains feed the twelve-mile-long glacier, which ploughs its way east, kept in check only by the undercutting currents of the Copper River. In mid-summer (mid-June to mid-July) stay alert as you wait for ice to calve into the river, as large chunks periodically break off, creating powerful ten-, twenty-, or even forty-foot-high waves which have been known to wash small icebergs into the day-use area and salmon into the trees. People have been injured, so you might feel safer on the viewing platform – on high ground away from the river's edge – from where you may also see harbor seals chasing salmon up the river. Wherever you stand, this is about as close as you are going to get to a large calving glacier – it is a magnificent and underrated sight.

Travel details

Trains

Whittier to: Anchorage (1 daily; 2hr 20min).

Buses

Valdez to: Delta Junction (on demand; 5hr 30min); Fairbanks (on demand; 7–8hr); Glennallen (on demand; 3hr 15min).
Whittier to: Anchorage (1 daily; 1hr 20min).

Ferries

Cordova to: Valdez (1 daily; 2hr 45min–7hr); Whittier (1 daily; 3hr 15min–6hr 30min).

Valdez to: Cordova (1 daily; 2hr 45min–6hr); Whittier (1 daily; 2hr 45min–6hr).
Whittier to: Cordova (1 daily; 3–6hr); Juneau (2 monthly; 38hr); Valdez (1 daily; 2hr 45min–6hr).

Flights

Cordova to: Anchorage (2–3 daily; 50min); Juneau (1 daily; 2hr); Seattle (1 daily; 6hr); Yakutat (1 daily; 45min).
Valdez to: Anchorage (2–3 daily; 40min).

Southwest Alaska

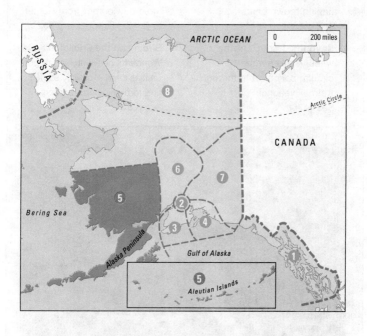

CHAPTER 5   # Highlights

✳ **Kodiak Island** Fascinating
Russian and Native history,
plus the chance to explore
the only real road system
in the Southwest.
See p.343

✳ **Bear-viewing at Brooks
Falls** Watch leaping salmon
run the gauntlet of hungry,
gaping brown bears.
See p.360

✳ **Savonoski Loop** Devote a
week to this gorgeous
circular canoe route through
Katmai National Park.
See p.360

✳ **Valley of 10,000 Smokes**
Spend a few days hiking in this
desolate landscape of sculpted
volcanic ash within Katmai
National Park. See p.361

✳ **Aleutians ferry trip** See
whales, dolphins, a string of
snow-capped volcanoes, and
tiny remote villages on this
three-day journey from Homer
to Dutch Harbor. See p.362

✳ **Birding on the Pribilof Islands**
Wonderful bird-watching opportunities in an excitingly stark
and forbidding environment.
See p.374

△ Horned puffins on the Pribilof Islands

Southwest Alaska

Even by Alaska's standards, few places are as isolated as the Southwest, a vast region that stretches over two thousand miles from Anchorage along the Alaska Peninsula and out to the tip of the Aleutian Chain. Fewer than 25,000 people call the whole Southwest Alaska region home, and its rugged terrain may explain why. From its southern shore, the Alaska Peninsula rises steeply to its snowy backbone, the Aleutian Range, and then drops away to the north towards the swampy lowlands of Lake Clark and Katmai national parks. Further west the peninsula tapers off until breaking up into the string of Aleutian Islands, each the top of a volcano rising from the sea bottom, together comprising 27 of the US's 47 active volcanoes.

The weather bears much of the blame for the Southwest's inhospitable reputation, as arctic winds whip up ferocious seas and warm currents from Japan generate dense fogs that can hang around for days. Yet those who can stick it out are often very well compensated – fishermen working two short seasons in these rich waters can haul in over $100,000 a year – a temptation that's hard to resist.

With these quick returns, there's a sizeable group of transient workers who fly into Kodiak or Dutch Harbor from the Lower 48, stay six weeks, then head somewhere warm until the next seasonal opening. Visitors come, too, but the high cost of transportation keeps numbers low. Only the truly dedicated and those with an adventurous spirit make the effort to experience Southwest Alaska, something that, to some, adds to the region's appeal.

Those who do visit are justly rewarded, not least by the striking topography of almost fifty **volcanoes**, many of them classic snow-capped cones: Spurr, on Anchorage's doorstep; Redoubt and Iliamna in Lake Clark National Park; Augustine, an island at the mouth of Cook Inlet; Novorupta in Katmai National Park; Shishaldin, at the end of the Alaska Peninsula, which has been erupting regularly for much of the last decade; Makushin on Unalaska Island; and many more.

At more than ten thousand feet, Redoubt and Iliamna are two of the region's tallest volcanoes, overlooking **Lake Clark National Park**, where exclusive fishing lodges allow avid anglers to hook salmon on their way upstream from Bristol Bay. The fish share the water with rafters and experienced canoeists, who tackle one of the three designated National Wild Rivers within the park's bounds. People also come to fish for salmon in **Katmai National Park**, but most folks prefer to see the fish eaten by the hungry brown bears congregating around Brooks Falls. If you can score a position on the platform, there's a chance of getting the ultimate in Alaskan wildlife photography: a snap of an open-jawed bear about to snag a leaping salmon.

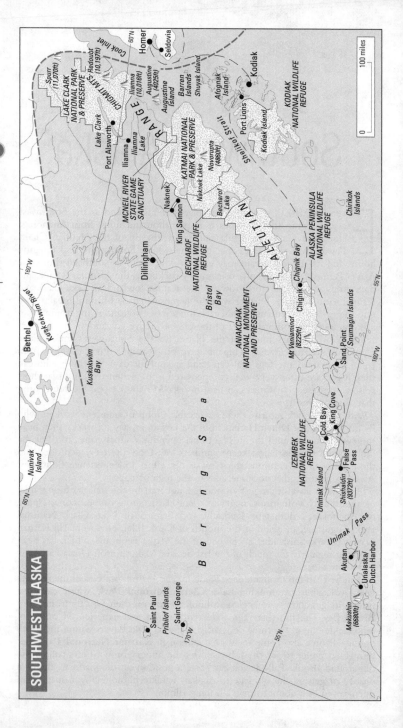

SOUTHWEST ALASKA

Homer
Seldovia
Spurr (11,070ft)
Redoubt (10,197ft)
CHIGMIT MTS
Cook Inlet
LAKE CLARK NATIONAL PARK & PRESERVE
Iliamna (10,016ft)
Augustine (4025ft)
Augustine Island
Barren Islands
Shuyak Island
Afognak Island
Kodiak
Lake Clark
Port Alsworth
R A N G E
KODIAK NATIONAL WILDLIFE REFUGE
Iliamna
Iliamna Lake
KATMAI NATIONAL PARK & PRESERVE
Novarupta (4860ft)
Port Lions
Kodiak Island
MCNEIL RIVER STATE GAME SANCTUARY
Naknek
Naknek Lake
Shelikof Strait
Bethel
King Salmon
Becharof Lake
Kuskokwim River
BECHAROF NATIONAL WILDLIFE REFUGE
A L E U T I A N
Dillingham
ALASKA PENINSULA NATIONAL WILDLIFE REFUGE
Chirikok Islands
Kuskokwim Bay
Bristol Bay
ANIAKCHAK NATIONAL MONUMENT AND PRESERVE
Chignik Chignik Bay
160°W
Nunivak Island
160°W
Mt Veniaminof (8225ft)
Sand Point
Snumagin Islands
55°N
B e r i n g   S e a
King Cove
Cold Bay
IZEMBEK NATIONAL WILDLIFE REFUGE
False Pass
Unimak Island
Shishaldin (9372ft)
Saint Paul
Pribilof Islands
Saint George
Unimak Pass
Akutan
Unalaska/Dutch Harbor
170°W
Makushin (6680ft)
55°N

0   100 miles

Both parks can only be reached by expensive flights; the rest of the Southwest, however, is accessible by ferry, with frequent services visiting **Kodiak Island**, with its concentration of enormous Kodiak bears. This is where the Russians set up their first capital, while enslaving the Native Aleut people to ensure a profitable supply of sea otter pelts. The ferry continues further southwest, calling at tiny fishing ports en route to **Unalaska/Dutch Harbor**, at the start of the Aleutian Chain; here, California gray whales can sometimes be seen migrating north to the Bering Sea in April and south to Mexico in September. The rest of the long Aleutian Chain, strung out beyond Dutch Harbor, is barely inhabited, expensive to get to (Alaska Airlines charges $1300 round-trip from Anchorage to Adak via King Salmon) and usually well off the tourist itinerary, though specialist bird-watching trips occasionally venture out here.

To the north, the **Pribilof Islands** stand apart from the Aleutian Chain, their treeless tops covered with lush grass and wildflowers in spring. There's a windswept beauty to the place, but the few visitors who make it here come specifically to admire the sea cliffs, alive with thousands of nesting birds, and the rocks and beaches below, usually packed with basking seals.

Kodiak Island and the archipelago

On most days an ethereal mist wreaths the green hummocky hills of **Kodiak Island**, a ragged, once-glaciated slice of the state adrift in the Gulf of Alaska. At a hundred miles long and sixty wide, it ranks as the largest island in the US.

Most of the residents are tucked into the top-right corner around the town of Kodiak, leaving the rest of the island to roughly three thousand of the biggest brown bears in the world. Weighing in at anywhere from 800 to 1500 pounds, they are so large they even get a distinct name, **Kodiak bears**. Their size is a product of their rich diet: so abundant are the salmon here that the bears often only bother with the fattiest, most nutritious parts (the skin and the roe) and discard the rest. With such a comfortable lifestyle, it is hardly surprising that the island supports as many Kodiak bears as there are grizzly bears in the whole of the Lower 48. Most of the bears are deep within the **Kodiak National Wildlife Refuge**, which encompasses the entire western two-thirds of Kodiak, all of neighboring Uganik Island, and parts of Afognak Island to the north. The refuge is also home to Sitka black-tailed deer, mountain goats, red foxes, Roosevelt elk, and plenty of bald eagles, but not a single moose. Come during the salmon runs between mid-June and early September for the best chance of seeing bears, and set aside a good wad of cash for the flights required.

Some history

Human settlement began with the Alutiiq people, who have occupied sites around here for upwards of seven thousand years, gradually developing a sophis-ticated culture based on fishing and hunting. That all changed in the middle of the eighteenth century when **Russian fur traders** arrived and, by forcefully separating families, kidnapping, and even burning villages, forced the Natives to hunt sea otters for sale rather than for their own needs. So profitable was the trade that by 1784 the enterprising Siberian merchant **Gregorii Shelikov**, along with his wife and over a hundred Russian men, established Alaska's first white settlement at Three Saints Bay, halfway down the east coast of Kodiak Island. After a couple of years, word of his ruthless methods got out and he was recalled to Russia, only to be replaced in 1790 by **Alexandr Baranov**.

After a tsunami nearly destroyed the Three Saints Bay settlement, Baranov set up Pavlovsk at St Paul Harbor, the current site of Kodiak, as the new Russian-American Company headquarters. Pavlovsk's golden period only lasted a decade, and as the region's sea otters were killed off the focus of Russian interest shifted towards Sitka, where Baranov moved his capital of Russian Alaska in 1808. For more on Alaska's Russian period, see p.145.

Today Kodiak Island has some wonderful kayaking and good hiking, all within easy reach of the historic town of Kodiak, which is attractively set on an island-studded bay. Add in a busy fishing fleet, a few good festivals, plus the possibility of surfing at road-accessible beaches, and you can easily fill a few enjoyable days, possibly supplemented by some remote kayaking around **Shuyak Island** further north. Be warned, though, that the **weather** throughout the archipelago is cool and wet most of the summer, with low clouds covering Kodiak Island.

Kodiak

The town of **Kodiak** was transformed on March 27, 1964, when the huge earthquake that rocked Southcentral and parts of Southwest Alaska caused a thirty-foot tsunami to sweep over the town. The wave was so powerful that fishing boats were washed onto dry land, one fisherman reporting to a state trooper, "It looks as though I'm behind the Kodiak schoolhouse, about six blocks from the waterfront;" a plaque on Lower Mill Bay Road still marks the spot. Much of the town was destroyed in the process, but land uplifted in the quake created a new flat surface that turned out to be perfect for the

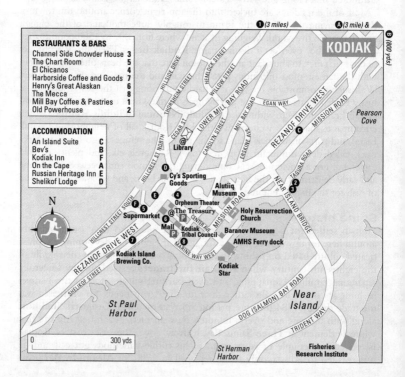

KODIAK

RESTAURANTS & BARS

Channel Side Chowder House 3
The Chart Room 5
El Chicanos 4
Harborside Coffee and Goods 7
Henry's Great Alaskan 6
The Mecca 8
Mill Bay Coffee & Pastries 1
Old Powerhouse 2

ACCOMMODATION

An Island Suite C
Bev's B
Kodiak Inn F
On the Cape A
Russian Heritage Inn E
Shelikof Lodge D

0   300 yds

reconstruction of downtown, largely modern with a couple of Russian-era buildings contributing the only architectural interest.

Despite the sucking power of the wave as it retreated between Kodiak and the offshore Near Island, Kodiak's fishing harbor survived and is as busy as ever, with almost seven hundred boats calling it home. King crab used to be the big-money catch, but it has been mostly fished out, and today the boats seek salmon, halibut, Dungeness and Tanner crab, and bottom fish, such as gray cod, pollock, and sole. The day's catch is brought to channel-side canneries, such as the one built around the *Star of Kodiak*, a World War II ship brought here after the tsunami as emergency accommodation and subsequently converted for fish processing.

After its days as the capital of Russian Alaska, Kodiak ticked by quietly until World War II, when the **US navy** moved in and set up a huge base south of town, constructing a "decoy Kodiak" topped with lights to draw enemy fire away from the blacked-out town. During the war, 25,000 people lived here, but the population has now dropped to around 10,000, with most living off fishing and fish processing. In the past twenty-odd years, high wages have attracted workers from the Philippines, Laos, Vietnam, Mexico, Hawaii, Samoa, and elsewhere, and Kodiak has taken on a fairly cosmopolitan tenor.

Although quite easy to reach from Homer, Kodiak sees relatively few tourists, and it can be refreshing to wander the streets, stopping in to the excellent Baranov and Alutiiq **museums**, checking out Near Island's Fisheries Research Institute, and visiting the moody clifftop forest of **Fort Abercrombie State Historic Park**.

Getting there and arrival

The *Tustumena* and *Kennicott* **ferries** from Homer tie up at the dock right in the heart of town beside the AMHS office (Mon–Fri 8am–5pm, Sat 8am–4pm; ☏486-3800 or 1-800/526-6731). Through most of the summer there are three ferries a week: on Sunday and Monday the ferry is in town for only a couple of hours before heading back to Homer, but on most Wednesdays you'll have a full five hours to explore. This makes a round-trip from Homer a great short cruise, especially if you see whales and the other marine mammals that frequently show themselves around the Barren Islands north of Kodiak. Every other Wednesday in summer, the *Tustumena* continues west along the Alaska Peninsula to Unalaska/Dutch Harbor (see p.365), after first spending the day in Kodiak.

ERA Aviation (☏487-4363) and Alaska Airlines (☏487-4363) jointly dispatch eight **flights** a day from Anchorage to Kodiak airport. Fares vary quite a bit, but they can often be as low as $250 round-trip with Alaska Airlines; both airlines have excellent Web specials on some weekends. Flight delays due to bad weather are not uncommon. The airport is five miles southwest of Kodiak town, and with only a very infrequent local bus service (see p.346) you'll probably want to catch one of the waiting taxis, or call A & B Taxi (☏486-4343), and pay around $15 into town.

Information and getting around

The main **visitor center**, 100 Marine Way (mid-June to mid-Sept Mon–Fri 8am–5pm, Sat & Sun dependent on ferries; mid-Sept to mid-June Mon–Fri 8am–noon & 1–5pm; ☏486-4782, ⓦwww.kodiak.org), is downtown right by the ferry dock. For information on the **Kodiak National Wildlife Refuge**, call at their visitor center (late May to early Sept Mon–Fri 8am–7pm, Sat & Sun noon–4pm; early Sept to late May Mon–Fri 8am–4.30pm; ☏487-2600, ⓦkodiak.fws.gov). It is currently at 1390 Buskin River Rd, four miles south of town and close to the airport, but by 2008 it should have moved to a new site downtown near the ferry dock. It is an essential stop before any trip into the refuge and worth a call anyway for the mounted animals and a video about the island and its wildlife.

The downtown sights are all accessible on foot, without recourse to the KATS **bus** system ($3; ☎486-8308), which operates just two weekday services (Mon–Fri 6.30–7.45am & 5–6.20pm) on a route from the big Safeway three miles northeast of town through the main shopping and residential areas to the airport and back. To explore outside the center, therefore, you really need to either **rent a car** or a **bike** (for both see Listings, p.350), or consider joining Kodiak Tours (☎486-3920 evenings) for a **bus tour** of the town and surroundings (half-day $50, full day $90). On ferry days you can choose a distilled highlights tour (2hr; $25).

Accommodation

As in most of Alaska, you'll need to book in advance to secure a room during the peak season, June through August. Kodiak has no hostel, and the eleven percent local taxes hike up the already high room rates, so those on a tight budget will want to make use of the two nearby **campgrounds**.

Along the roads **outside town**, accommodation is fairly limited, though there is plenty of freelance short-term camping beside beaches, and one more formal spot at Pasagshak (see below).

Chartering a float-plane opens up access to seven public-use **cabins** ($30) inside the Kodiak National Wildlife Refuge. Each comes with a kerosene heater, a pit toilet, and sleeping platforms for at least four people; you'll need to carry everything else, including a cooking stove. In practice, it can be hard to secure a cabin, as they are made available by lottery several months in advance – visit the website to enter. If spaces remain after the lottery, the cabins are let on a first-come, first-served basis; for details, contact the refuge visitor center. Alternatively, there are a couple of state-run cabins on Afognak Island (☎486-6339, ⓦwww.alaskastateparks.org; $35).

Around forty **wilderness lodges**, almost all sublimely remote and equipped with canoes and kayaks, also dot the archipelago. Many are pitched towards the rod-and-gun set, but will also cater to birders, wildlife photographers, and those who just want a few days' complete relaxation. All require float-plane access and most charge $300–400 per person a day; the Kodiak visitor center has a full list, and you can check out many of their websites through the "Wilderness Lodges" section of ⓦwww.kodiak.org.

Hotels, motels, and B&Bs

An Island Suite 720 Rezanof Drive ☎486-2205, ⓦwww.ptialaska.net/~keegan. Comfortable, self-contained mini-apartment with channel views and full kitchen. ④

Bev's Bed And Make Your Own Darn Breakfast! 1510 Mission Rd ☎486-0834, ⓦwww .bevsbedandbreakfast.com. B&B with four rooms (two with private bathroom) in a house an easy walk from downtown. There's a living room with TV/DVD, a communal kitchen where you are free to cook your own meals, and breakfast ingredients are included. Guests and hosts have separate entrances. ③

Kodiak Inn 236 Rezanof Drive West ☎486-5712 or 1-888/563-4254, ⓦwww.kodiakinn.com. The closest Kodiak gets to an upscale hotel, this *Best Western* has eighty pleasant and well-equipped rooms, plus a restaurant and bar. ⑥

On the Cape 3476 Spruce Cape Rd ☎486-4185, ⓦwww.onthecape.net. Attractive B&B three miles north of downtown Kodiak, with ocean-view rooms, a large deck, hot tub, and a buffet breakfast. ⑤

Pasagshak River Accommodations Mile 8 Pasagshak Rd ☎486-6702, ⓦwww .pasagshakriver.com. Fully self-contained two- and three-bedroom homes 45 miles from Kodiak town and close to the beach. Always popular with salmon-fishers, it is one of the few places in this area to get a roof over your head. $90 a night per person. ⑦

Russian Heritage Inn 119 Yukon St ☎486-5657, Ⓦwww.russianheritageinn.com. Decent enough motel-style rooms with private bath, cable TV, and microwave and refrigerator, plus some rooms with full kitchen. Kitchen room ⑥, standard room ④

Shelikof Lodge 211 Thorsheim Ave ☎486-4141, Ⓦwww.shelikoflodge.com. Kodiak's cheapest hotel rooms, and pretty decent ones, too, with TV, on-site bar and restaurant, and free airport shuttle. ⑤

Camping

Buskin River State Recreation Site 4.5 miles southwest of town. Close to the airport, this campground lies adjacent to the Kodiak National Wildlife Refuge Visitor Center and its associated nature trail. Fire rings, picnic tables, and potable water. $10 per site.

Fort Abercrombie State Historical Park 4 miles north of town. The best of the local campgrounds, with sites dotted among Sitka spruce and World War II fort remnants, fire rings, picnic tables, and potable water. $10 per site.

Pasagshak River State Recreation Site 45 miles south of town. Casual beachside camping spots close to a fishing stream. There's an outhouse and hand pump, but no other facilities. Free.

The Town

The *Explore Kodiak* magazine (free from the town's visitor center) contains a detailed walking tour around town, but you miss little by limiting yourself to the highlights covered here. Opposite the visitor center stand Kodiak's two most architecturally harmonious buildings, both Russian in design and execution. Straight ahead is **Erskine House**, a white-weatherboard building with green trim, built around 1808 as a fur warehouse and office for the Russian-American Company, making it not only the oldest building in Alaska but the oldest extant structure on the West Coast of North America. It houses the **Baranov Museum**, 101 Marine Way (late May to early Sept Mon–Sat 10am–4pm, Sun noon–4pm; early Sept to late May Tues–Sat 10am–3pm; $3; Ⓦwww.baranov.us), a small but intriguing collection of Native and Russian artifacts, including intricate woven grass baskets, a one-kopek note printed on sealskin, and a three-seat *baidarka* made from sea lion hides. One room is filled with high-quality furniture from the Russian era, illustrating just how much money was being made from the sea otter pelts. Elsewhere, there's a corner devoted to local Alutiiq boy Benny Benson, who designed the Alaska state flag (see p.272).

Behind Erskine House is the **Holy Resurrection Russian Orthodox Church** (free tours late May to early Sept Mon–Sat 11am–3pm and by appointment; services all year Thurs 6pm, Sat 5pm, and Sun 9am), another weatherboard structure, prim and white but for two flamboyant blue onion-dome cupolas. Sadly, it isn't authentic, the original having burnt down in 1943, but does contain some interesting treasures: a 1790s icon brought from Russia, ornate candle stands, and the reliquary of St Herman, a Russian missionary to Alaska who became the first canonized Orthodox saint in North America. You can see this monk's hat and thirty-pound chain of office, and if you're here around the second week in August, join three hundred other attendees in the annual boat pilgrimage to Monk's Lagoon on nearby Spruce Island, where he spent his later years. To the right of the main church entrance lie some of the West Coast's first bells, cast here between 1794 and 1796, and there's a small gift shop (same hours as church) packed with Russian icons, nested dolls, porcelain, and the like.

Across the street, the **Alutiiq Museum**, 215 Mission Rd (June–Aug Mon–Fri 9am–5pm, Sat 10am–5pm; Sept–May Wed–Fri 9am–5pm, Sat 10.30am–4.30pm; $3; Ⓦwww.alutiiqmuseum.com), plays a crucial role in preserving the history of Kodiak's Native people by facilitating interaction between the local Native community, anthropologists, and archeologists. When the Russians arrived in Alaska, they assumed the Alutiiq people were the same as the Aleut they'd encountered further west, but the Alutiiq actually have far greater cultural and linguistic associations with the Yup'ik further north. Some confusion is perhaps excusable since Kodiak has long been something of a cultural crossroads, as evident from archeological sites that date back 7500 years. Some of these sites have come under threat since the *Exxon Valdez* disaster; hose spraying during the beach cleanup washed away precious evidence of ancient peoples, and newly uncovered sites were vandalized.

One positive outcome of the oil spill was funding for the establishment of the Alutiiq Museum. Though the entire collection is huge, there are only a few artifacts on display at any time, inviting a studied appreciation of each item. Cases separate pieces into those associated with men's work, principally hunting and skin sewing, and those with women's work, such as food preparation and making clothing. There's also a lovely example of a skin kayak, plus the obligatory stuffed Kodiak brown bear. If all this sparks some interest, and you can spare a day or two, consider joining the museum's community **volunteer archeology program**, working at a dig somewhere out on the road system during the day, then returning to Kodiak in the evening.

Near Island and Pillar Mountain

A narrow channel separates Kodiak from **Near Island**, reached over the modern Fred Zharoff Memorial Bridge (aka "The Bridge to Nowhere"), renamed for an Alaska state senator and Native leader who died in 2001. Until then it was known as the Hoser Bridge, for the Kodiak fire department's Dalmatian which, shortly after the bridge's completion, took a suicide leap off the middle span.

Near Island is now home to Kodiak's second commercial fishing harbor, St Herman's, the float-plane dock, and the **Kodiak Fisheries Research Center**, 301 Research Court (Mon–Fri 8am–5pm; free), easily reached from town in twenty minutes on foot. There isn't a lot to see, but the building stands on a lovely, ocean-side site, and the displays are carefully presented, particularly the cylindrical aquarium stocked with several species of crab, assorted starfish, colorful anemones, mussels, and more. Behind is the touch tank, an explosion of purples, reds, blues, and oranges; dip your hand in to feel the silky-smooth sea cucumbers and inspect at close quarters the scarlet blood star. Notice, too, the panel showing where various species of salmon spend their lives before returning to Alaskan rivers to spawn.

With wheels you might fancy driving up the anonymous gravel road to the top of **Pillar Mountain** (1270ft) immediately behind town. The wide selection of radar and communications towers on top aren't especially pretty, but turn your back on them and you can see down to the town and harbor, and inland across the lumpy interior.

Fort Abercrombie State Historical Park

By far the best short outing from town is to **Fort Abercrombie State Historical Park**, four miles northeast of downtown. The prominent headland of Miller Point is now shrouded in towering, moss-draped Sitka spruce, but this was once an important defense position developed after the Japanese attack on Pearl Harbor in 1941. Stroll through the woods, and you will come across moldering, but neatly labeled, World War II remains: ammunition magazines, searchlight bunkers, observation platforms, and the shattered mounts for a couple of eight-inch guns. It is a great place to idle away some time, with orchids and wildflowers blooming in spring, and an opportunity to view bald eagles, puffins, and humpback whales (mid-May to mid-Aug) migrating past the **Miller Point headland**. Here you'll also find the largest of the ammunition bunkers, at the **Kodiak Military History Museum** (May & Sept Sat & Sun 1–4pm; June–Aug Fri–Mon 1–4pm; $3; ⓦwww.kadiak.org), which concentrates on World War II history, especially communications in this remote outpost. There's also a small visitor center (Mon–Fri 8.30am–5pm; ⓣ486-6339) and walking tracks that lead around **Gertrude Lake**, good for tidepooling and even swimming for the very hardy.

Kayaking and fishing

The Kodiak archipelago has some of the finest **sea kayaking** around. Near Island and the smaller islands around it, just across the channel from the town, have all sorts of narrow straits and shallow coves where you can bob about, looking down through crystal-clear water at brilliantly colored starfish and anemones. Alaskan Wilderness Adventures (ⓣ486-2397, ⓔakwild@ptialaska .net) runs excellent paddling trips (half-day $75, full day $100; minimum 2 people), as does Orcas Unlimited (ⓣ539-1979, ⓦwww.orcasunlimited.com), charging a little more but also offering mother-ship-supported longer trips ($360 per 24hr) with meals provided.

There are so many people prepared to take you **fishing** it is hard to know where to start, but Kodiak Fish Konnection (late May to late Sept; ⓣ1-888/283-2464, ⓦwww.kodiakfishkonnection.com) will show you a full day of salmon- or halibut-fishing for under $200, including processing (gutting, filleting, freezing, and packing) what you catch. If they don't do the sort of thing you're after, they'll put you in touch with someone who does.

Kodiak is also said to have some of the best roadside salmon-fishing in the state: the Alaska Department of Fish and Game, 211 Mission Rd (ⓣ486-1880, ⓦwww.adfg.state.ak.us), has a list of guides, knows the regulations, and can sell you a license. Cy's Sporting Goods, 117 Lower Mill Bay Rd (ⓣ486-3900, ⓦwww.kodiak-outfitters.com), sells all the gear you'll need, including locally made flies, and has all the latest on where fish are biting; they also organize fly-ins.

△ Fishing boats in Kodiak harbor

Eating, drinking, and entertainment

The range of restaurants in Kodiak is adequate for a few days, and **grocery** prices from Food For Less downtown are just ten percent higher than in Anchorage. About the only regular entertainment is seeing a **movie** at the Orpheum Theatre, 102 Center St (T 486-5449), or watching the **Kodiak Alutiiq Dancers** (around $15; call T 486-4449 for times), who perform an hour-long celebration of traditional dance in the Kodiak Tribal Council hall downtown at 312 W Marine Way. Look out for the **microbrews** of the island's own Kodiak Island Brewing Co, which sell on tap around town and by the bottle from their brewery at 338 Shelikof St (T 486-2537). If you're interested, stop by for a brief free tour (daily noon–7pm).

Channel Side Chowder House 450 E Marine Way T 486-4478. Appealing daytime café with windows and a sunny deck right over the channel. Good for espresso, pastries, cinnamon rolls, and great seafood dishes, from hearty bowls of chowder ($4) to fish and chips of halibut, salmon, or scallops ($9–14). Closed evenings.

The Chart Room 236 Rezanof Drive West, inside the *Best Western* T 486-8807. Kodiak's most formal dining; enjoy harbor views along with $40 king crab legs or $24 crab-stuffed halibut. Don't miss the photos of the 1964 tsunami aftermath in the hallway.

El Chicanos 103 Center Ave T 486-6116. Reliable Mexican meals are dished up either inside or out. The menu is filled with the usual suspects – enchiladas, burritos, and their kin – for $11–13, but they also do plates of *chorizo*, eggs, rice, and beans ($12) and for the brave, *menudo*, a kind of tripe soup.

Galley Gourmet T 1-800/253-6331, W www .kodiak-alaska-dinner-cruises.com. Combine sightseeing and eating aboard the characteristic old *Sea Breeze* launch for a gourmet 3–4hr dinner cruise based around local seafood. May & June $95, July–Sept $120; phone for reservation and directions to meeting point.

Harborside Coffee and Goods 216 Shelikof St T 486-5862. Just the spot for hanging out over an espresso, soup, or cinnamon roll, to watch the harbor activity out the window.

Henry's Great Alaskan 512 Marine Way T 486-8844. A combined sports, bar and restaurant with microbrewed beer and a good range of salads, sandwiches, burgers, and dinners, such as halibut and fries, all around $14.

The Mecca 302 Marine Way T 486-3364. Typically jumping bar often with live local music and even the occasional touring band.

Mill Bay Coffee & Pastries 3833 Rezanof Drive East, 3 miles northeast of town T 486-4411, W www.millbaycoffee.com. The best café-style eating on the island, with sofas and mismatched furniture, where you can sip good espresso or sate yourself with chicken Caesar salad ($10), quiches, and a sumptuous array of French pastries. There's even outside seating for those rare sunny days.

Old Powerhouse 516 E Marine Way T 481-1088. Predominantly Japanese seafood restaurant with great views over the channel and excellent box-lunch specials for around $8. Closed Mon.

Listings

Air-charter companies Andrew Airways T 487-2566, W www.andrewairways.com; Bear Quest Aviation T 1-888/304-2327, W www.bearquestaviation .com; Kodiak Air Service T 486-4446, W www .kodiakair.com; Sea Hawk T 1-800/770-4295, W www.seahawkair.com.

Banks There are several around town, including Key Bank, 422 E Marine Way, in The Mall. All banks and supermarkets have ATMs.

Bike rental 58°North, 1231 Mill Bay Rd (T 486-6294, E thowland@ptialaska.net), charges $35 for a full 24hr.

Books Several places around town have free book swaps, including *Harborside Coffee and Goods* (see above). For new books visit The Treasury, 104

Central St (T 486-0373), or head out to The Next Page, 3833 Rezanof Drive East (T 481-7243), handily sited beside *Mill Bay Coffee & Pastries*.

Car rental The best deals are Rent-a-Heap, inside Port of Kodiak Gifts in The Mall, 508 Marine Way (T 486-8550, E carrent@ptialaska.net), which charges $37 a day plus 37¢ a mile for a compact, and Budget, same address and at the airport (T 487-2220, E budget@eagle.ptialaska .net), which rents unlimited-mileage compacts for $60.

Festivals In late March or early April, there's the Pillar Mountain Golf Classic (T 486-2931, E folgers@ak.net), a one-hole par-70 course in which you have to hit 1400ft up Pillar Mountain

Hiking on Kodiak Island

Hiking on Kodiak is limited to forest walks and a few hillside trails near Kodiak town. Those smooth green hills might look tempting for off-trail exploration, but foot-tangling grasses and thickets of willow and alder make it very heavy going once you leave a defined path. The best map is *Kodiak Audubon's Hiking & Biking Guide* ($12 from town and National Refuge visitor centers), though they also produce an inferior *Hiking on Kodiak* leaflet ($5).

Out in the **Kodiak National Wildlife Refuge** hiking trails are few, and you'll be pretty much making it up as you go along. If you fancy engaging the services of a guide, you'll find a list of operators at the refuge visitor center.

Remember that Kodiak weather is fickle even by Alaskan standards, so you must be well prepared. If you need to rent (extra) gear, contact Kodiak Kamps (☏486-5333).

Barometer Mountain (5 miles round-trip; 3–4hr; 2500ft ascent). The most popular hike on the island climbs to the summit of this 2452-foot peak along the steep east ridge, with views improving all the way up. The trail starts almost opposite the end of the airport runway a hundred yards south of a sharp bend in Chiniak Road. After heading into the brush, it switchbacks up to a fork where you branch right along a gravel road for five hundred yards until the path up the ridge heads off to your left.

North End Park (half a mile one way; 20min; 100ft ascent). Easy shoreline trails starting beside the Zharoff Bridge on Near Island, ideal for an evening stroll and for salmonberry picking in July and August.

Pillar Mountain (5 miles round-trip; 2–3hr; 800ft ascent). A moderate hike to the summit, beginning on the left side of Pillar Mountain Road, just past the quarry a third of the way up the mountain. From the summit a second trail leads three miles southwest towards the substation, where a gravel road leads down to the highway a mile or so north of the airport.

Pyramid Mountain (4 miles round-trip; 3–4hr; 2200ft ascent). This hike starts at the ski area on Anton Larsen Bay Road, a couple of miles past the golf course. From the parking lot it climbs steeply through brush to a broad shoulder on alpine tundra. The views are great from here, but the more adventurous will want to press on to the top.

in the depths of winter snow, with ball-spotters allowed but no radio communication or dogs; Memorial Day weekend draws enthusiasts from Anchorage and elsewhere for the Kodiak Crab Festival (☏486-5557, ⊛www.kodiak.org /crabfest.html), with all manner of races, a blessing of the fishing fleet, crab eating, and music; and on Labor Day weekend there's the Kodiak State Fair.

Internet access Free for an hour at the library (see below; no WiFi) and also for reasonable rates at The Treasury (see "Books", above).

Laundry Dillard's, 218 Shelikof St, has laundry, shower facilities, and WiFi.

Library 319 Rezanof Drive West (Mon–Fri 10am–9pm, Sat 10am–5pm, Sun 1–5pm).

Medical assistance Kodiak Island Medical Center, 1915 Rezanof Drive East ☏486-3281.

Post office The main post office is at 419 Lower Mill Bay Rd (Mon–Fri 9am–5.30pm), but the Food For Less supermarket has a handier branch inside (Mon–Sat 10am–1pm & 2–6pm). The **General Delivery** zip code is 99615.

Taxes Kodiak has a six percent sales tax and an additional five percent bed tax, not included in accommodation price codes.

Travel agency US Travel, 340 Mission Rd ☏486-3232.

Around the island and the archipelago

Outside the main town, Kodiak Island gets pretty quiet. There are a few small communities dotted along the indented coastline, but most are only accessible by boat or float-plane. Kodiak's **road system** barely tops a hundred miles (mostly paved) and doesn't really contain any essential sights, but if you've come this far it is worth renting a car and exploring, especially if you strike clear, sunny weather. To see more than just the roads you'll need to go **flightseeing**, and most flights set off with the express aim of sighting some of the island's huge **bears**, observed from riverbank platforms erected for the purpose.

Kodiak Island is the largest in the archipelago, but several more islands warrant attention for the superlative kayaking all about. **Afognak and Shuyak islands** are the most obvious and accessible destinations.

Along the road system

You can easily explore the island's road system in a day, though the rocky coastlines, accessible beaches, and fossil-hunting opportunities may tempt you to venture out for longer. Bear in mind that there are few places to stay and even fewer to eat, so come prepared, especially if you fancy **camping** out for a few days. There is only one semi-formal campground, but you can pitch a tent or park an RV in numerous spots along the road provided you respect people's private property. Pick up the CVB's *Explore Kodiak* brochure, which contains a mile-by-mile rundown on these "Backcountry Byways."

Five miles south of town, the airport marks the main junction of the island's road system. Here, **Anton Larsen Bay Road** branches northwest and winds twelve miles over a low mountain pass to Anton Larsen Bay, where there's a small dock used by residents of **Port Lions**, a village just across the water but hidden behind a headland. It is a pretty drive, but there's not a great deal to see, except for Kodiak's golf course a couple of miles along, an odd vision of verdure in this untamed land.

At the airport junction, **Chiniak Road** runs south past the entrance to the former military base at Women's Bay, now the nation's largest **coast guard base** with over two thousand personnel patrolling the fishing grounds and providing search and rescue for the whole of Southwest Alaska. About ten miles south of town, you'll pass the *Rendezvous* bar and see the last of the Sitka spruce trees that blanket the eastern third of the archipelago. The road now breaks into more open country past Bell's Flat (once the island's dairy farm) and hugs the coast, where there's occasional beach access and bald eagles nesting in cottonwood trees. *Halsin Bay Inn* at Mile 28 is mostly a bar but also serves reasonable diner meals; despite its name, it has no accommodation. A patch of farmland at the head of Halsin Bay heralds the Pasagshak Road junction (Mile 30). Chiniak Road continues along the coast through a scattered residential area where you'll find Kodiak Island Winery, Mile 36.2 (☎486-4848, ⓦ www.kodiakwinery.com), one of the very few wineries in the state that's open to the public. Their tasting room (June–Aug daily 1–5pm) gives you a chance to sample wines made from salmonberries, rhubarb, blackberries, and whatever can be collected from the wild. The road ends at Mile 42, where the *Road's End Restaurant* (☎486-2885) does a great halibut sandwich, and the Chiniak airstrip, in service from World War II until 1967, lies surrounded by abandoned bunkers and gun emplacements.

Pasagshak Road runs eight miles south from the Pasagshak Road junction to **Lake Rose Tead**, swimming with red salmon in August and home to a variety of birds, especially swans, throughout the year. Nearby, **Pasagshak State Recreation Site** is good for beach walking and has free beachside camping with an outhouse and hand pump close by. For greater comfort, seek out *Pasagshak River Accommodations* (see p.346). The road then continues three miles to Pasagshak Beach, where Kodiak's **surfers** come for the best waves and beachside camping (no facilities). Three miles on, the road enters the **Kodiak**

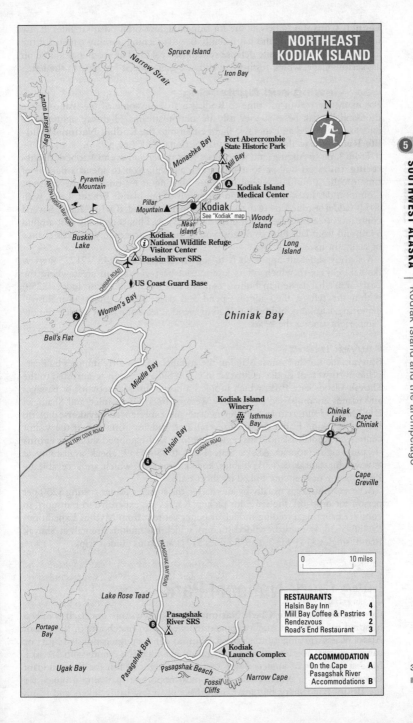

NORTHEAST KODIAK ISLAND

Spruce Island

Iron Bay

Narrow Strait

Anton Larsen Bay

N

Monashka Bay

Fort Abercrombie
State Historic Park

Mill Bay

Pyramid
Mountain

Pillar
Mountain ▲

Kodiak Island
Medical Center

Kodiak
See "Kodiak" map

Near
Island

Woody
Island

Kodiak
National Wildlife Refuge
Visitor Center

Long
Island

Buskin
Lake

Buskin River SRS

US Coast Guard Base

Women's Bay

Chiniak Bay

Bell's Flat

Middle Bay

SALTERY COVE ROAD

Kodiak Island
Winery

Isthmus
Bay

Chiniak
Lake

Cape
Chiniak

Halsin Bay

CHINIAK ROAD

Cape
Greville

PASAGSHAK BAY ROAD

Lake Rose Tead

Portage
Bay

Pasagshak
River SRS

Kodiak
Launch Complex

Ugak Bay

Pasagshak Bay

Pasagshak Beach

Narrow Cape

Fossil
Cliffs

0   10 miles

RESTAURANTS

Halsin Bay Inn	4
Mill Bay Coffee & Pastries	1
Rendezvous	2
Road's End Restaurant	3

ACCOMMODATION

On the Cape	A
Pasagshak River Accommodations	B

Launch Complex, a private site for launching low-orbit polar satellites. It saw its first launch in 1998 and has recently been launching dummy targets for the latest version of the missile defense system (see p.473). The road ends a mile on at Narrow Cape, where fossil-filled cliffs are accessible at low tide to the left.

Bear-viewing and flightseeing

For many, the reason to come to Kodiak is to view some of the island's three thousand Kodiak bears as they fish the salmon streams. Highway sightings are rare, so you'll need an expensive flight either into the **Kodiak National Wildlife Refuge** or to the coast of Katmai National Park (see p.356).

From June to August (and sometimes September and even October), **flightseeing tours** go out on four-hour runs, allowing you to spend a fair bit of time on the ground at several locations, viewing at reasonably close quarters. Common destinations are both in the south of the island: **Frazer Lake**, with a fish ladder a mile down the Dog Salmon River, and **Karluk Lake**. Several companies (see Listings, p.350) offer their services. Flights typically cost around $450, and from late June to August you've got at least a ninety percent chance of seeing bears.

A slightly different approach is to join Kodiak Treks (☎487-2122, ⓦwww .kodiaktreks.com), which offers low-impact bear-viewing in areas where the bears aren't habituated to human contact. You fly into the base lodge ($250) within the refuge, then ideally spend 3–5 days ($275 a night all-inclusive) exploring, kayaking, and fishing. Plan to spend at least one night at their remote camp, right among the bears.

Shuyak Island

Shuyak, the northernmost island in the archipelago, lies forty minutes by floatplane northwest of Kodiak. Cloaked in virgin Sitka spruce, it is entrusted to the Shuyak Island State Park, which protects a deeply incised network of passages and islands encompassed by Big Bay, Western Inlet, Carry Inlet, and Shanigan Bay. This is ideal territory for intermediate and experienced **kayakers**; pick up the sea-kayaking leaflet detailing several loop paddles from one of the visitor centers on Kodiak Island. This region has four well-equipped shoreline **cabins** sleeping eight (contact Alaska State Parks ☎486-6339, check availability at ⓦwww.dnr.state.ak.us/parks/cabins/kodiak.cfm; $75), which are accessible by kayak. Some of them are linked by short trails.

Access to Shuyak is usually by air charter, the smallest planes costing $250 per person for drop-off, the same for pickup. Kayaks are expensive to transport, so consider bringing a folding model, or better yet rent from Mythos Expeditions (☎486-5536, ⓦwww.thewildcoast.com), which has multiday rentals at Shuyak Island (singles $141 for 3 days, doubles $171) and runs guided trips.

Lake Clark National Park

Considering that **Lake Clark National Park** (ⓦwww.nps.gov/lacl) is only a hundred miles west of Anchorage and has scenery to match any in the rest of Alaska, it is surprisingly little visited. With no dense congregations of bears or calving glaciers, it is left off many itineraries, and yet this is quintessential Alaska. Modest numbers of anglers come to remote lodges to fish for the abundant sockeye salmon in what is one of the most important spawning grounds for the Bristol Bay fishery, but apart from that only a few hardy hikers and teams of rafters taking on the three federally designated National Wild Rivers seem to get up this way.

The park gets its name from the 42-mile-long **Lake Clark** in its southwest and features two conical snow-capped volcanoes – **Redoubt** (10,197ft) and **Iliamna** (10,016ft) – both visible from Anchorage and dominating the western horizon along the Kenai Peninsula's Cook Inlet coast. They form part of the Pacific Ring of Fire (aka the circum-Pacific seismic belt) and are sporadically active: in 1990 Redoubt spewed clouds of ash that briefly closed Anchorage airport. The volcanoes lie between Cook Inlet and the **Chigmit Mountains**, a jagged and glacially sculpted geological jumble where the Alaska Range meets the Aleutian Range. Glaciers still peel off the slopes, feeding rivers that either cut into the wild interior of the park or tumble steeply through Sitka and white spruce to the coastal cliffs.

It is a spectacularly diverse park with a remarkable range of plant communities, from coastal rainforest to boreal forest typical of Interior Alaska and even alpine tundra. Fauna is equally varied, from the seabird rookeries on the Cook Inlet sea cliffs to the moose, black and brown bears, Dall sheep, and caribou of the park's interior.

Hiking and rafting

The only community inside the park is **Port Alsworth**, on the southern shores of Lake Clark, which is where the park's one bona fide trail leads to the **Tanalian Falls** (2.5 miles one way) and on to **Kontrashibuna Lake** (3.5 miles one way). After that you're on your own. Keen hikers prepared to follow an unmarked route over rugged terrain can tackle the **Telaquana Trail** (50 miles one way), which follows an old Dena'ina route later used by trappers and miners during the early 1900s. It runs north from Lake Clark through boreal forest and across alpine tundra and requires fording glacial rivers that can at times be impassable. For recent trail conditions, talk to a park service representative before you head out, but keep in mind that nothing should be taken too literally; weather here is unpredictable and can turn quickly.

Lake Clark National Park is perhaps most visited for its multiday **rafting trips** on three National Wild Rivers. Rafters' primary activity on these rivers is watching the scenery, with occasional chances to tackle Class III and IV. All rivers are raftable from June to September (with the highest water being in July and early Aug), and all require float-plane access and egress. The *Lake Clark Inn* in Port Alsworth (see p.356) rents rafts for $95 a day.

The easiest of the rivers is the **Mulchatna River** (Class II–III), usually run from Turquoise Lake (about thirty miles north of Lake Clark), from where it descends into a shallow and rocky bed through the Bonanza Hills for a couple of days, then eases to a gentle float down to its confluence with the Chilikadrotna River, taking perhaps five days in all. The **Chilikadrotna River** (Class III) is a slightly tougher four- to five-day proposition running sixty miles down from Twin Lakes on the western flanks of the Alaska Range.

The put-in for the **Tlikakila River** (Class III–IV) is Summit Lake, a good hiking area on the eastern edge of the park that is easily reached direct from Kenai or Anchorage. From there it is 51 miles down to Lake Clark through a densely forested valley with occasional sections of Class III and one section of potentially Class IV (depending on water levels), though this can be portaged.

The weather in the park is cool, rainy, and unpredictable, so come prepared for anything, including bugs, which tend to be less brutal in August and September, the best months for hiking and rafting – if there's enough water.

Before traveling to Lake Clark, get detailed information and advice by contacting the Port Alsworth **field headquarters** (daily 8am–5pm; ☎781-2218). Stop in once you reach Port Alsworth for interesting natural history displays and video programs.

Almost everyone **flies** into the park, either by air taxi first to Port Alsworth and then out into the wilder sections of the park, or by private transport directly to one of the expensive lodges. *Lake Clark Inn* (☎781-2224, ⓦwww .lakeclark.com; ◉) flies to Port Alsworth direct from Anchorage for $325. They offer accommodation, meal packages, and all sorts of rentals and guide services, as does *The Farm Lodge/Lake Clark Air* (☎1-888/440-2281, ⓦwww.lakeclarkair.com), which also has an unguided river-float escape ($1555 per person) including airfares, two nights' accommodation, meals, and Chilikadrotna drop-off and pickup. Raft rental is extra.

Katmai National Park

Although there are several places in Alaska where bears congregate in large numbers, only **Katmai National Park** (ⓦwww.nps.gov/katm), more than two hundred miles southwest of Anchorage, combines the bear-viewing with wonderful scenery, relatively easy access, convenient accommodation, and a stock of other activities in case viewing bears begins to pale. None of this comes cheap, but it is hard to put a value on standing twenty yards from a large brown bear as it perches atop the five-foot Brooks Falls ready to chomp on any sockeye salmon that is foolish enough to leap within striking distance.

Throughout July the Brooks River is so thick with sockeyes that up to forty bears might be scattered along its mile-and-a-half length. This is also the busiest time for visitors, who arrive en masse again in September when the bears gather at Brooks Falls to feast on dying fish. You won't see bears catching fish in mid-air at this time, but you will see enormous bears fattened up for winter, sometimes topping a thousand pounds. Bear activity is low or nonexistent in June and August.

For many years, Katmai was known only for the most violent volcanic eruption of the twentieth century, when **Novorupta** (Latin for "newly erupted") spewed out seven cubic miles of ash and pumice for three days beginning on June 6, 1912. The cloud of ash drifted as far as North Africa, and northern hemisphere temperatures dropped a couple of degrees, effectively creating a year without summer. People a hundred miles away in Kodiak were wading knee-deep through volcanic ash and couldn't see their outstretched hands for two days. Close to Novorupta, intensely hot ash settled to a depth of up to seven hundred feet, blanketing the volcanic gases and vaporizing streams. As the steam and gases forced their way to the surface, they created an unearthly landscape described by *National Geographic* geologist Robert Griggs, in 1916, as looking like "all the steam engines in the world, assembled together, had popped their safety valves at once and were letting off surplus steam in concert." As the Novorupta fireworks emptied the underground magma chamber, the summit of nearby **Mount Katmai** collapsed to form an almost perfectly circular crater lake. Two years later the **Valley of 10,000 Smokes** became the centerpiece of the Katmai National Monument.

As the underground temperatures subsided and the gases escaped, the number of active vents diminished until none was left. The park languished until the

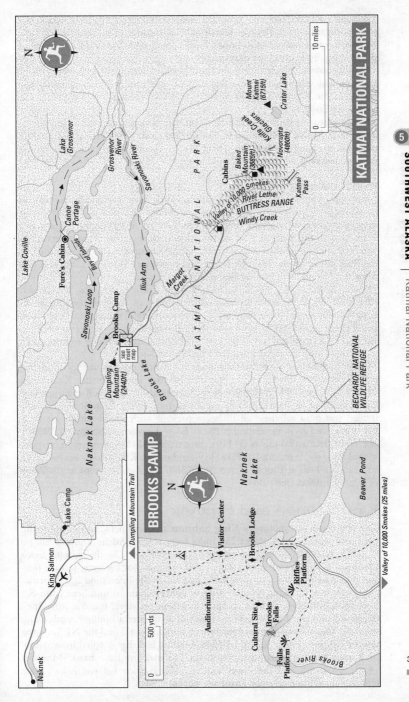

KATMAI NATIONAL PARK

BROOKS CAMP

N

Dumpling Mountain Trail

500 yds

0

Naknek Lake

Visitor Center

Brooks Lodge

Auditorium

Cultural Site

Brooks Falls

Riffles Platform

Falls Platform

Brooks River

Beaver Pond

Valley of 10,000 Smokes (25 miles)

N

10 miles

0

Mount Katmai (6715ft)

Crater Lake

Knife Creek Glaciers

Novarupta (4860ft)

Baked Mountain (3685ft)

Cabins

Katmai Pass

Valley of 10,000 Smokes

River Lethe

BUTTRESS RANGE

Windy Creek

Margot Creek

KATMAI   NATIONAL   PARK

Savonoski River

Grosvenor River

Lake Grosvenor

Canoe Portage

Lake Coville

Fure's Cabin

Bay of Islands

Savonoski Loop

Iliuk Arm

Brooks Camp

see inset map

Dumpling Mountain (2440ft)

Brooks Lake

Naknek Lake

Lake Camp

King Salmon

Naknek

BECHAROF NATIONAL WILDLIFE REFUGE

357

1940s, when Ray Petersen set up five remote fishing camps in the park, the most popular being at **Brooks Camp**. The abundance of sockeye salmon here had been equally attractive to brown bears, which, once humans started visiting the site, rapidly became the main attraction.

Now Brooks Camp is the single most popular bear-viewing spot in Alaska, and one that warrants at least a few days of your time, whether camping and hiking in the Valley of 10,000 Smokes or spending more time kayaking the Savonoski Loop.

If seeing bears is your sole objective, you may want to enter the lottery for an opening at **McNeil River State Game Sanctuary** (see box, p.362) on the northeastern fringe of Katmai, where bears are equally concentrated, though without the press of visitors.

Practicalities

Almost everyone visiting Katmai National Park does so from Anchorage on an all-inclusive package or a connecting sequence of flights to Brooks Camp, thereby avoiding unnecessary time spent in the small town of King Salmon, five miles outside the western edge of the park. With the appropriate reservations you'll be met upon your arrival at the King Salmon airport, driven a mile to the float docks on the Naknek River, and flown into Brooks Camp. It is also possible to fly in from Homer (see p.299).

Alaska Airlines (℡1-800/252-7522, ⓦwww.alaskaair.com) jets and PenAir (℡1-800/448-4226, ⓦwww.penair.com) twin-props **fly** from Anchorage to King Salmon several times daily, usually for around $400 round-trip. From there you'll pay around $165 round-trip to fly to Brooks Camp by air taxi: try Katmai Air, run by Katmailand (see below), who also allow you to book right through to Brooks Camp from Anchorage for $575 round-trip.

Once at Brooks Camp the only accommodation options are to camp (see p.361) or stay at *Brooks Lodge*, operated by park concessionaire Katmailand (℡243-5448 or 1-800/544-0551, ⓦwww.katmailand.com). You can't just find your own way to Brooks Camp and book into *Brooks Lodge* independently; instead you must purchase an inclusive package with round-trip flights from Anchorage and accommodation at *Brooks Lodge* (but not meals): day-trip ($549), one night ($826), two nights ($1119), three nights ($1414), three-night off-peak special (June 1–20 & Aug 10–25; $1119), and others. Katmailand also has kayak and canoe rentals at Brooks Camp (see p.360) and runs bus trips to the Valley of 10,000 Smokes (see p.361).

King Salmon and Naknek

The small bush community of **King Salmon**, scattered between its airport and the broad tidal Naknek River 250 miles southwest of Anchorage, was once a Cold War military base and is now the main service town for the region. There's no reason to be here except to stage a trip to Katmai or for some remote fishing. If you have an hour to spare here, stop in for the interesting and informative displays at the King Salmon **visitor center** (June to mid-Sept Mon–Sat 8am–5pm, Sun 9am–noon & 1–5pm; mid-Sept to May Mon–Sat 9am–5pm; ℡246-4250), right by the airport terminal, or wander a hundred yards along the street to the King Salmon Mall where, upstairs, you'll find the **NPS visitor center** (Mon–Fri 8am–4.30pm; ℡246-4250), which has detailed information on Katmai and Lake Clark national parks. The mall also has a **bank** (Mon–Fri 10am–5pm) with an ATM. Next door is *Eddies Fireplace Inn*, with a bar, diner, espresso corner, and coin-op **Internet access**.

Accommodation in King Salmon is expensive, although if you have a sturdy, bug-proof tent and are bear-aware you can easily find a quiet spot to camp. The cheapest rooms are at *Antlers Inn*, just behind the mall (℗246-8525 or 1-888/735-8525, ℮antlers@bristolbay.com; apartments ❸, rooms ❺), which has self-contained apartments as well as smaller rooms that share bathrooms and a small communal kitchenette. They also have a camping area (free) with shower facilities ($8) and a barbecue. Alternatively try *King Ko Inn* (℗1-866/234-3474, ℗www.kingko.com; ❼), which has fairly new and comfortable cabins. Local taxes add ten percent to room rates.

Eating in King Salmon is pricey and options are limited to *Eddies Fireplace Inn* and *King Ko*, which has pasta dishes ($20), steaks, salmon, and halibut meals ($20–30), and a lively bar. If you are self-catering and haven't brought everything you need from Anchorage (which you should do), pick up **groceries** from the limited supply at the AC Value Center supermarket/deli/liquor store beside the mall.

Fourteen miles downstream, the Bristol Bay fishing village of **Naknek** is the scene of the world's largest sockeye run, with some twenty million fish passing between mid-June and the end of July (peaking in the first two weeks of July). Around seventy percent of all the world's red salmon are caught in Bristol Bay and three quarters of those are caught in and around Naknek. Once the fishing season opens in late June, commercial fishing boats are gunwhale-to-gunwhale trying to be first to get their nets in the water, and both King Salmon and Naknek are alive with fishermen. To get there, contact Redline Taxi (℗246-8294), which charges around $20 for the ride from King Salmon or **rent a truck** from *King Ko Inn* ($85 a day).

Brooks Camp and around

Bears are all over Katmai National Park, but your best chance of seeing them in any number is at **Brooks Camp**, 47 miles east of King Salmon. It is essentially just a lodge, campground, and ranger station on the north side of the Brooks River, plus a couple of bear-viewing platforms on the south bank – one right by Brooks Falls. The whole place is compact enough to walk everywhere.

△ Brown bear at Brooks Camp

Since activity revolves entirely around the presence of bears, Brooks Camp is only open to the public from June 1 to September 17. On arrival you must attend the School of Bear Etiquette, a twenty-minute **orientation program**, partly to help you avoid having to deal with bears and partly to instill some common-sense rules so that the nearly three hundred sightseers and photographers present at any given moment can go about their business in relative harmony. It takes place at the **visitor center** (call the King Salmon visitor center for information), which also runs a program of afternoon and evening walks and talks.

Your first day is likely to be spent hanging around **Brooks Falls**, watching and photographing up to a dozen bears. Extensive new boardwalks opened in 2005 have made viewing easier, though rangers still have to limit the time people can stay on the platform so that everyone gets a chance. There's considerable jockeying for position as video cameras are poked between ranks of professional photographers and their tripods.

Things tend to be quieter early and late in the day when day-trippers are absent. You can spend the middle of the day tackling the **Dumpling Mountain Hike** (8 miles round-trip; 4–5hr; 2400ft ascent), which follows the only formed trail hereabouts and climbs to the mountain's summit, passing an overlook about halfway.

Kayaking and **canoeing** are superb ways to see more of the area, either on the Savonoski Loop (see box, below) or on shorter trips using boats booked in advance from *Brooks Lodge*: double kayaks $16 an hour, $60 a day; canoes $12/$40. There's plenty of interest for a couple of hours' paddle, but if you are equipped for camping you could head twenty miles to the Bay of Islands, one to

Savonoski Loop

Anyone with experience in backcountry camping and moderate kayaking or canoeing skills shouldn't have too much trouble completing the **Savonoski Loop**, an 86-mile lake and river paddle which can be done in as little as three days by fit kayakers, although most people take four to seven days. That said, it is a true wilderness experience and help may be days away, so you'll need to be able to handle the braided Savonoski River, which has sweepers but no whitewater. There's also one strenuous portage, and high winds can whip up across the lakes, so you need to be prepared to pitch camp and wait for bad weather to pass.

Everyone follows a clockwise course from Brooks Camp into the north arm of Naknek Lake and the **Bay of Islands**, myriad small islands with great camping spots, separated by crystalline water with good pike- and trout-fishing. Accommodation is available at *Fure's Cabin* (reservations through NPS visitor center in King Salmon; free), an original 1920s fur-trapper's cabin located at the start of the two-mile portage to **Lake Grosvenor**. At the southern end of Lake Grosvenor you enter the Class I **Grosvenor River**, which typically has excellent wildlife-viewing. Along the Class I–II **Savonoski River** the wildlife is most likely to be bears: you're advised to press through this section in one day to avoid camping among them. To complete the loop back to Brooks Camp you've then only got to cross **Iliuk Arm**, which is exposed and best traversed along its south shore. Pick a campsite away from the mouth of Margot Creek, which also has a reputation for bears.

You can rent canoes and kayaks at Brooks Camp but you might find it cost-effective to go for one of the **packages** run by Lifetime Adventures (☎1-800/952-8624, ⊛www .lifetimeadventures.net). They offer an unguided loop with a round-trip flight from Anchorage to Brooks Camp plus use of folding kayaks for $750, and run guided trips for $1700 including everything but food.

two days' paddle away, or ten miles to the islands around the mouth of Margot Creek, another area known for bears. Either camp on the islands or take them in on one very long paddling day.

If you don't have time for paddling but want to explore the area, **flightseeing** trips from Brooks Camp ($138 per person, minimum two) typically fly over the Valley of 10,000 Smokes and Novorupta volcano, providing a speedy alternative to a self-propelled adventure.

Fishing is stupendous around here, and many visitors are happy to spend their day with rented gear (spin and fly rods $12 a day, waders $9) or taking guided trolling trips for lake trout and arctic char ($175 a half-day); renting a boat on Naknek Lake ($260 a day per boat); or employing a river guide for rainbow trout-fishing ($50 an hour, $200 a day).

The only **rooms** at Brooks Camp are those available on package deals (see p.358) at *Brooks Lodge*, which fills up almost a year in advance for the prime viewing month of July. Everyone else stays at the **campground** ($8 per person), which has fire rings and bear-resistant food caches and also fills up early: book online or by phone (T 1-800/365-2267 6am–6pm Alaska time, W www.reservations.nps.gov).

If you are **cooking** your own meals, you'll need to bring a camp stove and an empty fuel bottle; white gas (but not propane) is available in Brooks Camp at the Katmai Trading Post, which also stocks a few snacks, film, and fishing gear, but little else. **Meals** are available only at *Brooks Lodge*, where they lay on all-you-can-eat buffet affairs (breakfast $12; lunch $18; dinner $28) open to all. The lodge also has a bar with seating ranged around a large central fireplace.

The Valley of 10,000 Smokes

If you've forked out the cash to get to Brooks Camp, it's a shame not to also visit the **Valley of 10,000 Smokes**, a virtually plant-free expanse of red, yellow, and tan wasteland some three miles wide and twelve long, deeply incised by river-carved gorges a hundred feet deep. It is reached along a 23-mile dirt road by Katmailand's Natural History Tour (8.30am–4.30pm; $88 round-trip, $51 each way for multiday hikers), which uses a 4WD bus for the ninety-minute run from Brooks Camp to Three Forks Overlook, where there's a wonderful view over the desolate landscape and a shelter to protect you from the wind and the volcanic ash it carries. The on-board ranger then leads an instructive three-mile round-trip hike (700ft ascent) down the **Ukak Falls Trail** to the confluence of Knife, Lethe, and Windy creeks, and the spectacular falls themselves. The tour is often full throughout the summer, so it pays to sign up at *Brooks Lodge* when you arrive.

To really explore the area, spend a few days **hiking**, best done in late August and early September when the weather is relatively benign, most snow cover has melted, and bugs are at their least menacing. After the bus ride to Three Forks Overlook, most hikers spend their first day heading southeast through the Valley of 10,000 Smokes to reach (in 5–7hr) some abandoned US Geological Survey **huts** (free; no reservations) on the flanks of Baked Mountain. One sleeps four, the other six and they are weatherproof but otherwise very basic: the only water supply is snowmelt from patches found nearby. By setting up a base camp you are then free to explore the half-mile-wide crater of **Novorupta**; **Mount Griggs** with its nested craters from successive eruptions; the 2600-foot **Katmai Pass**, which was used as a mail route during the Nome gold rush; and the turquoise, ice-encrusted crater lake of **Mount Katmai**. This last option requires crampons, an ice ax, and glacier navigation skills, and if you have these you may also want to play around on **Knife Creek Glaciers**, now stagnant and

If you want to see a lot of bears without the crowds, you could try your luck at visiting **McNeil River State Game Sanctuary**, 110 miles west of Homer, an enclave in the northeastern corner of Katmai National Park. From early July to mid-August, brown bears come to feast on chum salmon struggling up **McNeil River Falls**, a mess of rocks and whitewater a mile inland from Cook Inlet. Here you might easily see twenty or thirty bears at one time and perhaps a hundred over the course of a day. In June slightly smaller numbers (around 15–20) congregate for the sockeye run at **Mikfik Creek** a few miles away.

The trouble is, you are unlikely to experience this, because only ten people are allowed to come here on any one day (between June 7 and Aug 25), with spaces given only to winners of an annual lottery. What's more, each space is valid for four days, so the turnover is low. If that is not deterrent enough, you have to pay $25 simply to enter the lottery (where your chances are around one in ten), then a further $350 ($150 for Alaska residents) for the permit if your name is drawn, plus around $600 round-trip for the flight from Homer. If you are staying overnight you'll have to be self-sufficient for camping at McNeil River, and should bring hip waders. There are also three standby places (again distributed by lottery: $25 for the application; $175 nonrefundable fee for the standby permit; $75 for Alaskans) so that there are people on hand if someone fails to show or doesn't take their full quota of four days. Enter the lottery before March 1 of the year of your visit either online or by mail sent to ATTN: McNeil River Application, Alaska Department of Fish & Game, Division of Wildlife Conservation, PO Box 228080, Anchorage, Alaska 99522-8080. A full set of lottery rules and an application form can be found at Ⓦwww.wc.adfg.state.ak.us/mcneil.

slowly melting since the 1912 collapse of Mount Katmai robbed them of their nourishing icefields. Make your way back to Three Forks Overlook to grab the return ride to Brooks Camp with Katmailand's Natural History Tour.

With the rapid erosion in the area, conditions change quickly, so you'll need to get the latest information and route guides from the NPS visitor centers in King Salmon and Brooks Camp. They can sell you the Trails Illustrated *Katmai National Park and Preserve* topo map ($10), tell you where you can get water, and warn you about hazardous river crossings, since very deep, narrow gorges can often fill up and appear to be shallow pools, the bottom invisible through the silty water. Ferocious ash–laden winds occur quite frequently, so, along with a strong tent, you'll want protective goggles or wraparound sunglasses and perhaps a bandana to breathe through. Bear-resistant food canisters can be obtained free of charge from the NPS visitor centers in Brooks Camp and King Salmon (but aren't really necessary if you only plan to stay at the Baked Mountain huts).

The Alaska Peninsula and the Aleutian ferry trip

Beyond the vast national parks of Lake Clark and Katmai, and west of Kodiak, lies the **Alaska Peninsula**, a slender arm reaching out to Asia and separating the Bering Sea from the North Pacific Ocean. It ends 650 miles southwest of Anchorage, but the mountainous spine effectively continues as the **Aleutian Islands** (*al-OO-shun*), an 1100-mile-long necklace of volcanic islands along the seam of the American and Pacific plates that stretches to within five hundred miles of Russia's Kamchatka Peninsula. The whole arc of the Alaska Peninsula and Aleutian Islands is an isolated, windswept, and almost treeless place where fierce gales, earthquakes, and volcanic activity add a spectacular component to a region as often as not cloaked in silent mist.

Few people live out this way. The Native Aleut (*AL-ee-oot*) wrested a living from the sea around small villages throughout the region, before Russian fur traders established more substantial towns as bases for their operations. Most of the small towns are now populated by a mixture of Natives, white Alaskans, and a few dozen fishing workers from all corners of the world.

Ultimately, it was the Japanese occupation during World War II of the two westernmost islands, Attu and Kiska, and the subsequent military buildup that brought the first modern development to the region, which was further consolidated by the fishing industry. Now almost every community here lives off the sea, with subsistence fishing and hunting in the remaining Native villages and commercial fishing from **Unalaska/Dutch Harbor** – the US's most productive fishing port – and smaller ports along the peninsula.

There are only two realistic ways to visit this area. You can fly direct from Anchorage to Dutch Harbor, where you could easily spend a week, though two or three days is more likely; or take the **three-day ferry journey** to Unalaska/Dutch Harbor aboard the *Tustumena* from either Homer or Kodiak. It briefly calls at all the isolated fishing communities along the southern shore of the Alaska Peninsula, giving a real sense of just how isolated these places are. Unless you've a highly developed sense of adventure, and a fat wallet, you probably won't see any of the Aleutians beyond Dutch Harbor, though birding fanatics occasionally take specialist cruises out to the more distant islands to add Asiatic accidentals to their life list.

The Aleutian ferry trip

Any trip to Alaska should have at least one real adventure, and the best value has to be riding the **AMHS ferry** *Tustumena* along the southern coast of the Alaska Peninsula to the beginning of the Aleutian Chain. Twice a month from mid-April to early October the ferry leaves Homer (on Tuesday evening) for Kodiak, then continues west for the two-and-a-half-day trip to Unalaska/ Dutch Harbor, arriving early Saturday morning. The town warrants more of your time than the five or six hours' turnaround time, but the only solution is to stay for a while and then fly back to Anchorage; it'll cost you more, but it may be preferable to spending another three days on the boat getting back to Homer or Kodiak (especially if the weather forecast is foul).

Along the journey the ferry sails parallel to the treeless grassy lowlands of the Alaska Peninsula, which periodically rise up to lofty volcanoes, some of which let out small eruptions from time to time. Catch it all through a fine patch with calm seas and blue skies and it can be glorious, but the "Trusty Tusty," as the ferry is often called, has to regularly weather rough waters and can spend the whole journey easing its way through dense fog with the coastline barely discernible; bring a good book just in case. There's no guarantee of good weather, but the June, July, and August sailings are probably the best bets. At this time, there's also a **naturalist** on board helping interpret the creatures you might encounter along the way: sea otters, assorted birds, and probably dolphins and whales.

The *Tustumena* is no cruise ship, but a working ferry with a mission to call in at the half-dozen fishing ports along the way to drop off vehicles, people, and supplies. All the villages have airfields, but the ferry remains the lifeline, and half the pleasure is in chatting to those on board as you sail through the night to get to the next godforsaken fishing community. The ferry seldom stops for long, but the hour or two you spend in port is enough to make a brief inspection and be on your way.

The ferry passenger **fare** from Homer to Unalaska is currently $340 each way ($284 from Kodiak), with Alaska Airlines charging around $400 (14-day advance purchase) for the one-way fare back to Anchorage.

The *Tustumena* is one of the smaller ferries in the AMHS fleet, but it's still big enough to have a car deck, restaurant with meals at fair prices, and cabins (a two-berth from Homer to Unalaska costs $350, on top of your individual passenger fares). There is a small solarium with limited space for tents, but no reclining chairs. If you don't mind the discomfort, you can save money on a cabin by sleeping on the floor and taking full advantage of free showers, microwave, and hot water for tea, noodles, or whatever you bring with you.

Chignik and Sand Point

From Kodiak the ferry heads northwest between Kodiak and Afognak islands, threading through Whale Pass to reach the **Shelikof Strait**, which separates Kodiak from the Alaska Peninsula. From there it swings southwest, conveniently making the only open-water passage through the night. By morning you're hugging the coast, jagged white mountains stretching as far as you can see on the starboard side. Towards noon the ferry enters Chignik Bay, surrounded on three sides by mountains (snow-capped in spring and early summer) and approached past the soaring spires and plateau rock of Castle Cape. The hour-long stop in **Chignik** (pop. under 200) is all you need to go ashore and briefly inspect the outsides of the fish-processing plants and the few dozen houses strung along the shore. Ask for directions to the **bakery** if you fancy a donut or scone.

It is another nine hours to **Sand Point**, reached at about 10pm. It sits on Popof Island, where the community was first established in 1898 by a San Francisco fishing company. It now has a permanent population of around a thousand, giving it the feel of a real town. There's even a bar, and since you should have a couple of hours in port there is time enough to hike into town, look at the bald eagles that are almost always in the trees, and join the locals for a game of pool in the *Sand Point Tavern*.

King Cove and Cold Bay

An overnight passage brings you to **King Cove**, yet another small community entirely dependent on fishing and fish processing. The hour layover is just long enough for a brisk walk into town, where (as in many remote communities) the school is by far the biggest and best-kept building. Nearby there is a Russian Orthodox church, modern in execution but equipped with icons and exterior bells moved here in the 1980s from the now abandoned town of Belkofski, twelve miles to the southeast.

The shortest hop on the whole trip passes through a narrow channel surrounded by beautiful mountains and the conical form of Frosty Peak to **Cold Bay**, a tiny place that claims to be the second windiest in the US, and with only ten sunny days a year it is easily the cloudiest. It is a settlement with a level of importance that outweighs its hundred-strong population. In 1941 this became Fort Randall, a major base from which the war in the Aleutians was orchestrated. During the army's occupation, as many as twenty thousand troops were stationed here in Quonset huts (long, semicircular sheet-metal huts used in World War II installations), some contributing to the construction of the third longest airport runway in the state. Cold Bay is now an alternative airport when Anchorage is socked in, and even, it is said, a last-ditch alternative landing zone for the space shuttle. This ability to handle big planes has brought controversy to the region: residents of King Cove have demanded the construction of a twenty-mile road to Cold Bay so that in poor weather, when their own small airport is closed, they can still fly out from the larger airport. Medical emergency is cited as the reason, though cynics suggest that easy access to good hunting is a stronger driving force. None of this would be contentious except that the proposed road would cross critical wetlands within the **Izembek National Wildlife Refuge**. In place of the proposed road, a hovercraft service between King Cove and Cold Bay started up in September 2006, but King Cove residents continue to push for the road's construction.

The refuge attracts dozens of species of birds, but was originally set aside for Brant geese, virtually the entire North American population of 130,000 feeding on the world's largest eelgrass beds during the spring and fall migrations. Catch one of the fall ferry sailings and you may also see some of the 50,000 Canada geese that migrate through here.

During the ferry's two-hour layover you can walk along the half-mile wharf to Cold Bay's Izembek National Wildlife Refuge headquarters **visitor center**, which has a relief map of the area and heaps of info on the refuge. To visit the refuge itself, join the free, hour-long **tour**, organized on the ferry, to Grant Point on Izembek Lagoon. Currently, a lottery is held to allocate the limited number of seats on the bus.

False Pass and Akutan

Later that afternoon you'll hit tiny **False Pass**, which marks the entrance to the 150-foot-wide channel between the end of the Alaska Peninsula and the easternmost of the Aleutian Islands, **Unimak**. For centuries Aleut had used the channel to travel between the Bering Sea and the Gulf of Alaska, and the Russians followed suit, but large American ships found the strait too perilous and named it False Pass to encourage shipping to go around the western end of Unimak Island. The community that built up around the early twentieth-century cannery took on the name of the pass and now supports under a hundred people.

Around 5am next morning the ferry makes its last stop before Unalaska at **Akutan**, which hunkers below the dormant, 4275-foot Akutan Volcano. The settlement was established in 1878 as a fur-storage and trading port, though cod fishing soon took precedence. The residents here were evacuated to Ketchikan during World War II and few returned, but those who did have recently been nursing their dying language, which looks to be on the cusp of recovery.

With only half an hour in port you barely have time to see the historic **Alexandr Nevsky Chapel**, a Russian Orthodox structure built in 1918 to replace an 1878 original. In fact you can see it well enough from the boat.

Unalaska/Dutch Harbor

In a state full of remote spots, it is hard to outdo **Unalaska/Dutch Harbor**, twin towns separated by a thread of seawater and located on a foggy, wind-swept, and treeless Aleutian island rising out of the North Pacific, eight hundred miles southwest of Anchorage. The nearest town of any size is Kodiak, nearly six hundred miles away, and yet here you'll find the twelfth

5

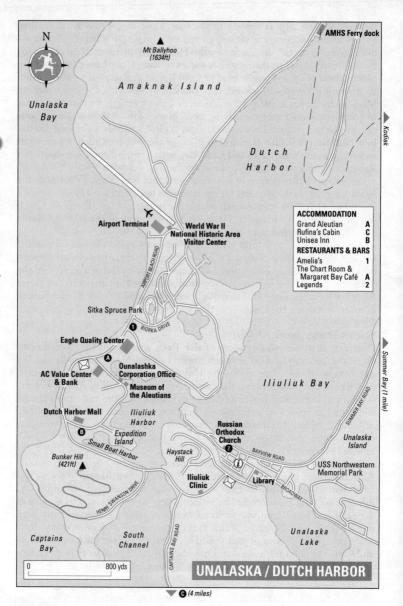

► Kodiak

► Summer Bay (1 mile)

N

Mt Ballyhoo
(1634ft)

A m a k n a k   I s l a n d

*Unalaska
Bay*

*D u t c h
H a r b o r*

AMHS Ferry dock

Airport Terminal

**World War II
National Historic Area
Visitor Center**

ACCOMMODATION	
Grand Aleutian	**A**
Rufina's Cabin	**C**
Unisea Inn	**B**
RESTAURANTS & BARS	
Amelia's	**1**
The Chart Room &
Margaret Bay Café	**A**
Legends	**2**

Sitka Spruce Park

❶

BIORKA DRIVE

AIRPORT BEACH ROAD

Eagle Quality Center

A

**AC Value Center
& Bank**

**Ounalashka
Corporation Office**

**Museum of
the Aleutians**

I l i u l i u k   B a y

*Unalaska
Island*

Dutch Harbor Mall

B

*Iliuliuk
Harbor*

*Expedition
Island*

Small Boat Harbor

**Russian
Orthodox
Church**

❷

BAYVIEW ROAD

SUMMER BAY ROAD

*Haystack
Hill*

ℹ

**USS Northwestern
Memorial Park**

*Bunker Hill
(421ft)*

HENRY SWANSON DRIVE

**Iliuliuk
Clinic**

Library

BROADWAY

*Unalaska
Lake*

*Captains
Bay*

*South
Channel*

CAPTAINS BAY ROAD

0		800 yds

UNALASKA / DUTCH HARBOR

▼ **C** *(4 miles)*

most populous locale in Alaska, as big as Homer and bigger than heavyweight
names such as Seward, Cordova, and Skagway. The reason is simple: this has
been the United States' most productive fishing port for the past decade or
so, both in terms of weight and dollar value. The 4000-strong town almost
doubles in size for the winter fishing and crabbing season, when storm-tossed
trawlers and 600-foot-long factory ships periodically call in to offload their

Unalaska or Dutch Harbor?

The airport is designated Dutch Harbor, but ferries officially dock at Unalaska. In truth, no one much cares whether you call the contiguous settlement **Unalaska** or **Dutch Harbor**, and the terms are used pretty much interchangeably. To locals, the settlement on the island of Amaknak is Dutch Harbor, now linked by the "Bridge to the Other Side" to Unalaska Island and the town of Unalaska, which is where mail for both "towns" arrives.

catches. From August to November, and again from January to March, the season is open on some of the world's richest fishing grounds – salmon, crab, cod, pollock, yellowfin, mackerel – and the town is alive with Mexicans, Filipinos, Russians, Vietnamese, Americans up from the Lower 48, in fact just about anyone who's after a quick buck.

Short-stay profiteering and the eternally erratic nature of the fishing industry do little to foster a developed community, and there's a certain frontier spirit to the place, but less than you might imagine. Taxes on fishing-boat catches have made Unalaska a wealthy town, so most of the roads are paved, health and public services are maintained to a high standard, and you can sleep in a top-class hotel. Even the fish-processing factories are conveniently tucked away from view (many in Captains Bay), and only the container port gives any kind of an industrial tenor to the place.

In summer, when most visitors arrive, the commercial fishery gives way to lively bouts of **sportfishing**, primarily for huge halibut. In the past few years, the world record has twice been broken around Dutch Harbor, and the record now stands at a whopping, barn-door-sized 459 pounds, caught here in 1996. There's plenty of **hiking**, **mountain biking**, and **kayaking** to take advantage of, and wildlife fans will appreciate the whales passing by each spring and fall, the sea mammals that amass in huge numbers hereabouts, and the unusual seabirds that turn up. Birders come especially to see the **crested auklet**, which is seldom found anywhere else.

There's interest, too, in the legacy of three nations – Aleut, Russian, and American – which have combined to leave a fascinating history, though not a great deal of tangible evidence. The Aleut have been here for close on nine thousand years, but Russian fur traders suppressed much of their culture. The US military helped complete the near-genocide during World War II (see box, p.368) and left behind hilltop bunkers and the shells of Quonset huts still visible in the hills. Fortunately, something of Aleut culture has been preserved in the **Museum of the Aleutians**, and local language and culture is again being taught at the town's schools.

Some history

Evidence from archeological digs around Unalaska indicates that the **Unangan** people (see box, p.368) have lived here for around nine thousand years, but recorded history doesn't begin until **Stephan Glotov** led a crew of fur buyers here in August 1759. They stayed for three years and laid the groundwork for what became a key link in the chain of Russian settlements along the American coast as far down as northern California. Ultimately, their main legacy was the Russian Orthodox Church, which remains the most important religion among the Aleut.

Under the US government, Dutch (as it is often known) became the base for seal harvesting in the Pribilof Islands and subsequently a **coal-supply depot** for Yukon-bound ships during the Klondike gold strike. As prospectors flocked to the beaches of Nome a few years later, Dutch was where boats amassed as they waited for the ice to break up in Norton Sound. Then when fuel oil replaced coal, the need for restocking the bunkers disappeared, and the town declined until 1939, when the government started fortifying the area against possible attack by Japan. It came on June 3–4, 1942, when this became the only place in the US besides Pearl Harbor to be **bombed during World War II**. Altogether over a hundred civilians and servicemen were killed and much of

The Aleut: kayaks, slavery, and internment

The **Unangan** people – or Aleut as they've become known since Russian times – had lived for centuries in this barren, treeless land, relying almost entirely on the ocean, using their finely honed hunting skills, expertly crafted iqax (kayaks), and unmatched knowledge of the sea. In their semi-subterranean sod-and-driftwood huts, they spent long winter nights around the seal-oil lamp creating some of the most finely woven baskets seen anywhere, stitching seal gut into wonderfully light and waterproof hunting jackets, and perfecting their sophisticated knowledge of medicine, acupuncture, and even the art of mummification.

They lived in tenuous balance with their environment until the arrival of the **Russians**, who came in the 1750s seeking sea otter pelts to sell on the Chinese market at exorbitant prices. The Russians virtually enslaved the Aleut, holding family members hostage in order to force the men to hunt. Within fifty years of Russian contact, the original population of about 15,000 had been decimated by disease, warfare, starvation, and enslavement. The situation only started to improve when the presence of the Russian Orthodox Church led to more benign treatment of, and better conditions for, the Aleut.

After the US purchase in 1867, the territorial authorities initially continued the virtual enslavement of the Aleut to harvest Pribilof island seals, then largely neglected them. The Aleut regained some degree of self-determination by returning to their traditional lifestyle, occasionally supplementing their income by working for wages on fox farms. The US government only started to take interest again when the US entered World War II, and preparations were made to move the Aleut from what was now considered a prime Japanese target. The **evacuation** took place after the Japanese bombed Dutch Harbor and captured the islands of Attu and Kiska in June 1942, and it would set the stage for another shameful chapter in the US government's far from exemplary history in dealing with its Native people.

Ostensibly for their own safety, Aleut on Atka, Umnak, Sedanka, Unalaska, and Akutan islands, plus those on the Pribilof islands of St Paul and St George, were shipped to Southeast Alaska. Almost nine hundred of them were housed in abominable conditions in old and dilapidated herring and salmon canneries, which were not insulated for winter use. Only the goodwill of the local Tlingit provided them with the means to fish and the transport to attend church. The radical change in climate, unfamiliar surroundings, primitive housing, and negligible medical care took its toll and in some places a quarter of evacuees died during the three-year **internment**. Some Aleut had been left on Attu and Kiska, and 42 were captured by the Japanese. Of these, over a third died during their internment on Hokkaido.

In 1943 some men were allowed to return and were put to work harvesting fur seals, but most waited in the camps until 1945. On their return they discovered their homes looted and destroyed and whole villages burned. Many villages were never rebuilt, and some islands remained under military control, principally Adak, about halfway along the chain. The military base on Adak was still in operation until 1995 when it was finally handed over to the local Native corporation, a small but significant step in the restitution of the Aleut people.

the town was flattened. Subsequently, Dutch was the headquarters of the battle for the Aleutians, sometimes known as "The Forgotten War." Almost all the roads you now see were built then, and up to 40,000 troops were stationed here. During their offensive, the Japanese seized the westernmost Aleutian islands of Attu and Kiska. Although they intended it as a diversion from the real battle at Midway, the Japanese dug in when they realized how intent the Americans were on regaining their territory, and were only ousted eleven months later in an intensely bloody, and largely pointless, battle.

Military involvement aside, Unalaska/Dutch Harbor was still a small town until the 1970s when super-lucrative crab fishing, and the get-rich-quick attitude that it engendered, turned it into the most productive seafood port in the nation. As successive fisheries declined, different species were targeted, and the boom and bust cycle has been repeated several times. A quota system has now been introduced in the hopes of stabilizing the situation, though fishing seasons are still short and frenetic.

Arrival and tours

There's no better way to reach Dutch Harbor than on the AMHS **ferry** *Tustumena* (see p.363), which arrives every two weeks (mid-April to early Oct only) early Saturday morning. It stays in port a little over five hours, so if you are heading back on the boat the best bet is to join Extra Mile Tours (mid-May to mid-Sept daily; ☎581-6171, ⓦwww.unalaskadutchharbortour.com), which has a ferry-day special tour (2hr; $65 including museum entry) visiting the main sections of town. On other days there's a general tour (2hr; $50) eschewing the museums in favor of the surrounding countryside via some rough roads.

Alaska Airlines and PenAir (both ☎1-800/448-4226; ⓦwww.alaskaair.com, ⓦwww.penair.com) run daily **flights** direct from Anchorage and charge $440–540 each way, depending on demand. There are occasional low-priced specials: shop around, especially if your dates are flexible. The airport is just over half a mile north of the *Grand Aleutian Hotel*; taxis wait outside, or you could walk.

Getting around and information

The twin towns are spread out, but fairly flat, so it is quite possible to **get around** on foot. If arriving with awkward luggage, you may want to engage the services of one of the many taxi companies. If you're staying at the *Grand Aleutian*, or even just going there for breakfast, the hotel minibus will give you a free ride from your arrival point. Rental cars are available from Northport Rental (☎581-3880) and BC Vehicle Rentals (☎581-6777, ⓔchecker@arctic.net), both at the airport, for $55 a day for a compact and $85 for a pickup or Explorer, all with unlimited mileage.

Hiking and camping permits

Almost all the land hereabouts is owned by the Native Ounalashka Corporation (locally known as "The O.C."). Before **camping**, **hiking** away from the roads, or even **exploring** the World War II remains on Mount Ballyhoo and Bunker Hill, you must obtain a **permit**, either 24-hour (individual $6, family $10) or weekly (individual $15, family $20). These can be obtained from the Ounalashka Corporation, 400 Salmon Way, Margaret Bay Subdivision (Mon–Fri 8am–5pm; ☎581-1276, ⓦwww.ounalashka.com), or more conveniently from the World War II visitor center (see p.372).

Close to the airport you'll find the two supermarkets, each with a bank and ATM, and the main **post office** (Mon–Fri 9am–5pm, Sat 1–5pm). Other tourist facilities congregate in Unalaska, including the **visitor center** on Burma Road (Mon–Fri 8am–5pm, ferry days 9.30am–1pm; ☎581-2612 or 1-877/581-2612, ⓦwww.unalaska.info), another post office branch, the **Iliuliuk Clinic**, 34 LaVelle Court (☎581-1202), and the **library** (Mon–Fri 10am–9pm, Sat & Sun noon–6pm), which has free **Internet access**.

Accommodation

High- and moderate-standard **accommodation** is available in Unalaska, but nothing comes cheap, and rooms are subject to an eight percent tax.

Once you have obtained a **permit** (see box, p.369), it is possible to **camp** almost anywhere. The trouble is, it is hard to find anywhere that is flat, dry, protected from the wind, and relatively inconspicuous on these bald hills. You also need to take account of the weather, which can whip up winds of 70mph in no time; locals even suggest taking balloons which, when partly inflated and inserted between the outer rain fly and inner layer of your tent, help keep the two separated. At least there are no bears to worry about.

Grand Aleutian 498 Salmon Way ☎581-3844 or 1-866/581-3844, ⓦwww .grandaleutian.com. An imposing, three-story, four-star hotel that's the acme of luxury in these parts. With over a hundred comfortable rooms and several restaurants and bars, it is so out of keeping with the general tone of the area that it's sometimes referred to as the "Grand Delusion." Free ferry transfers. ❼
Rufina's Cabin Mile 4.5 Captain's Bay Road; contact the visitor center on ☎581-2612. Peaceful

and cozy self-catering cabin sleeping four, remotely set by the shores of Captain's Bay (you'll need a vehicle to get out here). There's no running water but a generator provides power, and it is fully furnished. ❸
Unisea Inn 188 Gilman Way ☎1-866/581-3844, ⓦwww.grandaleutian.com. Decidedly faded but slightly cheaper sister of the *Grand Aleutian*. Clean and with its own sports bar and grill. Free ferry transfers. ❺

The Town

Easily the most imposing building in Unalaska is the **Russian Orthodox Cathedral of the Holy Ascension**, its green onion-dome tower endlessly reproduced on postcards and tourist brochures, usually with one of the town's abundant **bald eagles** regally perched on top of the triple-bar cross. It ranks as the oldest existing Russian Orthodox church in the state, built on the site of a church constructed in 1808 and a later model jointly built by Father Ivan Veniaminov and the local Aleut in 1826. The current structure was built in the mid-1890s and survived considerable neglect to rise gloriously restored in 1996. Inside is one of the finest collections of **religious art** in Alaska: almost seven hundred icons and relics, amassed over the years as the other half-dozen village churches on Unalaska Island closed when the villages were abandoned. There are currently no tours, so the best way to see inside is to attend a **service** (Sat 6.30pm & Sun 10am). Adjacent is the small **Bishop's House**, which was originally built in San Francisco in 1882 and subsequently reassembled here. It has been awaiting restoration for some years and is not open to the public.

The cathedral looms over Unalaska's sweeping arc of gravel beach, which is backed by the heart of downtown. Stroll to the far eastern end of the beach where there's a memorial to the **USS Northwestern**, a retired freighter pressed into use during World War II as civilian accommodation, but bombed by the Japanese. After burning for five days the boat was later scuttled, and its steel

△ Church of the Holy Ascension, Unalaska

prow can still be seen rising above the waters at the head of Captains Bay. The propeller was recovered for the fiftieth anniversary of the attack and now forms the centerpiece of the memorial. Beyond here, Summer Bay Road leads three miles to Summer Bay, where there's good beach walking, a small lake, and a hike across an isthmus to Agamgik Bay (see p.373).

West of downtown Unalaska, the "Bridge to the Other Side" crosses South Channel onto Amaknak Island, once five separate islands now joined by landfill. Here you'll find the **Museum of the Aleutians**, 314 Salmon Way (June–Sept Tues–Sat 9am–5pm, Sun noon–5pm; Oct–May Tues–Fri 11am–5pm, Sat 9am–5pm; $5; Ⓦ www.aleutians.org), built on the existing foundations of a World War II warehouse. Inside, temporary displays augment the permanent collection, which aims to interpret the history and culture of Unalaska Island and the Aleutian region. Foremost among the exhibited works is *Woman of Ounalashka*, an original pencil sketch of an Aleut woman done in 1778 by John Webber, artist on Captain Cook's third expedition. Long in private hands, it was bought by the museum after major community fundraising efforts. Along with fine grass basketry and a trio of seal-gut parkas (one incorporating a kayak spray skirt), it helps flesh out the coverage of local Aleut habitation. The Margaret Bay archeological dig (done here in the 1990s) also revealed artifacts including a 4000-year-old pumice mask, seal-bone harpoon points dating back two thousand years, and a seal-gut wallet handmade in the 1930s.

There's coverage, too, of the Russian involvement in the area, the herring salteries that flourished in the 1920s, and the World War II military buildup, represented here by the lower two-thirds of a Tlingit-style totem pole carved by bored servicemen stationed on Kiska.

Apart from the World War II remains (see p.372), the only other point of interest is **Sitka Spruce Park**, a short walk to the north, containing the last three trees of the Sitka Spruce Plantation, planted by Russian settlers around 1805.

World War II remains

Amaknak Island is where you'll find the majority of the remains from the World War II military buildup. It is fascinating to explore here, and amazing how much has been left lying around. It all forms part of the **Aleutian World War II National Historic Area**, which maintains a comprehensive **visitor center** (Thurs–Sun 1pm–6pm; $4; T 581-1276, W www.nps.gov/aleu) in the Aerology Building a short walk from the airport. This is the perfect starting point for a survey of the area, not only to obtain the necessary permit (see box, p.369) but also to browse the abundance of info on the region, the battle for the Aleutians, and the removal of Aleut to Southeast Alaska.

The upper floor overlooks the airport runway and is set up much as it would have been in World War II, with mannequins huddled over radios, typewriters, teleprinters, and war charts, with the chatter of Morse code in the background. Panels tell of the life of servicemen stationed in this bleak outpost, lauded among the troops as "where there's a woman behind every tree." The joke, of course, is that there are no trees.

The most accessible World War II ruins are around the 421-foot summit of **Bunker Hill** (aka Hill 400), topped by its distinctive gun emplacement. Turn down Harry Swanson Drive, which runs around the base of Quonset huts, then up the hill past the remains of the huts, ammunition stores, and tunnel entrances. It takes only about fifteen minutes to hike up the road to reach the summit, with its commanding views, concrete bunkers, and circular turntable for directing the 155mm guns at anything approaching.

North of the airport, around the flanks of **Mount Ballyhoo**, you'll see more remnants of military activity during World War II, mostly abandoned but in some cases incorporated into modern functions: for instance, an old torpedo-production facility is now a six-lane bowling alley. The best of the remains are at the northern headland of Mount Ballyhoo, about five miles from the airport and most easily reached along a road that climbs steeply just beyond the AMHS ferry dock. Here you can spend a happy hour or two groping through tunnels, poking around crumbling shelters, or simply admiring the view from the gun emplacements.

Hiking, biking, and kayaking

With miles of treeless terrain right on the town's doorstep, there is plenty of scope for hiking, either along the small number of accessible trails or off wherever you please. There's also an extensive network of old World War II roads that make wonderful mountain-biking territory. Bring a sturdy tent and other camping gear, and you increase the scope of your explorations immeasurably.

June is a good month for **hiking**. Snow still clings to the mountaintops, the 120 varieties of wildflower are magnificent, and the summer grass is not yet too tall. July and August are likely to have better weather (and juicy salmonberries and blueberries), although you still need to keep to the ridge if you want relatively dry feet. You should also carry a compass since the fog comes in quick and thick. Also note that, despite an extensive cleanup in recent years, there is still a slim possibility you may come across **unexploded ordnance** left over from World War II; don't disturb any rusted-up bits of metal. After all these warnings, it is comforting that there are no bears, and the bugs aren't too bad.

The easiest of the local hikes is up **Mount Ballyhoo** (4 miles round-trip; 3hr; 1600ft ascent), which rises behind the airport and offers views to

Makushin Volcano and the rest of Unalaska Island. You can extend the hike by continuing north along the ridge to Ulakta Head. The **Agamgik Bay Trail** (8 miles round-trip; 3–5hr; 500ft ascent) is also worthwhile, though it starts an inconvenient four miles from town at Summer Bay, reached along Summer Bay Road.

The twin towns have 38 miles of regular roads, and many more miles of disused paths from World War II, challenging terrain that is perfect for **mountain biking** using hardtail machines rented from Aleutian Adventure Sports (☎581-4489, ⊛www.aleutianadventure.com) for $25 a half-day and $35 for the full day. The same company also rents kayaks (single $65 a day, double $85) to experienced paddlers, and leads a wide range of excellent **guided kayak trips**, including the novice-level Harbor and Captains Bay tours (3–4hr; $55 and $65 respectively), the more demanding paddle northwest to Wide Bay (10–12hr; $145), and four- to six-day extended trips ($550–1100). **Guided hiking** and mountaineering excursions take place through the summer months, with visits to Akutan Volcano and the nearby hot springs, as well as the snowcapped 6680-foot summit of Makushin Volcano on Unalaska Island (each trip 4 days; $1100).

Halibut-fishing and birding

Birders and halibut-fishers usually fly in on Anchorage-based packages, a couple of the best offered in conjunction with the *Grand Aleutian Hotel* (see p.370), which provides accommodation and meals in Dutch Harbor. Their Whiskered Auklet tour comes in three variations, each a day charter out to see these rare birds, along with tufted and horned puffins, petrels, jaegers, and all sorts of marine mammals: two nights for $745, three nights for $1085, and four nights for $1424.

The hotel's Halibut Heaven (June–Aug) is a three-night sportfishing package for $1279, with one-night increments up to a total of seven nights for $2636, charters provided each day. If you are here and just fancy a day spent **halibut-fishing**, expect to pay around $190 (minimum two people) on the F/V *Lucille* (☎581-5949, ⊛www.unalaskahalibutfishing.com), which also runs trips out to the Ruby Islands for whiskered auklet-viewing.

Eating, drinking, and entertainment

Unalaska is reputed to have a cost of living almost thirty percent higher than Anchorage, so you can expect **eating** to be pricey. The best way around this is to prepare your own food with groceries from the huge Eagle Quality Center near the *Grand Aleutian*, which has good deli and bakery sections and sells espresso.

Amelia's E Point Road at Airport Beach Road ☎581-2800. Convivial restaurant with an extensive menu specializing in hearty breakfasts from 6am and Mexican dishes such as chicken *mole* ($15). Steak and fish dinners mostly $20–25.

The Chart Room *Grand Aleutian Hotel* ☎581-3844. The classiest dining in town, with views over Margaret Bay. It is particularly noted for its seafood, perhaps best sampled at their Wednesday night seafood buffet ($29). Also check out the Sunday brunch (10am–2pm; $23).

Legends Bayview ☎581-1271. Until recently this bar went by the moniker "The Elbow Room", once declared the second roughest bar in the US, with tales of near-constant fights and people left bleeding out in the snow. It is considerably toned down now (at least in summer when most visitors arrive and most fishermen are away) but is always lively and packed on the weekend.

Margaret Bay Café *Grand Aleutian Hotel* ☎581-3844. Upscale breakfast and lunch café with harbor views and a wide menu including toothsome *huevos rancheros* ($9) and eggs Benedict ($10).

The Pribilof Islands

Nature enthusiasts salivate over visiting the **Pribilof Islands**, an archipelago of two inhabited volcanic crests – St Paul Island and St George Island – and assorted islets rising from the bed of the Bering Sea nine hundred miles west of Anchorage and two hundred miles north of Dutch Harbor. A bleak stretch of treeless, tundra-covered hills, the Pribilofs are saddled with the wet and misty weather typical of the Aleutians and an average summer temperature below fifty degrees. Unappealing as this may sound, the islands have two major draws: an incredibly rich gathering of raucous seals and some of the most densely packed **seabird cliffs** found anywhere.

The islands were uninhabited when Russian Gavriil Pribylov discovered the fur-clad bounty he was looking for in 1786. It wasn't long before Aleutian Islands Natives were effectively enslaved and shipped to the Pribilofs to harvest the seals, in time reducing seal numbers to the brink of extinction. Nonetheless, pickings were still healthy enough for the United States to look to the islands to recoup some of their costs after the 1867 purchase from Russia. The US initially continued the harsh treatment of the Aleut, manipulating nearly every aspect of their lives, and during World War II forced the Pribilof Aleut to evacuate to Southeast Alaska (see box, p.368). Since their return to the islands, the Aleut have managed to gain some degree of self-governance.

By 1910 seal numbers were down to around 125,000 and stayed low until 1957, when the United States, Japan, Canada, and the Soviet Union created the North Pacific Fur Seal Commission to control indiscriminate killing. Seal harvesting finally stopped in 1986 and now every summer some 700,000 northern fur seals (over half of the world population) vie for space at the breeding rookeries on the rocky beaches, accompanied by harbor seals, Steller's sea lions, walruses, and sea otters. Camouflaged viewing hides have been set up along the beaches, and if your attention should waver, you can always wander along the hiking trails to other positions with a better angle on the nesting seabirds that cram onto every available ledge and squeeze into impossible crevices. The islands attract around two million birds from over two hundred species: mostly murres, puffins, fulmars, kittiwakes, cormorants, and auklets, but also small numbers of Asiatic vagrants that turn up mostly in May. Come a little later in the season and the endless summer days bring out blankets of wildflowers. Only the most curmudgeonly of city types could fail to be impressed by this spectacular convergence of birds, seals, and flowers, but the cost of getting and staying here puts many off.

Most visitors end up on **St Paul**, which at fourteen miles by eight is the larger of the two inhabited islands, supporting a population of seven hundred Aleut, the world's largest such community. Their spiritual center is the **SS Peter and Paul Church**, its plain exterior giving little hint of the rich Russian Orthodox interior, all icons and fuchsia carpet. Basic roads and hiking trails ring the island and provide access to half a dozen bird cliffs and seal-viewing areas.

St George has under two hundred Aleut residents, its own impressive church, **St George the Martyr**, and a few seals. It excels, however, when it comes to seabird cliffs, some of which rise a thousand feet from the crashing waves. It's small enough to hike around and find your favorite viewing spot.

Practicalities

The Pribilofs can be reached independently on scheduled flights from Anchorage with PenAir (☎1-800/448-4226), which has three or four direct flights a week to each island in summer. With round-trip fares of almost $900 and the islands' limited scope for independent travel, though, organized tours are usually more practical. The most frequent (and easiest to squeeze into a tight schedule) are those operated by Alaska Birding & Wildlife Tours (☏1-877/424-5637, ⓦwww.alaskabirding.com), which from mid-May to late August has trips including flights from Anchorage to St Paul, accommodation at the *King Eider*, and a naturalist guide: stay durations range from two nights ($1406) to seven nights ($2420) including everything except meals. The Pribilof weather frequently disrupts flight schedules for days at a time, so be sure to allow some flexibility in your schedule and have some spare cash for extra nights you may spend at the *King Eider*.

Accommodation on the islands is scarce and neither allows camping. On St Paul Island the only **place to stay** is the plain but comfortable *King Eider* (☏546-2477; ⓺) with shared bathrooms. Meals are available from the cafeteria of the local fish-processing plant and will set you back around $40 a day. On **St George Island** you can sleep at the historic ten-room *St George Tanaq* (☏272-9886, ⓦwww.stgeorgetanaq.com; ⓼), which has shared bathrooms and a kitchen where you can prepare food, best brought over from Anchorage but available locally at a price. There are **no restaurants** on St George.

Travel details

With the exception of a fourteen-mile road from King Salmon to Naknek, no roads link the towns of the Southwest. Transport is predominantly by air, although the *Tustumena* sails to Kodiak from Homer three or four times a week and continues along the Alaska Peninsula to Unalaska/Dutch Harbor twice a month in summer.

Ferries

Chignik to: Kodiak (every two weeks; 18hr); Sand Point (every two weeks; 9hr 15min).

Cold Bay to: False Pass (every two weeks; 4hr 25min); King Cove (every two weeks; 2hr).

Dutch Harbor to: Akutan (every two weeks; 3hr 30min); Chignik (every two weeks; 37hr); Cold Bay (every two weeks; 16hr); King Cove (every two weeks; 19hr); Kodiak (every two weeks; 61hr); Sand Point (every two weeks; 27hr).

King Cove to: Cold Bay (every two weeks; 2hr); Sand Point (every two weeks; 6hr 30min).

Kodiak to: Chignik (every two weeks; 18hr 30min); Cold Bay (every two weeks; 42hr); Dutch Harbor (every two weeks; 61hr); False Pass (every two weeks; 48hr); Homer (3–4 weekly; 7–13hr); King Cove (every two weeks; 39hr); Port Lions (weekly; 2hr 30min); Sand Point (every two weeks; 30hr).

Port Lions to: Homer (1–3 weekly; 10hr); Kodiak (1–3 weekly; 2hr 30min).

Sand Point to: Chignik (every two weeks; 9hr 15min); King Cove (every two weeks; 6hr 30min).

Flights

Anchorage to: King Salmon (5–8 daily; 1hr–1hr 20min); St George (4 weekly; 4hr 30min); St Paul (4 weekly; 3hr).

Dutch Harbor to: Anchorage (4–6 daily; 3hr).

King Salmon to: Anchorage (5–8 daily; 1hr–1hr 20min); Brooks Camp (4–8 daily; 20min).

Kodiak to: Anchorage (7–10 daily; 1hr).

6

Denali and the western Interior

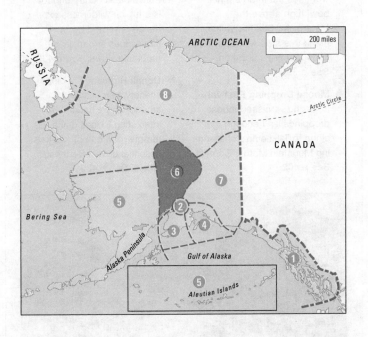

CHAPTER 6

Highlights

* **Eklutna Historical Park** Wander amid the colorful "spirit house" graves flanking a striking onion-domed Russian Orthodox church. See p.382

* **Independence Mine** Beautifully preserved mine workings set in an alpine bowl high above the Matanuska-Susitna Valley make this a perfect spot for midsummer exploration. See p.395

* **Moose Dropping Festival** If tossing varnished moose droppings isn't enough, get along to Talkeetna's challenging Mountain Mother Contest. See p.402

* **Mount McKinley flightseeing** A flying visit to North America's tallest peak is an essential part of any trip to the Interior and is enhanced by a glacier landing. See p.405

* **Hiking in Denali's backcountry** Exploring Denali National Park's backcountry on foot is a full-on wilderness experience rewarded by lonely landscapes and majestic mountain views. See p.430

* **Denali Highway** Fabulous scenery, hardly a soul around, and a handful of interesting lodges make this remote road one of Alaska's essential drives. Better still, bike it. See p.439

△ The Park Road, Denali National Park

Denali and the
western Interior

nterior Alaska is the Alaska of popular imagination – a land of wild and untamed beauty spreading west from the Canadian border. For the most part, it is a low plateau of permafrost swampland feebly drained by small streams. Anywhere in Alaska, you'll feel the presence of the mountains, either as a barrier to where you're trying to go or as an icy backdrop to broad river valleys. Nowhere is this more true than around **Denali and the western Interior**, where the Alaska Range arcs in a great crescent with its crown, Mount McKinley, forming the centerpiece of **Denali National Park**.

Originally, this was **Athabascan** country, populated by Native Americans who share their heritage with the Navajos and Apaches of the American Southwest. Their presence is still strong in the area, though they mainly keep to themselves in villages off the beaten track; you're more likely to run into the somewhat sanitized vignettes of their lifestyle occasionally presented in dance-halls for tourists. Over the past century the region has been settled by miners, hunters, and trappers, and while towns have grown up to serve the scattered communities, the pioneer spirit shows itself in the hardy, modern-day sour-doughs who have chosen it as their home. Most of the significant communities lie along the **Alaska Railroad**, which first linked Anchorage and Fairbanks in 1913, although since 1973 the almost-parallel **George Parks Highway**, named after a former governor, has driven most development.

In the lowland **Matanuska–Susitna Valley** (aka Mat-Su Valley), the depression-era farming colony that kick-started Alaska's limited agricultural tradition will be of interest to some, but the hills will surely draw you on, principally to **Hatcher Pass** and the ruin of **Independence Mine**, magnificently cradled in an alpine bowl. But this is small potatoes compared with what's to come: the mammoth, 20,320-foot **Mount McKinley**. Screaming up from the tundra at just two thousand feet above sea level, making it a whopping 18,000ft tall from base to peak, Mount McKinley boasts the greatest vertical rise of any mountain on dry land and is the highest point in North America. It is known to many as **Denali**, probably a Dena'ina word for "the Great One," and to say that it dominates the Alaska Range is an understatement. There are few other ranges in the world where the highest peak is fifty percent taller than those around it, and none where that peak is the highest on a continent. The giant mountain dictates local weather patterns, with moisture-laden winds from the coast forced up over it and into colder altitudes where they dump thousands of tons of snow – the raw material for a dozen regional glaciers – into the area. In the summer Denali is obscured by clouds two days out of three, and your best chances of a good view are from the wonderfully oddball village of **Talkeetna**, home of the famed Moose Dropping Festival, a base for flightseeing and, in spring, alive with Denali summit aspirants. North of the Alaska Range is the heartland of **Denali National Park**, Alaska's single greatest draw thanks to its unparalleled wildlife-viewing, though you need only a pinch of determination to leave the crowds behind for a wilderness hiking experience that is little short of spiritual. Before the creation of the George Parks Highway (or just Parks Highway), the only road access to Denali was the **Denali Highway**, now a scenic dirt road hemming the southern skirts of the Alaska Range. With very little habitation, few visitors, and a refreshing lack of rules and restrictions, it is a wonderful place to spend a day or two exploring.

Uniquely for Alaska, the Anchorage–Fairbanks corridor is fairly easy to get around, with the fast Parks Highway, a train line, and several bus companies operating along sections of the highway. That said, services are sparse, especially

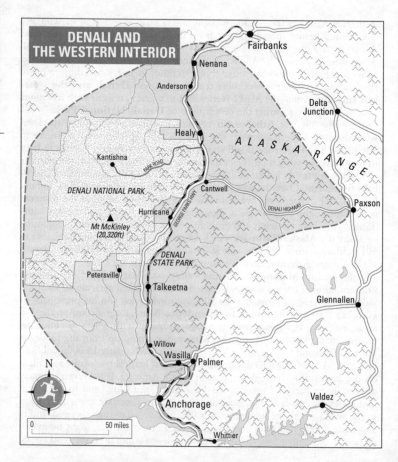

DENALI AND
THE WESTERN INTERIOR

Fairbanks
Nenana
Anderson
Delta
Junction
Healy
Kantishna
PARK ROAD
ALASKA RANGE
DENALI NATIONAL PARK
Cantwell
DENALI HIGHWAY
Hurricane
GEORGE PARKS HWY
Paxson
Mt McKinley
(20,320ft)
DENALI
STATE PARK
Petersville
Talkeetna
Glennallen
Willow
Wasilla
Palmer
N
Valdez
Anchorage
0   50 miles
Whittier

outside peak season; having your own transport is definitely a bonus, giving you the freedom to travel at your own pace and wander down whatever backroads you find.

Eklutna and around

Star-struck by the region's major highlights, many visitors race past **EKLUTNA**, but it is a mistake to ignore this hamlet 25 miles north of the state capital. Long before Anchorage existed, this Native settlement had become the most important village in Cook Inlet through trade with the Russians. Athabascan and Russian influences combine intriguingly at the Eklutna Historical Park, while across the Glenn Highway the impressive Thunderbird Falls mark the access road to the boating, biking, and hiking nexus of Eklutna Lake.

Thunderbird Falls and Eklutna Lake

An exit at Mile 25 of the Glenn Highway accesses **Thunderbird Falls**, a lovely 200-foot, two-leap cataract at the end of a mile-long trail through birch forest. Wilder scenery is on hand at the end of the paved, ten-mile Eklutna Lake Road to Eklutna Lake, a brush-ringed reservoir in the heart of the Chugach Mountains that provides half of Anchorage's tap water and is also popular with local windsurfers. It is bordered by the sizeable *Eklutna Lake Campground* ($10 includes parking fee; pump water and fire rings), a summer-only ranger station, and the **Eklutna Lake Recreation Area** (parking $5 a day; ⓦwww.dnr.state .ak.us/parks/units/chugach/eklutna.htm), where Lifetime Adventures (mid-May to mid-Sept Mon–Fri 11am–7pm, Sat & Sun 10am–8pm; ☎746-4644, ⓦwww.lifetimeadventures.net) rents kayaks (single $30 for a half-day, double $33) and bikes ($20–25 for a half-day, $30–35 full day) plus camping gear. The Peddle and Paddle combo ($75 full day) allows you to kayak to the other end of the lake and bike back.

Most activity is along the gentle **Eklutna Lakeside Trail** (12.7 miles one-way; 4–5hr; 300ft ascent), open to all-terrain vehicles (ATVs) from Sunday to Wednesday, but restricted to bikers and hikers on Thursdays, Fridays, and Saturdays. The "trail" follows a roadbed once used by the military to access the Eklutna Glacier for winter training, and runs for seven miles to the head of the lake (often using a narrowed cycle track to avoid road washouts), then beyond to the end of the roadbed at the calming Serenity Falls (Mile 12). From here hikers can continue along **Eklutna Glacier Trail**, which turns rockier and tougher as you approach the snout of the Eklutna Glacier across glacial gravel bars that were under hundreds of feet of ice as little as fifty years ago, before the glacier retreated. Here, the Mitre and Benign Peak rise over six thousand feet above you, and views of steep canyon walls and waterfalls abound. Before Serenity Falls, the Lakeside Trail provides access to two additional trails: five miles along Eklutna Lake, you can strike off north up the arduous **Bold Ridge Trail** (7 miles round-trip; 4–6hr; 2500ft ascent), a rigorous climb to open, explorable tundra; and, at the 10.5-mile mark, the narrow **East Fork Trail** (12 miles round-trip; 6–8hr; 700ft ascent) fords multiple streams while following the

Yosemite-like East Fork of the Eklutna River below Bashful Peak (8005ft), the highest in Chugach State Park. Yet another option, the steep and rugged **Twin Peaks Trail** (5 miles round-trip; 4–5hr; 1500ft ascent), tackles the mountainside north of the campground to reach fall berry-picking grounds and great lake views from above the tree line.

You'd do well to spend a night in one of the simple **backcountry camping** areas, such as the *Eklutna Alex Campground* at Mile 8.8 of the Lakeside Trail and the *Kanchee Campground* at Mile 11, both free, with fire rings and nearby stream water. Alternatives include the eight-person *Yuditnu Cabin* ($40 per night off-peak, $50 peak; reserve through APLIC in Anchorage ☎1-866/869-6887, Ⓦwww.nps.gov/aplic) at Mile 3 and the lovely *Serenity Falls Cabin*, Mile 12 (reserve online or in person through DNR Public Information Center, Suite 1260, 550 W 7th Ave, Anchorage ☎269-8400), where you can rent individual bunks (single $10 off-peak, $15 peak per night, double bay $25/35) or the whole thirteen-person cabin ($115).

Eklutna Historical Park

Turning left at the next exit, at Mile 26 of the Glenn Highway, you'll come almost at once to the Russian Orthodox Church of St Nicholas, a low, log-shaped structure with a shingle roof sporting three triple-barred crosses that ranks as the oldest standing building in the Anchorage area. Constructed by Russian settlers at the start of the nineteenth century, the church now forms the centerpiece of the **Eklutna Historical Park** (mid-May to mid-Sept daily 10am–6pm, last tour 5.15pm; $5; ☎688-6026), a fascinating blend of Russian and Athabascan cultures, with a cemetery densely packed with the state's finest collection of **spirit houses**. There are more than eighty of these barely waist-high huts, their yellow, red, blue, green, or even candy-striped pitched roofs topped with crenellated, technicolor

△ Athabascan spirit houses

crests. Rather than adopt the familiar headstone, Orthodox Russian Athabascan tradition requires that a new blanket be placed over the deceased's grave and a three-bar Orthodox cross planted at its foot. Forty days after burial, the honoree's family builds a spirit house over the grave using the family's traditional colors to identify the interred person. A small spirit house placed within a larger one is said to indicate joint burial of a mother and her child, and a house surrounded by a picket fence declares that the dead person was neither Tanaina (a local spelling of Dena'ina, denoting the Athabascans of Southcentral Alaska) nor Russian Orthodox. There's also a small exhibition and gift shop, and a newer wooden church, built in 1962 and now used for services.

The Mat-Su Valley

Too often overlooked by the same tourists who, speeding north from Anchorage to Denali, miss out on Eklutna, the glacially contorted **Mat-Su Valley** in fact consists of two valleys, shaped by the erosive powers of the Matanuska and Susitna rivers and spotted with lakes, open plateaux, and towering mountains. It is a huge area divided by the rugged granite forms of the **Talkeetna Mountains** which, despite only just topping seven thousand feet, are an impressive sight, particularly under fall's first dusting of snow.

This vast catchment contains just two substantial towns. **Palmer**, the more appealing of the two, is the result of a grand experiment in cooperative farming. Its prim town center is surrounded by dairy farms dotted with Midwest-style **colony barns**, scenically framed by the snow-capped ridges of Pioneer Peak. **Wasilla** is less inviting, the embodiment of a regional boom that, between 1990 and 2002, saw the region's population increase by 64 percent and encouraged unchecked suburban sprawl. If your time is limited, take a quick whirl through the Palmer backroads to check out the colony barns, then follow one of the loveliest alpine drives in the state to **Hatcher Pass** and the dramatic remains of the **Independence Mine**.

Both Palmer and Wasilla have small visitor centers, but the main **Matanuska-Susitna CVB** (mid-May to mid-Sept daily 8.30am–6.30pm; closed in winter; ☎746-5000, ⊛ www.alaskavisit.com) is located at Mile 35.5 of the Parks Highway, a couple miles north of the flyovers where the Parks and Glenn highways part company.

Palmer

For thousands of years, glacial silt was carried by the Matanuska River and deposited in the Matanuska Valley, creating the most fertile land in Alaska, upon which arose the small farming community of **Palmer**, 42 miles north of Anchorage. Though the soil's richness was recognized early on, and the Alaska Railroad linked Palmer to Anchorage in the 1920s, the city's great leap forward only came in 1935 when, as part of his New Deal, President Franklin D. Roosevelt drew up the unusual Matanuska **Colony Program**. The plan involved bringing some two hundred families from the drought-stricken Midwest states of Minnesota, Wisconsin, and Michigan to resettle here on forty-acre tracts. The government gave $3000 loans to help the settlers build homes, clear land, and eat until their first crop came in. In return the government received $5 an acre for the land and ran a highly un-Alaskan cooperative system whereby the crops grown became the property of the colony, which shared the profits. Though glad to escape their dusty farms back home, many

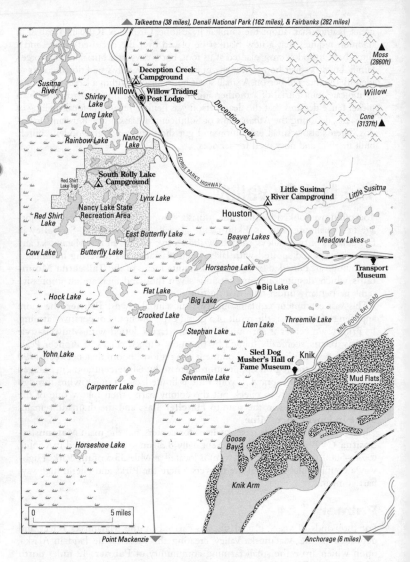

Moss (2860ft) ▲

Susitna River

Shirley Lake

Willow

Deception Creek Campground

Willow Trading Post Lodge

Deception Creek

Willow

Long Lake

Cone (3137ft) ▲

Rainbow Lake

Nancy Lake

G EORGE PARKS HIGHWAY

South Rolly Lake Campground

Red Shirt Lake Trail

Lynx Lake

Little Susitna River Campground

Little Susitna

Nancy Lake State Recreation Area

Houston

Red Shirt Lake

East Butterfly Lake

Beaver Lakes

Meadow Lakes

Cow Lake

Butterfly Lake

Horseshoe Lake

Transport Museum

Hock Lake

Flat Lake

Big Lake

Big Lake

KNIK GOOSE BAY ROAD

Crooked Lake

Liten Lake

Threemile Lake

Stephan Lake

Yohn Lake

Sled Dog Musher's Hall of Fame Museum

Knik

Sevenmile Lake

Mud Flats

Carpenter Lake

Horseshoe Lake

Goose Bay

Knik Arm

0 ____ 5 miles

felt the disapproval of the original valley homesteaders, who believed the newcomers were getting something for nothing.

The settlers eschewed the Alaskan log-cabin norms because the local logs proved too small, and constructed frame houses and gambrel-roofed barns of their home states, each with jutting eaves supporting winch jibs. Throughout the second half of the twentieth century, improved transportation made goods shipped in from Seattle and elsewhere increasingly competitive and farms were steadily sold off or subdivided; however, the "colony barns" and their associated grain silos remain a feature of the region today. Much of the state's best farmland is now prime real estate for residential and commercial development: although Alaskan supermarkets stock local dairy products, most of their ingredients now come from the Lower 48.

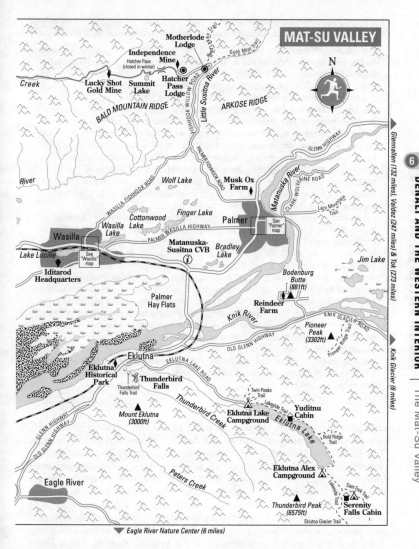

There is one agricultural enterprise that is still economically viable, though neither legal nor particularly visible to the casual observer. The region is renowned throughout Alaska for its **Matanuska Thunderfuck**, reputedly some of the strongest marijuana anywhere.

The town and around

In keeping with its origins, Palmer could still pass for a small Midwestern town with its gleaming water tower, its neatly maintained train station with preserved saddle-tank loco (though there are no passenger services), and a grid of small streets with shops and a steady trickle of pedestrians. Almost everything worth

Mat-Su's mega-veggies and the Alaska State Fair

The happy convergence of twenty hours of summer sunlight and a deep, rockless bed of loess (a type of glacial soil) allows the Mat-Su Valley to produce **gargantuan vegetables**, notably freak cabbages weighing in at close to a hundred pounds, as well as six-pound onions, eight-pound carrots, and once a single pea pod weighing a quarter of a pound. The record pumpkin for the area is an astounding 1019 pounds.

In late summer and fall, produce that is merely huge can be bought from pick-your-own farms all round the district – peaches, apples, and other fruit work out at bargain prices – but to see record-breakers you'll need to go to Palmer's **Alaska State Fair** (day tickets $8; ☎1-800/850-3247, ⓦwww.alaskastatefair.org), held on the ten days leading up to Labor Day at the State Fairground two miles south along the Glenn Highway. There's a train station at the fairground, built for a possible commuter service to Anchorage, but it's currently used only for transport between the fair and Anchorage. Look for the schedule in local newspapers and on the railway's and State Fair's websites.

Just about every sector of the Alaskan economy and arts scene is represented; in fact, it is hard to find a band playing anywhere else in the state when the fair is on. Expect everything from staples like monster-truck displays, rodeo, and lumber-jacking competitions to Native dance and blanket-tossing, and oddball events like the Husband Holler, the potato-stacking contest, and a competition in which the organizers grow a potato patch, then contestants dig as fast as they can striving to fill their two-gallon bucket first. Some kind of historical authenticity is lent by the homesteading events like wood-splitting and water-hauling, but the highlight for the valley growers is the giant vegetable weigh-off. If you're too early for the State Fair, try to catch Palmer Colony Days on the second weekend of June, with a parade, craft fair, and live music and entertainment; the Palmer Pride Picnic on July 28 at the old railroad depot, with giant veggies, free music, and presentation of the citizen of the year award; or, failing that, the Friday Fling open-air markets (Fridays May–Aug 11am–6pm), also at the old railroad depot, with veggies, arts and crafts for sale, and free music and entertainment.

seeing lies outside town, but you can pass a pleasant few minutes in the small, new **Palmer Museum of History and Art**, 723 S Valley Way (May–Sept daily 9am–6pm; Oct–April Mon–Fri 10am–4pm; donations; ☎746-7668, ⓦwww .palmermuseum.org), which has no art as yet but does have good coverage of history from Native times through the gold rushes to the colony, including a diorama of a colonist home in the basement. The museum shares its premises with the **visitor center** (see p.388), outside of which is a demonstration patch of oversized vegetables (see box, above), though they don't reach Brobdingna-gian proportions until late August. With a leaflet from the visitor center you can follow a self-guided walking tour of the Historic District, which boasts thirteen buildings on the National Historic Register (fourteen until the Mata-nuska Maid creamery burnt down in 2003). Following East Elmwood Avenue, you pass the **Colony Memorial**, a sculpture dedicated to the 202 families who first settled here, and the **Colony House Museum**, 316 E Elmwood Ave (May–Aug Tues–Sat 10am–4pm; $2), a nicely restored and furnished example of the type of house built here in 1935. Just beyond, the First School, now the Mat-Su Borough offices (with modern windows that remove any sense of history), stands opposite the Presbyterian "Church of a Thousand Trees."

On the other side of town, off the road to Wasilla, the **West Coast and Alaska Tsunami Warning Center**, 910 S Felton (☎745-4212, ⓦwcatwc.arh .noaa.gov), was built here in 2003 because Palmer was identified as the safest location in Southcentral Alaska. It offers free tours all year on Fridays at 1, 2, and 3pm; after a Powerpoint-style presentation on tsunamis worldwide, you can then take a look at the center's control desks and displays. It receives about two alerts a day, mostly insignificant, but the largest tsunami recorded, which hit Lituya Bay in Southeast Alaska in 1958, had waves reaching 1680ft above sea level. The Fairweather Fault, parallel to the continent off Southeast Alaska, is a so-called strike-slip fault, triggering few tsunamis; however, the Aleutian Fault is a dip-slip fault, which causes lots of them, some taking only three hours to reach Hokkaido.

The place that really draws visitors to these parts is the **Musk Ox Farm** (mid-May to late Sept daily 10am–6pm, June & July to 7pm; tours every half-hour; $8.50; ☎745-4151, ⓦwww.muskoxfarm.org) on Archie Road at Mile 50 of the Glenn Highway, seven miles north of Palmer, where you are guided past a few dozen of these ancient, straggly beasts grazing on the lush pasture. They're often pretty inactive in the warmth of a Mat-Su summer day – the best time is early morning, when they may even kick a soccer ball about – but they manage to look cute enough in a dopey sort of way. They aren't just here for tourists to pet, though. In the early 1950s, anthropologist John Teal envisaged helping the people of the Arctic to maintain some financial independence by setting up a cottage industry based on **qiviut**, the uniquely warm and soft under-wool shed each spring by musk oxen. These ancient animals had been extinct in Alaska from 1856 until the federal government introduced 34 specimens from Greenland in 1930 and set about breeding them and reintroducing them into the wild; three thousand of their descendants now roam the Arctic tundra. Since 1969, qiviut gathered at this farm has been spun into fine yarn and sent, undyed, to scattered western Alaskan villages, where knitted garments are produced using patterns unique to that village and based on motifs once common on its people's clothing and baskets. The garments are sold through the shop here at the Musk Ox Farm and at Oomingmak Musk Ox Producers Cooperative in Anchorage (see "Shopping," p.246). They often sell out, but you might not find yourself too disappointed at missing out on that $300 fawny-brown shawl. The gift shop, also selling T-shirts, fleece tops, and walrus-ivory carvings, is in a red colony barn along with an interesting historic display on John Teal and his business.

Domesticated wild animals are also on display some seven miles south of Palmer on one of the original colony farms, now operating as the **Reindeer Farm**, Bodenburg Butte Road, 0.7 miles west of Mile 11.5 of the Old Glenn Highway (May–Sept daily 10am–6pm; $6; ☎745-4000, ⓦwww.reindeerfarm .com), where hand-feeding and photo-taking is very much the order of the day. You can also ride horses here with Kim's Scenic Tours (☎745-4000). The journey out here is made considerably more worthwhile by the short hike up **Bodenburg Butte** (see box, p.388), which starts along Bodenburg Butte Road, almost opposite the farm.

A further three miles south, the Old Glenn Highway crosses the Knik River, and the eleven-mile Knik Glacier Road runs up beside the river past the **Pioneer Ridge** trailhead (see box, p.388) towards Knik Glacier, which can be visited on four-hour airboat tours run by Knik Glacier Adventures ($65 per person, three-person minimum; ☎746-5133, ⓦwww.knikglacieradventures .com) or Hunter Creek Adventures ($70 per person; ☎745-1577, ⓦwww .knikglacier.com). The glacier – the centerpiece of the 17,000-acre Lake George National Natural Landmark – is retreating and very recently created the lake, three miles long and four hundred feet deep.

Unfortunately, without your own transport, all of these out-of-town attractions can be difficult to reach; it's worth checking with the shuttle companies.

Palmer's proximity to farms and other towns makes it an unusual **hiking** area in the Alaskan context, but the trails listed here (and those in Hatcher Pass; see box, p.397) easily justify an extra day or so in the area. For informaton contact Mat-Su Borough on ☎745-9572 or ⓦwww.matsugov.us/recservices/trailshomepage.cfm.

Bodenburg Butte (2 miles round-trip; 1hr–1hr 30min; 800ft ascent). The shortest of the local hikes. The steep ascent is eroded and not that inspiring, but you soon rise out of the aspens for great views of farmland, the Knik Glacier, and the surrounding mountains. The trailhead is right by the Reindeer Farm (see p.387). Parking $3 per car.

Lazy Mountain Trail (5 miles round-trip; 3–5hr; 3600ft ascent). The best and most convenient hike near Palmer offers outstanding views of the valley and farmland. Parts can be pretty steep, but worth the effort. Turn the trail into a full day of hiking by combining it with others described in the free *Lazy Mountain & Morgan Horse Trails* leaflet available from the Palmer visitor center. To reach the trailhead, take Arctic Avenue east across the Matanuska River, then at Mile 15.9 take a left onto Clark–Wolverine Road and a right onto Huntley Road after a mile. The trailhead is at the end of Huntley Road, a mile or so along.

Pioneer Ridge Trail (12 miles round-trip; 6–8hr; 5100ft ascent). A fairly tough day-long hike requiring reasonable fitness to slog through underbrush up a steep hillside, though it eases as it reaches alder thicket and becomes almost gentle on the sub-alpine tundra approaching the ridge below Pioneer Peaks. Progress beyond here requires rock-climbing skills and gear, but it is still a rewarding hike with long views to the north and west, and the chance to see Dall sheep, moose, and black bears. The trailhead is at Mile 3.8 of Knik Glacier Road; parking $3 per car.

Practicalities

Mascot Dispatch (☎376-5000, ⓦwww.matsutransit.com) runs **buses** (Mon–Fri only) seven times a day from Wasilla ($2) and at 5.45pm from Anchorage ($2.50); buses have bike racks, making this the only sane way to take a bike along the stretch of the Glenn Highway from Eagle River to the Mat-Su, where drivers seem unwilling to share the road with cyclists. Mascot's buses from Anchorage will drop you at the Carrs supermarket on the Glenn Highway, while their buses from Wasilla make eight other calls across town. Get off at the library for the **visitor center**, 723 S Valley Way at Fireweed Ave (May–Sept daily 9am–6pm; Oct–April Mon–Fri 10am–4pm; ☎761-3500, ⓦwww.palmerchamber.org), which is close to some good central **accommodation**. The basic but clean and cable-equipped *Pioneer Motel*, 124 W Arctic Ave (☎745-3425; ❸), is easily outdone by the ⅔ *Colony Inn*, 325 E Elmwood Ave (reservations at the *Valley Hotel*, 606 S Alaska St ☎745-3330 or 1-800/478-7666; ❺), a lovingly restored teachers' dormitory from the colony days, with a dozen attractive rooms dressed in unfussy period decor. Ten of the rooms come with a Jacuzzi, while the other two have shower only. The *Valley Hotel*, built in 1948, has more basic rooms with cable TV and private bath (❸) plus a liquor store and 24-hour coffee shop. There are several good B&Bs hereabouts, not least the very friendly and welcoming *A-Lazy Acres*, Helmaur Place (☎745-6340; ❹), seven miles northeast of town up on Lazy Mountain; consider, too, staying at *Hatcher Pass Lodge*, up by the Independence Mine (see p.397). **Campers** should make for *Matanuska River Park*, 350 E Arctic Ave ($10 for two tents/vehicles, RVs $15), with wooded sites, showers for $2, and a day-use area all located half a mile east of town on the Old Glenn Highway; or *Homestead RV Park*, just north of the Parks Highway junction at Mile 36.2 on the Glenn Highway (☎1-800/478-3570, ⓦwww.homesteadrvpark.com;

tents from \$12, full hookup from \$23), which offers WiFi and modem Internet access and laundry. More or less opposite is the Kepler-Bradley State Recreation Area, where camping by Matanuska Lake costs \$10 (tents only); you can rent boats and canoes, and the snow clears very early in the year, making it popular for early-season biking.

There are several **places to eat** in the vicinity, but the only one worth seeking out is 𝔸 *Vagabond Blues Café*, 642 S Alaska St (☎745-2233), a cool, bohemian place with a huddle of old worktables (one dedicated to chess-playing) for sipping good coffee or tucking into great salads and soups, all vegetarian. On weekends this is the place to come for live music, usually acoustic and sometimes with a small cover charge. *The Inn Café*, 325 E Elmwood Ave (☎746-6118), in the *Colony Inn* building, is comparatively demure, but they bake their own pies and pastries, and serve lunch (Mon–Fri) with affordable specials (\$9); there's also dinner on Fridays only, with specials for \$11 or entrees such as New York steak or Cajun shrimp stir-fry for \$18–23, and a reasonably priced Sunday brunch (9am–2pm).

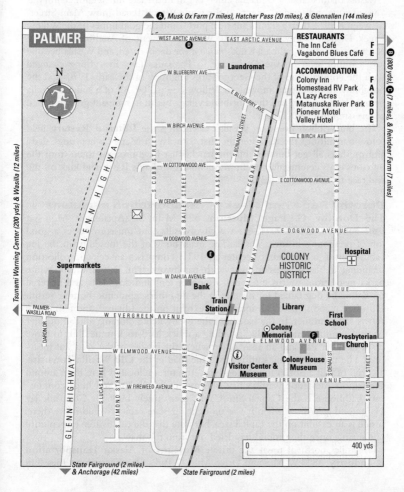

▲ **A**, Musk Ox Farm (7 miles), Hatcher Pass (20 miles), & Glennallen (144 miles)

PALMER

N

WEST ARCTIC AVENUE   EAST ARCTIC AVENUE   **D**

Laundromat

W BLUEBERRY AVE

E BLUEBERRY AVE

W BIRCH AVENUE

E BIRCH AVE

W COTTONWOOD AVE

E COTTONWOOD AVENUE

W CEDAR   AVE

W DOGWOOD AVENUE   **E**

E DOGWOOD AVENUE

Hospital

Supermarkets

COLONY
HISTORIC
DISTRICT

W DAHLIA AVENUE

Bank

E DAHLIA AVENUE

**Train
Station**   7

Library

W EVERGREEN AVENUE

**First
School**

**Colony
Memorial**   **F**

W ELMWOOD AVENUE   E ELMWOOD AVENUE

**Presbyterian
Church**

GLENN HIGHWAY

ⓘ
**Visitor Center
& Museum**

**Colony House
Museum**

W FIREWEED AVENUE   E FIREWEED AVENUE

S LUCAS STREET   S DIMOND STREET   S BAILEY STREET   COLONY WAY   S DENALI ST   S EKLUTNA STREET

S COBB STREET   S BAILEY STREET   S ALASKA STREET   S BONANZA STREET   S CEDAR AVENUE   S DENALI STREET

VALLEY WAY

GLENN HIGHWAY

PALMER-
WASILLA ROAD

DARON DR

◄ Tsunami Warning Center (200 yds) & Wasilla (12 miles)

B (800 yds), **C** (7 miles), & Reindeer Farm (7 miles) ►

RESTAURANTS
The Inn Café   F
Vagabond Blues Café   E

ACCOMMODATION
Colony Inn   F
Homestead RV Park   A
A Lazy Acres   C
Matanuska River Park   B
Pioneer Motel   D
Valley Hotel   E

0   400 yds

State Fairground (2 miles)
& Anchorage (42 miles) ▼   State Fairground (2 miles) ▼

Downtown Palmer has a **laundry** with showers at 127 S Alaska St; a **library** with free **Internet access** at 655 S Valley Way; and a **post office** on S Cobb Street at W Cedar Avenue. The town levies a three percent sales **tax** plus a five percent bed tax, not included in our accommodation price codes. You'll find a Wells Fargo **bank** (with ATM) at 705 S Bailey St.

Wasilla, Knik, and around

A first glance at **Wasilla** (Wa–SILL-a), forty miles north of Anchorage, captures all that is wrong with the kind of urban sprawl so prevalent in America today: countless strip-malls line almost eight miles of the Parks Highway, and the only indication of a town center is the train station. The blight, though, is only skin-deep, with some beautiful lakes just off the highway and a couple of good museums nearby. Provided you've got wheels, it can make an agreeable place from which to explore the Mat-Su Valley; after all, you're only ten miles west of Palmer, and Hatcher Pass is close at hand.

Wasilla (named after a Dena'ina chief) began in the late nineteenth century as a waystation and service center on the Carle Wagon Road (now Main Street) between Knik – then a significant tidal port – and the gold mines of the Willow Creek District below Hatcher Pass. With the advent of Anchorage and the construction of the railroad, Knik's *raison d'être* disappeared, and Wasilla became just a minor stop on the Anchorage to Fairbanks line. Everything changed with the construction of the George Parks Highway in the early 1970s and the possibility of the capital moving to Willow (see p.399). All of a sudden Wasilla became hot property, and the moribund village began its rampant growth fueled by overspill from Anchorage.

The blue-ribbon event on Wasilla's calendar is the **Iditarod Restart**, held (snow permitting) the day after the first Saturday in March, when dogs, sleds, and mushers all get bundled off the trucks that have brought them from the previous day's ceremonial run from Anchorage to Eagle River and kick off the real race from here (see p.392).

Dorothy Page and Alaska Transportation museums

The **Dorothy G. Page Museum**, 323 Main St (April–Sept Mon–Sat 9am–5pm; $3; ℗373-9071, ℗www.cityofwasilla.com/museum), does a good job of presenting historic Wasilla. The main body of the museum (in the log cabin built as a community center in 1931) comprises an eclectic collection including a Native sealskin coat with patchwork trim, a translucent white parka made from walrus intestines, a pioneer tent and dog-sleds, and material on Balto, the dog famed for his role in the diphtheria epidemic-busting Serum Run (see p.558). There's an interesting exhibit on the Iditarod, and temporary shows each summer. In the basement there's a wildlife diorama and all manner of gold-mining paraphernalia including a mock hard-rock mine akin to those up at Hatcher Pass and an assay office where the quality of the gold was measured. The most diverting stuff is across the road in the **Old Wasilla Townsite**, a corral of half a dozen mostly log-built structures relocated here from around the region. Alongside Wasilla's first one-room schoolhouse and huge community bathhouse is the Capital Site Cabin, prematurely built for Governor Jay Hammond at Willow when it was thought the state capital would move there; inside is an exhibit on the capital saga, but note that the cabins aren't open until late spring, once the ground has dried out from the thaw.

Five miles north of town, the private **Museum of Alaska Transportation & Industry**, 3800 W Museum Drive, Mile 47 Parks Hwy (May–Sept Tues–Sun

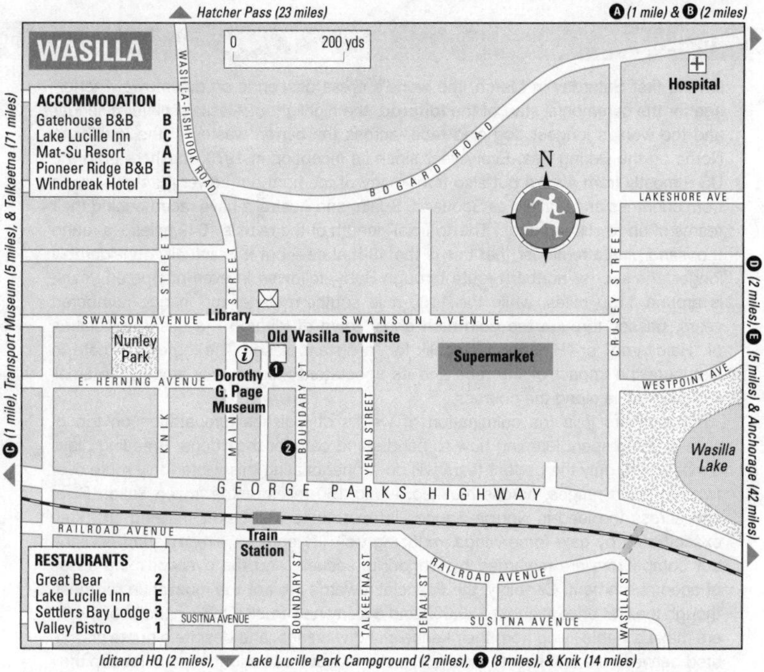
WASILLA
Hatcher Pass (23 miles)
A (1 mile) & B (2 miles)
0 200 yds
ACCOMMODATION
Gatehouse B&B B
Lake Lucille Inn C
Mat-Su Resort A
Pioneer Ridge B&B E
Windbreak Hotel D
Hospital
BOGARD ROAD
WASILLA-FISHHOOK ROAD
LAKESHORE AVE
N
KNIK STREET
MAIN STREET
CRUSEY STREET
SWANSON AVENUE
Library
Old Wasilla Townsite
Nunley Park
Supermarket
Dorothy G. Page Museum
E. HERNING AVENUE
BOUNDARY ST
YENLO STREET
WESTPOINT AVE
Wasilla Lake
GEORGE PARKS HIGHWAY
RAILROAD AVENUE
Train Station
RESTAURANTS
Great Bear 2
Lake Lucille Inn E
Settlers Bay Lodge 3
Valley Bistro 1
SUSITNA AVENUE
TALKEETNA ST
DENALI ST
WASILLA ST
C (1 mile), Transport Museum (5 miles), & Talkeetna (71 miles)
D (2 miles), E (5 miles) & Anchorage (42 miles)
Iditarod HQ (2 miles), Lake Lucille Park Campground (2 miles), 3 (8 miles), & Knik (14 miles)

10am–5pm; Oct–April Sat 10am–5pm; $8; ⓣ376-1211, ⓦwww.museumofalaska.org), hoards just about everything imaginable related to transport in the state: a Native umiak, homesteading sleds, Anchorage's first motorized pump fire engine, the first hang-glider to be launched off the summit of Denali, and a line of restored railroad locomotives and carriages. The industry section covers gold-mining, precision tools, ham radio, and much more. Outside are Dakota and Phantom airplanes, and more in need of restoration, plus old wooden boats, tractors, and other agricultural implements. The breadth of the coverage may overwhelm, but you can approach the deeply passionate and knowledgeable owner to give everything some context.

Knik

From the train station back in Wasilla, Knik Goose Bay Road runs fourteen miles southwest to the tiny settlement of **Knik** (ka-NICK), a former Russian mission site and fur-trading post, and then, starting in 1898, a transport and supply hub for the gold mines of the Interior. The construction of the Knik Goose Bay Road in the 1950s demolished the original town, and only two original buildings still stand. Stop along the way at the **Iditarod Headquarters**, Mile 2 Knik Goose Bay Rd (mid-May to mid-Sept daily 8am–7pm; mid-Sept to mid-May Mon–Fri 8am–5pm), the state's foremost shrine to the Iditarod Sled Dog Race (see box, p.392). In the main room (essentially a gift shop) one wall is a giant scrapbook of newspaper clippings reporting the Iditarod's history to 1983; there's also a sled with the traces that attach to the dog team and the large bag for carrying gear. Numerous trophies – including the winner's trophy used until 1999 – are displayed, and the 23-minute video *Beyond Courage*, one of many for sale here, plays on request, successfully capturing the

On the first Saturday in March, the world's press descends on downtown Anchorage for the ceremonial start of the **Iditarod**, the highlight of Alaska's winter calendar and the world's longest dog-sled race, across the barren wastes of the Interior to Nome on the Bering Sea. Every year since its inception in 1973, mushers from the US – mostly from Alaska but also from many of the northern Lower 48 states – and from countries as far afield as Scotland, Spain, and Australia have raced behind their teams of up to sixteen dogs. The "official" length of the race is 1049 miles – a round thousand plus a reminder that this is the 49th state – but it is actually considerably longer: the shorter northern route through Ruby, followed in even-numbered years, is around 1150 miles, while the 1180-mile southern route, run in odd-numbered years, passes through the gold-rush ghost town of Iditarod – a mispronunciation of "Halditarod" or "Hidedhod," Ingalik for "a distant place." The routes alternate to distribute the impact of the race and its spectators more evenly among the small villages that lie along the courses.

For mushers it is the culmination of weeks of logistical preparation on top of several years spent learning how to handle and care for their dogs. Breeding plays a major part; only the perfect team will do for negotiating this winter-only route over two mountain ranges, across muskeg, along 150 miles of the frozen Yukon River and across the iced-in Norton Sound. Temperatures well below freezing are often exacerbated by gale-force winds, reducing visibility on days already short on light, but competitors are rewarded by wonderful scenery and the overwhelming sense of accomplishment. Certainly, the financial rewards are not the motivation for most, though the first prize is about $50,000 and a shiny new truck. Only a handful of mushers make a viable living from their kennels and winnings, and despite a purse distributed between the first twenty mushers, just a few of these might hope to recoup their costs for running the race, which typically exceed $15,000 for maintaining a support crew and supplying dog food along the route.

Getting it all started

The Iditarod's genesis was an early twentieth-century winter mail and supply route linking fledgling gold towns from the ice-free port of Seward through the Interior mining camps to Nome. The route was used for distributing mail and food and for exporting gold. By the late 1960s, four decades of reliable air transport had done away with the need for regular dog-sled routes to remote communities, and the advent of affordable snowmobiles was threatening to hammer the final nail in commercial dog-sledding's coffin. Then in 1967, historian **Dorothy Page** sought to enliven the Wasilla–Knik Centennial commemoration by running a dog-sled race, a 27-mile sprint from Knik to Big Lake for a purse of $25,000. She soon joined forces with local musher **Joe Redington, Sr** (1917–99) – the "Father of the Iditarod" – and together they began promoting their idea of retracing the old mail route and capturing the spirit of the Serum Run (see box, p.558), on which a diphtheria antitoxin was whisked across the Interior to Nome by a relay of dog teams during an epidemic in 1925.

Finally, in March 1973, the first full-blown Iditarod set off along what is more or less today's route from Knik to Nome. Twenty-two mushers (around half the contestants) astounded doubters by completing the course that year. Though the Iditarod was first and foremost a race, in the early years it was also an endurance event: simply completing the course was regarded as an honorable achievement. Today, everything has become much more organized and professional, with some critics even complaining that the true musher spirit of the race has given way to a carefully managed series of short sprints. The criticism is overly harsh, but some purists prefer the rigors of the Yukon Quest (see "Winter in Fairbanks" box, p.503), or other long races such as the Kuskokwim 300.

Racing today

Since 1983 the race has had a circus-like **Ceremonial Start** in Anchorage, from where dog teams set off at two-minute intervals across snow dumped by trucks along 4th Avenue. Spectators can even bid to ride eleven miles in a sled's "basket," or passenger seat, as an "Iditarider." One enthusiast recently paid $7500 to ride with four-time winner Jeff King. The auction ends on the third Friday of January; place your bids on ☏1-800/566-7533 or ⊛www.iditarod.com.

The absence of a suitable route north of Eagle River means that teams are then trucked 35 miles to Wasilla for the staggered restart the following morning (or 62 miles to Willow if there's not enough snow in Wasilla). The last checkpoint accessible by road is Knik, fourteen miles southwest of Wasilla, but there is more than just wilderness up ahead. The trail is forged by enthusiastic snowmobilers, and checkpoints are attended by volunteers supported by a fleet of bush planes ferrying race organizers and veterinary staff. Far fewer women compete than men, but from 1985 to 1990 all but one race was won by a woman, four of them by Susan Butcher, whose record has been beaten only by five-time winner Rick Swenson. Swenson holds victories in three separate decades and missed first place by just one second in 1978. In 2003, Norwegian Robert Sørlie became the first non-American to win the Iditarod, repeating his feat in 2005.

The **race record** of 8 days, 22hr, 46min was set by Swiss-born Big Lake resident Martin Buser in 2002, but the race normally takes ten or more days. **Prizes** aren't only awarded at the finish line, though. The first musher to Unalakleet wins $2500, the first to the Yukon River gets $3500 and a seven-course meal from the chef of a top Anchorage hotel, and the first to the halfway point hauls in $3000, though this prize is considered a jinx – only five of its recipients have subsequently gone on to win at Nome. In recognition of one of the great mushers of the Serum Run, the Leonhard Seppala Humanitarian Award is presented to the musher who exhibits the most concern for his animals, according to the votes of fellow mushers.

In fact, **animal care** is a sensitive issue. Iditarod teams are made up of twelve to sixteen dogs of about fifty pounds each, bred to share a load of a few hundred pounds at 6–12mph over marathon distances. They can win or lose the race for a musher, so most competitors take their dogs' health very seriously; the occasional canine death, however, has led to accusations of mistreatment, some documented by the Sled Dog Action Coalition (⊛www.helpsleddogs.org), which promotes awareness of sled-dogs' quality of life. Race regulations require mushers to always have a supply of booties for the dogs' feet and they enforce compulsory layovers, two of eight hours and one of 24, at certain points along the route. Rules also insist that each sled carry a heavy sleeping bag, an ax, snowshoes, a cooking stove, a pot, a veterinary notebook, and dog food at all times – the last remaining nod to the original race's self-sufficiency, which has largely given way to frequent supply pickups. If you want to know more about sled dogs – and judge for yourself their living conditions – you can visit several kennels, mainly in the Big Lake area (see p.398).

Over the years the Iditarod has developed its own lore. As the mushers leave Anchorage, the "Widow's Lamp" is lit in Nome and attached to the official finish line, the Burl Arch. To honor all who complete the course, it remains lit until the arrival of the last musher, known as the "red lantern" (a term borrowed from cycling's Tour de France) – a link to the days when dog teams were the only means of transport in the area and a guiding light was hung in the window of roadhouses.

The official Iditarod website, loaded with information on the race's history, the course, and past winners is ⊛www.iditarod.com.

△ An Iditarod team races toward Nome

spirit of the race. In the second ("Video") room there's a BLM display on the history of the sled trail (which the Bureau manages as a National Historic Trail), winners' photos, and the current trophy, the Redington Cup. Look, too, for the immortalized sled dog Togo, who led the final sprint across the ice into Nome during the Serum Run, and Andy, Rick Swenson's lead dog in four of his record five wins, both stuffed and displayed nearby. Outside, a bronze statue remembers the "Father of the Iditarod," Joe Redington, Sr, who died in 1999. Nearby, beside a replica Iditarod checkpoint cabin, you can meet dogs from the Redington Kennels (daily 9am–5pm in summer; free) and board a wheeled sled ($10) towed along a wooded course.

If the Iditarod Headquarters has whetted your appetite for more history and memorabilia, continue twelve more miles to Knik itself; the unsigned **Knik Museum and Mushers' Hall of Fame** (June–Aug Fri–Sun 2–6pm; $2; to visit off-season call ☎745-4751) is just below the pullout at Mile 13.7 (the access to Knik Lake). Once a pool hall, its lower floor is packed with pioneer artifacts that seem little different from appliances your grandmother might have used, illustrating just how young Alaska is. The more interesting material is upstairs in the Iditarod Hall of Fame, an homage to the race, which swishes right past the door of the museum each year. Trophies, cups, and medals abound along with maps of the two main routes, some excellent photos of mushers in action, charcoal drawings of the winners up to 1984, and the winning sled from the first full-blown Iditarod in 1973, a lightweight, sporty-looking affair.

From Knik you can continue for 26 miles through flat boggy country (where the state tried and failed to set up a dairy industry) to Point Mackenzie, from where there should be a ferry to Anchorage by mid-2008.

Practicalities

Trains and Park Connection **buses** stop at, or close to, the train station, and you can reach Wasilla with Mascot ($2.50; ☎376-5000, ⊛www.matsutransit .com) – the two morning services from the Anchorage Transit Center stop at WalMart, well to the east of town, but the evening service takes you (via Palmer) to Carrs downtown; Mascot also runs seven times a day to Palmer ($2). The Airport Valley Shuttle (☎373-4359, ⊛www.airportvalleyshuttle .com) runs from Anchorage airport to anywhere in Wasilla five times a day

($22 one-way, $38 round-trip). Mascot also links Wasilla and Palmer seven times a day ($2). However, unless you have your own vehicle, you'll probably find yourself stranded a fair distance from anywhere you want to be, though you could walk to the Dorothy Page Museum and visit the town's simple **visitor center** inside (same hours). For more mobility, you can **rent a car** or truck at Valley Car Rental, 435 Knik St (☎1-888/649-1880, ⓦwww.valleycarrental.com).

Accommodation is reasonably priced, and often right by the lakes off the highway. From mid-May there's camping at *Lake Lucille Park Campground* (just beyond the Iditarod Headquarters; $10 for two tents/vehicles). The lakeside *Mat-Su Resort*, 1850 Bogard Rd (☎376-3228, ⓦwww.alaskan.com/matsuresort; ❹), offers comfortable rooms along with pedal-boat and jet-ski rental, and sometimes hosts **live music**. Further along the same road, about a mile and a half from the train station, nestles the equally appealing *Gatehouse B&B*, 2500 Bogard Rd (☎1-888/866-9326, ⓦwww.gatehousealaska.com; ❸), whose lakefront cabin is the most congenial spot to rest your head. Heading west on Fairview Loop Road, which leaves the Parks Highway further east at Mile 38, turn left onto the Old Matanuska Road and continue for a mile and a half to ⚘ *Pioneer Ridge B&B*, 2221 Yukon Circle (☎1-800/478-7472, ⓦwww.pioneerridge.com; suites ❻, shared bath ❸–❹). One of Alaska's best-known B&Bs, it's set in a converted milk barn with a couple of lovely large suites, themed rooms (go for the Iditarod one), a cozy, separate cabin, and a spacious lounge and viewing room, with panoramic views of the surrounding valleys and mountains. The best hotel in Wasilla is the spacious *Best Western Lake Lucille Inn*, 1300 W Lake Lucille Drive (Mile 43.5 Parks Hwy; ☎1-800/528-1234, ⓦwww.bestwesternlakelucilleinn.com; ❻), where half the rooms have balconies overlooking the lake; there's a gym, sauna, and Jacuzzi, plus canoe and paddle-boat rentals. It's very reasonably priced in winter, when there's illuminated ice-skating on Lake Lucille. The cheapest hotel rooms are just east of town at the *Windbreak Hotel*, Mile 40.5 Parks Hwy (☎376-4484, ⓦwww.windbreakalaska.com; ❷), which has ten clean, simple rooms and a café renowned for sating serious appetites with low-cost specials.

Outside the hotels, **eating** is largely a matter of choosing your favorite franchise, though there are a few alternatives. *Kaladi Brothers Coffee*, 591 East Parks Hwy, draws coffee-drinkers with **free WiFi**. For coffee, cakes, soups, burgers, sandwiches, and quiche of the day, visit ⚘ *The Valley Bistro*, 405 E Herning Ave (☎357-5633; Mon–Sat 7am–8pm, Sun 10am–4pm), opposite the Dorothy Page Museum in the oldest building in town, constructed in 1917 as a dry goods store; also try the nearby *Great Bear*, 238 N Boundary St (☎373-4782), for burgers, salads, soups, substantial entrees ($15–18), and tasty made-on-site microbrews. You may prefer to drive out to *Lake Lucille Inn* for a relaxing meal on a deck overlooking the lake; choices include beef teriyaki ($26), stir-fried scallops ($24), and sandwiches and burgers (from $9). At Mile 8 of the Knik–Goose Bay Road, the *Settlers Bay Lodge* (☎357-5678, ⓦwww.settlersbaylodge.com) serves dinner (Wed–Sun 5–10pm) with great views across Knik Arm.

Hatcher Pass and Independence Mine

Even if you don't plan to stop in the Mat-Su area, set aside half a day to drive to Hatcher Pass and the Independence Mine, high above the treeline among the shattered granite peaks of the Talkeetna Mountains. An asphalt road leads up to the mine and is kept open all year as far as *Hatcher Pass Lodge*, just a mile short of the mine. To the west of here the Hatcher Pass Road (mid-June to Sept) twists and turns for 31 mostly unpaved miles, climbing through the high tundra of the 3886-foot pass (Alaska's second highest driveable pass after Atigun Pass, north of Fairbanks), then dropping through a dramatic valley with a burbling stream and numerous beaver-dammed pools. The rugged road over the pass can make it slow going (RVs and trailers are strongly discouraged), but it is an excellent drive and a great **cycling** route.

The mine and around

The roads up here were built for wagons serving hard-rock gold mines now preserved in the **Independence Mine State Historic Park** (always open but generally accessible without skis or snowshoes from early June to early Sept; $5 per vehicle; ⓦwww.dnr.state.ak.us/parks/units/indmine.htm), a cluster of semi-dilapidated houses and mine workings spread 3500ft up in a beautiful alpine bowl twenty miles north of Palmer. It is a spectacular place: the fragile timbers and winding gear cast long shadows in the late afternoon sun while the silver and red paintwork of the old bunkhouses stands in dramatic contrast to the blue of the sky and the snowcapped peaks.

In 1897 prospectors found gold in Grubstake Gulch, well downstream of the mine, and surmised its source lay high in the mountains. In 1906 Robert Hatcher found the first hard-rock gold in the Willow Creek district and soon miners were ferreting along tunnels in search of thick quartz veins. Large-scale investment soon put the grubstake placer miner out of business, and before long the whole area was riddled with holes and humming with activity.

In 1937 the Independence camp and mill were built as the first year-round mine in the district, but in 1942 the government decreed that gold mining was not essential to the war effort and drafted the miners. The mine reopened in 1946 but never regained its former profitability and closed in 1951, leaving everything where it stood. Over the decades much was allowed to artfully rot away, but since the 1980s various bunkhouses and workshops have been restored. The former manager's house is now the **visitor center** (early June to early Sept daily 10am–7pm; ☏745-2827) and the place to head for some history and fascinating photographs. Guided tours (early June to early Sept 1.30 & 3.30pm, also 4.30 on weekends and holidays; $5) give you a chance to explore inside three of the buildings that are otherwise out of bounds. If you choose to wander around unescorted, you can go inside the **Assay Office**, now a museum with displays of mining and assaying techniques, and stand in the portal of the **Water Tunnel** to feel the underground air, naturally kept at a chilly 38°F.

The Palmer–Fishhook and Wasilla–Fishhook roads head north from their respective towns and join to become Fishhook–Willow Road (also known as Hatcher Pass Road) two miles before the bridge over the Little Susitna River, where a viewing area (Mile 8.5) contains informative panels on the Castle Mountain Fault, which crosses the river here. At Mile 10.9 you can camp ($10/vehicle) at the Government Peak picnic area, beyond which the road continues climbing through some gorgeous country, with the tumbling waters of the river framed by rocky spires poking up through aspen and cottonwood. The *Motherlode Lodge*, Mile 14 Palmer–Fishhook Rd (☏1-877/745-6171, ⓦwww.motherlodelodge.com;⑤), offers a comfortable bed and continental breakfast, as well as fine dining on weekends and bar food from noon Thursday to Monday. It's known for its jazz club on the last Sunday of each month (3–6pm), and marks the start of **Gold Mint Trail** (see box, below) with camping ($10/vehicle) allowed at the trailhead.

A mile before the mine lies 🍴 *Hatcher Pass Lodge*, Mile 18 Fishhook–Willow Rd (☎745-5897 or 745-1200, ⊛www.hatcherpasslodge.com; cabins ❼, rooms ❹), a group of modern and roomy cabins with limited facilities (but with a separate sauna building) clustered around an A-frame restaurant (open all day, all year) balanced on the rim of the valley looking down to Palmer far below. The rooms are very popular among locals for the **telemark and Nordic trail skiing** and snowmobiling in winter, as is the restaurant, where the stupendous view easily justifies the slightly inflated price of coffee, soup, gourmet pizza, pasta, steak, and assorted sandwiches (some vegetarian). A groomed cross-country ski trail about eight miles long starts here (pay $5 at the lodge), and there are plenty of ungroomed trails (but watch out for snowmobiles), plus a downhill run that starts at Mile 16 and rejoins the road at Mile 12. You can sled at Mile 13 and the Fishhook Trailhead (Mile 16.5), but the snowmobile trail from Fishhook Trailhead to Gold Mint Trailhead is closed to sleds, skis, and snowboards. There are plans to consolidate these areas with a ski center opposite the Government Peak picnic area.

Hatcher Pass and the Lucky Shot Gold Mine

To continue over Hatcher Pass (typically open early July to mid-Sept but some-times longer) to **Willow**, take the unpaved road to the left at Mile 21, just below *Hatcher Pass Lodge*, which climbs steeply a couple of miles up to the pass and then drops down to **Summit Lake**, a beautiful high-country tarn at the heart of the Summit Lake State Recreation Site. This is the region's prime spot for paragliding, and there's usually someone out flying on breezy summer weekends.

Hiking and biking around Hatcher Pass

Hatcher Pass, and the area around the Independence Mine in particular, invites freelance exploration: equip yourself with food, drink, sunscreen, and a camera and head for the hills. Dangerous old mine workings and loose rocks are hazards, but if you keep your eyes open and act sensibly, you can have a fabulous afternoon up here. Lower down you can access a couple of more formal trails from Fish-hook–Willow Road, all best hiked from mid-June to September when there is unlikely to be snow.

This area is open for **camping** in designated sites or half a mile or more from the road. Take a cooking stove as you won't find much firewood; day parking costs $5/vehicle.

Gold Mint Trail (18 miles round-trip; 6–8hr; 500ft ascent). An easy and delightful trail which follows the Little Susitna River – keep it on your right heading up – through a gently sloping valley past the ruined remains of the Lonesome Mine and on to the river's source at Mint Glacier. The first four miles are good for biking, but you may find it too brushy after that. The trailhead is opposite the *Motherlode Lodge*.

Reed Lakes Trail (7 miles round-trip to Lower Reed Lake; 3–5hr; 1800ft ascent). Another fairly easy hike, though one section is steep and involves some boulder hopping. It starts along a broad track (good for biking for the first 1.5 miles), then climbs to the head of the valley and Lower Reed Lake. The upper lake is another mile on beyond a waterfall; you could even continue up 2000ft of steep talus to Bomber Pass, the small gap in the ridge directly above the upper lake, to Bomber Glacier, strewn with the remains of a B-29 Superfortress that crashed here in 1957 (about two more miles). The trailhead is just over a mile up Archangel Road, which leads up Archangel Valley half a mile uphill from *Motherlode Lodge*.

From here the road descends four miles to the **Lucky Shot Gold Mine** (☎746-0511, ⓦwww.luckyshotgoldmine.com), which was worked from 1918 until 1950. Unlike at Independence Mine, here you can go underground on one-hour tours (June–Aug Thurs–Sun 11am–7pm; $10).

Descending further along the road, you join the cascading Willow Creek through lovely open mountain scenery and past beaver ponds before eventually reaching the George Parks Highway.

Along the George Parks Highway: Big Lake, Nancy Lake, and Willow

Between Wasilla and Fairbanks, some three hundred miles north, lie the Alaska Range, Denali National Park, a lot of spruce forest, and some beautiful lakes. The most popular of these is **Big Lake**, on a side road fifteen miles west of Wasilla (at Mile 52.3, marked by three big fireworks emporia, banned nearer to Anchorage), a large sheet of water lined by log houses and vacation homes typically with a float-plane or boat tethered alongside. It's popular with weekenders from Anchorage, but there are prettier and quieter lakes not far ahead; the main reason to stop is to visit some of the **sled-dog kennels** here and in the Willow area. At Martin Buser's Happy Trails Kennels (8.5 miles from the Parks Hwy at Mile 4.5 West Lakes Blvd; mid-April to mid-Oct daily tours 10am, 2pm & 6pm; $35, under-13s $15; ☎892-7899, ⓦwww.buserdog.com) you can take a multimedia tour along the Iditarod Trail with commentary by four-time Iditarod winner Buser (who is often present – but don't ask if he still keeps the body of his beloved lead-dog in the freezer). You can watch a mushing demo, pet puppies, and visit the new gift shop. Cheaper and less glitzy options include Plettner Kennels, at Mile 53 Parks Hwy (June–Aug Mon–Sat 10am, 1pm & 4pm; $20, child $10, free for under-6s; ☎892-6944, ⓦwww.plettner-kennels.com), with rides in a wheeled sled for an extra $20; and Dream a Dream Dog Farm, Mile 64.5 Parks Hwy (daily: mid-April to mid-Sept 9am–6pm, presentations 11am, 3pm and 6pm; $45; ☎1-866/425-6874, ⓦwww.vernhalter.com), run by Yukon Quest-winner Vern Halter, with an Iditarod presentation, kennel tour, and a walk in the woods with some puppies, plus $20 for a sled ride. Campers may want to rest up at the small, simple, and quiet *Rocky Lake State Recreation Site* ($15) four miles from the Parks Highway (turn right at Mile 3.1 Big Lake Rd) or the large, wooded, and peaceful *Little Susitna River Campground* ($10; tap water), Mile 57.3 Parks Hwy, at the hamlet of **Houston** (just south of Millers Market, known for its soft-serve ice cream). You could also press on to **Nancy Lake State Recreation Area**, accessed by a good gravel road off the Parks Highway at Mile 67.3. The low, tree-covered ridges and hummocks provide glimpses of an almost unfathomable network of small lakes and sloughs linked by small creeks. If you are equipped with camping gear and mosquito repellent, this is perfect country for canoeing and a little fishing or easy hiking; it's also popular with skiing and snowshoeing enthusiasts in winter, when the road is plowed to Mile 2.2. The large *South Rolly Lake Campground*, in an attractive lakeside setting at the end of the Nancy Lake Parkway 6.5 miles off the highway, is the place to base yourselves either for the day (late May to early Sept; parking $5) or overnight ($10 camping fee includes day-parking; well water, outhouse, and fire rings). There's also the six-bed *Bald Lake Public Use Cabin* ($45 off-peak, $60 peak), a fifth of a mile's walk from Mile 2.5. **Hikers** should find the nearby trailhead for **Red Shirt Lake Trail** (6 miles round-trip; 3–4hr; negligible ascent), the pick of several well-marked local trails, which sticks to higher ground and ends up at a primitive campsite by Red Shirt Lake. Here you can use **canoes** secured at the lakeside, which must be rented from Tippecanoe at their hut by the *South Rolly Lake Campground* ($20–26 for 8hr, $27–33 per 24hr day, $62–68 for 3 days, $72–78 for up to 7 days, no credit cards; ⊕495-6688, ⊛www.paddlealaska.com). Canoeing here provides access to four highly popular backcountry **cabins** (four to eight people, $30 off-peak, $45 peak a night; reserve through the State Parks office at Finger Lake ⊕745-3975), each with a wood stove but little else: bring everything but your tent. One cabin by South Rolly Lake and three by Nancy Lake can be reached by trails as well as by water, and there are also ten remote campsites. The State Parks office carries information on all these sites.

The waterways here could keep you entertained for a week or more, but most visitors will be satisfied with the popular **Lynx Lake Canoe Route**, a two-day loop that starts at the Tanaina Lake Canoe Trailhead (Mile 4.6 Nancy Lake Parkway) and pieces together fourteen lakes by means of short, well-signed portages. Primitive campsites and four backcountry cabins (including an especially eye-catching one beside James Lake that sleeps seven) dot the route, which can be extended almost infinitely.

Willow and north to Talkeetna Junction

Periodically, pretty much everyone except Juneau residents raises the issue of moving the state capital to somewhere more accessible. Every few years a referendum is defeated, but in the mid-1970s – when the state was flushed with the promise of untold oil riches – this process went further than usual, and **Willow**, at Mile 69 on the Parks Highway, was selected as the preferred site for the new state capital. Its location between Anchorage and Fairbanks, and proximity to the rail line and newly completed highway, swung the decision away from other contenders. Opponents distorted the projected costs into the billions, however, and the electorate soundly defeated the funding referendum in 1982. Read John McPhee's book *Coming into the Country* for extensive coverage of the issue. Since Willow's brief flirtation with greatness, it has become better known for the survivalists holed up in the surrounding woods.

Despite these past ambitions, you'll barely notice the town as you drive through, and on a clear day you are much more likely to gaze out at Denali, visible here for the first time. Nonetheless, Willow refers to itself as "Alaska's State Capital – of recreation," a half-joking promotion of its boundless opportunities for fishing and winter activities. Though shared by several other towns, its claim to be "Alaska's dog-mushing capital" is a justified one, with numerous successful kennels hereabouts, including that of DeeDee Jonrowe, currently the state's top female musher. The restart of the Iditarod takes place here when there's not enough snow in Wasilla, as occurred from 2004 to 2006.

Willow strings along the highway from Mile 61 to 80, but its heart is at Mile 69 where you'll find a grocery, an ATM, gas, and a post office – the very definition of small town. As the town is close to the western approach to Hatcher Pass, you might want to spend the night here before crossing over, and the best **place to stay** is the lakeside *Willow Trading Post Lodge* on Willow Station Road (east from Mile 69.5 Parks Hwy; ⊕495-1695), a traditional roadhouse with simple cabins (summer rates from $95 for two to $165 for nine), space for RVs ($18) and tents ($9), laundry, and a bar. The restaurant sells reasonably priced and filling meals (most dishes $14–16), though gourmands are better served at the *Pioneer Lodge*, Mile 71.1 Parks Hwy (⊕495-1000), an RV park with a lively bar and a restaurant that produces surprisingly good food. RVs can stop on the north side of the river at the *Willow Creek Resort*, identifiable by its alpacas

(T 495-6343; $26 full hookup and shower); campers can pitch tents here ($16) or at the rear of the *Pioneer Lodge*.

North of Willow and the turnoff for Hatcher Pass (at Mile 71), everything gets pretty quiet for a while. From Mile 88.1, Hidden Hills Drive leads 4.5 miles east to ⅄ *Gigglewood Lakeside Inn* (T 1-800/574-2555, W www.gigglewood .com; ⑤), one of the finest B&Bs in the region in terms of furnishings, setting, and service, with two cottages and an upstairs suite for four; at Mile 88.2 you'll find the welcoming *Sheep Creek Lodge* (T 495-6227, W www.sheepcreeklodge .com), open all year. They have nonsmoking, recently refurbished en-suite rooms (⑥), fine new cabins (④), RV camping from $15, and excellent food. In winter the area around the lodge is a destination for snowmobiling, evidenced by the separate bridges beside the highway for the machines. At Mile 96.5 there's camping at the Montana Creek State Recreation Area ($18/vehicle); otherwise just continue on to Mile 98.7, where a side road (and good parallel cycle track) leads you to one of Alaska's most inviting towns, Talkeetna.

Talkeetna

With dirt roads, log cabins, and an international flavor lent by the world's mountaineers congregating here to take on Denali, **Talkeetna** makes for an unusual and essential stop. The intimate downtown area, two blocks long and one wide, is the social center for the town's six hundred residents, some of whom can often be seen playing their fiddles and guitars for an ever-present canine audience. It's a perfect place to kick back for a day or two and stroll through the woods or along the sandy river banks.

Rumor has it that this eclectic hamlet was the model for Cicely in the early 1990s TV series *Northern Exposure*, and residents claim they can identify the source of every character – except for the retired astronaut. To its credit, Talkeetna doesn't use this as tour-bus bait, but that's not to say the visitors aren't coming. Several years as a hot destination on the travelers' grapevine have attracted the tourism mainstream, spawning a head-in-a-moose photo opportunity and an

△ Downtown Talkeetna

abundance of tacky souvenir shops. Some years back, the big tour-company lobbyists got a new bus-accessible train station built on the edge of town, and since then there's been a minor boom in new lodges and adventure tour operators. The road into town is even being widened and improved, but resistance from private-minded locals keeps buses barred from the main street.

Poking around town or walking out to some of the local lakes during the day and then returning for a good evening chinwag in the bar is a great way to get a feel for the area. But to really take advantage of Talkeetna's location, use it as a base to get into the nearby wilderness, either by boat or plane; luckily, there's no shortage of experts to provide advice and logistics. The biggest attraction is **flightseeing around Mount McKinley**, though if you can time it right, drop by for the Moose Dropping Festival (see box, p.402).

6

Some history

Talkeetna – from *K'Dalkitnu*, "river of plenty" in Dena'ina – lies at the confluence of the Talkeetna, Chulitna, and Susitna rivers, where the search for gold brought early prospectors in 1896. By 1910, Talkeetna had established itself as a riverboat station, providing supplies to miners and beaver trappers, and would have slipped into obscurity were it not for its brief revival in 1915 as the local headquarters for the construction of the new Seward-to-Fairbanks railroad. With the completion of the line, **President Warren Harding** visited Nenana to drive in the golden spike, then stopped by Talkeetna on his way south. He died a few days later, apparently from flu complicated by overwork and sheer exhaustion, but Talkeetna residents take a perverse pride in variously claiming that he was supplied with poisoned tobacco, was fed a dodgy stew at the *Fairview Inn*, or that the conviviality of the place induced him to indulge in one too many drinks. For the next few decades, all Talkeetna had was this manufactured claim to infamy; the population steadily declined until road access arrived in 1964.

Arrival and information

In summer the daily northbound **train** from Anchorage and a southbound one from Fairbanks and Denali stop at the station, half a mile south of the center, where Talkeetna Taxi & Tours (℡733-8294) can run you into town for a small fee; in winter the weekly flagstops (see p.43) stop at the section house in the center of town. Northbound travelers who can't afford the full journey from Anchorage to Fairbanks should catch a bus to Talkeetna, then ride the train from here to Denali – the most spectacular section of the journey.

Arriving by road, you turn off the Parks Highway at Talkeetna Junction (Mile 98.7), then drive fourteen miles into town. Most shuttle buses shoot straight along the Parks Highway, dropping off at Talkeetna Junction, from where it is usually easy to hitch into Talkeetna. Alaska Park Connection (daily from Anchorage; $41; ℡1-800/266-8625, ⓦwww.alaskacoach.com) comes as far as the *Talkeetna Alaska Lodge*, a couple of miles from the center. The Talkeetna Sunshine Shuttle (℡1-800/770-7275, ⓦwww.alaskashuttles.com) will run you from the Junction to Talkeetna for $7 (round-trip $13), connecting as well to Anchorage ($52/92), Denali ($45/85), and Fairbanks ($71/128). During the climbing season (late April to mid-July) you can ride door to door from Anchorage to Talkeetna (stopping en-route at Carrs supermarket in Wasilla) with Talkeetna Shuttle Service ($65 one-way, $125 round-trip; ℡1-888/288-6008, ⓦwww.denalicentral.com), which picks up once or twice daily from the capital's airport, hostels, and hotels. Also mainly for climbers, Denali Overland

Talkeetna's festivals are better than most – and certainly weirder. Topping the bill is the summer's biggest celebration, the **Moose Dropping Festival** (T733-2487), a fundraiser for the Historical Society on the second weekend in July. The very mention of the event allegedly caused one outraged Florida resident, who apparently mistook a noun for a verb, to reach for the phone and demand that the Chamber of Commerce tell him how far they actually drop the poor moose. The festival, in fact, focuses on the brown nuggets that are revealed in their millions with the spring snowmelt and are then sold throughout the town (complete with a heavy coat of varnish) for use as earrings, necklaces, and brooches. Leave space in your luggage for these essential items, especially Talkeetna's iconic moose-dropping-on-a-stick, the "lollipoop." (Several on the same stick is known as a "shish kapoop.") In addition to these prized lumps of Alaskana, the festival features craft stalls, dancing, drinking, and a **moose-dropping toss**, somewhat akin to a penny toss, played on a moose-shaped board with those shellacked ovoid excreta.

The festival wouldn't be complete, though, without the **Mountain Mother Contest** (on Sunday), in which contesting mothers sling a ten-pound baby doll on their backs, don hip waders, and set off on a course involving archery, carpentry, fly-casting, diaper-changing, cream-pie-making, and a simulated river-crossing using a log and stepping stones while carrying groceries. Fast mothers have completed the course in under four minutes.

The town comes together again on the first weekend in December when the Talk-eetna Bachelor Society hosts the **Wilderness Woman Competition** (T733-3939), designed to "select the lady who best exemplifies the traits most desired by a Wilder-ness Man." Competing "bachelorettes" struggle to complete a series of wintertime tasks – chopping wood, driving a snowmobile through an obstacle course – to reach the kitchen where she then prepares a sandwich and delivers it (along with a beer) to her bachelor, who sits watching football on TV. The event culminates in the Bachelor Auction and a Bachelor Ball at the *Fairview Inn*.

The more traditional **Talkeetna Bluegrass Festival** (four days in mid-Aug; $35; Wwww.talkeetnabluegrass.com) has become too large for the town that bears its name and now takes place at Mile 102 on the Parks Highway.

Transportation (T1-800/651-5221, Wwww.denalioverland.com) runs by reservation from Talkeetna to Anchorage or Denali (both $75/140 per person for four or more).

A couple of gift shops in town provide information, but pretty much everything you need is right in front of your eyes. The Talkeetna Denali Visitor Center (mid-May to mid-Sept 9am–9pm; winter phone only; T1-800/660-2688, Wwww.talkeetnadenali.com) can assist you with accommodation and tour reservations. Mountaineers and those gripped by the climbing lore of the Alaska Range should drop by the **Talkeetna Ranger Station** on B Street at W 1st (mid-April to early Sept daily 8am–6pm; early Sept to mid-April Mon–Fri 8am–4.30pm; T733-2231, Wwww.nps.gov/dena/home/mountaineering), a comfortable spot staffed by well-informed mountain enthusiasts and stocked with mountaineering magazines and other information for planning your days ahead in Denali.

Accommodation

Talkeetna has never been the sort of place where visitors expect to be pampered. The rustic charms of the *Talkeetna Roadhouse* are more in keeping with the spirit of the place, but a recent clutch of new **hotels** and luxury cabins is resetting the tone. Still, there is plenty of reasonably priced and welcoming accommodation as well as several **campgrounds**, though some campers choose to pitch illegally on the river flats beyond the legit campground at the western end of Main Street.

During the season, **climbers** can often find space to doss down in the hangar of the outfit they're flying with: ask in advance.

Hotels and B&Bs

Fairview Inn Main St ☎ 733-2423, ⊛ www .mtdenali.com. This old inn, built in 1923 as an overnight resting point along the railroad, is exactly halfway between Fairbanks and Seward. It has been only minimally modernized since then, with seven smallish rooms all with shared bathrooms. Nice as these are, be warned that the bar swings most nights until the early hours, so it can get loud; but once it closes you don't have far to stagger. ❷

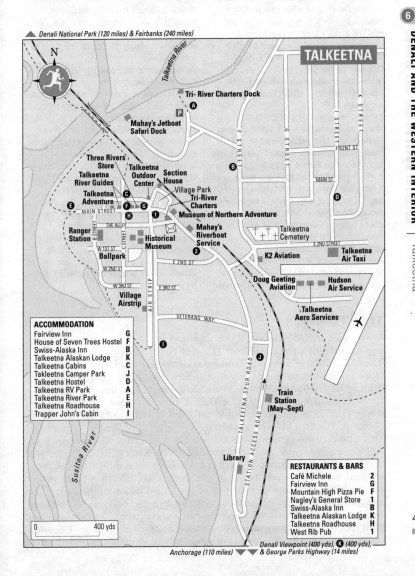

▲ Denali National Park (120 miles) & Fairbanks (240 miles)

N

TALKEETNA

Talkeetna River

Tri- River Charters Dock **A**

Mahay's Jetboat Safari Dock **P**

F STREET
G STREET
I STREET
K STREET

FRONT ST.

B

MAIN ST.

Three Rivers Store
Talkeetna River Guides
Talkeetna Outdoor Center
Section House
Village Park
Tri-River Charters

Talkeetna Adventure
E **F** **G**
H **1**

— MAIN STREET —

Museum of Northern Adventure

D

B STREET
THE ALLEY
C STREET

Ranger Station

Historical Museum

W 1ST ST.

Ballpark

W 2ND ST.

W 3RD ST.

Village Airstrip

AIR STRIP

Mahay's Riverboat Service
2

Talkeetna Cemetery

E 2ND STREET

K2 Aviation

Talkeetna Air Taxi

E 2ND ST.
E 3RD ST.

Doug Geeting Aviation

Hudson Air Service

Talkeetna Aero Services

VETERANS' WAY

I

J

TALKEETNA SPUR ROAD

Train Station (May–Sept)

Susitna River

Library

STATION ACCESS ROAD

ACCOMMODATION

Fairview Inn	G
House of Seven Trees Hostel	F
Swiss-Alaska Inn	B
Talkeetna Alaskan Lodge	K
Talkeetna Cabins	C
Talkeetna Camper Park	J
Talkeetna Hostel	D
Talkeetna RV Park	A
Talkeetna River Park	E
Talkeetna Roadhouse	H
Trapper John's Cabin	I

RESTAURANTS & BARS

Café Michele	2
Fairview Inn	G
Mountain High Pizza Pie	F
Nagley's General Store	1
Swiss-Alaska Inn	B
Talkeetna Alaskan Lodge	K
Talkeetna Roadhouse	H
West Rib Pub	1

0 ——— 400 yds

Denali Viewpoint (400 yds), **K** (400 yds),
Anchorage (110 miles) ▼▼ & George Parks Highway (14 miles)

Swiss-Alaska Inn F St ☎733-2424, ⓦwww
.swissalaska.com. Large inn with comfortable,
spacious rooms with small TVs, handily close to
town and with its own restaurant (see p.409). ❹

🏃 Talkeetna Alaskan Lodge Mile 12.9
Talkeetna Spur Rd ☎1-888/959-9590,
ⓦwww.talkeetnalodge.com. Modern hotel built of
raw logs and river stones high on a ridge behind
town with wonderful views of the Alaska Range.
Even if you're not staying, it is worth popping up
for a drink or a bit of relaxation beside the central
fireplace. The attractive rooms have all facilities,
including satellite TV, coffeemaker, and dataport
(plus WiFi in public areas), but you'll have to
reserve well in advance to get one of the $370-
plus Denali-view rooms in the main lodge. ❾
Talkeetna Cabins C St ☎1-888/733-9933,
ⓦwww.talkeetnacabins.org. Roomy four-berth
cabins right downtown with full kitchen, lounge,
and satellite TV. ❼
Talkeetna Roadhouse Main St ☎733-1351,
ⓦwww.talkeetnaroadhouse.com. Talkeetna's other
old inn dates to 1917, with simple but tidy rooms
sharing baths. With no bar, it doesn't have the robust
atmosphere of the *Fairview*, but easily makes up for
it with very hospitable staff and a cozy lounge, which
in spring and early summer is full of climbers planning their summit strategy. They have single rooms,
doubles, and a couple of larger, deluxe rooms, which
share a bathroom with a clawfoot tub. Closed on
weekdays from mid-Sept to mid-April. Deluxe ❹,
doubles ❷, singles and bunks ❶
Trapper John's Cabin D St ☎1-800/735-2354,
ⓦwww.alaska.net/~trapperj. A wonderfully rustic
cabin near the Susitna River, with full kitchen and

rustic outhouse, an easy walk from downtown. It
sleeps up to four, but can be taken by two, and
breakfast is included in the price. ❹

Hostels and camping
House of Seven Trees Main St ☎733-7733
or 243-3456, ⒺPatm_ak@hotmail.com. More
accurately the House of Six and a Half Trees, this
friendly new hostel next to *Mountain High Pizza Pie*
has a bunkhouse (❶) and private (❸) and family
rooms (❹).
Talkeetna Camper Park Talkeetna Spur Rd
☎733-2693, ⓦwww.talkeetnacamper.com. The
most convenient RV parking, located on the road
into town and offering electrical ($21) or full ($26)
hookup.
Talkeetna Hostel International I St ☎733-
4678, ⓦwww.talkeetnahostel.com. Welcoming
house in the woods about a ten-minute walk from
downtown, with clean, comfortable dorm bunks
for $27, a private double room for $75, tent sites,
a small but well-equipped kitchen, bikes to rent,
and free Internet access. Late May to Sept. Room
❸, bunks ❶
Talkeetna River Park This tent-only campground
at the western end of Main Street costs $12 per
two-tent site, paid to the summertime host.
Talkeetna Roadhouse (see above). This charismatic old inn maintains a four-berth bunk room
($21), with sheets and towels provided.
Talkeetna RV Park ☎733-2604, ⓦwww
.talkeetna-rv.com. Large campground and RV
park in the woods a short walk from town, with
showers, laundry facilities, and boat launch. $13
per site.

The Town

As you walk around town you'll notice plaques on over a dozen historic buildings, all detailed on the *Talkeetna Historical Society Walking Tour* leaflet (free).
These are available from the **Talkeetna Historical Society Museum**, one
block south of Main Street (May to mid-Sept daily 10am–6pm; March, April,
& Oct–Dec Fri–Sun 10.30am–6.30pm; $3; ⓦwww.talkeetnahistory.org), a clus-
ter of four buildings including **Ole Dahl Cabin**, the oldest building in town,
dating from 1916. Inside you'll find the usual collection of pioneer artifacts,
photos of Talkeetna old-timers, coverage of the antics of local bush pilots, and
plenty on the construction of the railroad. The highlight is the topographically
accurate twelve-square-foot scale **model of McKinley**, based on years of
detailed aerial photography by Bradford Washburn, an authority on just about
anything to do with the mountain (see box, p.406). Excellent examples of
the work, which earned him the title of the "Ansel Adams of the North," are
arranged around the walls, and there are more up at the *Talkeetna Alaskan Lodge*
(see Accommodation, above). Look, too, for the biographies of Denali heroes,
press clippings, and letters, such as one from the widow of Frederick Cook (see
box, p.406) asking for the opinion of rambunctious mountaineer and longtime

Denali guide Ray Genet on her husband's summit claim. His reply is instructive. Throughout the summer the free ranger program features hour-long talks on the mountain's conquerors using the McKinley model as a prop.

Climbers die almost every season on the mountain, adding to the nearly one hundred names on the memorial in the **Talkeetna Cemetery**, a salutary reminder that despite the climbing traffic, the presence of two ranger stations on the West Buttress route, and specialist rescue helicopters permanently on call, the mountain always has the last say. The cemetery contains the grave of "the climber's pilot," Don Sheldon, and is the spiritual resting place of Genet, whose body remains on Mount Everest.

On the road into town, the **Museum of Northern Adventure** (May to mid-Sept daily 10am–6pm; $2) displays two dozen waxwork dioramas depicting archetypal Alaskan lifestyles, as well as dolls, carvings and pottery; note the letter to the Presley estate for permission (refused) to display a moose-dropping Elvis. Across the road (behind the post office) the **Sheldon Community Arts Hangar** is home to the Denali Arts Council (no fixed hours; ☏733-7929), which sponsors exhibitions of local art at the North Wall Gallery and shows a thirty-minute video (May–Sept daily 2pm and 3pm) on Don Sheldon, the legendary bush pilot who owned the hangar. You may also catch a rehearsal for the evening's performance – perhaps a play, musical, or concert.

On a clear day – roughly one in three in summer, more in winter – don't miss the hike (or drive) to the **viewpoint**, a mile south along Talkeetna Spur Road, from where the Alaska Range, even sixty miles away, looks simply magnificent.

Outdoor activities

As more and more people come to Talkeetna, entrepreneurs are busy devising ways to keep visitors entertained. The well-established flightseeing, jetboating, rafting, and fishing trips are now being supplemented by horseback riding and even dog-sled rides.

The **Alaska Railroad** runs the Talkeetna–Hurricane flagstop service (mid-May to mid-Sept Thurs–Sun & holidays at 11.45am; $78), a diesel railcar that makes a five-hour jaunt north to Hurricane and back. Though primarily run for local residents heading off to their cabins in the woods, it makes for an entertaining and scenic day out of town. There are no reservations and no food is available, so pack what you need.

If you just want to go your own way, but need to buy **camping and mountaineering supplies** or pick up some USGS topo maps, visit Talkeetna Outdoor Center (see "Rafting," p.408).

Flightseeing

You might have to wait around for a couple of days until the weather plays ball, but an essential part of any visit to Talkeetna is a **flightseeing trip** to Mount McKinley. Don't delay until you get to Denali; you are closer to the mountain here, and the weather tends to offer better viewing from the south side of the range. Half a dozen air-taxi companies, mostly with offices on Main Street as well as at the airstrip (see Listings, p.410), run four- to five-passenger bush-plane flights and offer similar packages at competitive prices: shop around and see who offers you the best deal. Planes book up rapidly in summer, can be hard to fill after mid-September, and in May are mostly reserved by climbers who fly to the mountain from here. **Talkeetna Airstrip** itself is now on the National

Of the great mountains of the world, Denali (North America's highest peak at 20,320ft) is not particularly high: dozens of Andean peaks are higher, and if it were moved to the Himalayas Denali would barely rate a mention. Nonetheless, its subarctic location makes it one of the world's coldest mountains, and its extreme and unpredictable weather conditions raise its profile to the point where Denali is regarded as one of the world's most difficult mountains to climb. That very difficulty, and the sheer lonesome majesty that makes it one of the most sought-after peaks, has engendered a long and fascinating history of summit attempts and heroic conquests.

Some history

No one, certainly no European, had ever stepped on the slopes of Denali until the early twentieth century, but interest in conquering the mountain quickly reached fever pitch. In 1903, Alaska district judge and future congressman **James Wickersham** rounded up four local lads, equipped them with primitive climbing gear, and led them to above eight thousand feet on the north side of the mountain, where what is now known as the Wickersham Wall halted their progress. A couple of months later the explorer **Frederick Cook** led an exhausted party up to 11,300ft feet. In 1906 he telegrammed to the world that he had just successfully summited Denali on his second attempt, backing it up with a photo of himself on the peak and a detailed summit diary. The speed of his ascent immediately alerted the mountaineering community to possible deception, but he became the toast of American society, which was even more enthusiastic about his equally dubious claims to have beaten Robert Peary to the North Pole in 1909 (although it's now thought Peary didn't make it either). Pertinent questions were soon being asked, and Cook's reputation was already in tatters when, in 1910, Belmore Brown settled the matter by replicating Cook's "summit" photograph on an 8000-foot peak twenty miles from Denali.

As Brown took his photo he didn't realize that Denali's North Peak – 850ft lower than the South Peak – had already been scaled by a group of Kantishna-based gold miners now known as the **Sourdough Expedition**. In what is still regarded as one of the most extraordinary mountaineering feats ever, four prospectors – led by an overweight 50-year-old Welshman, **Tom Lloyd** – with no technical mountaineering experience and only the most rudimentary gear, succeeded in proving not only that Cook's claim was false, but that locals could outclimb anyone from "Outside." According to the *Fairbanks Daily News-Miner*, they carried "less 'junk' with them than an Eastern US excursion party would take along for a one-day's outing in the hills"; certainly they wore only normal winter clothes and ate little but bacon, beans, and caribou meat. Nonetheless, they reached the North Peak without major incident and planted a fourteen-foot spruce trunk which they had hauled up to use as a flagpole. The Stars and Stripes they had hoped would be visible from Fairbanks wasn't, and in the light of the Cook farce their claim was widely disbelieved.

All speculation was laid to rest in 1913 when respected Episcopal missionary Archdeacon **Hudson Stuck** led a shoestring expedition of four men that not only vouched for the Sourdoughs' success – the spruce pole was still upright three years on – but also entered the record books as the first to reach the true summit. Doubters were satisfied and interest in the conquered mountain waned to the point that it was nearly twenty years before anyone summited again, and almost forty before anyone thought of climbing it any other way than via the Muldrow Glacier route from the north, which had been used by all successful early expeditions.

In 1947, **Bradford Washburn** entered the scene and succeeded in climbing Denali along with his wife Barbara – the first woman to summit. But Washburn's real contribution was his detailed surveying work, which identified the West Buttress Route, first climbed by a party led by Washburn in 1951. What made this route possible was the novel practice of glacier landings, allowing climbers and equipment to be deposited at 7200ft on the Kahiltna Glacier, on Denali's southwest side. Washburn's success was followed by numerous others, and the West Buttress Route became firmly established as the preferred line of attack. The next twenty years perfected the approach and coincided with mountaineering's transformation into a mainstream sport: by the mid-1970s, every weather window from mid-April through the end of July saw parties setting off for the mountain.

Since then new routes have been pioneered and increasingly contrived "firsts" have been attempted: the first winter expedition in 1967, the first solo ascent in 1970 (by Naomi Uemura, who also made the first winter solo ascent in 1984, but died on the descent), the first hang-glider descent in 1976, and the first sled-team ascent in 1979. Meanwhile, even people who would barely class themselves as mountaineers were attempting Denali by engaging **guides**. One of the first guides was **Ray "the Pirate" Genet** – a veteran of the first winter ascent on which he earned his nickname for the skull and crossbones he used to mark his clothing – who, together with **Don Sheldon**, bush pilot *par excellence*, helped scores of climbers reach the top. Genet died while guiding on Everest in 1979; in 1991 his son, Taras, at the age of 12 became the youngest climber to summit Denali. Ten years later this record was broken by the 11-year-old Galen Johnston. The oldest climber summited at 71.

Climbing Denali today

Over the years the level of mortality, the high public profile of the mountain, and its administration by Denali National Park have caused considerable controversy, and it has taken the efforts of numerous working groups to finally settle on a system of administration that preserves the sense of adventure while providing a tolerable level of safety.

It's hard to find fault in the park's cautious stance, especially as more (and increasingly inexperienced) climbers take on Denali. In 2005 there were a record 1340 attempts and 775 successes; among the failures were two deaths and 13 rescues. If the number of attempts gets much higher the NPS expects to cap it; in the meantime, half a dozen authorized guiding services, listed on the Denali National Park website (see below), charge close to $5000 for an attempt at the West Buttress Route, taken by eighty percent of Denali's summiteers.

Today all climbers must register their intentions at least sixty days in advance of their climb and pay $200: details are available online (@www.nps.gov/dena/planyourvisit/mountaineering.htm) and in *Mountaineering: Denali National Park and Preserve*, a free booklet in eight languages available from the Talkeetna Ranger Station (see p.402). Almost all summit attempts start with a flight – roughly $300 round-trip with gear – from Talkeetna to the Kahiltna Glacier at 7200ft where the Park Service maintains a base camp (flown in by the army in mid-May) throughout the climbing season. Radio contact with Talkeetna improves safety on the mountain and allows climbers to call for a flight out when needed. The emphasis is very much on self-reliance, but emergency assistance is available at a medical camp at 14,200ft, where staff used to spend much of their day picking up climbers' trash – typically over a thousand pounds a season. Now climbers are issued an individually tagged "clean mountain can" (with methane release valve), and there's a $100 fine for leaving human waste on the mountain, and $150 for trash. The presence of rangers on the mountain and scores of others scrabbling for position at regular campsites could lead to overconfidence, but as veteran climber Jonathan Waterman writes, "The fact that the West Buttress Route is not technically difficult should not obscure the need to plan for extreme survival situations . . . the West Buttress route is a terribly underestimated climb."

Register of Historic Places, and new interpretive signage on the early history of aviation in Alaska is being installed.

There's a choice of three different circuits, all flying over the confluence of the Susitna, Chulitna, and Talkeetna rivers, then across the Peters and Dutch hills in Denali State Park to the Alaska Range itself. The most **basic package** (1hr; $140–150) links the Tokositna and Ruth glaciers on the southeast side of the mountain, and flies up Great Gorge, a 9000-foot-deep, vertical-walled canyon filled with almost 4000ft of ice. The mid-priced flight (1hr 15min; $175–190) includes the above itinerary but also loops around the back of the 14,573-foot Mount Hunter to the 7200-foot base camp on the Kahiltna Glacier – the fifty-mile-long tongue of ice that slices through the Alaska Range, separating Mount McKinley from the second-highest peak in the range, Mount Foraker. If you can afford it, go for the grand tour (1hr 30min; $200–210), which climbs higher up the Kahiltna and then makes a complete mountain circuit with views of the 14,000-foot Wickersham Wall and the main body of Denali National Park on the north side of the range. When snow conditions permit, you can add a **glacier landing** (additional 30min; $60–65) either on the Kahiltna Glacier (typically April to early July) or at the Don Sheldon Amphitheater (April–July and occasionally into Aug), a glacial cirque at the head of the Ruth Glacier.

Some operators also offer a **summit overflight** (1hr 20min; $215–235), which includes all of the above plus a bird's eye view of the tops of Denali, Foraker, and Hunter; these use low-winged twin-engine planes (as opposed to the high-winged single-engine planes used for lower flights) so views may be obscured, and glacier landings are not possible.

Jetboat trips and fishing

For a little gentle adventure, sign up with Mahay's Riverboat Service (mid-May to Sept; ☎1-800/736-2210, ⓦwww.mahaysriverboat.com), which runs a fifty-seat **jetboat** on some of the area's shallow, braided rivers, almost scraping gravel bars and hoping to catch sight of moose and bald eagles. The Jetboat Safari (2hr; $50) leaves several times a day and includes a fifteen-minute guided nature walk, while the Wilderness Safari (4hr; $95) heads further upstream to the former townsite of Curry, which was the overnight stop for Alaska Railroad passengers until 1947, when the *Aurora* same-day service was introduced between Anchorage and Fairbanks. The more committed can opt for either the Talkeetna Canyon (4hr; $125) or the Devil's Canyon (6hr; $175) trip, both in the smaller jetboats needed to negotiate the Class III whitewater.

Mahay's also runs **fishing trips**, either guided (5hr for $135, 8hr for $185) or unguided, where they rent you some gear ($25 a day) and drop you seven miles upstream ($45), returning later for you and your salmon and trout; Tri-River Charters (☎733-2400, ⓦwww.tririvercharters.com) provides similar service.

Rafting

A more peaceful alternative to the jetboats is rafting with Talkeetna River Guides, Main Street (☎1-800/353-2677, ⓦwww.talkeetnariverguides.com), which offers the gentle two-hour natural-history float trip (mid-May to mid-Sept daily 8.30am, 11am, 2pm & 5.30pm; $69), and a four-hour run on the Chulitna River (7am & 1pm; $115) which includes a little gold-panning. Rafters after more adventure can try fly-in overnight trips such as three days on the Chulitna River ($695), where there's pristine salmon-fishing, or the Talkeetna River ($1250), taking in the Talkeetna Canyon, fourteen miles of Class III and IV water, claimed to be the longest whitewater stretch in its class in North America, and certainly Alaska's prime whitewater trip. The Talkeetna Outdoor Center, behind the *Fairview Inn* (☎1-800/349-0064), runs a somewhat similar trip on the Talkeetna for $875 and may even have better last-minute deals. Denali View Raft Adventures, 15669 E Coffee Lane (☎733-2778, ⓦwww.denaliviewraft .com), offers two-hour trips on the Talkeetna for $60, or four hours on the Susitna for $95, plus a four-hour Susitna raft/train combo for $155.

Other activities

Should the bucolic surroundings inspire you to see more, join D&S Alaskan Trail Rides (☎745-2208, ⓦwww.alaskantrailrides.com) for guided **horseback riding** (1hr for $57, 2hr for $87) through the woods to good Denali viewpoints. Prefer dogs? Talkeetna Sundog Kennel (☎1-800/318-2534, ⓦwww.sundogkennel.com) will drive you from their office on Main Street to the nearby kennels where you'll meet the dogs and enjoy a four-mile **dog-sled ride**, either in a wheeled buggy in summer ($50) or a proper sled in winter ($60).

Beyond their bread-and-butter McKinley flights, the air-taxi companies will turn their hands to just about anything that involves flying. Talkeetna Air Taxi in particular specializes in tailored one- and two-day **glacier treks**, snowshoeing, and high-country skiing with all equipment provided. Backcountry trips can also be organized, flying you to a base camp for a few days. Prices depend greatly on numbers, the need for guides, and flying time, but $1000 per person for three days' snowshoeing, trekking, and glacier skiing is typical.

Eating and drinking

Many spots close quite early in Talkeetna, so the pickings are often slim. As for evening **entertainment**, it tends to revolve around the bars at the *Fairview Inn* and the *West Rib*.

Café Michele Talkeetna Spur Rd ☎733–5300, ⓦwww.cafemichele.com. The town center's finest dining in an airy room with a tempting menu of organic dishes and a good wine list (from $22). Lunches are modestly priced (gringo chili, $13), though you'll pay more for dinner entrees ($18–29), which might be soy-ginger king salmon ($25), roasted half-chicken ($22), or basil walnut chicken pasta ($19).

Fairview Inn Main St ☎733-2423. A classic, small-town Alaskan bar, with rough-wood floors and sepia-toned walls hung with beaver pelts, that's very much the place to be. Portraits of former bar-proppers line the walls while a broad cross-section of tall-talking Talkeetna characters entertain visitors. Most weekends and some weeknights there's top-flight Alaskan live music (usually $5); if not, there is always the bar piano and guitar.

Mountain High Pizza Pie Main St at C ☎733-1234. The happening new place, serving subs ($7.50), flatbread sandwiches ($9–10), and a range of pizzas (from $13), with eight beers on tap, and a covered beer garden to enjoy it all in. Spring noon–10pm, summer daily 11.30am–11pm.

Nagley's General Store Main St. Basically a grocery store but one that sells good cheap espresso, deli sandwiches, and ice cream along

with fishing gear and animal furs. Built c.1920, it also must be one of the last places in America still selling cigarettes individually. Upstairs there's a gift store and ATM.

Swiss-Alaska Inn F St ☎733-2424. The inn's restaurant serves hearty breakfasts (their omelettes are particularly good), steak, and seafood dinners ($15–23), with specialties such as Wiener schnitzel and German sausage salad ($9), and a token veggie dish.

Talkeetna Alaskan Lodge Mile 12.9 Talkeetna Spur Rd ☎733-9500, ⓦwww.talkeetnalodge.com. In addition to breakfast, lunch, and dinner in the *Base Camp Bistro*, the *Foraker Dining Room* (from 5pm daily) offers the best Alaskan ingredients such as king crab legs, halibut with mango salsa, or venison, plus desserts and fine wines – all at the highest prices in town.

🏃 **Talkeetna Roadhouse** Main St ☎733-1351. Featuring Talkeetna's best bakery and a great daytime café, the *Roadhouse* pleases guests with breakfasts (until 1pm) of sourdough hotcakes served with real maple syrup, or eggs, bacon, home-fried potatoes, and toast – the $7 half-plate is plenty for hearty eaters, the $10 full plate is for McKinley returnees. For lunch build your own sandwiches or try the cheese pinto beans on a grilled corn muffin with salsa ($6). Closes at 3pm but reopens in the evening (5–10pm) for light snacks, dessert, and coffee.

West Rib Pub & Grill Main St ☎733-3354, ⓦwww.westribpub.info. Decent diner food with a pleasant deck for warm days where an outdoor grill turns out burgers and sandwiches ($7–9 with nightly burger and beer specials). The bar inside has the town's finest selection of craft beers, including Guinness on tap and top Alaskan microbrews.

Listings

Air-taxi companies Fly Denali ☎1-866/733-7768, ⓦwww.flydenali.com; Hudson Air Service ☎1-800/478-2321, ⓦwww.hudsonair.com; K2 Aviation ☎1-800/764-2291, ⓦwww.flyk2.com; Talkeetna Aero Services ☎1-888/733-2899, ⓦwww.talkeetnaaero.com; Talkeetna Air Taxi ☎1-800/533-2219, ⓦwww.talkeetnaair.com.

Banks The nearest bank is in Wasilla, over an hour away, but there are ATMs at Nagley's General store on Main St and at the Tesoro gas station at Talkeetna Junction.

Gas Three Rivers, Mile 10 Talkeetna Spur Road (credit cards only) and at Talkeetna Junction.

Internet access The library (Mon–Sat 11am–6pm; ☎733-2359), a mile south along the spur road, has free Internet access (20min) and WiFi.

Laundry and showers Mabuhay Washi-Washi, on Talkeetna Spur Rd opposite Mahay's, has a coin-op laundry ($9.50/load) and showers.

Medical Talkeetna Family Medical Clinic is at 125 First St (Mon–Thurs 9am–noon, 2–5pm; ☎733-2708); the more modern Sunshine Clinic, with 24hr on-call service, is at Mile 4.2 Talkeetna Spur Rd (Mon–Sat 9am–5pm; ☎733-2273).

Post office Mon–Fri 9am–5pm; the **General Delivery** zip code is 99676.

Taxes The town imposes a two percent sales tax and a five percent bed tax, not included in our accommodation price codes.

Taxi Talkeetna Taxi & Tours ☎733-8294.

Denali State Park

From Talkeetna Junction the Parks Highway continues north, passing through Trapper Creek between Miles 107 and 133; at the junction of the Petersville Road, Mile 115, the Trading Post has the last gas until Cantwell, and the last affordable gas until Nenana. There's a motel, RV park, and B&B nearby, not to mention Wal-Mike's gift shop. The Trapper Creek Museum, a log cabin with exhibits on the 1920s gold rush in Petersville, now a ghost settlement, is less than a mile to the west. From Mile 132 to Mile 169 – still close to two hours' drive short of the entrance to Denali National Park – you're in **Denali State Park**, a land of braided rivers, a thousand lakes, and tundra-capped hills rising above the spruce forests. There's none of the rigid organization of the national park (which shares a similar name but remains a completely separate entity) and far fewer people come here, yet the state park sports many of the same attributes – great McKinley views and abundant moose, grizzlies, and black bears. There is little infrastructure here (and nowhere nearby to get information), so unless you come prepared for hiking and camping you may find it too much trouble. With the national park beckoning, you could easily pass through.

If you choose to stop, there are a few hikes worth leaving time for and a couple of campgrounds to use as bases, but stock up on groceries and any hiking maps and information you might need before you arrive. The key geographical feature for most park users is the 4500-foot K'esugi Ridge, which runs along the eastern edge of the highway and is followed by a sequence of hiking trails.

In the southern reaches of the park the highway passes the *Mount McKinley Princess Wilderness Lodge*, Mile 132.5 (☎1-800/426-0500, ⓦwww.princesslodges.com), used from May to September to house cruise-ship passengers, and *Mary's McKinley*

View Lodge, Mile 134.4 (☎733-1555, ⓦwww.mackinleyviewlodge.com; ⑤), with decent diner-style meals and very reasonable rooms, some with Denali views. Just north at Mile 135.2, **Denali Viewpoint South** has a huge turnout where signs point out the high points – Mount McKinley, Mount Hunter, and Moose's Tooth – and the glacial highlights – the Ruth, Buckskin, and Eldridge glaciers, between 14 and 38 miles long and up to four miles wide. The *Lower Troublesome Creek Campground*, Mile 137.2 ($10 per vehicle for walk-in sites; pump water), is just south of the trailhead for the **Troublesome Creek Trail**, which leads to the large *Byers Lake Campground*, Mile 147.1 ($10 per site; pump water), the most organized around with a camp host in summer, a public-use cabin ($45 off-peak, $60 peak for up to six persons; reservations ⓦwww.dnr.state.ak.us/parks/cabins), and excellent swimming and grayling- and trout-fishing. Also here is the Alaska Veterans Memorial with a visitor center and viewpoint, but for the best McKinley views seek out the superb *Lakeshore Campground* (free; lake water), accessed by either walking 1.8 miles along the **Byers Lake Loop Trail** or paddling across the lake. At the lake, Denali Southside River Guides (ⓦwww.denaliriverguides .com) offer fly-fishing and kayak and canoe rentals.

Yet more mountain views reveal themselves from **Denali View North**, Mile 162.7, a large parking lot where you can overnight ($10 per vehicle) either in your RV or in a tent pitched at some nice walk-in sites. Before leaving the park you pass the Little Coal Creek Trailhead, Mile 163.8, the northern terminus of the **K'esugi Ridge Trail**.

Cantwell and Broad Pass
The Parks Highway begins its gradual climb in Wasilla, but five miles after leaving Denali State Park it starts a steeper ascent at Hurricane Gulch, Mile 174. A 260-foot-tall single-span bridge crosses the gulch, and there's a big parking

---

Hikes in Denali State Park

Hikers hoping to tackle the park's longer trails must bring all camping gear (including a stove and fuel, as no backcountry fires are allowed) and be competent with a map. Topo maps are available from the Alaska Public Lands Information Office in Anchorage, where you can also get the free, schematic *Denali State Park* leaflet. Note that the two longer hikes described below are both one-way, though hitching back along the Parks Highway is seldom a problem, or you could even arrange for one of the Anchorage–Denali buses to pick you up.

Byers Lake Loop Trail (4.8-mile loop; 2–3hr; negligible ascent). Gentle and scenic stroll around the lake starting and finishing at the *Byers Lake Campground*. Late May to Sept.

K'esugi Ridge Trail (27.4 miles one-way; 2–3 days; 4000ft ascent). A magnificent trail starting at the *Byers Lake Campground* and climbing rapidly above the tree line, where you stay right until the descent to the Little Coal Creek Trailhead (Mile 163.9), although you can also escape halfway along to Ermine Hill trailhead (Mile 156.5). If all that isn't enough, you can add 1000ft of climbing to take in the summit of Indian Peak, close to the northern end of the trail. Mid-June to Sept.

Troublesome Creek Trail (15.2 miles one-way; 7–9hr; 2000ft ascent). Black bears gorging on salmon in July and August earned the name for this creek, which is followed from just north of the *Lower Troublesome Creek Campground* before the moderate climb up onto open tundra, pocked with small lakes. The views are spectacular, though you'll need to keep your eyes on the ground to follow the rock cairns leading back into the forest and down to the *Byers Lake Campground*. This can be combined with the K'esugi Ridge Trail to make a 36-mile expedition. June–Sept.

area to the northwest for admiring the views, but in truth they're much better from the train over the railroad bridge, which is some nine hundred feet long and three hundred feet high. At this point the highway begins a rapid climb to Broad Pass, Mile 201, where both the train line and the highway pass through a rent in the Alaska Range. From here on, all waterways flow north into the Yukon River and then west to the Bering Sea, including the fledgling Nenana River, which gently eases down through open country, where you're likely to see caribou. Eventually the river reaches **Cantwell**, Mile 210, where the Parks Highway meets the **Denali Highway** (see account starting on p.439), which heads 135 miles east to Paxson through remote country with limited services. If you're headed that way, fill your tank and your stomach at one of the two roadside diners near the junction of the two highways. The usual RV parks and lodges lie just off the highway, and in the village two miles west are the *Cantwell Lodge* (T1-800/768-5522, Wwww.cantwell-lodge.com; ❹ en suite, ❸ shared bathrooms), a 1930s roadhouse with Internet café, and *Blue Home* (T768-2020, Wwww.cantwell-bluehome.de) on Caribou Avenue (ignore the Private signs), a B&B with a double and a twin room (❹), also selling the German owner's leatherwork. Nearby, Atkins Guiding & Flying Service (T768-2143) offers flights from $100 per passenger per hour, and has a bunkhouse with outhouse.

The Parks Highway continues 27 miles north to the Denali National Park entrance, passing through a narrow defile which opens out onto long views of Mount Fellows with its ridgeline rocks said to look like a musher and her sled dogs. Thirteen miles before the park entrance you pass **Carlo Creek**, then six miles later reach **McKinley Village**. Both are really just clusters of places to stay but make feasible bases for forays into the park: accommodation and restaurants in both settlements are listed in the following account.

Denali National Park

The six million acres of **Denali National Park**, 240 miles north of Anchorage, hold a special, almost holy, place in the minds of Alaska's visitors – a vast wilderness carved out of the Alaskan heartland, preserving an entire ecosystem. This is where 450,000 people a year come to see big game: bears browsing in the low brush, moose chomping on aquatic weed at Wonder Lake, a lone wolf loping along a river bar, or a herd of caribou disappearing into the infinity of the Teklanika Valley. Scenes like these bring home the sheer scale of the place; the park is about the same size as Massachusetts, or half the size of Wales, and a round-trip along the road from the park entrance to Wonder Lake, right in the heart of the park, takes a full twelve hours.

For most, Denali's grail is the sight of the 20,320-foot **Mount McKinley**, equally known by its Athabascan name, **Denali**, "the Great One." It simply towers over its neighbors, most barely rising above 12,000ft, and even its 17,400-foot neighbor, Mount Foraker, is dwarfed firmly in second place. These are the king and queen of the **Alaska Range**, a mountain fastness still locked in the last ice age. This 600-mile crescent of jagged snowcapped peaks, which arcs through the Alaskan Interior to form the backbone of Denali National Park, still spews glaciers left and right. To the south the Ruth and Kahiltna glaciers have gouged out deep canyons on their fifty-mile passage to the vegetated lowlands, while to the north the Muldrow crooks its arm around 7000-foot foothills and melts away to become the McKinley River, one of the dominant features of the central wilderness area of the park.

Visiting Alaska without seeing Denali is unthinkable to most people, and therein lies the park's major problem. The place has become such an icon that few question why they are going and what they expect when they get there. Inevitably, some visitors come away disappointed after spending hours on a bumpy, dusty bus ride only to catch distant glimpses of caribou and moose, or upon discovering that Mount McKinley isn't even visible from the park entrance, remains shrouded in cloud for two days out of three in summer, and is often better viewed from Talkeetna.

Spectacular as the scenery is, nowhere is it more spine-tingling than along the Denali Highway, which spurs off the George Parks Highway 27 miles to the south of the Park Road, where the access to scenery is much simpler and the crowds incomparably thinner. Indeed, although Denali affords a chance to roam across trackless tundra, if it's backcountry hiking you want, then pretty much all of Alaska is out there waiting for you.

If you set expectations properly and carefully plan your visit, however, a visit to Denali can be supremely rewarding. If you only have a few hours, then just drive the first fifteen miles of the Park Road, stopping to observe any wildlife you may come across. At Savage River there's a two-mile walk so you can say you've hiked in Denali. On a longer visit, it really pays to reserve campsites and shuttle buses in advance (see p.418). Doing so, you can avoid much of the lining up and waiting around in the visitor access center and can progress smoothly into the park. With a night spent in a park campground you'll get a real feel for the place, but the full rewards are only gained through spending several days hiking and camping in the backcountry.

Denali's scenic splendor is made wonderfully accessible by the **Park Road**, ninety miles of gravel that winds from lowland **taiga** to alpine **tundra** on its passage through half a dozen river catchments and over as many high passes. Private vehicles are banned beyond the first fifteen miles; visitors must board a system of shuttle buses, which grind along offering a wonderful vantage for spotting and photographing wildlife almost undisturbed by human presence. The limited number of shuttle buses causes lines to form around the park entrance, but the system's minimal environmental impact preserves the sanctity of the land and makes its wilderness so uniquely appealing. For both human safety and animal protection, bus etiquette demands that you stay in the bus when animals are about, but otherwise you can, and should, get off sometime and explore away from the road.

Some history

The caribou, Dall sheep, and moose so prized by photographers were once quarry to Athabascan Indians. Hunters followed the herds through the Alaska Range foothills in the summer months, picking berries and gathering plants along the way, then descended to the river valleys in the colder months. Towards the end of the nineteenth century, long before there were roads, railroads, or even bush planes anywhere near Denali, gold prospectors entered the area. One Princeton-educated hopeful, William Dickey, came here in 1896 and reported to the *New York Sun* the existence of a huge mountain (estimating it to be over 20,000ft high); he named it after William McKinley, Republican nominee for the presidency. Having heard that James Wickersham discovered traces of gold on his 1903 summit attempt, prospectors in 1905 found their El Dorado in Kantishna and a full-blown stampede ensued, sprouting a tent city and then a boom town. Like so many gold towns, it barely lasted out the winter, but the

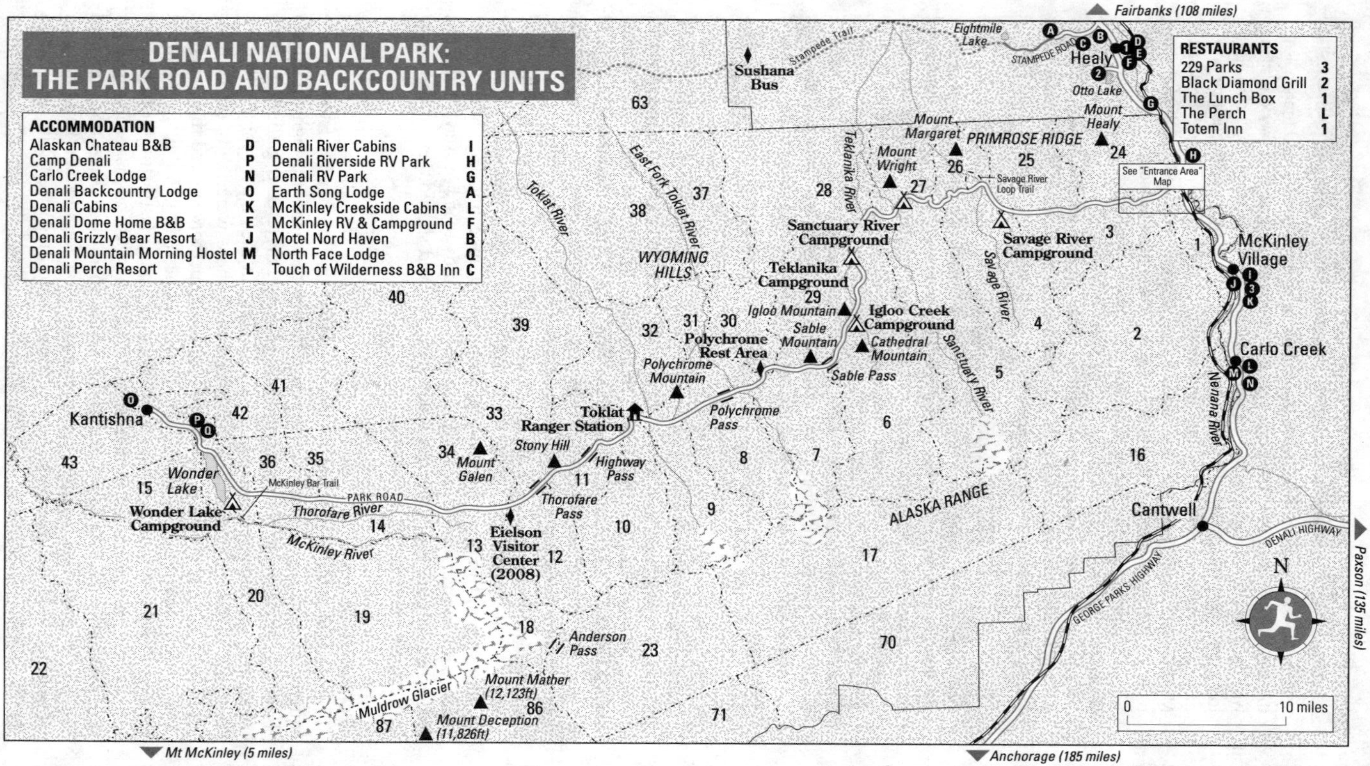

DENALI NATIONAL PARK:
THE PARK ROAD AND BACKCOUNTRY UNITS
ACCOMMODATION
Alaskan Chateau B&B D
Camp Denali P
Carlo Creek Lodge N
Denali Backcountry Lodge O
Denali Cabins K
Denali Dome Home B&B E
Denali Grizzly Bear Resort J
Denali Mountain Morning Hostel M
Denali Perch Resort L
Denali River Cabins I
Denali Riverside RV Park H
Denali RV Park G
Earth Song Lodge A
McKinley Creekside Cabins L
McKinley RV & Campground F
Motel Nord Haven B
North Face Lodge Q
Touch of Wilderness B&B Inn C
RESTAURANTS
229 Parks 3
Black Diamond Grill 2
The Lunch Box 1
The Perch L
Totem Inn 1
Fairbanks (108 miles)
Anchorage (185 miles)
Paxson (135 miles)
Mt McKinley (5 miles)
Sushana Bus
Stampede Trail
Eightmile Lake
Stampede Road
Healy
Otto Lake
Mount Healy
Mount Margaret
PRIMROSE RIDGE
Mount Wright
Savage River Loop Trail
See "Entrance Area" Map
Teklanika River
Toklat River
East Fork Toklat River
WYOMING HILLS
Sanctuary River Campground
Savage River Campground
Savage River
Teklanika Campground
Igloo Mountain
Igloo Creek Campground
Sable Mountain
Cathedral Mountain
Sable Pass
Sanctuary River
Polychrome Rest Area
Polychrome Mountain
Polychrome Pass
Toklat Ranger Station
Stony Hill
Highway Pass
Thorofare Pass
Mount Galen
Kantishna
Wonder Lake
Wonder Lake Campground
McKinley Bar Trail
PARK ROAD
Thorofare River
McKinley River
Eielson Visitor Center (2008)
Anderson Pass
Mount Mather (12,123ft)
Mount Deception (11,826ft)
Muldrow Glacier
ALASKA RANGE
McKinley Village
Carlo Creek
Nenana River
Cantwell
DENALI HIGHWAY
GEORGE PARKS HIGHWAY
N
0 10 miles
1
2
3
4
5
6
7
8
9
10
11
12
13
14
15
16
17
18
19
20
21
22
23
24
25
26
27
28
29
30
31
32
33
34
35
36
37
38
39
40
41
42
43
63
70
71
86
87

area did catch the attention of one **Charles Sheldon**, an East Coast naturalist intent on studying Dall sheep. Deploring the construction wreckage and unfettered hunting around Kantishna and the threat of further development thanks to the Alaska Railroad, and recognizing the unique nature of a virtually untouched ecosystem north of the Alaska Range, he lobbied Washington for the creation of a national park. In 1917 this central area between the ranges and stretching from Kantishna to the Nenana River was designated as McKinley National Park, the first in Alaska. Access was provided in 1923 by the railroad, which brought 34 visitors to stay in tents at the Savage River Tourist Camp (relocated 54 miles west to Eielson in 1939 to avoid competition with the new McKinley Park Hotel), and in 1957 by the Denali Highway from Paxson, but it was the completion of the George Parks Highway in 1972 that really sealed the park's future as Alaska's premier tourist destination, visitor numbers doubling to 88,615 in that year alone. In the same year, the Park Road, built from 1922 to 1938, was closed to private cars, with shuttle buses taking their place.

In 1980 the park was extended from 2 million to 6.2 million acres, acquiring Kantishna but putting an end to gold mining there, which had never completely died out since the town's demise. In recognition of the mountain's Athabascan moniker, the park was renamed Denali National Park and Preserve, but despite petitions and hundreds of newspaper columns, the mountain officially remains Mount McKinley. The pre-1980 land, or "Old Park," is designated as wilderness and closed to snowmobiles and fly-ins; the additions are open to snowmobiles for "traditional" activities only.

Arrival, orientation, and information

Undoubtedly the finest way to arrive at Denali is by rail. **Trains** pull into Denali Park station and are met by a phalanx of courtesy buses run by individual hotels. If you're not being met by a bus to your accommodation, you'll need to unravel the complexities of the shuttle buses (see box, p.420), which stop at the rear of the train station parking lot close to the new Denali Visitor Center.

All **long-distance buses** pick up and drop off at the Denali Visitor Center, and most will let you off at any of the local hotels. If you alight at the Visitor Center you'll have to master the shuttle buses to get any further into the park.

If you are planning to travel beyond Mile 15 of the Park Road, you should call at the Wilderness Access Center to pay the park **entrance fee** of $10 per person ($20 per family; valid 7 days).

Orientation

Getting into Denali National Park involves spending at least some time on the eastern fringe, in and around the nameless huddle of buildings known variously as Denali Park, Nenana Canyon, or **Glitter Gulch**. This is where you'll come to dine, book rafting and flightseeing trips, and perhaps stay.

About a mile south of Glitter Gulch (Mile 237.3) the Park Road cuts west and winds ninety miles right through the heart of the park to the former gold mines of Kantishna. Most of your time in the park will be spent close to this road, initially along the first two miles, an amorphous region known as the **entrance area**. Here you'll find the Wilderness Access Center, a campground, a post office, grocery store, the train station, and the Denali Visitor Center. The demand for accommodation close to the entrance of the park is so great in summer that a couple of other clusters of hotels have popped up along the George Parks Highway: **McKinley Village**, seven miles south of the entrance

6

Mount McKinley so dominates its surroundings that it creates its own distinct **weather**, turning the moist drafts coming off the Gulf of Alaska into rain and, at higher elevations, snow. This affects the weather along the Park Road, but north of the Alaska Range precipitation is low – around fifteen inches a year – limiting the amount of snowfall. Nonetheless, it can snow in any month of the year along the Park Road. June, July, and August are liable to have the best weather, but also the most bugs. May generally avoids the worst of the mosquito season and basks in long days, though snow cover may limit your movements. In September it is getting colder and darker, but the fall colors and berry picking easily compensate.

From early June to early September, Denali is at full tilt; then everything just shuts down for the rest of the year. Unless we specify otherwise, you can assume that all trips, tours, hotels, and restaurants mentioned in and around Denali are only guaranteed to be open through the summer season. The **shoulder seasons** (essentially the last two weeks of May and middle two weeks of Sept) are grayer; some things are operating and others not. As the winter snows melt, the Park Road becomes accessible to cyclists, and eventually the Park Service opens it to private vehicles as far as Savage River (usually by mid-April) and Teklanika (by early May). Hotels and restaurants start to open, then on about May 20 the season starts: the visitor centers are fully operational, shuttle buses start shuttling, private vehicles are limited to the first fifteen miles of the Park Road, and everything moves into top gear (though the Park Road won't open all the way to Wonder Lake until mid-June). The buzz of activity continues until mid-September, when shuttle buses stop and many hotels and restaurants close or reduce their menus. Then, for a four-day period, the road is open to those who have won the **road lottery** (see p.418). If the snow holds off after September 18 this can be a good time to visit, as private vehicles are again allowed to drive as far as Teklanika.

In winter Denali is hard but beautiful. The moose, wolves, and owls are still about, the aurora is often on display, and both the mosquitoes and the bears are sleeping. The road is plowed to the Park Headquarters; beyond here, however, the only way in is by snowshoe, ski, or dog team; the Sled Dog Trail runs parallel to the Park Road for around 85 miles. Snowmobiles are not permitted within the original extent of the park, and there are no services except for the unstaffed *Riley Creek Campground*. One excellent (if pricey) way to explore the park in winter is on multiday **dog-sled tours** with Denali Dog Sled Expeditions (see Basics, p.33) based at *Earth Song Lodge* (see p.420), or *Denali West Lodge*, Lake Minchumina (℡1-888/607-5566, ⓦwww.denaliwest.com), reached by air taxis and a scheduled flight from Fairbanks three days a week ($145) with Evert's Air Alaska.

Before heading into the park in winter, make sure you call at the Murie Science and Learning Center at Mile 1.3 (mid-Sept to early May daily 10am–4pm, foyer open 24hrs; call center managed by Park Headquarters Mon–Fri 8am–4.30pm; ℡683-2294), to let them know your itinerary and when you are likely to return; the park fee is collected here during open hours. Rangers lead snowshoe hikes at 1pm on Saturdays and Sundays until late March (with snowshoes, gaiters, and parkas available free; ℡683-9532), and stage Winterfest on the last weekend in February, with free events such as ski and snowshoe tours, and snow and ice sculpture competitions.

area, and **Healy**, a still functioning coal-mining town twelve miles north, with some of the best accommodation options.

Information

Park formalities all revolve around the **Wilderness Access Center** (**WAC**; Mile 0.6; early May daily 10am–4pm; mid-May to late Sept daily 5am–8pm;

closed in winter; ☏683-9274, ⓦwww.nps.gov/dena), where you'll need to go to book campsites and shuttle buses and access the backcountry. Here you can also pick up free copies of the schematic *Denali Park Map* and *Alpenglow*, a visitor guide (published in summer and winter editions) with comprehensive coverage of park facilities and ranger programs, as well as a guide to the various shuttle buses, campgrounds, and so forth. The standard National Geographic *Trails Illustrated* **maps** are sold in the WAC's gift shop (as well as jerky, compasses, water bottles, bug spray, boots, socks, and so on), but for more detailed maps you'll need to duck into the ANHA bookshop (near the Denali Visitor Center), which also sells wildlife books, videos, T-shirts, and some crafts.

In 2005 the park opened the **Denali Visitor Center** (mid-May & mid-Sept 8am–6pm; late May to early Sept 8am–8pm), close to the train station. It may look like an oversized log cabin, but it has won awards for its sustainable design, using recycled and locally sourced renewable materials and minimizing water and energy consumption. With exhibits on Charles Sheldon, life beneath the snow, plate tectonics, and Native artifacts, plus the free twenty-minute *Heartbeat of Denali* video (every half-hour from 8.30am) and a bookshop, baggage store, and restaurant nearby, it is designed to relieve the load on the Wilderness Access Center, which continues to be the place to organize campgrounds and shuttle buses. Across the WAC parking lot, the **Backcountry Information Center** (mid-May to mid-Sept daily 9am–6pm; ☏683-9510) is the place to arrange permits for overnight backcountry trips.

Finally, the **Murie Science and Learning Center** (daily: mid-May to early Sept 8am–4.30pm; mid-Sept to early May 10am–4pm; ☏683-1269, ⓦwww .murieslc.org), at Mile 1.3 of the Park Road immediately after the turn to the Denali Visitor Center and rail depot, organizes summer camps and courses for teachers, and serves as the winter visitor center (see box, opposite); it has an exhibition area with pelts and skulls, and interactive terminals which can lead those interested to some real science. Here you can buy checklists of the park's plants, birds, and mammals (50¢), and guides to the wildflowers and birds of Denali, plus Adolph Murie's books on the grizzlies and other mammals of Denali (based on his walks of around 1700 total miles from 1939 to 1941) and Margaret Murie's classic *Two in the Far North*. It's much less frenetic than the Denali Visitor Center but otherwise fairly missable.

Getting around

To relieve congestion and preserve the natural qualities of the park, most of it is open only to official shuttle buses, bicycles, and foot traffic. If you aren't traveling by car but decide to stay around Healy for a day or two, you might find it handy to **rent a car** locally or just use taxis to get back and forth between the park and your accommodation (for both see Listings, p.434).

Grappling with the various **shuttle buses** can be intimidating at first but with the aid of our box (p.420) you should quickly grasp the basic points: the green buses are run by the Park Service and are designed to link the campgrounds, train station, Wilderness Access Center, and Denali Visitor Center, while various courtesy buses link Glitter Gulch or McKinley Village to the Denali Visitor Center. Shuttle buses that run into Denali along the Park Road must be booked either at the WAC or in advance (see box, opposite).

Driving Denali
Drivers can explore the first fifteen paved miles of the Park Road as far as Savage River (see p.428), usually by mid-April – call ☏683-2294 for information on road

Various tours, as well as **campgrounds** – *Riley Creek*, *Savage River*, *Teklanika River*, and *Wonder Lake* – and the **shuttle buses** used to reach them, can all be reserved in advance, saving a lot of time at the Wilderness Access Center and unnecessary nights spent near the entrance area.

By **phone**: bookings up to a day in advance of your arrival can be made by phone (in US ☎1-800/622-7275; international ☎272-7275) between 7am and 5pm (Alaska time) from mid-February to mid-September. Pay by Visa, MasterCard, AmEx, or Discover.

By **fax**, **mail**, or **online**: any time after December 1 the previous year, but at least a month before your travel date (or two days prior by fax on ☎264-4684), you can send your requests to Doyon ARAMARK, VTS/Campground Reservations, 241 W Ship Creek Ave, Anchorage, AK 99501. You can download a form from ⊛www.nps .gov/dena detailing the information required: number of adults and children (with ages), desired dates and alternatives, credit card number and expiry dates. You can also book online at ⊛www.nps.gov/archive/dena/home/visitorinfo/camping/reservations.html or ⊛www.reservedenali.com. The entrance fee ($10 for individuals, $20 for a family) should be included in any payments (check or money order).

conditions. For further exploration, you'll have to abandon your vehicle in the *Riley Creek Campground* overspill parking area (not the Denali Visitor Center or Wilderness Access Center lots) and make use of the shuttle buses. **RV drivers** can get special dispensation to drive to the *Teklanika River Campground* (see p.423).

Depending on snow conditions, the road is often open to drivers as far as the Teklanika River (Mile 30) for a couple of weeks in early May and again after mid-September. Better still, you could enter the **road lottery**, which allows four hundred vehicles to drive the entire length of the Park Road to Kantishna on each of four consecutive days in mid-September. There are usually around 6000 applicants for the 1600 places, but if you feel lucky, then write in the first half of July to Road Lottery, Denali National Park, PO Box 9, Denali NP, AK 99755, enclosing a check or money order for the $10-per-car lottery fee and giving your name and address along with your preferred dates.

Cycling in Denali

One of the best ways of getting around is by **mountain bike**. You don't entirely avoid the tyranny of the Wilderness Access Center, as you'll still need to book campsites, but making your way along the Park Road at your own pace has obvious advantages. Certain rules restrict your movements, so you won't be allowed to stray off designated roadways and can only leave your machine overnight in the bike racks at the *Sanctuary River*, *Igloo*, and *Teklanika River* campgrounds (and possibly at the *Eielson Campground*) while you head off for a few days into the wilderness (with the appropriate permit, of course). On the plus side, you can hoist your bike onto a camper bus (see box, p.421) at no extra charge, get off where you want, then ride from there, even using a sequence of buses and campsites to explore the whole road. Some cyclists make full use of the long summer evenings by riding the Park Road at night, after the last shuttle bus to the park entrace has passed around 10.30pm.

During the spring and fall when there are no buses running and road closures are in effect, cyclists are permitted to ride beyond closed gates, though you must still use designated campgrounds and are not allowed to camp beyond Mile 30.

Bike rental is available from Denali Outdoor Center at Mile 240 Parks Hwy or half a mile west of Mile 247 on Otto Lake Road in Healy (☎1-888/303-1925 or ⓦwww.denalioutdoorcenter.com), which charges $7 an hour or $40 for the first day and $35 for subsequent days.

Accommodation

The greatest concentration of places to stay is a mile north of the park entrance in **Glitter Gulch**, conveniently located among the restaurants and shops along the George Parks Highway and easily accessible by frequent shuttle buses to and from the park. The trouble is that in Glitter Gulch you have to decide between overpriced camping (see box, p.422) and paying at least $150 for a double room (more likely $200) in a resort. These are run by the cruise lines and offer relatively good value as an extension to a cruise, but not for walk-ins.

With your own wheels, you'll find better rates by heading twelve miles north to the small town of **Healy** for its competitively priced B&Bs and motels. Consider, too, the small cluster of places near *McKinley Village Lodge*, seven miles south of the park entrance; although shuttle buses are too infrequent to encourage much to-and-froing, you can get by with a strong will. We've listed a couple of places even further south along the George Parks Highway around Carlo Creek, including the region's only **budget hostel**.

Other than camping, the only accommodation **inside the park** is at **Kantishna**, ninety miles west of the park entrance at the end of the Park Road. It is not an especially attractive area by Denali standards, but access to genuine wilderness is second to none. There are four resorts, all very expensive and all offering comfortable accommodation, gourmet breakfast and dinner, a wide range of activities, and complimentary bus travel from the park entrance (fly-ins extra), which bypasses the Wilderness Access Center bottleneck. One-night visits are discouraged, so you may need some flexibility to fit in with the resorts' fixed schedules, and will probably need to book several weeks in advance.

The Park Service allows **RVs** into three of its Denali sites – *Riley Creek*, *Savage River*, and *Teklanika River* (see box, p.422) – and, if this is your mode of transport, you should really do everything you can to secure a place in one of them. Failing that, you're left with the commercial sites that line the George Parks Highway, almost all of them little more than gravel parking lots with hookups but few concessions to aesthetics. The best are several miles south of the park or in Healy, twelve miles north.

Glitter Gulch

Denali Bluffs Hotel Mile 238.4 ☎1-800/276-7234, ⓦwww.denalibluffs.com. The least ostentatious of the cruise resorts: 112 rooms with two double beds, satellite TV, coffeemaker, and hairdryer, and many with balconies facing the Alaska Range. Breakfast, lunchboxes, pizza, and dinner are served alongside microbrews at the hotel's *Mountaineer Pub and Grill*. ⑧

Denali McKinley Salmon Bake Mile 238.5 ☎683-2733, ⓦwww.thebakerocks.com. An all-day restaurant/all-night bar, so not the quietest, but there are fully furnished en-suite rooms and shared-bathroom economy cabins ($74) here. All are nonsmoking and pet free. ⑥

Denali Rainbow Village RV Park Mile 238.6 ☎683-7777, ⓦwww.denalirvrvpark.com. Gravel parking lot right in the middle of Glitter Gulch; you can pitch a tent, though it's hardly ideal. $20 dry, $32 with electricity and water. Showers are $2 extra.

Denali Riverside RV Park Mile 240.5 ☎1-866/583-2696, ⓦwww.denaliriversiderv.com. A fairly basic gravel RV site, with laundry and tours available; tents $16, dry $20, water/electricity $30, pull-through $35.

Healy and north of the park entrance

🏃 **Alaskan Chateau B&B** Mile 0.9 E Healy Spur Rd ☎683-1377, ⓦwww.alaskanchateau.com. Comfortable and unpretentious cabins open year-round, all with private bathroom, satellite TV, fridge, microwave,

Shuttle buses operate from the third week in May to the middle of September. You must wear a seatbelt and bring your own carseat for children under four years or forty pounds; some buses take wheelchairs, which have to be pre-booked. The tour buses tend to operate for an extra week at either end of the season, when they drop their rates slightly. Tour buses generally feature running commentary on park sights, while shuttle drivers are less loquacious but may point out a critter here or there. Park Road shuttles are listed here in order of importance to most readers.

Entrance area

Courtesy Shuttle (free; no reservations). The *Denali Princess Wilderness Lodge* and *McKinley Chalet Resort* run frequent courtesy shuttles, which are free to all. All circuits visit Glitter Gulch and the Denali Visitor Center, and the Red Line also goes to McKinley Village.

Riley Creek Loop (green; free; no reservations). A continuous run between the *Riley Creek Campground*, the Wilderness Access Center, the Denali Visitor Center, Murie Science and Learning Center, Horseshoe Lake Trailhead, and the train station. Schedules are posted at bus stops.

Sled Dog Demo (tan; free; no reservations). Runs two miles from the Denali Visitor Center to the Park Headquarters forty minutes before the daily sled-dog demos at 10am, 2pm, and 4pm. Note that there is no vehicle parking at the Park Headquarters.

Shuttles along the Park Road

Park Shuttle (green; Savage River free, Toklat $19 round-trip, Wonder Lake $33.25, Kantishna $36.25). Often known simply as "the Shuttle," this is the primary means of entering the backcountry. It leaves the Wilderness Access Center every half-hour for Toklat (3hr one-way) and every hour for Wonder Lake (5hr), with a few continuing from early June to Kantishna (6hr). Schedules are well organized – even providing late train arrivees with a round-trip evening service to Polychrome Pass to see the late-day light against the mountains. To maximize your time in the park and your chance of seeing early-bird wildlife, try to get on one of the early buses (they start at 5am) and return on a late one (the last leaves Toklat at 6.30pm and arrives back at the Wilderness Access Center at 9pm). **Reservations are essential** outbound but

coffeemaker, and toaster (and one with full kitchen and a separate living area), plus the only car rental between Wasilla and Fairbanks. Take the E Healy Spur Rd from Mile 248.8, and turn right after 0.9miles. ④–⑥

Denali Dome Home B&B 137 E Healy Spur Rd ☎1-800/683-1239, ⊛www.denalidomehome.com. Large geodesic dome with huge lounge areas and great views of the Alaska Range. The seven rooms all have DVD players and private bath (one has a sauna), and the breakfast is fantastic. Jacuzzi and Internet are available. Turn off the Parks Highway at Mile 248.8, then right after 0.5 miles. Year-round. ⑥

Denali RV Park Mile 245.1 ☎1-800/478-1501 or 683-1500. Desolate RV park located six miles north of Glitter Gulch, offering dry sites for $15 and full hookup for $28. There is no provision for tents,

but they do have pay showers, laundry, family units (⑤), and simple motel rooms with private bath (③).

Earth Song Lodge Mile 4, Stampede Rd, Healy ☎683-2863, ⊛www.earthsonglodge .com. A cluster of charming, comfortable cabins (all with bathroom and coffeemaker, plus heating for winter visitors) with beautiful mountain views and access to a communal lodge with its own library. There's a good chance of spotting wildlife out of your window, and you can even tour the on-site sled-dog kennel. Breakfast, dinner and box lunches are available at the adjacent *Henry's Coffeehouse*, where there's fair-trade espresso, a PC (and WiFi), and a slideshow at 8pm most nights; you can also buy Divas of Denali crafts. Stampede Road runs west from the George Parks Highway at Mile 251.1. Two-bedroom cabins ⑦, standard cabins ⑥

coming back it is first-come, first-served (guaranteed seat on the bus you went out on); buses will sometimes pick up campers if there's space.

Savage River Shuttle (green; free). A subspecies of the Park Shuttle, leaving from the *Riley Creek Campground* and the Wilderness Access Center but only going as far as Savage River (Mile 15; 50min). No reservations.

Camper Bus (green; $24.25). Buses with extra space designed to get both back-country hikers and those using the campgrounds into the park from *Riley Creek* and the Wilderness Access Center. These run five times a day, are only available to those with campground reservations or backcountry permits, and usually have a less comprehensive commentary than the shuttle buses. They won't usually pick up non-campers as they have an obligation to campers encountered along the way. Each camper bus can carry two bicycles at no extra cost to their owners, and your fee is valid for any number of trips during your entire stay west of Mile 20. A reservation is required for your first trip into the park; after that they'll pick you up if they have room.

Tours

Kantishna Wilderness Trails (red and white; early June to early Sept; $129; ☎1-800/230-7275, ⓦwww.denaliwildlifetour.com). A marathon day driving the entire 95 miles from the main hotels to Kantishna and back (13 hours in all) with lunch, gold panning, and a dog-sled demo at the *Kantishna Roadhouse*. Sadly, there is limited time for wildlife stops; you can also take the bus one way and fly out with Kantishna Air Taxi (see p.427).

Natural History Tour (tan; $60; ☎1-800/622-7275, ⓦwww.reservedenali.com). Five-hour guided bus ride as far as Primrose Ridge (Mile 17) with a natural history angle. Park entrance fee and snack included. Runs twice daily from main hotels and the Wilderness Access Center; disabled facilities available. Try for the Grand Slam: all the state's large furry animals – bears, wolves, caribou, moose, Dall sheep – in their natural habitat.

Tundra Wilderness Tour (tan; $90; ☎1-800/622-7275, ⓦwww.reservedenali.com). Full-day (6–8hr) drive along the Park Road as far as Toklat River (Mile 54) stopping frequently to observe wildlife. Box lunch and park entrance fee included. Runs twice daily from main hotels and the Wilderness Access Center.

McKinley RV & Campground Mile 248.5 ☎683-2379 or 1-800/478-2562, ⓔrvcampak@mtaonline.net. The best RV park hereabouts and good for campers, too; sites are all in the trees and there is a coin-op laundry and showers ($2.50). Tent sites $20, power and water $29.

Motel Nord Haven Mile 249.5 ☎1-800/683-4501, ⓦwww.motelnordhaven.com. High-standard motel just north of Healy, with large rooms the match of any twelve miles further south. Each is equipped with queen bed, phone, dataport and TV, and there are free newspapers, tea and coffee, and a continental breakfast (summer only). Year-round. ⑤

Touch of Wilderness B&B Inn Mile 2.9 Stampede Rd ☎1-800/683-2459, ⓦwww.touchofwilder-nessbb.com. One of the most attractive places to stay in the area, with outside hot tub, Internet, kitchenette (with free hot drinks), and a great

breakfast included; dinner and bag lunch also available. ⑦

South of the park entrance: McKinley Village and Carlo Creek

Carlo Creek Lodge Mile 223.9, thirteen miles south ☎683-2576, ⓦwww.carlocreek.com. On the original homestead lot, with 32 acres of woodland, there are four cabins with shared bathrooms (③) and five en suite (④), plus camping ($12/tent plus $4/person; RV $14 plus $5 for electrical hookup), with unlimited showers included.

Denali Cabins Mile 229, eight miles south ☎1-877/233-6254, ⓦwww.denali-cabins.com. Spacious cabins in a nice grassy area with a couple of hot tubs, just far enough away from the park to see the prices drop a little and within walking distance of the lovely *229 Parks* restaurant. Courtesy van available. Suite ❻, full cabin ❺, duplex cabin ❹

Denali Grizzly Bear Resort Mile 231, six miles south ☎1-866/583-2696, ⓦwww.denaligrizzlybear .com. The most appealing commercial campground anywhere near Denali, set in the trees close to the Nenana River and open mid-May to the end of September. There are central cooking shelters (though no pans or crockery), coin-op showers, Internet access, a store, and a shuttle ($8 to the park entrance area) that leaves from across the road at *McKinley Village Lodge*. Lowest rates are for campsites ($20 for up to four; water and electrical hookup $6 extra), then there are tent cabins ($28, with no linen, heat or water), and then a range of regular cabins (❶–❻), some with cookstoves and showers and sometimes quite luxurious. In addition, there's the new *Cedar Hotel*, with 54 rooms (❼), some disabled-accessible and all with a deck over the Nenana, two double beds, cable TV, coffeemakers, and hairdryers.

Denali Mountain Morning Hostel and Lodge Mile 224.5 ☎683-7503, ⓦwww .hostelalaska.com. One of the best hostels in the state, in wooded seclusion thirteen miles south of the park entrance but with a bargain shuttle service ($3 a day). Accommodation is in spacious dorms or separate cabins, there's an efficient kitchen, Internet access, all manner of games, and the hosts will do everything to facilitate your Denali visit. They even rent full kits for camping in the park. Private cabins ❸, private rooms ❷, bunks $25.

Denali Perch Resort Mile 224.5, twelve miles south ☎1-888/322-2523, ⓦwww.denaliperchresort.com. A tight cluster of relatively low-cost cabins at Carlo Creek, made all the more appealing by their proximity to *The Perch* restaurant (see p.434). Cabins without bathroom (❸) sleep four and come furnished with raw-log furniture and sofa, with linen and breakfast provided. Those with bathroom (❹) are larger with an extra bed in a loft.

Campgrounds in Denali

The difficulty with camping in Denali is getting a place in one of the campgrounds through a booking system (see box, p.418) that is as infuriating as it is effective at controlling access to sites in the park. All sites at *Riley Creek*, *Savage River*, *Teklanika River*, and *Wonder Lake* campgrounds can be reserved in advance, with any remaining sites available from the Wilderness Access Center up to two days in advance. Once you have booked your first night in any Denali campground you can then book up to fourteen consecutive nights at any site where there is space. When you enter the Wilderness Access Center you'll see a board listing the campgrounds along with the number of sites available for the next two nights (ie tonight and tomorrow night): in midsummer your preferred sites may be full, and you will have to either camp elsewhere for a night or two or spend your first night in a hotel or commercial campground. Line up at the WAC very early the next morning as there are often dozens of people waiting for campsite reservations. Staying at campgrounds can also be combined with backcountry camping (see p.430), with a total maximum park stay of fourteen nights.

Once you're booked in for your first night you should find it pretty easy to reserve further nights at that or any other campground, even the much sought-after *Wonder Lake*, because you will have priority. Hikers without vehicles often have an easier time than drivers since they can self-register at the walk-in section of the *Riley Creek Campground* (that key first night), then trot down to the WAC to reserve the slightly less competitive walk-ins for the remainder of their stay.

For campgrounds from *Sanctuary River* west you'll have to pay the campsite **registration fee** ($4), which covers your entire stay at any one campground; changing sites means another $4 registration fee at each place.

Of the six campgrounds, all except *Sanctuary River* and *Igloo Creek* have potable tap water and all are equipped with either flush, chemical, or pit toilets. *Riley Creek* is open all year, *Wonder Lake* doesn't open until June (depending on snow cover), and the others are open from late May to September. Vehicles are only permitted at *Riley Creek*, *Savage River*, and *Teklanika*, which, along with *Wonder Lake*, have a free program of **ranger talks**, which varies each night (7.30–8.15pm).

The following campsites are listed in order of distance from the George Parks Highway:

Denali River Cabins Mile 231, six miles south
☎1-800/230-7275, 🌐www.denalirivercabins
.com. Some of the best rooms in the immediate
area: all new cedar cabins with showers, linked
by wooden walkways that drop down to the riverside deck and sauna. There's a hot tub and big
lounge area, too, but dining options are limited,
with only a choice between the restaurant at
McKinley Lodge and the *Denali Roadhouse*
restaurant and bar. Otherwise you'll need to
catch the shuttle into Glitter Gulch. Rates drop
thirty percent in May and September. Riverside
❼, others ❻

McKinley Creekside Cabins Mile 224.5, thirteen
miles south ☎1-888/533-6254, 🌐www
.mckinleycabins.com. By Carlo Creek, rooms and
cabins all with private bathroom and coffeemaker,
some with microwave and fridge. The *Creekside
Café*, part of the cabin complex, serves breakfast,
cinnamon rolls, lunch, and dinner, and has a
nearby campfire area. ❹

Inside the park: Kantishna

Camp Denali & North Face Lodge ☎683-2290,
🌐www.campdenali.com. *Camp Denali* is undoubtedly the best place to stay inside the park bounds
and the only one with views of McKinley. It was
the first lodge here, founded in 1951 by pioneering
conservationists Celia Hunter and Ginny Hill Wood,
who met delivering planes during World War II and
went on to save Creamer's Field in Fairbanks in
the 1970s . The camp's ecological ethos runs from
homegrown vegetables in the restaurant to naturalist tours often led by visiting experts. *Camp Denali*
comprises seventeen cabins strewn over a ridge,
each with separate outhouse, and lovely communal
lounge areas. It's not licensed to serve alcohol,
but you can drink your own (wine) anywhere but
in the restaurant. Less than a mile away is *North
Face Lodge*, a traditional hotel with a block of fully
plumbed rooms without McKinley views. Both lodges
are open early June to early September with mini-

Riley Creek Mile 0.5 (146 sites; May–Sept walk-in $12, drive-in $19; Oct–April free).
Large, vehicle-accessible family campground among the woods at the eastern
extremity of the park that's often full of RVs. It is far superior to the commercial RV
parks along the highway and comes equipped with a sewage dump station. No water
in winter; get it from the Murie SLC or melt snow.

Savage River Mile 13 (33 sites plus 3 group sites; $18). Drive-in tent and RV site
accessible without using the shuttle system, and offering distant views of Mount
McKinley from its position high and dry above the river. Good hiking onto Primrose
Ridge.

Sanctuary River Mile 23 (7 sites; $9). Primitive, wooded, tent-only site overlooking
the river that makes a good hiking base. It is the first campground that requires use
of the camper bus for access, only has river water (which needs treating), and open
fires are not permitted.

Teklanika River Mile 29 (53 sites; $16). Large site currently open only to vehicle
campers, who are given a pass (unrelated to the road lottery) to drive here but
must then leave their vehicle here for a minimum of three nights before driving out.
They can explore further west using the Teklanika Pass ($22.50), which allows one
reserved seat on either the camper bus or Park Shuttle, then unlimited use of those
buses on a space-available basis. Has been closed to tents in recent summers due
to wolf activity; call the WAC for current status.

Igloo Creek Mile 34 (7 sites; $9). Small, secluded, and quiet site requiring use of
the camper bus for access. No piped water and no open fires. Like the *Teklanika
River* site, it has been closed in recent summers due to wolf activity; call the WAC
for more information.

Wonder Lake Mile 85 (28 sites; $16). The jewel in Denali's crown. A beautiful
campground with well-distributed campsites laid out across the sparse taiga,
almost all of which have sweeping views of the Alaska Range with McKinley's
14,000-foot Wickersham Wall right in front of you. Arrive early in the day to avoid
being relegated to the less fashionable sites without the grand view. Access by
camper bus.

mum stays of three nights (Fri–Sun; $1300) or four (Mon–Thurs; $1740); a week's stay costs $3045. Rates include transport from the train depot, meals and lodging, guided outings, evening lectures, loan of sports gear, and the park entry fee. There's also the *Parkside Guesthouse*, a more intimate Arts and Crafts-style place, with free laundry and WiFi (ⓖ). **Denali Backcountry Lodge** ☎1-800/841-0692, Ⓦwww.denalilodges.com. Without the fabulous views that *Camp Denali* has, but with similarly immediate access to wonderful surroundings. Accommodation is in cedar cabins with private facilities, arranged around a spacious lodge, and there's a stack of self-guided walks and structured activities such as hikes, gold-panning, naturalist presentations, and so on. Rates for double occupancy are from $700 per person for four days, including excursions. ❾

Activities in and around the park entrance

With a vast proportion of Alaska's visitors making their way to Denali at some point, it is hardly surprising that a considerable industry has built up to tap this rich vein. Except for the very organized travelers who have everything booked in advance, in high season almost everyone spends half a day around the entrance area sorting out plans or simply waiting for a campsite or backcountry unit to become available. There are a few walks (see box, p.426) to keep you entertained, but you'll soon find yourself kicking your heels. Daytime relief comes in the form of **rafting** the Nenana River, **flightseeing** along the Park Road, **horseback riding** (see Listings, p.434), or attending the forty-minute **sled-dog demonstration** (daily at 10am, 2pm & 4pm; free). The Park Service still maintains kennels and patrols the park in winter with dog teams, so hop on the free shuttle from the Denali Visitor Center to see dogs put through their paces hauling a wheeled sled. It is a well-orchestrated show, and you can't help but smile at the dogs' huge enthusiasm at the prospect of a run.

In the evening the **Cabin Nite**, at *McKinley Chalet* in Glitter Gulch (nightly 5.30pm & 8.30pm; $46; ☎683-8200), draws quite a crowd to its "dinner theater," which features a cabaret-style performance and the waitstaff dishing up heaps of ribs and salmon while in character. Leave your critical faculties at home, and it can be quite fun. At the *Denali Princess* resort, the Music of Denali Dinner Theater show (6 & 8.30pm; $49) is similar, and there's also the Climbing Denali multimedia show (10am, 1.30pm; 45min; $6). If something scuppers your wildlife-viewing plans in the park, there's some compensation in visiting the **Northern Lights Theater** (daily at 9am, 1pm, 5pm, 6pm, 7pm & 8pm; $6) for a 35-minute film on the aurora projected onto a 34-foot screen and set to symphonic music.

Rafting

Half a dozen rafting companies (all but one based in Glitter Gulch) cover two stretches of the Nenana River several times a day. Upstream from Glitter Gulch, the seven-mile **Wilderness** section (Class I and II; 1hr 30min to 2 hours on the water) makes a pleasant drift on a sunny day, but is unlikely to reveal much remarkable wildlife. The lower **Canyon** section (Class III, and sometimes IV in high water) is altogether more thrilling – definitely a whitewater run. Oared rafts and more maneuverable paddle rafts (see Basics, p.68) are used for the two-hour run from Glitter Gulch through the Nenana Canyon to Healy. You will get wet, and the river is always very cold – around 38°F in June – so all companies kit you out in a **dry suit**; in addition, bring thermal underwear and a fleece if you have them.

Typically, you can expect to pay $55–70 for either or $80–95 for the four-hour combination. One reputable and fun local company catering predominantly to independent travelers and small groups is Denali Outdoor Center (☎1-888/303-1925, Ⓦwww.denalioutdoorcenter.com), or try AK

△ Rafting the Nenana River near the Denali entrance

Raft Adventures & Bike Denali, at the *McKinley Chalet*, Mile 238.5 (☎683-3200, ⓦwww.denalinationalpark.com); Denali Raft Adventures on the Glitter Gulch boardwalk at Mile 238.5 (☎1-888/683-2234, ⓦwww.denaliraft.com); or Nenana Raft Adventures, Mile 248.5 George Parks Hwy, Healy (☎683-2628) and by the Nenana River bridge in Glitter Gulch (Mile 238; ☎1-800/789-7238, ⓦwww.raftdenali.com). Most companies take anyone over 5 years of age on the Wilderness run, 12 for the Canyon. In addition,

Denali Outdoor Center runs a whitewater kayak school and operates **inflatable-kayak tours** (daily 8am & 1.30pm; $75) in self-bailing, blow-up boats on the Wilderness section. Having to control your own vessel is a much more challenging proposition than riding in a raft, but anyone with reasonable physical fitness can participate.

Flightseeing

The shortest and most competitively priced flights to Mount McKinley leave from Talkeetna, south of the Alaska Range, but a couple of local companies fly from Glitter Gulch and Healy and give the Talkeetna set a good run for their money. Denali Air at Mile 229.5 (☎683-2261, Ⓦwww.denaliair.com) charges $285 for a flight of just over an hour, overflying the Park Road, turning up

Entrance area hikes

There are essentially two types of hiking in Denali: arduous backcountry hiking (see p.430), and the relatively gentle strolls along smooth, well-managed paths around the entrance area or "frontcountry". The latter suffer to some degree from proximity to Glitter Gulch and NPS service areas, but otherwise make for good hikes with a fair chance of seeing some wildlife. Some of these are used for free daily **ranger-led hikes** (consult the *Alpenglow* visitor guide), and all make good filler while you are waiting to get access to the park proper. Hikes below are ordered roughly from northeast to southwest on the Denali National Park: Entrance Area map (opposite).

Horseshoe Lake Trail (1.5 miles round-trip; 1.5hr; 200ft ascent). The most popular of the entrance-area walks is a jaunt through taiga forest to a placid, beaver-dammed, oxbow lake, best done in the early morning or late evening when wildlife takes over. Starting where the Park Road crosses the train tracks, trace the rails north for a hundred yards, then cross and follow the signs on the right; after a fine viewpoint over the lake there's a steepish drop to the lakeside.

Taiga Trail (1 mile one-way; 30–60min; 150ft ascent). Links the Denali Visitor Center to the start of the Mount Healy and Rock Creek trails.

Mount Healy Overlook Trail (4.5 miles round-trip; 2–4hr; 1700ft ascent). While it's the most strenuous of the entrance-area hikes, this one is easy at first as you gradually pull out of the trees to a scenic overlook (2 miles round-trip; 1hr; 500ft ascent). The second half follows unimproved trail getting progressively tougher to the finish, just below a rocky bluff from where it is possible to see the whole of the Riley Creek catchment, and McKinley on a clear day.

McKinley Station Trail (1 mile; 30–60min; 200ft ascent). A short trail from the site of the *Morino Roadhouse* (near the visitor center) under one of the few remaining original railroad trestles to *Riley Creek Campground*.

Meadow View Trail (0.25 mile; 10–20min). Links the Rock Creek and Roadside trails to make a 0.8-mile loop from the Denali Visitor Center.

Spruce Forest Trail (0.25 mile; 10–20min). A short loop from the Denali Visitor Center, with interpretive panels.

Rock Creek Trail (2.3 miles one-way; 1hr 30min; 400ft ascent). A pleasant trail away from the road, best done on your return from the sled-dog demo at Park Headquarters; alternatively, combine it with the easier **Roadside Trail** (1.5 miles one-way; 1hr; 300ft ascent) close to the Park Road. You can also turn off this onto the Morino Loop Trail (0.4 mile; 25min), providing a direct link to *Riley Creek Campground*.

A multi-use trail also runs east alongside the road from the Denali Visitor Center to the post office (1.7 miles), linking to the pedestrian-only **Jonesville Trail** (0.4 mile), from opposite Riley Creek Mercantile down to the new cycle bridge across the Nenana River to Glitter Gulch.

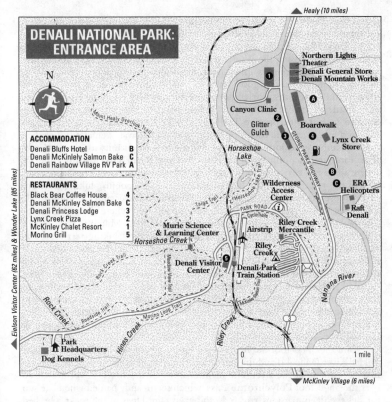

Healy (10 miles)

DENALI NATIONAL PARK: ENTRANCE AREA

N

Northern Lights Theater
Denali General Store
Denali Mountain Works

Canyon Clinic

Glitter Gulch

Boardwalk

Lynx Creek Store

Horseshoe Lake

ERA Helicopters

Wilderness Access Center

Raft Denali

Murie Science & Learning Center

Riley Creek Mercantile

Airstrip

Riley Creek

Denali Visitor Center

Denali Park Train Station

Nenana River

Park Headquarters
Dog Kennels

ACCOMMODATION
Denali Bluffs Hotel — **B**
Denali McKinley Salmon Bake — **C**
Denali Rainbow Village RV Park — **A**

RESTAURANTS
Black Bear Coffee House — **4**
Denali McKinley Salmon Bake — **C**
Denali Princess Lodge — **3**
Lynx Creek Pizza — **2**
McKinley Chalet Resort — **1**
Morino Grill — **5**

0 ——— 1 mile

McKinley Village (6 miles)

the Muldrow Glacier and heading for the Wickersham Wall. Fly Denali (☎1-866/733-7768, ⓦwww.flydenali.com) and Talkeetna Aero Services (☎683-2899, ⓦwww.talkeetnaaero.com) also have Healy operations with similar offerings; Kantishna Air Taxi (☎683-1223, ⓦwww.katair.com) offers fly-ins to Kantishna as well as flightseeing and charters; and ERA Helicopters (☎1-800/843-1947, ⓦwww.flightseeingtours.com) runs fifty-minute helicopter trips covering less ground for $245, as well as heli-hiking.

Exploring the park

After booking in advance or lining up in the Wilderness Access Center to obtain shuttle bus tickets, campground reservations, and maybe even a backcountry allocation, you're finally ready to explore the park. This could be as simple as driving the first fifteen miles of the Park Road to Savage River or hopping a shuttle bus to Wonder Lake, or it may be a complex combination of bus journeys, campground visits, and days spent exploring the park's wilder areas.

The Park Road

Almost everyone who visits Denali National Park uses the shuttle buses that ply the **Park Road**, a ninety-mile strip that winds its way into the heart of the park, providing access to the backcountry. The road – asphalt to Mile 15 and gravel thereafter – runs at right angles to the rivers, twisting and climbing from one watershed to another over six passes, each topping three thousand feet. That might sound a modest elevation, but even in July and August it is not unknown for these to be temporarily blocked by fresh snow.

The Park Road leaves the George Parks Highway and climbs from the Nenana River, passing the Wilderness Access Center, train station, and Murie and Denali visitor centers in the first two miles. Spruce forest gives way to willow around Mile 7 – good territory for spotting moose – and between miles 9 and 12 you get a brief glimpse of Mount McKinley, the last you'll see of it until just before Eielson. Just before Mile 13 the wheelchair-accessible **Savage Cabin Interpretive Trail** (a 0.3-mile loop) leads past a 1925 cabin still used by rangers and their dog teams in winter. Private vehicles (other than the September road lottery winners and those with permits for the *Teklanika River* campsite) can only go as far as the **Savage River checkpoint**, Mile 15, where there is a two-mile loop hike along the river, and a shorter wheelchair trail to the river bar. Shuttle buses continue past the popular hiking territory of Primrose Ridge and descend to the Sanctuary River and campsite (Mile 22). Across a low pass you reach the Teklanika River, where there is a campsite (Mile 29) and a huge rest area used by all shuttles (Mile 30), with lots of outhouses and a viewing platform. Again, this is good hiking territory. The small *Igloo Creek Campground* (temporarily closed) nestles between Igloo and Cathedral mountains, both impressive lumps of rock that make challenging destinations for those so inclined. By the creek, just two hundred feet from the Park Road, a dinosaur footprint (cast and displayed at the Denali Visitor Center) was discovered in 2006; for the previous three years, experts had wondered why there were so many in similar rocks on the North Slope but not here. A second was found at Double Mountain, about ten miles south of the *Sanctuary River Campground*.

Beyond the 3800-foot **Sable Pass**, a long bridge crosses the East Fork of the Toklat River (Mile 44) and finishes at the Polychrome Rest Area, often used for hikes beginning at the river. The main channel of the Toklat River lies ahead over the 3500-foot **Polychrome Pass**, which seems aptly named when late sun catches the deep maroons, rust reds, and even faint blues of the rocks. The bed of the **Toklat River** provides more opportunities for lowland river-walking in country noted for its caribou as well as grizzlies and Dall sheep; then the road climbs up to **Highway Pass** (Mile 58), the highest point on the road at 4100ft. A couple of miles further on you round **Stony Hill** to a superb view of Denali in its full glory, all 18,000ft of it truly lording over the surrounding mountains. Just beyond **Thorofare Pass** you descend to **Eielson Visitor Center**, Mile 66 (closed until 2008 for renovations), with a temporary bus turnaround at Fish Creek (Mile 63). Until the visitor center is reopened there's an information center in a tent at Toklat (Mile 53), where buses stop for half an hour. The moderate-to-strenuous Thorofare Alpine Trail (1 mile each way; 2hr; 1800ft ascent) leads up Mount Thorofare from opposite Eielson; it's a "social trail" (see p.431) that has now been officially adopted.

In a region full of spectacular scenery, the next few miles are some of the most scenic, with the heart of the Alaska Range framing the vegetated face of the **Muldrow Glacier**, which comes within a mile of the road. You traverse rolling terrain dotted with beaver ponds favored by moose as you descend gradually beside the broad, gravel-bedded expanse of the Thorofare and McKinley rivers to **Wonder Lake** (Mile 86). Without some serious hiking, this is as close to the mountain as you can get, but it presents the ubiquitous postcard shot of the mountain reflecting alpenglow across the waters of the lake. If you want easy hiking, the **McKinley Bar Trail** (5 miles return; 2–3hr) leads south from the campground to the McKinley River.

The road continues to **Kantishna** (Mile 91), an old gold-mining inholding with a handful of backcountry lodges (see Accommodation, p.423). The settlement is promoted well in brochures and sounds quite interesting but fails to live up to its promise. "No Trespassing" signs are everywhere, generators run much of the time, and though the lodges are undoubtedly luxurious, this may not be the Denali you were after.

Day-trips into the park

If time is tight, or you just want to supplement your other park escapades, then drive to **Savage River**, fifteen miles along the Park Road (there's no need for permits, tickets, or even park entrance fees). There are a number of pull-outs where you can park (but not overnight) and trudge off across the tundra, and on a clear day you can get a distant view of Mount McKinley near Mile 12. Even with this limited penetration you're still likely to see moose, especially in the late afternoon; bears, caribou, and Dall sheep, however, tend to stay deeper in the park. Those without cars can achieve much the same by riding the **Savage River Shuttle** (see box, p.420), which goes as far as the *Savage River Campground*.

If you've made it this far, it's definitely worth taking at least one bus ride beyond Mile 15 of the Park Road. The cheapest option is the **Park Shuttle** (see p.420), which runs right out to Wonder Lake near the end of the road in the center of the park. It is a wonderful trip but at eleven hours for the full there-and-back journey you may find that going as far as Toklat (7 hours round-trip) is enough.

Leave early enough, and you can engage in a little shuttle-bus surfing, hopping off when something strikes your fancy, hiking up a ridge or across the tundra for a few hours, then leaping on the next one that has room – although in the height of summer there isn't much space available, and you may well find yourself stranded for an hour or so. The rule is that you must pay for westbound travel and you get eastbound bus rides free. Remember that there is nowhere to buy anything in the park: take a good stock of food and drink for the day, along with binoculars, a camera with plenty of film, insect repellent, and sunglasses.

In addition to the Park Shuttle, there are a couple of other ways of spending your day in the park, either on one of the **bus tours** (see box, p.420) or on a free **ranger-led walk**, either one in the entrance area or "front country" (daily; 2hr), usually to Horseshoe Lake, or the more strenuous Discovery Hike (daily until early Sept; 1.5–6 miles, 3–5hr plus bus travel time), which requires sturdy hiking boots and the purchase of a Fish Creek bus ticket ($24.25) to get into the park.

Overnight stays in the park

Spending the day in the park riding the buses and going for the odd stroll is a wonderful experience, but you'll gain a much greater sense of the place if you're prepared to spend a few nights in one of the **campgrounds** (for reservation information see box, p.418). Not only does this give you the opportunity to get out on foot and do some serious hiking, but you'll also see animals in a more natural environment, away from the Park Road and its busloads of shutter-snapping visitors.

Drivers can use their own vehicles to get to *Riley Creek*, *Savage River*, and (with a permit) *Teklanika River*, but for all other sites you'll need a place on the **camper bus**, usually less packed than the Park Shuttle. **Cyclists** can use their bikes, but for the more distant sites it might be better (or at least a lot easier) to use the camper buses as well. Those without gear can **rent equipment** from Denali Mountain Works (see Listings, p.434).

There is no reason why you have to stick exclusively to campgrounds: one of the best ways to stay in the park is to combine campgrounds with backcountry camping. In fact, spending a few days in the backcountry (see below) can be an entertaining way to bide your time while you wait for a particular campground to become free. Having a reservation for a backcountry unit gives you the freedom to then book a sequence of nights both at campgrounds and in backcountry units, up to a maximum of fourteen nights.

Hiking and camping in the backcountry

The ease of access, availability of piped water, and the presence of park rangers make the campgrounds appealing, but the essence of Denali only truly reveals itself if you go **backcountry camping**. You'll have to show a fair bit of determination and flexibility, but it's worth the extra effort and there is no charge beyond the park entrance fee.

The park has been divided into 87 **backcountry units**, 41 of which have a daily quota of between two and twelve overnighting campers. These 41 lie within the original (pre-1980 expansion) Mount McKinley National Park, a thirty-mile-wide strip northwest of the central Alaska Range now designated as Denali National Park's **wilderness area**. If you want to stay inside the wilderness area but outside the designated campgrounds, you'll have to get yourself on this quota, something done in person at the Backcountry Information Center. There are no advance reservations for backcountry units.

Anyone intending to spend the night in the backcountry must first view the backcountry simulator video (25min), which teaches you about dealing with bears, or, more to the point, how to avoid having to deal with them; watch this at the Backcountry Information Center between 9am and 6pm or at the Wilderness Access Center from 7am to 9am and 6pm to 8pm – be sure to sign the clipboard. Next, consult the Quota Board, which lists the number of free spaces in each backcountry unit. You can only make **reservations** one day in advance (for example, reserve on Friday for Saturday night), and even though there may be nights available two days hence, you can't book them unless you already have a booking for tomorrow night. Once you've secured the first night, you can go ahead and reserve up to fourteen continuous nights (a maximum seven nights in any one unit, and no more than thirty nights combined), so arrive at the Backcountry Information Center early, accept what you can get for the first night or two, then home in on your desired area after that. Smaller groups have a better chance, and lone campers (a discouraged breed, for safety reasons) can often get something at short notice. The BIC has information on the backcountry units and topo maps, and we've given a few pointers on p.432.

Once in the backcountry, you can keep returning to the road and using the camper buses to access the next unit you have booked, but too much chopping and changing can easily wreck the continuity of your wilderness experience and it is usually preferable to concentrate on one area, hiking well away from the Park Road. If you're able, try to arrive without too many preconceptions of where you want to hike, and just make the best of what you can get.

With your backcountry reservations made, you'll be handed a free **bear-resistant food container** (see Basics, p.60), which is yours for the duration of your backcountry stay. Tuck it under your arm and amble over to the Wilderness Access Center to book onto a camper bus that will get you to within striking distance of your unit.

Chances are that hiking in Denali will be unlike anything you've experienced before. Forget the usual advice about sticking to the trail and avoiding cutting switchbacks: there are **no managed trails** in the main body of the park, so no switchbacks to cut. You'll have to repeatedly decide which line will afford easiest passage, then constantly reappraise your decisions while negotiating **tundra** – likened by some to hiking on foam-rubber basketballs on a waterbed. It is a continual process and, the physical difficulties aside, much more tiring than following a trail. Take heed: if twenty-mile treks across moors or along sierra trails are your norm, you'll need to revise your daily estimates down to five or six miles, at least until you learn the rhythm of the land.

This is a land where **following ridgelines** often provides the easiest passage. But if you don't want to go up – and you can quite quickly reach the snow line even in the height of summer, adding to the obstacles you're already grappling with – then your best bet is to follow one of the many rivers, which means getting your feet wet. With few exceptions it is hard going, but the rewards can be great: miles of wilderness barely touched by humans, with only the animals to keep you company; slopes drenched in spring wildflowers; or a larder of berries in fall.

In light of this, we have intentionally avoided suggesting any routes to follow. The rangers won't suggest any either; after all, the whole point of hiking in Denali – and its most inviting feature – is that you can make it up as you go along. This seems alien at first. You'll occasionally come across what are known as "social trails" where others have gone before you and worn a passage, and it takes a force of will not to follow them. You and anyone else in your party should find a unique route to avoid creating "social trails," which scar the landscape and detract from that exciting feeling of isolation. For the same reason, when it comes to camping, select an apparently unused spot and never stay for more than two nights.

Aside from all the usual considerations of bear safety and backcountry travel (for both, see Basics, p.60), it goes without saying that any party going into the backcountry needs at least one competent **map reader**. Backcountry rules dictate that you must camp more than half a mile from the Park Road and out of sight of it. Without some competence with topographical maps, you may find a huge mountain or impassable river between you and your planned camping spot.

Eating and drinking

Eating is expensive in and around Denali, but there is quite a range of options. Campers and those taking long day rides into the park on the shuttle buses will need **groceries**. If you're prepared to lug them from Anchorage or Fairbanks, then you'll open up your culinary options considerably (particularly with fresh fruit and vegetables, which are almost unknown in Denali's shops) and save yourself some money, but you can buy some food here. Riley Creek Mercantile, Mile 0.5 Park Rd (open 7am–11pm in summer), and two stores in Glitter Gulch all sell more or less the same limited range of goods at similar prices, and Denali Mountain Works sells freeze-dried camping meals. There are espresso bars at Riley Creek Mercantile, the Wilderness Access Center, the *Morino Grill*, and the main resort hotels. Most hotels will provide you with a box lunch.

Most of the places listed below are in Glitter Gulch, though we've also listed the best in Healy and points south of the park entrance.

Backcountry units

Denali National Park is a patchwork of 87 lots, or **backcountry units**. Forty-one of these have camper limits due to their popularity; the remaining 46 units, some of which have been omitted from this account, make up the park's outer additions and preserve and are quota-free. Every backcountry unit has its own character, advantages, and limitations, all of which can take some time to work out, especially under pressure from other visitors packed into the Backcountry Information Center trying to do the same. Our approach here is to lay down a few general points to guide you in the right direction. Units are marked on our park map (see p.414), but for more detail, consult *The Backcountry Companion* (available for viewing in the BIC), which has descriptions of each unit, and National Geographic's 1:200,000 *Denali National Park and Preserve* Trails Illustrated map ($10), the best general map showing terrain and unit boundaries. Most of the original park, a thirty-mile-wide strip along the Park Road, is classified as wilderness (except the Willow Lake and Kantishna Day Use Areas), while the 1980 additions are open for customary and subsistence use; to the far southeast and southwest the Denali National Preserve is a region of the park open for both subsistence and sport hunting, trapping, and fishing.

When planning your trip, first make a note of regions permanently or temporarily closed to protect animal breeding habitats: maps at the Backcountry Information Center make this clear. For your first night you will need to look at the 29 units that border the Park Road; the slow pace of travel in Denali and the sheer size of each unit dictates that your first and last backcountry night will be in one of these. For extended trips, carrying all your food can become a chore, one fortunately eased by provision of bear-proof food caches at campgrounds and the Toklat Rest Stop, where you can stash extra supplies.

The order of the following descriptions follows the road westbound.

Units 1, 2, 3, 24 & 25: The five units closest to the entry area are accessible without using the camper bus but a little noisy with air traffic. This area was less recently glaciated than the rest of the park and therefore has a denser cover of vegetation, so you may need to stick to the units' ridgetops and river valleys for the easiest passage. Great fall berrying, wonderful colors, and possible sightings of black bears and moose.

Units 16 & 17: South of the Alaska Range and wetter than other units. Normally accessed from outside the park near Cantwell through Unit 16 but can be reached through Unit 2 over Windy Pass.

Units 4 & 5: Gradually narrowing river valleys with some thick brush and possible high crossings into neighboring units.

Units 26 & 27: Plenty of dry high-country hiking (Mount Wright, Mount Margaret, and Primrose Ridge), bountiful wildflowers, and sheep plus walks along Savage River Canyon. Drinking water can be scarce in parts.

Units 6, 7, 8, 29, 30 & 31: Mixed area of broad rivers, accessible high country (Igloo, Sable, and Cathedral mountains), and rolling hills of varying colors and textures

---

229 Parks Mile 229.7 ☎683-2567, ⓦwww.229parks.com. Using organic, free-range, and locally sourced ingredients as much as possible, this beautifully designed place always has a vegan and several veggie dishes on the menu, alongside soups and salads ($6–18), a lamb burger ($14), halibut tacos ($20), silver salmon with barbecue sauce ($24), and rack of elk ($34). There's also a good wine list with microbrews. Open for coffee and pastries 7–11am and for dinner 5–10pm.

Black Bear Coffee House Mile 238.6, Glitter Gulch ☎683-1656. A tiny log cabin with a sunny deck (and an attached cyber-lounge) serving good coffee and cakes, plus soup, bagels, and build-your-own sandwiches for $7. Open 6.30am–10.30pm.

Black Diamond Grill Mile 1 Otto Lake Rd, Healy ☎683-4653. A relaxed, licensed restaurant at Healy's golf course that's worth the journey out from Glitter Gulch for beautifully prepared and

that offer very rewarding hiking. Some dry tundra and great views of the Alaska and Outer ranges.

Units 70 & 71: Accessible from the Parks Highway southwest of Cantwell, but very boggy, brushy going.

Units 28, 37, 38 & 39: Multiday-hiking territory only accessible from neighboring units. A vast and little-visited region of large rivers and spruce forests harboring black bears.

Units 9, 10 & 32: Wide, braided valleys with spectacular glaciers at the headwaters but sometimes difficult river crossings. Steep slopes limit crossings between valleys.

Units 11 & 33: Be prepared to get your feet wet in interesting little canyons, or stick to the rolling and rugged hills with loose, exposed rock. Tough going but outstanding views.

Units 12, 13 & 18: Easy hiking close to Eielson visitor center (currently closed, but should reopen in 2008) and lovely views of nearby glaciers, but quickly getting tougher, especially crossing the Muldrow Glacier or heading across the Thorofare River up into the steep mountains, glaciers, and scree of Unit 18.

Units 34, 35 & 36: Plenty of rolling wet and dry tundra with some heavy brush and beaver pools making for hard going in the low country. Follow ridges and knolls or aim for the summit of Mount Galen. Wonderful views of the whole Alaska Range and Mount McKinley.

Units 14 & 15: Mosquito-ridden swampland with heavy brush makes hiking difficult but offers great views of the Alaska Range. Access to units 19, 20, & 21 across the McKinley River is tricky. No camping in the day-use area around Wonder Lake.

Units 19, 20, 21 & 22: These are all south of the McKinley River, making access to them very challenging. You'll need glacier-travel skills to cross the Muldrow Glacier or be prepared for a complex and often dangerous waist-deep crossing of the McKinley River. All are rugged, with glaciers coming down to the lowlands and rigorous hiking required. Units 20, 21, and 22 require expedition logistics (flying in supplies, for instance) and thus have no quotas (see p.430).

Units 40, 41, 42 & 43: Lowland tundra with taiga high up and some thick brush to contend with, but uplifting Alaska Range views if you're on the south side of the hills. Some difficult river crossings and private property around old gold claims.

Unit 23: Only reachable via Units 13 and 18 over Anderson Pass; all rock and ice and only for serious mountaineers, so no quota.

Units 44–47 & 72–87: The backbone of the Alaska Range (including Mount McKinley in unit 45); they require expedition logistics and thus have no quotas. Permits should be obtained through the Talkeetna ranger station (☎733-2231).

6

DENALI AND THE WESTERN INTERIOR | Denali National Park

presented food at reasonable prices. Lunch on their herb-crusted prime rib sandwich ($9) or come in the evening for prosciutto-wrapped prawns on seasonal greens ($11) followed by chicken in pesto cream on parmesan risotto ($18). Otto Lake Road runs west off the Parks Highway at Mile 247.1. Open daily 7.30am–10pm in spring, 6am–11pm in summer.

Denali McKinley Salmon Bake Mile 238.5, Glitter Gulch ☎683-2733, ⓦwww.thebakerocks.com.

A favorite on the tour-bus schedule, so it fairly churns them through, but still provides a good salmon-bake dinner ($19), halibut dinner ($21), and salmon, halibut, and ribs combo ($23), as well as omelettes, sandwiches, burgers, soups, and salads. There's usually live music (cover charge $2–7), with free shuttle buses through the night to and from nearby hotels and resorts. Open from 5am in high summer, 6 or 7am shoulder seasons.

Denali Princess Wilderness Lodge Mile 238.5, Glitter Gulch ☎683.2282, ⊛www.princesslodges .com/denali_lodge.cfm. A sprawling resort complex including the *River Run Deli & Espresso* (5am–6pm) for light breakfasts, baked goods, and ice cream, the *Base Camp Bar & Bistro* (10.30am–midnight) for bar food, *Rapids Restaurant* (5am–8.30pm) for sandwiches and takeouts, and the *Summit Restaurant* (5am–10pm) for soups or salads, steamed clams ($12), salmon ($23), or steaks ($23–28).

The Lunch Box Healy ☎683-6833. Great takeout meals like chicken teriyaki or shrimp stir-fry, as well as hot dogs and fries, plus lunch boxes (all $10 or less). Open late May to late Aug Mon–Fri 11am–2pm, 4–7pm (lunch boxes can be picked up from 6.30am).

Lynx Creek Pizza Mile 238.4, Glitter Gulch ☎683-2547. Scrumptious pizza (from $16, or by the $4 slice) competes for your attention with Caesar salads ($9) and sandwiches. Wash it all down with draft microbrews, then stick around for more grub, suds, and often music until midnight.

McKinley Chalet Resort Mile 239.1, Glitter Gulch ☎683-8200. Eating at all levels in Holland-America's large hotel complex, from a good espresso bar (daily 5am–11pm); the *Courtyard Café* with burgers, sandwiches, and a salad bar (daily 4.30–10.30am, 11am–2.30pm, 5–10pm); and the upscale *Nenana View Grille* (6–10.30am, 11am–2.30pm, 5–11pm) with its open-plan kitchen dishing up standbys like soup, salad, and pizza, a grilled vegetable tower ($11) or crabcake sandwich ($13) for starters, wild mushroom risotto ($20), halibut and apple-lentil stew with parsnip puree and confit of minted butternut squash ($27), salmon on toasted couscous ($29), and reindeer tenderloin ($36).

Morino Grill At Denali Visitor Center ☎683-9225. Gastronomically uninspiring but always popular with park visitors. Open for coffee from 8am and from 11am to 7pm for burgers, pizza, and panini ($8–9), sourdough stew or seafood chowder ($7), and grills ($9).

🏃 **The Perch** Mile 224, 11 miles south at Carlo Creek ☎1-888/322-2523, ⊛www .denaliperchresort.com. Three eateries in one. The daytime bakery serves cinnamon rolls, coffee, and desserts, and the *Panorama Pizza Pub's* the place for pizza, burgers, soup, sandwiches, and packed lunches plus live music; both are right by the highway. An excellent restaurant (5–9pm) is perched on a bluff with views down to Carlo Creek from the picture windows and large deck. It is open year-round serving a full menu throughout the day: eggs Benedict for $9, pasta dishes from $16, and steak and crab legs ($25–28).

Totem Inn Mile 248.7 Parks Hwy, Healy ☎683-6500, ⊛www.thetoteminn.com. Lively bar with live music through summer (generally Wed–Sun; $3–5) and an hourly free shuttle from Glitter Gulch whenever there's a band on. Family meals and pizza served all day, plus WiFi.

Listings

Banks Wasilla and Fairbanks have the closest banks to Denali, but the Lynx Creek Store has an ATM, as do the *Princess* and *McKinley Chalet* resorts and both gas stations in Healy, 11 miles north of the park entrance.

Camping gear Denali Mountain Works, Mile 239 in Glitter Gulch (☎683-1542; 9am–9pm from late May), sells camping gear at reasonable prices and rents two-person tents ($18 for first day, then $9 a day, or $60 a week), sleeping bags ($12/$6/$42), and binoculars ($9/$5/$25), and fills your bottles with white gas. Bring a credit card for a deposit. Riley Creek Mercantile and the Wilderness Access Center shop also fill your bottles with bulk white gas at good prices.

Car rental Teresa's Car Rental (☎683-1377) rents late-model cars for $100 a day (including tax, free mileage, and transfers to and from the train station), though drivers without US insurance may not be allowed to rent: check first.

Gas Lynx Creek Store in Glitter Gulch sells gas in summer only (7am–11pm), and there's slightly less extortionate fuel year-round in both Healy and Cantwell.

Horseback riding To give your feet a rest, let the horses at Denali Saddle Safaris, Mile 4 Stampede Rd (☎683-1200, ⊛www.denalisaddlesafaris.com), take you through the northern reaches of the park, charging $59 for an hour-long taster, $99 for two hours, and $159 for a four-hour ride with views of Denali.

Internet access At the *Black Bear Coffee House* (see p.432) for $3 for each 15min (with a jack for laptops); and in Healy at the Chamber of Commerce (a third of a mile east from Mile 248.8 on Healy Spur Rd) and the Tri-Valley Library at Tri-Valley School, a bit further east (Sun–Wed afternoons only). The *Denali Princess* has free access (15min) for guests only outside the gift shop in the main lodge. Free WiFi is available at the resorts and the *Denali McKinley Salmon Bake* (one hour with a $10 purchase).

Laundry Riley Creek Mercantile and *McKinley Campground* in Healy, 11 miles north of the park entrance (tokens available 8am–10pm), have laundry facilities, as do the resorts for guests only.

Left luggage Lockers at the bus stop opposite the train depot cost $3 for up to 4 hours or $4/day for up to 14 days.

Long-distance buses Alaska Park Connection (☎1-800/266-8625, ⓦwww.alaskacoach.com) and Alaska/Yukon Trails (☎1-800/770-7275, ⓦwww.alaskashuttle.com) both pick up at the Visitor Access Center; Anchorage Denali Shuttle (Denali ☎683-3327, Anchorage ☎301-5436, ⓦwww.anchoragedenalishuttle.com) stops at the Canyon Clinic in Glitter Gulch.

Maps The Wilderness Access Center and the bookshop near the Denali Visitor Center stock maps. Most quad maps ($7 each) cover three or four backcountry sectors at one inch to the mile (1:63,360) but the National Geographic *Trails Illustrated* map (1:200,000; $10) will be more than enough for most visitors.

Medical assistance Denali Emergency Care is at the Canyon Clinic in the center of Glitter Gulch

(Mile 238.5; ☎683-4433 daily 9am–6pm, 24hr on-call service ☎911); the Healy Clinic, E Healy Spur Rd (Mon–Fri 9am–4pm; ☎683-2211), is located in the Tri-Valley Community Center, 11 miles north of the park entrance and half a mile east from Mile 248.8 on Healy Spur Rd.

Post office Next to *Riley Creek Campground* in the entrance area (Mon–Fri 9am–2pm, Sat 9am–12.30pm). The **General Delivery** zip code is 99755; also in Healy behind Keith's gas station, Mile 249.2.

Showers Riley Creek Mercantile (daily 6am–8pm) offers $4 unlimited-time showers.

Taxes Denali and Healy both impose a seven percent bed tax, not included in our accommodation price codes.

Taxis Healy's taxi companies run to the park entrance area for around $25 for two people; try Caribou Cab (☎683-5000). There's also the Denali Sunrise Shuttle (☎1-800/770-7275), which charges $5 to take you anywhere around the park entrance area ($9 round-trip), $7 from Healy or Cantwell to the park ($13), or $14 from Healy to Cantwell ($24), though at a time of their choosing, not yours.

North of Denali

From Denali it is 120 miles to Fairbanks, a journey which largely follows the course of the Nenana River to the town of the same name and then cuts across the hills flanking the Tanana River, claimed to be the world's longest glacier-fed stream; murky with mica-schist, it's avoided by salmon. For the first few miles trains crawl along the slowest section of their route while cars have an easier ride along the Parks Highway just above, as vehicles squirm through the Nenana Gorge, hugging the cliffs high above the rapids. The valley widens out at **Healy**, a coal-mining town since 1918 and now home to the open-pit Usibelli Coal Mine, hidden by a few rows of spruce, which gives its thousand residents the highest per-capita income in the US. It is mainly of interest to Denali visitors as a provider of affordable accommodation (see p.419) and food (see p.431), but you might choose to take the free **mine tour** (mid-May to end Aug Mon–Fri 10am & 2pm; ☎683-2226, ⓦwww.usibelli.com). Having reserved in advance, you need to go by car to the gate, call on the intercom for it to be opened, and then drive on the left side of the road for four miles past beaver ponds to the mine, where you'll be driven around to gasp at the size of the excavators and the holes they make, as well as the scale of the reclamation required. Almost $300 million of public money has been poured into building a new "clean coal" power station, but while the coal is very low in sulphur dioxide (which can cause acid rain) it is also very low in energy content, and the power utility has decided it can't afford to run the station, although it costs $7 million a year to keep it inactive.

Information and Internet access are available at the Chamber of Commerce (Mon–Fri 9am–6pm & often weekends; ☎683-4636), half a mile east on Healy Spur Road. Flagstop train service runs in winter only (summer trains stop only at the Denali Park station), further along Healy Spur Road.

There are delis at both gas stations, as well as the pricier Mountainview Groceries (8am–11pm in summer) at the junction of the Parks Highway and Healy Spur Road.

The Stampede Trail

One point of passing interest on the road north is the start of the **Stampede Trail**, a rugged track that heads west through the northern reaches of Denali National Park. It is mainly a winter and ATV trail to Kantishna in the heart of Denali National Park, but can be followed some of its distance in summer. The trail was built in the 1930s to access an antimony mine, but in recent times has gained a certain notoriety as the refuge and final resting place of Chris McCandless, the subject of John Krakauer's 1997 biography *Into the Wild* (see Contexts, p.606). After drifting across the States searching for some kind of inner peace in the wilderness, McCandless wound up, in the spring of 1992, in what is now known as the **Sushana bus**, a former Fairbanks city bus towed here by bulldozer in the 1950s. With few survival skills and no map, he seemed to want to live by force of will . . . and failed. He expired four months after his arrival, probably from eating poisonous berries combined with simple starvation.

The tale evidently strikes a chord, because the bus has become something of a point of pilgrimage, though not one you'd want to undertake without suitable consideration and preparation, and the story is now being turned into a movie directed by Sean Penn. Stampede Road spurs west off the Parks Highway (Mile 251.1) and runs eight miles (four of them dirt) to a trailhead. From here the bus is nineteen miles and two river crossings away. If you have a rugged, high-clearance 4WD you can cover a few more miles, but otherwise you must bike or walk. The same snowmelt-swollen Teklanika River that prevented McCandless's escape (although he should have been able to walk south to the Park Road) may well halt your progress about ten miles from the trailhead. Indeed, we only made it that far and thus haven't seen the shrine-like cache of survival gear – sleeping bags, first aid kit, food supplies, along with Krakauer's book and a copy of the original *Outside* magazine article it was based on – but rangers say it's all pretty trashed now and the bus itself is falling apart.

If you want to go, ask locally for advice, aim for late summer, and be prepared for a lot of bog-walking. Better still, go in winter on a **dog-sled tour** with Denali Dog Sled Expeditions (see Basics, p.33).

North towards Nenana

At Mile 276, the Parks Highway crosses to the right bank of the Nenana River and, eight miles on, passes a side road to the ballistic-missile early-warning station (no public access) at **Clear**, first established at the height of the Cold War in 1958. On the last weekend in July or first in August you might want to continue to **Anderson**, six miles west of the Parks Highway, for the **Anderson Bluegrass Country Music Festival** (℡582-2500, ⓦwww.americanbluegrass .com), a country and bluegrass extravaganza with regular acts from all over the state alongside Lower 48 headliners. You can stay at the spacious *Riverside Park RV & Camping* ($12 dry, $15 with electricity; dump station available), and eat and drink at the nearby *Dew Drop Inn*. On the highway, the *Clear Sky Lodge* at Mile 280 (year-round 11am–11pm daily; ℡582-2251) has some of the state's best steaks, and from Julius Creek (Mile 285.7) there are fine views back to Mount McKinley.

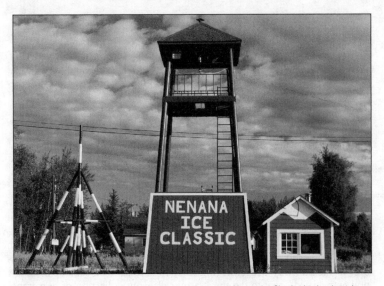
△ Nenana Ice Classic tripod and watchouse

Nenana

Alaskan winters are long, and break-up – the symbol of summer's imminent arrival, when icebound rivers finally thaw, allowing vast sheets of jagged ice to crash and flip their way to the ocean – is the most anticipated event of spring. Nowhere celebrates this better than the small town of **Nenana** (pronounced *Nee-nana* and meaning "good campsite between two rivers"), at the confluence of the Nenana and Tanana rivers, 67 miles north of Denali National Park (Mile 305). Every year from the beginning of February to the first week in April local citizens begin gathering entries for the **Nenana Ice Classic** (ⓦ www .nenanaakiceclassic.com), a huge statewide lottery in which people chance $2.50 on their estimate of the time and date that the ice will break up. The fun begins in the first week in March when a thirty-foot-high, four-legged "tripod" is hauled a hundred yards out onto the four-foot-thick ice of the Tanana River and firmly embedded there. In early April a flag-laden trip wire is attached to a clock that stops the moment the ice moves a hundred feet downstream. Back in 1917, railroad engineers wagered a total of $800 on the first such event: the pool is now usually close to $600,000, almost half going to the organizers (for taxes, salaries, and promotion) and local charities, and the rest ($270,500 in 2006) split among those who guess the right time. The earliest the clock has stopped was 3.27pm on April 20 in 1940; the latest was 11.41am on May 20 in 1964. During the summer the only place you can buy a ticket for the next year's event is in Nenana (at the visitor center, among other places); otherwise, drop your entry into one of the red boxes found everywhere from early February to early April.

For most of the year, the **tripod** stands next to the **watchhouse**, with its window theatrically framing the clock frozen at the trip time of the last break-up and the book of entries open to the winners' page. Standing beside what is the fastest navigable river in Alaska, it is hard to imagine that these broad rolling waters would ever freeze up, but freeze they do, and the subsequent break-up proved to be the major obstacle to engineers trying to complete the Seward to Fairbanks railroad. Freight and passengers crossed by ferry, or in winter on rails laid on the ice, until the 700-foot Tanana River Bridge, then the longest single-span bridge in the country, was completed early in 1923. A few months later President Warren Harding came to drive in the **golden spike** on the north side of the river. In 1967 the Alaska Native Veterans Honor Bridge was opened, the last road bridge over the Tanana River on its journey west.

Being at the junction of two rivers, Nenana was important long before the railroad came through, and from 1866 through to the mid-1950s wooden steamboats used to ply the thousand miles of navigable waterways throughout the Interior. Nenana still serves as a goods entrepôt with trains offloading onto barges that, through the 120 ice-free days of summer, supply remote villages with fuel, building materials, and vehicles. Recently the waterfront has been cleaned up a little and the dock moved just west, and you can stroll along learning some of the history and looking across the water at fishwheels (see Glossary, p.613) going about their automatic harvest. **St Mark's Episcopal Church**, just across the road from the watchhouse, is usually open and worth a few minutes of your time for the altar dressings, made of bleached and beaded moosehide by local Athabascan women.

A block west, the baggage room of the former train station is now given over to the **Railway Museum** (mid-May to Sept daily 8.30am–6pm; donation appreciated), easy to dismiss as a miscellaneous collection of bear traps, telegraph insulators, and railroad ephemera, but actually quite interesting for its material on the Ice Classic, including old entry books several inches thick. While you're in the vicinity it is worth briefly dropping into the **Alfred Starr Nenana Cultural Center**, a few blocks east on the waterfront (late May to early Sept daily 9am–6pm; free), which concentrates on Athabascan lifestyle and artifacts with a little on historical Nenana and dog-mushing for good measure.

Practicalities

Trains stop on request, but even without getting off you can still get a brief look at the town's main sites. As you wind through you go right past the Ice Classic watchhouse and tripod, catch a good view of town as you cross the bridge, then get a close-up of the plaque marking the spot where Harding drove in the golden spike, something you can't see from the road. For a more thorough investigation you'll need to drive, or arrive on the Alaska/Yukon Trails **bus**, which runs between Anchorage, Denali, and Fairbanks. The **visitor center** (late May to early Sept daily 8am–6pm; ☎832-9953) is located where the Parks Highway meets A Street, the town's main drag, which runs the gauntlet of trinket shops to the former train station. At other times of year you can get information at the Chamber of Commerce, at 3rd and Market (☎832-5410), the City Office (☎832-5441), or even the Ice Classic Office, on A between 1st and 2nd (☎832-5446, ⓦwww.ptialaska.net/~tripod). Should you decide to **stay**, *Rough Woods Inn*, on A Street at 2nd (☎832-5299; ❸), is the only place open all year, with spacious but ageing rooms, all en suite, and even larger suites with kitchenette (❸); or try *Bed & Maybe Breakfast* (☎832-5556, ⓔtripodgs@mtaonline.net; ❹) with four comfortable shared-bath rooms fashioned from the former stationmaster's apartment inside the train station – ask at the Tripod Gift Shop and Railroad Museum (daily 9am–6pm; ☎832-5272, ⓦwww.nenanaalaska.com). There's camping almost downtown at the *Nenana Valley RV Park & Campground*, 4th Street at C Street (☎832-5230), which also has rooms with shared bathrooms and a dorm at 211 E 4th St.

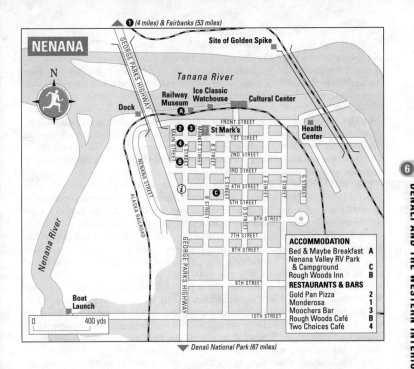

— at top of map:

● (4 miles) & Fairbanks (53 miles)

NENANA

N

Tanana River

Site of Golden Spike

Railway Museum **ⓐ**

Ice Classic Watchouse

Cultural Center

Dock

FRONT STREET

❷ ❸ St Mark's

Health Center

1ST STREET

❹

2ND STREET

ⓑ

3RD STREET

ⓘ

4TH STREET

ⓒ

5TH STREET

6TH STREET

7TH STREET

8TH STREET

9TH STREET

10TH STREET

GEORGE PARKS HIGHWAY

NENANA STREET

ALASKA RAILROAD

MAIN STREET

A STREET

B STREET

C STREET

D STREET

E STREET

F STREET

G STREET

Nenana River

Boat Launch

0   400 yds

ACCOMMODATION
Bed & Maybe Breakfast   A
Nenana Valley RV Park
  & Campground   C
Rough Woods Inn   B
RESTAURANTS & BARS
Gold Pan Pizza   2
Monderosa   1
Moochers Bar   3
Rough Woods Café   B
Two Choices Café   4

▼ *Denali National Park (67 miles)*

DENALI AND THE WESTERN INTERIOR | The Denali Highway

The **best burgers** for miles around are served at *The Monderosa*, four miles north of town at Mile 309 Parks Hwy (daily 10am–10pm in summer, closed Sunday in winter; ☎832-5243; no credit cards). In Nenana you'll find all you need along A Street: the *Two Choices Café* does well-priced **meals** in the Alaskan tradition; the *Rough Woods Café* offers homestyle cooking with daily specials and soup/sandwich combos, as well as Alaskan Amber beer; and *Moochers Bar* is a convivial place with an extensive liquor selection opposite *Gold Pan Pizza* (☎832-5856).

If none of this holds your interest, press on twenty-odd miles towards Fairbanks (now only 53 miles or an hour's drive to the north) to *Skinny Dick's Halfway Inn*, Mile 328, a bar and diner famed throughout the Interior for its extensive range of puerile T-shirts and souvenirs playing on the inn's name.

The Denali Highway

Nowhere in the area is the scenery more awe-inspiring than along the 135-mile-long **Denali Highway**, where access to wilderness is much simpler than in Denali National Park and the crowds incomparably sparser. The highway (typically open mid-May to September) runs through some of Alaska's finest landscapes along the south side of the Alaska Range. The land on either side of the highway is administered by the Bureau of Land Management (BLM), which allows locals and visitors a great deal more freedom to move about than the national park authorities do, giving easy access to great views and wildlife without the formal procedures. The road was originally built in 1957 (long before the Parks Highway was even proposed) to provide road access into Denali National Park from the Richardson Highway, but with the 1972 completion of the George Parks Highway, the Denali Highway was left mainly for recreation. If you're headed up the Parks Highway and not desperately eager to get to Fairbanks, it is well worth nipping up to Denali National Park and then doubling back to drive the Denali Highway to the eastern Interior.

There are no towns along the way, just a handful of roadhouses, and all but 24 miles are gravel. This is a sizeable deterrent to RV drivers and those who obey their car-rental agency's demands to stick to hard-surfaced roads, leaving the highway wonderfully free of traffic for everyone else. In particular, this is excellent **mountain-biking** territory: wonderful scenery, little traffic, and the freedom to camp where you want.

The road is broad and firm but bumpy in places, though this doesn't seem to stop locals hurtling along at a fair lick. The full 135 miles can certainly be traversed in half a day, but it is rewarding to spend a night or two out here either in one of the roadhouses or at one of the great campgrounds. You can even sleep beside the road, though all too often it is easy to tell where less considerate souls have done so before you; leave your spot cleaner than when you arrived. On the intervening days, stop a while to seek out trumpeter swans, moose, bald eagles, beavers, bears, and perhaps some of the 45,000-strong Nelchina caribou herd; or dip a line into one of the numerous lakes for grayling, char, and lake trout. **Hikers** mostly have to compete with ATVs on designated trails, but for a wilderness experience you can just make it up as you go along: pick a direction and go, but be prepared for wet conditions underfoot. Late season is best, when the willow flats and arctic birch shrubs are ablaze with yellows, reds, and oranges.

The one season when the Denali Highway is less than quiet is during the first three weeks of September, when it becomes "boys with toys" territory. This is **hunting season**, and everyone is out for moose or caribou: RVs lumber along towing trailers loaded mainly with four-wheeler ATVs, but also eight-wheeler amphibious vehicles, and even Everglades-style airboats – in fact, just about anything to get them to their quarry across this tough terrain. You'll see them parked up peering into their spotting scopes until something turns up, then they'll hop on their rig and hurtle off across the tundra hoping to beat the next guy to the kill. Presumably they get bored; the road signs here are more bullet-ridden than anywhere in the state, which is some achievement.

Remember that there is very little out here and you'll need to **come prepared**. Bring all the groceries you need and make sure your spare is good: expensive towing is available from Paxson (☏822-3330), Gracious House (☏259-1111), and Cantwell (☏768-2669), and there is tire repair at *Maclaren River Lodge*, but little else. **In winter** the road is impassable for ordinary traffic but becomes a popular route for snowmobilers, dog teams, and cross-country skiers.

Cantwell to the Maclaren River

Turning off the Parks Highway at **Cantwell** (Mile 210 Parks Hwy, Mile 135 Denali Hwy – see p.411), the paved road ends after three miles; the first reason to stop is at a viewpoint at Mile 124, from where Mount McKinley is visible on a clear day. Every few miles along this stretch there are good spots to roll out your sleeping bag in hopes of a crystalline dawn, but the first formal campground is the attractive *Brushkana Campground*, Mile 104.5 ($6; pump water). For a roof over your head, press on to *Gracious House Lodge*, Mile 82.5

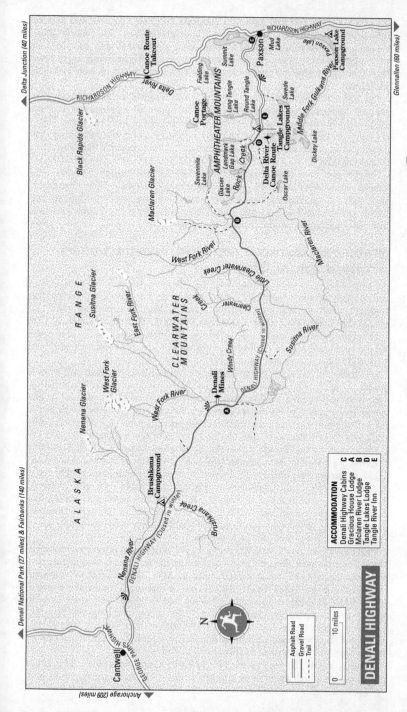

DENALI HIGHWAY

Asphalt Road
Gravel Road
Trail

0   10 miles

N

ACCOMMODATION
Denali Highway Cabins   C
Gracious House Lodge   A
Mclaren River Lodge   B
Tangle Lakes Lodge   D
Tangle River Inn   E

◄ Denali National Park (27 miles) & Fairbanks (140 miles)

◄ Anchorage (209 miles)

ALASKA

RANGE

CLEARWATER
MOUNTAINS

AMPHITHEATER MOUNTAINS

Nenana Glacier

West Fork Glacier

Susitna Glacier

Maclaren Glacier

Black Rapids Glacier

Nenana River

Brushkana Creek

West Fork River

East Fork River

West Fork River

Susitna River

Maclaren River

Little Clearwater Creek

Clearwater Creek

Windy Creek

Rock Creek

Susitna River

Cantwell

GEORGE PARKS HIGHWAY

DENALI HIGHWAY (Closed in winter)

DENALI HIGHWAY (Closed in winter)

Brushkana Campground

Denali Mines

Glacier Lake

Landmark Gap Lake

Sevenmile Lake

Oscar Lake

Dickey Lake

Swede Lake

Delta River Canoe Route

Tangle Lakes Campground

Round Tangle Lake

Long Tangle Lake

Canoe Portage

Fielding Lake

Summit Lake

Mud Lake

Paxson Lake Campground

Paxson Lake

Paxson

Middle Fork Gulkana River

Canoe Route Takeout

Delta River

RICHARDSON HIGHWAY

RICHARDSON HIGHWAY

▲ Delta Junction (40 miles)

Glennallen (60 miles) ►

(℡333-3148, Ⓦwww.alaskaone.com/gracious; ❹, private bath ❺; late May to mid-Sept), which has rooms with or without private bath, RV parking ($20), camping ($15), and showers ($5). You can eat a good **meal** here, too, drink at the *Sluice Box* bar, buy gas, get tires fixed, and even go **flightseeing** for an hour ($280 for up to 3 people) over the Susitna Glacier and past mounts Deborah and Hess.

The lodge makes a good base for exploring the **gold-mining district of Denali**, located up a six-mile dirt road that spurs off the highway at Mile 79.5, right by the Susitna River, the largest waterway in these parts. There is plenty of day-hiking here; make it up as you go along, but remember that existing gold claims are fiercely protected, and private property signs shouldn't be treated idly.

For the next forty miles you follow moraine-formed hummocks and eskers (glacial ridges) with long views south, though the Clearwater Mountains block your views of the Alaska Range to the north. Along the way, small hills are cut by narrow streams feeding kettle lakes, where you might spy trumpeter swans drifting gracefully or moose grazing on aquatic weed.

Maclaren Summit and the Tangle Lakes Archeological District

At Mile 43.5 of the Denali Highway, the Maclaren River Road runs twelve miles north to the Maclaren Glacier. A mile and a half further along the highway, where it meets the Maclaren River, is *Maclaren River Lodge*, Mile 42 (℡822-5444, Ⓦwww.maclarenlodge.com; cabins ❷–❺, rooms ❺; open all year – although there's no road access in winter). It offers decent food and a range of accommodation from bunks in an old miners' cabin sleeping six ($30 per person) to basic rooms and much nicer cabins.

Five miles on you reach the road's highest point, **Maclaren Summit viewpoint** (Mile 37; 4086ft), from where the entire Maclaren River watershed is spread out before you, the Maclaren Glacier tucked into the mountains to the north disgorging its milky waters through a broad landscape, dotted with kettle lakes, that could easily pass for a subarctic Wyoming. From Mile 37 tough cycle trails lead three miles north, and five miles south to Oscar Lake.

You now enter the **Tangle Lakes Archeological District**, which flanks the highway for the next twenty miles (Miles 38–16). Here, the acidic soils of the subarctic tundra have preserved a dense cluster of five hundred sites collectively recording ten thousand years of human occupation, much of it spent hunting bison. There are no real sites to visit, and ATVs are also entitled to tear up the trails, but if you are still keen on hiking, try to get hold of the free *Information Guide and Trails Map* to the area from local visitor centers and inns and look for trailheads at mileposts 37, 30, 24.6, and 16.

Dropping down from Maclaren Summit, you'll find magnificent views north through **Landmark Gap**, a glacial cut through the mountains used as a migration route by the Nelchina caribou herd. At Mile 22, the large and modern *Tangle Lakes Lodge* (℡822-4202; cabins ❸) has nice lakeside cabins and one larger affair ($200) sleeping up to twelve, ideal for birding groups who flock here in June to spot arctic warblers, Smith's longspurs, gyrfalcons, and long-tailed jaegers. Here you'll find a year-round restaurant serving breakfast, burgers, sandwiches, salads, and steak and seafood evening meals all at acceptable prices, rental canoes ($30 a day), and plenty of short hikes nearby – ask locally.

Virtually across the road is the *Tangle Lakes Campground*, Mile 21.5 (free; pump water), which sits in open country with wonderful mountain views, and

Keen paddlers with a sense of adventure and an appreciation of the Alaskan wilderness should seriously consider tackling either the **Delta River** or one of the two main routes on the **Gulkana River** system. They run through outstanding scenery, the low rolling tundra framed by the peaks of the Alaska Range, and all require some knowledge of topographic maps, wilderness camping ability, and enough paddling skill to negotiate sweepers and Class II rapids. The remote nature of these trips and the difficulty of some of the rapids make carrying some kind of hull-patching kit essential. Alaska Public Lands Information Centers in Anchorage, Fairbanks, Glennallen, and Tok (and local visitor centers) supply detailed leaflets on all three canoe routes, which can usually be run from early or mid-June to mid-September. The Gulkana is one of Alaska's best sportfishing streams, with flourishing trout, grayling, salmon, whitefish, lake trout, burbot, and whitefish populations.

Most rental outfits don't allow their canoes on rivers such as these, but you can **rent canoes** from Paxson Alpine Tours, who can also arrange for drop-off and pickup.

Delta River (29 miles; 2–3 days; Class I and II). The route starts at *Tangle Lakes Campground*, Mile 21.5 Denali Hwy, and follows a series of small, interconnected waterways through rolling tundra nine miles north to Lower Tangle Lake. Edging into the Amphitheater Mountains, a mile or so of Class II water is followed by a fifteen-foot waterfall which must be portaged using a half-mile marked trail. A little more Class II–III and twelve miles of Class I–II follow until a tributary makes the river glacially murky and braided to the pullout at Mile 212.5 on the Richardson Highway. It is possible to continue to Black Rapids at Mile 229 (an additional 17 miles; 1–2 days; Class III) but is only recommended for kayaks and rafts.

Main Branch Gulkana River (47 miles; 3–4 days; Class I, II & III). From *Paxson Lake Campground*, Mile 175 Richardson Hwy (see p.471), cross three miles of the lake to enter demanding Class II and III rapids before joining the Middle Fork for several miles of easy floating. After twenty miles you hit the Class III–IV Canyon Rapids (easily portaged on a quarter-mile trail), which are followed by nine miles of shallow and potentially damaging Class II and III water, then eighteen miles of Class I to the finish at the *Sourdough Campground*, Richardson Mile 147.5.

Middle Fork Gulkana River (76 miles; 6–7 days; mostly Class I and II). The boat launch at Mile 21.5 on the Denali Highway (*Tangle River Campground*) gives access to the southern sequence of Upper Tangle Lakes, negotiated with three short, unmarked, but easily determined portages. A fourth (2 miles) brings you to Dickey Lake (possible float-plane access to put-in; subtract 1–2 days from trip length) and the start of the Middle Fork, which descends through three miles of shallow water to a steep and rocky canyon (Class III–IV) requiring careful lining or a portage. After the canyon the river eases and joins the main Gulkana River (see above) down to the *Sourdough Campground* pullout.

acts as the starting point for running the Delta River and the Middle Fork of the Gulkana River (see box, above). To explore the beautiful subalpine **Tangle Lakes** themselves, rent canoes ($3 per hour, $24 for 24 hours) from *Tangle River Inn*, Mile 20 (℡822-3970, ⓦwww.tangleriverinn.com; two-person cabins $120, rooms ❸–❹; mid-April to Sept), which offers simple but comfy cabins and rooms, plus a deluxe bunkhouse with two beds per room for $30 per person, showers ($5), gas, and reliable, tasty diner fare. From Mile 16, at the eastern edge of the Archeological District, the very boggy Swede Lake Trail extends ten miles south to the Middle Fork Gulkana River, linking to another trail into the Alphabet Hills.

DENALI AND THE WESTERN INTERIOR | The Denali Highway

The final 21 miles of the highway are nice, smooth asphalt, descending into the Gulkana River Valley and leaving behind your final glimpse of the Alaska Range and the small Gulkana and Gakona glaciers. The views to the south are just as impressive, though, the dominant peaks of the Wrangell Mountains – Sanford, Drum, and Wrangell – easily visible from the viewpoint at Mile 13. The highway ends at **Paxson** (Mile 185 Richardson Hwy), where you'll find little more than *Denali Highway Cabins* (see p.471), an excellent base for the eastern end of the road.

Travel details

The most pleasurable way to get between Anchorage, Talkeetna, Denali, and Fairbanks is by train, which takes in the best of the scenery in comfort but at a price (see Basics, p.42). Buses (listed along with route descriptions in Basics, p.44) are faster, more frequent, and broader in their coverage. Again, the Anchorage–Denali–Fairbanks corridor is the busiest, with three companies doing a daily run in summer.

Trains

Denali Park to: Anchorage (1 daily; 7hr); Fairbanks (1 daily; 3hr 45min); Talkeetna (daily; 4hr 20min); Wasilla (1 daily; 6hr).
Talkeetna to: Anchorage (1 daily; 2hr); Denali Park (1 daily; 4hr); Fairbanks (daily; 8hr); Wasilla (1 daily; 1hr 30min).
Wasilla to: Anchorage (1 daily; 1hr 45min); Denali Park (1 daily; 4hr); Fairbanks (1 daily; 10hr 20min); Palmer (7 daily; 1hr); Talkeetna (1 daily; 1hr 30min).

Buses

Denali to: Anchorage (4 daily; 5–6hr); Fairbanks (1 daily; 3hr 45min); Talkeetna (1 daily; 3hr); Talkeetna Junction (4 daily; 3hr).

Nenana to: Anchorage (1 daily; 7hr); Fairbanks (1 daily; 1hr 30min).
Palmer to: Anchorage (3 weekly; 1hr); Glennallen (3 weekly; 2hr 30min); Whitehorse, Yukon (3 weekly; 17hr).
Talkeetna to: Anchorage (2–3 daily; 2hr); Denali (1 daily; 3hr).
Talkeetna Junction to: Anchorage (4 daily; 2hr); Denali (4 daily; 3hr); Fairbanks (1 daily; 7hr).
Wasilla to: Anchorage (4 daily; 1hr 50min); Denali (4 daily; 4–5hr); Talkeetna Junction (4 daily; 1hr 15min).

Wrangell-St Elias and
the eastern Interior

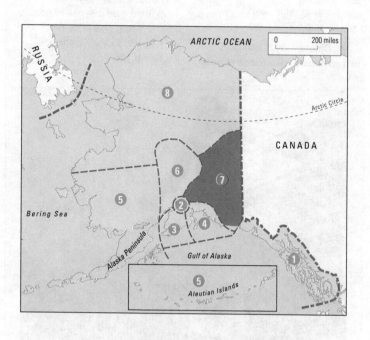

CHAPTER 7

Highlights

* **McCarthy and Kennicott** Twin settlements in the heart of the Wrangell-St Elias National Park with great scenery, wonderful old mill buildings, and bags of character. See p.457

* **Wrangell-St Elias flightseeing** McCarthy hosts some of the finest flightseeing in the state: huge mountains, vast icefields, and the remains of tiny gold-mining settlements. See p.460

* **Chicken** Try a little gold-panning, take a look at an old gold dredge, but most of all stick around for an evening in the *Chicken Creek Saloon*. See p.481

* **Eagle** Delightful former garrison town on the banks of the Yukon River. See p.483

* **Float through the Yukon-Charley** Mining detritus, old cabins, and the restored remains of ageing road-houses give a sense of how the Yukon was once the highway to the Klondike. See p.486

△ McCarthy Lodge

Wrangell-St Elias and the eastern Interior

Alaska's densest crush of mountains, the largest of its ice fields, and some of its vastest swaths of forest coexist around **Wrangell-St Elias and the eastern Interior**. Outside Alaska, Denali gets all the attention, but to those in the know the Wrangell-St Elias National Park is the state's real jewel, a trackless glacial wonderland where major mountain ranges ruck up against each other to create an almost impenetrable wilderness that stretches over the border into Canada. Tucked deep in the park are the beautifully complementary twin towns of Kennicott and McCarthy, the former the decaying wreck of a copper mine and stifling mill town, the latter a rumbustious place that still buzzes with life. Beyond these outposts, however, the park is incredibly remote: only two minor roads penetrate its interior and none of the region's major highways comes close. This isolation makes for a captivating journey, best enjoyed by taking a few days to adjust to the park's pace, and several more if you want to get out into the stupendous backcountry.

Along the park's western fringe, the **Richardson Highway** forms the backbone of the eastern Interior's road system, running from Valdez to Fairbanks. This was the first of the Interior highways and also the course chosen for the **Trans-Alaska Pipeline**. Access into the region from Anchorage is along the Glenn Highway, which meets the Richardson at workaday Glennallen, called the "Hub of Alaska" for its central location. From there the Tok Cutoff connects to the Alaska Highway at the crossroads town of **Tok**, a springboard for trips along the **Taylor Highway** into the Fortymile River region. Star attractions here are the oddball hamlet of **Chicken** and the Yukon riverbank town of **Eagle**, the Interior's first city, now a fascinating historical remnant.

People are hugely outnumbered by animals here: moose, Dall sheep, grizzly bears, and herds of caribou roam seemingly endless swaths of taiga and tundra. Day-to-day weather can vary enormously with even more severe seasonal variations: in winter temperatures can drop to -50°F for days at a time, while summer days reach a sweltering 90°F. The major problem during the warmer months, however, is large quantities of huge mosquitoes; don't set off without insect repellent.

The eastern Interior is a region that's easy to get around, though public transportation is infrequent, so you'll do well to get hold of a car. With your own

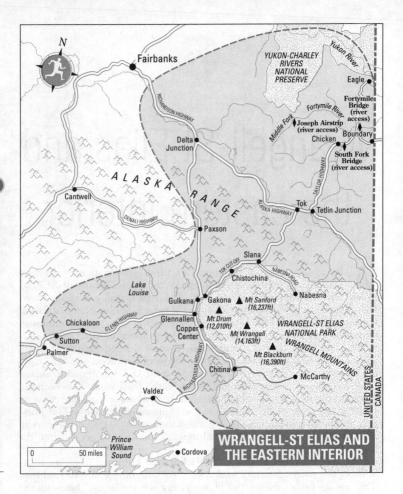

**WRANGELL-ST ELIAS AND
THE EASTERN INTERIOR**

transport you'll have the freedom to travel at your own pace and, if you are camping, it will allow much better access to roadside campgrounds.

The Wrangell-St Elias National Park

The **Wrangell-St Elias National Park** fills out the extreme southeast corner of the Alaskan Interior, on the point where four of the continent's great mountain ranges – the Wrangell, St Elias, Chugach, and Alaskan – cramp up against each other. At 13.2 million acres, it is bigger than Death Valley, Yellowstone, Grand Canyon, and Everglades national parks put together, and larger than Switzerland. It is a place that defies superlatives. Even the usually staid US National Park Service literature breaks out in a rash of (justifiable) hyperbole by saying, "Incredible. You have to see Wrangell-St Elias . . . to believe it." Everything in the park is writ large: peak after peak (including nine of the sixteen highest in the US, each over 14,000ft, and fourteen over 10,000ft), glacier after enormous glacier (some the size of small states), canyon after dizzying canyon – all laced together by braided rivers, massive moraines, and icy-cold lakes, with the volcanic 14,163-foot monster of Mount Wrangell still steaming in the background. It contains North America's longest mountain glacier, the 75-mile-long Nabesna, as well as the world's largest nonpolar icefield, the Bagley, close to 500 square miles in area and part of the Bering Glacier complex, which covers no less than 2250 square miles.

As if all this weren't enough, Wrangell-St Elias forms part of a contiguous cross-border wilderness with Canada's Kluane National Park Reserve and Tatshenshini-Alsek Park, as well as Alaska's Tetlin National Wildlife Refuge and Glacier Bay National Park, altogether forming the largest protected area on the planet that is recognized as a **World Heritage Site**.

Vegetation struggles to take hold in the higher reaches of the park, though it tenaciously hangs on enough to support mountain goats and Dall sheep. At lower elevations, the diversity goes wild: riparian fringes and wooded, silty lowlands are home to bears, moose, and three sizeable herds of caribou (although the Mentasta herd is seemingly being wiped out by wolves).

The park was created in 1980 and remains – in terms of access and development – in its infancy, with private landowners still holding large chunks of its putative territory. It sees less than a tenth of the visitors Denali gets, and though bush-plane landing sites stud the territory, only two roads penetrate the park. The **Nabesna Road** cuts into the northern fringes, but most visitors approach the park along the **McCarthy Road**, a sixty-mile epic along the Copper and Chitina rivers to freewheeling **McCarthy** and the copper-mining ghost town of **Kennicott**, with its thirty big, disused buildings now preserved as a National Historic Landmark. These are fascinating places, dramatically sited and wonderfully photogenic, but the appeal of the area lies equally in its access to stiff **hikes**, several easily accessible and others requiring a bush plane. There are eleven fly-in cabins, free and first-come, first-served, except for that at Esker ($25; ☏784-3295, ⊛www.nps.gov/wrst/planyourvisit/backcountry-cabins.htm).

Some history

In July 1900 two prospectors, **"Tarantula Jack"** Smith and **Clarence Warner**, started poking around the tributaries of the Chitina River in search of gold. They found none, but didn't go away empty-handed. Legend has

Kennicott or Kennecott?

Although explorer Robert Kennicott, part of the Abercrombie expedition in the 1860s, never came up this valley, he lent his name to the glacier that creaks off Mount Blackburn and the river it spawns. A slip of the quill, however, forever destined the mines and the mining company to the name Kennecott (although Kennycott was also used on occasion). Although the train station was known as Kennicott, the former post office was Kennecott, and the National Park Service has followed suit, naming the whole area Kennecott Mines National Historic Landmark. In practice, both names are widely used, but we've stuck with Kennicott for everything except the company, the mill, and the mines.

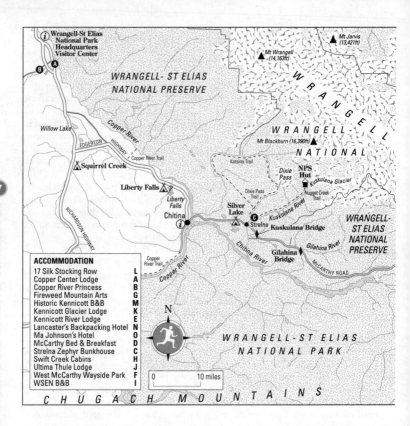

ACCOMMODATION

17 Silk Stocking Row	L
Copper Center Lodge	A
Copper River Princess	B
Fireweed Mountain Arts	G
Historic Kennicott B&B	M
Kennicott Glacier Lodge	K
Kennicott River Lodge	E
Lancaster's Backpacking Hotel	N
Ma Johnson's Hotel	O
McCarthy Bed & Breakfast	D
Strelna Zephyr Bunkhouse	C
Swift Creek Cabins	H
Ultima Thule Lodge	J
West McCarthy Wayside Park	F
WSEN B&B	I

it that they spotted what looked to be a promising patch of grazing well above the snow line close to the crest of a sawtooth ridge. As experienced prospectors with little interest in sheep pasture, it seems likely they knew full well that the green patch was something much more valuable than grass. Whatever the truth, they hightailed it up the slope and unearthed what became the **Bonanza Mine**, one of the continent's richest copper deposits, predominantly chalcocite, a phenomenally rich copper ore, which sometimes assayed at almost eighty percent pure copper and averaged thirteen percent, at a time when commercial mines in Utah and Arizona were getting two percent from their ore.

Mining engineer Stephen Birch bought their claim (and others nearby), and, with the backing of financier J.P. Morgan and the Guggenheim brothers, formed what was to become the Kennecott Copper Corporation. The mines were worthless without some means of getting the ore to smelters in the Lower 48, and the company set about the gargantuan task of building the Copper River & Northwestern Railway (see box, p.453). Work also began on what was to become the dedicated 600-strong company town of **Kennicott**. Everything had to be hauled in – mostly on sleds during the winter when the rivers froze – so that processed ore would be ready to ship out to Cordova when the first train arrived in 1911. Overnight, the Kennecott mines became the richest in the world.

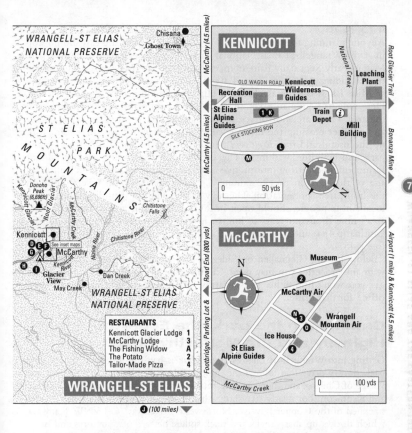

Chisana
Ghost Town

WRANGELL-ST ELIAS
NATIONAL PRESERVE

ST ELIAS

MOUNTAINS

PARK

Donoho
Peak
(6,696ft)

Chitistone
Falls

Kennicott

See inset maps

McCarthy

Glacier
View

May Creek

Dan Creek

WRANGELL-ST ELIAS
NATIONAL PRESERVE

RESTAURANTS
Kennicott Glacier Lodge 1
McCarthy Lodge 3
The Fishing Widow A
The Potato 2
Tailor-Made Pizza 4

WRANGELL-ST ELIAS

J (100 miles) ▼

KENNICOTT

Leaching
Plant

OLD WAGON ROAD   Kennicott
Wilderness
Recreation   Guides
Hall

St Elias
Alpine   **1 K**   Train   **i**
Guides   Depot
Mill
SILK STOCKING ROW   Building

L

M

0   50 yds   N

National Creek

Root Glacier Trail

Bonanza Mine

7

McCARTHY

Museum

N

2

McCarthy Air

N 3

O   Wrangell
Mountain Air

Ice House

St Elias
Alpine Guides   **4**

McCarthy Creek   0   100 yds

McCarthy (4.5 miles) ▲   *McCarthy (4.5 miles)* ▲

Road End (800 yds) ▲

Footbridge, Parking Lot & ▲

Airport (1 mile) & Kennicott (4.5 miles) ▲

WRANGELL-ST ELIAS AND THE EASTERN INTERIOR | Wrangell-St Elias

    Meanwhile, five miles down the tracks, business-minded John Barrett had leased his homestead land to the CR&NW for turntable and switching operations. With a flood of prospectors making for Skolai Pass and **Chisana** (pronounced *shu-shan-na*) for what turned out to be Alaska's last gold rush in 1914, Barrett was able to sell off more land, setting the stage for the development of **McCarthy**.

    The Great Depression of the 1930s sent copper prices spiraling down, and when the Chitina Bridge washed out in 1932, the mines closed. They reopened in 1935, but thirty years of frantic production came to an end in 1938: the last train arrived at Kennicott mines on November 11, apparently with instructions for the station agent to collect his papers and belongings in ninety minutes and climb on board the return service.

    Once the railroad bed was turned into a road a few years later, it became open season on looting anything not nailed down, and a fair bit that was. In the 1960s the Kennecott land was turned over to a faceless corporation that sold the managers' cabins to whichever hippies and recluses were interested. With the formation of the national park in 1980 and the Park Service's purchase of the whole site (except for the private inholdings) in 1998, the steady decay has been arrested, and visitors have begun to come in increasing numbers.

Information

Anyone planning to spend any time in the mountains to the east should stop in at the Wrangell-St Elias National Park Headquarters **visitor center** (late May to early Sept daily 8am–6pm; early Sept to late May in the administration building Mon–Fri 8am–4.30pm; ☎822-5234, ⓦwww.nps.gov/wrst) at Mile 106.8 on the Richardson Highway, just north of Copper Center. Here rangers help plan hikes, sell books and topo maps, and offer advice on the area. There are short hikes, including one to a good volcano viewpoint and another crossing the historic Valdez-Eagle Trail. While you're here, pick up the useful and free *K'elt'aeni* newsletter, which has all the latest on the park and activities within it. The center itself has great views of Mount Drum, offers diverting interpretive material, and shows some excellent footage of the park in the 22-minute *Crown of the Continent* (every hour on the hour; free) presentation. The new Native Culture Building, run by the local Ahtna people, should open in 2007 and exhibit artifacts covering the area's nine thousand years of human history. There's also a ranger center in Chitina (p.454) and a visitor center in the original train depot at **Kennicott** (see p.457).

Before leaving Glennallen or Valdez, you should fill your tank and stock up with any groceries you may need. Chitina generally has limited groceries and gas; you won't find either in McCarthy and Kennicott, or a **bank** or a **post office** for that matter.

Getting into the park: the Edgerton Highway and the McCarthy Road

Getting into Wrangell-St Elias National Park is half the fun. It takes a rugged backcountry drive that follows the smooth Edgerton Highway 33 miles to the village of Chitina, and thereafter the rough-dirt McCarthy Road to McCarthy and Kennicott. For nearly sixty bone-shaking miles, it twists along the former trackbed of the Copper River & Northwestern Railway (CR&NW Railway), which throws up sharp rocks and track spikes: beware of punctures and make sure your spare (preferably not the undersized, space-saving variety) is functional. Conditions vary with the frequency of grading, but at best it is slow going and can be an exacting drive.

Transport is a limiting factor. In general, rental agencies won't insure their vehicles for the journey, not that it seems to stop many people. Hitching can be a hit-or-miss affair, so you may need the services of Backcountry Connections (mid-May to mid-Sept Mon–Sat; ☎1-866/582-5292 in Alaska, ⓦwww.alaska-backcountry-tours.com). They pick up early in the morning from hotels and campgrounds around Glennallen and charge $109 for a same-day round-trip with four hours in McCarthy, $119 to spread it over several days; from Chitina the round-trip to McCarthy is $99 or $109. Mountain Kingdom Express (☎554-1188) does the same trip in reverse, starting in McCarthy and returning from Glennallen in the afternoon. An excellent alternative is to **fly to McCarthy**, perhaps with a bit of an aerial tour thrown in, obviating the need for a flightseeing trip once in McCarthy. In summer Wrangell Mountain Air (see p.461) flies into McCarthy from Chitina (May 15 to Sept 15 two or three times daily; $195 round-trip plus tax) or hooks up with Backcountry Connections to offer a fly/drive round-trip (also $195). Ellis Air Taxi (☎1-800/478-3368, ⓦwww.ellisair.com) flies from Anchorage via Gulkana on Wednesdays and Fridays, returning the same afternoon.

7

The "Can't Run & Never Will" Railway

The discovery of super-rich copper ore at Bonanza Ridge in 1900 offered the promise of great wealth, but presented a seemingly insurmountable physical challenge. Only two years earlier, hundreds of prospectors had died trying to reach the Interior gold-fields from the coast by crossing the Valdez Glacier, and the fledgling Valdez-Eagle Trail was inadequate and much too distant for transporting huge quantities of copper ore. In the spirit of the age, a railroad was chosen as the solution. Master railroad-builder Michael Heney (also responsible for Skagway's White Pass & Yukon Route; see p.198) was called in, and he plotted a 196-mile course up the Copper and Chitina rivers, through narrow canyons and across deep gorges precariously spanned by wooden-lattice trestle bridges, some of which survive today. Icebergs, rapids, shifting sandbars, and the howling Copper River wind all had to be taken into consideration, but undoubtedly the most challenging section was the 1550-foot span over the Copper River between the faces of two active glaciers – the Miles and the Childs.

Construction on the Miles Glacier Bridge – dubbed the **"Million Dollar Bridge"** (see p.338), though it actually cost appreciably more ($1.4 million, the equivalent of $29 million now) – began in earnest in the spring of 1908, but pessimists were not swayed and continued to refer to the Copper River & Northwestern Railway as the Can't Run & Never Will. Nonetheless, by March 1911 (in less than three years) the railroad was completed all the way to Kennicott and remained the premier Alaskan construction feat until the Trans-Alaska Pipeline was built in the late 1970s. The entire line cost $23 million to build and almost as much to maintain. Every year during spring break-up, careering ice would wipe out many of the river bridges, which would then be rapidly rebuilt. During its 27-year life the railroad hauled over $200 million in copper ore, but its operation halted for good in 1938. In 1941 the company magnanimously gave the CR&NW right-of-way to the state government, which eventually transformed its northern end into the McCarthy Road. Cordova boosters have long cherished ideas of putting in a highway along the Copper River to Chitina and then to the Richardson Highway, but hopes were dashed in 1964 when the Good Friday earthquake all but destroyed the Million Dollar Bridge; it has been repaired but hopes of opening a road north along the trackbed remain distant.

The Edgerton Highway to Chitina

The paved **Edgerton Highway** cuts off the Richardson Highway 36 miles south of Glennallen (Mile 82.6), and apart from the wonderful mountain scenery, there's little to distract you – though you may fancy the **Copper River Trail**, Mile 12.6 (7 miles round-trip; 3hr; mostly flat), which runs to the Copper River through excellent bird-watching territory. As far as Mile 17 you're passing through Kenny Lake, a homesteading settlement established in the 1960s, where you can stay at the *Copper Moose B&B* (☏1-866/922-4244, Ⓦwww.coppermoosebb.com; ❺) at Mile 5.8 or the *Wrangell Ranch B&B* (☏822-5797; ❹) at Mile 6; the helpful and friendly *Kenny Lake Mercantile* (☏822-3313, Ⓦwww.kennylake.com) at Mile 7.2 has rooms with shared bathrooms (❸) and camping (from $12 dry, $20 with electricity), plus groceries, an inexpensive **diner**, laundry, and gas. The small but beautifully formed *Liberty Falls State Recreation Site*, Mile 23.6 ($10 per vehicle; pump water), huddles by a cascading stream adjacent to the **Liberty Falls Creek Trail** (1 mile each way; 25min each way; 300ft ascent), which leads up through the spruce forest to a small ridge-end plateau with views of the cascading Liberty Creek and across the Copper River to the Wrangell Mountains.

The Copper and Chitina rivers join forces at **Chitina** (Chit-na), Mile 33, a hamlet locked in an aspen- and spruce-cloaked fold with an ancient, dilapidated appearance that belies its relatively recent genesis. It was born in 1910 as a way station for the CR&NW Railway and a transit point for rail passengers from Cordova taking the stage to Fairbanks and points inland; by 1914 it had restaurants, dance halls, and a movie theater. In the early 1940s the rails were pulled up and buildings removed to the extent that Chitina became virtually a ghost town, a point illustrated by one of the few local residents, who painted phantoms on the walls of the remaining buildings. The red and king salmon runs on the silt-laden waters of the Copper River still drew dipnetters every July and August, but it wasn't until the creation of the national park in 1980 and the upsurge in tourism that Chitina started to revive. One short row of original shop-fronts has been tastefully preserved, notably Spirit Mountain Art Gallery, which is worth a few minutes of your time for locally produced paintings and photography, plus quality Alaskan crafts. If it is open, call in at the national park **ranger center** (generally late May to early Sept daily 2–6pm; ☎823-2205), actually run by the Chamber of Commerce in the former home of a stagecoach-company manager, and bedecked with fascinating photos of old-timers working the riverboats that carried supplies during the railroad construction.

For a bite, try *Chitina Trading Post and Café*, serving breakfast, sandwiches, homemade pizza, and fruit pie. Nice **cabins** with radio-cassette, fridge, coffee-maker, and an outhouse, as well as a bunkhouse (❶), are available at *Chitina Guest Cabins*, Mile 32 Edgerton Hwy (☎823-2266, ⓦwww.pawandfeathers.com; ❺), where you also get a continental breakfast. ☀ *Gilpatrick's Hotel Chitina*, Fairbanks and Main (☎823-2244, ⓦwww.hotelchitina.com; ❻), was built in 1914 as the Arctic Brotherhood Hall and was later a cinema and then a hotel; after being jacked up and moved eight feet, it reopened in 2006 with small rooms with queen-sized beds and private bathrooms, as well as triples and one six-person room. The hotel also has the best restaurant in town (May–Oct 7am–11pm), with moderate prices. At the start of the McCarthy Road, *Chitina House B&B* (☎823-2298, ⓦwww.chitinahouse.com; ❻) has two double rooms and one twin in an original railroad bunk- and mess-house.

Bikers should consider detouring south along O'Brien Road (which can be driven by ordinary vehicles for about eight miles in dry conditions) which follows O'Brien Creek from the gas station at the east end of town and continues as the **Copper River Trail** (see box, p.456) – not to be confused with the identically named one above – but for everyone else the McCarthy Road beckons. The Chitina Fair, dominated by a giant-cabbage contest, is held on the first Sunday of September, and there's an Ice Fishing Derby on the first Saturday of April.

The McCarthy Road

The **McCarthy Road** (typically open May to mid-Oct) has a speed limit of 35mph, but if you've any respect for your rig you won't be troubling the state troopers. The road is gradually being widened and improved as part of a Parks Service strategy to take some pressure off Denali, but the sixty miles from Chitina to McCarthy are still likely to take you at least two, maybe three, hours as you climb from 500ft to 1500ft through spruce, cottonwood, and aspen.

The scenery is ruggedly mountainous, but you occasionally come across incongruous patches of private property where a roadside airstrip provides

Wrangell-St Elias National Park can also be accessed along the Nabesna Road, about eighty miles further north. Our account is on p.456.

access to a cluster of cabins, often with smooth lawns and brilliant flower beds. Just over a mile from Chitina the road crosses the Copper River (just south of its confluence with the Chitina) on the concrete bridge that in 1971 replaced a railroad trestle, which would frequently wash away at spring break-up. Silt from glaciers on the southern flank of the Wrangell Mountains makes ordinary fishing impossible, so this is one of only four Alaskan rivers where dipnetting and **fishwheels** are permitted; you may well see them in the water, if they're not obscured by the dust storms that howl up the Copper River. Fishwheels, which can catch up to a thousand salmon a day, were introduced from the Lower 48 around 1913, and are now used only for Native subsistence harvest; other Alaskans can only use dipnets here. On the east bank the free but often windswept *Copper River Campground* offers little temptation with the knowledge that you are now within Wrangell-St Elias National Park and can legally camp beside the road (though not on any private property). There is slightly more formal accommodation at the commercial *Silver Lake Campground*, Mile 10.7, which has tent sites and dry RV camping (both $10), does tire repair, and rents canoes and rowboats for lake trout-fishing ($5 per hour), and the *Strelna Zephyr Bunkhouse*, two miles north up Nugget Creek Road from Mile 14.5 (℡240-3055; ❸), a log cabin with just four bunks, a wood stove, and a sauna nearby: bring a sleeping bag. Nugget Creek Road also leads 2.5 miles north to the **trailhead** for the Dixie Pass and Nugget Creek trails (for both see box, p.462).

At Mile 17 the road teeters precariously over the **Kuskulana Bridge**, 238ft above the Kuskulana River. It must have been a nerve-wracking crossing before the metal guardrails were added in 1988. In the late 1990s the bridge was briefly the scene of a bungy-jumping operation that offered free goes to Alaskans jumping naked. The offer was stopped when it proved too popular, and the Department of Transportation finally closed down the outfit.

△ Gilahina Trestle Bridge, McCarthy Road

There's a pleasant, wooded camping spot (donations accepted) at Mile 27, with a couple of picnic tables and an outhouse, and beyond that an excellent example of an old wooden trestle bridge. The tumbledown form of the **Gilahina Bridge** (Mile 29) has tempted many a photographer: it is far from safe, so stay well clear. At miles 34.7 and 35.8 trailheads mark either end of the Crystalline Hills Trail, a 2.5-mile loop to the north that gives great views of the Chitina valley. Otherwise, the only reason to stop before the end of the road is the crafty *Fireweed Mountain Arts*, Mile 56.5 (☎554-4420), which sells artsy souvenirs and USGS maps, fixes tires, and offers a rental **cabin** (call for rates). From here it is just a couple of miles to the road end and the cluster of places to stay on the west side of the Kennicott River (see p.458). There's a fine illustration of the law of supply and demand here, with parking free half a mile west of the road end, but costing $10 a day right by the footbridge. On the far side of the river you have the choice of walking the half mile to McCarthy, calling a hotel for a free transfer, riding a bike (from the *Glacier View Campground*) or taking a shuttle bus.

Hiking and biking off the McCarthy Road

With McCarthy and Kennicott drawing you onward, it is tempting to charge headlong to the end of the McCarthy Road. Off-road cyclists, however, should consider turning off at Chitina and following the Copper River Trail, while hikers should leave the road at Mile 14.5 and follow Nugget Creek Road to the **trailheads** for the challenging Dixie Pass Trail and the appreciably easier Nugget Creek Trail. Consult the staff at the park headquarters (p.459) for appropriate maps and more detailed trailhead information.

Copper River Trail (3.5 to 20 miles one-way; 1hr to 2 days; mainly flat). Though access has been much curtailed by recent landslides, it is still possible to explore the first 3.5 miles of the old CR&NW trackbed south from Chitina by car, or about twenty miles by bike. The remainder of the road is officially closed, though remains in use by locals. The track flanks O'Brien Creek, then the surging gray water of the Copper River past some spectacularly crumbling old trestle bridges – now bypassed by the track – as well as a couple of places where the narrowness of Wood Canyon forces the route into two short tunnels. Mostly it is too flat to be an exciting walk, but makes great cycling country, with numerous places where you can throw down a tent for the night; you may also be able to shelter in the old station houses.

Dixie Pass Trail (24 miles round-trip; 2–4 days; 3300ft ascent). A fairly tough but popular there-and-back hike which offers one of the few backcountry experiences in the park that doesn't require a fly-in. The trail initially follows a well-defined streamside track, then requires a bit more route-finding to approach the 5100-foot Dixie Pass. The ascent of the pass is strenuous, and some make it a day-hike from their camp at the base, but committed types are rewarded by the chance to camp high on the alpine tundra with stupendous vistas all around. You can either retrace your steps to the trailhead, or make a long loop (45 miles in all; 5–7 days) by continuing north over Dixie Pass and down Rock Creek to join the **Kotsina Trail**, which follows the Kotsina River as it loops around the western end of Hubbard Peak to the trailhead.

Nugget Creek Trail (29 miles round-trip; 2–4 days; 1700ft ascent). An easy-to-follow hike (or bike ride), gradually climbing through the forest along an old mining road up the Kuskulana valley, eventually offering great views of the Kuskulana Glacier. It isn't that hard, though at the wrong time of year the bugs can be awful, and there are several boggy stream crossings. At the end is a poorly maintained NPS hut with bunks and a wood stove, which can be used as a base for further explorations up the valley and around old mine buildings. Return the same way.

McCarthy, Kennicott, and around

In their heyday Kennicott and McCarthy perfectly complemented each other, with McCarthy the licentious safety valve for the stiff-collared company town up the hill. Kennicott had all the amenities – hospital with dental office, grade school, recreation hall, ballpark, skating rink, and even a dairy – but McCarthy had the restaurants, pool halls, hotels, saloons, and brothels. The arrangement suited everyone: labor was short in the district, and the company knew that few disgruntled workers quitting Kennecott would make it past McCarthy with their pockets full and so would soon return to work. Kennicott was always "dry," but even during prohibition McCarthy flaunted the Feds' rules and stills were commonplace.

In some respects the distinction remains: **McCarthy** is still very much the social center of the district, and its restaurants, and especially its bar, always seem packed with the residents of this scattered hamlet. All around, ancient log cabins, frame houses pieced together from whatever was available, and assorted rusting hulks give the town a kind of junkyard beauty. Cars can only get across the Kennicott River in the frozen depths of winter, so traffic is negligible, and you can spend a couple of happy hours just ambling about, at some point directing yourself to the original CR&NW depot now transformed into the **McCarthy–Kennicott Historical Museum** (late May to early Sept daily 11am–6pm; donations encouraged), with models of boomtown McCarthy and the mine and material on life in the two towns, mining, and the coming of the railroad. While you're there, pick up the *McCarthy Self-guided Tour* brochure ($2) and use it to identify some of the town's more interesting buildings, such as the mill, the power plant, and the bunkhouses. McCarthy is expertly characterized in a poignant chapter in Pete McCarthy's book *The Road to McCarthy*, essential reading for an advance flavor of the place.

At some point, almost everyone spends at least half a day almost five miles up the main road at **Kennicott**, reached by shuttle bus along the road once traced by train tracks or on foot along the parallel Old Wagon Road. Kennecott's distinctive industrial buildings – all red with white trim – hug the mountainside on the moraine-strewn flanks of the Kennicott Glacier, and now all fall under the auspices of the **Kennecott Mines National Historic Landmark**. Back in the 1920s, when three hundred people worked here, the glacier was five hundred feet higher and completely obscured Fireweed Mountain across the valley, but the diminished hunk of ice now reveals magnificent mountain views as you hike up the tracks through town.

Since taking over in 1998, the National Park Service has been replacing roofs and generally stabilizing the rotting structures, but the work is far from complete and most of the buildings are off-limits and some will be allowed to collapse. The old Recreation Hall, near the entry from McCarthy, hosts educational programs and concerts, and the old train depot, at the bridge over National Creek, has been turned into a **visitor center** (late May to early Sept daily 9am–5.30pm; ☎554-2417); in 2008 a new visitor center will open in the former General Store and Post Office, just south. A free leaflet outlining a self-guided tour is available from the tourist office, but to really get inside the mill buildings you need to take one of the **excellent tours** (see p.452). Outside, you can still wander the hillside paths looking for that photogenic angle of the fourteen-story ore mill, the power plant, workers' bunkhouses, and numerous dilapidated cabins.

Arrival and getting around

Almost at the end of the McCarthy Road (Mile 58.5), a national park **infor-mation station** (late May to early Sept 9.30am–5pm; no phone) offers some local background (including information on shuttles, plus restrooms and free day-parking), but you might as well continue three-quarters of a mile to the Road End, a bleak and unsightly gravel parking lot ($10 a day). From there visitors must cross the Kennicott River using two successive footbridges: it is only half a mile to McCarthy, and a further four and a half miles to Kennicott. If you don't fancy the short walk into town, you could use the free phone by the bridge to call a Kennicott hotel, which should provide a free pickup. Another option is to call one of the **shuttle bus** services (McCarthy-Kenni-cott Community Shuttle and Wrangell Mountain Bus) that together provide a roughly hourly service throughout the day ($5 each way). Perhaps the best way to make the most of your time here is to **rent a bike** from *Glacier View Campground* ($25 a day; see below).

Accommodation

McCarthy and Kennicott are both sufficiently remote to keep prices high. Following their roots, Kennicott goes for the more refined approach, while McCarthy offers something altogether more rustic (though not lacking in comfort). If you've got the cash and don't mind lugging your gear over the footbridge, you'll prefer to stay in McCarthy or Kennicott, but there is a growing cluster of accommodation west of the Kennicott River, along the final mile of the McCarthy Road. All accommodation is marked on the map on p.450.

Those on a tight budget will want to **camp**, either at the *Glacier View Camp-ground* or (informally) beside the Root Glacier Trail a mile or so from the Kennecott Mill Building.

West of the Kennicott River

Fireweed Mountain Arts Mile 56.5 ☎554-4420, ✉fireweedmtnarts@starband.net. A small cabin a short walk into the woods with a wood stove, propane cooking, and a light breakfast, all for $50 a couple. Bring your sleeping bag. ❶

Glacier View Campground Mile 58.9 ☎554-4490, ⓦwww.glacierviewcampground.com. Commercial campground on a gravel lot with dry camping for tents and RVs (both $18) and a new cabin (❹). Showers ($5) are open to all, and there is mountain-bike rental for $25 a day. Late May to mid-Sept.

Kennicott River Lodge and Hostel Mile 59.4 ☎554-4441, ⓦwww.kennicottriverlodge.com. A modern log-built house with large common kitchen, sauna, a lounge and deck with good mountain views, and a series of comfortable cabins, some fitted with four bunks and a sleeping loft for two and charged at $28 per person; bring a sleeping bag for these (but not for the standard cabins or lodge), or rent for $2. Showers are free to guests and $10 for non-guests. Cabins & lodge ❹, bunks ❶

McCarthy Bed and Breakfast Mile 58.5 ☎554-4433, ⓦwww.mccarthy-kennicott.com/mccarthybb. Rooms and cabins, all en suite, with breakfast (perhaps on the screened gazebo), tours, and information; open all year. ❺

Swift Creek Cabins Mile 57 ☎554-4432, ⓦwww.swiftcreekalaska.com. A couple of cabins in the woods, sited on a bluff with great views, and each equipped with a small kitchen and relaxing porch. There's an outhouse and a semi-outdoor shower, plus a barbecue grill. ❹

West McCarthy Wayside Park Mile 59.6, right at the end of the road ☎746-0606, ✉syren@mtaon-line.net. Essentially a parking lot with tire repair and camping in the woods and beside the glacier moraine. Tent or RV $15. A water supply is planned, but it is best to bring your own.

WSEN (Wrangell-St Elias News) B&B Mile 58.6 ☎554-4454, ⓦwww.mccarthy-kennicott.com. Appealing B&B almost two miles down a side road a mile west of the Road End, with two cozy cabins and a converted trailer, plus a common bathhouse with flush toilet and shower. One cabin and the caravan have full kitchens, and a slightly cheaper cabin has only electricity and a coffeepot (but no running water). All have breakfast goodies supplied. ❸

McCarthy

Lancaster's Backpacking Hotel ☎554-4402, ⓦwww.mccarthylodge.com. The budget arm of *Ma Johnson's*, this recent conversion of a 1920s building offers simple shared-bath rooms fitted with bunks and going for $48 for one person, $68 for two. ❷

Ma Johnson's Hotel ☎554-4402, ⓦwww.mccarthylodge.com. The place to stay in McCarthy, built in 1923 and evoking an appropriate atmosphere with of-the-era decor. Rooms are small but pleasant with shared bathrooms, and a full breakfast, not included in room rates, is served over the road at *McCarthy Lodge*. ❻

Kennicott

17 Silk Stocking Row ☎554-1717, ⓦwww.17silkstockingrow.com. A former mine manager's home, beautifully restored though with some modern amenities – but you'll have to use the outhouse. ❺
Historic Kennicott B&B 14 Silk Stocking Row ☎554-4469. Comfortable B&B in a former mine manager's house, slightly less lovingly restored than the preceding, and outhouse-only as well. ❺

Kennicott Glacier Lodge ☎1-800/582-5128, ⓦwww.kennicottlodge.com. Easily the largest hotel around, offering comfortable, modern, shared-facility rooms, the best of which have balconies and glacier views. Rooms with private bath and two queen-sized beds are in the new South Wing, and rates include a transfer from McCarthy. Check the website for value packages including meals and a Kennicott town tour. Private bath ❽, shared bath ❼

Ultima Thule Lodge ☎688-1200, ⓦwww.ultimathulelodge.com. The ultimate Wrangell-St Elias backcountry experience, a luxury lodge (rebuilt in 2004 on a hillside site) 100 miles up the Chitina River from Chitina airstrip. Packages cost $1000 per person per night, for a minimum of four nights, or $5900 for a week, plus the flight in. A range of activities, including rafting, trekking, glacier exploration, fishing, wildlife-viewing, flight-seeing, and dog-sledding, is included.

Kennecott Tours

If you have the slightest interest in Alaska's industrial heritage, be sure to join one of the 2.5-hour **Kennecott Tours** (mid-May to mid-Sept 9.30am, 1.30 & 3.30pm; $25) run by St Elias Alpine Guides (May–Sept ☎554-4445, year-round in Anchorage 1-888/933-5427; ⓦwww.steliasguides.com) out of the Wrangell Mountain Air office, at the entry to Kennecott. This is the only way you can get into any of the major buildings. The highlights of the tour are the powerhouse, which powered the mill and provided underground steam-heating to prevent the town's walkways from freezing up, and the fourteen floors of the concentration mill, including the steps along the high-grade ore chute on which John Denver sang during a 1970s TV special – droll guides have dubbed the stairs the "John Denver Memorial Staircase."

Glacier hiking and ice climbing

From their office opposite *Kennicott Glacier Lodge*, St Elias Alpine Guides also run a highly professional mountain-guide service that leads unroped **glacier hikes** ($50 half-day, $95 full day), hikes up to Bonanza, Jumbo, and Erie mines ($95 a day), **iceclimbing** ($100 per day), **backcountry expeditions** ($125 per day), and fly-in hikes ($235–285 per day). Serious commitment is required for their longer adventures: ten days hiking the Chitistone Canyon ($2000 per person) with one guide to two customers, or a fourteen-day attempt on an unclimbed peak in the Wrangell Mountains ($3800–5300 depending on numbers; all experience levels welcome). There's a slightly more intimate and personal feel to the trips run by Kennicott Wilderness Guides (☎1-800/664-4537, ⓦwww.kennicottguides.com), which also works out of an office opposite the *Kennicott Glacier Lodge* and offers a more limited range of trips, with glacier treks ($55 half-day, $95 full day) and ice climbing ($110 full day). Trek Alaska (☎350-3710, ⓦwww.trekalaska.com) offers day hikes to the Root Glacier and old mines and longer backcountry treks, for instance on the Goat Trail or to Donoho Lakes, from $855 for four days.

The Pilgrims, the Feds, and the Motherlode

In Alaska there's a constant tension between the pro-development majority, the environmental preservationists, and the hermit set that wants to live simple lives in the backwoods. The state is full of people who have come from elsewhere for the wide open spaces and freedom to do their own thing. For some it is the opportunity to savor one of the world's largest virtually untouched landscapes; for others it is the opportunity to exploit its resources, unfettered by rules and regulations.

The "smaller government" mantra rings loud here, though some sort of local authority is usually encouraged if it means people are going to get schools and emergency services. State government is grudgingly accepted as a necessary evil, and one that provides for its people from oil revenues. But the federal government is always perceived as the heavy: it taxes your income, meddles in your life, and "locks up" land in national parks and preserves.

Nowhere does the conflict between such divergent views come into sharper focus than McCarthy, which has traditionally attracted people who don't want much to do with authority. Even so, there is heated debate about the state's role in development. Should the state pave the McCarthy Road? It would make access easier for residents but also encourage more tourists. Should vehicular access to the town from the road end be improved? The sort of tourists who make it to McCarthy generally appreciate the need to walk into town, but some residents want to get their four-wheelers across the footbridge (which the authorities continually try to prevent), and others want a proper road bridge.

The community has lived with these sorts of arguments for decades, and since 1980 it has also had to cope with being in the heart of the federally administered Wrangell-St Elias National Park. That has only been a problem since 1998, when the National Park Service purchased most of the Kennecott Mill and associated buildings and began to lay a heavier hand on its management of the area.

And then, in 2002, came the Hales, a highly devout, bluegrass-playing, hillbilly Christian family with sixteen kids – with names such as Bethlehem, Lamb, Hosanna, and Psalm – who call themselves **the Pilgrims** and moved onto an inholding within the national park thirteen miles northeast of McCarthy, thereby virtually doubling the region's year-round population. To get from McCarthy to their home beside the old Motherlode Mine they had to travel along an old miners' route through the national park, where the use of motorized transport is banned. There was no problem as long as the Pilgrims stuck to horse travel, but when one of their buildings burnt down and they decided to drive a bulldozer down the old track with a trailer-load of building materials, the Park Service put its foot down. An intense legal battle ensued, the Park Service and conservation groups fighting to protect the wilderness and pristine salmon breeding grounds threatened by the Pilgrims, and the Pilgrims and their rightwing supporters arguing for the inviolability of private property. Early in 2006 a federal appeals court upheld the district court's order blocking further bulldozing.

Some Alaskans saw the Pilgrims as good Christians trying to lead a simple, God-fearing life, but others just resented the fact that they had bought their land with eighteen Permanent Fund Dividend checks (see box, p.211) and had let themselves be hijacked by the anti-government land-use activists, who skilfully polarized the issue. Their doubts seemed justified when in September 2005 Robert Hale ("Papa Pilgrim") was indicted on thirty charges of child abuse relating to one of his daughters. He took off in a camper van but was arrested near Eagle River two weeks later.

Flightseeing

Several companies operate flightseeing trips from McCarthy's airport, from where fabulous scenery is visible straight away. And it only gets better as you fly higher and farther, with wave upon wave of snowy peaks harboring vast icefields. For spectacle alone, flights over Wrangell-St Elias match those around Denali from Talkeetna, and may just surpass them. For personal service, a relaxed atmosphere, and a very knowledgeable pilot, fly with McCarthy-based McCarthy Air (☎1-888/989-9891, ⓦwww.mccarthyair.com), which runs a thirty-minute taster ($60), although you should really fork out for an hour ($100, for up to seven passengers), which gives you a pretty good look around Mount Blackburn, glaciers, waterfalls, and old mine sites. To also see Canada's Mount Logan and the Bagley Icefield, you'll need the full ninety minutes ($140).

Also based in McCarthy, Wrangell Mountain Air (☎1-800/478-1160, ⓦwww.wrangellmountainair.com) starts with the skimpy Glacier Tour (35min; $90), and goes up to the much more satisfying Backcountry Tour (50min; $120), Mountain Tour (70min; $160), and the mammoth Grand Tour (90min; $195) over the Bagley Icefield and right around the Wrangell Mountains. They also offer a day tour from Gulkana, including two fifty-minute flights and tours of McCarthy and Kennicott ($329, or $260 flights only). Both companies will also drop you off for hikes in the vast backcountry (see box, p.462) with advice on a suitable itinerary, and pick you up when you're done.

Rafting

If the chilly glacial waters don't put you off, go rafting with Copper Oar, at the Road End parking lot (☎1-800/523-4453, ⓦwww.copperoar.com), which runs the Nizina Canyon trip (daily; 5–8hr; $265), with five miles on a Class II–III stretch of the Kennicott River followed by the spectacular scenery of the Nizina Canyon and a panoramic return flight. For more of a wilderness experience (with small portions of whitewater), you'll need to book ahead on trips like Chitina to Cordova (6 days; $2350) and the Source to the Sea Expedition (15 days; $4600).

St Elias Guides (see p.459) also does rafting trips offering Nizina Canyon (1 day; $275), the relatively gentle Chitina River (3 days; $990), and the massive trip down to the mouth of the Copper River (10 days; $3640).

Eating and drinking

The standard for dining establishments is surprisingly high, given the limited range of options, but for convenience sake you're unlikely to stray far from your accommodation for meals. In Kennicott the restaurant at the *Kennicott Glacier Lodge* is your only option, but down the hill the choice is wider and improving all the time.

Glacier View Campground Barbecue stand serving burgers ($8), hot dogs, and bratwurst, plus rib or pork chop specials on holidays like July 4 and Labor Day.

Kennicott Glacier Lodge Kennicott ☎1-800/582-5128. The only place to eat in Kennicott, serving breakfast ($8–12), lunch, snacks throughout the day, and an evening set menu for $25–30, for which reservations are recommended.

🏃 **McCarthy Lodge** McCarthy ☎554-4402. Casual but excellent restaurant festooned with mining paraphernalia. Soups and sandwiches are the norm for lunch (under $10), but they turn it on for their fixed-price three-course evening meals

($28). Otherwise try gourmet concoctions such as ale-battered halibut or fried risotto balls with a meat *ragú* (both $15). The selection is limited, but it changes nightly and is always good. The lodge also has a lively bar, open year-round and with occasional bands in summer, and an ATM.

The Potato McCarthy. Essentially a takeout burger joint, but everything is cooked fresh each morning and made to order, and they do a good espresso. Aside from the burgers, try the popular Potatohead burrito or the Spudnik.

Tailor-Made Pizza McCarthy. Serves superb pizza (starting around $15) on a mosquito-netted deck or around a wood-burning stove.

The Nabesna Road

Despite the mind-boggling immensity of the Wrangell-St Elias National Park, the only road access into the park aside from the McCarthy Road is the 42-mile-long **Nabesna Road**. This threads its way east between the Mentasta and Wrangell mountains into the northwestern corner of the park, ending at Nabesna, a privately owned (and therefore off-limits) former gold mine which was worked from 1923 to 1942; the road was built in 1933, allowing the removal of nearly $2 million of gold before the mine closed.

The Nabesna region is a far less developed corner of the park than the area around McCarthy, and there is considerable scenic pleasure in simply driving

Hikes around Kennicott and into the backcountry

Wonderful though it may be to simply wander around McCarthy and Kennicott, **hiking** will bring you much closer to the living, breathing wilderness. The views are breathtaking, especially if you choose, as many do, to take a short flight into the backcountry and begin hiking from there. Since there aren't any maintained trails, some mental preparation is required: read our comments in the Denali account (p.431). No backcountry permits are required, but you should complete an itinerary at a park office and leave it with someone trustworthy. No one will come looking for you unless someone requests a search – discussing emergency contingencies with your pilot is essential. You'll need a head net against mosquitoes and a bear-resistant food container, available on payment of a deposit from the visitor centers at Slana, Kennicott, and Copper Center.

You'll almost certainly be camping in the wilderness, though the Park Service people at the park headquarters will help you locate the eight free first-come, first-served fly-in **cabins** in this part of the park. Below, we've listed a couple of local trails – one easy, one less so – along with one backcountry suggestion, though there are dozens of others. Again, ask your pilot for ideas.

Root Glacier Trail (4–8 miles round-trip; 2–4hr; 200ft ascent). From Kennicott the track leads north through the main mill buildings and out onto the lateral moraine, giving excellent views of the surrounding mountains and the gleaming-white Kennicott Glacier. The ice is accessible in places, though for safety reasons you shouldn't stray far. There are some marginal **campgrounds** up here with an outhouse, bear-resistant food lockers, and untreated water from Jumbo Stream. Eventually, after the turn-off to the Root Glacier, the trail turns east to the Stairway Icefall and the remains of the Erie Mine bunkhouse (another two miles each way).

Bonanza Mine (13–16 miles round-trip; 4–7hr; 3800ft ascent). A wonderful hike initially following a 4WD road and soon rising high above Kennicott as you approach the substantial ruins of Bonanza Mine. The road to the tree line is only passable by the fittest and most determined **mountain bikers**, but if you're motivated to ride up there it is a superb, and fast, ride down (though keep an eye out for ascending hikers). Start by following the Root Glacier Trail and turn uphill as you leave the last of the houses, then continue past the end of the road (roughly halfway) on a rough track past a fretwork of gantries and wooden pylons perched on rocky bluffs, still carrying cables strung as they were when everyone left town. **Carry water**, especially if you are planning to camp up here.

Goat Trail (25 miles one-way; 3–8 days; 3000ft net descent). The park's most popular fly-in multiday hike, which follows the Chisana prospectors' route through the narrow Chitistone Canyon, twenty miles east of McCarthy, and past the 400-foot Chitistone Falls, the highest continuously flowing falls in Alaska. It is a strenuous venture with several deep river crossings between the airstrips at each end. Expect to pay $200 for drop-off and pickup.

the road, camping out a night or two, and maybe taking off on some remote hikes. In many ways the **hiking** here is more accessible than from McCarthy, where you really need to fly in to reach the superior trails. The trouble is, most routes are also used by off-road vehicles and can be boggy underfoot: check at the Ranger Station. The excellent Caribou Creek Trail leads north from Mile 19.2 for four miles and can easily be extended; at miles 29 and 30.8 you'll find the trailheads for the Trail Creek/Lost Creek Loop, offering day-hikes or a longer backpacking route over a ridge; and the Skookum Volcano Trail, from Mile 36.2, is a strenuous hike, only 2.5 miles long but climbing 2800ft through striking eroded volcanic rocks, where you should see Dall sheep.

The road is mostly gravel, but it is open all year and is generally in better condition than the McCarthy Road. Glacial stream crossings at miles 29 (Trail Creek), 30.8, and 34.3 sometimes make the road impassable to ordinary vehicles in hot weather and after heavy rain.

Slana and along the Nabesna Road

The Nabesna Road runs east from the Tok Cutoff at tiny **SLANA** (Mile 60), little more than a ranger station (Mile 0.2; late May to early Sept daily 8am–5pm, winter by appointment; ℡822-5238) and post office (Mile 0.8); the former is the place to call for advice on road conditions, park-related information, and the free *Nabesna Road Guide*. There's comfortable B&B **accommodation** at *Hart D Ranch*, Mile 0.7 Nabesna Rd (℡822-3973, Ⓦwww.hartd.com; ❻), also with space for tents and RVs ($25 dry, $32 with electricity), and at *Nabesna House*, Mile 0.8 (℡822-4284, Ⓦwww .nabesnahouse.com; ❸), with satellite TV and Internet access; but the lovely, rustic *Huck Hobbit's Homestead Retreat & Campground* (℡822-3196; cabins $20 per person, camping $5 per person) is more entertaining, with its cozy log cabins with wood stoves, campsites each with picnic table and fire ring, canoes for rent ($35 a day), and bargain meals. It is four miles east of Slana, then up a four-mile side road: the last mile can only be negotiated on foot or mountain bike or by ATV, so be sure to call ahead.

Beyond the end of the paved road, four miles from Slana, very few places offer any sort of facilities. Primitive **campgrounds** at *Dead Dog Hill*, Mile 17.8, *Rock Lake*, Mile 21.8, *Twin Lakes*, Mile 27.8, and *Jack Creek*, Mile 35.3, have outhouses and some sort of water supply, but if you come equipped you can pitch pretty much anywhere you find flat ground. One especially scenic spot is at Mile 16.6, with views across Kettle Lake to Mount Sanford (the fifth-highest in the US) and dozens of its neighbors. A quarter-mile north of the road at Mile 22, opposite Rock Lake, *Viking Lodge* is a new cabin that must be booked through Slana Ranger Station ($25; ℡822-5238).

At Mile 24.7 you cross the watershed divide from the headwaters of the Copper River (which flows into the North Pacific) to the headwaters of rivers flowing into the Yukon and the Bering Sea. Locals and the occasional visitor converge on *Sportsman's Paradise Lodge*, Mile 29 (℡822-5426, Ⓔdfrederick@starband.net; ❷), more for the convivial **bar** than the basic cabin accommodation or the very limited food and gas. You can press on to the end of the maintained road at Mile 42, where there's a rough airstrip and the rustic *Devil's Mountain Lodge* and *End of the Road B&B* (℡822-5312). You're still four miles from the Nabesna Mine site itself, where almost all the mine buildings are still standing and the owner's permission, acquired through the National Park Service, is required to enter.

The Glenn Highway to Glennallen

The **Glenn Highway** – and its logical and geographical continuation, the **Tok Cutoff** (see p.469) – is the shortest road route from Anchorage to the Lower 48, meeting the Alaska Highway at Tok, 328 miles to the northeast. The highway, named after the nineteenth-century explorer Captain Edwin Glenn, was opened in 1942 as an upgrade of the old track system that connected Anchorage to the then-under-construction Alaska Highway, and paved by 1952.

The entire road runs through sparsely populated country that, even on good asphalt, still feels very remote as you climb from one watershed to another over a series of low passes. Initially, you ascend beside the Matanuska River, which drains west to Cook Inlet, but you eventually end up beside the Tazlina Valley, which spills down the Copper River into Prince William Sound. There's some very fine scenery, too, with the Talkeetna, Alaska, and Chugach ranges soaring up on either side and immense glaciers poking out of the mountains.

The presence of a fast highway seems to encourage people to drive straight through in a few hours, and while there are few specific attractions there is a fair bit to see, with some perseverance. Wildlife may be more elusive than in Denali, but the animals are out there: the Dall sheep usually far up the roadside crags, bears in the woods, wolves crossing the tundra, moose in and around the small lakes, and caribou roaming the glacial river bars.

Sutton, Chickaloon, and the Matanuska Glacier

Leaving Anchorage, the Glenn Highway runs past Eagle River and Eklutna and into Palmer in the Matanuska Valley before swinging east. Pulling out of Palmer (Mile 42) on the Glenn Highway you first pass the junction with the Palmer–Fishhook Road (Mile 49.5, for Hatcher Pass and Independence Mine) and continue a dozen miles to **Sutton**, a small community which flourished in the 1920s around a rail siding from the days when this was coal country. The only reason to pause is the **Alpine Historical Park**, Mile 61.5 (mid-May to mid-Sept daily 9am–7pm; donation appreciated), a selection of relocated buildings on the former site of the Sutton Coal Washery, including the Chickaloon Bunkhouse and a coal museum in the old Sutton post office with material on the construction of the Glenn Highway and the local Athabascans.

From Sutton the highway winds along the Matanuska Valley, gradually climbing as you penetrate deeper into the mountains that tower on both sides. After fifteen miles a wide spot in the road with a post office, small store, and gas station constitutes **Chickaloon** (Mile 76.5), once site of a coal mine at the end of the Matanuska rail branch. It's home to Nova (T 1-800/746-5753, W www.novalaska.com), which runs the most popular **rafting** trip in Alaska – the four-hour Class III–IV **Lion Head** (June–Aug 9am & 2pm; $80 & $90 respectively) along the upper reaches of the Matanuska River, for which there is a minimum age of 12. Highly scenic and with a stop to explore the foot of the Matanuska Glacier, it is a wonderful trip made all the better by taking the evening run (mid-June to mid-July 7pm; $100) when the day's meltwater is at its peak – they even stop for a mid-trip burger. Downstream from Chickaloon township, the river relents to Class II, run on the gentle, family-oriented Matanuska trip (June–Aug; 2hr 30min; $75, kids aged 5–11 $40). Across the road from the Nova office sits *King Mountain Lodge* (T 745-4280), which has been serving down-home Alaskan meals for over fifty years, and has a bar full

7

△ Ice climbers on the Matanuska Glacier

of wise-cracking signs and a small stage for weekend bands. You can camp at the adjacent *King Mountain State Recreation Site* ($15; pump water) among the white spruce, some sites with river and King Mountain views.

The scenery just keeps getting better further up the valley and is made more inviting by the presence of the diminutive **Lower Bonnie Lake**, a day-use area two miles off the highway at Mile 83.2, which has good grayling-fishing throughout the summer.

Around Mile 100 you catch your first glimpse of the **Matanuska Glacier**, a 24-mile-long tongue of ice poking out of the Chugach Mountains. During the last ice age it stretched as far as Palmer, and though it has been chipped back considerably, it's still almost four miles wide at its terminus. Close contact can only be achieved by parting with $10 to drive to within three hundred yards of the foot of the glacier through *Glacier Park Campground*, Mile 102 (℡745-2534 or 1-800/253-4480; mid-May to mid-Oct). From the end of the road, you can hike onto the glacier and visit the office of MICA Guides (℡1-800/956-6422, Ⓦwww.micaguides.com), which runs guided **glacier treks** (1hr 30min for $35, minimum 4 people; 3hr for $70, minimum 2 people) and beginner **ice-climbing** trips (6hr for $130, minimum 2 people). There's dry camping for $10 per site at the nearby *Matanuska Glacier State Recreation Site*, which also has telescopes for viewing the glacier.

You'll find more distant, but still impressive, views of the glacier from the short hiking trails that thread along a bluff from *Matanuska Glacier State Recreation Site*, Mile 101.1 ($15 per site; pump water), or from the magnificent picture windows at the hunting-lodge-style *Long Rifle Lodge*, Mile 102.2 (℡745-5151 or 1-800/770-5151; ❸).They serve excellent homemade meals and have pleasant but functional rooms.

Tahetna Pass to Lake Louise

Excellent views of the Matanuska Glacier continue as you climb steadily east past Lion Head, a small mountain right in the middle of the valley named for its appearance from the east. Beyond Lion Head the valley opens out into country that's great for hiking or just sitting back with binoculars spotting wildlife. There are a couple of good **places to stay** in these parts. The lovely *Tundra Rose B&B*, Mile 109.5 (℡1-800/315-5865, Ⓦwww.alaska.net/~tundrose; suite ❺, cottage ❹), with its fabulous glacier views, is based around a log-built home with adjacent self-catering cottage and two-bedroom suite. Just below a hill renowned for its population of Dall sheep stands *Sheep Mountain Lodge*, Mile 113.5 (℡1-877/645-5121, Ⓦwww.sheepmountain.com; cabins ❻, bunkhouse ❶), with ten spacious, fully fixtured cabins, plus a bunkhouse (summer only; $60 plus tax for the first 4 people and $5 for each extra up to a total of 8). There's also a hot tub and sauna (free to cabin guests, bunkhouse users $5) and a modestly priced **restaurant** that is a substantial cut above the average roadside diner, serving classy homemade meals and drinks from a well-stocked bar.

Glance back for a view of Lion Head, then press on past the **Squaw Creek** viewpoint and trailhead (Mile 118.4), from where you can hike north for up to three days, to the 3000-foot **Tahetna Pass** (Mile 121), site of a couple of lodges and a gas station, and a good spot to look back at **Gunsight Mountain**, visible for miles approaching from the east, and distinguished by the missing-tooth serration on its summit ridgeline. The road passes the 1937 *Eureka Roadhouse*, the oldest on this highway and heart of one of the state's three most popular snowmobiling areas, to the 3321-foot Eureka Summit (Mile 129), the highest point on the Glenn Highway. Views now expand south to the ice-capped Chugach Mountains and north across flatter country pocked by myriad small lakes and threaded by narrow creeks, and you may see northern hawk owls sitting on trees and poles in the daytime. The road stays high for a time, until you reach the Little Nelchina River and the small, waterside *Little Nelchina River Campground*, Mile 137.5 (free; river water). At Mile 135 the *Slide Mountain Cabins & RV Park* (℡822-3883, Ⓦwww.rvparkalaska.com) has five cabins (❸–❺) and two simple rooms sharing a bathroom (❶) plus space for tents; at Mile 143.3 *Nelchina Lodge* (℡822-4555, Ⓦwww.nelchinalodge.com) has motel rooms (❹) and cabins (❷), all with microwave and coffeemaker.

Lake Louise

At Mile 159.8 a scenic gravel road spurs nineteen miles north to the shores of **Lake Louise**, a popular spot with vacationing Alaskans, chiefly for chilly swimming and lake trout-fishing, the latter best done in spring and early summer. Campers can stay right by the lake at the *Lake Louise State Recreation Area*, Mile 19.3 ($15 per vehicle or $5 for walk-in sites; pump water), the less hardy at *The Point Lodge*, Mile 17 (☎1-800/808-2018, ⓦwww.thepointlodge.com; ❺), which has its own family-style restaurant and a bar, and caters for those wanting to fish, boat, hike, and go flightseeing.

Glennallen and the central highways

Glennallen is effectively the hub of the central highway system, from which the major roads spoke out to just about everywhere of interest, including Wrangell-St Elias National Park to the southeast. Coming from Anchorage, you arrive on the Glenn Highway, which continues to Tok as the Tok Cutoff. Crossing the Glenn Highway is the Richardson Highway, following the original trail from Valdez, on the coast, to the heart of the state at Fairbanks.

Glennallen

Glennallen, 139 miles east of Palmer (Mile 187 Glenn Hwy), is far enough away from everywhere else that almost everyone passing through stops here, if only for gas and a bite to eat. Apart from wonderful views of mounts Sanford (16,237ft), Drum (12,010ft), Wrangell (14,163ft), and Blackburn (16,390ft) to the east, there's little reason to stay, though the town, being at the hub of the Interior highway system, has adequate lodging for long-haul drivers. Those needing transport into the Wrangell-St Elias National Park may also find themselves stopping overnight. The town straggles along the highway for a couple of miles east of the intersection of the Glenn and Richardson highways at **Glennallen Junction** (Mile 114.9 of the Richardson Highway, Mile 189 of the Glenn), where you'll find the Copper River Valley **visitor center** (summer daily 8am–7pm; ☎822-5555, ⓦwww.traveltoalaska .com). The only actual activity in town is walking the **Aspen Interpretive Trail**, from Mile 0.25 Co-op Rd, west of the post office, which leads north for a mile through aspen and white spruce forest into sedge meadow where you may see Alaska's only amphibian (thanks to its unique natural antifreeze), the wood frog.

Bus travelers using Alaska Direct buses will be dropped in Glennallen outside the *Caribou Hotel* (see p.468); Alaska/Yukon Trails passengers are dropped at Glennallen Junction and may have to walk or thumb into Glennallen. For information on both lines, see Basics, p.44.

For **buses into the Wrangell–St Elias National Park** along the McCarthy Road, contact Backcountry Connections or Mountain Kingdom Express (see p.452), which pick up in Glennallen and around the region. Alternatively, you can **rent a vehicle** to drive the McCarthy Road from Northwind Car Rental behind the Chevron at Mile 187 (☎822-5600, ⓔnorthwind@glennallenak.net) for around $80 a day.

Crack-of-dawn departures mean that those without their own vehicles will probably have to spend the night **camping** here, either at the *Northern Nights Campground and RV Park*, Mile 188.7, close to the visitor center (☎822-3199, ⓔnnites@yahoo.com; tent $12, full hookup $20), or just dossing down in any quiet spot available. The *Dry Creek State Recreation Site*, Mile 118, three miles north of Glennallen Junction ($10 per site; pump water), is better suited to drivers and comes with some quiet walk-in tent sites but lots of mosquitoes.

For a roof over your head you have the choice of **cabins and rooms** at the *Caribou Hotel*, Mile 186.6 (☎1-800/478-3302 in Alaska, ⓦwww .caribouhotel.com; ❸–❼), which has free coffee and Internet at reception, or a B&B such as *Fireweed Hill B&B*, behind Parks Place groceries at Mile 187.8 (☎822-3627, ⓦwww.alaska.net/~dmbowler; ❸). There is better **dining** further afield at Gulkana and Copper Center (see below), but Glennallen has some options, plus summertime espresso stalls beside the highway. You can fill your stomach adequately at the *Caribou Restaurant*, part of the *Caribou Hotel* complex, which serves the usual steak, halibut, and buffalo burgers, *Panther Pizza*, Mile 186.5, and the *Hitchin' Post*, Mile 187.3 (☎822-3338), which is noted for its $4 breakfast specials, but is otherwise a poor alternative.

If you've got to get a few things sorted, you'll find everything you need along the Glenn Highway: a **BLM office** (Mon–Fri 8am–4.30pm; ☎822-3217) at Mile 186.4, with leaflets and trail guides in racks outside; the **library** (Mile 186); the **pharmacy** and 24-hour emergency clinic of Cross Road Medical Center (☎822-3203) at Mile 186.5; the **post office** (Mile 186.9); a **bank** and **ATM** (Mile 187); and **laundry** and **groceries** (Mile 187.5).

South of Glennallen: the Richardson Highway

South of Glennallen, the Richardson Highway (see box, p.470) runs 120 miles to Valdez on the shores of Prince William Sound. Much of it crosses open country studded with permafrost-stunted spruce, often with stupendous views east to the snow-shrouded Wrangell Mountains. It is a solid, year-round paved road, occasionally dotted with roadhouses, some with cabins, plus primitive RV parks and campsites and usually fuel. That said, it is best to fill the tank and stock up with food if you're planning to make use of the lovely **campgrounds** along the way.

This is also the primary access route for the Wrangell-St Elias National Park, which maintains its headquarters **visitor center** at Mile 106.8 (see p.452). Stop for a great view of the mountains and a look at the film even if you're not headed into the park.

Copper Center

Swing briefly off the Richardson Highway between miles 106.1 and 100.1 along the Old Richardson Highway to visit the half-Athabascan hamlet of **Copper Center**, which boomed in 1898 when three hundred stampeders who made it over the Valdez and Klutina glaciers stopped here at the ferry crossing for the Copper River. They came to recuperate, but there was little comfort through the harsh winter and many died, their headstones still evident in the **Stampeders Cemetery** in town. At the southern end of the village, *Uncle Nicolai's Copper Rail Depot*, incorporating some 1914 CR&NW lineside cabins, is a bar (Mon–Sat 6–11pm) with a wonderfully detailed model of Kennecott out the back ($2 to non-patrons) plus a gift shop, laundry, and budget rooms (❷).

The heart of town beats around the 🎋 *Copper Center Lodge*, Mile 101 Old Richardson Highway (☎822-3245, ⓦwww.coppercenterlodge.com; ❺), an authentic descendant of the original 1896 roadhouse with smallish, fairly ordinary rooms, plus a good restaurant. Two log bunkhouses, formerly part of the lodge, now operate as the **George Ashby Memorial Museum** (mid-April to May Sat & Sun 10am–4pm; June to mid-Sept daily 11am–5pm; donations appreciated), packed to the rafters with memorabilia from the stampede and the copper years along with Athabascan basketwork, traps, ancient outboard motors, and a 1950s snowmobile, plus evocative photos of prospectors crossing the glaciers in 1898. Just north of the lodge, *The Fishing Widow* sells the best espressos and ices for miles around, and across the Old Richardson Highway is the 1942 log Chapel on the Hill. Heading west from Mile 102 Old Richardson Highway and crossing the main Richardson Highway on Klutina Lake Road, you'll soon come to the *Copper River Princess Wilderness Lodge* (℡1-800/426-0500, Wwww.princessalaskalodges.com; ●; mid-May to mid-Sept), a large hotel set high on a bluff. Even if you're not staying, call in for lunch or a drink and soak up the fabulous mountain views from the lounge, or ask for the free map of trails around the hotel.

Through the Chugach Mountains

A dozen miles south of Copper Center at Mile 88.7, it's worth turning off at a pipeline viewpoint if you haven't already seen it near Fairbanks; just south there's also a viewpoint for the volcanoes of the Wrangell range. At Mile 82.6 McCarthy-bound drivers turn east along the Edgerton Highway (see p.453), while those continuing south towards Valdez pass the forest-girt *Squirrel Creek State Recreation Site* ($10 per site; pump water), with some nice waterside sites at Mile 79.5 opposite a gas station selling snacks. At Mile 79 the current incarnation of the *Tonsina River Lodge* (℡822-3000, Wwww.tonsinariverlodge.com; ●) sits next to the disused 1929 lodge, moved here from Fort Liscum, across the bay from Valdez; there's space for RVs ($12) and tents ($5) and a diner (6am–11pm) with a Mexican menu and ATM, plus free WiFi and satellite TV. Although the pipeline runs parallel to the road for much of the way, it is most evident fifteen miles on around **Pump Station No. 12**, Mile 64.8, which forces the oil over the Chugach Mountains ahead. As you start to climb up towards **Thompson Pass**, you'll pass a couple of handy roadhouses: *Tiekel River Lodge*, Mile 55.9 (℡822-3259, Wwww.tiekelriverlodge.com; cabins ●, with private bath ●; March–Oct), which has dry RV and tent camping ($10) plus cabins and gas; and *Tsaina Lodge*, Mile 34.6 (℡835-3500, Wwww.alaska.net/~tsaina; cabins ●; March to early Sept), set amid majestic sawtooth ridges and offering a restaurant, bar, cabins, and a bunkhouse. The new *Alaska Rendezvous Lodge*, Mile 45.7 (℡1-888/634-0721, Wwww.arlinc.com), is open all year but is busiest during the heli-ski season (March to early May); it's a friendly youth- and activity-oriented place with sauna, massage, WiFi, and a lively restaurant. Rooms (●) are in a new lodge, but RV parking is free if you're skiing with them.

Northeast of Glennallen: the Tok Cutoff

A single road runs fourteen miles north from Glennallen to **Gakona Junction**, where you can continue straight on along the Richardson Highway bound for Delta Junction (see p.472), or turn right to travel along a section of the Glenn Highway known as the **Tok Cutoff**. The latter route runs along the Copper River, then sneaks over a low pass in the Mentasta Mountains into the

Thompson Pass, Keystone Canyon, and the run into Valdez are covered on p.328, and Chitina, McCarthy, and Kennicott on pp.452–461.

spruce forests around Tok, 125 miles away. There's not a lot to stop for along the way, and you can cover the distance in a little over two hours, though you could consider exploring the **Nabesna Road** into the northern reaches of the Wrangell-St Elias National Park (see p.462).

Like all such Alaskan roads, the Tok Cutoff is thinly peopled, with only the occasional roadhouse and gas station. The busiest section of the highway is the first five miles, where you'll pass through **Gakona**, centered around the *Gakona Lodge*, Mile 2 Tok Cutoff (☎822-3482, ⓦwww.gakonalodge .com; ❹), an authentic 1929 roadhouse on the site of an old ranch, with the affordable *Carriage House* restaurant next to the Gakona River. It is a mile on to River Wrangellers (☎1-888/822-3967, ⓦwww.riverwrangellers .com), which operates **rafting trips**, pretty much to order, on seven rivers in the Wrangell Mountains and Copper River Valley, such as the full-day trip ($190) on the Class III Tonsina River, famed for its fast, glacier-blue waters and high cliffs.

A few years ago the roadhouse in the hamlet of **Chistochina**, Mile 33, burnt down and hasn't been rebuilt, so you barely notice the place as you drive by, though there are a couple of B&Bs in the area if you need to stop.

The **Nabesna Road** (see p.462), which cuts off at the hamlet of Slana (Mile 60), provides the only diversion on the road north, passing a couple of **campgrounds**, both with pump water: the scenic streamside *Porcupine Creek State Recreation Site*, Mile 64.1 ($12 per vehicle), and *Eagle Trail State Recreation Site*, Mile 109.3 ($15). The latter has a mile-long nature trail and a 2.5-mile hiking trail to an overview of the Tok Valley with evidence of the old Valdez-Eagle Trail and the telegraph line that followed it. There is even scope to hike up Clearwater Creek for around eight hours to get into Dall sheep country. From here it is sixteen miles to the crossroads town of Tok (see p.476).

The Richardson Highway

The **Richardson Highway** is the oldest road in the Interior, yet in its full 368-mile journey from Valdez to Fairbanks it never passes through anything more than a small town. Its original construction was prompted by the abominable suffering of those who tried the Valdez Glacier route to the Yukon goldfields in the winter of 1898 (see p.469). The following year, Congress approved funds for the US Army to build a military road linking Fort Liscum in Valdez with Fort Egbert in Eagle, and Captain Abercrombie began surveying the route on April 21. Using sleds, packhorses, and mules in trying conditions made worse by harsh weather and mosquitoes, he soon had the Goat Trail cut through Keystone Canyon, bypassing the Valdez Glacier. In the few short months of summer, 93 miles of wagon road were forged and a further 114 miles were cleared and the streams bridged. The road was completed in 1900, but the gold-rush focus soon shifted to Fairbanks, and so did the main trail. The full journey from Valdez to Fairbanks could take up to two weeks, with travelers spending nights in roadhouses spaced a day's travel apart, which was particularly important during the winter when they had to journey in open carriages (the roads were so rough that closed carriages induced motion sickness) with only wolf robes and a charcoal brazier for warmth. General Wilds Richardson had the road upgraded to a wagon road in 1907, the Alaska Roads Commission improved it for automobile use in 1920 (although the first car had made its way from Valdez to Fairbanks in 1913), and the road was finally paved in 1957.

North of Glennallen: the Richardson Highway

North of Glennallen, the Richardson Highway runs fourteen miles to **Gakona Junction** and continues 137 miles to Delta Junction, initially traveling through open, rolling country peppered with small lakes feeding tiny streams that flow into the Gulkana River just to the west. **Campers** should consider stopping nineteen miles north of Gakona Junction at the BLM's large *Sourdough Creek Campground*, Mile 147.5 ($8 per site; pump water), within sight of the Trans-Alaska Pipeline's crossing of the Gulkana River. Sites are dotted among the sparse black spruce, and it comes equipped with a fishing deck, observation platform, and boat ramp where canoeists paddling the Gulkana (see box, p.443) pull out; there's also a mile-long trail (leaflet available). If you are not kitted out for cooking, you can still stop here and stroll a couple of hundred yards north to **eat** at the friendly *Sourdough Roadhouse* (☎822-7122), which has cabins and space for RVs (❹). The Richardson then begins to climb into the foothills of the Alaska Range, imperceptibly at first (passing trails west to the Gulkana River at miles 161 and 169), then more forthrightly as it rounds the 2641-foot Hogan Hill on the way to *Meier's Lake Roadhouse*, Mile 170 (☎822-3151), offering gas, groceries, showers, a mediocre restaurant, and boat rental for use on the nearby lake. Next door is the better *Atwater's Chateau Motel* (☎822-3151; ❹), although most rooms are occupied by construction crews in June and July.

At Mile 175 a side road leads a mile and a half down to the extensive, partly lakeside *Paxson Lake Campground* ($4 walk-in, $8 drive-in; pump water), with a dump station and a boat launch for the Gulkana River canoe trip to *Sourdough Campground* (see box, p.439).

Ten miles on, **Paxson**, Mile 185.3, marks the eastern end of the Denali Highway (see p.319), but comprises little more than the gas, basic food, and unappealing lodging at the dire *Paxson Inn & Lodge*. If you are looking for a **place to stay** (summer only), there's *Denali Highway Cabins* (☎822-5972, Ⓦwww.denalihwy.com; ❺) at the rear of the lodge, with some superb modern log cabins, each with private bath, TV, a small deck looking out towards Paxson Mountain, and the sound of the Gulkana River right outside. The owner, an avid birder and ecologist, runs Paxson Alpine Tours, which runs day hikes and the four-hour Evening Wildlife Float Trips ($45 per person, minimum 3 people) in a raft through the Paxson Wildlife Reserve, with the emphasis firmly on spotting nesting waterfowl and eagles, spawning sockeye salmon, moose, and whatever else might turn up.

From midsummer well into September, **red salmon** can be seen spawning right by the highway from a turnout (and outhouse) at Mile 190.2. The road then skirts Summit Lake, which is appropriately named, though with the mass of the Alaska Range stretching to the horizon in both directions you barely realize you are anywhere near a summit. In fact, the 3000-foot **Isabel Pass** lies just ahead with the **Gulkana Glacier** bearing down on it from the northeast. A 1.5-mile access road off Mile 200.4 of the Richardson runs to *Fielding Lake State Recreation Site*, where there's an appealing lakeside **campground** (free; lake water) and six-person cabin ($25 off-peak, $35 peak), with a boat ramp heavily used by fishers after lake trout, burbot, and grayling. The highway then follows the Delta River through a gap in the Alaska Range, where red and gray scree slopes cascade down the mountainsides, and continues to **Black Rapids Glacier**, Mile 225.4. It is now a retreating shadow of what it was in the winter of 1936–37 when this "Galloping Glacier" surged over three miles, almost overrunning the road: mounds of terminal moraine can be seen half a mile west of the highway. A 500-yard hike on the east side of the road leads to Black Rapids Lake, a good **fishing** hole. At Mile 227 *The Lodge at Black Rapids* (☎455-6158, ⓦwww.blackrapids.org), overlooking the Rapids Roadhouse (built in about 1902 and now being restored as an art gallery, gift shop, and museum), will give a great view of the glacier when it opens in June 2007.

The Delta Valley now broadens out past another appealing campground, the *Donnelly Creek State Recreation Site*, Mile 238 ($10 per site; pump water), and on to a couple of spectacular viewpoints: at Mile 241.3, where panels explain the genesis of the **Delta buffalo herd** (see below), which can often be seen in the distance across the river; and at Mile 244, where there are stupendous views south to the dominant peaks of the Alaska Range – Deborah, Hess, and Hayes. Four miles west, a short gravel road from Mile 247.9 leads to a trailhead for a well-worn but unmarked path leading up the north ridge of the 3910-foot **Donnelly Dome** (1900ft ascent), the alder and willow eventually thinning to reveal a great view of the Delta and Tanana rivers and the Alaska Range. Delta Junction is another eighteen miles on, beyond **Pump Station No. 9** (Mile 258), and the Fort Greely military base (see below).

Delta Junction and the road to Fairbanks

DELTA JUNCTION (Mile 1422 Alaska Hwy, Mile 266 Richardson Hwy) proclaims itself to be the end of the Alaska Highway, which starts 1422 miles to the southeast in British Columbia. Technically, this is accurate, as the remaining 98 miles of road to Fairbanks (the Richardson Highway) already existed when the Alaska Highway was completed in 1942. The Delta Junction CVB does brisk business selling "I completed the Alaska Highway" certificates; however, most people wait to celebrate their endeavors when they get to Fairbanks, a real city and a more fitting end to such an epic trip.

Still, Delta Junction makes a better spot to recuperate than Tok, with its attractive farmland homesteads stretching all the way east to the Clearwater River system. To the south the Granite Mountains rise up majestically, and if you are lucky in spring and fall, skeins of migrating geese might fill the skies.

Though close to the old Valdez–Fairbanks Trail, Delta Junction, established in 1904 as a telegraph station, didn't really come into its own until the 1920s. It was known then as Buffalo Center, the site chosen for the government's **buffalo importation program**, designed to establish a sporting herd in Alaska five hundred years after the species had died out here. In 1928, 23 Minnesota plains bison were released and immediately developed a taste for the local barley crop. They still occasionally wander onto farmland around harvest time, but since its creation in 1979 the 90,000-acre Bison Range, some twenty miles to the south of Delta Junction, keeps them occupied. Today the herd is around five hundred strong and can withstand a winter hunting season, during which 15,000 hunters pay $10 just to apply for one of the 65 permits, $450 each.

Since the founding of **Fort Greely** just south of town in 1942, Delta Junction has long had military influence. After its World War II service as a way station

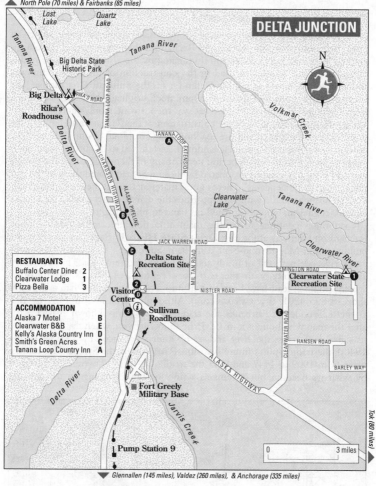

North Pole (70 miles) & Fairbanks (85 miles)

Lost Lake

Quartz Lake

Tanana River

DELTA JUNCTION

Tanana River

N

Big Delta State Historic Park

Volkmar Creek

TANANA LOOP ROAD

Big Delta

Rika's Roadhouse

RIKA'S ROAD

TANANA LOOP EXTENSION

A

ALASKA PIPELINE

RICHARDSON HIGHWAY

Delta River

Clearwater Lake

Tanana River

B

JACK WARREN ROAD

Clearwater River

C

Delta State Recreation Site

MILTAN ROAD

REMINGTON ROAD

Clearwater State Recreation Site

1

2

Visitor Center

D

NISTLER ROAD

3

i

Sullivan Roadhouse

E

CLEARWATER ROAD

HANSEN ROAD

ALASKA HIGHWAY

BARLEY WAY

Delta River

■ **Fort Greely Military Base**

Jarvis Creek

Tok (80 miles)

Pump Station 9

0   3 miles

RESTAURANTS	
Buffalo Center Diner	2
Clearwater Lodge	1
Pizza Bella	3

ACCOMMODATION	
Alaska 7 Motel	B
Clearwater B&B	E
Kelly's Alaska Country Inn	D
Smith's Green Acres	C
Tanana Loop Country Inn	A

Glennallen (145 miles), Valdez (260 miles), & Anchorage (335 miles)

for planes being sent to Russia under the Lend-Lease program, it was used for nerve gas research and also had a nuclear generator (operational from 1961 to 1971), which leaked in 1997. Its importance waned with the ending of the Cold War, and Fort Greely closed in 2001, only to be revived in 2003 for the new Ground-Based Midcourse Defense System (that's Star Wars to most people). One hundred **missile silos** (linked to a radar station on an old oil-rig off the Aleutian island of Adak) have been built and declared operational, although there's no sign that the system actually works. In addition, the new Pogo gold mine to the northeast of town and a possible natural gas distribution hub are helping the local economy diversify.

If you are in the vicinity around the last weekend of August, call ahead and check dates for the three-day **Deltana Fair**, a small-town agricultural fair with events such as the Cow Drop, in which a ten-by-ten checkerboard of two-foot squares is laid out and folk lay bets on where a cow will place its mark.

The town and around

Delta Junction lines the three main roads that make up the town, spreading out from the point where the Alaska and Richardson highways meet. This locus is marked by a microwave tower and dominated by the visitor center (see opposite), showcasing equipment used in the construction of the Alaska Highway and a pipeline scraper pig outside. Behind it sits the **Sullivan Roadhouse** (late May to mid-Sept Mon–Sat 9am–5.30pm; free), originally built eighteen miles from Delta Junction in 1905 on what was then a winter-only shortcut off the Valdez–Fairbanks route. With the construction of the Richardson Highway, the shortcut grew little used and the roadhouse lay abandoned from 1922 to 1996, when it was designated a historic landmark and moved to its current location. It has now been outfitted with period items, many of them originals – the double bed and stove in particular – donated by those who had looted them in the first place (or their descendants). There's good material, too, on the roadhouse tradition, all brought to life with excerpts from the diary of early roadhouse worker James Geoghegan, who also turned his hand to photography.

Roadhouses continue to be the main attraction nine miles north on the Richardson Highway at the **Big Delta State Historic Park** (site always open; buildings mid-May to mid-Sept daily 9am–5pm; free), a compact and manicured riverside park full of neatly tended c.1900 log buildings. They've missed a great opportunity with the two-story centerpiece, **Rika's Roadhouse**, which should at least have been turned into a museum, rather than a large gift shop (℡895-4201, Ⓦwww.rikas.com). Although established in 1904 by E.T. Barnette, founder of Fairbanks, the trading post became known as McCarty's after the man who bought it in 1905; the following year, when the army moved its signal post across the river and set up a ferry (replaced by a bridge in the 1940s), the trading post's future was sure. Rika Wallen, the Swede who ran the place from 1909 to 1947 and built the roadhouse in 1917, would be horrified by what it's become, but it remains a fine log-built building by the crossing

△ The Trans-Alaska Pipeline spans the Tanana River

of the Tanana River. Outside, things improve with assorted outbuildings, such as a Swedish-style barn, a spring house used as a cool store in summer, and a workshop now fitted out as a small **museum**, with artifacts from pioneer life. Here, too, is a WAMCATS telegraph station (see box, p.484) and a reasonable café/restaurant (mid-May to mid-Sept daily 9am–5pm). A couple of hundred yards north (Mile 275.4) the Alaska pipeline spans the Tanana River on a graceful 1200-foot suspension structure, the longest of its kind along the route.

Practicalities

That precious "I've driven the Alaska Highway" certificate can be obtained for a dollar at the **visitor center** (late May to early Sept daily 8am–8pm; ☎1-877/895-5068, ⓦwww.deltajunctionalaska.com) at the junction of the Richardson and Alaska highways. **Campers** are spoilt for choice here. Right in town you've got the wooded and convenient *Delta State Recreation Site*, Mile 267 ($10 per site; pump water), for tents only, and the better-equipped, RV-oriented *Smith's Green Acres RV Park and Campground*, 2428 Richardson Hwy, Mile 268 (☎1-800/895-4369, ⓦwww.greenacresrvpark.com), one of the most highly rated in the state, with full hookups for $26.50 and tent sites for $15, including showers. *Clearwater State Recreation Site*, eight miles north of Mile 1415 on the Alaska Highway ($10 per site; pump water), is even more appealing, beautifully tranquil as well as on the spring and fall migration routes of sandhill cranes and geese; and there's $5 parking space at Big Delta, beside Rika's Roadhouse, where there's a dump station.

For **rooms** try the spacious *Kelly's Alaska Country Inn* in the center of town at 1616 Richardson Hwy (☎895-4667, ⓦwww.kellysalaskacountryinn.com; ❹), where some rooms have kitchens; the *Clearwater B&B*, 3170 Clearwater Rd (☎895-4842, ⓔjay@davejay.org; ❸); *Tanana Loop Country Inn*, Tanana Loop Extension (☎895-4890; ❹), a log-built home on the New Hope commune six miles from town, with full kitchen access, plus Internet access and satellite TV; or the *Alaska 7 Motel*, Mile 270.3 (☎895-4848, ⓦwww.alaska7motel.com; ❹), which has rooms with satellite TV, bathtub, fridge, and coffeemaker (some with kitchenette).

If all you need is **groceries**, drop in at the IGA Food Cache, on the Fairbanks road, where you'll also find a great bakery, ice cream, and an espresso bar. More substantial fare is dished up across the street at *Buffalo Center Diner* (☎895-5989; 6am–10pm in summer), which has a range of buffalo burgers for around $10, and *Pizza Bella* (☎895-4841), by the visitor center. Alternatively, join Deltoids – as some locals call themselves – for steaks and burgers on the deck overlooking the river at *Clearwater Lodge* (☎895-5152), right by the *Clearwater State Recreation Site*. Local produce is sold at the **farmers market** by the Sullivan Roadhouse (Wed & Sat 10am–6pm).

Other everyday needs are catered for with a **post office** on the Richardson Highway a couple hundred yards north of the visitor center, a branch of Wells Fargo Bank with **ATM** by the Food Cache (there's another ATM at Mount McKinley Bank opposite *Pizza Bella*), a **laundry** two hundred yards north and, opposite, a **library** (Tues–Thurs 10am–6pm, Fri & Sat 10am–4pm, Sun noon–4pm) with a **book swap**. There's a health clinic (☎895-5100; 24hr emergency call-out) just north of the *Delta State Recreation Site*, Mile 267.

North of Delta Junction

The Richardson Highway chugs out of Delta Junction along the Tanana Valley, bound for Fairbanks almost a hundred miles north. It is sparsely populated country with only the odd roadhouse, a few simple campgrounds, and a lot of forest. After crossing the Tanana River nine miles north of town, right by Rika's Roadhouse (see p.475), you'll soon pass the turnoff to *Quartz Lake State Recreation Area*, three miles east of the Richardson Highway at Mile 277.8, a glassy lake stocked annually with rainbow trout, arctic char, and silver salmon, and supporting an ice-fishing shantytown in winter. There is lakeshore **camping** for $10.

With the exception of a few roadside viewpoints, there is really nothing to stop for unless you want to break your journey camping at one of the state recreation areas along the way. The best of these is *Harding Lake*, Mile 321.5 ($10; pump water), 1.5 miles off the highway with some quiet walk-in sites, lake swimming, volleyball, horseshoe and barbecue pits, and firewood for sale ($5). There's also the new and less developed *Birch Lake State Recreation Site* (Mile 305.2), with camping ($10 per vehicle) and a **cabin** ($25 off-peak, $35 peak) that's open only in winter, like most others in this area. Some thirty miles short of Fairbanks (Mile 334.8), you cross into the huge **Eielson Air Force Base** and drive parallel to the main runway, which is often busy, especially at times when half the world hates the United States: they're very touchy about that pipeline. Just after the entry flyover at Mile 341, the highway becomes dual-carriageway for its approach to Fairbanks, although the speed limit actually drops from 65mph to 55.

Almost the last open country before Fairbanks is **Chena Lakes Recreation Area**, Mile 347 Laurance Rd (always open; fee charged late May to early Sept; $4 per vehicle, $1 per bike), a set of dams and channels designed to prevent a repeat of Fairbanks' devastating 1967 flood. The road is paralleled for almost five miles by a bikeway on one side and a levee on the other, beyond which a floodable area is frequented by cranes, moose, and other wildlife. To the west is a recreation area with a lovely 2.5-mile nature trail, boating on Chena Lake (canoes $6 per hour or $24 per day; rowboats $8/$32), biking along the levees, and wooded **camping** ($10; pump water).

Tok and around

Most people have little reason to stop in **Tok** (pronounced *toke*), Mile 1314 Alaska Hwy, a scattered collection of RV parks, gas stations, motels, and diners at the junction of two major highways, also marked by a microwave tower. But for drivers arriving from Canada along the Alaska Highway, this is the first town of consequence and a thoroughly welcome opportunity to rest up, wash down the rig, fill up with Alaska-priced gas, and plan your next move. That said, there's certainly nothing to detain you for more than one night, and you may fancy cutting south along the Tok Cutoff (see p.469) towards Glennallen and the Wrangell Mountains, or following the Taylor Highway north to Chicken and Eagle. Heading for Fairbanks, it's an easy two hours to Delta Junction, a dead-straight run through spruce and silver birch with just a couple of lodges and RV parks along the way.

The settlement began life as Tokyo Camp, which provided workers' accommodation during the construction of the Alaska and Glenn highways in the early 1940s, and shortened its name during World War II. Although maintained as a way station on the highways, it got a boost in 1954, when the US Army built the now-defunct, eight-inch fuel supply pipeline from Haines through Tok to Fairbanks, and again in 1976, when four prominent 700-foot radio masts were built as a long-range aid to navigation.

Tok now acts as a service town for numerous Athabascan villages scattered around the vicinity (notably Tanacross at Mile 1326, where the Valdez-Eagle Trail crossed the Tanana River), but it thrives on passing visitors lured in by offers such as a free car wash with a tank of gas. Attractions don't rise much above the gift shops full of Alaska T-shirts and **Mukluk Land**, three miles west along the Alaska Highway at Mile 1317 (June–Aug daily 2–8pm; $5), where the minigolf, bouncy igloo, and gold-panning will keep the kids happy.

Practicalities

The Alaska Highway and Tok Cutoff meet at the town's main intersection, a stopping point for Alaska Direct and Alaska/Yukon Trails **buses** (see p.44 for details). Here you'll find the **Tok visitor center**, just west of Mile 1314 (early May to mid-Sept daily 8am–7pm; ℡883-5775, ⓦwww.tokalaskainfo.com), in what is reputed to be the largest wooden structure in the state. It's simply packed with information on the whole state and a selection of displays with stuffed animals, material on the 1990 fire, which nearly engulfed the town, and more. Next door is the **Alaska Public Lands Information Center** (mid-May to Aug daily 8am–8pm; Sept to mid-May Mon–Fri 8am–4.30pm; ℡883-5666/7, ⓦwww.nps.gov/aplic/center), stocked with specific material on wildlife and wilderness matters and showing wildlife films seven times a day. The Tetlin National Wildlife Refuge has a new headquarters at Mile 1.3 Borealis Ave (Mon–Fri 8am–4.30pm; ℡883-5312, ⓦtetlin.fws.gov), which dispenses information and also has a display of stuffed owls and a few books for sale.

If you just need food and cash, then Three Bears (Mon–Sat 7am–9pm, Sun 8am–8pm), almost opposite the visitor center, has a reasonable selection of **groceries**, free coffee, a branch of the Denali State Bank (Mon–Fri 10am–6pm), and an **ATM** (available whenever the shop is open). The **post office** (Mon–Fri 8.30am–12.30pm & 1.30–5pm) is just along the Alaska Highway towards Fairbanks.

RV parks abound in Tok, most charging $20–25 for full hookup, and all try to outdo each other, especially with WiFi facilities. The *Golden Bear Motel and RV Park*, Mile 124.3 Tok Cutoff (℡883-2561 or 1-866/883-2561, ⓔgoldenbear@aptalaska.net; ④), is consistently reliable, right in town, and has full hookup for $20, dry camping for $10, $3 showers, modern motel rooms, and good **espresso** at the *Grumpy Grizz Café*. The *Sourdough Campground & RV Park*, a mile and a quarter down the Glenn Highway towards Anchorage (at Prospector Way; ℡883-5543, ⓦwww.sourdoughcampground.com), has

Moving on from Tok

Drivers headed west towards Fairbanks should continue with our account of Delta Junction (p.472); those headed southwest to Glennallen, Anchorage, and the Wrangell-St Elias National Park should follow our account of the Tok Cutoff (p.469) in reverse order. The Alaska Highway to the Canadian border, and the Taylor and Top of the World highways to Eagle and Dawson City, are covered on the following pages.

Hitchhikers might expect that, as an important junction, it would be easy to thumb a lift from Tok, but for some reason it isn't. People have been known to wait days, and those bound for Canada can be turned back at the border. This may be a good time to engage one of the **bus services** (for the lowdown on routes, see Travel details, p.488), which stop close to the junction of the Alaska Highway and Tok Cutoff: Alaska Direct by Village Gas, opposite *Tok RV Park*, and Alaska/Yukon Trails by the visitor center.

wooded sites, unmetered showers, free WiFi, and laundry facilities; RV sites are open all year ($25 with electricity only), while in summer sites with water and electricity cost $26, full hookup is $30, and tent sites are $16. Dry RVers can also **stay free** at the site behind the *Gateway Salmon Bake* (see below) in return for the purchase of a meal. **Campers** wanting a little more tranquility can head eighteen miles northwest to *Moon Lake State Recreation Site*, Mile 1332 ($15 per site; pump water), with a boat launch, picnic area, good swimming, and even access for float-planes, which can often be seen tethered to the bank. Alternatively, go five miles east to the *Tok River State Recreation Site*, Mile 1309.3 ($15 per site; pump water), on the east bank of the Tok River, where there's a boat launch plus hiking and dog-mushing trails.

If you aren't camping, the cheapest **place to stay** is the *Tok Hostel* (☏883-3745, ✉tokstouts@hotmail.com; ❶; mid-May to mid-Sept), a rustic place in an ex-army tent with electricity, good hot showers (unless you're third in line), and two dorms ($10). It's neither in town nor well signposted – to find it head eight miles west along the Alaska Highway (Mile 1322.5), then 0.7 miles down Pringle Drive.

Winter Cabin B&B, Mile 1316.5 Alaska Hwy (☏883-5655, ✇www.alaska -wintercabin.com; ❸), is a far better bet with cozy and well-equipped wild-animal-themed log cabins in the forest 2.5 miles west of town. Next to the Three Bears grocery in the center, the *Snowshoe Motel* (☏883-4511, 1-800/478-4511, ✉snowshoe@aptalaska.net; ❹) includes breakfast and satellite TV, plus a good craft shop. At Mile 1314 *Burnt Paw Cabins* (☏883-4121, ✇www.burnt-tpawcabins.com; ❺, ❸ off-season) has sod roofs but modern interiors with TV, coffeemaker, hairdryer, and breakfast included.

Good all-you-can-eat **meals** of salmon, halibut, and reindeer are served all day at the *Gateway Salmon Bake*, Mile 1313.1 Alaska Hwy, for around $19 (summer only); the nearby *Fast Eddy's*, Mile 1313.3 (☏883-4411; from 6am all year to 11pm summer, 10pm winter), serves a broad selection of diner fare along with gourmet pizzas ($20 buys enough for two) and groaning plates of nachos ($8). **Internet access** is available at Chickadee Business Network at Caribou Books, the first building on the left on the Tok Cutoff (Mon–Fri noon–9pm).

Towards the Canadian border: the Tetlin National Wildlife Refuge

Heading southeast from Tok, the Alaska Highway runs towards the **Canadian border**, 92 miles away at Mile 1222. The initial arrow-straight twelve miles takes you past a burnt permafrost area, the *Tok River State Recreation Site*, Mile 1309.3 (see above), and the Coast Guard's Loran station to **Tetlin Junction**, Mile 1301.7, where the Taylor Highway heads north to Chicken, Eagle, and Dawson City in the Yukon.

Along most of the remaining 65 miles to the border, the Alaska Highway forms the northern boundary of the **Tetlin National Wildlife Refuge** (✇tetlin.fws.gov), broad marshy flatlands spotted with hundreds of miniature lakes. These feed the Nabesna and Chisana rivers, which make up the headwaters of the Tanana River, one of Alaska's major fluvial arteries. These wetlands are right on the migration flightpath and provide a perfect stopover for one of the highest densities of waterfowl in the state – 115 nesting species and 73 migrants – as well as large numbers of black and grizzly bears, moose, caribou, wolves, and beavers. The Alaska Highway provides access to the northern reaches of the refuge, along with various pullouts: interpretive panels at Mile 1228; Desper Creek (Mile 1226), with a canoe launch spot; Highway Lake

The Alaska Highway and the Canadian border

About the best way to earn a true appreciation of what Alaska is all about is to drive there through northern Canada along the epic **Alaska Highway** – formerly the AlCan and still sometimes known by that name. It will only give you the vaguest sense of what early prospectors and trappers were up against, but you'll at least realize just how far Alaska is from everywhere else: once you hit the Yukon Territory, you're still almost nine hundred miles from Fairbanks.

The 1422-mile Alaska Highway (85 percent of it in Canada) was built in response to the United States' entry into World War II. A route was selected to link a series of pre-existing air bases through the Canadian north and construction began on March 9, 1942 with coopted US soldiers (half of them African-Americans, who were not wanted in combat units) working from both ends in atrocious conditions: mosquitoes, mountains, swamps, frigid rivers, and astonishingly bad weather even for these latitudes. Incredibly, the two teams met less than seven months after starting, a magnificent effort costing $140 million. However, the highway was in a poor state for the next few years, and the bulk of the military supplies always came by sea. It is now paved throughout and is constantly being improved (and shortened). Travelers driving the Alaska Highway right through British Columbia and the Yukon should obtain a copy of the *Rough Guide to Canada*, though there's some coverage in this book in Basics (see p.28). Once on Alaskan turf, it is two hundred miles to the "official" end of the Alaska Highway at Delta Junction, where the road meets the Richardson Highway for the final 98 miles to Fairbanks.

Crossing the Canadian border

Alaska and Canada's Yukon share two border crossings: the important **Alaska Highway crossing** (open 24 hours all year), 92 miles east of Tok, and the summer-only **Top of the World Highway crossing** (mid-May to mid-Sept daily 8am–8pm Alaska time, 9am–9pm Yukon time), 122 miles northeast of Tok. Remember you'll have to **set your watch** back an hour heading to Alaska, forward an hour if Yukon-bound.

For those heading to Canada, a Yukon **road-condition** report can be found at ⓦwww.gov.yk.ca/roadreport or by calling ☏867/456-7623 or toll-free in Yukon 1-877/456-7623. Tok state troopers can give local highway information on ☏883-5111. You can call ☏474-0307 to check border opening hours, ☏867/862-7230 for Canadian Customs, or ☏907/774-2252 for US Customs.

(Mile 1225), with its beaver lodge at the east end; and Hidden Lake (Mile 1240), with a mile-long trail. You can **hike** and camp pretty much anywhere in the refuge, although Native corporations own some areas and permission is required. The refuge maintains two small free **campgrounds**, both on lakes and with great mountain views and wildlife-viewing, but with untreated water only: *Lakeview Campground*, Mile 1256.7; and *Deadman Lake Campground*, Mile 1249.3, with its quarter-mile boardwalk nature trail and ranger talks every evening from mid-June to mid-August (starts 7.30pm).

Eastbound travelers should call at the Tetlin National Wildlife Refuge's headquarters in Tok or, if it's closed, at APLIC (see p.477); coming from the Canadian border, call at the refuge's **visitor center**, Mile 1229 (mid-May to mid-Sept daily 8am–4.30pm), where you'll find free copies of the *Passages* newsletter, heaps of detailed hiking and camping information, and a welter of interpretive talks, books, and displays. You can pick up an hour-long audio cassette at either place to guide you along the highway, returning it at the other end. Mid-May to early June and September are the best times to visit, with relatively few mosquitoes and biting gnats, as well as plenty of migrating birds.

The Fortymile and the Taylor Highway

The **Fortymile gold district** butts up against Canada's Yukon Territory between the Yukon River (once the main thoroughfare for developers of the Klondike) and the Alaska Highway (now the main road artery through the region). This was the grandfather of all Alaskan goldfields, experiencing its rush in 1886 when the town of Eagle became the supply hub, connected to the Gulf of Alaska by the Valdez–Eagle Trail. As fortunes shifted elsewhere the trail fell into disrepair and the region languished until the completion of the Alaska Highway prompted the construction of the Taylor Highway in 1945–53, a new road into an old area, at least by Alaskan standards.

Mining still continues across the region, which is scattered with the detritus of pioneering attempts to make a living from the earth: sagging old cabins, dilapidated sluices, even rusting hulks of dredges. Look, but don't get too close and stick to recognized highways – these people are fiercely protective of their claims (and have guns).

If you're headed out this way, you'll need to resupply in Tok, a dull crossroads town that will be the first real opportunity to fill up your belly and find a soft Alaskan bed if you've just driven up through Canada. Heading into the Fortymile you enter caribou country (see box, below), a sparsely populated land with only a couple of places that deserve to be called towns: the likeable **Chicken**, with its welcoming bar and frontier spirit, and **Eagle**, one of Alaska's best-preserved historic towns, neatly perched beside the roiling Yukon River.

The Taylor and Top of the World highways

As soon as you reach Tetlin Junction, twelve miles east of Tok (where there's nothing but a café and some log cabins), and turn off the Alaska Highway onto the **Taylor Highway** (generally open mid-April to mid-Oct), the landscape immediately feels more remote. There's no human habitation whatsoever until you reach the quirky settlement of **Chicken**, sixty miles down the line. The asphalt ends here, after which the rusting hulks of gold dredges stand along the narrow, lumpy roads to remind you of what this area once meant to prospectors. The grievous impact of the wildfires of 2004 is also hard to miss: you'll pass through the wastelands left by the Porcupine and Chicken fires, then those of

---

Saving the caribou

As recently as 1920 the **Fortymile caribou herd** was the largest in the north, its domains spreading from Alaska over into the Yukon. Though much smaller today, the herd still moves northwest across the Taylor Highway in spring to spend the summer in the alpine zone, and in fall returns southeast to winter in lowland spruce.

The construction of the Taylor Highway, which gave hunters easy access to the animals' territory, dramatically reduced the herd's numbers; loss of habitat from wildfires has likewise taken its toll. By 1960 only 50,000 of the original half-million beasts remained, and lax hunting laws diminished them to a mere 6000 in the early 1970s. The adoption of stricter regulations allowed them to nearly quadruple their numbers in 1990, and from 1996 to 2001 they again approached 50,000 thanks to the controversial sterilization and relocation of wolves, their natural predators.

The Department of Fish and Game continues to monitor the populations of both predator and prey, "adjusting" the former as necessary to encourage growth of the herd – the ultimate goal being to increase the caribou's numbers enough so that roughly 1500 can be taken during the annual hunting season.

the Wallstreet and King Creek fires near Jack Wade Junction. Here the highway splits north to the former garrison town of **Eagle** and east to the Top of the World Highway into Canada and Dawson City, the final destination of the Klondike gold rush.

Most rental cars are banned on the gravel roads beyond Chicken, so you may have to use Alaska/Yukon Trails buses (see Travel details, p.488), which go through Chicken to Boundary and Dawson City, though not to Eagle. Hitching can be a dispiriting experience, though it is not impossible. These headaches may soon be eased by a continuation of the blacktop to the Canadian border, starting with the segment between Chicken and Jack Wade Junction.

The Taylor Highway, detailed in a free BLM leaflet found locally, follows a tortuous course from one drainage to the next, climbing above 3500ft three times – Mount Fairplay, Polly Summit, and American Summit – on its 160-mile journey to Eagle. The road to **Mount Fairplay Summit** (Mile 33) gives long views over mixed forests and myriad tributaries of the Fortymile River before descending across tannin-rich rivers the color of strong tea. The only **camping** place before Chicken is the fairly pleasant *West Fork Campground* ($8; pump water) at Mile 48.8 (on the West Fork of the Dennison River); there's a popular day-use area at Mile 64.2, with a boat launch on the Mosquito Fork.

Chicken

Having unearthed gold, early prospectors founded a tent city and decided to name it for the plump, poorly flighted, and tasty birds found in profusion hereabouts; but ptarmigan was too much for their collective lexicon, and they settled on **Chicken**, now a tiny settlement 66 miles along the Taylor Highway. With fewer than twenty permanent residents, there's not much to the place and little in the way of facilities besides fairly pricey gas and a post office on the highway. There isn't even a payphone in town, nor any roofed accommodation, but RVers are well catered for, and there's a great bar.

Downtown Chicken, on Airport Road (ⓦwww.chickenalaska.com), may just be the Alaska you're looking for, a classic piece of state history comprising no more than a Western-style wooden sidewalk linking a gift shop, the *Chicken Creek Café*, and, best of all, the wonderfully battered old ⚥ *Chicken Creek Saloon*, with a free pool table, a kick-it-to-make-it-go jukebox, and draft Silver Gulch beer from Fairbanks. You never know who you might meet in the bar – gold panners, hunters, curious tourists, geologists – but somehow everyone gets on, oiled by beer and the congenial Sue, who runs the whole show.

There is nowhere formal **to stay** here, but you can stagger out to your RV parked overnight on the dirt lot or throw up a tent on the grassy verge. Periodically, make for the *Chicken Creek Café* for chicken soup ($4), huge tooth-rotting cinnamon rolls ($3.50), or the nightly salmon bake ($16), with homemade dill tartar sauce; they usually close around 7pm, so come early.

Across Airport Road, **Chicken Gold Camp** (☏235-6396, ⓦwww .chickengold.com) is built around the Pedro Dredge, moved here in 1998 from its final working claim a mile up the river; tours cost $5. From 1958 to 1967 this was the largest dredge in the district, unearthing many mammoth bones and tusks, as well as plenty of gold. There's a tank where you can pan for gold ($5 all day), RV parking (dry $10, with hookup $15), cabins (❷), and an espresso bar, the *Chicken Creek Outpost*, also doing panini, ice cream, and soups, and providing wireless Internet access.

Just over the bridge at Mile 67 is *The Goldpanner*, a gas station, gift shop, and RV park (dry parking $10, water & electricity $15) which runs tours of the **Historical Town of Chicken** (June–Aug daily 9am & 1pm; $5). The now

Paddling the Fortymile

Driving the Taylor Highway through Chicken to Eagle gives you only a small taste of a prospector's lot in the time when all travel was done by river. Organized visitors can still sample something of this life by undertaking one of the multiday canoe journeys on the wild and scenic **Fortymile River**, a totally absorbing experience requiring considerable confidence in your abilities. You'll be spending at least one night (possibly a whole week) camping beside the river, seeing few people, and having no one to help you if you swamp your boat or lose your supplies. It is important that you recognize which rapids should be portaged: misjudgments can have grave consequences, though the river's popularity in summer means that someone will eventually happen along.

First step is to obtain detailed route **information** from APLIC in Fairbanks or the BLM's Tok Field Office (☎883-5121), next to the APLIC outpost. One free leaflet simply states the access points and float times, another adds more information on facilities and hazards along the way and a list of the appropriate inch-to-the-mile maps. If you haven't got your own gear, you'll need to look at **renting a raft or canoe** from Eagle Canoe Rentals in Eagle (mid-May to mid-Sept; ☎547-2203, ⓦwww.aptalaska.net/~paddleak/), which charges $160 per two-berth canoe and $350 per six-berth raft for four days. Alternatively, contact Tok-based Canoe Alaska (☎883-2628, ⓦwww.canoealaska.net), which rents canoes from Tok and does customized guided rafting trips on the Fortymile and the Yukon.

The most commonly run section of the river is from a put-in point at South Fork Bridge, east of Chicken at Mile 75 (for main access points, see the map on p.448), down to **Fortymile Bridge** (or O'Brian Creek Bridge; 38 miles; 10–16 hours' paddling time) passing after thirteen miles the few standing structures remaining from **Franklin**, a gold town abandoned only in 1948. A couple of miles above the pullout you'll probably have to line your boats through the Falls, a Class III–IV rapid portaged on the right. It's possible to start further upstream at Mile 49 (the bridge over the West Fork of the Dennison Fork) or Mile 64 (Mosquito Fork Bridge, upstream of Chicken), adding up to thirty miles and ten hours to the trip. Keen boaters may wish to continue from **Fortymile Bridge to Eagle** (101 miles; typically 3–5 days) past the abandoned Steele Creek townsite, negotiating Deadman's Riffle and Canyon Rapids (both Class II–III), paddling into Canada and then joining the Yukon River at the Fortymile townsite (deserted but being preserved) for the final fifty miles northwest to Eagle. Even more adventurous types can fly into the remote Joseph airstrip on the Middle Fork of the Fortymile River and paddle from there down to Fortymile Bridge (88 miles; 4–5 days), with four rapids up to Class III, and then continue to the Yukon River and Eagle. Contact 40-Mile Air at Mile 1313 Alaska Highway, Tok (☎883-5191, ⓦwww.40-mileair.com), or 6540 Airport Way, Fairbanks (☎474-0018), for fly-ins. You should also be aware that if you are planning to paddle below the Fortymile Bridge take-out down to the Yukon River and Eagle, you'll be crossing into Canadian territory and will need to **contact US and Canadian customs** (see p.479).

abandoned township lies just across the highway and is liberally festooned with private property signs. The track through it is actually public, but since all the interesting buildings are private you might as well take the tour, a fascinating hour-long stroll around dilapidated buildings now being colonized by willow, made all the more poignant if you've read Robert Specht's *Tisha*, the true story of Anne Purdy (née Hobbs), who taught at the **schoolhouse** here in 1927. Like all the other buildings, the schoolhouse was later put to an alternative use by the FE gold company, which mined the area until the late 1960s. As the winter of 1967 set in, they hauled out as usual, leaving all their gear ready for the next spring, but never returned. Everything remains in a state of partially arrested decay, scattered with enamel plates, incomplete record books, a *Glamour* magazine, and a wonderfully dated Sears catalog. The best-preserved building is the **hay barn**, later used as the dredge maintenance store and still sweetly smelling of hay and grease. Inside, copper gaskets hang on the wall, the repair schedule lies open on the bench, a working lathe sits in the corner, and all the pulleys still spin smoothly.

The Top of the World Highway and the road to Eagle
Beyond Chicken the highway starts to deteriorate noticeably, passing the BLM's Chicken Field Station, Mile 68.2 (June–Sept), which marks the start of a trail to a lovely overlook of the **Cowden Dredge** in Mosquito Fork (3 miles round-trip; 1hr 30min). The highway continues wending its way from one Fortymile tributary to another, at Mile 75.3 reaching the **South Fork Bridge**, main access point for the Fortymile Canoe Route (see box, opposite). You can **camp** seven miles up the road at *Walker Fork Campground*, Mile 82 ($8; pump water). Continuing past the rusting carcass of Jack Wade Dredge (1934) at Mile 86, you reach **Jack Wade Junction** at Mile 95.7, where the Taylor Highway continues north to Eagle and the **Top of the World Highway** spurs east towards Canada, appropriately running high along a broad subalpine ridge with expansive views down into the Fortymile mining district.

   Boundary lies nine miles along and consists solely of *Boundary Lodge* (no phone; ❶), a one-family operation with a cozy café, gas that's expensive but usually slightly cheaper than in Dawson, and a couple of simple cabins with beds and a wood stove, which sleep three – and as many as you can fit on the floor – for $40. From there it is four miles to the 141st meridian, which defines the US–Canadian frontier (for border formalities, see p.479), then 65 miles on to Dawson City.

Eagle
From Jack Wade Junction, the Taylor Highway becomes increasingly narrow and winding, passing Fortymile (or O'Brien Creek) Bridge, Mile 112.6, access point for the Fortymile Canoe Route, a 64-mile run to the Yukon River. At

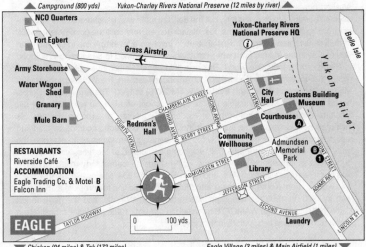

Campground (800 yds)   Yukon-Charley Rivers National Preserve (12 miles by river)

NCO Quarters
Fort Egbert
Yukon-Charley Rivers National Preserve HQ
Grass Airstrip
Army Storehouse
Water Wagon Shed
City Hall
Customs Building Museum
Granary
Courthouse
Mule Barn
Redmen's Hall
Community Wellhouse
Admundsen Memorial Park
CHAMBERLAIN STREET
SECOND AVENUE
FIRST AVENUE
THIRD AVENUE
FOURTH AVENUE
BERRY STREET
ADMUNDSEN STREET
Library
JEFFERSON STREET
SECOND AVENUE
ADAMS AVE
FRONT STREET
LINCOLN ST
Belle Isle
Yukon River

RESTAURANTS
Riverside Café   **1**
ACCOMMODATION
Eagle Trading Co. & Motel   **B**
Falcon Inn   **A**

N

EAGLE   TAYLOR HIGHWAY

0   100 yds

Laundry

Chicken (94 miles) & Tok (172 miles)   Eagle Village (3 miles) & Main Airfield (1 miles)

O'Brian Creek (Mile 113.3) you'll find 40-Mile Riverboat Tours, which has cabins. From American Summit (Mile 142) you'll be following the Valdez-Eagle Trail. **Eagle**, 94 miles north of Chicken on the south bank of the Yukon River, spent the middle years of the twentieth century neglected, but in the past twenty years has reinvented itself as the best-preserved town in the Interior. This is no museum, however; although small and isolated, it is very much alive, catering to prospectors and a few tourists in summer, and trappers in winter. Hugging an outside bend of the Yukon River only twelve miles downstream from the Canadian border, it is flanked by the pyramidal, 1400-foot Eagle Bluff, where the birds that gave the town its name formerly nested.

Eagle's core is little changed since 1905, the result of sixty years of neglect followed by forty years of preservation at the hands of the Eagle Historical Society, which was formed in the mid-1960s. They've done a wonderful job: all over town there are clapboard buildings restored and painted a fetching (but not original) white with green trim. The buildings are all brought marvelously to life on the society's tours, which have undoubtedly contributed to the group's worldwide membership, which at three hundred members is around twice the population of Eagle. Three miles to the east is the scattered community of Eagle Village; less than half of its population of sixty is native (Han Kutchin), but all live the subsistence lifestyle.

As the largest river-town between Dawson and the Arctic Circle community of Fort Yukon, Eagle supports an extensive bush community sequestered in the forests beside tributaries of the Yukon. Most now use mining and trapping only to supplement other sources of income, but in essence their lives aren't much different from those of the people so vividly described in John McPhee's *Coming into the Country* (see "Books" in Contexts, p.606).

Some history

Eagle started life as a trading post on Belle Isle in the middle of the Yukon in 1880 and subsequently moved to the south bank when the town site was

WAMCATS

As the Fortymile and Klondike gold rushes precipitated rapid population growth in the Alaskan bush, the need for improved communications increased. A post office had been established in Eagle in 1899, but the delivery route was treacherous: one messenger from Valdez took two months, lost eleven horses, and cost the government $3000 to deliver just three letters. The initial solution involved a telegraph line to Dawson and Whitehorse in the Yukon, from where messages were carried to Skagway and shipped to Seattle and the outside world. This was little better. Reluctant to rely on the Canadians, the government set about an "all-American" system, the **Washington–Alaska Military Cable and Telegraph System (WAMCATS)** in 1900. The Army Signal Corps, based in Eagle, was responsible for the construction, and the job fell to 21-year-old Lieutenant **William Mitchell**, later a vociferous advocate of airborne warfare. He instituted new ideas such as supplying the summer construction camps by sledding in supplies during the deathly cold winter and banning thermometers. In essence, the route followed the Valdez-Eagle Trail, still being completed at the time, which allowed better access for periodic maintenance, using sheds spaced at forty-mile intervals. It was completed to Valdez in 1902 and on to Seattle in 1904. Meanwhile another team was working from Nome, linking up with the Valdez-Eagle line to complete a 1500-mile web in 1903. In 1909 the telegraph was superceded by radio, and the garrison left Eagle in 1911, although WAMCATS remained in use until 1925, playing a critical role in the Serum Run (see box, p.558) in that year.

McQuesten's thermometer

Trader Leroy Napoleon "Jack" McQuesten left a huge legacy in the North. He never found much gold, but after scouting around the Tron-diuck River in the Canadian Yukon he decided he'd seen enough color to justify widespread interest and sent word south that there was gold to be found, thereby kick-starting the gold rush in the "Klondike" (his bastardized version of Tron-diuck, meaning "hammer-water," due to the stakes driven into riverbeds to hold fishtraps). He set up trading posts as a representative of the Alaska Commercial Company, including one at Fort Reliance on the Yukon, where he once tried his hand at plowing his land with two young moose. Here he financed prospectors and, to aid newcomers in judging their outdoor plans, instituted **McQuesten's Thermometer** (aka the Sourdough Thermometer). It comprised a series of four vials – mercury (freezing point -40°F), coal oil (-50°F), Jamaica ginger (-60°F), and Perry Davis's painkiller (-75°F) – in a rack outside along with a note instructing people to shake each bottle in turn. If the mercury was frozen it was too cold to be out on the trail at night, and even the daytime was dangerous if the coal oil was solid. When the ginger froze folks should stay in their cabin, and when the painkiller wouldn't budge you shouldn't stray from your stove.

surveyed in 1898. Unscrupulous land agents tried to talk up their prices with exaggerated reports of gold-rich streams hereabouts, even trying in vain to flog off a corner lot to Jack London, who passed through in June 1898. Nonetheless, eager prospectors came in numbers, and the town soon had a population of 1700. Lawlessness and a desire to control the Interior induced the US government to blaze the Valdez-Eagle Trail using soldiers stationed at Eagle's Fort Egbert from 1900.

The US government soon recognized Alaska's rising importance as a civilian center rather than simply a military outpost, and in 1900 Congress passed legislation for taxation, licensing, and the establishment of three judicial districts, one in Eagle. From here James Wickersham presided as US District Judge over almost half of Alaska, and a year later Eagle was incorporated as a city – the first in Interior Alaska. Anchorage wouldn't even be thought of for another sixteen years, and Fairbanks was just a mudbank in the Chena River.

Eagle played another major role in the civilization of the north as a critical node in the Washington–Alaska Military Cable and Telegraph System (see box, opposite). Though geographically remote, it was no longer isolated. In fact, in December 1905 this was the best-connected community in the Interior, a unique feature that lured explorer **Roald Amundsen** across four hundred miles of frozen rivers and mountain ranges by dog team. He came to announce to the world that, in the thirty months since he left his native Norway, he had successfully negotiated the Northwest Passage – the mariner's grail for much of the previous two centuries – and to beg his backers for more funds to continue the journey. It seems he liked Eagle (it had to be better than his sloop, locked in the polar ice of the Beaufort Sea for the nine-month winter), so he stayed a couple of months in a cabin off 1st Avenue on what is now Amundsen Street.

With the departure of Wickersham to burgeoning Fairbanks in 1904 and the closure of Fort Egbert in 1911 (though the telegraph and wireless operators stayed until 1925), Eagle began its steady decline in population: from around two hundred when the fort closed, to sixty-odd when the last sternwheeler paddled off in 1947 and a low point of only nine in 1953, at which point the completion of the Taylor Highway began to reverse the trend. The population now hovers below two hundred.

The Town

Eagle's waterfront is no longer the hotbed of activity it was in the town's stern-wheeler heyday, but it is still a place to which you are inexorably drawn. Stand on the rough promenade of Front Street and it feels as though the swirling silt-laden waters below are waiting to suck you all the way to the sea. You'll have to retreat a few steps to reach the geographical and social center of town, the **community well house**, an unmissable, pagoda-roofed frame structure built in 1903 and topped with a cupola housing a bell which can still summon the townsfolk to fight a fire. The windmill hasn't worked for years, and it's now a pump that provides water for the large proportion of residents who live without running water: you'll often see folk in trucks pulling up to fill drums from the gas-pump nozzle.

Next door stands **Wickersham's Courthouse**, on 1st Avenue at Berry Street, built in 1901 and with an upper floor laid out much as it would have been in those early days. The desk Wickersham last used in 1904 still contained his papers when the historical society began its restoration in 1975. Nowadays local guides from the society convene here for the absorbing three-hour **Historical Society Tour** (late May to early Sept daily at 9am; $5; or by appointment ☏547-2325, ⓦwww.eagleak.org), the only way you can get into the historic

Yukon-Charley Rivers National Preserve and paddling the Yukon

You'll need a fair degree of commitment to see anything of the **Yukon-Charley Rivers National Preserve**, a whopping 2.5 million-acre chunk of unglaciated Alaskan Interior flanking the Yukon River – and the entire 1.1 million-acre watershed of its major tributary, the Charley River – for 130 river miles from just below Eagle almost to Circle (see p.532). It is remote country almost devoid of human impact, though it was appreciably busier fifty to eighty years ago when sternwheelers forged their way up past Eagle to Dawson, and prospectors worked the area for paydirt. A few of their spiritual descendants remain, hardy types (only thirty in the whole park year-round, but more in summer) spinning out a subsistence lifestyle along the river or up the small tributaries. Most are reclusive enough that you won't see them, but you'll spot their nets, fish camps, and maybe a cabin or two, with the regular slap of Han Athabascan fishwheels as accompaniment.

The name Yukon means Great River, fully justified by its length of 1980 miles from its source just fifteen miles from the Pacific in the Yukon east of Skagway; near Eagle it's half a mile wide and over 35ft deep, flowing at 7–10 knots and bearing up to two hundred tons of silt a minute. For over two hundred days a year the river flows clear under six feet of ice, its surface used by snowmobiles and dog teams – the Yukon Quest dog-sled race comes right through here – but in summer the way to travel is by canoe. Paddling through the park, and along the Yukon River in general, is the only way to gain a sense of the region's interconnectedness: an appreciation of how much Dawson, Fortymile, Eagle, and Circle were part of a riverine continuum that can never be properly replicated by highways. The pleasure in traveling this country is the sheer sense of isolation, but you can fish while you drift, stop to hike up small streams, and pause to root around the few relics of the gold-rush era that remain: abandoned townsites, disused roadhouses, and the detritus of commercial gold-dredging, including the preserved Coal Creek Dredge in the heart of the park.

Practicalities

There are no roads or maintained trails in the Yukon-Charley, nor even any publicly maintained airstrips, so unless you take a bush flight into the upper Charley River, your only access is by boat. In Eagle, the Yukon-Charley Rivers National Preserve **visitor center** (mid-May to mid-Sept daily 8am–5pm; mid-Sept to mid-May call

buildings. The tour continues downstairs in a small museum devoted to Wicker-sham's tenure, Amundsen's visit, and operations at Fort Egbert, which, together with efforts to supply fuel for the riverboats, succeeded in completely denuding the surroundings. Eagle is still a border port, but it no longer has a permanent customs officer, obviating the need for the 1900 customs house, now turned into the **US Customs House Museum** (visited on the tour), with period furniture arranged among beautifully hand-drawn pilots' charts of the Upper Yukon. The tour continues to **Fort Egbert**, a collection of wooden buildings dotted on the grass at the end of the airstrip. The granary contains a Model T Ford and a Model B dump truck, both still used for the annual Fourth of July parade through town, and the adjacent mule barn is much as it was left, with four dozen stalls each marked with the name of its last occupant.

The tour varies a little depending on who is guiding that day, but might also include St Paul's log church (1900) or the plain, wooden hall of the Improved Order of Red Men, an organization dedicated to "friendship, brotherly helpful-ness, fraternal love, and good fellowship," though this didn't extend to the "red" men who lived in the district – it was strictly whites-only.

If you want to get out on the river, consider a **cruise** on Holland America/Gray Line's *Yukon Queen II* (mid-May to early Sept; in Dawson ☎867/993-5599 or

at the adjacent park headquarters Mon–Fri 8am–5pm; ☎547-2233, ⊚www.nps .gov/yuch) provides information and sells maps. In Fairbanks you can get informa-tion at APLIC (see p.495) or at the Preserve's headquarters, 201 1st Ave at Hall (☎547-2234). You can **rent a canoe** in Eagle from Eagle Canoe Rentals (mid-May to mid-Sept; ☎547-2203, ⊚www.aptalaska.net/~paddleak) for the float down to Circle (165 miles; 5 days; $175 per canoe). Alternatively, head to Dawson and hire a canoe at *Dawson City River Hostel* (☎867/993-6823; ⊚www.yukonhostels.com) for the float down to Eagle (105 miles; 3–4 days; $110 rental per canoe). Both trips can be undertaken at a steadier pace (canoes at an additional $25 a day), or you can take an epic combination from Dawson to Circle (270 miles; 9–10 days; $275). Canoes can be dropped in Circle, but you'll need to fly back to your starting point: this is best arranged beforehand with Circle Air (☎1-866/520-5223, ⊚www.circleair.com), which charges around $300 an hour for charters and also does fly-ins. A convenient alternative is to organize your trip from Fairbanks through GoNorth (see box, p.516), which runs Fairbanks-based trips flying into Eagle, letting you canoe down to Circle in 5–10 days, and then flying you back to Fairbanks, all for $345.

June to September is the window of opportunity, avoiding freeze-up (typically three weeks in mid-Oct) and break-up (usually two weeks in early May), when huge chunks of tumbling ice make river travel extremely perilous or impossible. Once on the river self-sufficiency is paramount. Obviously, you'll need to be a competent paddler – a midstream spill in such a broad, cold river can be lethal – and carry everything you need. You'll be **camping** on open beaches and river bars, where insects are kept at bay by the breeze, or at five free public-use **cabins** (available on a first-come, first-served basis), including one at the two-story, log-built *Slaven's Roadhouse*, built around 1930 and long deserted, but now converted for visitors' use. Through the summer *Slaven's* has a resident ranger who conducts free hikes of the Coal Creek Dredge. There's another four miles away at Coal Creek Camp, and three on the Yukon to the east.

Remember to leave a float plan at the park headquarters in Eagle (and let them know you're safe at journey's end), take along your fishing tackle, and stay bear-aware. March and April are also ideal for cross-country travel, on skis or snowshoes, but you'll need to be even more self-sufficient.

1-800/544-2206, ⓦwww.graylinealaska.com), which runs day-trips from Dawson to Eagle and back, leaving Dawson City at 9am (Yukon time) and departing Eagle at 2pm (Alaska time). Unfortunately, the trip is four hours each way, most spaces are filled by tours, and from this end the schedule only suits those who want to overnight in Dawson, but places (US$87 each way) are usually available and can be purchased at *Eagle Trading Company* (see below). Bicycles usually travel free, but call to check if there's space.

Practicalities

Most of the town's commercial activity revolves around the *Eagle Trading Company*, Front Street (☏547-2220, ⓦwww.eagletrading.com; ❸), a well-stocked grocery (with ATM inside) selling **gas** at inflated prices, operating a **motel** with comfortable spruce-paneled rooms, and letting functional **RV sites** by the river for $16, including showers. You'll need to book as far in advance as you can manage to stay at *Falcon Inn B&B*, 220 Front St (☏547-2254, ⓦwww.aptalaska.net/~falconin/; ❸), a modern log house with spectacular river views and tasteful decor that makes it one of the most appealing B&Bs in the Interior. The guests' lounge even has a wonderful turret and deck perfect for watching Eagle's daily routine or, with luck, the aurora. The town's peaceful BLM **campground** ($10; untreated river water) lies half a mile northwest of Fort Egbert on the route of a water-supply line that once supplied Fort Egbert from American Creek. Ferret around in the trees, and you'll come across the remains of structures where fires once heated the pipe to prevent it from freezing. Eagle's only **restaurant** (summer only) is the *Riverside Café*, Front Street, a good diner that is ideal for just sitting and watching the river roll by. Eagle is "damp," which means that there are **no alcohol sales** in town, but no one is going to stop you bringing a bottle or two in.

Travel details

With no train lines, Alaska's eastern Interior is most easily explored along the web of highways that link the region to Anchorage, Prince William Sound, Fairbanks, and Canada. Your own vehicle gives the most flexibility, but limited bus services do exist in the summer. Alaska/Yukon Trails and Alaska Direct (for details of both, see Basics, p.44) are the only two companies running between major towns, though Backcountry Connections and Mountain Kingdom Express (see p.452) run from Glennallen to McCarthy.

Buses

Chicken to: Dawson City, Yukon (3 weekly; 4hr); Fairbanks (3 weekly; 6hr); Tok (3 weekly; 1hr 30min).
Delta Junction to: Dawson City, Yukon (3 weekly; 7hr 30min); Fairbanks (6 weekly; 1hr 30min); Glennallen (on demand; 3hr); Tok (3 weekly; 2hr); Valdez (on demand; 5hr 30min).
Glennallen to: Anchorage (3 weekly; 4hr 30min); Chitina (1 daily; 1hr 30min); Delta Junction (on demand; 3hr); Fairbanks (on demand; 4hr 30min); McCarthy (1 daily; 4hr); Tok (3 weekly; 3–4hr); Valdez (on demand; 3hr 15min).
Tok to: Anchorage (3 weekly; 8hr 30min); Chicken (3 weekly; 1hr 30min); Dawson City, Yukon (3 weekly; 4hr 30min); Delta Junction (3 weekly; 2hr); Fairbanks (6 weekly; 3hr 30min–5hr 30min); Glennallen (3 weekly; 3–4hr); Whitehorse, Yukon (3 weekly; 8hr 30min).

Alaska in winter

Most people visit Alaska in summer, when snow and ice are found only in glaciers and on mountaintops. But to get a rounded impression of the state, you really need to visit in winter – roughly late October to the end of March – when lakes and rivers are solid, snow blankets the ground, and in the Far North the sea ice packs hard against the beaches. It is a magical time to visit, but with subzero temperatures and scarce daylight it can also be a challenging one. Consequently, most winter visitors have a specific, and hugely rewarding, mission in mind. Many come simply to gaze at the magical aurora borealis, though that can easily be combined with a little cross-country skiing or some ice fishing. Time your trip right and you can also witness the start or finish of the Iditarod or attend the World Ice Art Championships.

Aurora borealis

Most of Arctic Alaska's visitors miss out on the **aurora borealis**, which isn't visible during the short twilight periods otherwise known as summer nights. Make a trip in fall or winter though, and you'll be treated to one of the world's great natural phenomena. There's little to match the numinous wonder of reclining in a hot pool or huddling in your sleeping bag as myriad bands of pale blue, green, and pink light play across the sky above. Sometimes they'll appear for just a few minutes before fading away, but at others they may endure for hours, endlessly changing and never repeating.

Caused by the interaction between the earth's magnetic field and the solar wind (an invisible stream of charged particles constantly emitted by the sun), the aurora borealis can sometimes appear as far south as California, but is a regular occurrence around the Arctic Circle. Fairbanks offers some of the best viewing, where the lights are visible most nights during the winter months. For more on this natural wonder, see the box on p.506.

▼ Ice fishing on Little Diomede Island

Ice fishing

Fishing is big business in Alaska, and it doesn't head south when the lakes and rivers freeze: **ice fishing** is the vogue from December to March. Some brave souls even carry on into April, when much of the ice has become dangerously thin. On lakes around the state you'll see clusters of people on the three-foot-thick ice, usually with a pickup truck or snowmobile parked nearby. They'll drill through the ice, drop a line into the water, and settle into lawn chairs with a mug of something warm, hoping to hook an arctic char, lake trout, or coho salmon.

Most ice fishing happens on large lowland lakes common throughout the Interior: ask locally for the current favorite spots. If you have the proper gear, drill a hole (or find a recently used one), shovel away the surface snow for a few feet around it, then peer down into the water with a blanket or coat over your head. Sunlight penetrates the surrounding ice, illuminating the fish as they examine your bait.

▲ Snowshoeing

Skiing and ski-joring

The easiest way to get active in winter is on skis. Though Alaska has a handful of **downhill ski areas**, Girdwood's Alyeska resort being the most developed, locals typically gravitate toward **cross-country skiing**. By late October enthusiasts are waiting for a dump of snow big enough to cover the trails, which are groomed around towns and through forests all over the state.

Alaskans love their dogs, and many put their pooches to work **ski-joring**, similar to cross-country skiing but with a reined dog providing much of the forward locomotion.

The Iditarod

The mushers win the big prizes and the accolades, but the dogs are the real stars of the **Iditarod**. Teams of hardy, eager canines haul a laden sled through deep snow, over conifer-clad hills, and along frozen rivers roughly 1150 miles from Anchorage to the remote arctic town of Nome. Yes, it is mad, but it is the sort of madness that draws around sixty competitors from all over the world to Alaska every March.

With temperatures along the route often dipping well below 0°F, well-wishers are a rare breed, and even at the few remote villages along the way "crowds" are mostly officials and professional photographers. The Ceremonial Start in downtown Anchorage draws the biggest congregation of supporters, who watch the sleds make their way through town over trucked-in snow. Hopeful "Iditariders" can even compete for the chance to sit on a musher's sled for a few miles. The true race starts the next day from the nearby town of Wasilla, and visitors line the first fourteen road miles, after which the teams plunge into the wilderness. Many fewer fans make the effort to catch the race during the next section, but thousands fly into Nome for the finish a week or so later.

All mushers must carry a sleeping bag, snowshoes, an ax, and a cooking stove, but few expect to use them. Most just feed their dogs and get a few hours kip at the occasional checkpoint, then press on.

Aside from sheer endurance, tactics are crucial to a musher's success. Lagging racers may be virtually written off by the halfway mark, but, due to their steady pace and extra rest, sometimes end up passing the leaders just a couple days short of Nome. The fastest musher on record completed the race in just under nine days, and in 1978, the winner took first place by one second – a sled-dog nose. The slowest team ever reached the finish over 32 days after leaving Wasilla, but, following tradition, was given a champion's welcome into Nome. For more on the race and its history, see the box on p.392.

Ice carving

O'Grady Pond in Fairbanks produces superb blocks of ice. Virtually bubble-free, they're perfect for the **World Ice Art Championships**, the Olympiad of ice sculpting which takes place in March each year. Around twenty teams spend days arranging their quota of ten four-ton blocks, then feverishly chipping away in a bid for the top prize. They use chainsaws and grinders to outline their design, chisels and scrapers to add definition, then electric irons and hairdryers for the finishing touches.

The results are fabulous and often larger than life, many sculptures portraying mythical characters locked in mortal combat with dragons and serpents. You'll also see plenty of abstract shapes and those celebrated Alaskan icons, bears and bald eagles. Imaginative lighting makes everything sparkle in the crisp night air.

Visitors can wander around the sculpture park while the carvers are at work. Once the competition is over, the park stays open for another few weeks until the onset of spring weather slowly melts all that hard labor. Soon nothing's left except the memories – and photos at ⓦwww.icealaska.com.

8

Fairbanks and the
Arctic North

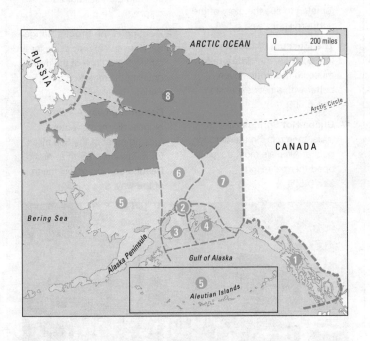

CHAPTER 8 # Highlights

* **Winter in Fairbanks** Come in late February and early March to catch the Yukon Quest sled-dog race, the ice carving competition, and the aurora at its best. See p.503

* **Aurora borealis** Make a special trip in March or hang around until mid-September (or later) to see the glory of the northern lights. See p.506

* **The Museum of the North** In Fairbanks, the state's best museum has gotten even better with a new expansion. See p.509

* **Chena Hot Springs** Hike the trails, then relax in the outdoor pool at Alaska's most developed thermal resort. See p.525

* **Nome** Camp on the near-Arctic beach with the gold dredgers and rent a car to explore the gorgeous roads round about. See p.554

* **Pinnell Mountain Trail** Excellent two-day ridgetop trail offering midsummer midnight sun and early fall aurora displays. See p.531

* **Floating in the Brooks Range** Set time and money aside for a rafting trip on one of the rivers draining the remote Brooks Range. See p.547

* **Dalton Highway** Alaska's biggest driving adventure, running most of the 500 miles from Fairbanks north to Arctic Deadhorse, and gravel much of the way. See p.537

△ Front Street, Nome

Fairbanks and the Arctic North

A journey to Alaska seems incomplete without time spent in the **Far North**, a region comprising the Alaskan Arctic and Fairbanks, the state's second-largest city and the hub of the north. It is stunningly dramatic, with long winter nights lit by the shimmering strands of the **aurora borealis**, extreme temperatures that demand extraordinary measures just so that people can live here, and settlements that all seem to claim some superlative: lowest temperature, most isolated cabin, or furthest-north something-or-other. The area is also where the legendary pipeline-building days of the mid-1970s were played out, with construction crews earning big money and then coming to town to squander fistfuls of cash nightly.

Today the North is actually wilder than it was a century ago. Abandoned cabins remain where gold-rush towns once bustled with activity, and bush planes have replaced sternwheel steamers as the transportation mode of choice. The heart of the region is **Fairbanks**, a flat, sprawling place that does a good job of balancing urban life with the needs of the cabin dwellers on its doorstep. If you've just spent some time in the Interior, you'll welcome city luxuries, and it's easy to spend a few days here making forays out to assorted gold-rush relics and soaking up the late evening sun as it glows on the Alaska Range. Before long you'll want to stray further, and the road system lends itself to easy trips to the resort at **Chena Hot Springs** and increasingly more challenging journeys to the semi-dormant town of **Circle**, the near-primitive **Manley Hot Springs**, or even the daunting 414-mile **Dalton Highway**, which runs along the route of the pipeline to **Deadhorse**, almost on the Arctic Ocean.

Fairbanks' roads will also take you to a few manageable hikes and easy canoe routes, but for the really challenging stuff – weeklong treks and float trips – you'll need to get out to the **Gates of the Arctic National Park** or the **Arctic National Wildlife Refuge**, which jointly encompass much of the **Brooks Range**. Beyond the Brooks Range, the 4000-strong Iñupiat town of **Barrow** clings to the edge of the land with only the ten-month-frozen sea between it and the North Pole. As a large Eskimo community, Barrow has a lot in common with **Kotzebue**, a springboard for the inland **sand dunes** beside the Kobuk River. Kotzebue is often visited jointly with its near neighbor **Nome**, a former gold town where miners flocked to sift

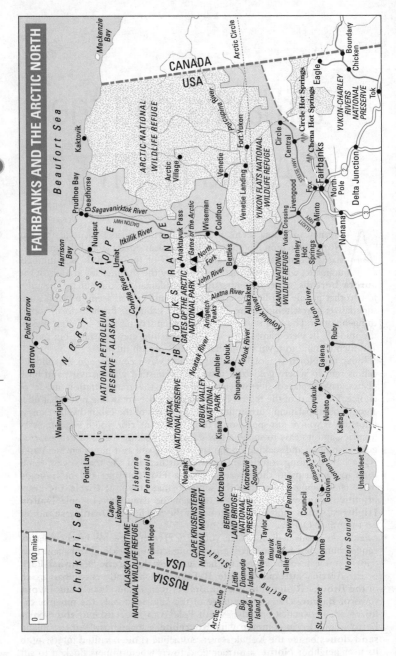

FAIRBANKS AND THE ARCTIC NORTH

the precious metal from its sands before eventually following the gold rush east to found Fairbanks.

Fairbanks is generally **snow-free** from sometime in May to late September or beyond, but to get the most out of the northern parks the best weeks are those in June and the first half of July.

Fairbanks

FAIRBANKS, 358 miles north of Anchorage, is the end of the road for most tourists and marks the ultimate conclusion of the **Alaska Highway** from Canada. If you've just driven the full 1500 miles from Dawson Creek in British Columbia, then some kind of celebration is in order. Catch it right and you can conduct your revelry under the ethereal glow of the **northern lights**, for this is aurora central, with sightings on some 240 nights a year.

Most visitors arrive in summer when nights aren't dark enough for aurora viewing, but they can watch residents play midnight baseball games in the 21 hours of natural light (and three hours of twilight). At this time, it can be disconcerting stumbling out of a bar at 2am into bright sunshine, but it is better than the dead of winter when Fairbanks receives only three hours and 42 minutes of direct sunlight daily and the population suffers from a high rate of depression.

Fairbanks lies just 188 miles south of the Arctic Circle and far from the moderating effects of the sea, a combination resulting in one of the most extreme temperature ranges found anywhere in the world. The thermometer can read over 95°F in summer, but temperatures of -40°F are not uncommon in winter when the average is -5°F and there's an average snowfall of 53.4 inches. Vehicle use in the winter is a problem: strategically placed electrical sockets enable engines to be plugged in and kept from freezing up, but frequent driving, and the fact that many people leave their engines running for extended periods, result in exhaust fumes condensing into a disgusting photochemical smog known as **ice fog**, which blots out the weak winter light. The pollution has forced many Fairbanksans, as they call themselves, to relocate from the city center into the surrounding wilderness, producing one of the most thinly populated cities imaginable and leaving plenty of room for even more vehicle use. Indeed, Fairbanks has more vehicles per capita than LA, and a network of four-lane freeways that could hardly be less friendly to pedestrians.

Fairbanks bills itself as Alaska's "**Golden Heart**," a moniker reflecting its geographical position and the sense of community that has managed to outlast the rapid urbanization. Of course, it also alludes to the city's history as a gold town, a status that draws tour buses to **Gold Dredge No. 8**, one of just two publicly accessible gold dredges in the state, **El Dorado Gold Camp**, and a couple of entertaining honky-tonk shows recalling those heady days. For more intellectual pursuits, the university's **Museum of the North** is among the best in the state, with entertaining shows on the aurora borealis and Native Alaskan sports, which the **World Eskimo–Indian Olympics** (Ⓦ www.weio.org) celebrates to the fullest each July.

Some history

Fairbanks was founded accidentally in 1901 by former miner **E.T. Barnette**. After serving five years in a Washington State prison for stealing his partner's gold, Barnette headed for Alaska and eventually found himself on the *LaVelle Young*, steaming up the Tanana River, bound for the Valdez-Eagle Trail where he hoped to set up a trading post. The river level was low, and Barnette talked the boat's captain into trying a "shortcut" up the equally shallow Chena River (pronounced "CHEE-na"). When he soon became grounded, the frustrated captain dumped Barnette's 130 tons of mining equipment and supplies on the bank where 1st Avenue now meets Cushman Street, and left him and his party alone in the wilderness two hundred miles short of their destination.

Meanwhile, hapless Italian émigré **Felix Pedro** (in fact Felice Pedroni; 1858–1910) – who three years earlier had discovered a wondrously rich stream and then lost it – had been stumbling around the Tanana Valley almost out of food when he spotted smoke from the departing *LaVelle Young* and headed towards it, eventually settling in with Barnette and company. Pedro continued his prospecting, and the following summer unearthed a couple of small finds. Barnette saw his chance to make a buck off eager gold seekers and dispatched his Japanese cook to Dawson City to spread "the Great Lie" about a rich strike, managing to convince three hundred prospectors to make the journey. Fortuitously, more gold was eventually found, and in 1904 thousands joined the **gold rush**, flocking to the new city of Fairbanks, named for the Indiana senator Charles Fairbanks, who later became vice-president under Theodore Roosevelt.

The city of Fairbanks was incorporated in 1903 with a population of 1200 plus 1800 miners in the hinterland, but it only established its supremacy over Chena, a few miles west, in 1904 when Judge James Wickersham moved his court here from Eagle. By 1909 it had a population of 3500 (plus 15,000 miners roundabout) enjoying electric light, a sewer system, fire and police departments, and a federal jail. From 1905 to 1906 a branch of the Valdez-Eagle Trail was built to Fairbanks: just five feet wide, only sleds could use it at first. In this climate, Barnette was able to make a fortune by charging extortionate prices (for which he was almost lynched) and by embezzling a million dollars from the Washington-Alaska Bank, hastening his 1911 departure from the town he had founded.

The early surface gold strike turned out to be a freak occurrence. Most of the gold was yards deep below frozen gravel – a mixed blessing because slow gold recovery sustained Fairbanks well beyond the two-year boom-and-bust cycle typical elsewhere. The population had fallen to 1150 before professional mining engineers came in the 1920s to exploit the deeper deposits using modern dredges that worked the rivers, scooping gold-bearing gravel with giant buckets, then spewing the spent "tailings" out the rear. Their heyday lasted only thirty years, but the evidence – vast piles of gravel and the occasional rusting hulk of a dredge – is hard to miss around neighboring Fox and Ester, and along the Chatanika River.

World War II bolstered the region's fluctuating population, as huge **military bases** were built to thwart possible Japanese attacks and provide a stepping-stone for almost eight thousand American planes on their way from Montana to Russia and the European battlefields as part of the **Lend-Lease program**. Fairbanks' Ladd Field (built in 1940 for cold-weather testing) was the point of handover to Russian pilots, who took the planes to Siberia via Nome, and was also key to the 1942–43 Aleutian campaign. Fairbanks then sputtered along until the city was chosen as the logistical headquarters for the construction of the **Trans-Alaska Pipeline** (see box, p.538). For four years in the mid-1970s, more than twenty thousand oil workers were based here. Generous wage packages, sometimes topping $1500 a week (not much less than the price of a small sedan at the time), fueled rapid expansion and generated a freewheeling atmosphere. Fairbanks became a byword for excess, infamous for its riotous 2nd Avenue bars and well-patronized brothels. Then the pipeline was finished, and so, it seemed, was Fairbanks: unemployment hit twenty percent, property prices crashed, and the city's economy collapsed. Things have since stabilized, but the scars remain, especially downtown, where empty parking lots have replaced blocks once solid with bars and bulging wallets. The military remains crucial to the city, with a Stryker armored infantry brigade based at Fort Wainwright since 2005, plus the huge Eielson air base to the east of the city.

Arrival, information, and city transportation

The daily Alaska Railroad **train** (weekly in winter) offers the most relaxing way to get here from Anchorage or Denali. It creeps through the suburbs of Fairbanks to arrive at a new station (☏458-6025), inconveniently sited at the junction of the Johansen Expressway and Danby Road over a mile northwest of downtown. Unless you are meeting a bus tour here, you'll need to take a taxi into town. **Long-distance buses** (see Listings, p.523, and Travel details, p.578) mostly drop off downtown outside the visitor center, some also calling at hostels and the main hotels.

You are most likely to use **Fairbanks International Airport**, four miles southwest of downtown, for bush- and float-plane flights into the Arctic, and if you're flying in long-distance. The MACS **bus** Yellow Line ($1.50) only takes half an hour to get from the airport (turn right as you leave the terminal) to downtown, but there are only eight services on weekdays, five on Saturday, and none on Sunday, so you may prefer to grab a **taxi** (around $12 to downtown).

Information

Buses arrive a few steps from the **visitor center**, 550 1st Ave (daily: late May to mid-Sept 8am–8pm; mid-Sept to late May 10am–5pm; ☏456-5774 or 1-800/327-5774, ⊛www.explorefairbanks.com), which is well equipped to handle general inquiries about Fairbanks and points north. Golden Heart Greeters are volunteers who will spend an hour or two with visitors to share their local knowledge and help them get more from their stay; contact the visitor center at least a week in advance. The visitor center also puts on walking tours, at 9.30am on Tuesdays and Thursdays ($10 per person) or by appointment (☏457-7834; minimum 5 people). A new information center, to the east of downtown by the Wendell Street bridge, is planned for 2008. For anything outdoorsy it is better to head to the nearby **Alaska Public Lands Information Center** (APLIC), lower level, 250 Cushman St (late May to early Sept daily 9am–6pm; rest of year Tues–Sat 10am–6pm; ☏456-0527), which covers everything related to recreational use of public lands in the northern third of the state. Excellent displays and free videos detail wildlife, land use, survival techniques, river rescue, and canoe-trip planning, and the helpful staff are good at helping channel your hiking and canoeing ambitions. Films on wildlife, the 1964 earthquake, the *Exxon Valdez*, and so on are shown at noon and 2pm, with talks on Saturdays at 2pm. They've also got stacks of relevant books for sale and the most popular topographical maps; for all other maps, visit the Map Office on the UAF campus (see Listings, p.524).

City transportation and tours

Even if you've made it this far without a vehicle, when you reach Fairbanks you should think seriously about **renting a car** (for local agencies, see Listings, p.523). For a city of only sixty thousand souls, Fairbanks is incredibly spread out and designed around the needs of drivers. By using buses and maybe renting a bike, it is possible to see most of Fairbanks, but services are painfully infrequent, and two or three people traveling together will soon find a car a very good investment, particularly once you start straying outside the city limits. Most rental agencies won't insure their ordinary vehicles on gravel-surfaced roads (though your own insurance may cover you; check before leaving home), so if you are planning to visit Manley Hot Springs or drive the Steese Highway to Circle, consider renting from Affordable, Northern Alaska, or GoNorth.

If money is tight, or you're traveling alone, you may find yourself drawn to the MACS **bus** system, with its hub at the **transit center**, on Cushman Street between 5th and 6th avenues (Mon–Fri 6.15am–7.45pm, Sat 9am–6.15pm; transit hotline ℡459-1011). There are five routes, most running every hour or so from around 7am to 7pm on weekdays, with restricted services on Saturday and none at all on Sunday. The most useful lines are: Yellow, from downtown past Pioneer Park and along Airport Way to the airport; Red, along College Road to the university campus; and Blue, past Pioneer Park and several shopping centers to the university. All buses have racks for bikes, which ride free. **Fares** are $1.50 per ride; $3 day-passes are available from the driver, and you can buy five tokens for $5 from the driver or from machines at supermarkets. The service is actually free from November to April, in an attempt to reduce the dreadful winter smog. Alpenglow's Fairbanks Shuttle (℡1-800/770-2267, Ⓦwww.alaskashuttles.com) will take you around town for $5 ($8 return) or to the airport or rail depot for $7, and offers tours to Ester, Fox, North Pole, and the musk ox farm. Alternatively, you could simply get around by **taxi** (for numbers see Listings, p.524).

Another option is to **rent a bicycle** (see Listings, p.523), although it is worth considering that even sights within the immediate vicinity of Fairbanks are widely scattered: Fox is eleven miles north, North Pole is fifteen miles southeast, and Ester is six miles northwest. Dedicated cycle trails are rare, but the Chena River Trail, from Fort Wainwright to the Chena River Recreation Site, is at last taking shape as a very useful crosstown route. The invaluable *BikeWays* map (available free from the visitor center) details multiuse paths, quiet roads with broad shoulders, and the expressways where bikes are not permitted, along with the location of hills. Bike-rental places will be able to point you in the direction of **mountain-bike** trails, mostly in the cross-country ski area known as Skarland Trails behind the university (maps from UAF's Wood Center; Ⓦwww.uaf.edu/trails) and in Birch Hill Recreation Area just north of downtown (map posted near the entry).

Accommodation

Fairbanks' accommodation is broadly distributed over an already spread-out city. With a few exceptions, non-drivers will want to stay **downtown** (roughly within twenty minutes' walk of the visitor center), where you'll have the best access to the bus system. **Hotels and motels** here are generally either pricey or drab, but fortunately there are a couple of good hostels and some excellent **B&Bs** at reasonable prices.

Having your own wheels opens up **suburban Fairbanks**, the domain of better-value motels, more good B&Bs and hostels, and some surprisingly sylvan campgrounds. Some of the best B&Bs and campgrounds lie beyond the city limits, often giving better access to the sights around Fairbanks.

Reservations are pretty much essential from June to August when **prices** are correspondingly high, especially during the Golden Days festival in mid-July (see box, p.513). With the exception of major festivals, such as the Ice Art competition (see box, p.503), the city is free of visitors through much of the **winter**, and hotel rates are about half those of summer.

Hostels

Fairbanks is not especially well supplied with hostels. Although there are a couple of decent places, neither is downtown.

Billie's Backpackers Hostel 2895 Mack Rd ☎479-2034, ⊛www.alaskahostel .com. Handily sited place that always seems to be packed, partly because Alaska/Yukon Trails buses finish various runs here. Comfortable and relaxing, with mountain bikes for rent and free Internet access. Dorms ($28) each have their own bathroom and kitchen, there is a barbecue area outside, and laundry and bag-storage facilities are available. Tent spaces $15 per person. Take the MACS Red bus to Westwood Ave.

Boyle's Hostel 310 18th Ave ☎456-4944. Bargain-basement hostel with dorms ($20), budget rooms, and tent space ($13) on a suburban street (near the MACS Red and Green bus routes) that will be unacceptably cluttered and too dark and dingy for many, though Mr Boyle is friendly and helpful. Low-cost laundry, some cooking facilities, and rattling bikes for rent. ❶

GoNorth Base Camp 3500 Davis Rd ☎479-7272, ⊛www.paratours.net. Based around a series of large fixed tents each with five beds ($24; bring a sleeping bag), this forest-girt place has a real outdoors feel with an open-sided (but with protection from bugs) kitchen and lounge that's great in good weather and OK when it's wet. There's camping, too, in your own tent or their teepee ($12), rental bikes ($10 for 6 hours, $18 for 24hr, $80 for a week), Internet (with Skype), and handy access to all the trips and equipment offered by GoNorth (see p.516). MACS Yellow bus. May to mid-Oct.

Hotels and motels

In summer almost all the hotels are packed with tour groups being paraded around the state after their cruise up the Inside Passage. Tour companies often book a handful of large, lackluster places scattered around town, none of which really warrants a mention. We've listed a few smaller, more personal places along with a range of the city's best motels.

Downtown

Ambassador Inn 415 5th Ave ☎451-9555. Family-run hotel with quite a few long-term residents and some fairly scruffy public areas, but it's central and the rooms, with cable TV and a full kitchen, are decently priced. ❹

Bridgewater 723 1st Ave ☎1-800/528-4916, ⊛www.fountainheadhotels.com. Decent tourist hotel with comfortable nonsmoking rooms, a café, and a nice lounge area with free Internet. The larger corner suites with bathtub and river views are the best, but they're in high demand. Mid-May to mid-Sept. ❺–❻

Golden Nugget 900 Noble St at 9th Ave ☎452-5141, ⊛www.golden-nuggethotel.com. Spartan but comfortable, this mid-range hotel is rather a period piece, with a restaurant and air-conditioned rooms with queen beds and cable TV, but not much of a view from any room. ❹

Springhill Suites 575 1st Ave ☎1-877/729-0197, ⊛www.springhillsuites.com. Modern but bland all-suites *Marriott* hotel right downtown complete with restaurant, indoor pool, exercise room, laundry, and free breakfast buffet. Rooms are spacious with fridge, microwave, cable TV, and dataport (plus free WiFi in the lobby). ❼

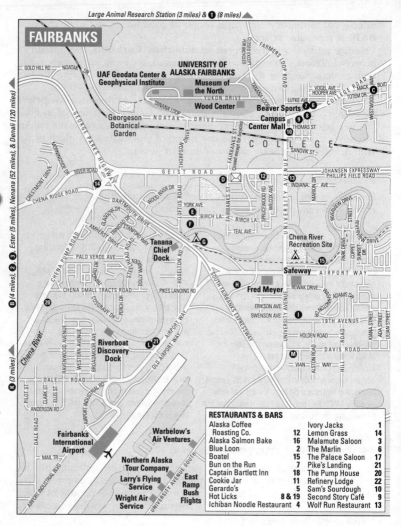

Large Animal Research Station (3 miles) & ❶ (8 miles) ▲

FAIRBANKS

UNIVERSITY OF
ALASKA FAIRBANKS

UAF Geodata Center &
Geophysical Institute

Museum of
the North

Wood Center

Beaver Sports

Georgeson
Botanical
Garden

Campus
Center Mall

COLLEGE

Chena River
Recreation Site

Safeway

Fred Meyer

Tanana
Chief
Dock

Chena River

Riverboat
Discovery
Dock

Fairbanks
International
Airport

Warbelow's
Air Ventures

Northern Alaska
Tour Company

Larry's Flying
Service

Wright Air
Service

East
Ramp
Bush
Flights

RESTAURANTS & BARS

Alaska Coffee		Ivory Jacks	1
Roasting Co.	12	Lemon Grass	14
Alaska Salmon Bake	16	Malamute Saloon	3
Blue Loon	2	The Marlin	6
Boatel	15	The Palace Saloon	17
Bun on the Run	7	Pike's Landing	21
Captain Bartlett Inn	18	The Pump House	20
Cookie Jar	11	Refinery Lodge	22
Gerardo's	5	Sam's Sourdough	10
Hot Licks	8 & 19	Second Story Café	9
Ichiban Noodle Restaurant	4	Wolf Run Restaurant	13

Wedgewood Resort 212 Wedgewood Drive
☎452-1442, ⊛ www.fountainheadhotels.com. Built
for pipeline workers in the 1970s, this sprawling
site now has HUGE suites with kitchenette; breakfast available in a café mid-May to mid-Sept only.
WiFi in the lobby. ❼

Suburban Fairbanks

College Inn 700 Fairbanks St ☎474-3666. Long-
term residents and the ageing infrastructure make
this a fairly dispiriting and charmless place to stay,
but it is cheap, handy for the university, and on the

MACS Blue and Red bus routes. Shared-bath rooms
come with towels and HBO, and there is a kitchen,
but no utensils, crockery, or cutlery. ❸

Golden North Motel 4888 Old Airport Rd
☎1-800/447-1910, ⊛ www
.goldennorthmotel.com. Friendly and spotless
motel with neat rooms (some with separate
lounge area) with cable TV, WiFi, and free continental breakfast. Located out towards the airport,
they do courtesy train and airport pickups and the
Yellow and Blue buses pass nearby. Large rooms
❹, economy rooms ❸

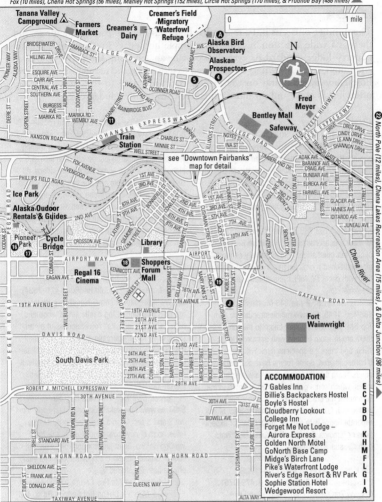

Fox (10 miles), Chena Hot Springs (56 miles), Manley Hot Springs (152 miles), Circle Hot Springs (170 miles), & Prudhoe Bay (486 miles)

North Pole (12 miles), Chena Lakes Recreation Area (15 miles), & Delta Junction (96 miles)

see "Downtown Fairbanks" map for detail

ACCOMMODATION	
7 Gables Inn	E
Billie's Backpackers Hostel	C
Boyle's Hostel	J
Cloudberry Lookout	B
College Inn	D
Forget Me Not Lodge – Aurora Express	K
Golden North Motel	H
GoNorth Base Camp	M
Midge's Birch Lane	F
Pike's Waterfront Lodge	L
River's Edge Resort & RV Park	G
Sophie Station Hotel	I
Wedgewood Resort	A

Pike's Waterfront Lodge 1850 Hoselton Rd ☎ 1-877/774-2400, ⓦ www.pikeslodge.com. A big, modern hotel near the airport (free shuttle) with a popular riverside restaurant. Rooms are large, with WiFi, microwave, and breakfast included, and there's a gym, sauna, and business center. Summer ⑤–⑧, winter ④

River's Edge Resort 4200 Boat St ☎ 1-800/770-3343, ⓦ www.riversedge.net. A large complex of boxy, modern cottages (open only in summer) with serviceable on-site restaurant and bar, and shuttles to all the major attractions. All cabins

come with two queen-sized beds and doors out onto a patio, though it is worth booking early to secure one with a riverfront setting. Fri & Sat ⑦, weeknights ⑥

Sophie Station Hotel 1717 University Ave ☎ 1-800/528-4916, ⓦ www.fountainheadhotels .com. Five minutes from the airport (with a free shuttle), with huge rooms, gym, WiFi and ethernet; breakfast costs $7 and is only served from 9am to 11am, but there's a nice restaurant for dinner. ⑤

B&Bs

The number of B&Bs in Fairbanks has boomed over the past decade or so, and there is a wide selection, ranging from simple homestays to places approaching country-lodge standard. As ever, they provide an appealing alternative to motels and hotels, and few owners are prepared to jeopardize the reputation of Alaskan hospitality by skimping on the breakfasts. Places close to the city center are often just as good and no more expensive than more secluded ones.

Downtown

Ah, Rose Marie 302 Cowles St ☏ 456-2040, ✉ ahrosemarie@yahoo.com. Justly popular B&B that's a little cramped but imaginatively decorated and well run by the charming John Davis. A hearty breakfast is served on the glassed-in front porch. Open all year; single rooms start at ❷, shared- and private-bath room ❸

All Seasons Inn 763 7th Ave ☏ 1-888/451-6649, ⓦ www.allseasonsinn.com. Attractive B&B inn on a central but quiet street with eight very comfortable air-conditioned rooms (one with disabled facilities) with cable TV, WiFi, cycle storage, and a great breakfast. ❻

Minnie Street B&B Inn 345 Minnie St ☏ 1-888/456-1849, ⓦ www.minniestreetbandb.com. Top B&B with every luxury taken to the nth degree: there are in-room phones with dataports (plus WiFi), and there's a spacious deck with hot tub and a barbecue area. Some rooms have a Jacuzzi while others share a bathroom, but you always get bath robes, which some guests even wear down to the communal full breakfast. There's also a business center with fax, copier, and Internet access, plus a separate house with garage that's ideal for expeditions or families. Room with Jacuzzi ❼, private bath ❻, shared bath ❺

Suburban Fairbanks

7 Gables Inn 4312 Birch Lane ☏ 479-0751, ⓦ www.7gablesinn.com. Popular and ever-expanding upscale B&B that is large enough to qualify as a small hotel; large rooms all with cable, VCR, and WiFi (and most with Jacuzzi) and flashy suites with a small kitchen. With the river just across the road, canoes and kayaks are free for guests ($35 per day for non-guests) and bikes cost $20 per day. Open all year; suites ❻, rooms ❺, with shared bath ❹

Forget Me Not Lodge – Aurora Express 1540 Chena Ridge Rd, about 8 miles west of downtown ☏ 1-800/221-0073, ⓦ www.aurora-express.com. A fun B&B partly in a lodge and partly in a set of old train carriages, with great views over Fairbanks towards the Alaska Range. Suites and carriage rooms ❺–❻, lodge rooms ❸

Midge's Birch Lane 4335 Birch Lane ☏ 388-8084, ⓦ www.alaskaone.com/midgebb. One of the best B&Bs in the city. It's neat, clean, and friendly, with access to a large lounge with fireplace, a piano, and stacks of Alaska books and videos. All rooms are comfortable and one has a large queen-sized bed, a walk-in wardrobe, private bath, and a deck that gets the afternoon sun. Breakfasts are excellent and may include blintzes or salmon quiche. A twenty-minute walk from the university. Private- and shared-bath rooms ❸

Out of town

Cloudberry Lookout 351 Cloudberry Lane, Mile 2.6 Gold Hill Rd ☏ 479-7334, ⓦ www.mosquitonet.com/~cloudberry. Welcoming B&B in a kind of log castle set in woodland with its own "aurorium" tower accessed by an impressive spiral staircase. Spacious rooms all have private bath, big windows, no TV, and lots of books; kitchen and laundry facilities are available. A tasty continental breakfast is included. March–Oct. ❺

Fox Creek B&B Mile 1.1 Elliott Hwy, Fox ☏ 457-5494, ⓦ www.foxcreekalaska.com. Just two rooms (for 3 and 5 people) in a secluded house twelve miles north of downtown and close to the *Howling Dog Saloon*. Quiet and comfortable, with big, cooked breakfasts. No credit cards. Open all year; private bath ❹, shared ❸

A Taste of Alaska Lodge 551 Eberhardt Rd, Mile 5.3 Chena Hot Springs Rd ☏ 488-7855, ⓦ www.atasteofalaska.com. Somewhere in between a B&B and a small country lodge, located on 280 acres on a ridge with a huge pond and wonderful views south to the Alaska Range. Comfortable rooms have cable TV, WiFi, and all the expected appointments, plus there's a hot tub and panning on their gold claim. Open all year; two-bedroom log house ❽, suites and rooms ❼

Trailhead Cabins Middle Fork ☏ 374-0717, ⓦ www.trailheadcabins.com. A real Alaskan experience awaits in these cabins, tucked just below the tree line on Haystack Mountain. It's a little inconvenient for Fairbanks (5 miles east from Mile 11.2 of the Elliott Hwy and 35 minutes' drive north of town), but makes a great base for exploring the North. The single-room cabins ($65) have a double with a single bunk above, and come with cooking facilities, breakfast requisites, an outhouse, and supply of water, but no shower or running water. The website has a map to the cabins and another of local trails in the White Mountains Recreation Area. ❷

Campgrounds and RV parks

Fairbanks is well served with places to park an RV, and many sites are pleasant for pitching a tent, though none is entirely RV-free. Campgrounds within the city limits are right on bus routes, though drivers can save a few dollars by staying a short drive out of town.

Suburban Fairbanks

Chena River State Recreation Site 221 University Ave at Airport Way ☎452-7275. A state parks campground by the Chena River that is surprisingly wooded and quiet for what is essentially a city campground. There are toilets, tables, a dump station, WiFi, volleyball courts, and even a boat launch. Walk-in tent sites for $10, dry vehicle slots for $15, and limited hookups for $22. On the MACS Blue bus route, and close to the Yellow airport bus; or follow the riverside cycle route to the center.

Pioneer Park 2300 Airport Way at Peger Rd ☎459-1095. Park your RV in the Pioneer Park parking lot and use their toilets, water, and dump station; no showers. $10 a night (four nights maximum). Take the MACS Blue and Yellow buses into town, or cycle the riverside trail. April–Sept.

River's Edge RV Park 4200 Boat St ☎474-0286 or 1-800/770-3343, ⊕www.riversedge .net. Fairbanks' largest RV park, adjacent to the *River's Edge Resort* (see p.499). Full hookup sites go for $30, tent sites are $19. The Yellow MACS bus stops outside. Mid-May to mid-Sept.

Tanana Valley Campground 1800 College Rd at Aurora Drive ☎456-7956, ⊕www.tananavalleyfair .org/campground.shtml. Peaceful, spruce-shrouded campground that's best for tenters and RVers who only want electrical hookups. Sites all come with tables and fire pits (wood sold), showers are free ($3 for non-guests), and there's a dump station, laundry, free Internet access, and a camp kitchen serving good meals throughout the day. Best of all, it is located midway between downtown and the university area on the MACS Red bus line (hourly or better). They also have free bikes for guests. Electrical hookups $16, dry RV sites $14, tent sites $10. Reserve a day or two in advance. Mid-May to mid-Sept.

Out of town

Chena Lakes Recreation Area Laurance Rd, Mile 347 Richardson Hwy ☎488-1655. Wooded camping and RV sites with no hookups located in an attractive recreation area seventeen miles southeast of Fairbanks. $10.

Ester Gold Camp Old Nenana Hwy, Ester ☎1-800/676-6925, ⊕www.akvisit.com/ester. Basic RV park without hookups, but with a dump station, showers, and a free coffee-and-muffin breakfast. Located at Ester (see p.514), half a mile from Mile 351 on the Parks Hwy, six miles northwest of town. Late May to early Sept. RV $15, tent $10.

Santaland RV Park 125 St Nicholas Drive, North Pole ☎1-888/488-9123, ⊕www.santalandrv.com. Reached from Fairbanks by shuttle, dry and tent sites cost $18 and full hookup pull-throughs $29; there's a dump station, cable TV, laundry, and private bathrooms.

The city and around

Downtown Fairbanks is on the up, with a rash of new building and a bit of civic pride finally taking hold. It's about time, too, as the absence of oil cash, which kept downtown buoyant in the 1970s, had turned once vibrant blocks into a depressing collection of neglected truck showrooms and parking lots gone to seed. Some of the old miners' cottages have been co-opted by small businesses – hairdressers, accountants, and graphic-arts companies. Still, downtown shouldn't take up much of your time: besides the visitor center, APLIC, and a couple of small museums, there isn't a great deal to divert your attention.

△ Downtown Fairbanks across the Chena River

The most concentrated area of genuine interest for visitors is on the city's northern flank along College Road towards the university. Outside of the school's first-class museum, sights tend to revolve around animals and nature: you can visit a waterfowl refuge, walk around the pleasant confines of the **Georgeson Botanical Gardens**, or drive north to view the musk oxen and caribou at the **Large Animal Research Station**.

There's an appreciably more kitschy approach at the forty-acre **Pioneer Park** complex, which showcases early Fairbanks buildings and the restored SS *Nenana* sternwheeler along with assorted kids' entertainments; it can be quite fun and most of it is free. In contrast, rides along the Chena River on the replica stern-wheeler *Riverboat Discovery* are bland and geared toward mass tourism, especially in terms of price.

The sights in Fairbanks might only keep you entertained for a day or so, but the city makes the best base for attractions in the immediate vicinity. No one with kids will be able to avoid visiting Santa at **North Pole**, fifteen miles to the southeast; fans of gold-rush poet Robert Service will want to spend an evening in **Ester**, six miles west; and the district's mining heritage can be experienced at one of three extensive sites in **Fox**, eleven miles to the north.

Downtown

Unless you've developed a deep interest in the machinations of Fairbanks' early civic leaders, skip the detailed self-guided downtown tour ($1 booklet from the visitor center) and concentrate on a few key sights, outlined here. The visitor center lies on the south bank of the languid Chena River where logs were once floated along for the construction of the town. It is now flanked by small patches of parkland, some long neglected, others overly tended. Foremost among the latter is **Golden Heart Plaza**, an open riverside area focusing on Malcolm Alexander's statue *Unknown First Family*, dedicated

Fairbanks' winter temperatures stay below 0°F for months on end, metal-snapping freezes below -40°F are expected and -60°F is not unknown, so it is no surprise that most visitors stay away from the end of September (when the temperatures are already getting nippy) until the end of April, when the last of the snow melts away. Still, a few hardy visitors do venture up this way, notably Japanese honeymooners, who put great store in consummating their marriage under the **northern lights** (see box, p.506), and those making pilgrimages to Fairbanks' two major winter events. Intending winter visitors should obtain the *Winter Guide* from the visitor center (also available at ⓦwww.explorefairbanks.com).

The Yukon Quest

The first of these events is the **Yukon Quest International Sled Dog Race** (ⓦwww .yukonquest.org), a thousand-mile classic between Fairbanks and Whitehorse, Yukon, over some of the wildest and most sparsely populated country anywhere. By most estimations it ranks second to the Iditarod in the sled-racing hierarchy (and is around a hundred miles shorter), but many mushers cite its infrequent checkpoints to support their claim that it is the tougher of the two races. It is less a series of sprints between checkpoints than a grueling endurance test requiring heavier loads and more sleeping rough on the trail, rigorously testing the self-sufficiency, determination, and dog-driving ability of the competitor. The race has been run in the second week of February (when river ice is at its thickest) since 1984 and alternates direction each year, starting in Fairbanks in even-numbered years. It largely follows the route of the Steese Highway from Fairbanks to Circle so, unlike the Iditarod, spectators can watch at various points. From Circle it then heads up the Yukon River through the Yukon-Charley National Preserve past Eagle to Dawson City, where there is a compulsory 36-hour layover before the final run into Whitehorse. Most competitors use teams of fourteen dogs and take ten to fourteen days, hoping to take home the first prize of around $30,000.

Fairbanks also hosts a number of shorter races, notably the **Open North American Sled Dog Races** (ⓦwww.sleddog.org), twenty-mile "sprints" which take place in March, starting and finishing downtown.

Ice art

Though the Yukon Quest is spectator-friendly, far more visitors come during the first two weeks in March for the **World Ice Art Championships** in the Ice Park on Chena Landing Loop off Phillips Field Road (reached by the Yellow bus). Sculptors come from around the world (Japan, China, and even Togo, among others) and strive to produce larger-than-life sculptures from blemish-free blocks of ice, harvested throughout winter from the adjacent O'Grady Pond. The chunks are fashioned using saws, picks, chainsaws, chisels, sanders, angle grinders, even electric irons into sculptures up to 35ft high. Along with prosaic natural subjects – polar bears, caribou, ice-fishing Natives – fantasy themes are popular, with images of medieval castles and jousting contests.

The event starts with the Single Block Classic, in which teams of two spend sixty hours shaping a single, solid 8000-pound block measuring 5ft by 8ft by 3ft. This is followed (after weekend's rest) by the Multi-Block Classic, where teams of four have five and a half days to transform ten 4600-pound blocks measuring 4ft by 6ft by 3.3ft. In the second half of the second week there's also the Fairbanks Open for novices, who hack at blocks 5ft by 3ft by 3ft. Competitors work through the day and night, with colorful lighting illuminating the works as they take shape, although judging is done under white light. The work remains on display through March at the Winter Carnival, where there's also a gift shop and Kids' Park with ice slides. The whole process, along with details of next year's contest, can be found at ⓦwww.icealaska.com, which also hosts a webcam that allows you to observe the artists' progress from the relative warmth of your home or hotel room.

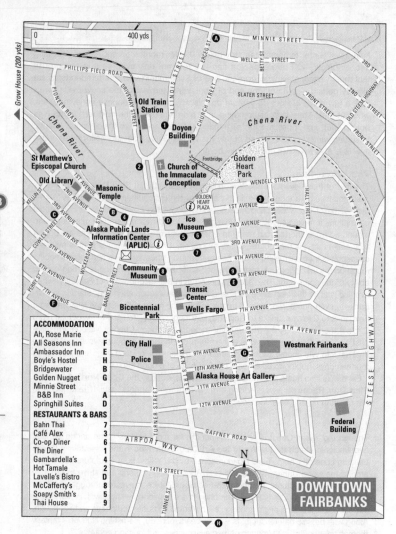

DOWNTOWN FAIRBANKS

0   400 yds

Grow House (200 yds)

Chena River

PHILLIPS FIELD ROAD

PIONEER ROAD

DRIVEWAY STREET

Old Train
Station

1 Doyon
Building

2 ✝ Church of
the Immaculate
Conception

St Matthew's
Episcopal Church

Old Library

Masonic
Temple

KELLUM ST

1st AVENUE

2nd AVENUE

3RD AVENUE

4TH AVE

5TH AVENUE

6TH AVENUE

7TH AVENUE

COWLES STREET

PERRY ST

WICKERSHAM

STREET

BARNETTE STREET

B **4**

C

F

Alaska Public Lands
Information Center
(APLIC) ⓘ

✉

Community
Museum **8**

Bicentennial
Park

City Hall

Police

TURNER STREET

AIRPORT WAY

14TH STREET

TURNER ST

GAFFNEY ROAD

12TH AVENUE

11TH AVENUE

10TH AVENUE

9TH AVENUE

CUSHMAN STREET

ERCCG ST

MINNIE STREET

WELL   STREET

BETTY ST

ILLINOIS STREET

CHURCH STREET

SLATER STREET

FRONT STREET

3RD ST

2ND STREET

OLD STEESE HIGHWAY

Chena River

Footbridge   Golden
Heart
Park

GOLDEN
HEART
PLAZA ⓘ

D

Ice
Museum

5 **6**

7

WENDELL STREET

1ST AVENUE

2ND AVENUE

3RD AVENUE

4TH AVENUE

5TH AVENUE **9**
E

6TH AVENUE

Transit
Center

Wells Fargo   7TH AVENUE

8TH AVENUE

DUNKEL STREET

HALL STREET

CLAY STREET

3

LACEY STREET

NOBLE STREET

G

Alaska House Art Gallery

Westmark Fairbanks

STEESE HIGHWAY

Federal
Building

2

N

A

H

to the "indomitable spirit of the people of Alaska's Interior." Immediately west, a plaque marks the spot where Fairbanks' founder, E.T. Barnette, was left stranded with his supplies in 1901. A short walk west along 1st Avenue takes you past the 1906 **Masonic Temple**, built as E.T. Barnette's home, then adapted with the addition of a second story for the Masons in 1913 and later used by President Warren Harding when he addressed the populace in 1923. Just beyond is the female equivalent, the Rebekah Lodge, built in 1913, and across Cowles Street the former library, built in 1909.

It isn't often you see a stained-glass depiction of an Alaskan sled dog or an Iñupiat on his way to church in the snow, but you can inside the 1947 **St Matthew's Episcopal Church**, 1029 1st Ave. It replaced the 1905 original built for Hudson Stuck, archdeacon of the Episcopal Church in Alaska from

1903 to 1920, a man noted primarily for being the first to reach Mount McKinley's summit (see box, p.406). Another glass shows him leaving for the mountain complete with a huge cross around his neck, which was later placed at the summit. You'll see the front page of the *Fairbanks Daily Times* announcing the ascent here in the church, and a range of historical photos in the hall behind. This whole stretch of 1st Avenue (originally Front Street) is being beautified and branded as Barnette's Landing. A couple of blocks further on there's a classic example of a **"grow-house"** at 1323 1st Ave, a basic log cabin that was extended out back with each new addition to the family, in this case four times.

Cross the Chena River on the Cushman Street bridge (until 1917 the crossing used to alternate between Turner and Cushman streets as it was rebuilt after break-up) to the prim **Church of the Immaculate Conception** (Mon–Fri 8am–4pm), which wouldn't look out of place in New England and has an ornate pressed-tin ceiling. The church was built south of the river in 1904 and moved across the ice to its current site during the winter of 1911, hence its nickname, the "Holy Rolly Church". Just east are the headquarters of the Doyon Native corporation, a modern block with a great selection of Native art on the first and second floors.

There are also a couple of museums downtown, notably the enjoyable **Fairbanks Community Museum**, in the former city hall at 410 Cushman St (Tues–Sat 10am–6pm; donation appreciated; ☎457-3669, ⓦwww .fairbankscommunitymuseum.com), which contains locally donated trapping, mining, and dog-sled-racing equipment, along with a mock-up of a trapper's cabin, assorted prospecting implements, and a handmade Athabascan birch sled lined up next to its modern racing equivalent as well as a 1967 Ski-doo snowmobile (capable of just 15mph). There's a revealing exhibition on life in Fairbanks in the winter (plus a temporary exhibition every summer), and the history display is being adjusted to give more coverage of Interior and Athabascan culture (and less of Dawson and the Iditarod). Check out the nice little diorama of Barnette's Cache in the spring of 1902, the early photo of 1st Avenue with its waterfront bars and cafés, and movie posters of such forgotten classics as *Red Snow*, *Alaska Seas*, and Abbott and Costello's *Lost in Alaska*. The museum incorporates the Dog Mushing Museum and acts as the public face of the **Yukon Quest** sled-dog race (see box, p.503), selling related books, videos, and T-shirts.

A similar winter theme is pursued at the **Ice Museum**, in the Deco former Lacey Street Theater at 500 2nd Ave (June to mid-Sept daily 10am–9pm; $8), a summertime chance to get a flavor of the annual Ice Art competition (see box, p.503). The impressive images screened in the half-hour slide show fall well short of the real thing, but you can see a few small sculptures by walking into two freezer rooms, one kept at the typical March daytime temperature of 20°F, the other maintained at the expected nighttime temperature of -15°F. It's also worth popping into KeyBank at 100 Cushman St, where historic photos and gold nuggets are displayed.

Along College Road and around the university

From the downtown area College Road (followed by Blue and Red MACS buses) arcs out along the northern flank of the city, and buildings become scarce after a mile or so, revealing the open fields of **Creamer's Field Migratory Waterfowl Refuge**, 1300 College Rd (unrestricted entry), at Creamer's Dairy.

The northern lights

It is impossible to witness such a beautiful phenomenon without a sense of awe, and yet this sentiment is not inspired by its brilliancy but rather by its delicacy in light and colour, its transparency, and above all its tremulous evanescence of form. There is no glittering splendour to dazzle the eye, as has been too often described; rather the appeal is to the imagination by the suggestion of something wholly spiritual...

Robert Scott

Words never fully capture the dynamic majesty of the **aurora borealis**, but Scott (writing of its southern-hemisphere counterpart, the aurora australis) comes close and, in *Arctic Dreams*, Barry Lopez perceptively writes of a "banner of pale light" appearing like "a t'ai chi exercise: graceful, inward-turning, and protracted." Everyone has their own explanation: one Inuit legend suggests the lights represent spirits playing ball with a walrus skull; another asserts they are spirits carrying torches to guide nomads to the afterlife; and a third sees the souls of their ancestors in these undulating gossamer strands. Ever hopeful, early prospectors saw them either as reflections of the mother lode or vapors from rich deposits as yet unfound. Galileo was loath to offer an explanation, but named them Aurora, after the Roman goddess of the dawn.

As you gaze at these celestial pyrotechnics you feel no need or desire to explain them. It is enough just to marvel as silken curtains of light miraculously materialize, then just as soon curl up and disappear, or hang around for hours on end folding back on themselves, delicately changing hue from rose pink to pale green and on to white, fading with the early light of dawn. The curtain effect isn't illusory; the band of light may hang from an altitude of three hundred miles down to forty miles above the earth and stretch for hundreds of miles, and yet be only a hundred yards wide.

The University of Alaska Fairbanks is at the forefront of research into the northern lights. Both are caused by an interaction between the earth's magnetic field and the **solar wind**, an invisible stream of charged electrons and protons continually blown out into space by the innate violence of the sun. The earth deflects the solar wind like a rock in a stream, the magnetic field channeling the charged particles down towards the earth's magnetic poles. Here the protons and electrons release some of their energy as visible light – much like a neon sign – the common yellowish

---

It was established in 1903 with three cows brought from Nome by the brother-in-law of the aptly named Charles Creamer, who operated it until 1966. Four years later, the state bought it and decided to continue the dairy's practice of spreading manure in spring (originally done to hasten snow melt), containing undigested grain that attracted migrant birds. The fields are still farmed and now provide a temporary resting place for several large species, including thousands of **sandhill cranes**, which leave their wintering grounds in Texas and New Mexico and pause here to recuperate in late April, some sticking around for the summer to breed here, others flying on to Siberia. Many return in fall to fatten up for the return flight south. **Canada geese** make a slightly shorter passage from the Pacific Northwest – the first V-shaped skeins heralding the arrival of spring – and you might also expect to see predatory peregrine falcons and bald eagles, along with pintails, golden plovers, and mallards. Visitors and locals park up beside College Road, training binoculars and telephoto lenses at the fields, but you may as well head to the house beside the dairy buildings, now an instructive **visitor center** (June–Aug daily 10am–5pm; Sept–May Sat noon–4pm). From there you can pick up one of two **trails** through the woods: the educational Boreal Forest

green produced by oxygen atoms, and the purples and rare deep reds caused by nitrogen.

While their manifestations may seem gentle, the forces involved are immense, occasionally blocking out radio communications and inducing magnetic fields in pipes, making them more susceptible to corrosion; even the oil pipeline is affected. The aurora's electrical charge can also cause power blackouts: on March 13, 1989, much of eastern Canada and the northeastern US was dark for six hours as a result of unusually powerful aurora activity. The aurora is now at the low end of an eleven-year cycle, and because the northern magnetic pole is drifting away from North America and may be in Siberia within fifty years, Alaska may lose its auroras, which would then be more visible in Siberia and Europe.

The northern lights are a circumpolar phenomenon, and it is only at times of extreme solar activity that they are seen at lower latitudes; in Fairbanks, however, they are almost continual. In summer there is too much daylight to see them clearly, but as the nights grow longer your chances of a good showing increase. The **best viewing** is when the sky is clear and the air chilly, preferably at the vernal equinox around March 20. At this time the worst of the winter temperatures have passed, and Fairbanks hotels do a roaring trade, some specializing in aurora packages aimed mostly at the Japanese, who have a particular passion for the lights, some believing that children conceived under the aurora will be successful in business.

For more information, consult the *Aurora Watcher's Handbook* by Neil Davis (University of Alaska Press), the UAF Geophysical Institute's aurora website (@www.gi.alaska.edu/cgi-bin/predict.cgi), which has a weekly aurora forecast with a map and a stack of other material pertaining to the phenomenon, or their auroral FAQs: @odin.gi.alaska.edu/FAQ.

Photographing the aurora isn't easy: expect to be disappointed with your results. If you're still keen, load up with a 200 or 400 ASA film, pick a time when the aurora is fairly stable, use a wide-angle lens, and go for exposures from one to thirty seconds using a tripod. Short exposures are usually better, but take notes and experiment on subsequent nights. You should also protect your camera from the cold, ground it to a large metal object so that static electricity doesn't cause streaks on the film, and wrap the camera in a plastic bag when you return inside to prevent damage from condensation.

Trail (2 miles) follows a packed-earth path and boardwalks through birch bog and out through grasslands regenerating after a fire; the seasonal Wetland Trail (1.4 miles) is best in early summer but worthwhile later to visit the bird-banding station where from August to mid-September you're likely to encounter songbird research in practice. If you can time it right, try to join one of the two-hour **nature walks** led by volunteer naturalists (June–Aug Mon & Wed 9am, Tues & Thurs 7pm; free; for subject matter call ☎452-7307).

A further trail leads east across the refuge to the **Alaska Bird Observatory**, 418 Wedgewood Drive (mid-May to Sept Mon–Thurs 9am–9pm, Fri 9am–6pm, Sat 10am–4pm; Oct to mid-May Mon–Fri 10am–5pm; ☎451-7159, @www.alaskabird.org), which conducts the refuge's banding operation, has a small display of mounted bird specimens and some active feeding stations, and is a must for keen birders, with its small library and shop, lists of recently seen birds, and arrival dates for migratory species. A Spring Migration Celebration is held on the last weekend of April, and the Sandhill Crane Festival in August. To reach the ABO, follow signs through the maze of the Wedgewood Resort, built for pipeline construction in the 1970s; you'll see an Alaskan flower garden in summer and ice sculptures in winter, plus an Aeronca Champ (a classic bush plane built in 1946), Mary Shields' sled from the 1974 Iditarod, and an early twentieth-century cabin. Another of Fairbanks' prime bird-watching spots is the **South Cushman Ponds**, around four hundred acres of wetlands (former gravel pits, now used mainly for dumping cars) south of the Tanana River levee between Lathrop Avenue and South Cushman Street. By 2010 this land should become the Tanana Lakes Recreation Area, with nature trails, boardwalks, camping, picnic areas, restrooms, fishing spots, and a boat ramp.

Half a mile west of the ABO is the Tanana Valley **Farmers Market** (May–Sept Wed 11am–4pm, Sat 9am–4pm; ⓦwww.tvfmarket.com), a forum for local growers to sell their produce along with crafts, freshly baked sourdough bread, and more. As much as anything, it is a local meeting place, drawing a typically oddball cross-section of Alaskans: bush-dwellers, students, neo-hippies, and suburbanites.

A couple of miles further along College Road there is a small knot of restaurants, cafés, bars, and shops that constitutes the suburb of **College**, at the foot of the ridge from which the **University of Alaska Fairbanks** commands great views of the distant Alaska Range. This is the state's original campus, established in 1915, and it still considers itself the most prestigious, though Anchorage now has a larger enrollment. The main reason to venture up here is to visit the Museum of the North (see opposite), though during the school year you might want to wander into the **Wood Center** and see what's happening around campus. You'll find campus cafés and bars, and a handy rides board; nearby are the Arts Complex and Alaska's largest library (open to all; see ⓦwww.uaf.edu/library for hours).

The **UAF Geophysical Institute**, Elvey Building, 903 Koyukuk Drive, presents a free educational program (June–Aug Wed 2.30pm; ⓣ474-7558) with slide show, aurora video, and a visit to the Alaska Earthquake Information Center. This is immediately followed by a walk through the adjacent **International Arctic Research Center** (same dates 3.30pm), a headquarters for scientists studying Arctic and global climates. You could even start with a virtual tour of the Arctic Region Supercomputing Center, showing off its 3-D imaging facilities, on Tanana Loop at the rear of the Rasmusson Library (same dates, 1pm; ⓣ450-8600, ⓦwww.arsc.edu).

Nearby, at the western end of the campus, a narrow track leads four hundred yards down through the fields to the **Georgeson Botanical Gardens**, W Tanana Drive (May–Sept daily 7am–8pm; $2; ⓣ474-1944). In spring and early summer, the gardens are filled with colorful flowers and lush leafy greens, and as the summer wears on, you'll see huge vegetables almost as large as those produced in the Mat-Su Valley. It is perfect for a sunny afternoon or evening, full of seats and shady bowers where you can breathe in the fragrant air and gaze at the Alaska Range. There's a small visitor center (May–Sept daily 10am–6pm), and free guided tours take place in summer (Fri 2pm).

Unless you join a city tour, you'll need your own transport to get to the **Large Animal Research Station**, north of the university on Yankovich Road, off Farmers Loop Road. A roadside parking lot with viewing platforms gives you the chance to see herds of caribou and musk oxen, all part of the university's research program into their nutrition, physiology, and behavior. For a true sense of the ongoing work, hook up with one of the one-hour guided tours (mid-May and mid-Sept Tues & Sat 1.30pm; late May to early Sept daily 1.30 & 3.30pm, Tues–Sat 6.30pm; late Sept Sat 1.30pm; $10; ⓣ474-7202, ⓦwww.uaf.edu/lars; reservations taken only for large groups) that meet outside the main gate. At peak times there may also be half-hour tours for $6; there's also a gift shop (late May to early Sept daily 9.30am–5pm), where you can buy wonderfully warm products made of qiviut or musk ox wool.

The Museum of the North

🦌 UAF's **Museum of the North**, 907 Yukon Drive (mid-May to mid-Sept daily 9am–7pm; mid-Sept to mid-May Mon–Fri 9am–5pm, Sat & Sun noon–5pm; $10; ☎474-7505, ⓦwww.uaf.edu/museum), is the best in the state. An architecturally daring extension (whose shape suggests crevasses, whales, and other Alaskan features) opened in 2005, finally allowing the museum to display its sizeable art collection, as well as providing lab space for dissecting whales and other large mammals. There's also room for temporary displays, a summer exhibition on an Alaskan theme, and coverage of life Outside, aimed more at locals. From the spectacular foyer (flanked by a café and a shop, which is one of the best in town for Native crafts), go upstairs to the "art bridge" skywalk, with huge views to the south, and the **Rose Berry Art Gallery**, which houses an eclectic mix of works, with Native artifacts alongside oil paintings. The entry ramp leads to three masterpieces – the iconic Sydney Laurence painting of Mount McKinley; an Iñupiaq parka made of ground squirrel, wolf, and wolverine fur; and the so-called **Okvik Madonna**, a seven-inch walrus-ivory carving that frankly hits the Laurence for a homer. Around two thousand years old, it was found in 1934 by legendary self-taught anthropologist Otto Geist buried in an abandoned village on the Punuk Islands, 270 miles southwest of Nome. It's the finest piece of carved Eskimo ivory in a public collection, a figurine holding what might be a child, a seal, or a small god; there's a hint of the *Mona Lisa* or of Cycladic goddesses from Paros in its ambivalence. There's also a fullsize outhouse (complete with quintessentially Alaskan blue styrofoam seat), a caribou skin parka, and various works of modern art. Next to the gallery, **The Place Where You Go To Listen** (a translation of an Iñupiat place name) is a small room housing an entrancing light and noise installation by composer John Luther Adams which responds in real time to its environment, including the position and phases of the moon, the angle of the sun, outdoor light levels and other weather conditions, the aurora (shimmering veils of "bells" ringing in the ceiling), and the area's near-constant seismic activity ("earth drums" near the floor). Back on the ground floor, the **Alaska Classics** gallery is crammed with over ninety paintings by the most popular Alaskan artists, notably Eustace Ziegler and Sydney Laurence, as well as Fred Machetanz, Ted Lambert, Rusty Heurlin, and Claire Fejes.

The pre-extension displays remain shoehorned into one large room, divided by region. The entry area is crowded with stuffed examples of just about every Alaskan animal as well as a huge-tusked mammoth skull and **Blue Babe**, a steppe bison found in the permafrost in a local placer mine. It died 36,000 years ago and, over time, the phosphorus in the tissue reacted with the iron-rich soil to produce an all-over blueish tinge. Nevertheless, the bone, marrow, and skin were so well preserved that the cause of death – at the claws of the now extinct American lion – could be determined.

Behind these massive beasts are sections devoted to major geographic regions of the state, the Arctic partly represented by a replica of the **Boulder Patch**, an underwater garden of marine flora, soft corals, and sponges found in the Beaufort Sea, which is frozen over for much of the year. The kelp that thrives here manages to store photosynthesized energy in the summer, which it then uses from November to April when the ice prevents sunlight from penetrating the depths. Elsewhere, there are palm-sized gold nuggets and a lump of solid copper the size of a small sofa from the Wrangell Mountains; assorted ephemera of early Fairbanks life; a car built in Skagway in 1905 with a one-cylinder marine engine; amazingly finely woven grass baskets from the Aleutians; engaging, if gruesome, footage of traditional whale- and seal-hunting alongside wooden snow goggles and a seal-gut parka with auklet-feather detail; and the *Forced to Leave* video on the appalling conditions suffered by the Aleut during their internment in Southeast Alaska in World War II: a powerful and moving indictment of US policy towards a group of its own people.

There are various multimedia shows in the new auditorium, among them free twenty-minute "explainer talks" on Alaskan wildlife or Native culture, art, and sports. There are also two fifty-minute shows, the first of which, *Dynamic Aurora*, is endearingly nerdy, explaining the physics of the northern lights with excellent digital animations but perhaps failing to fully convey their visual poetry. The other, *Winter in Alaska*, covers the natural phenomena of the state's most distinctive season, cultural adaptations to life in the cold, and a look at the activities that sustain Alaskans through the long winter. Both show at least twice daily in summer, and cost about $7 each, additional to the museum entrance fee.

There is perhaps a broader appeal to the **Northern Inua Show** ($6.50), a fast-paced, 45-minute live celebration of traditional Alaskan games. All major tribal groups are represented, though you are left without much of an impression of the distinction between the tribes. Many of the games are highly athletic, harking back to necessary honing of traditional hunting and survival skills: the "stick pull" is said to represent hauling hunted seals from the water and involves competitors sitting on the floor facing each other, the soles of their feet touching, with both holding onto a stick. The one who gets pulled up or lets go loses. These are included in the World Eskimo-Indian Olympics (see box, p.503), while others are simply for entertainment through the long winter nights – one, for example, based on a competitor making faces while others have to refrain from laughing as long as possible.

Pioneer Park

Somehow almost everyone winds up at **Pioneer Park**, Airport Way at Peger Road (park grounds always open, shops and museums open late May to early Sept daily 11am–9pm; free), a kind of low-key theme park reached by the Blue and Yellow MACS buses. The place seems unsure of what it wants to be, but acquits itself well enough in fine weather, especially if you've got kids, who will undoubtedly enjoy the play areas, miniature golf, and toy train ($2). Otherwise it is better to come in the late afternoon, take a quick tour of the buildings, and stick around for the **Alaska Salmon Bake** (see p.520) and perhaps the nightly show at the *Palace Saloon* (see p.522).

Pioneer Park (known as Alaskaland until 2001) was set up in 1967 as part of the state's centennial of the Alaska purchase and as a way to save some of Fairbanks' original log buildings. Some thirty historic structures have been preserved and lined up to form a pioneer street, though almost all the architectural and historical merit is camouflaged by the shelves of the trinket stores that now occupy the houses. It is still worth strolling along, pausing to duck into the period-furnished **Kitty Hensley House** (free), opposite the **Wickersham House Museum** (donations appreciated) in the one-time residence of Judge James Wickersham; the restored **Harding Car** that the president used when visiting Nenana in 1923 to drive the railroad's golden spike; and the **Pioneer Museum** (March to late May Fri–Sun 1–5pm; late May to early Sept daily 11am–9pm; free), with its material on early telegraph systems during the gold

△ World Eskimo–Indian Olympics, Fairbanks

rush, a small collection of foot warmers used in open stages and sleighs, and an 1897 Rand McNally map showing trails to the Yukon and Klondike goldfields, including winter river routes. The adjacent, 45-minute **Big Stampede Show** (6 times daily; $4) has the audience seated on a large turntable that revolves as fifteen scenes from the gold rush, painted on the walls by Rusty Heurlin, are spotlighted in turn.

Though beached and in need of a lick of paint, the **SS Nenana** sternwheeler (late May to early Sept daily 11am–9pm; guided tours on demand; $3, diorama only $2) lends the park a dramatic focus. Launched in 1933, she was the last and one of the most luxurious of the great wooden-hulled sternwheeler steamers, coming at the end of the era when the Interior waterways were the easiest (if not the only) way to get around in summer. But she was really a workhorse, carrying three hundred tons of cargo with a draft of just 3.5ft and pushing up to six barges, making the 770-mile run from Nenana to the mouth of the Yukon and back ten times in the five-month season. Until her conversion to oil in 1948, lumberjacks often worked with dog sleds through the winter to supply wood stockpiles. By 1955 air transport had rendered the steamers uneconomic, and the *Nenana* languished until rescued in 1967 for Pioneer Park; she's now the only large wooden sternwheeler left in the US, although there are others in Canada. For a deeper insight into how the *Nenana* and her sisters influenced the development of the Interior, look around the detailed, 300-foot-long Tanana/Yukon Rivers Historical Diorama, which shows a couple of dozen villages along the two rivers.

Volunteers at the new **Railroad Museum** (donations accepted), by the river at the northen edge of the site, have brought together artifacts from the Tanana Valley Railroad, notably Locomotive No.1, which started its career in the Yukon Territory in 1899 and moved here in 1905; it has now been fitted with a new boiler, cab, and running gear and plies a half-mile track a dozen times a year. Next door is the **Native Village Museum** (donations accepted), housing Athabascan cultural materials and a mural of life along the river; the **Pioneer Air Museum** ($2; ☎451–0037, ⓦwww.akpub.com/aktt/aviat.html), under the gold dome just to the south and with a Beechcraft 18 outside, displays other planes, photos of the Lend–Lease flights to Russia, and scraps from the crashed planes of Carl Ben Eielson, the founder of Alaska Airlines who died on a rescue mission to a ship icebound off Siberia, and Wiley Post, killed near Barrow (see p.570).

The riverboats

Unlike Pioneer Park's static *Nenana*, you and seven hundred others can actually ride on the **Riverboat Discovery**, 1975 Discovery Road, near the airport (mid-May to mid-Sept daily 8.45am & 2pm; $47; ☎1–866/479–6673, ⓦwww.riverboatdiscovery.com), a replica sternwheeler that packs in the tour groups for its slick and not overly thrilling three-and-a-half-hour cruises. The Binkley family takes pride in now having their fourth generation of riverboat captains at the helm for this narrated trip on which you'll call at a replica Athabascan fishing village, watch salmon being prepared for air-drying, be entertained by a bush pilot doing a short takeoff and landing beside the river, and see an Iditarod veteran demonstrate dog-sledding. If you can't be bothered getting out of your seat, you can watch it all on closed-circuit TV between visits to the snack bars and gift shop.

In recent years the **Tanana Chief** (mid-May to mid-Sept; ☎1–866/452–8687, ⓦwww.greatlandrivertours.com) has set up in competition using a 1984 replica sternwheeler, which plied the Mississippi until being brought north in 2000. With a far smaller boat, it is a much more intimate experience, taking a couple of hours to head downstream from the dock at 1020 Hoselton Rd to the confluence with the Tanana River and back. Their dinner cruise (6.45pm; $50) runs nightly, there's a Sunday brunch special (noon; $37), and you can skip the meals and take either cruise for pure sightseeing ($25).

Towards Fox

The only major route north from Fairbanks – and the access to most of the area's hot springs, canoe routes, and hiking trails – is the Steese Highway. This

8

Fairbanks festivals

In early February the Yukon Quest sled-dog race is in town, and the World Ice Art Championships take place over the first two weeks in March (see box, p.503), immediately followed by the revelry of the Fairbanks Winter Carnival. Summer gets into full swing at the summer solstice (June 20 and 21) with the Midnight Sun Fun Run, the 30,000-strong Midnight Sun street fair, and the **Midnight Sun Baseball Game**, a long-standing tradition from the gold days (first played around 1905) in which Fairbanks' semi-pro team, the Goldpanners, plays without artificial lights from dusk (around 10.30pm) until sunrise some two or three hours later. Around the middle of July the **World Eskimo-Indian Olympics** (Ⓦ www.weio.org) pits Native athletes against 25 grueling tests of skill, strength, and cunning, such as the "Ear Pull," in which a loop of string is passed around an ear of each contestant in a tug of war and the first to let the loop slip off or slacken loses; the "Knuckle Hop," a race in which competitors hop along on knuckles and toes; and the "One-Foot High Kick," where the contestant hops, kicks a foot up to touch a sealskin ball and lands on the same foot without falling over.

At much the same time, the town comes alive for **Golden Days**, a festival with all manner of games, parades, and events all ostensibly celebrating Felix Pedro's discovery of gold in the area (held the week between the second and third weekends in July). The last major event of the summer is the **Tanana Valley State Fair**, a traditional selection of rides, demonstrations, and giant-produce competitions held at the State Fairgrounds on College Road during the first week of August ($8). Up-to-date details of events can be found on the CVB's website, Ⓦ www.explorefairbanks.com.

is best reached from town by the Johansen Expressway, passing the former pipe yards, where forty-foot steel pipes were unloaded from trains, welded into eighty-foot tubes, and hauled by truck to the pipeline construction sites; the fields have now been covered by Wal-Mart, Home Depot, and similar big, box-like buildings. Following the Steese a couple of miles north, you reach the junction for **Birch Hill Recreation Area**, two miles east, a cross-country skiing area in winter (with a new ski lodge; open Mon–Fri noon–9pm, Sat 9am–6pm, Sun 11am–6pm) and a venue in summer for mountain-bike racing and Shakespeare plays (see p.521). Slightly further along the Steese Highway, the road to Chena Hot Springs diverts east. The highway continues north to the **Hagelbarger Road viewpoint**, with views of the Alaska Range, and the **Trans-Alaska Pipeline viewpoint**, Mile 8, where you can stand next to the pipeline, examine a section of the pipe and an old-style cleansing pig (see box, p.538), and glean information from the visitor center (late May to early Sept Mon–Sat 8.30am–5.30pm). Across the road, at least until April, are the **Twin Towers**, columns of ice (sometimes colored) up to 160ft high, created each winter by the Alaska Alpine Club (Ⓦ www.alaskanalpineclub.org) for ice climbing and general amusement.

Fox, eleven miles north of Fairbanks, appears to be an inconsequential road junction, with little of interest except for the *Howling Dog Saloon*, *Silver Gulch Brewery*, and the *Turtle Club* restaurant (listed on p.521). Fox, however, has long been the center of the Fairbanks mining district – over the years the most lucrative of all of Alaska's goldfields – so far yielding some seven million ounces of the metal. All around, the stripped hillsides, mounds of tailings, and abandoned heavy machinery betray the decades spent unearthing gold, while the "Keep Out" signs underline the continued search.

Felix Pedro first struck gold on what is now Pedro Creek, five miles northeast of Fox, setting in motion the establishment of Fairbanks and sparking the last of the major gold rushes. Loose flakes, relatively easily teased from streambed gravels, were soon gone, and miners turned to increasingly more troublesome and labor-intensive methods of extraction. In some cases, up to a hundred feet of frozen low-grade gravel had to be cleared away to reach ore-bearing layers. Several techniques were used, all requiring huge quantities of water, which grubstake miners couldn't obtain. Large mining companies eventually supplanted the grubstakers and funded the construction of the **Davidson Ditch**, which from 1928 until 1959 brought water from the Chatanika River using six miles of pipe and 83 miles of ditch, parts of it still visible along the Steese Highway.

Three local tours provide different perspectives on the eternal quest. **Gold Dredge No. 8**, Mile 9 Old Steese Hwy (mid-May to mid-Sept daily, tours hourly 9.30am–3.30pm; $21; ℡457-6058, ⓦwww.golddredgeno8.com), is the only place in Alaska where you can safely walk around the inside of an authentic gold dredge, in this case a steel-hulled affair operated from 1928 to 1959, devouring ton after ton of gold-bearing gravel from Goldstream and Engineer creeks. Operations finally came to a halt after statehood, when taxes rose and legal changes imposed by the federal government meant that employers could no longer exploit their workers to the same degree. Suffering from neglect, the dredge settled to the bottom of its pond, but remains impressive. An hour-long tour around the dredge's workings – sieves, separation tables, and gold-collection riffles – comes sandwiched between a video of 1940s dredging operations and an opportunity to try your hand with a poke (small bag) of gold-bearing gravel ($5). Additional pokes are available, and you can stay all day panning poorer gravel from a nearby heap if you wish; just don't expect to make a fortune. The bunkhouse, bath house, and office house a random collection of artifacts, including mammoth bones found in the gravel, and the workers' mess has now been converted into a dining room, where a basic, all-you-can-eat stew is served daily between 11am and 3pm ($9.75).

A more venerable method of obtaining gold from dirt is illustrated a couple of miles north at **El Dorado Gold Mine**, Mile 1.3 Elliott Hwy (mid-May to mid-Sept two-hour tours Tues–Fri & Sun 9.45am & 3pm, Mon & Sat 3pm; $30; ℡1-866/479-6673, ⓦwww.eldoradogoldmine.com), reached by riding a replica of the Tanana Valley Railroad train that once ran along Fox's main street. It now passes through a tunnel hewn from permafrost ground to reach the mining camp, where time-honored sluicing and separating techniques still used in small claims all over Alaska are demonstrated. It is all pretty light-hearted but quite informative, and there is, again, the opportunity to walk away with some gold at the end of the day. A free shuttle bus runs here from Fairbanks, picking up at various hotels and (forty minutes before the start of each tour) the visitor center. After the morning tour the bus continues to the *Riverboat Discovery* and returns for the afternoon tour of El Dorado, so it's possible to do both without a car as long as you don't mind a few lunchtime hours stranded at the riverboat's snack bar and gift shop.

Ester

During the day there is no reason to drive the six miles west of Fairbanks to the former gold-town of **Ester**. All you'll find are a few houses scattered in the woods and the remains of large-scale mechanized mining equipment from the town's boom time from the late 1930s until the 1950s. In the evenings, though, tour buses arrive for shows centered around the **Ester Gold Camp**,

Ester is widely known as the Ester Republic, not so much for leftwing politics as for its hippy and separatist attitudes, expressed in part by the satirical Stupor Bowl touch-football game. The neighboring areas of Goldstream and Murphy Dome are known for their "cabin hippies," mostly semi-feral students who live in basic cabins without power or running water (it's estimated in fact that a quarter of Fairbanksans live without running water, instead pumping it from Fox Spring or having it delivered for eight cents per gallon), although many have iPods and laptops that they charge at the university, and take showers in the Wood Center. The lifestyle has become so popular that "dry" cabins now cost $600 a month and more are being built, crowded onto small plots so that the essential sense of privacy has gone. The cabin hippies and indeed many other Fairbanksans are devotees of dumpster-diving, hanging around the municipal dumps, particularly on Farmers Loop Road just east of the university, to snatch up reusable trash.

Old Nenana Road (everything open late May to early Sept; ☏1-800/676-6925, ⓦwww.akvisit.com), a reconstruction of the original town which incorporates a couple of authentic early miners' cabins but has had so many false fronts and Western-style boardwalks added that everything you actually see is fake. The camp puts on "Service with a Smile" (nightly 9pm, additionally at 7pm Wed–Sat in July; $18), a cheesy, ninety-minute cabaret packed with gold-rush songs and poetry by Alaska's adopted son **Robert Service** (see box, p.204). The Bard of the North's best-known work is *The Shooting of Dan McGrew*, in which the action happens in the **Malemute Saloon**, a name revived for the rough-wood-and-sawdust bar where this nightly revue takes place. The saloon is actually quite modern, but incorporates part of the bar once installed in the *Royal Alexandra Bar* in Dawson City, on which Service reputedly jotted down some of his lines.

To make a night of it you could start off by dining at the *Bunkhouse Restaurant*, which offers an all-you-can-eat **crab buffet** (daily 5–9pm; $28, $18 without crab), then amble over to the Firehouse Theatre for the 45-minute "Crown of Light" **photosymphony** (daily 6.45pm & 7.45pm; $8), LeRoy Zimmerman's medley of aurora and nature photos set to ponderous classical music – a poor substitute for the real thing.

If you feel liable to indulge in one too many Dan McGrew or Lady Lou cocktails, then make use of the **bus** service (pickups from most major Fairbanks hotels in time for the *Malemute* shows; $2, reservations required), or arrange to stay either in the on-site RV park (see p.501) or the comfortable, if somewhat institutional, rooms at the *Gold Camp Hotel* ❸.

North Pole

For those who don't mind tourist-trap kitsch, **NORTH POLE**, just fifteen miles southeast of Fairbanks, is an essential stop. The town was first homesteaded in 1944 and subdivided in 1952 by local boosters who tried to entice toy manufacturers with the product label "Made in the North Pole." The idea didn't quite work out as planned, but one trader moved here, opened up **Santa Claus House** at 601 St Nicholas Drive – easily identified by the 42-foot Santa outside overlooking the Richardson Highway – and appointed the town the official home of Santa Claus (mid-May to mid-Sept daily 8am–8pm; mid-Sept to mid-May Mon–Sat 10am–6pm, Sun noon–6pm; ☏488-2200 or 1-800/588-4078,

@www.santaclaushouse.com). If a child addresses a letter to "Santa Claus, North Pole," it ends up here, and the kids' letters pinned up on a wall inside the gift shop are the most charming thing about the place. Inquiries about the spirits of the elves, the health of the reindeer, and the temperature up at the North Pole are commonplace.

You can arrange for a North Pole-franked letter from Santa to be sent in December for $7.50, the smaller kids can sit on Santa's knee, and there are cute reindeer in the compound out the back. To add to the entertainment value, street benches, lampposts, and other such fixtures are red and white, and street names stick to the theme: to see Santa, take the Santa Claus Lane or 5th Avenue exits from the Richardson Highway into St Nicholas Drive. You could also ride the Green Line bus there or call for a free shuttle pickup at Fairbanks hotels and RV parks. Behind Santaland is the Snowy River miniature railway ($2). North Pole's **Log Cabin Visitor Center** is on the north side of the Richardson Highway at Mission Road (☎488-2242; late May to early Sept).

Exploring the North: tour and bush-plane companies

We've discussed various trips throughout the text, but several companies operate a string of tours worth knowing about. We've listed the better ones below along with their most enticing trips.

40-Mile Air 6450 Airport Way ☎474-0018, @www.40-mileair.com. Flights to Big Delta ($88 plus tax) and Tok ($170).

Alaska Tickets and Tours ☎1-866/374-1999, @www.alaskaticketsandtours.com. A booking agency run by a pair of B&B owners who can arrange transport, tours, and accommodation anywhere from the Kenai Peninsula northwards.

Alpenglow Shuttle ☎1-800/770-2267, @www.alaskashuttles.com. $40 ($64 round-trip) to Chena Hot Springs, as well as these options, all round-trip and with a two-person minimum: $149 to Arctic Circle, $350 overnight to Dawson City, and $450 overnight to Anchorage via Valdez.

Frontier Flying Service 5245 Airport Industrial Rd ☎1-800/478-6779, @www.frontierflying.com. Important bush operator with regular services from the airport's main terminal to small communities all over the north and west of Alaska – Nome, Gambell, Kotzebue, Barrow, Deadhorse, Barter Island, Fort Yukon, and others. Having taken over Cape Smythe Air, it's ideal for Arctic adventurers keen to string together a series of visits to coastal towns such as Barrow, Point Lay, Point Hope, Kotzebue, and Nome, returning to Fairbanks or taking Alaska Airlines to Anchorage.

🏃 **GoNorth** 3500 Davis Rd ☎1-866/236-7272, @www.gonorthalaska.com. Professional year-round operation booking guided tours of all types throughout the Brooks Range and around Fairbanks, and helping organize a wide range of unguided trips. Whether you want a simple float down the Chena River or a major hiking expedition into Arrigetch Peaks in the Gates of the Arctic National Park, they'll help organize it from their base camp (see "Hostels," p.497). Standard trips include rafting the Middle Fork of the Koyukuk River (5 days; $1640), hiking in the Gates of the Arctic (6 days; $1975) or ANWR (10 days; $2900), winter backcountry skiing trips into Tolovana Hot Springs (5 days; $550), and much more. They also have RVs for trips up the Dalton Highway (see Listings, p.523) and rent gear such as canoes ($35 per day, $190 per week), whitewater canoes ($40/$200), road bikes ($22/$90), mountain bikes ($27/$115), and all manner of camping gear.

🏃 **Northern Alaska Tour Company** 3820 University Ave S ☎1-800/474-1986, @www.northernalaska.com. Well-organized operation running a slew of

Outdoor activities

Fairbanks presents an unparalleled opportunity to get out into the wilderness; a number of activities are firmly associated with Fairbanks itself, but the profusion of local bush-plane companies throws the **Arctic North** wide open to Fairbanks visitors. In general, we have covered the remoter canoe and backpacking trips in the appropriate sections of the chapter – in particular, see our accounts of the Gates of the Arctic National Park (p.547) and Arctic National Wildlife Refuge (p.552) – but to give a sense of the scope available, consult "Exploring the North," below.

Hiking and biking

Roaming alongside the Chena River or through Creamer's Field can be pleasant enough, but for more robust **hiking** you'll need to get out of town, preferably along either the Chena Hot Springs Road for the Granite Tors Trail,

flightseeing trips, some with remote landings, others using road transport for part of the journey. They do several trips to the Arctic Circle and Prudhoe Bay (covered in detail on p.540), as well as Anaktuvuk Pass Adventure (5hr; $399), flying to Anaktuvuk Pass for a village tour escorted by a Nunamiut Eskimo, and flying back to Fairbanks; Arctic Circle Air Adventure (5hr; $289), overflying the Arctic Circle and Gates of the Arctic National Park and spending a short time in Bettles; Arctic Circle Aurora Adventure (2 nights $519, 3 nights $569), a fly-drive trip to Coldfoot with optional excursions; Barrow Adventure (12–14hr; $435–535), a round-trip flight to Barrow with a village tour; Barrow Winter Adventure (13hr $549, overnight $629); the Brooks Range Adventure ($349), flying to Coldfoot Camp, visiting Wiseman, returning to Coldfoot to sleep, and then driving back to Fairbanks; and Arctic Ocean Adventure (3 days; $749), flying up to Deadhorse, taking a tour of the oil fields, then driving the Dalton back to Fairbanks. Optional extensions take in Barrow, Nome, and Kotzebue.

Trans Arctic Circle Treks 4825 Glasgow Drive ☎1-800/336-8735, ⓦwww.arctictreks .com. This outfit runs a wide range of excursions north including the "Cheechakos" minivan tour to the Arctic Circle (12hr; $149); the three-day Prudhoe-and-back "Oomingmak" road trip with an Arctic Ocean tour and overnights in Prudhoe and Coldfoot ($699, with all meals and lodging); and a three-day "North Slope" tour ($789), which includes a flight to Barrow, overnight and tour there, a flight to Prudhoe Bay, Arctic Ocean tour, and a road-trip to Fairbanks. They also offer fifteen-day tours to Kamchatka in Russia.

Warbelow's Air Ventures 3758 University Ave S, E Ramp, Fairbanks Airport ☎1-800/478-0812, ⓦwww.warbelows.com. These folks operate bush-mail flights to sixteen Interior villages (including three a day to Fort Yukon, Galena, and Tanana, and two to Anaktuvuk Pass and Bettles); you can take a 3–4 hour circuit on any of their mail flights for $255, or for $298 add on a tour of Fort Yukon with a Gwich'in guide. They also offer day-trips to Anaktuvuk Pass ($578).

Wright Air Service 3842 University Ave S, E Ramp, Fairbanks Airport ☎1-800/478-0502, ⓦwww.wrightair.net. Reliable and flexible company running charters and scheduled flights to villages mostly over the Arctic Circle. Stay-on-board village circuits vary depending on demand but the morning trip to Arctic Village ($330 round-trip) usually stops in Fort Yukon and Venetie. Other fares are $170 each way to Anaktuvuk Pass, $160 to Bettles, and $220 to Coldfoot.

Angel Rocks Trail, and Chena Dome Trail (for all see box, p.528), or still further away along the Steese Highway for the Pinnell Mountain Trail (see box, p.531). APLIC (see p.495) is the place to go for the latest information and brochures, and you can rent gear from Beaver Sports (see p.523).

Fairbanks is surprisingly poorly served for **mountain-biking** trails. The hiking trails are either unsuitable or biking is banned on them, leaving only bike paths through town and the ski trails at Birch Hill Recreation Area; for information contact Fairbanks Cycle Club (T459-8008, Wwww.fairbankscycleclub.org), which also has Tuesday evening road rides in spring and summer and stages the sixty-mile Chena Hot Springs Classic in late June. Further afield, try the fairly tough biking on the Angel Rocks, Stiles Creek, and Chena Dome trails in the Chena River State Recreation Area (see p.528).

Paddling

There is little whitewater around Fairbanks, so most of the paddling activity is canoeing along gentle rivers, perhaps dangling a line in the hope of hooking a fish, or even doing a mini bar crawl through Fairbanks. The handiest rental location is Alaska Outdoor Rentals & Guides (T457-2453, Wwww.2paddle1 .com) at Paddler's Cove, 1101 Peger Rd, by the river at the back of Pioneer Park, from where you can rent a single kayak (half-day $24, full $39), a double ($33/$47), or a canoe ($33/$47). With a couple of hours to spare, simply rent a canoe, paddle downstream past *The Pike's Landing* and *Pump House* restaurants (see p.521), and get picked up and brought back to base ($17 first boat, $7 extra boats). For a longer paddle, get dropped upstream and drift through downtown Fairbanks back to base, or paddle the eighteen-mile middle section of the Chena River from Nordale Road (drop-off $40 for one boat, $60 for two); these can also be done as guided trips (from $41). Further commitment is required to paddle some of the upper sections of the Chena River (see p.526), or down the Tanana to Nenana (see p.437), a sixty-mile trip covered in one long stint or two more relaxed days with a night camped on the riverbank. More distant possibilities include the Chatanika and Birch Creek canoe routes (consult APLIC for details).

Flightseeing

No matter how tight your budget, you really shouldn't miss out on a little **flightseeing**. If you feel you need to justify the expense, then visit one of the remote communities such as Bettles or Arctic Village, or take a whirlwind tour of a few of them on one of the **mail flights** that makes a circuit of three or four settlements, dropping off essential supplies and picking up the post. Another favorite approach is to take one of the **Arctic Circle overflights**, usually tracing the silver thread of the pipeline and issuing a certificate to verify the fact you entered Arctic airspace. The best of both these types of trip are listed in "Exploring the North" on p.516.

Other activities

If all the talk of gold around Fairbanks has fired your imagination, you can try your hand at **gold-panning** on the local streams with equipment and advice from Alaskan Prospectors, 504 College Rd at Blanche Ave (mid-April to mid-Sept Thurs–Sat 10.30am–5pm; winter Sat 10.30am–5pm; T452-7398), a treasure trove of minerals, books, maps, and gear that caters to just about all gold-digging needs. They sell a panning kit ($24) that includes a pan, magnet, collection vial, a sample bag of gold-bearing gravel, and instructions. Alternatively, they'll set you up for the real thing for about $30 and point you in the right direction.

You might also want to try learning something of **dog-mushing** at Alaskan Tails of the Trail ($28; ☎455-6469, ⓦwww.maryshields.com) with Iditarod veteran Mary Shields, the first woman to complete the course back in 1974. Over a couple of hours she'll show you the ropes and let you meet the dogs at her place off Goldstream Road, five miles north of town.

To actually try your hand at controlling a team of eager dogs you'll have to pay a little more; Paws for Adventure at Mile 3 Chena Hot Springs Rd (☎378-3630, ⓦwww.pawsforadventure.com) starts with a one-hour introduction for $80. Sun Dog Express, behind Beaver Sports at 1540 Hayes (☎479-6983, ⓦwww.mosquitonet.com/~sleddog) offers dog-sled rides from $15 for a quarter-mile to $80 for seven miles, plus a wildlife refuge tour at $100 for nine miles and a half-day mushing class for $250; Alaska Trail King Adventures, 35 miles south in Salcha (☎488-2535, ⓦwww.alaskatrailkingadventures.com), offers everything from a five-mile trip ($5) to a seven-night expedition ($3000).

In winter there's cross-country **skiing** at Birch Hill Ski Area (from 1.5 to 4 miles) and on UAF's Skarland Trails (3–12 miles, linking to Ester Dome), and downhill at Mount Aurora (see p.529) and Moose Mountain (☎479-4732, ⓦwww.shredthemoose.com; day $32, afternoon $27), off Murphy Dome Road. You can also see ski-joring, or dogs hauling skiers, on Creamer's Field.

Eating

Fairbanks is one of the few places in northern Alaska where you can escape from the culinary tyranny of salmon, halibut, and burgers. As long as your tastes aren't too exotic and you are prepared to drive around, you should be able to find pretty much anything you want here. And for no apparent reason, Thai seems to have become a Fairbanks specialty, and there are two or three Korean joints. Broadly, the cheaper places congregate around the western end of College Road towards the university, and the pricier places are further out, with the gaps being plugged by mid-range places and all the franchise joints you could ask for – especially along Airport Way. If you are thinking of bringing a jacket and tie, forget it. As long as your hiking boots are clean you'll not be turned away.

You'll find **grocery stores** in just about all the major malls: the most convenient are the Fred Meyer and Safeway stores, paired at the eastern end of College Road close to downtown, and also next to each other around the intersection of Airport Way and University Avenue (Safeway 24hr, Fred's 7am–midnight in summer). For the freshest vegetables head to the Farmers Market (see p.508).

Downtown

Bahn Thai 541 3rd Ave & 542 4th Ave (two entrances) ☎452-8424. A 2nd Avenue institution for a dozen years in its blue trailer, *Bahn Thai* has finally gone mainstream with a permanent location; a wide range of Thai dishes mostly costs $7–9.
Café Alex 310 1st Ave ☎452-2539. Fairbanks' first and only wine and tapas bar, where the trick is

to go with a group and sample widely from stuffed artichokes, mini pizzas, *queso fundido*, nutty wild rice salad, and more. They're $8–9 a plate and are served at the bar, in the main dining area, or in a cluster of intimate side rooms. Good wine by the glass, too. Closed Mon evening, Sat lunch, and all Sun.
Co-op Diner Co-op Plaza, 535 2nd Ave ☎474-3463. The best bet for all-day diner food ($7–10)

downtown, served either in booths or at the counter.

The Diner 244 Illinois St ☏ 451-0613. Reliable diner in the best old-fashioned tradition (though with a nonsmoking area) serving straightforward diner fare cooked to perfection and served with fried okra or half a dozen other sides. A full breakfast ($7–9) will set you up for the day, and even the single giant pancake ($2) is enough for most appetites. Early morning to 4pm daily.

Gambardella's Pasta Bella 706 2nd Ave ☏ 457-4992, ⓦ www.gambardellas.com. Fairbanks' best Italian restaurant is surprisingly well priced, especially considering that this is one of the city's finest spots. Weather permitting, diners spill out onto the terrace for lasagna ($10), eggplant parmesan ($10), and gourmet pizza ($8–25), all helped down with good Italian and American wines. They also have an extensive takeout menu. Closed for Sun lunch.

Gerardo's 701 College Rd ☏ 452-2299 & 3226 Airport Way ☏ 474-0409. Very friendly and very Italian, with Rat Pack music and plenty of garlic; the menu ranges from salads ($7) to pizza (from $14), halibut ($21), and steaks (up to $28). Evenings only.

Hot Tamale 112 N Turner Rd ☏ 457-8350. Authentic Mexican restaurant decorated in a kind of "cantina kitsch" style, with a full Mexican menu as well as steak sandwiches and fettucine Alfredo, though particularly noted for their all-you-can-eat $11 lunch and dinner buffets and their cheap beer.

Lavelle's Bistro 575 1st Ave ☏ 450-0555, ⓦ www.lavellesbistro.com. In the *Springhill Suites* hotel, an excellent wine bar (with 3000 bottles in the cellar and wine-wall); menu includes pizza (from $10), salads ($13), lasagna and meatloaf ($17), salmon (from $25), and lamb ($30), plus desserts from $6.50. Open daily 4.30–9 or 10pm, with live music Fri & Sat.

McCafferty's 408 Cushman St ☏ 456-6853. Relaxing and cheerfully decorated coffeehouse serving good espresso, soups, and cakes. Also open Friday and Saturday evenings for live music (often by the owners' own folk-pop band), not to mention the ukulele session at 6pm on Mondays. Mon–Thurs 7am–6pm, Fri 7am–11pm, Sat 10am–11pm, Sun 10am–4pm.

Soapy Smith's 543 2nd Ave ☏ 451-8380. Photos of the Klondike and an ancient kayak strung from the ceiling hardly make a convincing theme, but the food is pretty decent: barbecued ribs are $8.25, and they do a delicious California burger with shrimp, avocado, and Swiss cheese ($8.75), also available in vegetarian form. Closed Sun in winter.

Thai House 412 5th Ave ☏ 452-6123. A small but justly popular eatery serving the usual range of

Thai dishes, all beautifully prepared and at modest prices (around the $10 mark). The green and red curries with zucchini, peas, and peppers are especially good. Closed Sun.

Near the university

Alaska Coffee Roasting Co W Valley Plaza, 4001 Geist Rd ☏ 457-5282. Fairbanks' best coffee, roasted daily on the premises and served in a cozy café hung with interesting art and photos. There's a good selection of wraps, cakes, and muffins, too. Daily to 10pm.

Bun On the Run College Rd. Open for twenty summers in the Beaver Sports parking lot, an excellent takeout sandwich stand. Mon–Fri 7am–5pm, Sat 9am–3pm.

Cookie Jar Danby St ☏ 479-8319. A shame about its slightly industrial setting, but this is a friendly place serving great baked goods, all-day breakfast, soups, sandwiches, and burgers ($7–9). Halibut, lasagna (both $13), and steaks ($12–22) fill out the dinner menu. Mon 6.30am–8.30pm, Tues–Sat 6.30am–9pm, Sun 8am–7pm.

🏃 **Hot Licks** At the *Best Western*, 1521 S Cushman St, also May–Aug in a shack at 3453 College Rd, near University Ave ☏ 479-7813, ⓦ www.hotlicks.net. A Fairbanks institution selling excellent ice cream and shakes made from local cream and natural flavors, plus espresso.

Ichiban Noodle Restaurant 400 College Rd ☏ 455-9116. Splendid Japanese restaurant with great service, serving combos in bento boxes. Mon–Sat 11am–midnight.

Sam's Sourdough 3702 Cameron St at University Ave ☏ 479-0532. About the best greasy spoon in town, with the usual diner menu as well as reindeer sausage and eggs ($8.95) and Sharon's sourdough omelette ($9.25) – complete with ham, mushrooms, onions, olives, and sour cream.

Second Story Café 3525 College Rd ☏ 474-9574 ext 3. Pleasant café tucked above the excellent Gulliver's bookshop, serving wraps, sandwiches, bagels, biscotti, and coffee all at reasonable prices, plus free Internet access to boot. A rear deck catches the summer sun nicely. Mon–Fri 9am–8pm, Sat 9am–7pm, Sun 11am–5pm.

Suburban Fairbanks

Alaska Salmon Bake Airport Way ☏ 1-800/354-7274, ⓦ www.akvisit.com. Really hungry? Here's a stuff-in-as-much-salmon-halibut-and-ribs-as-you-can-for-$28 affair set on the flanks of Pioneer Park out among relic mining machinery (and mosquitoes in high summer). It is open for dinner (mid-May to mid-Sept daily 5–9pm), and there are shuttle buses ($3) from the bigger hotels.

Captain Bartlett Inn 1411 Airport Way ☎ 452-1888. A reasonably priced spot for a breakfast of, say, eggs Benedict ($8) or a lunch of burgers and wraps, inside or out on the sunny deck. May–Sept only.

Ivory Jacks 2581 Goldstream Rd, four miles northeast of the university ☎ 455-6665/6. Being a little out of town doesn't seem to stop this place being inordinately popular, as much for its late-night bar scene and frequent live bands as for the dining. Food ranges from crab-stuffed mushroom appetizers ($8) to half-pound cheeseburgers ($9), 12-inch pizzas ($17–20), and a halibut dinner ($18).

Lemon Grass 388 Chena Pump Plaza, Parks Hwy at Chena Pump Rd ☎ 456-2200. Another low-cost quality Thai restaurant that challenges *Bahn Thai* and *Thai House*. The decor of Thai musical instruments complements the very well-prepared dishes ($9–11), plus *Hot Licks* ice cream desserts. Closed Sun.

Pike's Landing 4438 Airport Way at Hoselton Rd ☎ 479-6500. A popular riverside complex with sports bar, large deck beside the Chena River, and some of Fairbanks' finest dining with jumbo black-tiger prawns ($22), pecan-crusted chicken ($20), and more. Lunchtime salads and sandwiches cost around $10, and there's a standout Sunday brunch ($19) with a huge spread and as many glasses of champagne as you could reasonably expect to drink.

The Pump House Mile 1.3 Chena Pump Rd ☎ 479-8452, ⊛ www.pumphouse .com. A local favorite and rightly so, this historic pump-house by the Chena River serves great food and comes stuffed with gold-mining paraphernalia (plus a pool table that followed the stampeders to Dawson City, Eagle, Circle, and Rampart, and a 1930 shuffleboard). The deck is the place to watch river life go by while tucking into burgers ($9) and

halibut nuggets ($13), mostly charged at half-price during happy hours (Sept–May 4–6pm & 10–11pm). The dining room is more formal, serving hearty portions of reindeer stew ($20) or musk ox meat-loaf ($21); you may not have space for one of the wonderful desserts. Late May–Sept 11.30am–1am daily; Oct to late May daily 4pm–midnight, also Sat from noon, Sun brunch from 10am.

Wolf Run Restaurant 3360 Wolf Run ☎ 458-0636. Still best known for coffee and dessert, it's also well worth stopping in for lunch, including a crab and mushroom cheesecake starter, quiche, ravioli Florentine, or Cornish game hen, served with soup or salad, plus soup-and-salad combos. Daily except Mon evening.

Out of town

Turtle Club Half-mile west from Mile 11 Old Steese Hwy, Fox ☎ 457-3883, ⊛ www.alaskanturtle.com. The *Turtle Club*'s reputation for the quality and quantity of its prime rib – $22 for the 12oz Foxy Cut, $24 for the 16oz Turtle Cut, $31 for the 24oz Miners Cut – extends throughout the North, but they also do delicious jumbo prawns weighing in at five to the pound. Evenings only. Reservations recommended.

Two Rivers Lodge Mile 16 Chena Hot Springs Rd ☎ 488-6815, ⊛ www.tworiverslodge.com. Although it is a bit out of town, this restaurant, with its stunning glassed-in dining area and lakeside deck, is well worth the trip. The menu offers a cosmopolitan blend of Alaskan and Mediterranean cuisines, with starters ($9–14) including confit of mushrooms, asparagus, escargot Pernod, and scallop vol-au-vent, and main courses including seafood or chicken ($25–29), filet mignon ($35), lobster tail or pheasant breast ($40), and vegetarian dishes ($21–24), all with home-baked bread and soup or house salad. There's also an extensive, mostly Californian, wine list. Open Tues–Sun evenings only.

Drinking and entertainment

You'll be disappointed if you arrive in Fairbanks expecting high fashion and up-to-the-minute music, but the city can provide a rollicking good time. Many visitors find themselves at one of the nightly cabaret revues at some stage, but there is usually a bar or two with a band thrashing away in the corner of a dark room. Perhaps more than any other large town, this is a place where Alaska's famed predominance of men is most apparent, and you'll never be short of a drinking partner in any of the numerous traditional Alaskan bars.

Check the Fairbanks *Daily News-Miner* for listings, especially on Thursdays, when the free *Fairbanks Square* also appears. Look out, too, for Fairbanks Shakespeare Theatre plays held in the Birch Hill Recreation Area or behind UAF's Museum of the North on the last three weekends of July (Thurs–Sat 7.30pm,

Sun 2pm; tickets $20; ☎457-7638, ⓦwww.fairbanks-shakespeare.org). At the Alaska Centennial Center in Pioneer Park, the Fairbanks Arts Association (☎456-6485, ⓦwww.fairbanksarts.org) puts on classic films for $3 (alternate Thursdays 7pm), free lunchtime concerts (Tues & Thurs noon), outdoor shows (summer only, Mon–Fri 7pm), and other events, and also runs a gallery selling works by local artists (daily 11am–9pm).

In Fairbanks

Boatel Geraghty St ☎479-6537. It calls itself a "sleazy waterfront bar," but there's nothing wrong with sipping a beer on the riverside deck on a summer evening.

Captain Bartlett Inn 1411 Airport Way. The inn's *Dog Sled Saloon* offers straightforward peanut-shells-on-the-floor drinking with a log-cabin interior and sports on big screens. May–Sept only.

The Marlin 3412 College Rd ☎479-4646. Poky, wood-paneled cellar bar at the cutting edge of Fairbanks' music scene with live bands – blues, jazz, and rock – most evenings from around 9pm; small cover charge, if any.

The Palace Saloon At Pioneer Park on Airport Way ☎456-5960 for reservations. Mock-up of a gold-rush-era music hall that plays host to the entertaining, if slightly cheesy, cabaret-style Golden Heart Review (late May to mid-Sept nightly 8.15pm with occasional extra shows at 6.30pm; $16). The show pokes fun at historic Alaskan life (specifically Fairbanks) through songs and stories, including a dog-mushing inter-pretation of the old Abbott and Costello "Who's on First?" routine. On weekends the review is usually followed by their considerably more risqué and topical Late Night Cabaret (typically mid-May to mid-Sept Fri & Sat 10.30pm; $10), which is limited to adults only.

The Pump House (See "Eating," p.521). The preferred watering hole for Fairbanks' smarter young set, who come to shoot pool or more likely hang out on the deck with a cocktail or two.

Out of town

Blue Loon Mile 353.5 Parks Hwy, Ester ☎457-5666, ⓦwww.theblueloon.com. A cavernous hot-spot five miles west of Fairbanks which hosts local and touring bands (or maybe a DJ) several nights a week; $5 cover unless a top name is in town. They also screen cult and mainstream movies that don't make it to the local multiplex (typically Tues–Sat 5.30 & 8pm; $5–6). Food served 5–11pm, bar typically closes late; closed Mon.

Howling Dog Saloon Mile 11 Old Steese Hwy, Fox ☎457-8780, ⓦwww.howlingdogsaloon.com. The wildest watering hole in the district and a local legend promoted as the farthest-north rock-and-roll bar in the world. It actually goes one better by having the bands perform (every Fri & Sat, plus blues on Wed and open mike on Thurs; usually no cover) on what is fondly referred to as the "Pope and the Dope" carpet, the red pile on which John Paul II met Ronald Reagan in 1984 when they both happened to be making pit stops in Fairbanks – the first meeting of an American president and a pope on American soil. If you're hungry, they'll dish up fine pizzas, but most come to drink in the wood-floored bar with pinball, flags of every nation, and knickers and bras hung from the moose rack. May–Oct from 11am to 2–3.30am.

Malemute Saloon Ester Gold Camp, Old Nenana Rd, Ester ☎479-2500. Nightly cabaret entertain-ment (see p.515) six miles west of Fairbanks, not far from the *Blue Loon*.

Refinery Lounge 2643 Old Richardson Hwy at 6th Ave, North Pole ☎488-0335. Typical dark bar with a large military clientele. It's a friendly spot with an entertaining weekend band (Thurs–Sat) playing Top 40 tunes and "No Country." No cover. From 11am Mon–Sat, noon Sun.

Silver Gulch Brewery Mile 11 Old Steese Hwy, Fox ☎452-2739. Not really a bar, but worth a mention for the Friday evening tasting session (5–7pm), which is something of a local meeting point with the chance to sample the product of the US's northernmost brewery.

Listings

Airlines Air North (to Canada) ☎1-800/764-0407; Alaska ☎1-800/252-7522; Northwest ☎1-800/225-2525; United ☎1-800/241-6522. See box on p.516 for a roundup of bush-plane services.

Art and craft shops Alaska House Art Gallery, Cushman and 10th Ave (summer Mon–Sat 11am–7pm; winter Tues–Sat 11am–6pm; ☎456-6449, ⓦwww.thealaskahouse.com), in the former home of artist Claire Fejes; Arctic Traveler's Gift Shop, 201 Cushman (daily to 5 or 6pm; ☎456-7080, ⓦwww .arctictravelers.com); Craft Market Giftshop, 5th & Noble (Mon–Sat 11am–6pm; ☎452-5495); New Horizons Gallery, 519 1st Ave (daily to 5 or 6pm; ☎456-2063, ⓦwww.newhorizonsgallery.com); The Art Works, 3677 College Rd (☎479-2563); Well Street Art Gallery, 1304 Well St (☎452-6169).

Banks and exchange Banks are located all over town (many of them drive-thru), all with ATMs, which also crop up in supermarkets and convenience stores. Downtown there's a KeyBank branch at 100 Cushman St; Wells Fargo at 613 Cushman St exchanges foreign bills.

Bicycle and canoe rental If you're not at one of the hostels that has bikes, rent mountain bikes from Alaska Outdoor Rentals & Guides (☎457-2453, ⓦwww.akbike.com), which has several locations around town, including 517 3rd Ave and their base on Peger Road, at the back of Pioneer Park (late May–Sept 11am–7pm). Rates are $8 an hour, $27 a day, or $99 a week, and they even have bikes set up for winter use (at increased rates). Also try 7 Bridges Boats and Bikes at the *7 Gables B&B*, 4312 Birch Lane (☎479-0751), which rents town and mountain bikes for $20 a day. Canoe and kayak rental (see p.518) is best from Alaska Outdoor Rentals & Guides or 7 Bridges. Beaver Sports, 3480 College Rd (☎479-2494, ⓦwww.beaversports .com), also rents bikes and canoes ($24 per day), services bikes, and has biking, camping, and canoeing gear for sale. For bike repairs go to Great Land Sports, 261 College Rd (☎479-8438).

Bookshop Gulliver's Books, 3525 College Rd (open daily to 6–9pm; ☎474-9574, ⓦwww .gullivers-books.com), offers the city's best selection of new and used books. They're also at Shopper's Forum Mall, 1255 Airport Way (☎456-3657). Try also Forget-me-not Books, 517 Gaffney (☎456-6212), selling second-hand books to raise funds for the Literacy Council of Alaska.

Buses (long-distance) Fairbanks has just two long-distance bus services, both operating roughly mid-May to mid-Sept, but call to check at the ends of the season, which may run longer or be cut short. Alaska Direct (☎1-800/770-6652) runs to Delta Junction, Tok, and Whitehorse ($155), departing Sunday, Wednesday, and Friday; and Alaska/Yukon Trails (☎1-800/770-2725, ⓦwww .alaskashuttle.com) has a daily run to Denali ($46) and Anchorage ($91), a thrice-weekly service between Fairbanks and Dawson City ($162), Yukon via Tok and Chicken ($108), and a reservation-only service from Fairbanks through Delta Junction and Glennallen to Valdez, all picking up at the visitor center, airport, and *Billie's Backpackers*.

Camping equipment Beaver Sports (see above) carries the best selection of camping and general outdoor gear, along with various guidebooks and maps.

Car rental International agencies all have desks at the airport; smaller local agencies frequently offer more competitive rates in return for slightly older vehicles and a poorer backup network. To get unlimited mileage and a courtesy pickup from your hotel expect to pay around $50 a day in July and August; phone around. Agencies include: Airport (☎456-2023, ⓦwww.alaskan.com/airportcarrental), Arctic (☎479-8044, ⓦwww.arcticrentacar.com), and U-Save (☎479-7060 or 1-877/979-7060). Only a few companies allow you to drive off paved roads: Affordable, 3101 S Cushman St (☎452-7341 or 1-800/471-3101), has cars from $45 with unlimited mileage and allows you to go everywhere except on the Dalton Highway. Arctic Outfitters (☎474-3530, ⓦwww.arctic-outfitters.com) will rent you a Ford Taurus for the run up the Dalton for $119 a day, including CB radio and 250 miles a day, 35¢ a mile above that, but you'll need your own insurance. GoNorth (☎1-866/236-7272, ⓦwww.gonorthalaska .com) offers a range of camper trucks ideal for exploring the Dalton and elsewhere and charges from $72 a day plus 30¢ a mile ($125 a day unlimited mileage) up to $126/$189 for a more luxurious and spacious model. There's an additional $45–99 preparation fee on top and a liability damage waiver will cost $18 a day. Adventures in Alaska RV Rental (☎458-7368, ⓦwww.adventuresakrv.com) has RVs from $200 per night or $1260 per week in summer, and gravel road-equipped rigs (cleared to go all the way to Deadhorse) from $310/2170.

Cinema The Regal 16, 1855 Airport Way (☎456-5113, ⓦwww.regalcinemas.com), screens mainstream releases, offering $3 off tickets on shows starting before 6pm; the *Blue Loon* in Ester (see p.522) shows more alternative and cult movies; and Fairbanks Arts Association (see opposite) and UAF's Summer Sessions put on classic films.

Emergencies Police, fire, and ambulance ☎911; Crisis Line ☎452-4357.

Hitchhiking As with any city it pays to get beyond the city limits before trying to thumb a ride: for the Richardson Highway the Green bus will take you to North Pole, and the Blue bus works best for the Parks Highway. To head north, take the Red bus to the Johansen Expressway. A sensible alternative is to try to get a lift by consulting the rides board in the Wood Center at the university.

Internet access *Gulliver's Books* (see above) offers 30min free use with a café purchase; the Noel Wien Library (see p.524) has free access bookable by the hour (or you can wait for a 15min slot); the Visitor Center allows 10min free access; at *College Coffeehouse*, 3677 College Rd (☎374-0468), has 15min free access with a purchase, then $2 for every subsequent 15min. In addition there's free WiFi at UAF, the *Pumphouse Restaurant*, *Pike's Waterfront Lodge*, and other hotels.

Laundry and showers B&C Laundromat, 3677 College Rd (daily 8am–9.30pm; ☎479-2696), and Cushman Plaza Laundry, 2301 S Cushman St (7am–midnight; ☎452-4430), both have competitively priced washing machines and showers for $3. Coin King, 431 Gaffney at Noble (☎452-6295), is a huge laundry. A dip (and shower) at Hamme Swimming Pool, 931 Airport Way (Mon–Fri 6am–9pm, Sat 9am–5pm; ☎459-1086, ⓦwww.co.fairbanks.ak.us), costs under $4.

Library The Noel Wien Library, 126 Cowles St at Airport Way (Mon–Thurs 10am–9pm, Fri 10am–6pm, Sat 10am–5pm, Sun 1–5pm; ☎459-1020). The MACS Blue bus passes close by. Don't miss the very stylized paintings and prints by Rockwell Kent (1882–1971), who only came to Fairbanks once, in 1935, but was inspired by Alaska throughout his career.

Maps The Alaska Public Lands Information Center (see p.495) handles most needs, and the Map Office, Room 204, International Arctic Research Center, N Koyukuk Drive, at the far end of the university campus (Mon–Fri 8am–5pm; ☎474-6960, ⓦwww.gi.alaska.edu/services/mapoffice),

sells USGS topographic maps for the whole state at 1:250,000 ($7) and 1:63,360 (one-inch) scales ($6) plus National Geographic maps and aurora photos.

Medical assistance Fairbanks Memorial Hospital, 1650 Cowles St ☎452-8181.

Money transfer Western Union has outlets at Fred Mayer and Safeway supermarkets (see map p.492).

Pharmacy Fred Meyer and Safeway supermarkets all have pharmacies (see map, p.498). The best is probably Fred Meyer, 3755 Airport Way (☎474-1433).

Photographic supplies Fairbanks Fast Foto, Shoppers' Forum Mall, 1255 Airport Way (☎456-8896), is a good camera shop selling all the usual stuff as well as slide and pro film. Alaskan Photographic, 551 2nd Ave, Suite 221 (☎452-8819) sells film, batteries, filters, and memory cards, and will repair digital and film cameras.

Post office 315 Barnette St at 3rd Ave (Mon–Fri 9am–6pm). For **General Delivery** use the 99707 zip code. UPS Shops are at 3875 Geist (☎479-2250) and 607 Old Steese Hwy (☎452-2221).

Road conditions Contact ☎511 or click your way to ⓦ511.alaska.gov.

Taxes A hotel tax of eight percent is charged and has not been incorporated into our price codes.

Taxis Ace Cab ☎460-4522; Alaska Cab ☎456-3355; Diamond ☎455-7777; Eagle/Yellow Cab ☎455-5555; Executive ☎455-8899; King Cab ☎452-5464.

Travel agency US Travel, 1211 Cushman St (☎452-8992), is open Mon–Fri 8am–6pm.

Around Fairbanks

Fairbanks' importance stems less from the appeal of the city itself than from its location at the hub of the only four significant roads to penetrate the Alaskan North, three of which end at **hot springs**. One is smooth blacktop all the way; the rest are dirt roads twisting and bucking through the white- and black-spruce forests that cloak the surrounding rolling hills. Since public transportation is not an option, you'll need a car to get around, or be prepared for some slow hitching.

Beyond the immediate environs of Fairbanks there is very little sign of human activity. Small communities occasionally throw up a roadhouse, and riverbeds have obviously been turned over by gold dredges, but after a very short time both seem like blots on the otherwise pristine landscape. Predominantly, this is country for **hiking**, **canoeing**, fishing, and, in winter, cross-country skiing and snowmobiling – all followed by a well-earned soak in a hot tub.

Easily the most accessible of these arterial spokes, and the only one you can explore in depth with the blessing of rental-car agencies (see our comments under "City transportation and tours" on p.496), is **Chena Hot Springs Road**, which follows the Chena River – a gentle canoe and raft route – past trailheads for three excellent hikes to the most developed of the region's hot springs.

The **Steese Highway** is longer and feels appreciably more remote as it threads its way northeast past the arduous but immensely satisfying two-day Pinnell Mountain Trail to the Yukon River. The only westbound road is the **Elliott Highway** across 160 miles of ridgetop forest to the charming community of **Manley Hot Springs**, with its ancient roadhouse and primitive tanks filled by a naturally heated stream. After the initial 73 miles of the Elliott you reach the last of the North's four roads, the Dalton Highway, which runs the remainder of the five hundred miles between Fairbanks and Prudhoe Bay on the Arctic Ocean.

There are no visitor centers of any consequence out here, so find out all you need in Fairbanks at the Alaska Public Lands Information Center (see p.495), which publishes a handy free leaflet detailing the points of interest along the Steese and Elliott highways. Fairbanks is also the place to stock up on any supplies you might need, rent your outdoor gear, and fill up with gas.

Chena Hot Springs and around

Of the spas around Fairbanks, **Chena Hot Springs**, sixty miles to the northeast, is the easiest to reach and the most developed. It is also the largest after considerable redevelopment in recent years. Weary miners and Fairbanksans have been coming out this way to ease their bones since 1905, when the Swan brothers publicized the rumored springs, apparently discovered earlier by Felix Pedro who had left behind the remnants of a campfire. Travel wasn't much easier for early devotees who regularly took two weeks to get here, but the situation gradually improved, and by 1912 the route was even passable by bicycles, and is now asphalt. It is easy enough to zip here in an hour or so, but the **Chena River State Recreation Area**, with some attractive campgrounds, some excellent hikes (see box, p.528), and a gentle canoe trip (see box, p.526), make this an appealing area to spend a day or two. And, of course, you can soak away your aches at the springs.

△ Chena Hot Springs near Fairbanks

The clear and very cold waters of the **Chena River** flow west through gently rolling wooded country, eventually joining the murkier Tanana River near Fairbanks. The narrower and more overhung upper sections are Class II and require some skill, but below the **Rosehip Campground** access point it is a gentle float trip for canoes, kayaks, and rafts, ranging from a couple of hours up to several days. The rapids may not be too challenging, but trees frequently fall into the river creating dangerous "sweepers" and log-jams that you need to be aware of: ask locally. You'll also need to scout ahead when the river braids confusingly, but it is mostly pretty easy going and wonderfully relaxing: fishing and looking for moose, brown bears, beavers, and river otters while lazing in the sun. With frequent access points you can do as much or as little as you want, even staying on the river to **camp**, either in established campgrounds or on river bars where the breeze keeps bugs at bay (though keep an eye on water levels if it has been raining).

Unless you've got your own gear, you'll want to **rent a canoe** in Fairbanks (see "Bicycle and canoe rental" on p.523) and either avail yourself of the agency's delivery service or (perhaps more cheaply) rent a car and be prepared to hitch back to your vehicle.

If you have some experience with Class II rivers and water levels are adequate (usually early to mid-summer), use the highest access point at the **Angel Rocks Trailhead**, Mile 48.9, and be prepared to line your canoe around log-jams and obstacles. After the bridge at Mile 44, the North Fork joins with the East Fork and the river widens and moves more slowly. Over the next seventeen miles down to *Rosehip Campground*, Mile 27 (8–13hr in all), there are five access points spaced thirty minutes to three hours apart. In general, the river gets progressively easier as you go, but if you're in any doubt, put in at *Rosehip* for the easy float to Grange Hall Road, Mile 20.8 (2–4hr). It is even possible to paddle into Fairbanks, taking a couple of days from Grange Hall Road.

For more **information**, visit APLIC in Fairbanks, discuss your plans with the staff, and pick up the free leaflets put out by Alaska State Parks and the US Army Corps of Engineers, both detailing access points, levels of difficulty, and expected float times.

There is no public transportation out this way, but given three days' notice *Chena Hot Springs Resort* (see opposite) can offer a **shuttle** (first person $80 round-trip, additional passengers $40). Hitching is feasible. Look out for moose on the road and in the ponds at miles 28, 32.8, and 41.5.

Along Chena Hot Springs Road

Twenty-six miles east of the Steese Highway (two miles beyond the Pleasant Valley grocery, café, and RV park), you enter the Chena River State Recreation Area and soon find yourself repeatedly crossing bridges, the main access points for paddling the Chena River. Along here, hikers should keep their eyes open for trailheads for the **walks** listed in the box on p.528.

There is very little **accommodation** along the road, except for **camping** at the excellent *Rosehip Campground*, Mile 27 ($10 per site; pump water), the slightly less inviting *Tors Trail Campground*, Mile 39.5 ($10 per site; pump water), and the lakeside *Red Squirrel Campground*, Mile 42.8 ($10 per vehicle; pump water); all are spacious and equipped with picnic tables and fire rings. At Mile 47.7 the *North Fork* cabin (☎451-2695; ●) is a five-minute walk from the road.

Chena Hot Springs

Only an hour from Fairbanks ($40 with Alpenglow Shuttle – see p.516), Chena Hot Springs has become the getaway of choice for Fairbanksans and visitors seeking a sybaritic day's relaxation. If you've experienced the more rustic hot springs elsewhere in Alaska, *Chena Hot Springs Resort*, Mile 56.5 (☎1-800/478-4681, ⓌW www.chenahotsprings.com; suites ❼, rooms ❺, cabins and yurts ❸), may come as something of a surprise, with numerous buildings containing hotel rooms scattered around a clearing in the forest. There's all manner of activities to keep you occupied, but the real stars are the hot pools themselves. The indoor chlorinated pool and an assortment of hot tubs are outclassed by the large outdoor Rock Lake (no under-18s), a chest-deep, sandy-bottomed lake of hot water with a massaging jet of spring water and a cooling fountain in the center.

The hotel's facilities and activities are all open to the public, as are the **pools** (daily 7am–midnight; $10 for a day-pass), which are free to hotel guests though not those staying at the campground and RV park. Rooms are comfortable and bland, but there are substantially more charming, rustic cabins without plumbing, simple yurts with three beds but no bedding, RV parking ($20; no hookups), and **camping** by the river ($20). It is always worth asking for discounts in spring and fall, and small groups can often land a large room at a very reasonable rate. When you've soaked enough you can have a massage ($55 per half-hour), rent bikes ($12 for 4 hours, $20 for 8 hours), go horse-back riding ($80 per hour) or rafting ($115 for 3 hours), and eat and drink in the restaurant/bar, which does sandwiches and salads (around $10) along with well-prepared mains ($20–25).

There's also the new ice hotel, known for licensing reasons as the **Ice Museum**, a Gothic-style palace of carved ice, complete with gargoyles and jousting knights, all by Steve Brice, nine-time winner of the World Art Ice Championship. Hidden in a utilitarian shed, it's chilled by geothermal energy and lit by cool LEDs. There's a bar (with glasses carved from ice, natch) and six rooms where, for the privilege of kipping in sleeping bags on reindeer hides, you pay $400 a room, but unless you're on honeymoon you'll probably just opt for a tour ($15), on the odd hours from 11am to 7pm, year-round.

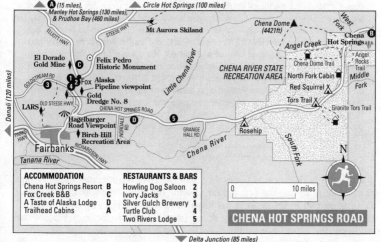

The **Chena River State Recreation Area** flanks thirty miles of Chena Hot Springs Road, encompassing the bald, spruce-flanked mountains on either side. Periodically, you'll see **granite tors**, gnarled rock pinnacles poking up from the ridges and providing the focus for a couple of lovely hikes. These were formed around eighty million years ago when molten rock forced its way through fissures, cooling over two million years into hard rock which has weathered less than the softer material that surrounded it.

APLIC in Fairbanks stocks free Alaska State Parks **information leaflets** on all these trails, which are restricted in summer to foot traffic except for Chena Dome Trail, on which **mountain biking** is permitted (though it is very challenging). Color-coded diamonds mark winter access (by bike, ATV, or snowmobile) to the public-use cabins, on trails which are boggy from May to September. Hikes are listed in order of their distance from Fairbanks.

Granite Tors Trail (15-mile loop; 6–10hr, 2700ft ascent). An excellent hike of moderate difficulty starting along boardwalks over muskeg, then climbing through thick woods and out onto alpine tundra past ancient granite outcrops rising up to sixty feet from the ground. You can do the hike in a day, camp out overnight, or sleep in the small free-use shelter at the midpoint (Mile 7.1); bring everything except a tent and expect to share the shelter with up to five others. It is a popular and highly scenic rock-climbing venue when dry; but if wet, misty weather brings out the best in the area, and the ghostly tors are wreathed in swirling clouds of fog, exaggerating the already dramatic landscape. The trailhead is at Mile 39.5. of Chena Hot Springs Road.

Angel Rocks Trail (3.5-mile loop; 2–3hr; 900ft ascent). The easiest of these trails, it follows a beaver-dammed creek, then climbs moderately to granite outcrops commanding a great view down the Chena Valley. It is especially striking in July when wildflowers are in full bloom. There are two alternative routes back to the trailhead (at Mile 48.9), and more ambitious hikers can continue from Angel Rocks to Chena Hot Springs (8.7 miles total; 3–4hr; 2000ft ascent in total), passing a free-use cabin at Mile 5.

Chena Dome Trail (29-mile loop; 2–4 days; 6000ft ascent). An arduous expedition (with a good viewpoint after one mile for the less committed) entirely encircling the Angel Creek drainage by means of a series of subalpine ridges separated by steep valleys and saddles. There are some wondrous views from the high points (Chena Dome at Mile 10.5 reaches 4421ft), and there is always a chance of coming across a bear or wolverine, though July wildflowers and August blueberries are more likely. In the valley below is the Angel Creek Trail, too boggy in summer to be any fun, but you can drop down from Mile 22.5 of the Chena Dome Trail to sleep at the *Upper* and *Lower Angel Creek* cabins, at Mile 3.6 and Mile 6.7 of the Angel Creek Trail (reserve in advance through the Department of Natural Resources' Public Information Center in Fairbanks, 3700 Airport Way at University Ave; ℡451-2705; Mon–Fri 8am–5pm; $20 off-peak, $25 peak per night) – still, it is far better to **camp** to avoid the descent. Keep in mind that there is little (or no) **water** along the trail: carry as much as you can and be prepared to treat whatever you can find. The trailhead is at Mile 50.5, and you've got a 1.4-mile road walk back to the trailhead from the end of the hike at Mile 49 of Chena Hot Springs Road.

Winter is peak season at *Chena Hot Springs Resort*. Room rates go up by one price code, reflecting the demand for viewing the aurora borealis. Dog-sledding ($50 to go two miles, or $195 for a two-hour lesson), rides on a snowmobile ($80 an hour), and cross-country skiing (rentals $7.50 an hour or $25 for the day) steal the scene from summer's hiking and biking.

Circle Hot Springs and around

Until recently, **Circle Hot Springs**, 135 miles northeast of Fairbanks, managed to achieve an agreeable balance between the overdevelopment of Chena Hot Springs and the simplicity of Manley Hot Springs. The *Arctic Circle Hot Springs Resort* has been officially closed since 2001, but the caretaker still usually allows access to the pool. Even if it does reopen, you'll need to weigh your desire for a steamy soak against a 270-mile round-trip that will definitely make you earn your dip. Unless you've shopped around you may find that your rental car isn't insured off blacktop roads and, even if it is, the trip is probably only worthwhile when combined with other activities: hiking the **Pinnell Mountain Trail**, canoeing Birch Creek (consult APLIC in Fairbanks for details), or undertaking a little **gold-panning** along the Chatanika River. If you are keen on panning, get details and buy equipment at Alaskan Prospectors in Fairbanks (see p.518). Around the turn of the twentieth century, sourdoughs on the Yukon headed to fresh prospecting grounds inland, blazing the Circle–Fairbanks summer trail along a sequence of ridgetops south of the Chatanika River. Today a section of this route (replaced in 1928 by the Steese Highway) is followed by the Circle–Fairbanks Historic Trail, a loosely defined hiking and horse trail. The annual Yukon Quest International Sled Dog Race (see box, p.503) now traces this trail in winter, using mostly frozen watercourses.

Along the Steese Highway: Fox to Central

North from Fairbanks the Steese Highway arrives at Fox (see p.512), from where it works its way northeast towards the Yukon River. Five miles from the junction it passes the **Felix Pedro Historic Monument**, which marks the spot where, in July 1902, Felix Pedro discovered gold in the region. The creek across the road is open for recreational panning; there is a nostalgic quality to dipping your pan in here, even if it has been worked over so often that you'll never find anything worthwhile. There is still gold around, though, most of it being pulled out of **Fort Knox Mine** a few miles further on. Opened in 1996, this is Alaska's largest gold mine, but output is declining as energy costs rise, and it is scheduled to close in 2010.

The highway then climbs steeply to **Cleary Summit**, Mile 20.3, a small ski area from where there are great views of the White Mountains to the north and Mount McKinley to the south. Mount Aurora Skiland (T389-2314, Wwww.skiland.org; for accommodation T389-2000, Wwww.mt-aurora.com) is three quarters of a mile south, with a single chairlift and four miles of cross-country trails; the Circle–Fairbanks Historic Trail starts three miles to the east of the summit and runs for 58 mosquito-plagued miles to Twelvemile Summit. On the road, a steep descent drops you into a land only just beginning to recover from the ravages of intensive gold mining. Historically one of the most active centers of gold extraction, the township of **CHATANIKA**, Mile 28, was once the terminus of the narrow-gauge Tanana Valley Railroad, which supplied the region from Fairbanks. There's little left of Chatanika now, but something of the glory days can be found in the artifacts strewn around *Old FE Company Gold Camp*, Mile 28 (T389-2414, Wwww.fegoldcamp.com; closed Mon–Wed in winter; cabins ❸, rooms ❷), formerly a 200-man camp centered around a 1921 bunkhouse which now operates as a **hotel**, bar, and good **restaurant** serving American and Italian cuisine, as well as a $12 Sunday brunch. It is well worth stopping for a meal or a few drinks, which may induce you to stay the night in the charismatic, well-kept shared-bath rooms upstairs, the appealing modern log cabins, or the more basic hostel ($27 for a bunk).

A mile up the road, *Chatanika Lodge*, Mile 28.6 (☎389-2164, ⓔchatanika .ak@att.net; ❷), also serves decent food and has functional rooms with shared bathrooms. Opposite, **Gold Dredge No. 3** looms from behind a heap of tailings like some beached galleon. The second largest dredge in Alaska, having produced a bounty of around $10 million since its installation in the 1920s, sits on private property, but no one is going to worry if you follow one of the short trails for a quick look.

A mile further on lies **Poker Flat Research Range**, UAF's rocket-launch facility; established in 1969 to study the effect on the ionosphere of nuclear war, since 1996 it's mainly been used by NASA. You can visit on a two-hour **tour** (June to late Aug roughly every second Thurs 1.30pm; free; ☎455-2110, ⓦwww.pfrr.alaska.edu), which starts at the gates.

In the thirty miles east of Chatanika there are two attractive **campgrounds**: the wooded, riverside *Upper Chatanika River State Recreation Site*, Mile 39 ($10 per vehicle; pump water), and *Cripple Creek Campground*, Mile 60 ($8; pump water), again by the river and with some walk-in sites. Cripple Creek, named after the more famous one in Colorado, was Alaska's richest stream, with gold worth $100 million ($2 billion now, with inflation) extracted from a ten-mile stretch. Both are access points for the Chatanika River Canoe Route (consult APLIC in Fairbanks for details), a gentle Class I–II float down to Mile 11 on the Elliott Highway, 45 miles from Cripple Creek.

At Mile 57.3, thirteen miles beyond the end of the asphalt, **US Creek Road** spurs north towards Nome Creek Valley, which borders the southern reaches of the White Mountains National Recreation Area; this area has been badly affected by recent wildfires, which also burnt the tundra and continued smoldering beneath the snow. A couple of hundred yards north are the remains of one of the pipeline sections of the **Davidson Ditch**, which supplied sluicing water to the Fox diggings (see p.512). The road then climbs over a thinly wooded ridge and drops down to Nome Creek, seven miles off the Steese Highway. The BLM's *Ophir Creek Campground* (four miles west down Nome Creek; $6; pump water) and *Mount Prindle Campground* (not so far to the east; $6; pump water) make good bases for recreational gold-panning, catch-and-release grayling-fishing, or just hanging out. They are mostly gravel plots designed for RVs, but they're lovely spots. Ophir Creek is at the confluence where Nome and Ophir creeks form Beaver Creek, a National Wild River; you can follow it by canoe through the White Mountains for seven to ten days before being taken out by plane from a gravel bar. From Mount Prindle Campground there's hiking up onto the alpine terrain of Mount Prindle, the highest in the White Mountains National Recreation Area at 5286ft.

As the Steese Highway climbs out of the Chatanika Valley, trees thin visibly until they virtually disappear at the watershed of **Twelvemile Summit**, Mile 85.5, finishing point of the Circle–Fairbanks Historic Trail and the Pinnell Mountain Trail (see box, opposite). The road then continues to the trail's start at **Eagle Summit**, Mile 107.3. It is a bleak spot with a long row of L-shaped poles marking the road ahead for snowplows. Eagle Summit has even been known to receive snow on the summer solstice, when the surrounding hilltops become favored spots for viewing the passage of the **midnight sun** as it brushes the horizon and begins its ascent for the new day. Both summits are good for experiencing tundra landscape, with a good chance of seeing caribou in late summer. From the Upper Birch Creek put-in at Mile 94.5 you can float down Birch Creek, another National Wild River with some Class III rapids, for 126 miles and seven to ten days as it loops south through the 1.2 million-acre Steese National Conservation Area, meeting the road again at miles 140.4 and 147.1, between Central and Circle, where it begins to meander through the Yukon Flats.

From Eagle Summit the Steese descends for twenty miles to the small junction town of Central past Mammoth and Mastodon creeks, where wonderfully preserved examples of these ancient animals have been discovered embedded in the permafrost before being carted away to museums. Rolling into **CENTRAL**, 127 miles northeast of Fairbanks, it is difficult to see just what it is central to, but back in the heady gold days this was the heart of the Circle Mining District, the place from which prospectors would disperse up the gulches to stake their claims. The region revived on the back of rocketing gold prices in the late 1970s and has since maintained a solid following of summertime miners pursuing the dream. An insight into the power of gold over the prospectors' psyche comes through from the **Central Mining District Museum** (late May to early Sept daily noon–5pm; $1), where staggering statistics of the quantity of gold pulled out of the surrounding hills are backed up by large nuggets and fascinating artifacts from the tough early years.

Only a few dozen souls permanently occupy Central, but this small town may nonetheless provide the creature comforts – simple **cabins**, straightforward diner food, and showers – you've been hankering after if you've just spent a couple of nights out on the Pinnell Mountain Trail. Choose between the *Central Motor Inn* (T 520-5228; ❸), where camping costs $12 and showers $3, and the adjacent *Crabb's Corner* (T 520-5599; rooms ❸, cabins ❷), which has cabins

---

Pinnell Mountain Trail

As you thread your way along an exposed ridgeline between Pinnell Mountain and Porcupine Dome on the **Pinnell Mountain Trail** (27.3 miles one-way; 2–3 days; 3200ft ascent), the 5000-foot elevation combines with the proximity to the Arctic Circle – just seventy miles to the north – to make the midnight sun visible from June 18 to 24. Understandably, this is the busiest time to be up here – particularly the summer solstice on June 21 – but at any time from mid-June to mid-September you'll find great views of the Alaska and Brooks ranges. After an initial climb the trail follows a high, windswept and treeless ridge seldom dropping more than a few hundred feet before scaling the next low mountain. It can get a little monotonous, but long views and the occasional caribou maintain interest, and the threat of bear encounters adds zest. If this sounds too intense, just hike the first couple of miles from either of the two trailheads for great views and palpable solitude.

The hike is perhaps best done over two or three days, spending the night in one or both of the emergency shelters (*Ptarmigan Creek* at 10.1 miles and *North Fork* at 17.8 miles), which are small but fully weatherproof (though not mosquito-proof) and can just about sleep six. Roof **rainwater** collected in a barrel outside can be used for cooking and is likely to be all you'll find along the way – come prepared. There can sometimes be **atrocious weather** up here, evidenced by the large number of posts and cairns that make the route discernable in a white-out, so it is a good idea to **bring a tent** – also advisable at popular times when the shelters may be full.

Leave your vehicle near the finish at **Twelvemile Summit** (2982ft), Mile 85.5, and hitch back to the start at the higher of the two trailheads, **Eagle Summit** (3685ft), Mile 107.3. The hitch can be a long and discouraging experience and is best not left until you are tired and hungry (and possibly wet and cold) at the end of your hike.

APLIC in Fairbanks stocks the BLM's useful *Pinnell Mountain Trail* leaflet, which includes a map detailed enough for hiking, though as a precaution you should always carry the appropriate topo maps.

with electricity (some with water) sleeping up to six (at a pinch), and free tent camping; showers are $3, laundry $2. Both have decent **restaurants** and sell gas, though it isn't cheap.

Circle Hot Springs

From Central, Circle Hot Springs Road spurs eight miles south to **Circle Hot Springs**, essentially just the *Arctic Circle Hot Springs Resort* (☎520-5113), founded back in 1909 but **currently closed**, although the caretaker may let you in. If he does, you can expect vast quantities of hot spring water filling a large outdoor swimming pool, which has traditionally been chlorinated because of heavy use. The tone of the place shies away from "health spa" and leans more towards having fun in the warm waters and simply getting away from it all, but there were various massage treatments available when it was open. The original 1930 building housed a restaurant, a bar, rooms with shared bathrooms, and a dorm, and there were cabins as well as space for RVs and camping. Camping is still available at Mile 6 Circle Hot Springs Road.

Without your own vehicle, **access** is limited to flights from Fairbanks with Warbelow's Air Ventures (Mon–Sat only; $110 each way; ☎474-0518 or 1-800/478-0812).

Circle

Beyond Central, the progressively deteriorating Steese Highway runs 35 miles to the Yukon River. In the days before a road was constructed to the oil fields of Prudhoe Bay, this was the farthest north you could drive in the US, falling fifty miles short of the Arctic Circle; of course, that didn't stop geographically challenged miners from picking **CIRCLE** for the name of the first supply post to be built on the Yukon River, established here in 1893. Until the rise of Dawson City during the Klondike rush five years later, Circle was known as the largest log-cabin city in the world, with a population of more than a

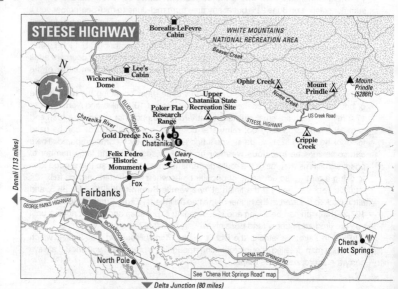

thousand and a waterfront a mile and a half long. It even had its own opera house, prompting some to dub it the "Paris of the North," though the long winters and hard-scrabble mining life quickly made that a laughable characterization. Only ninety people live here today, making a living from mining, fishing, and a bit of fur trapping.

The exodus to the Klondike pretty much cleaned out Circle, but its location on the river and role as a stopping point for steamers kept it alive. With much of the original townsite eroded away by the Yukon River, it is now a faintly dispiriting place, with none of the grace of its upstream neighbor, Eagle. Even the river – at this point some two and a half miles wide – is stripped of its majesty when viewed from Circle, as you only see one relatively small branch. But the river remains the lure: float trips through the Yukon-Charley National Preserve (see box, p.486) usually end here, and Circle City Charters (℡773-8439) runs **boat charters** (around $250 a half-day) for up to five people either upstream into the Yukon-Charley or downstream to Fort Yukon on the Arctic Circle through the **Yukon Flats National Wildlife Refuge** (Ⓦyukonflats.fws.gov). This lake-filled country, where the river braids out to over a sixty-mile breadth, is home to millions of geese, canvasbacks, swans, teal, scaup, and widgeon. The boat charters are run from the *Yukon Riverview Motel* (℡773-8439; ❸), which has basic motel rooms and public showers ($4). You can set up camp or park your RV nearby beside the boat launch, where there's an outhouse and tables, and then wander across to the Yukon Trading Post for expensive groceries, café food, and the bar.

Manley Hot Springs and around

Though recently straightened and improved, the **Elliott Highway** remains less than ideal, leading 160 miles north and west from Fairbanks through boreal

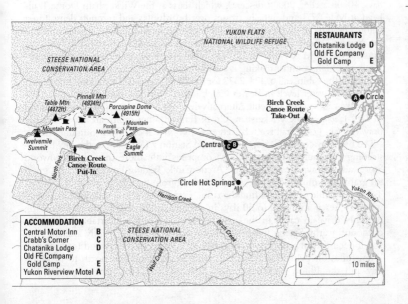

forest into what seems like nowhere. In fact it ends at the Tanana River, three miles beyond **Manley Hot Springs**, which is little more than a clearing in the woods with a classic roadhouse that claims to be Alaska's oldest continuously operated example of the archetypal hotel-cum-restaurant/bar. Nearby, a hot spring feeds tubs inside a greenhouse where grapes can be plucked off the vines trained above.

Along the Elliott Highway

The Steese Highway runs eleven miles north from Fairbanks to Fox, from where the **Elliott Highway** (officially open all year, but difficult after snow; contact Fairbanks Department of Transportation ☎451-5204) winds its way north, then southwest. The highway is now paved for the first seventy miles to Livengood, where the Elliott and Dalton highways part company, but it remains a four-hour run. If taken at a reasonable pace the road shouldn't provide any difficulty for ordinary cars, though services are almost nonexistent: stock up with crisp, **fresh water** at the Fox Spring, on the west side at Mile 0.3, and with **gas** in either Fairbanks, Fox, or at the *Hilltop Truck Stop*, Mile 5.5 (5am–midnight, gas 24hr; ☎389-7600) – there is no more until you reach Manley Hot Springs almost 150 miles on.

For most of the journey there is little reason to stop other than to linger over the gorgeous wilderness you're driving through. North of Fox, the Lower Chatanika River State Recreation Area harbors the waterside *Olnes Campground*, Mile 10.6 (free; lake water, which should be treated), with drive-up sites just over a mile off the highway. No longer state-maintained, it remains popular with Fairbanksans who come here to fish the lake.

The highway then approaches the western end of the **White Mountains**, an eye-catching limestone range that stretches off to the northeast. Much of the BLM's White Mountain National Recreation Area, which covers almost a million acres, is boggy and the majority of trails are only passable in winter. The one significant summer hiking trail is the arduous **Summit Trail** (40 miles round-trip; 4–5 days; 1000ft ascent, 2000ft descent), which starts at the Wickersham Dome Trailhead at Mile 27.7 and initially crosses over boardwalks and through dense forest before climbing up to the tundra of Wickersham Dome. It follows a ridge down to the *Borealis-LeFevre Cabin* by Beaver Creek (Fri & Sat $25, otherwise $20; reserve through the BLM ☎1-800/437-7021), but many prefer to turn back after camping in the high country, making it a two- or three-day hike. If you are intent on getting to the cabin, call ☎474-2372 for the BLM's recorded trail condition report in case high water levels in Beaver Creek (during spring snowmelt or heavy rainfall) make cabin access difficult. Alternatively it's just seven miles from the trailhead to *Lee's Cabin* on the Wickersham Creek Trail; all other cabins are for winter use only. The Ski Loop Trail is a relatively easy five-mile loop off the Summit Trail.

The highway continues north past Pump Station 7 (Mile 43) to the tiny homesteading community of **Joy**, which comprises little more than the Wildwood Store (also known by its old name, Arctic Circle Trading Post), Mile 49.3, good for grabbing a muffin and coffee or something from their huge stock of souvenir T-shirts. At Mile 62.5 you'll find the rustic *Fred Blixt Cabin* (Fri & Sat $25, otherwise $20; reservations up to 30 days in advance; call the BLM on ☎474-2250), the only drive-in cabin in the area, which sleeps five comfortably and has an outhouse nearby. Spring water, which should be treated, is readily available, but you'll need to bring white gas for the cooking stove and firewood for heating.

Ten miles on (Mile 73.1) the Dalton Highway continues north to Prudhoe Bay and the Elliott Highway turns left to Manley Hot Springs, passing the trailhead (Mile 92) for a fairly tough eleven-mile hiking trail leading south to **Tolovana Hot Springs**, where plastic pipes pour scalding hot and cold water into a cedar tub and two plastic ones; the temperature is regulated by removing the pipes as needed. There are a couple of rental cabins nearby with sleeping mats, gas cooking stoves, cookware, and lights but nothing else: one sleeps four (from $35 Mon–Thurs off-peak to $75 Fri–Sun peak), while the other sleeps eight (previous rates doubled). Use of the hot springs and adjacent cabins is by reservation (☎455-6706, ⓦ www.mosquitonet.com/~tolovana), and once booked you have the whole place to yourselves.

Around Mile 95 there are impressive views over **Minto Flats**, a state game refuge which spreads south of the predominantly Athabascan village of Minto, reached by a side road at Mile 110.

Manley Hot Springs

Manley Hot Springs, 160 miles northwest of Fairbanks, seems hacked out of the bush and consists of an airstrip, a general store with post office, a gas station, and a few houses clustered beside the placid tree-hung Hot Springs Slough. When gold was discovered at the nearby Tofty and Eureka goldfields in the early 1900s, miners came to clean up in freely available hot water and relished the fresh vegetables that could be grown in the warmer ground, a rare boon in Alaska. In 1902, J.F. "Daddy" Karshner set up a 320-acre market-gardening homestead around the springs – then known simply as **Hot Springs**. Four years later he was bought out by a man going by the alias of **Frank Manley**, who turned up with several hundred thousand dollars and a shady reputation from his Texas past. He was later forcibly returned there for horse thievery, but was eventually acquitted. Manley established the first resort, a log-built four-story affair with electricity, dance hall, billiard table, steam heating, and a "natatorium" for taking a dip at any time of year. It was an immediate hit with Fairbanks residents. The resort waned with Fairbanks' fortunes and finally burned down in 1913, but Manley's name lived on, and in 1957 it was attached to the name of the town. But don't go calling the place Manley (even if the road signs do), or you'll raise the hackles of older residents, not all of whom appreciated the change. As river traffic came to a halt in the early 1950s, Manley Hot Springs' fate looked bleak, but a gravel road allows for a trickle of tourist traffic; there's a proposal to extend the road west to Nome, but it'll take a long time.

The local population barely touches a hundred, and on a good Saturday night it seems they're all around the pool table and horseshoe bar inside the 1906 *Manley Roadhouse* (☎672-3161; rooms ❶, with private bath ❹, cabins ❸; mid-May to Oct), a wonderful chunk of Alaska's living heritage with good diner **meals**, beat-up chairs huddled around the oil-barrel stove and pianola, and rooms upstairs. The older rooms are small and share facilities, but their battered furniture and creaking floorboards are delightfully authentic; cabins sleep five. The patch of grass across the road makes a good **campground** ($5 per tent; pay at the roadhouse). There's also a cabin for rent by the hot springs (☎672-3231; ❷).

For the **hot springs**, head to the Bath House (open 24hr, year-round; $5 per hour per person paid to the amiable owner, Gladys, at the house just above; ☎672-3231), a verdant, heated greenhouse containing three simple concrete tubs supplied with cooled but untreated spring water. Grapes and Asian pears flourish here, and you are welcome to sample whatever is ripe as you loll back for a few hours. Essentially, once your group pays up the whole place is yours for an hour, though at busy times you might want to welcome others in. To reach the Bath House from the roadhouse, cross the bridge (once the Cushman Street bridge in Fairbanks) over the slough and take the third road on the left, about three hundred yards towards Fairbanks.

Arctic Alaska

Exactly what constitutes **Arctic Alaska** is hard to pin down, but it does encompass some of America's finest wilderness, fierce and shockingly desolate and yet shot through with an intricate, fragile beauty. To geographers it is anywhere north of the **Arctic Circle**, an imaginary line at 66° 33" above which the sun fails to set at the summer solstice (June 21), or rise on the winter solstice (December 21). For botanists the true Arctic begins at the tree line, where spruce give way to willows that creep along the ground, often for tens of yards, but never get off it. Meanwhile, ethnologists might argue that the Arctic is the preserve of the Iñupiat and Yup'ik peoples.

Whichever way you define the Arctic, it covers pretty much everywhere north of Fairbanks. This is the land of the midnight sun, where summer days are endless and intense low-angled rays can warm the air to almost 100°F. For three brief months the thin covering of snow melts, and the near-flat tundra thaws to a soggy, peaty landscape studded with myriad tiny lakes. Rainfall here is minimal, often less than in some parts of the deserts of the American Southwest, but much of the North is underlain by **permafrost** (see box, p.546), which impedes drainage enough to sustain the lakes. Bears, caribou, moose, and arctic foxes go through accelerated reproductive cycles in time for the arrival of the savage nine-month winter (spring and fall hardly exist), when snow blows across the tundra and the northern lights glow overhead.

Arctic Alaska is split by the **Brooks Range**, which extends almost the width of Alaska. It is the tail end of the continental dividing range that starts at the southern tip of the Andes and stretches right up through the Mexican cordilleras and the US and Canadian Rockies. To the south the Alatna, Chandalar, John, Koyukuk, and Sheenjek rivers drain through the Interior forests into the Yukon and out to the Bering Sea; to the north the Anaktuvuk, Colville, and Sagavanirktok rivers flow across the barren flatlands of the **North Slope** into the Beaufort Sea.

Despite the protection offered by a confusing patchwork of national parks, preserves, and wildlife refuges, much of this wilderness is under threat. Many of the more individualistic Alaskans object to the very idea of "tying up" land with such designations, but the greatest danger comes from the **oil lobbyists** and indeed the entire Alaskan political and media establishment. The face of the Far North has already changed with the exploitation of the Prudhoe Bay field and its satellites, as well as the construction of the pipeline. As reserves dwindle, oil companies are campaigning for access to other areas. Environmentalists argued against exploiting the National Petroleum Reserve – Alaska (NPR-A), an area the size of Indiana to the west of Prudhoe Bay set aside for the navy in 1923, but drilling is now underway. They have a stronger hand in protecting the Arctic National Wildlife Refuge (ANWR) to the east, although with the high oil prices of recent times there is considerable political pressure being applied to allow exploration in the refuge's northern coastal strip. The Bush administration has been very keen to get ANWR exploration authorized since 2003, but strident opposition in the Senate has always been enough to block it.

Exploring the region

The only road access into the Alaskan Arctic is along the 414-mile Dalton Highway to **Prudhoe Bay** (500 miles from Fairbanks, including the Steese and Elliott highways), which runs parallel to the Trans-Alaska Pipeline. Unless you are up for a heroic road trip in your own vehicle, it is best done as part of an organized tour taking in the Arctic Circle monument, the oil installation, the Arctic Ocean, and a lot of grand scenery. As it crosses the Brooks Range, the Dalton divides two of Alaska's largest and most remarkable protected areas, both conveniently visited directly by air from Fairbanks. To the west lies the **Gates of the Arctic National Park**, wonderfully remote hiking and canoeing country accessed through the tiny village of **Bettles**. To the east is the still more remote **Arctic National Wildlife Refuge**, also good for hiking and floating.

Much of the North is thinly populated, with only a few dozen tiny Native communities scattered across this vast area. The smaller hamlets are not really set up for visitors, so that really just leaves three towns to explore. There is an obvious draw to **Barrow**, the northernmost town on the continent; besides having the world's largest Eskimo population, it serves as the occasional stomping ground of polar bears. **Kotzebue** is smaller but has a higher percentage of Native Alaskans, lending it a more traditional feel. Located well inside the Arctic Circle, it is a good jumping-off point for trips to Kobuk Valley National Park. The onetime gold-rush town of **Nome** doesn't claim any superlatives, but it is perhaps the most immediately inviting of the three, with enough of a road system to encourage wider exploration. Nome also serves as the end of the roughly 1150-mile annual Iditarod sled-dog race from Anchorage.

The Dalton Highway to Prudhoe Bay

The Arctic location and remote nature of the **Dalton Highway** exert an almost irresistible pull, all 414 lonely, desolate miles of it from Livengood to the Arctic Ocean, three hundred miles beyond the **Arctic Circle**. It is certainly an adventurous journey, but all you get at the end of the road is Prudhoe Bay, miles of pipes, and the industrial camp of **Deadhorse**, which is nowhere near as exotic as it sounds. You can't even get to the Arctic Ocean except on a fairly perfunctory tour. For most of the year the Arctic pack-ice butts right up against the shore, and it's not uncommon to see polar bears roaming through Deadhorse. Things are different in summer, when you are more likely to be here, as both the bears and the ice floes are away over the northern horizon.

Those who like their wilderness pristine will be disappointed to learn that the **pipeline** runs above ground most of the way to Prudhoe Bay, though it quickly becomes a faithful companion pointing the way north. Both road and pipeline run down the center of a ten-mile-wide corridor managed by the Bureau of Land Management (BLM) and equipped with a few basic campgrounds. Along the way there are small lakes and streams that, when the snowmelt turbidity has dissipated (July to mid-Sept), offer good **fishing** for grayling, Dolly Varden, lake trout, and northern pike. Hiking is more problematic, with neither formal trails nor waymarked trailheads, though sections of the highway as it passes through

It is hard to overstate the importance of **oil** to the 49th state. Some jokingly contend that Alaska should break from the union and become an independent OPEC state, an idea that is not so far-fetched when you consider that Alaska produces seventeen percent of US oil and five percent of what the nation consumes. Alaskan taxes and royalties account for a third of the value of each barrel, an income that provides a whopping eighty percent of the state revenue. It is no surprise then that Alaska is virtually controlled by oil interests, and it is easy to get the impression that state politicians are little more than puppets for the oil companies.

Oil rises naturally to the earth's surface along the North Slope, historically providing lamp oil for Native Iñupiat and alerting hopeful white newcomers to the presence of deeper deposits. Years of exploration paid off in 1968 when the Atlantic Richfield Company (now part of ConocoPhillips) discovered a 23-billion-barrel reserve nine thousand feet under **Prudhoe Bay**. This constituted one of the world's largest finds, but the bay's location on the Arctic Ocean, where tankers could only penetrate the pack-ice for two months of the year, posed a problem. The solution was to build a $900 million pipeline running across the middle of the state to the northernmost ice-free port at Valdez. There was an immediate reaction from Alaskan Natives: the route of the planned pipeline would cut across areas claimed by Native groups and not covered by any treaty. Consequently, the 1971 **Alaska Native Claims Settlement Act** (ANCSA) was rushed through, offering land and cash in return for Natives relinquishing their claim on the remaining territory. Environmental concerns over damage to the tundra, disruption of animal migration routes, and the very idea of having a steel tube running hundreds of miles through untouched wilderness almost put a stop to the whole project, but the Arab oil embargo of 1973–74 finally forced the federal government's hand.

Over the years oil production has declined, and in the late 1990s the rallying cry of "No decline in '99" rang around halls of the Alaskan legislature in an effort to convince the state government to allow further exploration on the North Slope, particularly along the coast of the Arctic National Wildlife Refuge. At a time when oil prices were low, a report stated that there are "no economically recoverable amounts of oil" under ANWR if the price stays below $15 a barrel. On cue, the price of crude oil shot up towards $30 a barrel; the oil companies continue to apply pressure for more drilling, backed by many Alaskans as well as the Iñupiat-owned Arctic Slope Regional Corporation (ASRC), which stands to profit from royalties on any oil extracted, but opposed by the Athabascans living in the southern part of the refuge.

Even without new developments such as the Alpine, Kuparuk, and Ooguruk fields, production will continue until at least 2030, and with current high demand for natural gas, there is now talk of a parallel pipeline to exploit North Slope deposits. After all, Alyeska, the pipeline-operating company, has an obligation to restore the pipeline corridor to its original state once production ceases – something they want to put off as long as possible. Unfortunately for them it makes more sense to route the gas along the Alaska Highway to link up with the Canadian system and feed the gas down to Chicago, a $20 billion project that won't be complete before 2016 at the earliest. Proven gas reserves on the North Slope amount to 35 trillion cubic feet, equivalent to 10 billion barrels of oil (two-thirds of the total now taken out of the North Slope).

the Brooks Range present opportunities for freelance exploration, and if you are prepared to hike across tundra you can go wherever you want.

All around is federally managed wilderness: the **Yukon Flats** and **Arctic National Wildlife Refuges** to the east, and the **Kanuti National Wildlife**

The pipeline

The pipeline (ⓦwww.alyeska-pipe.com) is 800 miles long and in places looks like a four-foot-wide silver anaconda draped across the land. Altogether only 380 miles are buried: where it encounters permafrost, the pipeline gracefully emerges from the ground, rising onto ten-foot-high support brackets, and then embarks on a zigzag passage across the skyline, with kinks designed to accommodate earthquake movement as well as expansion and contraction in Alaska's extreme weather, which cools the oil from 145°F to 103°F by the time it reaches Valdez.

Pipeline construction began in November 1973, and employment peaked at over 21,000, with workers laboring away for wage packages of legendary proportions. With overtime and hardship bonuses, pipeline workers were pulling in up to $1500 a week (several times the national average at the time). Workers flocked up from the Lower 48 only to discover the work was long, hard, often lonely, and conducted in atrocious conditions, right through the Arctic winter.

The pipeline was finished in June 1977 at a cost of $8 billion, almost ten times the original budget, and the first oil was pumped from Prudhoe Bay on June 20, 1977. A Nenana Ice Classic-style lottery was conducted with $30,000 at stake for whoever could pick the exact time of the oil's arrival in Valdez – which turned out to be 38 days, 12 hours, and 56 minutes after it set off, thanks to all kinds of technical delays. Oil now makes the journey in about six days (averaging 5.5mph), its passage through a complex series of pumping stations and valves managed from Valdez.

More than five hundred **animal crossings** had been incorporated into the pipeline, some just short runs of buried pipe, others achieved by raising sections of pipe more than usual above ground. The jury is still out on the success of these measures: caribou congregate in spring around the pipe, where the grass tends to green up earlier, but tend to move away from the pipeline before calving, to areas with less food and a higher risk of predation.

Twelve **pump stations** were designed to move the oil along, each equipped with Rolls-Royce jet engines, but only eleven were built. As production has declined and the pipeline has become more efficient (for example with the addition of Drag Reducing Agent since 1979), six pump stations have been mothballed, with two more to follow as the system is automated and the jets are replaced by electric motors at pump stations 1, 3, 4, and 9. This will leave long sections without significant permanent staff, possibly compromising security. There have been small spills ever since the pipeline came on stream, but consequences of a major pipeline rupture were brought into sharp focus by the *Exxon Valdez* disaster (see box, p.322) and a 285,000-gallon spill caused by a bullet fired by a drunk in 2001. In response to the increasing risk of catastrophe, independent groups now monitor Alyeska's safety performance, continually highlighting weaknesses in the spill-response plan, leaking information on penny-pinching maintenance procedures, and generally driving home the idea that the pipeline is approaching thirty years of age (although it was only expected to last twenty years) and needs increased maintenance if a large-scale environmental disaster is to be avoided.

The most recent fiasco occurred in March 2006, a 200,000-gallon spill at Prudhoe Bay (flowing for three days before it was noticed) requiring a $6 million clean-up. BP had last cleaned that line in 1998, and the sludge build-up contributed to the corrosion and spill; the federal government forced BP to check all its pipelines, which were in such a poor state that the entire east side of the Prudhoe Bay field was shut down.

Refuge and **Gates of the Arctic National Park** to the west. With all this controlled land about, it is no surprise that there is plenty of **wildlife**. If you're lucky, the most impressive sight you'll see is the 30,000-strong Arctic caribou herd, which migrates in late April and early May through Prudhoe Bay to the

Kuparuk oilfields, the second-largest in the US, where the cows calve. The herd then returns to the Brooks Range in August for the abundant lichen. Grizzlies, Dall sheep, moose, and foxes are also present, and musk oxen sometimes congregate near the pipeline – binoculars are a boon.

Flights and tours to the Arctic Circle and Prudhoe Bay

Alaska Airlines flies large jets into Prudhoe Bay/Deadhorse airport once or twice daily from Anchorage. This will set you back about $670 plus tax if bought two weeks in advance – probably more than you want to pay to see an oilfield. Frontier Flying Service (℡1-800/478-6779, ⓦwww .frontierflying.com) flies direct from Fairbanks almost daily, but you'll pay around $665.

The venture seems more purposeful when combined with a road trip up the Dalton Highway, and by joining a **bus/plane tour** you won't wreck your vehicle and will (generally) avoid doing the same journey in both directions. Trips mostly involve driving up the Dalton in two days from Fairbanks, taking an Arctic Ocean tour at Prudhoe Bay, and then flying back to either Anchorage or Fairbanks. Some do the same in reverse, but go for the former if you can: two days on the road certainly heightens the drama of arrival.

Most companies run trips fairly infrequently, so it pays to inquire a week or two in advance (for contact addresses, see box on p.516). The widest range (and cheapest) of all-inclusive packages – including road transport, flights, and accommodation, but not food – is with Northern Alaska Tour Company, which runs the Arctic Ocean Adventure (3 days; $749), with a flight to Prudhoe Bay, then a minivan back down the Dalton with nights at Deadhorse and Coldfoot. There's an optional overnight extension flying to Barrow ($490 extra). If you want to rough it, try Dalton Highway Express (℡474-3555, ⓦwww .daltonhighwayexpress.com), which effectively runs a daily bus service

△ The Trans-Alaska Pipeline alongside the Dalton Highway

⑧

making the trip to Prudhoe Bay in sixteen hours. They charge $196 each way (bikes cost $60). Try Trans Arctic Circle Treks (℡1-800/336-8735, Ⓦwww .arctictreks.com) for an arduous three-day Prudhoe-and-back road trip with an Arctic Ocean tour and two nights in the Brooks Range ($699). A fly/drive option as well as Barrow and bush-flight extensions are available.

For those only wanting to visit the **Arctic Circle**, Northern Alaska Tour Company offers a number of variations starting with the full-day Arctic Circle Adventure (16hr; $139), driving up to the Arctic Circle and back. The Arctic Circle Fly Drive (11–12hr; $269) speeds things up by flying to Coldfoot and driving back or flying both ways (5hr; $289) with a couple of hours in Cold-foot or Wiseman. The Arctic Circle Native Culture Tour (14hr; $399) flies one way and includes a couple of hours in the Brooks Range village of Anaktu-vuk Pass. Alaskan Arctic Turtle Tours (℡1-888/456-1798, Ⓦwww.wildalaska .info) does day-trips to the Arctic Circle (12hr; $129 summer, $150 winter) and two-day trips to Prudhoe Bay ($549–799 depending on numbers). Trans Arctic Circle Treks (12hr; $129) and Alaska/Yukon Trails (10hr; $149) also run road trips to the Arctic Circle. Dalton Highway Express's Prudhoe Bay service will drop you at the Arctic Circle and pick you up again the next day ($70 each way).

Driving the Dalton Highway

From Fairbanks the route north follows the Steese and Elliott highways 84 miles to Livengood, where you'll find the start of the 414-mile **Dalton High-way** (open year-round but chains needed Sept–May), named for James Dalton, an Arctic engineer who played a major role in the early oil discovery and development of the North Slope. Old hands know it by its original working title, the North Slope **Haul Road**, named in honor of its fast, stop-at-nothing trucks and built in an astonishing five months in the summer of 1974 in preparation for the construction of the pipeline alongside.

For years the road was limited to pipeline traffic, but regulations were gradually relaxed until the whole road was finally opened to the general public in 1995. Nonetheless, there remains a distinct work-camp tenor along its length. There are no real villages or rest stops, just slightly remodeled work camps mostly comprised of prefabricated accommodation blocks. Don't expect much in the way of supplies either, and remember that everything you buy will have an Arctic price tag.

Driving the Dalton Highway mustn't be undertaken lightly, and you should seriously consider joining one of the bus tours. That said, conditions are improving with miles of fresh blacktop being added each year since 1999. Over two hundred miles are paved between Fairbanks and Deadhorse, but that still leaves almost three hundred miles of gravel. The word is that the entire road should be asphalt by 2008, but such dates have a habit of being continually put back. It'll take thirteen to sixteen hours to drive from Fairbanks to Deadhorse, and with possible delays due to wildlife sightings, weather, and construction, you should allow two days.

The problem is less the driving itself than the consequences if something goes wrong. There are only three places to buy gas on the Dalton – Yukon Crossing, Coldfoot, and Deadhorse – and between Coldfoot and Deadhorse is a 225-mile stretch with no services of any sort: towing fees can soon become astronomical. If you are determined, you'll either need your own car or be prepared to shell out for an expensive **rental vehicle**. Most companies don't allow their cars on gravel roads, and though you might choose to take the risk on the Steese or Elliott highways, this would be foolhardy on the Dalton. Your best bets are with sedans from Arctic Outfitters and campers from GoNorth or Adventures in Alaska, all covered under Fairbanks Listings on p.523.

Travelers' folklore has it that the Dalton is always in one of two states, muddy or dusty; worse still, the forty-odd eighteen-wheelers that ply the road each day supplying Prudhoe Bay have a nasty habit of hefting large rocks through windshields. June and July are the driest months, when wildflowers bloom and the caribou are on the coastal plain; in August there are often thunderstorms, especially south of the Yukon River, and it can snow from late August. For high-clearance trucks serving the oil community the road is passable **in winter**, but the cold (down to -50°F), darkness, and the general hostility of the environment pretty much rule it out for everyone else.

Whenever you go the rule is to **be prepared**. Allow for a couple of punctured tires (take two full-size spares with plenty of tread) and a cracked windshield, drive with your lights on and expect to wait a while for help if you need it. Some even carry a CB radio tuned to Channel 19 to pick up the conversations between truckers and tour-bus drivers but, in summer at least, there is a reasonable amount of traffic and it is enough to carry emergency supplies – food, water, sleeping bag, and perhaps a cooking stove. Cell-phone coverage ends about 35 miles out of Fairbanks. For more **information** visit APLIC in Fairbanks and pick up the BLM's free and comprehensive *The Dalton Highway* brochure (also at ⓦwww.blm.gov/ak/dalton), or check out the Coldfoot Interagency Visitor Center website (ⓦwww.aurora.ak.blm .gov/arcticinfo).

If you are thinking of **hitching** to Deadhorse, then persistence and patience will eventually pay off, usually with hunters, miners, and road crews but seldom with Prudhoe-bound truckers. Remember to take everything you'll need to camp out for several days. The occasional **cyclist** with a spoke loose also makes the journey, but it is tough, and mud and dust are a constant irritation. At least you can fix your own punctures, and once there you can get a ride back to Fairbanks with Dalton Highway Express (see p.540), which charges $60 just for the bike.

Designated campgrounds turn out to be the best places you can **camp**. You are generally free to camp anywhere along the highway, though in practice the only places sufficiently off the road are gravel parking lots.

Mile 0 to Mile 175

From its departure from the Elliott Highway at Livengood, the Dalton Highway sets off across a rolling landscape dotted with white and black spruce and strung with the gleaming pipeline. There's little reason to stop before Mile 56, where the road crosses the broad, dirty swirl of the **Yukon River** on the sloping, 2290-foot E.L. Patton Bridge, which has the pipeline strapped to its side. This is the only bridge over the Yukon downstream of Whitehorse in Canada.

Just over the bridge the grandly titled **Yukon Crossing** comprises a muddy (or dusty) expanse and the scruffy *Yukon River Camp* (☎474-3557; ❹), with shared-bath work-camp rooms, gas, and a café (summer only; 7am–9pm) serving a buffet to tour-bus passengers, as well as burgers ($9), salads ($11), and steak, fish, or pasta dinners ($16–20) to all comers. Adjacent, Yukon River Tours (☎452-7162, ⓦwww.mosquitonet .com/~dlacey/yrt.html) runs hour-long boat trips (June–Aug 3 daily; $25) downstream past hand-built fishwheels, with an environmentally and culturally oriented narrative. On the other side of the highway, the **BLM visitor contact station** (June–Aug daily 9am–6pm; no phone) provides information on the countryside flanking the Dalton.

The *Five Mile Campground* (free; water), actually four miles up the highway, sits on the site of an old pipeline-construction camp, right by *Teresa's Hot Spot Café* (June–Aug 10am–midnight; ☎451-7543; ❹), which produces great burgers served inside or out and has slightly dressed-up work-camp rooms at good prices; gas is sold here, as at Yukon Crossing.

North of the Yukon River the land begins to open out: trees become sparser, and the pipeline views get better. At Mile 97.5 the ancient forty-foot granite tor of **Finger Rock** pokes up from the bleak tundra, crooked as if warning of the perils of the road ahead. A short nature trail leads to a viewpoint overlooking the shallow pools that form the headwaters of the Kanuti River, the main watershed encompassed by the **Kanuti National Wildlife Refuge** (ⓦkanuti.fws.gov) to the west. With acres of relatively dry tundra, this makes a good spot for a couple of hours' hiking: pick a promising destination and go.

The highway enters the **Arctic Circle** at Mile 115 (200 miles and 4.5 hours from Fairbanks) and supports a series of explanatory panels and a viewing deck a short way up a side road, where everyone has their photo taken. There's a mosquito-ridden picnic area with wheelchair-accessible outhouses and barbecues among the aspen and black spruce, with a slightly breezier (and therefore less buggy) **campground** (free; water from Fish Creek a mile to the south) a quarter-mile up the hill. Unfortunately, the hills to the north preclude seeing the midnight sun from here, even on the solstice, so if this is what you've come for you'll need to press on to **Gobbler's Knob**, Mile 132, where there are panoramic views. About three miles further north, the former pipeline-constructors' **Prospect Camp** holds the record for the lowest temperature recorded in the United States: -80°F (-62°C) on January 23, 1971. There was once a campground here, and you can still find decent flat spots a mile off the road.

DALTON HIGHWAY: SOUTH

ACCOMMODATION
Arctic Gateway B&B — C
Boreal Lodging — B
Slate Creek Inn — D
Teresa's Hot Spot Café — E
Wiseman Gold Rush Camp — A
Yukon River Camp — F
RESTAURANTS
Teresa's Hot Spot Café — E

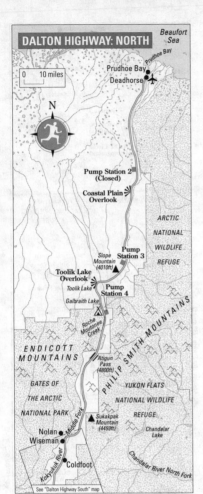

DALTON HIGHWAY: NORTH

Beaufort
Sea

0   10 miles

N

Prudhoe Bay
Deadhorse

Prudhoe Bay

Pump Station 2
(Closed)

Coastal Plain
Overlook

ARCTIC

NATIONAL

WILDLIFE

Slope   Pump
Mountain   Station 3
(4010ft)

REFUGE

Toolik Lake
Overlook

Toolik Lake   Pump
Station 4

Galbraith Lake

Roche
Moutonee
Creek

ENDICOTT
MOUNTAINS

PHILIP SMITH MOUNTAINS

Atigun
Pass
(4800ft)

GATES OF   YUKON FLATS
THE ARCTIC
                NATIONAL WILDLIFE
NATIONAL PARK

Sukakpak   REFUGE
Mountain
(4459ft)   Chandalar
               Lake

Nolan
Wiseman

Chandalar River North Fork

Coldfoot

See "Dalton Highway South" map

Coldfoot Camp

As the miles roll by, the open Arctic tundra gives way to the foothills of the Brooks Range, blunt, conical mounds skirted with white birch rising above broad, willow-studded glacial valleys. Gradually, the valleys deepen into the Middle Fork of the Koyukuk River (which offers Class I–II floating), and you hit the former highway-construction base of **Coldfoot Camp**, Mile 175. It bills itself as "the world's northern-most truck stop," and except for a couple of B&Bs at Wiseman (see opposite), Coldfoot is indeed your last chance for **accommodation**, **food**, and **gas** (open 24hr) before Deadhorse 239 miles on. Nothing comes cheaply, but unless you are camping, there isn't much choice. Most tours spend the night here, too. Coldfoot supposedly gets its name from prospectors moving north for more golden pastures and getting metaphorical cold feet around this point, but a literal interpretation suits equally: in 1989 the mercury stayed below -60°F for seventeen days in a row. It also gets hot here in summer: 1988 recorded a high of 97°F. In 1981 Dick Mackey leased space for the original truckstop, selling burgers from an old blue schoolbus; this was transformed by the truckers themselves, who got fed up with its limited facilities and started drop-ping off "surplus" building mate-rials on their southbound runs.

Workers' accommodation has also been transformed to create the *Slate Creek Inn* (in Fairbanks ☎474-3500, locally ☎678-5224, ⓦwww.coldfootcamp.com; ❼), with reasonably comfortable shared-bath twin rooms, a truckers' café known for its banana cream pie (open year-round, 5am–midnight), and a parking lot where you can camp ($15) and hook up an RV ($30). Showers are $10 extra, and there's laundry for $3. You'll also find very limited **groceries**, a **post office** (Mon, Wed & Fri 1.30–6pm), and phones. There are even flights to Anaktuvuk Pass ($149) or any feasible gravel bar in the Brooks Range with Coyote Air (☎1-800/252-0603, ⓦwww.flycoyote.com), and a float trip from Wiseman to Coldfoot down the Middle Fork of the Koyukuk River ($59) with Northern Alaska Tour Company (☎1-800/474-1986, ⓦwww.northernalaska.com).

You get an indication of Alaska's aspirations for making the Dalton Highway a tourist route by the presence of the **Arctic Interagency Visitor Center** (late May to early Sept daily 10am–10pm; ℡678-5209, Ⓦwww.aurora.ak.blm .gov/arcticinfo), which opened across the highway from Coldfoot Camp in 2003. Attractively designed, beautifully landscaped, and fitted with flush toilets, it is very un-Dalton in character, but it provides a welcome spot to get off the road, sit around the wood-burning stove to read up on the journey ahead, buy books and topo maps, obtain bear-resistant food canisters for backcountry trips, and attend nightly slide shows and talks (8pm; free). **Campers** are better served five miles north of Coldfoot at *Marion Creek Campground* ($8; June to mid-Sept; pump water and free firewood), where there are tables, fire pits, a summertime campground host, and great views of the Brooks Range, as well as a two-mile hike up the creek to a waterfall.

Wiseman to the North Slope

Miners prospecting in 1908 who weren't put off by the low temperatures of Coldfoot Camp chose to settle thirteen miles north at **Wiseman**, three miles off the highway from Mile 189, on the Middle Fork of the Koyukuk River – the "willow river". It is now a small, thriving cluster of log cabins hacked out of the spruce, supporting a dozen people year-round and a few dozen more who arrive for summer hunting, fishing, and gold extraction. Several original buildings have survived, one of which houses the **Pringle Roadhouse & Historical Museum** (June–Aug nominally daily 9am–1pm & 2–5pm but actually very sporadic; free), full of evocative old photos and assorted mining equipment. If you are not up for camping, Wiseman makes an appealing alternative to Coldfoot for **accommodation**: beyond the bridge in South Wiseman, *Boreal Lodging* (℡678-4566, Ⓔboreallodge@juno.com; cabin ❺, rooms ❸) has comfortable work-camp rooms with access to a well-equipped, cozy kitchen-cum-day room and a more luxurious cabin; *Arctic Getaway B&B* (℡678-4456, Ⓦwww.arcticgetaway.com; ❻ & ❹) has one large log cabin sleeping four and a smaller two-berth affair; and *Wiseman Gold Rush Camp* (℡479-3213, Ⓔfiddler04@gci.net; ❸) has tent cabins, useable from May to September.

Wiseman also makes a good jumping-off point for hiking into the eastern fringes of the **Gates of the Arctic National Park**, the only way to get far into the park without a costly flight. Consult APLIC in Fairbanks or the Coldfoot visitor center for details.

As you head north from Wiseman, views to the right are dominated by the great marble face of the 4459-foot **Sukakpak Mountain** (wayside Mile 204), which is traditionally thought of as the border marker between Iñupiat and Athabascan territory. There's an outhouse and parking area adequate for ad hoc **camping** at Mile 205 where the road again crosses the Middle Fork of the Koyukuk River. The sporadic trees in these parts look like frayed matchsticks, and they finally disappear altogether around Mile 235, the point where you start to climb the Brooks Range past lightly vegetated talus slopes cascading from snowcapped 7000-foot peaks. This is undoubtedly the scenic highlight of the journey as you breach the North American continental divide, cresting at the scenic **Atigun Pass**, Mile 244, which at 4739ft is the highest stretch of road in Alaska. It is also the highest point for the pipeline, which in recent years has been considerably rerouted in places prone to landslides.

Then the highway descends towards the North Slope, giving opportunities for rugged **hiking** up the valleys to the east. There are no trails, so choose a good day to pick your own way up Roche Moutonee Creek around Mile 266. The steep initial descent soon mellows as you enter a broad glacial landscape followed by gently shelving river valleys.

Pump Station No.4 heralds an excellent place to break your journey, the undeveloped *Galbraith Lake Campground*, Mile 275 (free; lake water), which is the last recognized campsite in the North. Along the side road leading west to the airstrip and campground there are good examples of permafrost polygons, which you can reach easily enough. People do park overnight at wayside viewpoints further on, but there is nowhere to camp at Deadhorse.

From now on the pipeline is almost always above ground, gleaming across the landscape in the low Arctic sun, especially around **Toolik Lake**, Mile 284 (no camping), where UAF operates an Arctic biology research camp. Dall sheep are often in evidence on the flanks of **Slope Mountain**, Mile 301, which marks the point where the Dalton joins the Sagavanirktok River on its journey to the Arctic Ocean at Prudhoe Bay. After Pump Station No.3 (Mile 312) you'll pass the former Happy Valley construction camp at Mile 334 (where you can camp, but not on the active airstrip), after which the highway is paved for 25 miles. You know you are onto the final straight when you hit the **Coastal Plain Overlook**, Mile 356, a low hilltop from where you can see the sixty miles of the North Slope fading away to the ocean while steadily losing six hundred feet of elevation. The sky seems endless, and the land begins to exhibit truly arctic phenomena – **pingos**, **polygons**, and **thaw lakes** (see box, below) – all caused by arcane facets of the annual thaw over hundreds of feet of permafrost. Most visible of these are the pingos, conical mounds rising as high as two hundred feet above the plain. You should also be able to see musk oxen, reintroduced to this area from Kaktovik in 1970.

Deadhorse and Prudhoe Bay

The end of the road is at **Deadhorse**, 860 miles north of Anchorage. You're still eight miles short of the Arctic Ocean and another 1200 miles from the North Pole – Alaska's southernmost town, Ketchikan, is closer to you. Deadhorse is a weird place, not really a town at all but an industrial area where venturing outdoors (and there is little reason to do this) risks stumbling onto restricted

Pingos, polygons, and permafrost

One of the defining features of the Alaskan North goes almost entirely unseen, though its effects can be very evident, particularly on the North Slope. Year-round temperatures are so low that most of the ground remains frozen as **permafrost**, stretching from a foot or so below the surface to a depth of up to 2200ft. This doesn't prevent life from gaining a foothold here, though; the weak summer sun manages to warm enough of the surface to form an **active layer**, one to ten feet deep, in which plants can take root and burrowing insects can go about their business.

The active layer freezes and shrinks slightly in winter, forming small vertical cracks in the earth. In spring these fill with meltwater and refreeze, a cyclic process that, over the years, forms an **ice wedge**, broad near the surface and tapering to a point perhaps thirty feet underground. There's often a hump on the ground above an ice wedge, and when several form next to one another they create a surface pattern made up of **polygons**, typically ten to seventy feet across. If the top of the ice wedge becomes exposed it may melt to form a **thermokarst lake**, or just a very wet active layer. As the active layer begins to freeze, it pushes up the ground to form a **pingo**, a rounded hummock on the surface that can grow, over several hundred years, to more than two hundred feet high. Eventually, the pingo will break through the insulating active layer, and the ice will begin to melt, gradually destroying all trace of the formation.

territory or getting bowled over by a fifty-ton truck. Nonetheless, the shallow lakes and flat tundra all around can be attractive enough on a warm evening: the median summertime temperature is only 40°F, but it feels warmer in the constant sun. Tucked in among the power plants, workshops, and aircraft hangars are a couple of sets of workers' rooms that have been converted into tolerably comfortable **hotels**.

The fence and checkpoint that mark the ultimate end of the Dalton Highway separate Deadhorse from **Prudhoe Bay**, the production facility where North Slope oil begins its six-day journey south to Valdez. There are few refinery-style flare stacks or sci-fi fractionation columns here, just a dendritic web of pipelines. But it's not just wasteland: in between lie acres of marshy grasslands and lakes seemingly undamaged by the industry all around. Quite likely it will appear as though no work is underway: most of the activity is in the winter when ice roads, built to protect the tundra, make transport easier than it would be across boggy permafrost.

Practicalities

After such a long journey to get here, there is just one way to get a real sense of closure. The only way you can see anything of Prudhoe Bay is to take the **Arctic Ocean Shuttle**, a two-hour tour (June–Aug several times daily; $39) offered by the *Arctic Caribou Inn*, which briefly drives past some of the oil operations, then visits a less-than-idyllic breakwater on Prudhoe Bay where you can dip your toe in the **Arctic Ocean**: full immersion is possible (and surprisingly common) from late July until early September when the pack ice melts away from the shore. For security reasons tours no longer visit Mile Zero of the pipeline and even for the "shuttle" you need to provide details of your driver's license or passport at least 24 hours in advance: call, fax, or email the *Arctic Caribou Inn*.

Accommodation is either at the *Prudhoe Bay Hotel* (☎659-2449, ⓦwww .prudhoebayhotel.com; private bath and TV ❼, shared bath ❻), which includes three buffet meals in its rates (non-guests pay $12 for breakfast, $15 for lunch, and $20 for dinner), or the *Arctic Caribou Inn* (☎1-877/659-2368, ⓦwww.arcticcaribouinn.com; late May to early Sept; room with private bath ❺). Neither spot is particularly salubrious, but they're decent by Haul Road standards; turn left entering Deadhorse to find them, between the airport and Lake Colleen, where waterfowl gather in summer. Both hotels have restaurants and there's an espresso stand at the *Prudhoe Bay Hotel*, but there are no other dining options in town. RVs can park up beside the *Arctic Caribou* ($15 with electricity, showers $10), but there is no designated campground. Both Deadhorse and Prudhoe Bay are "damp" areas, so there are no liquor sales, though you can bring your own.

The lone Brooks Range Supply general store on Old Spine Road (daily 10.30am–9pm; ☎659-2412) contains the **post office** (1–3.30pm & 6.30–9pm) and stocks the *Anchorage Daily News*, a very modest supply of **groceries**, hardware, and the North Slope's finest selection of Arctic work and survival wear, plus postcards, baseball caps, Native crafts, and *Dalton Highway Survivor* certificates.

Gates of the Arctic National Park

In the great American tradition of naming vast tracts of wilderness after a single geographic feature, the **Gates of the Arctic National Park** (no entry fee), two hundred miles northwest of Fairbanks, gets its name from Frigid Crags and

Boreal Mountain, a pair of peaks in the far eastern reaches of the park. As **Robert Marshall** was forging his way up the North Fork of the Koyukuk River in the 1930s, the wilderness advocate encountered "a precipitous pair of mountains, one on each side" and was immediately struck by how these sentinels framed the way north, the veritable "Gates of the Arctic." His early interest in preserving the region eventually led to the creation of the national park in 1980.

These "Gates of the Arctic" now form part of the nation's second-largest national park (after Wrangell-St Elias), occupying four times the area of Yellowstone, the largest park in the Lower 48, and linked by Noatak National Preserve to the Kobuk Valley National Park, creating a gigantic protected area. The park straddles the central Brooks Range, a labyrinth of rugged mountains rising in waves up to eight thousand feet, deeply incised by plunging U-shaped valleys that give the whole place an uncanny openness. It all comes cloaked in boreal forest, alder thickets, and a thin mantle of energy-sapping Arctic muskeg, a result of the permafrost that underlies the whole of the park. Such conditions don't support a great variety of animals, though on a longish trip you might reasonably expect to see brown bears, wolves, moose, Dall sheep, caribou, and wolverines.

Kobuk Eskimos and Koyukon and Kutchin Athabascans have lived in harmony with the land for centuries, as they continue to do in the Native villages of Allakaket, Anaktuvuk Pass, Evansville, Shungnak, and Kobuk, using the land for subsistence hunting, fishing, trapping, and gathering. Their ancestors, back in 1885, guided early white explorers and prospectors, who eventually turned up payable quantities of gold on the Koyukuk, sparking the rush of 1898. All of a sudden there were small paddle steamers and riverboats churning upstream from the Yukon River bound for trading posts at Bettles, Coldfoot, and Wiseman. For the next three decades miners scoured the southern flanks of the central Brooks Range with varying degrees of success, followed by the geological, geographic, and mineral-survey teams that brought Robert Marshall to the area. Much of the land here was only surveyed while planning the park – the last place in the US to be fully mapped – and few landmarks are named, even on the largest-scale topo maps. It remains wholly remote. There is only one Native village – Anaktuvuk Pass – within the bounds of the park, and eight others dotted around the perimeter, none claiming over four hundred souls. Within the park itself there are no facilities and no roads, not even tracks apart from those left by Dall sheep, the migrations of the 500,000-strong Western Arctic caribou herd (which has recovered after crashing to just 75,000 in the 1970s), and those made by subsistence hunters in pursuit.

Getting to the park

Wright Air Service and Warbelow's Air Ventures (see box, p.517) have regular daily flights from Fairbanks to Bettles (see p.550), charging around $320 round-trip. Northern Alaska (see box, p.540) runs their excellent-value, evening-only **Arctic Circle Air Adventure** (5hr; $289), giving you a flight north from Fairbanks along the route of the pipeline, then among the southern peaks of the park, low through the John River Valley to Bettles, and back to Fairbanks. *Bettles Lodge* (see p.551) offers a similar **Arctic Circle Day Tour** ($440), which includes lunch at the lodge and their Koyukuk River Tour (see p.551). By paying a bit more, you can also spend the night ($550 in total, based on double occupancy).

The biggest **wilderness operator** in the Gates of the Arctic is Bettles-based Sourdough Outfitters (☎692-5556, ⓦwww.sourdough.com), which offers a staggering array of guided, guide-assisted, and unguided trips for all seasons

– hiking, paddling in inflatable canoes, rafting, wildlife-viewing, and dog-sledding. The prices of guided trips include the flight from Fairbanks. Select from guided (9 days; $2000) and unguided (7 days; $430 per person assuming four passengers) backpacking to and around the Arrigetch Peaks, unguided canoeing on the headwaters of the Noatak (7 days; $800), and guided rafting on the John River (6 days; $2200). They also **rent gear** by the day with every fifth day free: rigid canoes ($25), small rafts ($35), canvas-wall tents ($15), sleeping bags ($5), and so on. Even if you are planning your own excursion, you might consider taking along a guide ($250 a day plus the guide's transport cost). Apart from providing peace of mind, the guide is usually bursting with information about the area's cultural significance, good fishing spots, or ways up apparently inaccessible peaks and saddles.

The folks at the *Bettles Lodge* (see p.551) also organize a smaller, but competitively priced, range of planned but unguided trips. Flights can also be arranged through Coyote Air in Coldfoot Camp (see p.544) or Brooks Range Aviation in Bettles, (☎ 1-800/692-5443, ⓦ www.brooksrange.com).

Exploring the park

To travel here you need to be completely self-sufficient, and since the scale and logistics are so mind-boggling, those who come tend to stay for a while. For full coverage of park land, pick up National Geographic's *Trails Illustrated* topo map ($10), easy to find in Fairbanks. Only around four thousand recreational visitors make it into the park each year (about what Denali gets in a day), and they stay an average of eleven days. For those prepared to make the commitment of time, energy, and money, it is a hugely rewarding place to be. Most people come to either **hike** or take a multiday **float trip** on one of six designated

△ Arrigetch Peaks, Gates of the Arctic National Park

National Wild Rivers – the Alatna, John, Kobuk, Noatak, North Fork of the Koyukuk, and Tinayguk – all possible under your own steam, but a good deal easier with guided or guide-assisted trips, mostly operated from Bettles. These trips concentrate on only a few spots, so much of the rest of the park remains entirely untouched – one research biologist apparently spent eleven five-month summer seasons here and saw only six people the whole time.

Even more than in most places in Alaska, your experience here will be dictated by **the weather**. Most visitors arrive after mid-June, when frozen rivers have completed their thaw, and move on by early September. Mosquitoes can be so bad in June, July, and early August that head nets are *de rigueur*, thus making late August and September particularly appealing, provided you're prepared for cooler temperatures and some rain. On average it snows eight or nine months of the year, and some years only July is snow-free. Throughout summer you'll seldom experience a completely dark night, and the park receives continuous sunlight for thirty days in June and July. Consequently, July basks in a relatively balmy average daily maximum of 70° (average daily minimum 46°F). Over the whole park rainfall is low, but most falls in late summer so you'll need to take proper protection for that time.

Access in summer is almost exclusively by float-plane from Bettles (reached by scheduled bush flights from Fairbanks). Before entering the park you'll be required to work through a "backcountry simulator" program in Bettles or Anaktuvuk Pass to ensure you are fully competent in outdoor skills. "Leave no trace" is the ethic: such is the delicacy of the Arctic environment that even minimal impact takes a long time to recover, so special care is needed in the more heavily visited areas. Two of the most popular **float trips** are on the headwaters of the Noatak River (5–9 days; Class I–II), among wonderful angular peaks and with possible access from Kotzebue (see p.566), and on the North Fork of the Koyukuk (5 days; Class I–III), with the entry point in the shadow of the Gates themselves, followed by a float down to Bettles. You are unlikely to be totally alone on these rivers, but adventure operators and bush pilots in Bettles can advise on more solitary rivers. Note that float trips are best in June and July when the water levels are high.

Hiking areas are more widely distributed. Essentially, you can arrange to be flown in pretty much anywhere there is water or a gravel river bar to land on, and then either use that as a base or hike to some pre-arranged pickup point. Again, there are more popular areas, but it is probably best to ask about places less frequented, if only to reduce impact on busier areas.

Keen hikers and rock climbers should head a hundred miles northwest of Bettles to the **Arrigetch Peaks**, the granite spires rising three thousand feet from the surrounding land that grace numerous Gates of the Arctic publicity brochures. The name – loosely translated as "fingers of an extended hand" – comes from a Nunamuit Eskimo legend of the Creator, who placed his glove on the land as a reminder of his presence.

Bettles

Bettles, 185 miles northwest of Fairbanks and 35 miles above the Arctic Circle, is an object lesson in how planes have changed life in bush Alaska. When gold was being sifted from the Koyukuk River around the turn of the twentieth century, Bettles stood on its bank as the highest point accessible to sternwheelers. Here supplies bound for Wiseman and Coldfoot were transferred to flat-bottomed scows that could negotiate the riffles upstream. Air travel took over after 1945, but the flattest land lay on a gravel bar five miles upstream. An airstrip was built and over the years the whole town relocated, leaving **Old**

Bettles moldering on its cut-bank, the willows, cottonwoods, and alders taking over the sagging remains of the cabins.

The population of Bettles and its contiguous Native twin, **Evansville**, only amounts to fifty-odd, and the airstrip is the center of town. There are no roads in or out (except in winter when an ice road is put in from Prospect Creek on the Dalton Highway) so everyone arrives and departs by plane. Unless you arrive with immediate plans to fly off to the park, you can suddenly feel stranded. A way out is to join *Bettles Lodge* for their two-hour **Koyukuk River Tour** ($65), which checks out former gold-prospecting sites and Old Bettles.

Summer is the busiest time in Bettles as the town fills with those bound for the Gates of the Arctic, but in March, viewing of the **northern lights** is the attraction and Japanese becomes the town's lingua franca; April and May are also popular with cross-country skiers and dog-mushers before the river ice breaks up.

Information, accommodation, and food

Before heading into the park, you'll need to pop along to the Bettles Ranger Station and **visitor center** (June to Sept daily 8am–5pm; Oct to May Mon–Fri 8am–noon, 1–5pm; ☎692-5495), just beyond the airstrip, where you can take the required backcountry **orientation program**, discuss your trip plans, and obtain the essential bear-resistant food canister.

On the way to the visitor center, you pass the 1948 *Bettles Lodge* (☎1-800/770-5111, ⓦwww.bettleslodge.com; rooms ❼, bunks ❶), effectively a bush truck-stop, with pilots dropping in for their morning coffee. It has a nice mosquito-proof veranda for knocking back a beer or two during the long evenings. **Accommodation** is either in the rustic lodge, where rooms share two central bathrooms; in less charming modern rooms, some with Jacuzzi; in a very basic bunkhouse ($20); or outside, where there's free camping (showers $5). The lodge also runs a day-trip ($420), with flights from Fairbanks and a boat ride on the Koyukuk River, and an overnight trip with accommodation and meals at the lodge ($500). The only other accommodation in town is *Spirit Lights Lodge* (contact Sourdough Outfitters ☎692-55567, ⓦwww.sourdough.com; ❸, ❼ with breakfast and dinner), modern self-catering cabins sleeping up to four.

You'll almost certainly be **eating** at *Bettles Lodge*, where the meals are decent (book for dinner; around $20), and burgers come at tolerable prices. There are also a couple of espresso vendors in the peak season.

Anaktuvuk Pass

The only settlement within the park is **Anaktuvuk Pass** (meaning "The Place of Caribou Droppings"), visited by some fly-in tours. Humans have been passing through the valley for at least seven thousand years, but it was only a seasonal camp until around fifty years ago, when the Nunamiut (Inland Iñupiat) established a permanent village, which now has a population of around three hundred. To discover the Nunamiut culture, head for the **Simon Paneak Memorial Museum** (and library; summer Mon–Fri 8.30am–5pm; ☎661-3413) in a log cabin near the village's northwestern corner. Artwork is for sale here, including the caribou-skin masks for which the village is best known. You'll also see some old sod houses including the post office. There's a park ranger station, open seasonally (☎661-3520, ⓦwww.nps.gov/gaar).

Warbelow's Air Ventures (☎1-800/478-0812, ⓦwww.warbelows.com) offers a full-day trip with a tundra tour for $549, flying in and out from Fairbanks;

Northern Alaska Tour Company (☏1-800/474-1986, ⓦwww.northernalaska.com) has a shorter Anaktuvuk Pass Adventure (5hr; $399); and Wright Air Service (☏1-800/478-0502, ⓦwww.wrightair.net) offers flights from Fairbanks for $170 each way.

Arctic National Wildlife Refuge

The **Arctic National Wildlife Refuge** (known as ANWR or "An-wah"; ⓦarctic.fws.gov) is something special, a profound wilderness where human impact is so slight that time ticks by at a perceptibly slower pace. It is the largest and northernmost of all America's wildlife refuges, encompassing the entire northeastern corner of Alaska. At almost twenty million acres, its enormous size enables it to present the full sweep of Arctic and subarctic ecosystems. Heavily wooded, serpentine river valleys dominate the south, notably those containing the Sheenjek, Ivishak, and Wind rivers, all three now designated National Wild Rivers. North of the Brooks Range (which bisects the refuge) lies the treeless expanse of the North Slope, patterned by innumerable lakes and braided river systems laden with arctic char and winding across open tundra through caribou-calving areas.

It is one of the last true wildernesses, so thick with wildlife in summer that it has been dubbed an Arctic Serengeti, with not a single introduced species. More than 170 bird species have been spotted here, with ducks, loons, geese, and swans in astounding numbers. It is also the most important polar bear denning habitat in the US and a critical calving area for the 130,000-strong **Porcupine caribou herd**. It was the protection of this herd that drew the attention of some of Alaska's earliest and most effective conservationists, **Celia Hunter** and **Ginny Wood**, who along with other like-minded souls met in Fairbanks in 1960 to establish the statewide Alaska Conservation Society. Ecologists Olaus and Margaret Murie lent weight to the campaign – Margaret later writing of their northern travels in *Two in the Far North* (see p.608) – and within months they had helped establish the Arctic Refuge, which doubled in size in 1980 to 19.6 million acres (the size of South Carolina). Unfortunately, such refuges have always had limited protection, and oil interests are now keen to offset declining reserves by surveying within the coastal strip of the Arctic Refuge (1.5 million acres, known as the 1002 or ten-oh-two). Public pressure from outside Alaska has so far limited exploration.

If oil production ever goes ahead, it will be the first time the hand of man has ever fallen heavily on this land. The Native Gwich'in have traditionally relied upon the caribou migrations for their survival, and trappers and hunters have built the odd riverside shack over the decades, but there is really nothing but wilderness: no roads or visitor facilities of any kind. If you do set aside the time and the considerable chunk of money needed to get into the reserve, you'll be on your own, except for some of the thickest swarms of Alaska's most voracious mosquitoes. That said, the Kongakut River, near the Canadian border, has a brief couple of months of relative popularity each summer as enthusiasts from both sides of the political fence come up to see just what it is they are fighting about.

Many of the companies operating trips into the Arctic Refuge do so through the small Gwich'in village of **Fort Yukon**, 140 miles northeast of Fairbanks and eight miles north of the Arctic Circle at the confluence of the Yukon and Porcupine rivers. The largest Athabascan village in Alaska, it lies on the southern edge of the Arctic Refuge and was one of the first Interior villages to find its way onto white men's maps when, in 1847, a Hudson's Bay Company trading post was established here. You can see a replica of the HBC post (fortified against the Russians, not the Natives), the Episcopal church (built in 1899) with its beautiful beaded altarcloth, and, near the river and former school, the home of Don Young, one-time tugboat captain, teacher, and mayor, who has been Alaska's sole congressman since 1973. It's becoming just as popular in winter, thanks to spectacular aurora displays, plus the vast open spaces to be discovered by snowmobile. There's bed and board at the *Sourdough Hotel* (☎662-2402); for more information call the city office at ☎662-2379.

Arctic Village (Vashra'ii K'oo to its 170 inhabitants) sits on the edge of ANWR; this area has been inhabited for 4500 years, but the Neets'aii Gwich'in people remained nomadic until guns became available a hundred years ago. Unlike the Eskimos of the Arctic coasts, this Athabascan group refused to participate in the ANCSA settlement, even though it would have shared in the $1 billion and 44 million acres on offer. They have maintained a poor subsistence lifestyle on their 1.8 million acres, a largely unspoilt environment though the warming climate has led to musk oxen moving south in the direction of their town, and spruce and willow have appeared on the tundra in the last decade. Present-day proposals to drill for oil in ANWR, and the threat to the caribou and their subsistence economy have made them even more determined to hold their ground. A succession of leading environmentalists has passed through and shared ideas with the locals, and the village now has a solar- and wind-powered shower and laundry block.

Getting there

Getting into the Arctic Refuge is neither easy nor particularly cheap, and staying means being totally self-sufficient – there's not much food about, and definitely no grocery stores. Most people who come here do so on a guided float trip with one of several companies (see p.516).

If you are heading into the refuge independently, you've got a choice of bush-plane companies, including Wright Air Service and Warbelow's Air Ventures (see box, p.516), that fly regularly to Fort Yukon from Fairbanks (an hour's flight, costing about $125 each way) and will advise on pilots for onward travel. If you just want a taster, join one of the trips run by Warbelow's: a regular bush-mail flight (3–4hr; $240), which briefly calls at Fort Yukon and continues to other small villages, or the Native Village Tour (3–4hr; $279), which starts with the bush-mail flight and adds on a 45-minute tour of the village. Larry's Flying Service (☎474-9169, ⓦwww.larrysflying.com) also runs a bush-mail flight with a one-hour village tour ($259). You can also fly into ANWR with Circle Air (☎520-5223, 1-866/520-5223) from Central; with Coyote Air (see p.544) from Coldfoot; or with Alaska Flyers (☎640-6513, ⓦwww.waldoarms.com), operating out of the *Waldo Arms Hotel* in Kaktovik.

Wilderness Birding Adventures (☎694-7442, ⓦwww.wildernessbirding.com), in Eagle River, offers five wildlife-oriented trips in ANWR: rafting on the Marsh Fork of the Canning River (12 days; $3400); rafting the Kongakut River (10 days; $3400); canoeing the Lower Kongakut and the Arctic Coast (9 days; $3200); a base camp trip (6 days; $2850); and the Gray-Headed Chickadee Float on the Canning River (7 days; $2600). Arctic Wild (☎1-888/577-8203, ⓦwww.arcticwild.com) has a wider range of trips, mostly rafting (typically 10 days for $3800) and a few backpacking trips (8 days for $2500). To the north on Barter Island, Kaktovik Arctic Adventure (☎640-6119, ⓦwww.kaktovikarcticadventures.com) offers rafting trips from June to August, whale-viewing in September, and polar bear-viewing from September to November.

Nome and around

Of all the towns in the Alaskan North, the former gold town of **Nome**, over five hundred miles northwest of Anchorage and a similar distance west of Fairbanks, has the greatest all-around appeal. The town's appearance may be unprepossessing, but it is a fascinating place with a diverting history and a slew of fun events throughout the year, not least the **Iditarod** sled-dog race, which finishes here in March. Though not connected to the Interior highways, Nome also lies at the hub of a relatively extensive road system which fans out across the **Seward Peninsula**, giving access to miles of bird-rich coastline, untold acres of undulating tundra periodically dotted with the detritus of gold mining, some secluded hot springs, and a couple of small towns, including the Iñupiat Eskimo village of Teller.

Ed Jesson and his "wheel"

Ed Jesson had a lust for gold, but despite coming north in 1896 he never made much money in the Klondike. Even his attempts at trading were ill-starred, so when news of the Nome rush reached Dawson City, he quickly sold his business and with his meager poke of gold prepared for the 1250-mile journey to Nome. His first move was to buy what he described as a "wheel," actually two wheels with broad tires, pedals, a white frame and no mudguards, for which he paid an extortionate $150. He had never ridden a bicycle before and spent the next week entertaining the locals with his attempts to learn.

Armed with food and seven of the latest newspapers he could get hold of, he set off through the snow on February 22, 1900, aiming to keep his wheels in the narrow tracks left by dog sleds, mainly on the frozen Yukon River. At times he took "headers" into snowdrifts and had to cope with temperatures as low as -48°F, which froze his tires, his nose, and his bearings. Still, as long as he could keep the bearings running free, the low temperatures helped the tires grip the snow and he was able to maintain a daily average of 45 miles, sometimes achieving 75 miles. He turned heads along the way, not least an Athabascan who, when asked to describe Jesson and his wheel, blurted "White man he sit down, walk like Hell!"

At 4pm on March 29, Jesson turned up in Nome, having taken just six rest days during the 35-day journey. He was tired, battered, and nearly snow-blind but proclaimed his "wheel" a great success, saying it "stood the trip in splendid shape and to my great surprise I never had a puncture or broke a spoke the entire trip." He thought it was, in some ways, better than a dog team. "It didn't eat anything and I didn't have to cook dogfeed for it," he enthused, and when conditions were right he was sometimes able to overtake dog teams. Aside from the renown he received for his accomplishment, he garnered praise for bringing the first news the town had seen for months. A dance hall was rented, the performers were given the night off, and the newspapers were read out loud. It was the first time people of Nome heard of the US victory in the Spanish-American War, which had ended in the Philippines three months earlier.

Unwittingly, Jesson had set an example, and the following winter over 250 prospectors made their way to Nome on wheels. Before long, Jesson moved on and finally found a fortune of sorts in the goldfields of Fairbanks in 1902. Just over a hundred years later, in 2003, three modern adventurers re-created his ride, finding the trails nearly void of the frequent usage that Jesson once inspired.

Locals say, "There's no place like Nome," and that is hard to deny. Once the greatest and most exuberant of Alaska's gold-rush towns, it is now down to fewer than four thousand people – about half white, half Eskimo – but retains a kind of subarctic Wild West feel, particularly along the main Front Street, its seaward side lined with what seems like an endless row of initially intimidating dark bars. The streets are dusty, the restaurants scruffy, and drab buildings which may not be old look like they've seen many a hard winter. Houses sit on stubby poles to prevent them sinking into the mire of thawed permafrost and are surrounded by gardens where grass has been replaced by the odd dredge bucket, parts of a dismembered snowmobile, and maybe an old freight container. Still, the town is attractively set on **Norton Sound**, which remains frozen from around mid-November through late May, but thaws to reveal Nome's golden beach – famed not for the quality of its sand but for the **gold** contained in it, which drew thousands at the end of the nineteenth century.

People still work the beach, and with no claims to stake, visitors are welcome to try their hand, though most of the 23,000 annual visitors are content to watch the professionals and explore the surroundings, relishing the 24-hour summer light that comes from being just a hundred miles shy of the Arctic Circle. Many hope to see animals, but despite the seasonally icy seas, you are very unlikely to see **polar bears** around Nome, though they sometimes make an appearance near the northern Seward Peninsula when the pack ice is firm. A much better bet are **reindeer**, which have been grazing across the peninsula since they were introduced over a hundred years back as a meat source. **Musk oxen** were reintroduced here in the 1970s from a growing herd near Delta Junction and now number around 1800. The Seward Peninsula is considered prime **birding** territory with 180 species either resident or paying a flying visit from late May to July, when Asiatic transients can be found. As the sea ice melts, the birds congregate along shore margins and in newly opened ponds, making shorebird- and waterfowl-spotting particularly good from the road system; it's also worth walking east to the mouth of the Nome River. The visitor center posts recent sightings on a bulletin board.

Some history

Long before the town of Nome existed, British navigators plotted the coastline, almost arbitrarily giving headlands and inlets the names of their patrons or home towns. The story goes that on a particularly uninspired day in the 1850s one officer spied the eminence on the northern shore of Norton Sound and merely marked "? Name" on his chart. Back home, cartographers mistook his scribble for C. Nome, and Cape Nome it became.

At the time, there were only a few Iñupiat encampments along the coast, and it looked likely to stay that way after the Reverend Hudson Stuck visited in the 1890s and declared, "A savage forbidding country, this . . . Seward Peninsula, uninhabited and unfit for habitation; a country of naked rock and bare hillside and desolate, barren valley, without amenities of any kind and coursed with a perpetual icy blast." It remained almost uninhabited until 1898, when the **"Three Lucky Swedes"** – actually two Swedes and a Norwegian – found gold below a mountain with a tall rock in the shape of an anvil. They called it Anvil Creek and the waterside settlement that formed four miles to the south became Anvil City. This was easily confused with the nearby village of Anvik, so the US Post Office forced a change and **Nome** took the name of the nearby cape.

Initially, the rush to Nome was no different from the dozens of others across Alaska over the last few decades of the nineteenth century. There were only 250 people here when, in July 1899, John Hummel, a prospector from Idaho who

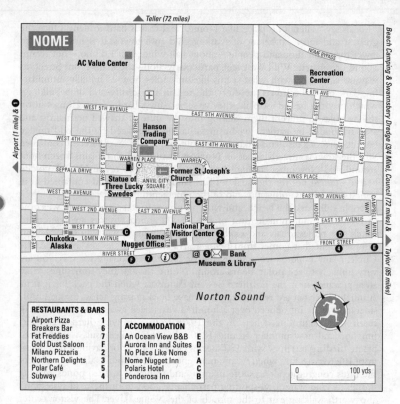

Teller (72 miles)

NOME

AC Value Center

Recreation Center

NOME BYPASS

WEST 5TH AVENUE — EAST 5TH AVENUE
E 6TH AVE
EAST D STREET
EAST E STREET
EAST F STREET
EAST G STREET

Hanson Trading Company

WEST 4TH AVENUE — EAST 4TH AVENUE
ALLEY WAY

SEPPALA DRIVE

Former St Joseph's Church
KINGS PLACE
STEADMAN STREET

WARREN PLACE
WARREN P.

Statue of "Three Lucky Swedes"
ANVIL CITY SQUARE

WEST 3RD AVENUE — EAST 3RD AVENUE
METTLER
MOORE WAY
CAMPBELL WAY
MINIX WAY

WEST 2ND AVENUE — EAST 2ND AVENUE
SPOKANE
LANES WAY

WEST 1ST AVENUE
LOMEN AVENUE
EAST 1ST AVENUE

Chukotka-Alaska

National Park Visitor Center
HUNTER
Nome Nugget Office
FRONT STREET

RIVER STREET
Bank
Museum & Library

Norton Sound

N

0   100 yds

RESTAURANTS & BARS

Airport Pizza	1
Breakers Bar	6
Fat Freddies	7
Gold Dust Saloon	F
Milano Pizzeria	2
Northern Delights	3
Polar Café	5
Subway	4

ACCOMMODATION

An Ocean View B&B	E
Aurora Inn and Suites	D
No Place Like Nome	F
Nome Nugget Inn	A
Polaris Hotel	C
Ponderosa Inn	B

Airport (1 mile) & ➊

was too sick to go to the rich creeks, realized that the ruby-colored sand at his feet was laced with gold. This beach made of gold soon became known as the "Poor Man's Paradise" since prospectors needed none of the usual miners' trappings; a bucket, a shovel, and a primitive rocker would suffice. There were no stakes to claim since the beach was open to all, and if another prospector left his diggings, you could move in. Better still, there was no desperate overland struggle as in Klondike, no icy passes to cross, and no frozen ground to thaw, just golden sands ready for sifting as soon as you stepped off the steamer. The pickings weren't especially rich, but three thousand prospectors arrived before winter ice halted the steamers, and many more arrived overland by any means possible, even cycling (see box, p.554).

By 1900 the beach was overrun with tents, some 25 miles of them with their owners standing shoulder to shoulder extracting paydirt – over $2 million worth in total. As you'd imagine, claim-jumping was rife, some of the best stories retold by Rex Beach in *The Spoilers* (see Contexts, p.608). The US census in 1900 recorded that one third of all non-Natives in Alaska were in Nome – a total of 12,488 people, though estimates put the real figure closer to 20,000, and some claim more like 40,000. No matter the actual number, it's undisputed that Nome was briefly the biggest city in Alaska. So much for the thoughts of Hudson Stuck, though he returned fifteen years after the founding of Nome and his opinions hadn't changed. He wrote, "[n]othing in the world could have caused the building of a city where Nome is built except the thing that caused it: the finding of gold . . . It has no harbor or roadstead, no shelter or protection of any kind; it is in as bleak and as exposed a position as a man would find if he should set out to hunt the earth over for ineligible sites."

Nome had the typical gold-town plethora of churches, bars, and brothels (not necessarily in that order), plus a French lingerie store and four piano movers, but by the time it was incorporated as a city in 1901 the population was already beginning to decline (especially as measles had killed between a quarter and half of the Native population in 1900). Still, it remained an important service town to mining communities around the Seward Peninsula and as the terminus for the **Iditarod Trail**, the original winter route across the Alaskan Interior from Seward through the short-lived gold town of Iditarod. Life in Nome ticked by, beleaguered by the occasional storm and fire that would damage the downtown area, until it hit the headlines again in 1925 with the diphtheria epidemic that would have killed hundreds but for the heroic exploits of those who took part in the **Serum Run** (see box, p.558).

Arrival, getting around, and information

To get to Nome you have to fly, and due to the high cost of tickets many choose to come on one of the Anchorage-based **package tours** run by Alaska Airline Vacations (mid-May to mid-Sept; ☎1-800/468-2248, ⓦwww .alaskaair.com/vacations): either a day-trip ($449) or a two-day affair with a night at the *Nome Nugget Inn* ($529 per person, based on double occupancy). These are from Anchorage, but you can add one or more Fairbanks legs for $110 each, a cost-effective option if you wish to include that city in your plans. The tours include an entertaining but predictable array of activities, from dog-mushing to gold-panning demos.

Flights with Alaska Airlines to Nome cost around $288 plus tax round-trip, if bought 21 days in advance (otherwise $650), although there are sometimes cheaper Web specials; you can also fly from Anchorage to Nome and return via Kotzebue (from $473), but to reach Barrow from Nome you'll have to make a stop in Fairbanks. Frontier Flying Service (☎1-800/478-6779, ⓦwww .frontierflying.com) flies from Fairbanks (except Saturdays), connecting to the Siberian Yu'pik villages of Gambell and Savoonga on St Lawrence Island.

The airport is just over a mile west of town: walk, stick out your thumb, or call a cab (try Checker Cab ☎443-5211 or Louie's Cab ☎443-6000), which will cost about $5. Once in town you can walk everywhere, though to explore the 300-mile road system (open June–Sept) you'll need either to **rent a car** (see Listings, p.561) or to join the entertaining Richard Beneville of Nome Discovery Tours (☎443-2814, ⓦwww.nomechamber.org/discoverytours.html), who conducts evening tundra walks ($40), 5.5-hour tours ($85) visiting the town, a gold mine, the Trains to Nowhere, and the tundra, and full-day tours ($150) to Council and Teller that see more of the road system.

The **Visitors Bureau**, 301 Front St (mid-May to mid-Sept daily 9am–9pm; mid-Sept to mid-May Mon–Fri 9am–6pm; ☎443-6624, ⓦwww .nomealaska.org), has everything you need to know about Nome and its environs, plus a selection of videos on the region and a stuffed musk ox. Anyone thinking of exploring the Bering Land Bridge National Preserve or any of the national parks, preserves, and monuments further north should call in at the **National Reserve Visitor Center**, 214 Front St (mid-May to mid-Sept Mon–Fri 8am–4.30pm, Sat 10–4.30pm; mid-Sept to mid-May Mon–Fri 8am–4.30pm; ☎443-2522, ⓦwww.nps.gov/bela). They have a stack of wet-day videos including material on reindeer-herding and traditional Native uses of Serpentine Hot Springs (see p.566).

Accommodation

Nome remains essentially a frontier town, and accommodation is expensive and generally not to a very high standard. There are central and modestly priced **B&Bs** and smaller hotels, but unfortunately there's nowhere really cheap: those on a budget will have to **camp** on the beach, an accepted (and often very pleasant) practice, around a mile east of the visitor center. It is free but the only facilities are a couple of outhouses: water can be obtained from a hose outside the visitor center, and there are **public showers** at the recreation center (see Listings, p.562).

The main busy season is from late May to August, but if you are thinking of coming to see the end of the Iditarod, you'll want to plan your accommodation up to a year in advance. Places fill up fast and you definitely don't want to arrive with nothing arranged. The eight percent tax has not been included in our price codes.

The Serum Run

As much as for gold, Nome is known for the **Serum Run**, a desperate attempt to save the lives of sick Nome residents by delivering an antitoxin. In January 1925 three Nome children were diagnosed with the highly infectious diphtheria, and memories of the influenza epidemic that killed 91 people seven years earlier soon panicked the community. Immediate quarantine laws were enacted, but with only a meager stock of ageing, half-spent antitoxin available, a call for external help was tapped out on the telegraph. Adequate supplies were dispatched from Seattle, but that was over a month's sail away; fortunately, 100 doses of antitoxin turned up in the Alaska Railroad's hospital in Anchorage, and thoughts turned to using one of Alaska's two planes, although it had been dismantled for the winter and both pilots were in the Lower 48. Nome had never been reached by air and winter conditions were atrocious, so it was decided to make use of an existing mail route down the frozen Tanana and Yukon rivers and deliver the serum 674 miles by dog sled. The glass vials (suitably insulated) were immediately sent by train to Nenana, where they were transferred to the first of a special relay of dog teams designed to cover the route much faster than the normal thirty-day ship passage. Instead of being relieved every 100–125 miles, mushers were mostly staged 18–40 miles apart, while champion dog-musher **Leonhard Seppala**, setting out from Nome to meet them, was allotted a ninety-mile leg across Norton Sound – almost double that of any other musher. Naturally, he needed his best team and rejected one of his weaker dogs, **Balto**.

As time went on the need for the serum intensified, but bad weather brought down the telegraph wires and made communication impossible. Several teams set out from Nome to relieve Seppala along the final leg and it was **Gunnar Kaasen**, his team led by the rejected Balto, who brought the serum through a whiteout into Nome just five days and seven and a half hours after it left Nenana. The vials were frozen but still useable, the epidemic was stemmed, and the nation rejoiced. The entire effort had to be repeated within days with a second batch of antitoxin.

All the mushers involved were rewarded with cash payouts and presented with a medal by President Calvin Coolidge, but, as the team that actually delivered the serum, Kaasen and Balto were feted with the greatest praise. This rankled Seppala, who had covered a record 84 miles in one day, especially when Kaasen and Balto were taken on national lecture tours and offered film roles, Kaasen was given $1000 by the manufacturers of the serum, and Balto even had his statue erected in New York's Central Park, where it remains today.

In recent years, Seppala's name has become the better known. Every year during the Iditarod – a race founded on the spirit of the Serum Run but following a quite different route as far as Ruby – the **Leonhard Seppala Humanitarian Award** is awarded to the musher who exhibits the most concern for his animals.

An Ocean View B&B 209 E Front St ☎ 443-2133, Ⓦ www.nomebb.com. Attractive B&B right beside the Bering Sea with a lovely communal lounge built around a stone fireplace. Shared- and private-bath rooms. ❹

Aurora Inn and Suites 302 E Front St ☎ 443-3838 or 1-800/354-4606, Ⓦ www.aurorainnome.com. Currently Nome's top-line hotel, featuring a sauna and large, comfortable rooms with cable TV, some with kitchenettes and sea views. They also have an "executive wing" at West 2nd Ave & West D St with larger suites. Apartments and kitchen rooms ❼, suites and standard rooms ❻

No Place Like Nome 605 Steadman St ☎ 443-2451, Ⓔ bente@nook.net. About the cheapest B&B in town, but it's a pleasant spot with five rooms. ❹

Nome Nugget Inn 315 Front St ☎ 443-4189 or 1-877/443-2323. Long-standing hotel, right by the Burl Arch (see below), that's patronized by tour groups despite the fairly basic, poky rooms with small private bathroom. Rooms do come, however, with cable TV, and some have sea views. ❺

Polaris Hotel 202 Bering St ☎ 443-2000 or 1-866/443-5778, Ⓔ polarisent.inc@gci.net. Although they do have private-bath doubles, this fairly scruffy and sometimes noisy hotel is only recommended for lone travelers not geared for camping: basic shared-bath singles, which don't really meet expected standards, go for $40. Private-bath doubles ❸

Ponderosa Inn 291 Spokane St at 3rd Ave ☎ 443-5737. Some of the nicest rooms in town, with fairly simple but tasteful decor, cable TV, and the option of a full kitchen. Suites ❻, rooms ❹

The Town

To get your bearings, follow the *Historical Walking Tour* brochure obtained free from the visitor center on Front Street. The tour starts outside by the finish line of the Iditarod, where the **Burl Arch** – usually stashed off down a side alley in summer – is wheeled into place in March to mark the end of the final sprint down Front Street.

Following Front Street with the huge boulders of Nome's protective seawall on your right, you pass the offices of the **Nome Nugget** (Ⓦ www.nomenugget .com), the town's newspaper, which claims to be the oldest in the state, though the *Wrangell Sentinel* challenges the claim. Always a good read, the weekly paper comes out each Thursday at a cost of 50¢ – the same as it was when it was founded in 1900, when the gold-rush economy inflated prices enormously. Diagonally opposite, below the library, sits the **Carrie M. McLain Memorial Museum**, 223 Front St (June–Sept daily 10am–6pm; Oct–May Tues–Sat noon–6pm; $1 donation appreciated; ☎ 443-6630), a small-town museum that packs in the history of the Serum Run (including the preserved body of Fritz, Leonard Seppala's less famous lead dog), stacks of photos and artifacts from the gold rush, a large ivory collection, and assorted changing exhibits.

Continuing in the same direction, you can **pan for gold** anywhere along the mile of beach between the end of the seawall and the former *Fort Davis Roadhouse* (now apartments). The nearby Country Store, 1008 E Front St (☎ 1-800/478-3297), sells gold pans (around $7 for a decent-sized 14" model) so you can join the beach miners. They spend the summers with their sluice boxes and suction dredges working the beach and the shallow coastal waters while camped in a motley collection of faded tents and draped tarps. Don't expect to get rich: this area has been well panned already, though you'll probably get a few flakes.

A measure of how little gold is left lies further on (about a mile from the visitor center) where the rusting **Swanberg Dredge** has lain idle beside the road since the 1950s. It is now the centerpiece of Swanberg Rocker Gulch Park, where you'll find explanatory panels and assorted mining paraphernalia scattered about.

Back in town the distinctive focal point is the slender spire of the former **St Joseph's Church** on Bering Street and Seppala Drive, thrusting upwards as if mocking the over-optimism of 1901, when there were perhaps twenty thousand souls to minister to; it now serves as a community hall, known as "Old St

△ Old St Joe's, Nome

Joe's." Blindingly white in the low subarctic sun, it casts its shadow over **Anvil City Square**, a wide expanse of grass with one corner graced by statues of the **Three Lucky Swedes**, none looking especially delighted with his good fortune.

In winter, don't miss the surreal **Nome National Forest**, created in the New Year when used Christmas trees are collected and set up on the pack ice, together with painted plywood cut-outs of people, animals, a few flamingos, and palm trees. The cut-outs are removed before break-up but the trees are left to drift out to sea and eventually sink. Additionally, the **Bering Sea Ice Golf**

Classic is held on the third Saturday of March each year, with golfers playing with bright orange balls on a six-hole Astroturf course laid out on the ice.

Eating and drinking

Eating in Nome is more a function than a pleasure, although as the largest town for hundreds of miles there is a reasonable choice of overpriced places to dine. Those on a tight budget may prefer to patronize the AC Value Center, about a mile north of downtown on Bering Street, with its deli, bakery, and **groceries**, or the Hanson Trading Company, also on Bering Street but closer to town. Both have provisions costing around forty percent more than in Anchorage.

The approach to **drinking** may be unsophisticated, but locals from Nome and the surrounding "dry" villages bring the Front Street bars enthusiastic patronage. Many a Permanent Fund Dividend has vanished in these bars, and a surprising number of people have also disappeared in PFD season, perhaps falling off the jetty when drunk or else meeting other misfortunes.

Airport Pizza 406 Bering St ⓣ443-7992, ⓦwww.airportpizza.com. *Airport Pizza*'s claim to fame is that it delivers. Free. Anywhere. By air. With help from Frontier Flying Services, half-baked pizza is delivered to bush villages several hundred miles away, but you can also enjoy it in Nome, from $16 for the basic cheese and tomato to $32 with fancy ingredients such as chorizo, artichoke hearts, sun-dried tomatoes, or spicy Thai peanut sauce. Mon–Fri 11am–10pm, Sat 2–10pm, Sun 2–9pm.

Breakers Bar 243 Front St ⓣ443-2531. Ever-popular drinker's bar that vies with the *Anchor Tavern*, just next door, for top conviviality honors.

Fat Freddies 305 Front St ⓣ443-5899. Reliable family-style dining at fairly decent prices.

Milano Pizzeria 250 Front St ⓣ443-2924. The best restaurant in town, offering pretty decent pizzas ($12–16 for a 13-inch), pasta, and Japanese dishes. There's also a well-priced lunch special for $9.

Northern Delights 245 Front St ⓣ443-5200. The town's only espresso café, also serving bagels and muffins.

Polar Café 205 Front St ⓣ443-5191. The best overall value of the downtown restaurants, with great sea views and all-day breakfasts of reindeer sausage, eggs, and hash browns ($9). It's also good for burgers and sandwiches ($6–10) and dinners of liver and onions ($12), or a plate of battered halibut and trimmings ($17).

Subway 135 Front St ⓣ443-1800. Not a very inventive option, but here *Subway* represents decent fare at a good price.

Listings

Airlines Alaska Airlines ⓣ443-2288; Bering Air ⓣ443-5464; Frontier Flying Service ⓣ443-2414, ⓦwww.frontierflying.com.

Banks Wells Fargo, 107 Front St (Mon–Thurs 10am–5pm, Fri 10am–6pm), has an ATM in the foyer.

Books Arctic Trading Post, 302 Front St (ⓣ443-2686), and Chukotka–Alaska Inc, 514 Lomen Ave (ⓣ443-4128), have the town's best selection of books on the region, the Iditarod, and more.

Car rental Stampede Rentals, at the *Aurora Inn* (ⓣ443-3838 or 1-800/354-4606, ⓔaurorainn @gci.net), rents 4WD pickups and SUVs for $95 a day with unlimited mileage and passenger vans for $115. Alaska Cab Garage (ⓣ443-2939) has competitive rates for similar vehicles.

Cinema Gold Coast Cinema, 135 Front St (ⓣ443-8200/82), offers a surprisingly comfortable environment for film-viewing.

Cycling Nome's road system is great for bikes, and if you're thinking of bringing yours, get in touch with Keith Conger, who runs Bering C Bikes, 500 Spinning Rock Rd (ⓣ443-4994, ⓔcong06@gci.net), located in the suburb of Icy View, a mile or so north of Nome. As well as operating a bike repair shop and offering general logistical support for kayaking and wilderness trips, Keith offers **van-supported bike tours** of Nome's road system, providing meals, backup, and local knowledge. Rates depend on numbers (though expect $150–200 a day), and you'll need to bring a bike with you. June and July offer the best weather.

Festivals The Nome calendar abounds in festivals, kicking off with a bunch of events designed to coincide with the Iditarod Sled Dog Race around the second and third weeks in March. Of these, most notable is the Miners & Mushers Ball and the Bering Sea Ice Golf Classic (third Sat), a six-hole charity tournament with huskies dressed up as caddies, arcane rules, and warming tots of vodka. At summer solstice, around June 21, Nome celebrates the longest day with the Midnight Sun street festival, which usually coincides with the Nome River Raft Race, using home-built rigs. With all this revelry you might be induced to enter the Polar Bear Swim in 35°F water with a certificate awarded for full immersion. And in September (Labor Day), there's a Rubber Duck Race and a Bathtub Race along Front Street, with water, bubbles, soap, a bath mat, and a bather in each tub.

Fishing There's reasonable salmon-, pike-, and grayling-fishing in the region's rivers. Nome Outfitters, 120 W 1st Ave (☏ 443-2880 or 1-800/680-6663), is the best contact for gear and local knowledge.

Internet access See Library, below.

Laundry There is no public laundry, so take your dirty smalls back to Anchorage.

Library The Kegoayah Kozga Library, 223 Front St (Mon–Thurs noon–8pm, Fri & Sat noon–6pm; ☏ 443-5133), has a free paperback swap and free **Internet access** booked by the half-hour.

Medical assistance Norton Sound Regional Hospital, at Bering St & E 5th Ave (☏ 443-3311), is open 24hr.

Post office 113 E Front St. The **General Delivery** zip code is 99762.

Shopping Nome is a good place to buy Iñupiat and Yup'ik crafts, with a good range at fair prices, and the person selling may know (or be) the person who did the work. Try the Arctic Trading Post, 302 Front St (☏ 443-2686); Ivory Jim's, 213 Front St; and Chukotka–Alaska Inc, 514 Lomen Ave (☏ 443-4128), which along with superb local Eskimo crafts stocks a fabulous treasure trove of books, Russian watches, dolls, T-shirts, and Lomonosov porcelain.

Showers Recreation Center, 208 E 6th Ave (Mon–Fri 6am–10pm, Sat closed, Sun 2–10pm; ☏ 443-5543), where your $5 entry fee gets you all-day use of racquetball courts, gym, weight room, sauna, and bowling alley.

Swimming In the sea if you dare (it is typically 40–50°F in summer), or at the high-school pool three miles northwest of town (☏ 443-5717), though it is usually closed in July and August.

Taxes Nome imposes a four percent sales tax, plus a four percent bed tax, not included in our accommodation price codes.

Around Nome

Though Nome is interesting itself, the real pleasure in visiting the Seward Peninsula is getting out on the three fascinating roads in the vicinity – three hundred miles in total – which is something you can't really do from any other Alaska bush community. Along the way you'll see stacks of mining castoffs, abandoned buildings from dozens of old claims, the rusting hulks of earth movers, unidentified ironmongery, and ditches dug across the hills to divert essential sluicing water to the diggings. It is even said that there are 44 dilapidated **gold dredges** visible from the road system, though it will take eagle eyes to spot them all. There is also plenty of **wildlife** to see, with bears, musk oxen often close to the road, ten thousand semi-nomadic reindeer roaming the peninsula, and rare birds blown over from Asia, including bristle-thighed curlew, bluethroat, and white and yellow wagtails.

Generally, the roads open in early to mid-June depending on the thaw and close once the snows arrive around the end of September. Other than a couple of stores in Teller and one bar on the Council Road, there are no services anywhere outside Nome, including gas stations, so go prepared. Of course, there is no public **transport**, so either bring your own bicycle or rent a car from Nome (see Listings, p.561).

To explore beyond the road system, you'll have to take to the air, either into the **Bering Land Bridge National Preserve** or across the Bering Strait to the **Russian Far East** and the garrison town of Provideniya.

Council Road

At the turn of the twentieth century, there were small gold towns all around Nome, but most died away as quickly as they formed. **Council**, 73 miles

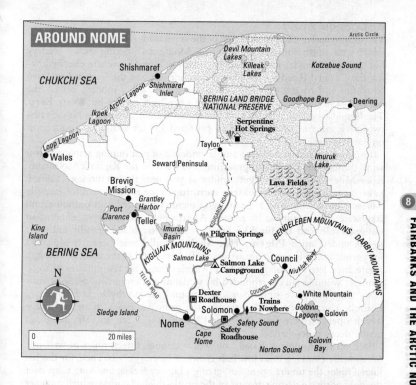

northeast of Nome, is one of the few survivors, with a few dozen summer residents and just a handful of hardy year-rounders. It is reached along **Council Road** (usually snow-free June–Sept), which heads east from Nome along the coastline, littered with beach shacks where miners work the sands and fishers dry their catch on driftwood frames. The road continues past the expansive viewpoint of **Cape Nome** at Mile 13 and the prime **birding wetlands** of **Safety Sound** at Mile 20 to the nearby *Safety Roadhouse*, a quirky bar that acts as the last checkpoint on the Iditarod before Nome. At Mile 31 the road turns inland by the roadside "**Trains to Nowhere**," a rusting line of steam locomotives built in the 1880s for the elevated railway in New York. They were brought here in 1903 for the Council City & Solomon River Railroad, but were abandoned in 1907 when the bridge connecting the railroad to the port on the coast was washed away in a storm. Standing picturesquely on the open tundra, they're a reminder of just how suddenly the boom turned to bust. A short distance on, the scattered remains of **Solomon** herald a stretch of heavily worked streambed, with several abandoned dredges in the next few miles as well as evidence along the hillsides of where channels were dug to direct water to mining camps. Beyond, the road climbs over a low range of hills to Council, unique in these parts for its stand of spruce: half of Nome comes out here before the road closes in the fall to snag their Christmas trees. The road ends at the shallow Niukluk River, where locals keep their skiffs for getting across to the far bank and Council (where there are no facilities for visitors). If you're intent on visiting what was the site of the Seward Peninsula's original gold find in 1897, be patient and you may be able to hitch a ride across with a local.

Kougarok Road

The longest and perhaps most scenic of the area's roads is the **Kougarok Road**, which cuts north through the Kigluaik Mountains offering snowy scenery, hot springs, and more mining detritus than you'll find anywhere else. Following the Council Road out of Nome, turn left just past the former *Fort Davis Roadhouse* and continue to *Dexter Roadhouse*, Mile 8.5, a modern bar on the site of a watering hole rumored to have once been owned by **Wyatt Earp**. The legendary gunslinger also built the Dexter Saloon, downtown Nome's first two-story structure, and managed to get fined $50 for assaulting a policeman on Front Street.

Beyond the roadhouse there's ample evidence of past mining activity as you wind through the foothills approaching a low pass in the Kigluaik Mountains. After Mile 30 the scenery gets wilder as you near the picturesque Salmon Lake, where there's wonderful **free camping** at the BLM's beautiful, lakeside *Salmon Lake Campground*, Mile 40, with picnic tables, grills, an outhouse, and lake water which should be treated. As you pull out of the mountains, an unsigned side road at Mile 53.5 branches seven rough and gravelly miles left to the undeveloped **Pilgrim Hot Springs** (call Louie Green ☎443-5583 for permission; it is almost always granted). At the end of the road, go through a gate, turn left, and follow the four-wheeler tracks for ten minutes or so to a simple wooden tank surrounded by wetlands and cottonwoods. Soak your cares away, but leave time to wander around the nearby locked clapboard Catholic church with its tiny steeple, the principal legacy of an orphanage which operated here from 1918 to 1941. Half a dozen ancillary buildings gently decay in its shadow.

Back on the Kougarok Road, you weave through fifteen miles of wetlands, occasionally climbing onto low hills crowned by craggy tors. Then, for the last fifteen miles, the tundra opens out, giving a big-sky feeling and long vistas over the only northern nesting ground of the bristle-thighed curlew, which migrates here from the South Pacific. The road ends at the Kougarok bridge, from where it is possible to set out on foot twenty miles to **Taylor**, a private summer mining camp 87 miles from Nome. Beyond Taylor an increasingly hard-to-follow trail leads a further twenty miles to Serpentine Hot Springs (see p.566), two to three days' walk from the road end.

Teller Road

The only substantial Native community accessible on the local road system is **Teller**, a 150-strong Iñupiat reindeer-herding and subsistence village 72 miles northwest of Nome. It is strung along a thin, attractive spit that separates Port Clarence from Grantley Harbor, but there really isn't a whole lot there. Unlike many Native communities, it is of fairly recent origin, founded as a trading center during the gold years around 1900. It was a barely viable community when, in 1926, bad weather forced Norwegian explorer **Roald Amundsen** to make an impromptu visit in his dirigible, *Norge*, after he completed the first transpolar flight, a seventy-hour, 3500-mile journey from Spitzbergen.

The two-hour drive from Nome is a lovely one, out along the **Teller Road** (generally open early or mid-May to mid-Oct), which runs past Nome's high school, where there is a sign marking the "Discovery Claim" close to the original 1898 gold find in Anvil Creek. Beyond the marker you contour around the hills a couple of miles in from the coast, then head further inland to open high country with spiky mountains. There is a fair chance of seeing **reindeer**, a species brought here to replace the longer-legged native caribou that died out here towards the end of the nineteenth century. As a way of

8

Even though Bering Air first broke through the "ice curtain" in 1988, and the nearest Russian town is only an hour from Nome, tourist **visits to Russia** are still difficult. Officials, academics, and Natives with relatives on the other side make the trip frequently, but the nearest town of any size, the military port of **Provideniya** (about 160 miles from Nome), remains a "closed" area. Throughout the 1990s it was gradually depopulated, and few people now live there, but a Cold War mentality remains. Unless you have some special reason to visit, there are plenty of better ways to spend your time and money within Alaska.

Should you still wish to go, there are a couple of possibilities. Contact Bering Air at Nome airport ($300 each way; ☎443-5464, ⓦwww.beringair.com), but note that it takes four or five weeks to organize a permission document to visit the Chukotka region before you apply for a visa ($100) and book your charter. Rules change frequently but Bering Air can put you in touch with the right people. They may also be able to arrange accommodation, usually in furnished apartments. Circumpolar Expeditions in Anchorage (☎1-888/567-7165, ⓦwww.arctictravel.net) offers a ten-day wildlife trip from Nome, and there are also a few cruises (see p.565).

trying to help the local Iñupiat regain some form of self-determination, the Reverend Sheldon Jackson (see p.146) imported a small herd from Russia and released them in 1892. After years of hunting them for meat, Native Alaskans were finally given formal ownership of all reindeer on the Peninsula in 1937, and since then have developed husbandry techniques to exploit the antler velvet for the Asian "medicinal" market. Of late, reindeer numbers have decreased as large numbers have run off with the migrating Western Arctic caribou herd.

Around Mile 35 you drop down again to the coastal strip, and then pass the old wooden Gold Run Dredge (Mile 54) artfully decaying on the far bank of the adjacent river, before the final run into Teller. To get beyond Teller you'll have to engage the services of **Grantley Harbor Tours** (☎642-3682, ⓦwww.grantleyharbor.com), which runs guided tours pretty much to order, along with a wildlife-viewing outing ($99) that also takes in a sample of Eskimo culture and a trip to the spot where Amundsen put down. For something a good deal more ambitious, contact Iditarod veteran **Joe Garnie** (☎642-2139), identifiable by the raucous kennel outside his house, who will teach you to run sled dogs while sharing the modern Iñupiat lifestyle of his home. Ideally, you'll want to devote ten days (at around $200 a day) so that you can learn the ropes for a few days in town before heading out to his cabin and sweatlodge sixty miles upriver, catching food for yourself and the dogs as you go. From mid-April to mid-May there's enough snow and 24-hour light, but you'll need to fly into Teller, as the road won't be open.

Bering Land Bridge National Preserve

During the ice-bound Pleistocene era around 13,000 years ago, the sea level dropped so much that the 55 miles of sea between the Seward Peninsula and Russia was dry land and, it is thought, Asiatic peoples, not to mention plants and animals, migrated into the unpeopled Americas. Evidence from Alaska's oldest known archeological site, the nine caves of Trail Creek (not open to the public), indicates that some of the first people to set foot on the North American continent strode across the low tundra that now forms the **Bering Land Bridge National Preserve** (ⓦwww.nps.gov/bela), seventy miles north of Nome and at its closest, just seventy miles from Asia.

There are no roads, no facilities of any kind, and hardly any people in this gently rolling and largely treeless landscape, so you'll need to come fully prepared. Access is by plane, though the lack of maintained airstrips limits your choices. The most popular destination is **Serpentine Hot Springs** ("Iyat" in Iñupiat, meaning cooking pot or place), a hundred miles north of Nome and forty miles beyond the end of the Kougarok Road. Once known as a place for teaching shamans, it became popular with miners in 1901. Here in a wide valley below Cretaceous tors, water up to 170°F wells up inside a bathhouse which is maintained by the Park Service along with the adjacent bunkhouse-style **cabin** (first-come, first-served; free). It sleeps at least fifteen and has a wood stove for heating and a propane stove for cooking; bring a sleeping bag and food. You can walk here from the end of the Kougarok Road (2–3 days each way) following an old ridgeline track, or fly into the short, rough airstrip with Bering Air (see p.569) for around $350 for a planeload of four, or twice that if you also want them to pick you up. Remember that there are bears up here and no trees for food storage, so you'll need to bring bear-resistant food canisters.

If you want to join the ranks of a very select group, you could try to bike in, though expect tough conditions and consult Keith Conger (see p.561) for advice and the latest reports.

In winter, a moderately popular snowmobile destination is the otherworldly **lava fields** in the southern quarter of the preserve. There are no trails, so you can just make it up as you go along, though the staff at the visitor centers in Nome and Kotzebue will advise on likely itineraries.

Kotzebue and around

The town of **Kotzebue** perches on the outer edge of the slender Baldwin Peninsula some six hundred miles northwest of Anchorage. It is just 26 miles north of the Arctic Circle, but for that reason alone it has become a fairly popular destination for tourists lured by 24 hours of daylight (from mid-May to the end of July) and some 37 days around the solstice when the sun never goes down at all. The place was long known as Qikiqtagruk, but takes its current name from Russian navigator Otto von Kotzebue, who charted the area while searching for the Northwest Passage in 1816.

With three thousand inhabitants, Kotzebue is second only to Barrow as the world's largest Eskimo community and is a predominantly Iñupiat town that blends tradition with a mainstream Alaskan outlook. The comforts that people expect from town life – shops, restaurants, and lodging – are here, all infused with the tenor of a Native "village" more akin to Barrow than to (relatively) nearby Nome. Three quarters of the three thousand residents are Iñupiat, and it is they who run the town, primarily through the Northwest Arctic Native Association (NANA), the regional corporation which represents Kotzebue and ten other villages spread over much of northwest Alaska, half-owns the huge Red Dog zinc mine ninety miles north of town, and manages a 6000-strong caribou herd. **Independent travelers** are poorly served here: unless you are bound for the **wilderness rivers** to the northeast, or have local friends, you'll soon find yourself with little to do and facing the prospect of an expensive night in a hotel. Without a boat or a plane there is no way out of town, and even walking the streets you might find that people are not as interested in you as you may be in them.

Though the seascape is attractive, Kotzebue isn't a pretty town. Indeed, it gives the impression of being temporary: the streets are unpaved, telephone wires hang loosely, and the whole town can look like a graveyard for shipping containers with every second home having one as a storage shed. Trash is blown up to fifty miles away by the steady wind, which also powers a new set of turbines. These details won't concern you, though, as you stroll along the beach in the golden light watching the **midnight sun** appear to roll along the tops of the hills across Kotzebue Sound.

Getting there and information

As with Nome, the only way to get to Kotzebue is to fly, and you'll likely use a taxi to get around the sights. An alternative is to organize your travels through Anchorage-based Arctic Circle Educational Adventures (☎276-0976, ⓦ www.fishcamp.org), which from mid-June to August runs *LaVonne's Fish Camp* (☎442-6013) on the coast near Kotzebue. It is a peaceful spot, frequently visited by locals out hunting or gathering, and is great for birding or just lazing around in the 24-hour light. Accommodation is in cozy cabins, family-style meals are served, and rates (typically $250–350 a day) depend on what you do since all trips are customized.

Alaska Airlines **flights** from Anchorage to Kotzebue cost around $315 round-trip if bought 21 days in advance, so it is worth considering an Anchorage–Kotzebue–Nome–Anchorage loop, which will cost about $473. Committed Arctic tourists could also fly with Frontier Flying Service (☎1-800/478-6779, ⓦ www.frontierflying.com), which serves all the coastal villages between Nome and Barrow, with connections to Fairbanks. The paved runway, incidentally, sits on six inches of styrofoam atop 2240ft of permafrost.

You'll probably walk wherever you want to go downtown, but there are few street signs and numbers and you may prefer to call Polar Cab (☎442-2233), Kobuk Taxi (☎442-3651), or B&D Taxi (☎442-2244), all of whom charge around $5 for adults.

The only source of tourist assistance in town is the **Innaigvik Education and Public Lands Information Center**, 154a 2nd Ave (summer only; Tues–Fri noon–8pm, Sat noon–4pm; ☎442-3760). At other times you can ask at the Western Arctic National Parklands headquarters, behind the post office at 333 Shore (Mon–Fri 8am–5pm; ☎442-3890, ⓦ www.nps.gov/nwak), which manages Cape Krusenstern National Monument, Kobuk Valley National Park, and Noatak National Preserve, but will help with local queries. In addition, the Selawik National Wildlife Refuge has an office at 160 2nd Ave (☎1-800/492-8848, ⓦ selawik.fws.gov), and the BLM has a Field Station at 207 5th Ave (☎442-3430). Free **Internet access** is offered at the Chukchi **library** on 3rd Avenue (Mon–Fri noon–8pm, Sat noon–6pm); there's a Wells Fargo **bank** with ATM at 2nd Avenue and Lagoon Street; and a **post office** on Shore Avenue near Mission Street.

The Town

NANA's Museum of the Arctic has closed and been demolished, so until a new NPS Visitor Center opens in 2008, there's little to do but wander the streets aiming for Shore Avenue (also known as Front Street), where much of the town's activity takes place. During the ice-free months of mid-June to mid-September, you'll see fuel oil and construction materials being unloaded from supply barges here. For the rest of the year everything comes in by plane. Head along 3rd Avenue to the junction of Mission Street, where two blocks are devoted to the town **cemetery**, complete with a few **spirit houses** (see p.382). The large building nearby is the Maniilaq Health Center, an impressive

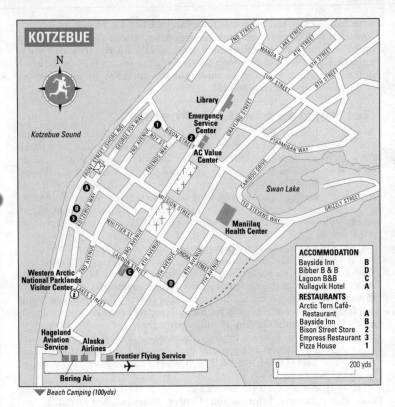

Beach Camping (100yds)

new hospital with a lobby (one floor up; Mon–Fri 9am–6pm; ☎442-3311/21) that is well worth a visit for its **excellent display of Native craftwork**: a beautiful seal-gut parka, a soapstone and ivory Madonna, an ulu knife with a handle of mastodon ivory, an exquisite box made of Dall sheep horn and baleen, and much more.

Accommodation, eating, and drinking

Accommodation is scant, with most groups using the *Nullagvik Hotel*, 308 Shore Ave (☎442-3331; ⓦwww.nullagvik.com; ⓿), which is comfortable enough though not great value for money; renovated in 1997, its 74 rooms have cable TV and some are air-conditioned. Almost next door you'll find the marginally cheaper but inferior *Bayside Inn*, just south on Shore Avenue (☎442-3600; ⓿), but you're better off at the *Bibber B&B* at 398 Lagoon St (☎442-2693; ⓔbibber@otz.net). There is no campground and free **camping** isn't particularly encouraged, nor is it a very appealing option, with the best spot being a narrow strip above the steeply shelving beach just south of the airport. If it is windy, tethering your tent can be a problem.

Eating options are as limited as accommodation and equally expensive. The *Nullagvik Hotel* has an **espresso bar** in its craft shop and the *Arctic Tern Café-Restaurant* (summer only), which has large picture windows overlooking the sea and serves good meals from a standard Alaskan menu. The *Bayside* also has a restaurant, open from 7am for breakfasts, sandwiches, pasta, burgers, steaks ($19–27), Chinese chicken, and Korean dumplings; lunch specials cost $10. There's also Chinese chow at the *Empress Restaurant* (T 442-4304; Mon–Sat 11am–11pm) and the *Bison Street Store* (T 442-2758; daily 11am–midnight), which also serves burgers, sandwiches, and pizza ($13–32). By the airline terminals *Arctic Blues Coffee & Gifts* (T 442-2554; Mon–Sat 7.30am–6.30pm) also offers **Internet access**. **Groceries** are available from the AC Value Center (Mon–Sat 8am–10pm, Sun 9am–9pm). It is also worth remembering that Kotzebue has a six percent **sales tax**, plus another six percent hotel tax, which are not included in our accommodation price codes. Kotzebue is a damp community with no alcohol sales, though you can bring a bottle or two in with you.

Around Kotzebue

Kotzebue may be a fairly limited destination in itself, but it does offer relatively easy access to some of the finest wilderness in the Alaskan Arctic, all encompassed by the Western Arctic National Parklands. Set aside $200 to see something of the **seabird oasis** of the Selawik National Wildlife Refuge, mostly tundra wetlands, the Noatak National Preserve with its **superb rafting rivers**, and the massive sand dunes stranded miles from the sea in the Kobuk Valley National Park. Other worthy options include flying from Kotzebue to the Bering Land Bridge National Preserve (see p.565) and, for committed paddlers, **sea kayaking** along the bird- and sea mammal-rich barrier islands of **Cape Krusenstern National Monument** (W www.nps.gov/cakr).

The single most alluring sight around these parts is the **Great Kobuk Sand Dunes** in the southern reaches of the **Kobuk Valley National Park** – Alaska's smallest and one of the country's least-known national parks (W www.nps.gov/kova). Located over a hundred miles inland and fifty miles north of the Arctic Circle, the dunes are an unlikely sight spread over 24 square miles and rising up to 250ft above the surrounding boreal forest, here at its northern limit. Formed from glacier-ground sand, they are thought to be the remains of a once much larger dune-field created when ancient retreating glaciers stripped the land of stabilizing vegetation. The northernmost dunes lie only a mile or so south of the Kobuk River, the easiest access point, especially for rafters (see below).

A great way to see the area is by scheduling a **flightseeing** outing, which may briefly stop at several villages. Bering Air (T 442-3943, W www.beringair.com) flies over the Cape Krusenstern National Monument to Kivalina ($173–192 round-trip) and to Kobuk via Ambler and Shugnak ($295–330 round-trip).

You probably won't want to spend time in the villages – Kiana, Ambler, Kobuk, and others – which are tiny and fairly insular. You'll feel very out of place in these communities unless someone is meeting you there, perhaps for a float trip on one of the remote and scenic rivers in these parts, which should be seriously considered by people with a taste for adventure and some time on their hands. Local operators offering boating and backpacking trips include Arctic Circle Adventure Tours (T 442-6013), Goodwin Tours (T 442-3557), and Noatak Tours (T 442-3944). In addition, Caribou Adventures, just south in Deering (T 363-2120, W www.caribou-adventures.com), will take you to fish camps and on birding trips. Gear rental is available at NW Backcountry Rentals (T 442-3944) and fly-ins are provided by Arctic Air Guides Flying Service (T 442-3030).

Some of Alaska's most satisfying **float trips** run through the Noatak National Preserve and the Kobuk Valley National Park. None is short and all require considerable logistical commitment; however, you could always join one of the very few commercial trips: try Utah-based Nichols Expeditions (☎1-800/648-8488, ⓦwww.nicholsexpeditions.com), which runs just one nine-day trip out of Fairbanks each summer for around $2700. Canoes, rafts, and folding kayaks are all acceptable means of transport on the rivers: either bring your own or get the latest on rental options in Kotzebue through the Parklands Visitor Center. Note that the flight prices below are the passenger fare; rafts, canoes, and gear will put you well over your personal luggage limit, and it may work out cheaper to negotiate a charter flight. In all cases, you'll need to be entirely self-sufficient on the river. There are no facilities except in the villages and you are unlikely to see many people, except during the fall hunting season when noisy boats head upstream to access prime caribou areas.

Access to the dunes is from the lower section of the **Kobuk River** ("Big River"; navigable June to late Sept; Class I) from Ambler to Kiana, a run of a hundred miles usually taking five to six days. Flights into Ambler and out of Kiana with Bering Air cost $293–325. To extend the trip by three or four days, start by flying into Kobuk, 45 miles further upstream. The truly committed can run the whole 270 navigable miles from Walker Lake in the Gates of the Arctic National Park (accessed from Bettles or Coldfoot) down to Kiana in fifteen to twenty days, although there are a few short upper sections where portaging or lining your boat is necessary.

The **Squirrel River**, a candidate National Wild River to the north of the Kiana Hills, is an easy Class I float (with good grayling-fishing), starting with a put-in at the North Fork confluence (just a thirty mile flight from Kotzebue); it takes four to five days to cover the 53 miles to Kiana, at the confluence with the Kobuk River. The **Salmon River**, a tributary of the Kobuk with its confluence downstream of the dunes, is another popular float. Trips often start at Ambler, where *Kobuk River Lodge & General Store* (☎445-2166) offers accommodation. Downstream from the Kobuk Valley National Park is **Kiana**, home to four hundred Iñupiat, where the locally-owned *Kiana Lodge* (☎475-2149, ⓦwww.alaskasheefishing.com) offers lodging and tours.

Like the Kobuk, there are several ways to approach the **Noatak River** (meaning "passage to the interior"; navigable June–Sept; Class I–II) with plenty of landing spots for float-planes, allowing you to do as much or as little as you please. This is the largest undisturbed watershed in North America, flowing 396 miles from the glaciers of Gates of the Arctic National Park; it is virtually empty except for seasonal rangers based by the river at Makpik, in the center of the preserve, and Kelly River, at its western end. Again, Bettles and Coldfoot are good starting points for flying into the headwaters, from where you could take sixteen to eighteen days to float 220 miles down to Noatak (served by both Frontier Flying and Bering Air), and another couple of days to the mouth, which is just fifteen miles across Kotzebue Sound from Kotzebue. Kayaks and canoes (but not rafts, which are too susceptible to high winds) could then pick a calm morning and paddle across to Kotzebue. For more details on these and other rivers, consult Karen Jettmar's *The Alaska River Guide* (see Books, p.611).

Barrow

Many people visit **Barrow**, five hundred miles north of Fairbanks, simply because it is the northernmost settlement on the continent, and just eleven miles from Point Barrow, the very tip of the United States. Though 330 miles north of the Arctic Circle, there are still eight hundred miles of ocean to the North Pole and for ten months of the year it is ice all the way. This far north the sun doesn't rise for two months in the middle of winter, but after the middle of May it doesn't set until the start of August. In these 82 days of relative warmth and midnight sun, the ice gradually breaks up and melts away just over the horizon.

But the appeal isn't just geographic. This is the largest Eskimo community in Alaska, with around 65 percent of the 4400 residents claiming Iñupiat heritage – you'll hear Iñupiaq spoken as much as English. The Iñupiat call Barrow Utqiagvik or Ukpiagvik, "the place where we hunt snowy owls" (although since traditional belief holds that you inherit the traits of the animals you eat, these clumsy birds aren't fed to children). It is also the administrative capital of **North Slope Borough**, a vast region of Arctic Alaska with another 4500 people distributed through eight widely scattered villages. The borough encompasses the North Slope oilfields and the royalties from oil sales make this the richest Native region. Yet Barrow can look depressingly utilitarian, little more than a shantytown. It's got warm homes, well-stocked supermarkets, and a frequent jet service to Fairbanks and Anchorage, but no amount of money can combat the isolation, fierce weather, permafrost, and the ever-present threat of polar bears on the prowl.

Barrow is only slowly gearing itself towards tourism, and many details of daily life that make the town special will be inaccessible to the casual visitor. A partial solution is to join one of the hotel-and-culture package **tours**, though this is still a somewhat mainstream experience. Fly here independently, and your moves are limited and fairly expensive, although there is an excellent museum, tours to Point Barrow with the hope of seeing polar bears, and plenty of good **birding** on the surrounding tundra.

The **timing** of your visit is all-important. In May, when the rest of the state is gearing up for summer, Barrow is still in the grip of winter: the sea ice doesn't usually break up and melt away until mid-July. May and early June is the spring whaling season, and it is white to the northern horizon. Mid-to late June heralds the end of whaling and half a dozen **Nalukataq** feasts, celebrating a crew's successful hunt, including a genuine blanket toss. Through May, June, and July, birders flock to Barrow for easy spotting on the treeless tundra, where birds nest on tufted

Whaling in the Arctic

Despite Barrow's wealth and modernity, **whaling** fundamentally defines the community. Whatever you may think about whaling elsewhere, it is hard to begrudge a people going about their lives much as they have for thousands of years. During the spring or fall whale hunt, it is easy to get swept along by the buzz that goes around town when word of a successful kill comes in from the ice. There are no factory whaling ships here, just small seal-skin boats and men with hand-held harpoons and guns, both fitted with nitrate bombs, twenty or thirty miles out across the ice. They try to harpoon a forty-foot, forty-ton bowhead as it passes – heading northeast in late April and May, southwest in late September and October – along one of the narrow breaks in the sea ice known as "leads." Successful kills are signalled by cell phone as well as the traditional flag, and up to fifty people gather to haul the whale onto the ice with a pulley system. Each village gets an annual quota based on the known population – Barrow, which is unique in having two whaling seasons each year, in spring and fall, is allotted 22, and can also take unused quota from other villages at the end of the season – but each strike is counted whether the whale is killed or not, so a poor season can be over pretty quickly.

mounds: eiders, snowy owls, jaegers, swans, and arctic terns are some of the feathery attractions. Winter begins to set in by the end of September; ice starts to form at the shore and spreads out to create a pack about ten feet thick. For most people winter is off-limits, though the fall whale hunt makes October a good time to visit if you want to see polar bears. **Kivgiq**, the "Messenger Feast," is a celebration of a successful whaling season, held over three days in January or February of alternate years; **Piuraagiaqta** is a week-long spring festival held in April.

Arrival and getting around

Most visitors arrive in Barrow on **package tours** jointly run by Tundra Tours (at the *Top of the World Hotel* ☏1-800/882-8478, ⓦwww.tundratours.com) and Alaska Airlines Vacations (mid-May to mid-Sept daily; ☏1-800/468-2248, ⓦwww.alaskaair.com/vacations). These hardly seem cheap but almost always work out to be the lowest-cost option, and include a town tour plus a "culture program" at the Heritage Center with storytelling, dances, and a blanket toss. The cheapest is the Day Tour ($449), though for the full midnight sun experience you'll want the Overnight Tour ($549), which gives you two full days in town and a night at the *Top of the World Hotel*. These tours run from Fairbanks, but you can add one or more Anchorage legs for $110 each, a good deal if you need to get back to Anchorage. There are also Fairbanks-based winter variations at similar prices with a tour to Point Barrow. Northern Alaska Tour Company (see box, p.516) offers similar day-trips from $435 and overnights from $485, plus $100 each way for Anchorage extensions.

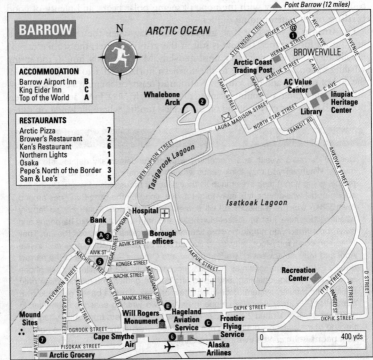

▲ Point Barrow (12 miles)

BARROW   N   ARCTIC OCEAN

BROWERVILLE

ACCOMMODATION
Barrow Airport Inn   B
King Eider Inn   C
Top of the World   A

RESTAURANTS
Arctic Pizza   7
Brower's Restaurant   2
Ken's Restaurant   6
Northern Lights   1
Osaka   4
Pepe's North of the Border   3
Sam & Lee's   5

Arctic Coast Trading Post

Whalebone Arch

AC Value Center

Iñupiat Heritage Center

Library

Tasigarook Lagoon

Isatkoak Lagoon

Hospital

Bank

Borough offices

Recreation Center

Mound Sites

Will Rogers Monument

Hageland Aviation Service

Frontier Flying Service

Cape Smythe Air

Alaska Airlines

Arctic Grocery

0   400 yds

▼ Freshwater Lake (1 mile) & Wiley Post Crash Site (16 miles)

For more flexibility, take one of several **flights** a day with Alaska Airlines, which cost upwards of $360 round-trip from Fairbanks, and at least $414 from Anchorage. You can book excursions with Tundra Tours or Arctic Tour Company (☎852-4512). Frontier Flying Service (Barrow ☎852-8333) has mail runs to villages such as Wainwright, Point Lay, and Point Hope, as well as Fairbanks and Kotzebue, connecting to Nome. The various airlines all have their own terminal buildings; the Alaska Airlines shed (open 8.30am–8pm) actually won an award for the best prefab metal building of 1988.

Getting around is easy. The airport borders the south side of town, and you can walk anywhere you need to go in about ten or fifteen minutes. If you've got heavy bags, engage the services of one of the half-dozen **taxi** companies, which all charge around $10 anywhere within Barrow and Browerville: Alaska Taxi (☎852-3000), Arctic Cab (☎852-2227), Barrow Taxi (☎852-2222), and City Cab (☎852-5050) are as good as any. There are very few roads around here, but **rental cars** are available from Ukpik Rentals (☎852-2700) for around $85 a day; the *King Eider Hotel* has rentals for guests only – see Ⓦwww.kingeider.net/kingrent.html.

There's free **Internet access** (though email is discouraged) at the Tuzzy Consortium Library (Mon–Thurs noon–9pm, Fri & Sat noon–5pm), right by the Iñupiat Heritage Center at Ahkovak Street and C Avenue; at 5146 Boxer St the world's northernmost Internet café, Polarbear PC (summer Mon–Thurs 1–11pm, Fri & Sat 1pm–midnight; hours reduced in winter) charges $5 per hour. **Banking** needs are met by Wells Fargo, 1780 Kiogak St (Mon–Thurs 10am–5pm, Fri 10am–6pm), with an ATM in a 24-hour lobby; there's another ATM in the AC Value Center.

Accommodation

The town's biggest **hotel** and the one where all the package tours stay is the *Top of the World*, 1200 Agvik St (☎852-3900, Ⓦwww.topoftheworldhotel.com; ❼), which has new deluxe and noticeably ageing standard rooms (at opposite ends of the price code) with the standard amenities, though no pool, gym, or sauna. Cheaper and very pleasant rooms can be found at the *Barrow Airport Inn*, 1815 Momegana St (☎852-2525, Ⓔairportinn@barrow.com; ❺), which caters mainly to business visitors and has some rooms with kitchenettes as well as cable TV, WiFi, and continental breakfast with fresh-baked bread. Barrow's newest hotel, the *King Eider Inn*, by the airport at 1752 Ahkovak St (☎1-888/303-4337, Ⓦwww.kingeider.net; ❼), has the nicest rooms in town (some with kitchenettes for $20 more), a guest sauna, and free coffee and muffins.

There is no budget accommodation in Barrow and beach camping is discouraged, not least because there are polar bears about for much of the year. Likewise, don't go out onto the ice alone. Fall is the busiest time for bears, when they're waiting for the ice to form, but they can come into town at any time. The town's polar bear patrol was closed down in 2003, but may have to be reactivated, as tundra grizzlies are beginning to appear in the area.

The Town

Barrow's airport goes by the grandiose title of the **Wiley Post/Will Rogers Memorial Airport**, in honor of pioneer aviator Wiley Post and entertainer, homespun philosopher, and all-round spokesman for rural America Will Rogers, who died in 1935 when their plane went down sixteen miles south of Barrow while they were searching for a new air route to Siberia. A concrete **monument** stands by the finger signpost at Ahkovak and Momegana streets, just west of the Alaska Airlines terminal.

△ Whalebone arch in Barrow

Continue west along Ahkovak Street towards the sea, and overlooking the beach you'll find a series of low **mounds** that are nothing much to look at but are the archeologically important remains of sod houses, with driftwood and whalebone struts visible in summer. Follow the beach to the northeast through what constitutes the center of town, and you'll eventually come to Barrow's original **whaling station**, now a restaurant, and beside it a **whalebone arch** that seems to feature on most postcards of Barrow.

To learn something of European and Eskimo whaling in this area, visit the **Iñupiat Heritage Center**, 5421 North Star St (Mon–Fri 8.30am–noon, 1–5pm, mid-May to mid-Sept Sat 2–4pm; $5; ℡852-4594, Ⓦwww.nps.gov /inup), a modern and well laid out museum that provides a wonderful evocation of the Iñupiat spirit, celebrating traditional and modern life in the eight villages of North Slope Borough. Passing under a model whale suspended from the rafters, turn right to the excellent "The People of Whaling" exhibit, which makes a persuasive case for traditional subsistence harvest. There's a pair of fine skin kayaks – one, a 1912 model, is long and thin for ocean travel; the other, from 1920, wider and more stable for river crossings. There's excellent material on subsistence living, particularly the annual bowhead hunts, with some superb photos of whale recovery and chopping up the muktuk, or blubber. Artifacts haven't been neglected, and there's a beautiful toboggan made from whale baleen and sealskin rope, exquisite gut parkas and the ivory needles used to sew them, and spirit masks presented next to angels carved from ivory. Elsewhere there are some fine stuffed birds, a gift store, and a community workshop, known as the Tradition Center, where you can look through a window at locals preparing their boats for whaling. It's also well worth tracking down the private **Joe the Waterman's Museum** (℡852-5131, or ask at *Pepe's*), a house packed with an eclectic collection of art, stuffed wildlife, sleds, carved ivory, baleen, mastodon bones, oosiks (walrus penis bones), and a bizarre assortment of metal items washed up on the beach that could be from nineteenth-century whalers or from last summer's barge.

Like Anchorage, Barrow now boasts a **scale model of the solar system**, with Pluto 4248ft from the sun (under a mile, as against 3.6 billion miles in reality). The sun and the first five planets are at Barrow's famous $62 million Ipalook Elementary School (the most expensive in the US), Saturn at City Hall, Uranus at the high school, Neptune just west, then Pluto opposite the weather station.

Outdoor activities and tours

The perfect complement to any trip to Barrow is the **Polar Bear Swim**, not a single event, but a summer-long chance (roughly mid-July to mid-Sept) to experience full Arctic submersion and receive membership of the Polar Bear Club ($10), a certificate, a patch, and the opportunity to buy a members-only T-shirt. See Fran Tate or any of the staff at *Pepe's* (see p.577).

Alternatively, **hike** out of town across the tundra, but go prepared to combat cold, wind, hunger, and mosquitoes, and ask locally about recent polar bear movements. Leave word of your plans with your hotel before making for destinations such as Point Barrow, Freshwater Lake, a mile south of town, and the two monuments where Wiley Post and Will Rogers crashed sixteen miles south of town. This last hike passes "Hollywood," the site of the filming of the early 1970s Disney movie *Track of the Giant Snow Bear*.

The prime destination out of town is **Point Barrow**, which was the start of the longest sustained sledge journey in the history of polar exploration:

the first surface crossing of the Arctic Ocean by its longest axis and the first expedition to the North Pole on foot. Wally Herbert, Allan Gill, Fritz Koerner, and Kenneth Hodges arrived in Spitzbergen in May 1969 (just before the first moon landing) after 464 days and 3663 miles, implicitly proving that Robert Peary didn't do it in 1909, since the distances he'd claimed to have covered would have been humanly impossible.

These days you still have to reach Point Barrow on foot (or on a tour), since the road covers only 12 of the 14.5 miles northeast from town. Before you reach the road end, stop at Ilisagvik Community College and the **Barrow Arctic Science Consortium** (BASC; T 852-4881, W www.arcticscience.org), on the site of the former Naval Arctic Research Lab. From the college's *Niggivik Restaurant* (which has free WiFi) corridors lead left to the Wildlife Department or right to the Environmental Studies Department, both hallways lined with posters and cuttings telling you all you could want to know about local environmental issues. The $100 million Barrow Global Climate Change Research Facility is now under construction, a massive project to belatedly prove to Washington that the Arctic is warming up fast (see p.598). The BASC has strong links with the community, which began when it gave 7466 acres in 1992 to establish the Barrow Environmental Observatory, protecting the only Steller's eiders still nesting in North America; in particular, there's an "open schoolyard" workshop every Saturday with talks by scientists on their work. There's also a webcam and radar on the town's highest building, giving real-time images of the ice (currently thinning by eight percent per decade) to help whaling crews decide if conditions are safe.

The so-called highway continues north past Dewline Road, where the DEW (Distant Early Warning) radar station is still in use, although run by civilian contractors; it's known as a good spot to see snowy owls and foxes and it's no problem to drive in and around the loop. You may also see a few spoof palm trees with baleen fronds planted hereabouts. The highway then passes the Pigniq village site and its remains of sod houses, now a summer camp for hunting duck and goose, and onto the spit between the Chukchi and Beaufort seas.

For some the attraction of being here is simply because it's the **northernmost point in the US**, but when the sea ice is in, especially after a successful whale hunt when the stripped carcass is dumped there, this becomes prime **polar bear** territory. This wouldn't be a good time to walk, but John Tidwell of Alaskan Arctic Adventures (T 852-3800 or 367-3449, E frozentoes94@yahoo.com) leads customized tours here (and elsewhere) in a caterpillar-tracked van or off-road vehicle, with the emphasis on viewing wildlife, such as arctic foxes, whales, seals, walruses, and loads of birds. The two-hour tour (Mon–Sat only) costs $130 for two people; get more together and costs per person go down.

From November to May, John's son, John, runs Alaskan Arctic Mushing Tours ($95 for one, $170 for two; T 852-6874), where you get a full two hours learning to run a **dog sled** and can even head off across the tundra viewing wildlife.

Eating and not drinking

Those on a tight budget should head for the AC Value Center, on Ahkovak Street at C Avenue in Browerville (Mon–Sat 7am–10pm, Sun 9am–9pm), the retail heart of Barrow, with everything from snowmobiles, furniture, and clothing to expensive **groceries** and even fresh flowers flown in daily from Anchorage. There's a **food court**, too, with a deli, pizzas, Mexican food, subs, and cinnamon rolls. Groceries are also available more centrally from Arctic Grocery, at the corner of Pisokak and Apayauk streets.

There's a decent selection of **restaurants**, all as pricey as you'd expect for such a remote location and all serving burgers, sandwiches, and breakfasts as well as their individual specialties. ⚓ *Pepe's North of the Border*, 1204 Agvik St (☎852-8200; 6/7am–10pm), serves genuine Mexican dishes under a ceiling strung with piñatas, with tacos starting from $4, a burrito plate for $18, burgers for $11, and steaks from $25 to $30. The best pizza is at *Arctic Pizza*, 125 Apayauk St (☎852-4222), which also has a huge range of salads, Mexican and pasta dishes, and even jambalaya, all served in an upstairs dining room with good sea views. *Sam & Lee's*, 1052 Kiogak St (☎852-5555), is decent for Chinese, as is *Ken's Restaurant* on Ahkovak St (☎852-8888), which also has the best bargain breakfasts in town ($8–12).

If you find yourself over in Browerville, pop into Charles DeWitt Brower's original whaling station, which now operates as *Brower's Restaurant*, on Stevenson St (☎852-3456; closed Sun), and enjoy views past the arched whale jawbones and out to sea as you sip an espresso or dine on American or Korean dishes, including surprisingly good burgers and pizza. Also in Browerville, *Northern Lights*, 5122 Herman St (☎852-3300; closed alternate Sundays), has Korean food as well, plus sandwiches, pizza, and steak, and good weekday lunch deals. *Osaka*, 980 Stevenson (☎852-4100; 7am–11pm/ midnight), serves Japanese dishes such as sushi (from $6), teriyaki chicken ($16), steaks (from $21), and Alaskan king crab ($27), as well as sandwiches and burgers.

Barrow is currently a damp community, so there are **no alcohol** sales, but you can bring in a liter of spirits, a gallon of beer, or two liters of wine without a permit.

Travel details

As the only large town covered by this chapter, Fairbanks is understandably the hub of all transportation networks. Its only train line, running south to Denali National Park, Anchorage, and Seward, has daily service in summer (roughly mid-May to mid-Sept) and weekly service in winter (north on Saturdays and south on Sundays). Buses (almost all mid-May to mid-Sept only) run parallel to the train line to Denali and Anchorage and also run east towards the Canadian border and southeast to Valdez. Planes fan out to just about every tiny bush community imaginable, the most important of which we've listed below.

Trains

Fairbanks to: Anchorage (1 daily; 12hr); Denali Park (1 daily; 3hr 45min); Talkeetna (1 daily; 8hr 10min); Wasilla (1 daily; 10hr).

Buses

Fairbanks to: Anchorage (1 daily in summer, 3 weekly in winter; 9–10hr); Chicken (3 weekly; 6hr); Dawson City, Yukon (3 weekly; 12hr); Delta Junction (6 weekly; 1hr 30min); Denali (1 daily; 3hr); Glennallen (on demand; 4hr 30min); Nenana (1 daily; 1hr 30min); North Pole (8 daily, not Sun; 40min); Talkeetna Junction (1 daily; 6hr 30min); Tok (6 weekly; 3hr 30min–5hr 30min); Valdez (on demand; 7–8hr); Whitehorse, Yukon (3 weekly; 15hr).

Flights

Barrow to: Anchorage (2 daily; 3hr); Fairbanks (2 daily; 1hr 20min).
Bettles to: Fairbanks (2–3 daily; 1hr 20min).
Fairbanks to: Anaktuvuk Pass (1–4 daily; 1hr 30min); Anchorage (10–12 daily; 1hr); Arctic Village (1–3 daily; 1hr 30min); Barrow (2 daily; 1hr 20min); Bettles (2–3 daily; 1hr 20min); Juneau (2 daily; 3hr–3hr 30min); Prudhoe Bay/Deadhorse (1 daily; 1hr); Seattle (6–9 daily; 3hr 40min–6hr).
Kotzebue to: Anchorage (3 daily; 1hr 30min); Nome (2 daily; 45min).
Nome to: Anchorage (3 daily; 1hr 30min–3hr).
Prudhoe Bay/Deadhorse to: Anchorage (1 daily; 1hr 40min); Barrow (2 daily; 1hr 20min); Fairbanks (1 daily; 1hr).

Contexts

Contexts

History

A laska's recorded history is both brief and frenetic, a recurring tale of the white man's exhaustive exploitation of the land followed by economic stagnation until the next big boom. The region's unrecorded history, however, goes back much further, and centers around four main groups of Native people and their sustainable relationship with nature.

The first people

Alaska has been inhabited longer than anywhere else in the Americas. The recent discovery of skeletons exhibiting Caucasoid features points to early colonization of the "New World" from Europe, perhaps over a frozen North Atlantic. This conjecture is highly controversial, and there is greater agreement that Asiatic people were the first to arrive, sometime after 15,000 years ago. One expert on early Native American migrations describes the body of archeological evidence as "a confusing morass of conflicting data and opinions," but it is known that during the most recent ice age, from 25,000 to 12,000 BC, the sea level dropped enough to occasionally reveal the Arctic continent of **Beringia**, now under the northern half of the Bering Sea and the southern limit of the Chukchi Sea. This "**land bridge**" was a flat, dry, intensely cold, windy, and generally inhospitable steppe-tundra several hundred miles wide. It existed for a geological blink of the eye, but long enough for many generations of proto-Aleut and Eskimo to make it their home as they followed herds of large herbivores such as bison and mammoths eastward. The romanticized image of noble hunters crossing the land bridge and tracking deer through a sylvan corridor overhung with vast glaciers is almost certainly just that. The oldest confirmed archeological evidence discovered so far – at Healy Lake near Fairbanks and the Mesa site on the North Slope – dates back only around 11,000 years, so it seems that eastern Beringia (modern-day Alaska) probably wasn't populated until the land began to flood at the end of the last ice age, forcing the people to higher levels.

That is where they stayed for millennia, their passage south to more temperate lands blocked by the great North American ice sheets. Some scholars contend that there was just one major migration from which all Native Americans descended, but linguistic and cultural evidence points to at least two distinct groups arriving a significant period apart but before the land bridge flooded. From the earlier migration developed the forest-hunting cultures, which spread throughout the Americas and gave us the Na–Dene language group, comprised of the **Tlingit** of Southeast Alaska, the **Athabascans** of the Alaskan Interior, and their close kin the Navajo and Apache of the American Southwest. The later migration developed into the **Aleut** and Alaska's two main Eskimo groups, the **Yup'ik** and **Iñupiat**, cultures reliant on sea mammals and genetically the most Asiatic of all Native Americans. They occupied geographically and climatically distinct regions from the Arctic to Greenland, forcing them to develop their own ways of shaping the land to their needs.

European exploration and occupation: 1640 to 1867

For the best part of 12,000 years, Native Alaskans forged their own destiny without interference from abroad, though the Yearbooks of China's Sung dynasty record that in 458 AD five Buddhist monks led by **Hwui Shan** sailed up the coast of the Kamchatka Peninsula, then east through the Aleutian Islands to mainland Alaska. No further details of their journey are known.

Significant impact on the affairs of Native Alaskans didn't come until late in the European "Age of Discovery," the region's high latitudes and short summers deterring all but the hardiest of explorers. Spaniard **Bartholeme de Fonte** made the first claim of discovery, having battled his way up from Spanish Mexico into the waters of the Inside Passage in 1640. He reported nothing of interest and almost a century passed until, in 1725, Russian czar Peter the Great sent a party led by Danish explorer **Vitus Bering** to search for whatever lay to the east of Russia. After traveling for almost three years, Bering confirmed the suspicion that Siberia and the Americas were separate, and gave his name to the sea that divides the two landmasses; dense fog, however, prevented him spotting North America. It wasn't until his third journey, in 1741, that he finally set foot on the Alaskan mainland near what is now Cordova. Bering fell ill shortly after this (and died on the way back to Russia), but his lieutenant, Alexis Chirikof, commanded the ship as far as Sitka before returning to Russia with news of huge quantities of **sea otters**, whose pelts were highly prized for fur hats. Over the next sixty years the Aleutian Islands were alive with Russian *promyshleniki* (private fur traders), who quickly found that the Aleut were far more efficient at killing otters than they were. The Russians effectively enslaved these Natives, forcing them to hunt the otters to the brink of extinction. In 1743 the Aleut staged a revolt but failed, and they resigned themselves to economic domination by the *promyshleniki* and cultural suffocation at the hands of Russian Orthodox missionaries. Over the years the religion worked its way into Aleut culture, forever altering this Native people's stories, traditions, and way of life. In the past few decades the Aleut have begun to revive their traditions, but the Aleutian Chain remains an Orthodox stronghold.

Soon the British, Spanish, and Americans were all after this sea otter bounty, the Spanish (a waning but still major sea power) sending expeditions up the coast from their Mexican base at San Blas. But apart from adding a handful of Spanish names to landmarks around Prince of Wales Island and carting off a few boatloads of furs, they failed to consolidate their claim to hegemony over the entire west coast of the Americas.

While the carnage continued, further exploration began for the **Northwest Passage**, a long-sought trade route connecting the North Pacific to the North Atlantic. In 1778 British explorer **James Cook** sailed north from Vancouver Island, charting and naming features all the way to Turnagain Arm in Cook Inlet, near present-day Anchorage. He then continued west along the Aleutian Chain and up the coast to Icy Cape on the Arctic Ocean, 250 miles north of the Arctic Circle, where the pack ice drove him back. Cook's lieutenant, George Vancouver, returned in the 1790s and claimed the coast for Britain. With meticulous precision, he also mapped the Inside Passage, creating charts that were still in use at the start of the twentieth century.

Though outsiders had been meddling in Alaska for more than sixty years, in 1784 Russia's **Gregorii Shelikov** established the first non-Native settlement at

△ Baranov Museum, Kodiak

Three Saints Bay on Kodiak Island. Eight years later, Catherine II granted him a monopoly on furs as head of the **Russian–American Company**. In stepped the company's manager, **Alexandr Baranov** (see p.145), the self-styled "Lord of Alaska," to oversee the expansion of Russian interests. In 1790, he moved Shelikov's settlement up the coast to Kodiak, where his original storehouse still stands. Within a decade his political guile and business acumen extended Russian influence throughout southern Alaska and even as far as Fort Ross in northern California. As seal and otter populations plummeted, he moved his operations to Southeast Alaska, establishing a fort there in 1799. Three years later aggrieved Tlingits, armed by the British and Americans, destroyed the fort, but in 1804 Baranov returned with a navy warship and re-established Russia's hold on the site, naming it New Archangel, later changed to **Sitka**. Through savvy trading and pragmatic treaties with the Spanish, British, and Americans, the Russians developed a considerable mini-empire and fashioned Sitka as "an American Paris."

The Russians' influence spread quickly, even to areas where none had ventured. **Tlingit** traders altered their routes to obtain pelts from Native communities far from any foreign outpost; they'd then sell them to *promyshleniki*, who would immediately take the goods back to Russia. The more entrepreneurial Tlingit families turned healthy profits and flaunted their wealth at traditional **potlatches** (see p.98), holding them more frequently and giving away goods with impunity.

From the 1820s to the 1850s the fur trade declined dramatically due to dwindling supply, and the Russians diverted their attention to troubles at home. Alaska was still a largely unexplored land, only given some shape on world maps after an 1824 treaty between Russia, Britain, and the United States defined what for the most part remain its current boundaries. Its size and untamed wilds had become such a drain on Russia's resources that the navy had to take control of the faltering Russian–American Company. Even mining engineer P.P. Doroshin's discovery of a few gold flakes in the Kenai River Valley wasn't enough to revive interest among Russians, who were preoccupied by poor relations with Britain after the Crimean War. Meanwhile, expansionary pressure from Britain through its Canadian territories, as well as from the United States through the newly opened Pacific Northwest, made it increasingly obvious that Russia might lose its Alaskan territory. So it started looking around for a buyer.

Seward's Folly: American Alaska from 1867 to 1896

Russia had first tried to interest the United States in Alaska as early as 1859, but Congress's reluctance and the eruption of the American Civil War left the matter unresolved. Meanwhile, Russia's hold on its territory was being eroded by its own inability to finance armed forces so far from home and by the British Hudson's Bay Company, which had established trading posts in the Alaskan Interior. In 1867 the Americans finally saw an opportunity, and on March 30 Andrew Johnson's secretary of state, **William Seward**, signed the **Treaty of Purchase** in Washington DC. On October 18, at a ceremony in the Alaskan capital of Sitka, the Russian government formally signed over the territory for a sum of $7.2 million, a paltry 2¢ an acre. Of course, the Russians didn't actually "own" the Alaska they were selling: no treaties had been entered into with the Natives, and none would be until the Alaska Native Claims Settlement Act (ANCSA) of 1971.

The Russian withdrawal was complete. After 120 years of contact, they left Alaska virtually unchanged except for a decimated sea mammal population, a smattering of triple-bar crosses, a few picturesque churches, and the Aleut race almost wholly converted to Russian Orthodoxy. The purchase price was undoubtedly low, but many Americans felt it was a waste of money and dubbed America's new land "**Seward's Folly**" or "Seward's Icebox." After all, the territory was largely uncharted, fur seals and sea otters were all but wiped out, there was only the vaguest hint of the territory's gold wealth, and oil would have been considered of little value even if its presence had been known. The federal government now owned one of its territories outright, a unique state of affairs that has informed much of what has happened since. Alaskans might like to think they are masters of their own domain, but every significant stage of Alaskan development has been carried out with the approval of the federal government.

That is not to say that the Feds had immediate control over Alaska. Initially, there was very little to administer: the Natives managed their own affairs, and no one else had much reason to go there. The United States took almost no notice of its new possession, holding a loose rein and allowing the frontier ethic to prevail. Before they left, the Russians had managed to stabilize the fur seal population on the Pribilof Islands in the Bering Sea, but in 1870 the American Commercial Company was given a monopoly in the region and resumed the slaughter. The company soon controlled much of Alaska's meager trade and still operates in bush Alaska today.

Meanwhile, naturalist **John Muir** visited Southeast in 1879 and 1880, fired with enthusiasm for Alaska's glaciers, whose role in shaping the mountain landscape had only recently been unraveled. His *Travels in Alaska* catalogs his mainly fair dealings with the Natives, but he was less complimentary about the role of the American missionaries he often traveled with. By 1885 one of these missionaries, **Sheldon Jackson**, had whipped up the proselytizing zeal of as many denominations as possible, and they agreed to divide up Alaska into a number of ecclesiastical monopolies (see p.146). Each denomination got some easily accessible spots and some remote tracts and committed themselves to converting the Natives without treading on each other's patch.

The US Army was responsible for keeping the peace in Alaska and, fearing a Native uprising, felt compelled to map as much of the territory as it could. Three **exploratory expeditions** were sent between 1883 and 1885: one up the Yukon River, one up the Copper River, and a third overland from the Copper River and across the mountains to the Tanana River. The largely peaceful nature of the Natives they encountered allayed the government's fears and quelled interest in further investigation. Meanwhile, in 1884 the federal government passed the **Organic Act**, effectively providing local government for Alaska. Until this was extended in 1900, Alaska made do with just a judge, an attorney, and a marshal, all stationed in Sitka and with virtually no influence anywhere else. It wasn't a favored posting, and those who ended up there were often incompetent, if not wantonly unjust and self-serving. Alaska languished until the discovery of gold.

An Alaskan Eldorado

Alaska traces its modern development only as far back as the gold rushes that swept across the northwest of the continent, mostly from 1880 to the early 1900s. They completely transformed the physical and social make-up of the region, driving Alaska from neglected territory towards eventual statehood.

The first big Alaskan rush came in 1880, when **Joe Juneau** and **Richard Harris** discovered gold on the site of present-day Juneau. Hundreds flocked here and the town grew rapidly, though most of the gain fell to big mining corporations who could exploit the hard-to-access gold. More than two decades later, the development here would lead Juneau to take Sitka's place as the capital of Alaska. Meanwhile, intrepid Interior prospectors had uncovered gold in the **Fortymile** district around Eagle, and this rush, together with Juneau's, sparked widespread interest in Alaska and the North. But everything until now had just been a curtain-raiser for the big show about to unfold in the Canadian Yukon: in 1896 "Skookum" Jim Mason, "Dawson" Charlie, and George Washington Carmack found gold on a tributary of the **Klondike** River and started a massive stampede through Alaska. For twelve months following spring 1897, over sixty thousand hopefuls set off from Seattle and other Pacific ports, many struggling along the treacherous Chilkoot Trail from Skagway, others trying the All-American Route from Valdez, and the better-off riding sternwheelers up the Yukon River.

Initial gold strikes were wildly exaggerated, and few fortunes were made. Most prospectors found little gold and blew the bulk of their earnings on extortionate supplies, abundant liquor, and good-time girls. Typically, the tent cities that sprung up virtually overnight alongside the diggings grew over the first year into shambolic wooden towns full of bars and brothels. By the second winter, when the easiest pickings had been taken, they lay virtually abandoned. Nonetheless, the Klondike gold rush opened up the Interior as never before. Few people had previously spent much time away from the coasts, but now

Gold has been enormously important to the development of Alaska, but the California goldfields of the 1840s and 1850s gave up five times as much as all the Alaskan goldfields together, and South Africa produces more gold in a single year than Alaska has in a hundred.

sternwheelers were plying the Yukon and smaller rivers, the **White Pass & Yukon Route railway** was built from Skagway, telegraph lines were established, and all-weather roads eventually replaced the winter dog-sled routes.

Alaska saw another rush in 1896, when gold was discovered around **Turnagain Arm**. Hope, Girdwood, and Sunrise City sprung up, but by 1899 interest had been siphoned off north to the Seward Peninsula where the beaches of **Nome** produced as much gold as the Klondike, and then to **Fairbanks** in 1902 for Alaska's last major rush. Mining has continued on a steadier scale ever since, occasionally buoyed by hikes in the price of gold, notably in 1934 and again in the early 1970s. Wherever you go in rural Alaska, you'll find people working their claims, ever hopeful of making that big strike next summer.

The gold rushes' **effect on the Interior Natives** was profound. Newcomers failed to respect Natives' "ownership" of the land, duped them, and treated them inhumanely. They introduced alcohol to Native culture, destroyed the environment, and imported diseases that weren't cured by Native medicines but responded impressively to white doctors' potions, thereby encouraging dependence. Yet Natives with an entrepreneurial bent made the best of these circumstances: the Chilkat Indians, aggressive businessmen who initially barred prospectors from their inland trails, eventually opened them up but charged impressive rates for their packing services. Nonetheless, the events of the gold-rush years heralded the end of Native societies as they had been known for centuries.

The federal government couldn't ignore Alaska any longer. Even if the rumors of lawlessness on the frontier were only half true, there had to be some form of local government. In response, a Civil Code was enacted in 1900, allowing for taxation, licensing, and the division of Alaska into three judicial districts, with judges at Sitka, Eagle, and St Michael. Communication between these three centers was at first so poor that Congress set the US Army to work building a network of telegraph cables known as the Washington–Alaska Military Cable and Telegraph System (WAMCATS; see box, p.484). Less than forty years after its purchase from Russia, Alaska was becoming well and truly American.

After the gold rushes

The changes initiated by the gold rushes were consolidated in the years immediately afterwards. By 1906 Alaska had a non-voting delegate in Congress. It attained territorial status in 1912, the first territorial legislature the following year giving women the right to vote (long before the federal government extended this basic right), and in 1916 Judge **James Wickersham** introduced the first Statehood Bill. Alaska was getting aspirations. Its infrastructure was improving, too: WAMCATS was linked directly to Seattle by 1904, the first car drove the Richardson Highway between Valdez and Fairbanks in 1913, and in 1914 the federal government put its weight behind a new railroad between

Seward and Fairbanks, in the process creating **Anchorage**.

At a time when almost everyone was fixated on gold, folk with a longer vision began to establish **salmon canneries**, the birth of an industry that was to become the mainstay of the Alaskan economy. The first cannery was built in 1878 at Klawock on Prince of Wales Island, and by 1900 there were fifty canneries operating between Ketchikan in Southeast and Bristol Bay on the Bering Sea.

With the easy pickings stripped from the goldfields, most people left, but others started to look around for a more settled **homestead** life. The 1861 Homestead Act that paved the way for opening the American West was not applied to Alaska until 1898, and even then many found it impossible to make a living from their allocated 160 acres in Alaska's short growing season and had to supplement their income by hunting and trapping. It was a lonely life, as communities were reliant on slow river travel in the summer and hazardous sled-dog routes in the winter. For four to six weeks during the spring ice break-up and again during the fall freeze-up, both of which made the rivers impassible, these pioneers were pretty much stuck. The situation began to change in the late 1920s with the advent of **bush planes**, which had more of an impact in Alaska than anywhere else in the US and remain an essential tool in large sections of the state. All of a sudden a village that had been a week's travel from Fairbanks could be reached in an hour; dog teams contracted to deliver the US mail started disappearing, and commercial sternwheeler services were reduced, though they didn't completely stop until the late 1950s.

For the next few decades, Alaskan events seldom featured in the national consciousness except for the **conquest of Mount McKinley** in 1913 (see p.406) and the Serum Run of 1925 (see box, p.558), when Nome was saved from a diphtheria epidemic by a heroic delivery of antidote by a series of dog teams. Native Alaskans in particular suffered for their lack of recognition by the federal government, though a 1922 court case paved the way for all US Natives' citizenship and voting rights. Despite their newly acquired legal status, Alaska's first peoples remained marginalized with a crumbling social structure, weak leadership, and increasing alcoholism. President Franklin Roosevelt took some notice of Alaska in 1935, when, as part of his New Deal, the **Matanuska Valley Colony** was established on some of Alaska's most fertile land around Palmer, just north of Anchorage. This remains the only real attempt at organized settlement in Alaska, and though not wholly successful, Alaska could at last begin to partly feed itself. Until this point there had been no large-scale agriculture in the territory, and everything that couldn't be obtained locally was imported from Seattle.

World War II and its aftermath

The United States' entry into World War II, after the Japanese bombing of Hawaii's Pearl Harbor in 1941, provided Alaska's next great leap forward. By 1940 war looked likely and Alaska's strategic importance and vulnerability were brought into sharp focus. The military machine swung into action – the first non-extractive industry to have an effect on the Alaskan economy – establishing military bases in Anchorage, Delta Junction, Dutch Harbor, Fairbanks, Kodiak, Nome, Sitka, and Whittier. The only way to get substantial quantities of materials and machinery up to Alaska was by sea, and the military wanted a safer and more easily protected route. The answer was the **Alaska Highway** (also known as the ALCAN), a 1500-mile road punched through the wilds of northern British Columbia and the Yukon Territory to Fairbanks in Alaska. It was an immense and logistically difficult project, and yet it was completed (in a primitive but useable condition) in seven short months in 1942. It is now much improved and remains the only road link to the Lower 48.

While the Alaska Highway was being built, the Japanese attacked the Aleutian Islands, which at their westernmost point are only a thousand miles from Japan. They bombed Dutch Harbor and occupied the two remote islands of Attu and Kiska – the only successful invasion of US soil in the war (see box, p.368). US territory was soon reclaimed, and military build-up continued, fueling a booming economy as the United States spent a total of a billion dollars to support up to 150,000 troops.

Apart from a brief postwar recession, boom times in Alaska continued with increased military spending and construction during the Cold War. This, along with the civilian benefits of the Alaska Highway, brought tremendous population growth and economic expansion: the timber industry got under way, and both mining and fishing became more regulated. Alaska's carefree youth was coming to an end.

Statehood and the Trans-Alaska Pipeline

Alaska became a territory in 1912 (the same year that New Mexico and Arizona became the 47th and 48th states), but this had little appreciable effect on the land and its people. Renewed calls for statehood came in the early 1950s when the impotence of local representation in Congress started to rankle; proponents, particularly those engaged in the over-fishing of salmon, claimed they needed statehood for protection from outside interests. Counterclaims that Alaska would be a financial burden on federal resources won out for a time, but in 1957 economically viable quantities of oil were discovered along the Swanson River on the Kenai Peninsula. Suddenly Alaska looked more appealing, and in 1958 Congress approved the **Alaska Statehood Act**. President Dwight Eisenhower declared Alaska the 49th state on January 3, 1959 (beating Hawaii to the title by eight months), and Alaskans could finally rid themselves of their perceived status as second-class citizens.

Until now, Alaskans had felt that a combination of limited funds and a small and thinly spread population had prevented them from truly taming their great land. Rural poverty was still the norm and though there was now a railroad linking the two biggest cities, Anchorage and Fairbanks, the road system was still rudimentary and planes were beyond the means of most residents – all difficult to imagine considering the four-lane highways and shopping malls of Alaska's urban centers today. Statehood brought a spirit of optimism manifested in accelerated population and economic growth. This took a body blow five years later with the 1964 **Good Friday earthquake** (see box, p.590), which left a scar on the psyche of the Alaskan people, but came with the silver lining of the post-quake reconstruction as railroads were realigned, streets repaired, and whole sections of some towns rebuilt.

Until statehood, the federal government had owned something like 99 percent of all the land in Alaska, the remaining one percent having been ceded to homesteaders. As part of the Statehood Act, and to help Alaska become

△ Aftermath of 1964 Good Friday earthquake, Anchorage

self-sufficient, the US government promised to transfer control of over a quarter of the land, and the state of Alaska was given 25 years to choose which areas it wanted. One of the earliest selections was large tracts of the North Slope, flanking the Arctic Ocean, where in 1968 the Atlantic Richfield company discovered huge **oil deposits beneath Prudhoe Bay**, thereby altering Alaska's financial destiny. The trouble was, the only feasible way to get the oil to market was by constructing an 800-mile pipeline right across the heart of the state. Environmentalists were immediately up in arms, but what worried the consortium of oil companies most was land ownership. The oil companies needed permission to cross land which was almost exclusively federally owned – and some of this territory was contested by newly resurgent Native groups who were demanding recognition of their first-people rights, a topic pointedly ignored at statehood. In the spirit of the late 1960s and early 1970s, Natives found a sympathetic ear in the federal courts and among the wider public. The government couldn't really approve pipeline construction until these Native claims were addressed. There was also a desire to at least partially right the wrongs meted out to Native Alaskans over two centuries of white intervention, and with all that oil waiting to be tapped, the government was keen to settle. Understandably, Native leaders played it for all they could get. In 1971, Nixon signed the **Alaska Native Claims Settlement Act (ANCSA)**, which extinguished Native land titles in return for almost $1 billion and 44 million acres – roughly a tenth of Alaska – spread among 60,000 people. At the time the settlement was widely regarded as the most generous and fair of any deal with aboriginal people, with every man, woman, and child getting $17,000. In hindsight, some believe the Natives were manipulated, their naive representatives sucked in by the machinations of big business and politics. Since ANCSA, oil companies have extracted over $150 billion from the North Slope, and the Alaska state government has received a third of that in taxes and royalties.

ANCSA drastically changed the economic status of Natives. The $1 billion was paid over a decade into twelve (later thirteen) regional corporations and over two hundred village corporations, all Native-administered bodies responsible for investing half the money and distributing the rest among their people. Instead of being communal owners of the land, the people now became shareholders in their corporations, so the act effectively forced Native Alaskans into a capitalist world they neither wanted nor were prepared for. As John McPhee writes in *Coming into the Country*, "the bluntest requirement of the Alaska Native Claims Settlement Act was that the natives turn white," and came at a time when the Native way of life was already under threat. Snowmobiles were replacing sled dogs, homes were getting modern conveniences, and the Native men working on the Trans-Alaska Pipeline could send back weekly remittances larger than the annual earnings of their village cousins. Binge drinking became the huge problem it still is today.

The regional corporations found themselves rich and immediately started buying up real estate, canneries, and businesses all over Alaska and beyond. A case in point is the Cook Inlet region's CIRI, which now owns sightseeing cruise companies in Prince William Sound and Kenai Fjords National Park, as well as hotels throughout Southcentral Alaska.

With Native opposition to the pipeline largely defused, the environmental challenge lost steam and eventually collapsed, and when oil prices went stratospheric as a consequence of the 1973 oil crisis, Congress gave the go-ahead. Construction of the **Trans-Alaska Oil Pipeline** began in 1974, and as thousands of workers and hundreds of millions of dollars started flowing into the state, Alaskan aspirations went through the roof. Everyone was riding the oil wave, not least the workers with their huge pay packets: Fairbanks was the base for much of the construction and sprouted bars and brothels to cope with hordes of suddenly wealthy men; Anchorage boomed as the Alaskan headquarters of most of the oil companies; and Valdez tripled in size for the construction of the deep-water oil terminal.

This period also marked a shift in the sociopolitical make-up of the state. The heritage of gold prospecting, hunting, trapping, and commercial fishing left a strongly **libertarian** streak through the state, manifest in an almost paranoid mistrust of any form of authority or government. This point of view, however,

The Good Friday earthquake

In the evening of March 27, 1964, Alaska was dealt a devastating blow when the most powerful earthquake ever recorded in North America rocked the new state's Southcentral region. Rating an astonishing Magnitude 9.2 – San Francisco's 1906 quake rated 8.2 – and lasting close to five minutes, the **Good Friday earthquake** flattened entire blocks of buildings, twisted railroad lines and roads, and pitched cars into shop windows with their tail fins pointing skyward.

Centered below Miners Lake on the northern edge of Prince William Sound, roughly eighty miles east of Anchorage, the quake and its numerous aftershocks were felt across Southcentral. An underwater landslide in Prince William Sound sent huge waves sweeping over Cordova, Valdez, Whittier, Seward, and Kodiak Island, accounting for 119 of the 134 deaths attributed to the quake. **Valdez** was so devastated that it was abandoned and had to be completely rebuilt four miles away on more stable ground. Further along the coast, **Kodiak** lost its harbor, and one unlucky fishing boat was pitched over waterfront buildings to be left high and dry two streets back. In Anchorage the twelve-foot drop between 4th and 3rd Avenues hints at the destruction, and **Earthquake Park** now stands on land which liquefied, virtually swallowing the suburb of Turnagain Heights. All the wrecked houses have long since been cleared away, but explanatory panels and a ruckedup landscape tell the tale.

Alaska is determined to exploit the huge quantity of natural gas contained within the North Slope oilfields. After thirty years of oil extraction, supplies of "black gold" are getting low, but between one and three percent of the world's natural gas reserve is believed to be still waiting below the surface.

A new pipeline to get the gas to the major markets in the eastern United States would cost around $25 billion, but that's peanuts compared to the potential profits to be made if natural gas prices stay high – and there's the rub. The state government wants to get the major oil companies to build the pipeline in return for a cut of the revenue, but no one seems to be able to decide exactly how much. The defeat of Governor Frank Murkowski in 2006 stalled negotiations and it remains to be seen what will happen under Governor Sarah Palin.

had always been softened by a broadly liberal outlook: Alaskans even voted to legalize marijuana for home use in the 1970s, though this was later rescinded. With the discovery of oil and the construction of the pipeline, many of the newcomers were Southerners – from Texas, Oklahoma, and elsewhere in the Bible Belt – and Alaska shifted from being a mostly Democratic state to repeatedly returning Republican congressmen and senators to office.

Reaping the oily rewards

The pipeline was completed in 1977 at a cost of $8 billion, making it the largest private construction job in history. The crews went home (though many individuals stayed) and the state settled back to reap the proceeds of the oil. But there was unfinished business. The 1971 ANCSA agreement had established the size of the Native land settlement, but the fate of other Federal lands had not been decided, something left for the 1980 **Alaska National Interest Lands Conservation Act (ANILCA)**. In this, Congress set aside almost a third of the state for new or expanded parks. In a sense it marked the maturing of an Americanized Alaska: the old freedoms (however illusory) were perceived as being eroded as the land was "tied up." All of a sudden there were rules about where you could go, where you could hunt, and how much fish and game you could take, though Natives were guaranteed access to park land for **subsistence hunting** and fishing. In contrast to the Feds, who were perceived to be undermining Alaska's sovereignty, the state garnered popularity by abolishing all individual state taxes in 1980 and, two years later, by paying the first installment of the **Permanent Fund Dividend** (see box, p.211) to all residents. In almost every year since, more than $1000 has been paid to each Alaskan.

Oil fueled massive growth in the mid-1980s, with Alaskans enjoying the highest income of any state. Coffers were bulging and money was lavished on all manner of civic institutions, such as the museum and performing arts center in Anchorage. As a consequence of the 1976 **Molly Hooch Decree**, the state was obliged to provide secondary schooling in any community that had an elementary school, and though no other state would have had the money to comply, the timing was right and Alaska went ahead with the program. Now even tiny settlements have a swanky school; indeed, it's often the finest building in the district, and one that's usually put to multiple uses – community hall, sports hall, movie theater, and so on.

Despite widespread belief to the contrary, such fortune couldn't last, and the bubble finally burst in 1986 when oil prices plummeted. The state budget was slashed by sixty percent, triggering a deep recession which halved housing prices and prompted around twelve percent of Anchorage's population to leave the state. But a recovery of sorts wasn't far behind, ironically riding on the back of the 1989 **Exxon Valdez disaster** (see box, p.322). When eleven million gallons of crude oil spilled from the *Exxon Valdez* tanker into Prince William Sound, many companies involved in the massive clean-up operation made a stack of cash, lending their executives the local nickname "spillionaires."

Present and future Alaska

Through the 1990s and into the new century, Alaska's traditional economic mainstays have been under threat. Oil remains the main source of Alaskan wealth and new fields are tapped every couple of years, but these are small and overall production is declining. From a peak of 2.1 million barrels per day (mbpd) in 1988, it dropped to under 1mbpd in 2006, and the projection for 2016 is less than 0.5mbpd. Oil companies are clamoring to open new areas for exploration. The most contentious of these is the coastal strip of the **Arctic National Wildlife Refuge (ANWR)**, which is thought to contain rich deposits currently inaccessible because of Refuge status and public pressure. Moves to have the area designated a national monument failed to put the Arctic Refuge outside oil-company reach, though with the Democrats taking over the Congress in 2006, George W. Bush is going to struggle to get exploitation started.

Oil still brings in eighty percent of Alaska's revenue, but while the skyrocketing world oil price in the last couple of years has swelled the state coffers, it only serves to delay the inevitable need to turn to other industries. Though similarly unsustainable, **forestry** has been a big earner for the past few decades, with activities concentrated in the nation's two largest national forests: the Tongass, which encompasses almost the entire Southeast, and the Chugach, covering much of Southcentral and the southern Interior. Falling world prices for spruce pulp and timber have hit the industry hard, though, and pulp and saw mills have closed all over Southeast. Many lay the blame firmly at the feet of the federal government, which owns the forests and has cut back on the sale of timber-cutting rights. During the Clinton years, the government was seen as bowing to pressure from environmental groups seeking the preservation of some of the world's largest tracts of untouched temperate rainforest. Bush has tried to revive the industry with looser legislation, but so far without much success.

Alaska's fishery is the other big earner, particularly the super-rich **salmon-fishing** industry, though annual catches are subject to wild swings. Over-fishing tends to get the blame for low returns, but poor years are often followed by bumper harvests. Still, supplies seem to be in ever greater demand, and the issue of international fish quotas came to a head in the summer of 1997, when Canadian fishers sought to stop Alaskans "poaching" what they perceived to be Canadian fish. Fishing boats surrounded the tourist-laden Alaskan ferry *Malaspina* in the Canadian port of Prince Rupert and held it hostage for three days, eventually releasing it when the matter was resolved in an out-of-court settlement.

Over the years, other fish species, along with king crab and tanner crab, have been all but wiped out by over-fishing, and the industry now has a system of

Most people have to wait until they're dead to get stuff named after them, but Alaska's senior US senator, **Ted Stevens**, has jumped the gun. In 1999, Anchorage's airport became the Ted Stevens Anchorage International Airport in recognition of the man's huge influence in bringing federal money to the 49th state. Stevens is one of the US's longest-serving senators, having been in the role since 1968, and for years he headed the powerful Senate Appropriations Committee, responsible for allocating over half a trillion dollars in federal funds each year.

He hasn't been shy about using his position to benefit Alaska. Indeed, he is the master of **pork-barrel politics**. When it comes time to push through a crucial bill that must pass, he'll regularly slip in a few dozen pet projects amounting to tens of millions of dollars: as chairman of the influential Defense Appropriations Subcommittee, he spends much of his time trying to put ANWR drilling into defense bills. Wags in Washington have dubbed his chase for tax dollars "Alaska's second gold rush."

Despite being one of the country's least populous states, Alaska gets around $8 billion in federal funding each year, the highest per capita in the US at roughly $12,000 per resident. Of course, it's negligible compared to the $200 billion California receives. Stevens even claims that Alaska has been short-changed, though for every tax dollar the state gives to the Federal government, it receives $1.80 back in funding. Depending on whom you ask, Stevens' activities are a source of either pride or acute embarrassment. Across the board, however, there's a grudging satisfaction in the good he does for the state and amusement in his barefaced favoring of all things Alaskan.

Things are no less murky back home, where Alaska runs a closed political shop. In 2002, Republican **Frank Murkowski**, who for years had been Alaska's second senator, became state governor and, with the right to appoint his daughter **Lisa Murkowski**. If that sounds a little dodgy, read on. In the summer of 2002, Murkowski knew that he might win the gubernatorial race. He also knew of the governor's prerogative to appoint a senator to any vacant position and that, because he wouldn't take office until a month or so after the election, the privilege would fall on the incumbent, Democrat Tony Knowles. Knowing he would have the support of the Republican-dominated state legislature, our Frank pulled political strings to tease through a law that would delay the appointment of a replacement for fifty days, long enough for him to take office. Knowles vetoed the bill, but Murkowski had enough backing to get the veto overridden, and into law it went. Soon after taking office, he appointed his daughter to his vacated post. Maybe his chickens were coming home to roost when he was voted out of office in 2006.

In addition to its two senators, Alaska has one congressional representative, Republican **Don Young**, who has held the post continuously since 1973. Now one of the highest-ranking Republicans in the House of Representatives, he chairs the Transportation and Infrastructure Committee and, like Stevens, is skilled at using his position to promote plum projects for his home state. Currently, he is championing a $200 million bridge from Ketchikan to its airport, and a bridge from Anchorage across Knik Arm to Point MacKenzie, which is projected to cost between $400 million and $1 billion. His efforts to sell taxpayers the Ketchikan "bridge to nowhere" recently earned him the Golden Fleece Award from Taxpayers for Common Sense, a government-spending watchdog. Young's response? "Very proud of that."

quotas which aim to set sustainable catch limits. Currently pollock is a huge money-spinner, and efforts are being made to ensure it doesn't succumb to the classic boom-and-bust cycle. More recently, foreign salmon-farming has become the Alaskan industry's biggest threat, pushing down the price of the state's wild salmon.

Since World War II, the **military** has been a big spender in Alaska, but with the end of the Cold War and progressive rounds of military belt-tightening, things look bleak. So far Alaska has escaped the worst of the spending cuts, but no one is expecting a bright future of bountiful military funding.

Alaska has thrived on these boom-and-bust economies, but all currently look to be on a downward spiral – though perhaps **natural gas** (see p.591) will be the next boom. With such an uncertain future, Alaska is attempting to stabilize its economy. The great hope is **tourism**, which has been expanding steadily over the past couple of decades and looks set to continue growing. Yet with such a short tourist season, and the prevalence of cruise-ship packages that see much of the profits leave the state, it seems unlikely that tourism can fill the void left by the decline of extractive industries.

Times of economic difficulty always highlight political divisions, and in Alaska those run deeper than almost anywhere else in the country. Speak to Alaskans and you'll hear a lot of libertarian rhetoric that borders on the survivalist. Anything that smacks of government interference is immediately pounced upon, and yet Alaska has the highest per-capita state spending in the country, pays an annual dividend of more than $1000 to every resident, runs the railroad and state ferry system, and owns almost a third of the state's entire surface area. Against these (whisper it) socialist tendencies there is the cherished lack of state income tax, though as oil revenues decline it seems likely that some form of taxation will eventually be imposed. Already, intentions to dip into the Permanent Fund aren't dismissed completely out of hand, sales taxes are spreading around the state, and it seems only a matter of time before income tax will become a reality.

Chronology

11,000 years ago ▶ Earliest record of human presence in Alaska.

1725 ▶ Peter the Great sends Vitus Bering to explore the North Pacific.

1728 ▶ Vitus Bering sails through the Bering Strait, naming St Lawrence Island.

1733 ▶ Georg Wilhelm Steller becomes the first naturalist to visit Alaska on Bering's second expedition.

1741 ▶ Bering sets foot on the Alaskan mainland on July 15 during his third expedition, but dies on the way home.

1745 ▶ Russian fur hunters spend winter in the Aleutian Islands; first European habitation.

1774 ▶ Spaniard Juan Perez sights southern end of Prince of Wales Island.

1778 ▶ English captain James Cook charts Alaska coast and reaches Unalaska.

1784 ▶ Gregorii Shelikov establishes first white settlement at Three Saints Bay, Kodiak.

1792 ▶ Catherine II grants Alaskan fur monopoly to Shelikov.

1795 ▶ The first Russian Orthodox church established in Kodiak.

1804 ▶ Russians establish settlement at modern-day Sitka.

1847 ▶ Hudson's Bay Company establishes Fort Yukon at the confluence of the Porcupine and Yukon rivers; Russian hegemony in Alaska challenged.

1849 ▶ Russian mining engineer discovers gold and coal on the Kenai Peninsula.

1857 ▶ Coal mining begins at Coal Harbor on the Kenai Peninsula.

1865 ▶ Extensive exploration of Alaska as Western Union Telegraph Company prepares to put telegraph line across Alaska and Siberia.

1867 ▶ US purchases Alaska from Russia.

1871 ▶ Gold discovered at Indian River near Sitka.

1880 ▶ Tlingit Kowee leads Richard Harris and Joseph Juneau to gold near Juneau; Juneau established.

1881 ▶ Presbyterians under Sheldon Jackson begin mission schools.

1884 ▶ Congress passes Organic Act providing a civil government for Alaska.

1890 ▶ Large corporate salmon canneries begin to appear.

1897–1900 ▶ Klondike gold rush.

1898 ▶ Gold discovered in Nome.

1900 ▶ Civil Code for Alaska enacted.

1902 ▶ Felix Pedro discovers gold near Fairbanks.

1906 ▶ Capital moved from Sitka to Juneau.

1910 ▶ The Sourdoughs make first ascent of North Peak of Mount McKinley.

1911 ▶ Sea otters given complete protection after international agreement between US, Great Britain, Canada, Russia, and Japan.

1912 ▶	Alaska given territorial status.
1915 ▶	Anchorage established as a construction camp for the Alaska Railroad.
1923 ▶	President Warren G. Harding comes to Alaska to drive the last spike in Alaska Railroad.
1935 ▶	Matanuska Colony Project brings New Dealers to Alaska.
1940 ▶	Beginning of military expansion.
1942 ▶	Japan bombs Dutch Harbor, invades Aleutians. ALCAN Highway built.
1959 ▶	Alaska becomes 49th state.
1964 ▶	Good Friday earthquake strikes Southcentral and parts of Southwest Alaska.
1968 ▶	Oil discovered at Prudhoe Bay.
1971 ▶	Alaska Native Claims Settlement Act (ANCSA) signed into law.
1976 ▶	Molly Hooch Decree requires secondary schooling throughout the state.
1977 ▶	Trans-Alaska Pipeline completed from Prudhoe Bay to Valdez.
1980 ▶	Congress passes Alaska National Interest Lands Conservation Act (ANILCA).
1982 ▶	First Permanent Fund Dividend (PFD) paid out.
1986 ▶	Oil price drops below $10 a barrel, initiating economic slump.
1989 ▶	The *Exxon Valdez* oil tanker spills eleven million gallons of crude into Prince William Sound.
1994 ▶	Federal trial awards $5 billion in restitution for the *Exxon Valdez* disaster.
1997 ▶	Canadian fishermen detain Alaskan ferry over fishing rights.
1999 ▶	SeaLife Center opens in Seward, partly funded by restitution from the *Exxon Valdez* disaster.
2002 ▶	Republican Frank Murkowski takes over from Democrat Tony Knowles as state governor.
2003 ▶	Drop in oil revenue causes budget blowout; imposition of a state income tax narrowly averted.
▶	Public pressure sees oil development in Arctic National Wildlife Refuge dropped from federal energy bill.
2005 ▶	Low oil revenues and poor stock market performance drop PFD to $845, the lowest since 1988.
2006 ▶	Governor Sarah Palin takes office after defeating incumbent Frank Murkowski.

Landscapes and wildlife

A visit to any Alaskan bookshop will reveal racks of books on the state's impressive geology, flora, and fauna, and indeed there is much to cover: mountain ranges, deep fjords, lakes, wetlands, and all sorts of species occupying those environments. What follows is a general overview of animals, plants, and landscapes you may encounter during your stay.

Glaciers, volcanoes, and earthquakes

Most people's expectations of the Alaskan landscape are based on Southeast Alaska, where ancient **glaciers** carved out deep **fjords**, now filled in by the sea to form the narrow channels of the Inside Passage. The pine- and spruce-cloaked islands here shelve steeply into deep water, and beaches are rare. In several places glaciers calve off icebergs directly into the fjords, but many glaciers have receded to the point where they no longer reach the water. The most rapidly shrinking glaciers are those in Glacier Bay, where they have receded seventy miles over the past two hundred years. Lichens only just manage a toehold on the most recently revealed rock near the glaciers; once land has been ice-free for around two hundred years, it achieves the mix of mature spruce and hemlock found all over Southeast.

Large sections of Southcentral, around Prince William Sound and on the Kenai Peninsula, have a similar topography, although here there's no narrow network of channels. Several tidewater glaciers are fed by large **icefields** high in the Wrangell, Kenai, and Chugach mountains, where enormous quantities of snow accumulate.

Further north, the Interior is sliced through by the **Alaska Range**, a jagged chain of icy peaks topped by **Mount McKinley**, the highest mountain in North America. Glaciers exist here, too, but precipitation is much lower than on the coast, and with less weight driving them downhill they tend to move much more slowly. Consequently, most Interior glaciers have accumulated so much surface debris they appear an unappealing brown – a sharp contrast to the clean and white glaciers of the coast.

Once winds reach northern Alaska, most of their moisture has been lost as snow over the coastal mountains and the Alaska Range, leaving nothing for the **Brooks Range**, the ultimate northern extension of the Rockies. Though glacially sculpted, there is no longer enough snowfall here to support large glaciers, and most of the mountaintops remain bare.

Most Alaskan mountain ranges are the result of the folding of the earth's crust, but in places this process is given a helping hand by **volcanoes**, around fifty of which form an orderly line from the highest, the 14,000-foot Mount Wrangell in the east, out along the Alaska Peninsula and right out to the western end of the Aleutian Islands. They add a certain grace to the skyline, particularly from the western shore of the Kenai Peninsula and from the ferry trip along the Alaska Peninsula to Dutch Harbor. Forty are active, and there's on average one eruption a year, although usually far from human habitation.

Effects of global warming

It's been clear for a while that glaciers in Alaska are retreating, as they are almost everywhere worldwide. This trend accelerated dramatically in the 1990s, when glacial meltwater from Alaska began to account for at least ten percent of the global sea-level rise. Less than a third of the glaciers present in Glacier Bay in 1850 are there now, and the bay itself has grown from five to sixty miles in length. Similarly, as Prince William Sound's Columbia Glacier retreats, a new fjord is being revealed.

Average temperatures in Alaska have risen by 3°F since 1950 (especially since the 1970s), and by about 5°F in the Interior. For the past two decades, average temperatures have increased twice as fast in the Arctic as in the rest of the world. Maximum temperatures are not increasing much, but there's been a 5–6°F increase in minimums, and the frost-free season is getting steadily longer (in Talkeetna, for instance, from an average sixty days in the 1930s to 120 now). Whereas temperatures in the Interior used to drop to between -40°F and -70°F perhaps three times each winter for a month or more, these spells now only last a few days.

As a result of the warmer climate, the **Arctic icecap** is shrinking in area by 8.6 percent per decade, forcing the Iñupiat people to take more risks in their whaling activities and endangering polar bears, which rely on stable ice floes for hunting seals. Each year from 2002 to 2005, the summer polar icecap was the smallest on record, and in September 2006 it was 2.3 million square miles, twenty percent below the long-term average. Snow cover in the Arctic is melting earlier in the year and causing less reflection of sunshine, leading to more warming – a devastating positive feedback loop. As a region with delicate ecosystems, a short growing season, and slow-growing plants, the Arctic will adapt to these changes far more slowly than other areas, where species grow faster and can move to higher ground, for instance, as the lowlands heat up.

The same feedback loop applies to **shrinking lakes** in the Interior, which are covered by less and less ice in the winter. As the region warms and dries, tree growth is slowing, tundra is greening, and permafrost is melting; both the tree line and the permafrost limit may move as much as two hundred miles north over the next century, producing huge challenges to engineers as roads buckle and buildings tilt

The volcanoes form part of the **Pacific Ring of Fire** where the North American and Pacific tectonic plates meet. It is the interaction of these two plates that causes Alaska's **earthquake** activity. It's said that in the twentieth century, a quarter of all the energy released worldwide by earthquakes came from Alaska. Little wonder then that an earthquake of over Magnitude 7 is expected on average every fifteen months, and three of the ten largest earthquakes ever recorded occurred in Alaska, the 1964 Good Friday quake (see box, p.590) coming in second (though some authorities suggest it may have been supplanted by 2004's Sumatra quake).

Forests, taiga, and tundra

Alaska has four main vegetation zones: temperate forest, boreal forest, taiga, and tundra. Most of the southern coastal regions are swathed in deep-green temperate **rainforests**, mainly comprised of huge **Sitka spruce** – the state tree – and **western hemlock**, with a little yellow and red cedar mixed in. With spruce commonly measuring up to eight feet in diameter, it's not surprising that loggers have been hard at work. Some areas have been clear-cut, most noticeably

due to seasonal variations in the soil's consistency. Plant species will be able to move north to replace the boreal forest in Canada, but probably not in Alaska, due to the sea and very high mountains blocking the way, so grassland – highly susceptible to fires – will probably be the dominant feature of the Interior in the long term. The summers of 2004 and 2005 were very smoky, with people wearing masks in Fairbanks, and satellite images show that trees stopped growing across the Interior because their ability to photosynthesize was hindered.

Forty-three percent of Alaskans say they are convinced the planet is warming – almost twice the national average. Republicans are more likely to think global warming is an entirely natural phenomenon than a result of human activity, but all Alaskans are aware of the changes that are taking place in their state. Some are happy with the prospect of a longer, more bountiful tourist season and the possibility of summer shipping in the Arctic, but others fear **widespread flooding** and increased storm damage. These are already serious problems in the Eskimo villages of the Bering and Chukchi seas, such as Shishmareff, where the vanishing sea ice leaves the coast exposed to storms that wash away the gravel bank on which the village sits; the town is likely to be entirely relocated at an estimated cost of $180 million. But what really makes Alaskans sit up and take notice is the effect on their totemic **salmon**: warm summers and more glacial melt are leading to increased turbidity in breeding lakes and rivers, and zooplankton populations – the main food of salmon fry – have already halved in some places, causing fry to grow to less than half their historical average size. Returning runs are both smaller and more erratic than in the past.

Alaska's politicians, however, are slower to take notice. Congressman Don Young simply doesn't believe in climate change, while Senator Ted Stevens supports the view that because the warming of the Arctic is happening faster than computer models predicted, it's not possible to draw any conclusions about what's going on and that taking action might in fact do more harm than good. Despite these dissenting opinions, there is ever more support in Alaska for the widespread conviction that carbon emissions from America's energy-consuming habits are at the heart of global warming.

on Prince of Wales Island, but for long stretches in Southeast rainforest covers every square inch of land up to the tree line. Closer inspection reveals an understory of low scrub made almost impenetrable by abundant **devil's club**, with its broad green leaves and five-foot stems covered in spines. Above the tree line, thickets of **willow** (which accounts for 33 of Alaska's 133 species of tree and shrub) and **alder** predominate before giving way to alpine tundra.

In clearings and along roadsides you'll see tall stems of **fireweed**, which chart the progress of summer. The bottom of the stem flowers early in summer and the flowering zone moves progressively up the stem, finishing with a flourish as the uppermost section blooms in late August. When it has gone to seed, it is said to be only six weeks until the first snowfall.

Southcentral Alaska also has its share of rainforest, though cedar doesn't make it this far north, and only spruce makes it as far as Kodiak, the western limit of the rainforest. North of Anchorage, dense woods continue only to the Matanuska Valley, where **boreal forest** (ninety percent of Alaska's woodland) takes over. Characterized by scattered stands of aspen, white spruce, cottonwood, lodgepole pine, and paper birch, it lacks the grandeur of the rainforest, but makes up for it with spectacular seasonal changes. In what seems like hours, the buds of the deciduous trees produce fully opened leaves, then turn to shades of gold in fall, which also goes by in a flash.

△ Caribou coexist with oilfields

Further north, particularly beyond the Alaska Range, you're into **taiga**, a Russian word meaning "little land of sticks." It is an appropriate description for a sparse landscape only periodically dotted with short white and black spruce, the latter taking decades to grow by a mere inch in diameter. The trees are usually interspersed with dwarf willow and **muskeg**, a kind of swampy peat bog that in wetter areas develops into a network of ponds linked by small, slow-moving streams.

Trees finally disappear altogether in the Brooks Range, where **moist tundra** takes over and runs all the way to the Arctic Ocean. Many of the taiga species are still in evidence, but are usually more stunted: nothing grows above knee height. As everywhere in the north, there are species of willow, which here might only be an inch high but spread for up to a hundred yards along the ground. On very flat ground the land becomes soggy **wet tundra**; the limited rainfall, unable to penetrate the underlying permafrost, collects on the surface, forming numerous lakes.

Anywhere in the state with hills high enough will allow you to climb out of the forest and into **alpine tundra**. Again the vegetation is very low on the ground, with heather and an abundance of wildflowers, including the state flower, the beautiful blue **forget-me-not**.

Wildlife

Alaska's charismatic big mammals are a key part of the state's image and a major draw for visitors. The vast wilderness allows them to wander fairly freely, thereby making them more visible and more natural in their behavior than their cousins to the south. Moose, in particular, are found all over the mainland, a fact to keep in mind while driving as they can do a lot of damage to your car. Bears are also plentiful and widespread, though generally more wary of humans and a potential threat if you're hiking or camping in the bush.

Marine mammals are abundant: sea otters paddle about southern fjords, whales migrate along the shoreline to spend summer in the Arctic, and seals and the polar bears that hunt them make tracks on the arctic ice. An increasing number of people come to Alaska to see the multitudes of birds that travel up the Pacific coast to breed on the tundra, and fish – especially salmon – remain a massive attraction in their own right.

For tips on wildlife-watching, see the *Watching wildlife* color section.

Bears

With the exception of the city centers, the mountaintops, and a few islands, Alaska is **bear** country. The **brown bear** goes by three names – **brown, grizzly, and Kodiak** – but is essentially the same species and is easily identified by its shoulder hump and broad, stubby face. Whatever the name, they've become something of an icon of all places wild. There are only around three hundred left in the Lower 48, but up here there are almost 40,000 of them.

In inland areas they're known as **grizzlies**, generally solitary animals each roaming over fifty square miles of territory to satisfy their mixed diet of berries, roots, willow shoots, ground squirrels, and occasionally something bigger, like a moose calf or caribou. Except during the mating season around July, solo males and mothers accompanied by cubs – which stay with them for two summers before being forced out on their own – are most conspicuous.

Large grizzly males can stand up to seven feet tall and weigh six hundred pounds, although this is small in comparison with their coastal kin, the **brown bears**. The presence of salmon-rich streams means that all a hungry brown bear has to do is wait for the salmon run, stand by the stream, and pluck out fish until sated. Later in the season this is even easier, as the salmon die and float downstream where the bears scavenge. Brown bears put on a huge amount of weight at this time, attaining up to twelve hundred pounds. The readily available food also reduces the amount of territory needed for each bear, and so at places such as Brooks Camp in Katmai National Park and Pack Creek near Juneau you'll see several brought together by the rich pickings. The biggest of all brown bears are **Kodiak brown bears**, on Kodiak Island; they're the world's largest land carnivores, occasionally reaching eleven feet and 1400lb.

Alaska also has 150,000 **black bears**, mostly around the coast where you'll see them foraging along the shore, but also inland where they prefer denser undergrowth, seldom venturing out onto open ground. They're usually much smaller than grizzlies but can't always be distinguished by their color, which varies from black through cinnamon brown to the rare blue-gray of the **glacier**

Photographing wildlife

Wildlife photography is a specialist's undertaking, and people routinely return from Alaska disappointed with their shots of vaguely bear-shaped smudges and featureless seas where whales had frolicked moments earlier. If you've any aspiration of producing quality images, follow these suggestions:

• Animals will generally be far from you, so you'll need a lens that zooms to at least 300mm.

• The long lenses necessary for decent close-ups make a tripod a good investment.

• Go shooting around dawn and dusk, when animals are most active; low light levels at these times of day mean you'll need a fast lens and a high ISO setting (400 or higher).

• If your camera allows continuous shooting, use that function to maximize your chances of a winning image – provided you have adequate film or card memory.

For more information about locating wildlife, see the *Watching wildlife* color section.

bear. The lack of a shoulder hump and a much pointier face than the grizzly's makes them easy to identify.

Polar bears are a different matter entirely. They inhabit the Arctic rim, scouring the marine ice for seals most of the year and only heading south onto land when the ice joins with the coast in winter. At up to eleven feet and reaching 1400lb, they are one of nature's great predators, sometimes killing and eating beluga whales, young walruses, and musk oxen. In winter, however, they can go many months without sustenance: in September or October, females dig a den in a snowbank and crawl inside, giving birth to cubs in November or December and feeding them until all emerge together in spring. Although their fur is white for camouflage against the snow, their skin is black to absorb the sun's warmth, and hollow hairs provide unequalled insulation in winter. In summer the bears can overheat rapidly and won't run far, although in a sprint they will easily catch a human.

Moose

Lugubrious-looking **moose** are a much more visible part of the Alaskan landscape than bears, and are found everywhere except the islands of Southeast, Kodiak, and the Aleutians. Alaskan moose are the largest of all moose, itself the largest member of the deer family. A bull (male) will weigh in at over 1200lb and stand five feet high at the shoulder. Size usually distinguishes bulls from cows (females), but a bull also grows an impressive set of antlers, usually known as a "rack" – up to 50lb in weight and 75in across, though 45 is more common – which is shed annually and regrown through the summer. Throughout most of the year, a cow will have one or two calves in tow, only chasing them away in spring when she is ready to give birth again.

Caribou and reindeer

Caribou are also members of the deer family, but are less than half the size of moose and live socially in huge herds that are constantly on the move. They graze on open ground for a while and then, at the slightest hint of danger, flit off across the landscape at great speed. This is their first line of defense against their main predator, wolves. Alaska's million or so caribou are found in over a dozen herds, mostly occupying areas far away from human habitation, especially north of the Brooks Range. They migrate throughout the year, in winter searching out areas with little snow cover so that they can use their broad hooves to scrape through to the limited grazing below – caribou means "scraping hooves" in the Maine Algonquin dialect. Uniquely within the deer family, the females also grow antlers, both sexes shedding them every year.

Caribou are very closely related to **reindeer**, a northern European and Asian subspecies – shorter and stockier – that has been domesticated. A number of animals were imported from Siberia late in the nineteenth century and their descendants are still found on the Seward Peninsula near Nome, though some have escaped and joined caribou herds.

Wolves

For centuries the **wolf** has been feared, despised, and hunted to extinction in many parts of the world, but extensive research over the past few decades – much of it in Alaska – is beginning to balance the prejudice with some respect for this complex animal. Wolves are found throughout Alaska, although their natural shyness and sensitivity to human development makes them hard to spot. Shaded from black to almost white, they tend to live in packs of six to twelve, and sometimes up to thirty, usually sticking to a home territory but ranging widely in search of caribou. It is this behavior that puts them in danger, since wolves are not protected in Alaska. Even those that normally live in protected areas, such as the wilderness sections of Denali National Park, often stray into unprotected areas and are shot. Of Alaska's roughly 8000-strong wolf population, around 1500 are shot or trapped each year, partly to manage caribou numbers, but also for sport.

Dall sheep

Dall sheep are the world's only wild white sheep. Although their color undoubtedly provides suitable camouflage in winter, it looks like a poor evolutionary move in summer, when you can spot them high in the hills from miles away. Their agility on steep terrain and a tendency to stick to high ground gives them some protection, as do the rams' distinctive curled horns, which grow a bit fiercer each year of their lifespan. Spending their days grazing on precipitous hillsides, they're easy to spot along the Seward Highway south of Anchorage, around the Copper River Delta near Cordova, and in Denali National Park.

Musk oxen

If you drive near Nome or slog your way up the Dalton Highway towards Prudhoe Bay, you've a reasonable chance of seeing wild **musk oxen**. Looking like shaggy buffalo, they live in herds of around twenty, grazing on grass, sedge, and other river plants in summer, and moving to higher ground in winter, when they dig under the snow for food. When threatened, the adults form a circle with their massive horns facing outwards and the young corralled inside, allowing them to resist predation by wolves but making them easy prey for human hunters. They were wiped out in Alaska in the nineteenth century but reintroduced in 1930, when 34 specimens were imported from Greenland and released on Nunivak Island in Southwest Alaska. Numbers grew and all other Alaskan herds were populated from there. The Seward Peninsula around Nome was seeded with 71 beasts, and the area now has more than nine hundred animals.

Birds

Alaska has exemplary birdlife. There have been some 440 species recorded here and some come in countless quantities, completely covering vast areas of wetlands.

Among the most sought-after of Alaska's birds is the **bald eagle**, a national symbol that remains relatively rare in the Lower 48 but is so abundant in Alaska that after a while you'll almost cease to notice them. The white-feather hood that gives them their bald appearance certainly lends a noble countenance, something enhanced by their unruffled posture as they sit in the trees, but they often eschew the noble art of hunting in favor of opportunistic scavenging. The familiar coloration – black body, yellow beak and talons, and a white head and tail feathers – doesn't appear until the birds are about five years old, but they can live to twenty years or more. **Golden eagles** are also in evidence, mostly in the Interior where they hunt for small mammals on the tundra.

Waterfowl and shorebirds make up a large portion of Alaska's summer bird population, and the numbers are staggering: over twenty million pass through the Copper River Delta each spring, including the world's entire population of

western sandpiper, and some 24 million nest and feed on the delta of the Yukon and Kuskokwim rivers between May and September, including sandhill cranes, black brants, the entire North American populations of emperor geese and spectacled eider, and assorted loons and ducks. Worth special mention are the world's largest waterfowl, **trumpeter swans**, with wingspans up to seven feet. They were once thought to be on the brink of extinction, until a large flock was discovered in the Copper River Delta, still the best place to see them.

Alaska's state bird is the **willow ptarmigan**, a poorly-flighted game bird similar to a large quail. They live throughout inland Alaska, mostly in high country where they burrow into snowdrifts to protect themselves from the cold and hungry wolves. They're even blessed with feathers on their legs and feet to protect them, but otherwise their survival mechanisms are poor: early pioneers found them easy to catch and good eating.

Marine life

Alaska is surrounded by a rugged shoreline that offers sanctuary to enormous numbers of marine mammals. In spring, northbound **whales** pass through en route to their summer feeding grounds in the Arctic Ocean, then return in fall on their way to their subtropical breeding territory. Others stay year-round, feeding on the abundant fish and crustaceans. And herein lies the conflict that is threatening sea mammal populations. Commercial fishing fleets are getting ever more efficient at emptying the sea of their target species, making it increasingly difficult for sea mammals to feed themselves. Quota systems attempt to strike a balance, but economic interests often prevail, especially in small communities where fishing is the sole livelihood.

A lot of Alaska's visitors spend a huge portion of their time casting a line into rivers in the hope of hooking a prize **salmon**, but this isn't all the rivers have to offer. Several varieties of **trout** are also prevalent, probably the largest and most sought-after being the **steelhead**, which normally weighs around ten pounds, fights hard once on a line, and tastes good. Others go for the smaller **cutthroat**, **rainbow**, **brook**, and **lake trout**, or the oddly named **Dolly Varden**, a type of char that gets its moniker from its pink spots, said to resemble a dress worn by the Dickens character of the same name from *Barnaby Rudge*.

Rivers in the far north are often devoid of salmon and trout, but are full of **arctic grayling**, a tasty little fish mostly weighing under a pound and distinguished by its sail-like dorsal fin. Of the non-anadromous fish, the best-known is the **halibut**, a flat fish that takes around eight years to mature and reaches an average 30lb in weight, although the record stands at 459lb. It has surprisingly few bones for such a big fish and has a delicate flavor that does not require much seasoning.

Salmon

If there is one creature that is discussed more than any other in Alaska, it is **salmon**, a fish that supports huge commercial operations and is the object of the state's main pastime. There are five species of Pacific salmon, all prevalent in Alaska and all going by two names, which are used interchangeably. Wherever you go in Alaska, there is an enormous quantity of information about the different types, their characteristics, and their **unusual life cycle**, which sees them spending a few years at sea and then returning to the stream they were born in to breed and then die.

The largest of the species is the **king salmon** (or chinook), a deep-bodied fish which can grow up to 97 pounds, though 11–40 pounds is more common – except in the Kenai River, which has a reputation for huge fish. They typically run fairly early in the season from mid-May to mid-July, and have a high fat content, giving a silken texture almost like smoked salmon. **Silver salmon** (or coho) have a similar full-bodied shape, but are much smaller, averaging 6–12 pounds, and run late, mostly in September right through to mid-November. **Red salmon** (sockeye) are widely considered to be the best-tasting and have brilliant-red flesh with a meaty flavor. As they swim up the rivers in June and July, their skin turns from a greenish-blue to a green head and deep-red body. They average around ten pounds. The most abundant of the five species are **pink salmon** (or humpback or humpies), which grow to around 4–6 pounds and have a pronounced hump on their back. They run from mid-August to mid-September, though many get caught before they ever make it into the rivers and are canned. Lastly, there's **chum salmon** (or dog), the lowliest of the breed and the species traditionally caught for feeding to sled dogs. They weigh 10–20 pounds and typically run from mid-August to mid-September.

Sea mammals

Kings of the sea are the whales, various species appearing seasonally off Alaska. **California gray whales** make their migration in April, when tourists are generally absent; **humpback whales** are more accommodating, usually passing through in May and September, with some hanging around for most of the summer. **Bowhead whales** migrate north to the Arctic in spring and fall, and are hunted for subsistence by the Iñupiat (see p.8); very slow-growing, they reach maturity after twenty years, the latest of any mammal, and harpoon heads dating from the 1880s are still found in whales killed nowadays.

Orca are particularly common in Alaskan waters; they're still commonly called killer whales by many Alaskans, though they are in fact the largest in the dolphin family. Usually around twenty feet long, they have a distinctive black and white patterning and a very pronounced dorsal fin. Pure-white **beluga whales** (sometimes known as belukha to distinguish the whale from the sturgeon) populate Cook Inlet, though numbers are in decline and sightings less frequent.

Another marine mammal in decline is the **Steller's sea lion**, named by Georg Wilhelm Steller, a naturalist aboard Bering's second voyage in 1733. It is a huge beast, with bulls weighing over a ton, which they achieve by eating lots of pollock. This bottom-dwelling fish has been caught in huge quantities in the past few decades (primarily for use as imitation crab), roughly corresponding to the drop in Steller's sea lion numbers. Those that are left favor rookeries on remote islands, and sightings are rare unless you make a specific journey.

The **northern fur seal** is a slightly smaller member of the same family, and it spends much of its time out at sea before returning each summer to the cramped beaches of the Pribilof Islands, where up to a million breed. Hunting of fur seals has been banned (except for subsistence harvest by natives of the Pribilof Islands) by international treaty since 1911, when the same protection was afforded the **sea otter**. Because of its supremely soft, virtually waterproof and immensely valuable fur, the sea otter was hunted very close to extinction, but a few survived in remote spots and numbers have increased dramatically from 1911. However, the Aleutian population has crashed from around 125,000 in 1986 to barely 40,000 now, possibly due to predation by orcas. Fortunately they're doing well in Southcentral Alaska, where they can be seen floating on their backs, hind flippers waving in the air like sails.

Books

M any of the following books are widely distributed in Alaska but have limited availability outside the state. If you are keen to buy before you travel, the easiest solution is to check booksellers on the Web such as ⓦwww.amazon.com or .uk, ⓦwww.barnesandnoble.com, ⓦwww .powells.com, and others. Alaskan booksellers with online retailing include: Alaska Natural History Association (☎274-8440, ⓦwww.alaskanha.org); Cook Inlet Books (☎1-800-240-4148, ⓦwww.cookinlet.com); and Title Wave (☎278-9283, ⓦwww.wavebooks.com). Where two publishers are given, these refer to US and UK publishers respectively; wherever we've cited a single publisher, it's the same publisher in both countries. Books that are out of print by a certain publisher are marked "o/p," though they may still be available through another publishing house; books that are especially recommended are marked with ⚓.

Travel and impressions

Jon Krakauer *Into the Wild* (Anchor/Pan). In 1992, in an abandoned bus just north of Denali National Park, idealistic young Chris McCandless died after repeatedly ingesting mildly toxic plant matter while pursuing high-minded but poorly thought-out dreams of self-sufficiency and aesthetic purity. Climber, author, and *Outside Magazine* contributor Jon Krakauer reconstructs the peregrinations of Chris's last couple of years and weaves them in with tales of like-minded adventurers and his own youth. A fascinating and unashamedly self-indulgent tale.

⚓ **Mark Lawson** *The Battle for Room Service: Journeys to All the Safe Places* (o/p /Picador). Denali, Fairbanks, and Barrow make for an entertaining chapter on Lawson's world tour of "activity challenged" and "differently interesting" places. Astute observations of both the state and those drawn to it.

Barry Lopez *Arctic Dreams* (Vintage/The Harvill Press). Lopez takes you forever deeper into the interstices of Arctic life and landscapes, weaving together philosophy, science, ethics, polar history, and ecology into a magisterial volume that is in turns poetic, pragmatic, and lyrical. It's essential reading for anyone visiting the Arctic North of Alaska or with even the faintest interest in Arctic ecosystems.

⚓ **Joe McGinniss** *Going to Extremes* (o/p /Pan). McGinniss ranks alongside John McPhee as a commentator on the turbulent mid-1970s oil-boom years, but takes a different slant. Whereas McPhee writes about what he likes, McGinniss writes about what he doesn't; some cheap shots perhaps, but funny and often just as true today as when it was written.

⚓ **John McPhee** *Coming into the Country* (Noonday). The single most accurately observed and sharply written volume on modern Alaska, even if it is over a quarter of a century since McPhee traveled in the Brooks Range, along the Yukon River, and through the Interior. His evocation of Alaska and the Alaskan character is both matchless and timeless.

John Muir *Travels in Alaska* (Mariner). A powerful collection of reflections on his trips to the Alaskan Southeast between 1879 and 1890, a time when very few Americans besides missionaries had been there. There are tediously long descriptions of forests and glaciers (their land-sculpting actions barely understood at this time), which are offset by his tremendous enthusiasm for the landscape and indomitable spirit of exploration.

Gary Paulsen *Winterdance: The Fine Madness of Alaskan Dog Racing* (Harvest Books). Entertaining and harrowing autobiographical account of Paulsen's seventeen-day ordeal as an ignorant novice undertaking the Iditarod sled-dog race.

Alastair Scott *Tracks Across Alaska: A Dog Sled Journey* (Atlantic Monthly/ Abacus). Wilder-the-better travel writing which transcends the genre. Scott arrived in Alaska with almost no knowledge of dog-sledding, but ended the winter making a month-long sled journey from Manley Hot Springs to Nome, a trip which he uses as the thread that links deep insights into the bush. Well worth seeking out.

History, society, and politics

Ernest S. Burch and Werner Forman *The Eskimos* (University of Oklahoma Press). Informative and well-written treatise on the traditional Eskimo way of life that is pan-Arctic in scope but with frequent reference to the Alaskan experience. Beautifully photographed, with an emphasis on some exquisite Eskimo crafts.

Brian M. Fagan *The Great Journey* (o/p /Thames & Hudson). Probably the best lay-reader's explanation of current anthropological and archeological theories about the origins of Native Americans. More information than most people need but a good read nonetheless.

Jay Hammond *Tales of Alaska's Bush Rat Governor* (o/p). Enjoyable and thoroughly readable autobiography of Alaska's Republican (but very independently minded) governor from 1974 to 1982 – the state's most formative oil-industry years. Outspoken, self-effacing, and seldom pulling punches, Hammond charts his life from bush pilot, trapper, and fishing guide on remote Bristol Bay to the chains of high office and the governor's mansion in Juneau.

Nick Jans *The Last Light Breaking: Living Among Alaska's Iñupiat Indians* (Alaska Northwest Books). A rare Alaskan voice amid all the impressions of outsiders, beautifully written and with insightful discussion of the Alaskan bush and Iñupiat Eskimos.

Roger Kaye *Last Great Wilderness – The Campaign to Establish ANWR* (University of Alaska Press). Definitive account of the tensions between the pro-development mindset and the idealistic urge to preserve pristine wilderness.

John Keeble *Out of the Channel: The Exxon Valdez Oil Spill in Prince William Sound* (University of Washington Press). Updated for the tenth anniversary of the spill, this is a sober and detailed account of everything that went wrong.

Claus M. Naske and Herman E. Slotnick *Alaska: A History of the 49th State* (University of Oklahoma Press). Probably the best all-around history of Alaska up to the early 1990s.

Don O'Neill *The Firecracker Boys* (St Martin's Press). Indictment of government action and arrogance over Project Chariot, a real-life plan to carve a new harbor out of the Alaskan coast, just north of Kotzebue, with six thermonuclear bombs.

Harry Ritte *Alaska's History* (Alaska Northwest Books). A handy, pocket history of the state, with plenty of photos and anecdotes, though a little superficial for history buffs.

John Strohmeyer *Extreme Conditions: Big Oil and the Transformation of Alaska* (Cascade Press). A damning 1993 study of how oil-inspired greed has altered the face of Alaska and still threatens to bring about the state's downfall. Too earnest at times, but an entertaining eye-opener.

Memoirs

Rex Beach *The Spoilers* (Indypublish.com). Firsthand tales of the Nome gold rush written in 1919 and currently only available in expensive reprints, though second-hand copies can be found.

Art Davidson *Minus 148°* (The Mountaineers). Huddled in a tiny snow cave at Denali Pass with temperatures at -50° and wind speeds reaching 150mph, the team making the first successful winter ascent of Mount McKinley in 1967 experienced a wind chill off the bottom of the scale, below -148°F. Drawing on the diaries and reminiscences of the others involved, Davidson has woven an Alaskan mountaineering classic, free of unnecessary jargon and with human frailty playing as important a part as selfless heroism.

Ray Hudson *Moments Rightly Placed: An Aleutian Memoir* (Epicenter Press). A kind of "Zen and the Art of Basket Weaving" title, in which Washington State native Ray Hudson tells of his years in Unalaska, during which he shocked the locals by taking up basket weaving – traditionally a woman's task. A sensitive and moving story of the transition from stranger to friend.

Beth Johnson *Yukon Wild* (Berkshire Traveler Press). The adventures of four Texas women who paddled two thousand miles down the Yukon River through America's last frontier. Sometimes wordy but always interesting.

Lael Morgan *Good Time Girls of the Alaska–Yukon Gold Rush* (Epicenter Press). Life and high times on the Alaskan goldfield as seen by the other kind of gold digger. An empathetically told series of true stories with a heap of fascinating detail and a good deal of humor.

Margaret Murie *Two in the Far North* (Alaska Northwest Books). A very readable memoir by one of Alaska's earliest conservationists that gives a real sense of how Alaska has changed over the decades, from her youth in Fairbanks in the 1910s, through trips into the Arctic in the 1920s and 1950s, to her involvement in the creation of national parks and wildlife refuges (especially ANWR) in the mid-1970s.

Jonathan Raban *Passage to Juneau* (Vintage/Picador). Raban continues his later-life maritime wanderings up the Inside Passage from Seattle, haunted by the ghost of British explorer George Vancouver and the spirits of two temperamental underwater Native American gods. It is a fascinating journey through history, literature, art criticism, and his own rites of passage, even if only part of it is actually in Alaska.

Kim Rich *Johnny's Girl* (Alaska Northwest Books). Intriguing and well-written tale of growing up in 1960s and 1970s Anchorage as the daughter of one of the major players in the fledgling city's small-town gambling and prostitution gangland. An interesting insight into Alaska's underworld machinations and their impact on modern Anchorage.

Ned Rozell *Walking My Dog, Jane* (Graphic Arts Center Publishing Co).

An account of the leading Alaskan science journalist's walk from Prudhoe Bay to Valdez, exploring the country and the self, with beautifully drawn encounters with many Alaskan characters along the way.

Jonathan Waterman *In the Shadow of Denali* (Lyons Press). Well-written personal odyssey touching on all aspects of Denali as a mountaineer's quarry and lifelong focal point. Subject matter jumps around – brief life stories, tales of mountain guiding, and work as a park ranger – but the whole still manages to convey a vivid impression of what the mountain means to its devotees. A good read for anyone already drawn to Denali.

Literature

Susan B. Andrews and John Creed (eds). *Authentic Alaska: Voices of Its Native Writers* (University of Nebraska). A rare chance to read Native Alaskan literature unfiltered by white eyes: forthright stories of life as it is lived today in rural Alaska.

T.C. Boyle *Drop City* (Penguin/ Bloomsbury). A vivid description of the wilderness around Fairbanks, with a commune of Californian hippies settling near a survivalist's holdout; it's not long before a clash of cultures occurs.

Kathryn Harrison *The Seal Wife* (Random House/Fourth Estate). An oblique view of Anchorage in 1915, as a meteorologist arrives and develops a sexual obsession with a mute Aleut woman that turns to a sort of love.

Sue Henry *Murder on the Iditarod Trail* (Avon Mystery). The first and perhaps best-known novel by this popular Alaskan murder-mystery writer. An easy and entertaining tale of intrigue on Alaska's 1150-mile dog race, with much of the background material factually correct. *Termination Dust, Dead North,* and *Sleeping Lady* are also worth checking out.

Ken Kesey *Sailor Song* (Penguin/Black Swan). Set in the early 21st century, when the bohemian Alaskan fishing village of Kuniak is invaded by a Hollywood film crew; Kesey satirizes everyone in this baroque epic, marred only by a weak ending.

Jack London *The Call of the Wild; White Fang* (Signet Classic/Wadsworth). Two classic tales describing London's view of the human condition portrayed through the life of a domestic dog progressively turning wild in the former, and pretty much the reverse process in the latter. Though mostly set in the Yukon during the Klondike rush, the scenes of hardship, camaraderie, and arduous dog-sledding translate to the Alaskan experience at the same time.

Wayne Mergler (ed). *The Last New Land: Stories of Alaska Past and Present* (Alaska Northwest Books). Modern anthology with excerpts of everything from Native legends and early exploration to the oil years and climbing Denali. A great starting point.

James A. Michener *Alaska* (Crest/ Random House). A lumbering brick of a book that's about what you'd expect from the master of rambling historic novels, partially redeemed by a guide to where fiction parts company from fact. Forget it and read John McPhee instead.

Robert Service *The Best of Robert Service* (Perigee). The best value for your money of all the Service poetry anthologies, including favorites such as *The Shooting of Dan McGrew* and *The Cremation of Sam McGee.*

Robert Specht *Tisha* (Bantam). One of Alaska's most popular reads, written as a romantic novel, but in fact a largely true story of Anne Hobbs, a 19-year-old white school-teacher who, in 1927, lived in Chicken and courageously insisted on treating everyone as equals, in the process falling in love with a half-Athabascan.

Dana Stabenow *A Deeper Sleep* (St Martin's Press). The fifteenth in a very successful series of thrillers featuring the Aleut detective Kate Shugak; between 1998 and 2001 Stabenow wrote four others about Liam Campbell, a state trooper in Southwest Alaska.

John Straley *The Woman Who Married a Bear* (Signet/Orion). The best of Alaskan crime fiction by Sitka-based Straley, telling tales of ineffectual private investigator Cecil Younger, who has a habit of being in the right spot as convoluted stories solve themselves. *The Curious Eat Themselves, The Music of What*

Happens, and *Death and the Language of Happiness* are also worth reading.

Barbara Vine *No Night is Too Long* (Penguin). Ruth Rendell takes on a *nom de plume* for this engaging psychological thriller mostly set in the Alaskan Southeast and Pacific Northwest. The denoue-ment is as convoluted and unguess-able as you'd expect from Rendell at her best.

Velma Wallis *Two Old Women: An Alaskan Legend of Betrayal, Courage and Survival; Bird Girl and the Man Who Followed the Sun: An Athabaskan Legend from Alaska* (Harper Perennial). Modern retelling of traditional Alaskan folk tales, simply told, but immediately engaging.

Susannah Waters *Cold Comfort* (Doubleday/Black Swan). Perhaps the first successful stab at climate change literature, a tale of a young girl and her cousin in Interior Alaska, both obsessed with the creeping symptoms of global warming.

Reference and specialist guides

The Alaska Almanac (Alaska Northwest Books). Definitive, annually updated Alaska fact book chock-full of everything from air services to the Yukon Quest Sled Dog Race, and with irreverent quips from Anchorage oddball comic Mr Whitekeys.

The Milepost (Vernon). Alaska's biggest-selling travel book, full of mind-numbing detail, including just about every stream crossing, pullout, and gas station on the entire Alaskan road system, mile by mile. You'll find the previous year's edition in Alaskan shops at a big discount.

Wildlife

Robert H. Armstrong *Guide to the Birds of Alaska* (Alaska Northwest Books). The pick of the introductory bird books to Alaska, with a section on identification, clear photos, and detailed material on habitat.

Rita M. O'Clair, Robert H. Armstrong, and Richard Carstensen *The Nature of Southeast Alaska* (Alaska Northwest Books).

Lively field guide to the plants, animals, and habitats of Southeast Alaska that eschews dry lists in favor of weaving together and interpreting the ecosystem. Highly readable and full of entertaining insights for the nonspecialist.

E.C. Pielou *A Naturalist's Guide to the Arctic* (University of Chicago Press). A practical, portable guide to the flora, fauna, and atmospheric phenomena of the Arctic.

Tom Walker *Alaska's Wildlife* (Graphic Arts Center Publishing Co). Beautifully presented coffee-table book with superb shots of the best of the state's fauna, taken by Alaska's premier wildlife photographer. The text includes discussion of how the shots were made.

Hiking, biking, mountaineering, and backcountry travel

Rosemary Austin *Mountain Bike Anchorage* (Near Point Press). Pocket-sized yet comprehensive guide to trails from Eklutna to Girdwood.

Richard Larson *Mountainbike Alaska* (The Bicycle Shop). Forty-nine trails in the 49th state, mostly in South-central Alaska.

Dean Littlepage *Hiking Alaska* (Falcon). A comprehensive guide to hiking throughout the whole state, with a hundred hikes spanning a range of abilities, each laid out with maps and elevation plans.

Shawn Lyons *Walk-about Guides to Alaska* (Publication Consultants). Volume I covers the Kenai Peninsula and Turnagain Arm; Volume II the Chugach Mountains; Volume III the Hatcher Pass area; and Volume IV the Talkeetna Mountains along the Glenn Highway. The most detailed and up-to-date guide to hiking in Southcentral Alaska.

Jon Nierenberg *Backcountry Companion: Denali National Park and Preserve* (Alaska Natural History Association). A fairly brief but clear and understandable introduction to Denali's backcountry units and their flora, terrain, and wildlife. Helpful for planning your backcountry travels.

R.J. Secor *Denali Climbing Guide* (Stackpole Books). Accurate and detailed guide to most of the routes up Denali. Well researched and perfect for the summit aspirant, but intriguing also for those who just dream.

Kristian Sieling *The Scar: South central Alaska Rock Climbing* (Global Motion). Definitive guide to the region's rock climbing, mostly covering Anchorage's after-work rock playground and the crags along the Seward Highway south of the city.

Canoeing, kayaking, and rafting

Andrew Embick *Fast & Cold: A Guide to Alaska Whitewater* (Falcon). The serious kayaker's guide to Alaska with all the big stuff – the Turnback Canyon of the Alsek, Devil's Canyon on the Talkeetna – included in detail and plenty of inspirational boating history and river-running accounts.

Karen Jettmar *The Alaska River Guide: Canoeing, Kayaking and Rafting in the Last Frontier* (Alaska Northwest Books). A general guide for river runners with little in the way of inspiration, but plenty of relevant information – simple diagrams, pointers to more detailed maps, access to put-ins and takeouts, craft suitability – and a few black-and-white photos.

Jim and Nancy Lethcoe *Cruising Guide to Prince William Sound* (Prince William Sound Books). Detailed coverage of sea kayaking in Prince William Sound divided into two volumes, covering the eastern and western areas.

Glossary of Alaskan terms

Alaska Day Commemorates the formal transfer of Alaska from Russia to the US in Sitka on October 18, 1867.

Aleut (pronounced "AL-ee-oot"). Native of the Aleutian Islands.

Alpenglow Rich pink hues around the mountains, particularly in the low winter light.

Alutiiq (pronounced "a-LOO-tick"). Academic but increasingly general term for Alaskan Natives living between the west end of the Alaskan Peninsula and Prince William Sound, including Kodiak Island.

AMHS Alaska Marine Highway System. The state-run ferries.

Anadromous Describes fish, such as salmon, that live in salt water but travel to freshwater locations to breed.

ANCSA Alaska Native Claims Settlement Act (see p.589).

ANILCA Alaska National Interest Lands Conservation Act (see p.591).

Athabascan (also Athapascan). Native of the Alaskan Interior.

Baleen Long, black, fibrous strips from the mouth of a baleen whale, used by Eskimos to make fine baskets and souvenirs.

Beluga (or more correctly belukha). Species of small, white whale.

Bidar, baidarka Russian terms for Eskimo skin vessels. A bidar is a large, open boat (see "Umiak"); the baidarka is a kayak with one, two, or three hatches.

Blanket toss Eskimo game using a walrus hide to toss an individual into the air. Originally used for spotting whales and other quarry over the horizon.

BLM Bureau of Land Management. A federal agency.

Bore tide A broken wave of foaming whitewater up to six feet high. A rare phenomenon that only occurs in perhaps sixty places around the world, two of them in Alaska (see p.256).

Break-up Two-week period in April or May when warmer temperatures, longer days, and melting snows build up pressure below the ice, then burst through, causing the resulting ice floes to thunder down the flooded Interior rivers. Signals the end of winter.

Bunny boots Thermal footwear made of double-skinned white rubber with an air layer in between, developed by the US Army in the Korean War and said to keep active feet warm in temperatures of -60°F.

Bush Rural Alaska away from the rail and highway systems.

Cabin fever Irritable and depressed state brought on by extended periods indoors during the long, dark Alaskan winter.

Cache A tiny food-storage cabin raised high above the ground on stilts, out of reach of bears and other animals. By extension, any food store.

Cannery Any waterside fish-processing plant. The original salmon canneries are largely a thing of the past.

Cheechako Pejorative jargon for a newcomer or first-time visitor who has not wintered in Alaska or mastered Alaskan ways.

Damp community Town where alcohol sales are banned but imports for personal use are permitted.

Dena'ina (pronounced "DEH-na EE-na"). Name of the Athabascan language and people of Southcentral Alaska around Cook Inlet.

DEW Line Array of Distant Early Warning sensors built across the North Slope in the mid-1950s to detect Soviet missiles.

Diamond dust Tiny ice crystals suspended in the winter air.

Dolly Varden Possibly the only fish named for a fictional character, in this case Dolly Varden from Dickens' *Barnaby Rudge*, who wore a pink-spotted dress, which the markings on this trout are said to resemble.

Eskimo General term for northern people; in Alaska this includes the Yup'ik and Iñupiat peoples, and in Canada the Inuvialuit and Inuit. Though the word is said to derive from an Algonquin word for "eater of raw flesh," it is not considered disparaging or offensive in Alaska.

Eskimo ice cream (aka *akutuq* in Iñupiaq and *akutak* in Yup'ik). Traditional dessert made from whipped seal oil, berries, and snow.

Fishwheel Mechanical fish harvester used in murky glacial rivers. Can catch up to a thousand salmon a day on a good run.

Flume Artificial channel for water, used in gold mining.

Freeze-up The opposite of break-up, usually in late October.

Frost heaves Undulations in the road surface or house foundations built on permafrost, caused by repeated annual freezing and thawing.

Gold dredge A piece of heavy machinery that scoops gravel from a riverbed and pumps it through sluices to remove gold and discard the leftover rock, or tailings.

Grubstake mining Process whereby a banker or trader would supply a prospector with the means – food, tools, etc – to pursue his prospecting with the understanding that the advance would be repaid many times over when he struck paydirt.

Haida (pronounced "HI-da"). Coastal Natives of the Southeast.

Homesteading Now largely defunct practice of giving settlers land in return for building a house and making the land "useful" within a certain period.

Honey bucket Outhouse slops receptacle in places where it is not possible to dig a pit.

Igloo Iñupiat Eskimo word for house or dwelling. In Alaska traditional houses were often made of driftwood and sod, rather than the ice used by Canadian Eskimos when out hunting.

Inuit See "Eskimo."

Iñupiaq Language of the Iñupiat.

Iñupiat Alaskan Eskimos in northwest Alaska as far south as Unalakleet. Distinct from Yup'ik.

Kayak Yup'ik and Iñupiat word for the familiar one-person, skin-covered boat.

Lower 48 The contiguous United States, a term often used disparagingly.

Mukluks Knee-length boots, made of sealskin or moose hide and bound with thongs; lightweight, warm, and perfect for cold snow.

Muktuk Whale blubber and the associated skin layer (usually from bowhead or Beluga whales) eaten as an Eskimo delicacy raw, pickled, frozen, or boiled and fermented.

Muskeg Mossy peat bogs that cloak much of Interior Alaska, often covered with short plants such as blueberries or crowberries.

Native Alaskan Refers to anyone born in the state, except when the "N" is capitalized, when it refers only to those with indigenous heritage.

North Slope Gently shelving Arctic flatlands north of the Brooks Range. Often used as shorthand for the oil industry around Prudhoe Bay.

Outhouse Outdoor toilet comprised of a hole in the ground surrounded by anything from a poorly built hut to a sturdier, more modern structure. The outhouse has been raised to both an art form (bookshops stock several outhouse picture books) and a sport, with several summer festivals featuring outhouse-carrying races.

Outside Everywhere that's not Alaska; see "Lower 48."

Outsider Not an Alaskan.

Panhandle Nickname for Southeast Alaska, derived from the shape of the state.

Permafrost Soil that remains frozen throughout the year.

Permanent Fund The state's invested profits from oil royalties and taxes. The Permanent Fund Dividend (see p.211) is paid annually.

Poke A small bag containing gold dust, or sometimes just gold-bearing gravel.

Potlatch A massive feast thrown by Southeast coastal Natives.

Qiviut (pronounced "KIH-vee-yoot"). Soft underhair of the musk ox that is knitted or woven into scarves and other garments.

Rack Set of antlers, generally used to refer to a moose rack.

RV Recreational vehicle or motorhome.

Ski-joring Cross-country skiing while being helped along by a dog on reins.

Skookum Native word for "strong," used favorably as a nickname, particularly during the early gold rushes.

Sled dog Any dog used to pull a sled. Most sled dogs in Alaska are not huskies.

Slough (pronounced "sloo"). Slow-moving backwater that loops off the main river.

Smolt Juvenile salmon large enough to enter and survive in salt water.

Sourdough Longtime Alaskan and what a cheechako becomes after

about thirty years. Derived from the long-lasting yeasty mixture carried by pioneers to lighten breads and hotcakes.

Subsistence Living off the land (and sea). Controversially, all Alaskans (not just Natives) have rights to undertake subsistence hunting and fishing.

Taiga Marginal subarctic landscape sparsely populated by spruce and birch.

Termination dust The first snow that covers the top of the mountain in the fall. So called because this is a sign of the termination of summer in Alaska.

Tlingit (pronounced "thling-get"). Major coastal Native people of Southeast Alaska.

Traces Reins used to attach a team of sled dogs to the sled.

Tsimshian (pronounced "SIM-shee-an"). Southeast Alaskan Natives originally from British Columbia.

Tsunami A seismic wave often misnamed a tidal wave.

Tundra A treeless expanse covered with low-lying plants.

Ulu, Uluaq The Iñupiat and Yup'ik words for a broad, semicircular knife, often also called a woman's knife.

Umiak Open sealskin boat about thirty feet long and fitted with a sail, often used as a support boat while men in kayaks hunted.

Williwaws Sudden gusts of wind caused by air building up on one side of a mountain, then bursting through into an otherwise sheltered area.

Yup'ik Eskimo people of central western Alaska.

Small print and
Index

A Rough Guide to Rough Guides

Published in 1982, the first Rough Guide – to Greece – was a student scheme that became a publishing phenomenon. Mark Ellingham, a recent graduate of English from Bristol University, had been traveling in Greece the previous summer and couldn't find the right guidebook. With a small group of friends he wrote his own guide, combining a highly contemporary, journalistic style with a thoroughly practical approach to travelers' needs.

The immediate success of the book spawned a series that rapidly covered dozens of destinations. And, in addition to impecunious backpackers, Rough Guides soon acquired a much broader and older readership that relished the guides' wit and inquisitiveness as much as their enthusiastic, critical approach and value-for-money ethos.

These days, Rough Guides include recommendations from shoestring to luxury and cover more than 200 destinations around the globe, including almost every country in the Americas and Europe, more than half of Africa and most of Asia and Australasia. Our ever-growing team of authors and photographers is spread all over the world, particularly in Europe, the USA, and Australia.

In the early 1990s, Rough Guides branched out of travel, with the publication of Rough Guides to World Music, Classical Music, and the Internet. All three have become benchmark titles in their fields, spearheading the publication of a wide range of books under the Rough Guide name.

Including the travel series, Rough Guides now number more than 350 titles, covering: phrasebooks, waterproof maps, music guides from Opera to Heavy Metal, reference works as diverse as Conspiracy Theories and Shakespeare, and popular culture books from iPods to Poker. Rough Guides also produce a series of more than 120 World Music CDs in partnership with World Music Network.

Visit www.roughguides.com to see our latest publications.

Many Rough Guide travel images are available for commercial licensing at www.roughguidespictures.com

Rough Guide credits

Text editor: Seph Petta
Layout: Pradeep Thapliyal
Cartography: Rajesh Chhibber
Picture editor: Mark Thomas
Production: Aimee Hampson
Proofreader: Diane Margolis
Cover design: Chloë Roberts
Photographer: Paul Whitfield
Editorial: **London** Kate Berens, Claire
Saunders, Ruth Blackmore, Polly Thomas,
Richard Lim, Alison Murchie, Karoline Densley,
Andy Turner, Keith Drew, Edward Aves, Nikki
Birrell, Alice Park, Sarah Eno, Lucy White, Jo
Kirby, Samantha Cook, James Smart, Natasha
Foges, Roisin Cameron, Joe Staines, Duncan
Clark, Peter Buckley, Matthew Milton, Tracy
Hopkins, Ruth Tidball; **New York** Andrew
Rosenberg, Steven Horak, AnneLise Sorensen,
Amy Hegarty, April Isaacs, Ella Steim, Anna
Owens, Sean Mahoney
Design & Pictures: **London** Scott Stickland,
Dan May, Diana Jarvis, Jj Luck, Harriet Mills, Nicole
Newman; **Delhi** Umesh Aggarwal, Ajay Verma,
Jessica Subramanian, Ankur Guha, Sachin Tanwar,
Anita Singh, Madhavi Singh, Karen D'Souza

Production: Katherine Owers
Cartography: **London** Maxine Repath, Ed
Wright, Katie Lloyd-Jones; **Delhi** Jai Prakash
Mishra, Ashutosh Bharti, Rajesh Mishra, Animesh
Pathak, Jasbir Sandhu, Karobi Gogoi, Amod
Singh, Alakananda Bhattacharya, Athokpam
Jotinkumar
Online: **New York** Jennifer Gold, Kristin
Mingrone; **Delhi** Manik Chauhan, Narender
Kumar, Rakesh Kumar, Amit Kumar, Amit Verma,
Rahul Kumar, Ganesh Sharma, Debojit Borah
Marketing & Publicity: **London** Liz Statham,
Niki Hanmer, Louise Maher, Jess Carter, Vanessa
Godden, Anna Paynton, Rachel Sprackett; **New
York** Geoff Colquitt, Megan Kennedy, Katy Ball;
Delhi Reem Khokhar
Special Projects Editor: Philippa Hopkins
Manager India: Punita Singh
Series Editor: Mark Ellingham
Reference Director: Andrew Lockett
Publishing Coordinator: Megan McIntyre
Publishing Director: Martin Dunford
Commercial Manager: Gino Magnotta
Managing Director: John Duhigg

Publishing information

This third edition published May 2007 by
Rough Guides Ltd,
80 Strand, London WC2R 0RL
345 Hudson St, 4th Floor,
New York, NY 10014, USA
14 Local Shopping Centre, Panchsheel Park,
New Delhi 110017, India
Distributed by the Penguin Group
Penguin Books Ltd,
80 Strand, London WC2R 0RL
Penguin Group (USA)
375 Hudson Street, NY 10014, USA
Penguin Group (Australia)
250 Camberwell Road, Camberwell,
Victoria 3124, Australia
Penguin Books Canada Ltd,
10 Alcorn Avenue, Toronto, Ontario,
Canada M4V 1E4
Penguin Group (NZ)
67 Apollo Drive, Mairangi Bay, Auckland 1310,
New Zealand

Cover concept by Peter Dyer.

Typeset in Bembo and Helvetica to an original
design by Henry Iles.

Printed in Italy by LegoPrint S.p.A

© Paul Whitfield and Tim Burford, 2007

No part of this book may be reproduced in any
form without permission from the publisher except
for the quotation of brief passages in reviews.

632pp includes index

A catalogue record for this book is available from
the British Library

ISBN: 978-1-84353-772-4

The publishers and authors have done their best
to ensure the accuracy and currency of all the
information in **The Rough Guide to Alaska**,
however, they can accept no responsibility for
any loss, injury, or inconvenience sustained by
any traveler as a result of information or advice
contained in the guide.

1   3   5   7   9   8   6   4   2

Help us update

We've gone to a lot of effort to ensure that the
third edition of **The Rough Guide to Alaska** is
accurate and up to date. However, things change
– places get "discovered", opening hours are
notoriously fickle, restaurants and rooms raise
prices or lower standards. If you feel we've got it
wrong or left something out, we'd like to know,
and if you can remember the address, the price,
the time, the phone number, so much the better.
We'll credit all contributions, and send a copy of
the next edition (or any other Rough Guide if you
prefer) for the best letters. Everyone who writes

to us and isn't already a subscriber will receive
a copy of our full-color thrice-yearly newsletter.
Please mark letters: "**Rough Guide Alaska
Update**" and send to: Rough Guides, 80 Strand,
London WC2R 0RL, or Rough Guides, 345
Hudson St, 4th Floor, New York, NY 10014. Or
send an email to **mail@roughguides.com**
Have your questions answered and tell others
about your trip at
www.roughguides.atinfopop.com

Acknowledgments

The **authors** would like to thank the staff at tourist offices all over the state, who have been unstintingly generous with their time and advice, and the operators of tour companies, hotels, hostels, and museums for their thoughts and assistance. Cheers, too, to the people of Alaska who have gone out of their way to help make sure this book is as accurate as possible.

This guide would have been far inferior without the editorial attentions of Seph Petta and the overseeing eye of AnneLise Sorensen. Thanks to them and the rest of the crew in the New York office, to photo editor Mark Thomas in London, and to the team in Delhi.

Paul Whitfield would like to give special gratitude to Cindy Rowland for cookies in Skagway, Len Laurence at the Inter-Island Ferry Authority, Barbara Fairbanks and Vernon Craig at AMHS, Tim Thompson at the Alaska Railroad Corporation, Michael Brandt at the White Pass & Yukon Route railway, and Karen Peterson on Prince of Wales Island. Big ups, too, to Marie of Rainwalker Expeditions in Wrangell, Ryn Schneider at *Alaska Island Hostel* in Petersburg, John Michener in Sitka, Lori Stepanski in Haines, Kristin Wilkinson in Skagway, and Jim Janssen at Girdwood Ski & Cyclery. Also greatly appreciated was research assistance in Katmai and Prince William Sound from Brett McGill, Colin Megson, Allan MacLachlan, and Richard Sullivan.

For that home on the road, a huge debt is owed to Colleen Shannon in Anchorage, who eased all sorts of logistical problems, always with a smile. And hello to the rest of the Anchorage crew for making fleeting visits fun, as well as to my new co-author, Tim, for stepping into the breach and being a delight to work with. Lastly, a big debt of gratitude to Irene for her great support, a sympathetic ear, and forbearance through long absences.

Tim Burford thanks above all Pat Campbell for an Alaskan home away from home; Susan Orlansky, Sarah Hurst, Ann Cunningham, Wendy Eakle, Laurie Ashby, Tucker and Ginger Spohr, Wayne Mattingley, Shawn Lyons, John Wolf and Becca Barnard for help, advice, and happy hiking; Vern Craig and Barbara Fairbanks (Alaska Marine Highway System) and Tim Thompson (Alaska Railroad); John Davis, Marnie Hazelaar, Mary Richards, Kelly Carlson Attlee, Rolf Meyer, Scot Baer and family, Evan Rainey and Jade Frank (Fairbanks CVB), and Craig Kenmonth (Frontier Flying) in Fairbanks; Barbara Paichert, Andy Baker, Susan and Mark Lutz, Glen Hemingson, Turi Fesler (Anchorage CVB), and Marsha Barton in Anchorage; June Miller in Whittier; Becky, Martin, Moe, Cheryl, Mimi, and David in Cordova; Vern Rauchenstein in Talkeetna; Tom Huddleston in Copper Center; and Paul, Andrew, AnneLise, Ella, Seph, and everyone else at Rough Guides New York.

The **editor** would like to thank Paul Whitfield, Tim Burford, Pradeep Thapliyal, Rajesh Chhibber, Umesh Aggarwal, Mark Thomas, Ella Steim, AnneLise Sorensen, Andrew Rosenberg, Steven Horak, and Christina Markel.

Readers' letters

Thanks to the readers who have taken the time to write in with comments and suggestions (and apologies if we've inadvertently omitted or misspelt anyone's name):

Tom Ball, Ruth Bowen, Simon Condliffe, Brigid Dodge, Ryan Fisher, Laura Pence

Photo credits

All photos © Rough Guides except the following:

Introduction

Cruise ship in Glacier Bay © Harvey Lloyd/Getty
Images
Humpback whale © Brandon Cole/Getty Images
Cycling on the Chilkoot Trail © Rich Reid/Getty
Images
Full moon rising over Silver Lake © Rich Reid/
Getty Images
Log cabin in Wrangell-St Elias National Park
© Ron Niebrugge/Alamy

Things not to miss

01 Glacier Bay National Park © Jeri Gleiter/Getty
Images
02 Hikers in Denali National Park © Mark
Cosslett/Getty Images
05 College Fjord Cruise © Ron Niebrugge/Alamy
06 Log walk at Mountain Mother contest,
Talkeetna © Paul Whitfield
07 Orthodox Church on Unalaska Island © Kevin
Schafer/Alamy
08 Independence Mine © Walter Bibikow/Jon
Arnold Images/Alamy
10 Aurora borealis © Fred Hirschmann/Getty
Images
13 Salmon navigating falls © Daniel J. Cox/Getty
Images
16 The Million Dollar Bridge © Ron Niebrugge/
Alamy
21 Hikers on the Chilkoot Trail © Alaska Stock
LLC/Alamy
25 Halibut hanging in the Kenai Peninsula
© Bruce Peter/Hemis/Alamy
26 Trains to Nowhere © Loetscher Chlaus/Alamy

Color section: Watching wildlife

Humpback whale breaching © Art Wolfe/Getty
Images
Grizzly bear and cubs © Tom Walker/Getty
Images
Moose © Paul Nicklen/Getty Images
Caribou © Johnny Johnson/Getty Images
Sea otter © Kenna Ward/Corbis
Grizzly in Denali National Park © Kim Heacox/
Getty Images

Color section: Alaska in winter

Skiers in the backcountry © Charlie Munsey/
Corbis
Aurora borealis © Steven Nourse/Getty Images
Ice fishing © Ira Block/Getty Images
Snowshoeing © Michael DeYoung/Corbis
Dog sled © Paul Souders/Corbis
Ice carving championships © James Marshall/
Corbis

Black and whites

p.173 Tracy Arm Fjord © Wolfgang Kaehler/Alamy
p.186 Haines © Paul A. Soulders/Danita
Delimont/Alamy
p.208 Moose approaching a front porch © Paul
A. Soulders/Corbis
p.234 Biking on the Coastal Trail © Alison Wright/
Corbis
p.252 Homer town © Maciej Tomczak/
phototramp.com/Alamy
p.261 The visitor center at Portage Glacier
© Tom Bean/Corbis
p.269 Mount Marathon © Alaska Stock LLC
p.285 Our Lord Russian Orthodox Church © Ron
Niebrugge/Alamy
p.300 Halibut Cove © Tom Bean/Corbis
p.324 Tanker loading in Valdez © Bill Brooks/
Alamy
p.330 Abandoned cannery, Eyak River
© Prettyfoto/Alamy
p.340 Puffins © Danita Delimont/Alamy
p.349 Boats in Kodiak harbor © Walter Bibikow/
Alamy
p.382 Spirit houses © Julie Eggers/Danita
Delimont/Alamy
p.394 Iditarod dog team © blickwinkel/Alamy
p.465 Ice climbers on the Matanuska Glacier
© Tom Bol/Stock Connection Distribution/
Alamy
p.490 Front Street, Nome © Norman Price/Alamy
p.502 Fairbanks © Walter Bibikow/Getty Images
p.511 World Eskimo-Indian Olympics © Paul A.
Soulders/Corbis
p.525 Chena Hot Springs © Alison Wright
p.540 Dalton Highway © John Schwieder/Alamy
p.549 Arrigetch Peaks © Brett Baunton/Alamy
p.560 Old St Joe's, Nome © Arco Images
p.574 Whalebone Arch, Barrow © blickwinkel/
Alamy
p.589 Good Friday earthquake, Anchorage
© Corbis
p.600 Caribou feeding near the Prudhoe Bay
oilfields © Paul Soulders/Danita Dalimont

Index

Map entries are in color.

INDEX

Map symbols

maps are listed in the full index using colored text

-----	International borders		⚓	Church (regional maps)
---	Chapter division boundary		⚑	Museum
═══	Road		⚘	Gardens
───	Unpaved road/track		⚑	Ski area
▥▥▥	Steps		⚑	Golf course
-----	Footpath		⊛	Swimming
━━━	Railway		〰	Surfing
──	Ferry route		⚘	Vineyard
--◆--	Tramway		P	Parking
✈	Airport		T	Toilets
✗	Airfield		⛽	Gas station
◆	Point of interest		@	Internet
⊙	Statue		⊞	Hospital
☀	Viewpoint		ⓘ	Tourist office
〰	Rocks		◉	Hotel
⌒	Arch		▣	Restaurant/bar
⬛	Shelter		★	Bus stop
⬟	Cabin		⊠	Post office
⛺	Campsite		▮	Building
⬥	Ranger station		✚	Church (town maps)
⬥	Customs		⊡	Cemetery
▲	Peak		▨	Park
⋍	Mountain pass		▨	National park
⚐	Waterfall		✕	Restricted area
〰	Spring		〰	Glacier
◠	Cave		⠿	Beach
⋀	Volcano		▨	Mud flats
⋀⋀	Mountains		〰	Lava flow
⛪	Monument		〰	Marsh